PRAISE FOR
THE REFORMATION AS RENEWAL

For centuries Protestants have had a clear sense of what it means to be "catholic." Surely, it was the church against which they defined themselves. What has been lost is the creedal language of "one, holy, catholic, and apostolic church" that the Reformers of the sixteenth century sought to recover, not upend. Matthew Barrett offers a rich theological and historical account of catholicity as the lifeblood of Protestantism—that is, not a movement of innovation, but a church in continuity with the historic faith. Barrett removes the layers of varnish of misunderstanding that have obscured what the Reformation was truly about. If Protestant churches were not catholic, they were merely the sects denounced by their opponents. This book is a crucial corrective to a historical tradition that has lost its sense of self.

—**Bruce Gordon,** professor of ecclesiastical history, Yale Divinity School

For a long time, the Reformation has been misrepresented by polemical scholarship. More sadly, modern Protestantism often supports the caricatures. Finally, we have a weighty, passionate, and well-informed riposte. This is a must-read for friend and foe alike.

—**Michael Horton,** J. Gresham Machen Professor of Systematic
Theology and Apologetics, Westminster Seminary California

Modern pundits and Roman Catholic apologists have long asserted that the Protestant Reformers were theological innovators who destroyed the unity of the one, holy, catholic, and apostolic church and unleashed toxins that contributed to our secular age. In this provocative and well-argued book, Matthew Barrett counters this misrepresentation by demonstrating that central theological contributions of Reformers such as Martin Luther and John Calvin were in broad continuity with Augustine and the Augustinian tradition as it was refracted through the writings of various scholastic theologians, including Thomas Aquinas. The Reformers were concerned to renew, not overturn, the one true church. Barrett's study is a *tour de force*, lending persuasive weight to Luther's brash statement: "We are the true ancient church and . . . you have fallen away from us."

—**Scott Manetsch,** professor of church history and the history of
Christian thought, Trinity Evangelical Divinity School

That we are not the first ones who think about the church is evident. That we can learn from the Reformation how to be church of Christ is made evident in this rich book. Barrett describes the Reformation as the Reformation of the church but does this through offering us a fascinating overview of the theological and intellectual history from Late Middle Ages up until the Council of Trent. Matthew Barrett writes directly from the sources and in conversation with the latest in early modern research and does this in an accessible style that stimulates to see how today we can make use all the wealth of insights of the Reformation era. A fine academic work for the classroom and far beyond.

—**Herman J. Selderhuis,** professor of church history,
Theological University Apeldoorn, president of REFORC

The Reformation as Renewal is a *tour de force* in the history and theology of the Protestant Reformation. Detailed and yet clearly written, covering both familiar and neglected territory, this massive text will serve for years to come as a rallying point for those seeking to cultivate (or rediscover) a classical Protestant identity. Barrett successfully demonstrates that the Reformation was a catholic enterprise, over and against the claims of the church of Rome as well as the shallow, dehistoricized tendencies of many contemporary Protestant circles.

—**Gavin Ortlund,** author, *Theological Retrieval for Evangelicals*

Far too long Protestants have imbibed from the fountain of the pop history of the Reformation, namely, that the Reformers rejected the "dark ages" and all things medieval. The truth of the matter is: history is more complex than this caricature. Barrett makes a compelling case that the Reformation has more in common with the early church and Middle Ages than most realize. The Reformation has genuinely unique attributes but is also rooted in the catholic, or universal, church. Barrett dispels the darkness of distortion, myth, and legend and shines the light of history, truth, and nuance to create a clear picture of where the continuities and discontinuities lie. This book is a must-read for all serious Protestants.

—**J. V. Fesko,** Harriett Barbour Professor of Systematic and Historical Theology, Reformed Theological Seminary, Jackson, Mississippi

With verve and erudition, writing from the perspective of the vibrant movement of Reformed catholicity, Matthew Barrett has written a stimulating introduction to the figures and controversies of Reformation era. He defends the Augustinian-Thomistic theology that was advocated by a number of first- and second-generation Reformers. Historically sensitive and theologically sophisticated, Barrett's argument is that the Reformers carried forward a church that was catholic but not Roman. So long as it doesn't entail the notion Roman Catholics are Roman but not catholic, his argument may offer promising ecumenical potential.

—**Matthew Levering,** James N. Jr. and Mary D. Perry Chair of Theology, Mundelein Seminary

This is an impressively comprehensive and compelling account of the Reformation as a movement for renewal and retrieval rather than wholesale revolution, which gives far more than the usual passing attention to important medieval precursors as well as the Roman counter-Reformation. A splendid tour-de-force of historical and theological writing.

—**Lee Gatiss,** lecturer in church history, Union School of Theology, author of *Light After Darkness: How the Reformers Regained, Retold, and Relied on the Gospel of Grace*

Highlighting the continuity of the Reformation with the classical orthodoxy of the patristic and medieval eras, Matthew Barrett invites the contemporary church to find renewal by traversing the "old, ancient paths." He beckons us to walk alongside Luther, Calvin, Zwingli, and many other Reformers on pilgrimage on these paths with medieval theologians, who, in turn, follow after the early church fathers. With his clear, engaging prose, Barrett provides us with both a splendid textbook for Reformation courses and a strong call to creedal catholicity.

—**Gwenfair Walters Adams,** professor of church history and spiritual formation, Gordon-Conwell Theological Seminary

In this panoramic achievement, Matthew Barrett proposes and defends the thesis that to be Protestant is to be catholic, but not Roman. Busting the myths that Protestantism is inherently antitraditional and promodern, a precursor of secularism, this book leaves no stone unturned and shows us that the Magisterial Reformers had no intention of departing from the Great Tradition bequeathed by the ancient church and transmitted by the best of the medieval thinkers. The Reformers sought to purge the church of unevangelical accretions precisely so that it would reflect catholic truth. This book is a must-read for all conservative Protestants.

—**Mark Mattes,** Lutheran Bible Institute Chair in Theology,
Grand View University, Des Moines, Iowa

The Reformation had elements of continuity and discontinuity with the medieval Latin tradition out of which it emerged. In many popular accounts, the elements of discontinuity are emphasized, while the continuities are perhaps ignored. Matthew Barrett has addressed this issue with great skill, showing that in a real sense, the Reformation had profound roots in medieval soil. It was not a movement of sheer novelty but the Catholic faith drawing on its own best resources, reforming its own abuses, and thereby offering a self-corrected and revitalized catholic faith to the church. Anyone concerned to dig deeper into this story will find many fascinating riches to ponder in this significant work.

—**Nick Needham,** church history tutor,
Highland Theological College

Matthew Barrett argues that the Reformers did not aim to start a new church but to renew the true "catholic" church—that is, the universal church that Christ is building in all ages and among all nations through his Word. Barrett's thesis is stimulating and his arguments robust. His evidence ranges from medieval scholasticism to the teachings of the Reformers. Though readers may differ in their approaches to medieval theologians, Barrett demonstrates that the Reformers confessed with sincerity their faith in the one, holy, catholic (universal), and apostolic church. Thus, he reminds us that the Reformers were examples of not neglecting the doctrinal heritage of the church but embracing *sola Scriptura* in a manner that is not radically sectarian but well informed by historical theology.

—**Joel R. Beeke,** president, Puritan Reformed Theological Seminary,
Grand Rapids, Michigan

The Reformation has been caricatured as carrier of three viruses, nominalism, secularism, and individualism, which many blame for the downfall of the West. In this volume Matthew Barrett does a fine job of undermining those pernicious narratives and calling attention to the self-consciousness of Reformation (and post-Reformation) churches as heirs of the best of the patristic and medieval church (i.e., as catholic). This volume is a welcome contribution.

—**R. Scott Clark,** professor of church history and historical theology,
Westminster Seminary California

In this excellent book, Matthew Barrett has argued for the catholicity of the Reformation. Professor Barrett eloquently articulates the important truth that the Reformation did not break wholly with the Christian church of previous ages but was rather in direct continuity with it. Catholicity is integral and essential to the project of Reformation. Well-argued and meticulously researched, this volume comes at a vital time for the church and the academy. This book is a must-read for all who are interested in the relationship between the Reformation and catholicity.

—**Christopher Cleveland,** associate professor of Christian thought,
Reformation Bible College

This book has the potential to change your understanding of the nature of the Reformation. Instead of seeing it as a repudiation of the mainstream of medieval Christianity and the beginning of something new, this book helps us see it as the rejection of late medieval scholasticism, the *via moderna*, and the recovery of an older Augustinian-Thomist tradition. Radical philosophical ideas central to the *via moderna* such as univocity, voluntarism, and nominalism were advocated by thinkers such as Scotus, Ockham, and Biel in the thirteenth to fifteenth centuries. What Barrett's painstakingly precise analysis shows is that elements of the *via moderna* found expression both in Roman Catholic and Protestant thinkers but were more formative in the post-Tridentine Roman Church. What dominated Protestant Scholasticism was the older Augustinian-Thomist ideas that had come under attack from advocates of the *via moderna*. On this basis, Barrett argues not only that the Reformers intended to be more catholic than Rome but also that they largely succeeded in doing so. The Reformation, therefore, is not the founding of a new religion or a deviation from the mainstream of tradition but rather the retrieval of the catholic roots of Christianity.

—**Craig A. Carter,** research professor of theology,
Tyndale University

This historical study of how to understand the Reformation is not for the faint of heart, or should I say, faint of mind. It is a deep dive into the self-understanding of those whom we denominate the Reformers of the sixteenth century. Its goal is to reaffirm the Reformation as a recovery of that rich tradition of biblical and patristic teaching that rightly merits the name catholic, and it admirably succeeds in doing so. Along the way, Barrett tackles not only some of the major theological issues of the world of the Late Middle Ages and the era of the Reformation, but also ably corrects some common misreadings of the Reformation from secular, Roman Catholic, and evangelical Protestant scholars. It is a splendid work and a must-read for anyone interested in the most important event in the last millennium of church history.

—**Michael Azad A.G. Haykin,** chair and professor of church history,
The Southern Baptist Theological Seminary

The
REFORMATION
as RENEWAL

The
REFORMATION
as RENEWAL

RETRIEVING THE
ONE, HOLY, CATHOLIC,
AND APOSTOLIC CHURCH

An Intellectual and Theological History

MATTHEW BARRETT

ZONDERVAN
ACADEMIC

ZONDERVAN ACADEMIC

The Reformation as *Renewal*
Copyright © 2023 by Matthew Barrett

Published in Grand Rapids, Michigan, by Zondervan. Zondervan is a registered trademark of The Zondervan Corporation, L.L.C., a wholly owned subsidiary of HarperCollins Christian Publishing, Inc.

Requests for information should be addressed to customercare@harpercollins.com.

Zondervan titles may be purchased in bulk for educational, business, fundraising, or sales promotional use. For information, please email SpecialMarkets@Zondervan.com.

Library of Congress Cataloging-in-Publication Data

Names: Barrett, Matthew, 1982- author.
Title: The Reformation as renewal : retrieving the One, Holy, Catholic, and Apostolic church / Matthew Barrett.
Description: Grand Rapids : Zondervan, 2023. | Includes bibliographical references and index.
Identifiers: LCCN 2022057654 (print) | LCCN 2022057655 (ebook) | ISBN 9780310097556 (hardcover) | ISBN 9780310097563 (ebook)
Subjects: LCSH: Catholic Church--Relations--Protestant churches. | Reformation--Causes. | Protestant churches--Relations--Catholic Church. | BISAC: RELIGION / Christian Church / History | HISTORY / Europe / Renaissance
Classification: LCC BR307 .B377 2023 (print) | LCC BR307 (ebook) | DDC 280/.042--dc23/eng /20230419
LC record available at https://lccn.loc.gov/2022057654
LC ebook record available at https://lccn.loc.gov/2022057655

Cover design: Bruce Gord | Gore Studio, Inc.
Cover image: Public domain
Interior design: Kait Lamphere

Printed in the United States of America

24 25 26 27 28 29 30 31 32 33 34 /TRM/ 15 14 13 12 11 10 9 8 7 6 5

*To Michael Haykin, who pursued me to support
my scholarship when I was young and unproven.
I have sought to model your humble generosity with my
students at Midwestern Baptist Theological Seminary*

"[We must] vindicate an absolute historical necessity to the Reformation, and to expose in its utter emptiness and nakedness the reproach, cast upon it by its enemies, as an uncalled for innovation. We go further, however, and affirm that *the entire Catholic Church as such, so far as it might be considered the legitimate bearer of the Christian faith and life*, pressed with inward necessary impulse toward Protestantism, just as Judaism . . . rolled with steady powerful stream, in its interior legal, symbolical and prophetical principle, directly toward Christianity, as the fulfillment of the law, the prototype of all its symbols, and the accomplishment of all its prophesies."
—Philip Schaff, *The Principle of Protestantism*

CONTENTS

PART 3:

The Formation of Reformed Catholicity

PART 4:

Counter-Renewal

FOREWORD

The pathway between scholarly breakthroughs and their popular reception is neither a swift nor a simple one. And this is nowhere more true than with the reception of theology within the church. This pathway between the insights of scholarship and the attitude of the church can seem long and arduous, especially since it is embedded within a broader culture of strong individualism with an antispeculative and pragmatic ethic. An understandable fear of novelty has often been akin to error or even heresy, and there has long been a deep suspicion of intellectuals and scholars in American conservative Protestantism, particularly in its evangelical variety.

There have been many exciting scholarly developments in the field of historical theology in the years since the Second World War. Heiko Oberman redrew the map from the late Middle Ages to the Reformation. As with all great scholars, he built upon the insights of an earlier generation, such as those offered by Joseph Lortz, who drew attention to the clear connections between late medieval theological paradigms and Martin Luther's Reformation theology. Unlike Lortz, Oberman set aside time-worn and time-hardened Catholic-Protestant polemics to assess late medieval nominalism and Martin Luther on their own merits. In so doing, he freed Reformation studies from the distorting effects of later ecclesiastical posturing and opened the field in new and fruitful ways for the next generation of scholars. His student, David C. Steinmetz, took up the challenge of theological genealogy as it had been developed by Oberman and applied it to the history of exegesis. Then, Steinmetz's student, Richard A. Muller, applied both approaches to Reformed Orthodoxy and extended the narrative into the early eighteenth century. The older theological approaches began to crumble as they faced the rising challenge of epistemology.

Oberman, Steinmetz, and Muller, along with their doctoral students and many other academics influenced by their work, effected a revolution in how the relationship between the Middle Ages, the Reformation, and the early modern period is understood in terms of intellectual and theological developments. It became clear that the accepted Protestant readings of, say, Aquinas were nonsense and unsustainable in light of the primary texts. The old paradigm of Reformation theology as a radical break was finally put to bed as it became clear that Reformation theology was built upon a medieval heritage (particularly

theology proper) even as it broke with that medieval heritage on aspects of soteriology, sacraments, and authority.

But historical scholarship was not only transforming scholarly understanding
of the Reformation. In the field of patristics the last twenty years have seen some
equally remarkable developments. Scholars such as Lewis Ayres and Khaled
Anatolios have reworked the scholarly understanding of Nicene orthodoxy.
We now have a much better grasp of what terms such as *hypostasis* and *ousia*
meant in the fourth and fifth centuries, and a deeper understanding of what
lay at the heart of the doctrine of the Trinity. Old clichés that drew sharp divisions between East and West, between the Cappadocians and Augustine, have
been put to the scholarly sword. Just as the Catholic-Protestant paradigm was
shown to be a distorting lens through which to understand the Reformation, the
division between Rome and Constantinople has now been revealed as similarly
problematic. Institutional divisions are stark and clear; intellectual relationships
are far more subtle and complex.

All of these scholarly developments inevitably have implications for the
church, especially Protestant and evangelical churches. Some of the implications are disturbing. As scholars such as James Dolezal, Matthew Barrett, and
Stephen Duby have appropriated the fresh insights into the classical doctrine of
God that lay behind the theology of such august Protestant documents as the
Westminster and Second London Confessions, it has become clear that much of
modern evangelical writing on this subject would not have been recognized as
orthodox by the Reformers and their heirs. While such deviation was no doubt
pursued in good faith, the rejections of simplicity, immutability, and impassibility—as classically understood—place much of contemporary evangelical
theology closer to the biblicist and highly problematic Socinianism of the early
seventeenth century than to the Trinitarian orthodoxy of the church catholic.
A return to orthodoxy on the doctrine of God is belated, but it can only benefit
the church. Socinianism was a dead end in the Reformation and can only prove
so again today.

Other implications are more positive. Protestantism long labored under
the accusation from Catholics that it represents a set of deviant innovations.
Now we know—and can prove—that this is not the case. To the extent that
Protestantism is confessional, to the extent that it is committed to the teaching
embodied in a document such as the Westminster Confession, it is catholic and
represents what Calvin and his contemporaries claimed it to be: not a repudiation of the church's tradition but an affirmation of the church's true tradition
over against the fallacious additions under which it had been buried.

Yet the path from scholarly breakthrough to church life is never easy or
straightforward. The works of the scholars I've mentioned is often highly technical. Their work frequently assumes both a wide knowledge of historical context and a deep familiarity with the history of scholarly debate. What is needed,
therefore, is for one of them to outline an accessible road map that makes the

salient points comprehensible to a wider audience and makes clear the implications of these fresh insights for Christians today.

This is why Matthew Barrett's new book is such a gem. It bears all the marks with which readers of his earlier work on the doctrine of God will be familiar. It is not overburdened with technical jargon, nor is it misleadingly simplistic. It builds upon the best scholarship, yet does so in a manner the layperson and student alike will find accessible. And it gently guides the reader into a deeper knowledge of the Reformation and its aftermath in a way that highlights the theological catholicity of the movement. It is a key tool for bridging that gap between scholarly research and the everyday life of the student and the church.

No doubt some of Barrett's claims will prove hard to swallow for those unfamiliar with the vast and compelling scholarship of the last sixty years. There is always a time lag on such things. Those who still peddle old and discredited caricatures of Thomas Aquinas, for example, will no doubt be around a while longer—careers in some quarters depend upon it. But careful reading of texts and thoughtful scholarship will, in the long run, defeat the tendentious polemics of a bygone age. Matthew's book is a gracious contribution to that process, for which we all now owe him a debt of gratitude.

Carl R. Trueman
Grove City College
Christmas 2022

1

THE CATHOLICITY OF
THE REFORMATION

With this [universal/catholic] Church we deny that we have any disagreement. Nay, rather, as we revere her as our mother, so we desire to remain in her bosom.

—John Calvin, Reply to Sadoleto

Luther was not breaking with catholic tradition but self-consciously retrieving the tradition, bringing to bear the deepest insights of Augustine and the great monastic teachers on a [late medieval] scholasticism out of touch with its own [Scholastic] roots.

—David S. Yeago, "The Catholic Luther"

R eturn to the Catholic Church."
      This summons to return to the mother church was addressed to Geneva in a letter written by Jacopo Sadoleto in the year 1539. Sadoleto was a cardinal who carried no little clout, an experienced theologian, a seasoned polemicist, and a representative of Rome. The timing of his letter to that small locale called Geneva was strategic: John Calvin had been exiled, no longer Geneva's pastor. And no longer under his direct influence—and the influence of the zealous William Farel—Geneva was ripe for a call back to the mother church. According to Sadoleto, the stakes were high: to depart from the Catholic Church could only end in everlasting death, but to return to the Catholic Church promised the reward of eternal life.[1]

Sadoleto could be very persuasive. Reformers like Calvin were schismatics, leading the Genevans away from the one, holy, catholic, and apostolic church into endless dissension. To depart from mother church was sacrilegious, Sadoleto warned.[2] The choice, then, was easy: either follow the Catholic Church and its fifteen hundred years of faithfulness to God or follow the "innovations" of the past two and a half decades, led by innovators like Calvin, whom the Genevans

---

1. Sadoleto, "Letter to the Genevans," 40.
2. Sadoleto, 43.

expelled.[3] According to the cardinal from Carpentras, the exiled pastor of Geneva had misled the Genevans, failing to teach them the ways of the ancient church, leading them astray into innumerable "novelties."[4]

Sadoleto's opinion was not merely his own but was shared by many in the papacy. The Reformers were heretics, introducing new doctrines into the church. For that reason, they were not catholic, but their modernizations betrayed the church universal. To make matters worse, they created discord when the Catholic Church stood for concord. "Truth is always one," Sadoleto reminded the Genevans, but "falsehood is varied and multiform."[5]

Although Calvin was no longer pastor of the Genevans, he was asked to respond to Sadoleto. His reply was a life preserver cast on the seas of a vulnerable Reformed Church, sustaining the Genevans under heavy and successive waves of pressure that called out, *"Return to Rome, return to Rome, return to Rome."* Return home. Yet Calvin's reply was also revealing; Sadoleto's summons forced the Reformer to explain the true intentions behind his program of reform. Sadoleto's bidding galvanized Calvin to answer the charge of novelty, a charge also lobbed at Luther in the early 1520s (see chapters 8–9). Was Sadoleto right that the Reformers—and all those who followed them—were leading Christians out of the one, holy, catholic, and apostolic church?

WHO IS CATHOLIC?

Calvin must have infuriated Sadoleto and the whole Roman Church by his reply. He told Sadoleto that the Reformation is not only catholic but *more catholic than Rome.* The Reformers were not peddling novelties, leading the people astray into heretical innovations. If anyone had strayed from the catholic heritage, it was Rome. By contrast, Calvin pursued reform because the Reformation he perpetuated and advanced was committed to *renewal.* The Reformers believed that their teachings, in contrast to Rome's, were not only faithful to the sacred Scriptures but allegiant to the catholic tradition that embodied those same biblical teachings. The doctrine the Reformation retrieved only needed retrieving because Rome failed to articulate such beliefs in a way that adhered to the catholic tradition without wavering. As Calvin said with fervidity, "With this [universal/catholic] Church we deny that we have any disagreement. Nay, rather, as we revere her as our mother, so we desire to remain in her bosom." Calvin said to Sadoleto, *We are more catholic than you.* "Our agreement with antiquity is *far closer* than yours," Calvin insisted. Therefore, Calvin clarified what the Reformation was about, namely, an attempt "to *renew* that ancient form of the Church, which,

---

3. Sadoleto, 40.

4. Sadoleto, 42, 43. Sadoleto was not as aggressive as other theologians could be. For example, he did express his own criticisms of abuses in the papacy (cf. *Consiliu de Emendanda Ecclesia*), and he did show good faith at times by extending himself toward dialogue with Reformers. Nonetheless, he remained committed to wooing Geneva back to Rome.

5. Sadoleto, 46.

at first sullied and distorted by illiterate men of indifferent character, was afterward flagitiously mangled and almost destroyed by the Roman Pontiff and his faction."[6]

Calvin's words—and his underlying claim—represent the essence of this book, the mechanism by which this project presents a fresh intellectual and theological history of the Reformation. In the words of T. H. L. Parker, "It was a belief common to the Reformers that they had on their side not only the Bible but also, on the major dogmas at issue, the Church fathers. It was not they who were the innovators; it was the Romanists."[7] That claim is often wielded for theological, even polemical paradigms, but the assertion should be a historical benchmark that captures the Reformation's *intent*, regardless of Protestant or Roman Catholic allegiances today. One need not be a Protestant to recognize this conspicuous historical truth: *the Reformers did not think the Reformation was primarily a revolution for new, modern ideas, but a retrieval and renewal of the one, holy, catholic, and apostolic church.*[8] Whether one thinks the Reformers were correct is a theological matter that is not the burden of this book. Whether the Reformers defined themselves by this theological conviction, however, is a historical matter, one that defined the Reformation as a whole. According to David Steinmetz,

> The goal of the reformers was not to supplant a dead or dying church with a new Christianity, as though God had written Ichabod over a moribund Christendom and repudiated his covenant. The goal of the reformers was a *reformed catholic church*, built upon the foundation of the prophets and apostles, purged of the medieval innovations that had distorted the gospel, subordinate to the authority of Scripture and the ancient Christian writers, and continuous with what was best in the old church. As they saw it, *it was this evangelical church, this reformed and chastened church, that was the church catholic. It was the innovators in Rome who could no longer pretend to be genuinely catholic and whose claim to be the custodians of a greater and unbroken tradition was patently false.* What the Protestants thought they offered was a genuine antiquity.[9]

---

6. Emphasis added. Sadoleto, 62.

7. Parker, "Introduction," 64.

8. That motive may have resulted in revolutionary consequences, but the motive itself and its accompanying reforming program was fixated on this catholic spirit.

9. Emphasis added. Steinmetz, *Luther in Context*, 129. And again, "The Lutheran program for the reformation of Christendom began with an appeal to Christian antiquity. There was, of course, nothing in the sixteenth century less revolutionary and more traditional than an appeal to the past. Sixteenth-century Christians, both Protestant and Catholic, shared a strong cultural assumption that what is older is better than what is new. That assumption applied not only to religion but to civic and cultural relations, art and architecture, law and custom, economic and agricultural practices—in short, to the whole range of activities and beliefs that gives human society its character. The modern notion that new things are generally better and ought, in a well-ordered society, to supplant what is older was, on the whole, an idea that had not yet found a home in sixteenth-century Europe. The cultural bias was in favor of what was sound, tested, ancient, and rooted in the collective experience of generations" (127).

A *reformed catholic church*—that label (and goal) captures the title and subtitle of this project.

The Reformers believed they had every right to claim allegiance to the church catholic (universal). On account of deviations within the church of Rome, specifically the papacy, the Reformers mustered their disciples to reform, retrieve, and renew the church's catholicity. Again, Calvin and his reply to Sadoleto is a window into their motivation. The church *catholic*—which Calvin defined as the "society of all the saints . . . spread over the whole world"—stands on three pillars: doctrine, discipline, and sacraments. The Reformers had labored to preserve each, said Calvin, linking arms with the church catholic who understood these marks according to their pure, scriptural meaning.

Rome, in contrast, had undermined such fidelity. "The truth of prophetical and evangelical doctrine, on which the Church ought to be founded, has not only in a great measure perished in your Church, but is violently driven away by fire and sword." Calvin asked, "Will you obtrude upon me, for the Church, a body which furiously persecutes everything sanctioned by our religion, both as delivered by the oracles of God, and embodied in the writings of holy Fathers, and approved by ancient Councils?" Calvin, at this point, reached a fever pitch: "Where, pray, exist among you any vestiges of that true and holy discipline which the ancient bishops exercised in the Church? Have you not scorned all their institutions? Have you not trampled all the canons under foot? Then, your nefarious profanation of the sacraments I cannot think of without the utmost horror."[10]

Calvin was convinced the Reformation was catholic at its core, and according to his own testimony, he was horrified by its distortion with more modern innovations. Calvin and the Reformers, says Bruce Gordon, "would have hated the idea of Rome being called Catholic."[11] Calvin considered his reforming program a renewal rather than a departure from the one, holy, catholic, and apostolic church. If anyone had strayed from true catholicity, it was Rome, said Calvin.

ROMAN BUT CATHOLIC?

Calvin's argument was not unique, as if catholicity was segregated to the Reformed wing of the Reformation. The German wing of the Reformation thought along the same lines: "Luther, who seems to have read and admired Calvin's letter [to Sadoleto], was in fundamental agreement with its argument."[12] For example, when Henry of Braunschweig accused Luther of betraying the church universal with innovation and heresy, Luther became furious. "They allege that we have fallen away from the holy church and set up a new church."

---

10. Calvin, "Reply to Sadoleto," 63.

11. Gordon, *Calvin*, xi.

12. "The Catholic church was riddled with innovations introduced over centuries of inattention and theological laxity. By submitting themselves to Scripture and the writings of the ancient fathers, the Protestant communities were purging themselves of such unwanted innovations and returning to a more ancient and therefore purer form of ecclesiastical life and thought." Steinmetz, *Luther in Context*, 128.

No, Luther said in response, "We are the true ancient church . . . you have fallen away from us."[13] Yet even outside Luther's reaction to Henry, numerous other assertions of catholicity among German Reformers existed.

For example, consider Philip Melanchthon, the Wittenberg professor of Greek, author of the *Loci Communes*, and architect of the Augsburg Confession, that foundational document of Lutheran concord. When Melanchthon commented on the meaning of the word *catholic* in the creed, he claimed that a Reformation church was a true representation of creedal fidelity. His argument relied on his definition of the catholic, universal church. The church "is an assembly dispersed throughout the whole world and . . . its members, wherever they are, and however separated in place, accept and externally profess one and the same utterance or true doctrine throughout all ages from the beginning until the very end," said Melanchthon. The church is invisible, dispersed across time and space, but a local, visible assembly knows whether it is part of this universal church by whether or not it confesses the one and the same true doctrine. In Melanchthon's estimation, the credibility of the Reformation did not depend primarily on the visible—kneeling before the Eucharist, venerating images of saints, going on pilgrimages to the Vatican—but the invisible truth of their doctrine.[14] The Reformers proclaimed "one and the same . . . true doctrine," and as that doctrine was heard and embraced within by faith alone, the reforming church knew they were part of the of assembly dispersed "throughout all ages."[15]

As for Rome, she claimed to be purely catholic, but her theological beliefs and ecclesiastical configuration proved otherwise, said Melanchthon: "It is one thing to be called catholic, something else to be catholic in reality." In other words, "Those are truly called catholic who accept doctrine of the truly catholic church, i.e., that which is supported by the witness of all time, of all ages, which believes what the prophets and apostles taught, and which does not tolerate factions, heresies, and heretical assemblies."[16] The papacy could accuse the Reformers of heresy, but the reforming church was on the side of orthodoxy. The papacy might be Roman, but it was not purely catholic, he concluded.

According to various Reformers, Rome defined catholicity in a far *too narrow sense*, tapering Christianity's catholicity to its institutional badges. The Vatican aligned its children under an institutional umbrella, but an umbrella confined to external distinctives such as apostolic succession, papal supremacy, transubstantiation, and indulgences. Outside its institutional walls no salvation was possible (which raised major questions about the entire Eastern church, at least in the minds of Reformers). Conformity, therefore, was paramount to soteriological, ecclesiastical fidelity. That conformity presupposed Rome was in continuity with the past, a continuity that included both her beliefs (from indulgences

---

13. *LW* 41:194.
14. Although I will argue in chapters 14–15 that Calvin did have a place for living icons.
15. *CR* 24.397–99.
16. *CR* 24.397–99. Cf. McGrath, *Reformation Thought*, 160.

to purgatory) and her organization (from papacy to supremacy). In the eyes of Rome, the Reformers transgressed that fundamental principle of continuity by introducing novel heresies. Therefore, excommunication was entirely appropriate. The church needed to expunge the unorthodox virus.[17]

In response the Reformers refused to delimit catholicity to such narrow, external—and *Roman*—confines. They could reject purgatory and penance alike because these were not products of the ancient church but recent accretions, even modern corruptions. A return to both Calvin and Melanchthon's words revealed a different standard of catholicity: sound doctrine.[18] Catholicity is a *theological* matter, they said. Their spiritual bond with the church universal was stronger than institutional externals. Although the Reformers desired—even craved—external, international concord, their ecclesiastical threads consisted of gospel continuity. By retaining Christ and his grace, the Reformers linked arms not only with the apostles but with the core of Christianity, both its patristic and medieval representatives.

While Rome had the political and ecclesiastical power to expel the Reformers, the Reformers were not so easily dismissed. They considered themselves members of the one, holy, catholic, and apostolic church, however small or challenged or powerless they might have appeared. Their intention from the start, as Luther's life demonstrated, was to reform the church *from within*, to bring about genuine *catholic* renewal by means of its own members. It was Rome's decision, not Luther's, to oust the "heretics." When threatened with expulsion, the Reformers were unwilling to sacrifice the staple of catholicity—professing one and the same true doctrine with the church from its beginning—for the sake of institutional unity. Unity—*catholic* unity—could not be sacrificed on the altar of conformity to Rome. For a unity substantiated by the catholicity of their doctrine was their direct line of continuity with the church universal, however hostile the church of Rome might become. Therefore, with Rome's accusation of innovation in mind, Melanchthon responded in his *Loci Communes* (1543) with this clarification: "I am not creating new opinions. Nor do I believe that any greater crime can be committed in the church than to play games by inventing new ideas, departing from the prophetic and apostolic Scripture and the true consensus of the church of God. Further, I am following and embracing the teaching of the church at Wittenberg and those adhering to it. This teaching unquestionably is the consensus of the catholic church of Christ, that is, of all learned men in the church of Christ."[19]

---

17. Alister McGrath says it so well: "Catholic opponents of the Reformation declared that Protestants had broken away from the Catholic church by introducing innovations (such as the doctrine of justification by faith alone) or by abandoning the traditional structures of the church (such as the papacy and the episcopacy).... It was clear to the Catholic opponents of the Reformation that this continuity had been destroyed or disregarded by the Reformers, with the result that Protestant congregations could not be regarded as Christian churches, in any meaningful sense of the word." McGrath, *Reformation Thought*, 160.

18. Again, McGrath: "Protestant writers argued that the essence of catholicity lay not in church institutions, but in matters of doctrine.... Historical or institutional continuity was secondary to doctrinal fidelity." McGrath, 160.

19. *LC 43*, 15.

Calvin, Luther, and Melanchthon were only a few in the immense chorus of Reformers who sang this same tune. As this book will make plain, the Reformation's insistence on catholicity was the blood that kept its heart pumping, from Luther to Melanchthon, from Bullinger to John Jewel, from Calvin to Cranmer, from Bucer to Vermigli. However, some old and new histories of the Reformation portray the sixteenth-century movement in categories that run counter to the Reformation's own testimony to catholicity.

INTERPRETATIONS OF THE REFORMATION

Over the last century, the Reformation's self-confessed identity (catholicity) has not always been appreciated or understood with accuracy. Consider several reasons why.

Lamenting the Reformation as Schism and the Seed of Secularism: The Secularization Narrative

Interpreted as a deviation from the church catholic and its view of God and the world, the Reformation has been labeled the birth mother of all that is schismatic and sectarian on one hand and all that is modern and secular on the other hand. Such an approach takes on many different shades.

First, some historians focus mostly on *schism* and blame the intrinsic divisiveness of the Reformation on various factors. For example, the Reformers taught the priesthood of believers, a doctrine that decreased the gap between clergy and laity. When coupled with the belief in *sola scriptura*, each Christian became his own arbitrator, deciding for himself what the Bible really said. This is Protestantism's dangerous idea, and it was not only revolutionary but also inspired revolution itself. Its effects were ravaging: ecclesiastical and political authorities were questioned, which at times led to rebellion and revolution.[20]

For others, the Reformation's schismatic nature stemmed from a posture of criticism that precluded catholicity from the start. Even the label *Protestantism* reveals a fixation with protest that is destructive for Christianity, past, present, and future. The Reformation, therefore, was tragic because it did not unite but divided Christendom.[21] Depending on how sympathetic this interpretation is toward Protestantism, it may even label the Reformers as schismatics.

---

20. Whether or not they are lamenting the Reformation as schism, some frame the Reformation as schism, or a break to start a new church: e.g., Ryrie, *Protestants*; McGrath, *Christianity's Dangerous Idea*; and McGrath, *Historical Theology*, 125.

21. Leithart, *The End of Protestantism*. Vanhoozer responds to Leithart's interpretation of the Reformation with the following correction: "However, contra Leithart, the fundamental gesture of Protestantism is not negative but affirmative. The Reformers did not view themselves as schismatics, nor were they. To protest is to testify *for* something, namely, the integrity of the gospel, and, as we will see, this includes the church's catholicity. It also includes prophetic protest (the negative gesture) whenever and wherever the truth of the gospel is at risk. Unity alone (*sola unitats*) is not enough unless the unity in question is a *unitas* of *veritas* (truth)." Vanhoozer then offers his own interpretation, one far more in line with this book: "the only true Protestant—a biblical, Christ-centered Protestant, whose conscience is indeed captive to the gospel—is a catholic Protestant." Vanhoozer, *Biblical Authority after Babel*, 15.

Blaming the Reformation for schism may be an ongoing, contemporary maneuver, but it is also as old as the Reformation itself. In the sixteenth century, Rome blamed the Reformers for schism in the church, and once the Council of Trent concluded, this accusation became formal, setting the trajectory for the centuries ahead. This interpretation—the Reformation as a schismatic sect—has been recapitulated by Roman Catholics since.[22]

Second, if some interpreters blame schism on the Reformation, others hold the Reformers accountable for an unwitting *secularism*.[23] The two interpretations are not unrelated. To hold the Reformers responsible for secularism, one must first decide that the Reformers were in some sense revolutionaries—religious revolutionaries but perhaps even political revolutionaries. The method of interpretation is not all that different either: the Reformers created this revolution by heralding the primacy of Scripture, which then gave every individual and every society the right to decide for themselves what they believed. The Reformers could not agree with each other, and the history of Protestantism since has followed suit with one denominational split after another. Hermeneutical pluralism has resulted in religious pluralism, as everyone claims to possess the only true interpretation of the text, and anyone can claim an exclusive legitimate application of Scripture to church and society. *Sola scriptura* is dangerous because it rebels against the authority of the church for the sake of the individual's rights. That, in turn, is a recipe for secularism, in which everyone becomes his own authority. Granted, the Reformers did not intend to create a secularist revolution. Yet as soon as they turned to the individual's interpretation of the Bible, they elevated a subjectivism that could only lead to modernity and the triumph of the self over received ecclesiastical beliefs.

Such an interpretation depends on a reading of the late medieval era as well. On one hand, this interpretation observes a true shift that started with Duns Scotus in the thirteenth century but culminated with the *via moderna* (modern way), as represented by William of Ockham in the fourteenth century and Gabriel Biel in the fifteenth century. The *via moderna* was a reaction against the *via antiqua* (old way), especially as it was embodied in Thomas Aquinas. As chapter 4 will explore, Thomas believed that the Creator and the creature can be properly related to one another by an analogy of being.[24] The incomprehensible God is infinite and eternal, while the creature is finite and temporal. He is pure actuality itself, while the creature is defined by a passive potency—God is being, but the creature is becoming. Therefore, predication must occur within the parameters of likeness.[25] For instance, the creature may possess love in his heart,

---

22. E.g., Denifle, *Luther et le Luthéranisme*, ch. 4.

23. Gregory, *Unintended Reformation*. For a more recent example of a scholar who sees himself carrying the baton of the Bred Gregory narrative, see Saak, *Luther and the Reformation of the Later Middle Ages*.

24. "The forms of the things God has made do not measure up to a specific likeness of the divine power; for the things that God has made receive in a divided and particular way that which in Him is found in a simple and universal way." Aquinas, *SCG* 1.32.2.

25. Predication is the "act of affirming something of a subject" or "assigning something to a class" or

but however pure that love may be, it only images the love of God. For unlike the creature's love, God's love is an infinite love, an eternal love, an immutable love, and a most holy love. Analogical predication assumes a Creator-creature paradigm of *participation*. Since God is simple (without parts), all that is in God *is* God. As Thomas said, "There is nothing in God that is not the divine being itself, which is not the case with other things."[26] God does not depend on another being for his being, but he is life in and of himself (aseity). Therefore, this self-sufficient God is the source of the creature's being and happiness. In him the creature lives and moves and has his being, as Paul told the Athenians, quoting their own Greek poets in Acts 17:28.[27] Participation, in other words, depends on the analogy of being.

For reasons that will be explored in chapter 5, Scotus rejected analogical predication for univocal predication instead (although Thomas was not the direct target). Univocal predication is "attributing the predicate to two or more subjects in a *completely similar sense*."[28] For Scotus univocal predication was a claim about the type of knowledge man has of God, not necessarily (or at least not primarily, as we will see) an ontological claim. Univocal predication seemed like an innocent move to Scotus and his disciples. However, to his critics substituting univocal for analogical predication was a serious, even colossal shift, one impossible to sever from ontology. Prior to Scotus, Scholastics like Aquinas spoke of the analogy of being in the same breath as God who is pure being—metaphysics and theology could not be segregated as they were with later Scholastics. For instance, if love is predicated to God in a "completely similar sense" as love in the creature, God becomes another being like all the other beings, only greater. Univocity of being does not necessarily entail a total dependence of the creature on the Creator, but now the creature can be his own, independent being in the world. His will may even be autonomous from God's will, introducing a competitive relationship between God and man, grace and nature, faith and reason in which both parties vie for influence and jurisdiction. As a result, the tapestry of the participation paradigm articulated by classical theism is severed.[29]

Scotus, followed by Ockham and Biel, also introduced a voluntarism that elevated God's will over his intellect and privileged his absolute power to do

---

"naming something as possessing some act or perfection or as belonging to some other act or perfection," may be univocal, equivocal, or analogical. Analogical predication is "attributing a perfection to an object in a sense partially the same and partially different from the attribute of the same when applied to some other objects." For both definitions, see Wuellner, *Dictionary of Scholastic Philosophy*, s.v. "predication."

26. Aquinas, *SCG* 1.32.3.

27. Acts 17:28.

28. Wuellner, *Dictionary*, s.v. "predication," emphasis added.

29. Thomas anticipated as much; see *SCG* 1.32.6. Some might object that univocity does not fall outside the boundaries of classical theism, only Aquinas's version of classical theism. However, Aquinas aside, demonstrating that univocity was acceptable to the Great Tradition from the church fathers to the High Middle Ages is a tall order, especially when evidence exists to the contrary (see White, ed., *The Analogy of Being: Invention of the Antichrist or Wisdom of God?*). Furthermore, the Reformed Orthodox of the sixteenth through eighteenth centuries often considered the analogy of being representative of classical theism on the whole. Muller has shown that the majority of Reformed Orthodox outright rejected Scotus's univocity of being. See Muller, "Not Scotist," 127–50.

anything at all (so long as the law of noncontradiction was not violated). In the hands of Ockham and Biel, the implications for salvation were momentous: God is not bound to reward an act of merit according to a fixed standard of righteousness and justice. Rather, God is free to enact a covenant that declares—simply by divine fiat and will—that *if* the sinner does his best, *if* he does what lies within him, then he will be accepted by God and rewarded with further distributions of grace (see chapter 5). This covenantal, voluntarist paradigm provoked the charge of Pelagianism (or Semi-Pelagianism at best) from the *schola Augustiniana moderna* (e.g., Thomas Bradwardine and Gregory of Rimini), who said it betrayed not only Scripture but the Augustinian view of grace that earlier Scholastics taught.

Behind Ockham's voluntarism resided nominalism.[30] In the Platonist tradition, its advocates were realists, convinced that reality is more than individual, particular things. Reality cannot be limited to that which is sensible, as if the world is merely material and mechanical. Rather, reality is structured by two tiers, a sensible world of becoming and an intelligible world of Being. Such a belief in transcendence entailed the existence of universals. To that end, Platonists developed a theory of Forms or Ideas: for example, there are red squares and blue squares, silver squares and gold squares, but their similarity can be explained by their participation in a perfect Form called square. By that logic, Platonists could posit the existence of transcendentals: goodness, truth, and beauty. Disagreements occurred over whether Forms or Ideas exist in a separate realm (Plato believed in transcendental universals) or subsist and inhere within concrete particulars (Aristotle believed in concrete, immanent universals). Nonetheless, they all considered themselves Platonists in this sense: they all agreed that reality is defined by the existence of universals—they were all *realists* even if they disagreed on a specific theory. Over against other ancient philosophies, Platonism believed in a transcendent reality that could not be reduced to materiality with all its limitations. A divine Being could exist who was not bound by the restrictions of space and time, a Being on which all else depends upon and participates in to live and move and have its being. Platonism's radical idea—realism—was not merely agreeable to the Great Tradition, as if it was merely a compatible philosophy to buttress Christian theology. Realism was far more: the true outlook on the sensible world and transcendent Being. As chapter 5 will explore, the Great Tradition—from the Cappadocians to Augustine, from Boethius to Thomas Aquinas—believed in a realist metaphysic. By a process of refinement, they *critically appropriated* Platonism in variegated ways to explain how reality participates in the likeness of God. For example, in an original synthesis Thomas Aquinas corrected and transformed Platonism, explaining the creature's participation in the likeness of the Creator by locating Ideas in the mind of God, yet he used Aristotelian vocabulary (e.g., act, potency) to explain his Christian transcendentalism. For reasons that will be explained in

---

30. Some believe it may be more precise to label him a conceptualist; see chapter 5.

chapter 5, however, Ockham considered universals illogical. In fact, universals are mere *nomina*, names we assign. As a result, individual things do not have to be substantiated by universals outside the mind. In the eyes of his critics, if Ockham's voluntarism redirected attention away from God's intellect to God's will, then his nominalism redirected attention away from universals to individual objects, the particulars, provoking his critics to charge him planting the seeds of subjectivism, skepticism, and secularism. Once more the participation paradigm was severed, this time by the blade of nominalism.

Everything said so far is an interpretation with historical precedent, and chapters 4 and 5 will labor to define the differences between the classical realism of fathers like Augustine to scholastics like Thomas Aquinas and the paradigm shift to univocity and voluntarism with Scotus and nominalism with Ockham and Biel. Although debated, Radical Orthodoxy is right that these late medieval scholastics bear a certain degree of blame for the advent of later modernity, even if the modern turn was only present in seed form.[31] The consequences of univocity, voluntarism, and nominalism are not to be dismissed. However, Radical Orthodoxy makes a controversial pivot when it then points its finger at the Reformers as if they were *the carriers* of this voluntarist, nominalist virus, or, to change metaphors, the farmers who spread the seeds that then sprouted in the modern era. The accusation is twofold: First, by virtue of their voluntarism, the Reformers said justification is now a legal transaction in which God, by the unilateral power of his will, simply *declares* the sinner righteous. Second, as a result, Radical Orthodoxy believes the sinner's intimate participation in God, on which he depends for his internal, holy transformation, is now questioned. In the spirit of nominalism, the Reformers substituted a legal fiction, an *external*, imputed righteous status for the *internal*, infused righteousness of their ancestors. The forensic triumphed over the medicinal, an exterior transaction for an interior renovation. The Reformers have been accused of severing the tapestry of participation—man is no longer made righteous but merely receives an announcement—introducing yet another wedge between God and man. That substitution may occur in soteriology, but it is merely one effect of exchanging a realist for a voluntarist, nominalist metaphysic.[32]

---

31. Although, as chapter 5 will explain, Radical Orthodoxy's representation of Scotus may need some correcting and further nuance to be accurate.

32. Different scholars have adopted this interpretation, but not always with the same emphasis nor always with the same aggressiveness. Still, a version of this narrative has been perpetuated by a host of contemporary thinkers, even if in different ways and to different degrees. Consider, Grummett, *Henri de Lubac and the Shaping of Modern Theology*; Milbank, *Theology and Social Theory*; Milbank, "Alternative Protestantism," 25–41; Milbank, Pickstock, and Ward, eds., *Radical Orthodoxy: A New Theology*; Dupre, *Passage to Modernity*; Dupre, *The Enlightenment and the Intellectual Foundations of Modern Culture*; Boersma, *Heavenly Participation* (11, 84–94); Boersma, *Nouvelle Théologie and Sacramental Ontology;* Taylor, *A Secular Age*; Funkenstein, *Theology and the Scientific Imagination*; Gregory, *Unintended Reformation*; Meyendorff, *Catholicity and the Church*, 75; Ward, "The Church as the Erotic Community," 167–204; Pickstock, *After Writing*, 156–57. For a critique, consult Cross, *Duns Scotus*; Adams, *Some Later Medieval Theories of the Eucharist*; Adams, *What Sort of Human Nature?*; and Horton, *Justification*, 1:311–35, who uses the label "Scotus story" taken from Horan, *Postmodernity and Univocity*, 7.

For example, John Milbank accuses the Reformers (especially Calvin) of destroying the catholic fabric of participation and as a result divorcing God from the sinner due to a unilateral gift of grace. Others have joined this chorus by labeling Calvin a voluntarist and nominalist, convinced he opened the door to the Enlightenment's radical dualism between divinity and humanity, faith and reason, Scripture and science.[33] The argument, however, can be applied to numerous other areas as well. For instance, by redefining Rome's sacramentalism, the mechanism for man's participation in God, the Reformers took away the Creator's ability to communicate his grace in and through the material realm, the Eucharist being one major example. Or consider the Reformation and hermeneutics: the Reformers, so it is claimed, set the literal sense of Scripture over against the spiritual sense. Without the participation metaphysic of classical realism, their hermeneutic was not primarily concerned with a divine authorial intent that inheres across the canon, as exemplified in the allegorical and christological hermeneutic of the church fathers. Instead, they preoccupied themselves with the human author and his grammatical-historical rendering of the text. *Sola scriptura*, imputed righteousness, the literal sense, and so on—here lie the symptoms of a voluntarist, nominalist paradigm that cannot retain participation in God and by consequence bakes into Christianity the secularism of a modern world. Perhaps we are justified to label this interpretation the *secularization narrative.*

The secularization narrative, however, overlooks how complicated and variegated both the medieval and Reformation eras could be, and it also overlooks the immediate heirs of the Reformation, namely, the Protestant Scholastics. Certainly a shift occurred in the late medieval era with Scotus, Ockham, and Biel, one that departed in significant ways from both the patristic era and the early and High Middle Ages, including earlier forms of Scholasticism (especially Thomism). As chapter 5 will reveal, that shift should not be underemphasized as if the changes were *merely* philosophical, as if the *via moderna*'s metaphysic had no theological, ecclesiastical, and cultural consequences. The secularization narrative is half right: the effects of this metaphysical shift left aftershock tremors well into modernity. However, a straight, unqualified line of transition between the nominalism of the *via moderna* and the Reformation must be challenged, since it is a line that involves both continuity and discontinuity, debt and rebellion. It is simply not true to say that the Reformers and their Protestant heirs absorbed and advanced those radical changes *in toto* and are therefore responsible for advancing the modern way as a precursor to secularism. While the reasons are many, consider three.

First, the secularization narrative's categories are not nuanced enough. One major reason the secularization narrative can be so persuasive is due to the rhetoric of the Reformers, especially the way they appear to set in stone an antithesis.

33. Milbank, *Theology and Social Theory*; Milbank, "Alternative Protestantism," 25–41; Milbank, "Only Theology Overcomes Metaphysics," 325–343; Milbank, Pickstock, and Ward, eds., *Radical Orthodoxy*; Oliver, "The Eucharist before Nature and Culture," 331–51; Ward, "The Church as the Erotic Community," 167–204; Ward, *Cities of God*, 161–67. One of the best critiques of these voices is Billings, *Calvin, Participation, and the Gift*.

The Reformers may appear to be sold out nominalists and voluntarists because they operated with a strong polemic against Rome that can seem like a hard dichotomy. As Michael Horton observes, "Critics often focus on 'dualism' as the tie that binds the Reformation to nominalism: church versus state, God's agency versus human agency, sacred versus secular, revelation versus reason, and so forth." Yet does such a charge assume too much, as if to differentiate is to sever altogether? The "charge assumes that *distinctions* are *separations*, which is certainly not characteristic of the Lutheran or Reformed treatment of these topics. In fact, more than Radical Orthodoxy, the Reformers affirmed the temporal city, common grace, and common callings in the world."[34]

Furthermore, even if the Reformers were influenced by voluntarism and nominalism, the following claims are all unfounded: (1) the Reformation as a movement should be defined by an absorption of voluntarism and nominalism; (2) the Reformers were marked by voluntarism and nominalism in equal measure; (3) the Reformers imbibed the voluntarism and nominalism system *as a whole*.[35] Granted, some Reformers were no doubt influenced by nominalism in a variety of ways. And yet, the historian possesses no little evidence that Reformers like Luther took issue with the soteriological outcome of a voluntarist and nominalist philosophy. As chapters 5 and 8 will explain at length, the German Reformation started because Martin Luther revolted against *Ockham and Biel's* voluntaristic, nominalistic justification theology, which he was taught and even tried to practice at first. When Luther named Ockham and Biel in his 1517 *Disputation against Scholastic Theology*, one thing was clear: Luther was not the same as before. Even if signs of voluntarism and nominalism persisted in other ways, which they did, Luther was adamant in his hostile stance against the voluntarist, nominalist soteriology of the *via moderna*. Now he was on a mission to warn his colleagues, which put him at odds with those who educated the young Luther. However, Luther became more convinced with each passing year that his protest put him in continuity with the church catholic, especially Augustine. One could even describe Luther's journey toward Augustine's theology of grace as a journey away from the Pelagian or Semi-Pelagian voluntarist, nominalist soteriology of the *via moderna*.[36] In the end, Luther believed his discontinuity with the *via moderna* in soteriology manifested a line of continuity with an older, more catholic heritage.

Second, the secularization narrative fails to consider the Reformation's relationship to classical theism and its orthodoxy, including the doctrine of God and its metaphysical underpinnings (i.e., classical realism). Claiming the Reformers abandoned the realist metaphysic of the *via antiqua* for the

34. Horton, 1:313.

35. See chapter 5 for a fuller treatment on the issue. Others have made this point, including Kolb, *Martin Luther,* 31; Rupp, *The Righteous God,* 87–101.

36. To what degree that change also meant a shift away from nominalism to realism in Luther's epistemology and metaphysic remains fruitful for further inquiry.

nominalist metaphysic of the *via moderna* is so startling because the first generation of Reformers did not even address such matters. Their focus was occupied by soteriological and ecclesiastical polemics. While accents may have been present, a mature treatment of metaphysics was not.[37]

Furthermore, even when someone like Luther made a sweeping condemnation of scholastic metaphysics, for example, the reader should remember that (1) Luther's context often specifies something or someone specific he was reacting against, and (2) the story of the Reformation does not rise and fall with Luther, as if influences of nominalism in the German Reformer mean other Reformers across Europe followed the same fate, let alone the Reformation as a whole.

As for second generation Reformers and their Reformed Scholastic heirs, it is simply not true that they jettisoned a classical theology proper, along with its realist metaphysic of participation. Nor is it true that they left behind Thomism entirely with its reliance on the analogy of being and instead sold out to the univocal predication that buttressed Scotus' voluntarism or the nominalism that fueled Ockham's soteriology, thereby rupturing the creature's participation in the Creator. As chapter 4 on Thomism will reveal, many second-generation Reformers as well as their Reformed Scholastic successors did not withhold their criticisms of Thomas Aquinas on infused righteousness and transubstantiation, disagreeing with the way he applied realism to these doctrines. However, in innumerable other areas they were influenced by Thomas, even indebted to Thomas. One such area was metaphysics and its consequences for theology, as they aligned themselves with Thomas's realist paradigm of participation and considered it essential to their agreement with Thomas's Trinitarian and christological orthodoxy.[38] That line of continuity was not limited to theology proper either but extended to other areas as well—hermeneutics, natural theology, providence, hylomorphist anthropology, Christian virtue and ethics, and so on. For this reason, chapter 4 will emphasize the innumerable ways Protestants of diverse stripes retrieved Thomism, a point historians like Richard Muller and David Steinmetz have proved at great length.[39]

That is no small point since Protestant Scholastics lived on the eve of modernity itself, if not within its early lifespan. If anyone should have been the carrier

---

37. "Although, Scotist as well as Thomist, nominalist, and Augustinian accents are evident among the Reformers of the first two generations, what we do not find is a fully developed metaphysics and certainly not any indication of how they might have dealt with the question of univocity of being." Muller, "Not Scotist," 130.

38. I am not claiming Thomism was the only metaphysic that claimed to adhere to orthodoxy and explain its rationale. Others, such as Bonaventure, disagreed with Thomas and offered an alternative metaphysic without turning to nominalism like Ockham (see Copleston, *History of Philosophy*, 2:250–92). Furthermore, as later chapters will assume, a variety of groups (e.g., monasticism, Renaissance humanism) influenced the Reformed Orthodox, for example. Nevertheless, as historians like Richard Muller and Carl Trueman have demonstrated, the Thomist metaphysic profoundly influenced the Reformed Orthodox in a way that proved strategic to their polemical and confessional writings. See chapter 4.

39. To be clear, this book's purpose is not to provide a critique of that misconception which blames the Reformers for bringing nominalism into modernity. The scholarship of Muller, Steinmetz, and others speaks for itself, and I need not reproduce it here. This book, rather, builds on their scholarship to cast the history of the Reformation in a better light—one of renewing the church catholic.

of a Scotus-Ockham metaphysic, blameworthy for cutting the cord of participation and giving birth to modernity, it should be them. And yet, in Muller's
sweeping survey of Reformed Scholastics—Zanchi, Daneau, Beza, Keckermann,
Crakanthorpe, Timpler, Maccovius, and so on—he concludes, "Scotist language of the univocity of being is not at all characteristic of Reformed orthodox
thought." Contrary to caricatures, the "documentary evidence points specially
toward a diverse reception of arguments concerning predication . . . and a positive interest in Thomist as opposed to Scotist formulations."[40] The language of
"interest" is not strong enough. They "echoed Aquinas by grounding the analogy
in a doctrine of participation," says Muller. "Against the negative approach of
Radical Orthodoxy and [Brad] Gregory, we offer a significantly firmer verdict.
Whatever one concludes concerning the implications of the univocity of being,
the claim that the concept invested itself in Protestant theology cannot be sustained, nor indeed that early modern Protestant thought evidenced a 'shift' away
from a 'metaphysics of participation.' In short, their claim that the absorption of
the concept of the univocity of being into early modern Protestantism accounts
for the perceived problems of twentieth and twenty-first century secular culture
is seen to be a sorry imposture."[41]

Perhaps the misconception perpetuated by the secularization narrative, then,
is due to an overreaction. For instance, could critics be overplaying signs of voluntarism and nominalism even in the first- and second-generation Reformers?
If Calvin or Peter Martyr Vermigli, for example, emphasized the sovereign will
of God in predestination or providence, that does not necessarily entail that
they were carriers of a voluntarism or nominalism in the same vein as Soctus,
Ockham, and Biel. While influence is possible (though direct influence is difficult to prove), it is also likely that the Reformers were just as influenced, if
not more so, by the Pauline and Augustinian emphasis on the power of God in
salvation, the latter having implicit overtones of realism. Likewise, if Luther and
Martin Bucer emphasized justification as a legal declaration, that is not to be
equated with Ockham and Biel's covenantal voluntarism by which God accepts
the sinner's best merit by divine fiat. The former rooted God's justification of the
ungodly in the actual righteousness of his Son, while the latter determined God's
acceptance of the sinner on the basis of a divine will that conditions approval on
man doing what lies within him (Pelagianism or Semi-Pelagianism).[42] One still
contains the threads of a participation fabric, however rearranged and refined;
the other has cut that fabric altogether. In short, nominalist voluntarists believed
in the sovereign will of God and the declaratory nature of his Word, but not
all who believed in the sovereign will of God and the declaratory nature of his
Word were nominalist voluntarists—such a fallacy should be avoided.

---

40. "There is also, contra [Brad] Gregory, no ground for claiming a nearly universal Suarezian metaphysics." Muller, "Not Scotist," 145.

41. Muller, "Not Scotist," 145, 146.

42. Consider Horton, *Justification*, 1:316, 322–33.

The contrast in these examples becomes all the more apparent when one considers how hostile Luther was to the soteriology that stemmed from Ockham and Biel's nominalist and voluntaristic metaphysic. The same can be said of Calvin's antagonism to the nominalists at Sorbonne. Meanwhile, others like Martin Bucer, Peter Martyr Vermigli, and Girolamo Zanchi could be explicit in their critical appropriation of a Thomistic metaphysic, however much it had to be modified to meet the outcome of their Reformed soteriology.

Furthermore, ascribing to a monolithic influence is simplistic; the Reformers were far more complicated. Luther, for example, was not influenced by one but many different streams of medieval thought. As chapter 2 will reveal, German mysticism moved Luther's piety. Since German mysticism cannot be separated from Neoplatonism, advocates of the secularization narrative must explain why Luther is a carrier of nominalist voluntarism when his spirituality is reliant on the realist metaphysic of Christian Platonism in a way not all that different from Augustine.[43]

Third, to claim, as the secularization narrative does, that Reformers like Calvin dismantled the participation paradigm by means of a unilateral declaration of forensic imputation fails to consider their justification theology in the context of the *ordo salutis* (order of salvation). For instance, the claim forgets that Calvin positioned his doctrine of justification within his broader, more encompassing doctrine of union with Christ. Calvin's corpus as a whole, but his *Institutes* in particular, reveals a weighty emphasis on participation through union with Christ. Yet rather than sanctioning participation to one corner of soteriology (justification), Calvin allowed union to define a *duplex gratia*, a double grace—justification *and* sanctification.[44] However primary the former is to the latter as its logical cause in the *ordo salutis*, Calvin considered both essential to a full understanding of the Christian's union with Christ, a union that is the avenue to participation with God. J. Todd Billings, among others, has led the way in correcting the misconception.

> One cannot simply label Calvin's doctrine of the double grace (*duplex gratia*) wholly forensic or simply reducible to a non-forensic account of "union with Christ." Calvin's view is irreducibly forensic, but a courtroom analogy of an external, forensic decree is not the exclusive image for his theology of union with Christ and the double grace. Rather, Calvin's theology of union with Christ is articulated with reference to participation, adoption, imputation, and the wondrous exchange. It is a multifaceted doctrine, utilizing both legal and transformative images.[45]

43. Horton, 1:318, also makes this point, pushing against Lortz's two volumes: *The Reformation in Germany*.

44. E.g., Calvin, *Institutes* 3.6.1, 3, 4; 3.7.3; 3.8; 3.9.4; see my forthcoming companion book on Calvin's *Institutes* (Zondervan Academic).

45. Billings, *Calvin, Participation, and the Gift*, 23. On justification's logical and causal priority to

Calvin did not abandon participation in his soteriology due to some over-powering influence of nominalism and voluntarism. In his own mind, he merely described participation in full color. He did not ignore its transformative and internal force, but merely located the transformative in sanctification instead. In other words, Calvin did have a participation paradigm, but it was multi-dimensional, elastic enough to incorporate *both* a forensic shade (justification) and a transformative effect (sanctification), yet without ignoring its eschatological outcome (ascent to the beatific vision).[46] Furthermore, even when Calvin did describe the forensic nature of imputation, he refused to portray the doctrine as impersonal and detached, merely exterior, without participatory measure (the very accusation lobbed at the Reformers). Calvin sounded nothing like the voluntarist-nominalist tradition when he wielded the concept of participation and said, "Christ, having been made ours, makes us sharers with him in the gifts with which he has been endowed. We do not, therefore, contemplate him outside ourselves from afar in order that his righteousness may be imputed to us but

---

sanctification in Calvin, see Fesko, *Beyond Calvin*; Horton, "Calvin's Theology of Union with Christ and Double Grace," in *Justification*, 1:72–96.

46. See *Institutes* 3.6–8, 11–14. In his impressive comparison of Aquinas and Calvin, Raith argues that the reader does not see "robust signs of participation" in Calvin's commentary on Romans until chapter 6. "This is due in large part to Aquinas's doctrine of justification as transformation rather than Calvin's extrinsic-imputational understanding of justification. We discover that Calvin's understanding of justification, combined with the *way* Calvin distinguishes justification from sanctification, mutes his participatory understanding of our salvation" (*Aquinas and Calvin on Romans*, 5). I do not take issue with the differences Raith highlights between Aquinas and Calvin. However, the claim about Calvin assumes from the start that participation is exhausted by transformation, as if the two are synonymous, precluding anything "extrinsic-imputational." Under that assumption the Reformation doctrine of justification will always appear antithetical to participation. But why define participation by such narrow parameters? In other words, why should participation be limited to the transformative alone? Criticisms of Calvin reveal that one's definition of participation at the start determines whether the Reformation is a threat to or advancement on the past. Yet reasons exist for considering the legitimacy of the latter. For example, consider Calvin's doctrine of adoption. Even in human experience, participation of an orphan in his/her new family is not limited to life in the family's new house, but that transformative relationality is entirely caused by and dependent on the judge's declaration in court that the child is no longer an orphan. To claim that this external, legal determination is irrelevant to or even antithetical to "participation" is illogical. Without it, participation loses its footing. How much more so with spiritual adoption into the family of God? In short, the strength of recent scholarship like J. Todd Billings (*Calvin, Participation, and Gift*) should not be dismissed: Reformers like Calvin recognized that in a book like Romans, participation incorporates *both* the forensic and the transformative, and for that reason the concept is advanced. In his astute study, Raith does recognize this point (also made by Billings), but considers it mute in the end for this reason: "What is the nature of our participation in God's activity of saving us if Calvin declares all our works condemnable *in se* even if pardoned and rewarded *in Christo*?" (5). The question is fair enough, but far from original; the Reformers and their Reformed heirs gave an answer. First, while the Reformers distinguished between justification and sanctification, they never severed them; the former grounds and causes the latter and the latter has no legal foundation without the former. Second, if justification and sanctification are not severed, then neither the forensic nor the transformative alone must bear the full weight of participation. Both contribute in unique ways. Third, why must one set a participation *in se* over against an external-imputational pardon *in Christo*, as if the latter cannot be participatory? Again, the illustration of adoption begs to differ: by the declaration of the judge the orphan is truly part of the family even before he has eaten a meal in his new house. Fourth, the Reformed did situate the forensic (justification) *in between* the transformative in the *ordo salutis*: first is regeneration, then conversion and justification, which leads necessarily to sanctification. Reformed participation, then, is not less but more transformative than critics think. Despite these criticisms, I do appreciate Raith's conclusion that "there exists a substantial amount of harmony between Calvin and Aquinas on a number of points pertaining to the topic of participation" (12).

because we put on Christ and are engrafted into his body—in short because he deigns to make us one with him."[47]

The secularization narrative's accusation that Reformers like Calvin have betrayed the realism of the Great Tradition (the *via antiqua*) with its classical conception of God and the world is ironic. Reformers like Calvin relied on the church fathers in a variety of ways to propose a participation paradigm that had manifold consequences for his Reformed soteriology and ecclesiology, the sacraments included.

> Calvin's theology of participation emerges from a soteriology which affirms a differentiated *union* of God and humanity in creation and redemption. Through his engagement with biblical and catholic sources (especially Irenaeus, Augustine, and Cyril of Alexandria), Calvin develops a wide-ranging and emphatic doctrine of participation. In prayer, the sacraments, and obedience to the law, believers are incorporated into the Triune life: as believers are made "completely one" with Christ by faith, the Father is revealed as generous by his free pardon, and the Spirit empowers believers for lives of gratitude. In this way, Calvin's strong account of divine agency enables, rather than undercuts, human agency in sanctification. Grace fulfills rather than destroys nature, so that believers may "participate in God," the *telos* of creation. Moreover, "participation in Christ" is inseparable from participation in loving relationship of social mutuality and benevolence, both in the church and beyond its walls. At every stage, Calvin's account of participation in Christ is grounded in a participatory vision of human activity and flourishing.[48]

Far from abandoning the concept of participation, a number of Calvin scholars now recognize that *union with Christ* is an essential motif for a Reformation vision of the entire Christian faith.[49] Even when the Reformers took issue with certain patristic or medieval streams, they aligned themselves with other patristic and medieval emphases to exhibit the catholicity of their sacramental soteriology and ecclesiology. In the estimation of the Reformers, a mixture of continuity and discontinuity with patristic and medieval predecessors did not mean a departure from the realist metaphysic of participation *in toto* but rather its refinement, bringing the concept to further maturity in light of Reformation soteriology and ecclesiology.

Or consider Calvin's Christology and its corresponding spirituality, both of which were framed in the category of participation. In his commentary on Colossians, Calvin asked what Jesus meant when he told his disciples that it is expedient for him to go up to the Father. Calvin denied that the Son was

47. *Institutes* 3.1.10.
48. Billings, *Calvin, Participation, and the Gift*, 17.
49. Also, union with Christ is not limited to Calvin's theological treatises but appears throughout his sermons and commentaries. See Billings, *Calvin, Participation, and the Gift*; Gatiss, *Cornerstones of Salvation*, 43–68.

subordinate to the Father since he was "endowed with heavenly glory," which means he ascended to the Father as one who "gathers believers into participation in the Father." Calvin then zoomed out to describe the entire purpose of the incarnation through the lens of participation: "For this reason Christ descended to us, to bear us up to the Father, and at the same time to bear us up to himself, inasmuch as he is one with the Father."[50] The pattern of descent for the sake of ascent has participation in the holy Trinity as its goal. In his *Institutes* Calvin called this descent-to-ascent the "wonderful exchange" (Luther, reflecting on Christ as Jacob's ladder, called it a happy exchange). By "becoming Son of man with us, he has made us sons of God with him; that, by his descent to earth, he has prepared an ascent to heaven for us."[51] In light of these passages and many other proofs of participation in Calvin, Julie Canlis writes, Calvin "makes both the *goal* and *means* of the Christian life to be participatory communion."[52] She further demonstrates that a variety of similarities exist between Calvin and Irenaeus, both "mediating the Platonic tradition of participation in a self-consciously Trinitarian context," and at points "re-fashioned Platonic participation" to articulate the Christian's communion with the triune God.[53] From Irenaeus to Calvin, "This is not a lineage that is necessarily in competition with the Plato-Augustine-Aquinas axis celebrated by Radical Orthodoxy, although its accents and corrections need to be recognized if contemporary Christianity is to benefit truly from a retrieval of participation."[54] Therefore, mere correction does not capture this axis but *renewal*.[55]

Examples could be multiplied, but the critical point is this: the secularization interpretation may be appealing, laying the blame at the feet of the Reformers as if they were perpetuators of the late medieval shift to voluntarism and

---

50. *Comm. Col. 3:1.*

51. *Institutes* 4.17.2.

52. Canlis, *Calvin's Ladder*, 4.

53. Canlis, *Calvin's Ladder*, 17; cf. *Adversus haereses*, III.19.1. Canlis believes Calvin does not merely add Christ to the ladder of Platonic ascent, but Christ "breaks open the circle and grafts it onto himself" (44). True enough, but Canlis also claims this is a new feature original to Calvin that improves on medieval mysticism and scholasticism. That claim is too ambitious since many medievals did "graft" the circle of participation onto Christ. Canlis contrasts Calvin with the medievals—communion versus naturalization, Christ versus anthropology—as if Calvin "relocated 'participation' from between impersonals (the soul in the divine nature) to personals (the human being in Christ, by the Spirit)." However, that contrast does not take into account the trinitarian nature of medieval notions of participation. Canlis has a point that Calvin makes Christ the controlling principle of participation, but that emphasis was not entirely missing from medieval theologians, some of whom even used allegory to describe participation through a Christological lens. The medieval participation paradigm was Christological as far as it was Trinitarian (e.g., Legge, *The Trinitarian Christology of St Thomas Aquinas;* Torrell, *Spiritual Master,* volume 2 of *Saint Thomas Aquinas*). To refine Canlis's analysis, if Calvin contributed something "new" it was not the addition of Christ but the way Calvin coupled participation to his *reformed* definition of union with Christ (which then eliminated the medieval notion of merit on the ladder of ascent). Nonetheless, Canlis is correct that Calvin was an "*heir* of a rich medieval mystical and theological tradition that had inestimable impact on him" (46). In that sense, Calvin modified and transformed Platonism with the best of them. For a fuller engagement with Canlis, see Muller, *Calvin and the Reformed Tradition*, 204, 238–43, 281.

54. Canlis, *Calvin's Ladder*, 18.

55. Canlis, *Calvin's Ladder*, 20.

nominalism, cutting the cord of participation between the Creator and the creature. However, the truth of history is far more complicated and nuanced. Not only do lines of continuity exist, but so do lines of serious discontinuity exist between the Reformers and the *via moderna*. To complicate matters further, significant lines of continuity exist between the Reformers and earlier eras of Scholasticism (from the eleventh to the fourteenth centuries), not to forget the church fathers in preceding centuries. Those lines of continuity are so strong that the Reformers, facing Rome's charge of novelty and heresy, could claim to swim in the stream of the one, holy, catholic, and apostolic church. If true, these lines of continuity defy a straight, tidy line from the faults of Scotus, Ockham, and Biel to the Reformers, as if the Reformation was the carrier of the new, even secular seeds of modernism.

Celebrating the Reformation as Modernism's Liberation or Radicalism's Opposition

The secularization interpretation continues to gain traction for those who lament the Reformation. This is ironic because the history of the nineteenth and twentieth centuries voiced a similar secularizing interpretation but with cause for great celebration. Beginning in the sixteenth century, Roman Catholics interpreted the Reformation out of a spirit of grief and anger. However, modern liberalism praised the Reformers for this innovative, radical secularization. Friedrich Schleiermacher reoriented theology around the individual's subjective feeling of absolute dependence, creating a new norming norm in the Christian experience.[56]

That reorientation was the ideal framework for Adolf von Harnack and his program of deconstruction, which resulted in the modification or abandonment of traditional dogmas. Liberalism appealed to the Reformation as if the Reformers were the first to set the Christian free from dogma, those unquestioned beliefs adopted on the basis of church authority. Liberated from the shackles of tradition and its ecclesiastical guards, the Reformers could read Scripture afresh, this time by means of critical methodologies. The Reformers, in other words, planted the seeds that eventually blossomed into an enlightened future where the individual no longer depends on or must submit to ecclesiastic authority but can explore and even trust his own, internal religious instincts.[57] The Reformation gave birth to modernism.

Yet whether lamentation or celebration, each of these interpretations (in various ways) returns to a common root problem: *sola scriptura*, the priesthood of all believers, personal and subjective interpretation, and the rejection of a sacramental worldview all combine to create a Reformation that represents the antithesis of catholicity. Its subjectivism has become the mother of schism and secularism alike.

---

56. Schleiermacher, *Christian Faith*, 738–49.

57. See, e.g., Paul Tillich, *Protestant Era*; Georg Wilhelm Friedrich Hegel, *Lectures on the Philosophy of History*; Ernst Troeltsch, *Protestantism and Progress: The Significance of Protestantism for the Rise of the Modern World*.

WHAT IS BIBLICISM?

To be Protestant is to believe in biblical authority. However, biblical authority and biblicism are not synonymous. Biblicism moves beyond believing in the final authority of the Bible to imposing a restrictive hermeneutical method onto the Bible. Biblicism can be identified by the following symptoms:

(1) Ahistorical mindset: Biblicism is a haughty disregard (chronological snobbery in the words of C. S. Lewis) for the history of interpretation and the authority of creeds and confessions, chanting an individualistic mantra, "No creed but the Bible," which in practice translates into "No authority but me." *Sola scriptura* is radicalized into *solo scriptura*. As a result, biblicism fails to let theology inform exegesis, which is designed to guard against heresy.

(2) Irresponsible proof texting: Biblicism treats Scripture as if it is a dictionary or encyclopedia, as if the theologian merely excavates the right proof texts, chapter and verse, tallying them up to support a doctrine. Biblicism limits itself to those beliefs explicitly laid down in Scripture and fails to deduce doctrines from Scripture by good and necessary consequence.

(3) Anti-metaphysics: Biblicism undervalues the use of philosophy in the service of exegesis and theology. Biblicism is especially allergic to metaphysics, failing to understand how the study of being should safeguard who God is (e.g., pure act) in contrast to the creature. As a result, biblicism conflates theology and economy, as if who God is in himself can be read straight off the pages of Scripture when these pages are often focused on historical events.

(4) Univocal predication: Biblicism assumes language used of God in the text should be applied to God in a direct fashion, as if the meaning of an attribute predicated of man has the same meaning when predicated of God. By consequence, biblicism risks historicizing God by means of a literalistic interpretation of the text.

(5) Restrictive revelation: Biblicism is a suspicion or even dismissiveness toward the diverse ways God's has revealed himself, limiting itself to the book of Scripture while shunning the book of creation. Biblicism is often suspicious towards natural theology.

(6) Overemphasis on the human author: Biblicism neglects the divine author's intent and ability to transcend any one human author. As a result, biblicism struggles to explain the unity of the canon and Christological fulfillment, nor does it provide the metaphysic necessary to explain attributes of Scripture like inspiration and inerrancy.

These points are taken from my forthcoming *Systematic Theology* (Baker Academic). For a critique of biblicism today and a call to return to the Reformation understanding of authority, see R. Scott Clark's *Recovering the Reformed Confession*. As for the origins of the word, "The earliest use of the word 'biblicism' in English occurred in 1827 in a work by Sophei Finngan in criticism of 'biblicism.' In 1874 J. J. van Osterzee defined it as 'idolatry of the letter'" (19).

Unfortunately, another stream of interpretation has prevailed, but this time from within the ranks of those who claimed to be the Reformation's own heirs. Evangelical Protestants may claim rights to the heritage of the Reformation more than any other Christian tradition. How ironic, then, that evangelical

Protestants have sometimes cultivated an interpretation of the Reformation that is not all that different from the historical assumptions of modern liberalism. If modern liberalism points to the Reformation to celebrate the genesis of the enlightened individual who dispenses with tradition to stand on the autonomous stool of reason, evangelicals have sometimes embodied this same presupposition toward the Reformers but for the purpose of perpetuating a modern biblicism instead. The story of the Reformation is retold in evangelical institutions and churches as if the Reformers were radicals, throwing off the shackles of tradition, as if the church had been corrupted and lost since the apostles. In the name of *sola scriptura*, the Reformers shed a corrupt church, breaking with the church of the Middle Ages to start their own undefiled church.

Such an interpretation latches onto and (re)interprets specific narratives. Luther marched up to the castle church door and, with the world watching, nailed his Ninety-Five Theses, beginning a revolution against all things Catholic. John Knox imitated all the other Reformers when he shouted down the female rulers of his day to throw off the political powers that kept the church under the clutches of temporal authorities and their Roman allegiance. I will call this interpretation the "oppositional narrative" because it sets the Reformation in opposition to the church catholic (universal) and takes fire at the medieval Scholastics in particular. The oppositional narrative gives gusto to the phrase the Dark Ages and portrays the Reformers with their fists high in the air, standing on the Bible alone to protest a church polluted in every way.[58] In this view, the Reformation is a *break* with the past.

Four major myths (though there are likely more) tend to characterize the oppositional narrative and threaten to stand in the road to block the Reformation's self-conscious pursuit of catholicity.[59] First, according to this interpretation, the Reformation was anti-tradition. The Reformers believed *sola scriptura*, and that meant the Bible was the only authority for the church. Tradition was their enemy and threatened to seduce the Christian away from the Bible as a rival authority. The Reformers believed the right way to interpret their

---

58. The oppositional narrative, however, predates contemporary evangelicalism. In the nineteenth century, Carl Christian Ullmann drove a wedge between medieval and reformational (see his two-volume *Reformatoren vor der Reformation*). Euan Cameron says the tide has changed only in the last four decades as scholars consider the vivacity of religious life in the late Middle Ages, yet he also warns against swinging the pendulum too far, as if all was well prior to Luther. Cameron, "Reconsidering Early-Reformation and Catholic-Reform Impulses," 5; and Cameron, *European Reformation*, 119.

59. To be clear, the oppositional narrative is more of a spirit, an attitude than anything else. The point is not whether an individual holds to every one of these points (some may embody only some), but whether the spirit of them is perpetuated. Furthermore, the oppositional narrative has found its way into diverse denominations and is not limited to Baptists or Presbyterians. For example, Jordan Cooper addresses those he calls "radical Lutherans," who argue that Martin Luther made a "radical departure" from medieval Scholasticism. In contrast, Cooper claims, "The Lutheran movement is to be viewed as a development of the theology of the church catholic, accepting the theological convictions of the early and medieval church, such as the basic assumptions of classical theism, which also includes certain essentialist metaphysical notions" (*Prolegomena*, 330). Cooper warns against projecting nominalism into Lutheran confessions or even Luther's own writings. For the "Formula of Concord accepts Aristotelian metaphysics as indisputably true . . . [and] in the Heidelberg Disputation itself, Luther affirms Platonic metaphysics, and thus most certainly does not identify such with a theologian of glory" (281).

Bibles was by themselves, without the interpretations of the church. Second, the Reformation was not only anti-Catholic (Roman Catholic) but also anti-catholic (universal church), as if the true gospel and the true church had been lost since the days of the apostles, only to be recovered in the sixteenth century and faithfully preserved by means of an intentional schism and split from the church. Third, the Reformation was anti-medieval, specifically anti-Scholastic. The Reformers thought Scholasticism represented everything wrong with the church, both its beliefs and its practices. Reformation theology should be set over against medieval theology, a complete alternative to Scholasticism's speculative, rationalistic, elitist, papalist, and natural theology. Fourth, the Reformation was anti-philosophy, convinced Christianity was antithetical to Plato and Aristotle. Luther considered reason the devil's whore because medieval theology had been corrupted by Greek, pagan thought.

The best evangelical academics avoid this oppositional narrative and have set fine examples of historical nuance, exemplifying accurate representations of the Reformation. However, among the evangelical masses, the oppositional narrative is prevalent—a default position, sometimes even perpetuated in Christian universities and seminaries. Those who slip into the oppositional narrative may do so for a variety of reasons, but two stand out: (1) They desire to distinguish their Protestant beliefs from Roman Catholics today (who are always the enemy), and so they assume Roman Catholicism must exercise a rightful monopoly over vast periods of patristic and especially medieval theology. That explains, from the oppositional standpoint, why the Reformers reacted with such protest; they had to overcome the Dark Ages and introduce the light of the Scriptures for the first time since the apostles. (2) The opposition narrative is especially strategic for the pastor or professor, church or institution, that shifts from the spirit of evangelicalism to fundamentalism. It is a way to still claim the Reformers—and by default a Protestant identity—while interpreting the Reformers as radical as the interpreter's own agenda in the present day, as if the Reformers would have been in favor of the radical changes at play in the interpreter's own contemporary empire or movement.

The opposition narrative, however, is plagued with historical problems. First, it embodies a similar interpretive spirit celebrated by Protestant liberalism, only with different results. For liberals this rebel interpretation was the dawn of a new day: the advent of modernism. For evangelicals this rebel interpretation was the dawn of a new day: the advent of biblicism. Yet both interpretations assume the Reformers had abandoned the past, broke with everything catholic, and pioneered a path that took the church all the way back to the apostles and pure Christianity. All had been dark since the apostolic age, but now the Reformers had arrived, ushering in the light of a new dawn.

Second, the opposition narrative is riddled with historical confusion. Its description of the Reformers may be a fitting representation of the radical wing, but it fails as an accurate representation of the Reformers. As chapters 10–11 and 13 will explore, Rome as well as the political powers of the sixteenth century did not always distinguish between the Reformers and those who originated from within the Reformation camp but later turned radical. The Reformers labored to clarify this confusion, explaining to magistrates and ministers alike that these radicals were schismatics and extremists, betraying the Reformation program.[60] In part this explains why the Reformers were so adamant to support the authorities in their punishment of radicals. The Reformers were not sectarians but orthodox, they insisted.[61]

Third, one reason the oppositional narrative struggles to see the Reformation through the lens of catholicity—as the Reformers themselves did—is due to an unbalanced, overriding, and misinformed theological vision of the sixteenth century. At the risk of oversimplification, the Reformers sacrificed their time and gave most of their energy to countering two strands within Rome's teachings: (1) soteriology (especially justification, the sacraments, and purgatory) and (2) ecclesiology (especially papal authority over Scripture, the church, and society)—most all other grievances fall under these two doctrinal domains. But if not careful, the historian might look at the avalanche of publications by the Reformers on these *loci* and conclude that the Reformation was nothing less than a total break with the church and, with it, the past, especially the medieval past.

That is a dangerous historical presupposition. Such an outlook is, for instance, as faulty as examining Augustine's battles with Pelagianism only to conclude that he did not assume the church's prior condemnation of Arianism. It is as faulty as looking at the first of the Scholastics, Anselm of Canterbury (see chapter 3), and his defense of classical theism only to assume he did not absorb the church's prior understanding of scriptural authority. In similar fashion, the historian should not look at the sixteenth-century Reformers and their polemics over soteriology and ecclesiology—polemics that eventually resulted in their excommunication from the only church that existed—only to assume that the Reformers must not have feasted at the widespread table of catholicity on a thousand other concerns. Richard Muller's warning is sobering: "It is worth recognizing from the outset that the Reformation altered comparatively few of the major *loci* of theology: the doctrines of justification, the sacraments, and the church received the greatest emphasis—while the doctrines of God, the trinity, creation, providence, predestination, and the last things were taken over from the tradition by the magisterial Reformation virtually without alteration."[62] *Virtually without alteration*—that

---

60. To clarify, historians often use a vocabulary that situates the radicals *within* the Reformation—i.e., the radical *wing* of the Reformation. That move is true enough as the radicals did emerge from within Reformation churches (Lutheran or Reformed) and were characterized by a protest of their own. However, the magisterial Reformers themselves did not usually consider the radicals true and faithful representatives of the Reformation. As their disciplinary measures document, according to magisterial Reformers the radicals "went out from us, but they were not of us."

61. "Luther's Reformation rejected with equal vigor the heteronomy of Eck and Cochlaeus, whose institutionalism caused them to ascribe absolute authority to the empirical church, and the autonomy of Münzer and Carlstadt, whose biblicism and individualism caused them to think that each man is his own authority in religious matters." Pelikan, *Obedient Rebels*, 33.

62. Muller, "Scholasticism in Calvin," 247.

claim deserves repeating. Muller's correction is behind the inspiration of this book and its fresh introduction to the Reformation's intellectual history.

Fourth, if Muller is right, then the oppositional narrative fails to recognize the Reformation's continuity with the church catholic and its centrality to their polemics with Rome and radicals alike. If Calvin's reply to Sadoleto reveals anything at all, it exposes how far the oppositional narrative falls short. In fact, if the oppositional narrative was adopted by someone like Calvin, he would have proved Sadoleto's point: the Reformation advocated innovative doctrines and therefore sits outside the one, holy, catholic, and apostolic church. Yet the Reformers did not set out to start a new church, let alone a new denomination; they intended to reform the only church they knew, a catholic church they still believed possessed and practiced legitimate marks of a true church (e.g., baptism), even if this church was polluted by the papacy's innovations and political machinations. For example, as the Reformers wrote to defend their catholicity to Charles V in preparation for Augsburg, Johannes Eck wrote 404 fiery theses asserting that the Reformers had no right to claim continuity with the church fathers. On the heels of Eck's charges, the proponents of the Augsburg Confession made a repeated effort to buttress its orthodoxy with the church universal. Others like Martin Bucer and Wolfgang Capito did the same.[63]

As for authority, the Reformers were not advocates of the contemporary fundamentalist mantra "No creed but the Bible" but were determined to retrieve a right view of tradition (ministerial) over against Rome's faulty view of tradition (magisterial). The Reformers stood on the supreme authority of the sacred Scriptures, but only a Scripture rightly interpreted by the church and with the church catholic (universal). The Reformation did oppose Rome's elevation of tradition as a source of infallible revelation—one equal to and sometimes an interpretive authority superior to Scripture. But the Reformers also opposed the radical Reformers' rejection of tradition as both an authority and source for theology and exegetical guidance. In contrast to both groups, the Reformers affirmed tradition as a ministerial authority for the church, holding the church accountable to its creeds and councils, guiding the church in a sound, orthodox interpretation of Scripture. As David Steinmetz observed,

> While it is true that the reformers were at first optimistic that it would be possible to teach and preach a theology that was wholly biblical, they rarely intended to exclude theological sources that were non-biblical. *Sola scriptura* generally meant *prima scriptura*, Scripture as the final source and norm by which all theological sources and arguments were to be judged, not Scripture as the sole source of theological wisdom.[64]

---

63. *BDS* 3:321–38. For this story, see Greschat, *Martin Bucer*, 94–95. For other examples of this fury throughout this book, see chapter 12.

64. Steinmetz, *Luther in Context*, 129.

In other words, *sola scriptura* did not mean Scripture was the *only* or *sole* authority—that was the position of radicals. Rather, *sola scriptura* meant that "only Scripture, because it is God's inspired Word, is the inerrant, sufficient, and final authority for the church."[65]

As for soteriology, the Reformers saw themselves as Augustinians; and as far as medievals embraced an Augustinian soteriology, the Reformers had little objection.[66] Numerous examples exist and will be pursued in this book. During the English Reformation, Thomas Cranmer's treatment of justification *sola fide* in the Anglican *Book of Homilies* (1547) makes numerous allusions to the patristic and medieval church for support.[67] Likewise, when Martin Chemnitz refuted the Council of Trent, he claimed that many church fathers taught justification by faith alone and used their voices to support the Lutheran claim to catholicity.[68] Granted, the Reformers would in time add to and refine Augustine's doctrine of justification where they believed Paul taught a forensic imputation rather than a moral infusion.[69] Nevertheless, the Reformers counted themselves indebted to Augustine because he ensured that grace remained primary, not only in predestination but in regeneration and conversion. Their criticisms notwithstanding, the Reformers also recognized that *sola gratia* was not limited to the patristic era

---

65. My definition comes from my book *God's Word Alone*, 23.

66. Although we cannot engage in a tour, I am aware that a vast land of literature exists that debates the meaning of *Augustinian* in the late medieval period. Heiko Oberman, for instance, has argued for an "Augustinian Renaissance" (e.g., "Headwaters of the Reformation," 40–88), while a contemporary like E. L. Saak opposes Oberman and proposes a "historical understanding as distinct from a theological or a philosophical understanding" (*Creating Augustine*, 21). In my estimation, Steinmetz (*Luther and Staupitz*, 13–15) offers a balanced, nuanced approach, capable of acknowledging five different uses of Augustinian: (1) "the theology of the Latin West in general"; (2) "the theology of the Augustinian Order" (as taught by its members); (3) "a party within the Augustinian Order which agrees with St. Augustine on a wide range of disputed issues and at a depth which is more profound than the merely nominal Augustinianism common to all medieval theologians" (e.g., right-wing Augustinians); (4) an embrace of Augustine's theology that "translates him into the theological vocabulary of one's own circle without dulling the bracing effect of his thought" (on doctrines like original sin and predestination, for example); (5) an "embodiment of a theological tendency [Augustinianism rather than Pelagianism for example] which in special cases may go beyond their original thinking." On this fifth point, the advent of the Reformation complicated Augustinianism further. For example, "In one sense it is possible to say that Thomas Aquinas is more Augustinian than Luther on the question of merit, if the standard is fidelity to the original teaching of St. Augustine. But one can also hold . . . that Luther is more Augustinian than Thomas, if the frame of reference is the more perfect embodiment of a tendency." This project operates under the assumption that the Reformers believed that fifth point was not only legitimate but good and necessary. They not only desired at points to fit Augustine's theology but they intended to bring it to culmination, even if by refinement or reform. In that sense, they were persuaded they were truly Augustinian, even more Augustinian than their opponents. That process began, for example, when Staupitz counseled a troubled, anxious Luther and put forward theological principles by which Luther could verify he was an Augustinian as opposed to a disciple of a nominalist like Biel. As Steinmetz explains, when Staupitz elevated a theology which "gives glory to God rather than to men," he "intended it as a principle which would exclude nominalist theologies of grace," which Luther then engrafted into Protestantism. "In all these principles it was important that Staupitz was an Augustinian rather than a nominalist" (15). Judging from the Reformers' own testimonies and polemics, Steinmetz is on target.

67. Consider the footnotes of Lee Gatiss, which prove as much, in Gatiss, *First Book of Homilies*.

68. See his first and second topics in Chemnitz, *Examination of the Council of Trent*.

69. E.g., for Luther see *Dokumente zur Luthers Entwicklung*, 192, 11.25–27; cf. Calvin, *Institutes* 3.11.15; Cameron, *European Reformation*, 151.

but could be heard from the lips of many medieval Scholastics because everyone at least desired to claim Augustine's legacy (whether some could or not is another question).

Therefore, the Reformers' correlation with medieval thought is not yes *or* no but yes *and* no. Medieval thought—during the Early, High, and Late Middle Ages—was not homochromous. As chapter 5 will reveal, at least in soteriology a shift occurred in the late medieval era with the advent of the *via moderna* (Ockham, Biel), a shift the Reformers believed betrayed many who represented the *via antiqua*, including the church fathers, medievals during the Early Middle Ages, and Scholastics during the High Middle Ages. The *via moderna*'s shift motivated the *schola Augustiniana moderna*'s accusation of Pelagianism at worst or Semi-Pelagianism at best. Luther himself was trained in the *via moderna*'s soteriology, and the year that ignited the Reformation (1517) was the same year Luther opposed the *via moderna* through a public disputation. In other words, the target for the Reformation's *soteriological* protest was specific. That does not mean the *via moderna* was the only target; as the soteriological debate moved from justification to the sacramental system, others like Peter Lombard came under attack. But it does mean that an oppositional narrative is simplistic. Despite the Reformers' broad polemical rhetoric against the "Schoolmen," careful scrutiny demonstrates that specific individuals and movements were the target, not necessarily the entire Scholastic, let alone medieval, era.[70] As chapter 4 will explain, the Reformers were indebted to Scholasticism in numerous ways.

As for philosophy, the Reformation may have reacted to the way a philosopher like Aristotle was *appropriated* by papal theologians to substantiate a theology of glory (as Luther called it), but the Reformers depended on ancient, patristic, and medieval philosophy, even instituting curriculum in their universities and academies to ensure it was taught to the next generation of Protestants. Philip Melanchthon was a stalwart in this regard, as was Peter Martyr Vermigli. A contextual reading of the Reformers and specific polemical statements against "reason" or "philosophy" reveals concerns with the misuse of reason or philosophy but not a wholesale rejection of Greek thought. If the Reformers did not presuppose certain epistemological and metaphysical commitments of Greek philosophy, their polemic against Rome would have been nonsensical, and Rome could have possessed further ammunition for their charge of heresy. Furthermore, the *type* of philosophical influence on the Reformers was not uniform. At points, some Reformers showed great reliance on classical realism. At other points, some Reformers were marked by the influence of nominalism and voluntarism. While the Reformers rejected the *via moderna*'s soteriology, some of them sympathized with the *via moderna*'s broader philosophy (i.e., nominalism), while others

---

70. For example, in chapter 4 we will consider Calvin's use of "Scholastic," which does not refer to all Scholastics of the medieval era but often refers to the Sorbonne professors in his own context, those *scholastici* (Latin) or *Sorbonnists* (French) that Calvin said had deviated in soteriology. Richard Muller's scholarship will be pertinent (Muller, *Unaccommodated Calvin*).

did not.[71] But a simplistic, even anachronistic, oppositional narrative fails to take these various complications into consideration.

On that point, fundamentalism and liberalism may appear strange bedfellows, but the oppositional narrative's portrayal of the Reformation as anti-Greek philosophy is uncanny in its similarities to the rhetoric of Adolf von Harnack's Hellenization thesis. Robert Louis Wilken's declaration on the death of such a misreading deserves repeating: "The notion that the development of early Christian thought represented a Hellenization of Christianity has outlived its usefulness. The time has come to bid a fond farewell to the ideas of Adolf von Harnack, the nineteenth-century historian of dogma whose thinking has influenced the interpretation of early Christian thought for more than a century."[72] In summary, the oppositional narrative's persistence within fundamentalism today is a flawed historical hermeneutic not because it is too conservative but because it is too liberal.

With these missteps pinpointed, how then should we proceed?

THE PARADOX: CATHOLIC SUBSTANCE, PROTESTANT PRINCIPLE

Despite the trend to blame the Reformation for everything from schism to secularism or the popular tendency to celebrate the Reformation as the bridge to modern liberalism or the golden age of oppositional radicalism, not all historians have walked down such interpretive paths. Respected Reformation historians have recognized that such narratives overlook the Reformers' own intentions and misunderstand the nature of their theological and ecclesiastical vision.[73]

For example, Jaroslav Pelikan, one of the celebrated historians of the last century, contributed toward a better narrative. He did not wish to deny the rebel spirit of the Reformation, but he refused to interpret the Reformers as anything but obedient rebels lest he overlook the catholic substance inherent within what he called the Protestant principle.[74] Without apology, such an outlook involves a *paradox* (though not necessarily a contradiction), but it is a paradox that unmasks the Reformation's true genius and unique contribution to history. Despite Rome's initial (and sometimes ongoing) rhetoric, which painted Luther as a heretic and schismatic, "Martin Luther was the first Protestant, and yet he was *more Catholic* than many of his Roman Catholic opponents." Far from a sideline issue, Pelikan thinks this "paradox lies at the very center of Luther's Reformation."[75] Such a bold claim is the heartbeat of this book as well.[76]

---

71. On this point, see Dieter, "Luther as Late Medieval Theologian: His Positive and Negative Use of Nominalism and Realism," 31–48.

72. He adds, "a more apt expression would be the Christianization of Hellenism, though that phrase does not capture the originality of Christian thought nor the debt owed to Jewish ways of thinking and to the Jewish Bible." Wilken, *The Spirit of Early Christian Thought*, xvi.

73. The breakthrough work was Lortz's two volumes: *The Reformation in Germany*.

74. These are his phrases. See Pelikan, *Obedient Rebels*.

75. Pelikan, 11, emphasis added.

76. That does not mean, however, that this book necessarily agrees with the contemporary ecumenical applications of Pelikan's thesis.

Before Pelikan is dismissed as a historian not enlightened by more modern interpretations, remember that Pelikan was no stranger to the plethora of Luther interpretations in the last century, including the Protestant liberal Luther mentioned already (as narrated by Adolf von Harnack).[77] In the twentieth century, historians and entire movements turned the Reformation and especially Luther into a wax nose. Each, however, missed the paradox so central to a right interpretation of the Reformation. That paradox can be seen in a variety of ways, some of which will be showcased in this book. For Pelikan, Luther's ecclesiology highlighted this paradox better than most.

> *Catholic substance*—means the body of tradition, liturgy, dogma, and churchmanship developed chiefly by the ancient church and embodied (but not exhausted) for Luther in the Roman Catholic Church of his day.
>
> *Protestant principle*—is a summary term for the criticism and reconstruction of this Catholic substance which Luther and his Reformation carried out in the name of the Christian gospel and with the authority of the Bible.[78]

Quoting Luther's *Lectures on the Psalms*, Pelikan captured Luther's motive in the early years of the Reformation: "Since he [Luther] saw himself as standing in the 'succession of the faithful' of all ages, including the Middle Ages, he was highly reluctant to break with the church which had mothered him." Luther expressed his protest *"not as a revolutionary, nor even as a protesting critic, but primarily as a member of the church, as one of its doctors and professors."* In other words, "He addressed his appeal from one member of the church to other members of the church for a consideration of that gospel which creates the church." Luther, therefore, must be differentiated from the radicals. They "may have left the church in order to find greater purity of doctrine or life elsewhere, but not Luther." Luther prized ecclesiastical fidelity instead. "He stayed where he believed his calling had placed him, and from that calling he spoke to the church of the peril which he saw threatening it. That peril he sought to correct, *not by separation but by proclamation, not by schism but by the word.*"[79]

How telling: despite Luther's many conflicts with Rome, it took the pope himself excommunicating Luther for the Protestant church we know today to be born. Luther was committed to the church and its renewal. From that angle, *Luther did not start a new church; the pope forced a new church by removing one of its own members.*[80] From Luther's standpoint, he did not create a new faith; the pope had rejected the ancient faith. From that perspective, Luther was not the founder of a new gospel; the pope declared his rejection of the old gospel.

---

77. See von Harnack, *History of Dogma*, 7:173. Pietism, liberalism, Barthianism—each had its own Luther, each contradicting the other. Pelikan, *Obedient Rebels*, 12.
78. Pelikan, 13.
79. Pelikan, 16, emphasis added.
80. Luther said exactly this in *LW* 41:193–96.

"Luther maintained that by this action [excommunication] the pope was declaring his unwillingness to put up with the gospel for which Luther was contending. To Luther this meant that the pope had condemned not merely Luther but the gospel itself."[81] And by condemning the gospel, the pope had condemned the church catholic. "Thus Rome turned its back on the church, while Luther remained with the church."[82]

Pelikan was not alone. In the last century, a stream of interlocked historians contributed to this correction, many of whom will be invoked in the chapters that follow (Schaff, Oberman, Steinmetz, Ozment, Muller, van Asselt, et al.).[83] For example, Steinmetz wrote,

> The Lutheran form of the appeal to the past rested on the conviction that many so-called ancient traditions of the Catholic church were not ancient at all but represented innovations introduced into Catholic life and thought at a later—often much later—stage of the church's history . . . the church promulgated as ancient, customs and ideas that could not be traced in unbroken succession to a period earlier than, say, the pontificate of Gregory VII or the codification of canon law by Gratian or the introduction of scholastic theology by Peter Lombard. . . . For Melanchthon and Calvin, though less so for Luther, the Reformation was almost as much an argument over the writings of the early Christian fathers as it was an argument over the meaning of Scripture.[84]

Steinmetz recruited a team of Reformation historians at the end of the twentieth century who proposed three corrections: (1) The Reformation was pluralist: since diversity defined the sixteenth century (Lutheran, Reformed, etc.), the historian should have a category for Reformations (plural). (2) The Reformation was *chronologically fluid*: modern readings defined the Reformation as a reaction, an interpretation that presupposed discontinuity, but a better outlook is a long sixteenth century (1400–1650). It is superior to define the Reformation as an "organic unity with the later Middle Ages rather than as a break with them." (3) The Reformation was *contextual*: the Reformation was not a revision or abandonment of most Christian doctrines (Trinity, creation, Christology,

---

81. Pelikan, *Obedient Rebels*, 18: "And so, in Luther's eyes, it was Rome that had left Luther, and not Luther that had left Rome. As long as the Roman Church would tolerate the gospel it remained the church for Luther, despite its error. But when it condemned the gospel and forced Luther out, it became sectarian. If, as Luther maintained, the church is where the gospel is, then it followed that by condemning the gospel Rome was condemning the church."

82. Pelikan, 18.

83. Schaff, *The Principle of Protestantism*, 53–128; Ozment, ed., *The Reformation in Medieval Perspective*; Ozment, *Age of Reform, 1250–1550*; Oberman, *The Harvest of Medieval Theology*; Steinmetz, *Luther and Staupitz*; Steinmetz, *Luther in Context*; Janz, *Luther and Late Medieval Thomism*; Farthing, *Thomas Aquinas and Gabriel Biel* (Farthing traces this line of thinking back to Heinrich Hermelink, *Die theologische Fakultät in Tübingen vor der Reformation, 1477–1534*); Zachman, "The Birth of Protestantism? Or the Reemergence of the Catholic Church?," 17–30; Cameron, *European Reformation*, 127; Muller, "The Problem of Protestant Scholasticism," 45–64; van Asselt, *Introduction to Reformed Scholasticism*, 1–9.

84. Steinmetz, *Luther in Context*, 128, 129.

incarnation, etc.). In context, the Reformation was concerned with practical questions of salvation, church, and society.[85] Without the medieval context the Reformation can appear to be a wholesale abandonment of Christianity, as if it was a departure from the church catholic and its faith. In truth, the Reformation's "ideas did not spring to life *ex nihilo* . . . or emerge full-blown from an 'objective' study of the Bible alone."[86]

Likewise, consider Luther scholar Scott Hendrix. "The reformation," he says, "was not a denominational split in which Protestant churches left the same Roman Catholic Church that had existed from the beginning of Christianity. Instead, Protestants (mainly Lutherans in Luther's view) preserved true Christianity and the true church that had always existed even though the Roman hierarchy, popes and bishops, betrayed it and defected, as it were, to a false church of heretics and the devil."[87] When Luther "listed marks of the false church," he included "indulgences, pilgrimages, private masses, purgatory, monasteries, and popes," all of which he labeled "novelties."[88] When Luther attempted to expose these novelties, he was excommunicated, which forced him to realize he might never be reconciled with the church he desired to reform from within.[89]

Nevertheless, Luther never stopped thinking of himself or the Reformation as part of the one, holy, catholic, and apostolic church. When Luther wrote his preface to the Revelation of Saint John and commented on that line from the Apostles' and Nicene Creeds, he confessed, "This article, 'I believe in the holy Christian church,' is as much an article of faith as the rest. Natural reason cannot recognize it even if it puts on all its glasses. The devil can cover it over with scandals and divisions such that you cannot avoid being offended. God, too, can conceal it behind faults and shortcomings of every kind, so that you too are fooled and pass false judgment on it. The church will not be known by sight but by faith."[90] The Reformation might look like a sect of heretics if judged by sight. However, if the Reformation is judged by faith, then its church has every right to claim that creedal, ecclesiastical identity, said Luther. The Reformers believed they had equal claim to the one, holy, catholic, and apostolic church as the papacy. At times they even dared to claim their tie was stronger. For they did not rely on a papal succession but traced their bloodline to adherents of sound doctrine, and that bloodline did not stop at the apostles but continued into the church of the patristic and medieval eras as well.[91]

---

85. Bagchi and Steinmetz, eds., *The Cambridge Companionn to Reformation Theology,* 3.

86. Janz, "Late medieval theology," 5.

87. Hendrix, *Martin Luther,* 268.

88. Hendrix, 268. Including "monasteries" needs qualification. Luther was concerned about the abuse of monastic practice in his own day, specifically as it related to a denial of *sola fide.* However, monasticism itself was not novel, reaching back into the early centuries of history. Calvin, therefore, praised the monasticism of the church fathers but criticized the corruptions that seeped within its late medieval variety (*Institutes* 4.13.8–13).

89. Hendrix, 268.

90. *LW* 35:410; WADB 7, 419–20.

91. To be clear, the Reformers did not think of the Reformation as a return to exhaustive continuity

To conclude, why does this interpretive emphasis matter? It matters a great deal, because if the Reformers' *own perception* is considered, then the story of the Reformation is not a story of a rebellious departure from the church catholic but a story of *renewal*. The Reformation should then be defined not according to its critics but on its own terms, as a movement of catholicity. What follows is *not* an attempt to mine the church fathers or medieval theologians to determine if the Reformers were right, which itself is a different project. Rather, what follows is a fresh, intellectual and theological history of the Reformation that listens to discern if the Reformers themselves interpreted their reform as a renewal of catholicity.

If so, then the Reformation could be labeled a renewal of *evangelical catholicity* or in the estimation of the Reformed wing of the Reformation, a renewal in *reformed catholicity*. Such phrases capture both the high reverence and priority to align with the church of the past. By means of a renewed attention to the sacred Scriptures these phrases also communicate a vital instinct to *reform* (even *transform*) whatever *loci* and practices Rome had misconstrued or added to the catholic faith.[92] The Reformers did not take an axe to the tree, throw the tree in the fire, and plant a new tree. Rather, the tree remained the same; they simply pruned its savage branches.[93]

If the Reformation did posture itself as a renewal of evangelical, reformed catholicity, a retrieval of the one holy, catholic, and apostolic church, then that is a story we endeavor to tell.[94]

---

with the past—that myth is not the claim of this book. At the same time, the Reformers did not think of their Reformation as a radical break with the past—a caricature this book seeks to remedy. To avoid the latter, whenever possible I will use the contrast between "Reformer and Rome" or "Protestants and papacy" rather than "Protestant and Catholic." I will also try to avoid "Roman Catholic" since that label can be somewhat anachronistic when describing the context prior to Trent.

92. The phrase "evangelical Catholicity" is used by Pelikan, *Obedient Rebels*, 25, who also likes to use the phrase "critical reverence" to describe the posture of the Reformers toward the past. I have inserted the word *transform* because historians like Berndt Hamm, Michael Welker, and Volker Leppin oppose the Reformation as a "breach" with the Middle Ages and instead acknowledge the "complex relationship of continuity and innovation." They observe "gradual growth while also taking sudden jolts in the process into account." Leppin, "Luther's Transformation of Medieval Thought," 116; cf. Hamm and Welker, *Die Reformation, Potentiale der Freiheit*.

93. Canlis uses this illustration to describe Calvin's relation to scholastics like Thomas Aquinas. "Calvin's evangelical project is more like pruning a tree that has grown wildly in one direction so that it will grow in another; nevertheless, it is the same tree." Canlis, *Calvin's Ladder*, 43.

94. I will not focus on all three periods of the sixteenth century: 1510s to 1530s, 1530s to 1550s, and 1550s to 1580s. Rather, for the most part I will limit myself to the first two to keep our focus on the genesis and early maturity of thought.

Part 1

THE REFORMATION'S CATHOLIC CONTEXT

We retain the Christian, orthodox, and catholic faith whole and unimpaired.... Nor do we approve of the Roman clergy who have recently passed off only the Roman Church as catholic.
— Heinrich Bullinger and the Second Helvetic Confession

It is incorrect to suppose that the Renaissance, humanism and the Reformation were by definition anti-scholastic.
— William J. van Asselt

2

SPIRITUAL ASCENT AND MYSTICAL DISSENT

The Reformation and Monasticism

The revelation he makes through the Holy Spirit does not only illuminate the understanding; it also fires with love.

—Bernard of Clairvaux, *Sermons on the Song of Songs*

No book except the Bible and St. Augustine has come to my attention from which I have learned more about God, Christ, man, and all things.

—Martin Luther, preface to the Complete Edition of a *German Theology*

THE RISE OF MEDIEVAL MONASTICISM

In the first two centuries, the church experienced sporadic persecution and clung to Jesus' words "If anyone would come after me, let him deny himself and take up his cross daily and follow me" (Luke 9:23). To be a Christian was to suffer. True, authentic dedication to Christ was tested when the heat of persecution intensified.

However, in the fourth century Christians were no longer persecuted, for the Edict of Milan (AD 313) permitted Christianity. Christianity was eventually adopted when Theodosius I sanctioned the religion to represent the Roman Empire. Yet the acceptability of Christianity presented the church with a dilemma. In the past, the church told and retold the stories of their martyrs. Martyrdom marked exceptional Christian devotion and even became a mark of authentic orthodoxy.[1] Now that Christianity was accepted by the state, receiving countless political and cultural freedoms as a result, the church struggled to determine what it meant to pick up its cross when there no longer was a cross to bear.

Some took to the wilderness, a ripe and rough environment to demonstrate

---

1. Luther was aware of this mark and wielded the suffering the Reformers experienced as an indicator of their catholicity. *LW* 41:193–96.

Christian fidelity, enduring natural but self-inflicted suffering—no accessible food, no roof to keep warm, and no entertainments to distract from prayer and meditation. In the wilderness, the Christian could imitate Christ, fasting for forty days, for example. By knowing the Savior's suffering, the monk drew closer to Christ. Some ascetic monks withdrew altogether, secluding themselves in caves as a way of denying themselves the physical pleasures of this world.[2] Christians back in society idolized these ascetics as the true saints, which only widened the divide between the average layperson and the Christian superior in spirituality. Some of these spiritual elites were clergy, but many were desert monks. The church fathers encouraged this reverence. Athanasius, for example, wrote *The Life of Antony*, a form of early Christian biography designed to model spiritual devotion.[3]

In time, exile from society for the purpose of spirituality was not only an individual affair but became a communitarian enterprise. For example, in the eleventh century, followers of Benedict of Nursia (ca. 480–ca. 547) dedicated themselves to the Benedictine Rule.[4] Benedict lived in total isolation at one point, secluding himself to a cave, but his rule involved the whole community, prescribing each monk's daily routine to the number of hours assigned to each task. Monasteries were founded to house those ready to devote every waking moment to disciplines like fasting, prayer, and physical labor. Working the property of a monastery with one's hands was not merely a means to maintaining property but a way to serve the creator of the earth.

SPIRITUAL ASCENT

At the heart of monastic experience was a spiritual vision of the Christian life that was mystical. The word *mystical* or *mysticism* is not original to the monastic movement itself but is recent in its invention. Although far from perfect, the word is unavoidable as a descriptor of monastic theologians during the eleventh and twelfth centuries and even beyond. The word captures the monastic focus on the Christian's spiritual ascension to God. Union with God was the goal of the soul, the culmination of spiritual ascent. In this fallen world, however, many barriers challenge that ascent (affluency, sexual appetite, etc.). Thus, to avoid spiritual descent, the Christian must cleanse himself of anything that could

---

2. "An early monastic motto held that those visited by men cannot be visited by angels." Ozment, *Age of Reform*, 83.

3. Monasticism started to flourish in the Constantinian era, but hermits and desert fathers like Antony are evidence it predates that era.

4. At the start, the Benedictine Rule distinguished between four kinds of monks: (1) Coenobites: "those who live in monasteries and do their service under a rule and an abbot." (2) Anchorites or hermits: "They go out from the ranks of the brothers to the single combat of the desert, without anyone's support; relying on their own strength and with God's help, they are able to fight against physical and mental temptations." (3) Sarabaites: The "most detestable kind of monks . . . who have not been tested like gold in the furnace by any rule and have not learned from experience; instead, softened like lead, they still keep faith with the world in what they do." (4) Gyrovagues: "They spend their whole lives wandering around different regions . . . indulging their own desires and caught in the snares of greed." The gyrovagues were worst of all. The rule then made its case for the Coenobites. Benedict of Nursia, *Rule of Benedict*, 7–8.

detract from union with God. From a positive vantage point, such an ascent requires contemplating God and loving God with unparalleled devotion. For that reason, God has given the Scriptures, his spiritual bread for hungry souls. By reflecting on the Scriptures, the Christian can contemplate God himself since the Scriptures are his words, reveal his character, and show the way to heavenly bliss. Contemplation is not merely an individual affair but is refined by the corporate life of monastic discipline..[5]

Since the monastic life afforded the Christian a wholesale, around-the-clock opportunity to climb this ladder of spiritual ascent, the monastic experience was considered far superior to life as a civilian. The monk's rigorous, consuming devotion created a class of Christians separated from most other Christians distracted by practical and material priorities like marriage and children. "Inevitably, therefore, a sense of elitism can frequently be discerned in monastic mystical writing, reflecting the extent to which the monk has turned his back on the world and has committed himself to a specialized religious existence."[6] Bernard of Clairvaux, for example, compared monks to angels since they dedicated themselves body and soul to God rather than to a woman.[7]

To join a convent was considered a sacred sacrifice. The monk relinquished all the comforts and cares of the world for a life of holiness. Paradise was closer at hand for the monk than the civilian since the former had left everything to follow Christ with all the suffering that devotion entailed. Even the priest who ministered among the people was considered inferior to the monk who was untouched by the world and wholly devoted to a life of spiritual contemplation and ecstasy. As the spiritually elite, monks had far more access to the supernatural, and their experiences were sometimes defined by their harmony with angels and fights against demons, as well as their reception of miracles and visions.[8]

Many different orders defined the Middle Ages, orders that have been labeled "families," including Benedictines, Augustinians, Carmelites, hermits (including the Carthusians), Dominicans, Franciscans, Cistercians, and Cluniacs.[9] The Cistercians, Dominicans, and Franciscans will occupy our attention. The Dominicans and Franciscans, for example, were considered two of the original mendicant orders and two of the most influential, defining mystic spirituality for centuries. The Reformation was both indebted to monastic spirituality and a reaction to presuppositions latent in the spiritualist mentality.

THE CISTERCIANS IN WHITE

Distinguished by their white robes, the Cistercians were founded at the end of the eleventh century and were defined by their quest for asceticism, their

---

5. Davies, "Later Medieval Mystics," 222.

6. Davies, 222.

7. *Sermo de diversis* 37; quoted in Schaff, *History of the Christian Church*, 5:316.

8. Schaff, 5:314–17.

9. Schaff, 5:330–426.

allegiance to the Benedictine Rule, and their pursuit of monastic reform.[10] With a reputation for cultivating the soil, they prided themselves on their physical labor, and in time they acquired sizable plots of land, increasing their visibility and influence. In the twelfth century, Cistercians could be found all over Europe, from England to Germany to Italy, and were allies to the papacy in the Crusades and Inquisition. Unlike the Dominicans, however, the Cistercians were not primarily preachers. Unlike some of the Franciscans, the Cistercians did not host up-and-coming Scholastic scholars.[11] However, their greatest spiritualist monk—Bernard of Clairvaux—did possess Scholastic inclinations, although even his intellectual bent was coated by the superiority of a spiritualist layer.

Bernard of Clairvaux

Bernard of Clairvaux (1090–1153) received his name from the monastery he established in Clairvaux. Bernard advanced reform through his innumerable sermons and spiritualist publications. Bernard defied the simplistic dichotomy that sets all of monastic mysticism against Scholastic thought.[12] He embodied both, defending orthodoxy with theological acuteness that matched the precision of Scholasticism's best representatives. At the same time, Bernard did not limit himself to the Scholastic style, a style often convenient in the heat of polemics, but he pursued an experiential theology, one he articulated in a poetic discourse few could rival.[13] Bernard's style was less common among later Scholastics, who preferred a dialectic tone. As Bernard himself said, "There (in the schools) we hear what wisdom teaches; here we receive it into ourselves. There we are taught, here—deeply moved. Instruction produces knowledgeable men, whereas association [in religious life] produces wise men. . . . There one arrives at wisdom; here one penetrates into it."[14]

Bernard is often praised as a model mystic, paradigmatic for medieval spirituality that followed. Consider, for example, his book *On Loving God* and Bernard's thesis: "You wish then to hear from me why and how God ought to be loved. I answer: The cause of loving God is God himself."[15] Bernard commanded the Christian to love God, but he also reminded the Christian from the start that love for God is a gift from God himself. Bernard did not hesitate (as would other mystics) to enlist Aristotle's help. The reason "God is the cause of loving God" is that "he is both the efficient and the final cause." In other words, "He himself provides the occasion. He himself creates the longing. He himself fulfills the desire."[16]

---

10. Sometimes they were called gray monks because they wore brown prior to adopting a white robe.
11. Schaff, *History of the Christian Church*, 5:337–42.
12. Stiegman, "Bernard of Clairvaux, William of St. Thierry, the Victorines," 132.
13. For Bernard's works, see *Sancti Bernardi Opera*.
14. Bernard of Clairvaux, *Sup. Cant.* 23.14 (I, 147.22–148.13); cf. Leinsle, *Introduction to Scholastic Theology*, 115.
15. Bernard of Clairvaux, *On Loving God* 1.1 (p. 174).
16. Bernard of Clairvaux, *On Loving God* 6.22 (p. 191).

THE DICHOTOMY BETWEEN SCHOLASTICS
AND SPIRITUALISTS RECONSIDERED

Chapters 3–4 will be dedicated to the rise of Scholasticism, whose spirit can be felt in that famous mantra "*Credo ut intelligam*," "I believe so that I may understand." This mantra was voiced by Anselm, the first of the Scholastics, and embodied by each of the major Scholastics after him. Scholasticism has sometimes been set in opposition to monasticism and its spirituality. When the Scholastics are set side by side with medieval spiritualists, a new mantra can be heard from the latter: "*Credo ut experiar*," "I believe that I may experience." Historian Steven Ozment captured the contrast:

> Whereas the scholastic program of study proceeded from question to argument, the monastic program moved from reading to meditative prayer and contemplation. Universities trained scholars to form questions from their reading. . . . Such a regimen encouraged pedantry, scholarly factions, and verbal battles over where truth lay. In the cloisters monks and nuns read to prepare themselves for meditation, which gave way not to disputation, but to prayerful reflection. . . . For the new monastic orders of the twelfth century theology was immediate practical wisdom, not abstract dogmatic knowledge; it was a way of living, not a body of doctrine, something to be realized in love and contemplation, not by dialectical reasoning. Hugh and Richard of St. Victor, like Bernard, believed that the end of theology was affective union with God, not a creedal statement or great theological *summa*. It was a cardinal principle of medieval spirituality that impractical wisdom—ideas and doctrines that do not edify individuals and society—is useless and properly spurned. (Ozment, *The Age of Reform*, 81, 82, 89)

Although Ozment was right to draw a contrast, stretching the divide between Scholastics and spiritualists so far is not wise. For example, Ozment overlooked the fact that the Scholastic Anselm began and ended his *Proslogion* with prayer. Also, Emero Stiegman warned against exaggeration: "Monastic theology can be differentiated from that of the Schoolmen in its source, its objective, and its method—though it is easy to exaggerate the differences of these two modes of religious thought and, perhaps unwisely, to disengage them" ("Bernard of Clairvaux, Williams of St. Thierry, the Victorines," 129). Not only did Scholasticism and monasticism overlap for centuries, but more than a few major representatives were both Scholastic and spiritualist. Bonaventure is a case in point. Still, a spiritualist theme cannot be avoided, even among those who are easily located in the Scholastic vein. As chapter 3 will demonstrate, the first Scholastic, Anselm, treated theology proper from start to finish as faith's quest not only for understanding but for present and future joy, a bliss that is found by means of contemplation, prayer, and devotion. Likewise, a chief Scholastic like Thomas Aquinas believed the aim of his pursuit for theological answers was the beatific vision. As he said in his *Compendium of Theology*, "God is goodness itself, which is the cause of love. . . . Therefore, in the vision of God, who is goodness itself and truth, as comprehension is necessarily present, so is pleasure or pleasurable enjoyment, as Is. 66:14 says: 'You will see, and your heart will rejoice'" (Aquinas, *Compendium of*

Theology, 165). Thomas believed theology leads to contemplation, and its end is nothing less than union with God.

Therefore, overstretching the contrast between Scholastics and spiritualists risks overlooking theological as well as spiritual similarities. Such a sharp contrast is also not wise because many Scholastics, such as Anselm and Thomas, taught monks and considered their calling a spiritual, even monastic enterprise in many respects. It is appropriate to look back and locate certain medieval figures, especially those given to a far more mystical than intellectualist approach to Christianity, within a spiritualist instead of a Scholastic vein. However, many medievals cannot be restricted to one camp or the other. For that reason, monastic spirituality's more radical representatives and their criticisms of Scholasticism deserve attention; nevertheless, a stricht dichotomy cannot be enforced between spiritualists and Scholastics. Monasticism will then serve as a backdrop for the advent of the Reformation, and its influence on the Reformation will be assessed. After all, Martin Luther himself experienced his Reformation breakthrough *within* the monastic life, although the German Reformer then turned to critique components he believed could be harmful.

If God creates love within the Christian, then how should the Christian love God in return? "The way to love him is without measure."[17] Bernard had little patience for the wandering mind, which he said, "is always rushing about in empty efforts among the various and deceptive delights of the world" and consequently "grows weary and remains dissatisfied." Bernard compared such a person to a man who is hungry but does not know how to eat. "It is like a starving man who thinks that whatever he is stuffing himself with is nothing in comparison with what remains to be eaten; he is always anxiously wanting what he has not got rather than enjoying what he has."[18] They will never find "happy fulfillment," said Bernard, because they "delight in the beauty of the creature rather than of the Creator (Rom 1:23)." They "lust for each and every experience more than they desire to come to the Lord of all." Yet when the Christian turns to the source of all things—the God of all—then and only then will he find everlasting rest by clinging to God, as the psalms so often say.[19]

The goal of the Christian life, then, is to ascend into the life and love of God. One does not ascend merely by gaining knowledge; rather, ascent comes by desire. Faith is not mere assent to religious facts but a religious experience itself.[20] The affections, therefore, are instrumental, a vehicle by which the Christian knows and loves God and ascends into the life and love of God.[21]

Bernard distinguished between four degrees of love that moderate the nature

---

17. Bernard of Clairvaux, *On Loving God* 1.1 (p. 174).

18. Bernard of Clairvaux, *On Loving God* 6.18 (pp. 188–89).

19. Bernard of Clairvaux, *On Loving God* 6.19 (p. 189).

20. Experience—not only nature and Scripture—is an avenue for divine revelation. See Stiegman, "Bernard of Clairvaux, William of St. Thierry, the Victorines," 138.

21. Since the Christian's experience is the bedrock for knowing God and ascending to God, Bernard does posit a power to the freedom of the will. Stiegman, 136ff.

(and the success) of this spiritual ascent. The first degree of love is a basic, "bodily love, by which man loves himself for his own sake." The second degree of love occurs when man "loves God, but . . . for his own sake, not God's." The third degree occurs when man loves God but not for man's own sake; rather, he loves God for God's own sake. "It is in this way that the taste of his own sweetness leads us to love God in purity more than our need alone would prompt us to do." With that motive we should speak to our flesh and say, "Now we love God not because he meets your needs; but we have tasted and we know how sweet the Lord is," says Bernard.[22] The fourth degree of love occurs when "man loves himself only for God's sake."[23]

What does the destination of this spiritual ascent look like? For Bernard it reaches its culmination when the Christian has little thought of himself and finds his identity in God. "To lose yourself as though you did not exist and to have no sense of yourself, to be emptied out of yourself (Phil. 2:7) and almost annihilated, belongs to heavenly not to human love."[24] Bernard's reference to Philippians 2 is key, the reason why the incarnation became a center point for Bernard's spirituality. In Christ—the God-man—the world witnessed carnal love. God made his magnetic love known to humanity by taking the form of humanity itself, all for the purpose of drawing humanity into this same divine love. Christ is an example of this selfless, humble love that seeks not its own interests but the interests of others.

If the Christian takes on the servant mentality of Christ, he will discover a love altogether superior to any love in this world. "To love in this way is to become like God." Bernard used the illustration of a barrel of wine: if a tiny drop of water is released into the large barrel of wine, the water is swallowed up and takes on the wine's red color, even the wine's grape flavor. Likewise, with "those who are holy, it is necessary for human affection to dissolve in some ineffable way, and be poured into the will of God."[25] Here is the beatific vision and the fourth degree of love. Such a love is discovered "when no entanglements of the flesh hold him back and no troubles will disturb him, as he hurries with great speed and eagerness to the joy of the Lord (Mt 25:21; 25)." Not just anyone could experience this fourth degree of love. It was reserved for the most devout and sacrificial martyrs, for example. Free of the body, they were "wholly immersed in that sea of eternal light and bright eternity."[26]

Christ's centrality to Bernard's spiritual vision of the Christian life is conspicuous in his *Sermons on the Song of Songs.* As a young monk, he became sick. He had worked so hard that his body felt the effects and demanded a break.

---

22. Bernard of Clairvaux, *On Loving God* 9.26 (p. 194).
23. For these four degrees of love, see Bernard of Clairvaux, *On Loving God* 8.23–9.30 (pp. 192–97).
24. Bernard of Clairvaux, *On Loving God* 9.27 (p. 195).
25. Bernard of Clairvaux, *On Loving God* 9.27 (p. 196).
26. Bernard of Clairvaux, *On Loving God* 9.28–30 (pp. 196–97). That does not mean Bernard has no place for the physical, future bodily resurrection, which he treats at length.

During his time of retreat in the monastery, Bernard met and talked with William of St. Thierry. Together they walked in the garden and found refreshment by contemplating the Song of Songs. From 1135 to his death, Bernard then preached on the Song of Songs.

Using the fourfold method of interpretation, Bernard considered the Song of Songs a book consumed with the marriage between Christ and his bride, the church. The Christian finds "supreme happiness" when he arrives at knowledge of the Holy Trinity. For the "Father is not known without the Son and the Son is not known without the Father. . . . [and] where Father and Son are known fully, how can their goodness, which is the Holy Spirit, not be known?"[27]

> So when the Bride asks for a kiss she begs to be flooded with the grace of this threefold knowledge as much as mortal flesh can bear. She asks it of the Son, for he is to reveal it to whom he wills (Mt 11:27). Therefore the Son reveals himself to whom he wills and he reveals the Father when he does so. It is undoubtedly through the kiss that he makes this revelation, that is, through the Spirit. . . . But in giving the Spirit through whom he reveals, he reveals him as well. In giving he reveals him; in revealing he gives him. The revelation he makes through the Holy Spirit does not only illuminate the understanding; it also fires with love [Rom 5:5].[28]

Bernard's last sentence is a prime example of a spiritualist *telos*. The Spirit does illuminate the mind, the basis for all monastic study and inquiry. However, the Spirit also fires up the affections with love. Here is the road map for the soul's ascent to God and union with God.

Hugh of St. Victor and Richard of St. Victor

Others, such as Hugh of St. Victor (ca. 1096–1141) and Richard of St. Victor (d. 1173), were not dissimilar to Bernard. They, too, described spiritual ascent as union with the Trinity, and they, too, pursued monastic reform but within the Victorine heritage. Likewise, they both held Scholastic rigor in one hand and experiential piety in the other hand. Hugh of St. Victor, for example, wrote a *summa* of Christian theology long before Thomas Aquinas. Some historians have credited Hugh of St. Victor not only with "keeping Victorine theological reflection within the lines of Catholic orthodoxy" but also with "ensuring the general acceptance of what developed into the scholastic method."[29] And yet

---

27. For Bernard the "Holy Spirit is the love and goodness of both [the Father and Son]." Bernard of Clairvaux, *Sermons on the Song of Songs*, Sermon 8, 1.3 (p. 237). "And so the Father, kissing the Son, pours into him in full the mysteries of his divinity, and breathes the sweetness of love [the Spirit]." Sermon 8, 6.6. On the details that led Bernard to contemplate Song of Songs with William of St. Thierry, see *Sermons*, 209.

28. Bernard, Sermon 8, 2.5 (p. 238).

29. Stiegman, "Bernard of Clairvaux, William of St. Thierry, the Victorines," 143.

Hugh's conception of the Christian life—as his spiritual exegesis models—was no less contemplative than Bernard's.[30]

The same can be said of Richard of St. Victor. Richard defended Trinitarian orthodoxy, for example. He said nothing new when he followed Augustine by describing the Trinity within the parameter of divine love. Yet Richard added his own mark by using the concept of love itself to explain why there must be three divine persons instead of one or two. If not a plurality of persons, then how can love be gratuitous? The "fullness of gratuitous love resides in the Father, the fullness of due love [resides] in the Holy Spirit, the fullness of both gratuitous and due love [resides] in the Son."[31]

Richard's logic, which moved from a plurality of human persons to a plurality of divine persons, informed his understanding of spiritual ascent. Since the Holy Spirit is described in Scripture as the gift of love, his mission must be the infusion of divine love into those whom the Spirit indwells. "The Holy Spirit, then, is given by God to man when due love residing in the divinity is inspired into the human soul. In fact, when this Spirit enters the rational soul, he inflames its sentiments with divine ardor and transforms it by communicating to it a character similar to his own, in order [to enable] it to express back to its own Creator the love it owes him."[32]

Despite the prominence of the Cistercians in the eleventh and twelfth centuries, they were overshadowed by the Mendicant orders—the Dominicans and the Franciscans—in the thirteenth century.

THE DOMINICANS IN BLACK

The Dominicans were named after their founder, Dominic Guzman (ca. 1170–1221). Dominic was from Spain, but early on he left his home in Calaroga in Castile to become a missionary. Dominic encountered the Waldensians and Cathars in Languedoc, but rather than joining them, he resolved to stay within the confines of the Catholic Church. Nevertheless, Dominic saw enormous value in their commitments to poverty and preaching and dedicated himself to a lifestyle of begging for food as a thirteenth-century street preacher, eager to tell the destitute about the gospel of Jesus Christ. Dominic represented a clear deviation from prior monastic methodology. Previously, the spiritualists *withdrew* from society to devote themselves to God, but Dominic *returned* to society to spread the good news, either locally to reach the nominal or internationally to reach Muslims. His reversal in methodology and mission marked a new age for monasticism.[33]

---

30. To see both, consult Hugh of St. Victor's *Mysteries of the Christian Faith* and his *Didascalicon*.

31. Richard of St. Victor, *On the Trinity* 6.14 (pp. 219–20).

32. Richard of St. Victor, 6.14 (pp. 219–20). To see Richard's description of spiritual ascent, consult his book *Mystical Ark*.

33. Schaff, *History of the Christian Church*, 5:420; Needham, *Two Thousand Years of Christ's Power*, 2:348.

Dominic petitioned the Fourth Lateran Council (1215) for support, but Pope Innocent III declined. Dominic was not a dissenter like the Waldensians and Cathars, but the founding of another order seemed superfluous to Innocent, who advised Dominic to join the existing Augustinians instead. However, Innocent's successor, Honorius III, did not feel the same way as his predecessor. Dominic had proved himself loyal to the church, and his emphases on begging and preaching even served the church. In 1216 Honorius sanctioned the new order, and in 1217 Dominic and his Dominicans were commissioned as friars.[34] Distinguished by their black garments, the Dominicans now had papal sanction to preach in society. They may have started in southern France, but they soon spread to numerable countries exercising their missionary methods. In the years and decades after their establishment, Dominican monks traveled all over Europe and created colonies and convents from Spain to Germany, from Italy to England. Their reputation can be defined by three marks (although not limited to these three).

First, the Dominicans were dedicated to scholarship. Unlike friars in other orders, Dominican friars were not hostile to Scholastic methods and Scholastic theology, as exemplified in their most famous theologian, Thomas Aquinas (see chapter 4). However, the Dominican dedication to theological study did put their order at a crossroads. In the past, orders put their friars to manual labor. As mentioned, labor was considered beneficial to the logistical needs of the order, even a spiritual discipline. But as any student of theology knows, the study of theology takes considerable time, especially Scholastic theology, which involves precise articulation. Theological study and manual labor now competed with one another, the two impossible to reconcile. The Dominicans decided theology must take precedence, at least in their order.

Second, the study of Scripture and theology was not an end in and of itself but a means to proclamation. The Dominicans not only preached to their own but to those in society. Their style of proclamation could be passionate since they pursued the conversion of their hearers. Yet such zeal could take the form of hostility toward heretics as well.

Third, the Dominicans participated in the Inquisition. Not a few Dominicans became marksmen, targeting heretics in question. Three decades into the thirteenth century, the Dominicans leveraged significant power within the Inquisition, leading its cause in major European countries, intent on eliminating any deviance from catholic Christianity.

The Dominicans often operated among high-class society. Although they supported commitments to poverty, they were never seriously divided by debates over poverty. The same cannot be said of the Franciscans.

---

34. In Latin *frater* means "brother."

THE FRANCISCANS IN GRAY

If the Dominicans were set apart as the friars in black, the Franciscans were distinguished as the friars in gray. Confusing a black with a gray garment may appear a minor offense, but a medieval Christian was not as easily forgiven for confusing the competing ideologies of these divergent orders.

The Franciscans took their name from Francis of Assisi (1182–1226).[35] While Dominic Guzman and the Dominicans originated from Spain, Francis and the Franciscans hailed from Italy. Francis became renowned; his undying devotion to Lady Poverty was exceeded by few since he committed himself to a lifetime of begging. Francis and the Franciscans were called *mendicants*, a Latin word that conveys the begging disposition. With Lady Poverty, Francis and the Franciscans after him traveled from town to town preaching. They believed this model—poverty and preaching—was based on the practice of the apostles themselves, and for that reason they received the label *vita apostolica*.[36]

Francis was not sympathetic with Scholastic theology. The Christian faith should produce a simple life characterized by trust in God. The educated theories of medieval Scholasticism were irrelevant to the conditions of the destitute in society, the very ones Francis was passionate to serve by virtue of his own poverty. The Rule of Francis taught its disciples that poverty was central to Christian living and community. Naturally, the Franciscans did not purchase land or monasteries or church sanctuaries.

Dominic failed to recruit the support of Innocent, but Francis did not, which contributed to the growing success of his disciples. What persuaded Innocent to support a new order? A dream. One night in the year 1210, the pope was sleeping when he was ushered to Saint John Lateran (Rome) without warning. The church was in crisis, practically crumbling. Then Francis appeared, lifted Saint John Lateran by his own two hands, and hoisted the church above his head, establishing its stability and longevity. When the pope woke from his dream, he granted the Franciscans legitimacy with enthusiasm, which fueled the order's establishment in Italy and many other European countries.

Pope Innocent III may have been motivated by more than just a dream. The Cathars had created no small amount of resistance, which Innocent had to squash due to its dissenting, even heretical nature (see chapter 7). From Innocent's perspective, the Cathars exemplified how precarious a heterodox movement could become outside the jurisdiction of the church. Even more so if the laity resonated with—let alone glorified—that spiritual movement's sacrifice, exposing the wide contrast between the affluency of the pope over against Lady Poverty. Within that context Innocent could squash one group of spiritualists with a crusade while establishing another group of spiritualists as an order. Accomplishing both demonstrated that spiritualist allegiance to the

35. The Franciscans were also called Little Brothers and Friars Minor.
36. Steinmetz, *Luther in Context*, 127.

papacy would be blessed while spiritualists dissenting from the papacy would be cursed. Innocent proceeded with that vision: he launched his crusade against the Cathars (the Albigensian Crusade) and sanctioned the Franciscan order.[37]

What initially appeared a blessing—the sanction of the pope—created controversy. Francis had started the Franciscans with Lady Poverty as his guide and goal. Now that the pope was involved, the Franciscans were presented with an opportunity to become an establishment, which guaranteed the long-term survival of the Franciscans. In contrast to dissenting groups who struggled to survive persecution, an order sanctioned by the church could thrive and even reach new heights of power.

Yet bureaucracy was distasteful to Francis, a spiritual man, not a politician. Despite Francis's original intentions for the Franciscans, Pope Honorius III pressed formalization. Francis's original vision was disappearing, which led him to step down in 1220. Francis's suspicions were right; the next year Francis's rule was surpassed by the rule of Ugolino, the pope's cardinal, a rule that dethroned Lady Poverty and found ways for adherents to own property without technically owning property, a rule that replaced Francis's ultimate appeal to conscience with absolute obedience to papal authority.[38] The order originally ruled by Francis's simple spirituality was overcome by more ambitious churchmen.

Leaving the order he had established was no barrier, however, to Francis's fame in 1224. According to reports, blood oozed from his hands and feet, even his side. Francis was not the victim of some injury; he was bleeding like the crucified Christ. These miraculous marks, or *stigmata,* qualified Francis for sainthood. In the end, Francis died a hermit, still devoted to the basic principle of his mystical experience: poverty, begging, preaching, fidelity to conscience, and most of all, a simple faith in God. Before he died, he finished his *Testament,* reiterating these pillars of Christian living but, above all, holy poverty, reminding his followers of his rule. To the very end, Francis feared his rule could be corrupted by the papacy. "I make it an imperative demand of obedience that no brother dare accept any privilege from the Roman curia, either by himself or through an intermediary, for a church or any other place using the pretext of the needs of preaching or a refuge from persecution."[39]

The shift that began with Cardinal Ugolino continued after Francis died. For example, while Francis and his vision of the spiritual life was antithetical to Scholasticism, later Franciscans embraced Scholasticism. The "newly founded Dominican and Franciscan Orders attempted a *rapprochement* between Christianity and classical philosophy which gave fresh impetus to the Christian

---

37. Ozment, *Age of Reform,* 99.

38. On "conscience" in the thought of Francis, see Needham, *Two Thousand Years of Christ's Power,* 2:343–45. On the issue of property ownership, especially under Pope Gregory IX, see Ozment, *Age of Reform,* 109.

39. Francis of Assisi, *Brother Francis,* 52.

mystical tradition."[40] Many Scholastics of the High and Late Middle Ages—Alexander of Hales, Bonaventure, Nicholas of Lyra, Duns Scotus, William of Ockham—were Franciscans, demonstrating to what extent the Franciscan order had evolved by the advent of the Reformation.

Yet not all Franciscans were alike, with some far more apocalyptic than others. Consider two examples: Bonaventure and Joachim of Fiore. Although Joachim died fifteen years before Bonaventure was born, Bonaventure will be considered first to contrast his later, more moderated mysticism with the more apocalyptic mysticism of Joachim and the Franciscans who carried Joachim's eschatological vision forward.[41]

Bonaventure

Bonaventure (ca. 1217–74)—or Giovanni di Fidanza—was a superlative Scholastic who was also a dedicated spiritual mystic.[42] General of the Franciscan order starting in 1257, he wrote works such as *The Journey of the Mind to God*, laying a theological foundation for Franciscan mysticism. Bonaventure retreated to Mount Alverno to consider in solitude how he might experience spiritual ascent. Bonaventure said he withdrew to this quiet habitat "to satisfy the yearning of my soul for peace." In silence he reflected on the example of Francis and considered how Francis himself achieved a state of contemplation. *Journey* is Bonaventure's findings, written as a manual to others on the same spiritual quest. He illustrated the nature of ascent by the six-winged seraph who rises high, flying into the presence of God. The six stages or steps of illumination define the soul's enlightened ascent.[43]

Bonaventure's *Journey* should not be read as if he pursued an innovative spiritual quest. His outline for spiritual accent was indebted to those before him, patristic and medieval. Augustine was a major influence on Bonaventure, as were medieval Cistercians like Bernard of Clairvaux. Richard of St. Victor and Giles of Assisi should not be overlooked either, since they, too, put forward their own "steps" up the ladder of spiritual ascent. Bonaventure was influenced by Francis as well, as is plain when his *Journey* appeals to the seraph, the same heavenly creature Francis saw when he received his stigmata.[44]

Like Augustine and Anselm before him, Bonaventure defined happiness as

---

40. Davies, "Later Medieval Mystics," 223.

41. Comparing the two, Stephen Brown thinks their language is similar. "Yet, Bonaventure's use of layered language has a certain discipline that rules over, guides, and enriches his symbolism and metaphors. This discipline restrains him from the extreme interpretations found among the Spiritualist writers and the Franciscan brethren who followed their lead." See "Introduction," in Bonaventure, *Journey of the Mind to God*, x.

42. Some date the birth of Bonaventure later: ca. 1221.

43. Bonaventure, *Journey*, 1.2.

44. Bonaventure was influenced by books such as Bernard's *On Consideration* and Richard's *Mystical Ark*. For a comparison of Richard, Giles, and Francis with Bonaventure, see "Introduction," in Bonaventure, *Journey*, x–xv.

"nothing else than the enjoyment of the Supreme Good," but since the "Supreme Good is above us, no one can enjoy happiness unless he rise above himself, not, indeed, by a bodily ascent, but by an ascent of the heart." Did Bonaventure think such an ascent must originate from man's own powers? He did not. For "we cannot rise above ourselves unless a superior power raise us." To receive this divine aid, the Christian must humble himself with a "devout heart, that is by sighing for it in this vale of tears by fervent prayer." Prayer is key, instrumental to spiritual ascent from start to finish. Bonaventure followed the lead of Dionysius and his *Mystical Theology* when he said that prayer is the "mother and origin of every upward striving of the soul."[45]

To ascend to God, whom Bonaventure, in a Scholastic key, labeled the First Principle, Christians must "pass through vestiges which are corporeal and temporal and outside us." Once Christians have moved past the material world, they then enter their own minds. For Bonaventure the mind was the *imago Dei*. That connection between the mind and the image of God matters at the end of his treatise because the mind's destination is Christ, *the* image of the invisible God. Christ therefore is not only the destination but the road itself—or in Bonaventure's language, *the ladder*, an allusion to the book of Genesis and Jacob's ladder.[46] This ladder has six steps of ascent, and like the six days of creation, these six steps are well ordered and equipped to usher the soul out of darkness and into light.[47] These six steps of enlightenment—"the quiet of contemplation"—are as follows:

First, we "may behold God in the mirror of the visible creation . . . by considering creatures as vestiges of God."[48] Bonaventure enlisted faith and reason, both of which open the eyes to see a world fashioned by God's Word (Heb. 11:3). "Therefore, from visible things the soul rises to the consideration of the power, wisdom, and goodness of God."[49]

Second, we "may behold God in the mirror of visible creation . . . [by] seeing Him *in* them; for He is present in them by His essence, His power, and His presence."[50] By synthesizing the apostle Paul, Augustine, and Aristotle, Bonaventure described the five senses as doors that lead the soul to the material so that a person can witness the spiritual. God does not merely work through creation, but he manifests himself in creation. Indebted to Aristotle, Bonaventure wrote in a vein not all that different from Thomas Aquinas. "For creatures of this visible world signify the invisible things of God: partly, because God is the Origin, Exemplar, and End of every creature."[51]

45. Bonaventure, *Journey* 1.1.
46. Bonaventure, *Journey* 1.9.
47. Bonaventure, *Journey* 1.3–4.
48. Bonaventure, *Journey* 2.1.
49. Bonaventure, *Journey* 1.13.
50. Bonaventure, *Journey* 2.1.
51. Bonaventure, *Journey* 2.12.

Third, by "entering into ourselves, [we] see God through a mirror . . . upon the face of *our mind*, in which the *image* of the most Blessed Trinity appears in splendor."[52] Bonaventure was channeling Augustine's *De Trinitate*, conspicuous in the Franciscan's appeal to memory, intelligence, and will to identify the Trinity's reflection in the *imago Dei*. Bonaventure, never straying too far from Scholastic principles, was persuaded that natural, rational, and moral philosophy could buttress such a connection.[53]

Fourth, we "contemplate the First Principle not only by going through us, but also within us." The previous step revealed how close God is to the soul; yet the First Principle can be perceived "within" as well. However, a barrier stands in the way: the senses in a fallen world. "Distracted by many cares, the human mind does not enter into itself through the memory; beclouded by sense images, it does not come back to itself through the intelligence; and drawn away by the concupiscences, it does not return to itself through the desire for interior sweetness and spiritual joy. Therefore, completely immersed in things of sense, the soul cannot re-enter into itself as the image of God."[54] Bonaventure used the illustration of a man who has fallen down and cannot get back up. Someone must "lend a hand to raise him up." So, too, with the soul.

Who is that someone? The incarnate Christ. By assuming flesh, he became the sinner's mediator, so that "if we wish to enter again into the enjoyment of Truth as into Paradise, we must enter through faith, hope, and love of the Mediator between God and men, Jesus Christ, Who is like *the Tree of life in the midst of Paradise*."[55] By hope and love, Bonaventure intended a longing and an affection, an authentic disposition. The result is a reformation of the image and a transportation of the soul upward, one that not only enlightens but perfects. Bonaventure labeled this upward movement hierarchical and called Christ the "Hierarch" because he is the one who "purifies, enlightens, and perfects His spouse, that is, the whole Church and every sanctified soul."[56]

For Bonaventure an indivisible connection exists between spiritual ascent and biblical interpretation. His hermeneutic even grounded his spiritual vision. The Hierarch (Christ) and the hierarchical process (ascent) moves in pace with the story line of sacred Scripture. Consider Bonaventure's three laws:

---

52. Emphasis added. Bonaventure, *Journey* 3.1.

53. Consider, for example, natural philosophy. "Metaphysics deals with the essences of things; mathematics, with numbers and figures; and physics, with natures, powers, and diffusive operations. Thus the first leads to the first Principle, the Father; the second, to His Image, the Son; and the third, to the gift of the Holy Spirit." Bonaventure, *Journey* 3.6.

54. Bonaventure, *Journey* 4.1.

55. Emphasis added. Bonaventure, *Journey* 3.2.

56. "It comes down into our heart when, by the reformation of the image, the theological virtues, the delights of the spiritual senses, and the uplifting transports, our spirit becomes hierarchical, that is, purified, enlightened, and perfected." Bonaventure, *Journey* 4.4.

LAW, PRINCIPAL PART, SPIRITUAL MEANING

Law	Principal Part	Spiritual Meaning
The Law of *Nature*	Law of Moses *purifies*	*Tropological*: purifies for righteousness of life
The Law of *Scripture*	Prophets *enlighten*	*Allegorical*: enlightens for clearness of understanding
The Law of *Grace*	Gospel (evangelical doctrine) *perfects*	*Analogical*: perfects through spiritual transports and the most sweet perceptions of wisdom[57]

These three laws do not sit on a static plain, but alongside the drama of the biblical story, they culminate in the "love of Christ," which Bonaventure considered the perfecting mechanism that transports the spirit upward.[58]

Fifth and sixth: so far Bonaventure's journey has transitioned from outside (vestiges in creation) to inside (*imago Dei*), but in his last two steps of ascent, the journey moves "above"—the light of God on the mind.[59] For a Scholastic like Bonaventure, moving "above" means contemplating the Being (essence) of God in all its perfections. The Old Testament is instrumental to such an end: ascending souls must fix their "gaze primarily and principally on Being Itself, declaring that the first name of God is *He Who is* . . . [and] *I am Who [I] am*."[60] Marshaling the classical doctrine of God articulated by the church fathers and medieval theologians before him, Bonaventure described God as the most perfect and pure being, indeed, Pure Act itself.[61] His being is simple, without parts or composition, indivisible and incorruptible. Quoting Anselm almost verbatim, Bonaventure said this "highest good is unqualifiedly that than which no greater can be thought."[62] Bonaventure reasoned that perfect-making attributes must follow, perfections that preclude any limitations.[63] Apart from divine aseity, eternity, immutability, and omnipotence, God cannot be the one Paul referenced in Romans 11:36: "from him and through him and to him are all things."

---

57. All three of these were described by Bonaventure, but the layered diagram is my own. Bonaventure, *Journey* 4.6.
58. "Filled with all these intellectual lights, our mind like the house of God is inhabited by Divine Wisdom; it is made a daughter, a spouse, and a friend of God; it is made a member, a sister, a co-heir of Christ the Head; it is made the temple of the Holy Spirit; faith laying the foundation, hope building it up, and sanctity of soul and body dedicating it to God." Bonaventure, *Journey* 4.8.
59. Bonaventure, *Journey* 5.1.
60. Emphasis added. Bonaventure, *Journey* 5.1.
61. E.g., John of Damascus and Boethius.
62. Although brief, Bonaventure even paid tribute to the ontological argument. Bonaventure, *Journey* 6.2.
63. It is difficult to miss the similarities between Bonaventure and Augustine. In a statement that echoes the *Confessions*, Bonaventure wrote, "For being itself is both the first and the last; it is eternal and yet present; it is most simple and yet the greatest; it is most actual and still most changeless; it is most perfect and nonetheless immense; it is supremely one and yet pervades all things." Bonaventure, *Journey* 5.7 (cf. 5.8).

That basic premise, so foundational to spiritual ascent, hinges on Bonaventure's classical conception of theology proper.[64]

After establishing God as pure act, the basis on which ascent can occur, Bonaventure returned to divine simplicity once more to establish the unity of the Trinity. This transition from divine perfections to divine persons oscillates on Bonaventure's choice descriptor: God as the Good. "If, therefore, you are able to behold with the eye of your mind the purity of that goodness which is the pure act of the Principle . . . you can see that through the utmost communicability of the Good, there must exist a Trinity of the Father, the Son, and the Holy Spirit. By reason of Their supreme goodness, the three Persons must necessarily have supreme communicability; by reason of their supreme communicability they must necessarily have supreme consubstantiality."[65] If the Son is consubstantial with the Father in divinity, then he is, as Paul said, the image of the invisible God (Col. 1:15). "For, if an image is an expressed likeness, then when our mind contemplates in Christ the Son of God, Who is by nature the image of the invisible God, our humanity so wonderfully exalted, so ineffably united, and when at the same time sees united the first and the last, . . . it has already reached something that is perfect." According to Bonaventure's three laws, the last is the law of grace that leads the pilgrim to the gospel, a gospel that has power to perfect. If Genesis is read within this analogical framework, then everything falls into place: "Thus it [our mind] arrives at the perfection of its illuminations on the sixth step, as God did on the sixth day."[66]

To be sure, Bonaventure did not think that this ascent can begin (step 1) or end (step 6) without divine aid, namely, God's grace. Bonaventure used the contrast between light and darkness to describe the fallen state of humankind. By "turning away from the true light to a changeable good, he [Adam] and all his descendants were by his fault bent over by original sin, which infected human nature in a twofold manner: the mind with ignorance, and the flesh with concupiscence." Ignorance explains why Bonaventure so often contrasted blindness with sight, darkness with light. "The result [of original sin] is that man, blinded and bent over, sits in darkness and does not see the light of heaven, unless grace comes to his aid—with justice to fight concupiscence, and with knowledge and wisdom to oppose ignorance." Grace has come with the incarnate Word, whom Bonaventure called wisdom, grace, and truth.[67]

---

64. Divine simplicity is indispensable to Bonaventure's perfect being theology. For a being with composition cannot be "supremely one." The consequences are devastating for spiritual ascent. Since his being is "supremely one and yet pervasive, it is *all in all*, even though all things are many and it is itself but one. And this is so because through its most supremely simple unity, its most serene truth, and its most sincere goodness, it contains in itself all power, all exemplarity, and all communicability. Hence *from him and through him and unto him are all things*, for He is all-powerful, all-knowing, and all-good." Bonaventure, *Journey* 5.8.

65. By this logic, he listed supreme likeness of nature, supreme coequality, supreme coeternity, supreme mutual intimacy (perichoresis), supreme identity, and absolute indivision of substance. Bonaventure, *Journey* 6.2.

66. Bonaventure, *Journey* 6.7.

67. Bonaventure seemed quite concerned to be Pauline at this point. Bonaventure, *Journey* 1.7.

Divine grace is necessary, but so is participation. Grace precedes and prepares the way for participation in divinity. "He, therefore, who wishes to ascend to God must first avoid sin, which deforms nature. He must bring the natural powers of the soul under the influence of grace, which reforms them, and this he does through prayer; he must submit them to the purifying influence of justice, and this, in daily acts; he must subject them to the influence of enlightening knowledge, and this, in meditation; and finally, he must hand them over to the influence of the perfecting power of wisdom, and this in contemplation."[68]

Bonaventure concluded his *Journey* with a Scholastic investigation into the being of God, but he framed his entire project as a spiritual exercise more than an intellectual endeavor. The pilgrimage of ascent may involve speculation but never without devotion.[69] "In this passing over, if it is to be perfect, all intellectual activities ought to be relinquished and the loftiest affection transported to God, and transformed into Him." Bonaventure used the word *mystical* to describe the experience, and, with Dionysius, offered this advice: "Abandon the sense, intellectual activities, and all visible and invisible things—everything that is not and everything that is—and, oblivious of yourself, let yourself be brought back, in so far as it is possible, to union with Him Who is above all essence and all knowledge. And transcending yourself and all things, ascend to the superessential gleam of the divine darkness by an incommensurable and absolute transport of a pure mind."[70]

In the mind of Bonaventure, spiritual ascent was not unrelated to the Franciscan commitment to poverty. Yet Bonaventure rescued Lady Poverty from a literalistic interpretation by advocating for a spiritual poverty as the true goal of the Franciscan vision. However, the Franciscan order was not without its own dissenting Reformers. As the order shifted, some protested, calling for a return to Francis's original vision of Lady Poverty.[71] Over against conventual types, the Spiritual Franciscans raised their voices, not only motivated by the rejection of all property but by an eschatology convinced that the last epoch in God's plan of redemption was at hand. The end was near. Prior to Bonaventure, the Franciscan who inspired this more radical apocalyptic mysticism was Joachim of Fiore.

---

68. Emphasis added. And again, "For just as no one arrives at wisdom except through grace, justice, and knowledge, so it is that no one arrives at contemplation except through penetrating mediation, holy living, and devout prayer." Bonaventure outlined three steps: (1) "Since grace is the foundation for righteousness of the will, and for the penetrating enlightenment of reason, we must first of all pray." (2) "We must live holily." (3) "We must gaze at the spectacles of truth, and by gazing at them, rise step by step until we reach *the mountain height where the God of gods is seen on Zion.*" Bonaventure, *Journey* 1.8.

69. "Wherefore, it is to groans of prayer through Christ Crucified, in Whose blood we are cleansed from the filth of vices, that I first of all invite the reader. Otherwise he may come to think that mere reading will suffice without fervor, speculation without devotion, investigation without admiration, observation without exultation, industry without piety, knowledge without love, understanding without humility, study without divine grace, the mirror without divinely inspired wisdom." Bonaventure, *Journey*, pp. 1–3.

70. Bonaventure, *Journey* 7.5.

71. Bonaventure tried to unite the two sides, but he was more sympathetic to the conventual mindset. See Ozment, *Age of Reform*, 103, 110; and Moorman, *A History of the Franciscan Order*, 154.

Joachim of Fiore

The eschatology of the Spiritual Franciscans was not born in isolation. They were influenced by Joachim of Fiore (1135–1202) before them, also an Italian.[72] Joachim became a Cistercian as a youth and eventually an abbot himself, but then grew frustrated with the monks under him because of their lack of dedication. Joachim was ambitious: when Francis was only ten years old, Joachim of Fiore was busy establishing his monastery. Francis was still a youth when Joachim recruited the approval of Pope Celestine III.

Joachim's vision was unique because he did not interpret history or his present day like everybody else.[73] His reading of history was Trinitarian, assigning the Old Testament and its fear of the law to the Father, the New Testament and faith in the gospel to the Son, and the new era of love to the Spirit. The agent to usher in this new spiritual era was none other than the monastic order with its communitarian structure, much in contrast with the era of the Son ruled by authoritarian clergy. But the present condition of the monastic order was unacceptable in God's sight, polluted by its worldly compromise and ambitions. Needed, said Joachim in *Everlasting Gospel*, was a new monastic order, one that understood these three epochs and was unafraid to confront the corruption of the church. According to Joachim, this new era was nearly at hand, and his followers set themselves to prepare the way, like John the Baptist clearing a path for Christ. When was the new era of the Spirit set to arrive? In AD 1260.

Spiritual Franciscans heeded Joachim's call.[74] Seeing the polluted witness of the Franciscans, they set themselves to reform the order to Francis's original intentions, convinced the new era would descend as a reward. Joachim never lived long enough to see his predictions come true, but the Spiritual Franciscans were confident their reformed order was the one Joachim envisioned, the order to usher in the new epoch in AD 1260.

Debate between Conventual and Spiritual Franciscans grew fierce throughout the latter half of the thirteenth century but came to a head in the first two decades of the fourteenth century. Pope John XXII's sympathies resided with the Conventual Franciscans, which did not scare the Spiritual Franciscans but galvanized them to oppose the pope. Since he stood against them, he must be the Antichrist who, according to the book of Revelation, would lead the church astray.

---

72. Some date his birth as early as 1132.

73. The following works by Joachim are relevant: *Liber de concordiae Novi et Veteris Testamenti*; *Expositio in Apocalypsim*; *Psalterium decem chordarum*.

74. The Spiritual Franciscans had many leaders, some first generation, others second generation. E.g., Pisan Franciscan, Gerard of Borgo San Donnino (see his *Introduction to the Eternal Gospel*), Peter John Olivi (see his *Commentary on the Apocalypse*).

THE CONDEMNATION OF JOACHIM'S TRINITARIANISM

Joachim of Fiore's views were condemned by the papacy for several reasons. First, his communitarian vision of monasticism during the era of the Spirit as the successor to the priestly era of the Son was an obvious threat to the authority of the papacy. While Joachim did not advocate violence, the papacy still interpreted his reading of history through an insubordinate lens. Second, by assigning persons of the Trinity to only one epoch of history, Joachim risked tritheism. Classical Nicene Trinitarianism emphasized each person's distinction by virtue of personal properties (unbegotten Father, begotten Son, spirated Spirit) and believed it was then fitting to say that each person could appropriate a work of salvation that was consistent with his eternal relation of origin (e.g., the Father sends the Son to become incarnate). Nevertheless, they also emphasized that no matter what era of history was in view or what work of salvation was under consideration, all three persons of the Trinity operated as one. The external works of the Trinity are indivisible. The persons act as one because they are one in essence, each a subsistence of the simple, inseparable divine nature. However, Joachim appeared to violate the simplicity of the Trinity by segregating persons from one another entirely, restricting them to specific epochs. Furthermore, Joachim appeared to conflate God in himself with what occurs in history. As Ozment said, "In Joachim's vision, the unfolding of secular history, the history of salvation, and the trinitarian nature of God were one process" (Ozment, *Age of Reform*, 104). For these reasons, Joachim's theology was condemned by the Fourth Lateran Council (1215).

When the pope heard about his new role in the book of Revelation, he responded with his own verdict in one papal bull after another, starting in 1317, dismantling the Spiritual Franciscan view of poverty and property. True Christian obedience is not a matter of abandoning and condemning property ownership but a matter of spiritual sacrifice. Furthermore, the bulls condemned Joachim and his followers, shaming their interpretation of history. The Spirit has always been and continues to be present in the church wherever salvation is found. Thirsting for a higher experience of the Spirit, one that brings eternity into the present may be right. However, the key is not a prophecy but discipline. "The medieval church did acknowledge that a few could rise beyond the bounds of time and experience a genuine 'third age' in the present life. This was not, however, by Joachite prophecy but by rare mystical experience. Mysticism made it possible for individuals to pass momentarily beyond the limitations of the present age and touch eternity," said Ozment. "In the fourteenth century, mysticism became to the poverty movement of the twelfth and thirteenth centuries what monasticism had been to martyrdom in the early Christian centuries: the continuation in a new form of an ideal that had ceased to be practicable. Those who could not be impoverished in fact would become so in mind and in spirit."[75]

What happened to the Spiritual Franciscans after the release of Pope John's bulls? No longer were these Spiritual Franciscans reforming their order from within the confines of the Catholic Church; they were now heretics to be hunted down. And who better to capture and burn these *Fraticelli*, little brothers, than the Inquisition itself? Since the Inquisition was supplied agents by the Dominicans, the Spiritual Franciscans grew to despise the Dominican order.

Despite fierce persecution, the Spiritual Franciscans hid themselves across Europe and somehow managed to survive the reign of Pope John XXII. Two centuries later, the same year Martin Luther posted his Ninety-Five Theses, Pope Leo X decided that the Franciscan order had been cursed by conflict long enough. The two warring sides—Conventual and Spiritual—must exist independently of one another, ruled by their own leaders. Little did Pope Leo realize that the Franciscan order had already influenced a German friar about to set the church aflame with further controversy.[76]

LATE MEDIEVAL GERMAN MYSTICISM

By the fourteenth and fifteenth centuries, the disunity of the papacy of the past and the increasing corruption of its churches became impossible to conceal. Disenchanted, many across Europe desired a fresh and far more devout spiritual experience. That yearning was present in Germany and found a voice among the Dominicans. Eager for a better spiritual path, Meister Eckhart and John Tauler emerged in the fourteenth century, followed by Thomas à Kempis in the fifteenth century. The explosion of mysticism along the Rhine River was surprising. Much of the ecclesiastical action was occurring in other European countries. Yet out of the little town of Bethlehem a piety emerged that became contagious.

This new German pietism lacked uniformity. Unlike the monastic orders, it had neither an official institution nor structure nor a single leader or faculty of professors but was caught and carried on by example, proclamation, and literary output. It shared similarities with the older medieval mystics and their orders. It, too, put matters of the heart in first place in the life of the Christian. It, too, withdrew from the world for the sake of spiritual ascent. It, too, practiced the mortification of the flesh and looked to the incarnate Christ as the path to mystical union with God.

Yet late medieval German mysticism differed in some respects as well, not so much in beliefs but emphases. For example, the new German mystics claimed

---

75. Ozment, *Age of Reform*, 115. On each of Pope John's bulls, as well as the critical response to the bulls by Michael of Cesena and William of Ockham, see 113–14. Also consult Leff, *Heresy in the Later Middles Ages*, 1:208.

76. Luther was influenced by Nicholas of Lyra (see ch. 3). Needham, *Two Thousand Years of Christ's Power*, 345–46.

regeneration as the primary doctrine and experience that should define Christian identity, a foundation for spiritual initiation and the driving force behind sanctification and the final unification of the soul with divinity itself. Their emphasis on the new birth also led some German mystics to abandon the methods and ambitions of Scholasticism, either in whole or in part. And although they did not oppose the church, they did consider its stress on externals (e.g., church offices, sacraments, flagellation) subordinate to what mattered most: the conversion of the heart and its love for Christ.

To prioritize the internal focus of Christian spirituality, the new German mystics took to the vernacular, using language the laity could understand. The church, by restricting itself to Latin, could perform its external rites but sometimes struggled to invest the significance of those rites within the heart of the recipient. The German mystics overcame that barrier by communicating their message in the language of the people and in a way that was as simple as it was spiritual.[77]

Eckhart, Tauler, Suso, and *A German Theology*

Mysticism pervaded Europe, but its roots in Germany were strong and sometimes moved far outside the boundaries of the church. For example, consider Meister Eckhart, also known as Eckhart von Hockheim (ca. 1260–ca. 1327/28). Eckhart was trained as a Dominican from his youth, and at the turn of the fourteenth century, he traveled between Germany and France, serving in both academic and pastoral roles, advising monastic orders of all different types. Eckhart was a Scholastic, but like other Scholastics (Bonaventure, Hugh and Richard of St. Victor, et al.) he did not consider his Scholasticism at odds with his mystic spirituality. However, Eckhart did not model the type of synthesized balance so central to the *Summa Theologiae* of Thomas Aquinas. Thomas knew the benefits but also the limitations of Greek philosophy; Eckhart, by contrast, did not, at least from the perspective of his critics.[78]

For example, Eckhart advocated for the birth of humanity in eternity. Before humans existed on earth, they existed in eternity and upon death return to their eternal state. "By virtue of this eternal birth," said Eckhart, "I have been eternally, I am now, and I shall be forevermore."[79] For Eckhart, birth in eternity substantiates a human's union with the eternal God. Humans were united to God in eternity, and now, in their present state, they journey back to union with God.

---

77. These differences and more are chronicled in greater detail by Schaff, *History of the Christian Church*, 5:240–42.

78. "The German Dominican school of which he was a leading figure showed the influence in particular of Neoplatonist texts, such as the *Book of Causes*, and Avicenna's highly platonizing way of reading Aristotle's *De Anima*. One of the chief characteristics of this school was the tendency to combine philosophical and theological positions in a comprehensive understanding of the unity of truth: all that is true, whether in knowledge, in Scripture or in nature, flows from a single fount, a single root." Davies, "Later Medieval Mystics," 225; quoting *LW* 3:4–5.

79. *Deutsche Mystiker des 14. Jahrhunderts: Meister Eckhart*, 2:281; cf. Ozment, *Age of Reform*, 128–33, for a synopsis of Eckhart's view.

WOMEN AND MEDIEVAL MYSTICS

Universities were limited to men in the Middle Ages. Since the academic parlance of the university was Latin, the majority of women could not read academic works. That did not mean, however, that they could not learn the ideas in the air. For example, Meister Eckhart preached to women and received a notable following as a result. Women eager to spread mystic ideas took to the vernacular. "Women's spiritual writing often shows a greater degree of innovative originality than that of men, who were working more closely within set patterns of thought and expression" (Davies, "Later Medieval Mystics," 227). By default, if a woman wanted to transcend the limits of an educational system restricted to men, she had to be bold, even daring and defiant.

Some women, such as Mechthild of Magdeburg (b. 1212) and Julian of Norwich (ca. 1342–1416), even became leading mystics in their day. Julian paid special attention to the ways Scripture used feminine descriptors to describe the compassion and love of God and Christ. "A mother's is the most intimate, willing and dependable of all services, because it is the truest of all. None has been able to fulfil it properly but Christ. . . . The human mother will suckle her child with her own milk, but our beloved Mother, Jesus, feeds us with himself, and, with the most tender courtesy, does it by means of the Blessed Sacrament, the precious food of all true life" (*Julian of Norwich*, 169–70).

Those who do not feel united to God here and now may wonder how they can achieve such a human-divine reunion. Eckhart's advice is to look *within*, to examine the soul where a spark can be found. This spark is "like the divine nature." This spark is not limited by the confines of this temporal world— "Untouched by any createdness, by any nothingness"—but moves us beyond our physical experience to our heavenly origin.[80] By some miracle, this spark was not extinguished by Adam's fall but continued in all his children. It can be seen whenever creatures do what is good, and it calls each of them back to God, back to their existence prior to this earth.

While other mystics exercised spiritual disciplines to subdue their mind, will, and emotions to God, Eckhart argued for a union far more ontological. For example, the sixth century philosopher Boethius represented many church fathers before him and many medieval theologians after him when he said our participation in the likeness of God is the means to eternal happiness. "Since it is through the possession of happiness that people become happy, and since happiness is in fact divinity, it is clear that it is through the possession of divinity that they become happy. . . . Each happy individual is therefore divine." But then Boethius qualified, "While only God is so by nature, as many as you like may become so by participation."[81]

---

80. Davies, ed., *The Rhineland Mystics*, German Sermon 28 (p. 31); cf. Davies, "Later Medieval Mystics," 226.
81. Boethius, *The Consolation of Philosophy*, 3.10 (p. 71).

However, Eckhart's work did not seem to retain the Creator-creature distinction by means of participation. By finding their way back to their eternal home, Christians are absorbed into divinity itself. They emanated from God and, upon mystical reunion, emanated back into God. "In the breakthrough to God I discovered that God and I are one," Eckhart said.[82] Existence in the present world, then, is awkward and uncomfortable, even undesirable. It is not natural; the Christian must transcend it and overcome it to reestablish union in the Godhead. The Christian must separate himself altogether, even to the point of seclusion—*Abgeschiedenheit.*[83]

For the medieval critic, Eckhart's view violated the Creator-creature distinction so fundamental to the patristic view of God. From nearly every corner of the medieval world—from Dominicans to the Franciscans—Eckhart was accused of pantheism. For it is difficult to see how the Creator and the creature do not become one and the same when participation is erased. The papacy did not approve either; in 1329 the papacy listed twenty-eight reasons Eckhart's view was heretical.

Despite Eckhart's controversial theology, his mysticism was influential, perpetuated by Germans such as Johann Tauler (1300–1361) and Heinrich Suso (ca. 1295–ca. 1360/66), although they did not disseminate some of Eckhart's radical conclusions on the divine nature. Tauler's emphasis on internals (new heart; regeneration) over externals (pope and sacraments), his default to a simple faith as opposed to Scholastic intricacies, and his belief in the power of the spoken word in the vernacular all deeply affected young Martin Luther in the sixteenth century.[84] Eckhart's mysticism also influenced the Friends of God both in Germany and Switzerland, who contributed one of the most prominent works of mysticism, *A German Theology* (*Theologica Germanica*).[85] Who wrote *A German Theology* remains evasive, but it left an undeniable impression on young Martin Luther, who said he placed the *German Theology* next to the Scriptures and Augustine. We will return to the subject of mysticism and the Reformers at the end of this chapter. For now, the reason why *A German Theology* influenced a young Reformer like Luther had everything to do with its simple instruction from the New Testament on the way to salvation. That way to salvation is none other than Christ. Although sinners are dead in Adam, they are made alive in Christ. Born again, they have been liberated. Rather than positioning works as a qualifier to justification, *A German Theology* introduced works as the glad obedience of those set free, which could be one reason Luther was so drawn to

82. Eckhart, quoted in *Deutsche Mystiker des 14. Jahrhunderts*, 2:284; 1.11–22; cf. Ozment, *Age of Reform*, 130.

83. Schaff, *History of the Christian Church*, 5:238 (cf. 6:259). Over against those who try to defend Eckhart from the pantheism accusation, Ozment said, "The point of Eckhart's work, however, and certainly its effects on others beyond his control, was not to exalt the distance creation had placed between God and man, but to overcome it. . . . In the final analysis, Eckhart begrudged all reality beyond the eternal birth; for him, man was meant to be in God, not to live as a creature in the world." Ozment, *Age of Reform*, 132.

84. Schaff, *History of the Christian Church*, 6:258–59.

85. See Ozment, *Age of Reform*, 87, esp. comments on *German Theology* and Luther. For Tauler's influence on Luther, see Leppin, "Luther's Roots in Monastic-Mystical Piety," 55–60.

the book, along with its Christ-centered focus. Nevertheless, it may be premature to label *A German Theology* a forerunner text of the Reformation.[86]

THE *DEVOTIO MODERNA*

A German Theology was not the only influence on the Reformers. The *devotio moderna* (modern devotion) informed sixteenth-century spirituality as well. If Germany was home to the mysticism of Eckhart, Tauler, Suso, and the *German Theology*, the Netherlands was the launching pad of the *devotio moderna* in the fourteenth century, due in large part to Gerard Groote (1340–84), a layman in the church. Groote, however, was no typical layman; he had a passion for preaching. Groote was well educated too, his affluency providing him the opportunity to study across Europe, including France, Germany, and the Netherlands. He could have become a follower of Meister Eckhart, for example, but Groote was not persuaded by Eckhart's brand of mysticism. He did believe, nevertheless, that any theological education should have piety as its end. That telos characterized Groote's Brethren of the Common Life. The single-minded focus on piety was infectious; after Groote's death in 1384, his form of spirituality continued into the fifteenth century and spread internationally. Yet the Modern Devotion was not a dissenting spirituality but operated within the life of the church and parallel monastic orders, attempting to reform the lives of clergy and laity alike.

The success of the Modern Devotion continued with a German: Thomas à Kempis (1380–1471). Although he was a German by birth, in his youth Thomas à Kempis was accepted into the monastic life of Mount Saint Agnes. He was born the same year Groote died, and although he never did learn from Groote firsthand, Groote's mysticism influenced him more than anyone else's spirituality.[87] Yet Groote was not the only influence on Thomas à Kempis; Augustine and Bernard of Clairvaux can also be heard across his writings. Nevertheless, Thomas à Kempis did chart a vision of the Christian life that distinguished his view of spiritual ascent.

That vision is apparent in his classic work of spirituality, *The Imitation of Christ*. The book was written sometime between 1420 and 1427, and each chapter consists of sayings, almost proverbs, followed by a dialogue between Jesus and a disciple. In the opening chapter, Thomas à Kempis made a hard contrast between the life of learning (likely an allusion to Scholasticism) and the life of piety. The Christian life is not the former but the latter, occupied day and night with meditating on the life of Jesus in order to conform to his example. Although Thomas à Kempis was not against learning per se, he was suspicious because it can displace piety. "What good does it do you to be able to give a learned discourse on the Trinity, while you are without humility and, thus, are displeasing to the Trinity? Esoteric words neither make us holy nor righteous;

---

86. Schaff observed how the Roman Catholic Church in the seventeenth century praised the book just as much as Luther. Schaff, *History of the Christian Church*, 6:295.

87. E.g., Thomas à Kempis, *Prayers and Meditations on the Life of Christ*.

only a virtuous life makes us beloved of God. I would rather experience repentance in my soul than know how to define it." Thomas à Kempis then criticized Scholasticism: "If you knew the entire Bible inside out and all the maxims of the philosophers, what good would it do you if you were, at the same time, without God's love and grace?"[88] If ever there was a mystic who championed deeds over creeds, it was Thomas à Kempis.[89]

Pervasive throughout *Imitation of Christ* is a constant disdain for the things of this world (the visible, the material) in contrast to that which is spiritual (the invisible, immaterial). Withdrawal is a repeated exhortation, extraction from the sinful nature of the flesh and anything in this world that might jeopardize God's benevolence. "Therefore, withdraw your heart from the love of things visible and turn yourself to things invisible. Those who yield to their sensual nature dishonor their conscience and forfeit God's grace."[90]

The chapters that follow this introductory admonition address innumerable topics pertaining to Christian living, but at the core of each is a primary concern for transformation, an inner change that mortifies the flesh by means of self-control and fosters a genuine love for Christ above all. Thomas à Kempis was suspicious of formalism or overreliance on externals, a religiosity that matters little if the heart of the person is not right. He said, "Wearing a monk's habit and having one's head tonsured produces little change in the monk himself. What truly distinguishes the real religious are his change in outlook on life and the complete control of his passions." That contrast was an admonition for those monks who used the monastery for self-gain. "He who seeks anything in the monastery other than God and his soul's salvation will find nothing but sadness and misery, and he who strives not to be the least of all and the servant of all, will not enjoy peace very long."[91]

The way forward was (1) a renunciation of all worldly cares and (2) a dedication to contemplating God. Thomas à Kempis looked for examples among the Carthusians and the Cistercians, but the desert fathers were the most perfect models in these two respects. "In earthly things they were poor, but in grace and virtue they were opulent. Outwardly they were in want, but inwardly they regaled in God's consoling grace."[92] We have yet to assess the Reformation continuity and discontinuity with monastic spirituality. Yet the contrast between

---

88. Thomas à Kempis, *Imitation of Christ* 1.3. Later he targeted Scholasticism: "Why should we concern ourselves with such philosophical words as *genera* and *species*? He whom the eternal Word teaches is set free from a multitude of theories" (3.2; p. 6).

89. "If we were as diligent in uprooting vices and planting virtues as we are in debating abstruse questions, there would not be so many evils or scandals among us nor such laxity in monastic communities. Certainly, when Judgment Day comes we shall not be asked what books we have read, but what deeds we have done; we shall not be asked how well we have debated, but how devoutly we have lived." Thomas à Kempis, 1.3.5.

90. Thomas à Kempis, 1.1.5.

91. Thomas à Kempis, 1.17.2.

92. "These holy Fathers are given as models to us religious and their examples more powerfully spur us on to advance in holiness than the multitude of the lukewarm can entice us to become lax." Thomas à Kempis, 1.18.3, 4 (p. 23).

Thomas à Kempis and Martin Luther on the desert fathers is vivid already. For Thomas à Kempis, modeling these desert fathers required solitude and silence, withdrawal from the world, a practice the young Augustinian monk Martin Luther knew well. When Thomas à Kempis described the cloister life that he thought was exemplary, he might as well have described Luther's experience. "They rarely go out and they live a retired life; their diet is poor and the habit they wear is coarse; their hours of labor are long and they speak very little; they extend their vigils late into the night and they rise early. They spend a great deal of time in prayer and in reading, but in all things, these religious always keep themselves under discipline."[93]

However, as Luther reached Reformation convictions—such as the priesthood of believers—he advised a modified scheme. Thomas à Kempis exclaimed, "How undisturbed a conscience we would have if we never went searching after ephemeral joys nor concerned ourselves with the affairs of the world! What great peace and tranquility would be ours if we had severed ourselves from useless preoccupations, put our trust in God, and thought only of divine things and our salvation!"[94] Luther disagreed. Enter the world, he said to the average layman, with every confidence that your vocation—from farmer to clerk to nursing mother—is not some "useless preoccupation" but just as worthy of God's pleasure and just as useful in God's kingdom as the priest in the cathedral or the monk in the monastery. As Luther said in 1521, monastic vows are "no better than working on a farm or any other kind of manual work."[95]

Furthermore, although Thomas à Kempis did not major on penance, purgatory, and the fires of hell like a sixteenth-century preacher such as Luther's early nemesis Johann Tetzel, nevertheless, these beliefs were still present. A "strict life with hard penances," said Thomas à Kempis, "will then bring you more pleasure than any worldly delight." Failure to abide by such hard penances, however, is damning. "If a modicum of suffering now makes you uneasy, what will hell's fire do to you?"[96] The Christian must "remain faithful and fervent in good works," and then God will give the appropriate reward.[97] That model of faithfulness never sat well with Luther. Faithfulness is not found in ourselves but in Christ. Justification by imitation relies not on the righteousness of Christ but on the righteousness of sinners who model themselves after Christ.[98]

---

93. Thomas à Kempis, 1.25.8 (p. 42).

94. Thomas à Kempis, 1.20.4 (p. 28). "But the saints of God and all the faithful friends of Christ scorn what pleases the flesh and what thrives and flourishes in this world, and have directed all their hope toward eternal things. All their desires tended heavenwards, to things invisible and everlasting, lest the love of things visible should drag them down and bind them here below" (1.22.4). He also advocated for an infused grace into the soul. See 3.54.8.

95. *LW* 44:295.

96. Thomas à Kempis, *Imitation of Christ* 1.24.6 (p. 38).

97. Thomas à Kempis, 1.25.1 (p. 39).

98. Luther "could even oppose the *imitatio Christi* piety of the later Middle Ages, noting sarcastically that a successful imitation would require Christians to be born of a virgin, have brown eyes, and walk on water. Such an imitation piety is the antithesis of what Luther regards as a proper theology of vocation; namely, his

MYSTICS CRITICAL OF SCHOLASTICS: GERSON AND NICHOLAS

Mystics may have been defined by renunciation of the world and contemplation of God, but that did not mean all mystics contemplated God the same. Some mystics grew critical of the Scholastic approach to contemplation, for example.

The Franciscans' later adherents (e.g., William of Ockham) may have shifted from suspicion of Scholasticism toward an embrace of the Scholastic method. However, not every spiritual tradition moved in that direction. For example, at the turn of the fifteenth century in France, Jean Gerson (1363–1429) set his mystical theology over against Scholastic thought in his book *On Mystical Theology*. Gerson had stood by and watched as followers of Scotus and Ockham debated ad nauseum with followers of Thomas Aquinas at the University of Paris. Weary of these intellectual debates, Gerson concluded that the way to God could not be the path of reason. Rather, the way to God must be paved by the emotions. The soul's journey to God did not travel through the head but the heart. Gerson did not jettison theology altogether, but he did believe spirituality was the proper focus of the Christian faith and life.

By implication, a doctrine's importance was largely determined by its relevance to Christian spirituality. Key components of the Trinity, like eternal generation and eternal spiration, had little use. They were speculative. Gerson advocated dispensing with complex theological inquiry and sticking to the Bible. Gerson detested advanced theological vocabulary, proposing instead that theologians must limit themselves to language laypersons can follow. In practice, Gerson's biblicist method meant distancing the Christian faith from theological debates to focus instead on the moral instructions of the Bible that tell the Christian how to live. Gerson recommended that theological education be reconfigured so that at least half of the student's time was spent on Christian living. Books assigned to students were to focus on the mystical experience of God; theological tomes and treatises on the endless disputes over eternal divine matters were to be suppressed.[99]

Gerson's revisionist program resulted in the priority of preaching over theological discipline. His student Nicholas of Clémanges (ca. 1363–1437) accelerated such an emphasis so that theology's main purpose became the pulpit. Deeds over doctrine, love over logic—here lay the minister's method as he approached his people. Anything else was pointless. Following Gerson's lead, Nicholas cultivated an anti-intellectualism that became standard in reactions against Scholasticism.[100]

---

conviction that Christians are called to serve God in their own space and time and not in the space and time of the apostles." Steinmetz, *Luther in Context*, 139.

99. See Gerson, *Oeuvres completes*, 1:113; 2:26–38; 3:242–43; as cited in Ozment, *Age of Reform*, 73–78. On the specific historical sources Gerson selected for his revised curriculum, see 76–77. For treatments of Gerson, see Connolly, *John Gerson*.

100. Nicholas of Clèmanges, *De studio theologico*, 475–79. "In Nicholas we find strong anti-intellectual tendencies, which became typical of much late medieval and Reformation criticism of scholasticism. Actually, Nicholas only expanded on a religious anti-intellectualism that was bone and fiber of the medieval spiritual

DISSENT: THE WALDENSIANS

The move away from medieval Christianity's more academic setting is apparent with the Waldensians, who took their name from Peter Waldes (Valdes), or Waldo, in Lyons, France, who lived during the twelfth century and beginning of the thirteenth century. Waldo decided he needed to read both the Bible and the patristics at great length to determine what it really meant to follow Christ. As an affluent man, he afterward concluded that imitation of Christ had to be taken with earnestness. To demonstrate his allegiance, he gave everything he possessed to the destitute of society, a type of worldly abandonment also imitated by his followers. Waldo even left behind his family for this purpose.

As for the church, Waldo adopted an oppositional stance to the papacy by denying the supremacy and perfection of the pope and instead elevating the Bible as the church's final authority. Many of the doctrines the Reformers rejected in the sixteenth century were already jettisoned by the Waldensians of the twelfth century. For example, the Waldensians did not believe Christians should pray for their dead loved ones in purgatory. In fact, the Waldensians did not even believe in purgatory. Nor did they believe Christians or priests should make oaths. Neither did they accept the restrictions against translating the Scriptures but devoted themselves to translating the Scriptures into French so that average laypersons did not have to rely on Latin, a language they probably did not know. The Waldensians were not, however, an academic guild. After vowing poverty, they took to lay preaching. Sometimes their lay sermons took aim at the doctrines and practices of the church.

The Waldensians sought sanction from Alexander at the Third Lateran Council (1179), but the self-commissioned nature of their ministry and lay preaching was met with disapproval by Pope Alexander III. Back in Lyons, the archbishop wanted proof the Waldensians were not a heretical sect. In 1180 Waldensius wrote *The Profession of Faith of Valdes* to defend his orthodoxy and catholicity. He started his *Profession* affirming the Trinitarian vocabulary of the creeds: "Let it be known to all the faithful that I, Valdes, and all my brethren ... believe ... that the Father, the Son, and the Holy Spirit are consubstantial, coeternal, and co-omnipotent; and that each person of the Trinity is fully God, all three persons one God, as is contained in the creeds, the Apostles' Creed, the Nicene Creed, and the Athanasian Creed."[101]

Waldensius then followed the structure of the creeds, moving from the Trinity to creation and ultimately to the incarnation. Most revealing was Waldensius's unqualified confession, "We believe in one church, catholic, holy, apostolic, and immaculate, outside of which no one can be saved." Waldensius did not view himself or his followers as outside the church but as those within the church,

---

traditions and had fostered dissent and reform throughout the Middle Ages. For Nicholas, preaching excelled study, the parish the university, practice the life of the mind, as love excelled knowledge. He strongly suspected that impractical genius and unapplied knowledge, common marks of the pure scholastic, were refined iniquity." Ozment, *Age of Reform*, 79.

101. *CCFCT* 1:772.

no less catholic than anyone else, albeit attempting a reform to ensure the church remained apostolic. To further confirm his allegiance, Waldensius signed his name to the sacraments: "We do not in any way reject the sacraments which are celebrated in it [the church]. . . . We firmly believe and absolutely affirm that the eucharist, that is, the bread and wine after consecration, is the body and blood of Jesus Christ and in this nothing more is accomplished by a good priest, nothing less by an evil one." As for the office of the priest, Waldensius was once again affirmative. "We humbly praise and faithfully venerate the ecclesiastical orders, that is, the episcopate and the priesthood."[102]

Despite Waldensius's *Profession*, the Council of Verona (1184) excommunicated the Waldensians. Exiled, the Waldensians managed to survive in other French and Italian territories, ensuring their endurance until the advent of the Reformation itself.

INTOLERANCE FOR DISSENT: FOURTH LATERAN COUNCIL, INNOCENT, AND THE CATHARS

At the turn of the twelfth century, the power of the papacy rose to new heights.[103] In large part, this unprecedented power was due to the political and ecclesiastical ambitions of Lothario Conti, otherwise known as Pope Innocent III.[104]

Innocent's papal supremacy (1198–1216) took the seat of the pope to a new level when he adopted the title "vicar of Christ." Popes prior to Innocent identified themselves as vicars of Peter, representing the apostle and wielding his keys to the kingdom. But Innocent moved beyond Peter to Christ himself, claiming the pope was the representative of Christ on earth. By virtue of this title, Innocent was challenging the Holy Roman Emperor and every king and governor, situating himself as the supreme ruler on earth. Innocent was not only making an ecclesiastical statement but a political one. Every king and emperor was subservient to the pope's power. His superiority was second to none.

Innocent was ready to back up his self-declaration as well, targeting England, France, and Germany. If he could subjugate these most powerful countries, the scope of Innocent's rule could become expansive, leaving no rivals. Innocent spared no ecclesiastical weapons in the process, threatening to excommunicate anyone who challenged his ascent to power. For example, when King John of England backed Stephen Langton as the new archbishop of Canterbury, Innocent blackmailed King John. Either King John backed a cardinal that met Innocent's approval or Innocent would ban all church services. That was no small threat: what clergyman dared risk disobedience to the pope?

King John was not intimidated, and he continued to support Stephen

---

102. Waldensius, *The Profession of Faith of Valdes, 1180,* 1:772–73.

103. To learn more about Innocent, consult Needham, *Two Thousand Years of Christ's Power,* 2:325–32.

104. Ozment included Alexander as well: "This was the period in which popes Alexander III (1159–81) and Innocent III (1198–1216) transformed the papacy into the political and commercial power attacked by reformers down to the Reformation." *Age of Reform,* 98–99.

Langton. Innocent responded with an interdict, and for the next six years the doors of churches across England remained closed. The interdict, however, only infuriated King John even more, hardening the stalemate. When Innocent saw that King John still refused to bend, he condemned John to an eternity in hell. Excommunication by the pope was the worst punishment a soul this side of heaven could receive, because outside the church there was no salvation. But Innocent's excommunication also had political ramifications. Innocent called for a crusade against King John. If he had to, Innocent would recruit kings from all over until a new king sat on England's throne. King John was now helpless, forced to submit himself to Innocent if he had any hope of continuing as king. When he did, churches reopened and John retained his throne, but it was a throne owned by the pope. Innocent's rise in power over England was but one case among many. Innocent used similar tactics over Germany and France.

Toward the conclusion of Innocent's reign, the pope summoned the Fourth Lateran Council (1215). Now that entire countries were subservient to the pope, not only bishops but royal representatives were sent on behalf of kings. Several key decisions were made that set the future trajectory of the papacy.

First, the council declared that salvation could not be located anywhere outside the Catholic Church. "There is indeed one universal church of the faithful, outside of which nobody at all is saved, in which Jesus Christ is both priest and sacrifice."[105]

Second, the council marked the public sanction of transubstantiation. Christ's "body and blood are truly contained in the sacrament of the altar under the forms of bread and wine, the bread and wine having been transubstantiated, by God's power, into his body and blood, so that in order to achieve this mystery of unity we receive from God what he received from us."[106]

Third, the council identified the priest as the one who effects this miracle since he possesses the power of Peter's keys by virtue of his ordination. "Nobody can effect this sacrament except a priest who has been properly ordained according to the church's keys, which Jesus Christ himself gave to the apostles and their successors." Likewise with the sacrament of baptism: "But the sacrament is consecrated in water at the invocation of the undivided Trinity—namely Father, Son, and Holy Spirit—and brings salvation to both children and adults when it is correctly carried out by anyone in the form laid down by the church."[107]

Fourth, the council asserted the penance system by attaching it to the

---

105. *CCFCT* 1:741.
106. *CCFCT* 1:741–42. Aristotle distinguished between substance and accidents. On the one hand, an object has a nature, an essence, a substance. Its substance is not necessarily visible but may be invisible to the eye. Its substance is essential to its identity and purpose. On the other hand, an object also has accidents. Accidents are external, sometimes visible, and nonessential. An accident can be removed or even change, and the substance of a thing remains. In the thirteenth century, the council used Aristotle's distinction concerning physics to justify their theory of transubstantiation in theology. When the bread and wine are consecrated by the priest, they said, the accidents remain unchanged. The bread still looks like bread, even tastes like bread. Likewise the wine. Nonetheless, at the moment of consecration, the substance is changed, transformed into the body and blood of Christ. As later chapters will observe, this was a misuse of Aristotle's distinction.
107. *CCFCT* 1:742.

sacrament itself: "If someone falls into sin after having received baptism, he or she can always be restored through true penitence. For not only virgins and the continent but also married persons find favor with God by right faith and good actions and deserve to attain to eternal blessedness."[108]

The reign of Pope Innocent not only incorporated councils but crusades. The elevation of his office to a place of supremacy precluded the possibility of tolerance toward dissent. At the start of the thirteenth century, a group known as the Cathars had attracted considerable attention. In doctrine, the Cathars were the Gnostics of the High Middle Ages. Their name was a message itself: *we are the elect, the pure and only true Church.*[109] The Cathars were also characterized by their fight for economic independence from the established church.

The existence of the Cathars infuriated Pope Innocent. However, the Cathars were international, not only practicing in Italy (where they were called Paterenes) but especially in southern France (where they were called Albigensians). Yet the murder of the pope's legate in Albigensian territory gave Innocent sufficient reason and motive to commission a crusade that promised to extinguish the Albigensians (as well as the Waldensians) once and for all. With the greedy assistance of northern France at his side, Innocent started the Albigensian Crusade (1209–29). The crusade was long and brutal—a massacre, to be more precise— and one that did not offer mercy to the guiltless. By the end of the two decades, southern France had nothing left to show for itself.

The crusade was successful in its consolidation of papal power. Hunting down heretics proved not only ecclesiastically advantageous but politically expedient, ensuring in a short amount of time that foreign territories moved to the beat of papal authority. During the Albigensian crusade, Innocent made strategic use of the Inquisition, repositioning its power toward the papacy.[110] Papal legates were sent out like spies, trained to sniff out the slightest whiff of a secret meeting, Cathar or Waldensian, and then torture and punish the religious perpetrators, sometimes even putting the dissenter to death. By 1227 the papacy had created an entire division devoted to the castigation of religious dissent. Agents of the Inquisition not only possessed considerable power but freedom, answering to the pope alone.[111]

Pope Innocent III had no tolerance for dissent. It mattered not whether it

---

108. *CCFCT* 1:741–42.

109. On the debate over the historicity of the Cathars, a detailed history of Cathar conflict with Innocent, and a history of other dissenters like the Petrobrusians, see Needham, *Two Thousand Years of Christ's Power*, 2:335–38.

110. "During the pontificate of Pope Alexander III (1159–1181), the Inquisition appeared as an instrument of coercive episcopal authority to ensure diocesan discipline. Pope Innocent III (1198–1216) centralized it in the papacy, and it became henceforth a judicial proceeding carried out by papal legates chosen from the established monastic or mendicant orders." Ozment, *Age of Reform*, 95.

111. "The activities of the inquisition forced dissenting movements (like the Waldensians) to meet in secret. This is the main reason why we know so little about the history of religious dissent in medieval Catholic Europe, compared with what we know of the history of the Catholic Church itself." Needham, *Two Thousand Years of Christ's Power*, 2:340.

was doctrinal or spiritual heterodoxy.[112] Popes like Innocent, however, not only tolerated but supported monastic orders that could guard Catholic doctrine and practices and assist in punishing dissenters.

MONASTIC ORDERS AND THE PAPACY

The monastic life's popularity in the Middle Ages is hard to overemphasize, an esteem due to spiritual reasons no doubt but practical and material benefits as well. The Middle Ages were characterized by threats that ranged from starvation to unemployment, from plagues to warfare. Convents became safe havens from innumerable struggles, microcommunities that provided food, spiritual care, and education in theology, philosophy, and the arts. In some cases, convents became hubs of affluency. Convents cultivated their own property and harvest, benefiting everyone inside, and gave opportunities for skilled monks to become practitioners in the arts, painting frescos, sculpting statues for convents and churches alike, even building cathedrals. Those monks with extraordinary intellects could become theologians and philosophers, and some, like the monks of Cluny, even produced several popes.[113]

Due to their relationship with the papacy, monastic orders gained incredible power and influence in ecclesiastical and political affairs. In the early Middle Ages, one could be a monk without becoming a priest. That changed starting in the eleventh century; to become a monk was all but a guarantee of priesthood.[114] As its constituency grew, the papacy realized that the monastic orders could be leveraged to advance its program, both in the church and in the world. Rome granted monastic orders a variety of privileges, and in return monks supported the ambitions of the papacy. Sometimes those ambitions were doctrinal; popes recruited monks to lead the Inquisition and the elimination of heresy. Sometimes those ambitions were political; popes counted on monks to support the papacy's desired dominion over magistrates.

That arrangement elevated the authority of monks above other ecclesiastical offices, creating tension between monks on one hand and prelates and bishops on the other hand. However, with power and influence came an identity crisis. The mutual benefiting relationship between monks and popes was nothing short of ironic.[115] Monks originally represented a withdrawal from the world. Now they supported the papacy's reach for political power in the world and in exchange for special exemptions. To critics, especially the sixteenth-century Reformers, that smelled like compromise and tasted like hypocrisy.

---

112. Ozment, *Age of Reform*, 95.
113. Popes included Gregory VII, Urban II, and Pascal II. Schaff, *History of the Christian Church*, 5:313, 331.
114. Schaff, 5:313.
115. Schaff, 5:325–27.

MYSTICISM AND THE REFORMATION

The Reformation is not often remembered for its spirituality. Yet in increasing measure Reformation historians are now recognizing that the Reformers did possess and pass on a spiritual vision. With sixteenth-century reform came a transforming vision of the Christian life, a vision just as significant as its renewed vision for theology and ecclesiology. Whether that vision was indebted to the medieval mystics, however, remains a complicated matter. As in chapters 3 and 4's study of Scholasticism, the answer is neither a simple yes or no. A better answer is more nuanced, one that recognizes streams of continuity and discontinuity.

Continuity

On one hand, the Reformation was not a total break with the mysticism of the past. One could even argue that the Reformation emerged from the soil of mysticism, even if such a claim needs qualification.[116]

For example, consider late medieval mystics in Germany. *A German Theology* and mystics like John Tauler had a major influence on young Luther. In 1508 Luther read Tauler's sermons and took them to heart as he contemplated his own struggles over Christian obedience and devotion. In a letter to Spalatin, Luther could not praise Tauler enough; neither could Melanchthon, who considered Tauler without rival on matters of the heart.[117] In 1516 Luther crossed paths with another German mystical treatise by an unknown author, and Luther was so inspired that he published the book as *A Spiritually Noble Little Book*.[118] The book Luther acquired, however, was incomplete. When he discovered a more complete version, he published it in 1518 as *A German Theology*. Luther gave the book supreme praise: "No book except the Bible and St. Augustine has come to my attention from which I have learned more about God, Christ, man, and all things."[119]

Luther wrote a short preface to the book, one that revealed the connection in Luther's mind between his reformation (which had only just begun) and *A German Theology*. As mentioned, one of the strengths of the new German mystics was their accommodation to the common Christian by means of the vernacular and simple prose. Luther recognized that the movement before him did not have the prestige of the papacy and its institution; of course, neither did an Augustinian monk in Wittenberg, which made the comparison so fitting. Yet none of this bothered Luther; the Reformer used these weaknesses to claim divine support. "When one contemplates God's wonders it is obvious

---

116. See the argument of Schaff, *History of the Christian Church*, 5:241. More recently, see Leppin, "Luther's Roots," 49–61.

117. Schaff also pointed out that the next generation of Reformed thinkers, which included Calvin's successor Theodore Beza, did not share this high opinion of Tauler but considered him a "visionary." Schaff, 6:261.

118. *WA* 1:153.

119. *LW* 31:75.

that brilliant and pompous preachers are never chosen to spread his words [Ps. 8:2]." Do not be irritated by the unassuming German, Luther advised. For "this noble little book, poor and unadorned as it is in words and human wisdom, is the richer and more precious in art and divine wisdom."[120]

The year was 1518, which makes Luther's next comment remarkable. Luther considered this little German treatise a window into his own catholicity. Luther remarked that he and the Wittenberg theologians had been accused of speaking "disgracefully, as though we want to undertake entirely new things." As early as 1518, Luther felt the sting of Rome's accusation that he was teaching novel beliefs, leading people away from the church's catholic heritage. Luther, however, put the burden of proof back on Rome, asking why this old book, *A German Theology*, was absent from the curriculum of the universities. By retrieving this work of theology and spirituality, Luther claimed he was the one reaching back to his ancient roots. "Let anyone who wishes read this little book, and then let him say whether theology is original with us or ancient, for this book is certainly not new." With a punch to his adversaries, retrieving this old book also explained where ancient truths could be found: not in Italy, but Germany. "God grant that this little book will become better known. Then we shall find that German theologians are without a doubt the best theologians. Amen."[121]

Were early Reformers like Luther influenced by the *devotio moderna* as well? That question is debated, but Ozment's assessment moves beyond those debates to pinpoint the contribution of the Modern Devotion: "While the Modern Devotion may in some ways be said to have anticipated and aided the reform movements of the sixteenth century, its main achievement lay in the revival of traditional monasticism on the eve of the Reformation. It demonstrated that the desire to live a simple communal life of self-denial in imitation of Christ and the Apostles was as much alive at the end of the Middle Ages as it had been in the primitive church."[122]

If correct, then the variegated spiritualist traditions of the High and late Middle Ages should throw into doubt that popular assumption that on the eve of the Reformation the church was a spiritual graveyard, lifeless and full of darkness. The evolution and vivacity of monastic life demonstrates quite the opposite: from the laity to the clergy there was a serious, steady dedication to the life of the soul in the Middle Ages. The reaction of the Reformers had far more to do with the corruption of pope and papacy and the system of soteriology that turned lucrative by virtue of the indulgence system. That is not to say the Reformers never took issue with popular piety or monastic spirituality. They did. Martin Luther's crisis started *within* an Augustinian monastery. The monastic view of Christian conversion and the Christian life, when coupled with

---

120. *LW* 31:75.
121. *LW* 31:76.
122. Ozment, *Age of Reform*, 97.

Rome's penance and indulgence system, proved just the right context for Luther's reconsideration of his Christian pilgrimage. At the same time, the Reformers continued to retrieve the mysticism of the Middle Ages even after their evangelical awakening. Medieval piety underlined not only their theology but their spirituality as they drew on representatives like Bernard to advance their vision for the Christian life.[123]

Discontinuity

Thus, Luther's high praise for Tauler and *A German Theology* did not mean that the Reformer retrieved German mysticism in its totality or without criticism. Even though Tauler was critical of ritualism in the church, he nevertheless remained a faithful servant of the church and embraced many of its beliefs (e.g., Mary as mediator), which Reformers like Luther found repugnant.[124]

Luther never did become a mystic himself, retaining serious critiques of its shortcomings. For example, some mystics rested their notion of God and their path to knowing him on a subjective experience, one that assumed a spiritual ascent based on works of penance. Each monk was expected to confess his sins to his abbot. Transparency was rewarded when the abbot absolved the monk. Still, the temporal punishment for sin remained, demanding penance. The monk was required to perform specific acts that satisfied the penance requirement. The severity of these works of satisfaction depended on the seriousness of the sin. In towns, churches practiced the same between their clergy and laity. However, only the monk dedicated himself to such a system of penance day and night. As chapter 8 will reveal, Martin Luther's early Reformation development was born out of that monastic context. Young Luther joined an Augustinian monastery and became a serious practitioner of its penance system.

Therefore, as much as Luther appreciated *A German Theology*, he knew from his own experience that the mystic's soteriological presuppositions could not satisfy. Rather than turning inward (to subjective experience), Luther looked outside himself to the objective righteousness of Jesus Christ.[125] By turning outward, to Christ, by faith, the believer had a far better foundation for knowing God and receiving all the grace, mercy, and love he has in store for every child united to his Son.[126]

---

123. Whether the Reformers should be called mystics is debated; see Leppin, "Luther's Roots," 59.

124. On Tauler's Mariology, see Schaff, *History of the Christian Church*, 6:261–62.

125. "Unlike these [mystics], he [Luther] never became subjective in his approach, but continued to emphasize at every step the doctrine which resulted from his own experience and study, namely, justification by faith. Christ's redemptive act always remained for him a reality, appropriated by a sinner solely by faith through the mercy of God." Grimm, "Introduction," in *LW* 31:73–74.

126. Grimm, 31:74. Harold Grimm did not believe Luther's departure from mysticism was limited to *sola fide*. Luther took issue with the mystic's *Gelassenheit* as well. "Luther rejected the mystic conception of love as essentially 'the sweetness' of the loved one and stressed the active love which suffers and labors for the loved one. This emphasis upon the moral activity of a child of faith stands in sharp contrast to mystical passivity (*Gelassenheit*), contemplation, and ecstasy." Grimm, "Introduction," in *LW* 31:74.

THE JUDGMENT OF MARTIN LUTHER ON MONASTIC VOWS

As mentioned, monastic orders and the papacy had close relations, often (but not always) supporting one another. It may be tempting to read Luther's early protests as restricted to the papacy, but the institution itself was a type of umbrella under which monastic spirituality (and its soteriology) lived and breathed. In the early 1520s, Luther knew that to strike at one was to punch at the other. For example, in 1521 Luther published *The Judgment of Martin Luther on Monastic Vows*. He called the monastic vow a "most pernicious invention" and a "most dangerous thing because it is without the authority and example of Scripture."[127] He announced that "all monks be absolved from their vows," which Luther said are "worthless in the sight of God."[128] Then Luther turned, as he often did, to his most serious charge: the monastic vow is satanic, a doctrine of devils.[129]

Luther's strong accusation was not based merely on his belief that monastic vows were absent from Scripture. He used strong language in his accusation because the monastic vow was an enemy of justification *sola fide*: "They take their vows and live their lives under nothing but the faithless and blasphemous idea that man is able to obtain grace and remission of sins by his natural works."[130] Monks in Luther's day believed that the vow was a "work of supererogation and perfection which has no like or equal," and therefore the monk in the monastery possessed a far superior vocation (and a far shorter path to heaven) than the farmer in the field or the mother nursing her child.[131]

Luther worried that monastic vows, if interpreted within the penance system of his day, could lead to a justification theology determined by merit.[132] "Faith in Christ cannot tolerate grace and justification coming from our own works or the works of others, for faith knows and confesses continually that grace and justification come from Christ alone." If a vow was taken, it must be taken under an entirely different premise, one that does not think vows are "necessary for righteousness, salvation, and the remission of sins." Luther believed, "Faith alone is necessary."[133] Vows, by contrast, threatened the basis of justification (*solus Christus*) and the instrumental cause of justification (*sola fide*). "Is it not clear that those who take their vows in the belief that they will live good lives and earn their salvation by this way of life, and that they will wipe away their sins and become rich in good works, are blasphemous Jews and apostates from the faith, indeed, who rather blaspheme and deny the faith? They attribute to their laws and good works what properly belongs to faith alone."[134]

---

127. *LW* 44:252.
128. *LW* 44:282.
129. *LW* 44:285, 289.
130. *LW* 44:288 (cf. 281).
131. *LW* 44:295.
132. One should not assume all monks from past eras committed the error Luther targets. For example, Augustine himself was a monk.
133. *LW* 44:286.
134. *LW* 44:280.

Luther did place a high premium on works, but their place is not before but after justification *sola fide*. Good works "do not really pertain to the remission of sins and a serene conscience, but are the fruits of a forgiveness already granted and still present, as well as of a good conscience."[135] Luther was convinced as well that the best monks of the patristic and medieval periods agreed. Consider Bernard of Clairvaux, for example, whom Luther quoted at length. Bernard was a monk, but he did not consider his vow a work, a merit that substantiated his right standing with God. Instead, Bernard "put all his faith in Christ and despaired absolutely of his own works." Even on his deathbed, as he considered his many good deeds, he trusted in none of them for the afterlife. Bernard "takes no pride in his vow of poverty, obedience, and chastity; in fact, he calls his life wasted. . . . He is aware of the judgment of God before whom no one stands save Christ alone and his righteousness. It was for that reason he abandoned his own righteousness and betook himself to Christ, declaring that his own righteousness was wasted."[136]

LUTHER, BERNARD, AND CATHOLIC SPIRITUALITY

Luther did not think Bernard was the exception either, since "the rest of the saints" followed the same model. Luther enlisted the Fathers and contrasted them with monks of his present day who "make a great show of works which the fathers condemned, and under the pretext of the example of the saints the godless teach a departure from the faith."[137] Luther was claiming, in other words, that his condemnation of merit-based vows was not novel but aligned with the church catholic. Luther's catholicity was supported not only by the example of Bernard on his deathbed but by the many fathers who came before him. Whereas monks of Luther's day had distorted the monastic intention by misusing vows to make humans good, as if they could somehow attain righteousness by this dedication and devotion.

Luther qualified that he was not, in principle, against vows. "The vow is and remains a human invention. Yet it is not altogether ridiculous. Voluntarily to vow subjection of this kind for only a given time is not without worth."[138] For example, Luther might be open to a vow if it sounded like this: "I vow to thee obedience, chastity, and poverty, together with the whole rule of St. Augustine until death. I do it of my own free will, which means that I would be free to change my mind if it seemed good."[139] Such a vow is said out of voluntary

---

135. *LW* 44:279.

136. *LW* 44:290. Some claim Luther abandoned mystical piety after his evangelical turn, but his use of Bernard here says otherwise. Leppin goes further to say Luther's mystical side was even foundational for his theology of the cross. Leppin, "Luther's Roots," 53.

137. *LW* 44:291. And again, "Bernard and many others have been saved. But in these cases, the poison did them no harm because of the faith in Christ with which they were filled" (44:288–89).

138. *LW* 44:312.

139. *LW* 44:311.

service—the fruit of faith. In this case, the monk who makes the vow is master rather than slave to his vow.

Luther, however, was concerned that many vows were not being taken under the liberating sunshine of Christian freedom, but instead enslaved their speakers, reversing the natural Christian order.[140] They were imposed as a means to merit justification, and once taken they became compulsory, burdening the monk with an impossible weight of living up to his vow and all the perfection it demands.[141] For Luther, justification by faith alone liberates sinners so that they live for Christ with a conscience no longer burdened. "Christian or evangelical freedom, then, is a freedom of conscience which liberates the conscience from works. Not that no works are done, but no faith is put in them. For conscience is not the power to do works, but to judge them. . . . Christ has freed this conscience from works through the gospel and teaches this conscience not to trust in works, but to rely only on his mercy."[142]

By turning vows into instruments of merit, popes and canon laws "ensnare consciences in their works and take them away from Christ, after having first destroyed their freedom as well as any teaching or knowledge of freedom."[143] For that reason, Luther had no patience with vows as a form of works, as if "necessary for righteousness and salvation." The liberated conscience, by contrast, looks to the "works of Christ alone, works which were poured out over us and freely given to us in baptism." Luther used a powerful contrast in a proverb to capture his point: "To those who believe in Christ there are no works so bad as to accuse and condemn us, but again, there are no works so good that they could save and defend us. But all our works accuse and condemn us. Christ's works alone protect and save us."[144]

In summary, whatever works are accomplished must be "done freely and for no reward, to the benefit and advantage of our neighbor, just as the works of Christ were done freely for us and for no reward." Then and only then will our works no longer be "works of the law but of Christ working in us through faith and living in us in everything we do."[145]

Luther was speaking as a monk who tried the system and found it wanting. He took the vow but found its obligation a crushing burden on his conscience because it imposed a system of merit that he could not achieve no matter how perfect his efforts. Yet his newfound wisdom—Christian liberty—was not his own invention. He blamed the "Roman Antichrist" for introducing such "idolatry": "While in former times the monks were celibates and lived in poverty

---

140. Luther's concern should not be read across every order. For example, the Franciscan Rule advocated for obedience as long as it did not violate the conscience or the rule itself.

141. *LW* 44:315.

142. *LW* 44:298.

143. *LW* 44:300.

144. *LW* 44:301.

145. *LW* 44:301.

and obedience of their own free will, their successors eventually turned their voluntary and evangelical example into a compulsory vow." Nevertheless, God preserved a remnant of monks who understood *sola fide* and Christian liberty. "St. Bernard and others kept vows of chastity, obedience, and poverty, but not because of the vows. Instead, they observed the ancient example of the fathers and of the gospel."[146] In that tradition of catholicity Luther put forward his program for reforming monastic vows.

THE SUBSTITUTE: MARRIAGE AND FAMILY AS MICRO-CHURCH

By the sixteenth century, the pure intentions of older, medieval monks like Bernard of Clairvaux were corrupted. "In central Europe," said Steinmetz, "clerics who found the celibate life too demanding were permitted to live in a sexual relationship with a housekeeper contingent on the payment of an annual tax to the bishop." The Reformers knew this clerical arrangement firsthand. For example, "Heinrich Bullinger, the Protestant Reformer of Zurich, was the child of such an informal clerical family. Nevertheless, in spite of the fact that such arrangements were given a quasi-official sanction, the housekeeper was still regarded by the townspeople as the priest's whore."[147]

Seeing such corruption, Luther threw a dark shadow over monastic vows. Did he provide a substitute in return? The Reformers were usually mindful that whenever a wall was torn down, a new and better one had to be erected; otherwise chaos could follow. When Calvin and his Company of Pastors removed confession to a priest based on the penance system, they replaced it with pastoral visits in the home so that families could confess their sins and receive pastoral guidance in preparation for the Lord's Supper (see chapter 15). Luther was a practitioner of the same method long before a second-generation Reformer like Calvin. He argued against the abuse of monastic vows and protested the immorality of priests. Yet he replaced monastic celibacy with the Protestant vision for the family, elevating the God-ordained beauty of marriage and children (see chapters 8–9).[148] No longer were monks the spiritually elite of Western Christendom; every husband and wife should exhibit Christ's love for his church, since each Protestant home is a micro-version of the assembly of the saints.[149]

Luther's response to monastic vows is but one example of the Reformation's complicated relationship with monasticism, a relationship that shows signs of continuity as well as discontinuity—*sic et non*. Other examples may accentuate the relationship as well. Consider preaching.

---

146. *LW* 44:316.
147. Steinmetz, *Luther in Context*, 131.
148. "In place of saints who were models of sexual self-denial and asceticism, the Protestants substituted the minister's family as a model of the Christian home." Steinmetz, *Luther in Context*, 132.
149. I say "Western" Christendom because the East did reconcile monasticism with the family of a priest.

PREACHING AS SACRAMENT:
FROM *LEUTPRIESTER* TO PREACHING PASTOR

The false idea that the Reformation introduced expository preaching for the first time deserves a slow and painful death. As evident in the previous survey of the Dominicans and Franciscans, itinerant preaching played a major role in cultivating the apostolic model (along with poverty). Sometimes an entire order was defined by preaching, as the initials O.P. (Order of Preachers) became attached to the name of a Dominican, for example. "'Preach the Word'" explained Steinmetz, "was as much a Dominican or Augustinian slogan as it was Lutheran or Reformed.... The laity in several late medieval cities in the Holy Roman Empire had laid aside funds to pay for a *Leutpriester*, a priest whose principal function was to preach on Sundays and feast days, leaving the ordinary liturgical services to the parochial clergy." This appreciation for a *Leutpriester* was not lost on the Reformers; many of them knew it well because not a few Protestants first emerged from within mendicant orders, from Martin Bucer to Robert Barnes, among others.[150]

What, then, was the contribution of the Reformation to preaching? *The Reformation's contribution was not so much the introduction of preaching, as if it were an invention, but the centrality of preaching under a refined theology of grace.* "However important the preached Word was to the mendicants and the late medieval princes of the pulpit, it was still ancillary to the sacraments." Steinmetz concluded, "The sermon could be nothing more than an invitation to baptism, penance, and eucharist, where alone saving grace was dispersed. It was not the preacher in the pulpit, however eloquent, but the priest at the altar, however inarticulate, who stood at the center of medieval worship."[151]

Yet such a contrast should be nuanced: the Reformers were serious about administering baptism and the Lord's Supper, both of which they called sacraments and kept within the regular rotation of ecclesiastical liturgy. However, Steinmetz's point is, as a rule, insightful. The major difference between medieval and reformation churches was not the presence of preaching so much as its sacramental nature. Steinmetz went so far as to claim that Luther turned preaching into a third sacrament.[152]

Luther was not alone in that respect. Even if Bullinger and Calvin did not call preaching a sacrament, they treated it as such. They were convinced that

---

150. Steinmetz, *Luther in Context*, 133.

151. "It was not by the foolishness of preaching but by the Word joined to the elements of bread and wine and water that God saved the faithful of every generation. The sermon moves sinners to the sacraments but is not itself a sacrament." Steinmetz, *Luther in Context*, 133–34.

152. "The power of the keys, the power to bind and loose from sin, was exercised through the preaching of the gospel. No sacramental power as such was thought by him [Luther] to reside in ordination or in ecclesiastical offices. Office bearers were authorized by the Word they carried. They had no authority that was not the authority of the gospel they preached. It was through the preached Word that God justifies sinners and pardons sin. Even the sacraments of baptism and eucharist were redefined as the visible Word of God.... For them it is the pulpit, not the altar, that is the throne of God and the sermon, not the eucharist, that is the ladder that links heaven and earth." Steinmetz, *Luther in Context*, 134.

the Spirit accompanied the proclamation of the Word, regenerating, converting, and sanctifying sinners. The Word, therefore, had the power to create new life and possessed the authority to discipline its recipients not because the preacher was something special but only because his mouth was the instrument through which God himself spoke, made alive, and admonished his people.

CONCLUSION

Many other examples—from confession to catechisms—could be provided, but the complicated matrix of continuity and discontinuity is evident. The student of the Reformation is on safe ground to answer yes and no. The Reformation was not, as some say, an annihilating renovation, let alone a radical revolution, dispensing all that came before and substituting a completely new system of faith and practice. A better, more accurate analysis says the Reformation ratified a revision but one that created a renewal, that is, a renewal of the old, ancient paths, patristic and medieval, rather than a wholesale abandonment. "The Reformation began as an argument among Catholic insiders; it continued as an argument between Catholics and former Catholics until well past the middle of the century."[153] That changed when Reformers were condemned by Trent, yet even then they persisted in their claim that they were far more catholic than Rome.

Some, however, have assumed that the Reformation's claim to catholicity could not have applied to Scholasticism. In the next two chapters, a more nuanced picture of the sixteenth century tells a different story.

---

153. Steinmetz, *Luther in Context*, 141.

FAITH SEEKING UNDERSTANDING

The Advent of Scholasticism

> *I do not try, Lord, to attain Your lofty heights, because my understand-*
> *ing is in no way equal to it. But I do desire to understand Your truth a*
> *little, that truth that my heart believes and loves. For I do not seek to*
> *understand so that I may believe; but I believe so that I may understand.*
>
> —Anselm, *Proslogion*

> *First, it must be understood that scholastic language was a common*
> *inheritance for all theological discourse among the sixteenth-century*
> *reformers.*
>
> —Frank James III

> *All of the scholastic thinkers . . . whether medieval or Protestant, assumed*
> *the priority of Scripture over reason and philosophy.*
>
> —Richard Muller

I n the Early Middle Ages, theologians were often located in monasteries (see chapter 2). The monastery was the haven not only for spiritual life but for intellectual stimulation as well. The modern dichotomy between the heart and mind would have been foreign to a monk. Therefore, the monastery became an ideal place to pursue a theological *and* spiritual quest for God. The interest in theological education spurred monastery schools (e.g., Cluny and Le Bec), and such schools became the womb that gave birth to Scholastic theologians of the eleventh century.[1] Scholastics were born out of cathedral schools as well. Notre Dame, for example, is famous to this day as a university, but in the medieval era it was a cathedral that educated many a Scholastic. As a result, the novice had to choose between monastic and cathedral opportunities. Yet cathedral schools gained momentum by the twelfth century, eclipsing monastic schools.[2]

---

1. Historians debate when Scholasticism began. Many call Anselm the first Scholastic. However, signs of the Scholastic method can be traced to Boethius. For its early history, see Leinsle, *Introduction to Scholastic Theology,* 16–73.
2. Vos, "Scholasticism and Reformation," 102. Tracing Scholasticism's origins, Leinsle identifies several

With the turn of the thirteenth century arrived the proliferation of the medieval university, and now a student could embark on an intellectual quest without necessarily becoming a monk. Europe housed many universities in cities like Bologne and Oxford, for example. But with time Paris became the premier university for the study of theology, complimented by its cathedral, Notre Dame. The proliferation of schools in the High and late Middle Ages was accompanied by the advent of "Schoolmen" (*scholastici*).[3]

The Scholastics wrote some of the simplest yet most sophisticated systems of theology in the history of Christianity, from Anselm's *Proslogion* to Peter Lombard's *Sentences* to Thomas Aquinas's *Summa Theologiae* and *Summa Contra Gentiles*. Scholasticism is often misunderstood and caricatured, however, as if Scholasticism is restricted to specific philosophical or theological content. While much of Scholasticism (though not all) was anchored to classical Trinitarian orthodoxy and the philosophy of realism that supports its participation metaphysic (see chapter 3), nevertheless, Scholasticism refers first and foremost to a *method*.[4]

The method of Scholasticism, which will become plain as Scholastics are introduced, was nothing if it was not thorough. No rock was unturned, as the length of their manuscripts and the thoroughness of their questions and answers demonstrate. The methodical nature of Scholastic prose and argumentation was due in part to the revival of *dialectics*. The word *revival* is key; after a sixth-century philosopher like Boethius (480–ca. 524/26), philosophy became dormant until the eleventh century, although there were exceptions (e.g., John Scottus Eriugena, Pseudo-Dionysius).[5] When philosophy revived, so did the dialectic method. De Rijk defines the Scholastic method as follows:

> a method applied in philosophy (and in theology) which is characterized, both on the level of *research* and on the level of *teaching*, by the use of an ever and ever recurring system of concepts, distinctions, definitions, propositional analysis, argumentational techniques and disputational methods, which had originally been derived from the Aristotelist-Boethian logic, but later on, on a much larger scale, from the indigenous terminist logic [i.e., "the logic of properties of terms and the uses of terms in propositions."].[6]

schools in the early Middle Ages: "(1) public schools, (2) cathedral schools, (3) personal schools, (4) monastery schools for externs, (5) monastery schools for interns, (6) schools for special disciplines." *Introduction to Scholastic Theology*, 34–35.

3. Vos introduces two phases: the Christian university from 1200 to 1500 and the confessional university from 1500 to 1800. With the latter in view, Vos can refer to a "reformational scholasticism." "Scholasticism and Reformation," 103, 105.

4. Van Asselt, *Introduction to Reformed Scholasticism*, 56–72; McGrath, *Reformation Thought*, 60.

5. Various scholars have tried to explain why. Thomas Williams proposes two reasons: (1) German tribes roamed, conquered, and destroyed towns and monasteries, and (2) philosophy took a back seat to literature and history. See Williams, *Reason and Faith*, 96. On the rise of the dialectic method, see Leinsle, *Introduction to Scholastic Theology*, 38.

6. de Rijk, *Middeleeuwse wijsbegeerte*, 111 (*PMA* 85); Vos, "Scholasticism and Reformation," 106–7.

That word *logic* is critical. The dialectic method is all about precision in its prose, which explains why Scholasticism made many distinctions by defining and differentiating between theological and philosophical terms and concepts (see chapter 4 on the use of Aristotle's works for this purpose). These nuances were aids, designed to guide the philosopher-theologian's faith toward understanding. But these distinctions were also pathways to a solution.[7] As the Schoolmen encountered difficult exegetical, theological, historical, and philosophical dilemmas, terms, distinctions, and logic itself all introduced a type of clarity and coherence that exposed faulty answers (and fallacies) and revealed right answers. The purpose was not to create truth but to understand truth for the sake of strengthening faith in God and love for God. Therefore, the method was not an end in itself but a means to ascend in one's spiritual quest to gaze at the beauty of God.

The outcome of dialectics was a well-rounded, all-inclusive vision for Christianity. To some later Renaissance humanist critics (see chapters 3–4), such distinctions were considered extreme, debating infinitesimal questions irrelevant and impractical to the real matters of Christianity.[8] Since some of the questions that Scholastics entertained were hypothetical, various Renaissance humanists considered Scholasticism an exercise in speculation that was anything but profitable for Christian piety and spirituality. However, Scholasticism is better understood and appreciated when its motives and context are considered, both of which go a long way toward explaining Scholastic methods.

Those motives and context will rise to the surface as sample Scholastics are introduced, but a central motive should be recognized from the start: the Scholastics cared about truth and they believed that Christianity, if constructed systematically, could present a clear and coherent account of truth. The Scholastics considered the Christian faith logical and capable of consistency, even concord. That belief, and the task it proposed, required a Scholastic method dedicated to logical rigor that could aid students in the study of sacred Scripture as well as historical texts. Scholastics posed questions, entertained false answers, then refuted error by positing anywhere between two and ten theses in response, only to answer the strongest objections. The goal was to construct an intellectual cathedral, one that not only confessed the faith but displayed the beauty of its logic and cohesiveness from start to finish.[9] The construction of this intellectual cathedral involved biblical commentary—the Scholastics were rigorous scriptural exegetes. Indeed, the Scholastic method was applied at its start to better understand the biblical text. With that exegetical aim in view,

---

7. That is not to say Scholasticism was mere method, as if its method never influenced its theological conclusions. See Muller, "Scholasticism in Calvin," 251.

8. McGrath, *Reformation Thought*, 60.

9. Étienne Gilson often describes Scholasticism as building "cathedrals of the mind" (*Spirit of Mediaeval Philosophy*).

theology was defined in reference to the *sacra pagina*.[10] Yet it also required the tools of both theology and philosophy. But in the Scholastic mind, exegesis and theology were interwoven, inseparable and indispensable to the unified mission of the theologian: *faith seeking understanding*. That mission was patristic at its core, Augustinian in its roots, even if the manner of appropriating such a mission looked different for the Scholastic theologians.

As the university provided a budding intellectual home for Scholasticism, the Scholastic method shined bright in the university curriculum by means of four stages:

1. *Lectio*—a lecture and commentary on a text considered an authority
2. *Meditatio*—a meditation in which the student reflected on how that text and its teaching should be applied
3. *Quaestio*—a major question submitted for consideration
4. *Disputationes*—a disputation in which scholars engaged one another over a difficult or controversial question[11]

These four created an intellectual environment fruitful for achieving clarity and coherence, consistency and credibility. The *quaestio* stage, however, developed into a method in and of itself. Peter Abelard utilized the *quaestio* to establish whether a text was authoritative (determined by a text's correspondence to truth). Later Scholastics like Lombard and Thomas Aquinas turned to the *quaestio* method to investigate both sides of a question, drawing on a variety of sources to evaluate what position was more favorable. Because of its inspiration, sacred Scripture was the source possessing the highest authority, yet subordinate authorities were also considered, both patristic and medieval.[12]

In the thirteenth century, disputations were organized by teachers who wrote theses for students to discuss and debate. At the end, the teacher himself interceded to shed more conclusive light on whatever ambiguity the dispute retained. On holidays, disputations could also be arranged for the purpose of treating a topic of special interest, and the public was invited to attend and even ask questions of their own.[13]

The many Scholastic theologians and their diverse beliefs and colossal contributions cannot be surveyed here. Yet for the purposes of (1) capturing the spirit and theology of the Scholastics, and (2) understanding what aspects of their method and theology inspired the Reformers, some of the most notable Scholastics deserve attention. My approach will not be exhaustive but illustrative.

---

10. Vos, "Scholasticism and Reformation," 107.
11. For an elaboration of each, see Vos, "Scholasticism and Reformation," 107.
12. Van Asselt, *Introduction to Reformed Scholasticism*, 63.
13. These were called *disputationes de quodlibet*. For this process as outlined, see Van Asselt, 58–59.

THE REFORMATION'S USE OF *QUAESTIO* AND *DISPUTATIONES*

Since many of the Reformers were educated in medieval universities, they were products of the Scholastic method. Like everyone else, those Reformers who pursued a doctorate were required to write a commentary on Peter Lombard's *Sentences*, for example. Pieter Rouwendal observes the purpose of such a commentary: "Generally speaking, it was assumed that the truth no longer had to be discovered, since the biblical authors and the church had already done that. The truth only had to be elucidated, systematized, and defended" (*Introduction to Reformed Scholasticism*, 63).

Even when Reformers objected to the theological content of Scholastic positions, they did not protest Scholasticism as a method. For instance, in 1517 Luther's *Disputation against Scholastic Theology* assumed the *disputationes* method, and his Ninety-Five Theses were posted for academic discussion, following medieval protocol. As for the Geneva academy, students were called *scholastici*. Even when they were defending their Reformed theology, they did so in the context of academic *disputationes*.

Although Calvin never did receive the type of formal Scholastic training as other Reformers, nevertheless, he was familiar with the *quaestio* method, as the structure of his *Institutes* reveals (see Rouwendal, *Introduction to Reformed Scholasticism*, 61).

Reformed Scholastics continued to perpetuate this method, as is plain in Petrus van Mastricht's *Theoretical-Practical Theology* and Francis Turretin's *Institutes of Elenctic Theology*.

ANSELM OF CANTERBURY

Anselm (1033–1109) was born in Italy, but he spent much of his lifetime in France and England.[14] Anselm's relationship with his father was so tense that when his mother died, Anselm left his father altogether. Passing over the Alps, Anselm suffered from hunger but survived and made his way to France. Years went by as Anselm traveled in pursuit of a teacher, not an uncommon method for the eleventh century as students searched for instructors with a good reputation. Anselm's name surfaced in Normandy where in 1059 the Benedictine abbey of Le Bec became his new home.

Le Bec and Lanfranc

Why Le Bec? Lanfranc (ca. 1005–89) was prior at Le Bec, a teacher with a reputation for his spiritual and theological acumen, considering faith's pursuit of understanding. Anselm's mind sprouted within this tradition of faith seeking understanding. Those who caricature the Scholastics as dry, logic-chopping rationalists have never really met and understood Anselm. Like Augustine before

---

14. The details that follow and a fuller account of Anselm's life and writings can be found in Davies and Evans, "Introduction," 1–26; Visser and Williams, *Anselm*, 3–12.

him, Anselm's pursuit of knowledge was inseparable from this first Schoolman's quest for spiritual happiness. Contemplation for Anselm was a life of prayer and study together. That explains why Anselm could begin a treatise in prayer, fill it with philosophical reasoning over the divine essence, only to conclude with reflections on how such theological discoveries lead to joy both in the present and in the life to come.

With Lanfranc at the helm, the Benedictine abbey at Le Bec was appealing for other reasons as well. Like most monasteries, Le Bec trained monks, but Le Bec also welcomed young students from families of nobility, which turned Le Bec into an intellectual hub for theology and philosophy, one with growing acclaim among elites of French society. In addition, Le Bec made real intellectual contributions that engaged heated controversies of the day, giving Le Bec a credibility that was exhilarating for young students.

For example, Lanfranc modeled dialectics over against two other approaches. When the dialectic method returned in the eleventh century, it was embraced, but disagreement emerged over its power. Some put so much confidence in dialectics that they dispensed with doctrines of the faith when those doctrines did not match reason's rationale (e.g., Berengar of Tours used reason to dispense with transubstantiation). Others, however, were suspicious toward an overreliance on dialectics, so they fortified the authority of traditional doctrines over against dialectics and became skeptical, even hostile, toward an overreliance on reason. Whether a doctrine or belief was logical was irrelevant in their estimation (e.g., Peter Damian's obscurantism). Lanfranc, however, did not side with either of these approaches. He wrote against Berengar and concluded that reason should not be judge and jury, deciding what *loci* stay and which ones go. Yet he also did not appreciate the default, defensive instinct to protect the authoritative position at all costs when reason exposed legitimate faults. Lanfranc tried to model a better way by utilizing dialectics to move past ambiguity in debates and make his own apologetic for orthodoxy.[15] Reason in the service of theology, said Lanfranc. Anselm observed Lanfranc, and such balance later became evident in his own writings.

In 1060 Anselm took another step forward: he became a monk. Anselm did not go to Le Bec with the intention of becoming a monk, but under the influence of Lanfranc he was drawn into the monastic life and the spiritual benefits it promised for the soul committed to contemplation. When Lanfranc left Le Bec three years later, Anselm rose in the ranks and became a budding teacher himself, succeeding Lanfranc as prior.[16] At heart Anselm was a teacher, but not a teacher in the tradition of Peter Damian, who discarded the rationale behind

---

15. All three positions are outlined in greater detail by Williams, *Reason and Faith*, 98–111.

16. Despite the fact that Anselm was originally an external student, his approach focused instead on those who were monks. "Anselm did not encourage 'external' pupils. He was interested in training the minds of the monks of Bec in ways which would foster their spiritual as well as their intellectual development." Davies and Evans, "Introduction," vii.

a doctrine. Anselm not only insisted his students know what they believed but *why* they believed. "Faith seeking understanding"—*fides quaerens intellectum*—that mantra guided Anselm as he studied the Scriptures and church fathers, developing a special affinity for Augustine.

Monologion

Even before Anselm started writing, he had a powerful influence on his students because of his dialectical method. These monks already knew what to believe on the authority of Scripture and the church, which challenged Anselm to use reason alone and explain why they should believe what they believed. These monks did not need another book telling them what the Scriptures and the Fathers said. They wanted to know the rationale, the logic behind these beliefs. In 1075 they asked Anselm to start with God's being, his divine essence itself.

> Some of my brethren have often and earnestly asked me to write down, as a kind of model meditation, some of the things I have said, in everyday language, on the subject of meditating upon the essence of the divine. . . . They specified . . . the following form for this written meditation: nothing whatsoever to be argued on the basis of the authority of Scripture, but the constraints of reason concisely to prove, and the clarity of truth clearly to show, in the plain style, with everyday arguments, and down-to-earth dialectic, the conclusions of distinct investigations.[17]

Anselm declined. The task was far too daunting for his feeble talents, he said. They reassured Anselm he need not feel such a burden because they only wanted an accessible work. Any theologian who has tried to take the deep things of God and make them accessible will resonate with Anselm's response: "For the easier they wanted it to be to use, the harder they made it to produce." Under persistent (and loving) pressure, Anselm capitulated and wrote his monologue or *Monologion*, expecting only his students to read his little book. However, the little tract became one of Anselm's first and most enduring Scholastic works.

Monologion begins by taking on the challenge Anselm's students posed. First, he stated what he would prove and then how he would prove it. "Of all the things that exist, there is one nature that is supreme. It alone is self-sufficient in its eternal happiness, yet through its all-powerful goodness it creates and gives to all other things their very existence and their goodness." But how would Anselm prove this to the person who had "never heard of, or does not believe in, and so does not know, this"? Anselm followed the rules set by his students. He said, "I think that they can, even if of average ability, convince themselves, to a large extent, of the truth of these beliefs, simply by reason alone."[18]

---

17. Anselm, *Monologion*, prologue, 5.
18. Anselm, *Monologion* 1.

Interpreters have sometimes misunderstood Anselm, as if he were a *rationalist*. He was not. Rather, Anselm believed the Christian faith is *rational*. In other words, Christian beliefs are logical and sound, reasonable and consistent. They can even be harmonized, together forming a compatible paradigm of thought. The charge that Anselm was a rationalist also ignored the source of reason. When Anselm summoned reason, he did not embark on a man-centered quest, as if he was an Enlightenment man, dispensing with God and authority to determine truth by his own powers and capabilities. Quite the opposite, *Anselm summoned reason because reason is from God, and reason, in its most perfect form, is God*. On that score, Anselm was merely mimicking the patristics before him who used the word *Logos* to describe God (e.g., Justin Martyr). Anselm was confident, then, that he could use reason to speak of divinity itself.[19]

How then did Anselm reason? He accentuated the coherence of the divine perfections, from God's immutability to his justice, from his timeless eternality to the simple nature of the Trinity. Divine simplicity was focal for Anselm. Simplicity is the historic, orthodox belief that God is not made up of parts; rather, God's essence *is* his attributes and vice versa. In short, all that is in God is God. For his attributes are identical with one another. After demonstrating that God is the supreme, perfect being, Anselm raised the question of simplicity, asking whether God's supreme nature can be a composite of many good things. If God is a composite, however, he cannot be one, and if he is not one, he is divisible by parts and dependent on these parts for his existence. In no way could he then be the Supreme Being.

> A composite requires, for its existence, its components and owes its being what it is to them. It is what it is through them. They, however, are not what they are through it. A composite, therefore, just is not supreme. If, then, the supreme nature is a composite of many goods, what belongs to a composite necessarily belongs to it also. But truth's whole and already manifest necessity destroys and overthrows by clear reason this, falsehood's blasphemy.
>
> Since, then, the supreme nature is not composite at all, and yet really is all those good things, it is necessary that all those good things are not many, but one. So any one of them is the same thing as all of them (the same thing as all together and as each individually). So to call the supreme nature "justice" or "essence" signifies the same thing as the others (together and individually). So whatever is predicated of the supreme substance with respect to essence is one single thing. And just so, therefore, whatever the supreme substance is, it is with respect to essence, in one and the same way and respect.[20]

---

19. Williams believes this is why Anselm used the phrase "reason of faith." "The reason of faith derives from God. God himself is supreme reason, so truths about the divine nature will be supremely rational truths." Williams, *Reason and Faith*, 104.

20. Anselm, *Monologion* 17.

Anselm's argument is not only instrumental to the preservation of God's incorruptible nature, but it is essential, as late sections of his *Monologion* reveal, to the unity of the Trinity and the equality of Father, Son, and Spirit.[21] For the persons of the Godhead are not parts that are divisible from one another, nor are they parts that can be greater or less in relation to one another. Instead, the one, simple, and undivided essence subsists in three persons. As chapter 4 will reveal, all the sixteenth-century Reformers stood on this foundation, a foundation Anselm helped pave with his dialectic mind.

When Anselm finished his *Monologion*, he sent it to his spiritual and intellectual mentor, Lanfranc, seemingly expecting a positive, supportive response. Anselm was disappointed; Lanfranc did not appreciate *Monologion*. Abundant citations from the Scriptures and the church fathers, Augustine most of all, were missing. Lanfranc did not welcome Anselm's effort to explain, by means of reason alone, what the monks should believe and why they should believe. Anselm, however, was not ignorant of the Scripture or the Fathers, as his many other writings demonstrate. Instead, he was taking the dialectic method with utmost seriousness. To his disappointment, the one who taught him this method did not value the extent of its application. A more careful reading of *Monologion* does reveal that Augustine and the truths of Scripture pervade *Monologion*, even if Anselm was intentional not to quote them. Anselm even said in the prologue,

> I have been unable to find anything which is inconsistent with the writings of the Catholic Fathers, and in particular with those of the Blessed Augustine. If, then, someone thinks that I have said here anything which is either too modern, or which departs from the truth, I would ask them not to denounce me as an arrogant modernizer or a maintainer of falsehood. Rather I ask that they first make a careful and thorough reading of the books *On the Trinity* of the aforementioned learned Augustine and then judge my little treatise on the basis of them.[22]

While Anselm's appropriation of the dialectic method may have been progressive for his day, the content of his argument conformed to orthodoxy. And yet by means of his dialectic style, Anselm did not just affirm the faith but exhibited its coherence. Lady philosophy was summoned to serve theology.

Proslogion

Despite his mentor's dissatisfaction, Anselm believed his arguments were correct. Nevertheless, some discontentment lingered. Anselm gave a chain of arguments, as he called them, in his *Monologion*, showing how one link connected to another. Now he was curious: could he locate a single argument to prove (1) that God exists and (2) that he is the supreme good? The outcome:

---

21. Anselm, *Monologion* 26–80.
22. Anselm, *Monologion*, prologue (p. 6).

Anselm's *Proslogion*, his allocution, written sometime during 1077 and 1078. If *Monologion* is brief, *Proslogion* is shorter still, a mere twenty-six chapters, some chapters only one paragraph long. Yet it is this small treatise that has been discussed and debated by most major philosophers and theologians since.

Proslogion has a spiritual accent to it from start to finish. Reason is summoned as before but this time within the context of a mind that rises up to contemplate God. In other words, before Anselm began his argument, he was sure to play it in a doxological key. In the medieval and monastic mind, the theologian often utilized the *lectio divina* method, a method that resisted a sharp division between theology and prayer. The theologian moved into theological contemplation by means of a prayerful, holy reading of texts.[23] Anselm was a prime practitioner in his *Proslogion*. His approach, though no less rigorous in its use of reason than the *Monologion*, first pays heed to Isaiah 7:9.[24] Anselm crafted his argument but within the paradigm of faith itself, a faith that seeks understanding, rather than vice versa.

> I acknowledge, Lord, and I give thanks that You have created Your image in me, so that I may remember You, think of You, love You. But this image is so effaced and worn away by vice, so darkened by the smoke of sin, that it cannot do what it was made to do unless You renew it and reform it. I do not try, Lord, to attain Your lofty heights, because my understanding is in no way equal to it. But I do desire to understand Your truth a little, that truth that my heart believes and loves. *For I do not seek to understand so that I may believe; but I believe so that I may understand* [credo ut intelligam]. For I believe this also, that "unless I believe, I shall not understand" [Isa. 7:9].[25]

Anselm's two emphases—*Credo, ut intelligam* (I believe so that I might understand) and *Nisi credideritis, non intelligetis* (Unless you believe, you shall not understand)—proceed from the anthropology of Augustine. Anselm acknowledged the *imago Dei* but then admitted the devastation caused by sin. The image exists after the fall, but it is effaced. The smoke of sin, he said with poetic prose, has cast a dark shadow. The result is inability—the sinner cannot do what God created him to do. Divine grace is necessary, for unless God renews the image, the darkness remains. Here the charge that Anselm was a rationalist is shown again to be without warrant. Apart from renewal the mind remains in darkness, and even with renewal, Anselm admitted God remains lofty and man and his reason small and low to the ground. His understanding was so small in comparison with the infinite God he contemplated. Nevertheless, the image did mean something: renewed and reformed, the image admitted a desire to

---

23. Baxter, *The Medieval Mind of C. S. Lewis*, 52. Baxter is indebted to Armstrong, *Medieval Wisdom*, 165–190; Robertson, *Lectio Divina*, 134; Leclercq, *The Love of Learning and the Desire for God*.

24. And he begins with Psalm 13, answering the fool who says there is no God.

25. Anselm, *Monologion* 1, emphasis added.

understand. Where did that desire come from? Faith. Yet faith was present only by God's grace, a faith that desired to know its Maker and Savior. It was a faith that hungered for understanding not because understanding is an end but only because it is a means to a much greater end. As Anselm explained by the end of *Proslogion*, that greater end is joy, a happiness found in heaven, a happiness that is none other than God himself.

Anselm prayed, asking God to grant him "understanding to faith" so that his faith might understand why God must exist. Anselm then asserted his reason for why God must exist: "Now we believe that You are something than which nothing greater can be thought."[26] Later generations became enamored with defending or refuting Anselm's ontological argument for the existence of God.[27] Their fixation is all the more remarkable considering Anselm devoted only four chapters (four paragraphs) before transitioning to define the attributes of this perfect being. Anselm's argument did not need to be verbose to be profound —the reason it is profound has much to do with his conception of the mind and reality.

A painter, explained Anselm, plans ahead of time what he will paint, envisioning his craft and its outcome in his mind. With the picture in his mind, he then begins painting, and when finished he sits back and admires the real thing. If that is true of a paint job, how much more so with the mind's inescapable conception of a divine being who is perfection itself? Even the fool, said Anselm, knows this much. He is "forced to agree that something-than-which-nothing-greater-can-be-thought exists in the mind, since he understands this when he hears it, and whatever is understood is in the mind. And surely that-than-which-a-greater-cannot-be-thought cannot exist in the mind alone. For if it exists solely in the mind, it can be thought to exist in reality also, which is greater." Anselm concluded that existence in the mind alone is an impossibility.[28]

Anselm's argument for God's existence assumes that God is not merely a being among other beings. Indeed, he *is* being itself while the creature must participate in the likeness of his being. He is, in other words, *Supreme Being*, and by nature of his excellency and perfection he must exist. He is his existence.

> And You, Lord our God, are this being. You exist so truly, Lord my God, that You cannot even be thought not to exist. And this is as it should be, for if some intelligence could think of something better than You, the creature would be

---

26. Anselm, *Proslogion* 2.

27. Anselm was not unopposed in his own day. Consider the response of Gaunilo of Marmoutiers, *Pro Insipiente (On Behalf of the Fool)* as well as Anselm's *Reply to Gaunilo*, both in *The Major Works*, ed. Evans and Davies, 105–22.

28. "If then that-than-which-a-greater-cannot-be-thought exists in the mind alone, this same that-than-which-a-greater-*cannot*-be-thought is that-than-which-a-greater-*can*-be-thought. But this is obviously impossible. Therefore there is absolutely no doubt that something-than-which-a-greater-cannot-be-thought exists in the mind and in reality." Emphasis added. Anselm, *Proslogion* 2.

above its Creator and would judge its Creator—and that is completely absurd. In fact, everything else there is, except You alone, can be thought of as not existing. You alone, then, of all things most truly exist and therefore of all things possess existence to the highest degree; for anything else does not exist as truly, and so possesses existence to a lesser degree.[29]

The ontological argument is brief, and his next concern is what *kind* of perfect being God must be, one that is better to exist than not exist. By establishing God's perfections, Anselm believed he only further solidified his *a priori* argument for this God's existence. "Thus, then, truly are You perceptive, omnipotent, merciful, and impassible, just as You are living, wise, good, blessed, eternal, and whatever it is better to be rather than not to be."[30]

The rest of Anselm's *Proslogion* describes what perfecting attributes must follow if this God is someone than whom nothing greater can be thought. Although Anselm proceeded from this one argument, he linked a chain of arguments together, one perfection logically entailing the next. With each one, Anselm was pressed to demonstrate that he who is a perfect being, by definition, cannot be corrupted by limitations. The Creator is domesticated by the creature whenever a creaturely limitation is predicated to God. If that occurs, then he is no longer someone than whom nothing greater can be thought; and if he is no longer someone than whom nothing greater can be thought, then what reason can explain his existence? Anselm was now in the position of answering objections.

For example, God cannot be corrupted, nor can he lie, let alone turn the truth into a falsehood. This would mean he must not be omnipotent after all. And if he is not omnipotent, then he cannot be the perfect being; and if he is not the perfect being, then he must not exist. Anselm's answer exposes the flaw in such an argument. "Or is the ability to do these things not power but impotence? For he who can do these things can do what is not good for himself and what he ought not to do. And the more he can do these things, the more power adversity and perversity have over him and the less he has against them. . . . Therefore, Lord God, You are the more truly omnipotent since You can do nothing through impotence and nothing can have power against You."[31]

One of the most striking features of the *Proslogion* is its style: logical prose written in the form of a prayer. Although Scholasticism was caricatured as speculative rationalism in later centuries, not helped in the least by some prejudiced humanists, the father of Scholasticism himself evaded such a stereotype. He may have climbed the upper recesses of logic when he reconciled justice and mercy—"Truly, then, you are merciful because You are just." However, when he reached the top, he shouted with praise because such logic led him to contemplation of

---

29. Anselm, *Proslogion*, 3.
30. Anselm, *Proslogion*, 11.
31. Anselm, *Proslogion*, 7.

the gospel. "O boundless goodness which so surpasses all understanding, let that mercy come upon me which proceeds from Your so great abundance! Let that which flows forth from You flow into me!" said Anselm, begging God to lavish his infinite grace.[32] Likewise, when Anselm reached the heights of God's incomprehensibility, he did not boast in his accomplished rationality. Instead, he was speechless before the inexplicable mystery that he, a mere creature, could understand anything at all. "What purity, what simplicity, what certitude and splendour is there! Truly it is more than can be understood by any creature."[33] Echoing the apostle Paul, who said God dwells in light inaccessible, Anselm humbled himself—his reason included—before the effulgence of God's ineffable beauty. "My understanding is not able [to attain] to that [light]. It shines too much and [my understanding] does not grasp it nor does the eye of my soul allow itself to be turned towards it for too long. It is dazzled by its splendour, overcome by its fullness, overwhelmed by its immensity, confused by its extent. O supreme and inaccessible light; O whole and blessed truth, how far You are from me who am so close to You!"[34]

At the end of his *Proslogion*, Anselm's contemplation had reached its culmination: joy. Or as Anselm called it, the fullness of joy. "What joy there is indeed and how great it is where there exists so great a good! O human heart, O needy heart, O heart experienced in suffering, indeed overwhelmed by suffering, how greatly would you rejoice if you abounded in all these things!" Anselm was convinced his contemplation of this perfect being was the answer to everyman's question: *Where can I find happiness?* And what is his answer? In someone than whom none greater can be conceived. In him joy is complete. Anselm sounded like Augustine, who said, "You stir man to take pleasure in praising you, because you have made us for yourself, and our heart is restless until it rests in you."[35] Anselm's prayer at the close of his *Proslogion* matches Augustine's and returns the father of Scholasticism to his starting point: faith seeking understanding. In humility, Anselm recognized his understanding was small, yet he rejoiced in anticipation knowing that one day faith, love, joy, and hope will be complete. Until then he contemplated the blessed Trinity.

I pray, O God, that I may know You and love You, so that I may rejoice in You. And if I cannot do so fully in this life may I progress gradually until it comes to fullness. Let the knowledge of You grow in me here, and there [in heaven] be made complete; let Your love grow in me here and there be made complete, so that here my joy may be great in hope, and there be complete in reality. . . . Until then let my mind meditate on it, let me tongue speak of it, let my heart love it, let my mouth preach it. Let my soul hunger for it, let my flesh thirst for it, my whole

32. Anselm, *Proslogion*, 9.
33. Anselm, *Proslogion*, 14.
34. Anselm, *Proslogion*, 16.
35. Augustine, *Confessions*, 1, 1 (1).

being desire it, until I enter into the "joy of the Lord" [Matt. 25:21], who is God, Three in One, "blessed forever. Amen" [Rom. 1:25].[36]

Archbishop of Canterbury

Anselm's endeavor to write and publish his *Proslogion* coincided with his advancement in the monastery, and in 1078 Anselm was promoted to abbot of Le Bec. However, Anselm wanted nothing to do with this office. Administration could only deter him from his heart's true desire: contemplation of God for the sake of spiritual communion with God. As his many letters reveal, Anselm was as devoted to loving God as he was to contemplating God because he saw the two as inseparable. Anselm never wavered from the spirit captured in the rule of Saint Benedict.[37] He was a monk first, then a theologian and philosopher, but surely not an administrator, let alone an ecclesiastical politician. The latter, in his opinion, was full of temptation, leading the monk away from a Godward gaze to preoccupation with this world's affairs. Anselm feared time in prayer would only be forfeited as a result. But as his reputation grew, leadership became inevitable, and Anselm reluctantly accepted his new position as abbot out of a sense of duty. Obedience, after all, was also essential to the rule of Saint Benedict.

As the name of Anselm spread across Europe in the 1080s, Anselm also became a target for attack. While his *Monologion* and *Proslogion* were written out of didactic motives, his *On the Incarnation of the Word* was written to defend his orthodoxy and counter the charges of the French theologian and philosopher Roscelin of Compiègne. Roscelin disliked Anselm's illustrations for the Trinity and accused Anselm of tritheism, although Roscelin's disdain may be due more to a misunderstanding than an accurate representation of Anselm's position. The point of Anselm's language was lost in translation.[38] Although Anselm attempted to appease Roscelin, the critic was insatiable in his attacks, never satisfied with Anselm's answers. However, the exchange came to a sudden halt when Anselm's mentor, Lanfranc, died in 1089.

In 1093 Anselm followed in the footsteps of his old master Lanfranc and, despite his reluctance to take up office, became archbishop of Canterbury.[39] Despite the renown of the office, Anselm lamented the political dilemmas he could not escape, too often caught between the ambitions of pope and king. For example, when he became archbishop, he could not retrieve his pallium from Rome since the English king William Rufus refused to accept Urban II as pope. When Anselm realized the bishops under him were allegiant to the king, not to the pope, Anselm considered whether he must leave England for Italy.

---

36. Anselm, *Proslogion*, 26.

37. See his many letters to this effect. Cf. Evans, *Saint Anselm of Canterbury*, 8–9.

38. For specifics, see Evans, 14–15.

39. "There was a peculiar irony in this, for it was usual for a show of protest to be made as a token of modesty and to confirm that the new bishop had a proper sense of his own unworthiness of office. But there can be no question of the sincerity of Anselm's protests, and it was no small comfort to him in later years, when he discovered that he had inadvertently allowed a secular lord to intrude upon spiritual jurisdiction." Evans, 15.

PETER ABELARD ON THE TRINITY

In the humility of faith seeking understanding, Anselm believed reason could be instrumental to understanding God's existence and divine attributes. Nevertheless, he did not think natural reason could arrive at doctrines like the Trinity apart from Scripture. By contrast, Peter Abelard (1079–1142) said non-Christian philosophers did understand something (though not everything) about the Trinity by means of reason alone. After writing three books on the Trinity, Abelard concluded that God had manifested the doctrine of the Trinity to pagans so that they could use their reason to embrace the doctrine. Others like Bernard of Clairvaux were sure to expose Abelard as heretical. Abelard was condemned by Pope Innocent II in 1141.

He was torn: on one hand, his pastoral loyalty sided with the welfare of his sheep, the English congregation. On the other hand, the English people were ruled by William, and William expected Anselm's allegiance. Influence from a foreign power like the pope could easily throw suspicion on Anselm. Anselm could be charged with treason. Staying was daunting because the bishops loyal to the king had no intention of submitting themselves to Anselm if his orders were even vaguely influenced by Urban in Rome.

When Anselm's flight was imminent, the king relented and agreed to cooperate, permitting the bishop of Albano to retrieve Anselm's pallium in 1095. The gesture forced the king to put aside his fight with Urban temporarily. However, the gesture was too late, incapable of recovering Anselm's full confidence in the king. The push and pull taxed Anselm to the point of exhaustion and desperation. "I am so harassed in the archbishopric that if it were possible to do so without guilt, I would rather die than continue in it."[40]

As Anselm expected, whatever armistice was achieved did not last. In 1097 the peace collapsed once more. William left England for Wales, and when he saw the pathetic state of the soldiers under him, he blamed Anselm, as if the archbishop had sabotaged the king's mission by a debauched selection process. When Anselm asked yet again for permission to travel to Rome—Anselm believed mediation from Urban was the best route—he was denied as before. This time, however, Anselm did not wait for the king to return. He left anyway. He knew his allegiance to Urban put his archbishopric in jeopardy before, but now he understood it had no future.

The journey from England to Italy, all the way to Rome, was dangerous. The long travel put Anselm's health at risk. Plus, the archbishop on the run had to hide along the way, taking alternative routes so that he was not captured by the

---

40. Anselm, quoted in Davies and Evans, "Introduction," viii. On the battle between the bishops and Anselm, see Evans, *Saint Anselm of Canterbury*, 20.

king's soldiers. Nevertheless, he knew that if he could make it to Rome, Urban could protect him. On the way, Anselm returned to the same mountains where he was raised as a boy. The abbot of Telese ensured Anselm's recovery.

Cur Deus Homo and On the Procession of the Holy Spirit

As Anselm recovered from the journey, his return to the mountains gave him the quiet and solitude he once enjoyed as a monk. That peace afforded him the opportunity to return to his writings and apply the Scholastic method so successful in his *Proslogion*. The book Anselm was so eager to pick up again and finish was his *Why God Became Man—Cur Deus Homo*.[41] Back in the early 1090s, Anselm had talked with one of his former monks, Gilbert, about evangelism among the Jews, eager as Anselm was to persuade them that Jesus was the Son of God. Anselm's evangelistic zeal found precedent in the church fathers. For example, ante-Nicene father Justin Martyr wrote his *Dialogue with Trypho, a Jew*, exploring the apologetic (and hermeneutic) Christians should utilize when refuting Jews, always with an eye to their conversion. Gilbert wrote *Dialogue* to continue that apologetic effort. Like Justin, Gilbert knew that one of the main stumbling blocks for Jews was the incarnation. Anselm and Gilbert had many talks discussing how they might persuade the Jews. At rest in the mountains, Anselm now had the opportunity to return to the topic with his project, *Cur Deus Homo*. Since Anselm said from the outset that he was writing to persuade the unbeliever, some have suggested that he must have had the Jew in mind. Anselm's relationship with Gilbert supported that suggestion.

Cur Deus Homo exemplifies Anselm's Scholastic method. To become "well-grounded in the faith," the Christian must dedicate himself to "the investigation of its logic," or what he called "the logical principles of our faith." Anselm previously applied his method—faith seeking understanding (Isa. 7:9)—to theology proper, but now he applied his method to the center of the faith: the incarnation and atonement. Doing so, he said, is encouraged by God's revelation: "The Sacred Page invites us to explore its rationale—he [Isaiah] is plainly encouraging us to pay more attention to understanding, while teaching us the sort of method by which we must proceed towards it." Jesus also confirmed this quest when he said he would be with his church until the end of the world (Matt. 28:20). His presence means he will "not cease to bestow his gifts within it." Faith in pursuit of understanding is one of those gifts, and the church has been summoned to rise up and "contemplate the logic of our beliefs."[42]

Cur Deus Homo is divided into two books. Book 1 has an apologetic mission. "The first book contains the objections of unbelievers who reject the Christian faith because they think it militates against reason, and the answers given by the faithful." Anselm was determined to reply to the unbeliever's objections by

---

41. Anselm also wrote *On the Virgin Conception and Original Sin* around the same time he finished *Why God Became Man*.

42. Anselm, *Why God Became Man*, Commendation, 260–61.

demonstrating how reason itself confirms the truthfulness of redemption's logic. As Anselm said, "Eventually it proves, by unavoidable logical steps, that, supposing Christ were left out of the case, as if there had never existed anything to do with him, it is impossible that, without him, any member of the human race could be saved."[43] Anselm summoned reason to exhibit the rationale behind the necessity of the Son's incarnation.

As for the second book, "similarly, the supposition is made that nothing were known about Christ, and it is demonstrated with no less clear logic and truth: that human nature was instituted with the specific aim that at some stage the whole human being should enjoy blessed immortality, 'whole' meaning 'with both body and soul.'" Anselm was resolved to explain why such immortality can only be the consequence of a redemption by a God-man. He promised to show "that it was inevitable that the outcome concerning mankind which was the reason behind man's creation should become a reality, but that this could only happen through the agency of a Man-God." Book 2 concludes with a strong emphasis on the necessity of incarnation. Anselm showed "that it is from necessity that all the things which we believe about Christ have come to pass."[44]

Anselm dedicated *Cur Deus Homo* to Pope Urban II, which was fitting since Anselm had remained faithful to the church in the face of the king's opposition. The two could not have been more different: the king's affluent lifestyle clashed with Anselm's humble, spiritual simplicity.[45] Despite these differences, the relationship between Anselm and Urban became strategic as the two moved forward. For example, as Anselm's *Monologion*, *Proslogion*, and *On the Incarnation of the Word* validate, Anselm was a model of Christian Trinitarian orthodoxy in the West, a foundation on which the entire Reformation later stood for its theology proper. Yet diversity within orthodoxy persisted over the controversial affirmation of the filioque clause. The question was whether the phrase "and the Son" should be added to the Nicene Creed so that it read, "The Spirit proceeds from the Father *and the Son*." The Eastern church said no, but the Western church said yes. The reasons were as political as they were theological, resulting in the unfortunate schism between East and West during Anselm's lifetime (AD 1054). On the heels of this schism, the Council at Bari met, and Urban invited Anselm to give his theological opinion. The invitation was not insignificant since not only Western but Eastern leaders were present. Here was a monumental opportunity for Anselm to bridge the divide, but could he accomplish such a feat? Using his Scholastic logic, Anselm made his case for the *filioque*, trying hard but failing to persuade the East.[46] Anselm did not succeed in bridging the divide between East and West, but the profundity of his argument succeeded

---

43. Anselm, *Why God Became Man*, Preface, 261.
44. Anselm, *Why God Became Man*, Preface, 262.
45. Evans, *Saint Anselm of Canterbury*, 22.
46. Out of Anselm's address came a larger treatise in defense of the *filioque* called *On the Procession of the Holy Spirit* (AD 1102).

in bridging Western Trinitarianism from Scholastics to the Reformers. Not only did the Reformers pride themselves on their Trinitarian orthodoxy, but many of them considered themselves in step with the Western case for the *filioque* as a more precise articulation of Trinitarianism. Whether they knew it or not, they owed their Trinitarian rationale to the Scholastic rigor of Anselm.

In between King and Pope

At last Urban ensured that Anselm made his way to Rome in 1098. One year later the scene in England and Rome changed when both Urban and William died, the former succeeded by Paschal II and the latter succeeded by Henry I. Controversy came with these new appointments, putting Anselm once more in between king and pope. The controversy foreshadowed later debates in the sixteenth century over the scope of magisterial and ecclesiastical jurisdiction. In Anselm's time the controversy came down to this question: What authority should the king exercise in the investiture of bishops? Henry I was convinced he had every right to intercede. Previously, Anselm agreed with that position under King William. Now Anselm disagreed.[47] His changed viewpoint put him in conflict with the king once more. "Anselm [now] thought that in loyalty to the Pope he ought to dispute the rights the King was claiming in the investiture of bishops. It was uncontentious that a king had a right to invest a new bishop with the lands or temporalities of his see. But it was becoming common for kings and emperors to go further into the sacramental domain and try to invest them with the spiritualities too, by giving them the ring and staff of their pastoral office."[48]

In 1103 Anselm appeared before Paschal II in Rome, and the pope commissioned him to return to England. That decision was met with sharp opposition by Henry I. Anselm had clout, and Henry I was not about to let Anselm into his land when the Scholastic sided with the pope rather than the king. If Anselm wanted back in, he must return to the king's side. Despite this initial impasse, negotiations followed in France and headway was achieved. During this process, Anselm traveled to Normandy and then to Bec, where the king visited him and reached an agreement: Anselm could return to England as archbishop (1106).[49]

Unfortunately, Anselm's future was bleak due to his increasing illnesses. However, his theological plans were still ambitious, too ambitious to reach fulfillment. He did manage to complete his *De Concordia—The Compatibility of God's Foreknowledge, Predestination, and Grace with Human Freedom*,

---

47. When did Anselm change his view? Probably when Urban brought Anselm to Rome. "In 1099 a Vatican council was held in which Urban addressed himself to the Investiture Context and pronounced with the Council a sentence of excommunication against laymen who 'gave' pastoral charge of church to the clergy who were to serve in them, and those who received such 'investiture' from them. Anselm found these events disturbing. He perceived that he might be said, however, innocently, to have consented to such an investiture himself when he was [first] made archbishop." Afterward, Anselm stayed in Lyons. Evans, *Saint Anselm of Canterbury*, 22.

48. Davies and Evans, "Introduction," x.

49. For details surrounding the negotiation, see Evans, *Saint Anselm of Canterbury*, 23–24.

a work most relevant to the coming Reformation of the sixteenth century.[50] In one sense, finishing his life with *De Concordia* was fitting for the father of Scholasticism. One of the great philosophers of Christianity, Boethius (ca. 480– 524), also wrote on the subject before he was executed.[51] Prior to Boethius, the subject was famously engaged by Augustine in his debates with the Pelagians and Semi-Pelagians over predestination, original sin, and the nature of grace itself. Therefore, the capstone of Anselm's career was a doctrinal controversy that paramount theologians and philosophers wrestled with since the patristic era.

The end of Anselm's life was near, but he was not ready to part with this world. He still had plans to write on the origin of the soul, a most complex subject that Anselm did not think had been addressed adequately in the history of the church. The father of Scholasticism never did apply his method to anthropology. His mind was willing, but his body was fragile. At the age of seventy-six, Anselm died as the future hope of the eschaton was read to him (Luke 22).[52] Less than one decade into the twelfth century, future Scholastics had to find its way without him.

Did the theology of Anselm, so early on in the history of Scholasticism, pose a total contrast with the Reformation, or did the heart of Anselm's theology—the gospel of Jesus Christ—pave a foundation for the Reformation? Consider the following case study to answer that question.

Case Study: Incarnation and Satisfaction

The sixteenth-century Reformers were adamant defenders of *solus Christus* in their polemics with the papacy. Justification depended on an atonement by which Christ paid it all. Christ substituted himself for sinners and satisfied the wrath of God, which sinners deserved. Upon faith in Christ alone, the ungodly are forgiven not in part but in whole. Furthermore, upon faith the righteousness of Christ is imputed to them as well. For not only did Christ suffer in the sinners' stead, but he lived on the sinners' behalf, obeying the law to perfection, something sinners failed to accomplish. His flawless record of obedience is reckoned to believers, granting all those with faith in Christ the assurance of eternal life.

The medieval Scholastics did not align exactly with the Reformers on redemption applied, as evident when the medieval affirmation of infused righteousness is contrasted with the Reformation's doctrine of imputed righteousness. However, the Reformers did align in some significant ways with notable Scholastics on redemption accomplished—the objective, historic work of Christ as mediator on the cross. That alignment may not have been exact (as will be seen), but it was remarkable in its congruity. The Reformers stood on

---

50. Anselm, *De Concordia*, 435–74.
51. Boethius, *Consolation of Philosophy*, esp. bks. 4 and 5.
52. Evans, *Saint Anselm of Canterbury*, 24–25.

a foundation that was paved not only by the church fathers but the medieval Scholastics. That foundation explains why the Reformers could take issue over transubstantiation (see chapter 8), which they believed violated the sufficiency of Christ's sacrifice (*solus* Christus). However, the Reformers did not challenge Rome's basic and essential affirmation of the cross as an atonement, even a satisfaction for sin.

As the father of Scholasticism, Anselm's interpretation of the incarnation and atonement as a satisfaction contributed to this catholic foundation, a foundation prepared by certain church fathers and inherited by the Reformers. The purpose of *Cur Deus Homo* is identified from the start: Anselm summoned reason to demonstrate the credibility of Scripture and its belief that only a God-man could reconcile God with man. As Anselm articulated this doctrine of reconciliation, he also turned to the nature of the cross. "What we have to investigate, therefore, is the question: 'By what rationale does God forgive the sins of men?'" The answer depends on the nature of sin. Sin may be many things, but its offensive quality is plain in the way it steals God's *honor*. Created in his image, the creature is made to honor God. Therefore, when the creature's will acts in a way that is displeasing to God, he or she *dishonors* God.[53] That dishonor is not an individual affair alone but disrupts the moral order established by the Creator for his creation. "There is nothing more intolerable in the universal order than that a creature should take away honour from the creator and not repay what he takes away."[54]

The consequence of this dishonor is serious: the sinner is left in a state of guilt.[55] The only proper response to such dishonor is to repay the honor lost; more than that, one must go above and beyond and "pay back more than he took, in proportion to the insult which he has inflicted." Anselm gave several practical examples of this system of repayment in human society and concluded that nothing less is required in a heavenly society between God and man. "Therefore, everyone who sins is under an obligation to repay to God the honour which he has violently taken from him, and this is the satisfaction which every sinner is obliged to give to God."[56]

Cannot God merely forgive sin without requiring honor's restitution? Is that not more merciful? Anselm disagreed. "To forgive a sin in this way is nothing other than to refrain from inflicting punishment. And if no satisfaction is given, the way to regulate sin correctly is none other than to punish it. If, therefore, it is not punished, it is forgiven without its having been regulated. . . . But it is not fitting for God to allow anything in his kingdom to slip by unregulated."[57]

---

53. "Someone who does not render to God this honour due to him is taking away from God what is his, and dishonouring God, and this is what it is to sin. As long as he does not repay what he has taken away, he remains in a state of guilt." Anselm, *Why God Became Man* 1.11.

54. Anselm, *Why God Became Man* 1.13.

55. Anselm, *Why God Became Man* 1.11.

56. Anselm, *Why God Became Man* 1.11.

57. Anselm, *Why God Became Man* 1.12.

SIN FROM EVE, BUT A SAVIOR FROM MARY

Anselm did not think Eve was inconsequential to sin's remedy, but instead thought hope comes through woman: "just as the sin of mankind and the cause of our damnation originated from a woman, correspondingly the medicine of sin and the cause of salvation should be born of a woman. Moreover, women might lose hope that they have a part in the destiny of the blessed ones, in view of the fact that such great evil proceeded from a woman: in order to prevent this, it is right that an equivalent great good should proceed from a woman, so as to rebuild their hope" (*Why God Became Man*, 2.9). Anselm was not blaming Eve, but he spent most of his time pointing out all that was wrong in Adam. Eve played "a part" in the tragedy. However, hope is a woman's womb. Anselm did not think it was accidental that God chose a woman to be the God-bearer. He had great respect for Mary because through her humanity found hope once more.

Such a slip would compromise his own holy character, as well as the moral order he has established in the world, an order that is supposed to reflect his righteousness.[58] To avoid forfeiting his righteous character, a retributive punishment must be distributed. "If it is not fitting for God to do anything in an unjust and unregulated manner, it does not belong to his freedom or benevolence or will to release unpunished a sinner who has not repaid to God what he has taken away from him.... [Therefore, it is a] necessary consequence that either the honour which has been taken away should be repaid, or punishment should follow. Otherwise, either God will not be just to himself, or he will be without the power to enforce either of the two options; and it is an abominable sin even to consider this possibility."[59]

The tragedy of humanity is heightened by Anselm's confession that all those in Adam cannot pay the infinite debt of their dishonor. Anselm returned to the garden and targeted Adam because he was supposed to be "God's deputy, in a position between God and the devil, the intention being that he might overcome the devil by not consenting when the devil recommended sin by means of persuasion." If Adam had confounded the devil's persuasion, Adam would have honored God, but instead he was conquered. "He did this in accordance with

---

58. Furthermore, such a slip could raise sin itself up to God and lower God himself down to the level of sin, as if no law exists anymore. "Everyone knows that the righteousness of mankind is subject to a law whereby it is rewarded by God with a recompense proportional to its magnitude.... If, however, sin is neither paid for nor punished, it is subject to no law." That lack of accountability is catastrophic: "Sinfulness is in a position of greater freedom, if it is forgiven through mercy alone, than righteousness—and this seems extremely unfitting.... *it makes sinfulness resemble God.* For, just as God is subject to no law, the same is the case with sinfulness." Anselm, *Why God Became Man* 1.12, emphasis added.

59. Anselm, *Why God Became Man* 1.12, 13. Anselm said later, "Consider it, then, an absolute certainty, that God cannot remit a sin unpunished, without recompense, that is, without the voluntary paying off of a debt, and that a sinner cannot, without this, attain to a state of blessedness, not even the state which was his before he sinned." Anselm, *Why God Became Man* 1.19.

the will of the devil and contrary to the will and honour of God."[60] To be exact, Adam stole the honor God was due. The tragedy compromised all the blessed happiness God had in store for Adam. "Man, therefore, neither ought nor can receive from God what God planned to give him, unless man returns to God all that he has taken away from him."[61]

Can man return to God all the honor he has stolen? He cannot. For all of Adam's children are "born in sin." They are bound by an inescapable "incapacity," a term Anselm used repeatedly to underline man's spiritual inability to pay his debt (the honor he has robbed from God). That incapacity does not excuse man, however. "Not at all. It serves, rather, to increase his guilt, since he has brought the incapacity upon himself." In other words, "a person who has of his own accord bound himself by a debt which he cannot repay, has thrown himself into this state of incapacity by his guilt. As a result, he is unable to repay what he owed before his sin, that is, an obligation not to sin, and the fact that he is in debt as a consequence of his sin is inexcusable."[62] To make his situation worse, man refuses to return the honor God is due, which makes him a wrongdoer. "No wrongdoer, moreover, will be admitted to a state of blessed happiness, since blessed happiness is sufficiency in which there is no want and, correspondingly, this state is appropriate for nobody except a person in whom there is such pure righteousness that there is no wrongdoing in him."[63]

Anselm has set up his reader. The answer to his inquiry is Christ and Christ alone, the God-man. Only he can be the one in whom there is pure righteousness and therefore the only one who can make satisfaction for sin.[64] That satisfaction must not only be met by one who is unstained by Adam's sin; it must be met by the Word made flesh. Anselm refuted many of the major christological heresies (though without naming them), explaining that the two natures cannot be changed, mixed, or intercontaminated, thus aligning himself with the Definition of Chalcedon. "In order, therefore, that a God-Man should bring about what is necessary, it is essential that the same one person who will make the recompense should be perfect God and perfect man. For he cannot do this if he is not true God, and he has no obligation to do so if he is not a true man."[65]

---

60. Anselm said Adam was "conquered by persuasion alone, not under forcible compulsion" so as to avoid the charge of coercion. Anselm, *Why God Became Man* 1.22.

61. Anselm, *Why God Became Man* 1.23.

62. Anselm, *Why God Became Man* 1.24.

63. Anselm, *Why God Became Man* 1.24.

64. Anselm spent much energy demonstrating that the incarnation is voluntary. If it is not, then salvation is not by grace but the result of compulsion. Christ, however, did not come for his own sake but for humanity's sake, demonstrating that the incarnation represents no compulsion. Christ chose to "put himself under an obligation to bring his good beginning to fulfillment." Anselm, *Why God Became Man* 2.5.

65. "Given, therefore, that it is necessary for a God-Man to be found in whom the wholeness of both natures is kept intact, it is no less necessary for these two natures to combine, as wholes, in one person.... For otherwise it cannot come about that one and the same person may be perfect God and perfect man." Anselm, *Why God Became Man* 2.7.

Why not exactly? If, on one hand, the God-man is not man, then he cannot claim to represent humanity in his satisfaction for sin nor pay the debt on humanity's behalf. In other words, "he will not have an obligation to give recompense on behalf of this race, because he will not be from it." He must be, therefore, a "member of the same race" to pay recompense on behalf of that race. "Therefore, just as, starting from Adam and Eve, sin has been engendered in all human beings, similarly, no one except either these two themselves, or someone descended from them, has an obligation to pay recompense for the sin of mankind. . . . Therefore, it is necessary that the man through whom the race of Adam is to be restored should be taken from Adam's progeny."[66]

On the other hand, if the God-man is not God, then he cannot restore the honor due to God. The dishonor robbed God; only one who is God can return that honor. He must offer a satisfaction that is so "sublime and so precious that it can suffice to repay the debt owed for the sins of the whole world, and infinitely more besides."[67] If Jesus is not the *God*-man, then his death is not of infinite worth. Yet if he is who he says he is, then he owes no debt and can offer himself for the debt of others. Christ owed no debt, yet he "gave his life, so precious, no, his very self; he gave his person—think of it—in all its greatness, in an act of his own, supremely great, volition."[68]

To be clear, Anselm did not think Christ was paying such a debt to the devil; this set Anselm in contrast to one patristic stream that interpreted the cross as a ransom to Satan. To explain his reasoning, Anselm introduced the Nicene tradition's doctrine of inseparable operations—*opera Trinitatis ad extra indivisa sunt.*[69] Anselm, too, affirmed that the external works of the Trinity are undivided. For example, Augustine said that since the Trinity is one in essence, the "Father, and the Son, and the Holy Ghost are inseparably united in themselves." Therefore, "all the works of the one God are the works of the Father, of the Son, and of the Holy Ghost."[70] Anselm agreed and applied this orthodox belief to the cross as a restoration of honor not merely to the Father but to the entire Godhead, the Son included. How could the Son be included when he was the one offering satisfaction? "That honour, to be sure, belongs to the whole of the Trinity. It follows that because Christ himself is God, the Son of God, the offering he made of himself was to his own honour as well as to the Father and the Holy Spirit; that is, he offered up his humanity to his divinity, the one selfsame divinity which belongs to the three persons."[71]

---

66. Anselm, *Why God Became Man* 2.9 (p. 323).

67. These are the words of Boso, Anselm's dialogue partner, but Anselm agrees. Anselm, *Why God Became Man* 2.18.

68. Anselm, *Why God Became Man* 2.18.

69. For the development of inseparable operations as a mark of Nicene orthodoxy, see Ayres, *Nicaea and Its Legacy.*

70. Augustine, *Homilies on the Gospel of John* 20.13 (*NPNF*¹ 7:137).

71. Anselm, *Why God Became Man* 2.18.

If the incarnate Son has given back the honor due to the whole Trinity, then the payment for sin's debt is a payment to God, not the devil. God is no one's debtor, especially Satan's. Satisfaction was "the action of the man of whom we have spoken . . . [and] God did it, in view of the unity of his [Christ's] person." However, it is "not the case that God needed to come down from heaven to conquer the devil, or to take action against him in order to set mankind free." Anselm explained why:

> Rather, God demanded it of man that he should defeat the devil and should pay recompense by means of righteousness, having previously offended God through sin. Certainly God did not owe the devil anything but punishment, nor did man owe him anything but retribution—to defeat in return him by whom he had been defeated. But, whatever was demanded from man, his debt was to God, not to the devil.[72]

For Anselm, Christ conquered the devil who conquered Adam in the garden. However, that victory over the devil was not accomplished through a debt paid to the devil himself. Instead, the devil's power was relinquished when Christ restored honor to the Holy Trinity and mankind was set free from sin and its guilt as a result, which is the only leverage the devil had over mankind.

Underneath this Godward satisfaction is a subtle but persistent emphasis on the atonement as an act of substitution. When Anselm concluded *Cur Deus Homo* he was sure to underline its significance in the voice of the Father and the Son. "What, indeed, can be conceived of more merciful than that God the Father should say to a sinner condemned to eternal torments and lacking any means of redeeming himself, 'Take my only-begotten Son and give him on your behalf,' and that the Son himself should say, 'Take me and redeem yourself.'"[73] Throughout *Cur Deus Homo*, Anselm framed man's fall and rise within the sphere of blessed happiness lost and regained. Adam's fall was so devasting because all his progeny cannot "repay to God what he owes," and therefore "will be incapable of being blessedly happy." However, in Christ blessed happiness returns and is multiplied. The believer has every reason to hope since he will receive "that final mercy, whereby, after this life, he makes a human being blessedly happy."[74] Yet that blessed happiness is contingent on the forgiveness of sins and the repayment of debt. Christ alone—the God-man—can pay that debt. That answer was the nucleus of Anselm's apologetic response to "satisfy not only Jews, but even pagans." And that answer, and all its logic in between, has "proved" the truthfulness of the Old and New Testaments, Anselm concluded.[75]

---

72. Anselm, *Why God Became Man* 2.19.
73. Anselm, *Why God Became Man* 2.20.
74. Anselm, *Why God Became Man* 1.24.
75. Anselm, *Why God Became Man* 2.22.

PETER LOMBARD

As important as Anselm is as the first of the Scholastics, his work did not become the standard textbook on which the Reformers of the sixteenth century cut their teeth. That honor went to Peter Lombard instead, whose importance is difficult to exaggerate.

Prior to Scholasticism, theological prose took a certain form. In the East, for example, Gregory of Nazianzus's famous Trinitarian treatise took the form of orations and Athanasius's *On the Incarnation* was a concise but profound theological essay. In the West, Augustine's *Confessions* had the flavor of autobiography (though much more) and Boethius's *Consolation of Philosophy* took the form of a dialogue. Scholasticism benefited from each of these genres, quoted many of these authors, and engaged their theological and spiritual programs. As Scholasticism developed, however, it added a genre of its own, contributing its own mark to this mosaic of Christian literature, one that was far more didactic for the theological student and budding scholar.

THE SCHOLASTIC DEDICATION TO THE BIBLE: THE *GLOSSA ORDINARIA*

In the twelfth century, the Vulgate included a commentary on the scriptural text. In preceding centuries all the way back to the patristic era, a word in the Bible that was ambiguous to the reader was often accompanied by a *gloss* or *glossa*. As time passed, not only was a word used to clarify the meaning, but a comment was added as well. Eventually comments turned into commentary with an explanation of the meaning of the text and its message. As Scholastics rose up in universities in the eleventh century, for example, they contributed their own glosses, becoming glossators. By the twelfth century, teachers assigned the *Glossa Ordinaria* to help students understand the text. Some of these students became scholars themselves, who then studied and wrote on the *Glossa* themselves. In view of its patristic and medieval pedigree, the *Glossa Ordinaria* carried credibility, even authority, influencing not only theologians but canon law itself.

At the risk of oversimplification, Lombard imitated what glossators accomplished but with *loci* instead, providing patristic commentary but over theological topics. Just as students commented on the *Glossa* for their studies, so, too, did students write commentaries on Lombard's *Sentences*. At the turn of the sixteenth century, some of these commentators on the *Glossa* and *The Sentences* became Reformers.

For a list of exegetes who contributed and preserved the apparatus, see Swanson, "The *Glossa Ordinaria*," 156–67.

Theologians in the past often crafted their theology in the monastery. With the rise of the Schoolmen, theologians could now surface in the halls of the university. In the classroom, a theologian could be lecturing to the next generation of archbishops and archdeacons, as well as the next great university theologians.[76] Method, therefore, was not insignificant. Both in publication and in lecture form, the theologian became the instructor, raising some of the most stirring questions about human existence and the human plight, drawing from sacred Scripture and tradition.

Students were expected to attend lectures and read assigned texts designed to provide instruction in exegesis and theology, both of which were considered complementary and inseparable from one another. To learn exegesis and its history, a lecturer assigned the *Ordinary Gloss* (*Glossa Ordinaria*), a collection of patristic commentary on the scriptural text. To learn theology as well as its history, a lecturer assigned Peter Lombard's *Four Books of Sentences*. Yet the two—exegesis and theology—were two currents in the same river. "Medieval theologians did not draw a sharp distinction, as we would, between biblical exegesis and dogmatic theology. The words 'theology' and 'sacred page' could be used interchangeably, since biblical interpretation was by definition theological and dogmatic theology exegetical."[77]

Such an approach to biblical exegesis and theology can be credited to Peter Lombard (1100–1160), at least in part.[78] Lombard was born in Italy, but under the influence of Bernard of Clairvaux, he decided to travel to France. Lombard spent a good part of the 1130s studying theology at Rheims and Paris. Some think Lombard even learned from Hugh of St. Victor during this time.[79] He then spent the 1140s and 1150s teaching theology in Paris. In a colossal feat, Lombard wrote commentaries on nearly the entire Bible, but his commentaries were saturated in theological reflection. Take, for example, Lombard's commentary on the Psalms. "Rather than glossing the Psalms to incite devotion, he extracts doctrine from them, mainly ethical and sacramental."[80]

Four Books of Sentences

Many of these theological commentaries later became the bedrock for Lombard's comprehensive and systematic work in theology.[81] From 1147 to 1151 Lombard systematically addressed mysteries of the Christian faith.[82] These opinions or sentences formed Lombard's *Four Books of Sentences*, a work indebted to

---

76. "Most parish priests never saw the inside of a university and were trained for their work in a more rudimentary way at a local level." Steinmetz, "Scholastic Calvin," 19.

77. Steinmetz, "Scholastic Calvin," 21. "In order to become a Master of Theology a candidate needed to become first a Bachelor of the Bible and then a Bachelor of the Sentences" (22). Consider Luther's own education in chapter 8.

78. Some historians believe Peter Abelard (1079–1142) taught Peter Lombard in Paris.

79. Colish, "Peter Lombard," 168.

80. Colish, "Peter Lombard," 168. The same insight could be deciphered from Peter Lombard's commentary on Paul's epistles, his *Collectanea*. "Peter's *Collectanea* reflects quite thoroughly the interplay between his exegesis and systematic theology" (169).

81. Some were written in the late 1130s before Lombard started teaching in 1142.

82. Whether Lombard was a student of Peter Abelard or not, Lombard's most influential work is striking in its resemblance to Abelard's *Sic et non*. For a critical edition, consult Lombard's *Sentences, Magistri Petri Lombardi Sententiae in IV libris distinctae*, 5.

the labors of Hugh of St. Victor and Peter Abelard, though his theology does not wholly commit to either but is a type of *via media*. The purpose of the project was not only formative but polemical, an attempt to fortify the faith against heresy.[83] The four books were organized as follows:

Book 1: The Mystery of the Trinity
Book 2: On Creation
Book 3: On the Incarnation of the Word
Book 4: On the Doctrine of Signs

The contribution of *The Sentences* was not limited to content but was defined by format, specifically *method*. To understand the significance of method, consider Lombard's first book on the Trinity and his ninth "distinction." In chapter 2, Lombard turned his attention to the coeternity of the Son and formatted his treatment as follows:

1. Here on the coeternity of the Son with the Father. (Lombard stated the church's belief.)
2. The argument of the Arians. (Lombard stated the heretic's challenge to the church's belief.)
3. The Catholic response of Augustine. (Lombard quoted Augustine's *De Trinitate*.)
4. Augustine's objection against the heretic. (Lombard quoted Augustine once more.)
5. Ambrose's response to the same, strengthened by authority. (Lombard enlisted a second church father, Ambrose, and quoted his *De fide*.)
6. Ambrose used reason against the heretic. (Lombard concluded by recruiting reason to settle the conflict.)
7. Ambrose's attack against the heretic. (Lombard allowed a patristic the last polemical word on the matter.)[84]

To a degree, the above structure is restricted (to Ambrose and Augustine, the latter most often cited by Lombard), but in many other chapters Lombard summoned a host of patristic voices as evidence. For example, only two chapters later Lombard asked "whether it ought to be said that 'the Son is forever generated' or 'was forever generated.'"[85] To answer this basic orthodox belief, Lombard provided extensive quotations from Gregory, Augustine, John Chrysostom, Origen, and Hilary of Poitiers.

Lombard was not citing church fathers at random; his quotations were strategic. When he quoted Gregory on eternal generation, he cited Gregory's

---

83. Leinsle, *Introduction to Scholastic Theology*, 60, 99–100.
84. *Sentences* 1.9.2.
85. *Sentences* 1.9.4.

comments on 1 Corinthians 1:24. Likewise, when he quoted Augustine, he quoted Augustine's commentary on Psalm 2:7. Lombard did the same with each church father so that his answer was not only a scriptural answer to the question but one with the support of patristic interpretation. However, Lombard prioritized Augustine's opinions above all, quoting the church father not only for paragraphs but sometimes for pages. At certain points in Lombard's *Sentences*, all other fathers disappeared as Augustine became the voice that monopolized his imagination.

By the time Lombard finished, his answer was accompanied by an overwhelming symphony of voices. Lombard not only put forward the scriptural witness but the testimony of the church catholic and its stance over against heresy. Lombard's format was accessible for the student and lecturer alike, forcing each to wrestle with apparent contradictions in Scripture and tradition. Lombard's *Sentences* did not depart from the priorities of the patristic era; *The Sentences* attempted to take those priorities with great seriousness by arranging *loci* systematically, giving each its due attention.

That meant, however, a shift in genre. At least with Lombard, the student was not reading a hymn, sermon, or polemical tract, but a systematic presentation of theology that organized doctrines and then encouraged the student to reconcile diverse or even contrary answers. In an Augustinian vein, *The Sentences* were structured according to (1) *frui*, that which you love for its own sake, as an end in and of itself, like God, and (2) *uti*, that which you love, like creation, as a means to loving something else, like God. Since book 1 presents the Trinity, its focus is *frui*. Since book 4 presents the sacraments (signs), its focus is *uti*. And since book 2 treats creation and book 3 incarnation, they present both *frui* and *uti*.[86] The movement from *frui* to *uti* was a Scholastic strategy designed to orient the student's methodology properly, conceptualizing theology first and foremost around God and then all things in relation to God.

In the Scholastic era, the student sat down to hear his teacher lecture on Lombard's *Sentences*. Why *The Sentences* instead of reading a particular church father instead? *The Sentences* were not a mere repristinating of the past, as if Lombard's work assumes that all that came prior to the Scholastic era formed a unified body or consensus. Surely a harmony did exist on core doctrines of orthodoxy. However, many of the questions Lombard raised had yet to be answered in comprehensive fashion, nor were they officially decided by the church. On these pages, Lombard's originality shines through as he introduced streams of thought yet to be reconciled. Lombard sometimes presented these unanswered questions in a way that revealed his opinion, nudging the reader toward a resolution, pushing future generations to reach concord previously unachieved.[87]

---

86. Sometimes the language of *signa*, or signs, and *res*, or things, is used instead. See Steinmetz, "Scholastic Calvin," 20.

87. "Peter often finds new ways of conceptualizing questions that other thinkers had raised but failed to resolve. At other times he polemicizes on issues on which no contemporary consensus existed. He sometimes

When Lombard is read in this way—acknowledged for his broad synthesizing of disciplines from exegesis to philosophy—his *Sentences* become exciting terrain. While modern readers may feel like the *Sentences* are a wilderness of endless patristic meandering, medieval readers entered a jungle full of delicious fruit and encountered exotic animals they were challenged to tame. As the lecturer explored this terrain, he did not merely regurgitate Lombard's *Sentences* but provided his own commentary, interpretation, and assessment. Those with ingenuity might have even asked questions not addressed by Lombard or addressed only in part. After posing these new questions, the teacher might have offered his own solution to the theological dilemma he raised.[88] Lombard, in other words, was a launching pad, sending the reader to the past but also into the future. That launching pad sent students back to the history of theological interpretation, East and West. In short, this academic practice ensured both catholicity and canon were held hand in hand.

That process also guaranteed precision and logic, not only pressuring the student and lecturer alike to be accurate but also exposing anything less than coherency and consistency in solving the dilemma. Sometimes questions pressed up against the heights of mystery, but critics of Scholasticism often forget that many questions pressed into the weeds of church ministry and the Christian's eternal destiny. Steinmetz captured the pastoral motive: "Scholastic masters, while grounding their arguments in the Bible and tradition, hoped so to pattern the minds of their students with the logic of Christian faith that they could witness to the gospel without losing themselves in unresolved contradictions, logical absurdities, imprecise definitions, or maudlin sentimentality. Clear thinking about theological issues was an important skill for a university don to cultivate. It was an equally important skill for a bishop, entrusted with the care of souls."[89]

To matriculate at the highest levels of theology, the advanced student had to write his own commentary on Lombard's *Sentences*. For that reason, theologians after Lombard lectured and wrote commentaries on Lombard's *Sentences*, including some of the most impressive Scholastics, such as Thomas Aquinas and Duns Scotus. On Lombard they cut their teeth, making a name for themselves. And on the eve of the Reformation, the soon-to-be Reformers were writing commentaries and lecturing on Lombard's *Sentences* just the same. If Lombard's formulation places great emphasis on a retrieval of orthodox commitments, from a Nicene Trinitarianism to a Chalcedonian Christology, then why did the first

plays a major role in the emergence of a new consensus, or at least articulates the terms in which questions continued to be debated. In addition to making apt use of philosophy and the liberal arts, where he deems them helpful, Peter draws heavily on canon law, especially in his sacramental theology. This, too, gives Lombardian theology a fresh, broad-gauged, and distinctive look." Colish, "Peter Lombard," 170.

88. Steinmetz, "Scholastic Calvin," 20.

89. Steinmetz, "Scholastic Calvin," 21. For example, "How, asked some scholastic masters, could a Catholic boy and girl, each of whom had been cleansed from original sin by the sacrament of baptism, communicate an original sin they did not have to their baby?" (20).

Reformers not extensively address such *loci*?[90] If the Reformers did not address major doctrines of orthodoxy, their silence is not due to disagreement with their Scholastic predecessors. They felt no need to question the orthodoxy of their Scholastic heritage lest their own catholicity be called into question by Rome. By presupposing orthodoxy, the Reformers considered themselves in lockstep with the church catholic.

As for their treatment of soteriology and ecclesiology (the sacraments included), we might label their relationship a *critical appropriation*. As far as Scholastics like Lombard and Thomas imitated Augustinianism (predestination, original sin, *sola gratia*, etc.), the Reformers found themselves in general continuity. However, where seeds of future papal ecclesiology were sown, the Protestants were convinced the tradition before them needed reform, that is, a return to a purer patristic conception. For example, consider a short case study in Lombard and the sacraments.

Case Study: The Sacraments—Eucharist and Penance

Following Augustine, Lombard defined a sacrament as a "visible form of an invisible grace."[91] As an invisible grace, the sacraments do not merely point to a greater reality (as if a mere sign), but they prove effective, distributing grace to make the sinner righteous. "For a sacrament is properly so called because it is a sign of God's grace and a form of invisible grace in such manner that it bears its image and is its cause. And so the sacraments were not instituted only for the sake of signifying, but also to sanctify."[92] Lombard numbered these sanctifying sacraments at seven: (1) baptism, (2), confirmation, (3) bread of blessing (Eucharist), (4) penance, (5) extreme unction, (6) orders, and (7) marriage. While each cannot be treated at length, consider Lombard's understanding of two sacraments that set the scene for the sixteenth-century reaction—Eucharist and penance.

Eucharist

Lombard and both patristic and medieval theologians assumed that the purpose of baptism was nothing less than the washing away of sin's guilt. Yet the temporal punishment for sin committed after baptism remains.[93] After baptism,

90. To qualify, Peter may have transferred the *core* of a Nicene doctrine of God and a Chalcedonian Christology, but he did stray at points from certain components of the broader classical tradition. "He objects to platonizing theologies of all kinds. He opposes immanentalist and emanationist views of the deity and has no use whatever for negative theology." Colish, "Peter Lombard," 168.

91. *Sentences* 4.1.2.

92. *Sentences* 4.1.4. Colish observes how Peter departed from Hugh of St. Victor by this "redefinition of sacraments in generation, not just as visible signs of invisible grace but as signs that resemble what they signify and that mediate divine grace, making it effective in the inner lives of the recipients." Colish categorizes Peter's definition as "Victorine." Colish, "Peter Lombard," 178.

93. Lombard quoted Isidore to this effect: "And so, although the guilt of sin is taken away, the temporal punishment still remains, so that the life which will be free from all punishments should be more zealously thought." Isidore, *Sententiae*, bk. 1, ch. 22, n. 3; Lombard, *Sentences* 4.4.6.

one receives confirmation, which is followed by reception of the Eucharist, a strategic but subsequent sacrament to initiation at baptism. "Baptism extinguishes the ardour of the vices; the Eucharist restores us spiritually."[94] To apply this spiritual restoration, however, the Eucharist must undergo a change in substance. Lombard described this transubstantiation as follows: "When these words ['This is my body. . . . This is my blood'] are pronounced, the change of the bread and wine into the substance of the body and blood of Christ occurs."[95] To deny this change is heresy. For the skeptic is not only denying the change in the elements but is questioning (and limiting) the power of God himself.[96] Since God is unlimited in power, Christ's "true body, is on every altar wherever the Eucharist is celebrated." That body may be "veiled by the form of bread and wine" but "invisibly he is on the altar."[97]

Does such a mystical consecration mean that anytime the Eucharist is given on the altar a sacrifice occurs, an immolation? "To this, it may briefly be said that what is offered and consecrated by the priest is called sacrifice and oblation, because it is a remembrance and representation of the true sacrifice and the holy immolation made on the altar of the cross. And indeed Christ died only once, namely on the cross, and there he was immolated in himself; but he is daily immolated in the sacrament, because in the sacrament is made a remembrance of what was done once."[98] That daily immolation on altars across Rome and wider Europe does not mean, however, that Christ is multiplied into many Christs in many places. "No, but there is one Christ everywhere," said John Chrysostom, "being here in his fullness, and there also. Just as what is offered everywhere is one body, so also it is one sacrifice."[99]

The daily immolation is necessary as well since sin is committed daily and needs an offering. Its regular distribution underlines its continual, even effectual power, which takes a twofold form, one negative and the other positive: "the remission of venial sins and the perfecting of virtue."[100] Lombard followed through on this twofold purpose, noting that the former explains why the Eucharist is a "medicine for our daily infirmity" while the latter explains why it serves to increase virtue within, charity in particular.[101]

Penance

If baptism is the first plank of salvation after sin has shipwrecked the soul, the sacrament of penance is the second plank. Baptism had a twofold effect on

---

94. *Sentences* 4.8.1.
95. *Sentences* 4.8.4.
96. *Sentences* 4.10.1.
97. *Sentences* 4.10.1.
98. *Sentences* 4.12.5.
99. John Chrysostom, *Homiliae in epistolam ad Hebraeos*, hom. 17, n. 3, on Heb. 10:1; Lombard, *Sentences* 4.12.65.
100. *Sentences* 4.12.5.
101. *Sentences* 4.12.6.

the sinner. First, baptism washed away guilt and punishment, *culpa* and *poena*. Second, removing the person from a state of sin, baptism also moved the sinner into a state of grace. That movement can occur because baptism not only removes guilt and punishment but infuses a habit of love—*habitus charitatis*.[102] Now that the sinner has been returned to a state of innocence, he has a renewed disposition. Yet subsequent sins return the baptized to an infected, diseased state, plagued by guilt, sins that then require a temporal punishment. Sin after baptism causes a second shipwreck. Nevertheless, penance—or *poenitentia*, taken from *poena* (punishment)—is the needed rescue. To switch metaphors, penance is the necessary medicine. For "if anyone has corrupted by sin the clothing of innocence which he received at baptism, he may repair it by the remedy of penance." Penance serves to renew what was lost since baptism. "The first plank is baptism, in which the old man is laid down and the new one is put on; the second, penance, is the one by which we rise against after having fallen, while the old nature which has returned is driven away and the lost newness is again taken up. Those who have fallen after baptism can be renewed by penance," concluded Lombard.[103]

To clarify, penance is not as potent as baptism. Baptism can remove both the guilt of sin and the temporal penalty that results from sin. Penance, by contrast, cannot remove guilt. It can, nevertheless, reduce the punishment of sin. When a person sins after baptism, if he or she is contrite and confesses, then the priest can absolve the sinner from guilt. Yet the temporal punishment remains and must be satisfied by means of penance.[104]

Lombard was persuaded that support for the practice of penance could be found in the Vulgate's translation of Matthew 3:2, where Jesus commanded, "Do penance, for the kingdom of God is at hand." As chapter 6 will reveal, humanists like Erasmus and Reformers like Tyndale took issue with the Vulgate's translation, persuaded by the Greek that Jesus was not referring to some system of penance but to repentance from the heart. Lombard, too, gave significant credence to the necessity of repentance, even calling on the ungodly to abandon their sins with tears of sorrow.[105]

Unlike abuses on the eve of the Reformation that promoted indulgences without requiring repentance in the heart, Lombard was quite serious about its necessity. He even defined penance as a "virtue by which we bewail and hate, with purpose of amendment, the evils we have committed, and we will not commit again the things we have bewailed." If Lombard had lived alongside the young Luther, he might have protested abuses of the sacrament as well. "True penance," he insisted, "is to sorrow in one's soul and to hate vices."[106] Although Luther's

102. Wengert, *Martin Luther's Ninety-Five Theses*, xv.
103. *Sentences* 4.14.1. Lombard credited Jerome with labeling penance the second plank after shipwreck.
104. For a clear overview of the penance process on the eve of the Reformation, see Wengert, *Martin Luther's Ninety-Five Theses*, xvi.
105. *Sentences* 4.14.2.
106. *Sentences* 4.14.3.

protest evolved and matured, his initial protest in 1517 was not far removed from Lombard's belief in genuine repentance of the heart.

Nevertheless, Lombard did advocate for a type of penance that Luther tried as a monk and found crushing. Lombard not only considered penance's positive outcome—a renewal after baptism—but also considered penance's negative means to that outcome. Penance is a type of vengeance, a vengeance on oneself for sin.[107] To be truly remorseful, pain must be inflicted to pay the temporal punishment for sin. For God is just, and he requires a fitting satisfaction in return.

Since man is made up of heart, mouth, and hand, Lombard identified three corresponding components to true penance: "compunction of heart, confession of the mouth, satisfaction in deed."[108] As for compunction of heart, the penitent "should be sorry not only that he sinned, but also because he deprived himself of virtue."[109] Following this pattern of three, penance occurs in three stages of life:

1. Before baptism, namely for previous sins
2. After baptism, for the graver sins that are committed afterward
3. Daily penance for venial sins, which pertains to both the humble and the perfect[110]

If the penitent cannot pay the temporal punishment for sins by means of penance in this lifetime, then the next lifetime offers a preliminary stage for purging by fire. God, after all, "does not leave a crime unpunished."[111] All that is wood, hay, and stubble (1 Cor. 3:12–13) will "find a fire of transitory tribulation, to burn the flammable constructions which they have brought with them." By flammable constructions, Lombard, following Augustine, meant venial sins, "which are burned in the correcting fire . . . blotted out after this life."[112]

Lombard's understanding of the sacraments, and penance in particular, occurred during the High Middle Ages—the twelfth century. As it developed across the next four centuries, it matured into an intricate formula for this life and the afterlife. Consider the following five stages:

1. First plank after shipwreck: sacrament of baptism
   Baptism transitions the sinner from a state of sin to grace. Baptism (nonrepeatable) washes away original sin. Baptism has the power to remit both guilt (*culpa*) and punishment (*poena*) and infuse a habit of love (*habitus charitatis*).

---

107. *Sentences* 4.14.3. Lombard appealed to Pseudo-Augustine for support.
108. *Sentences* 4.15.7.
109. *Sentences* 4.16.2.
110. *Sentences* 4.16.3.
111. *Sentences* 4.20.2.
112. *Sentences* 4.21.2. Lombard went on to qualify, however, that such purging may be slower in some than others.

2. Post-baptismal sin: sin after baptism requires satisfaction (penance).
3. Second plank after shipwreck: sacrament of penance (repeatable)
   a. *Contrition:* penitent; real sorrow for sin[113]
   b. *Confession (and absolution):* confess sins to a priest, who grants absolution for guilt.
   c. *Satisfaction:* priest prescribes works of satisfaction to pay for temporal penalty of sin. Works of satisfaction include fasting, giving alms to the poor, prayers, pilgrimages, masses, indulgences, abstaining from communion, and so on. For example, an indulgence draws from the treasury of merit (surplus merit from Mary and saints) and is transferred to the recipient, decreasing some or all (plenary) temporal punishment for sins.
4. Death and purgatory
   Purgatory is for purgation (*purgatorium*), a place to suffer the remaining temporal punishment for sin and a place to purge sin until made holy.
5. Heaven

Chapter 8 will tell the story of indulgences and why they became instrumental, an avenue for the fulfillment of penance and advantageous to the papacy. By the sixteenth century, the Christian knew each of the following stages, stages that structured life from cradle to grave, defining the religious experience of king and peasant, clergy and laity alike.

ALEXANDER OF HALES AND BONAVENTURE

A Scholastic like Anselm solidified his career in England as archbishop of Canterbury. However, the Scholastic epicenter after Anselm was located in Paris, France, where Peter Abelard, Peter Lombard, Alexander of Hales, and Bonaventure all taught, even if they were not French by birth (like Abelard) but Italian (Lombard, Bonaventure) or English (Alexander of Hales). In the days of Abelard, a student interested in theology turned his eyes toward Notre Dame. However, in time what began as a school in a cathedral turned into a university, so that many of the best Scholastics found their careers situated at Paris University.

For example, Alexander of Hales (1185–1245) was an established archdeacon in England when Paris came calling. Alexander spent the latter half of his career teaching theology students at Paris University, and they so grew in their esteem for Alexander that his reputation was unsurpassed by any other theologian in the university. He was characterized to a degree by a bold academic spirit.

---

113. Not all medieval theologians considered contrition necessary, but some said attrition (fear of punishment) was sufficient. Due to the overwhelming power of sin, the expectation of contrition was too high. Nevertheless, attrition could be transformed into contrition by confession. "Hearing the priest's absolution in confession infused a person with a habit of love, changed a person's attrition into contrition and moved him or her from a state of sin to a state of grace." Wengert, *Martin Luther's Ninety-Five Theses*, xvii.

Prior to Alexander, lecturers assigned the Scriptures to their students and provided an interpretation as they discussed various *loci*. But Alexander was innovative, proposing a new model that assigned Lombard's *Sentences* to his students instead. Alexander was committed to the Scriptures, of course, but he moved his students beyond Scripture readings to theological and philosophical inquiry. This simple curricular decision was more significant than Alexander could have imagined. From Alexander to the Reformation era, Lombard's *Sentences* became the filter and the foil for any student of theology. A brilliant commentary on *The Sentences* might just make one a premier theologian. Yet Alexander distinguished himself not only by his curricular innovations but also by his theological distinctives, sometimes in ways that resisted the instincts of his choice textbook by Lombard.

One of Alexander of Hales's most promising talents at Paris University was a student from Italy named Bonaventure (ca. 1221–74), whom we met in chapter 2. Alexander not only influenced Bonaventure's academic studies but his monastic experience as well.[114] With Alexander, the Franciscans were introduced to Scholastic methods and reasoning, all the while retaining other emphases, such as preaching, especially since Alexander's influence was not limited to the university but penetrated the monastic order when he became a friar. The perpetuity of Scholastic influence is manifested in the train of Scholastics that followed Alexander's lead, including Bonaventure, Duns Scotus, and William of Ockham.

Alexander's two domains (Paris University and the Franciscan order) and his dual projects (theology and piety) reverberated in Bonaventure, one of the quintessential combinations of Scholasticism and mysticism. As for the former, Bonaventure was one of the superior Scholastic minds of his day. Like other Scholastics, Bonaventure was an exegete, lecturing and writing numerous commentaries on books of the Bible. For Bonaventure, and other Scholastics as well, the Scriptures were inspired by God and therefore authoritative for theology, making these sacred Scriptures the wellspring of biblical and theological interpretation.

Based on the exegesis of biblical books, Scholastics like Bonaventure were confident they could develop a theological outlook, one that incorporated the insights of the text but also history (especially patristic history) and philosophy.[115] Bonaventure studied the Fathers, East and West, with the same dedication he gave to his study of the Scriptures. And like Peter Lombard before him, Bonaventure found a special affinity for the theology of Augustine.[116] For over two decades Bonaventure carried on Alexander's tradition by lecturing in theology at Paris University (1248–55). If Alexander had lived long enough, he would

---

114. Bonaventure's academic studies can be dated to 1243–45.
115. Michael Robson says, "Scriptural studies laid the foundation for the study of scholastic theology." Robson, "Saint Bonaventure," 188.
116. Robson estimates 3,050 citations of Augustine in Bonaventure. Robson, 189.

have been proud to discover that Bonaventure not only assigned Lombard's *Sentences* but wrote his own commentary on *The Sentences* as well as a handbook to theology called *Breviloquium* (1256–57), his original work. Bonaventure's theology was influenced not only by Augustine but by Anselm, echoing the latter's interpretation of the atonement through the lens of honor and satisfaction.[117]

Besides his works devoted to answering questions concerning Nicene Trinitarianism and Chalcedonian orthodoxy, Bonaventure also explored the interplay between theology and philosophy in the late 1260s.[118] Yet unlike other Scholastics such as Thomas Aquinas, Bonaventure did not exhibit the same level of sympathy toward the revival of Aristotelianism. Although Bonaventure defended philosophy, it did not have the same level of prominence as all the other disciplines. Bonaventure even countered those who used Aristotle to argue for an eternal creation and the determinism of the human will.[119] And yet even Thomas Aquinas did not follow Aristotle everywhere. Augustine before him utilized the realism of Platonism but nevertheless knew when Platonism contradicted special revelation and needed refinement. Likewise, Thomas did the same, though his critical appropriation of Platonism was filtered through Aristotle's grammar, producing an original synthesis (see chapters 4–5). Bonaventure, however, allowed extreme appropriations of Aristotle to steer him away from the philosopher in many respects, which set Bonaventure apart from other Scholastics.

As mentioned, Bonaventure carried on Alexander's legacy not only as a Scholastic but as a devotee of the Franciscan order. He committed to the order as early as 1243, two years prior to Alexander's death. However, Bonaventure's success among the Franciscans far extended his master's passing, becoming minister general in 1257, leaving the lectern of the university behind to devote himself to the fraternity. In one sense, Bonaventure's influence on the Franciscan order took more permanent form than Alexander's due to Bonaventure's biography of Francis of Assisi, his commentary on the Franciscan rule, and especially his mystical classic *The Journey of the Mind to God* (see chapter 2).[120] "Speculation without devotion" misses the point of theology, which is the pursuit of righteousness and eternal life itself.[121]

That pious intention led Bonaventure to lament the immoral motivations of priests and friars in his own day who secured ecclesiastical or monastic offices for selfish gain instead of godliness and love for Christ. That pious intention

---

117. Many of the works mentioned by Bonaventure can be located in *Doctoris Seraphici S. Bonaventurae opera omnia*.

118. See his *Disputed Questions on the Mystery of the Trinity* and his *Disputed Questions on the Knowledge of Christ*, for example.

119. See Bonaventure's *Collations on the Seven Gifts of the Holy Spirit*.

120. *Itinerarium mentis in Deum*. For his spiritual writings, see *The Threefold Way*; *On the Perfection of Life*; *On Governing the Soul*; *The Soliloquium: A Dialogue on the Four Spiritual Exercises*. For his more polemical books related to spirituality, see *Disputed Questions on Evangelical Perfection* and *Defense of the Mendicants*.

121. *Itinerarium mentis in Deum*, prol., no. 4, p. 296; quoted in Robson, "Saint Bonaventure," 188.

also led Bonaventure to warn Christians against approaching the altar without due preparation. As a believer in transubstantiation, Bonaventure worried that sinners violated the body and blood of Christ with their lack of repentance.

Although it is debated, some believe Bonaventure set the trajectory for late medieval Scholastics (e.g., Ockham) and their separation, even bifurcation between reason on one hand and faith and love on the other hand. Did Bonaventure's elevation of experience over reason in the soul's quest for God create a crack in the foundation that allowed late medieval Scholastics to wedge reason and faith apart until they were completely separated from one another? Whether Bonaventure is the origin of such a dichotomy will continue to be debated.

Yet before we can explore that gap, we will first recognize in chapter 4 the union between reason and faith in the thought of a chief Scholastic like Thomas Aquinas. Chapter 4 will counter popular caricatures by acknowledging the Reformation's debt to Scholasticism and the Reformers' critical appropriation of Scholasticism.

4

THOMAS AQUINAS AS A
"SOUNDER SCHOLASTIC"

*The Reformation's Critical
Retrieval of Scholasticism*

*The Reformation altered comparatively few of the major loci of
[Scholastic] theology: the doctrines of justification, the sacraments, and
the church received the greatest emphasis, while the doctrines of God, the
trinity, creation, providence, predestination, and the last things were
taken over by the magisterial Reformation virtually without alteration.*
— Richard Muller, "Scholasticism in Calvin"

*The story of Thomas Aquinas and Protestantism has yet to be written,
and it is not identical with the story of Thomas and Luther.*
— David Steinmetz, *Luther in Context*

The fear of scholasticism is the mark of a false prophet.
— Karl Barth

Bonaventure died in 1274, the same year Thomas Aquinas (1225–74) died.
If Anselm was the first of the Scholastics in the High Middle Ages and
Bonaventure was Scholasticism's mystical connoisseur, Thomas may be its
most influential theologian when subsequent centuries are taken into account,
ushering Scholasticism into an age of intellectual maturity across exegetical, theological, and philosophical lines.[1] His influence, however, was by no
means obvious in the years after his death as he became a target of criticism.
In 1277 the dirt over his tomb was still fresh when concepts derivative from
Thomas were denounced in Oxford. Thomas had devoted much of his career
to Paris only for ecclesiastical authorities to damn his teaching that same year.

---

1. Stanglin is bolder still, labeling Thomas the "most influential theologian after Augustine" (*Letter and
Spirit of Biblical Interpretation*, 103).

Despite the lukewarm (and sometimes hostile) reception, both in his own day and right after, the hands of time have produced a different verdict. Thomas was not only canonized in the fourteenth century, but his biblical scholarship, his theological synthesis, and his philosophical analysis have endured, informing variegated religious traditions.

For our purposes, Thomas will receive more attention than most because (1) the late medieval Scholasticism of Scotus, Ockham, and Biel (the *via moderna*) was a shift away from some (though not all) core components of High Scholasticism as perpetuated by individuals like Thomas; and (2) the sixteenth-century Reformers, whether they always knew it or not, had far more in common with Scholastics like Thomas than they did with a medieval theologian like Scotus and theologians of the *via moderna* like Ockham and Biel, who became the primary targets of Luther's 1517 protest (see chapter 5). As the end of this chapter will reveal, the Reformers had significant disagreements with Thomas (on infused righteousness and transubstantiation, for example). Nevertheless, Reformers like Luther, Melanchthon, and Calvin were more indebted (and possibly influenced) by Thomas than they ever knew, and numerous other Reformed theologians like Bucer, Vermigli, Zanchi, and others were quite cognizant of their debt. To avoid popular Protestant caricatures of Thomas, the following will limit itself to Thomas as a biblical exegete, his harmonization of theology and philosophy, and the fidelity of his orthodoxy. Nevertheless, a budding garden of research in the last half century continues to demonstrate the influence of Thomas on the Reformers and Reformed Orthodoxy in innumerable other doctrinal domains as well.

Thomas Aquinas
Matthew Barrett,
The Nelson-Atkins
Museum of Art

THOMAS AS BIBLICAL EXEGETE AND THEOLOGIAN OF ORTHODOXY

Thomas was an Italian by birth, and as a boy his parents took him to Monte Cassino (1230–31) to live in the Benedictine abbey.[2] The abbey was advantageous to parents looking to educate their children. If a child grew into a promising young talent, he might even rise in the ecclesiastical ranks for a promising career. However, the plan changed when the abbey was caught in the middle of battle between emperor and pope. Thomas was taken to Naples to attend the

---

2. For the details that follow and far more in-depth explorations of Thomas's life and thought, see Davies, *Aquinas*. For an analysis of Thomas's theology, consider Davies, *Thought of Thomas Aquinas*.

new university instead, which proved instrumental to the young man's development since he read for the first time philosophers like Aristotle, Averroes, and
Maimonides, all of which he returned to in his later publications.

Rather than remaining in the Benedictine order, for some enigmatic reason
Thomas was drawn to the Dominicans instead from 1242 to 1244. Perhaps it
was their dedication to preaching the Scriptures? Judging by Thomas's commentaries on the Bible later on, that may be a viable reason for the change. Or
perhaps the transition to the Dominicans was attractive because they took teaching with prodigious seriousness, encouraging their monks to pursue the life of
the mind. Whatever the reason, his family was not amused. They had sent him
to Monte Cassino to become a member of the Benedictines. Details are few, but
it is possible his mother was embarrassed. The Dominicans were not exactly a
prestigious order. When she learned Thomas had no intention of relenting, she
traveled first to Naples and then to Rome to set her son back on the Benedictine
plan. When she did not find Thomas, she recruited her other sons to find and
capture their brother and lock him up at home (they were wealthy, and the family owned several homes).

According to one legend, his family conspired, hiring a prostitute, who entered
Thomas's quarters to tempt him. But Thomas, seeing the trap for what it was,
picked up the tongs from the fire and chased the prostitute out of his quarters
and returned to prayer and study as before. House arrest frustrated Thomas, but
at least he could continue his private studies. In the end, the family kidnapping
did not work but only made the Dominican life even more alluring, so that in
1246 he was released and found himself among the Dominicans as he intended
all along. Over the next decade Thomas traveled back and forth between Paris
and Cologne, continuing his studies. During this time, Thomas was influenced
by Albert the Great (ca. 1200–1280), both through his lectures and by his direct
mentorship, until Thomas was ready to become a teacher himself.

Thomas is often described as a philosopher. However, Thomas was a biblical
scholar first and foremost. As David Steinmetz said, "Thomas Aquinas was
not more Scholastic when he presided at disputations concerning the nature of
truth than when he lectured on the literal sense of Job."[3] Although it is difficult
to assign an exact date to the genesis of Thomas's commentary on Isaiah, it is
probable he wrote this commentary even before his teaching career in Paris. He
also wrote commentaries on the book of Job in Paris. Exegesis continued to be
Thomas's priority in the lectern. He began his teaching career in Paris by lecturing on books of the Old Testament, but he wrote commentaries on numerous
books of the Bible by the time of his death. In that sense, Martin Luther and
Thomas had much in common, both starting out as scriptural exegetes, a task
that never left them no matter what polemical waters they waded into later in life.

---

3. Scholastic theology pursued its own vision of the exegetical task. It was not identical with the humanist
vision, but it was not altogether different either." Steinmetz, "Scholastic Calvin," 23.

As products of the medieval university, not only did Luther and Thomas alike lecture on the Bible, but they also lectured on Lombard's *Sentences*. Back in Naples, Thomas had already started reading ancient sources, but his lectures on Lombard brought him into direct engagement with patristics across various *loci*, Augustine in particular. Thomas proved he was one of the bright minds in Paris, and in 1256 Thomas received the title master of theology, which qualified him to supervise and participate in debates and disputations.[4]

Taken as a whole, Thomas's days in Paris were pivotal to his future theological contribution. Consider two examples. First, Thomas not only lectured on Lombard but went as far back as Boethius, writing a commentary on his *De Trinitate*, a commentary that exhibited Thomas's extensive knowledge of Nicene orthodoxy. Thomas later built on that foundation to write his own treatment of the Trinity in his *Summa Theologiae*. The sixteenth-century Reformers all assumed the credibility of this Nicene foundation that Thomas helped preserve and even mature.

Sometime prior to 1260 Thomas decided to leave Paris. From France he traveled to Italy and was content teaching students in Orvieto. During all this transition, Thomas continued to be prolific even across disciplines, validating his contribution as a true systematic thinker. For example, in Orvieto Thomas developed an ambitious commentary on the Gospels (*Catena Aurea*) that recruited and consolidated patristic exegesis, evidencing his advanced grasp of Scripture and the history of theological interpretation.[5]

In 1265 Thomas left Orvieto for Rome, and Santa Sabina became his new base of operations. The Dominicans commissioned Thomas, asking him to create a house where theological learning could take place under Thomas's oversight. They recognized such learning had suffered, and they needed a Dominican like Thomas to do the needed repairs. The year 1265 was also the start of his summary of theology, his *Summa Theologiae* (ca. 1265–73). Thomas never finished his *Summa Theologiae*, a work that became his magnum opus. Nevertheless, what he did finish was extensive, from theology proper and Christology to the *imago Dei* and the beatific vision. Thomas also explored Christian virtues, the nature of ethics, and the pursuit of happiness. On one hand, he retrieved and synthesized classical Christian orthodoxy and Augustinian soteriology, to which the sixteenth-century Reformers were indebted. On the other hand, he articulated a sacramental system and ecclesiology that the papacy later expanded and

---

4. Thomas engaged two types: Disputed Questions was an opportunity to ask and answer some of the hardest questions in Christian faith and philosophy with the goal of arriving at a sense of understanding and perspicuity. These disputes could occur in a university or an order. A second type Thomas engaged was the Quodlibetal Disputations, which were not entirely different from Disputed Questions but did tend to be more specific, an up-close look at sacred and ancient texts. Disputed Questions was what it sounded like. Someone raised a question (or perhaps theses), an answer followed, then typically an objection to the answer, followed by an answer to the objection. As a master of theology, Thomas led these Disputed Questions, guided the debate, and then pronounced his own answer.

5. Cf. the five volume *Catena Aurea*, edited by John Henry Newman.

turned official, even though he was by no means the only theologian to plant such seeds, as Peter Lombard has already demonstrated.

Thomas did not stay in Rome long but returned to Paris in 1268. His last two years in Paris produced his large commentary on the Gospel of John (1270–72). Out of his many commentaries, his Johannine reflections brought together Thomas the exegete and Thomas the Nicene Trinitarian.[6] Whether the text was John 1 or John 5, Thomas moved through John's narrative but not without articulating John's attestation to Jesus' eternal relation of origin (generation from the Father) and its importance for eternal life through the gospel of Jesus Christ. Even though Luther did not labor to maintain the same Scholastic approach as Thomas, Luther's numerous sermons on John were not entirely different, as Luther's other writings on the creeds demonstrate as well (see chapters 9, 18).[7]

Thomas did not limit himself to the Johannine corpus, but sometime during his time in Rome, Paris, and Naples—1265 to 1273—he wrote his commentaries on Paul's epistles. These Pauline reflections reveal a mature Thomas, now toward the end of his life, one committed as ever to Augustinianism and the primacy of grace. Although, as will be seen, Thomas was far more comfortable with Augustine's concept of infused righteousness, much in contrast to Luther's later commentaries on Paul and his belief in an imputed righteousness.

After Paris, Thomas made his way to Naples in 1272, again commissioned by the Dominicans to start another house or *studium*. In 1272 and 1273, the Psalms captured his attention, and Thomas benefited from Augustine's commentary on the Psalms as he considered his own exegesis of the Psalter. Thomas the intellectual should not overshadow Thomas the churchman. In Naples Thomas's preaching guided the church, introducing the core of Christian orthodoxy as articulated in the Apostles' Creed. His sermons also taught church members how to pray as they followed his exposition of the Lord's Prayer.[8] None of this was a belated effort to benefit the church. Almost a decade prior Thomas dedicated himself to writing on the liturgy for the Feast of Corpus Christi (1264).

In 1273 Thomas's writing, including his *Summa Theologiae*, came to an abrupt halt. Many have speculated why. Whatever occurred, he still felt that he was able to advise others; the following year he traveled to be present for the second Council of Lyons (1274). However, he never did have the chance to participate in the ecumenical discussions at Lyons. On his way there an unexpected sickness overtook him, confining him to his deathbed in Fossanova, and he died in the Cistercian abbey.

---

6. See Aquinas, *Commentary on the Gospel of John*. For Thomas's Nicene Trinitarianism, see Emery, *Trinitarian Theology of St Thomas Aquinas*.

7. See *LW* 22, 23, 24, 69.

8. To qualify, Thomas's work on the Apostles' Creed and the Lord's Prayer can be dated as far back as 1268, though it continued through 1273.

NATURAL THEOLOGY, REASON, AND THE *SUMMA CONTRA GENTILES*

To understand the significance of a Scholastic like Thomas, the *Summa Theologiae* deserves attention, both for its scriptural and theological syntheses. However, his *Summa Contra Gentiles* should also be considered to understand the way philosophy served theology in the mind of Thomas.[9] Starting while still in Paris, he wrote his work to equip missionaries with an apologetic for Christianity against the unbeliever.[10] Older interpretations of the *Summa Contra Gentiles* believed Thomas's main purpose (or at least one of them) was to write an apologetic against Islam, one that missionaries could use. Thomas does mention Islam, but historians now question whether an apologetic against Islam was his main motive.[11]

Across the *Summa Contra Gentiles*, Thomas referenced Aristotle, referring to him simply as "the Philosopher." The *Summa Contra Gentiles* from 1259 to 1265 was but the beginning of Thomas's philosophical corpus. From 1267 to 1273 Thomas wrote and published numerous commentaries on Aristotle. Moreover, Thomas's contributions on the whole were informed by the realism of both Plato and Aristotle, resulting in a participation metaphysic which overcame the weakness in both philosophers and served to complement his biblical and theological conception of God and the world.[12] Chapter 5 will explore the Great Tradition's critical appropriation of Platonic realism in more depth, but to understand why Thomas's original synthesis of Plato and Aristotle was so advantageous, first consider Aristotle's long absence from theology and philosophy.

The Rediscovery of Aristotle and the Move toward Clarity and Coherence

With certain exceptions, such as Origen's *First Principles* or John of Damascus's *The Orthodox Faith*, many of the treatises in the patristic and early medieval eras were contextually driven by a variety of theological controversies. But with the patristic foundation in place, the Scholastics took a step forward by constructing a cohesive system of theology and philosophy that aimed for internal consistency. Logic and reason were key to this enterprise. For classical Christianity, Thomas included, the human person is a composite of body and soul, but unlike the animals the human person has a rational soul that is the form of the body, one defined by intellect and will. By using the intellect God implanted within the *imago Dei*, one may arrive at a natural theology by observing God's revelation of his existence, attributes, and divine providence through the natural order.

---

9. See Regan, *Philosophical Primer on the Summa Theologica*.

10. Thomas wrote numerous polemic works as well: see his *Against Those Who Impugn the Cult of God and Religion* (1256), *On the Perfection of the Spiritual Life* (1269–70), *On the Unicity of the Intellect against the Averroists* (1270), *Against the Teachings of Those Who Prevent Men Entering the Religious Life* (1271), and *On the Eternity of the World* (ca. 1271).

11. For an example of Thomas's engagement with Islam, see *SCG*, 1.6.4. On Thomas's motive, see Davies, *Thomas Aquinas's* Summa Contra Gentiles, 3–16.

12. See Morello, who demonstrates that Thomas was indebted to Neoplatonism; *The World as God's Icon*, 37–66.

The task of utilizing the tools of reason was twofold: (1) Scripture indicated that God had made himself known to humankind in the created order. The Scholastics interpreted natural revelation with great earnestness, asking what man can know about God by virtue of the natural order, a realm that includes not only creation at large but the human mind and its capacity for reasonable observation. (2) Even those truths that can only be known by means of supernatural revelation (e.g., the Trinity and the gospel) can nevertheless be further understood by virtue of human reason. Some things can only be known by faith; nevertheless, true faith seeks understanding. The Scholastics were not rationalists—as if faith is withheld until understanding is satisfied. Projecting the rationalism of modernity back into medieval Scholasticism is anachronistic. The Scholastics were not fideists either, as if they advocated a leap of blind faith that completely contradicts reason. Their project avoided both extremes. Faith was fundamental, even essential. Apart from faith—a faith that is dependent on God's self-revelation—understanding stays at bay. But the God who grants faith also opens the door to apprehension (though never comprehension), a door that hinges on the bolts of reasonable observation. While the doctrines of the Christian faith remain a mystery, faith matures when it pursues understanding. Reason, therefore, is instrumental if faith is to pursue wisdom at any level. Furthermore, reason is certainly strategic for theologians serious about presenting a coherent rationale for what they believe and why.

Long before the advent of Scholasticism, the church fathers revealed their commitment to faith seeking understanding as well, a mantra not original with Anselm but reaching back to Augustine. That commitment gave them every reason to listen not only to Christian but non-Christian voices. Wisdom invited the church fathers—East and West—to critically appropriate the methods, theology, and philosophy of Greek luminaries from Plato to Aristotle to Plotinus. As chapter 5 will explore, Augustine recognized ways the realism of Platonism clarified, complemented, and corresponded with Christianity. Like other fathers, Augustine was not afraid to disagree with Platonism, aware that human reason had its limits and fallibilities. Yet Augustine also recognized that Platonism could be a handmaid to Christianity if refined, assisting the Christian intellectual with a systematic presentation of the faith, even serving to substantiate a Christian apologetic.[13] Although he dispensed with excesses inconsistent with Christian thought (e.g., preexistence of the soul), Augustine retrieved and redeemed other components of Platonism that served to advance Christianity's logical credibility (the existence of universals, participation in the likeness of God, ascent and the beatific vision, etc.). To be more precise, the Great Tradition did not merely select random beliefs within the Platonist tradition that fit Christianity. Rather, the Great Tradition understood that Platonism was a revolutionary outlook on reality itself, a transcendental

---

13. Kristeller, *Renaissance Thought*, 75–76.

reality to be exact. Committed to anti-materialism, anti-mechanism, and anti-nominalism, Platonism believed universals were real, so that all the goodness, truth, and beauty of this world participates in the Good, the Truth, and the Beautiful. Such a transcendent outlook made room for a belief that came to age with Christianity, a belief in divinity unbound by the limitations of matter. He is not a mere being among other beings but is one who *is* being in and of himself, one in whom we must participate to live and move and have our being. In summary, Platonist philosophy was not merely convenient for classical theology but put forward a transcendent reality so true that Platonism became the perennial, reigning model for late antiquity. Platonism's realist, participation metaphysic, therefore, was knitted into the very fabric of the Great Tradition. Platonism's belief in incorporeal reality was indispensable to Christianity's transcendentalism, even if Platonism had to be *refined* to serve the creature's communion with his Creator. As Augustine says (see chapter 5), Platonism provided a map of true reality; Christianity then demonstrated how to arrive at the destination—Christ.[14]

Yet Platonism was a rich tradition. In chapter 5 we will discover that the transcendental realism of Plato was not the only theory advantageous to Christian theology and apologetics. The concrete realism of Aristotle's Platonism proved instrumental as well, but not in its fullest form until the medieval era. Despite Aristotle's prominence in his own day, his writings struggled to survive in the West. There are many reasons why. In the period after Aristotle, his writings were not universally distributed. Locked away in his own school's library, Aristotle's works did not spread into the hands of wider society or easily move across geographical borders. As a result, in the centuries that followed, only small traces of Aristotle's works and ideas can be found. If not for the Neoplatonists during the third through sixth centuries, Aristotle's legacy might have remained in the shadows.[15]

In addition, the West faced a language barrier. Aristotle's works did not struggle for survival in the East because the East thrived in the Greek language. Along with Plato's corpus, Aristotle's writings were never lost by the East but enjoyed circulation and engagement. However, Aristotle's works had to be translated into Latin for the West. The need for translation challenged the accessibility of Aristotle's literary corpus. As a result, Aristotle was absent from major patristic and medieval church fathers in the Latin West, Augustine included.[16] Still, small remnants of Aristotle remained. Boethius, the sixth-century philosopher-theologian, did translate some of Aristotle's works from Greek into Latin. Yet not until many centuries later did Aristotle's entire corpus make its way into Europe by means of an ironic turn of events. In the twelfth century,

---

14. I am indebted to personal correspondence with John Peter Kenney for this point.

15. "During that period [third to sixth centuries], Aristotelianism disappeared as a separate school tradition, yet the Neoplatonists themselves were committed to a synthesis of Plato and Aristotle." Aristotle's writings survived in the Byzantine, Arabic, and Latin traditions. For an overview of each, see Kristeller, 26ff.

16. The "Western Latin Middle Ages," said Kristeller, "had its foundation in Roman, and not in Greek antiquity." Kristeller, 29.

those despised enemies of Christianity—the Muslims—expressed great interest in Aristotle's thought. A Spanish Muslim by the name of Averroes, for example, helped Aristotle make his way into Arabic. He wrote one of the most impressive and longstanding commentaries on Aristotle as well. In the thirteenth century, Arabic translations made their way into Latin, opening the door for Aristotle's entire corpus to find a home in Europe. With the reception of Aristotle in Europe, scholars made additional attempts at translation, but they bypassed Arabic and returned to the Greek text itself to ensure accuracy.[17]

From the High to the late Middle Ages, competing philosophical systems— from Thomism to Scotism to Occamism—engaged the corpus of Aristotle, assuming Aristotelian categories. Diverse schools had serious disagreements in philosophy, but many of them presupposed the validity of Aristotelian techniques in an effort to contest one another.[18] The tools of Aristotelian philosophy crossed monastic boundaries as well. A common reading of medieval history says Aristotelianism was a Dominican heritage that the Franciscans did not share. That sweeping caricature is not altogether false, but it cannot be applied in too strict a fashion since even notable Franciscan Scholastics such as Bonaventure and Duns Scotus were influenced by and relied on Aristotle's thought (even if to different degrees and for different ends).[19]

Paul Kristeller clarifies that the "Aristotelianism of the later Middle Ages was characterized not so much by a common system of ideas as by a common source material, a common terminology, a common set of definitions and problems, and a common method of discussing these problems."[20] The reappearance of Aristotle was no mere recovery of an ancient text, but a gateway to a world of systematic exploration and explanation. "What was involved was not merely the influx of additional philosophical sources and ideas, both Platonist and Aristotelian." The consequences for theology were significant: "Much more important was the novel tendency to transform the subject matter of Christian theology into a topically arranged and logically coherent system."[21]

A logically coherent, perennial system made Aristotle attractive, more attractive than some other philosophers whose thought was fragmentary. In short, the Scholastics took a page from Aristotelian logic to advance an apologetic for

---

17. Needham, *Two Thousand Years of Christ's Power*, 2:268. Note Needham's overview of Averroes's influence on Siger of Brabant. For a treatment of Averroism, see Gilson, *History of Christian Philosophy in the Middle Ages*, 387–401.

18. Kristeller, *Renaissance Thought*, 33–37. To do so, however, each school of thought had to consult the authoritative twelfth-century commentary by Averroes. On the debate over Averroes's influence, Kristeller concluded, "If we understand by Averroism the use of Averroes' commentary on Aristotle, every medieval Aristotelian including Aquinas was an Averroist."

19. "A better way to explain the difference is to say that the Franciscans were much more in the spirit of Augustine than the Dominicans tended to be. As Augustine did, the Franciscans tended to emphasize the role of the will and the role of love more than the role of the intellect and the role of knowledge. In particular, they tended to have a more radical view of the freedom of the will—both God's will and the human will—than the Dominicans did." Williams, *Reason and Faith*, 309.

20. Kristeller, *Renaissance Thought*, 32.

21. Kristeller, 77.

Christian beliefs that was clear and coherent, precise and logical, but most of all consistent as a true portrayal of transcendent reality itself. Scholastics were not attempting to invent new truth; rather, they were committed to better understanding truth out of a posture of faith. The goal was not unjustified speculation but devotion. Theology's *telos* was not information but the beatific vision. As Thomas said, referencing both Aristotle and Boethius, the wise man seeks certitude so that he will know the truth and enjoy the goodness and beatitude it brings.[22]

On the most basic level, Aristotle provided Scholastics like Thomas with three tools useful for constructing a Scholastic method and theology: (1) terms, (2) distinctions, and (3) logic. In his books *Categories*, *On Interpretation*, and *Prior Analytics*, Aristotle classified words so that terms and concepts could be defined, and a coherent argument could follow. Syllogism became instrumental to determining whether an argument was sound.[23] In his book *Topics*, Aristotle also put forward various avenues for reasoning—from inductive to deductive methods. And in his book *On Sophistical Refutations*, Aristotle exposed diverse logical fallacies. Furthermore, Aristotle was not only a master at logic but at physics and metaphysics, as well as poetics, ethics, and politics, writing books named for each of these disciplines. In *Physics* and *Metaphysics*, for example, Aristotle identified four causes (efficient, formal, material, and final), which not only served to demonstrate the necessity of an efficient or First Cause (or Unmoved Mover) but then served to confirm (and even celebrate) purpose or *telos* in the world by means of final causality. In *De Anima*, Aristotle improved upon Plato by studying form and matter only to conclude the human person is a composition of both, the soul being the form of the body (hylomorphism). And in *Nicomachean Ethics* he explained what the good life or happy life should look like if humanity were governed by virtue (prudence, justice, temperance, and courage).[24]

Naturally, each became advantageous for theology. For example, knowing the difference between essential and accidental as well as genus and species became fundamental to differentiating the Creator from the creature. For nothing can be accidental to a Creator who is simple (without parts), nor can genus or species place parameters around a God who is infinite in being, as if he exists on the same plain as his creation, merely a being among other beings. Moreover, knowing how form and matter correlate, for instance, went a long way toward explaining the existence and sophistication of reality, including the human person who is a composite of soul and body. Additionally, knowing why everything finite is in the process of becoming, defined as it is by passive potency, helped differentiate the mutable creature from an immutable Creator. God, as pure actuality (*actus purus*), is life in and of himself (*a se*), complete and sufficient in

---

22. Aquinas, *SCG* 1.3.1. On the influence of Aristotle on Aquinas, see Emery and Levering, *Aristotle in Aquinas's Theology*.

23. Here is a common example of a syllogism: (1) All men are mortal beings. (2) Socrates is a man. (3) Therefore, Socrates must be a mortal being.

24. For each of these works, see Aristotle, *Complete Works of Aristotle*.

his infinite perfection, eternal and immutable, invulnerable to the fluctuation of parts and passions, a God of being not becoming. Furthermore, Aristotle's four causes not only could be appropriated to explain God as the creator of the cosmos (efficient causality), but for what purpose he made man in his image (final causality).[25] The possibilities were endless, and Christianity was the beneficiary of such clarity and coherence.

Did utilization of Aristotle mean Scholastics were blind adherents to the philosopher? Not at all. For example, Thomas "was not so loyal to the opinions of Aristotle that he did not abandon them when what he regarded as better opinions could be found elsewhere." Steinmetz concludes, "Philosophy was the Scholastic theologian's tool, not his principal subject matter."[26] In other words, Scholastic theologians like Thomas "made free use of the philosophers, not as a substitute for divine revelation and never willingly in contradiction to it. Philosophy was a good gift of God to human beings made in the rational image of God and like God capable of creative thought."[27] To witness such discernment firsthand, chapter 5 will unveil ways Thomas developed an original synthesis of Plato and Aristotle, discontent as he was with Plato's failure to locate Ideas in the mind of God, dissatisfied as he was with Aristotle's unwarranted suspicion towards participation.

To consider how Thomas used this tool, the format of the *Summa Contra Gentiles* deserves brief attention.

Participation: The Wise Man's Pursuit of Goodness, Truth, and Beatitude

The *Summa Contra Gentiles* begins with Proverbs 8:7 and a call to the wise man, but Thomas knew his first task was to define what makes someone wise. Thomas referenced Aristotle's *Topics* and then his *Metaphysics* in the opening sentences: "The usage of the multitude, which according to the Philosopher is to be followed in giving names to things, has commonly held that they are to be called wise who order things rightly and govern them well. Hence, among the other things that men have conceived about the wise man, the Philosopher includes the notion that 'it belongs to the wise man to order.'" Order always involves an end, a *telos*, and "it belongs to the wise man to consider the highest causes" of that end, such as, for example, the origin of the cosmos.[28]

An end must have a "first author or mover," but the "first mover of the universe is an intellect"—God himself. If God is the first mover, then the universe's ultimate end is "the *good* of the intellect." To be more specific, "This good is truth. Truth must consequently be the ultimate end of the whole universe, and the consideration of the wise man aims principally at truth." Now Thomas was ready to connect this basic Aristotelian logic to Christianity and its gospel.

25. For a far more detailed outline of Aristotle's works in relation to Scholasticism, see Van Asselt, *Introduction to Reformed Scholasticism*, 26–44. Also, for an introduction to the Great Tradition's appropriation of Aristotle, see the Davison, *The Love of Wisdom*, 32–52.

26. Steinmetz, "Scholastic Calvin," 23.

27. Steinmetz, "Scholastic Calvin," 23.

28. *SCG* 1.1.1.

As John's Gospel teaches, the Truth and the Wisdom is none other than Jesus Christ, whom John labels the *Logos*, a concept he borrowed from Greek philosophy. "Divine Wisdom testifies that He has assumed flesh and come into the world in order to make the truth known: 'For this was I born, and for this came I into the world, that I should give testimony to the truth' (John 18:37)." First philosophy, for Thomas and for Aristotle, can be nothing less than the science of truth. By truth, however, Thomas did not mean just any truth. He was referring to *the Truth*, that "which is the origin of all truth."[29]

The intention of Thomas in his *Summa Contra Gentiles* therefore is the pursuit of wisdom since God made all things in wisdom (Ps. 103:24). Following Proverbs and Ecclesiastes, that is Thomas's definition of philosophy. For this pursuit is "more perfect, more noble, more useful, and more full of joy" than any other human pursuit.

The reason the pursuit of wisdom is more perfect than other pursuits has much to do with *participation*: the wise man has a "share in true beatitude."[30] To pursue wisdom is to pursue participation in the blessedness of God.[31] For Thomas philosophy and theology were inconceivable apart from the notion of participation. God *is* being itself, receiving his life from no one since he is life in and of himself (*a se*) and without measure. By contrast, all else is created and finite and therefore receives being from him who is the source of being itself. As Paul said to the Athenians, quoting their own heritage, "In him we live and move and have our being" (Acts 17:28). As Thomas said in his treatment of creation, "God alone is essentially a being, whereas all other things participate in being."[32] Thomas elaborated elsewhere and said, "Every thing, furthermore, exists because it has being. A thing whose essence is not its being, consequently, is not through its essence but by participation in something, namely, being itself. But that which is through participation in something cannot be the first being, because prior to it is the being in which it participates in order to be. But God is the first being, with nothing prior to Him. His essence is, therefore, His being."[33]

Reason's Role, Reason's Limitations

Thomas's pursuit of goodness, beauty, and truth requires reason, but what is reason's role in this quest, and does it have limitations? The truth reason seeks

---

29. *SCG* 1.1.2.

30. *SCG* 1.2.1.

31. For a full treatment of participation in Thomas, see Wippel, *The Metaphysical Thought of Thomas Aquinas*, 94–131; Davies, *The Thought of Thomas Aquinas*, 33–35, 98–100.

32. *SCG* 2.53.4. Thomas defends participation by an appeal to God as pure act. See 2.53.3–5.

33. Thomas believed the divine name "I AM WHO I AM" in Exodus was proof. *SCG* 1.22.9. Andrew Davison defines participation in its most general sense as a notion that "rests in perceiving all things in relation to God, not only as their source but also as their goal, and as the origin of all form and character." Participation, then, is fundamental for the *imago Dei*. For "notions of likeness and exemplarity lie close at hand, and an inclination to celebrate the variegated particularity of things, as a creaturely expression of the goodness and beauty of God." Naturally, Davison considers a "realist" metaphysic, with its affirmation of universals, essential to that claim, a point we will explore in chapter 5. Davison concludes, "Approaching the world in terms of sharing and receiving should be the bedrock of a Christian understanding of reality, and of Christian doctrine." *Participation in God*, 1.

has two modes. "Some truths about God exceed all the ability of the human reason. Such is the truth that God is triune. But there are some truths which the natural reason also is able to reach. Such are that God exists, that He is one, and the like. In fact, such truths about God have been proved demonstratively by the philosophers, guided by the light of natural reason."[34]

Thomas assumed the fundamental distinction—a distinction taught by Protestants after him—between truths of supernatural revelation and truths of natural revelation. Reason serves each, but in different ways. As for natural revelation, "the truths about God have been proved demonstratively by the philosophers, guided by the light of the natural reason."[35] As for supernatural revelation (the truths of faith), these truths may be further understood and defended with reason, but they are given to mankind only by supernatural revelation. Reason may be instrumental, but it cannot be foundational. Only supernatural revelation can tell us truths beyond reason, like that the divine essence subsists in three persons named Father, Son, and Holy Spirit. "For the human intellect is not able to reach a comprehension of the divine substance through its natural power." The intellect uses the senses to make reasonable observations, but "sensible things cannot lead the human intellect to the point of seeing in them the nature of the divine substance; for sensible things are effects that fall short of the power of their cause."[36] In summary, while our intellect's use of the senses can lead us to the conclusion that a First Principle exists, discovering that the First Principle is Trinity is beyond its powers.

Thomas wishes everyone would use reason and pursue philosophy that is "directed towards the knowledge of God," especially that branch called metaphysics since it "deals with divine things" (for Thomas, divorcing metaphysics from his definition of God was inconceivable). However, Thomas was not naive but quick to add that many intrinsic and extrinsic barriers stand in the way of reason's proper use. Some of these are practical (most cannot devote their days to contemplation but must labor instead), but some are intellectual and moral (falsehood is mixed within man's reason). These barriers and others show why knowledge of God must go beyond reason itself. "If the only way open to us for the knowledge of God were solely that of the reason, the human race would remain in the blackest shadows of ignorance."[37] To begin with, Thomas recognizes natural theology's extrinsic parameter: he quoted Paul to emphasize the depravity of the mind and its effect on reason. "Gentiles walk in the vanity of their mind, having their understanding darkened" (Eph. 4:17–18).[38] Even the philosophers knew man must move beyond the "pleasure of sensible things to virtue," if they were to "find much sweeter enjoyment in the taste of these higher goods."[39]

---

34. *SCG* 1.3.2.
35. *SCG* 1.3.2.
36. *SCG* 1.3.2; cf. *ST* 1a. 12, 13.
37. *SCG* 1.4.4.
38. *SCG* 1.4.7. He quotes Isaiah 54:13 as well.
39. *SCG* 1.5.2.

Aristotle, for example, opposed Simonides for telling mortals to limit themselves to what is mortal. "Man should draw himself towards what is immortal and divine as much as he can."[40] That draw will lead him to the experience of intense joy and the soul's perfection. "Therefore, although the human reason cannot grasp fully the truths that are above it, yet, if it somehow holds these truths at least by faith, it acquires great perfection for itself."[41]

These limitations to reason offer many benefits. One of them is *humility*. The truths of supernatural revelation exceed reason and therefore serve to curb presumption, which Thomas said is "the mother of error." Thomas is often caricatured as attributing too high a power to reason, but in truth this is the position Thomas labored to demolish. "For there are some who have such a presumptuous opinion of their own ability that they deem themselves able to measure the nature of everything." Thomas had little patience for these fools, as he affectionately called them. "So that the human mind, therefore, might be freed from this presumption and come to a humble inquiry after truth, it was necessary that some things should be proposed to man by God that would completely surpass his intellect."[42]

Thomas did not believe the two modes of truth conflict with one another. The truths from faith, like the Trinity, are not self-evident to reason alone; they require supernatural revelation. However, articles of faith are not contrary to reason but compatible with reason.[43] Likewise, those truths known by natural reason (i.e., mixed articles), like the First Cause or Principle, are consistent with and confirmed by God's supernatural revelation.[44] After all, God is the author of both modes of truth. The same God who reveals himself through the natural order has manifested himself through his Son and his gospel. Like a teacher instilling knowledge in his students, "the knowledge of the principles that are known to us naturally has been implanted in us by God, for God is the Author of our nature."[45]

Some grossly misinterpret Thomas as if he thought natural theology was sufficient for faith. That misrepresentation is due to a prejudiced assumption, as if Thomas thinks belief in God's existence is definitive for faith itself. However, Thomas did not even consider belief in God's existence faith itself. "For Aquinas," clarifies Davies, "belief in the existence of God does not constitute faith and is not, strictly speaking, even a part of faith. It is part of the *preambular fidei*, the preambles of faith, or what faith presupposes."[46] For Thomas, faith concerns the articles of faith instead, which can be summarized in the Nicene Creed's witness to the Trinity and the salvation accomplished by Christ.[47]

---

40. Aristotle, *Nicomachean Ethics* 10.7 (1177b 31); as quoted in *SCG* 1.5.5.
41. *SCG* 1.5.5.
42. *SCG* 1.5.4.
43. "That which we hold by faith as divinely revealed, therefore, cannot be contrary to our natural knowledge." *SCG* 1.7.1.
44. *SCG* 1.7.1.
45. *SCG* 1.7.2.
46. Davies, *The Thought of Thomas Aquinas*, 275.
47. *ST* 1a. 2.2; 2a2ae. 1.8.

Furthermore, Thomas did not tolerate the assumption that says God gave humanity a natural knowledge that contradicts the truths of supernatural revelation. Reason may be "imperfect" and "inadequate" to "manifest the substance of God." Nevertheless, man's reason is an effect that has a cause and therefore bears a likeness to its cause. As effects so often fail to do, reason may not "always reach to the full likeness of its cause." After all, the context for reason's knowledge is sensible things. Nonetheless, both sensible things and reason itself retain their likeness. That likeness alone, Thomas concluded, is insufficient for the truths of faith—Thomas readily recognized natural theology's intrinsic parameter. "Yet it is useful for the human reason to exercise itself in such arguments, however weak they may be, provided only that there be present no presumption to comprehend or to demonstrate." Thomas then held out the reward: joy. "For to be able to see something of the loftiest realities, however thin and weak the sight may be, is, as our previous remarks indicate, a cause of the greatest joy."[48]

A Posteriori: Pure Actuality and the Five Ways

By treating faith and reason as a congruity (rather than a dichotomy) with one another and by subordinating reason to faith, Thomas lifted a burden from the theologian's back—one can almost hear Thomas exhale a sigh of relief. He put reason in proper perspective, not weighing it down with the weight of proving articles of faith—due to natural theology's extrinsic and intrinsic parameters. Instead, reason is a handmaid, serving to demonstrate mixed articles, namely, the truths of natural revelation made plain by the many effects in this world that depend on a First Cause.[49]

Therefore, as Thomas summoned reason to establish natural theology he did not do so under the assumption (or presumption) that it must *convince* the adversary. Reasonable observation of natural revelation may testify to the existence of God's divine nature and invisible attributes. Yet Sacred Scripture, which carries the gospel in its womb, is necessary for the adversary to become God's friend. Otherwise, he will never participate in the life of the holy Trinity. "The sole way to overcome an adversary of divine truth is from the authority of Scripture," says Thomas. "For that which is above the human reason we believe only because God has revealed it."[50] So again, Thomas warned against forcing reason to do too much.

Nevertheless, natural theology is instrumental for *answering* the adversary, giving good reasons for those beliefs that are accessible through natural revelation. Reason brings forward "arguments that . . . make divine truth known."[51] In other words, Thomas puts forward "probable arguments" that allow human

---

48. *SCG* 1.8.1. Thomas's point was not original to him, but echoed Hilary of Poitiers's *De trinitate*.

49. For a treatment of this faith-reason dynamic in Thomas, see Wippel, *The Metaphysical Thought of Thomas Aquinas*, 379–99.

50. *SCG* 1.9.2.

51. *SCG* 1.9.2.

reason to "investigate about God."[52] Thomas was aware that some say God's existence cannot be demonstrated, as if only faith must be relied on for God's existence. However, if Paul was correct to say that the "invisible things of God . . . are clearly seen, being understood by the things that are made" (Rom. 1:20), then the creature has every right to "arrive at causes from their effects."[53] Granted, "we are not able to see His essence," but "we arrive at the knowledge of His being, not through God Himself, but through His effects."[54]

Since Thomas reasoned from effects observable in the natural order to a First Cause (an *a posteriori* argument), he did not adopt Anselm's *a priori* approach to God's existence, which moved from the cause itself to effects.[55] Although he broke from Anselm, Thomas believed his five inductive arguments drew from the philosophers and church fathers before him. The next chapter will unveil the intuitiveness of Thomas's instinct since Augustine maintained proofs from complexity to simplicity and from particulars to universals, exercising the realist metaphysic of Christian Platonism.[56] Yet among the Platonist philosophers Aristotle was most relevant to Thomas since the Philosopher "proceeds to prove that God exists" by beginning with motion.[57] Thomas begins the same way as he makes five arguments from:

1. motion to the unmoved mover
2. causation to a first uncaused cause
3. contingency to a necessary being
4. degrees of perfection to the Perfect Being
5. ordered finality to divine understanding[58]

Behind these five proofs is a most critical distinction between act and potency.[59] All things creaturely are defined by passive potency. The things of creation must be moved to reach their potential; the things of the world must be acted upon to achieve completion. In short, they must be changed, even caused by something or someone else to arrive at their full capacity. That principle applies to the human person as well, which explains why participation is so integral. "What does not act with the whole of itself is not the first agent, since it does not

---

52. *SCG* 1.9.3.

53. *SCG* 1.12.6.

54. *SCG* 1.11.5.

55. For his critique of Anselm (whom he does not mention by name), see *SCG* 1.11. Here is one of his main objections: "For assuredly that God exists is, absolutely speaking, self-evident, since what God is is His own being. Yet, because we are not able to conceive in our minds that which God is, that God exists remains unknown in relation to us" (1.11.2).

56. For a survey of the Fathers, see Levering, *Proofs of God*, 27–47. For a full treatment of the five ways in Thomas, see Wippel, *The Metaphysical Thought of Thomas Aquinas*, 442–500 (cf. 391–99 for a comparison of Thomas and Anselm); Gilson, *The Christian Philosophy of St. Thomas Aquinas*, 59–83 (cf. 46–58 for a comparison of Thomas and Anselm); Davies, *The Thought of Thomas Aquinas*, 21–32.

57. Thomas is aware of the nuances between Plato and Aristotle on motion, for example. *SCG* 1.13.10.

58. *SCG* 1.13. cf. *ST* 1a. 2, 3. Also see his rationale for moving from effects to a cause in *ST* 1a. 12, 12.

59. *SCG* 1.13.9.

act through its essence but through participation in something."[60] Apart from receiving and sharing in God's life, the human person will suffer. By nature, the creature depends on the Creator. The same, however, cannot be said of the Creator. "The first agent, therefore, God, has no admixture of potency but is pure act."[61] As eternal life in and of himself, the Creator is *a se,* self-existent and self-sufficient. Therefore, he is not a being who is in the process of becoming, but he is being itself. While he causes and changes all things, he is not changed by anyone or anything.[62] On that basis, Thomas's five arguments fall into place because only a God who is pure actuality can be the unmoved mover, the first uncaused cause, the necessary being, the perfect being, and divine wisdom and understanding itself. A "being that is only in act"—pure act—can explain the motion of all creatures who are in the process of becoming, moving from potency to act themselves.[63]

The Way of Remotion, Analogical Predication, and Pure Actuality

If God is eternal and incomprehensible, immutable and *a se,* pure actuality itself, then the way to know God is by way of remotion. "For, by its [the divine substance's] immensity, the divine substance surpasses every form that our intellect reaches. Thus we are unable to apprehend it by knowing *what it is*. Yet we are able to have some knowledge of it by knowing *what it is not*."[64]

This method is in operation whenever the creature describes God in the negative—God is not a body, God does not change, God is without passions, God is not dependent. In other words, "by such negations God will be distinguished from all that He is not."[65] Negation safeguards God in himself from the creature creating his own little tower of Babel, as if he, but a finite creature, can climb up into the essence of God to contain and control knowledge of the Infinite. As Thomas explains in his *Summa theologiae,* the "*infinite cannot be contained in the finite. God exists infinitely and nothing finite can grasp him infinitely.*"[66]

The way of remotion assumes a participation paradigm. "Since, then, that which is found in God perfectly is found in other things according to a certain diminished participation, the basis on which the likeness is observed belongs to God absolutely, but not to the creature." Therefore, "it is more fitting to say that a creature is like God rather than the converse."[67] Thomas is protecting Genesis 1 and 2 to ensure the creature is made in God's likeness, not vice versa. Participation and the *imago Dei,* however, assume a specific mode of predication.

---

60. *SCG* 1.16.5.
61. *SCG* 1.16.5.
62. "God is absolutely impassible and immutable . . . He has, therefore, no part of potency—that is, passive potency." *SCG* 1.16.6.
63. *SCG* 1.16.7.
64. *SCG* 1.14.2.
65. *SCG* 1.14.3.
66. *ST* 1a. 12, 7.
67. *SCG* 1.29.5.

The type of predication appropriate must properly conceive of the creature's participation and only one type of predication can manage that responsibility. Consider three options. First, *univocal* predication. Suppose monks are assembling into their monastery on a bright but misty Sunday morning for worship and a little orphan whom they have taken into their care looks up at Dominic and says, "Monk." His first word. Then he looks to the right and points to Gabriel and exclaims, "Monk." His second word. The child is using the word *monk* in a univocal fashion. Though different individuals, Dominic and Gabriel are both monks in the same way with the same meaning.

According to Thomas, if univocal predication was used of God and man, the Creator could only be conflated with the creature. Suppose Dominic the monk is reflecting on the mercy of God and feels deep within his soul that he is an undeserving sinner. That conviction leads him to praise God and say, "God is love." Afterward he is tired from praying, returns to his cell, and notices his cat is sleeping on his bed. When he sits down, the cat purrs and wraps its tail around Dominic's arm. Dominic says to the cat, "You are so lovely." In Thomistic thought "love" cannot be used of God and the cat in a univocal way. Thomas explained why: "Now, the forms of the things God has made do not measure up to a specific likeness of the divine power; for the things that God has made receive in a divided and particular way that which in Him is found in a simple and universal way. It is evident, then, that nothing can be said univocally of God and other things."[68]

Thomas's logic has everything to do with God's simplicity (God is without parts, without composition). Love is something the cat may or may not be. But love in God simply *is* God. God does not merely possess love, but he *is* love. And unlike the cat, God is love without measure, infinite in his perfections. Love, in other words, is not accidental to God for "all things are predicated of God essentially."[69] For according to divine simplicity, "there is nothing in God that is not the divine being itself, which is not the case with other things."[70] Socrates is a man because he participates in humanity. He is not a man because he *is* humanity.[71] On the other hand, all that is in God *is* God. He does not need to participate in love as if to possess love when he *is* love itself. Univocity, therefore, threatens the fabric of participation, as if it applies not only to the creature but to the Creator. "But nothing is said of God by participation, since whatever is participated is determined to the mode of that which is participated and is thus possessed in a partial way and not according to every mode of perfection."[72]

Now consider *equivocal* predication. Suppose Dominic the monk has an accident one day in the garden when he slips on a sharp rock and falls. Gabriel is

68. *SCG* 1.32.2.

69. *SCG* 1.32.7 (cf. 1.32.3–7).

70. "Whatever is predicated of many things univocally is either a genus, a species, a difference, an accident, or a property. But . . . nothing is predicated of God as a genus or difference . . . Nor . . . can there be any accident in God . . ." *SCG* 1.32.3.

71. *SCG* 1.32.7.

72. *SCG* 1.32.6.

nearby learning philosophy in the monastery when he hears the terrible fall. Before rushing out the door to help his friend he puts on his coat because he is aware the seasons have changed, and fall is imminent. The word *fall* is used in an equivocal fashion, meaning two things are nothing alike—one an accident and the other a season. Thomistic thought rejected equivocal predication in reference to the Creator and the creature, as if there is only unity of a name but nothing similar. By contrast, said Thomas, "there is a certain mode of likeness of things to God."[73] Thomas believed such a conviction follows since man and woman have been made in the *imago Dei*.

The last category is *analogical* predication.[74] Suppose Dominic the monk bursts into Gabriel's cell with news that the two of them will travel to Canterbury, appointed to represent the monastery before the archbishop. Gabriel, however, is lacking in zeal because he has no idea what Canterbury is like. Seeing Gabriel's expressionless face, Dominic takes Gabriel to a tree outside his cell and with a knife carves into the trunk the image of the cathedral. The carving in the tree is not Canterbury (univocal) but neither does the carving lack any likeness to Canterbury (equivocal); it resembles something of Canterbury even if it is a faint, weak similarity. Of course, when Gabriel arrives at Canterbury the carving in the tree is no longer needed. He sees reality for himself.

None of this means the carving in the tree is not important. Prior to his journey, Gabriel's knowledge of the real thing (Canterbury) depended on the type, the carving in the tree—what Thomas called "order of knowledge." Yet Gabriel knows that the real Canterbury is the basis on which Dominic carved the image of the cathedral in the tree—what Thomas called the "order of being/name/reality." Thomas used a different illustration: an animal and its health. "Thus, the power to heal, which is found in all health-giving things, is by nature prior to the health that is in the animal, as a cause is prior to an effect; but because we know this healing power through an effect, we likewise name it from its effect. Hence it is that the *health-giving* is prior in reality, but animal is by priority called *healthy* according to the meaning of the name."[75]

Likewise with God. If univocal predication conflates the Creator and the creature and equivocal predication removes any point of reference between the two, analogical predication assigns similarity (like Dominic's carving of Canterbury) but without compromising the distinction (the carving is not Canterbury). For example, consider the word *love* again. God and the creature are not love in the same way (univocal), nor is it true that love in the created realm has nothing to do with the love of the Creator (equivocal). Rather, the

---

73. *SCG* 1.33.3.

74. Thomas will also treat analogical predication in *ST* 1a. 13, 5.

75. Emphasis original. "For the order of the name follows the order of knowledge, because it is the sign of an intelligible conception. When, therefore, that which is prior in reality is found likewise to be prior in knowledge, the same thing is found to be prior both according to the meaning of the name and according to the nature of the thing." *SCG* 1.34.5.

creature reflects and participates in the love of God, yet he recognizes that God's love is infinite, eternal, and immutable while his is not.

Again, none of this means that the image or the copy (in creation) of the real thing (God) is insignificant. Thomas followed Aristotle's concrete realism (see chapter 5), which said that our knowledge must go through the senses since universal forms subsists in particulars. We look at the sensible in the world around us, and our knowledge works its way from the effects to their cause (Thomas was mindful of Romans 1:20).[76] That explains why Thomas could put so much import in his argument for God's existence based on causation. As the First Cause, he is the reason for all that exists (order of being/reality). Nevertheless, our reason makes contact with the natural world (the effects) and is drawn upward to the Creator (the cause)—this is the order of knowing. And that logic applies not only to nature itself but to the pinnacle of the created order: man and woman. For they have been made in God's likeness.[77]

Analogical predication was indispensable to Thomas, the framework through which the creature properly participates in God's likeness. Paul was right to agree with the Greeks who said, "In him we live and move and have our being" (Acts 17:28). The Creator and the creature do not compete with one another for jurisdiction, nor is the creature's will at creation set over against the Creator's. Thomas did not tolerate a world in which the creature is autonomous. Rather, the creature's existence and happiness depend on and derive from the Creator. While the creature participates in the Creator, the Creator has his being from no one. Infinite and eternal, simple and immutable, he is life in and of himself—*a se.* As pure actuality itself, he is being not becoming. Suffering no deficiency, he *is* absolute perfection. He is, therefore, the fountain of life (Ps. 36:9). For this reason, Thomas could not fathom a soteriology in which the sinner is not completely dependent on the primacy and efficacy of divine grace, as will be seen soon enough.

Thomas's participation paradigm was not limited to book 1 of *Summa Contra Gentiles*, which contained his arguments for God's existence and perfections. In books 2–3, Thomas also reasoned that if God is the First Cause of creation, then his divine providence ensures that we live and move and have our being in him. By means of his divine providence the creature participates in the goodness of his Creator. For Thomas, both the nature of creation and divine providence implemented a moral framework accompanied by a natural law that explained virtue and vice. When book 4 turned to doctrines like the Trinity, Christology, soteriology, and the sacraments, Thomas stayed faithful to his opening affirmation of truth's two modes. Thomas quoted Scripture throughout books 1

---

76. As he will also say in his *ST* 1a. 13, 8: "Now God is not known to us in his own nature, but through his works or effects . . ."

77. See Williams who uses the fitting illustration of a photograph (*Reason and Faith*, 247–57). For a thorough treatment of analogy of being in Thomas, see Wippel, *The Metaphysical Thought of Thomas Aquinas*, 65–93, 501–75; Gilson, *The Christian Philosophy of St. Thomas Aquinas*, 97–109; Davies, *The Thought of Thomas Aquinas*, 58–79.

through 3, but in book 4 Scripture's authority became paramount as Thomas presented truths that transcend reason and can only be revealed by supernatural revelation. His participation paradigm continued but now explained how the creature (now sinner) was reconciled to his Creator (now Savior) through union with Christ by means of the Spirit's participatory power.

Thomas's Critical Appropriation of Aristotle

The above points that begin Thomas's *Summa Contra Gentiles* are worth belaboring to ensure the interpreter of the Reformation does not meet Luther's theologians of glory and assume Thomas must be one of them. As chapter 5 will stress, Luther had a bad opinion of Thomas (due to Gabriel Biel's misrepresentation of Thomas), but Luther's theologians of glory were Scotus, Ockham, and Biel. In the sixteenth century, however, the Reformers, whether they always knew it or not, rested their theological program on this patristic and medieval "analogical" metaphysic. Although John Calvin did not usually engage Thomas directly, nevertheless, he, too, explained how the finite creature can have knowledge of an infinite, incomprehensible Creator. Calvin appealed to the patristic concept of *divine accommodation* to describe God as the one who lisps to reveal himself. Calvin's concept of accommodation depended upon the analogy of being, which was basic to a classical (and Thomistic) distinction between the Creator and the creature.[78]

Whatever the vocabulary, these metaphysical maneuvers depended on an Aristotelian understanding of predication and causation. By the sixteenth century, Aristotle's vocabulary and concepts were embedded deep in the curriculum of universities across Europe, from Italy to France to Germany. Humanists and Reformers alike were indebted to numerous Aristotelian notions. For example, the Renaissance, says Kristeller, was "still in many respects an Aristotelian age which in part continued the trends of medieval Aristotelianism, and in part gave it a new direction under the influence of classical humanism."[79] Humanism had its criticisms of Aristotle, but its entire project depended on Aristotelian presuppositions, even if some of those presuppositions were adapted for the humanist outlook (see chapter 6).

Can the same be said of the Reformation? Some Reformers were educated in the methods and ideas of Scholasticism, which depended on the style and structure of Aristotle's vocabulary and logic. Even if some Reformers, such as Luther, protested Aristotle's influence at first (see examples in chapter 4), the Reformers depended on the basic presuppositions of Aristotelian logic and used them throughout their disputations. Despite Luther's sporadic and hostile dismissal of Aristotle, Aristotle was not removed from the universities either. Even German universities influenced by Luther retained Aristotle. The irony of Luther's protest is that his right-hand Reformer, Melanchthon, labored to ensure

---

78. See Zachman, "Calvin as Analogical Theologian," 162–87.
79. Kristeller, *Renaissance Thought*, 47.

that Aristotle remained embedded within the Wittenberg curriculum.[80] And even Luther himself praised Aristotle and his natural law ethic, understanding its importance for the temporal realm.[81] As will be seen, Melanchthon was anything but unique. Other Reformers not only kept Aristotle in the curriculum but preserved his insights in their biblical and theological literature.

CONCISE, CLEAR TRAINING FOR THE NOVICE: *SUMMA THEOLOGIAE*

Modern interpreters have developed a fixation on Thomas the philosopher. Certainly, Thomas was one of the great philosophers of the Middle Ages, if by philosopher we mean someone who wrestled with the harmony of faith and reason, someone who applied reason to advance epistemology and metaphysics for example. However, Thomas would not have recognized the title *philosopher*, which in his day referred to a non-Christian thinker.[82] As seen already, Thomas was a Dominican preacher and biblical exegete. He was also a master of patristic literature, which he often used to interpret the Scriptures. If Thomas reflected on his outpost, he might have described himself as a catholic theologian. As Brian Davies says, "There can be no doubt that Aquinas was primarily a theologian" and one who "takes himself to be chiefly concerned with the Christian faith."[83] That claim needs little support. The *Summa Theologiae* not only certified Thomas's theological acuteness but his ability to achieve theological synthesis and in a style that was as didactic as it was lucid.

Thomas's Scholastic Style

Renaissance humanists like Erasmus could be vicious in their criticisms of Scholasticism. According to Erasmus, the Scholastics pedaled speculative questions that were incomprehensible to most Christians and irrelevant to Christian faith and practice. Since Erasmus, this criticism has continued in that infamous caricature that says the Scholastics obsessed over speculative questions like how many angels can dance on the head of a pin. The Scholastics never did ask such a question. Whatever one thinks of the humanist criticism, a careful examination of Scholastic motives and methods tells a different story.

At the beginning of Thomas's *Summa Theologiae*, he told his reader why he wrote his *Summa* the way he did: "[I wrote] in a style serviceable for the training of beginners." Thomas considered his *Summa* a handbook for novice Christian students. Eager to retain their attention and instruct them in first principles, Thomas wrote his *Summa* in a style they could comprehend and follow. Did Thomas,

---

80. Kristeller, 35.

81. Haines, *Martin Luther and the Rule of Faith*, 3; cf. *WATR* 3:698.10–17, no. 3904; 6:345.28–33, no. 7031; WA 40, 3:608.11–24. For another use of Aristotelian categories, see *LW* 24:341–42.

82. Davies, *Thomas Aquinas's* Summa Contra Gentiles, 6. For a more extensive analysis of Thomas's ideas, see Davies, *The Thought of Thomas Aquinas*; Kretzmann and Stump, *Cambridge Companion to Aquinas*.

83. Davies, *Thomas Aquinas's* Summa Contra Gentiles, 6.

as the caricature says, pursue endless, speculative questions concerning hypotheticals? Thomas said his purpose was the direct opposite. He even confronted those writers who pursued irrelevant questions that bored their readers to death, persuaded these theologians do not practice a "sound educational method." "We have considered how newcomers to this teaching are greatly hindered by various writings on the subject, partly because of the *swarm of pointless questions* . . . partly because repetitiousness has bred boredom and muddle in their thinking." By contrast, Thomas applied a different method: "Eager, therefore, to avoid these and other like drawbacks, and trusting in God's help, we shall try to pursue the things held by Christian theology, and to be *concise and clear,* so far as the matter allows."[84]

Thomas's prefatory comments have led scholars to speculate on his intended readership. Judging by the advanced material in the *Summa,* as well as Thomas's metaphysical presuppositions, some say the readership must have been students and scholars with advanced training. However, if Thomas's prefatory remarks mean anything, and if his ministry at the time is taken into consideration, it is more likely Thomas had in view the average Dominican needing theological training. Thomas started his *Summa* in Rome (1265) when he was assigned to Santa Sabina, charged with repairing the state of theological education (which was poor) among the Dominicans. Who were these Dominicans? "They were not academic stars like Albert and Aquinas." Brian Davies suggests that they "were mostly working friars who needed help when it came to their primary tasks—preaching and hearing confessions." Thomas did not stay in Rome forever, and the writing of his *Summa* did continue after his leave of Santa Sabina. However, Thomas remained a scholar committed to writing theology for those busy in the work of ministry. Thomas is "nowadays commonly thought of as a university professor," but he "spent only around seven years of his Dominican life working in a university." The rest was spent in the context of the Dominican order, teaching the "common brothers" what to believe and why so that they could attend to the care of souls. Some believe Thomas considered this task so important that it is the reason why he stopped his commentary on Lombard's *Sentences.*[85]

Concision and clarity are apparent throughout the *Summa,* which is structured by "articles," each article represented by a question. The format breeds perspicuity: First, Thomas posed the question. Second, he supplied the opposing answers and enlisted a scriptural passage or church father that could be quoted in support. Third, he provided the correct answer, usually with a quotation from Scripture or sometimes a church father. Fourth, he gave his "reply," which contained on average anywhere between two and five points (though sometimes more depending on the difficulty of the article/question). For example, consider the doctrine of eternal generation so essential to the Nicene Creed:

---

84. Emphasis added. Aquinas, *ST,* "Foreword" (p. 3). All references to the *Summa Theologiae* are taken from the Blackfriars edition reissued by Cambridge University Press.

85. Davies, *Thomas Aquinas's Summa Theologiae,* 9, 10, 11. Davies is largely in agreement with the thesis of Leonard Boyle, although even Boyle recognizes the argument is circumstantial, though still a good one.

ARTICLE 2. IS THERE IN GOD A PROCESSION WHICH CAN BE CALLED "GENERATION"?

THE SECOND POINT: 1. It seems that procession in God cannot be called "generation." For generation is the change from not existing to existing, and its opposite is decay; in both processes there is a material subject. But such ideas do not apply to God. Therefore there can be no generation in God.

... [Thomas provides three objections.]

ON THE OTHER HAND there are the Psalmist's words: *Today I have begotten thee* [Ps. 2:7].

Reply:

1. The procession of the Word within God is called "generation." ... The notion of generation does apply to the procession of the Word in God. ...

2. ... Hence the Word comes forth as subsisting in the same nature, and is called "begotten" and "Son" in a strict sense. That is why, when referring to the coming forth of divine wisdom, Scripture makes use of words connected with the generation of living things, for example, "conceiving" and "giving birth." For it is said in *Proverbs* [8:24], about divine wisdom personified, *The ocean's depths were not yet and I had already been conceived; before the mountains I was given birth.*

... [Thomas gives three replies to the original objections.][86]

The doctrine of eternal generation is one of the greatest mysteries of the Christian faith. Yet Thomas's Scholastic structure, as well as his exposition of Scripture, add clarity, holding the student's hand as the student seeks further understanding. By the end, Thomas had answered the hardest and most common objections, some historical, some contemporary.

Scripture and the Science of Theology

The *Summa Contra Gentiles* began by outlining two modes of truth: truths known by natural revelation (like the existence of God and his perfections) and truths revealed only by supernatural revelation (like the Trinity and the incarnation). The *Summa Contra Gentiles* was reason's pursuit of a natural knowledge based on God's natural revelation, though book 4 does engage those articles of faith as revealed by the sacred Scriptures. *Summa Theologiae* does not leave reason behind; reason is instrumental to understanding the coherence of Christian theology.[87] However, the *Summa* does turn its attention to articles of faith revealed

---

86. *ST* 1a. 27, 3.
87. "All the same holy teaching also uses human reasoning, not indeed to prove the faith, for that would take away from the merit of believing, but to make manifest some implications of its message. Since grace does not scrap nature but brings it to perfection, so also natural reason should assist faith as the natural loving bent of the will yields to charity. St Paul speaks of *bringing into captivity every understanding unto the service of Christ.* Hence holy teaching uses the authority of philosophers who have been able to perceive the truth by natural reasoning, for instance when St Paul quotes the saying of Aratus, *As some of your poets have said, we are of the race of God.*" *ST* 1a. 1, 8.

in Scripture. Scripture is nothing less than the inspired Word of God, as Paul said in 2 Timothy 3:16, a passage Thomas enjoyed quoting to confirm not only Scripture's divine origin but its sufficiency and clarity for Christian theology and practice.[88] "Divinely inspired Scripture, however, is no part of the branches of philosophy traced by reasoning. Accordingly it is expedient to have another body of sure knowledge inspired by God." This body of knowledge is a "necessity for our welfare," but it must be a body that is made up of divine truths "surpassing reason" and "signified to us through divine revelation." Previously Thomas's *Summa Contra Gentiles* focused on faith seeking *understanding*. Now Thomas turned his attention to *faith* seeking understanding. For faith is the only proper response to revelation: "Reason should not pry into things too high for human knowledge, nevertheless when they are revealed by God they should be welcomed by faith."[89]

Christian theology is nothing less than a science that "takes on faith its principles revealed by God."[90] Since theology is based on revelation, it is like "an imprint on us of God's own knowledge, which is the single and simple vision of everything."[91] For that reason, theology carries a certitude that other disciplines do not possess. Other sciences originate "from the natural light of human reason which can make mistakes, whereas sacred doctrine's is held in the light of divine knowledge which cannot falter." Where uncertainty is present, the fault lies not with God's knowledge or revelation but with man's reception. "Doubt about the articles of faith which falls to the lot of some is not because the reality is at all uncertain but because human understanding is feeble. Nevertheless, as Aristotle also points out, the slenderest acquaintance we can form with heavenly things is more desirable than a thorough grasp of mundane matters." Since this acquaintance with heavenly things comes by means of divine revelation, theology gathers together all the sciences to its service, much like an architect employs construction workers.[92] For Thomas, theology was "mainly concerned with the divine things which are, rather than with things men do," and therefore a theoretical science. Theology "deals with human acts only in so far as they prepare men for that achieved knowledge of God on which their eternal bliss reposes."[93] As far as theology is aimed at this end, Thomas said sacred doctrine can be called a practical science because "its aim is eternal happiness" itself.[94]

---

88. Did Thomas believe Scripture was inerrant? He quoted Augustine to that effect. "In this sense St Augustine wrote to St Jerome; *Only to those books or writings which are called canonical have I learnt to pay such honour that I firmly believe that none of their authors have erred in composing them. Other authors, however, I read to such effect that, no matter what holiness and learning they display, I do not hold what they say to be true because those were their sentiments.*" *ST* 1a. 1, 8; quoting Augustine, *Epist.* 82, 1. PL 33, 277.

89. *ST* 1a. 1, 1.

90. *ST* 1a. 1, 2.

91. *ST* 1a. 1, 3.

92. Does that mean theology lacks sufficiency? Thomas said no. "That it turns to them [other sciences] so is not from any lack or insufficiency within itself, but because our understanding is wanting, which is the more readily guided into the world above reason, set forth in holy teaching, through the world of natural reason which the other sciences take their course." *ST* 1a. 1, 5.

93. *ST* 1a. 1, 4.

94. *ST* 1a. 1, 5.

In sum, Thomas's approach and definition of theology was Augustinian. Augustine said that wisdom is "knowledge of divine things."[95] Theology therefore is a type of sacred doctrine or holy teaching that "goes to God most personally as deepest origin and highest end," said Thomas. Theology can only reach such heights, however, because it depends not on reason alone but on God's self-revelation in sacred Scripture. The theologian can go to God personally "not only because of what can be gathered about him from creatures (which the philosophers have recognized, according to the epistle to the Romans, *What was known of God is manifest in them*) but also because of what he alone knows about himself and yet discloses for others to share." The task of the theologian is to *share*, for theology is a "holy teaching" that is nothing less than "wisdom in the highest degree."[96]

The Fourfold Sense of Scripture

If theology depends on God's self-disclosure in sacred Scripture, then the interpretation of Scripture (hermeneutics) is instrumental for theology. Thomas did not hesitate to recognize Scripture's various uses of language and genre. For example, Scripture (and theology too) employs metaphorical language. "Holy Scripture fittingly delivers divine and spiritual realities under bodily guises." That would make sense to an Aristotelian like Thomas since the recipients of divine revelation live in a world governed by the senses; indeed, he was part of that sensible world. Therefore, "all our knowledge takes its rise from sensation." How fitting then for Scripture to deliver "spiritual things to us beneath metaphors taken from bodily things."[97]

That is good news for the uneducated, said Thomas. How kind of God to accommodate the uneducated by conveying spiritual truths in metaphors that all can understand.[98] Even when someone cannot understand the metaphor, they can turn to a different Scripture passage where the same truth is explained with greater clarity.[99] Thomas believed God chose to communicate spiritual truths through figurative language on purpose to help the believer but also to guard the church against the unbeliever. The figurative language is both "a challenge to those eager to find out the truth" and a "defence against unbelievers ready to ridicule; to these the text [Matt. 7:6] refers, *Give not that which is holy to the dogs*."[100] In addition, figurative language is appropriate in light of who we are in contrast to who God is. "For in this life what he is not," Thomas said, "is clearer to us than what he is." The way of remotion means he uses "the likeness of things

---

95. Augustine, *De Trinitate* 12, 14. PL 42, 1009; quoted in *ST* 1a. 1, 6.
96. *ST* 1a. 1, 6.
97. *ST* 1a. 1, 9.
98. Thomas quoted Romans 1:14 to this effect and said, "The uneducated may then lay hold of them [spiritual things], those, that is to say, who are not ready to take intellectual truths neat with nothing else." *ST* 1a. 1, 9.
99. "In fact truths expressed metaphorically in one passage of Scripture are more expressly explained elsewhere." *ST* 1a. 1, 9.
100. *ST* 1a. 1, 9.

farthest removed from him" so that "we can more fairly estimate how far above our speech and thought he is."[101]

With the validity of figurative language established on the basis of the Creator-creature distinction, Thomas was ready to introduce the fourfold meaning of Scripture—the Quadriga. These include (1) historical or literal, (2) allegorical, (3) tropological or moral, and (4) anagogical. Augustine of Dacia famously summarized all four senses when he said,

> *Littera gesta docet, quid credas allegoria, moralis quid agas, quo tendas anagogia.*

> The letter teaches events, allegory what you should believe, morality teaches what you should do, anagogy what mark you should be aiming for.

According to medieval scholar Henri de Lubac, the catchy summary was a type of "theological compendium for the use of the 'simple.'"[102]

The fourfold meaning was not original to medievals; they were simply retrieving, though at times adapting, a hermeneutic considered a staple of the church catholic. The method originated among the church fathers, though two different lists of senses circulated. De Lubac has demonstrated that both lists were present in Origen. "More than any other figure in the fields of hermeneutics, exegesis, and spirituality, he would be the grand master."[103] Although, Augustine does compete with Origen for that title.

Thomas, however, never cited Origen or Augustine when he introduced the fourfold meaning in his *Summa*. That does not mean he was unaware of Origen, other church fathers, or the medieval reception of the fourfold meaning. For example, Thomas did acknowledge Hugh of St. Victor, commenting out of curiosity that Hugh listed only three senses: historical, allegorical (which included anagogical), and tropological.[104] Yet overall, Thomas felt no pressure to defend the fourfold meaning; he was quite comfortable assuming its credibility, as did many precritical, premodern interpreters. Thomas considered the fourfold meaning essential to preserving the spiritual truths the divine author intended to communicate. The divine author's communication occurred through a human author (whether Moses or Job, Isaiah or Matthew), but transcended any single human author as well, moving across the entire canon of Scripture, culminating in the incarnation of Christ, the *telos*.

---

101. *ST* 1a. 1, 9.

102. Quoted in Henri de Lubac, *Medieval Exegesis* 1:1. For a short study, see Smalley, *The Study of the Bible in the Middle Ages; Stanglin, The Letter and Spirit of Biblical Interpretation, 77–111.*

103. De Lubac, *Medieval Exegesis*, 1:159.

104. *ST* 1a. 1, 10. Thomas was influenced by Gregory the Great and may have been well acquainted with Gregory's use of multiple senses, although Gregory listed three instead of four: "First we lay the foundation in history; then by following a symbolical sense, we erect an intellectual edifice to be a stronghold of faith; and lastly, by the grace of moral instruction, we as it were paint the fabric in fair colors." Gregory the Great, *Ep.* 5.53a, in *Gregory the Great*, 1:193.

The relationship between each of these four senses is especially relevant for a book on the Reformation. Interpreters have sometimes assumed medievals were fixated on allegory, forsaking the literal sense or at the least giving it little import. This oppositional reading then jumps to the Reformation and concludes that the Reformers despised such a method and brought the church back to the literal sense, rejecting one or all of the other remaining senses. Such an interpretation is erroneous, lacking nuance in its understanding of medievals and Reformers alike.

To begin with, Thomas affirmed the fourfold meaning, but he did give the literal sense priority and was not quiet about it, either. The spiritual sense, which includes the allegorical, moral, and anagogical senses, "is *based on and presupposes* the literal sense."[105] For Thomas, the literal substantiated the spiritual sense(s). For example, when Thomas described the three spiritual senses, he never did so apart from their literal foundation.

> *Allegorical sense* is brought into play when the things of the Old Law signify the things of the New Law.
> *Moral sense:* The things done in Christ and in those who prefigured him are signs of what we should carry out.
> *Anagogical sense:* The things that lie ahead in eternal glory are signified.[106]

Thomas concluded, "Consequently holy Scripture sets up no confusion, since all meanings are based on one, namely, the literal sense. . . . Nothing necessary for faith is contained under the spiritual sense that is not openly conveyed through the literal sense elsewhere."[107]

Modern interpreters have been dismissive of Thomas's hermeneutic: how can multiple senses be present in a single human author who has only one intended meaning? That objection would have been bizarre to Thomas because it assumes (as moderns so often do) the absence of a divine author and his authorial intent. The objection assumes the inability of the divine author to transcend any single human author, to intend something more, above and beyond the human author's knowledge and context. *Sensus plenior* may be rejected by moderns who refuse to presuppose divine authorship, but to Thomas biblical interpretation and Christian theology were an impossibility apart from such a concept.[108] As Thomas said, "Now because the literal sense is that which the author intends, and the author of holy Scripture is God who comprehends everything all at once in his understanding, it comes not amiss, as St Augustine observes, if many meanings are present even in the literal sense of one passage of Scripture."[109]

---

105. Emphasis added. *ST* 1a. 1, 10.
106. *ST* 1a. 1, 10.
107. Thomas contrasted Augustine with Vincent the Donatist as an example. *ST* 1a. 1, 10.
108. Thomas need not use the exact phrase *sensus plenior* to assume its legitimacy.
109. With Augustine's help, Thomas clarified that the literal sense includes history, etiology, and analogy. Aquinas, *ST* 1a. 1, 10.

The omnipotence, omniscience, and omnisapience of the divine author explains why the biblical interpreter can and should consider the ways the literal sense is a foundation on which the allegorical, moral, and anagogical are built.

The Measure of Orthodox Christianity and Its Broad Continuity

To grasp a correct understanding of Thomas's Scholastic method on subjects like faith and reason and Scripture and interpretation, we have devoted brief attention to the way Thomas started both his *Summa Contra Gentiles* and his *Summa Theologiae*.[110] One critical misconception about both the *Summa* and medieval Scholasticism in general should not be overlooked otherwise ignorance will result in gross misrepresentation of Scholasticism and the Reformation. Although the Reformation reacted against medieval doctrines like infused righteousness, transubstantiation, or purgatory—doctrines that are significant and worthy of strong debate—nevertheless, those were a small portion, even a minority of the larger medieval framework that depended on orthodoxy. Consider the structure and content of Thomas's *Summa*:

In total Thomas wrote 512 questions in his *Summa Theologiae*. Out of those 512, only 16 treated faith and only 34 treated the saints (Mary included) and the seven sacraments. That means only approximately 10 percent of the entire *Summa* addressed those major doctrines considered most controversial during the sixteenth century, doctrines that Protestants could not affirm and remain Protestant (see boldface items in table). Even if one is generous and includes ancillary doctrines like original sin or mysticism, the percentage only rises by 1 percent. And that addition is generous since it is complicated by Thomas's Augustinian soteriology (see below). If nuance is considered—for example, the Reformers took issue with *specific aspects* of medieval soteriology and ecclesiology—the 10 percent drops.

When the scope of the *Summa* is taken into consideration, the continuity between the Scholastics and the Reformers dwarfs their discontinuity. For example, in *Prima Pars* Thomas treated the knowledge of God, the inspiration of Scripture, the existence of God, divine perfections, the Trinity, creation *ex nihilo*, the *imago Dei*, the human soul, divine providence, angels, and more. By and large, the Reformers did not need to address these *loci*, some of which were essential to orthodoxy. To do so in front of Rome could have thrown into question their own orthodoxy. By contrast, Rome and Reformers alike agreed on classical theism's articulation of these tenets. Even *Tertia Pars*, which does include questions on Mary and the sacraments, consists of large sections devoted to Chalcedonian Christology. Again, the same conclusion follows. The point deserves emphasis: *Scholastics like Thomas constructed a massive foundation grounded in classical Christian orthodoxy, and the Reformers never felt the need to*

---

110. We will not capture the scope of the *Summa* here, but see Davies's fine work: *Thomas Aquinas's Summa Theologiae.*

address a majority of its loci *because to disagree was to diverge from orthodoxy itself and its accompanying theological parameters. Their silence should not be taken as divergence but conformity, a quiet testimony to their catholicity.* That should change current perspectives which so major on discontinuity that the massive amount of continuity is either neglected or denied. Failure to see broad continuity is a failure to read Thomas in the context of his entire corpus.

SUMMA THEOLOGIAE

Prima Pars (1a. 1–119) 119 articles 23% (of Summa)	Prima Secundae (1a2ae. 1–114) 114 articles 22%	Secunda Secundae (2a2ae. 1–189) 189 articles 37%	Tertia Pars (3a. 1–90) 90 articles 18%
Theology	End happiness	**Faith**	The incarnate Word
Existence and nature of God	Human acts	Consequences of faith	The grace of Christ
The names of God	Principles of morality	Hope	The one Mediator
Knowledge in God	Love and desire	Charity	**Our Lady**
The will and power of God	Pleasure	Consequences of charity	The childhood of Christ
The Trinity	Fear and anger	Prudence	The life of Christ
Father, Son, and Holy Ghost	Habits	Justice	The passion of Christ
Creation	Virtues	Injustice	The resurrection
Angels	Gifts and beatitudes	Religion	**The sacraments**
Cosmogony	Sin	Consequences of religion	**Baptism and confirmation**
Man	Original sin	Social virtues	**The Eucharist I**
Human intelligence	Effects of sin	Courage	**The Eucharist II**
Man made in God's image	Law	Temperance	**Penance**
Divine government	The old law	Parts of temperance	
The world order	**The gospel of grace**	Mysticism and miracle	
		Activity and contemplation	
		The pastoral and religious lives	

One could object that the quantitative continuity between Thomas and the Reformers is irrelevant since Thomism is a *system* and its rotten parts spoil the whole. That common argument, however, faces a major historical obstacle: many Reformers and Protestant Scholastics from the sixteenth to the eighteenth centuries operated under the exact opposite assumption. As we shall see, the Reformed Orthodox, for instance, never hesitated to critique Thomas on doctrines like soteriology or ecclesiology while embracing his teaching on innumerable other doctrines. More important still, they considered their system the appropriate *refinement* Thomism needed. The Reformed Orthodox were not atomistic, randomly picking points of agreement, but they considered their system the proper *fulfillment* of that system Thomas inaugurated. As mentioned, Thomas applied classical metaphysics to orthodoxy with no little success; the Reformers saw no need for correction but perpetuated that legacy. They only believed that legacy could be more consistent if they distilled Thomas's system and introduced its logic to a more accurate understanding of soteriology and ecclesiology as well. Their dogmatics was a culmination more than a breach, a sanctification more than a condemnation.

That correction in place, consider a case study: Thomas the Augustinian. Although innumerable case studies could exemplify the continuity between Thomas and the Reformers, this one is strategic, revealing the complicated nuance needed when comparing the Reformers to the Scholastics. This case study presents one disagreement that did occur between Scholastics and Reformers. However, the irresponsible temptation to assume complete discontinuity must be resisted. For even when discontinuity is present, significant continuity is not absent.

CASE STUDY: THOMAS THE AUGUSTINIAN

The "oppositional narrative" of the Reformation sets Scholastics over against the Reformers and assumes that Thomas Aquinas represents the essence of what the Reformers stood against. But a more holistic, responsible reading of both the Reformation and Thomas reveals a different discovery: while there are certainly significant aspects of Thomas's thought that the Reformers found dissatisfying (e.g., infused righteousness, transubstantiation), the Reformers shared a large degree of continuity with Thomas, his orthodoxy most of all. To reiterate, the Reformers had far more in common with Thomas than they did with the late medieval Scholastics they targeted most often (see chapter 5). What was the reason for this basic and broad continuity? Besides Thomas's fidelity to orthodoxy, one reason must be his persistent Augustinianism. If the Reformers were transparent on anything, it was their unembarrassed dependence on Augustinianism for their vision of Reformation.

Predestination

For example, consider Thomas on predestination, a doctrine that reveals his Augustinian instincts.

First, like the doctor of grace himself, Thomas positioned predestination under the larger category of divine providence. For if providence is "to arrange things to an end," then predestination is simply one type, the arranging (or sending) of souls to an eternal end.[111]

Second, predestination is eternal rather than temporal, occurring in the mind of God, but its execution has an "effect" on those external to God. Predestination is "like the plan, existing in God's mind, for the ordering of some persons to salvation." Predestination is "actively in God" but "passively . . . in the persons predestined." Like Augustine, Thomas is eager to protect God from a predestination that makes him dependent on the human agent. *God* is the one who predestines; sinners are merely the recipients of his grace. Predestination, therefore, is one of God's "immanent activities . . . like understanding and willing," because it remains in the "doer." Predestination, in other words, "does not put anything into the predestined." Yet the execution of predestination "reaches out into external things and produces an effect there." Predestination is "a prevision of God's benefits," said Thomas, quoting Augustine. "Foreknowledge is not in the things foreknown, but in the foreknower. Neither, then, is predestination in the predestined, but in the one who predestines."[112] Positioning predestination in the mind of God led Thomas toward a most Augustinian article.

Third, any doubt that Thomas was an Augustinian can be corrected by Thomas's affirmation of reprobation. For Thomas, like Augustine, predestination included not only the election of some to salvation but the reprobation of others to condemnation. "God loves all men and all creatures as well, inasmuch as he wills some good to all: all the same he does not will every sort of good to each. In that he does not will to some the blessing of eternal life he is said to hold them in hate or to reprobate them."[113] To explain how God can love all in a general sense but some in a special, saving sense, Thomas warned his readers against a univocal understanding of divine and human love.[114] "When we love things our will does not cause them to be good; it is because they are good already that we are roused to love them; therefore we choose someone to love, and our choice precedes our loving. With God the converse is true." To articulate why, Thomas highlighted the unconditionality of divine love. "For when [God] chooses to love another and thereby wills him good, his will is the cause of the other being singled out and so endowed. Clearly, then, the notion of God's special loving logically precedes that of his choosing, and that of his choosing that of his predestining. Therefore all the predestined are picked loves." To reconcile God loving all people in a common, general sense and some people in a special,

---

111. "Accordingly the planned sending of a rational creature to the end which is eternal life is termed predestination, for to predestine is to send. And so it is clear that predestination as regards what it does objectively is a part of Providence." *ST* 1a. 23, 1.

112. *ST* 1a. 23, 2.

113. However, reprobation does not excuse the culpability of the ungodly. "God's reprobation does not subtract anything from the rejected one's own ability." *ST* 1a. 23, 5.

114. Thomas distinguished between election and dilection. *ST* 1a. 23, 5.

saving sense, Thomas distinguished between God's antecedent will and consequent will. "God wishes all men to be saved by his antecedent will, which is not downright willing, but willing in a qualified sense, not by his consequent will, which is committed willing."[115]

Fourth, if predestination is eternal, occurring in the mind of God, then the love that predestines the elect is unconditional, grounded in the will of God, not in anything humans do. Here Thomas relied not only on Augustine but on Paul, Romans 9 in particular. Thomas was aware that the Pelagians would counter by appealing to free will, but he reminded them that even free will is predestined by God. If it were not, then grace is man's doing instead of God's gift. "Were anything on our part the reason for predestination it would lie outside predestination considered as an effect. Yet what is from freewill and what is from grace are not distinct, no more than what is from a secondary cause and what is from the first cause." Augustine recognized the importance of secondary causes but never severed secondary causes from participating in God, their First Cause. "God's providence procures its effects through the operation of secondary causes. Hence what is through freewill is also from predestination." Man, therefore, cannot look at anything in himself—including free will—as if it is the basis of God's choice. "Whatever there is in man ordering him to salvation is entirely compromised in predestination as a total effect, even down to his very preparing himself for grace."[116] If everything stems from grace, then not even foreknowledge can condition God's choice. God's foreknowledge of man's choice to accept grace cannot be the cause of his electing decision. "The good use of grace foreknown by God is not the reason for conferring it, except, as we have explained, according to the turn of final causality."[117] Thomas was adamant that God's will, not man's, is the cause of this eternal choice. "His so willing is the sole ground," said Thomas, much like building a house "depends on the mere will of the builder."[118]

Fifth, since election and reprobation are God's choices, he is glorified in both, though in different ways. "God wills to manifest his goodness in men, in those whom he predestines in the manner of mercy by sparing them, in those whom he reprobates in the manner of justice by punishing them."[119]

First Cause, Creation and the *Donum Superadditum*

Final causality was critical for Thomas's understanding of creation, being a logical entailment of God as First Cause and a guarantee that creation was

---

115. *ST* 1a. 23, 5 (cf. 1a. 19, 6). To see this distinction utilized by a Reformed Scholastic, consult the fourth topic on God's decree in Turretin's *Institutes*.

116. *ST* 1a. 23, 5.

117. *ST* 1a. 23, 5.

118. How did Thomas reply to the charge that God is unfair? "On this account we cannot complain of unfairness if God prepares unequal lots for equals. This would be repugnant to justice as such were the effect of predestination a due to be rendered, not a favour. He who grants by grace can give freely as he wills, be it more be it less, without prejudice to justice, provided he deprives no one of what is owing." *ST* 1a. 23, 5.

119. *ST* 1a. 23, 5.

imbued with purpose—eschatology framed Thomas's participation teleology from beginning to end. For those made in the likeness of God, final causality reaches its apex in the beatific vision, where eternal blessedness and happiness is found in God. However, the Creator is infinite and incomprehensible to created man, who is but finite. To comprehend is to "contain something," but the "infinite cannot be contained in the finite; God exists infinitely and nothing finite could grasp him infinitely."[120] Something supernatural must be added to man in his natural state since it is "impossible that any created mind should see the essence of God by its own natural powers." God *is* his existence, but those created by God *share* in existence—Thomas was committed to a participation metaphysic.[121] If "no creature *is* its existence" but must "share in existence," then "no created mind can see the essence of God unless he by his grace joins himself to that mind as something intelligible to it."[122] According to Psalm 36:9—"In your light do we see light"—the mind's eye can only "see God" by means of illumination. "Hence there must be some disposition given to the understanding beyond its own nature so that it can be raised to such sublimity. Since as we have shown, the natural power of the intellect is not sufficient to see the essence of God, this power of understanding must come to it by divine grace."[123] For Thomas, ultimate happiness is found in seeing and participating in the divine nature (2 Peter 1:4; 1 John 3:2), so he defines grace as God's gift to unite us to himself.[124] Therefore, even prior to the fall, the grace of God is instrumental, ensuring finite man's faculties are ordered towards God. Man was created good but since he is finite, he is capable of change, and change could forfeit his stability in a state of righteousness. Thomas established the real presence of God in the garden; otherwise, natural man will not arrive at his supernatural *telos*.[125]

Thomas followed Augustine in the *City of God*, who said that grace before the fall explained both man's need for God and man's rebellion against God. "Now man could not even trust in the help of God without God's help; but this did not mean that he did not have it in his power to withdraw from the benefits of divine grace by self-pleasing."[126] Augustine posited the necessity of an *auxilium sine quo non*, meaning Adam and Eve needed an "assistance without which a desired result cannot occur."[127] Life with God was the desired outcome, but without grace, man

---

120. *ST* 1a. 12. 7.

121. On the basis of God's name in Exodus—I Am—Thomas says, "the existence of God is his essence" (*ST* 1a. 13. 11).

122. *ST* 1a. 12. 4.

123. *ST* 1a. 12. 5.

124. "For him it [grace] is the work of God in human beings raising them above their human nature to the point where they become sharers in the divine nature." Davies, *The Thought of Thomas Aquinas*, 264 (cf. 262).

125. "Grace, according to Aquinas, operates at the subjective, transformative level, enabling men and women to reach the supernatural end for which they were intended. He denies that it is a substance because that would displace the soul [*ST* 1a2ae. 110.2.2]. Instead he asserts that it is a quality imparted to the soul by God in order to heal and elevate it." Trueman, *Grace Alone*, 100.

126. And again, "it was not in man's power, even in paradise, to live a good life without the help of God, yet it was in his power to live an evil life." *City of God* 14.27.

127. The exact meaning: "an assistance without which not." Muller, *Dictionary*, s.v.

and woman could not continue in communion with God. Nevertheless, prior to the fall such grace could be obstructed by transgressing the command of God not to eat of the tree of the knowledge of good and evil.[128]

Therefore, a superadded gift—*donum superadditum*—of grace at creation served to assist man's nature, keeping finite man from changing, moving from a state of righteousness to corruption. However, the exact nature of the *donum superadditum* was debated. Thomas maintained the Augustinian emphasis on the primacy of grace by claiming the superadded gift was inseparable from man's constitution, even given to man at creation itself. In other words, never was there a time when Adam was without it. The *donum superadditum* could be distinguished in the mind of the theologian but in Adam's experience such a gift was inseparable from his existence at the start.

By contrast, certain Franciscans created a gap between the creation of man and the *donum superadditum*—from Bonaventure to Scotus. Scotus so severed the two in time that he conditioned superadded grace on man's merit, thereby opening himself up to the charge of Pelagianism. Consider the contrast:

Augustine and Thomas Aquinas: "The *donum superadditum* was part of the original human constitution and . . . its loss was the loss of the original capacity for righteousness. Since the superadded grace was not merited in the beginning, it cannot be regained by merit after the fall."

Duns Scotus and the Franciscans: "The *donum superadditum* was not part of the original constitution or original righteousness of human beings but was to be considered truly as a gift merited by a first act of obedience on the part of Adam performed by Adam according to his purely natural capacities (*ex puris naturalibus*). Since Adam could, by doing a minimal or finite act, merit the initial gift of God's grace, his fallen progeny might, by doing a minimal act, also merit the gift of first grace (see *meritum de congruo*)."[129]

Some Reformed Scholastics in the sixteenth and seventeenth centuries did believe a type of grace preceded the fall, which allowed them, like Thomas, to emphasize finite man's dependence on his Creator. To say otherwise might sound as if creation is necessary and man does not participate in God or need his divine accommodation.[130] However, instead of a *donum superadditum*, most

---

128. Therefore, such grace should not be confused with *auxilium quo*. Muller, *Dictionary*, s.v.

129. Muler, *Dictionary*, s.v.

130. Trueman, *Grace Alone*, 102. For example, consider Francis Turretin, *Institutes* 8.3.15 (1:578). More recently, Perkins demonstrates that some in the Reformed tradition (like Junius) used the language of grace to explain how Adam was supposed to depend on God and obey his law during his status under the covenant of works (others like Ussher did not). However, even this language of grace may be more directed to God, specifically his act to establish a covenant itself, than towards a *donum superadditum* for the sake of obedience. More research is needed to add clarity to such a lacuna. However, see the fine work of Perkins, *Catholicity and the Covenant of Works*, 48–116.

adopted a *donum concreatum*, a concreated gift.[131] Their position was far closer to the Augustinian-Thomistic position than the Scotus-Franciscan view since it refused to sever grace from man's constitution, as if the former was contingent on the latter. And yet some of the Reformed believed the union had to be even more inseparable than Augustine and Thomas imagined. The gift was not merely superadded at creation but "given in the original human constitution" itself. The *donum concreatum* was not original to the Reformers and their heirs, however, but was taught by Henry of Ghent, for example, and can be defined as follows:

> *Henry of Ghent and the Reformed Scholastics:* "The Protestant argument was the *donum gratuitum*, the utterly free gift, of *iustitia originalis* was part of the original constitution of humanity and therefore a *donum concreatum*. . . . By extension, the loss of the *iustitia originalis* in the fall was the loss of something fundamental to the human constitution that could be resupplied only by a divine act and was not, as the semi-Pelagian tendency in late medieval Scotism and nominalism indicated, something superadded that could be regained by a minimal act of human obedience."[132]

If the gift is not superadded but original, built into the natural constitution of man himself, then how much greater the loss of original righteousness at the fall?

The difference between the superadded gift (Thomism) and a concreated gift (Reformed) is not insignificant, but both camps were an ally against Scotism and later Ockham and Biel (see chapter 5). While the Thomists and Reformed refused to sever the gift from man's constitution, ensuring the primacy of grace, Scotism did not hesitate to sever the two, conditioning the gift on man's merit.

Original Sin

The Augustinianism of Thomas not only kept Pelagianism and Semi-Pelagianism at bay when he articulated man's state of integrity but the doctrine of original sin served a similar purpose. "All who are born of Adam can be considered as one man by reason of sharing the one nature inherited from the first parent, even as in political matters all belonging to one community are reckoned to be like one body, and the whole community like one person."[133] Due to Adam's fall, the one common nature inherited from Adam places all of humanity under divine judgment, which explains why Paul could say in Ephesians 2:3, "We . . . were by nature children of wrath."[134]

---

131. E.g., *LW* 1:164–65.

132. Muller, *Dictionary*, s.v.

133. *ST* 1a2ae. 81, 1. Later Thomas appealed to Romans 5:12. See 1a2ae. 81, 3.

134. *ST* 1a2ae. 81, 3. *How* does Adam's posterity inherit their father's nature? "Because the power of semen cannot cause it, a rational soul is not transmitted with the semen by generation. Yet the semen does act as dispositive cause, so that what is transmitted from parent to child through the power of the semen is human nature, and together with nature the sickness of nature." For a newborn child becomes a partaker in the sin of the first parent by the fact that he takes human nature from him through a kind of generative impulse." Later

THOMAS AQUINAS'S CRITIQUE OF ARISTOTLE

A common misconception has said Thomas Aquinas simply baptized Aristotle, who then corrupted Christian theology. That myth is easily dismantled by a careful reading of Thomas. For example, Aristotle believed that the way a person becomes good is by submitting to laws that are good. Aristotle's point may contain truth if he was merely referring to the civil realm, but Thomas strongly disagreed if Aristotle's point was transferred into soteriology. In his *Commentary on Romans*, Thomas was adamant in his anti-Pelagian instinct. He insisted man is so perverted by original sin that God's electing grace is effectual, conquering the opposition of the sinful nature. Furthermore, before any activity on man's part, God must infuse grace. Yet is faith itself a gift? "God's justice is said to exist through faith in Christ Jesus, not as though by faith we merit being justified, as if faith exists from ourselves and through it we merit God's justice, as the Pelagians assert; but because in the very justification, by which we are made just by God, the first motion of the mind toward God is through faith" (3.3).

Thomas carried this disagreement with Aristotle into his treatment of virtue and the Christian life. Aristotle viewed the magnanimous man as someone who knows that he is great, but Thomas regarded the magnanimous man as humble, convinced he is nothing at all.

Here is a point of caution: in contrast to the *via antiqua* and Thomas Aquinas, the *via moderna* could at points be far more bound to Aristotle. As chapter 5 will reveal, Thomas was willing to depart from Aristotle if the philosopher conflicted with his Augustinian soteriology.

On Thomas's divergence from Aristotle, see Horton, *Justification*, 1:106; Kapic, *You're Only Human*, 104–7; Chesterton, *The Dumb Ox*, 90.

Since original sin is a contamination of man's nature, Thomas followed Augustine and concluded that original sin involves a habit or *habitus*. By habit Thomas meant a disposition in one's nature.[135] Due to original sin, human nature is now infected. Thomas used the analogy of bodily illness to convey his point: when a person is sick, that person has a "discorded disposition of the body upsetting the balance in which good health consists." That logic follows with original sin: "Original sin is called a *sickness of nature.*" This sickness involves a deficiency. Just as a "privation" of good health is the result of physical sickness,

---

Thomas asked "whether or not original sin is rather in the soul," to which he answered, "Original sin can in no way be in the body as in its subject, but only in the soul." Thomas explained the relation between original sin and the body by means of Aristotelian categories: "The original sin of all men existed in Adam as in its first principal cause, according to St Paul's text, *in whom all have sinned*. As in its instrumental cause original sin is in the semen. The reason for this is that original sin is transmitted to offspring together with human nature through the power of the semen" (1a2ae. 83, 1).

135. Thomas said, "Habit means a modification of a nature composed of many elements, according as it bears itself well or ill towards something, and chiefly where such a disposition becomes as it were second nature, as in the case of sickness or health. In this way it is that original sin is a habit. For it is a disordered disposition growing from the dissolution of that harmony in which original justice consisted." *ST* 1a2ae. 82, 1.

so a "privation" or original righteousness and justice is the result of the soul's sickness. Such a privation highlights the "disordered disposition" in human nature.[136]

Forensic categories are not missing from Thomas's description of original sin, either. Again, Thomas followed Augustine, who said, "Concupiscence is the guilt of original sin." Thomas utilized Aristotelian categories to distinguish between types of causation to explain facets of original sin. For example, "Original sin materially is concupiscence, yet formally it is the lack of original justice." Without original justice, nothing subjects the will to God. So "the lack of original justice subjecting the will to God is what is formal in original sin."[137] To argue this claim, Thomas appealed to the father of Scholasticism. Original justice "first of all concerns the will, for it is *uprightness of will*, as Anselm says."[138] Likewise with original sin. The will is not immune from devastation, which is why Thomas could describe original sin as a disordered disposition. "Original sin, therefore, primarily affects the will."[139]

The pervasive effect of original sin on the soul did lead Thomas to ask whether the nature of man is obliterated altogether. In usual Scholastic style, Thomas's riposte is nuanced. The answer depends on the definition of human nature as "good." Thomas said the answer is threefold:

1. There are the principles constitutive of nature together with the properties derived from them, for example the powers of soul and the like.
2. Since it is from this nature itself that man has an inclination to virtue, as previously indicated, this inclination is itself a good of nature.
3. The gift of original justice can be termed a good of human nature in the sense that in the first man it was bestowed as a gift to all mankind.[140]

How does original sin affect each? "Of these goods, the first is neither destroyed nor lessened through sin. The third has been totally removed by the sin of the first parents. But the middle one, man's connatural inclination to virtue, is lessened through sin."[141] Consider each:

First, the "principles constitutive of nature" are not destroyed by original sin. If they were, then human nature itself, along with all its faculties (the rational soul, which includes will and intellect), would be exterminated and the human person in the process. After the fall, the human nature, though corrupt, remains a human nature. His intellective soul still separates man from beast, a mere sensory soul.[142]

---

136. "This disordered disposition does have the character of a habit, whereas the disordered disposition in an act does not. For this reason it is possible for original sin, but not actual sin, to be a habit.... Nor should it be said that original sin is a habit either infused or acquired by an act (except of the first parent, not of anyone else); it is a congenital habit arising from a vitiated origin." *ST* 1a2ae. 82, 1.

137. *ST* 1a2ae. 82, 3.

138. Thomas was quoting from *De Conceptu Virginali* 3 (PL 158, 436). *ST* 1a2ae. 82, 3.

139. *ST* 1a2ae. 82, 3.

140. *ST* 1a2ae. 85, 1.

141. *ST* 1a2ae. 85, 1.

142. "If the inclination were lessened in the first way, eventual eradication would necessarily result, namely

Second, Thomas said inclination to virtue is "lessened through sin." As will become plain, Thomas rejected those who thought man did not require God's assisting grace (Pelagians) or that man did not need God's assisting grace for the initiation of justification (Semi-Pelagians). God's grace is primary, even effectual and irresistible because of the depravity of man. Thomas believed "obstacles" or "hindrances" stand in the way of Adam's progeny.[143] When the "powers of the soul" are dissected into reason, will, appetite (e.g., courage), and concupiscible appetite (e.g., temperance), original sin has wounded them all (Thomas liked the word *wound* to describe this sorry state). Actual sins only further the damage. "Because of sin the reason, especially with regard to moral decision, is blunted; the will becomes hardened against the true good; sustained virtuous activity becomes increasingly difficult; concupiscence grows in ardour."[144] Thomas said virtue is "lessened through sin," which the Reformers may not have considered damning enough, at least a Reformer like Luther in his *Bondage of the Will*. And yet Thomas did elaborate and say, "The will becomes hardened against the true good," an elaboration the Reformers might have appreciated.

Third, even if the Reformers turned to fiercer language to describe this hardening of the will, nevertheless, they were in lockstep when Thomas said original righteousness has been "totally removed" by original sin.

Toward the conclusion of his reflections on original sin Thomas became more than transparent about the consequences that follow once original justice is lost. These are twofold: first, human nature is corruptible; second, punitive damages follow.[145] As for the latter, the world has felt the effects ever since Adam. "Like the withdrawal of grace, the withdrawal of original justice is a penalty. Death, then, and all the evil consequences for the body, are particular penalties for original sin. While they were not intended by the one who sinned, they do fall under the order of divine punitive justice."[146]

How serious is a denial of original sin to a Scholastic like Thomas? To deny original sin is to deny the Catholic faith, since the saving message of Christianity assumes man's fallen state requires a remedy that God alone can provide. "The denial of this truth implies the error that not all would be in need of redemption through Christ."[147] The Pelagian position is not a mere alteration to the Augustinian doctrine of original sin but a wholesale alternative to the Christian religion and its saving message. Appealing to Paul's logic in Romans 5, Thomas contrasted the condemnation humanity receives in Adam with the redemption

---

the destruction of human nature.... Accordingly the root of the inclination is neither destroyed nor lessened, as has been said." *ST* 1a2ae. 85, 2.

143. *ST* 1a2ae. 85, 2.

144. *ST* 1a2ae. 85, 3.

145. On the former, Thomas said, "Once, therefore, original justice was lost through the sin of the first parents, just as human nature was injured in soul by the disordering of the powers, so also it became corruptible by reason of the disturbance of the body's order." *ST* 1a2ae. 85, 5.

146. *ST* 1a2ae. 85, 5.

147. *ST* 1a2ae. 81, 3.

transmitted through a second Adam, namely, Christ. "Just as the sin of Adam passes to all who are begotten of him corporally, so also the grace of Christ passes to all who are begotten of him spiritually."[148]

How is the sinner *spiritually* begotten of Christ? The answer explains how the work of Christ is applied to the sinner infected by original sin. The "grace of Christ passes to all who are begotten of him spiritually *by faith and baptism* and this not only to remove the sin of the first parent but also all actual sin and to lead them to glory."[149] The inclusion of baptism in the remedy for original sin is a standard medieval assumption since original sin involves not only guilt (removed by baptism) but the "tinder of sin," which explains original sin's ongoing effects. "Original sin is taken away by baptism as to its guilt, since the soul recovers grace for the life of the spirit. Original sin remains, nevertheless, as to the '*tinder of sin*,' which is the disorder of the lower powers of the soul and of the body."[150]

Before the application of grace is considered, however, the remedy for original sin—the efficacy of Christ's passion—deserves attention.

Atonement

In the eleventh century, Anselm positioned the passion within a satisfaction framework, but one that surged on the concept of honor stolen and honor repaid. Thomas also positioned the passion within a satisfaction framework, and in that sense the two Scholastics agreed, especially when contrasted with ransom-to-Satan theories or moral influence and example theories of the atonement. Yet unlike Anselm, Thomas did not turn to dishonor and honor as his controlling mechanism but advanced the argument for satisfaction by paying more attention to the nature of divine justice in the atonement.

Bernard and Abelard

Before we explore Thomas's atonement theology, we should acknowledge the significance of his contribution both in his time and for the Reformation. To begin with, not every patristic or medieval theologian defined the atonement as a substitution and satisfaction like Thomas did, at least not with such impetus. Bernard of Clairvaux's twelfth-century debate with Peter Abelard is a case in point. Bernard advocated for a ransom theory, and when Peter Abelard rejected the ransom theory, convinced it was illogical and contradicted God's righteousness and justice, Bernard accused him of heresy—*nova haeresis*.[151] In his *Commentary on the Epistle of Paul to the Romans*, Abelard did affirm an objective ground for the cross, contrary to Bernard's mischaracterization of Abelard.[152]

---

148. *ST* 1a2ae. 81, 3.

149. *ST* 1a2ae. 81, 3, emphasis added.

150. *ST* 1a2ae. 81, 3.

151. The atonement was not the only reason Bernard charged Abelard with heresy. For a full account, see Leinsle, *Introduction to Scholastic Theology*, 117–119. Leinsle engages Bernard of Clairvaux, *Ep.* 190.26 (VIII, 38.16); 189.2–3 (VIII, 13–14); 192 (VIII, 43, 17–19); 190.2 (VIII, 18.25); 330 (VIII, 267.11–12).

152. Abelard, *Commentary on the Epistle to the Romans*.

Abelard did not, in other words, restrict himself to an entirely subjective theory of the cross. He did use substitutionary language, drawn from Romans; otherwise he could not explain why the ungodly is liberated from sin's punishment.

Even if it is not accurate to classify Abelard's entire program in subjective categories, nevertheless, Abelard did transition from this objective emphasis to a highly subjective emphasis. For Abelard, the cross was an example—but not just any example, an example of divine love. Abelard marveled at the divine love put on display at the cross because it is so self-less. Christ laid down his life for others (objective aspect of the cross), which should inspire humanity everywhere to love as selflessly as Christ (subjective aspect of the cross). At the cross, God showed us his selfless love, which makes the ungodly love him as the God who is love. Seeing this love then galvanizes the sinner to turn away from his love for sin and love God instead. Whether the accusation is true or not, Abelard was accused of Pelagianism for his view of the cross.

The Bernard-Abelard context accentuates Thomas's contribution a century later. Thomas did not assume either a ransom view or an example view of the atonement, but instead presented the cross as a substitution. Turning to the apostle Paul, Thomas also accentuated the biblical notion of propitiation to explain how a God infinite in righteousness could justify the ungodly. Thomas did not always reference propitiation in direct fashion, but the concept served as an undercurrent, driving the logic of substitution. For Thomas, Christ was Isaiah's suffering servant, pierced on behalf of Adam's children to appease a divine justice that was nothing less than retributive. Whether they always knew it or not, the Reformers had an ally in Thomas. While differences between the Reformers and Thomas are often enlarged, this line of Augustinian continuity cannot be ignored.[153]

Satisfaction and Propitiation

The genesis of Thomas's atonement theology did not take for granted the qualifications that substantiated Christ's substitution: Christ is the God-man. "The dignity of Christ's flesh should not be reckoned merely from the nature of flesh, but according to the person who assumed it; it was, in fact, the flesh of God, and on this account of infinite value."[154] With the infinite value of Christ established, Thomas appealed to texts such as 1 John 2:2—Christ is "the propitiation for our sins." Thomas was convinced that Christ "by his suffering

---

153. Some (not all) Roman Catholics today will argue that the Reformation's appeal to penal substitution was novel, as if the concept was foreign to the catholic heritage, Thomas included. Some will go further, blaming penal substitution on the Protestant proclivity to nominalism and voluntarism (since penal substitution is occupied by forensic themes). However, this interpretation is motivated more by anti-Protestant polemics than a nuanced reading of history. While the Augustinian-Thomistic tradition may not have communicated penal substitution with the same level of detail as Protestants in the sixteenth and especially the seventeenth century, the concept itself is present. Furthermore, as chapter 1 mentioned, theologians across the Great Tradition did not consider an emphasis on the forensic a virus that could only infect classical realism.

154. *ST* 3a. 48, 2.

made perfect satisfaction for our sins."[155] To understand why the passion is a satisfaction, Thomas first turned to Scripture to understand the variety of ways Christ's crucifixion is described.

First, Thomas considered Paul's words to the Ephesians—Christ "gave himself up for us, a fragrant offering and sacrifice to God" (Eph. 5:2)—and concluded that the cross must be a true *sacrifice*. Interpreting the passion as a sacrifice is not only Pauline but entirely Augustinian. Augustine's rhetorical question is most appropriate: "What could be so acceptably offered and received as the flesh of our sacrifice, made the body of our Priest?"[156]

Second, if the passion is a sacrifice, then it must also be a *redemption*. As Peter told the church, "You were ransomed from the futile ways inherited from your forefathers, not with perishable things such as silver or gold, but with the precious blood of Christ, like that of a lamb without blemish or spot." (1 Peter 1:18–19). Redemption presupposes a bondage, and man's bondage is irresolvable apart from Christ. For Scripture says those who commit sin are slaves to sin (John 8:34; 2 Peter 2:19). Thomas said, "Because, then, the devil had overcome man by inducing him to sin, man was delivered into the bondage of the devil." Therefore, "Christ's passion provided adequate, and more than adequate satisfaction for man's sin and debt, his passion was as it were the price of punishment by which we are freed from both obligations."[157]

Punishment is key to a Thomistic interpretation of the cross. By means of the Johannine concept of propitiation, Thomas presented the cross as a satisfaction of divine judgment against sin.[158] The vocabulary of propitiation was not pervasive in Thomas, but the concept was insinuated throughout Thomas's explanation of satisfaction's necessity. By satisfying the penalty for sin—the wrath of a just God—Christ's death acts as a price paid. Or to use scriptural language, Christ paid a *ransom*. "Satisfaction offered for oneself or for another resembles the price whereby one ransoms himself from sin and from punishment," said Thomas. "Now Christ offered satisfaction ... by giving the greatest of all things, namely himself, for us. For that reason, the passion of Christ is said to be a ransom.... Hence man is said to be redeemed by Christ's passion inasmuch as he was freed from sin by Christ, who satisfied for him by his suffering."[159]

To whom did Christ pay this ransom price? Thomas aligned himself with that patristic and medieval stream that said the ransom was paid to God himself. The sinner is not indebted to Satan, but the sinner is "principally indebted to

---

155. *ST* 3a. 48, 2.

156. Augustine, *De Trinitate* 4, 14. PL 42, 901. Quoted in Aquinas, *ST* 3a. 48, 4.

157. *ST* 3a. 48, 4. In 3a. 48, 5, Thomas expanded by mentioning both original sin and actual sin. Christ's sacrifice treats both. "Through Christ's passion however we are delivered not only from the sin of the entire human race both as regards the sin and the debt of punishment (for Christ paid the price of our ransom), but also from our own sins, provided we share in his passion by faith, love, and the sacraments of faith."

158. There is no question Thomas had divine judgment and wrath in view. See *ST* 3a. 48, 4, where Thomas surveyed Scripture's testimony to God's hatred toward sin and the remedy of an appeasement by means of the passion.

159. *ST* 3a. 48, 4.

God" because God is his "sovereign judge." As for Satan, he may enslave the sinner but only as executioner, not as sovereign judge. Thomas quoted Chrysostom to this effect and concluded, "As far as God was concerned, justice demanded the ransom of man; it did not require ransom to be paid to the devil." Therefore, Christ is "not said to have offered his blood, the price of our redemption, to the devil, but to God."[160]

If Christ's blood, by virtue of his humanity, was offered to God, not Satan, then the cross should be interpreted as the accomplished work of the entire Trinity. For God the Holy Trinity is the recipient of this debt payment. Using Aristotle's fourfold causality, Thomas explained, "Thus the payment and the price paid both pertain immediately to Christ in his capacity as man, but to the whole Trinity as to the first and remote cause, since Christ's very life belongs to the Trinity as to its first and remote cause, since Christ's very life belongs to the Trinity as to its first author, and it was the Trinity which inspired Christ the man to suffer for us." Thomas concluded, "Christ as man therefore, is, properly speaking, the immediate Redeemer, although the actual redemption can be attributed to the entire Trinity as to its first cause."[161]

If the whole Trinity is the First Cause, then Christ's passion must be the efficient cause. Thomas broke efficient causality into two categories: principal and instrumental. "God is the principal efficient cause of man's salvation. But since Christ's humanity is the instrument of his divinity, all Christ's acts and sufferings work instrumentally in virtue of his divinity in bringing about man's salvation." For that reason, the passion is the efficient cause of salvation, although this passion "derives from the Godhead an infinite power."[162]

Since the sacrifice of the passion is a true propitiation, as Romans 3:25 says, the ungodly have been reconciled to God, no longer his enemies but his friends, even his children. They have been liberated from the "guilt of punishment" because Christ has made satisfaction; they have been set free from sin's slavery because Christ's death is their redemption.[163] How that redemption is applied by the Spirit remains to be seen.

The Primary Mover and the Primacy of Grace

If Thomas was Augustinian in his affirmation of original sin and the necessity of satisfaction at the cross, undercurrents of propitiation included, then he was equally Augustinian in his emphasis on the *primacy* of divine grace. Thomas asked whether "man can will and do good without grace," and again, whether "man can love God above all things by his natural endowments alone without grace." In answer to both questions Thomas gave a negative response.[164] He joined

---

160. *ST* 3a. 48, 4.
161. *ST* 3a. 48, 5.
162. *ST* 3a. 48, 6.
163. *ST*, 3a. 48, 6.
164. *ST* 1a2ae. 109, 2 and 109, 3.

Augustine to condemn the Pelagian presumption that man does not need God's grace to meet the commandments.[165] A healing, assisting grace is necessary: "Human nature needs divine assistance" from the giver of grace himself.[166] In the "state of spoiled nature man cannot fulfil all the divine commandments without healing grace." Thomas found Augustine's appeal to the Holy Spirit faithful to the biblical description of the image of God: "It is the Spirit of grace who does this, so as to restore in us the image of God in which we were made by nature."[167]

Thomas believed the correlation between scriptural commentary and Aristotelian categories—categories that complement and clarify the biblical text—supports the primacy of grace. His defense of grace and its necessity was one of those correlating moments. Thomas enlisted the testimony of Jesus, who said, "No one can come to me unless the Father who sent me draws him" (John 6:44).[168] Earlier Thomas emphasized that God must be the "primary mover."[169] Now Thomas elaborated on Jesus' words by returning to this concept once more to showcase man's total reliance on God to move him, turn him, and convert him by his divine grace. Unless God is the primary mover, man cannot be renovated within.[170] When Thomas faced the question of human freedom, he did not forfeit God as primary mover but used the concept to explain the nature of human freedom. Even when man prepares himself "to receive the light of grace" he cannot do so "except by the gratuitous assistance of God moving him within." In other words, "Man's turning to God does indeed take place by his free decision; and in this sense man is enjoined to turn himself to God. But the free decision can only be turned to God when God turns it to himself, as it says in *Jeremiah, Turn me, and I shall be turned; for thou art the Lord my God*, and in *Lamentations, Turn us, O Lord, to thee, and we shall be turned*."[171] Yet again, Thomas returned to Aristotelian categories to underscore these Old Testaments texts: "For a man to be moved by God there is no need for any other prior motion, since God is the primary mover."[172]

With the preeminence of assisting and healing grace established—grace is required for "man to rise up"—Thomas put forward a type of *ordo salutis* that disclosed the sequence of salvation. Contrary to the Semi-Pelagianism of later Scholastics in the *via moderna* (see chapter 5), rising up is not something that

---

165. *De haeresibus* 88, PL 42, 47; *ST* 1a2ae. 109, 4.

166. *ST* 1a2ae. 109, 2.

167. *De spiritu et littera* 29, PL 44, 229 ; *ST* 1a2ae. 109, 4.

168. *ST* 1a2ae. 109, 6. Later Thomas appealed to John 15:5, "Without me you can do nothing." Thomas concluded, "Man can do nothing unless he is moved by God.... And so, when man is said to do what is within him, this is said to be in his power in so far as he is moved by God."

169. *ST* 1a2ae. 109, 2.

170. "And so it is only by way of God's converting him that man is turned to God.... It is clear that man cannot prepare himself to receive the light of grace except by the gratuitous assistance of God moving him within." *ST* 1a2ae. 109, 6.

171. See Jer. 31:18; Lam. 5:21. *ST* 1a2ae. 109, 6.

172. And again, "It is the part of man to prepare his mind, since he does this by his free decision; yet he does not do this without the assistance of God moving him and drawing him to himself, as was said." *ST* 1a2ae. 109, 6.

"precedes the illumination of grace," said Thomas. Rather, "when man tries to rise from sin by a free decision moved by God, he receives the light of justifying grace."[173] Insinuated is a type of order that prioritizes grace in light of the sinner's depravity and inability:

1. God infuses assisting, healing, illuminating grace. Grace is operative.
2. Moved by habitual grace, the sinner rises up and exercises meritorious acts of free choice. Grace is cooperative.
3. The remission of sins (infused gift of justifying grace).[174]

This *ordo* was explicit in the thought of Thomas when he said, "In this natural order, the infusion of grace comes first; next the movement of free choice directed to God; third the movement of free choice directed at sin; four the forgiveness of sins."[175] Augustine was uncompromising when he said that grace must be present from start to finish, and Thomas followed that *ordo:* grace "precedes us to heal us, it follows us to make us strong once healed; it precedes us to call us, it follows us to make us share in glory."[176]

When Thomas parsed grace, he distinguished between two types: operative and cooperative.[177] Operative grace is God's doing. He is the first and primary mover; the sinner is the one moved. "For the enactment or operation of some effect is not attributed to what undergoes movement but to the mover."[178] Operative grace is interior. God moves on the will so that it becomes good instead of evil. Likewise, he moves on the mind for the same effect.[179]

173. Thomas was adamant that none of this happens according to the light of nature. "Natural reason does not suffice as a source for that health which is found in man through justifying grace; its source is grace, which is taken away by sin. And so man cannot be restored by himself, but he needs the light of grace to be infused in him again, like a soul infused into a dead body when it is raised to life again." Aquinas, *ST,* 1a2ae. 109, 8.

174. *ST* 1a2ae. 109, 8. To nuance further, later Thomas distinguished between divine assistance and the habitual gift: "grace can be understood in two senses. Firstly, as the divine assistance by which God moves us to will and do good; secondly, as the habitual gift implanted in us by God. In both senses grace is satisfactorily divided into operative and cooperative grace" (1a2ae. 111, 2). Thomas then specified that assisting grace can move the soul toward good without preparation on man's part while God's gift in the form of habit can involve preparation. "In the first sense [God's gift in the form of a habit], some preparation for grace is demanded in advance, since no form can subsist except in matter disposed for it. But if we speak of grace in the sense of the assistance of God moving man towards the good, no preparation as it were anticipating the divine assistance is required on man's part; rather, whatever preparation there might be in man derives from the assistance of God moving the soul towards the good." Thomas stressed that even free choice is due to God's movement. "In this sense, that good movement of free choice itself, by which a man prepares to receive the gift of grace, is the action of a free choice moved by God; and in this respect man is said to prepare himself, according to the text of *Proverbs, It is the part of man to prepare his mind.* The principal agent is God moving the free choice; and in this sense it is said that *man's will is prepared by God,* and *man's steps are directed by the Lord*" (1a2ae. 112, 2).

175. *ST* 1a2ae. 113, 8. In 2a2ae. 6, 1. Thomas also said faith is infused by God.

176. *De Natura et Gratia* 31, PL 44, 264; quoted in *ST* 1a2ae. 111, 3.

177. "Grace, operative and cooperative, is the same grace, but it is distinguished by its different effects," Thomas qualified. *ST* 1a2ae. 111, 2. Later he used the categories of prevenient and subsequent (1a2ae. 111, 3). In other words, Thomas does not think grace is divided, but he merely desires to contemplate grace from our human vantage point in different ways. See Davies, *The Thought of Thomas Aquinas,* 269.

178. *ST* 1a2ae. 111, 2.

179. "There is first the interior act of the will; and as regards this act, the will behaves as moved and God

Cooperative grace differs: "In that effect in which our mind is both a mover and is moved, the operation is attributed not only to God but also to the soul." Cooperative grace, therefore, involves an external component.[180] Thomas appealed to Augustine, who said, "It is by his operation that we will; but once we will, it is by his cooperation with us that we bring our action to completion."[181]

Augustine's emphasis on *God's cooperation with us* means Thomas's distinction between operative and cooperative should not be caricatured as if the former is God's initiation and the latter is man's initiation. Aquinas "does not even think that the co-operation involved in co-operating grace is co-operation on the part of the one who has grace. For him, co-operative grace is a matter of God co-operating with us," says Brian Davies.[182]

Thomas should not be confused with Louis de Molina in the sixteenth century, who said grace is "merely a help for us to do what we finally do on our own." Such a position, warns Davies, "is emphatically not Aquinas's position" since his "line is that grace is wholly the work of God." The difference is plain in the divergent ways Thomas and Molina define free will. For Molina free will is "something permitted by God but not caused by him." For Thomas, if God is the first mover, then the will of man cannot be autonomous, as if it could operate apart from God's causation. "Aquinas does not think of human freedom as a case of God leaving us alone to get on with things. For him, my actions are caused by God without ceasing to be free. And this, he says, is the case when grace is present. In his view, grace is the result of God's action in me drawing me to himself. It is not just a help to my acting on my own." Davies concludes, "It is what there is when I am wholly the end product of what God is doing. And, for this reason, Aquinas insists that *only* God is the cause of grace."[183] Unless God wills, man's will can do nothing, and when man's will does operate, God's grace alone is credited.

Much later in the *Summa* Thomas followed through on this commitment by also insisting that God must be the cause of faith itself. Over against Pelagianism, "since in assenting to the things of faith a person is raised above his own nature, he has this assent from a supernatural source influencing him." That supernatural source, of course, is God, which explains why Thomas said the "assent of faith" must have God as its cause, who moves "us inwardly through grace."[184]

Previously, Thomas attributed the notion of habit to original sin. Now, to counter its debilitating effects, he introduced habitual gift or the "gift of habitual

---

as mover, especially when a will which before had willed evil begins to will the good. And so, when God moves the human mind to this act, grace is called operative." *ST* 1a2ae. 111, 2.

180. "And since for this act too God helps us, both by confirming the will within so that it might achieve its act and by providing the means of action without, grace is called cooperative in respect of this act." *ST* 1a2ae. 111, 2.

181. *ST* 1a2ae. 111, 2; quoting Augustine, *De Gratia et Libero Arbitrio* 17, PL 44, 901.

182. Davies, *The Thought of Thomas Aquinas*, 270. Davies has in view Molina's *Concordia liberi arbitrii cum gratiae donis, divina praescientia, praedestinatione et reprobation* (1588).

183. Davies, *The Thought of Thomas Aquinas*, 267 (cf. 268).

184. *ST* 2a2ae. 6, 1. Cf. Davies, *The Thought of Thomas Aquinas*, 283.

grace."[185] Habitual grace has a twofold effect: being and activity. Thomas used the illustration of heat. An object must first heat up to warm up its surroundings. "Thus habitual grace, inasmuch as it heals or justifies the soul, or makes it pleasing to God, is called operative; but inasmuch as it is the principle of meritorious action, which proceeds from free choice as well, it is called cooperative."[186] Cooperative grace is critical in order for the believer to become righteous. "God does not justify us without us, since while we are being justified, we consent to God's justice by a movement of free choice." And yet Thomas qualified that even our choice is due to grace. "But that movement is not the cause but the effect of grace. Thus the whole operation belongs to grace."[187] Not the cause but the effect—this basic philosophical distinction serves to protect the gratuity of grace itself. When coupled with the Psalms—"The Lord will give grace and glory"—no one can point to self as the cause of grace. "No being can act beyond the limits of its specific nature, since the cause must always be of a higher potency than its effect. Now the fit of grace surpasses every capacity of created nature, since it is nothing other than a certain participation in the divine nature, which surpasses every other nature. And so it is impossible that a creature should cause grace."[188] For Thomas, the concept of participation framed his understanding of God as Savior as much as it informed his affirmation of God as Creator.

Later it would be plain that Thomas's position was misrepresented to Luther by Gabriel Biel, and consequently Luther thought ill of the Scholastics, Thomas Aquinas included. Biel misinterpreted Thomas, as if Thomas taught no differently than Biel himself, who has been labeled Semi-Pelagian by some and Pelagian by others. Biel's position will be explored in chapter 5, but Biel believed that if man does what he can—does his best—God will then infuse him with grace. As evident already, Biel and the *via moderna* dispensed with the primacy of grace so prominent in Thomas by conditioning assisting grace on man's works. Yet what makes Biel's misrepresentation of Thomas even more disconcerting is this irony: Thomas addressed "doing what one can" long before Biel and was emphatic in his outright rejection of such a position. For example, Thomas raised the question, "Is grace necessarily given to someone who prepares himself for grace or does what he can?" But a "meritorious act of free choice," said Thomas in reply, is "already informed by grace."[189]

Gabriel Biel should not have drawn from the tradition of Thomas, who was no Semi-Pelagian. Yet Thomas, like Augustine before him, did think

---

185. *ST* 1a2ae. 109, 9. Later Thomas defined grace as a quality in the soul, identifying God as the efficient cause. See 1a2ae. 110, 1 and 2.

186. *ST* 1a2ae. 111, 2. Elsewhere Thomas said a "habitual gift is infused by God into the soul." "All the more, then, does he infuse supernatural forms or qualities into those whom he moves towards obtaining an eternal, supernatural good, whereby they may be moved by him sweetly and promptly towards obtaining the eternal good. Thus the gift of grace is a kind of quality" (1a2ae. 110, 2).

187. *ST* 1a2ae. 111, 2. Although Thomas liked to attribute everything to grace by utilizing the Johannine concept of love as well. He wrote, "What is pleasing to God in man is caused by the divine love" (1a2ae. 110, 2.).

188. *ST* 1a2ae. 112, 1. Thomas was quoting Psalm 83 (84):12.

189. *ST* 1a2ae. 112, 3.

justification was transformative. Although the Reformers prized Augustine's (and by default Thomas's) bulwark for the primacy of grace, nevertheless, it was a transformative definition of justification (and merit's role to that end) that left the Reformers discontent due in large part to their distinction between justification and sanctification.

Justification and Charity

To be accurate, forensic elements are not absent from Thomas's doctrine of justification.[190] At the start, he looked to Romans 3:24 and concluded that justification is the forgiveness of sins, reconciliation with God.[191] Justification means the nonimputation of sin, which stems from nothing but the love of God.[192] In short, "justification of the unrighteous takes place when God moves man to justice; for it is he *who justifies the unrighteous* [Rom. 4:5]."

How God moves the sinner to justice, however, does require justification to be transformative and sanative, that is, a moral renewal within, not merely a forensic declaration from without. God "infuses the gift of justifying grace in such a way that at the same time he also moves the free choice to accept the gift of grace," said Thomas. There is a "certain *transformation* of the soul when justifying grace is infused into it."[193] Since justification involves transformation by means of infusion, faith must be defined as a movement that is "informed by charity." In the "justification of the unrighteous, there is also a movement of charity together with the movement of faith."[194] What requirements, then, must be met for God to justify the unrighteous? Thomas listed four:

1. Infusion of grace
2. Movement of free choice directed toward God by faith
3. A movement of free choice directed toward sin
4. The forgiveness of sin[195]

On one hand, creating within the unrighteous a disposition necessary for God to infuse that first grace into the soul may be accomplished either in an instant or over time, "gradually and by successive stages." On the other hand, justification itself is instantaneous.[196] Thomas wrapped these requirements for justification within his causal paradigm. Movement entails a cause and effect. Since infused grace must be prior to the movement of the will, grace is always the cause, free choice the effect.[197]

---

190. I am not alone in this observation. See Needham, "The Evolution of Justification," 587–622.
191. Our attention is on his *Summa Theologiae*, but also consult *Commentary on Romans*, 1.2–3, 6, 2.2–3, 3.2, 4.1–2; 5.1–6; 6.1; 8.6, 9.2–3.
192. *ST* 1a2ae. 113, 2.
193. *ST*, 1a2ae. 113, 3. Emphasis added.
194. *ST* 1a2ae. 113, 4.
195. *ST* 1a2ae. 113, 6. Thomas called numbers 2 and 3 a "double movement" (1a2ae. 113, 5).
196. *ST* 1a2ae. 113, 7.
197. *ST* 1a2ae. 113, 8.

YOUNG VERSUS SEASONED THOMAS AQUINAS

Thomas was quite aware that the early Augustine thought that the "commencement of faith was due to us," and Thomas himself seemed to see his own story as through a mirror. For the young Thomas, too, thought something similar. But like Augustine, Thomas abandoned this way of thinking and elevated grace to the seat of primacy. Whether Augustine or Thomas, the most mature theologians of the church considered retractions a sign of humility, convinced the best theologians were always in the process of maturing (see Aquinas, *ST* 1a2ae. 114, 5).

Where did Thomas locate merit in this fourfold order? His answer returns the reader to his definition of grace. With Romans 11:6 in view—"If it is by grace, it is no longer on the basis of works"—Thomas defined grace as a "gratuitous gift." Sin is an impediment, one "which prevents him from meriting grace." Thomas said without apology, "Thus it is clear that no one can merit the first grace for himself." Faith, therefore, "cannot merit the first grace."[198] Thomas sounded not all that different, on this score, from Luther after him.

But what about the sinner who has received the first grace? Although Thomas did affirm merit—which put him at odds with the Reformers—he was adamant such merit cannot come before grace, nor can it operate independently of grace. "By his will man does perform works meriting eternal life; but, as Augustine said . . . for this there is need that man's will should be prepared by God through grace."[199] Infused with grace, man does exercise his will, yet Thomas insisted that every "good work performed by man proceeds from the first grace as principle and source."[200] A meritorious work can be considered from two perspectives: as far as a work of merit "proceeds from free choice"—that is, "considered in its substance"—there "can be no equivalence, because of the greatest of inequality."[201] "But if we consider the meritorious work so far as it proceeds from the grace of the Holy Spirit, then it is meritorious of eternal life by equivalence." Citing John 4:14, Thomas appealed to Jesus' words to the Samaritan woman when he claimed that the water he gives wells up into life everlasting. The "value of the merit is assessed by the power of the Holy Spirit moving us to eternal life," and the "price of the work is assessed by the worth of grace, by which man, having

---

198. "Man is justified by faith, therefore, not as though by believing he merits justification, but in the sense that he believes while he is being justified; because, as was said above, the movement of faith is required for the justification of the unrighteous." *ST* 1a2ae. 114, 5.

199. *ST* 1a2ae. 109, 6.

200. *ST,* 1a2ae. 114, 5.

201. "But there exists a fitness, on account of a kind of proportionate equality; for it seems fit that God should make return, in proportion to the excellence of his power, to a man who works in the degree of his own power." *ST* 1a2ae. 114, 3.

become a sharer in the divine nature, is adopted as a son of God, someone to whom the inheritance is owed by the very right of adoption" (Rom. 8:17).[202]

If the merit that leads to eternal life does not occur outside the movement of the Holy Spirit, then neither should it be defined apart from charity itself, which Thomas considered merit's principal source. The "merit of eternal life belongs primarily to charity, and only secondarily to the other virtues, inasmuch as their acts are directed by charity." Faith, therefore, is "meritorious only if faith *works through love*, as it says in *Galatians* [5:6]." That explains why Paul could say that he profited nothing—even if his own body was sacrificed to the flames—if he had not charity (1 Cor. 13:3). For the "acts of fortitude and endurance" cannot be "meritorious unless one performs them out of love."[203]

RECONSIDERING THE RELATIONSHIP BETWEEN SCHOLASTICISM AND THE REFORMATION

This chapter has explored but a small measure of Thomas's *Summa*. Next to the sacraments, Thomas's treatment of soteriology—predestination and justification—was a major *loci* under debate during the Reformation. However, the evidence reveals that an "oppositional narrative" cannot work. Aspects of Thomas's doctrine of justification—for example, infused righteousness—clashed with the Reformers. Still, the broader contours of Thomas's soteriology were Augustinian, which the Reformers retrieved over against the *via moderna*. Even stronger continuity existed between Thomas and the Reformers in the domain of the atonement. Thomas departed from ransom theories to defend the atonement as a satisfaction with overtones of propitiation, an interpretation of the cross the Reformers later regurgitated and considered essential, even definitive, for their reforming program.

Moreover, as the next chapter will reveal, it was not high medieval Scholastics like Thomas so much as late medieval Scholastics like Ockham and Biel who shifted away from Augustinian soteriology, as is plain in Luther's *Disputation against Scholastic Theology* (see chapter 8). When Thomas's treatment of predestination is set side by side with Luther's *Bondage of the Will* or Calvin's *Institutes* or Calvin's polemical tracts against contemporaries like Bolsec and Pighius (see chapters 14–15), a striking similarity emerges between the Reformers and Thomas. That similarity is due to the Augustinianism they hold in common.[204]

This nuance can be labeled Thomistic Augustinianism and should be combined with our earlier discovery—the majority of the *Summa Theologiae* and *Summa Contra Gentiles* is presenting classic Nicene and Chalcedonian

---

202. As for the Spirit, he is "the sufficient cause of eternal life, who dwells in man; and so he is called *the pledge of our inheritance*" (2 Cor. 1:22). *ST* 1a2ae. 114, 3.

203. *ST* 1a2ae. 114, 4.

204. "If one compares Calvin's doctrine of predestination with the teaching of Thomas Aquinas and Duns Scotus, one will undoubtedly be impressed by how close they were to each other, in large measure because each remained close to Augustine." Steinmetz, "Scholastic Calvin," 27.

orthodoxy. That combination is revealing: the Reformers had far more in common with "sounder" Scholasticism than they had in opposition—in fact, the Reformers themselves used this language of "sounder" to speak of Scholastics like Thomas. The "oppositional narrative" not only fails to read Thomas as an Augustinian, but it also fails to read Thomas as orthodox. This orthodox foundation was articulated, tabulated, and defended by the church fathers and codified in their creeds and councils, but it was protracted, perpetuated, and extended with prodigious, systematic precision and clarity by Thomas. Therefore, when the Reformers assumed an orthodox doctrinal baseline, they likewise assumed their continuity not only with the patristic pedigree but with the Scholastic preservation of that orthodox tradition, a preservation indebted in large part to Thomas.[205]

Due to the oppositional narrative, it is unusual—even considered comical—to label Luther or Calvin "Scholastic." Yet this assumption relies on an antithesis: the Reformation represented a departure from Scholasticism. The return of Scholasticism among the Reformed Orthodox of the seventeenth century, so the argument goes, was a betrayal of the sixteenth-century fathers. Thus, the Reformers would have lamented the return to Thomism by their sixteenth and seventeenth century heirs.[206]

That assumption, however, has been challenged as Reformation scholarship has further investigated the connection between Scholasticism and the Reformation. Due to the research of historians such as Armand LaVallee, Willem van Asselt, David Steinmetz, and Richard Muller, a slow and steady push against the oppositional narrative is now apparent. Reconsidering the relationship has even motivated these scholars to look at a figure like Calvin, for instance, and conclude that it is now appropriate to use a label like "Scholastic Calvin."[207] Some have done the same with Peter Martyr Vermigli. And, bold as it

---

205. They are indebted in part, but not exclusively, for we should not overlook the influence of others like Lombard whose *Sentences* were the textbook for many Reformers in the universities. Nevertheless, Aquinas's reputation grew with time, as is plain with his retrieval by Reformed Scholastics and eventually the 1879 encyclical *Aeterni Patris*.

206. This argument is assumed in many institutions today, especially evangelical institutions, and it is prevalent in the church. It can also be seen in academic treatments. For an example, see Spykman, *Reformation Theology*. He blamed the "pseudo-Protestant" return to Scholasticism in the seventeenth century on its preoccupation with responding to Rome. "As a result, much of the heritage regained in the sixteenth century was lost during subsequent centuries. Protestant theology came under heavy pressure from a resurgent Thomism." He went on to say that the Reformed Scholastics abandoned the methods and theology of Luther and Calvin. "As a result, instead of growth, stagnation set in" (24). From a historical point of view, Spykman not only ignored the debt the sixteenth-century Reformers owed to the best of medieval Scholasticism, but he failed to identify the type of Scholasticism they were really countering, namely, the late medieval variety encapsulated by the *via moderna*. Spykman also neglected to observe how different polemical challenges (e.g., Socinianism) might explain why seventeenth-century Protestant Scholastics turned to the resources of medieval Scholasticism, specifically Thomism. Assaults on the classical doctrine of God, for instance, required such a retrieval, whereas the Reformers had the luxury of assuming a theology proper in continuity with the past. Lastly Spykman couldn't prove "stagnation" was the product of either medieval or Protestant Scholasticism. Historians have been keen to point out the opposite, noting the renewal that resulted from this method.

207. Steinmetz, "Scholastic Calvin," 26. Cf. Muller, *Unaccommodated Calvin*.

may seem, some have even challenged the "anti-Thomism" reading of Luther. To understand why, the following will begin with Luther, transition to Bucer and Zanchi, then Calvin and Vermigli, but then conclude with a more topical outlook, using natural theology and the fourfold sense of Scripture as further case studies. We will conclude by observing Reformed Scholasticism's discernable debt to Thomas.

Luther, Anti-Thomist? Dangerously Misleading

Chapter 5 will devote attention to the last of the Scholastics, Gabriel Biel. He is the late medieval theologian Luther read as a student and then targeted in his *Disputation against Scholastic Theology* (1517).[208] Since Biel's soteriology was built on the foundation Ockham laid, Luther naturally took aim at Ockham as well in his *Disputation*. Chapter 5 will underline this critical point: despite Luther's sporadic, sweeping use of a word like *Scholastic* or even *Thomist*, the young Luther had specific late medieval Scholastics in view (Ockham, Biel), not necessarily the entire Scholastic tradition. To elaborate, the late medieval Scholastics that defined the *via moderna* shifted from the Augustinian soteriology of Scholastics in the High Middle Ages like Anselm and Thomas Aquinas, among others. This shift, and its betrayal of Augustinian soteriology, was one of the major factors that sparked the German Reformation.

Historians have little reason to believe Luther had firsthand acquaintance with the writings of Thomas Aquinas.[209] In a breakthrough study, John Farthing has systematically examined Gabriel Biel's use of Thomas Aquinas.[210] The significance

---

208. *LW* 31:2–16.

209. Steinmetz gave a detailed account of historians who debated Luther's knowledge of Thomas. "Some historians, particularly Hennig and Grane, have pointed out the significance for Luther of the clash in 1518–1519 with such Thomist defenders of the Roman Church as Sylvester Prierias (1456–1523) and Thomas de Vio Cardinal Cajetan (1468–1534). Hennig in particular argued that Luther had met the theology of Thomas Aquinas in Cardinal Cajetan, its best and most authoritative interpreter, and rejected it. In his own day, however, Cajetan was opposed by Bartholomew Spina and Ambrosius Catherinus, both avowed Thomists, who, unlike Hennig, thought that Cajetan had strayed from the path of authentic Thomism." In addition, even historians debate Cajetan's reliability as a Thomist. "Recent historians have also been divided over the role of Cajetan as an interpreter of Thomas. Scheeben, Mandonnet, Limbourg, Grabmann, and Caro have defended the reliability of Cajetan's reading of Thomas, while Gilson, Maurer, Pesch, McSorley, Jenkins, and Janz have expressed more or less serious reservations. Janz, for example, believes that Luther could not have heard the authentic voice of Thomas on grace and free will through Cardinal Cajetan, who diverged significantly from Thomas in his more optimistic assessment of the capacities of fallen human nature. On those questions, John Capreolus was closer to the original spirit and intention of St. Thomas than was Cajetan." One might object that Luther could have received an accurate presentation of Thomism at Wittenberg under Martin Pollich of Mellerstadt (d. 1513) and Andreas Bodenstein of Carlstadt (1480–1541). But Steinmetz countered with proper chronology: "We should not overlook the fact that Luther's understanding of Thomistic theology had already been influenced by the interpretation given to Thomas in Occamist theology [as channeled through Biel and Pierre d'Ailly]. . . . Whatever Luther owed to his colleagues and his enemies, it was in the school of William Ockham and not in the school of John Capreolus or Cardinal Cajetan that he first encountered the theology of Thomas Aquinas." Steinmetz, "Luther among the Anti-Thomists," 47–48. The litany of disagreeable historians is surveyed in Janz, *Luther and Late Medieval Thomism*, 123–25.

210. Consider book 2 of Biel's *Epithome et collectorium ex Occamo circa quatuor sententiarum libros*, as well as Biel's *Canonis misse expositio*, I–V. Also consult Biel's *Collectorium circa quatuor libros Sententiarum*, I, II, III, IV-1, IV-2.

of Farthing's conclusion cannot be overstated: although Biel gave an accurate representation of Thomas on a range of theological topics, on the subjects of sin, grace, and justification Biel misrepresented Thomas in fundamental ways, as if Thomas embodied a soteriology no different from Biel and the *via moderna.* The young Luther assumed Biel's representation of Thomas was accurate, which explains in part why Luther did not hold Thomas or Thomism in high estimation. As far as justification is concerned, Luther did not know the real Thomas. Instead of representing Thomas as the Augustinian he was in matters of nature and grace, Biel passed down a Thomas who sounded as Semi-Pelagian as himself.

Farthing's study is far too intensive and expansive to capture here.[211] However, his findings are invaluable, even indispensable to recognizing Luther's misperception of Thomas due to Gabriel Biel. Consider five *loci:*

FIVE THOMISTIC *LOCI* MISREPRESENTED BY GABRIEL BIEL

Free Will	
Misrepresents Thomas Biel thinks Thomas sees a certain motion of the human will as a requisite predisposition for the infusion of grace.	*Truth* What he [Biel] fails to note is Thomas's conception of the will itself as being disposed or prepared by the prior operation of grace.
Need for Predisposing Grace	
Misrepresents Thomas Biel suggests that Thomas reduces the help that one needs in order to be able to prepare oneself for grace to nothing more than the *concursus generalis* by which the Prime Mover is ultimately involved in every creaturely act. . . . Biel—ignoring the critical distinction between habitual grace and special gratuitous help—makes use of Thomas's language as a pretext for claiming that Thomas sees no need at all of a special gift of predisposing grace.	*Truth* Such a position is excluded by Thomas's insistence that to prepare oneself for grace is to be turned toward God, which happens only *as a result* of God's inner work in the sinner's faculty of free choice (Jeremiah 31.18; Lamentations 5.21). . . . [Thomas] insists that the sinner depends upon God to provide not only the "habitual gift" (corresponding to Biel's *gratia infusa)* but also the inner movement by which his soul is prepared to receive it.
Sin	
Misrepresents Thomas Overlooked by Biel	*Truth* Biel overlooks Thomas's emphasis on the effect of sin as an impediment that prevents the sinner from meriting an eternal reward.

---

211. The following points (and wording) can be located in Farthing, *Thomas Aquinas and Gabriel Biel,* 151–80. Other than the Latin, emphasis is added.

Merit	
Misrepresents Thomas Biel thinks "Thomas agrees with him in allowing that the sinner can merit grace *de congruo.* . . . 'By doing what in him lies' (*faciendo quod in se est*) the sinner merits grace *de congruo. . .* the grace by which he is justified."	*Truth* Thomas categorically denies . . . that the first grace can be merited. . . . There can be no merit at all on the part of one in whom sanctifying grace is not already operative. . . . When Thomas speaks of congruity in connection with "man's meritorious work" . . . he is not—as Biel supposes—talking about the works performed while one is still in a state of mortal sin. . . . Thomas makes it abundantly clear that these purely natural faculties are insufficient, apart from the healing influence of grace, to make the sinner capable of meriting anything at all from God.
Infused Grace and Love	
Misrepresents Thomas Biel teaches that the *viator* may receive grace—no longer healing so much as decorative or, at most, invigorating— only on the condition that he love God above all things *ex puris naturalibus.*	*Truth* Biel, of course, reverses the logical priority observed in Thomas's teaching that one loves God only on the condition that he first receive the gift of healing (enabling) grace.

These five *loci* are but a few of the many ways Biel unwittingly misrepresented Thomas to Luther.[212] Unfortunately, the stakes were high; Biel had misrepresented Thomas to Luther on a central issue, the very issue over which the Reformation occurred: justification. Historical theology gone wrong was never so costly than when Biel gave Luther the impression that the Scholastics believed sinners could do their best and put forward the initial step to merit their own justification.[213] No wonder Luther's *Disputation against Scholastic Theology* reacted against Thomism. Luther was Augustinian, but judging by Biel's misrepresentation, Thomas appeared Pelagian at worst or Semi-Pelagian at best. The irony

---

212. Other historians of the Reformation have come to identical conclusions as Farthing. For example, David Steinmetz wrote, "It is simply not true [as Biel thinks] that Thomas teaches that sinners can merit the grace of justification, not even by merits of congruity. While Biel, following the Franciscan tradition in theology, makes a temporal distinction between merits of congruity (which rest on the generosity of God) and merits of condignity (with rest on the inherent worth of the agent's activity), *Thomas does not.*" Steinmetz reached a startling but accurate conclusion: "The general effect of Biel's interpretation is to move Thomas in a more Pelagian, even in a more voluntaristic direction, and away from the more Augustinian, more ontological framework in which he properly belongs." Steinmetz, "Luther among the Anti-Thomists," 55.

213. "Again the effect of this interpretation is to associate Thomas—wrongly, as it turns out—with certain semi-Pelagian tendencies in Biel's view of how the sinner is actively involved in meriting his own justification." Farthing, *Thomas Aquinas and Gabriel Biel*, 166 (cf. 175). Should Biel bear all the blame? Probably not. A look at Cajetan produces similar results: a misrepresentation of Thomas in Semi-Pelagian terms (180).

is this: when Luther reacted against the Thomists in favor of Augustinianism instead, Luther was actually positioning himself closer to *true* Thomism. If only Luther had known.[214]

Some historians think the Reformation never would have happened if Luther would have read the real Thomas for himself.[215] If Luther only knew that the Thomas channeled through Biel's Semi-Pelagian paradigm was a misrepresentation, Luther might have been satisfied with a retrieval of Thomas.[216] Could it be the case that knowledge of Thomas, predominantly on predestination, atonement, and grace, might have buttressed the best in Luther's reaction to the *via moderna*, keeping Luther from swinging the pendulum to the other extreme (i.e., the heresy of a Protestant view)?

Resting historical interpretation—especially the entire genesis of the Reformation—on hypotheticals can result in a shaky foundation, especially when the rapidly evolving theology and fluctuating personality of a Martin Luther is in consideration. In one sense, this hypothetical will remain forever a mystery. In another sense, the question may not be as hypothetical as it seems. Thomas was, after all, a committed Augustinian in much of his theology. As seen already, Thomas's articulation of predestination, the atonement, and grace was laced with Augustinian overtones. However much Luther appreciated and retrieved Augustine, he may have done the same with Thomas.

Nevertheless, it may be a step too far to assume knowledge of Thomas would have prevented the Reformation, particularly the Reformation as a terrible misfortune. First, young Luther did have knowledge of Augustine, yet Augustine did not stop but only enhanced Luther's zeal for reform. The same might be said of Thomas. Second, even if Luther had a more accurate perception of Thomas on predestination and *sola gratia*, for instance, Luther still would have taken issue with Thomas's transformative rather than forensic view of justification, much as Luther took issue with Augustine. Luther might have found a medieval ally in Thomas due to the latter's emphasis on the primacy of grace, but it is unlikely Luther would have adopted Thomas wholesale. As much as Luther praised and credited Augustine, Luther still acknowledged that Augustine's *sola gratia* theology lacked a forensic account of justification that made way for imputed righteousness (as opposed to infused righteousness). The same reaction to Thomas from Martin Luther is most probable. As significant as an Augustinian view of predestination and grace may have been, the Reformation hinged on further soteriological advancement. After all, numerous theologians in the sixteenth century considered themselves committed Augustinians but did not convert to

---

214. Biel, however, was not the only one who misrepresented Thomas Aquinas to Luther. Luther's colleague Andreas Karlstadt did as well. See Janz, *Luther and Late Medieval Thomism*, 111–22.

215. E.g., Lortz, *Die Reformation in Deutschland*. The question was asked by Steinmetz, "Luther among the Anti-Thomists," 47.

216. Steinmetz was not convinced Luther went to the source and read Thomas himself, at least not at any length nor without the filter of Ockham and Biel. *Luther in Context*, 47–48.

the Reformation (Luther's own Staupitz was one of them). Furthermore, even aside from varieties of Scholastic soteriology, Rome's ecclesiology also posed a conflict that made the Reformation inevitable (see chapter 17). Luther still would have taken issue with Thomas on transubstantiation or Rome's papal polity, for example.

All that said, the hypothetical is curious, perhaps even suspicious, but not to be easily dismissed. The contrast between an Augustinian like Thomas and a Semi-Pelagian like Biel is stark. A young Luther aware of the real Thomas might have reacted to Biel and Ockham *but with the support of Thomism*. Lortz thinks that knowledge would have appeased Luther's restless anxiety. Yet it is also possible that knowledge might have granted Luther more grist for the protesting mill. If so, the monk who set the church aflame with controversy would not only have been an Augustinian but a Thomist. Considering the evidence, the Luther that protested the *via moderna* and its Semi-Pelagian soteriology was more of a Thomist than he ever knew.

With Luther in sight, one final question remains: if Luther's real target in 1517 was late medieval soteriological departures from the core of Scholasticism's Augustinianism (e.g., Anselm, Thomas), then was Luther himself indebted to this core? Despite Luther's rhetoric against "Scholastics," the evidence shows (1) his target was typically a specific strand of the Scholastics (*via moderna*) and (2) he was indebted to the Scholastics even after his famous *Disputation against Scholastic Theology*. Luther used numerous Scholastic distinctions across his polemics but also in his positive construction of theology, which makes the historian wonder whether Luther returned to Scholasticism in some sense. With Luther's appropriation of Scholastic methods in view, did Luther ever leave Scholasticism in its entirety? However unwitting Luther may have been, perhaps the Wittenberg Reformer—in all his vehemence against "Scholastic doctors"—was actually a practitioner of his own Scholastic approach.

That conclusion may seem outrageous—Luther's rhetoric could be rancorous —until one considers the plethora of ways Luther relied on Scholasticism after 1517.

- Luther used the Scholastic hierarchy of authority (Scripture, patristics, Scholastics) even in his polemic against Scholastics (see Luther's *Sermon on Indulgences and Grace*).
- Luther depended on an Ockhamist evaluation of transubstantiation as mediated through Pierre d'Ailly (see Luther's *Babylonian Captivity of the Church*).
- Luther relied on key Scholastic distinctions even for his soteriology—grace and gift; suffering but victorious (see *Against Latomus*).
- Luther borrowed from Aristotle and the Scholastic use of Aristotle to defend the Christian as simultaneously just and a sinner (see his *Lectures on Romans*).

- Luther borrowed from Aristotle, as well as the Scholastic use of Aristotle, to argue for an external, alien righteousness that is then given to the sinner (see Luther's 1538 *Lectures on the Psalms*).
- Luther appropriated the Scholastic differentiation between *necessitas coactionis* and *necessitas immutabilitatis* in his definition of free will against Erasmus (see *Bondage of the Will*).[217]

We have by no means exhausted the examples of medieval, even Scholastic reliance and influence. For example, consider Luther's Christology on two fronts. First, twentieth-century theologians—including modern Lutherans like Jürgen Moltmann—assumed that Luther's rhetoric in support of a *theology of the cross* over against a *theology of glory* must mean the Reformer dispensed with the metaphysic of the church fathers and the Scholastics.[218] For example, since Luther believed Christ was revelation's point of departure, Luther did not limit Christ's suffering to his humanity but considered it essential for his divinity. Naturally, Luther must have abandoned classical theology's adherence to divine impassibility, which Luther believed was responsible for creating theologians of glory during Scholasticism. However, a deeper investigation conveys the opposite conclusion: Luther did not see his commitment to God's impassibility— and a classical doctrine of God—as irreconcilable but instrumental both to his affirmation of an incorruptible God and the righteousness God gives so freely in the gospel of his Son. Luther was not rescuing the church from the corrupting influence of Hellenism, an interpretation David Luy calls the divergence thesis. Rather, Luther adhered to a Chalcedonian Christology that utilized the best concepts of philosophy to defend orthodoxy (including the Platonism of Aristotle). Like Chalcedon, Luther believed the person of the Son is the "proper referent for all Christological predicates, but the divine nature (per se) does not and, indeed, cannot suffer." Luther was self-consciously in agreement with certain Scholastics who said the person of the Son is the referent for incarnational suffering, but only by virtue of assuming a human nature, thereby precluding suffering in his divine nature.[219] Luther's belief in impassibility means the diver-

---

217. I am summarizing Bagchi's findings: "Sic Et Non: Luther and Scholasticism," 11–14. For Luther's use of d'Ailly, see *WA* 6:508–12 (*LW* 36:28–35). For Luther's use of soteriological distinctions, see *WA* 8:88.3–6 (*LW* 32:201); *WA* 8:107.38–40 (*LW* 32:229). For Luther's use of Aristotle to defend the Christian as just and a sinner, see *WA* 56:441.24–442.14 (*LW* 25:433). For Luther's use of Aristotle for alien righteousness, see *WA* 30:518.7. Bagchi's observation on Luther and the Eucharist is important. Others have investigated further. For example, Cross says, "In his [Luther's] anxiety to distance himself from certain Scholastic doctrines—in particular transubstantiation . . . Luther seems at first sight to reject the nominalist two-name theory of predication, according to which a necessary condition for the truth of a predication is that subject and predicate supposit for the same thing. As we shall see, this is not in fact his considered view. What he objects to, as I shall show, is the argument from the two-name theory to transubstantiation. As he makes abundantly clear, he believes that the two-name theory . . . supports rather than undermines both his own Eucharistic theology and his Christology." Cross, *Communicatio Idiomatum*, 40.

218. Moltmann, *The Crucified God*, 65–75.

219. *LW* 22:327–328. Or as Luy says, Christ suffers "but only on account of the human nature, which he assumes." Luy, *Dominus Mortis*, 228. Other examples related to his Christology could be accentuated. For

gence thesis and its appeal to Luther for a communication of attributes from the divine to the human nature should be reconsidered, which leads to a second example.

Second, a common assumption is that Luther departed from medieval Christology and instead proposed an innovative *communicatio idiomatum*, as if the divine attributes were mixed with and absorbed by the human nature of Christ. However, further research shows that such a Christology was associated with a colleague of Luther's named Johannes Brenz instead (see chapter 10). In other words, Brenz added to Luther's Christology the idea that divine attributes can be predicated to the human nature of Christ for the sake of furthering the Lutheran understanding of the Eucharist. Brenz was far more innovative while Luther's methods remained entrenched in medieval categories. As Richard Cross says, "Luther's Christology is in most respects quite Medieval.... Luther typically employs the technical apparatus of Scholasticism—particularly a version of Ockhamist semantics—to explicate Christological problems.... Luther gives a far more Scholastic account of the metaphysics and semantics of the hypostatic union than is generally supposed. The way in which he frames his questions, and the way in which he answers them, is thoroughly Scholastic both in form and content."[220]

To be sure, at times Luther truly thought he was refuting a Scholastic like Thomas Aquinas, when in truth he misunderstood the Scholastic. His *Bondage of the Will* is a case in point. With no little irony, Luther criticized distinctions like necessity of consequence versus necessity of consequent or necessity of force versus necessity of immutability. "It has been pointed out that Luther misunderstood both these distinctions, and that in fact his own position was closer to that of Aquinas, which he believed he was rejecting."[221] And yet at other points in *Bondage of the Will*, Luther was aware that he was in agreement with Scholastic categories. "Luther's use of the scholastic method as an antidote to scholastic theology was meant seriously, not ironically."[222] For example, Luther decried Scotus, Ockham, and Biel but did so by using their own methods of disputation and theses for debate.

In summary, the complex continuity-discontinuity dynamic between Luther and Scholasticism should not be oversimplified. Still, it is fair enough

---

instance, Luther reacted against the soteriological nominalism of Ockham and the *via moderna*, yet Luther's Christology was indebted to Ockhamist methods. Furthermore, Theodor Dieter has shown that Luther still presupposed *some* tenets of nominalism, expressing not only negative but also positive evaluations. Dieter, "Luther as Late Medieval Theologian," 31–48.

220. "Luther, for example, had a standard Ockhamist education; it is hard to imagine that Brenz did—and if he did, his thinking at any rate offers no evidence of any real understanding of Scholastic Christology." Cross, *Communicatio Idiomatum*, 37. Quotations above from 33, 34, 37. Cross's argument can be situated within other studies of Luther and his Christology, including Haga, *Was There a Lutheran Metaphysics?*; Dorner, *History of the Development of the Doctrine of the Person of Christ*; White, *Luther as Nominalist*; and Luy, *Dominus Mortis*. Cross is countering studies like Lienhard, *Luther*, and Pannenberg, *Jesus*.

221. Bagchi, "Sic Et Non," 13.

222. Bagchi, 14.

to conclude that Luther revolted against certain aspects of Scholastic theology (e.g., soteriology) even while he depended in significant ways on other Scholastic conclusions and methods.[223] Therefore, the contrast between Scholasticism and the Reformers may not be "completely false," says Steinmetz, but it is "so inaccurate as to be dangerously misleading."[224] Why is the contrast so dangerously misleading? The caricature positions Scholasticism on the side of unbiblical speculation, even rationalism, and positions the Reformers (Calvin in particular) on the side of biblical conviction and exegetical devotion. The caricature segregates Scholasticism to the side of ambiguity and obscurity but the Reformers to the side of clarity and relevancy. The strict discontinuity caricature assumes the Reformation program must bypass a major epoch of the church— Scholasticism—to return to orthodoxy. That assumption reads the Reformation outside the confines of its own quest for catholicity. For that reason alone, *the typical contrast between Luther and all that is medieval is dangerous because it puts a muzzle over Luther's own confessional claims to catholicity, which we will return to in future chapters.*

Martin Bucer and Girolamo Zanchi: Appropriating Thomism

At the end of his short study evaluating Biel's misrepresentation of Thomas and Luther's misinformed accusation that Thomism succumbed to Pelagian or Semi-Pelagian soteriology, David Steinmetz advised Reformation historians that the relationship between the Reformation and Thomas Aquinas cannot be narrowed to Luther's experience. "Of course, not everyone in the Protestant camp agreed with Luther." The Reformed wing of the Reformation was no doubt influenced by Thomism. "There were Thomists who were converted to the Protestant cause and who remained, to a greater or lesser degree, Thomists all their lives: theologians like Martin Bucer, Peter Martyr Vermigli, and Jerome (Girolamo) Zanchi." Nor was Lutheranism immune from Thomistic influence. Some of Luther's own colleagues appreciated Thomas. "Even Philip Melanchthon could read Thomas with profit when he wrote his lectures on the gospel of John."[225] Luther's misinformed evaluation of Thomas is unfortunate, but the Reformed wing of the Reformation did not suffer the same fate. While an extensive investigation has already been accomplished by others, a brief survey of first and second generation Reformers as well as their heirs will prove instructive.

As medieval men, the Reformers were not always aware of Scholasticism's every influence on their methods and conclusions. Some Reformers, however, were more aware than others, such as Martin Bucer, the spiritual father to Calvin, especially during Calvin's exile in Strasbourg. Entering such an academic

---

223. In other words, "while *theologia scholastica* was always to be opposed to the *theologia crucis*, the *modus loquendi scholasticus* was not always for Luther contrary to the *modus loquendi theologicus*." Bagchi, 13.
224. Steinmetz, "Scholastic Calvin," 18.
225. Steinmetz, "Luther among the Anti-Thomists," 58.

order like the Dominicans, young Bucer was trained as a Thomist.[226] Bucer also studied the philosophy of Aristotle. The program was rigorous: three years studying logic (*studium logicale*), followed by two years studying natural science, metaphysics, and ethics (*studium naturalium*).[227] However, Bucer was not without help: he not only read Aristotle but owned Thomas Aquinas's annotations on books like *On the Soul* and *Metaphysics*, for example.[228] Aristotle's philosophical foundation paved the way for his theological study of Scripture and the Scholastics. Historians have discovered an inventory of Bucer's library dating to 1518, and half of his library was filled with books by or about Thomas Aquinas![229] Bucer studied each of Thomas's theological works and read numerous commentaries on them as well.

Did Bucer leave behind his Thomism when he converted to the Reformation? He did not, however much he dispensed with those parts irreconcilable with Reformation theology. Instead, he continued to refine Thomism *for the sake of the Reformation*, even labeling Thomas the "prince of the scholastics."[230] Consider several examples. First, in the 1520s, still fresh in his evangelical conversion, Bucer wrote a book called *That No One Should Live for Himself but for Others, and How We May Attain This*. The resemblance to the *Summa Theologiae* of Thomas Aquinas is uncanny. Bucer followed Thomas's lead, structuring his book based on Thomas's movement from the Creator to the *imago Dei* to Christ and the Christian life.[231] Yet not only did Bucer mimic Thomas's outline, but he followed his theology as well, putting forward the law as that which is ingrained within all those made in God's image. God's law on the conscience of humankind is the basis on which all people should support a society in which neighbor loves neighbor. In other words, Bucer echoed Thomas's natural-law ethic to explain what society should look like in the sixteenth century.

Second, in Bucer's commentaries (e.g., Romans) as well as his theological treatises, Scripture was his final court of appeal, holding a place of primacy. Yet Bucer did not consider Scripture and reason antithetical to one another. He believed reason was instrumental to a proper interpretation of Scripture and essential to forming a coherent theological argument. Therefore, Bucer advocated for the use of Scholasticism's syllogisms, persuaded such a method was indispensable to a university education and even the Reformation's case for catholicity. "By using

---

226. As were other Reformers. For example, Wolfgang Capito was trained in Scholastic theology and philosophy at Freiburg. Cameron, *European Reformation*, 129.

227. Greschat estimated that Bucer fulfilled this program from 1510 to 1514. Greschat, *Martin Bucer*, 16. The details that follow were outlined by Greschat.

228. Greschat noted that Bucer also owned Lefèvre d'Etaples's commentary on *Nicomachean Ethics*. Greschat, *Martin Bucer*, 16.

229. That number is remarkable considering Bucer was immersed in humanism as well, which is another reason the historian should not drive a wedge between Scholasticism and humanism (see ch. 14). This point is also made by Greschat in *Martin Bucer*, 18 (cf. p. 25 where he described the makeup of Bucer's library).

230. To see why, consult Parker, "Saint Dionysius," 126; McGraw, *Reformed Scholasticism*, 102.

231. Consult *BDS* 1:30–60, 150–200, 297–350. The only difference is the combination of the first two parts. See Greschat, *Martin Bucer*, 56.

this [Scholastic] method," says Spijker, "Bucer intended to defend the catholicity of Reformation theology in relation to that of Rome."[232]

As chapter 13 will explain, some who were born from the womb of the Reformation had gone radical. Bucer knew Anabaptists who, in the name of reform, jettisoned anything that smelled like Greek philosophy, as if Plato or Aristotle could only corrupt Christianity. Rome considered these sectarian maneuvers fruit from the poisonous evangelical tree. To avoid association, Bucer was eager to demonstrate that Protestants could and should use classical philosophy as exemplified by the medieval Scholastics. As Bucer reflected on his training among the Dominicans, he considered their Scholastic methods and resources timely instruments in his hands, tools that could demonstrate the coherence and consistency of the Reformation's truth claims. To be exact, Bucer was indebted to the "realism of the *via antiqua* in the Thomist-Aristotelian tradition."[233] The metaphysic and epistemology of classical realism as filtered through Thomas was not lost on Bucer. For that reason, Thomas Aquinas became an ally in the cause of Reformed catholicity. Bucer used the Scholastic method "to defend the catholicity of Reformation theology in relation to that of Rome."[234]

Third, Bucer's apologetic for catholicity via Thomas Aquinas showed itself both in his commentaries and in his polemics. For example, Bucer wrote one of the most thorough commentaries on Romans in the sixteenth century. Although Bucer differed from Thomas on the exact nature of justifying grace, the commentary is littered with direct and indirect similarities and even references to Thomas. For instance, consider election. Bucer and Thomas agreed on the unconditional nature of election, and they both appealed to God's inscrutable and just will as the ultimate explanation. Bucer also referenced Thomas when he defined human freedom—"The will by which we choose what reason through mature deliberation perceives and judges to be more advantageous."[235] And like Thomas, Bucer proceeded to establish the will's total dependency on the primacy of God's mercy.[236] Bucer did differ from Thomas—he did not treat predestination in differentiation from election and he emphasized divine goodness more than justice when explaining the mystery of election. Nevertheless, the core of their doctrine exhibited continuity due to their common Augustinian tradition.[237] Therefore, Bucer never hesitated to critically appropriate Thomas to the advantage of his Reformation theology.

Bucer's polemics also showed signs of influence. In 1542 Bucer defended

---

232. Spijker, "Reformation and Scholasticism," 84.

233. Hazlet, "Bucer," 106.

234. Spijker, 85. Cf. Bucer's *Praefatio ad Romanos*, 31. Spijker is building on the work of Leijssen, "Martin Bucer und Thomas von Aquin," 266–96. Bucer also appealed to Thomas when he was presenting the Reformation to King Francis I; Greschat, *Martin Bucer*, 105.

235. "Recte itaque Thomas Aquinas liberum arbitrium, voluntatem intelligit qua eligimus, quod ratio consultatione conducibilius esse deprehendit et arbitrate est." Bucer, *Metaphrases*, 400. Bucer is referencing Thomas's *Expositio in Omnes Sancti Pauli Epistolas*.

236. For far more examples, see Steinmetz, *Calvin in Context*, 147.

237. Steinmetz, *Calvin in Context*, 151.

the Reformation in a letter to Albert Pighius, the same Pighius who attempted to woo the Genevans back to Rome when Calvin was exiled. In his letter, Bucer argued that the Reformation was not novel but was consistent with the church catholic, from the apostles to the church fathers to medieval Scholastics like Thomas Aquinas. That same year, Bucer entered a sharp exchange with Bartholomaeus Latomus, once again defending the Reformation *church* as a true church because it, too, was part of the church universal. Latomus accused Bucer of innovation, as if the evangelical church under Bucer had apostasized, but Bucer denied that his evangelical commitment meant opposition to "the entire ancient and proven church, and that everything about us is new or was thought up recently."[238]

Bucer may have been a spiritual father to Calvin, but Calvin was not his only son. As the Reformed community developed and matured, looking to Bucer for leadership, many also looked to the Italian Girolamo (Jerome) Zanchi (1516–90) as the natural theological heir of Bucer's program.[239] Like Bucer, Zanchi received an education that introduced him to the Platonism of Aristotle and its critical reception in the theology of Thomas.[240] When Zanchi left the Augustinian canons for the Aigistomoam house, he met Vermigli. Under Vermigli's care, Zanchi started reading Reformation theology and was persuaded. However, the 1550s were tumultuous; Protestants were persecuted in territories under the watchful eye of the papacy. To escape arrest by the Inquisition, Zanchi fled to Geneva and benefited from Calvin's teaching. Next, Zanchi taught students the Old Testament in Strasbourg, and in the 1560s he arrived in Heidelberg, filling Ursinus's vacancy at the university.

In Heidelberg Zanchi baptized (and cleansed) his Thomism in the waters of the Reformation and began to compose a *summa* of his own.[241] The first two volumes on the Trinity and divine attributes were published in the 1570s, but the volumes on creation and sin were published posthumously, leaving the project unfinished.[242] Notable throughout is Zanchi's debt to Thomas. For example, the parallel between Zanchi's structure to Thomas's *Summa* is uncanny. Zanchi draws from Thomas's theology at liberty, retrieving analogical predication, divine simplicity, natural law, concurrence in divine providence, the immortality of the soul, and especially Thomas's Augustinian definition of predestination and the primacy of grace.[243]

Zanchi disagreed with Thomas on the nature of justifying grace (e.g., infused

238. Bucer, *Scripta duo adversaria*, BB 78, p. 4; cf. Greschat, *Martin Bucer*, 196.
239. Spijker, "Reformation and Scholasticism," 94.
240. All these details are chronicled in Goris, "Thomism in Zanchi's Doctrine of God," 123–24.
241. Zanchi's *De religione Christiana fides—Confession of Christian Religion*. Cf. Lindholm, "Jerome Zanchi's Use of Thomas Aquinas," 75–89.
242. *Zanchi opera omnia theologica*. The second volume was devoted to divine attributes and was called *De natura Dei seu de divinis attributis (DND)*.
243. E.g., *DND* 7, 22, 25–26, 61–85, 171–74, 335–68, 553–54, 651–54, et al. Goris, "Thomism in Zanchi's Doctrine of God," 132–34; Donnelly, "Calvinist Thomism," 444–46.

qualities, merit); nevertheless, Zanchi found the *via moderna* to be the true provocation of Reformation, betraying the realism of Thomism for a nominalist Pelagianism (see chapter 5). At least Thomas attributed merit to the grace of God; Ockham and Biel granted man's will the ability to do his best prior to God's grace. Furthermore, whatever faults Lombard, Thomas, and Gregory of Rimini may have possessed, they at least understood the unconditional nature of divine election, while William Ockham and Gabriel Biel conditioned God's choice on foreknowledge of man's merit.[244] The latter was advocated by Albert Pighius in the sixteenth century, whom Zanchi not only encountered but Calvin refuted in his *Bondage and Liberation of the Will*. Yet Calvin's treatment was not as influential as Zanchi's Thomistic predestinarian theology (along with Vermigli's) when the Synod of Dort assembled to respond to the Arminians or Remonstrance of the seventeenth century.[245]

In short, Zanchi provided an extensive exegetical critique of Thomas for failing to define justification in forensic, imputational categories. Yet he was balanced enough to understand Thomas's error was still wrapped within Augustinianism in contrast to the unforgivable error of Semi-Pelagianism or even Pelagianism so prominent in the *via moderna* soteriology of Ockham and Biel. In addition, Zanchi was not narrow in his evaluation but broadened his horizon to conclude that Thomas was profitable across the scope of Christian theology, especially for Zanchi's defense of an orthodox theology proper and Christology. "Zanchi's primary ambition was to be a catholic by teaching what the Scripture has revealed and to learn from the church's best Scholastics, among whom Aquinas was the purest."[246]

The Scholastic Calvin

On the surface, John Calvin was not all that different from Luther in his rhetorical derision of Scholastics. Yet Calvin did not receive formal training in theology like Luther, Bucer, and Zanchi, and thus Calvin never experienced the same level of pressure as Luther did to embrace the *via moderna* soteriology of his instructors. Those peers interested in theology traveled to the University of Paris for formalized training by the best theologians of the day, but Calvin did not. Instead, he submitted to his father's wishes to study law. For these reasons, the relationship between Calvin and Scholasticism is rarely explored, and when it is many assume it must be one of hostility, as if *Scholastic* and *Calvin* are two words destined to be antithetical by nature.[247]

The reason many draw such a conclusion is not only due to their mistaken assumptions about Calvin but Scholasticism itself. They assume Scholasticism was "invariably arid, speculative, subservient to Aristotelian philosophy,

---

244. *DND* 421, 652–54. Cf. Goris, "Thomism in Zanchi's Doctrine of God," 134–35.
245. Donnelly adds that Francis Gomarus was a student of Zanchi. See "Calvinist Thomism," 448.
246. Lindholm, "Jerome Zanchi's Use of Thomas Aquinas," 87.
247. Steinmetz, "Scholastic Calvin," 18.

philosophical rather than biblical, absorbed with trivial questions, and devoted to logic-chopping."[248] Calvin's commentaries and *Institutes* by contrast are characterized by clear, biblical priorities. However, such a description of Scholasticism is a colossal caricature. The more Calvin developed in his historical knowledge, the more he uncovered Scholastic distinctions profitable for his own theology, distinctions he grew to depend on in polemics as well. How peculiar to criticize Calvin for lacking philosophical integration, partitioning him off as only a theological exegete, when some of the most famous Scholastics before him engaged philosophy no more than Calvin did.[249]

No reasonable interpreter can deny that Calvin was critical of the "Scholastics." While his rhetoric may not have reached Luther's pitch, Calvin was not shy about using the label *Scholastic* in a derogatory manner.[250] Yet who were these infamous Scholastics? Calvin did not usually identify them, which is one reason the McNeill-Battles edition of Calvin's *Institutes* is so misleading, inserting Thomas's name where Calvin never mentioned him, as if Thomas was Calvin's Scholastic nemesis.[251] Yet the "Scholastics" Calvin criticized were not always the typical figureheads (Anselm, Thomas, et al.). Instead, these targets of disdain originated from Calvin's homeland, nominalists from the late medieval period operating in the Sorbonne.[252] The Sorbonne Scholastics, in other words, were not the heirs of the *via antiqua* and its realism but the *via moderna* and its nominalism, considered by critics to be Pelagian at worst and Semi-Pelagian at best (see chapter 5). "What appears to the casual reader to be a blanket condemnation of Scholasticism may prove in certain cases to be nothing of the kind, but to have a quite local point of reference. Calvin may condemn an entire phylum in order to squash a single specimen."[253]

---

248. Steinmetz, "Scholastic Calvin," 18.

249. "Calvin discovered that some philosophical distinctions, including many of the distinctions drawn by the schoolmen, were too useful to be discarded lightly. If one objects that there is still very little philosophy in Calvin's late theological and exegetical writings, the obvious reply is that there is even less in Peter Lombard's." Steinmetz, "Scholastic Calvin," 18. For examples of Scholastic commitments to commentary on the sacred Scriptures, see Leinsle, *Introduction to Scholastic Theology*, 16–118.

250. At the same time, some editions of Calvin's *Institutes* may be misleading. The McNeill-Battles edition, complains Ballor, "regularly adds specific references to Thomas's work that do not appear in Calvin's own work, leaving the impression that there is more direct engagement and opposition between Calvin and Thomas than the text actually sustains." Ballor, "Deformation and Reformation," 38. Cf. Raith, *Aquinas and Calvin on Romans*, 13.

251. Raith, *Aquinas and Calvin on Romans*, 13; cf. *Institutes* 3.2.8; 3.14.11. Raith's experience has been my own as well.

252. LaVallee, "Calvin's Criticism of Scholastic Theology." Some, like Reuter, have tried to connect Calvin to a Scholastic education by claiming Calvin studied under John Major. Reuter, *Das Grundverständnis der Theologie Calvins*. That claim has been thrown into serious question by Ganoczy, *Le jeune Calvin*. For an overview of the debate and other contributions to it, consult Muller, "Scholasticism in Calvin: Relation and Disjunction," 247–49. Muller is especially informative, tracing Calvin's language from his Latin to his French edition of his *Institutes*, demonstrating the specific targets Calvin has in mind.

253. Steinmetz, "Scholastic Calvin," 26. Cf. *Institutes* 3.23.2. Muller, after tracing how Calvin's criticisms evolve in the French edition of the *Institutes*, writes, "If the language of the French text is accepted as Calvin's meaning, the critiques are often quite specific and, indeed, quite contemporary—and no longer directed against such luminaries of the Scholastic past as Bonaventure, Aquinas, or Duns Scotus. In addition, Calvin

In addition, Calvin's views were sometimes identical with Scholasticism when he thought they were contrary to Scholasticism. Consider an example: the Scholastic distinction between God's absolute and ordained power. When Calvin addressed this distinction in his *Institutes*, he "misstated what the Scholastics meant by the use of this distinction, restated what he regarded as the correct answer (which was more or less what the Scholastics taught when they drew the distinction), and concluded, quite wrongly, that he and the Scholastics were worlds apart."[254] But in truth, they were not. Calvin was promoting a Scholastic position all the while claiming his view was contrary to the Scholastic position. A similar phenomenon occurs in Calvin's commentary on Job.[255] Calvin was frustrated with the way the Sorbonne theologians (mis)used absolute power, convinced they had compromised divine simplicity in the process. Notice, Calvin was so frustrated because a standard Scholastic committed to a classical understanding of God—divine simplicity—was compromised by late medieval Scholastics in France.[256] Was Calvin really frustrated with Scholasticism as a whole, or was he frustrated with modern Scholasticism that deviated from a purebred Scholasticism to which Calvin himself was unconsciously committed?

In a host of other cases, it is unclear whether Calvin was aware he was borrowing distinctions and even methods from his Scholastic fathers. To summarize the findings of Richard Muller and company, consider a litany of instances:

- To define providence, Calvin distinguished between the hidden will of God and the manifest or revealed will of God, a distinction that can be traced from the Scholastics back to Augustine.
- In a unique acknowledgment, Calvin did accept the Scholastic distinction between types of necessity (e.g., consequent necessity, necessity of the consequence) and considered these appropriate for defining the divine decree.
- Calvin arrived at an essentialist interpretation of divine aseity and eternity in his exegesis of Exodus 3:14, which mirrored the classical orthodoxy of the Fathers and was perpetuated by Scholastics like Bonaventure and Thomas Aquinas.
- When describing the atonement of Christ, Calvin distinguished between the sufficiency and the efficacy of Christ's satisfaction, yet another Scholastic distinction. Calvin was forthright, recognizing its Scholastic roots.
- Calvin identified Christ the Mediator as the immediate object of faith, a move that was explicit in Giles of Rome and Gregory of Rimini.

clearly tended to reserve his most angry and specified polemic for his French audience." Muller, "Scholasticism in Calvin," 264. Cf. Van Asselt with Rouwendal et al., *Introduction to Reformed Scholasticism*, 66.

254. Calvin "made an honest mistake and misrepresented the scholastics unwittingly." Steinmetz, "Scholastic Calvin," 27.

255. Calvin, *Sermons sur le livre de Iob*, CO 34.339. Cf. Steinmetz, *Calvin in Context*, 40–52.

256. "What is notable here is . . . the fact that Calvin opposes this particular 'scholastic' or Sorbonnistic teaching with equally 'scholastic' assumptions concerning the divine simplicity and the essential identity of the divine attributes." Muller, "Scholasticism in Calvin," 253.

- Sounding a lot like Thomas Aquinas, but also Augustine and Lombard, Calvin differentiated between three aspects of faith: knowledge, will or assent, and trust. And like the Scholastics, Calvin taught that all three must be present for saving faith.[257]
- When Calvin was defining God's two kingdoms, he at least borrowed from the Scholastic—and Aristotelian—differentiation between that which is momentary and that which is transcendent, even Aristotle's distinction between accident and substance.[258]
- On predestination, Calvin (and Martin Bucer) interpreted Romans 9 no differently than Thomas Aquinas: election is unconditional; God's will is the ultimate explanation for eternal choice. To explain why God chose some and not others, each has a slight difference in emphasis (Thomas: justice; Bucer: goodness; Calvin: honor), but the "substance" of their position is the same since they all abided by Augustinian exegesis.[259]

These examples do not exhaust remnants of Scholasticism in Calvin but consider one of the above examples: faith. First, when Calvin was defining faith and justification, he made direct use of Aristotle's four causes (efficient, material, formal/instrumental, and final), drawing on Aristotle's *Physics* and *Metaphysics*.[260] That move was not original either since other Reformed theologians applied Aristotle's four causes to election as well, naming God's good pleasure the efficient cause, Christ the material cause, the preaching of the word the formal cause, and the glory of God the final cause.[261] Although Calvin and Thomas Aquinas had their differences over justification, nevertheless, Calvin followed in Thomas's wake, whether he realized it or not, by borrowing a Scholastic method to substantiate the Protestant viewpoint.

Second, the point at which Calvin and Thomas seemed to disagree most is but a difference in language, not content. A close investigation reveals that

---

257. This summary is my own, but to see these points explained, consult Muller, "Scholasticism in Calvin," 253–63. For example, consider the following: On the hidden will of God, see *Institutes* 3.24.17. On the definition of faith, Muller has in view Augustine, *In Ioannem,* 29:6; Peter Lombard, *Sententiae,* 3.23.4; and Aquinas; *ST* 2a2ae. 2, 2. Muller, "Scholasticism in Calvin," 256. On types of necessity, see *Institutes* 1.16.9; 2.12.1. On an essentialist interpretation (of Ex. 3:14), see *Institutes* 1.10.2. On sufficiency and efficiency distinction, see Calvin, *Commentarius in Iohannis Apostoli epistolam,* CO 55.310; Calvin didn't think the distinction worked in 1 John 2:1–2, but he did think it was a legitimate theological distinction. On Christ as the object of faith, Calvin thought the Schoolmen only "identify God as the object of faith *simpliciter.*" *Institutes* 3.2.1–2. But Muller counters, "On the one hand, Calvin's point that scholastic theology drew attention away from Christ, is a truism of Reformation era polemic—on the other hand, it falls considerably short of being a description of scholastic theology either in general or in particular. Few medieval scholastics claimed, without qualification, that God is the object of faith." Muller, "Scholasticism in Calvin," 254.

258. "Calvin used the Aristotelian distinction between substance and accidents to distinguish between the temporal affairs of life, which pass away, and the world itself, which will be restored and transformed in accord with its original eschatological purpose." Tiuninga, *Calvin's Political Theology and the Public Engagement of the Church,* 357.

259. Steinmetz, *Calvin in Context,* 150, 151.

260. Calvin, *Institutes* 3.14.17 and 3.14.21.

261. Muller, *Dictionary,* causa, s.v.

Thomas required knowledge for faith as much as Calvin. Alvin Vos has demonstrated that "Aquinas holds that faith is a firm belief and Calvin holds that it is a sure and certain knowledge, but what may appear to be a basic disagreement is in fact a mere semantic difference—a discrepancy in their use of the verb *to know*—rather than a difference in substance."[262] Calvin's disdain of implicit faith is better directed at deviating Scholastics in the sixteenth century than any and every Scholastic of past centuries.[263]

The abundance of examples leads Muller to conclude, "Calvin's assault on Scholastic distinctions, therefore, often occurs within the bounds of rather traditional constructions that he shared with many medieval theologians."[264] Yet the legitimacy of a "Scholastic Calvin" may also be sustained by the Genevan ministry itself—the Reformers even applied Scholasticism to evangelical ministry. On first appearance, the Geneva church seemed worlds away from a medieval university like Paris. As noted earlier, Scholastics were training the next generation of archbishops and archdeacons. By contrast, Geneva set its sights on educated laity, although Calvin's Company of Pastors and the Geneva Academy (governed by Beza) might inch closer in the Scholastic direction. But overall, the two appear at odds. Upon closer examination, however, Calvin's methods show signs of continuity. Calvin preached by glossing through a text, commenting on verses out loud, a method that resonated with medieval listeners.[265] Calvin not only preached utilizing this Scholastic method but wrote commentaries and encouraged readers to consult the theological rationale in his *Institutes*, an approach not all that different from Scholastics like Lombard or Thomas Aquinas, who did the same even if in a monastic or university setting.[266] Granted, Calvin was ministering in the church, not the university; he was a pastor, not a professor in the traditional medieval sense of the word. And yet Calvin's didactic priorities and his teaching methods created a school-like environment. Indeed, the Schoolman in Calvin saw the nature of the church itself through such a lens. Granted, Calvin preached sermons in the vernacular. "Nevertheless, the fact that Calvin regarded the church as both mother and school, meant that in his view all Christians, no matter how limited their capacity, had a theological task

---

262. Vos, *Aquinas, Calvin, and Contemporary Protestant Thought*, 161 (cf. 4). Compare Calvin's *Institutes* 3.2 with Aquinas, *ST* 1a2ae. 109, 1; 1a. 1, 8; 2a2ae. 2, 1–4; 2a2ae 4, 2; 6, 1.

263. Vos, *Aquinas, Calvin, and Contemporary Protestant Thought*, 161. On related topics (e.g., merit), Calvin seems to misdirect his aim. Calvin's "engagement with Aquinas on merit reflects the judgments of Calvin's more immediate opponents rather than Aquinas himself. When Aquinas's and Calvin's commentaries on Romans are read together, we discover that most if not all of Calvin's warnings in his commentary about the theology of the schoolmen do not apply to Aquinas's positions, while Calvin's principal positive affirmations are embraced by Aquinas as well. . . . Calvin interprets Romans within a broad tradition of thought that includes Aquinas. The similarities should come as no surprise given Aquinas's and Calvin's shared appreciation for Augustine, but they cannot always be traced back to Augustine." Raith, *Aquinas and Calvin on Romans*, 9; cf. Raith, "Calvin's Critique of Merit, and Why Aquinas (Mostly) Agrees," *Pro Ecclesia* 20 (2011): 135–166.

264. Muller, "Scholasticism in Calvin," 254.

265. Parker, *Calvin's Preaching*, 80, 132; Muller, "The Problem of Protestant Scholasticism," 52.

266. On Calvin's glosses, see Steinmetz, "Scholastic Calvin," 29.

to discharge.... The church was a school, not only for an elite, but also for quite ordinary people."[267] *In short, Calvin took what Scholastics did in the classroom and transferred their method of learning into the church.* "The local parish became less a sacred space for the celebration of religious mysteries than an assembly room for the theological education of the laity."[268]

To add to Steinmetz's initial observation, Calvin's school-like approach to the church might also stem from his Reformation commitment to the priesthood of all believers. If so, "Scholastic Calvin" is an appropriate oxymoron, or to be more accurate, *paradox*. The *Scholastic* Calvin provided learned lessons from the text with theological import, while the Scholastic *Calvin* applied such a medieval approach to the average Christian, ensuring an open channel of theological education from clergy to laity. If correct, then Calvin, whether he knew it or not, served as the bridge between the Reformation church and the Scholastic university. Yet historical investigation says Calvin did know it; he was self-aware. Not only did Calvin receive the compliment from time to time that his own lectures were "Scholastic," but when he wrote about the Geneva Academy, he boasted that he and his colleagues were raising up *scholastici*.[269] Calvin could use the word *Scholastic* in a negative sense (especially when his Sorbonne nemeses were in view), but he could also use the word in a positive sense, even as a label of pride, exhibiting his continuity and catholicity. And his *Institutes* reveal that even Calvin could advise his readers to listen and learn from the "sounder Schoolman," including Thomas Aquinas.[270]

Some have speculated whether Martin Bucer—one of the greatest influences on the young Calvin—directly introduced Calvin to Thomism. No evidence supports such a speculation. Rather than looking for a "common school tradition," a better answer is found in a "common Augustinian heritage."[271] As far as Calvin was indebted to Augustine—and his debt was deep—he was indebted to Thomas and any other Scholastics committed to Augustinian exegesis and theology.

Peter Martyr Vermigli: Reformed Thomist

Although history has favored the reception of Calvin, in the sixteenth century the Italian humanist and Reformer Peter Martyr Vermigli (1499–1562) was no less significant a Reformer. Contrary to contemporary assumptions, Calvin held no monopoly as *the* Reformed voice of the century. Vermigli gained a reputation

---

267. "They could not sidestep their theological responsibility by relying on implicit faith and claiming, as they had once done in the old church, that they believed whatever the church taught. That was far too indolent a faith." Steinmetz, "Scholastic Calvin," 29.

268. Steinmetz, "Scholastic Calvin," 30.

269. Muller attributes this label to the logic and methods of disputation, and also observes how Beza "praised the Academy as a *republica scholastica*." Muller, "The Problem of Protestant Scholasticism," 51.

270. *Institutes* 3.14.11.

271. Steinmetz, *Calvin in Context,* 151.

for both his exegesis and his theological and philosophical erudition; some historians even credit Vermigli with codifying the Reformed Orthodoxy of the next generation.[272]

On one hand, Vermigli was grounded in the Italian humanist endeavor, exercising ressourcement within his own platform.[273] He not only surrounded himself with humanists but read the patristic corpus—Augustine in particular—to retrieve the exegetical and theological insights of the church fathers. He also devoted himself to the discipline of philology, which allowed him to study sacred texts—biblical, patristic, and medieval—in the original languages.[274]

On the other hand, Vermigli grounded himself better than most Reformers in the Scholastic heritage *and* critically appropriated his heritage in service of the Reformation. Young Vermigli learned the Scholastic method and its corresponding theology in his formative days at the S. Giovanni di Verdara monastery and the University of Padua. Yet Vermigli did not study just any and every Scholastic; he studied the Scholastic his Dominican teachers considered unparalleled: Thomas Aquinas.[275] Committing to the evangelical camp, however, did not entail repudiating the influence of Thomism. If refined, Vermigli considered Thomism and the Reformed religion compatible, the latter building on the metaphysical foundation of the former. Vermigli's training in Augustinian Thomism gave him an advantage: he knew it so well that he could consider where it might complement his evangelical faith. For example, Vermigli was far more capable of identifying points of compatibility between faith and reason than Calvin.[276] In the estimation of Muller, "Vermigli, trained at Padua as a Thomist, manifests a willingness to deal with the complex questions of the relationship of faith—which is a rational disposition of the soul—to rational argumentation, within the context of his thoroughly Augustinian anthropology." The result was an added sophistication that surpassed other Reformers at points: "Vermigli maintains the *sola gratia* of the Reformation but also develops a more sophisticated view of the theological and philosophical functions of reason than Calvin ever attempted."[277]

Unfortunately, whenever Scholasticism has been caricatured as an Aristotelian corruption of Christianity, a rationalism that overruled a pure, exclusive focus on the Bible, Vermigli has been blamed for introducing a Reformed Scholasticism into the Reformation, one that departed from the Reformation's biblical focus.[278] Not only has such a "Calvin vs. the Calvinist" generalization

272. James, "Peter Martyr Vermigli," 63. Also see James's larger work, *Peter Martyr Vermigli and Predestination.*

273. Anderson, "Peter Martyr Vermigli," 65–84.

274. James, "Peter Martyr Vermigli," 69.

275. Vermigli was influenced by Gaspare Mansueti da Perugia and Alberto Pascaleo da Udine. James, "Peter Martyr Vermigli," 64.

276. Muller makes this point. Muller, *PRRD* 1:106.

277. Muller, *PRRD* 1:106; cf. *The Peter Martyr Reader,* 5–79, 107–123.

278. E.g., see Armstrong, *Calvinism and the Amyraut Heresy.* For a more nuanced definition of

been challenged successfully by recent historians such as Richard Muller, but this negative opinion of Vermigli assumes the Italian theologian was an uncritical receptor of all things Aristotelian or Thomistic. For reasons too many to number, such an opinion falls short. Vermigli was as astute as he was prudent, identifying numerous areas in which the Reformed faith was influenced by Thomas and dare not deviate lest it lose the pedigree of its catholicity. Some of these included metaphysics, epistemology, ethics, hermeneutics, bibliology, Nicene Trinitarianism, Chalcedonian Christology, creation, anthropology, eschatology, and more.[279]

Vermigli did identify chinks in Scholasticism's soteriology and ecclesiology. However, instead of abandoning the entire suit of armor, Vermigli perfected it, putting forward a sanctifying effort. Since Vermigli was committed to biblical authority, as were his Scholastic predecessors, he never considered his appropriation of Scholasticism for the sake of the Reformed religion a conflict. "Vermigli's method of biblical interpretation was not a rejection of Scholastic methodology but a *reconfiguration* of Scholastic and humanist approaches in the service of new theological convictions."[280]

As mentioned at the start of this chapter, critics tend to play Reformed Orthodoxy against the Reformation because they fail to see that medieval Scholasticism was unique for its methodology in the university, a method that did not elevate reason above Scripture but utilized reason in the service of understanding Scripture. If Scholasticism is defined with accuracy, then Vermigli's contribution shines through. Vermigli was not corrupting the Reformation but utilizing the tools of Aristotle and Thomas to sharpen exegesis. As for theology, Vermigli was Augustinian through and through. As mentioned, Augustinianism was channeled through Thomas. As far as the Reformation appropriated Augustine—which it did to no little extent—it appropriated Thomas by default, if not in whole at least in part. In that light, Thomism influenced the Reformation movement to one degree or another, even if someone like Vermigli was far more intent on refining Thomistic philosophy and theology within evangelical contours.

In summary, if it is fitting to call the Genevan Reformer the "Scholastic Calvin," then it may be fitting to title the Italian Reformer the "Reformed Thomist."[281]

Scholasticism as well as a more sympathetic handling of Vermigli, see Donnelly, *Calvinism and Scholasticism in Vermigli's Doctrine of Man and Grace.* For an outline of the debate, see James, "Peter Martyr Vermigli," 65.

279. James, "Peter Martyr Vermigli," 66, points to Vermigli's *In primum, secundum, et initium tertii libri ethicorum Aristotelis ad Nichomachum . . . commentarius doctissimus,* 292–96.

280. Emphasis added. James, "Peter Martyr Vermigli," 72.

281. James calls Vermigli the "pioneer of Calvinist Thomism." James, "Peter Martyr Vermigli," 63. I use "Reformed Thomist" instead because I do not want to give the impression that Calvin somehow set the Thomistic example for Reformed thought moving forward. James himself avoids that assumption when he identifies other evangelical Thomists, such as Theodore Beza and Girolamo Zanchi, drawing from the research of Donnelly's *Calvinism and Scholasticism.*

BROAD THEMATIC CONTINUITY

A more topical or thematic approach also unveils varying degrees of continuity between the sixteenth century and Scholasticism. Consider only two examples: natural theology and the fourfold meaning of Scripture.

Case Study 1: Natural Theology

The last two chapters have been attuned to Anselm's *a priori* argument and Thomas's *a posteriori* argument for God's existence, the latter drawing on patristic luminaries such as Augustine. As historians have long observed, natural theology enjoyed a continual presence from the church fathers to the Scholastics, a fact that will be elaborated upon in the next chapter to explain a departure that occurs with late medieval theologians like Ockham.[282] However, some Reformed thinkers in the twentieth century have concluded that the Reformers severely criticized or even abandoned the natural theology of their medieval predecessors, including natural theology's metaphysical and epistemological structure. Calvin, more than most, has been turned into a foil for this argument, an argument that has spread in variegated forms from Karl Barth to Otto Weber to Cornelius Van Til.[283] This oppositional narrative has even influenced the contemporary translation of Calvin's *Institutes*. Calvin kept at bay Scripture citations in his opening chapters so that he could give proof of God's existence, but McNeill and Battles have written into the text over forty biblical passages, which only serve to mask Calvin's argument from natural theology.[284]

History, however, disagrees with this revisionist interpretation. First, consider how Calvin situated knowledge of the Creator within a participation paradigm. Appealing to the goodness of God's providence, Calvin did not believe the creature will understand what honor we owe to God if he does not comprehend that God is the source, the fountain of all goodness. For "not only does he sustain this universe (as he once founded it) by his boundless might, regulate it by his wisdom, preserve it by his goodness, and especially rule mankind by his righteousness and judgment, bear with it in his mercy, watch over it by his protection; but also that no drop will be found either of wisdom and light, or of righteousness or power or rectitude, or of genuine truth, which does not flow from him, and of which he is not the cause."[285] God's sustaining care, in other words, is evidence that he is the cause of all goodness humanity enjoys. "Again, you cannot behold

---

282. For a survey of the Fathers, see Levering, *Proofs of God*, 27–47.

283. J. V. Fesko has provided a critique in his "Introduction," xxv. He engages: Barth, *Natural Theology*, 94–107; Barth, *The Knowledge of God and the Service of God According to the Teaching of the Reformation*; Van Til, *Defense of the Faith*, 210; Van Til, *Common Grace and the Gospel*, 93–94. Others include: Lange, "Reformation and Natural Law," 56–98; Dooyeweerd, *In the Twilight of Western Thought*, 116; Dooyeweerd, *Reformation and Scholasticism in Philosophy*, in *The Collected Works of Herman Dooyeweerd*, 1:15. Fesko also critiques contemporary theologians who follow this interpretation (e.g., John Frame). Besides Fesko, consider Muller's critique of Otto Weber's *Foundations of Dogmatics* in *PRRD* 1:270–278.

284. Calvin, *Institutes* 1.1–5. Cf. Fesko, "Introduction," xxiii.

285. Calvin, *Institutes* 1.2.1.

him clearly unless you acknowledge him to be the fountainhead and source of every good."[286]

Second, as the pinnacle of the created order, those made in the likeness of God exhibit natural revelation's presence within themselves. Each person has a "natural instinct, an awareness of divinity," including "more backward folk and those more remote from civilization." Cicero, the "eminent pagan" as Calvin called him, is a case in point. As Calvin said, there is "no nation so barbarous, no people so savage, that they have not a deep-seated conviction that there is a God."[287]

Recent revisionists claim Calvin denies that man *after the fall* can derive a knowledge of God from creation. Calvin had strong words for humanity's suppression of this knowledge (he does not hesitate to use the language of idolatry). However, the fall never moved Calvin to be so extreme as to deny that pagans like Cicero can recognize a "deep-seated conviction that there is a God." For example, Paul writes to the Romans and says, "For his invisible attributes, namely, his eternal power and divine nature, have been clearly perceived, ever since the creation of the world, in the things that have been made. So they are without excuse. For although they knew God, they did not honor him as God or give thanks to him, but they became futile in their thinking, and their foolish hearts were darkened" (1:20–21). Calvin interpreted Paul's phrase "they knew God" as follows: God "declares here, quite obviously, that God made a knowledge of his majesty flow down into the spirits of all men: which is to say that he has shown himself so much, by his works, that they are forced to see that which they do not seek by themselves, that is, that there is a God."[288] In other words, culpability assumes they do possess a natural knowledge of God's existence by means of God's natural revelation. "If natural theology were impossible [for Calvin]," clarifies Muller, then "idolatrous man would not be left without excuse."[289]

In fact, even when Calvin echoed Paul (in Rom. 1:23) and said fallen man has exchanged the immortal God for an image or an idol resembling mortal man, he thought such distortion proof from the created order itself that man was made to worship God. Man "prefers to worship wood and stone rather than to be thought of as having no God," and "clearly this is a most vivid impression of a divine being."[290] Therefore, however strenuous the resistance to the true God may be,

---

286. Calvin, *Institutes* 1.2.2.

287. Calvin, *Institutes* 1.3.1.

288. Calvin, *Epistle to the Romans*, 26. This translation is from the French by David Haines, who says that the word *flow* is from the "French word *descouler*," which "gives the notion of a river running down a mountain" (*Natural Theology*, 38). Van Til conflicts with Calvin when he interprets Romans 1:19–21 as if only prefallen man is in view (*An Introduction to Systematic Theology*, 100). For a critique, see Haines, *Natural Theology*, 21–48, 171–82.

289. Muller, *PRRD* 1:274. Muller has in mind Calvin, *Commentary on Psalms*, Ps. 19:1 in loc. (*CTS Psalms*, I, 308; *CO*, 31, col. 194); Ps. 19:7 in loc. (*CTS Psalms, I*, 317; CO 31, col. 199); *Commentary on Acts*, 14:17 (*CTS Acts*, II, 19); *Commentary on Acts*, 17:22 (*CTS Acts*, II, 154). Muller is opposing the Barthian interpretation of scholars like Parker, *Knowledge of God*, 34–36; Dowey, *Knowledge of God in Calvin's Theology*, 73–75; Weber, *Foundations of Dogmatics*, 1:117–18, among others.

290. Calvin, *Institutes* 1.3.1.

no person is capable of escaping the knowledge of God in the created order that he must assume in the first place to be an idolater. For even "the boldest despiser of God is of all men the most startled at the rustle of a falling leaf," explains Calvin. "Whence does this arise but from the vengeance of divine majesty, which strikes their consciences all the more violently the more they try to flee from it?"[291]

Calvin's affirmation of the universal, natural knowledge of God leads him to affirm a *sensus divinitatis* that cannot be eradicated no matter how hard fallen man tries. "Men of sound judgment will always be sure that a *sense of divinity* which can never be effaced is engraved upon men's minds." Again, even pagan philosophers understood and embraced the sense of divinity and considered it indispensable to natural theology. Calvin found an ally in Plato's philosophy for example: "Plato meant nothing but this when he often taught that the highest good of the soul is likeness to God, where, when the soul has grasped the knowledge of God, it is wholly transformed into his likeness."[292]

A natural knowledge of God not only sits within the creature but stands before his eyes in the creation as well. The seed of religion is sown in the mind but also revealed daily "in the whole workmanship of the universe."[293] The creation is a theater of God's glory.[294] Granted, no one can see God's essence and live. For God is incomprehensible. Yet God has accommodated himself by means of his *works*. God's works in creation and providence, for example, are the proper medium for knowing he exists, a point no different from Thomas and Augustine.

> We know the most perfect way of seeking God, and the most suitable order, is not for us to attempt with bold curiosity to penetrate to the investigation of his essence, which we ought more to adore than meticulously to search out, but for us to contemplate him in his works whereby he renders himself near and familiar to us, and in some manner communicates himself. . . . As Augustine teaches elsewhere, because, disheartened by his greatness, we cannot grasp him, we ought to gaze upon his works, that we may be restored by his goodness.[295]

Therefore, the natural order is a reflection in which we see the image in which we were created. "The reason why the author of The Letter to the Hebrews elegantly calls the universe the appearance of things invisible is that this skillful ordering of the universe is for us a sort of mirror in which we can contemplate God, who is otherwise invisible."[296]

Calvin's affirmation of natural revelation and with it, natural theology—from

---

291. "Indeed, they seek out every subterfuge to hide themselves from the Lord's presence, and to efface it again from their minds. But in spite of themselves they are always entrapped." Calvin, *Institutes* 1.3.2.
292. Calvin, *Institutes* 1.3.3.
293. Calvin, *Institutes* 1.5.1.
294. Calvin used this language in *Institutes* 1.6.2.
295. Calvin, *Institutes* 1.5.9.
296. Calvin, *Institutes* 1.5.1.

Plato to Augustine—never denies the need for what Calvin called the spectacles of faith.[297] Calvin placed no little emphasis on natural theology's intrinsic parameter (a revelation of God's existence and perfections but not articles of faith, such as the Trinity) and extrinsic parameter (man's rebellion). However, those parameters did not lead Calvin to deny the legitimacy of natural theology altogether, only to understand its contribution within proper limits. Due to these parameters the light of nature requires the light of God's Word *for salvation*, but that does not eliminate the light of nature's instrumentality *for a knowledge of God's existence, perfections, and divine providence in creation.*[298] For God is the author of two books, the book of nature and the book of Scripture, and Calvin does not hesitate to appeal to the former to develop a natural theological argument, even if he does not use the grammar of "natural theology" like his heirs in the decades and centuries that followed.

To clarify, the continuity between Calvin and the patristic and medieval practitioners of natural theology does not mean Calvin merely republished their arguments in his own idiom. And yet, continuity with his patristic and medieval predecessors persists because Calvin (1) not only utilized natural theology but (2) wielded *a posteriori* arguments, as is plain in his use of natural theological arguments from Cicero and the Stoics.[299] For example, J. V. Fesko observes the way Calvin appealed to the Greek conception of natural law (preconception; *prolepsis*) to explain why the Gentiles do what the law requires by nature (Rom. 2:14).[300] In addition, Calvin's approach to natural theology in his Romans commentary is similar to his *Institutes* where he mentioned the philosophers and modeled their strategy, namely, an argument that moved from the beauty of the body to its Maker, a method that was conspicuous in Cicero and Aristotle alike.[301]

Despite these continuities between Calvin and the Augustinian tradition, Calvin's view does differ in this sense: creation makes it plain *that God is* but the sinner twists *who God is.* "Human reason perceives that God exists," but nonetheless "misperceives what God is like."[302] Blindness can only be remedied through saving faith which sees God with new eyes through the spectacles of Scripture. While agreeing with Calvin that sin distorts this natural knowledge, most other Reformers said more about the content of natural knowledge: not only does natural knowledge perceive that God is but who God is (e.g., perfections and providence).

In the judgment of Calvin's contemporaries, Paul does not stress an acute noetic impairment because of sin or distinguish sharply between what is revealed in

---

297. Calvin, *Institutes* 1.5.14.
298. Calvin, *Institutes* 1.6.1.
299. Calvin, *Romans*, esp. Rom. 2:14–15. Cf. Fesko, "Introduction," xxiii.
300. E.g., Calvin is engaging Cicero's *De Naturam Deorum.*
301. Calvin, *Institutes* 1.5.3; Fesko, "Introduction," xxiii. Cf. Aristotle, *Physics*, 8.2.
302. For Steinmetz's emphasis on Calvin's contrast between offering and receiving, see *Calvin in Context*, 32. Cf. *Institutes* 1.6.1.

nature and what is perceived by fallen human reason. The thrust of Paul's argument, indeed, runs in the opposite direction. The point that Paul makes is not how little the Gentiles knew, but, considering the circumstances, how much they did know and how little use they made of it.[303]

Steinmetz enlists a litany of Reformers who diverge from Calvin in their reading of Romans 1—from Luther to Melanchthon, from Bucer to Bullinger, from Zwingli to Oecolampadius, from Musculus to Vermigli, and many more. A survey of Reformed Orthodoxy in the sixteenth through eighteenth centuries produces similar results on the whole (Leigh, Turretin, Owen, Witsius, etc.).[304] Calvin and the Reformed alike affirmed natural knowledge and its distortion by sin, but whereas Calvin thought natural knowledge of God's *nature* was misperceived, other Reformers and many of the Reformed Orthodox thought this knowledge may be perceived, for they cannot misconstrue what they do not perceive.[305] To be clear, that difference did not mean the Early and High Reformed Orthodox then concluded that natural theology was *the basis* of supernatural theology, as scholars like Weber have assumed. Rather, natural theology was *instrumental*, with reason remaining a handmaid to the revelation of the Word.[306]

The Reformed Scholastics of the late sixteenth and seventeenth centuries operated in continuity with the Reformers even if it was more necessary to treat natural theology at greater length to write confessions and systems of theology to codify Reformed theology. The Belgic Confession of 1561, Francis Junius's *A Treatise on True Theology* in 1594, Johann Heinrich Alsted's *Theologia Naturalis* at the start of the seventeenth century, the Westminster Confession in 1647, Francis Turretin's *Institutes* of the seventeenth century—these are only a few examples that manifest Reformed Scholasticism's steady testimony to natural theology, much in line with the Augustinian-Thomist tradition.[307] Many of these theologians and confessions appealed to texts like Psalms 19:1–6 and 89:1–13; Job 38; Romans 1:19–25 and 2:14–15; and Acts 14:15–17 and 17:22–33 to accentuate Scripture's own confirmation of natural revelation and with it a justification of natural theology. In summary, the Reformation and its heirs did practice natural theology and in a way that put them, by their own admission, in "broad continuity" with the church catholic.[308]

---

303. "Calvin is a believer in natural theology, otherwise man cannot be held culpable, yet he knows its external parameter." Steinmetz, *Calvin in Context,* 30.

304. Muller, *PRRD* 1:278–310.

305. Steinmetz, *Calvin in Context,* 31. E.g., Melanchthon, *Commentarii,* 71, 74; Zwingli, *In Evangelican,* 409; Oecolampadius, *In Epistolam b. Pauli Apost. Ad Rhomanos Adnotationes,* fols. 12r-15r; Musculus, *In Epistolam Apostoli Pauli ad Romanos,* 30–31; Vermigli, *In Epistolam S. Pauli Apostoli ad Romanos,* 57–67; et al.

306. Muller, *PRRD* 1:310; contra Weber, *Foundations,* 1:217.

307. For an overview of natural theology in these documents, see Fesko, "Introduction," xxiv-xxxi.

308. Fesko, "Introduction," xxv; cf. Muller, *PRRD,* 1:271. Fesko and Muller both demonstrate that it was not until the period of late orthodoxy that certain Reformed theologians begin to move natural theology beyond its intrinsic and extrinsic parameters.

Case Study 2: The Fourfold Meaning of Scripture
and the Catholicity of Hermeneutics

A common assumption is that (1) the medievals dispensed with or ignored the literal sense of Scripture for the sake of the spiritual sense, but (2) the Reformers abandoned this wild hermeneutic and returned the church to the literal sense. This reading is often driven by modern prejudices and is inaccurate for a variety of reasons.[309]

First, medieval interpreters did not abandon the literal sense. As the Quadriga demonstrates, the literal sense was considered indispensable. Allegory teaches "what you should believe, morality teaches what you should do, anagogy what mark you should be aiming for" but the "letter teaches events."[310] For medieval biblical commentaries, the literal sense was considered essential, presupposed whenever the other senses were operative. Yet some medieval interpreters went further, convinced the spiritual sense was *based on* the literal sense. As we witnessed in a scholastic like Thomas Aquinas, he did not hesitate to empower the literal sense with a governing authority in his use of the allegorical, moral, and anagogical.

Thomas was not a maverick either. Others after Thomas took a similar approach, such as Nicholas of Lyra (1270–1349), who also affirmed the fourfold sense but chose to underline the literal sense.[311] Even those who featured the allegorical prominently still operated under the assumption that the literal sense is a bedrock on which the other senses rise up. Gregory the Great in the sixth century, Alcuin in the eighth century, Hugh of St. Victor in the twelfth century—each used the illustration of a house to capture the way the *littera* is the foundation on which *allegoria*, *tropologia*, and *anagogia* are built.[312] The illustration fits the purpose of allegory itself, which in their estimation builds on the historical milieu of the text to then transport the reader to Christ, the *telos* of the text in its wider context (i.e., the canon). That *telos* is not imposed on the text by the interpreter but is the revelatory intention of the divine author himself, who rises above any individual human author to create a unified canon

---

309. For a survey of moderns who are dismissive of precritical exegesis or play into the caricatures mentioned above, see Muller, "Biblical Interpretation in the Era of the Reformation," 3–6. Muller blames Frederic Farrar in particular, though he also identifies many others. Muller concludes, "It is certainly the case that the neat lines historians have tended to draw between the Middle Ages and the Renaissance, or between either the Middle Ages or the Renaissance and the Reformation, or between the Reformation and the pre-Reformation eras, were by no means visible in the sixteenth century" (5).

310. De Lubac, *Medieval Exegesis*, 1:1.

311. Nicholas of Lyra, *La metamorphose des dieux*, 1 (1957), 372, quoted in De Lubac, *Medieval Exegesis*, 1:1. Also see Herrmann, "Luther's Absorption of Medieval Biblical Interpretation," 76, who considers Luther's criticisms of Lyra's "double-literal sense" hermeneutic. As for d'Etaples, who rejected the "traditional four-fold method of exegesis for the sake of a single, spiritual-literal (Christological) sense is idiosyncratic, but it grows out of the broader trends among medieval scholars who increasingly associated the spiritual meaning of the Scriptures with its literal sense" says Herrmann. Luther not only read d'Etaples but appeared appreciative.

312. Historians do acknowledge, however, that some did place more emphasis on the allegorical. See Spicq, *Squisse d'une histoire de l'exégèse latine au moyen âge*; Schreiner "Through a Mirror Dimly: Calvin's Sermons on Job," 177; Muller, "Biblical Interpretation in the Era of the Reformation," 9.

that culminates in Christ. The spiritual sense has no foundation apart from the literal sense, but the literal sense is incomplete without the spiritual sense. For the capstone of the spiritual sense is Christ; therefore, a disregard for the spiritual sense is not worthy of *Christian* interpretation.

Furthermore, such a christological ambition results in a most biblical outcome: the salvation and sanctification of the reader, which rises to the surface of the text with the moral and anagogical senses. Exegesis was a participatory endeavor. With that sanctifying outcome in mind, medieval interpreters followed the hermeneutical example of the church fathers, from Irenaeus to Origen, from John Cassian to Augustine.[313] True, certain Antiochene theologians (e.g., Theodore of Mopsuestia, Basil of Caesarea) did criticize the use of allegory among the Alexandrians, but historians now warn against a sharp contrast between two "schools" for many reasons. For instance, the Antiochenes did not deny a spiritual sense in the text, but assumed its legitimacy in their desire to reform allegory.

Second, the Reformers criticized allegory, but they were not against allegory *per se*, only its abuses. Apart from such nuance, the historian cannot make sense of the Reformers who condemned allegory one moment only to utilize it to interpret the Old Testament the next.[314] Luther and Calvin are prime examples. Each criticized allegory but continued to employ the method to interpret the whole canon through the lens of the gospel of Jesus Christ. Their criticisms were directed against those who used allegory to justify heretical or novel doctrines. Yet instead of abandoning allegory, many Reformers refined or even redefined the catholic method for the sake of their Reformation theology. Commenting on Luther's evolving use of allegory, Robert Kolb observes how Luther "changed his use of allegory from application to illustration, but he also replaced it as a primary tool with a concrete, historically oriented focus on God's promise in Christ."[315]

Unfortunately, after modernity some of Luther's heirs have assumed Luther had nothing to do with that catholic hermeneutic, the analogy of faith. As if the analogy of faith was a novel product of Protestant Scholasticism in the subsequent centuries—we could call this the Luther versus the Lutherans outlook. However, a survey of Luther's sermons reveals his constant appeal to the Creed to interpret the text. In other words, Luther brought the Creed to the text from the start of his hermeneutic adventure, ensuring he (1) interpreted Scripture as Scripture interprets Scripture and (2) interpreted Scripture according to orthodoxy rather than heresy.[316]

313. See Boersma, *Scripture as Real Presence*, 1–26, 56–80.

314. Kolb examines *WA* 2:550.8–552.32 and draws the same conclusion (*Martin Luther*, 46–47). Also compare *LW* 5:346–347 with 1:86–87. For Calvin, see *Institutes* 2.5.19. Cf. Chase, *40 Questions About Typology and Allegory*, 222–223; Carter, *Interpreting Scripture with the Great Tradition*, 185.

315. Kolb, *Martin Luther*, 46–47 n. 17. Haines makes Kolb's point as well: *Martin Luther and the Rule of Faith*, 7–8; cf. *WATR* 2:487.27–28, no. 2493.

316. Haines gives ample evidence in *Martin Luther and the Rule of Faith* (over against Derek Cooper, Sujin Park, et al.).

Protestant misinterpretations of Reformation hermeneutics have been prejudiced by modernity. "As a result of the Enlightenment turn, Protestant exegetes increasingly saw the analogy of faith as a logical fallacy (*petition principii*, it assumes the conclusion); they replaced it with the standards of historical criticism and reason." Todd Haines observes the irony: "In contrast, the Reformers would see the standards of historical criticism and reason as circular reasoning that assumes its conclusions and does not understand the Bible as a book authored by the Holy Spirit."[317] The Reformers may have tailored the Quadriga for their Reformation theology (e.g., law and gospel, justification *sola fide*, priesthood of believers), but unlike moderns they were lockstep with medieval interpreters because they always assumed the indispensability of divine authorial intent and therefore a spiritual sense. Anything less meant the Scriptures—the Old Testament in particular—could no longer be, as Luther said, the swaddling clothes of baby Jesus.

Anxiety over an allegorical method severed from the literal sense was not unique to the Reformation. The same medieval theologians who insisted on the foundational nature of the literal for the spiritual sense (Rupert of Deutz, Thomas Aquinas, Hugh of St. Victor, etc.) also warned against separating allegory from the literal sense.[318] As far as the Reformers considered the literal sense the foundation of the spiritual sense they followed in the stream of scholastics like Thomas.

Third, the Reformers exhibited a variety of hermeneutical opinions among themselves—they were not monolithic. Luther's christological exegesis of the Psalms (in which the fourfold sense was prominent) and Zwingli's allegorical interpretation of the Old Testament stand in stark contrast to Martin Bucer's criticisms of allegory and his default retreat to Erasmian humanism.[319] Such diversity should guard against sweeping generalizations that pit the Reformers over against the Scholastics as if the Reformers themselves were of one hermeneutical mind. More to the point, remnants of the fourfold sense in Reformers like Luther, Calvin, and Zwingli should also caution against a sharp contrast between the Reformers and medieval interpreters themselves. As McGrath says, "It is difficult to sustain the thesis that the distinctive foundational ideas of the Reformation themselves arose on account of a novel hermeneutic, even in the case of Luther himself."[320] On that score, the absence of

---

317. Haines, 17–18.

318. Chase, *40 Questions About Typology and Allegory*, 90–91.

319. For Luther's Christological hermeneutic, see *WA* 55/2:6.25–8.2; *WA* 10:7; cf. Kolb, *Martin Luther and the Enduring Word of God*, 125. McGrath even ties the contrast to differing spiritualities, Martin Bucer aligning himself with the *devotio moderna* and its *imitatio Christi*. McGrath, *The Intellectual Origins of the European Reformation*, 171.

320. McGrath, 174. As for Luther, Herrmann argues that Luther was not against the fourfold method per se; rather, he believed the method needed to be complimented further by the distinction between law and gospel. Luther was indebted to the medieval method, but he also established a "new framework" with "creative adaptations of traditional methods as he reoriented Augustine's interpretation of Paul to the hermeneutical

a novel hermeneutic does leave open the real possibility that the Reformation's interpretation of Scripture is far more catholic than critics have assumed.

Catholicity remained embedded within their hermeneutic because they insisted on interpreting the Bible according to the *analogia fidei*, the analogy of faith, a move both patristic and medieval. Consider Luther for example. For Luther, the analogy of faith or the rule of faith consisted of the following:

1. Ten Commandments
2. Apostles' Creed
3. Lord's Prayer (Our Father)
4. Sacraments

Combined, they form the "ancient, true Christian catechism" of the Christian faith, which explains why Luther lamented how few preachers in his day knew how to preach—they did not even know the catechism themselves.[321] Theological education needed reform so that those who knew the catechism were considered the true doctors of Holy Scripture.[322]

Luther, therefore, did not stand against all allegory but allegory that conflicted with the catechism. As Luther himself said, "When we condemn allegories we are speaking of those that are fabricated by one's own intellect and ingenuity, without the authority of Scripture. Other [allegories] which are made to agree with the analogy of faith not only enrich doctrine but also console consciences."[323]

Fourth, if far more continuity exists between medieval and Reformation interpreters than has been recognized, then the misconception that the Reformers departed wholesale from medieval exegetes may be based on an anachronistic reading of history—as if the hermeneutic of the Reformers is modern, a product of the Enlightenment to be exact. Although historians include the sixteenth century in the "early modern" era, we should be hesitant to apply a "modern" label to the hermeneutic of the Reformers. Whatever criticisms they voiced of medieval interpretation the Reformers remained *precritical* interpreters of Scripture.[324] For all their vocalized critique of allegorical excess, they never left the spiritual sense behind, a hermeneutical maneuver unimaginable until the rise of modernity.

Richard Muller is instructive. He warns other historians against the common assumption "that the exegetical methods of the Reformers are a prologue to modern critical exegesis and that the hermeneutical assumptions of the Reformation were far more akin to those of twentieth-century biblical interpreters than

---

problem that Origen and others had tried to address." His hermeneutic is defined by both "relevance and catholicity." Hermann, "Luther's Absorption of Medieval Biblical Interpretation," 84.
  321. *WA* 23:486.1.
  322. *WA* 11:60.1.
  323. *LW* 27:311.
  324. Steinmetz, "The Superiority of Pre-Critical Exegesis," 27–38.

to those of the medieval exegetes." This assumption fails to acknowledge the obvious: the Reformers were late medieval men (they were not familiar with our modern divisions of history). They assumed a "precritical model" that had far "more in continuity with trajectories of medieval biblical interpretation than with tendencies in modern and so-called 'critical' exegesis."[325] When moderns witness a Reformer emphasizing the literal sense, they must be careful they do not project the restrictions of a strict historical-grammatical mindset that came much later back into Reformation hermeneutics. "The transition from the Middle Ages to the Reformation was not, certainly, a transition from precritical to modern 'critical' exegesis."[326] For example, Muller considers Calvin and Luther's exegesis of the Old Testament hard evidence that the Reformers stood in continuity with the fourfold sense of Scripture. His historical insight into the literal sense deserves full consideration:

> The "literal" meaning of the text, for Calvin, held a message concerning what Christians ought to believe, what Christians ought to do, and what Christians ought to hope for. This paradigm seems suspiciously familiar. It is clearly not at all like the modern, higher-critical paradigm for biblical interpretation. It asks that the exegete move past the rather bare grammatical meaning of the text to doctrine, morality, and hope—in short, from *littera* to *credenda*, *agenda*, and *speranda*. . . . The sense of the text is focused in its literal meaning, but the underlying assumption that the meaning of the text is ultimately oriented to the belief, life, and future of the church retains significant affinities with the *quadriga*, the basic pattern of the so-called "allegorical exegesis" of the Middle Ages. . . . [Likewise] all Luther's commentaries, whether early or late, consistently address doctrinal and moral issues—*credenda* and *agenda*. . . . The point of these observations is not to claim either Luther or Calvin as a proponent of the *quadriga*. Rather, the point is to note a fundamental continuity of exegetical interest that remained the property of precritical exegesis as it passed over from the medieval fourfold model into other models that, in one way or another, emphasized the concentration of meaning in the literal sense of the text. The *quadriga*, after all, was never merely an allegorical interpretation. The history of medieval exegesis, moreover, evidences a shift toward the letter. Even so, Luther, Calvin, and their contemporaries did not simply trade allegory for literal interpretation. They strengthened the shift to letter with increased emphasis on textual and philological study, and then proceeded to find various figures and levels of meaning, indicating *credenda*, *agenda*, and *speranda* embedded in the letter itself. This passage from the fourfold exegesis toward an exegesis emphasizing the literal

---

325. Muller, "Biblical Interpretation in the Era of the Reformation," 8.

326. Muller does explain what kind of transition he thinks occurred: "It was a transition, however, from a precritical approach that could acknowledge spiritual senses of the text beyond the literal sense to a precritical approach that strove to locate spiritual meaning entirely in the literal sense." Muller, "Biblical Interpretation in the Era of the Reformation," 14.

meaning of the text, therefore, marks a continuity—not a contrast—between sixteenth-century biblical interpretation and the exegesis of at least the preceding four centuries.[327]

Continuity, not contrast—the Reformers did take issue with certain excesses that put too much emphasis on the allegorical instead of the literal in their opinion. Nothing in this chapter denies their worries over exuberance. However, from a historical perspective the Reformers still remain on the *precritical* side of the hermeneutical divide. For like their medieval predecessors the Reformers believed in a divine author, presupposed his divine authorial intent, and affirmed the divine author's ability to move above and beyond any single human author's understanding to communicate Christ across the canon. The mediums through which the divine author has chosen to do so are diverse, but they include typology and allegory (not all medieval interpreters distinguished between these two). Even in their emphasis on the literal sense their exegesis moved toward the spiritual sense, as evident in their moral and christological reading of the Old Testament in light of the New Testament.

Such broad continuity (as opposed to contrast) is another feature of the Reformation's catholicity. When David Steinmetz put forward ten theses that governed the Reformation's hermeneutic, he was strategic, concluding with this final thesis: "Knowledge of the exegetical tradition of the church is an indispensable aid for the interpretation of Scripture."[328] However much the Reformers critiqued the interpretive tradition before them, they always did so under the assumption that their exegesis was *catholic*.

The Reformers interpreted the Bible *with the church*.

SCHOLASTIC SOIL FOR A REFORMATION GARDEN

Instead of interpreting Scholasticism as the wilderness and wasteland that the Reformers escaped to enter the promised land, these brief studies demand a more accurate illustration. Scholasticism was a *soil*, a mixed and diverse soil to be sure, but one responsible for a lush garden cultivated by its heirs. Much of this soil provided nutrients from orthodoxy that the flowers of the Reformation drew upon to sprout. However, in this the soil weeds sprouted as well, at least in the estimation of the Reformers. And these weeds, such as the penance system, grew alongside the flowers. It took a forceful gardener (Luther) to uproot those weeds, but it is a mistake to assume that the Reformers considered all the soil poisonous to the garden they then sought to prime and nurture.

Students of the Reformation who understand the method and spirit of pure

---

327. Muller, "Biblical Interpretation in the Era of the Reformation," 12.

328. Steinmetz, "Theology and Exegesis: Ten Theses," 382; cf. Muller, "Biblical Interpretation in the Era of the Reformation," 7. I find theses 1 and 6 supportive to my argument as well: "1. The meaning of a biblical text is not exhausted by the original intention of the author. . . . 6. The gospel and not the law is the central message of the biblical text."

Scholasticism will notice its traces across the landscape of the sixteenth century.[329] Brief attention has been given to Luther, Calvin, Bucer, Zanchi, and Vermigli, as well as themes such as the fourfold sense of Scripture, but many other Reformers and themes could be enlisted as well. Throwing off the "oppositional narrative," Protestants today are now revisiting the Reformers to discover afresh the pervasive Scholastic, specifically Thomistic influence on the sixteenth century.

For example, Philip Melanchthon lived in the shadows of Luther's fiery rhetoric against Scholasticism and voiced criticism of his own. Yet with time even Luther's colleague could not avoid a more nuanced and even positive evaluation of Thomas, calling him "reasonable among the recent ones" in the *Apology of the Augsburg Confession*.[330] Melanchthon, in his first edition of *Loci Communes* (1521), did not hesitate to criticize medieval theologians and sidelined a treatment of theology proper and Christology in the name of taking a more redemptive-historical approach. However, as Melanchthon taught on Romans and lectured on anthropology a natural theology emerged that affirmed the unregenerate person's use of reason in logic, ethics, and physics, as evident in ancient philosophers like Socrates, Plato, and Aristotle. Melanchthon's natural theology was presupposed when he ensured Aristotle's philosophy and ethic became essential reading in the university. Melanchthon kept Aristotle as a pillar in Lutheran education, and others like Martin Bucer and Peter Martyr Vermigli did the same in Reformed education via the Aristotelianism of Thomas Aquinas.[331]

In addition, in 1537 Melanchthon lectured on the life of Aristotle, and in 1538 the humanist in Melanchthon wrote four volumes on dialectic, reaching the conclusion that Aristotle's philosophy was indispensable for developing a clear, coherent method, as well as dispelling the irrational argument of heretics. By the 1540s Melanchthon had felt the pressure of sectarians, such as certain anti-Trinitarians and various Anabaptists. Therefore, by his third edition in 1543–44 the Reformer had expanded his *Loci Communes* to exhibit the Reformation's catholicity, covering the doctrine of God and Christology to demonstrate the Reformation's conformity to patristic and medieval orthodoxy.[332] Despite Luther's sharp words against Aristotle, Melanchthon introduced a classical metaphysic that shaped Lutheranism for the future. As Rober Kolb observes, "His use of Aristotelian principles within his own rhetorical-dialectical system of analysis determined the manner of argumentation among Wittenberg students

---

329. One of the best surveys of the literature is by Sytsma, "Sixteenth-Century Reformed Reception of Aquinas," 121–43.

330. Melanchthon, "Die Apologie der Konfession," 152. If Melanchthon utilized Aristotelianism, why was he not vocal as a Reformed Thomist? Historians debate the answer, but some believe the answer may have to do with association. Melanchthon's friend Joachim Camerarius said that "when Melanchthon studied in Tübingen Aristotle was associated with the *via moderna* rather than the *via antiqua*," explain Swensson and VanDrunen ("Introduction," 10). They are following Oberman, *Werden und Wertung der Reformation*, 424.

331. Muller says Melanchthon's decision is due to his belief in the continuance of the *imago Dei* after the fall. Muller, *PRRD* 1:102; cf. Kusakawa, *The Transformation of Natural Philosophy*.

332. Melanchthon, *Loci Communes* (1543–44). Catholicity was not the only reason, however. Van Asselt, *Introduction to Reformed Scholasticism*, 89–91.

and pointed the way to a Lutheran return to the employment of metaphysics at the turn of the seventeenth century."[333]

Among the Swiss, Ulrich Zwingli preached a sermon on divine providence on the cusp of the Marburg Colloquy (1529), and he echoed the spirit of Scholastics from Anselm to Thomas when he not only described God as the supreme good—whose nature is true, simple, immutable, and omnipotent—but as the primary cause, an Aristotelian notion if there ever was one.[334] "For all his radical theology," Zwingli "had been a student of the medieval Scholastics and believed himself an inheritor of the legacy of the church fathers."[335] One of Zwingli's closest theological allies, Johann Oecolampadius (1482–1531), was forthright with those he ministered to in Basel that the theology of late medieval Scholastics like Duns Scotus was at points irreconcilable with the theology of the Reformation; Oecolampadius then pointed to earlier Scholastics like Thomas Aquinas as a superior model.[336] When Heinrich Bullinger preached in Zurich, he appealed to Thomas in his sermons in a variety of ways, demonstrating that he never actually broke with his early Thomistic education.[337]

In Cambridge, England, the Reformer William Whitaker (1548–95) also appealed to Thomas Aquinas but with special attention to his commentaries for the sake of defending the authority and clarity of Scripture in his *Disputatio de Sacra Scriptura*, utilizing Thomistic arguments against Rome.[338] And Richard Hooker (1554–1600) appropriated Thomas Aquinas's understanding of natural law not only to establish the credibility of his own orthodoxy but to advance his ecclesiology.[339] And in Scotland, even a Reformer like John Knox, perhaps the most aggressive opponent of medieval papalism, turned to a "conventional Scholastic set of syllogisms" to challenge the Mass, and drew from his training in "Aristotelian syllogisms" to advance his argument in his *First Blast*.[340]

---

333. Kolb, "Confessional Lutheran theology," 69–70. For an example, consider how the Formula of Concord used Aristotle's "accidents" to refute Flacius who made sin essential to human nature (75).

334. On "primary cause," see Zwingli, *On the Providence of God*, in *On Providence and Other Essays*, 132. When Zwingli distinguished between created and uncreated powers, he recruited support from antiquity, sacred and otherwise: "Moses, Paul, Plato, Seneca are witnesses," he said. Eliciting their support in various ways, Zwingli built his argument in support of a deity whose reign is as unsurpassable as it is unchangeable. "There is then, nothing which is not ruled by the Deity, nothing so high or powerful that it can avoid the sway of our Deity, nothing so lowly or humble that it is abhorrent to His care. All this will be set forth more at length.... It is enough in the present chapter to have shown that wisdom, goodness, and might ... are what necessarily constitute Providence, and that Providence is the eternal and unchangeable government and direction of all things in the universe" (138).

335. Gordon, *Zwingli*, 8 (cf. 17).

336. Ballor, "Deformation and Reformation," 35; Herzog, *Das Leben Johannes Oekolampads und die Reformation der Kirche zu Basel*, 1:105.

337. Ballor, "Deformation and Reformation," 35; Bullinger, *Decades*, 1.9:160–1; 5.6:239; 5.6:239; 5.9:443; 5.9:464.

338. Whitaker, *Disputatio Deo Sacra Scriptura*. Cf. Sytsma, "Thomas Aquinas and Reformed Biblical Interpretation," 48–74.

339. Hooker's *Lawes* in volume 1 of the *Works of Richard Hooker*. Cf. Kirby, "Richard Hooker and Thomas Aquinas on Defining Law," 91–108.

340. Dawson, *John Knox*, 61, 144.

While innumerable other Reformers could be investigated—some presupposing Scholasticism more than others—denying the Reformation's subtle but formidable reliance on Scholasticism may be common but cannot be wise. Scholasticism is the soil in which the Reformation garden grew its roots. In histories of the Reformation, credit is given to the sun's rays (humanism) and the rainfall that followed (cleansing papal abuses), but without the soil (Scholasticism) the garden had little chance of survival. However critical some Reformers may have been, the Reformation garden presupposed, even depended on a Scholastic soil apart from which its claims to catholicity could only ring hallow.

PROTESTANT AND REFORMED SCHOLASTICISM

Out of the richness of that Scholastic soil came the Reformation, but that soil proved so rich that heirs of the Reformation also sprouted and blossomed, resulting in the longevity of Protestant Scholasticism from the late sixteenth century into the eighteenth century. Three reasons explain its rise to prominence:

1. Undergraduate education in the sixteenth and early seventeenth century still rested on Aristotle; the Renaissance Aristotelianism of the Protestant academics conditioned the minds of students to a Scholastic type of theology.
2. Religious controversies led theologians back to Scholastic thought categories for more ammunition after they had shot off their store of scriptural proof texts.
3. Individual Protestant theologians more and more appropriated Scholastic attitudes, categories, and doctrines as they tried to systematize theology.[341]

Protestant Scholasticism transcended Lutheran and Reformed divides, as both camps retrieved the method of Scholasticism and, to different degrees, its theology as well.[342] For example, Lutherans did not necessarily follow their founding father's rhetoric, as is plain in Johann George Dorsch, who was convinced that the Lutheran confessions were in alignment with the best features of Thomism. In 1656 he said Thomas was a "confessor of the evangelical truth according to the Augsburg Confession."[343]

Protestant Scholasticism found a home in the Reformed Church as well. Reformed Scholasticism was defined, in part, by its method. Following the form of the medieval Scholastics, the Reformed Scholastics used the *quaestio* approach,

---

341. Donnelly, "Calvinist Thomism," 442 (cf. 450).

342. The influence of Thomas is not limited to Lutheran and Reformed Scholastics, but can also be observed within Anglicanism (e.g., Richard Hooker). Kirby, "Richard Hooker and Thomas Aquinas on Defining Law," 91–108.

343. Johann Georg Dorsch, *Thomas Aquinas, dictus doctor angelicus, exhibitus confessor veritatis evangelicae Augustana confessione repetitae*. Cf. Svensson and VanDrunen, "Introduction," 1. Also consult John Gerhard's *Loci Theologici* (1610). Muller warns against the assumption that Aristotelianism controlled either medieval or Reformed Scholasticism (*PRRD* 1:37).

a style that allowed them to be precise. Three components were incorporated as well: (1) dialectic discourse, (2) systematized structure, and (3) Aristotelian distinctions—although the third mark should not be misconstrued as foundational when it was merely instrumental.[344]

However, form was not the only trademark or concern, but a means to an end. Above all, they desired a Reformed faith that was marked by catholicity. The broader label of Reformed *Orthodoxy* can be used to capture the *content* their method produced. Nevertheless, Reformed *Scholasticism* as a label is not identical with Reformed *Orthodoxy*. Yet when the Reformed Orthodox did choose to utilize the scholastic method, the "primary goal in doing so was to develop a method of teaching confessional Reformed theology that was suitable to theological schools."[345]

With the deaths of second-generation Reformed theologians such as John Calvin and Peter Martyr Vermigli, Reformed Orthodoxy was born and may be divided into three eras:

1. Early Orthodoxy: ca. 1565–1640
   Theologians: Theodore Beza, Franciscus Junius, Zacharias Ursinus, Caspar Olevianus, Jerome Zanchi, Lambert Daneau, William Perkins, Amandus Polanus, Franciscus Gomarus, John Davenant, William Ames, etc.
   Confessions and Catechisms: e.g., Scots, Belgic, Second Helvetic, Heidelberg
   Synods: Synod of Dort, etc.
2. High Orthodoxy: ca. 1640–1725
   Theologians: Johannes Cocceius, Gisbertus Voetius, Francis Turretin, Edward Leigh, John Owen, Stephen Charnock, Wilhelmus á Brakel, Peter van Mastricht, Herman Witsius, Thomas Boston, etc
   Confessions: Westminster Confession of Faith, Savoy Declaration, Formula Consensus Helvetica, London Baptist Confession, etc.
3. Late Orthodoxy: ca. 1725–1790
   Theologians: Johann Stapfer, Herman Venema, John Gill, etc.[346]

Out of these three eras, High Orthodoxy represented a most mature retrieval of medieval Scholasticism to defend the Reformed faith against external and internal threats.[347] Reformed Scholastics did participate in ongoing polemics with Lutherans (over the Lord's Supper and the christological controversy of the *communicatio idiomatum* for example), but they also engaged a wide variety

---

344. Costello, *The Scholastic Curriculum*, 8.
345. McGraw, *Reformed Scholasticism*, 97.
346. Various dates have been suggested, but I am following Muller, *PRRD*, 1:31–32.
347. Muller, *PRRD*, 1:65–66; Asselt and Dekker, eds., *Reformation and Sscholasticism*, 13; McGraw, *Reformed Scholasticism*, 99.

of old and new challenges with (1) Roman Catholicism, (2) anti-Trinitarianism (Italy, Poland), (3) Socinianism, (4) Arminianism, and (5) Deism.[348]

A past generation of historians tried to cast the post-Reformation Reformers as if they departed from their sixteenth-century forefathers—otherwise known as the Calvin versus the Calvinist thesis (e.g., Basil Hall, R. T. Kendall, Brian Armstrong, Rogers and McKim).[349] However, many historians have demonstrated the futility of that interpretive grid.[350] One should not assume, for example, that the Reformers were biblical, while their children turned rationalists. Nor should one believe the caricature that the Reformed Scholastics posed a central dogma (e.g., predestination) only to deduce an entire system rationally. Rather, the children of the Reformation faced a new context in which the building blocks of the previous century now required assembly so that Reformed churches could rely on an entire system of theology to give proof of their continuity with patristic and medieval orthodoxy. "The selectivity of the Reformation in its polemic had to be transcended in the direction of a reformed catholicity," observes Muller.[351] The Reformers were no doubt indispensable to the genesis of Reformation theology, but their heirs were "responsible for the final form of such doctrinal issues," and the Scholastic method proved instrumental to that task.[352]

> Where the Reformers painted with a broad brush, their orthodox and scholastic successors strove to fill in the details of that picture. Whereas the Reformers were intent upon distancing themselves and their theology from problematic elements in medieval thought and, at the same time, remaining catholic in the broadest sense of that term, the Protestant orthodox were intent upon establishing systematically the normative, catholic character of institutionalized Protestantism, at times through the explicit use of those elements in patristic and medieval theology not at odds with the teachings of the Reformation.[353]

---

348. Peter Martyr Vermigli exemplified a Reformed Scholastic response to many of these groups. See his *Dialogus de utraque in Christo natura* and *Epistolae duae ad ecclesias Polonicas*. Donnelly, "Calvinist Thomism," 443–44.

349. Hall, "Calvin against the Calvinists," 19–37; Kendall, *Calvin and English Calvinism to 1649*; Armstrong, *Calvinism and the Amyraut Heresy*; Rogers and McKim, *The Authority and Intepretation of the Bible*. This line of argument is found in older studies too: Gründler, *Thomism and Calvinism in the Theology of Girolamo Zanchi*. Gründler has been refuted by Donnelly, "Calvinist Thomism," 441–455.

350. For responses to Calvin versus the Calvinist caricature, see Van Asselt and Dekker, *Reformation and Scholasticism*, esp. Muller's chapter, "The Problem of Protestant Scholasticism," 45–64. Muller critiques McGrath, *Reformation Thought*, 120–30, and Armstrong, *Calvinism and the Amyraut Heresy*, 32, for example, but he also lays blame at the feet of Karl Barth and Barthianism for painting the Protestant Scholastics as deductive rationalists.

351. Muller, *PRRD* 1:28.

352. Muller, *PRRD* 1:37.

353. Muller, *PRRD* 1:37. "Protestant scholasticism represents the academic answer to a demand that Christian doctrine be elaborated within the bounds of a body of dogmatic norms, the churchly confessions.... Protestant scholasticism is, in part, the result of the educational as well as the theological-confessional institutionalization of the Reformation." Muller, "The Problem of Protestant Scholasticism," 62.

Reason was important to that task, yet reason was not foundational but merely instrumental, a faith seeking understanding, not vice versa; Scripture remained the cognitive foundation (*principium cognoscendi*), which explains why their dogmatics presupposed rigorous exegesis.[354] Yet dogmatics was their ambition since their Reformation predecessors did not usually write comprehensive systems of Reformed belief. Calvin's *Institutes,* explains Muller, was "no more than a basic instruction in the doctrines of Scripture and not a full system of theology written with the precision and detail of the systems of Calvin's own Roman Catholic opponents."[355] However, by the end of the sixteenth century full systems were born with the rise of Reformed Scholasticism. Likewise, whereas Reformation confessions sometimes limited themselves to doctrines under polemical pressure, later Reformed confessions establish a more extensive landscape of Reformed theology.[356]

Reformed Scholastics wielded Aristotle and Thomas Aquinas alike to refute their opponents and to codify their Reformed catholicity. To qualify, their retrieval of the Thomistic stream of medieval Scholasticism was not mere duplication but critical appropriation—an adoption of a "modified Thomism" evident in early figures like Vermigli and Zanchi.[357]

Furthermore, Thomism was not the only influence; they utilized aspects of other preceding streams, such as Renaissance humanism as well.[358] Nevertheless, a modified Thomism presented them with a metaphysic and epistemology that could further support and clarify the Reformed religion. They were not compromising the program of the early Reformers but bringing that program to maturity, even codification by answering new challenges.[359]

For example, John Patrick Donnelly has demonstrated the many ways Reformed Scholastics appealed to Aristotelian and Thomistic metaphysics to refute Rome. For example, Peter Martyr Vermigli used Thomism to counter Stephen Gardiner on the subject of transubstantiation.[360] Girolamo Zanchi did the same to refute Domingo de Soto (1494–1560) and the Council of Trent on subjects like nature and grace, free will and original sin.[361] In other words, even as early as the sixteenth century, they believed they could arrive at a purer Thomism by virtue of their evangelical commitments, not in spite of

---

354. Muller, "The Problem of Protestant Scholasticism," 59.

355. Muller, *PRRD* 1:33.

356. Muller, *PRRD* 1:33.

357. Muller, *PRRD* 1:65.

358. Muller, *PRRD* 1:37, 73. Some Early Orthodox also engaged Ramism, though that proved controversial, as evidenced in Beza's opposition to Ramism (1:62). Some were influenced by Ockham's division of theology into theoretical and practical as well (1:96).

359. Donnelly, "Calvinist Thomism," 452.

360. Peter Martyr Vermigli, *Defensio doctrinae . . . Eucharistiae . . .* , 116–65. Donnelly points out that Gardiner was wielding instead a Scotist philosophy ("Calvinist Thomism," 443).

361. Zanchi, *Opera Theologica* 4.35, 58–59, 92, 101–3, 191; cf. Donnelly, "Calvinist Thomism," 451. Even when Zanchi critiques Thomas, he still separates Thomas and says he is "purer than the other scholastics on the doctrine of grace" (*Opera Theologica* 2.344–45).

them, as is plain in their ironic use of Thomism against their Roman Catholic counterparts.

Yet critical appropriation of Thomism was not limited to polemics but defined the construction of their dogmatics as well. For instance, Reformed Scholastics from Patrick Gillespie to Francis Turretin to John Owen retrieved medieval Scholasticism's Trinitarianism. However, they did so in a way that was advantageous for Reformed covenant theology. They presupposed and sometimes outright retrieved the Thomistic articulation of inseparable operations and Trinitarian appropriations but for the sake of articulating the covenant of redemption, the covenant of works, and the covenant of grace.[362] To be accurate, it may be best to speak of a Trinitarian covenant theology to emphasize the way Reformed Scholasticism used its continuity with Nicaea and medieval Scholastic Trinitarianism to further its soteriology.

Historians like Donnelly even use a label like "Calvinist Thomism" to describe these eras because in "most of this vast area of theology there was no sharp conflict between Thomism and Calvinist orthodoxy."[363] That continuity is axiomatic within Puritanism as well. While not all Puritans were Reformed Scholastics, notable Reformed Scholastics were Puritans, such as John Owen (1616–1683). His creative and regular retrieval of Thomas has surfaced with the recent revival of Owen studies.[364] That appropriation should not be surprising. As a student Owen was taught by Thomas Barlow and John Prideaux, both of whom required Owen to read a wide range of medieval scholastics.[365] Although Owen was critical of medieval Scholasticism for a short time, over the course of his career he appreciated medieval Scholasticism and found it advantageous for polemics in his own day.

Out of the many Scholastics Owen studied, Thomas proved a special ally. Owen quoted Thomas, but his retrieval of Thomas was far more intrinsic to his exegesis, theology, and philosophy, as seen in his use of Thomistic concepts, principles, and logic.[366] In *Thomism in John Owen* Christopher Cleveland gives three examples.[367] First, the doctrine of God. Owen appealed to Thomas's description of God as pure act (*actus purus*) to defend divine simplicity against Arminians and Socinians in his day who threw it into question with a divine will they insisted could be thwarted.[368] Second, consider Christology. Owen explicitly

362. Gillespie, *The Ark of the Covenant Opened*; Cf. McGraw, *Reformed Scholasticism*, 103.
363. Donnelly, "Calvinist Thomism," 451.
364. Cleveland, *Thomism in John Owen*; Rehman, *Divine Discourse*; Trueman, *John Owen*; Trueman, *The Claims of Truth*.
365. Rehnman, *Divine Discourse*, 20–37, 124–127; Cleveland, *Thomism in John Owen*, 18–19. In 1661 Owen criticizes Scholasticism in his *Theologoumena*. However, the surrounding years—1642–1679—reveal his positive assessment.
366. See *Discourse on the Holy Spirit* for indirect use. For direct quotation, see *Christologia* (*Works* 1) and *The Doctrine of the Saints' Perseverance* (*Works* 11). Cf. Cleveland, *Thomism in John Owen*, 3.
367. Each of these are outlined by Cleveland, *Thomism in John Owen*, 4–5 (but throughout his entire study). References below follow his outline, though I've rearranged the order.
368. Owen, *A Display of Arminianism*, in *Works* 10:44; Owen, *Vindiciae Evangelicae*, in *Works* 12:70–71.

sided with Thomas over against Peter Lombard and rejects the belief that the human nature of Christ is an accident merely added to the divine nature, which cannot explain the hypostatic *union*. Following Thomas, Owen instead argued that the Son of God assumed a human nature to his person.[369] Third, consider sanctification. Owen disagreed with Thomas who said justification is defined by infused habits of grace (as opposed to imputation).[370] However, that disagreement did not move Owen to reject the concept of infused habits altogether. Owen discovered that Thomas had merely placed infused habits in the wrong doctrinal domain. So Owen moved the concept of infused habits out of justification to explain the new principle of grace in *regeneration* and its continual renewal of the believer in *sanctification*.[371] In summary, Trueman may be referring to John Owen, but his observation could be applied to many other Reformed Scholastics in the sixteenth and seventeenth centuries: John Owen "drew deeply upon the medieval metaphysical tradition, with a particular liking for the thought of Thomas Aquinas."[372] With John Owen Thomism was refined.

The Reformed Scholastics revealed their Thomistic influence by their philosophical commitments as well, a point to revisit in the next chapter. Etienne Gilson was correct to hold the nominalism of the *via moderna* responsible for the dichotomy between faith and reason. However, certain Roman Catholics who followed Gilson went further and blamed the Reformers and their Protestant Scholastic heirs for carrying that nominalism into modernity.[373] As mentioned in chapter 1, historians and theologians since have assumed the same. However, the assumption is a faulty one since the majority of Reformed Scholastics during the era of High Orthodoxy were transparent in their criticisms of Scotus (e.g., univocity of being, voluntarism, contingent divine knowledge) and Ockham (e.g., nominalism), finding refuge in the realism of the Augustinian and Thomist traditions instead. As Richard Muller has said, the Reformed Orthodox were decisively "Not Scotist." As for Ockham, as the Reformed Orthodox retrieved Thomism the majority sided with the realism of the *via antiqua* over against the nominalism of the *via moderna*.[374] Peter Martyr Vermigli, for example, "refers to twenty medieval Scholastic authors, particularly Peter Lombard and Aquinas," observes Donnelly. But he "never cites with approval a nominalist work."[375]

---

369. Owen, *Christologia*, in *Works* 1:224–231.

370. Owen, *Doctrine of Justification by Faith*, in *Works* 5:12, 64.

371. Owen, *Discourse on the Holy Spirit*, in *Works* 3:329, 468–469.

372. Trueman, *John Owen*, 22.

373. Examples: Joseph Lortz, Philip Hughes, Louis Bouyer, John Todd. See the critique of Donnelly, "Calvinist Thomism," 454.

374. Muller, "Not Scotist," 127–150; Sebastian Rehnman, *Divine Discourse*; Trueman, *John Owen*, 24. Trueman is responding to Antonie Vos, "Scholasticism and Reformation," 113–114, who assumes the Reformed were Scotists. Also see Cleveland, *Thomism in John Owen*, 16–17. However, certain Late Reformed Orthodox theologians did move beyond their predecessors's commitment to Aristotle by entertaining philosophies of the Enlightenment (Cartesian, Lockean, Ramist, etc.). Wallace, *Shapers of English Calvinism, 1660–1714*, 167–199; Goudriaan, "Theology and Philosophy," 27–64; McGraw, *Reformed Scholasticism*, 107.

375. Donnelly, "Calvinist Thomism," 443 (cf. 452–55). For example, consult Vermigli, *Philosophical Works*, a sampling of his works on reason, human psychology, epistemology, providence, and more.

As Peter Martyr Vermigli embodied a Thomistic retrieval in his church (Lucca) many, including John Diodati, Benedict Turrettini, and Francis Turrettini, traveled to Geneva where they modeled the same. The library at the Geneva academy was filled with works in Thomism, though the same could not be said about nominalism.

In summary, however much first-generation Reformers may have been tinged by sporadic influences of nominalism (itself a contested claim), the late sixteenth century and seventeenth century Reformed Scholastics were far more at home in the realism of Christian Platonism that spanned the Great Tradition, particularly the Aristotelian and Thomistic variety. John Owen is a case in point, a committed realist in the tradition of Thomism.[376]

Preserving the continuity between the Protestant Scholastics and (1) the Reformation and (2) the medieval Scholastics is no mere historical quibble but a historical paradigm that properly connects the Protestant identity to its ancient past. Put negatively, to sever Protestant Scholasticism from its Reformation and medieval heirs is to lock Protestantism out from the premodern world, thereby eliminating its own claims to catholicity.[377]

WHAT, THEN, PROVOKED REFORMATION?

If the Reformers were not only critical but also positive in their appropriation of the best methods and conclusions of Scholasticism, then what exactly provoked reformation?

That question is somewhat simplistic, as if one era of church history is to blame. The Middle Ages occupied over one thousand years—half of church history—and Scholasticism fills but a portion of that time span. Furthermore, the Middle Ages are not a monolithic era either; even Scholasticism itself was diverse (as will be seen in chapter 5).

That diversity does not deny that the Reformers took issue with important aspects of the Early and High Middle Ages. Even still, as this chapter and future chapters will reveal, the Reformers' criticisms were not directed at a *majority* of Christian doctrines—scriptural inspiration, Trinity, attributes of God, arguments for God's existence, divine providence, creation *ex nihilo*, anthropology, Christology, atonement, ethics, eschatology, and so on—especially those essential to remaining orthodox.[378] Rather, the Reformers' criticisms were directed at two broad *loci* in particular: (1) soteriology (justification, penance, purga-

---

376. Cleveland, *Thomism in John Owen*, 17.

377. "If reformed scholasticism is cut off from scholasticism in general and if one tries to understand both, without the background of medieval *philosophia christiana*, one prevents oneself from understanding centuries of European and Western thought." Vos, "Scholasticism and Reformation," 108.

378. To be extra clear, I am not saying that every Reformer agreed with every doctrine in every point. Christian theology is complex enough for disagreements to occur no matter the doctrine. What I am saying is this: overall, soteriology and ecclesiology were the *loci* that provoked critique, not the many other doctrines considered more or less agreeable and even indispensable to the Reformation's catholicity. Hence, a broad continuity persisted.

tory, etc.) and (2) ecclesiology (papal authority, polity, sacraments, transubstantiation, etc.). As far as the Scholastics went astray on soteriology, the Reformers withheld few criticisms. Yet ecclesiology expanded beyond Scholasticism to the medieval evolution of the papacy, as chapter 7 will explore, also presenting a point of division.

Therefore, the historian commits a significant blunder by assuming that the spark that lit the fire of the Reformation was Scholasticism *in toto*. What instigated the Reformation in Germany was a novel and far more radical movement known as the *via moderna*. The *via moderna* was a product of *late* medieval thought, with the rise of Scholastics like William of Ockham and Gabriel Biel. Whether Luther always knew it or not, the source of his soteriological crisis was not so much the pure Scholasticism of the High Middle Ages but the decadent Scholasticism of the late Middle Ages.[379] *Decadent* was the evaluation among those in the *late* Middle Ages who claimed Augustine's theology of grace (e.g., Bradwardine, Rimini) to counterattack the *via moderna*. For the soteriology of the *via moderna* was a conscious rejection of earlier Scholastics like Thomas Aquinas who, whatever his faults, nonetheless considered grace primary, much like Augustine himself.

With accusations such as the charge of Pelagianism being lobbed like grenades on the *via moderna*, we now explore this curious shift, which may be the hinge on which this story turns.

---

379. The language of "decadent" Scholasticism is shared by Vos, *Aquinas, Calvin, and Contemporary Protestant Thought*, 171.

5

PROVOCATION FOR REFORMATION

The Via Moderna, *Nominalism, and the Late*
Medieval Departure from the Realism of
Thomistic Augustinianism and Its Soteriology

Men like ... Thomas [Aquinas] do not belong exclusively to Rome. They
are partres and doctores to whom the entire church owes a great debt.
—Herman Bavinck, *Reformed Dogmatics*

It was virtually a truism among the Protestant scholastics that the earlier
medieval scholasticism of Anselm and Lombard was more congenial
to the Reformation and less troubled by philosophical and speculative
questions than the scholasticism of the later Middle Ages, particularly
from the time of Duns Scotus onward.
—Richard Muller, *After Calvin*

The Occamistic system is radically uncatholic.
—Joseph Lortz

This chapter is one of the most important chapters in this book because it is
one hinge on which its argument turns. It should be read in tandem with
the last chapter's evidence for the retrieval of medieval Scholasticism by the
Reformers and their Reformed Scholastic heirs. This chapter is so important
because it identifies the provocation of Luther's Reformation.

First, this chapter will reveal that Scotus but especially Ockham and Biel
represent a radical break with the soteriology of Augustinian Thomism and the
via antiqua. The justification theology of Augustine and Thomas may not go
all the way to the Protestant understanding (e.g., imputation), but this tradition was unwavering in its commitment to *sola gratia*, which explains why the
Reformers were so indebted. By contrast, the *via moderna* opened the door to
Semi-Pelagianism or even Pelagianism, and this school in which Luther was
nursed became the soil for his early protest.

Second, the Reformation has been accused (by schools like Radical Orthodoxy as well as recent historians) of cultivating the nominalism original to Ockham and friends. As a result, the Reformation has been blamed for abandoning the realist conception of participation (see chapter 1), thereby opening the door to modernity's divide between the sacred and the secular. However, this chapter, as well as parts 2 and 3, will lay a foundation that demonstrates such a thesis could not be more mistaken. Such an interpretation is correct to lay blame at the feet of Ockham's nominalism. However, the Reformers reacted *against* the nominalist soteriology of the *via moderna* as represented by Ockham and Biel. By contrast, the Reformers did in fact put forward a strong participation theology with their doctrine of union with Christ, a doctrine that made room for the *duplex gratia*, the double grace of justification and sanctification.[1]

Granted, some Reformers were influenced by nominalism in epistemology and metaphysics, but even these Reformers still reacted against nominalism's soteriology, placing themselves instead within the Augustinian heritage. Nevertheless, many second-generation Reformers and a majority of Protestant Scholastics did reject the univocity of Scotus and the nominalism of Ockham, recognizing its incompatibility with their classical realist conception of God and the world as manifested in their Augustinian soteriology.[2]

In short, the Reformation's reaction *against* the nominalist soteriology of the *via moderna* (see chapter 8) is proof that in the minds of the Reformers they remained catholic while the *via moderna* was radically uncatholic.

CLASSICAL REALISM AND THE GREAT TRADITION

To understand why Scotus, Ockham, and Biel represent a break with the *via antiqua* in major ways, a brief venture into classical philosophy is essential.[3] The goal in what follows is not to provide an exhaustive or meticulous examination of Platonism. Nor is the aim to examine the differences between variations of Platonism, which should be acknowledged but not overplayed.[4] Rather, this chapter's approach is humble, merely identifying certain threads of *continuity* that help explain why the Great Tradition (East and West) critically appropriated the metaphysic of the Greeks. From the church fathers to the Scholastics of the High Middle Ages, many in the Great Tradition transformed Platonism (resulting in what many historians call Christian Platonism).[5] To clarify, Platonism was not merely adaptable to Christianity, a philosophy that happened to be a convenient fit for theology, something they could pick at as an advantageous supplement.

---

1. I wrote this chapter (and chapter 8) prior to the release of Michael Horton's *Justification* (vol. 1). I was pleased to discover we draw similar conclusions in our research, and I have tried to mention his contribution briefly.

2. This point has been demonstrated by Muller, "Not Scotist: Understandings of Being, Univocity, and Analogy in Early-Modern Reformed Thought," 127–150.

3. What follows is in no way comprehensive, but merely gives a context to understand why a tear occurs in the fabric of the *via antiqua*'s participation metaphysic.

4. Consult Gerson, *Aristotle and Other Platonists*, 1–23.

5. Hampton and Kenney, eds., *Christian Platonism*, 1.1, 1.2, 1.3, 1.4, 1.5, 1.6, 2.1, 2.2, 2.3, 2.4.

Rather, the Great Tradition understood that Platonism had become the perennial philosophy of late antiquity because it offered a revolutionary, even unrivaled perspective that explained transcendent reality. Unlike nominalism, Platonism's belief that universals are *real* (hence, realism) ensured the goodness of this world, for example, was not left to material, mechanical processes but participates in the Good, which transcends the limitations of finitude. Realism also created space for transcendent divinity and all the perfections entailed (pure actuality, infinitude, timelessness, immutability, omnipresence, etc.). Furthermore, by positing a transcendent reality Platonism provided a map for the soul's ascent, ensuring the soul can participate in something beyond that which is material by means of contemplation, ultimately arriving at communion. Platonism was variegated in its theories over universals, but its realism was knit into the very fabric of the Great Tradition: to be a Christian was to be a transcendentalist. Not any philosophy would do—one looks in vain for Christian Epicureans. But Platonism, for all its serious flaws, displayed the power of natural revelation (Ps. 19:1–6). By critically appropriating Platonism the Great Tradition fortified the *realist* metaphysic that could substantiate participation in a transcendent reality. Yet that realist metaphysic proved inadequate to the nominalism of the late medieval era, a nominalism that led the *via moderna* to a soteriology the Reformers considered Pelagian at worst and Semi-Pelagian at best.

Plato

Plato used a variety of illustrations to capture a philosophy most indebted to his master Socrates. Consider his illustration of the cave. Imagine a group of prisoners in a cave who are fixated on shadows moving and dancing on the wall in front of them. They believe the shadows are real, but they do not know that there is a short wall behind them where a fire blazes as puppets are held up to cast shadows. They are so convinced the shadows are real that they conform their existence around these shadows, entertaining themselves and making bets to see who knows what the shadows will do next. Suppose one of the prisoners became suspicious, escaped, and walked outside of the cave, only to discover the real world. At first, he would cover his eyes, blinded by the sun, but over time his eyes would become illuminated by the sun. But if he returned to the darkness of the cave in his joy to tell others about the sun outside, those in the cave would mock him and perhaps even kill him for questioning the shadows.[6] To Plato, this martyr was Socrates, killed for questioning the shadows.

As the cave illustrates, for Plato the natural, sensible world is in the process of change, a world of Becoming, much in contrast to the intelligible world of Being, which is unchanging in its eternal, incorporeal perfection. In this world

---

6. For Plato's use of the cave allegory, see bk. 7 of his *Republic*. But for his understanding of creation, see *Timaeus* 20, 28–31, 37–46, 87, 90. Also consider his perception of the afterlife in *Gorgias*. For a more thorough overview of Plato and Platonism, see Gerson, *From Plato to Platonism*, 11–14; Copleston, *History of Philosophy*, 1:142–216; Markos, *From Plato to Christ*, 1–118.

of change, the human person sees but shadows of that perfect, unchanging, and transcendent reality. The shadows are but copies that imitate reality. Truth, goodness, and beauty may be experienced in the world of Becoming, but they are shadows that participate in their corresponding Ideas, which exist within the world of Being: the Truth, the Goodness, and the Beauty.[7] Plato believed the Good was the ultimate Idea (or Form). As subsistent Ideas that explain the universal similarity of particulars, they may also be labeled transcendentals.[8]

To know that world of Being, one must not limit oneself to the confines of the material realm, where the lust of the flesh weighs the soul down from contemplating its true home in the world of Being. The world of becoming is known by sensation but can only result in opinions and speculations. The world of Being, however, is known by the mind's eye. Hence the significance of philosophy; the soul must utilize reason to contemplate the Good in all its beauty. Illuminated by the Good, the result is true knowledge. With every degree of illumination, we are liberated from our fixation on lesser goods in the material world of Becoming, as we leave the darkness of the cave and its shadows to participate in the light of the sun in the world of Being.[9] Plato, therefore, had a strong conception of the beatific vision, in which a person ascends the ladder of truth, goodness, and beauty until he at last sees God.[10]

Plato was unique in his day because he believed in a Creator God—a Craftsman—who was the origin of all things, patterning the world after the Ideas.[11] The Ideas, in other words, act as exemplary causes, but they exist external to the Creator God. Plato described the Creator God as a personal Father who fashioned the world out of love to bless others.[12] While other philosophers like Protagoras said man is the measure of all things, Plato said God is the measure of all things. Indeed, in him we live and move and have our being—Plato was so enduring because he set in motion a participation metaphysic. Plato criticized the Greek gods because they were vulnerable to change and passions, even immoral. With a little manipulation, they could even be bribed. By contrast, Plato believed divinity must be immutable and impassible, good and just. Those who pursue wickedness will be punished in hell, but those who live the virtuous life—the just man—will be rewarded.

Plato's belief in universals was both timely and prophetic, especially when the

---

7. Plato sought to reconcile the many with the one. *Republic* 6.

8. A "universal" is "some one thing common to many which can be in many or be predicated of many." An "idea" is "the form or likeness of a thing existing apart from the thing itself" or "the exemplary form or mental type which the agent deliberately imitates in production; model." A (Platonic) "form" is a "subsistent Idea or Model supposed to exist as one of its kind in a separate universe, and in which things in this world participate as multiple copies and degrees of the Idea's perfection." And a "subsistent form" is a "form that can (or does) exist and act independently of matter." Wuellner, *Dictionary*, s.v.

9. Plato, *Republic* 7.

10. Plato, *Republic* 7, 10.

11. On Plato's description of the craftsman, consult *Timaeus* 28–37, 42, 46, 87, 90.

12. *Timaeus* 20, 30, 31, 37.

historian considers rival theories in ancient Athens, from the monistic materialism of the Stoics to the distant corporal deities of the Epicureans and their annihilation of final causality. Other philosophies, in other words, cut the cord of participation between the Creator and the creature. Plato, however, was convinced that Ideas exist and transcend this world and explain how this world of becoming participates in the world of Being. For example, consider beauty. As Socrates said in Plato's *Phaedo*, "When something is found to be beautiful, then it is beautiful because it participates in the absolute beauty."[13] Or consider the universal "holiness." Holiness can describe and define a variety of objects and persons in this world. A priest is holy, set apart for the Lord. A sanctuary is holy, the place where God's presence descends. A tree and the ground under it can be holy, as Moses discovered when God asked him to take off his sandals. Yet holiness is not limited or circumscribed by a priest or a sanctuary or a tree. Holiness is a Form or Idea that transcends any object or person, that archetype in which all copies participate for their likeness. Each particular participates in its Form or Idea, even though the Form or Idea itself is not dependent on a particular, existing in an independent realm.

Aristotle

Plato's theory of universals made him a realist, though in comparison with his student it may be best to call him a realist of transcendental universals. Aristotle (384–322 BC) carried his master's baton, teaching and elaborating on Plato's views in his Lyceum, but with a special talent for mapping Plato's original outlook onto a more systematic framework. By Aristotle's own testimony, Plato and Aristotle were in wide agreement on the grand contours of this realist metaphysic, despite contemporary caricatures that pit the two against each other.[14] As Thomas Williams explains, "Platonists and Aristotelians alike agreed that sensation is of particulars, whereas understanding is of universals. . . . Without universals, there will be no distinction between sensation and understanding." Without universals not even predication itself can function. The "universal entity gives objectivity to this predication."[15]

Furthermore, Aristotle advanced an understanding of metaphysics that explained the perennial value of first principles. For Aristotle, metaphysics is "Wisdom *par excellence,* and the philosopher or lover of Wisdom is he who desires knowledge about the ultimate cause and nature of Reality, and desires that knowledge for its own sake. . . . Wisdom, therefore, deals with the first principles and causes of things, and so is universal knowledge in the highest degree."[16] For example, Plato's world of Becoming is so defined by change

---

13. *Phaedo*, 100c.
14. Gerson, *From Plato to Platonism*, goes a long way to correcting such caricatures.
15. Williams, *Reason and Faith*, 328.
16. Copleston, *History of Philosophy*, 1:288. Metaphysics becomes the "study of being *qua* being" (290).

because everything exists in a state of potentiality—a state of passive potency—still in process of becoming complete in its actuality, perfect in its capacity. Composed as we are of act and potency, we are dependent on something outside ourselves, even changed by something outside of ourselves to make us complete.[17] That something or someone must be complete himself—pure act or pure actuality—lacking imperfection due to the motion and mutation caused by passive potency.[18] Those things subject to passive potency may exist but do not have to exist, and if they do exist, they must be caused by another. Yet someone "whose very substance is actuality" exists by absolute necessity without a First Unmoved Mover.[19]

Thus, Aristotle posited a Creator God who is the First Act and Unmoved Mover, and whose existence can explain all the movement—change—in the world because he alone is invulnerable to motion or change.[20] In Aristotle's own words, what we require is a "mover which moves without being moved, being eternal, substance, and actuality."[21] Aristotle's four causes—formal, material, efficient, final—defy an endless regress of change. Rather, they presuppose the existence of a First Cause, who is himself uncaused and therefore without change.[22] Aristotle is after First Philosophy, which in his mind depends upon divinity. Such an inseparable connection explains why Aristotle believed he was conducting theology itself.[23] For theology not only has an efficient cause but leads to final causality itself, the *telos* of humanity's existence, namely, participation in the likeness of God.

Aristotle, like Plato, understood the implications of a realist metaphysic for the purpose of humanity: contemplation. If divine truth, goodness, and beauty are the foundation for all the goodness, truth, and beauty in this world, then the "act of contemplation is what is most pleasant and best." For the object of contemplation is divinity. "If, then, God is always in that good state in which we sometimes are, this compels our wonder." Such wonder is fitting since "God *is* in a better state. And life also belongs to God; for the actuality of thought is life, and God is that actuality; and God's essential actuality is life most good and eternal." Therefore, we may say that "God is a living being, eternal, most good, so that life and duration continuous and eternal belong to God."[24] Aristotle was no skeptic (in contrast to the naturalism of the Epicureans).[25]

---

17. Aristotle, *Metaphysics* 9.4–6.12.6.
18. Consult Wuellner, *Dictionary of Scholastic Philosophy*, s.v. "potency" and "act."
19. Aristotle, *Metaphysics* 12.6, 7.
20. Aristotle, *Metaphysics* 12.6–8.
21. Aristotle, *Metaphysics* 12.7.
22. For Aristotle's description of the four causes, see *Physics* 2.
23. Aristotle, *Metaphysics* 6.1; 11.7; cf. Copleston, *History of Philosophy*, 1:291; Tyson, *Returning to Reality*, 52.
24. Aristotle, *Metaphysics* 12.7.
25. "Aristotle was from the start always thinking about the ongoing project that is Platonism." Gerson, *From Plato to Platonism*, 129. Likewise see Gerson's elaborate proof for continuity in *Aristotle and Other Platonists*.

The School of Athens, Raphael
Public Domain

Despite Aristotle's general agreement with the broad contours of Plato's realist metaphysic, one difference was visibly captured by the Renaissance artist Raphael in his famous fresco *The School of Athens*. As Plato and Aristotle walk side by side, the great thinkers of the past surrounding them, Plato points his finger up while Aristotle points out (or down). Aristotle agreed with his master on the existence of universals—this is one reason why Lloyd-Gerson is correct to call Aristotle a Platonist.[26] However, Aristotle disagreed with Plato on the location of the Ideas, revealing his suspicion toward Plato's theory of participation. Aristotle worried that Ideas could become autonomous, as if they could exist independent of the natural order in a separate sphere. As Aristotle said, it is "impossible that the substance and that of which it is the substance should exist apart; how, therefore, can the Ideas, being the substances of things, exist apart?"[27] To meet that concern, Aristotle deviated from Plato's theory of participation, modifying Plato's realism by postulating the existence of the Ideas in particulars. Using the vocabulary of *Forms*, Aristotle said that Ideas/Forms exist in things by way of immanence, which for him was reasonable since knowledge is obtained through observing the sensible world (whereas for Plato the genesis of knowledge occurs in the mind). Forms are real, but they subsist in the concrete, that is, the particulars themselves. Rather than pointing up, positing two worlds, one above with Ideas and one below

26. Gerson, "The Perennial Value of Platonism," 22; Gerson, *Aristotle and Other Platonists*, 24–46.
27. *Metaphysics* 1.9.

with their many manifestations, Aristotle pointed outward, convinced Forms inhered within sensible things. To summarize the difference, if Plato believed in a "transcendental universal," then Aristotle believed in a "concrete universal."[28]

From Decline to Revival

After Plato and Aristotle, a variegated Platonist tradition evolved in the centuries that followed. Interpretations vary but some historians lament these centuries as an era of decline, at least in comparison with the purer pedagogy of Plato and Aristotle.[29] If true, then in the century before Christ and in the centuries after Christ—roughly 80 BC to AD 220—the rise of Middle Platonism represents a resurgence. The contributions of Antiochus of Ascalon, Eudorus of Alexandria, Plutarch, Atticus, Albinus, Apuleius, Maximus of Tyre, Celsus, and many others may be diverse, and their originality debated, but by their own estimation they embodied a retrieval of Platonism's original vision. Moderns may label them Middle Platonists, but they simply called themselves Platonists. The rise of Middle Platonism influenced the advent of Jewish Hellenist philosophers like Philo of Alexandria as well. Philo has drawn attention for his attempt to bring Greek philosophy into conversation with the Jewish religion over a variety of shared commitments, from the soul's ascent to a transcendent God to the existence of Platonic Forms within the *Logos* (as justified by an allegorical interpretation of the Hebrew Scriptures). By identifying commonality between Platonism and the Hebrew canon, even the defense of the former with the latter, Philo became a bridge that led Middle Platonism into an era of Neoplatonism, which flourished in the third century AD.[30]

When Neoplatonism surpassed Middle Platonism, time revealed the former as the great attempt to arrive at a synthesis of the Platonist past. The label *Neoplatonism* is most unfortunate, a derogatory and biased word used for the agenda of modern German philosophy.[31] Neoplatonists like Plotinus, Porphyry, Iamblichus, Proclus, and others certainly did not think of themselves in an original sense, and they would have objected with great vehemence at anyone who claimed they deviated from Platonism's most proper parameters. They considered themselves faithful Platonists, however varied their philosophies may have been.[32] As manifested in Plotinus (ca. 204/5–269/70), the contribution of Neoplatonism was its attempt to combine Plato and Aristotle's best insights while filtering out their oversights.[33]

28. Copleston, *History of Philosophy*, 1:386.

29. E.g., Tyson, *Returning to Reality*, 97.

30. A treatment of Middle Platonism is not possible here, but see Dillon, *The Middle Platonists*, 52–415; Copleston, *History of Philosophy*, 2:457–62, 309.

31. See the nineteenth century in particular: Gerson, *Aristotle and Other Platonists*, 2.

32. Gerson, *From Plato to Platonism*, 227–54. Also see Gerson's treatment documenting points of harmony between Neoplatonism and its predecessors in *Aristotle and Other Platonists*.

33. Space does not permit me to explore so-called Neoplatonism, but for a test case, see Plotinus, *Enneads* 1.6.1–9; 3.2–3; 6.9.2–3, 5–6, 9–10. For a survey of Neoplatonism as well as primary sources, see Wallis, *Neoplatonism*, 47–159; Dillon and Gerson, *Neoplatonic Philosophy*. I will explore Plotinus's contribution (with an eye towards Augustine) in my forthcoming *Doctrine of God* (Baker Academic).

THE PLATONISM OF PLOTINUS

Like Aristotle before him, Plotinus (AD 204–270) considered himself a follower of Plato's philosophy, notwithstanding attempts today to use a label like Neoplatonism to define Plotinus and his school of philosophy. Nevertheless, Plotinus did adapt Plato's philosophy with originality of his own. While there may be points of discontinuity with Plato, a more balanced approach positions Plotinus as instrumental to the maturity of his master's philosophy.

For example, Plotinus drew on Plato's concept of the One (cf. *Parmenides*) and in continuity with Aristotle, Plotinus considered the One *pure act*. Invulnerable to passive potency, the One is simple, *a se*, timeless, immutable, and impassible. And in a tradition that was still ambiguous about the nature of infinitude (Aristotle associated infinitude with the lack of finality), Plotinus put forward a positive and original affirmation of infinitude that conveyed completeness and perfection (5.5–11; 6.7–18; cf. Morello, *The World as God's Icon*, 30–31). Differentiating the One from all that is contingent and compositional, Plotinus said the One is beyond being itself (*Enneads* 6.9.2). The doctrine of simplicity became instrumental to that end: "The One, that is, the principle of all beings, is simple" (6.9.5). Since the One is simple, the One does not merely possess goodness, as if it must participate in a goodness external to itself. Rather, the One *is* good, which leads Plotinus to reflect on the One's aseity.

> Further, any multitude, as long as it has not become a unity, is deficient. Its substantiality is deficient relative to being a unity, whereas the One is not deficient of itself. For it is itself. By contrast, what is many needs all the things it is and each of these things, being with the others and not in itself, is in need of all those other things, and brings about a deficiency both in terms of a unity and in terms of being a whole. If, then, there must indeed be something entirely self-sufficient, the One alone must be the kind of thing which is deficient relative neither to itself nor to anything else. It seeks nothing, so that it may be, nor that it may be in a god state, nor so that it may be established in the intelligible world. As it is the cause of other things, it does not get what it is from other things. How can its good be outside it? Thus its good is not an attribute of it; for it is it itself (6.9.6).

Deficiency characterizes those beings who are divisible because they are dependent, but fullness characterizes the One because his goodness is his essence. As pure actuality, he is complete in every way and therefore he never needs to participate in the goodness of something else but all else participates in the goodness of the One. On that basis, Plotinus called the One the principle: "The principle of all things is in no need of all things. Anything in need, is in need because it desires the principle. If the One were in need of something, it would be seeking to be not the One, so it would be in need of what will destroy it. But everything that is said to be in need, is in need of its good, that is, what preserves it." According to Plotinus, the One is the giver of goodness but not the receiver, for the latter assumes there is some deficiency within the One, some potentiality that needs actualization. "Thus, there is no good for the One, and so it does not have a will for anything. It is beyond good, and is good not for itself but for other things, insofar as other things can participate in the Good" (6.9.6).

Building on Plato's illustration of the sun, Plotinus elaborated by introducing his concept of emanation. "For everything beautiful is posterior to the One, and comes from it, just as all daylight comes from the sun" (6.9.4). The One emanates an Intellect, and this Intellect is the image of the One. However, the One precedes the Intellect because the One is simple and beyond being whereas the Intellect is complex. "So the One is not Intellect, but prior to it. For Intellect is something, whereas the One is not something, because it is prior to every Being, since it is not Being. Indeed, Being has in a way the shape of Being, whereas the One is shapeless, without even an intellectual shape. For the nature of the One, being generative of all beings, is to be identified with none of them. It is, then, not a 'this', not quality or quantity, neither Intellect nor Soul" (6.9.3). Lloyd Gerson observes, "Plotinus will reject all the attempts of Middle Platonists to conflate the Good or One and the Demiurge or Unmoved Mover. He argues for an irreducible hierarchy of distinct principles, Good, Intellect, and Soul" ("The Perennial Value of Platonism," 24).

Plotinus located the Forms with the Intellect in the intelligible realm. For example, consider beauty. All the beauty in the world is the offspring of Intellect. When the soul ascends to the Intellect the soul sees the Form of Beauty. Quoting Plato's *Republic,* Plotinus said, "the 'place' of the Forms is intelligible Beauty, whereas the Good that transcends that and is the 'source and principle' of Beauty." Therefore, "Beauty is in the intelligible world" (1.6.9). Plotinus's understanding of the One, the Intellect, and the Soul is defined by a hierarchy and can be illustrated in elementary fashion:

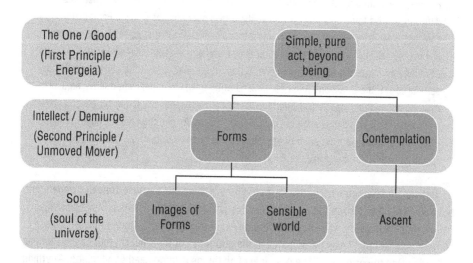

As illustrated, emanation does not reach its cessation with the Intellect, but the Intellect emanates the Soul which is responsible for crafting the world. "Anyone who thinks that beings are governed by chance and spontaneity, and are held together by corporeal causes is far removed from god and the conception of unity. . . . they should understand the nature of Soul, both its other attributes, and that it comes from Intellect, and that it has a share in reason from Intellect, and thereby acquires virtue" (6.9.5). Since the Forms are identified with the Intellect and the Soul emanates from the Intellect, the Soul may infuse the world with images of the Forms. Plotinus even hinted at a doctrine of providence when he acknowledged that the Soul not only crafts but sustains and governs the world according to its understanding of the Ideas in the Intellect (3.2–3). However, the Soul is inferior to the One and the Intellect. While the former are timeless, the latter exists within time since it crafts the sensible world. Plotinus denies that the Soul is beyond being, like the One.

Plotinus's contribution is twofold, says Gerson. First, "Plotinus repeatedly draws upon the fundamental principles [of Plato] both to respond to opponents of Platonism and to solve problems unknown to Plato." Second, Plotinus uses "Aristotelian insights to articulate and defend the Platonic system" ("The Perennial Value of Platonism," 25).

As the apostle John exemplified the refinement of Greek ideas (e.g., *Logos*), so too the church fathers in the East and the West engaged Plotinus's Platonism. They were critical of Plotinus when he departed from Christianity (e.g., see Aquinas's correction of Platonic hierarchy below) but unashamed in their appropriation of Plotinus's Platonism when it exhibited a continuity that could be further refined to advance Christianity's transcendentalism. For examples, consult Andrew Radde-Gallwitz's essay, "The One and the Trinity," 53–78. Also consider Plotinus's affirmation of the beatific vision and the soul's ascent to contemplation in *Enneads* 1.6.4–8 and 6.9.9–11. For a critical edition of *The Enneads*, consult Lloyd P. Gerson's edition with Cambridge University Press.

The need for synthesis was longstanding. Aristotle's representation of Plato was not entirely fair since Plato did not posit a "local separation" between Ideas and sensible things but merely the independence of Ideas.[34] Furthermore, Plato did not say the Ideas were autonomous in the sense that they were severed from one another either, especially the Good itself.[35] However, Aristotle did identify the weakness in Plato's theory: "Whatever Plato might say or write, he is forced perhaps in spite of himself to make Forms into individuals," says Lloyd Gerson.[36] And yet, Aristotle's explanation needed supplementation as well. According to Copleston, by "rejecting Platonic exemplarism, he also betrays the inadequacy of his own theory, in that he provides no real transcendental ground for the fixity of essence."[37] Maintaining *both* the transcendental and the concrete with adequate care proved a fruitful conundrum for Neoplatonism's contribution.

Neoplatonism found a remedy by addressing both weaknesses. To begin with, Neoplatonists refused to dispense with Plato's exemplary causes, but they located the exemplary causes in God himself since the "Divine Essence is the ultimate Exemplar of all creatures."[38] Later, both Augustine and Aquinas capitalized on this Neoplatonist maneuver by locating exemplary causes in the mind of God. In the end, Neoplatonists were able to retain exemplary causes by laying

---

34. Copleston, *History of Philosophy*, 1:294.

35. Gerson, *From Plato to Platonism*, 109.

36. Gerson, *From Plato to Platonism*, 110.

37. Aristotle used his own criteria for participation ("immanent form") to judge Plato's inadequate. Copleston, *History of Philosophy*, 1:294.

38. Copleston, *History of Philosophy*, 1:297.

a transcendental foundation. At the same time, they did not necessarily sever abstract universals from the concrete particulars. Since God is the exemplary cause of all creatures, he can be known by his effects on sensible objects. Therefore, a person may live in the sensible world of particulars, grasping onto knowledge of abstract universals *in things*, contemplating universals in their own mind. Since universals are real—dependent as they are on the transcendent (i.e., the divine mind)—they may be abstracted from the sensible world due to the universal's concrete immanence. Thomas Aquinas later capitalized on this process of abstraction with his principle of individuation.[39] The universal, however, is not merely a concept in a person's mind.

Christian Transcendentalists and Critical Appropriation

The Great Tradition was not ignorant but appreciated that Platonism and its realism had become the perennial philosophy of late antiquity.[40] Nevertheless, examples like Augustine and Aquinas will reveal that the Great Tradition also understood the need to *refine* Platonism, taking its map of reality towards its true destination in Christ. In other words, the Great Tradition did not crudely transfer raw Platonism into Christianity, as if they lacked discrimination and corrupted the latter (the Hellenization thesis of Adolf von Harnack and Protestant liberalism).[41] Words like *critically* in "critically appropriated" and *Christian* in "Christian Platonism" accomplish the heavy lifting. Platonism, if left to itself, held to beliefs that contradicted Christianity. For example, Plato explained the origin of the soul by preexistence in the world of Being. The soul enters the material world through a human body but with an innate understanding of the world of Being. However, the body is a barrier to recollecting such knowledge, resulting in ignorance. Classical Christianity taught that the soul is the form of the body, which God created good in the beginning, but for Plato the soul must escape the body. The Christian Scriptures do have a negative evaluation of the flesh over against the Spirit (Rom. 8:5; Gal. 5:17; 1 Pet. 2:11; 1 Jn. 2:16) but always in relation to the fall; sin is not original to the flesh but a corruption that is reversed in redemption and new creation. Like Plato, the Christian Scriptures also teach a spiritual ascent (e.g., Jacob's Ladder in Gen. 28:10–22). That ascent will result in a disembodied state at death, but that state is intermediate, awaiting the resurrection of the body. Plato had no category for the resurrection (let alone an Incarnation) but only transmigration in his explanation of the afterlife. Plato did believe in a sinful nature, but unlike Christianity it was not his primary concern.

---

39. Copleston, *History of Philosophy*, 1:298, 301. After Thomas, Scotus reacted against the principle of individuation and considered it precarious (491). To understand the realism of Thomas, consult Gilson, *Thomist Realism and the Critique of Knowledge*.

40. Some like Augustine even speculated as to whether Plato had read Old Testament authors, an opinion generally rejected by scholars today.

41. Harnack, *History of Dogma*, especially volumes 4 and 5. For a critique of Harnack, see Wilken, *Spirit of Early Christian Thought*, who argues against the Hellenization of Christianity and instead proposes the Christianization of Hellenism, though Wilken recognizes such a label doesn't do justice to Christianity's Jewish roots.

As a result, the answer to man's plight was *recollection* (of the world of Being), not primarily a *regeneration* and *reconciliation* (by the Word who is Being).[42] Ignorance was the ultimate problem Plato desired to remedy.[43]

Other examples could be listed, but these sample differences required the Great Tradition to criticize Platonism's shortcomings. However, criticism was not the Great Tradition's last word. It could not be. With the rest of late antiquity those in the Great Tradition were committed transcendentalists. They considered how they might bring Platonism's transcendent map of reality to *fulfillment*, redeeming its participation metaphysic like only classical theism can. They imitated Paul in Acts 17:28 when he quoted the Greeks who said, "In him we live and move and have our being," and "We are indeed his offspring." The Greeks had Zeus in view, but Paul did not hesitate to redirect their participation metaphysic to its rightful deity—"the unknown god" of Christianity.

If one word captures the way Christians, following Paul, considered Platonism serviceable to Christianity if refined then it may be the word *participation*. Creation's participation in the likeness of its Creator is not "*merely* a sacramental sharing . . . in the life of God," nor a necessary emanation lest God's aseity be compromised—indications of emanation in Platonism had to be corrected.[44] The Great Tradition's emphasis on analogy of being and analogical predication played a significant role in avoiding that mistake. Identity (univocity of being) is precluded since the Creator—unlike the creature—is infinite and eternal, indivisible and independent, incorporeal and incomprehensible. The creature's participation is not necessary for God (he did not have to create in the first place), but gratuitous, stemming from his boundless generosity and goodness.[45] Therefore, only God's existence is necessary since his essence is his existence, and his existence is his essence. He is the fountain of life because he alone is eternal life in and of himself (aseity). For that reason, God alone deserves to be worshipped and enjoyed for his own sake, while everything else in creation is but a means to that ultimate purpose. As for God's presence in the world, it should not be interpreted as a sign that his infinite disparity has been forfeited, but as an indicator of the participatory or sacramental nature of creation. As Boersma says, "The sacramentality of the relationship implies that, although God is present in his creation, and though creation participates in the eternal Word of God, the sacramental reality (*res*) of the Word infinitely transcends terrestrial objects."[46]

---

42. That difference also stemmed from a contrast between Platonism's innate knowledge (*cognitio innata*) and the patristic and medieval belief in implanted knowledge (*cognitio insita*). The latter could explain the seed of religion (*semen religionis*). Thus the need to *critically* appropriate Platonism. Muller, *Dictionary*, cognitio insita, s.v.

43. For a fuller treatment of discontinuity, see chapter 7 of Markos, *From Plato to Christ*.

44. Boersma, *Heavenly Participation*, 70.

45. Boersma, *Heavenly Participation*, 71.

46. "The infinite difference tween the Creator and the creature implies the rejection of the pantheism that lurks in straightforward Neo-Platonism." Boersma, *Heavenly Participation*, 72.

Augustine and the Nicene Fathers

The Great Tradition's critical appropriation of Platonism is apparent in both the East and the West.[47] In the West, Augustine believed Platonism was right about universals, except Augustine refined Platonism by locating these universals in the divine intellect. When God created the world, for example, he already had the universal Idea we call humanity in his mind. The consequences for morality should not be overlooked: if God creates the world with a universal Idea of humanity in his mind, then the dignity and virtue of humanity is not arbitrary. Likewise, neither is the moral law that governs humanity whimsical.[48] God's commands align with who he has made man to be, and who he has made man to be aligns with God's own moral character or essence since man is made in the image of God, a theme that presupposes and pervades Augustine's apologetic for Christianity in his *City of God*.

Platonism was also personal for Augustine. In his *Confessions*, Augustine recounted the story of his conversion, detailing how God used Platonism to correct his Manichaean misconception of divinity (as material), removing the cognitive barrier to the incomprehensible, infinite, and incorporeal God of the Scriptures.[49] The opening of Romans became lucid as a result: "After reading the books of the Platonists and learning from them to seek for immaterial truth, I turned my attention to your 'invisible nature understood through the things which are made' (Rom. 1:20)."[50]

Later in life Augustine wrote *The City of God*, celebrating the Platonist conception of God as the supreme deity, the origin of all things, the light of our knowledge, and the source of our blessedness. Outlining many more philosophies, Augustine said he was justified to elevate Platonism above others (e.g., Epicureanism, Stoicism) that explain the cosmos by matter alone, even reducing the Creator to a material being. The Platonists have been "raised above the rest by a glorious reputation they so thoroughly deserve" because "they recognized that no material object can be God" and "raised their eyes above all material objects in their search for God."

> They realized that nothing changeable can be the supreme God; and therefore in their search for the supreme God, they raised their eyes above all mutable souls and spirits. They saw also that in every mutable being the form which determines its being, its mode of being and its nature, can only come from him who truly is, because he exists immutably. . . . For him existence is not something different from life, as if he could exist without living; nor is life something other than intelligence, as if he could live without understanding; nor understanding something other than happiness, as if he could understand without being happy. For him, to exist is the same as to live, to understand, to be happy.[51]

47. Boersma (*Heavenly Participation*, 72) demonstrates that *analogia entis* is present not only in the West (Augustine, Aquinas), but the East (Athanasius, Cappadocians). Cf. Elders, *The Metaphysics of Being of St. Thomas Aquinas in a Historical Perspective*, 170–89.
48. Copleston, *History of Philosophy*, 3:50.
49. *Confessions* 7.
50. *Confessions* 7.10. Likewise see *City of God* 8.
51. Augustine, *City of God* 8.6.

That clarification also assisted Augustine with avoiding Christological heresy. Augustine admits, "I had a different notion, since I thought of Christ my Lord only as a man of excellent wisdom which none could equal. I thought his wonderful birth from a virgin was an example of despising temporal things to gain immortality for us, and such divine care for us gave him great authority as teacher."[52] However, the Platonists introduced Augustine to the concept of *Logos*—word or reason—preparing him for the Gospel of John and the Epistle to the Philippians. "In reading the Platonic books I found expressed in different words, and in a variety of ways, that the Son, 'being in the form of the Father did not think it theft to be equal with God', because by nature he is that very thing."[53] Although the Platonists did not teach Augustine about Christ, they did provide him, however unwittingly, with a natural theology that prepared the way for Christ. By consequence, Augustine was not seduced by Christological heresies, from Arianism to Apollinarianism. "I began reading [the apostle Paul] and found that all the truth I had read in the Platonists was stated here together with the commendation of your grace."[54] Platonism knew the goal, but not how to get there through Christ. Rather than ascending to heaven through a humble Mediator, they prided themselves on their ascent to divine knowledge. "The philosopher is his own savior," they said. The gospel gave Augustine the map needed to reach the homeland the Platonists could only gaze at from afar.[55]

Yet Augustine's highest praise surfaced when he considered the Platonist goal of contemplation—they knew no divide between metaphysics and the spirituality of the soul. Happiness is reached when one participates in the Good, the source of infinite life, a striking parallel to Christianity that locates the blessed life in the believer's union with God.[56] "All those schools must be ranked below those philosophers who have found man's true Good not in the enjoyment of the body or the mind, but in the enjoyment of God." In comparison, "it is like the eye's enjoyment of light." And the Platonists knew this eye's enjoyment more than most: "Plato defined the Sovereign Good as the life in accordance with virtue; and he declared that this was possible only for one who had the knowledge of God and who strove to imitate him; this was the sole condition of happiness. Therefore Plato has no hesitation in asserting that to be a philosopher is to love God, whose nature is immaterial." Augustine ranked Platonism the highest philosophy because, for all its flaws, it above all others considered true philosophy nothing less than the love of wisdom, convinced the soul is destined to ascend to the One who is wisdom without measure. "And that is why he [Plato] will have it that the true philosopher is the lover of God, since the aim of philosophy is happiness, and he who has set his heart on God will be happy in the enjoyment of him."[57]

52. *Confessions* 7.19.
53. *Confessions* 7.9.
54. *Confessions* 7.20, 21.
55. John Peter Kenney, "Augustine and the Platonists," in *Augustine and Tradition: Influences, Contexts, Legacy*, ed. David G. Hunter and Jonathan P. Yates (Grand Rapids: Eerdmans, 2023), 127–52.
56. Augustine, *City of God* 8.8.
57. And "no one is happy without the enjoyment of what he loves." Augustine, *City of God* 8.8.

This is why we rate the Platonists above the rest of the philosophers. The others have employed their talents and concentrated their interests on the investigation of the causes of things, of the method of acquiring knowledge, and the rules of the moral life, while the Platonists, coming to a knowledge of God, have found the cause of the organized universe, the light by which truth is perceived, and the spring which offers the drink of felicity.[58]

Augustine said the Platonists admonished him to "return into myself" and search with his "soul's eye." Although he found a "region of dissimilarity" (Plotinus), he saw "immutable light higher than my mind." God raised him up to see that "what I saw is Being, and that I who saw am not yet Being." His pride defeated, his inner self revealed his need to participate in the absolute source of reality: "You gave a shock to the weakness of my sight by the strong radiance of your rays, and I trembled with love and awe." The Platonists helped Augustine turn in, but when he peered into his "innermost citadel," he was turned upward to see God (Ps. 29:11).[59]

Augustine may have been one of the greatest minds to critically appropriate Platonism to display the philosophical credibility of Christianity, but he was not unique by any means. Not only fathers in the West, but fathers in the East presupposed Christian Platonism as well and even made explicit use of its logic to buttress the biblical and theological coherence of classical, Nicene orthodoxy, a point scholars now recognize more and more.[60] "By the time of the Council of Nicaea in 325 CE," says Lloyd Gerson, "self-declared Christians who wanted to reflect philosophically on their religion did so almost exclusively within a Platonic context."[61] In his survey of the Eastern fathers of the fourth century, Andrew Radde-Gallwitz has corrected the misconception that says Platonism inspired Arianism while Nicaea was anti-Platonism. Platonism was not absent from the writings of Arians, but "it is not Arianism as such that was Platonist."

Arius and those labelled "Arians" were no more especially Platonizing, and were in important respects less so, than their Nicene opponents. Nor was anti-Arianism implicit or covert anti-Platonism. In one or two cases, anti-Platonism was implicit or covert anti-Arianism, *but generally the pro-Nicenes identified greater continuity between their own doctrine and that of their Platonist sources than between their opponents and the Platonists.*[62]

58. Augustine, *City of God* 8.10.
59. *Confessions* 7.10. On the theme of returning "into myself," see Cary, *Inner Grace.*
60. Notable in East and West: Irenaeus, Gregory of Nyssa, Gregory of Nazianzus, Origen, Boethius, Dante, and Aquinas. See Gerson, *Platonism and Naturalism*; Gerson, "The Perennial Value of Platonism," 13–33; Radde-Gallwitz, "The One and the Trinity," 53–78; Edwards, "The Bible and Early Christian Platonism," 143–61; Kenney, "Platonism and Christianity in Late Antiquity," 162–82; Markos, *From Plato to Christ*, 119–214; Tyson, *Returning to Reality*, 90–124.
61. Gerson, "The Perennial Value of Platonism," 13.
62. Radde-Gallwitz, "The One and the Trinity," 65.

For example, the Fathers utilized the Platonist concept of participation to ensure Christ is not subordinated to the Father. The creature participates in the likeness of God by grace, said Athanasius. However, "the Son does not exist by participation" since he is the eternal "Wisdom and Word of the Father in whom all things partake." The Son is "same-in-substance" with the Father "not foreign-in-substance" since he is the "the deifying and illuminating power of the Father," explains Athanasius.[63] Gregory made a similar argument in his polemics against Eunomius.[64]

Aquinas's Synthesis: Divine Ideas and Participation

In the Middle Ages, a variety of theologians grew out of this tradition, yet not without improvements of their own. For example, Thomas Aquinas was indebted to variations of Christian Platonists before him like Augustine, Pseudo-Dionysius, and Boethius.[65] In his *Summa Theologiae* Thomas built on this realist tradition when he erected a mature participation metaphysic that appropriated the strengths and supplemented the weaknesses of Plato and Aristotle alike. In one sense, Thomas sympathized more with the realism of Aristotle than Plato, agreeing with the former who said the Forms/Ideas do not exist in an independent domain but subsist in concrete particulars, which enabled Thomas to develop an epistemological theory of abstraction. In another sense, Thomas was more sympathetic to Plato's realism because the philosopher's motive to affirm participation and ground it in a *transcendent* reality was an instinct most compatible with Christianity's transcendentalism.[66] Therefore, Thomas disagreed with the deficiency of participation in Aristotle. Thomas used Aristotle's vocabulary of act and potency for the sake of defending participation, a Neoplatonic maneuver that Aristotle would have found disagreeable. Aristotle used the language to describe "change or motion of individual substances." Thomas repurposed act and potency to explain how the created order—defined by a passive potency—reaches its telos only by participating in the likeness of its Creator, who alone is pure actuality.[67]

To understand why, Thomas's definition of Ideas should be clarified first before a brief exploration of his doctrine of creation. Thomas agreed with Augustine that the Ideas are in the mind of God. They do not exist in their own right (Plato), but they exist in the intellect, namely, the *divine* intellect.[68] Thomas described God

---

63. Athanasius, *On the Synods* 51; as quoted in Radde-Gallwitz, "The One and the Trinity," 70.

64. Gregory of Nyssa, *Against Eunomeius* I.276.

65. To consider the ways Dionysius, Augustine, and Boethius influenced Thomas, see te Velde, "Participation," 122–139.

66. Some have said Thomas's method and philosophy resulted in the death of Platonism, but recent scholars have demonstrated that Thomas was a type of Christian Platonist himself. See Rudi A. te Velde, "Participation: Aquinas and His Neoplatonic Sources," 122–142; Boersma, *Heavenly Participation*, 36.

67. Morello, *The World as God's Icon: Creator and Creation in the Platonic Thought of Thomas Aquinas*, 19. Thomas is sometimes painted as if his retrieval of Aristotelianism is a rejection of Platonism. However, Morello demonstrates otherwise. To see Thomas's criticism of Aristotle's suspicion towards participation, see his *An Exposition of the On the Hebdomads of Boethius*. To see how Thomas repurposes act and potency, see *SCG* 2.53.

68. In reply to Plato: "Therefore, to posit the forms of things as existing in themselves outside the divine intellect does not suffice for God to understand a multitude of things; these intelligibles must be in the divine intellect itself." Aquinas, *SCG* 1.1.52.

as an Architect, who has Ideas in his mind, the blueprint for reality. For instance, "The form of the house already exists in the mind of the architect. This can be called the idea of the house; because the architect intends to make the house to the pattern of the form which he has conceived in his mind." (For Thomas, "*Idea* in Greek corresponds to *forma* in Latin.") The illustration of an architect allowed Thomas to define the divine Ideas as indispensable to Christianity's confession of a Creator: "Now since the world is not made by chance, but is made by God acting as an intellectual agent, . . . there must be in the divine mind a form, to the likeness of which the world is made; and that is what we mean by an Idea."[69]

Participation, therefore, depends on these divine Ideas. Divine Ideas are God's knowledge of how all things participate as the likeness of his essence. "Now the divine essence can be known not only as it is in itself, but as it can be participated in some degree of likeness by creatures."[70] Thomas used the word *imitable* to explain the correlation: "In this way then God, in knowing his essence as imitable in this particular way by this particular creature, knows his essence as the nature and Idea proper to that creature."[71] Furthermore, since God *is* his essence (simplicity), he knows how all things participate in him by simply knowing his essence (all effects can be known by knowing their First Cause; the likeness is known by knowing its reality).[72] Thomas may logically distinguish the divine Ideas to analogically predicate the "likeness of which the world is made."[73] Nevertheless, the divine Ideas are the divine essence itself for God is simple. In the words of Thomas, "God in his essence is the likeness of all things. Hence an Idea in God is simply the divine essence."[74]

To understand how Thomas supplemented the weaknesses in both Plato and Aristotle, consider his commentary on John and the interplay between the divine Ideas and Christology. Thomas acknowledged that for Plato the Ideas were "subsistent," meaning they exist "separately in their own natures." Therefore, "material things exist by participating" in these subsistent Ideas. Thomas, however, identified a problem: if the Ideas exist separately in their *own* natures, then they are also independent from God.[75] That problem also posed a difficulty for the Christian

---

69. Thus, the "likeness of the form must be in the agent." *ST* 1a. 15.1.

70. For Thomas, "Every creature has its own nature in so far as it participates in some way the likeness of the divine essence." *ST* 1a. 15, 2.

71. *ST* 1a. 15, 2.

72. "An effect is adequately known when its cause is known. So 'we are said to know each thing when we know the cause' [Aristotle, *Posterior Analytics*, I, 2 (71b 3)]. But God Himself is through His essence the cause of being for other things. Since He has a most full knowledge of His essence, we must posit that God also knows other things." Aquinas, *SCG* 1.1.49.

73. "We cannot help using language which implies that they are distinct; but actually they are ontologically identical with the divine essence, being simply the divine essence known by God as imitable externally (that is, by creatures) in different ways." Copleston, *History of Philosophy*, 3:49.

74. *ST* 1a. 15.1. Thomas anticipated the objection that a plurality of divine ideas must contract divine simplicity. "It is not contrary to the simplicity of the divine intellect to know many things; but it would be contrary to its simplicity were the divine intellect informed by a plurality of knowledge-likeness. Hence many Ideas are in the divine mind as objects of God's knowledge. . . . God by one act knows many things . . ." (1a. 15, 2).

75. For example, Plato prioritized the primacy of the Good as that which exists above being, but Thomas prized the primacy of Being since the Good is not a subsisting nature of its own but God himself *is* the Good. Since God is being, Thomas said God *is* Good, as one might expect from a God who is simple (without parts). Te Velde, "Participation," 130–32.

understanding of Christ and creation. In other words, Thomas feared that Ideas with their own independent natures could only keep the *Logos*—the one through whom all things were created—external to God, as if the *Logos* originated from a different nature than God. Yet Thomas thought John 1:1 solved the dilemma: "So lest you supposed, as did Plato, that this Idea through which all things were made be Ideas separated from God, the Evangelist adds, *and the Word was with God.*"[76]

Yet another fear surfaced: an essential division between God and the *Logos* could even make the *Logos* subordinate to God. But again, the apostle John can borrow the Greek concept of *Logos* yet without absorbing hierarchy within God (e.g., Plotinus). With help from the Eastern fathers Thomas explained, "Other Platonists, as Chrysostom relates, maintained that God the Father was most eminent and first, but under him they placed a certain mind in which there were the likenesses and ideas of all things. So lest you think that the Word was with the Father in such a way as to be under him and less than he, the Evangelist adds, *and the Word was God.*"[77]

So far Thomas has solved the deficiency in Plato, but what about Aristotle? Plato's student "thought that the ideas of all things are in God, and that in God, the intellect, the one understanding, and what is understood, are the same."[78] However, Thomas did not merely baptize Aristotle's theory of Ideas as if correction was not necessary. True, the Ideas are in God which weaves a tight cord of participation between the Creator and the created, better explaining how Ideas in God then subsist in concrete particulars. "Nevertheless, he [Aristotle] thought that the world is coeternal with him [God]." Thomas overcame this deficiency in Aristotle (a coeternal world) once more by appeal to John 1:1. The apostle retrieves the Greek idea of *Logos* but avoids Aristotle's mistaken assumption when John identifies the *Logos* with God himself. "Against this the Evangelist says, *He*, the Word alone, *was in the beginning with God*, in such a way that *He* does not exclude another person, but only another coeternal nature."[79] Contrary to the subordinationism of Eunomius for example, the *Logos* is not "entirely unlike the Father" since the *Logos* does not have a different nature but is eternally generated from the Father's divine nature. The procession of the Son from the Father is not an external operation, but immanent and intrinsic. The apostle, therefore, can differentiate the *Logos* from creation since the created order is neither coeternal with God nor consubstantial with God. While those in creation must participate in God for life, the *Logos* is not subject to the inferiority of participation since he is a Son by nature, not grace. He is begotten, not created. Just as he is light from light (Nicaea), so too did the church fathers say he is life from life, as Jesus says in John 5:26.

Furthermore, the unity in being between the Son and the Father is not only supported by John's description of the *Logos*, but the apostle's critical

76. Aquinas, *John*, ch. 1, p. 29.
77. Aquinas, *John*, ch. 1, p. 29.
78. Aquinas, *John*, ch. 1, p. 29.
79. Aquinas, *John*, ch. 1, p. 30.

appropriation of the Greek concept further clarifies how divine knowledge works. Previously Thomas said God knows all Ideas by knowing his own essence since the divine Ideas are the divine essence (God is simple).[80] And who is one with the Father in essence but the Son, who is the Word or Wisdom of God? "So, God makes nothing except through the conception of his intellect, which is an eternally conceived wisdom, that is, the Word of God, and the Son of God." In other words, if God creates the world according to divine ideas, and if these divine ideas are in the mind of God, then who is the mind of God except the Word of God? Thomas agrees with Augustine, who provides the answer: "The Word is the art full of the living patterns of all things."[81] The Word, therefore, is the Exemplar. "Thereby it follows that the conception of the divine intellect as understanding itself, which is its Word, is the likeness not only of God Himself understood, but also of all those things of which the divine essence is the likeness." Thomas concluded, "In this way, therefore, through one intelligible species, which is the divine essence, and through one understood intention, which is the divine Word, God can understand many things."[82] God knows how all things participate in him (divine Ideas) by knowing his divine essence. The Father "can understand many things" through his Word because the Word is true God of true God, the Son who is begotten from the Father's divine essence rather than created (Nicaea). For the Word did not participate in God like creation, but the Word was God. By means of the Word all things participate in the likeness of God. Thomas's quotation from Psuedo-Dionysius was fitting: "Therefore, in knowing itself, the divine wisdom knows all things."[83]

Thomas's Christology aside, how did Thomas's realist metaphysic (with its fusion of Plato and Aristotle's best insights) inform his *Christian* doctrine of creation? First, if God is subsistent being (simple), then he can be the first cause of all things. "Plato held that before the many you must place the one" and Aristotle believed that "the supremely real and true is the cause of everything that is real and true."[84] On that logic, anything that has its being by participation must be caused by God who is uncaused himself, a God who exists by necessity. Something has "real existence" because it has an efficient cause, who is God. Otherwise, it does not and cannot exist. If Romans 11:36 is right—"For from him and through him and unto him are all things"—then God is not only the efficient cause ("from him") and the exemplar cause ("through him") but the final cause ("unto him") of all things, though he is not the material cause.[85]

Second, God's goodness is the final cause, which explains the ultimate *telos* of the creature's participation. While things in this world are both acting and acted upon

---

80. "The divine essence is the likeness of all things." *SCG* 1.1.53.

81. Aquinas, *John*, ch. 1, p. 34; quoting Augutine's *De Trinitate* 6.10, no. 11; PL 42, col. 931.

82. *SCG* 1.1.53.

83. Pseudo-Dionysius, *De divinis nominibus* 7, 2 (*PG*, 3, col. 869B); as quoted in Aquinas, *SCG* 1.1.58.

84. *ST* Ia. 44, 1.

85. *ST* Ia. 44, 1, 3, 4. Thomas adds, "Since God is the efficient, exemplary, and final cause of everything, and since primary matter is from him, we infer that the origin of all things in reality is single" (Ia. 44, 4).

and therefore remain incomplete, God alone acts without being acted upon because he is complete—pure act. His completeness means he is free to "communicate his own completeness, which is his goodness." He creates without needing anything in return. "He alone is supremely generous, because he does not act for his own benefit but simply to give of his goodness."[86] Creation is not necessary but an altruistic work of God, a free communication of his goodness.[87] Without need of his own, he does not create out of preexisting material but out of nothing—*ex nihilo.*

Third, creation *ex nihilo* displays not only the freedom and goodness of God but also his power. "A cause's strength is assessed not only by the substance of the thing made but also by the manner of its making. . . . Hence, even though the creation of a finite effect does not demonstrate infinite power, its being made from nothing certainly does." Thomas returned to the distinction between act and potency to explain: "For if an efficient cause's power must be increased in proportion to the potentiality's distance from actuality, then surely when no potentiality is present, as with creative causality, this power must be infinite."[88] For finite beings, we create out of something because passive potency is not absent but present. However, God—as pure actuality—need not rely on anything to create. Creation *ex nihilo* is only possible because he is a God who is *a se*, complete in and of himself. Therefore his fullness of life means he can create by his own infinite power alone. Thomas refined Platonism by retrieving a First Cause and clarified that if such a First Cause is both complete in his goodness and infinite in his power, creation cannot be out of something but nothing. As such, creation is not a "change" that occurs since change presupposes something already exists, something not caused by him.[89]

Fourth, Thomas refined Platonism by eliminating any hierarchy within God in the work of creation since creation is the *indivisible* operation of the simple Trinity. "Hence creation is God's action by reason of his existence, which is his very nature, and this is common to the three Persons. So that creative action is not peculiar to any one Person, but is common to the whole Trinity."[90] Over against Middle Platonism's merge of the Good with the Creator (Demiurge), Plotinus introduced a taxis: the First Principle is the Good (One), the Intellect is the Creator (Demiurge), and the Soul is the soul of the cosmos.[91] Christian

---

86. *ST* Ia. 44, 4.

87. *ST* Ia. 47, 1. That also explains why God created so many different things in the world. He "brought things into existence so that his goodness might be communicated to creatures and re-enacted through them. And because one single creature was not enough, he produced many and diverse, so that what was wanting in one expression of the divine goodness might be supplied by another, for goodness, which in God is single and all together, in creatures is multiple and scattered. Hence the whole universe less incompletely than one alone shares and represents his goodness." Thomas then says God "acts through a form as held in the mind." Those forms do not dispel his simplicity, however. "Since, therefore, it is not against God's singleness and simplicity that he should understand many things. . . . The truth remains that although he is the One he can also make the many" (Ia. 47, 1).

88. *ST* Ia. 45, 5.

89. *ST* Ia. 45, 2.

90. *ST* Ia. 45, 6.

91. It is right to call Plotinus a Platonist, but his introduction of this triad does demonstrate the original contribution of his own, though Plotinus is using Aristotle's grammar to create his own Platonist system. Gerson, "The Perennial Value of Platonism," 24–25.

Platonists such as Clement of Alexandria, Augustine, Cyril of Alexandria, Basil of Caesarea, and eventually Thomas Aquinas either assumed or acknowledged Platonism's triad, but corrected it by clarifying that the three must be *persons* without hierarchy or essential divisibility.[92] Again, by correcting and transforming Platonism, they simply followed the example of apostles like John, who used a Greek concept—*Logos*—to designate the only begotten Son as the one who was both with God and was God, through whom all things were created.

Map for Reality: Realism

Historians have demonstrated at great length that Christian Platonism defined the Great Tradition in innumerable ways, even variegated ways, many of which this project cannot begin to explore.[93] Our purpose will be a mere focus on the ways the nominalism of the *via moderna* departed from the realist, participation metaphysic of the Augustinian and especially Thomistic heritage. Nevertheless, for the sake of clarity Lloyd Gerson has identified five marks that define the Christian Platonist tradition, or what he calls Ur-Platonism.[94] These marks ask, What must be true about God and the world to believe and defend the truth claims made by God in his two books of revelation, the book of nature and book of Scripture?[95] When worded that way, these marks may be labeled the "building blocks for early Christian doctrine."[96] They are as follows:

1. Anti-materialism. Christian Platonism claims that bodies and their properties are not the only things that exist.
2. Anti-mechanism. Christian Platonism maintains that the natural order (including, therefore, physical events) cannot be fully explained by physical or mechanical causes.
3. Anti-nominalism. Christian Platonism argues that reality is made up not just of individuals, each uniquely situated in time and space, but that two individual objects can be the same in essence (e.g., both being canine) while still being unique individuals (distinct dogs).
4. Anti-relativism. Christian Platonism rejects the notion, both in terms of

---

92. Clement of Alexandria, *Stromateis* 5; Augustine, *Confessions* VII.ix.13; Cyril, *Against Julian* 8.33; cf. Radde-Gallwitz, "The One and the Trinity," 56–57 (note as well his treatment of Theodoret of Cyrrhus). Also consult, Salvatore R. C. Lilla, "The Neoplatonic Hypostases and the Christian Trinity," 127–89.

93. Nevertheless, consult the twenty-one historians who chronicle the ways East and West critically appropriate Platonism in Hampton and Kenney, eds., *Christian Platonism*.

94. Proto-Platonism.

95. In one sense, the post-Enlightenment interpreter unfamiliar with the continuity of pre-Enlightenment Christianity could assume that Christianity and Christian Platonism are two separate streams. That is often assumed in the common objection that Platonism is being foisted upon Christianity, as if Christianity is forced to fit the Platonist worldview or even corrupted by the Platonist worldview. That assumption is mistaken, however. The designation "Christian Platonism" merely identifies the metaphysical framework that must be in place so that Christianity—and its many transcendental beliefs—is possible in the first place. Stated otherwise, Christian Platonism does not demand that the Christian impose an unnatural and foreign grid on its sacred text, but it's logic is original to the text.

96. Boersma, *Five Things Theologians Wish Biblical Scholars Knew*, 43.

knowledge and morals, that human beings are the measure of all things, suggesting instead that goodness is a property of being.

5. Anti-skepticism. Christian Platonism maintains that the real can in some manner become present to us, so that knowledge is within reach.[97]

These five take on a polemical posture, so a positive description of Christian Platonism and its participation metaphysic should complement them. The word *participation* is the key to that positive description because unless God *is* being, he alone cannot be the one in whom we live, and move, and have our being, as Paul said quoting the Greeks (Acts 17:28). And without participation everything else evaporates, from creation *ex nihilo* to divine providence, from union with Christ to communion at the table.[98] Nonetheless, these five points do serve an indispensable purpose: they create boundaries and identify those building blocks so foundational to Christianity. And with the third building block in view, this tradition can also absorb a more specific label like *classical realism*. For universals are indeed real, not mere names.

The label Christian Platonism never denies that it is necessary to distinguish between Plato's realism of transcendental universals and Aristotle's realism of concrete, immanent universals, or the diverse ways Augustine and Thomas critically appropriated their realist metaphysic. In fact, the label is elastic for that purpose, encompassing diversity within a realist tradition. But the label does serve a positive purpose as well, a purpose that identifies the reason the Great Tradition considered Platonism revolutionary. "Platonism mattered to early Christian thinkers not because they needed a congenial philosophy to ground their theology, but because Platonism was the driver in an epic revolution in human thinking about reality in general and the divine in particular," says John Peter Kenney. "This was the emergence of the radical idea of transcendent reality, of a level of intelligible being entirely distinct from space, time, and materiality. This is why Platonism swept through the Roman world and became the regnant mode of philosophy." Yet Platonism's radical idea of a transcendent, infinite, omnipresent One (e.g., Plotinus) swept through the Nicene world as well. "It looks to us like Platonism—as it was in one sense—but it had become an increasingly common and established metaphysical understanding of reality adopted across the ancient intellectual world. So the 'greatest generation' of Nicene theologians of the fourth century were Christian Platonists from our perspective, but it might also be said that they were Christian transcendentalists."

Modern (and postmodern) philosophers and theologians may be prone to misunderstand and criticize Christian Platonism because they only look to

---

97. These five points are Boersma's, and he is summarizing the more elaborate description in Gerson, *From Plato to Platonism*, 11–14. Gerson does recognize that someone can be a nominalist and still be antimaterialist (e.g., Ockham). Yet his point is directed elsewhere and should not be overlooked: "If, though, we begin to explore logical or explanatory connections among the five 'antis,' the range of positions begins to narrow" (14).

98. Tyson makes the point about *koinonia* quite well: *Returning to Reality*, 134.

reduce it to a set of systematic doctrines (which they will not find). However, this common approach sets off in the wrong direction, forgetting from the start that Platonism is a philosophy, a *mode* for contemplating reality that is more of a way of life (think Socrates). "This sometimes frustrates commentators who want to nail down a complete list of Platonist (or Christian Platonist) doctrines like any other school," observes Kenney. "But the central teachings of Platonism are really intended to advance the soul in its search for wisdom and to provide a map for the soul's journey to true reality. But it does not offer a detailed description of its terrain." Therefore, participation is the very tapestry of true reality. For Platonism, "participation is the notion that the soul can share in the higher level of reality it seeks to know. All true knowledge of the divine, the eternal, and the really real is an exercise in communion."[99] The Great Tradition then knit this true notion of participation within the very fabric of the realist metaphysic until it defined everything from divine providence to union and communion with Christ to the beatific vision itself. However, certain late medieval theologians cut the tapestry of participation and dispensed with the fabric of a realist metaphysic altogether.

DUNS SCOTUS, VOLUNTARISM, AND UNIVOCITY

Scholasticism's diversity may be most apparent with John Duns Scotus (ca. 1265/66–1308). Little is known about his early life except that he studied at Oxford, Cambridge, and Paris. Like others, he sharpened his intellectual teeth on Lombard's *Sentences* and gained a reputation for his lectures on each of Lombard's books.[100] In time each of the three universities benefited from Scotus's insights, and his lectures became respected and consulted commentaries. As for his monastic affiliation, Duns Scotus was a committed Franciscan, though he made no secret about his disagreement with past Franciscans on points of doctrine. His transparency created some difficulty as the Franciscans at the end of the twelfth century and the first half of the thirteenth century were influenced by Bonaventure only now to be swayed by Scotus during the second half of the thirteenth century. Furthermore, Scotus was vocal in his constant critique of Bonaventure, a reminder that Thomas Aquinas was by no means the only one Scotus criticized.[101] Eventually Ockham would draw their attention during the first half of the fourteenth century, leaving Franciscans divided in their allegiances at times, though many went the way of Ockham's *via moderna* by the eve of the Reformation.[102]

Scotus deserves attention because he is one of the most significant scholastics after Thomas Aquinas. Yet Scotus has also captured the interest (and disdain)

---

99. John Peter Kenney to Matthew Barrett, personal correspondence, December 2022. For an elaborate treatment of Kenney's point, see his chapter "Platonism and Christianity in Late Antiquity," in *Christian Platonism*, 162–82. Kenney's insight follows a long line of historians. For example, Philip Schaff said, both in the patristic era and in the sixteenth century Platonism "excited a longing for something higher and better than all that was offered by the present." *The Principle of Protestantism*, 65.

100. Probably between 1297 and 1307.

101. Cross, *Duns Scotus*, 5.

102. Janz, "Late medieval theology," 9.

of many because he is a bridge from one form of scholasticism to another. Scotus proved both original and controversial in some respects. With no little severity he took aim at Bonaventure, Henry of Ghent, and Thomas Aquinas, and he considered Thomas's system perilous, though his hostility was more directed at changing philosophy moving forward than dwelling on its past.[103] Scotus's shift is of critical importance because it set a trajectory that proved explosive on the eve of the Reformation with the advent of late medieval scholastics like William of Ockham and Gabriel Biel.

Condemnation of 1277

The details of Scotus's education escape the historian, but his learning at the University of Paris occurred within a polemical context that had been recently characterized by a voluntarism. For example, on March 7, 1277, the three year anniversary of Thomas Aquinas's death, Stephen (Etienne) Tempier, bishop of Paris, published his *Condemnation*. The *Condemnation* featured hundreds of theses that denounced the philosophical and theological beliefs of a group on faculty (although Tempier did not name individuals).[104] Ambiguity persists over who was the object of the *Condemnation's* wrath. The theology faculty had ongoing frustrations with the faculty of Arts for overstepping their discipline, which could have been a possible factor.[105] Judging by the theses themselves, Aristotelian philosophy was one of the targets of Tempier's contempt. Since Thomas retrieved Aristotle, Thomism was targeted as well by default. Thomas was dead by then, but his thought lived on in students and scholars alike at the University of Paris.[106]

Tempier criticized reliance on reason, specifically dependence on an Aristotelian use of reason, and advocated instead that philosophy should be kept separate from theology due to its significant limitations. Philosophy, for example, cannot claim to know exactly how or why God acts the way he does, as if reason can explain such a mystery. According to God's absolute power, God may act (and does act) in ways that defy natural explanation. Since nothing can limit God's freedom in creation, the laws of nature, logic, and reason can never box God in by demanding that he must act by necessity. God is free to act however he wants to act even if his actions resist justification or transgress our human sense

103. Copleston, *History of Philosophy*, 2:483–86.

104. His 1277 *Condemnation* was preceded by his disdain towards thirteen propositions in 1270 which taught monopsychism and cosmic eternality but rejected immortality, denied free will but also divine providence. For the *Condemnation* itself, see Hyman and Walsh, eds., *Philosophy in the Middle Ages*, 583–91. For context, see Nieuwenhove, *An Introduction to Medieval Theology*, 306–9; Wippel, "The Condemnation of 1270 and 1277 at Paris," 169–201; Gilson, *History of Christian Philosophy in the Middle Ages*, 387–427.

105. Williams, *Reason and Faith*, 292. Space does not permit a venture into types of Aristotelianism, but one should be aware of Latin Averroism and how its reception painted the context in the decades leading up to 1277. Consult Gilson, *History of Christian Philosophy in the Middle Ages*, especially part 9.

106. Critiques of various philosophical positions was not uncommon. For instance, in the background of the Averroistic controversy Bonaventure critiqued Averroism in his *Collationes de decem praeceptis* (1267). For that story, see Gilson, *History of Christian Philosophy in the Middle Ages*, 402–3.

of rationality and even morality.[107] Therefore, philosophy is severely inadequate, or at least it should be in Tempier's estimation.

Tempier's *Condemnation* betrays a subversive voluntarism-nominalism as well as a distrust in reason-metaphysics, but was one the cause of the other? That question has created some debate, but historian Rik Van Nieuwenhove proposes that the "split between faith and reason as we have come to know it in modernity is not the result of voluntarism and nominalism; it is the other way around; the critique of natural reason . . . led to growing metaphysical skepticism, voluntarism and nominalism."[108] As for the *Condemnation,* it proved prophetic, signaling the fiery winds of metaphysical doubt to come. Thomas insisted on the harmony of faith and reason, theology and philosophy, but Tempier trumpeted the disposal of such a paradigm, taking the first hack at the tapestry of Thomas's participation fabric. Philosophy, of course, continued in the centuries ahead, but operated by different rules, including:

1. Philosophical argumentation becomes more logical and semantic rather than metaphysical.
2. Theological writings are less systematic but prefer to consider distinct aspects from Peter Lombard's *Sentences.*
3. Reason employed appears decidedly more analytical rather than synthetic-intellective.[109]

A turn towards an analytical mindset, says Nieuwenhove, even resulted in skepticism towards theology itself, as if reason must be segregated to philosophy and faith confined to revelation.[110]

That divide is the backdrop to the university of Paris at the end of the thirteenth century, just on the eve of Duns Scotus's arrival. Tempier's attack only escalated in 1286, for example, when the Franciscan John Peckham took the *Condemnation* to its logical outcome by attacking Thomas Aquinas himself. Is not Thomism responsible for "destroying with all its strength what Augustine teaches?"[111] Bonaventure, by contrast, has remained Augustine's true heir and his program is the way forward, concluded Peckham.

Evidence does not demonstrate Tempier's direct influence on Scotus. Nonetheless, the general voluntarist outlook was entertained in the university setting and may have left an impression on the young thinker who engaged theology at Paris at the start of the fourteenth century. Furthermore, although Scotus was occupied with all sorts of metaphysical and epistemological questions,

107. See Thijssen, "Condemnation of 1277"; cf. Williams, *Reason and Faith,* 292–93.
108. Nieuwenhove, *Medieval Theology,* 307.
109. Nieuwenhove, 308.
110. Nieuwenhove, 308.
111. *Registrum Epistolarum Fatris Johannis Peckham Archiepiscopi Cantuariensis,* 111.871. Nieuwenhove believes the attack on natural reason furthered the divide between theology and spirituality. For how much blame Bonaventure should receive, consult Nieuwenhove, 309.

he abandoned Thomas's marriage between metaphysics and theology. The two should be kept separate from one another because their subject is not the same. Since metaphysics is about being and theology is about divinity, Scotus disagreed with Thomas when he said theology is a theoretical science. For theology, if separated from metaphysics, is limited to matters of faith, whereas metaphysics operates under reason. Richard Cross summarizes the consequence: "none of the principles or axioms of theology are shared by any other kind of study: metaphysics or natural science . . . So nothing that we can know about God by natural reason belongs to the study of theology."[112] Theology is not, as Thomas said, contemplative (or speculative)—a simple gaze at truth. Rather, theology is practical.[113] Such a definition was present in Bonaventure, but Scotus also advanced the priority of the practical, which led him to conclude that theology is not ultimately after knowing God—that is a contemplative or speculative approach. Instead, theology is concerned with love, that is, a love of God.

Scotus's separation of theology from philosophy had consequences, including a widening gap between philosophy and spirituality. While Thomas was clear that theology is a science that is primarily theoretical rather than practical, nevertheless, he did not sever one from the other, as if knowledge and love could be partitioned off in separate spheres (see chapter 4).[114] In other words, the dichotomy between knowledge and love "signals a well-known bias of Scotus: the primacy of love and will over intellect," to which we now turn.[115]

Voluntarism

Scotus incubated a voluntarism that elevated the divine will to a state of unparalleled, enigmatic sovereignty. For Scotus, God possesses contra-causal freedom (or what is today labelled libertarian freedom). Since his will is never determined by something or someone else, he can always choose otherwise.

---

112. Cross, *Duns Scotus*, 8. Cross does not think Scotus and Thomas are far apart, but I think Scotus creates a gulf between theology and metaphysics that Thomas would not have appreciated.

113. *Rep. Par. I-A*, Prol. Q. 2 nos. 152, 173–74, 208; Prol. Q. 3 nos. 218, 226–27 (cf. Nieuwenhove, 312, who also surveys Scotus rejection of subalternation). Also consult *Lect. Prol.* 4.1–2, n. 163, 164 (Vatican, 16:54 = *WM*, p. 137); *Ord. prol.* 5.1–2, nn. 310, 314, 332 (Vatican, 1:204–205, 207–208, 217); cf. Cross, 9.

114. Theology is "more theoretical than practical, since it is mainly concerned with the divine things, which are, rather than with things men do." Theology "deals with human acts only in so far as they prepare men for that achieved knowledge of God on which their eternal bliss reposes" (*ST* Ia. I, 4). To clarify, theology is *more* theoretical than practical. As long as the theoretical is primary, Thomas was comfortable incorporating a practical element because theology's end is the beatific vision itself. "Now in so far as sacred doctrine is a practical science, its aim is eternal happiness" (Ia. I, 5). Additionally, the priority of the theoretical over the practical is one of form. "In the order of generation the disposition precedes form, though absolutely speaking and by its nature the form is prior" (2a2ae. 182, 4). Therefore, the moral virtues "do not have the essential part, because the goal of the contemplative life is the consideration of truth." However, moral virtues "do have their place in the contemplative life as dispositions" (2a2ae. 180, 2). In the end, Thomas did not sever the contemplative from the active, although he gave priority to the former. For this reason, he could sympathize with Gregory the Great: "Gregory makes the contemplative life consist in the *love of God*, since through loving him we are aflame to gaze on his beauty. . . . The love of God impels us to the vision of the first principle, who is God" (2a2ae. 180, 1).

115. Nieuwenhove, 313.

Contra-causal freedom is exhibited in divine power itself. According to Scotus, God's ordained power (*potentia ordinate*) confirms that God will accomplish that which he has ordained to occur. However, according to his absolute power (*potentia absoluta*) God can do whatever he pleases. No limitations can be placed on God's freedom. God cannot contradict himself or his own holy character; nor can he change or violate truths self-evident and necessary. Beyond these parameters, however, God owes no explanation for his decisions. His choices are indiscriminate; his omnipotence answers to no one. Whatever is possible, God can accomplish, even if it makes little or no sense to our human reason or morality.

For example, if God wanted to create unicorns to rule the earth instead of human beings, he could have. If God wanted to send an elephant to redeem humanity instead of his own Son, he could have. If God wanted to give Israel the command, "You shall not ride on the backs of camels," instead of "You shall not murder," he could have. Whatever God decides, his decision is good and fitting. More to the point, nothing can determine God's choice. As long as he does not transgress the law of noncontradiction, his freedom is as absolute as his power. God wills what God wills. No determinative reason can be provided. He may establish the law and morality with it, commanding his people how to treat others (e.g., "You shall not murder. You shall not commit adultery. You shall not steal. You shall not bear false witness against your neighbor"). But God's nature is not constrained by those neighbor-oriented commands, although he may choose to abide by them. Therefore, he is free to will the opposite of those same commands. As Scotus said, "Without contradiction the will could will the opposite, and thus it could justly will such."[116]

To qualify, commands that are God-oriented (e.g., "You shall have no other gods before me," "You shall not make for yourself a carved image," "You shall not take the name of the LORD your God in vain") do reflect God's nature. For Scotus, such commands are not indifferent to God. "These laws are binding on God, since God is intrinsically just, and thus bound by duties expressed in necessarily true propositions." At the same time, anything beyond laws that bind God to his nature could be otherwise. According to Scotus, "there are no *other* constrains on what God can command. So no moral principles concerning actions whose objects are creatures are necessarily true."[117]

God's knowledge (or intellect), therefore, does not govern his will, but *his will governs his knowledge (or intellect)*. If his intellect did control his will, then God would be bound, restricted to do what he is determined to do by his knowledge of the world. That was an impossibility for Scotus. God's intellect may be instructive for his will, but his will is always free to do as it pleases. "As Scotus

---

116. Scotus does qualify, "Otherwise it could will something by its absolute power and not do so justly, which seems incongruous." *Ord.* 4.46.I.n. 8 (Wadding, 10:252 = *WM*, p. 247); cf. Cross, 93.

117. "This does not mean that there are not many such moral principles that are contingently true, true unless God decides to command otherwise. Thus . . . a divine command is not necessary for the truth of these moral principles. They hold automatically unless God commands otherwise." Cross, 91–92.

pictured it," says Thomas Williams, "God's intellect presents him with all the logical possibilities. God is fully informed about everything he *can* do. But nothing in what God *knows* determines what he *will* do. It's God's will, rather than his intellect, that has the final say."[118]

Scotus's priority of will to intellect and especially the self-governing activity of the will apart from the intellect is a notable departure from Thomas Aquinas. "It was characteristic of Aristotelian thinking to make the will a mere appendage to the intellect. The will was regarded as an 'intellectual appetite,' a kind of desire or inclination that follows the intellect's perception of the good." As Williams explains, "The will basically did by nature whatever the intellect judged to be the best course of action."[119] For Thomas, that order was critical, ensuring God's actions were not unjust, his will always conforming to his moral character. Scotus disagreed: such an Aristotelian-Thomistic scheme forfeits the freedom of the will, both for God and for man, as if the will is a puppet to the intellect's rationality, a mere appetite of the mind's opinions.

The distinction by Scotus (and Ockham after him) between God's ordained and absolute power was not original. In centuries past other medieval theologians had drawn on the distinction to make sense of Scripture passages that appeared to contradict themselves. Yet they always set in place parameters based on their classical realist metaphysic. God's ordained power does not actualize something immoral (you shall murder) since it stems from a will in God that is absolutely holy.[120] However, the way Scotus and especially Ockham utilized the absolute power of God was quite different and controversial. Rather than appealing to God's absolute power to explain the range of possibilities within God's reach, God's absolute power was utilized in a radical fashion, as if God could or would do that which violated his ordained will.[121]

Scotus, of course, denied that his emphasis on the divine will led to its arbitrary exercise, but critics wondered what parameters could keep the will from becoming capricious, especially if God can contradict right reason itself.[122]

---

118. Williams, *Reason and Faith*, 297.

119. Williams, *Reason and Faith*, 298. "The central element of Scotus's theory of human freedom is his denial that the will is 'intellectual appetite'; that is, his denial that the will is merely a capacity for rational desire.... Aquinas had held that the will is intellectual appetite.... The will always chooses what the intellect judges to be the best option.... Scotus, by contrast, identifies two fundamental inclinations in the will, and only one of them is intellectual appetite. He calls the two inclinations the 'affection for advantage' and the 'affection for justice'" (298–99). Williams believes Scotus retrieved this distinction from Anselm's *On the Fall of the Devil*, even though Scotus's appropriation was for different reasons, to serve his own argument.

120. E.g., Aquinas, *ST* 1.25.5; cf. Nieuwenhove, *Medieval Theology*, 340.

121. Cross differentiates Scotus's position, however, from modern versions of divine command ethics (*Duns Scotus*, 90–91). Yet for a more critical evaluation, see Boersma who outlines four consequences (critiques) that result from Scotus and Ockham's appeal to God's absolute power: *Heavenly Participation*, 79. On Scotus's denial of an arbitrary will, see Copleston, *History of Philosophy*, 2:530.

122. Wolter has defended Scotus from the charge of making God arbitrary ("Native Freedom of the Will as a Key to the Ethics of Scotus," 158), but Williams offers a critique, demonstrating that Scotus's God is characterized by some degree of indifference to explain his freedom to contradict right reason ("A Most Methodical lover?" 169–202). The passages in view include *Rep. Par. I-A*, d.41 sol. Q. no. 55; d.44 q. 2 no. 31; IV.d.14. q.1.8. Cf. Nieuwenhove, *Medieval Theology*, 313.

Even a defender of Scotus like Williams thinks a degree of indifference is inevitable. Further, as will be seen, the implications appear innumerable. If nothing intrinsic defines the way things are but the only explanation is God's will and that will can be otherwise for any particular reason, then what should the Bible reader make of sin, the merit of Christ, grace in the sacraments, virtue and vice? Are each of these good or evil because there is something good or evil that defines them or are they good and evil only because God willed them to be so?[123] Scotus would not have appreciated such a criticism, but in the eyes of his critics, value itself no longer appeared essential but accidental.

Univocity of Being and the Weakening of Divine Simplicity and Ineffability

Scotus has become a turning point in Scholasticism for another reason: he rejected the participation paradigm embodied in the analogy of being, which created no little debate over language for God and the Creator-creature distinction.[124] Lest Scotus be misrepresented, Scotus's turn to a univocal theory was not in direct reaction to Thomas Aquinas.[125] Rather, Scotus's primary target was Henry of Ghent (c. 1217–1293), whom he believed had capitulated to equivocation in the worse way.[126] As chapter 4 observed, equivocal occurs when a "term or proposition" has "two or more wholly different meanings, with mere resemblance of words or sounds employed."[127]

Yet Scotus's reaction to Henry also revealed his departure from Thomas's *analogia entis*, analogical referring to a "resemblance without identity" or "any imperfect likeness between two or more beings that are compared with each other."[128] Like Thomas, Scotus did recognize the difference between the Creator and the creature, and he did not think finite man could know the infinite essence of God.[129] To be clear, Scotus did have a place for a concept of analogy, but he considered its legitimacy dependent on the concept of univocity. "I say

---

123. Voluntarism explains why, says Nieuwenhove, Scotus is an occasionalist as to the sacraments, denying their instrumentality, and no supporter of eudemonistic virtue ethics. His departure from an Aristotelian, Thomistic framework has significant consequences then for ecclesiology and ethics. Nieuwenhove, *Medieval Theology*, 321, who is engaging Williams, "Reason, Morality and Voluntarism," 73–94.

124. Scotus continued by enlisting another reason the *via remotionis* would not work, and this time his reason concerned the Christian life. "Neither are negations the object of our greatest love." Scotus, *Man's Natural Knowledge of God*, 15.

125. Scotus engaged a variety of medieval intellectuals before him, including Giles of Rome and Godfrey of Fontaines. To be clear, when Scotus does choose to disagree with another medieval thinker, he may or may not disagree with other aspects of their philosophy or theology. The same point should be applied to Scotus's engagement with ancient philosophers (e.g., Aristotle, Avicenna, Avicenna).

126. See *OX* I, 8, 3, no. 16 (in contrast to Henry of Ghent's *Summae quaestionum*). Cf. Copleston, *History of Philosophy*, 2:503–4; Cross, *Duns Scotus*, 4–5; Horton, *Justification*, 1:136. Space does not permit me to give a presentation of Henry of Ghent, but consult Horan, *Postmodernity and Univocity*, 163–68. Leff and Muller believe Henry paves a pathway to a more critical outlook (*Medieval Thought*, 241; cf. Muller, *PRRD* 1:93).

127. Wuellner, *Dictionary of Scholastic Philosophy*, s.v.

128. Wuellner, *Dictionary of Scholastic Philosophy*, s.v.

129. "He cannot be known naturally by any created intellect precisely as 'this essence.' . . . For there is univocation only where general notions are concerned." Scotus, *Man's Natural Knowledge of God*, 26.

that God is thought of not only in some concept analogous to that of a creature, that is, one entirely different from what is predicated of a creature, but also in some concept univocal to himself and to a creature."[130] Scotus believed predications can portray more than similarity; identity is possible since being itself is the immediate object of the mind.[131] If a word has the same meaning when used of two different objects then univocity occurs. Univocity is "the state or condition of a concept or term that is identical in its reference to different concepts or objects."[132] Therefore, something is univocal when "only one meaning" is in play or when something is "applied to one or to many in an identical meaning."[133]

Thomas Williams summarizes Scotus's understanding of univocity as follows: "Notwithstanding the irreducible ontological diversity between God and creatures, there are concepts under whose extension both God and creatures fall, so that the corresponding predicate expressions are used with exactly the same sense in predications about God as in predications about creatures."[134] For example, consider "being." Being is not equivocal but univocal, having the same meaning when applied to God and man. "The concept of being affirmed of God," explained Scotus, "is univocally common to him and to a creature."[135] The only question is whether being is infinite or finite, a difference that determines the semantic way an attribute is predicated, either towards divinity or humanity.[136]

Scotus is so apologetic about univocity because without it how can man know anything about God at all. Metaphysics and natural theology depend on the legitimacy of univocity of being for Scotus.[137] In the aftermath of the *Condemnation* and its separation of philosophy and theology, reason and faith, univocity becomes all the more indispensable for metaphysics.[138] Yet univocity, according to Scotus, is indispensable to theology as well. As Scotus reasoned, "Unless 'being' implies one univocal intention, theology would simply perish." Scotus considered the Trinity a case in point: "For theologians prove that the

---

130. *Ord.* I, dist. 3, pars 1, q. 1–2, no. 26 (Vatican 3:18).

131. Copleston, *History of Philosophy*, 496, 501.

132. Wuellner, *Dictionary of Scholastic Philosophy*, s.v.

133. Wuellner, *Dictionary of Scholastic Philosophy*, s.v.

134. Williams, "The Doctrine of Univocity Is True and Salutary," 577.

135. *Rep. Par. I-A*, d.3 q.1 no. 32; Nieuwenhove's clarifies, "Creaturely being is not univocally predicated of God's being. . . . univocity theory is a semantic or cognitive rather than a metaphysical theory" (*Medieval Theology*, 314–15).

136. Cross qualifies, "Accepting the univocity theory does not commit Scotus to the claim that *all* theological statements are univocal. In fact, Scotus wants to defend the claim that most theological statements are analogical. But he does not think that analogy is possible without univocity" (*Duns Scotus*, 34).

137. Broadie, "Duns Scotus and William Ockham," 263; Williams, "The Doctrine of Univocity Is True and Salutary," 578–80.

138. And yet, univocity of being did not lead Scotus in the direction of Anselm's *a priori* argument for God's existence. God's existence is not self-evident, but the creature must look at created effects. Yet Scotus was not in favor of Thomas's *a posteriori* method either, persuaded a true *proof* is not possible, only *possibility*. Contingency in the finite precludes certainty via cause and effect. *Rep. Par. I-A*, d. 2 p. 1 q. 1–3 no. 21, 28; cf. Nieuwenhove for this point, who thinks in the end Scotus has to circle back to Anselm's *a priori* argument to make his case (*Medieval Theology*, 317–18). Nieuwenhove engages King, "Duns Scotus on Metaphysics," 15–68.

divine Word proceeds and is begotten by way of intellect, and the Holy Spirit proceeds by way of will. But if intellect and will were found in us and in God equivocally, there would be no evidence at all that, since a word is begotten in us in such and such a fashion, it is so in God—and likewise with regard to love in us—because then intellect and will in these two cases would be a wholly different kind."[139]

Or consider the attributes of God, such as love for example. Scotus recognized that God is infinite, and the creature is finite. Yet for any comparison between Creator and creature to work, there must be univocity in being. God's love may be immutable and the creature's love mutable; nevertheless, the concept of "love" itself must have the same (univocal) meaning; otherwise, the analogical contrast cannot function to begin with. Love may be connoted of a Creator who is eternal, and love may be connoted of a creature who is temporal, but unless the concept of love stands on its own (univocal) foundation, differences between the Creator and creature remain nonsensical (and equivocity is the inevitable outcome).[140]

Or consider some of Scotus's own examples, such as "being" and "wisdom." A category like "being," a category that is impartial, can be used in a univocal manner, regardless of whether the recipients are different kinds of beings: one simple, the other complex; one *a se*, the other dependent; one eternal, the other temporal; one infinite, the other finite; and so on. One being may be compared to another being even if the two are different (God and man) because the concept of "being" itself is the same. Univocal predication is therefore possible if being in God and being in humanity has the same meaning.[141]

Likewise with wisdom. Scotus writes,

In order to conceive "wise," therefore, it is necessary to have a conception of some prior subject, because I understand this property to be verified existentially. And so we must look beyond all our ideas of attributes or quasi-attributes, in order to find a quidditative concept to which the former may be attributed. . . . Because this notion [of wisdom] includes formally no imperfection nor limitation, the imperfections associated with it in creatures are removed. Retaining this same notion of "wisdom and "will," we attribute these to God—but in a most perfect degree. Consequently, every inquiry regarding God is based upon the supposition that the intellect has the same univocal concept which it obtained from creatures.[142]

139. *Lect.* I.3.1.1-2, n. 113 (Vatican, 16:266–67); cf. Cross, *Duns Scotus*, 36.
140. This leads Broadie to conclude that in the mind of Scotus, "analogy presupposes univocity." See Broadie, 250–65.
141. Scotus, *Man's Natural Knowledge of God*, 20–21, 27. Broadie explains that for Scotus this univocal reasoning does involve an "intellectual act of abstraction." Broadie, "Duns Scotus and William Ockham," 255.
142. Scotus, *Man's Natural Knowledge of God*, 19, 25. Compare to Ockham's treatment of univocal: *Quodlibetal Questions* 2.4; 5.14.

If the attribute of wisdom in the Creator and the creature escapes univocal predication, then Scotus saw no reason why wisdom, as opposed to some other random thing, like a stone, must pertain to God.

> If you maintain that this is not true, but that the formal concept of what pertains to God is another notion, a disconcerting consequence ensues; namely that from the proper notion of anything found in creatures nothing at all can be inferred about God, for the notion of what is in each is wholly different. We would have no more reason to conclude that God is formally wise from the notion of wisdom derived from creatures than we would have reason to conclude that God is formally a stone. For it is possible to form another notion of a stone to which the notion of a created stone bears some relation, for instance, stone as an idea of God.[143]

Scotus's case for univocity also meant he was not favorable toward the *via remotionis*, a method which described God by precluding all that cannot be ascribed to God. If the theologian only says what God is not (apophaticism), then he has not actually said what God is at all. By contrast, a positive, affirmative statement must be possible—*via affirmationis*.[144] Thomas Aquinas did not limit himself to negative statements alone; nevertheless, he still saw value in the *via remotionis* and gave it priority. What set Scotus apart was his wholesale rejection of the *via remotionis*. He found the notion nonsensical since even a negative statement depends on something positive (kataphaticism). He wrote, "There is no need to make the distinction that we cannot know what God is: we can only know what He is not. For every denial is intelligible only in terms of some affirmation. It is also clear that we can know negations of God only by means of affirmations; for if we deny anything of God, it is because we wish to do away with something inconsistent with what we have already affirmed."[145]

On the one hand, Scotus intended his doctrine of univocity to be a semantic advantage, not necessarily a descriptive endeavor of the Creator or the creature's ontology. For this reason, Scotus was comfortable treating "being" in metaphysics prior to or even apart from any particular being (God, man, etc.) in theology. As Horan explains, "unlike his predecessors, Scotus does not hold that God should be the starting point of metaphysics, nor does he hold that God is the

---

143. Scotus, *Man's Natural Knowledge of God*, 25.

144. Williams, *Reason and Faith*, 308. To be clear, Scotus's arguments for God's existence are indebted to Aristotle. Thomas and Scotus both made similar cases for divine causation by moving from the effect back to its cause. However, Thomas's rejection of univocity was anathema to Scotus. Even still, Scotus did not react against Thomas's epistemology because he detested Thomas's case for the Unmoved Mover, the First Cause. Instead, he reacted against Thomas's epistemology because he did not think it preserved God as the Unmoved Mover, the First Cause, as it should. Nevertheless, it may be a step too far to say Scotus's maneuver did not affect his picture of God; later Thomists were convinced Scotus compromised the God he sought to preserve when he embraced univocity (see p. 303). For the broader context of his metaphysic, see Williams, ed., *The Cambridge Companion to Duns Scotus*, esp. chapters by Ross and Bates, King, Mann, and Noone.

145. Duns Scotus, *Man's Natural Knowledge of God*, 15.

subject of it. The subject of metaphysics is being as the primary transcendental."[146] With that starting point in place, Scotus did not believe univocity threatened the Creator's distinction from the creature. Scotus's univocity theory was merely a semantic maneuver that substantiated knowledge of God.

On the other hand, even advocates of Scotus's univocity theory believe significant ontological consequences follow for natural theology and serious theological consequences follow for revealed theology (though they consider these positive rather than negative ramifications).[147] First, consider God's simplicity. Scotus's univocity theory entailed a rejection of divine simplicity as defined by many in the Great Tradition, Thomas Aquinas in particular. They said God is without parts, meaning his essence is his attributes and his attributes his essence, and likewise his attributes are identical with one another. Univocity, by contrast, entailed redefining simplicity in a weaker sense: the attributes are essential to God's essence but nonetheless are dissimilar.[148] A formal difference between God's attributes follows from univocity because "being" must be predicated of God and man, the Creator and the creature, in the same sense. As Cross explains, "the basic lexical definitions of some of the terms applied to God are exactly the same as the lexical definitions of those terms when applied to creatures. . . . Scotus makes the point by arguing that, if these different divine attributes were not distinct in God, then (given his univocity theory) they would not be distinct in creatures either." Scotus must weaken simplicity to make room for univocity, whereas Thomas did not have to weaken simplicity due to his adoption of analogy of being. "So univocity, as understood by Scotus, entails a weak account of divine simplicity, according to which the divine attributes are distinct from each other."[149]

Second, consider God's ineffability. "The theological result of all this," says Cross, "is that the doctrine of divine ineffability, so strongly stressed by Aquinas and (to a lesser extent) by Henry of Ghent, is greatly weakened in Scotus's account." Cross then delivers a bold conclusion: "The difference between God and creatures, at least with regard to God's possession of the pure perfections, *is ultimately one of degree.*"[150] According to a defender of Scotus like Cross, the

---

146. Horan, *Postmodernity and Univocity*, 176.

147. Even Horan, who is adamant in rejecting Radical Orthodoxy's claim that Scotus's univocity theory is an ontological statement, nevertheless does acknowledge that Scotus is "anticipating ontological inquiry or metaphysical explication, setting the stage as the foundation and condition for such investigation." However, he is convinced such inquiry has "less to do with *existence* as such and more to do with *relationality*" (*Postmodernity and Univocity*, 187).

148. *Ord.* I.8.1.4, n. 192 (Vatican, 6:192). Cross defines Scotus's doctrine of simplicity this way: God's "attributes are nevertheless *different* attributes, and they satisfy Scotus's criteria for a *formal* distinction . . . Simplicity, for Scotus, entails no more than that a simple being cannot have *really* distinct parts . . ." (*Duns Scotus*, 43). And again, "there will be a formal distinction between God and his attributes. God and his attributes are inseparable, but the definition of no divine attribute will fully encompass the divine substance" (44). On the formal distinction in Scotus, see Nieuwenhove, *Medieval Theology*, 318–19, and *Rep. Par. I-A*, d.45 q.1–2 no. 32.

149. Cross, *Duns Scotus*, 43. Cross has in view *Ord.* I.8.1.4, n. 193 (Vatican, 4:261–62). Cross himself makes the same point about Thomas and his "strong account" of simplicity (44–45).

150. Emphasis added. Cross, *Duns Scotus*, 39.

distance between the Creator and the creature may be the difference between infinite and finite; nonetheless, the difference is merely quantitative. Univocity of being places the Creator and the creature within the same plain; the difference in their "being" is one of degree.

Sin and the autonomy of the will

Some have doubted whether Scotus's voluntarism and univocity theory influenced his theological conclusions in domains like sin and salvation, but such doubt does not give Scotus enough credit as a systematic thinker.

To begin with, Scotus departed from the Augustinian and Thomistic pessimistic posture towards humanity's nature after the fall, which later put him in conflict with the Reformers.[151] "Scotus's account of original sin," says Cross, "is in every respect weaker than the standard Augustinian one accepted by most of his contemporaries. The supernatural gifts of unfallen humanity were minimal, and their loss has only the smallest effect on human existence."[152] For Scotus, sin is an external, forensic transgression rather than an internal, moral disease that has spoiled man's nature.[153] Man may be haunted by the guilt of a sinful action because God has threatened judgment and man may persist in habits that orient him towards wickedness instead of righteousness. In other words, man commits acts of sin that deviate from God's laws. However, Scotus was not committed, like the Augustinian-Thomistic tradition, to a definition of sin that runs deep, so deep that a sinner's actions can ultimately be explained by the pollution of his nature.[154] For Scotus, the sinner is not actually sinful, and the will, as a result, is free rather than necessitated by a pervasively corrupt nature. "Sinfulness is no more than liability for punishment . . . Persons can certainly have morally bad qualities or habits; but *sinfulness* cannot be one of these."[155]

Chapter 4 observed how Scotus's understanding of prelapsarian grace departed from both Henry of Ghent and Thomas Aquinas. As for Adam prior to the fall, Scotus rejected the *donum concreatum* of Henry of Ghent, who said human nature was made good and that goodness is God's gift implanted within man's nature. Scotus also rejected the *donum superadditum* of Augustine and Aquinas, who said grace is added to human nature at creation, only to be lost by the first sin. Instead, said Scotus, Adam's nature did not need grace in the first place to merit the added grace he desired. The *donum superadditum* was "not part of the original constitution or original righteousness of human beings but

---

151. Although, Scotus and the Reformers did share some points of similarity, such as the forensic nature of forgiveness, for example.

152. Cross, 83.

153. "Human sinfulness, according to Scotus, is not some kind of real quality inhering in the sinner. Actual sin does not cause any lasting state in the sinner. Sin is just a lack of rectitude in an *act*, not in a *person*." Cross, 95.

154. Scotus, *Ord.* 2.37.1, n. 6, 22; 2.37.2, no. 22; 4.14.1, n. 3, 6. Cf. Cross, *Duns Scotus*, 83–100; Horton, *Justification*, 1:137–39.

155. Cross, *Duns Scotus*, 96.

was to be considered truly as a gift merited by a first act of obedience on the part of Adam performed by Adam according to his purely natural capacities (*ex puris naturalibus*)."[156]

Yet more can be said: original righteousness or justice did not have the potential of equipping man with some quality that could keep death at bay. The body would have diminished regardless. However, as long as Adam refused iniquity, the body would not meet death but only experience corruption. God would have withheld death by rewarding Adam's merit with the vision of God.[157] Scotus, therefore, did not consider original righteousness or justice synonymous with sanctifying grace. Contrary to Thomas, Scotus denied Adam sanctifying grace in the garden. Sanctifying grace was absent, though it could have been Adam's if he had obeyed God.[158]

What, then, is original sin for Scotus? While Scotus had little patience for the Augustinian account of original sin (and concupiscence), he provided little data for a working definition of his own. Yet Cross ventures one: "Scotus's theory has no such straightforward account. On his theory, original sin is just a *privation*— the lack of original justice—and certainly not a positive quality, whether spiritual or bodily."[159] And for Scotus, the lack of original righteousness or justice is the loss of tranquility.

If Cross is right—that "Scotus tries to minimize the effects of the Fall"—we might expect such a minimization to surface when Scotus turned his attention to Adam's children and the pathway to grace. "Since Adam could, by doing a minimal or finite act, merit the initial gift of God's grace," observes Richard Muller, "his fallen progeny might, by doing a minimal act, also merit the gift of first grace (see *meritum de congruo*)."[160] To qualify, Scotus did not believe the sinner could merit "the *very first gift of such grace* (given standardly in the sacrament of *baptism*)" which is received "as a result of the merits of Christ."[161] Yet assuming baptism has occurred, the sinner does not necessarily need sanctifying grace to move towards God. For example, congruous merit may occur as long as attrition is present, but attrition does not include sanctifying grace like contrition does.

Has Scotus succumbed to the Pelagian heresy? Two reasons keep advocates of Scotus from answering in the affirmative:

1. Scotus does not believe that a congruously meritorious action such as attrition could ever be *sufficient* for grace. At the instant at which grace is given,

156. Muler, *Dictionary*, s.v.

157. Cross, *Duns Scotus*, 98.

158. Cross says this hypothetical is an inference from Scotus's logic (though he believes an accurate one). Cross also observes that Scotus is betraying Thomas Aquinas but following Peter Lombrd. Consult *Rep.* 4.1.5, n. 4 (Wadding, 11:571ᵇ); cf. Cross, *Duns Scotus*, 98.

159. As evidence, Cross enlists *Ord.* 2.3032.1–4, n. 6 (Wadding, 6:946–47).

160. Muller, *Dictionary*, s.v.

161. Cross, *Duns Scotus*, 106. Cross has in view *Ord.* 2.5.I, n. 2 (Wadding, 6:505); *Rep.* 4.2.I, nn. I, I (Wadding, 12574ᵃ, 577ᵃ).

the sinner could fail to receive it. But the Pelagian claim is that the sinner can earn grace without divine aid; in other words, that the sinner's actions are *sufficient* for grace.

2. This merit is done in cooperation with Christ. God has decreed that our cooperation is required if we are to receive the reward, and that our cooperation, although not in any sense equal to the reward, is meritorious. . . . there is a sense in which contrition is necessary for the restoration of grace. . . . At the instant at which grace is given to the sinner, the act that was attrition becomes an act of contrition by the addition of grace. If contrition is not present, however, the gift of grace is immediately lost.[162]

Both the ability of man to reach a state of attrition apart from sanctifying grace and the ability of man to resist and lose grace after contrition reveals the type of freedom Scotus attributed to man. Here is the intersection where his doctrines of univocity and voluntarism cross paths with his anthropology and soteriology.[163]

First, consider the intersection of voluntarism and free will. Richard Cross says Scotus defines free will as voluntaristic, meaning "the will is a radically free, self-determining cause."[164] Scotus's "account of freedom of the will is the first serious attempt to defend an account of what philosophers today call 'contra-causal' freedom." Contra-causal freedom may also be labelled libertarian freedom, a freedom that presupposes indeterminism.[165] Cross identifies two features: "that a free power is a self-mover, a sufficient cause of its own actions; and that a free power can refrain from acting even when all the conditions necessary for its acting obtain."[166] Contra-causal freedom—and the indeterminism presupposed—means that even after the fall the will of man is not determined by an internal factor, like the corrupted nature inherited from Adam, but remains capable of moving itself, however burdened it may be by the habit of sin.

Second, consider the intersection of univocity and free will. The turn to univocity means God's will and the sinner's will have the potential to operate independent of one another, as evident in the sinner's ability to resist and even lose grace. The creature and the Creator may differ—as finite differs from infinite—but being is nonetheless predicated of both in a univocal sense. By consequence, a strong degree of autonomy follows for man if God is but another being (though a perfect one) in whom man may or may not participate. For example, one may choose the path of merit, a path that invites reward, but a person may also act

---

162. I am quoting Cross, *Duns Scotus*, 106–7. On Scotus and attrition, see Horton, *Justification*, 1:142.

163. To be transparent, some scholars such as Williams do not see an explicit connection between voluntarism and univocity in Scotus, though Williams personally does. "The Doctrine of Univocity Is True and Salutary," 582. However, other scholars appear more willing to draw the connection in Scotus, seen most when Scotus addresses soteriology.

164. Cross, *Duns Scotus*, 89.

165. Cross, *Duns Scotus*, 6.

166. Cross, *Duns Scotus*, 85; cf. *In Metaph.* 9.15, n. 2 (Wadding, 4:796ᵃ–97ᵇ = *WM*, p. 147). Scotus "argues that there is an indeterminacy of 'superabundant sufficiency,' and that something indeterminate in this sense 'can determine itself.'" *Duns Scotus*, 86; cf. *In Metaph.* 9.15, n. 5 (Wadding, 4:798ᵃ = *WM*, p. 153–55).

irrespective to God, exercising his will in an autonomous fashion that refuses to cooperate with God.

In Scholastic soteriology God first creates a habit (quality) within the soul (see chapter 4). Since he is the one to create such a habit or quality, the habit itself is supernatural in origin. Scotus does not question whether God infuses habitual grace so that it inheres within and transforms the sinner, but he does break from some earlier Scholastics by questioning whether God *must* infuse habitual grace to accept the sinner. [167] For earlier Scholastic theologians, habitual grace was necessary to create change, a transformation that leads to justification itself, a belief that stems from the Augustinian tradition. Scotus, however, deviates from a strict adherence to this medieval belief. Faithful to his voluntarist commitment, Scotus believes God can justify the sinner regardless of habitual grace's presence or transforming effect. Appealing to the will of God, Scotus sees justification as a forensic act, whereby God decides he will not judge the sinner according to his guilt. Even if no change has occurred within due to habitual grace God can act in a unilateral fashion and grant the believer a new status.[168] In short, remission may take precedence over infusion, the forensic over the medicinal.

Naturally, such a priority worried the church. Even if Scotus affirmed the importance of internal transformation as well as the significance of the sacraments to achieve such change, nevertheless, their absolute necessity was now questioned. By default, the church's place in the salvation of the believer was threatened as well, no longer considered strictly necessary. Furthermore, as much as Scotus guarded his position from Pelagianism, questioning a dependency on habitual grace for justification had a way of inviting the accusation. Scotus only furthered suspicion when he insisted God does not judge our acceptance by the worth of the habit of grace within us. Rather, the habit is only worthy because God decided it was worthy. His decision is not determined by the value of the habit in and of itself. "God could in principle damn someone with the habit. . . . God could have chosen to accept people without such a habit."[169] That same logic continues with actual grace as well, as Scotus throws its necessity into question by means of his voluntarist view of justification.[170] In the end, Scotus denies

---

167. Scotus "argues that there is no reason why God could not accept someone without a habit of grace. . . . Thus, God could will my beginning to be justified, even without the creation of a habit of grace. . . . Scotus is clear that a habit of grace is not necessary for justification." Cross, *Duns Scotus*, 108, 109, 110; cf. for example *Ord.* 1.17.1.1–2, n. 160 (Vatican, 5:215).

168. "On this account, the remission of sin involves essentially no more than God's willing non-punishment . . . The remission of sins does not bring about any real change in the sinner. For the same reason, then, there seems nothing to prevent there being a change in status with regard to justification without the creation or destruction of a habit of grace." Cross, *Duns Scotus*, 109.

169. Cross, *Duns Scotus*, 110.

170. Cross also believes voluntarism is behind these conclusions: "And, likewise, his decision with regard to which acts to accept as meritorious is made irrespective of the natural moral values of those actions. God's decision to save people by means of a habit of grace is likewise contingent. God could have chosen to accept people without such a habit. Again, it is difficult not to be struck by the *contingency* of all this. God's freedom from any external constraint—his being wholly unconditioned—is the basic presupposition behind Scotus's account." Cross, *Duns Scotus*, 111. Cross has in view *Ord.* 4.14.1, n. 3 (Wadding, 9:7).

the charge of Pelagianism. However, to be technical, God could accept a sinner apart from habitual grace. God may not have, but according to the voluntarism of Scotus God could "have chosen the Pelagian way," exclaims Cross.[171] The Pelagian possibility is real for Scotus as long as God remains free in the voluntarist sense.

The First Modern?

Other examples of controversy could be outlined yet the two examples discussed—voluntarism and univocity of being—model a change of course in Scholasticism with Scotus.[172] The danger in that shift has been debated ever since Scotus.[173]

For example, consider Radical Orthodoxy's interpretation of Scotus in the last century.[174] From the church fathers to the Scholastics of the High Middle Ages, the world was interpreted within the framework of participation. Since the creature's being is derivative, he lives and moves and has his being in his Creator, who alone is pure actuality. In other words, his being must participate in the being of his Maker for his existence and happiness. However, Scotus's doctrines of voluntarism and univocity ruptured participation, creating a secular space that eventually breathed life into modernity and its skepticism.

First, Radical Orthodoxy criticized Scotus for severing theology from ontology. Scotus segregated "being" to metaphysics, as if it is a category that can be defined apart from revelation's definition of God. However, such a divorce of disciplines is an impossibility since metaphysics is concerned with arriving at a first principle and who is the first principle but God? As long as metaphysics is occupied with being it must submit itself to revelation's understanding of divinity. Being is not antecedent to God let alone independent from God but defined by God himself. An autonomous metaphysic was substituted for a participation metaphysic.[175]

Second, Scotus's separation between metaphysics and theology meant he could define "being" as univocal rather than analogical. As Milbank says, "'God is good' means that he is good in the same *sense* that we are said to be good,

---

171. Cross, *Duns Scotus*, 110.

172. E.g., For instance, Thomas denied the immaculate conception of Mary, but Duns Scotus made a great effort to refute Thomas and advise his Franciscans to advance the doctrine. In 1387 Thomists were even thrown out of the University of Paris for their rejection of the immaculate conception as Thomism itself entered a period of ostracization only to experience revival in the fifteenth century that ensured major universities had Thomists on faculty. Examples of faculty who followed the way of St Thomas—*in via sancti Thomae*—include John Capreolus. Janz, "Late Medieval Theology," 6.

173. I will limit myself to certain voices, but also consider interpretations of Scotus by Sweetman, "Univocity, Analogy, and the Mystery of Being according to John Duns Scotus," 73–87; King, "Scotus on Metaphysics," 15–68; Noone, "Universals and Individuation," 100–128.

174. Radical Orthodoxy will sometimes rely on the interpretation of Scotus by Gilson (*John Duns Scotus*, 1–300), though Gilson has proved controversial in his reading of Scotus.

175. Milbank, *Theology and Social Theory*, 306; Milbank, *The Word Made Strange*, 9; Smith, *Introducing Radical Orthodoxy*, 97.

however much more of the quality of goodness he may be thought to possess."[176] In other words, Scotus flattened out being until God and man exist on the same plane. For Radical Orthodoxy the shift to univocity tempts idolatry because being now subsists in the creature no different than the Creator, only to a lesser degree since the creature is finite and the Creator infinite.[177] A radical autonomy follows for the creature since he no longer participates in God on the basis of an analogy of being. Again, a secular space uncanny in its resemblance to a future modernity is the outcome, a space in which the creature can exist independent of the Creator.

Third, if being is the same in reference to Creator and creature, the former becomes unknowable for the difference is an infinite one along the same plane of existence. In the estimation of Radical Orthodoxy, the turn to univocity has an inevitable outcome: equivocity. In the words of Catherine Pickstock, "By withdrawing the means through which creatures might distinguish themselves ontologically from God through figuring or analogically drawing near to Him, the distance between the infinite and the finite becomes an undifferentiated and quantified (although unquantifiable) abyss."[178] Ironically, Scotus's quest for a semantic mechanism by which the creature can know God led him to a univocity theory, but in the end his position terminates in an equivocity theory, the very theory he criticized Henry of Ghent for advocating.

Radical Orthodoxy's criticisms of Scotus have been carried forward by various intellectuals.[179] However, contemporary advocates of Scotus have contested Radical Orthodoxy's claims on several grounds, convinced Scotus has been misrepresented and the supposed secular consequences of his position do not follow.[180]

First, the priority of being in Scotus—a priority that allows Scotus to address being in purely metaphysical categories, apart from revelation and theology—does not mean that God's being is substantiated or constituted by something that precedes him. As Cross says, "for claiming that God falls under the extension of a concept—*being*—is very different from claiming that God somehow requires being for his existence, as it were."[181]

Second, Scotus's statements on being are not intended to say something theological about the Creator's divinity. Whereas Thomas defines being in direct reference to God (and draws a theory of participation by consequence), Scotus

176. Milbank, *Theology and Social Theory*, 305; cf. 304.

177. Milbank, *The Word Made Strange*, 44, 47.

178. Pickstock, *After Writing*, 123. To consider how Pickstock advances Milbank's criticisms of univocity in Scotus, also consult the following: "Modernity and Scholasticism: A Critique of recent Invocations of Univocity," 3–47; "Duns Scotus: His Historical and Contemporary Significance," 543–74; "The Univocalist Mode of Production," 281–325.

179. Cunningham, *Genealogy of Nihilism*; "The Difference of Theology and Some Philosophies of Nothing," 289–312; Hyman, *The Predicament of Postmodern Theology*; Ward, *Cities of God*; et al.

180. Cross, "Scotus and Suárez at the Origins of Modernity," 65–80; Cross, "'Where Angels Fear to Tread': Duns Scotus and Radical Orthodoxy," 7–41; Williams, "The Doctrine of Univocity Is True and Salutary," 575–85; Horan, *Postmodernity and Univocity*.

181. Cross, "Where Angels Fear to Tread," 26–27. Also see Horan, *Postmodernity and Univocity*, 116–21.

does not. Scotus and Thomas have different purposes in view. When Scotus uses the concept of being he has no intention to say something specific about the attributes of various types of beings, whether God or man or animals. "All that it tells us is that there is a concept under whose extension both God and creatures fall, just as there is a concept under whose extension both cats and dogs fall."[182] Therefore, defenders of Scotus are not alarmed when critics accuse Scotus of flattening participation, as if God and the creature are set on the same plane. Scotus's univocity theory is merely a *semantic* point of departure, not a statement about the ontology of either God or man.[183] As Horan observes, "When Scotus speaks of 'infinite being,' he is not speaking of degree in a proper sense, but rather a mere abstraction . . . such a qualification (that of an abstract transcendental) tells us *nothing* about God or creatures in themselves, beyond the existence of a genus-like concept under which both God and creatures fall."[184]

Third, defenders of Scotus are not worried the scholastic collapses the Creator-creature distinction because Scotus assumes (even prioritizes) divine infinitude and still maintains some notion of participation even if it is subtle. Scotus, to be precise, does not conceive of divine infinitude—or what has been labelled an intensive infinity—in quantitative measurements because he does not think God is divisible.[185] For this reason, defenders of Scotus do not appreciate the charge of idolatry. Furthermore, Scotus does not utilize the language and concept of participation to the great extent of someone like Thomas Aquinas. Nevertheless, claims Cross, Scotus does not abandon "the underlying claim that things owe their perfections to God, and that they in important respects resemble him."[186] Therefore, claims that Scotus is a gateway to a secular space where God is absent are unfounded.[187]

In evaluation, both interpretations of Scotus raise legitimate concerns but not without the need for correction or at least balance. On the one hand, Radical Orthodoxy has not always given a fair representation of Scotus, and Scotus advocates exposed points of correction, both in the sources used and the methodology wielded.[188] Furthermore, Radical Orthodoxy may place too much weight on the shoulders of Scotus himself, as if he alone is responsible for the secularization that occurs in modernity. Even if we grant that Scotus's paradigm was a radical shift, Scotus could not have anticipated the nihilism and skepticism of modernity, and he would not have agreed with such a suspicious stance towards truth and morality.

---

182. Cross, "Where Angels Fear to Tread," 15. Also see Horan, *Postmodernity and Univocity*, 108–13.
183. Cross, "Scotus and Suárez at the Origins of Modernity," 77; Williams, "The Doctrine of Univocity Is True and Salutary," 577; Horan, *Postmodernity and Univocity*, 173.
184. Horan, *Postmodernity and Univocity*, 114.
185. Cross, "Where Angels Fear to Tread," 23–24. Also see Horan, *Postmodernity and Univocity*, 114–16.
186. Cross, "Where Angels Fear to Tread," 33.
187. Williams, "The Doctrine of Univocity Is True and Salutary," 580; Horan, *Postmodernity and Univocity*, 116–21.
188. I do not agree however with Horan who goes so far to say that representatives of Radical Orthodoxy have a "malicious intent" or are "disingenuous." *Postmodernity and Univocity*, 145–46.

On the other hand, defenders of Scotus also need greater discernment for several reasons.[189] First, the scholars of Radical Orthodoxy are not the only ones who have pointed to Scotus as the first modern or at least criticized Scotus for planting the seeds of modernity. Defenders of Scotus act as if the Scholastic will be interpreted in a positive light if only Radical Orthodoxy does not read its criticisms of modernity back into Scotus. However, others who do not label themselves representatives for Radical Orthodoxy have still recognized a radical shift in Scotus's thought. For example, Matthew Levering has concluded that Scotus introduced "a deracinated form" of participation.[190] Vos says Scotus "reconstructed the doctrine of God at the end of the thirteenth century."[191] And Hans Urs von Balthasar labels Scotus the first true modern for similar reasons.[192] According to a variety of authors who may or may not have the same agenda as Radical Orthodoxy, Scotus was not merely shifting epistemological pieces on deck but sinking the metaphysical ship of classical theism. Even older historians like Heiko Oberman insinuate that Scotus prepared the way for the nominalism of the *via moderna* (Ockham, Biel), even if Scotus still operated with the borrowed capital of the *via antiqua* and its realism.[193]

Second, those who have rehabilitated Scotus are often advocates of Scotus's views as well. They dismiss criticisms of Scotus's theory of univocity, but they are committed to univocity themselves. They do not take the negative consequences of univocity seriously, but they consider univocity full of positive entailments instead. Naturally, Scotus is not the villain but the hero, moving the tradition to a new and improved paradigm. Commitment to Scotus does not make advocates necessarily wrong, but their cast of Scotus as hero rather than villain must be considered in light of their precommitments to his position, especially when they deny any and all modern proclivities in Scotus however small.

Third, representatives of Radical Orthodoxy have been criticized for evaluating Scotus in the shadow of Thomas Aquinas (and his analogy of being), as if doing so does not give Scotus's univocity a fair hearing. Of course, it is important to evaluate a theologian's paradigm on its own terms. At the same time, Scotus's context itself was characterized by a Thomistic atmosphere, though Thomas was not the only influence on the century. As demonstrated, the events that led to criticisms of Thomas in the universities created a dynamic climate, one Scotus was born into and at points could not help but engage. Furthermore, in

---

189. The following are not defenses of Radical Orthodoxy. I am not a representative of Radical Orthodoxy, but an outsider looking in. Rather, I offer these points as a way forward, a way to even move beyond Radical Orthodoxy itself.

190. Levering, *Participatory Biblical Exegesis*, 18–25.

191. Vos, "Scholasticism and Reformation," 113. As the last chapter revealed, however, I do not agree with Vos when he then concludes that Protestantism is the child of Scotism. For other critics of nominalism, see especially Gilson, *History of Christian Philosophy in the Middle Ages*; Lortz, *Die Reformation in Deutschland*; Leff, *Bradwardine and the Pelagians*; Leff, *Gregory of Rimini*; Leff, *William of Ockham*.

192. Balthasar, *The Glory of the Lord*, 6–28; cf. Nieuwenhove, *Medieval Theology*, 311.

193. Oberman, *Luther*, 117.

the centuries ahead, univocity and analogy did surface as competing paradigms and sixteenth but especially seventeenth century theologians—Roman Catholic and Protestant—did evaluate univocity in light of Thomas's doctrine of analogy.

Fourth, and related to the previous point, the deviation of Scotus's paradigm shift and its potential for provocation in the centuries after Scotus should not be underestimated. Scotus may have been well-intentioned when he confined his univocity theory to the semantics of his epistemology rather than the ontology of divinity, or when he sanctioned univocity on the whole to metaphysics as opposed to theology.[194] However, such a move assumes these disciplines can be sharply divided from one another, which itself is a deviation from some earlier Scholastics. From Boethius to Anselm to Thomas, Scholastics recognized these distinctions, but they also believed their epistemological and metaphysical convictions entailed a specific theology, even a doctrine of God, and vice versa. Unlike Scotus, their definition of "being" was inseparable from the one who is the Perfect Being. As a result, being was not a mere semantic category irrespective of various species of being. Natural theology, with its inquiry into being, operated under the authority of a natural *revelation*, which considered God the First Being. Therefore, being was never isolated and abstracted but defined according to the creature's being and its participation in the being of God. Mere semantics was an impossibility; mere abstraction was implausible. For many Scholastics, being did say something about God. And if God is being in and of himself, then a definition of being occurs under the auspices of who God is first and foremost. Philosophy was conducted from a specific posture: faith seeking understanding—*fides quaerens intellectum*. Scotus may have agreed with that mantra, but his consistency was questioned as soon as he separated being as a category that could be abstracted prior to and apart from a Scholastic understanding of God who is being itself (hence the Great Tradition's strong account of divine simplicity in conducting metaphysics).

If earlier Scholastics were correct in their refusal to separate semantics from the ontology of theology proper, then the historian can understand why later Scholastics in the Thomist tradition—as well as later Protestant Scholastics who retrieved the Thomist tradition (see chapter 4)—considered univocity a serious error. For if univocity does have ontological consequences, then the Creator-creature distinction has been flattened. God and those in his likeness exist on the same plane. While that plane may be defined by a Creator who is infinite and a creature who is finite, nevertheless, the difference is not one of kind but degree, not one of quality but quantity, despite Scotus's protest. And the creature's participation in the Creator now appears weak at best if not dispensable at worst. Thomas anticipated this entailment long before Scotus promoted univocity.

---

194. To be fair, Cross and Williams do acknowledge that Scotus's epistemology may have ontological entailments. Nevertheless, they do not consider those entailments worrisome.

Everything, likewise, that is predicated univocally of many things belongs
through participation to each of the things of which it is predicated; for the species is said to participate in the genus and the individual in the species. But nothing is said of God by participation, since whatever is participated is determined to
the mode of that which is participated and is thus possessed in a partial way and
not according to every mode of perfection. Nothing, therefore, can be predicated
univocally of God and other things.[195]

Again, this criticism does not pretend Scotus himself advocated such a confla-
tion between the Creator and the creature; he no doubt denied it. However, in
Scholastic theology a critique did not merely address the position itself but its
entailments, however much the advocate may disagree with the consequences an
opponent considered inevitable. Drawing out those entailments was not considered poor scholarship but careful scrutiny when considering a position's logical
coherency or lack thereof.

Furthermore, the deficiency of univocity logic became apparent to other
Scholastics when Scotus's univocity resulted in a weak doctrine of divine
simplicity. For if God's attributes are essential but nonetheless dissimilar to
one another, then critics will wonder how God is not downgraded, leveled to
the same domain as the creature. Simplicity appears to be a harmony in God
between differentiated attributes (although an essential harmony), but such a
weak definition of simplicity can be assigned to angelic beings as well, a point
Scholastics readily recognized in their treatment of angels. As mentioned
already, the motive behind Scotus's weak account of simplicity is a univocity of
being between the Creator and the creature so that what is distinct in God is
also distinct in the creature, a point defenders of Scotus articulate. According
to the critic, however, a weak account of simplicity cannot avoid domesticating
God so long as differentiation of attributes in the creature match differentiation
of attributes in the Creator, being meaning the same thing in both parties. The
creature's participation in the Creator, by consequence, lacks justification. After
distinguishing between substance and accident Thomas made a similar point in
his *Summa Contra Gentiles*:

Now nothing is predicated of God and creatures as though they were in the same
order, but, rather, according to priority and posteriority. For all things are predicated of God essentially. For God is called being as being entity itself, and He is
called good as being goodness itself. But in other beings predications are made
by participation, as Socrates is said to be a man, not because he is humanity itself,
but because he possesses humanity. It is impossible, therefore, that anything be
predicated univocally of God and other things.[196]

195. *SCG* 1.32.6.
196. *SCG* 1.32.7.

Likewise, in his *Summa Theologiae* Thomas explained why univocity cannot make sense of a complex creature's participation in a simple Creator.

> It is impossible to predicate anything univocally of God and creatures. Every effect that falls short of what is typical of the power of its cause represents it inadequately, for it is not the same kind of thing as the cause. Thus what exists simply and in a unified way in the cause will be divided up and take various different forms in such effects—as the simple power of the sun produces many different kinds of lesser things. In the same way, as we said earlier, the perfections which in creatures are many and various pre-exist in God as one.[197]

Thomas used the example of "wisdom" (as did Scotus after him) but to explain why being cannot be predicated of God and man in the same sense.

> Thus when we say that a man is wise, we signify his wisdom as something distinct from the other things about him—his essence, for example, his powers or his existence. But when we use this word about God we do not intend to signify something distinct from his essence, power or existence. When 'wise' is used of a man, it so to speak contains and delimits the aspect of man that it signifies, but this is not so when it is used of God; what it signifies in God is not confined by the meaning of our word but goes beyond it. Hence it is clear that the word 'wise' is not used in the same sense of God and man, and the same is true of all other words, so they cannot be used univocally of God and creatures.[198]

For these reasons (and others), the majority of Reformed Scholastics of the sixteenth and seventeenth centuries decided against Scotus's univocity theory and sided instead with the realism of the Thomist tradition (see chapter 4).[199]

Last, when Scotus's univocity theory intersected with his voluntarist proclivities, the stage was at least set for the *via moderna* in the fifteenth century and its provocative Pelagian turn. Such a criticism does not claim that Scotus himself advocated Pelagianism, which he clearly denied. Rather, such a criticism is convinced Scotus sets in place the priorities of voluntarism, priorities with major soteriological ramifications. As mentioned, these voluntarist priorities have led defenders of Scotus to acknowledge a hypothetical Pelagianism that Scotus himself could not preclude from the realm of soteriological possibilities. Defenders of Scotus do recognize that the Scholastic departed (or at least weakened) the Augustinian doctrine of original sin. When Scotus's weak account of original sin was coupled with a voluntarist definition of human freedom (contra-causal or libertarian freedom), Ockham and Biel's belief that God will decide (in the voluntarist sense) to reward the sinner if he does his best, if he does what lies within

---

197. *ST* 1a. 13, 5.
198. *ST* 1a. 13, 5.
199. Muller, "Not Scotus," 127–50.

him is not far removed. How direct the correlation may be between Scotus and Ockham is a lacuna future historians will have to explore.

In addition, defenders of Scotus acknowledge that the Scholastic is the first to put forward a full account of contra-causal freedom. They should not be so surprised, then, when critics consider voluntarist freedom a means to cultivating human autonomy, an autonomy so radical it severs the cord of participation between the Creator and the creature or the Savior and the sinner. Scotus himself did not intend to create a secular space for man. Yet critics committed to the Augustinian heritage from which Scotus deviated are not unreasonable to ask whether Scotus's redefinition of human freedom does not at least plant the seeds for an autonomy that modernity was content to water.[200] The radical nature of voluntarist freedom in Scotus should not be underestimated.

To conclude, defenders of Scotus do observe subtle ways remnants of a participation metaphysic remained intact within Scotus's corpus. Nevertheless, defenders of Scotus are also transparent that participation is not as focal in Scotus as earlier Scholastics. If critics of Scotus are correct that Scotus's doctrines of voluntarism and univocity—especially in view of contra-causal freedom—throw participation into question, then the contrast between Scotus and the Great Tradition before him may be far more striking than they believe.

> For the Great Tradition, earthly realities existed not just for themselves but for the sake of a greater purpose. Augustine, for example, maintained that only God should be enjoyed for his own sake. The life of the triune God was the only ultimate end. Since all other realities had their being only inasmuch as God graciously granted participation in his own being, those realities could never be ultimate in character. Created objects and earthly ends had never more than penultimate significance; they were always ordered to something greater—the life of God himself.[201]

Once Scotus's voluntarist-univocity doctrine is combined with Ockham's nominalism, Boersma is persuaded they form the "two blades of a pair of scissors that cut that tapestry by severing the participatory link between earthly sacrament (*sacramentum*) and heavenly reality (*res*)."[202] Yet the second blade proved sharper still.

---

200. We have not ventured into ethics, but the application of voluntarism to Scotus's ethical theory has also proved controversial. Defenders of Scotus deny that the Scholastic's position is synonymous with more modern versions of divine command theory. However, others, like Nieuwenhove, believe Scotus's ethic is "closer to Kant's understanding of morality than to Thomas Aquinas's" and "the divine command ethic, when secularized, results in a subjectivist ethics, in which we effectively construe values rather than recognize them" (*Medieval Theology*, 322).

201. Boersma, *Heavenly Participation*, 69. After acknowledging diverse interpretations, Boersma uses different language than I have used to make a similar point: "with Scotus there appears an initial flattening of the infinite horizons of the sacramental ontology of the Great Tradition" (*Heavenly Participation*, 75).

202. Boersma, *Heavenly Participation*, 69. Ockham and nominalism "has received a generally negative assessment among such important historians as Gilson, Feckes, Knowles, Lortz, Iserloh, and Leff. According to the critics of nominalism, its philosophy and theology are atomistic, skeptical, and fideistic. This understanding . . . has been challenged by many scholars, chiefly E. A. Moody, Paul Vignaux, Gerhard Ritter, Philotheus

WILLIAM OF OCKHAM: FOUNTAINHEAD OF NOMINALISM, GUARDIAN OF VOLUNTARISM

William of Ockham (ca. 1287/88–ca.1348/49) was born around two decades after Duns Scotus. Although William was born in England instead of Scotland, he shared many similarities with Duns Scotus: he, too, was a Franciscan, studied at Oxford, and lectured on Lombard's *Sentences*. Unlike Duns Scotus, however, William of Ockham had a volatile relationship with the pope, John XXII, who eventually excommunicated Ockham. As chapter 7 will detail, the controversy that led to Ockham's excommunication concerned the Franciscan vow of poverty, the nexus between ecclesiastical and secular authority, and Ockham's accusation that the pope was a heretic. That charge was ironic: Ockham was in Avignon because he faced heresy charges himself from 1324 to 1328 due to his controversial theology and philosophy.[203] Ockham's intellectual contribution, or his radical deviance from the classical realist tradition before him, is not irrelevant to his suspicious reputation either. Ockham was indebted to Scotus in a variety of ways, but he was severe in his criticism of Scotus's moderate realism, and in a moment of irony he even used Aristotle himself to advance his attack.[204]

Ockham was a bridge between the voluntarism of Scotus and the voluntarism of Gabriel Biel. He, too, defended God's freedom in absolute terms—*potentia absoluta*. Ockham's continuity with Scotus over against Thomas Aquinas served to perpetuate a voluntarist tradition inherited by Biel (with soteriology implications that provoked Martin Luther). However, Ockham's conclusions on a variety of other matters also resisted Thomas (and sometimes Scotus) and proved to be a major deviation from classical realism's epistemology and metaphysics. Consider two: Ockham's nominalism and Ockham's razor.[205]

Ockham, Universals, and Natural Theology

Each of the five benchmarks of Christian Platonism depend on the existence of universals. Ockham, however, attacked the third distinctive: the belief that "reality is made up not just of individuals, each uniquely situated in time and space, but that two individual objects can be the same in essence (e.g., both being canine) while still being unique individuals (distinct dogs)." In doing so, he questioned a core pillar of realism (including the realism of Scotus before him).[206]

Boehner, Erich Hochstetter, Léon Baudry, Heiko A. Aboerman, Leif Grane, William J. Courtenay, and Albert Lang." Steinmetz, *Calvin in Context*, 42–43.

203. John Lutterell expressed concerns with Ockham's commentary on Lombard's *Sentences*. Ockahm wrote many other controversial works on salvation, the papacy, and the religious-secular divide. Consult *On Predestination and Future Contingents, De imperatorum et pontificium potestate, Dialogus, Opus Nonaginta Dierum, Quodlibetal Disputations*.

204. Copleston, *History of Philosophy*, 3:46, says Ockham's philosophy is not a "development" but a "strong reaction" and perpetual attack on Scotus. Copleston calls Ockham an original thinker and the "fountainhead" of nominalism.

205. For the material that follows, consult Ockham, *Philosophical Writings*.

206. Ockham was not the only one to go the direction of nominalism; Peter Abelard did as well. Tyson, *Returning to Reality*, 72.

The idea of universals was illogical, Ockham said. Particulars do not have to be substantiated in universals. Universals are only *nomina*, mere names or concepts or terms (*termini concepti*) that people use even though they have no objective reference point to an actual universal. For this reason, Ockham has been labeled a nominalist, even though the label itself is a much later invention and does not always account for nominalist varieties.[207] Nevertheless, the label is adequate since Ockham considered the idea of universals unnecessary. For example, "humanity" is not destroyed simply because one human dies. In Ockham's words, "One man can be annihilated by God without any other man being annihilated or destroyed. Therefore there is not anything common to both, because (if there were) it would be annihilated, and consequently no other man would retain his essential nature.... No universal is anything existing in any way outside the soul; but everything which is predicable of many things is of its nature in the mind, whether subjectively or objectively; and no universal belongs to the essence or quiddity of any substance whatever."[208]

Or consider the human intellect. For example, the intellect does not depend on a universal entity for knowledge of objects in this world. The senses can take in the experience of a particular car, for example, and know what cars are like wherever cars are driven. A transcendent idea of *carness* is irrelevant. The sensation that occurs in driving a particular car can be extended to driving in any other car. The concept of a car is sufficient, capable of extension to all experiences with cars. A universal entity—carness—is not necessary.[209] How then does Ockham explain the cohesiveness of reality? (Why is my experience in one car similar to my experience riding in another car?) Ockham answered with the principle of parsimony: two things share commonality not due to a third thing (a common, universal nature); rather, the two things by themselves are similar since only particulars exist.[210] As a theist, however, Ockham also offered a more supernatural explanation. As a voluntarist committed to a radical conception of God's absolute power, Ockham's answer was the will of God.[211] God decides there shall be commonality, so there is. But such continuity is not explained by universals.

207. On varieties of nominalists, see Gilson, *History of Christian Philosophy in the Middle Ages*, 499–520; Spade, "Ockham's Nominalist Metaphysics," 100–117.

208. I *Sent.*, 2, 4, D and 2, 8, Z; cf. Copleston, *History of Philosophy*, 3:57–58. Copleston added the clarification, "It [universal] is not, however, a fiction in the sense that it does not stand for anything real: it stands for individual real things, though it does not stand for any universal thing. It is, in short a way of conceiving or knowing individual things." Yet Ockham should not be confused with Thomas: "St. Thomas gave a metaphysical explanation of the similarity of natures; for he held that God creates things belonging to the same, things, that is, with similar natures, according to an idea of human nature in the divine mind.... Although St. Thomas and William of Ockham were fundamentally at one in denying that there is any *universale in re*, the former combined his rejection of ultra-realism with the Augustinian doctrine of the *universale ante rem*, whereas the latter did not."

209. "There are no universal entities, but concepts are universal, in the sense that they can apply to many things.... For Ockham, it's not that we apprehend universals; it's that we apprehend particular things in a universal way. Our minds, in a sense, create the universality that things themselves do not possess." Williams, *Reason and Faith*, 330–31.

210. Consult Scotus's use of haecceity (*haecceitas*) as well. Nieuwenhove, *Medieval Theology*, 337; Adams, *William Ockham*, 111; cf. *Ord.* I, d.2 q. 6.

211. Boersma, *Heavenly Participation*, 81.

The consequences for epistemology and metaphysics were many. For instance, one's encounter with sensible things does result in an image of those things in one's mind, as if its form can be abstracted from its matter, as Thomas supposed.[212] Abstraction, on the basis of universals, is a moot point. Likewise, when a person thinks about God, he thinks of mere concepts.[213] In other words, cognitive constructions and representations are in view, not God. Ockham did not merely preclude God's unity but the attributes that define his supremacy, such as his "infinite power or the divine goodness or perfection." Ockham concluded, "What we know immediately are concepts, which are not really God but which we use in propositions to stand for God"—what can be labeled *quid nominis*.[214] Consequently, the philosopher should not claim he can prove anything about God from nature and natural reason. To claim he has certain, sure, definitive knowledge is to claim he has moved beyond nominal construction, which is an impossibility.[215]

Ockham still believed we could know things about God, but if that knowledge came from philosophy, then it could only be probable, not certain. The only way certain knowledge is achieved is by faith, that is, through revelation itself. As a result, Ockham rejected proofs for the existence of God put forward by classical realists such as Thomas Aquinas and his five ways. Reasonable observation could not demonstrate God's existence or attributes such as eternity, infinitude, aseity, immutability, omnipotence, and omniscience. Creating the world *ex nihilo* was also outside the reach of reasonable observation.[216] Ockham went so far as to criticize any attempt to demonstrate through nature and reason that effects in this world have God as their cause.[217]

In the end, Ockham's nominalism questioned natural theology as a project altogether, at least as traditionally construed. Furthermore, Ockham's denial of universals—his attack on realism—could be aggressive as well. He did not think universals were merely unnecessary but that they were dangerous, a threat to God's freedom. If universal Ideas exist in God's mind (Augustine) and if they are identical with his essence (Thomas), then God's act of creation is determined rather than free, as if everything from human nature to moral law must be the way it is and cannot be otherwise.[218] In Ockham's mind, he was not undermining theology proper but saving it from the various forms of realism within Christian Platonism from Augustine to Thomas, along with its Greek imposition of universals. A denial of universals was essential to preserving a voluntarist view of God's absolute power.

---

212. Nieuwenhove, *Medieval Theology*, 338.

213. Some think Ockham's position could be called conceptualism. Ockham did not deny the cognitive entertainment of universals as concepts, but their existence in reality outside the mind (in the realist sense). See Boersma, *Heavenly Participation*, 80 n. 24.

214. I *Sent.*, 3, 2, F.

215. Ockham will appeal to conservation instead. Copleston, *History of Philosophy*, 3:87.

216. *Prol. Sent.*, 2, D, D. Cf. Copleston, *History of Philosophy*, 3:85–85–92.

217. I *Sent.*, 35, 2, D. Cf. Copleston, *History of Philosophy*, 3:85–92.

218. Copleston, *History of Philosophy*, 3:50.

Ockham's denial of universals appeared innocent to sympathizers, but his critics thought his nominalism was catastrophic.[219] The last of the five marks of Christian Platonism is anti-skepticism. Critics of Ockham were convinced that his denial of universals could only result in skepticism.[220] Without universals there can be no objective, sure footing on which all knowledge can stand. To avoid skepticism in the end, human knowledge must have an objective, transcendent reference point that is not limited to particulars. The mind itself must make a connection to that which is beyond sensations. If not, then the participatory connection between human knowledge and universal objectivity in the essence of God is severed.

Consider holiness once more. If universals do not exist, then what universal reference point—like an eternal, simple, and infinite God—can substantiate all the temporal, compositional, and finite instances of holiness perceived by the senses in this world? The priest may be holy, the sanctuary may be holy, and the tree may be holy, but none of these share with another the same identical universal called *holiness*. Each is holy in itself and for itself, independent of anything outside itself. In the eyes of anti-nominalists, such a world without universals lets subjectivism reign, allowing someone (God or man) to determine the meaning and significance of any particular nature since no individual thing has an objective reference to a governing universal entity.[221]

Worse still, if nominalism is applied to orthodoxy, specifically its historical articulation of the Trinity, how can Ockham avoid heresy? If universals have no objective existence, then what keeps the persons from becoming mere names, mere individuals? According to critics, Ockham stripped the Trinity of its "ontological reality" so that the "charge of tritheism (three Persons) seems valid."[222] Nieuwenhove observes how that same logic eliminates divine ideas. The long, varied tradition of Christian Platonism in the East and West believed in universals and therefore divine ideas. As we learned from Thomas Aquinas, divine ideas are essential to mapping the creaturely realm. As an architect, God created the world through his divine ideas, which explains the participation between type and archetype. The divine ideas are exemplars, even exemplary causes that substantiate the creature's participation in the Creator.[223] By contrast, Ockham thinks God bypasses divine ideas altogether and acquires direct knowledge of creation, operating on a univocal plain.[224] Participation through divine ideas is no longer feasible or necessary. The "transcendental dynamic" has been cut down, a dynamic present not only in Thomas but across the medieval landscape, from "authors as diverse as Augustine, Eriugena, Anselm, the Victorines and Bonaventure."[225]

219. Ockham, however, is one example of nominalism. Oberman explained how various shades existed. Oberman, *Masters of the Reformation*, 27.
220. Contemporary examples of this criticism are many, but see Gillespie, *The Theological Origins of Modernity*, 19–33; White, *The Trinity*, 34.
221. Williams, *Reason and Faith*, 333.
222. Nieuwenhove, *Medieval Theology*, 339.
223. Muller, *Dictionary*, causa exmplaris, s.v.
224. Nieuwenhove, 340.
225. Nieuwenhove, 344.

Yet the consequences of Ockham's position transcend creation and extend into the church. For when Ockham's nominalism and voluntarism meet, he no longer feels obligated to assign an intrinsic value to the sacraments. The sacraments are a means of grace because God wills that they be so; they are not a means of grace because they serve as an instrumental cause, bringing the sinner into participation with the Savior. On that basis, transubstantiation became an absurdity to Ockham.[226] Furthermore, God is free, and should he decide tomorrow that the sacraments are extinct, he may do so. His inhering presence suffers no loss if the sacraments are replaced. And if transcendentals spiral into irrelevancy, the church is vacated of a virtue ethic. That fear stemmed from Ockham's voluntarism, which had little patience for Thomas's natural law ethic. However premature a divine command ethic may be, signs of its presence surface when Ockham surveyed history. According to God's absolute power, he may and does dispense with one law in one age only to create another law (or even the opposite of the previous law) in another age. Ockham denied that God is arbitrary; nonetheless, God can change his moral commands.[227]

In its most radical form, subjectivism gives birth to skepticism because knowledge of any universal nature is impossible. Critics saw Ockham's rejection of natural theology and its arguments for God's existence as proof. Such an outlook, if taken to its logical end, has little room for a divine being who is the source of all that is universal, said critics. Once knowledge of universals is forfeited, and with it any sense of objectivity, how can knowledge of God—the source of all universals and the ground of all objectivity—be retained? Ockham never took his position in this direction, nor did he intend to be a skeptic. In his estimation, he was merely being a reliable logician.[228] Yet later critics believed Ockham unwittingly opened the door to such a mindset all too eagerly pursued in the centuries that followed.

Moreover, critics also wondered whether Ockham's nominalism had severed theology and philosophy, faith and reason. Ockham rejected universals and man's ability to demonstrate by reasonable observation of the natural order God's existence and attributes, convinced as he was that such matters had to be taken by faith. Ockham may not have intended to create a chasm between philosophy and theology, but critics believed he had regardless. Even a historian intent on resisting prejudices against the *via moderna*, like Heiko Oberman, has observed Ockham's nominalism and said, "If abstract concepts are allowed to develop lives of their own, the link between thought and reality becomes either

---

226. Consult *Quodlib.* VI.I art 2 and Nieuwenhove, 342, who engages McCord Adams, *William Ockham*, 1278–79; Leff, *William of Ockham*, 473.

227. Nieuwenhove, 341.

228. Copleston said Ockham was "willing to retain something of the language of the theory of divine ideas, doubtless largely out of respect for St. Augustine and tradition; but he emptied the theory of its former content" (*History of Philosophy*, 3:50). Copleston believed Ockham's use of the language meant he did not reject the theory of universals in its entirety but interpreted it to align with his paradigm (3:92).

speculative or dangerously ideological—and usually both at once."[229] The close marriage between faith and reason from Augustine to Anselm to Thomas had now been breached.

Ockham's Razor: The Widening Divide between Faith and Reason

The divide Ockham created between faith and reason can be traced back to his principle of *ontological parsimony*. By means of the principle of parsimony, Scotus advocated for austerity in intellectual thought, especially when handling a subject like metaphysics. Ockham discouraged the Scholastic search for terms, concepts, arguments, and theories, all of which had to be substantiated to establish the bigger claims of metaphysics. In contrast, Ockham advised cutting and consolidating (hence the term "razor"), limiting metaphysics to those arguments Christianity cannot do without, theistic assertions essential to explaining everything else that exists in the world. In short, Ockham advocated for a type of minimalism that reduced Christianity to that which is absolutely indispensable. Ockham's razor contributed to his rejection of universals (and his unwitting bent toward skepticism, at least in the eyes of his critics). Once universals were shredded by Ockham's razor, they were considered anything but essential. As mentioned already, universals were superfluous for human knowledge and understanding.

The integration of faith and reason did not survive his razor either. Again, many within the classical realist tradition believed philosophers like Plato and Aristotle were not to be dismissed in the long view of divine providence. Herman Bavinck captures the posture of the Great Tradition towards Greek philosophy: "The pagan world, especially in its philosophy, is a pedagogy unto Christ; Aristotle, like John the Baptist, is the forerunner of Christ. It behooves the Christians to enrich their temple with the vessels of the Egyptians and to adorn the crown of Christ, their king, with the pearls brought up from the sea of paganism."[230] Despite the shortcomings of Platonist philosophy, it became instrumental as God prepared the way for the full revelation of the Christian faith in Christ, as exemplified in John's use of the *Logos* or Paul's quotation of Greek poets in the Areopagus.[231] As evident with Augustine's conversion, the Fathers believed the tools of Greek philosophy can serve the Christian faith by demonstrating the coherence and credibility of major doctrines. When put to the test, Christian beliefs are compatible with reason. That confidence proved helpful in apologetics. The Christian Platonist, for example, could argue for the existence of God with the tools of classical realism, demonstrating the legitimacy of theism by means of their own system of thought. Natural revelation gave the Christian intellectual permission to use reason alone to confirm the existence of God from nature, for example. The apostle Paul assumed as much when he wrote to the Romans, "For since the creation of the world God's invisible qualities—his

---

229. Oberman, *Luther,* 117.
230. Bavinck, "Calvin and Common Grace," 441.
231. To clarify, I do not mean Greek philosophy was the equivalent of the Old Testament.

eternal power and divine nature—have been clearly seen, being understood from what has been made, so that people are without excuse" (1:20 NIV).

On that basis, Thomas Aquinas presented his five ways to know God exists, and one of the most notable was his argument from effects in this world to a first cause (the argument from causation). Scotus, too, engaged and supported Thomas's theistic program, even if he departed from Thomas on issues like univocal predication. The Great Tradition, in other words, used the tools of Aristotle's philosophy because they believed reasonable observation of creation could substantiate and defend the Creator's existence, though always in ways consistent with and confirmed by God's revelation in Scripture. As for beliefs like the Trinity or the incarnation, the Great Tradition recognized that these were not beliefs that could originate from reason alone but come to God's people by means of supernatural revelation. Nevertheless, even these revealed beliefs are not contrary to but consistent with reason. Therefore, reason can serve faith by showing the logical coherence of these doctrines even if reason is not their birth mother.[232]

Ockham, however, was not amused. He, too, utilized Aristotelian philosophy; he was no fideist. Yet Ockham did not put confidence in reason's ability to prove Christian beliefs. For example, he was not convinced by arguments for God's existence by means of reason.[233] He was not persuaded by Thomas's argument for a first cause, for example, because he saw no reason to deny an infinite regress. Ockham, of course, believed God was the First Cause, but he believed based on faith, not reason. Reason cannot prove such truths; natural theology is useless for such a purpose.

Nor did Ockham reserve any assurance that reason should remain agreeable with faith. Contrary to Augustine, Anselm, and Thomas, Ockham thought reason and faith could be incompatible with each other. Ockham experienced this conflict himself when "relations" in the Trinity failed to survive the blades of his razor, even though relations was a concept indispensable to orthodox Trinitarianism and its defense of the Son's eternal generation from the Father. Ockham had to choose, and in such a situation the choice goes to faith, not reason.[234]

---

232. For instance, the tools and grammar of Aristotelian philosophy were appropriated at Nicaea and Chalcedon to defend the eternal generation of the Son in the fourth century and the hypostatic union in the fifth century against numerous heresies.

233. Ockham, *Quodlibetal Questions* 1.1; 2.1; 2.2; 4.2. Ockham did find one argument from reason persuasive: in a hierarchy of beings, there must be a supreme, perfect being. Yet even then reason falls short since a more superior being at the top of the hierarchy does not have to be a divine being nor a certain type of divine being. See Williams, *Reason and Faith*, 342. Also, Ockham had other reasons for resisting Thomas and Scotus, such as Ockham's denial that theology is a science. This, too, motivated Ockham's skepticism and segregation of faith and reason (340). Cf. Freddoso, "Ockham on Faith and Reason," 326–49.

234. Williams qualifies: "Ockham is not accepting anything like the two-truths theory of the integral Aristotelians. He's not saying that something can be true in philosophy but false in theology, or vice versa. Yet he is, in his way, saying something almost as radical. He's saying that reason, operating on its own, can come to believe on the best possible evidence that something is true—even though Christian theology shows definitively that it's false. What reason believes in such a case will be false, period—not just false in philosophy, but false period—but reason itself will have no way of discerning that it's false. Only someone whose natural powers have been elevated by faith will be able to see that it's false; an unbelieving philosopher will simply be stuck. In saying that, Ockham is setting himself apart from the tradition not only of Aquinas and Scotus, but of Augustine, Anselm and Abelard." Williams, *Reason and Faith*, 345.

PROTESTANT FRUIT ON THE THOMISTIC TREE

Was nominalism anti-Augustinian? For much of the twentieth century, historians assumed nominalism was anti-Augustinian. That assumption seemed reasonable since many nominalists happened to depart from an Augustinian view of grace. For example, historians considered the debate over nature and grace between the *via moderna* (represented by figures such as Ockham and Biel) and the *schola Augustiniana moderna* (represented by figures such as Thomas Bradwardine and Gregory of Rimini). As will be seen in chapter 8, that debate in various ways reincarnated the old controversy between Pelagius and Augustine. Nominalism was equated with the *via moderna* and associated with the Pelagian (or Semi-Pelagian) tradition. By contrast, realism was equated with Augustinianism and associated with the *schola Augustiniana moderna*.

However, in the latter half of the twentieth century, Reformation scholars changed course, now convinced that such a paradigm was flawed because it could not account for nominalist strands of thought within *both* camps. Some representatives in both schools had nominalist commitments and agreements, even though they were in total conflict with one another over nature and grace. That discovery revealed that some late medieval Scholastics could defend an Augustinian view of grace all the while rejecting certain aspects of realism (like universals). In their mind at least, their philosophical view of universals was a different debate than their theological position on original sin and divine grace. The former concerned metaphysics and epistemology, the latter soteriology. McGrath goes so far as to say, "Thus both schools rejected the necessity of universals—but thereafter could agree on virtually nothing" (McGrath, *Reformation Thought*, 4th ed., 65).

However, the historian should be careful not to swing the proverbial pendulum too far. Granted, some representatives of both the *via moderna* and the *via Augustiniana moderna* were nominalists in metaphysics and epistemology despite disagreements in soteriology. Furthermore, all can agree that examples of nominalists can be found within the *via Augustiniana moderna*. However, were those in the *via Augustiniana moderna* consistent to hold nominalism in their metaphysical and epistemological hand while holding Augustinianism in their soteriological hand? That is a question theologians and philosophers must determine. From a historical perspective, one should acknowledge that notable Reformers and post-Reformation Reformers did not think these two positions could be held hand in hand. Thomistic realism proved far more compatible and advantageous for Reformed Orthodoxy. "The theology of Vermigli and Zanchi, together with parallel developments within Lutheranism, shows that when Protestants came to recast their theology into a Scholastic form, they rather consistently avoided nominalism as a base. Insofar as the roots of Protestant Scholasticism go back to the Middle Ages, they tend to go back to the *via antiqua* and Thomism. Protestant fruit grows quite well on the Thomistic tree, even better than on the bad nominalist tree" (Donnelly, "Calvinist Thomism," 454).

In the end, a way forward must make two observations: (1) nominalists can be found among both the *via moderna* and the *via Augustiniana moderna;* nominalism did not automatically make someone suspicious in their soteriology. (2) However, as the Reformation faith was codified many of the Reformed Orthodox did dispense with nominalism because they connected its consequences from metaphysics and epistemology to theology itself. Such a transition in the sixteenth and seventeenth centuries is another reason one should be suspicious of blaming the Reformers or their heirs for the spread of nominalism and with it, modernity's secularism.

For a survey of older literature critical of Ockhamist nominalism and a survey of literature reacting with a positive assessment, see Steinmetz, *Calvin in Context*, 42–43. Steinmetz labels the latter a "revisionist assessment of nominalism."

Ockham's consolidating approach risked eliminating principles unsubstantiated by philosophy but nonetheless essential to Christian theology. Thomas Williams, who is a fair and generous interpreter of Ockham, nevertheless concludes that Ockham's razor did "destabilize the medieval synthesis of faith and reason, because Ockham is in effect saying that the best philosophy, as it stands, can't be pressed into the service of Christian doctrine." That was a bold move on Ockham's part since the majority of the Great Tradition before him— from the Cappadocians to John of Damascus, from Augustine to Boethius, from Anselm to Thomas—believed philosophy can and should serve theology. Reason is compatible with faith. Yet in order "to elucidate Christian doctrine, he [Ockham] has to admit principles or entities that the best philosophy, left alone, would reject."[235] Due to his voluntarism, Ockham did not restrict God's will to logic; therefore, Christian beliefs need not be compatible with reason.[236]

Augustine, Anselm, and Thomas presided over a marriage between faith and reason; Ockham facilitated the papers for a divorce. Ockham put forward a radical program, one that was a definitive exodus from the *via antiqua*, the old or ancient way. Although Ockham did not consider himself a skeptic, his approach to faith and reason opened the door to skepticism in the opinion of his critics. Furthermore, when Ockham's skepticism was coupled with his perpetuation of voluntarism—a voluntarism that set the stage for a reincarnation of Pelagianism or Semi-Pelagianism (e.g., Gabriel Biel)—it is hard to overemphasize the collateral damage in soteriology. Here were the seeds of a provocation that demanded Reformation.

For example, in his *Quodlibetal*, Ockham's voluntarism and nominalism together inform his theology of justification. With the distinction between God's absolute and ordained power established, Ockham asked whether a person could be saved apart from created grace and charity. His response accentuated both the autonomy of the divine and human wills. For "a human being is able by the absolute power of God to be saved without created charity. . . . Whatever

---

235. Williams, *Reason and Faith*, 325.
236. "The doctrines do not seek assent from the intellect, but rather the surrender of the will." Van Asselt with Rouwendal et al., *Introduction to Reformed Scholasticism*, 66. Nieuwenhove believes Ockham is not that far from Kant (*Medieval Theology*, 344).

God is able to do by the mediation of a secondary cause in the genus of efficient or final causality, he is able to do immediately by himself.... Therefore, he is able to give eternal life without such grace to someone who does good works."[237] Ockham anticipated that his statement could invite the accusation of Pelagianism, so he distinguished his view from the heresy: "For Pelagius held that grace is not in fact required in order to have eternal life, but that an act elicited in a purely nature state merits eternal life condignly. I, on the other hand, claim that such an act is meritorious only through God's absolute power accepting it [as such]."[238] The difference was slight. For Pelagius, man's merit itself was worthy of eternal life (condign merit). For Ockham, man's merit was accepted simply by fiat of the divine will. As he would add later, by virtue of God's absolute power, no infusion of created grace is strictly necessary for the remission of man's guilt and punishment.[239] Here is the reason why Luther so distrusted Ockham's appeal to God's absolute power: Ockham said that grace is not necessary for the remission of sins. Nevertheless, by virtue of his *ordained* power, God has in fact willed the necessity of grace, so that no one "will ever be saved ... without created grace ... no human being will ever elicit or be able to elicit a meritorious act without such grace."[240]

In conclusion, Ockham left behind the realist, participation paradigm of the *via antiqua* and its manifestation in the thought of Scholasticism during the High Middle Ages. By means of his voluntarist, nominalist outlook, he conditioned divine election on man's merit. But in the estimation of Ockham's critics, his claim to move outside the Pelagian camp was at best only a retreat into Semi-Pelagianism. Here was the beginning of a modern way—*via moderna*—setting the stage for one of its most ardent successors on the eve of the Reformation, Gabriel Biel.

THE *VIA MODERNA* VERSUS THE *SCHOLA AUGUSTINIANA MODERNA*

Gabriel Biel (d. 1495), commonly recognized as the last of the Scholastics, arrived on the eve of the Reformation. Yet the issues he was addressing originated before his time with the collision of two medieval schools of thought. Although Biel developed his own justification synthesis, his covenantal and voluntarist preunderstanding was not novel but inherent in the *via moderna*. Over the span of multiple centuries, the *via moderna* took form in the thought of William of Ockham, Robert Holcot (ca. 1290–1349), and Pierre d'Ailly (ca. 1350/51–1420), among others.[241]

---

237. Ockham, *Quodlibetal Questions* 6.2.2 (thesis 1).
238. Ockham, *Quodlibetal Questions* 6.2.2 (thesis 2). For context, see Wood, "Ockham's Repudiation of Pelagianism," 350–74.
239. Ockham, *Quodlibetal Questions* 6.4 (thesis 1).
240. Ockham, *Quodlibetal Questions* 6.2.2 (thesis 2). Cf. 6.4 (thesis 1).
241. Consult, e.g., Holcot, "Lectures on the Wisdom of Solomon," 142–50.

Matriculating from universities such as Heidelberg, Biel was an engaged academic, yet his attention was particularly devoted to life in the church, being himself a priest and a known preacher. Such a pastoral emphasis stemmed from his background in the *devotio moderna*, the Brethren of the Common Life.[242] That fact is not irrelevant, for Biel's insistence on man's ability, as captured in the slogan *facere quod in se est*, was pastorally motivated. Only if man possessed the spiritual ability "to do his very best," or, literally, "to do that which lies within him," could reconciliation with his Maker be attainable. As Heiko Oberman put it, "Biel's concern is to provide a way to justification within the reach of the average Christian."[243]

The *schola Augustiniana moderna*, on the other hand, perceived the *via moderna* as a return to Pelagianism. The modern Augustinian school consisted of theologians such as Thomas Bradwardine (ca. 1290–1349), Gregory of Rimini (ca. 1300–1358), and Hugolino of Orvieto (after 1300–1373). Bradwardine is especially fascinating for his own conversion out of Pelagianism. A student-turned-lecturer at Merton College, Oxford University, he would later be chancellor of Saint Paul's, London, and eventually archbishop of Canterbury in Avignon. It was during his years at Saint Paul's that he wrote a book he titled *De causa Dei contra Pelagium* (*The Cause of God against Pelagius*) in 1344.[244] In that work, Bradwardine reflected on his own personal experience, having been absorbed by what he believed was Pelagianism at Oxford, only to discover *sola gratia* through a text like Romans 9.[245] Bradwardine became a formidable nemesis of Robert Holcot, whom the former encountered in Durham.[246]

Despite the force of Bradwardine's critique of the *Pelagiani moderni*, historians often point to another theologian from the Order of the Hermits of Saint Augustine at the University of Paris, Gregory of Rimini, as the theologian responsible for the revival of Augustinianism. Bradwardine and Gregory of Rimini together formed an "academic Augustinianism," but Gregory gave

---

242. Oberman, *Forerunners*, 137.
243. Oberman, *Harvest of Medieval Theology*, 157.
244. See Bradwardine, *De causa Dei contra Pelagium*, 1.42. One of the best studies is Leff, *Bradwardine and the Pelagians*, 69.
245. Bradwardine wrote, "Idle and a fool in God's wisdom, I was misled by an unorthodox error at a time when I was still pursuing philosophical studies. Sometimes I went to listen to the theologians discussing this matter [of grace and free will], and the school of Pelagius seemed to me nearest the truth.... In the philosophical faculty I seldom heard a reference to grace, except for some ambiguous remarks. What I heard day in and day out was that we are masters of our own free acts, that ours is the choice to act well or badly, to have virtues or sins and much more along this line.... Every time I listened to the Epistle reading in church and heard how Paul magnified grace and belittled free will—as is the case in Romans 9, 'It is obviously not a question of human will and effort, but of divine mercy,' and its many parallels—grace displeased me, ungrateful as I was." Then something changed: "However, even before I transferred to the faculty of theology, the text mentioned came to me as a beam of grace and, captured by a vision of the truth, it seemed I saw from afar how the grace of God precedes all good works with a temporal priority [God as Savior through predestination] and natural precedence [God continues to provide for his creation as 'First Mover'].... That is why I express my gratitude to him who has given me this grace as a free gift." Bradwardine, *De causa Dei*, 2.32, p. 613, quoted in Oberman, *Forerunners*, 135; cf. Oberman, *Masters of the Reformation*, 66.
246. All such details can be found in fuller form in Oberman, *Forerunners*, 136.

it momentum as a movement.[247] Frank James III notes how it was Rimini who reintroduced Augustine's predestinarianism. Coupled with the release of Augustine's works from 1490 to 1506, academic Augustinianism transformed into a pastoral Augustinianism with Johann Staupitz (d. 1524), the mentor of the young Luther. Not limiting himself to the university setting, Staupitz infused the pulpit with an Augustinianism accessible to the late medieval Christian.[248] The soteriology of Rimini eventually influenced certain Reformers, such as Peter Martyr Vermigli, the Italian Reformer whom Thomas Cranmer recruited to come to England (the extent of Bradwardine's direct influence on the Reformers is contested).[249]

The example of Gregory of Rimini has led historians to three conclusions: (1) anti-Pelagian rhetoric was present in the fourteenth-century university setting, which means the historian must consider to what degree Pelagianism or Semi-Pelagianism was influential; (2) although everyone claimed Augustine, anti-Pelagians like Rimini believed they embodied the true interpretation of Augustine while other interpretations were illegitimate; (3) at least in the fourteenth century, theologians could be Augustinian in their soteriology but still be sympathetic to Ockham in their epistemology and metaphysic. For example, in his philosophy Rimini exhibited nominalist sympathies and for that reason historians have included him within the *via moderna*; however, on the basis of his soteriology historians have assigned Rimini to the *schola Augustiniana moderna* (Luther followed Rimini's dual citizenship in some ways as well).[250]

Some have assumed that late medieval Augustinianism must be superior to the Augustinianism of Scholasticism in the High Middle Ages. Yet that assumption has been demonstrated false. As Janz explains, even theologians during the fifteenth century acknowledged that "the *fundamentum* of such an anti-Pelagian protest is without doubt present in Thomas's emphasis on the sovereignty of grace, at least in his mature writings." Furthermore, we should not hold against an earlier century a context that was not their own. "Thomas and Bonaventure were not driven to a vigorous anti-Pelagian protest by their contemporaries," but that does not mean they were less pure in their Augustinianism for lack of antagonists.[251] The influence of each school cannot be minimized. For instance, not

---

247. Oberman went so far as to say the *schola moderna Augustiniana* had its true genesis with Gregory of Rimini. Oberman, *Masters of the Reformation*, 70–71; Oberman, *Forerunners*, 151–64. Trapp called Gregory of Rimini "the first Augustinian of Augustine." Trapp, "Augustinian Theology of the Fourteenth Century," 181. Also see Janz, *Luther and Late Medieval Thomism*, 163.

248. Steinmetz, *Misericordia Dei*, 30–34; Janz, *Luther and Late Medieval Thomism*, 164; Oberman, *Werden und Wertung der Reformation*, 389.

249. James, "Peter Martyr Vermigli," 205. Also see Donnelly, *Calvinism and Scholasticism in Vermigli's Doctrine of Man and Grace*; James, *Peter Martyr Vermigli and Predestination*; James, "Peter Martyr Vermigli," 62–78; James, "A Late Medieval Parallel in Reformation Thought," 157–88; Leff, *Gregory of Rimini*. On Rimini's influence on Luther and Calvin, see Oberman, "Headwaters of the Reformation," 40–88; McGrath, "John Calvin and Late Medieval Thought," 58–78; Spieler, "Luther and Gregory of Rimini," 160.

250. Janz, *Luther and Late Medieval Thomism*, 165; Oberman, *Luther*, 118.

251. Janz, 165.

only was the *via moderna* the position that Reformers like Luther were taught to embrace, but representatives as late as Biel would leave a notable impression on sixteenth-century Roman theologians and councils as well. For example, Biel's soteriology is inherent within the theology of Luther's arduous opponent Johann Eck, as well as within the Council of Trent (1545–63).[252] Writing to Frederick the Wise, Luther said concerning his 1519 debate at Leipzig with Eck, "In debating with me he [Eck] rejected Gregory of Rimini as one who alone supported my opinion against all theologians."[253] Aligning himself with an Augustinian like Gregory in 1519 was but the outcome of Luther's stance two years earlier as he rigorously set his aim on Biel, who serves in this chapter as the appropriate foil to understanding Luther's departure from the *via moderna*.

BIEL'S COVENANTAL, VOLUNTARIST ACCOUNT OF JUSTIFICATION

The starting point to comprehending Biel's doctrine of justification properly is the divine *pactum*.[254] Such a starting point may not be, at first glance, immediately relevant. For instance, in his sermon "Circumcision of the Lord," Biel spent most of his effort explaining infused grace and defining meritorious actions. Not until the end did he briefly introduce the "rule" or "covenant." Nevertheless, this covenant was critical to Biel's *processus iustificationis*.

According to Biel, "God has established the rule [covenant] that whoever turns to him and does what he can will receive forgiveness of sins from God. God infuses assisting grace into such a man, who is thus taken back into friendship."[255] The covenant established is voluntary on God's part and gracious in its inception. Recognizing that man has lost his way, God deliberates, leading him to initiate an agreement in which the possibility of eternal life might become a reality. Yet not only is the covenant voluntary in the sense that God chose to institute a rule he did not have to establish, but it is voluntarist in nature as well. The covenant is God's way of accepting man's works, even if they be unworthy in and of themselves. Biel put forward a parable to convey this point:

> Let us say that there is a most lenient king who shows so much mercy to his people that he publishes a decree saying that he will embrace with his favor any of his enemies who desire his friendship, provided they mend their ways for the present and the future. Furthermore, the king orders that all who have been received in this fashion into his friendship will receive a golden ring to honor all who are dedicated to his regime, so that such a friend of the king may be known to all. *The king*

---

252. See Oberman, *Forerunners*, 137.

253. *LW* 31:322.

254. To see how the *via moderna* connects and contrasts with prior medieval perspectives on justification, see Needham, "The Evolution of Justification," 587–623. Also consult McGrath, *Iustitia Dei*. However, Needham believes McGrath may emphasize too much discontinuity across the medieval era.

255. Biel, "Circumcision of the Lord," 173.

gives to such a man by way of delegation of his royal authority such a position that every work done to the honor of the king, regardless of where performed or how large or small it is, shall be rewarded by the king above and beyond its value. And to give him extra strength to perform this kind of meritorious work, precious and powerful stones are inserted in the ring to encourage him who wears it, so that his body does not fail him when he needs it but increases in ability to gain further rewards the more the body is exercised and accustomed to resist every adverse force.[256]

That phrase "lenient king" is most telling. Leniency is the prime characteristic of the covenant that God inaugurates. His enemies deserve not his friendship. Nevertheless, should they be determined to "mend their ways," and should they perform works that honor the king to the best of their abilities, it matters not whether those works are inherently worthy, reaching the perfect standard of divine justice. The leniency of the king and his contract means that he will accept such works regardless. Such works may even be rewarded above and beyond any inherent value they possess. The king has that right or authority by virtue of his royal office. With that scheme in mind, it is appropriate to label Biel's covenantalism voluntarist in nature.

The Intellectualist Approach: Thomas Aquinas

The *via moderna* intentionally parted ways with the intellectualism of Thomas Aquinas (ca. 1225–74), in which the divine intellect held primacy over the divine will.[257] For the medieval intellectualist, prioritizing the divine intellect meant that the inherent value of man's merits mattered. God did not necessarily reward *above and beyond* the inherent value but *according to* the inherent value of one's works; otherwise his own justice could be thrown into question. Approaching justification through an intellectualist framework avoided the charge that God's *liberum arbitrium* was arbitrary—a dangerous and incriminating charge in the Middle Ages.[258]

Distinguishable, as well, is the *iustificationis* embraced by an intellectualist. For Thomas, justification involved not merely the forgiveness of sins but an ontological transformation, one that involved the habit of grace being infused into man's soul, a habit necessary for man to be pleasing to God. With the habit of grace infused, man might cooperate (exercising his free will), being made righteous and in order to be made righteous.[259] As his nature is changed by habitual

---

256. Biel, "Circumcision of the Lord," 173, emphasis added.

257. To be technical, Thomas considered will and intellect identical in view of divine simplicity, but he distinguished them to discern God's ways.

258. Why dangerous? McGrath answers, "Thomas rejected the opinion that *iustitia Dei* is merely an arbitrary aspect of the divine will. To assert that *iustitia* ultimately depends upon the will of God amounts to the blasphemous assertion that God does not operate according to the order of wisdom. Underlying *iustitia* is *sapientia*, discernible to the intellect, so that the ultimate standard of justice must be taken to be right reason." McGrath, *Iustitia Dei*, 85.

259. "By every meritorious act," said Aquinas, "a man merits the increase of grace, equally with the consummation of grace which is eternal life." *ST* 1a2ae. 114, 8. I hesitate to use the word *cooperate* because it might

grace—a substance supernatural in orientation—man becomes more and more satisfactory in the eyes of God (i.e., *gratia gratis faciens*). Thomas wrote in his *Summa Theologiae*, "God infuses a habitual gift into the soul," an infusion of "certain forms or supernatural qualities into those whom he moves to seek after supernatural and eternal good, that they may be thus moved by him to seek it sweetly and readily." The "gift of grace," he reasoned, "is a certain quality."[260] The ontological transformation that habitual grace manufactures is the preliminary ground on which God is then justified in his justification of the ungodly.

For Thomas, such an infusion is both gracious and prevenient. Enabled by infused grace, man's acquired merit is rewarded, complimented according to the measure of value it possesses. Justice is a priority in this schema; God is obligated to bestow the just reward that every act of grace-inspired merit deserves. Thomas outlined the step-by-step logic of grace when he wrote in *Summa Theologiae*, "The first is the infusion of grace; the second, the free-will's movement towards God; the third, the free-will's movement towards sin; the fourth, the remission of sin."[261] Thomas's *ordo* can be outlined as follows:

1. Gratuitous infusion of grace
2. Moral cooperation: doing the best one can with the aid of grace
3. Reward of eternal life as a just due[262]

Thomas did not always prioritize grace over man's freedom. Earlier in his career, he wrote a commentary on Peter Lombard's *Sentences*, in which he (to be anachronistic) sounded like Biel centuries later. Man was to do his best, and his best would be rewarded by grace, a grace that would prepare him for justification. Man's best did not meet God's perfect standard, but God would accept it anyway because of his sovereign generosity.[263] Later on, as his *Summa Theologiae* and *Summa contra Gentiles* evidence, Thomas reversed the order, claiming instead that grace must come first if works are to follow at all.[264] It is essential to observe at this point that the *iustificationis* involves an *ordo* in which infused grace holds primacy to the movement of the will, thereby excusing Thomas not only of Pelagianism but Semi-Pelagianism as well.[265] As McGrath observes, *facere quod*

give the impression that Aquinas was a synergist in the way that many in the late medieval or post-Reformation eras were synergists. Aquinas's Augustinian predestinarian theology would preclude such an assumption. So the language of cooperation above is merely meant to acknowledge the role of man's acquired merits.

260. *ST* 1a2ae. 110, 2. For similar themes, see Aquinas, *Commentary on the Letter of Saint Paul to the Romans* 1.3, 1.6, 2.3.

261. Aquinas, *ST* 1a2ae. 113, 8 (cf. 1a2ae. 113, 7).

262. Ozment, *Age of Reform*, 233.

263. E.g., Biel, *In II Sententiarum*, d. 28, q. 1, a. 4 and 4um; Biel, *In IV Sententiarum*, d. 17, q. 1, a. 3–4. See Biel, *Collectorium circa quattuor libros sententiarum*.

264. Oberman, *Forerunners*, 130. Contrary to some who think Aquinas was contradicting himself, McGrath demonstrates that a change in Aquinas's view of nature and grace had occurred (*Iustitia Dei*, 110–11).

265. E.g., Aquinas, *ST* 1a2ae. 112, 3; 1a2ae. 109, 6, ad2um.

in se est now takes on a different meaning: "doing what one is able to do when aroused and moved by grace."[266] Yet in contrast to the doctrine of the sixteenth-century Reformers, justification for Thomas remained a transformation, one in which the individual was made righteous in his inner nature, not a strictly forensic declaration, as the Reformers would argue at a much later date.[267]

The Voluntarist Approach: Scotus, Ockham, and Biel

By contrast, the voluntarist conception would differ completely. Duns Scotus and English Franciscan William of Ockham believed that Thomas had demolished God's freedom. The notion that God is restricted or obligated to reward works inherently worthy undermines God's freedom to reward works above and beyond what they are worth. God can and does reward however he sees fit; as God, he is free to do so. The freedom and sovereignty of the Divine will entail that something is only good because God says it is good. If the liberality of God's choice is to be prioritized, then God is not to be held accountable to an external standard of justice, but justice itself is to be defined according to whatever God chooses to accept as just.[268]

In that vein came the perceived genius of Biel's covenantal conception, though its covenantal flavor is not original to Biel but is present in *via moderna* representatives like Holcot. Through the establishment of a voluntary *pactum*,

---

266. McGrath, *Iustitia Dei*, 112.

267. McGrath stresses such a point, arguing that it is a misinterpretation of Aquinas to take that final step—remission of sin—and assume justification is forensic. "Some commentators have misunderstood Thomas's occasional definition of justification solely in terms of remission of sin, representing him as approaching a forensic concept of justification. It will be clear that this is a serious misunderstanding. Where Thomas defines justification as *remissio peccatorum*, therefore, he does not exclude other elements—such as the infusion of grace—for the following reasons. First, justification is thus defined without reference to its content, solely in terms of its *terminus*. Such a definition is adequate, but not exhaustive, and should not be treated as if it were. Second, Thomas's understanding of the *processus iustificationis* means that the occurrence of any one of the four elements necessarily entails the occurrence of the remaining three. The definition of *iustificatio* as *remissio peccatorum* therefore expressly *includes* the remaining three elements." The four elements McGrath references are (1) the infusion of grace, (2) the movement of the free will directed toward God through faith, (3) the movement of the free will directed against sin, and (4) the remission of sin. McGrath has in mind *ST* 1a2ae. 113, 8; 1a2ae. 113, 6; 1a2ae. 113, 6, ad1um. McGrath, *Iustitia Dei*, 64.

268. McGrath explains, "Gabriel Biel insists upon the priority of the divine will over any moral structures by declaring that God's will is essentially independent of what is right or wrong; if the divine will amounted to a mere endorsement of what is good or right, God's will would thereby be subject to created principles of morality. What is good, therefore, is good only if it is accepted as such by God. The divine will is thus the chief arbiter and principle of justice, establishing justice by its decisions, rather than acting on the basis of established justice. Morality and merit alike derive from the divine will, in that the goodness of an act must be defined, not in terms of the act itself, but in terms of the *divine estimation of that act*. Duns Scotus had established the general voluntarist principle, that every created offering to God is worth precisely whatever God accepts it for.... Applying this principle to the passion of Christ and the redemption of humankind, Scotus points out that a good angel could have made satisfaction in Christ's place, had God chosen to accept its offering as having sufficient value: the merit of Christ's passion lies solely in the *acceptation divina*." McGrath, *Iustitia Dei*, 86. In view are the following works: Biel, *Canonis missae expositio* 23E, 1.212; Biel, *In I Sententiarum*, d. 43, q. 1, a. 4 cor., in Biel, *Collectorium circa quattuor libros sententiarum*, 1:746.5–7; Biel, *In II Sententiarum*, d. 27, q. 1, a. 3, dub. 4, in Biel, *Collectorium circa quattuor libros sententiarum*, 2:253.7–9; Duns Scotus, *Opus Oxoniense*, bk. 3, d. 19, q. 1, n. 7. For an extended treatment of Scotus's position, see Cross, *Duns Scotus*, 15–61. To see Ockham's position, consult his *Quodlibetal Questions*, vols. 1–2, *Quodlibets 1–7*.

God obligates himself rather than being obligated by the inherent value of man's merit via habitual grace. That covenantal obligation preserves the libertarian freedom of his will, for he chooses if and how he will reward man's effort, and it need not be according to the weight of its value. In that sense, Biel believed his view to be *more* gracious than challenging views. If God is not bound to bestow the inherent value according to some external standard but is free to go above and beyond, then his reward for man's deeds can exceed their worth. The worth or value of man's merits is assigned or ascribed but cannot be inherent, innate, or inborn.

Furthermore, this view avoids Pelagianism since man doing his best is not meant to merit God's grace *de condigno* (merit of condignity), as his deeds are unworthy in and of themselves as full merit, but rather *meritum de congruo* (merit of congruity), that is, half merit.[269] It is not "that man's moral efforts unaided by grace are fully meritorious of God's rewards (*de condigno*) but rather that they are graciously regarded by God as half merits or merits in a metaphorical sense (*de congruo*). The relationship between God's bestowal of grace and sinful man's best effort rests on 'contracted' rather than 'actual' worth and is a result of God's liberality in giving 'so much for so little.'"[270] Nevertheless, there was a theological catch for Biel. The voluntarist nature of the covenant may mean God goes "above and beyond," but that is only true should persons do their best. To be fair to Biel, the point was stated by him far more positively. To receive God's reward, all people need to do is their best, even if their best does not add up to God's perfect standard. If they do their best, infused grace will subsequently matriculate. Hence we return to that previous statement from Biel: "God has established the rule [covenant] that whoever turns to him and does what he can will receive forgiveness of sins from God. God infuses assisting grace into such a man, who is thus taken back into friendship."[271] Biel's *ordo* can be outlined as follows:

1. Moral effort: doing the best one can on the basis of natural moral ability
2. Infusion of grace as an appropriate reward
3. Moral cooperation: doing the best one can with the aid of grace
4. Reward of eternal life as a just due[272]

Behind these four steps in Biel's *ordo,* however, is an anthropological assumption on which salvation itself hinges.

---

269. Muller, *Dictionary*, s.v.

270. Oberman, *Forerunners*, 129. By *de condigno* Oberman referred to a full merit; by *de congruo* he referred to a partial merit. Oberman, *Masters of the Reformation*, 98.

271. Biel, "Circumcision of the Lord," 173.

272. Ozment offered a more detailed diagram of Ockham's and Biel's order: "(1) Moral effort: doing the best one can on the basis of natural moral ability; (2) Infusion of grace as an appropriate reward; (3) Moral cooperation: doing the best one can with the aid of grace; (4) Reward of eternal life as a just due." Ozment, *Age of Reform*, 234.

Biel's Anthropological Assumption: *Actum Facientis Quod In Se Est*

There is, however, one major assumption—and in the eyes of Biel's nemeses, the Achilles' heel of Biel's position—namely, that one is able to do one's best to begin with. Infused grace is a subsequent reality, conditioned on one doing what lies within. Biel had a strong anthropological optimism, one that would be characteristic of adherents to the *via moderna* system overall. God may graciously establish a covenant whereby he accepts man's best, however unqualified his best may be. Yet Biel assumed that man has a "best" to offer. Consider the power he credited to man's will in his work *In II Sententiarum*: the soul, by removing an obstacle in front of a good movement to God through the free will, is able to merit the first grace *de congruo*. This is so because God accepts the act of doing "what lies within its powers" [*actum facientis quod in se est*] as leading to the first grace, which is thus not on account of God's generosity. The soul, by removing this obstacle, ceases from acts of sin and consent to sin; it thus elicits a good movement toward God as its principal end and does "what lies within its power" [*quod in se est*]. Therefore, God accepts, out of his generosity, this act of removing an obstacle and a good movement toward God as the basis of the infusion of grace.[273]

Such phrases as *actum facientis quod in se est* and *quod in se est*—phrases that originated not with Biel but with his Franciscan master Alexander of Hales—are revealing.[274] In man's power is the ability to "merit the first grace *de congruo*," a point we shall return to. Although the covenant may be prevenient, the first grace is subsequent to man's merit. Man's "good movement toward God" serves as the condition for future grace, the "basis of the infusion of grace." Free will, then, is very much alive, so much so that one wonders to what extent, if any, it has been affected by the fall.

To be accurate, however, Biel did believe humans are fallen creatures, corrupt in their nature. Biel's emphasis on man's corruption was stronger than that of other medieval Schoolmen. "More than Duns Scotus and Occam," said Oberman, "Biel stresses that man's original nature has been corrupted by original sin; man is not only *spoliatus a gratuitis* but also *vulneratus in naturalibus*." Oberman elaborated, "Man's miserable condition after the fall is not only due to a vertical imputation by God, but also to a horizontal continuation of infirmity, through an infection in which all mankind partakes and through which the will is wounded, so that it is more inclined to evil than to good deeds."[275]

Biel was, unfortunately, unclear as to the specifics. He "does not elucidate the exact relation of the potential disorder of man's created nature before the fall to

---

273. *Ex sua liberalitate.* Biel, *In II Sententiarum*, d. 27, q. unica, a. 3, c. 4, in Biel, *Collectorium circa quattuor libros sententiarum*, 2:517.1–8. The Latin translation comes from McGrath, *Christian Theology Reader*, 367.

274. Oberman, *Harvest of Medieval Theology*, 132. Hence, Oberman summarized Biel: "After the fall man is still able to detest sin and seek refuge with God with his own powers, without the help of any form of grace. This, of course, does not exclude God's general *concursus* in every deed, good, bad or indifferent, since without this 'natura' energy man would not be able to act at all" (175).

275. Oberman, *Harvest of Medieval Theology*, 128.

the corruption of that nature—the law of the flesh reigning over man—after the fall."[276] What is clear is that the will is not so corrupted or wounded that it cannot perform meritorious acts. Man's will may be wounded and in need of repair, but it is not so wounded that freedom has been lost, that is, a freedom to act righteously, even if imperfectly. Apart from such freedom, man cannot do his best or what lies within him, which is necessary if he is to be rewarded with infused grace and merit divine justification. Original sin's grip, Oberman observed, is not ontological but psychological in its effect:

> Though man may be said to be in a miserable position, enslaved by the law of the flesh which requires that there be a healing aspect to the process of justification, his will is nevertheless free, original sin being a certain outgrowth of natural difficulties which can therefore be healed with natural medicines. Original sin has primarily a psychological, not an ontological impact on the free will of man; it destroys the pleasure of eliciting a good act and causes unhappiness and fear, thus changing the direction of the will. This does not, however, interfere with the freedom of the will as such. This presentation prepares us for Biel's psychological prescription for those who would like to reach the level of the *facere quod in se est* and thus dispose themselves for the infusion of grace.[277]

On that basis, we may seriously doubt that Biel was "Thomistic or Augustinian," an assertion Oberman also found "groundless," despite Biel's own claims.[278]

Grace Defined: The Impediment to Flight Lessened

Notwithstanding the heavy stress on the freedom of the will after the fall, Biel believed that he was far from bordering on Pelagianism. The grace God gives as a reward to those who do what lies within them originates not from man but from God.

After quoting Romans 11:6 in his sermon "The Circumcision of the Lord," Biel then claimed, "Because nature cannot make something out of nothing, that which is created comes from God alone. If grace could come from the creature, a grace which would suffice unto salvation, then any creature would be able to save himself by his own natural powers, that is, do what only grace can do. That is the error of Pelagius."[279] And again: "Now we must see just what this grace is by which the sinner is justified and what is actually accomplished in us. The grace of which we speak is a gift of God supernaturally infused into the soul. It makes the soul acceptable to God and sets it on the path to deeds of meritorious love."[280] Biel then proceeded to structure the majority of his sermon under three headings.

---

276. Oberman, *Harvest of Medieval Theology*, 128.
277. Oberman, *Harvest of Medieval Theology*, 129.
278. Oberman, *Harvest of Medieval Theology*, 130–31.
279. Biel, "Circumcision of the Lord," 168.
280. Biel, "Circumcision of the Lord," 168.

First, "God makes acceptable for this reason alone, that it is present in and is part of that nature which can be beatified, that is, man." Biel appealed to Scotus to explain how "grace is an enrichment of nature that is pleasing to God's will. Grace makes human nature acceptable to God by adorning it not with an ordinary acceptation but with that special acceptation by which man is according to God's decision ordained toward life eternal. For to be acceptable, to be beloved by God and to be His friend, means to be in such a state that one will attain eternal life unless one loses this state through sin."[281]

Second, "And because grace makes the sinner acceptable to God it follows that it also justifies him." Biel then broke justification down into two aspects: (1) "remission of guilt" and (2) "acceptation to eternal life, since it is impossible for one who is going to be accepted to eternal life to be at the same time condemned to eternal punishment." To be forgiven of one's guilt was, for Biel, a requirement of entering paradise.[282]

Biel did seem to distinguish between an infused grace that invites justification ("remission of guilt" and "acceptation to eternal life") and an infused grace that arrives after initial justification to continuously cultivate good works throughout the Christian life. Quoting Romans 3:24 to support his claim, Biel wrote, "But if grace is infused into someone who is already justified, that which it accomplishes is not justification. An example would be the grace once given to the holy angels and now daily given to those who are upright of heart, who through their good works earn an additional gift of grace above and beyond the grace already in them."[283]

Third, "Thus God makes these our works meritorious and acceptable for eternal reward, not actually all our works but only those which have been brought forth by the prompting of grace."[284] If any act is to be ultimately meritorious, in Biel's framework, it must be, he said, "brought forth by the prompting of grace." Hence, not all acts qualify. But those acts prompted by grace should result in love for God above all else.[285]

Biel did follow in the footsteps of Lombard, listing two components of a meritorious act: *liberum arbitrium* ("free will") and the grace of God. "There is no human merit that does not depend partly on free will. The principal cause of meritorious moral action, however, is attributed to grace. But grace does not determine the will. The will can ignore the prompting of grace and

---

281. Biel, "Circumcision of the Lord," 168.
282. Biel, "Circumcision of the Lord," 169.
283. Biel, "Circumcision of the Lord," 169.
284. Biel clarified, "It is assumed of meritorious work that the person who performs it is accepted, since the acts of a person who has not been accepted or of an enemy cannot please God." Biel, "Circumcision of the Lord," 169.
285. Biel explained, "This grace prompts us to love God above all things and in all things, that is, to seek after the glory of God as the goal of every action, and to prefer the ultimate good, God, ahead of one's self and everything else. Therefore, all those things which are not directed consciously or unconsciously toward God do not come from the prompting of grace and therefore are surely not worthy of eternal life." Biel, "Circumcision of the Lord," 169.

lose it by its own default. The prompting of grace is toward meritorious acts for the sake of God. Therefore, the act as such stems primarily from grace. This is the case because it is performed by someone who has grace in accordance with the prompting of grace."[286] Indispensable to a meritorious act is *liberum arbitrium*. Biel did label grace essential, even the "principal cause of meritorious moral action." Nevertheless, he qualified that the will is never necessitated or determined by grace but can resist and defeat grace. Subsequent grace in the life of those who've done their best and been rewarded by infused grace can even be lost altogether. Grace may prompt but not efficaciously.[287]

Biel called grace the principal cause, but what exactly is grace? When Biel used the word *grace*, he had in mind "love" or "infused love." Love and grace, he said, "are exactly the same."[288] (On this point he differed, by his own admission, from Scotus, who distinguished love from grace.) Furthermore, grace is a "habit, although it is not acquired but infused." Biel explained,

> Grace accomplishes in the soul something similar to the effects of a naturally acquired habit, although in a far more perfect fashion than an acquired habit. The naturally acquired habit is a permanent quality in the power of the soul which stems from frequently repeated acts. This habit prompts and urges the man to repeat the same act. . . . But grace elevates human power beyond itself, so that acts which had been turned by sin toward evil or inward toward one's self now can be meritoriously redirected against the law of the flesh and toward God. Grace leads, assists, and directs in order that man may be prompted in a way which corresponds with divine charity. And thus grace weakens the remaining power of sin, not—as many doctors say—because it forgives or wipes out sins, but because it strengthens human power.[289]

Being a preacher, Biel used the illustration of a bird trying to fly with a stone attached. Under such conditions, the creature can "scarcely fly away," but "if this bird's wings were strengthened, then we would say that the impediment to flight had been lessened, although the weight of the stone had not been lessened."[290] Similarly, grace infused into man strengthens him to overcome sin that weighs him down. Biel stressed, quite strongly, that this infused grace is a gift from the triune God: "By this grace we are able to remain without difficulty in His friendship, and to grow continually through good works. On such a foundation we can

---

286. And again: "Moreover, without grace it is absolutely impossible for him to love God meritoriously. Such is the rule established by God that no act should be accepted as meritorious unless it be prompted by grace." Biel, "Circumcision of the Lord," 170.

287. Biel appealed to Augustine for support, especially Augustine's illustration of a rider and a horse. It is doubtful that Augustine would have agreed with how Biel appropriated him. Biel, "Circumcision of the Lord," 170.

288. Biel, "Circumcision of the Lord," 171.

289. Biel, "Circumcision of the Lord," 171.

290. Biel, "Circumcision of the Lord," 172.

easily overcome the onslaughts of the devil, the world, and flesh, and gain a great reward in store for us."[291]

The Condition of the Covenant

Despite Biel's toil to emphasize the indispensability of God's infused, assisting grace, he ended his sermon, as noted earlier, with a *major* theological qualifier, brief though it may be: "Thus God has established the rule [covenant] that whoever turns to him and does what he can will receive forgiveness of sins from God. God infuses assisting grace into such a man, who is thus taken back into friendship."[292] For a sermon that so stresses the import of infused grace, this may appear to be a surprising way to end. Infused, assisting grace may be necessary for justification, but owing to the covenantal arrangement, Biel viewed man doing what he can as a *preliminary step* toward the reception of such grace at all. If man "does what he can," then he "will receive forgiveness," and God will infuse "assisting grace" into him. That is the condition of the covenant, and the parable of the golden ring narrated already seems only to confirm that covenantal condition.

As gracious as it may be for God to infuse grace into man (like a bird suddenly strengthened in its wings by a power outside itself), nevertheless, whether man receives the infused grace at all depends on him doing his best. When Biel said that meritorious acts rely on two factors—*liberum arbitrium* and grace—the former, according to the nature of the covenant, is decisive for procuring the latter. Not only can the Christian lose grace after justification because of the stubborn disinclination of the will, but it is possible (likely?) that some may not receive infused grace at all if they fail to do their best in the first place, though Biel never said so in that many words. In short, as gracious as grace may be for Biel once the gift is given, whether the gift is given (and the covenant put into action) is an altogether different matter, one that depends entirely on man turning to God at the start.

From *Meritum De Congruo* to *Merita De Condigno*

Heiko Oberman, the leading medievalist historian to examine Biel's justification theory, produced an elaborate chart that sets Biel's soteriology within an ecclesiastical framework. For our purposes, it is the condition of the covenant (*facit quod in se est*) that is relevant and has thus been stressed in bold.

Oberman's visualization of Biel's justification process is illuminating for a variety of reasons. First, Oberman reminded interpreters that for Biel there was, in the sacrament of baptism, a habit of grace "infused and substituted for original righteousness." Tragically, man's "relapse" into a "state of mortal sin" undermines such a habit of grace. After baptism, grace is compromised, and a further infusion is needed, though one that depends on man doing his best according to the *pactum* arrangement.

---

291. Biel, "Circumcision of the Lord," 173.
292. Biel, "Circumcision of the Lord," 173.

[OBERMAN'S] SCHEMA I: A CHART OF THE INTERRELATION OF JUSTIFICATION AND PREDESTINATION

THE ELECT [predestinati]	FALL	SACRAMENT OF BAPTISM	THE SINNER'S DISPOSITION	THE SACRAMENT OF PENANCE	ETERNAL REWARD
Those foreknown to fulfill the requirements set in God's eternal decrees [iustitia dei]	Original sin [spoliatus a gratuitis, vulneratus in naturalibus]	Habit of grace	He Does His Very Best [facit quod in se est]	The Decisive Transition	Acceptation
	State of mortal sin The virgin Mary exempted	Infused and substituted for original righteousness →	Not necessarily aided by prevenient grace [gratia gratis data]	Confrontation with the preached Word [lex nova] →	Good works produced in state of grace are necessarily by God's commitment—second decree—accepted as full merits [merita de condigno]
		Usually a relapse into a state of mortal sin	Ordinarily [regular-iter] facere quod in se est is the basis [causa] for infusion	Acquired faith [fides acquisita] →	They determine man's status in purgatory or heaven
			The Virgin Mary, the Apostle Paul, and some others are exceptions to this rule	Supreme love for God [amor dei super omnia] →	[N.B. The status in purgatory can also be influenced by indulgences acquired from the treasure of the Church and applied to members of the Church Militant which encompasses not only the living but also the dead who are not beati.]

(continued)

THE ELECT [predestinati]	FALL	SACRAMENT OF BAPTISM	THE SINNER'S DISPOSITION	THE SACRAMENT OF PENANCE	ETERNAL REWARD
			God's general assistance [*influential generalis*] is necessary for all acts, both good and evil	**God has committed himself—first decree—to reward those who are doing their best** →	Immediately of eventually *gloria* →
				Semi-merit [meritum de congruo] →	
				Restoration of the state of grace in anticipation of [*in proposito*] lor at time of absolution [*gratia gratum faciens*] by infusion of faith, hope and love	

[OBERMAN'S] SCHEMA I. CONTINUED . . . THE REPROBATE

THE REPROBATE [*presciti*]	FALL	SACRAMENT OF BAPTISM	THE SINNER'S DISPOSITION	THE SACRAMENT OF PENANCE	ETERNAL WORD
Those foreknown not to fulfill the requirements set in God's eternal decrees [*iustitia dei*]	Original Sin [*spoliatus a gratuitis, vulneratus in naturalibus*]	Habit of Grace	**He Does Not Do His Very Best [non facit quod in se est]**	*demerita*	Rejection
	State of mortal sin	Infused and substituted for original righteousness →	Remains in a state of mortal sin; or if temporarily in a state of grace, he is in a state of sin at the time of his death		Guilt is punished by eternal damnation [*culpa* → *pena damnationis*]
		Usually a relapse into state of mortal sin	Guilt [*culpa*]		
			God's general assistance [*influential generalis*] is necessary for all acts, both good and evil		

Second, and perhaps most importantly, Oberman confirmed that *facit quod in se est* is (ordinarily, *regulariter*) the *causa*, or basis, for infused grace in Biel's mind. Grace "does not prepare the sinner for the reception of this justifying grace since *grace is not the root but the fruit of the preparatory good works.* . . . This *facere quod in se est* is the necessary disposition for the infusion of grace and implies a movement of the free will, which is at once aversion to sin and love for God according to Eph. 5:14."[293] Within the context of the penance system, "God has committed himself—first decree—to reward those who are doing their very best."[294]

Such a "reward" produces *meritum de congruo*, and the "state of grace" is recovered—either before or during absolution "by infusion of faith, hope, and love." It is *meritum de congruo* that flowers into *merita de condigno*, as agreed on by God himself in his multilayered *pactum* (multilayered because *merita de condigno* is located in God's "second decree"). Therefore, the ordering of *meritum de congruo* and *merita de condigno* is critical, the former being conditioned on man's best works but the latter being acquired as one does one's best within a state of infused grace. "Once this genuine love for God's sake is reached, the last obstacle is removed and the road to acceptance is paved by the eternal decrees of God according to which this *facere quod in se est* is first *de congruo* rewarded with the infusion of grace, while then, secondly, acts performed in a state of grace are rewarded *de condigno* with acceptance by God."[295]

PELAGIAN OR SEMI-PELAGIAN?

Since the covenantal condition (*actum facientis quod in se est*) results, if performed, in the gift of infused grace, some interpreters of Biel have labeled this grace a "reward" for prior merit. Though the following description by Steven Ozment focuses on Ockham (in contrast to Thomas), it can be equally applied to Biel:

> In opposition to [Thomas and company] making salvation *conditional* upon the presence of a *supernatural habit of grace*, Ockham argued that one could perform works acceptable to God simply *by doing the best one could with one's natural moral ability.* Not only did Ockham believe it possible for those lacking such a habit to love God above all things and detest sin, but he argued further that God found it "fitting" to *reward with an infusion of grace* those who did so. Whereas

---

293. Oberman, *Harvest of Medieval Theology*, 140, 152. Oberman added a key clarification as to how Biel understood "grace": "The most important point to be kept in mind for the further presentation of Biel's doctrine of justification is the conclusion that when Biel discusses the necessity of grace in the process of justification, its relation to man's free will, and its relation to the *ex opera operato* efficacy of the sacraments, he has always the *gratia gratum faciens* in mind—by which the sinner is made acceptable to God—and is not thinking of another kind of grace, traditionally often called *gratia gratis data*, the grace of divine vocation, by which the sinner is provided with the proper disposition for the reception of the *gratia gratum faciens*. Biel denies that the sinner would be incapable of providing such a disposition with his own power by doing good works" (140).

294. Oberman, *Harvest of Medieval Theology*, 152.

295. Oberman, *Harvest of Medieval Theology*, 184.

Aquinas... had required the presence of such grace *before* any positive relationship with God could exist, Ockham [and Biel] made the reception of grace a reward for *prior moral effort*.... Ockham appeared to free divine acceptance from absolute dependence on infused habits of grace only to make God's will dependent on the good works man could do in his natural moral state. Unassisted ethical cooperation now preceded, as a condition, the infusion of grace, which, with subsequent ethical cooperation, won man salvation. To the traditional mind such an argument was Pelagianism.[296]

Or consider Oberman, whose conclusion is just as affirmative though more nuanced. Oberman concluded that for Biel, "sin has not made it impossible for man to act without the aid of grace."[297] Yet Biel "can speak in what appears to be such bold Pelagian language about the respective contributions of free will and grace as regards the moral quality of an act because he feels that he brings the full biblical doctrine of grace to bear on the relation of good deeds and meritorious deeds."[298]

Additionally, the *pactum*, by design, is meant to be gracious: "The gratuitous character of God's remuneration is therefore not based on the *activity* of the habit of grace nor on the *presence* of the habit of grace, but on God's decree according to which he has decided to accept every act which is performed in a state of grace as a *meritum de condigno*."[299] As Biel revealed in his commentary on the Mass, "The infusion of grace is granted to the sinner when he does his very best, not on grounds of a previous pact, but on grounds of God's generosity. Biel invites his auditors and readers to find God's overriding love and sovereignty expressed in the most articulate way, not in the full merit of justice, but in the semi-merit of generosity."[300]

Given the complexity of the *pactum*—a *pactum* initiated by God out of his generosity yet conditioned for its success on man doing his best—Oberman concluded that Biel's doctrine of justification is "at once *sola gratia* and *solis operibus*!" *By grace alone*—because if God had not decided to adorn man's good works with created and uncreated grace, man would never be saved. *By works alone*—because not only does man have to produce the framework or substance for this adornment, but God by the two laws of grace is committed, even obliged to add to this framework infused grace and final acceptance. Once man has done his very best, the other two parts follow automatically. The emphasis falls on "justification by works alone"; the concept of "justification by grace alone" is a rational outer structure dependent on the distinction between *potentia*

---

296. Emphasis added. Ozment, *Age of Reform*, 40–41.

297. Oberman, *Harvest of Medieval Theology*, 164.

298. Oberman, *Harvest of Medieval Theology*, 166.

299. Oberman, *Harvest of Medieval Theology*, 170.

300. Strictly speaking, then, Biel "rejects the idea that a sinner is able to earn the first grace *de condigno*: neither with an act that precedes nor with an act caused by this first grace can he do so." I might add, according to Oberman's chart, that *meritum de congruo* is another matter. Oberman, *Harvest of Medieval Theology*, 171.

absoluta and *potentia ordinata*.[301] Oberman chided past historians (e.g., Vignaux, Weijenborg) for allowing Biel's "outer structure" (i.e., the *pactum*) to excuse the Pelagian feel of Biel's inner structure (i.e., man doing his very best). "*It is therefore evident*," Oberman said confidently, "*that Biel's doctrine of justification is essentially Pelagian.*"[302]

McGrath, however, disagrees with Oberman. To understand why, it is necessary to regress briefly into McGrath's portrait of Biel. According to McGrath, Biel's doctrine of *liberum arbitrium* can be summarized as follows:

1. The human free will may choose a morally good act *ex puris naturalibus*, without the need for grace.
2. Humans are able, by the use of their free will and other natural faculties, to implement the law by their own power but are unable to fulfill the law in the precise manner that God intended (that is, *quoad substantiam actus*, but not *quoad intentionem praecipientis*).
3. *Ex puris naturalibus* the free will is able to avoid mortal sin.
4. *Ex puris naturalibus* the free will is able to love God above everything else.
5. *Ex suis naturalibus* the free will is able to dispose itself toward the reception of the gift of grace.

In view of points 1 and 5, why would McGrath disagree with Oberman? McGrath believes the *pactum* itself removes the Pelagian and Semi-Pelagian charge, for the existence of the *pactum* is proof that God has taken the first initiative. All that is required of man is a "minimum human response to the divine initiative" in this *pactum*.[303] If the charge of Pelagianism or Semi-Pelagianism means "that the *viator* can take the initiative in his own justification, the very existence of the *pactum* deflects the charge; God has taken the initiative away from humans, who are merely required to *respond* to that initiative by the proper exercise of their *liberum arbitrium*."[304]

---

301. Oberman, *Harvest of Medieval Theology*, 176–77.

302. Oberman, *Harvest of Medieval Theology*, 177. Later Oberman observed how Biel's Pelagianism makes a doctrine of predestination nonexistent: "As we can gather from the absence of any discussion of predestination in his sermons, this doctrine does not really function in Biel's theology. This should not surprise us. It is the traditional task of the doctrine of predestination proper to form a protective wall around the doctrine of justification by grace alone—a doctrine which does not necessarily imply justification by faith alone. Since we have found that Biel teaches an essentially Pelagian doctrine of justification, absolute predestination is not only superfluous but would even be obstructive. And seen against the background of his doctrine of justification, we can well understand that foreordination would in Biel's hands have to be transformed into foreknowledge" (196).

303. McGrath explains, "As Biel himself makes clear, his discussion of the role of individuals in their own justification must be set within the context of the divine *pactum*. The requirement of a minimum response on the part of the humans of the divine offer of grace is totally in keeping with the earlier Franciscan school's teaching, such as that of Alexander of Hales or Bonaventure. Biel has simply placed his theology of a minimum human response to the divine initiative in justification on a firmer foundation in the theology of the *pactum*, thereby safeguarding God from the charge of capriciousness." *Iustitia Dei*, 100.

304. McGrath, *Iustitia Dei*, 101.

Furthermore, the presence of the *pactum* itself in Biel's soteriology is absent in historic Pelagianism. Biel and Pelagius, therefore, cannot share a strict alignment. The Pelagian controversy did not have "so sophisticated a concept of causality as that employed by the theologians of the *via moderna*, expressed in the *pactum* theology, so that the applications of epithets such as 'Pelagian' to Biel's theology of justification must be regarded as historically unsound."[305]

Additionally, and perhaps most significantly for McGrath, the charge of Pelagianism is historically untenable since Biel himself was not under suspicion for heresy nor seen as contradicting prior councils. McGrath indirectly accuses Oberman of anachronism, judging it unfair of him to apply "one era's understanding of 'Pelagianism' to another."[306] What criteria would have been used in Biel's day to judge whether he was Pelagian? "The sole legitimate criteria . . . are the canons of the Council of Carthage—the only criteria which medieval doctors then possessed."[307] Biel simply did not have knowledge of or access to the minutes of the Second Council of Orange. McGrath concludes that if "Biel's theology is to be stigmatized as 'Pelagian' or 'semi-Pelagian,' it must be appreciated that he suffered from a historical accident which affected the entire period up to the Council of Trent itself."[308]

Such a debate between historians is relevant to the Reformation because it informs the type of theology Luther reacted to in his *Disputation against Scholastic Theology*. On one hand, McGrath makes a fine point about the Council of Carthage, as well as the Second Council of Orange. It would be unfair to hold an individual or movement accountable to documents not possessed. McGrath is also correct that Biel's introduction of the *pactum* defies a strict parallel between the *via moderna* and Pelagianism. The presence of a *pactum* does mean that God's initiation precedes man's, something that Pelagianism cannot say, at least not in the exact same way.

On the other hand, McGrath overlooks several factors and may be guilty of overreacting to Oberman. First, while McGrath accuses others of anachronism, McGrath himself does not entirely pay attention to the historical context and soil in which Biel's theology grew. If the *via moderna*, and with it the theology of the *pactum*, does not begin with Biel but can be traced back to Ockham and Holcot, then it is far too generous to conclude that the charge of Pelagianism crosses a line or would be foreign if lobbed against Biel. One need only revisit the controversy between Holcot and Bradwardine to note the title of Bradwardine's polemical book of 1344: *De causa Dei contra Pelagium*. Even without access to documents from the Second Council of Orange, Bradwardine's work demonstrates that theologians in the fourteenth century (even before Biel) still assumed, and sometimes asserted outright, a certain criterion for whether one

305. McGrath, *Iustitia Dei*, 101.
306. McGrath, *Iustitia Dei*, 100.
307. McGrath, *Iustitia Dei*, 100.
308. McGrath, *Iustitia Dei*, 100.

had crossed the heretical line. That is a reminder that even if confessional and conciliar documents are absent, the theological content of past theologians or councils is not necessarily lost but often continues. Furthermore, simply because Biel was not charged with the Pelagian heresy in his day does not mean his view is innocent. If that were a valid criterion, then any figure in the history of the church to escape public accusations must be considered orthodox.

Second, and perhaps most important, is how McGrath downplays the role of *liberum arbitrium* in Biel's *processus iustificationis*. To call *quod in se est* a "minimum human response to the divine initiative," as if mankind is "merely required to *respond* to that initiative by the proper exercise of their *liberum arbitrium*," is not only to overplay the power of the *pactum* prior to infused grace but is also to underplay the magnitude of *liberum arbitrium*. McGrath believes that the positioning of the *pactum* at the start of the *processus iustificationis* eliminates Pelagian tendencies. Yet that is a failure to see how and when the *pactum* actually functions.

It is true that God has taken the initiative by establishing an agreement to reward man's very best. However, that is all it is—an agreement, a promise, a pledge—until man does so. Stated otherwise, the *pactum*, as Oberman's chart demonstrates, is never actualized if *non facit quod in se est* ("he does not do his very best"). This is the most common oversight in those who believe Biel escaped Pelagian or Semi-Pelagian tendencies. It is the reason why Oberman admonished older historians. Seeing the "outer structure" (as Oberman called it) of the *pactum*, they glossed over what we might label the "inner structure," namely, man doing his very best. As generous as the *pactum* may be, it is not and cannot functionally be applied until man does what lies within his power. In that sense, at least according to the "inner structure," it is man who is primary, not God, for God's *pactum* is conditioned on man's best.

It follows that although the *pactum* may have chronological priority, man's *liberum arbitrium* has causal priority, for whether God rewards man with infused grace depends entirely on man's undetermined choice. The *pactum* may issue a promise, but whether it is fulfilled or finds its application in man rests on *liberum arbitrium*—and not just any free act but man's *best* free act. Ironically, Biel's covenantal scheme may have intended to protect a voluntarist conception of God, but in the end, it conditioned divine sovereignty on human choice.

Therefore, the charge of Pelagianism is not far off the mark, even if the specifics of its alignment are contested. Suppose one softens the label to Semi-Pelagianism because of the introduction of the *pactum*; it is still difficult to avoid just how conditioned that *pactum* is on man's best merits. Looking back on the *processus iustificationis* of the ungodly, one might conclude that only Semi-Pelagianism applies to Biel since the *pactum* took effect when man did his very best. However, when one reflects on the pilgrimage of the *unjustified*, one realizes that as promising as the *pactum* may have sounded in theory, in reality it meant little since man never did his very best. To play off Biel's imagery, the bird never left the ground. Man's *liberum arbitrium* had the last word. Long before Biel, Thomas Aquinas identified the Pelagian heresy only to counter it by claiming that matter "does not move itself to its own perfection; therefore it must be moved by something else."[309] It is difficult to see how Biel could agree when the *pactum* does not actually move anyone but only promises divine movement should man move himself to the best of his abilities.

WHAT TYPE OF SCHOLASTICISM PROVOKED THE REFORMATION?

Whether Biel was Semi-Pelagian or Pelagian, he had no little influence on a sixteenth-century student named Martin Luther.

Luther's theological education was birthed out of the womb of the *via moderna* (see chapter 8). Luther was influenced by a variety of professors, many of whom were disciples of Gabriel Biel. Erfurt was crowded with such disciples, including Arnoldi of Usingen, Jodocus Trutvetter, and Bartholomaeus Arnoldi of Usingen. Johann Nathin also deserves attention since he was a student of Biel himself, or at least a student who encountered Biel's teaching firsthand.[310] Nathin completed his doctoral degree at Tübingen, and it is most probable that Nathin was present at Biel's lectures.

When Luther studied under Nathin, Nathin assigned Biel's dogmatic works.[311] Like his teacher, Luther absorbed Biel's nominalist, voluntarist soteriology in the process. Much later Philipp Melanchthon said Luther so absorbed Biel that even after his evangelical turn Luther could still recite from memory long portions of Biel's corpus.[312] So influential was Biel via Nathin that when Luther started lecturing on the Psalms (1513–15), it was Biel's soteriological assumptions that rose to the surface.[313] For instance, Luther wrote, "The doctors rightly say that, when people do their best, God infallibly gives grace. This cannot be understood as meaning that this preparation for grace is *de condigno* [meritorious], as they are incomparable, but it can be regarded as *de congruo* on account of this promise of God and the covenant (*pactum*) of mercy."[314] Yet Luther wrapped *quod in se est* within the voluntarist framework as well: "Righteousness (*iustitia*) is thus said to be rendering to each what is due to them. Yet equity is prior to righteousness, and is its prerequisite. Equity identifies merit; righteousness renders rewards. Thus the Lord judged the world 'in equity' (that is, wishing all to be saved), and judges 'in righteousness' (because God renders to each their reward)."[315]

---

309. Thomas Aquinas, *SCG* 3.149.1.

310. Hendrix, *Martin Luther*, 36. On each of these disciples, see Oberman, *The Dawn of the Reformation*, 94–95.

311. Hendrix, *Martin Luther*, 36.

312. *WA* 1:44.15; 45:34; cf. Oberman, *Luther*, 138.

313. Elsewhere Luther confirmed he was under the influence of Ockham: *WA* 6:195. 4; cf. Oberman, *Luther*, 120.

314. Martin Luther, *Psalmenvorlesung*, in *WA* 4:262.4–7 (cf. 3:288.37–289.4). This translation is McGrath's, in *Iustitia Dei*, 116. Cf. Martin Luther, *First Lectures on the Psalms II*, in *LW* 11:396.

315. Luther, *Psalmenvorlesung* (Glossen), in *WA* 55.1:70.9–11. McGrath comments, "Luther here

Progressively, sometimes slowly, Luther took issue with Biel, a turn that occurred as Luther transitioned from lecturing on the Psalms to lecturing on Romans (1515–16), Galatians (1516–17), and Hebrews (1517–18).[316] His lectures at the University of Wittenberg on Romans were the first of the three to signal a shift. The *via moderna* was not spoken of as favorably as before now that Luther sounded more Augustinian. The sinner is not active in the *via moderna* sense—doing his best or doing what lies within—but passive in the reception of divine grace.[317]

Any hostility to the *via moderna* that remained in seed form in the years 1515–16 reached its full potential by 1517. Luther went from skeptical to critical, believing that the *via moderna* soteriology he had been fed was not only incompatible with a Pauline anthropology and soteriology but also that the root cause of his frustrations originated from the late medieval system. Although Franz Günther defended a set of theses that year as a requirement to earning his bachelor's degree, it was Luther who wrote the theses for public appearance at the University of Wittenberg. These theses, which now bear the title *Disputation against Scholastic Theology*, were presented on September 4, 1517. Harold Grimm observed that they emerged from Luther's "commentary on the first book of Aristotle's Physics," which he wrote for the purpose of "dethroning the god of the scholastics."[318]

As mentioned in chapter 1, a common misinterpretation of the Reformation assumes the Reformers reacted against all that is medieval, especially against all that is Scholastic—an oppositional narrative. The truth, however, is far more nuanced. The Reformers did not reject Scholasticism as a whole, despite their own polemical use of the word *Schoolmen*. A close look at their writings—such as Luther's *Disputation against Scholastic Theology*—reveals a reaction to *late* medieval Scholasticism. Luther did not target every corner of Scholasticism—which would be odd considering different Scholastics held different positions on a range of theological and philosophical issues.[319] Instead, Luther targeted late medieval Scholastics, such as Duns Scotus, William of Ockham, and especially Gabriel Biel. These are the Scholastics he claimed to dethrone.[320]

---

produces the key aspects of Biel's understanding of *iustitia Dei*: *iustitia* is understood to be based upon divine equity, which looks solely to the merits of humans in determining their reward within the framework established by the covenant. The doctors of the church rightly teach that, when people do their best (*quod in se est*), God infallibly gives grace (*hinc recte dicunt doctores, quod homini facienti quod in se est, Deus infallibiliter dat gratiami*). Luther's theological breakthrough is intimately connected with his discovery of a new meaning of the 'righteousness of God,' and it is important to appreciate that his earlier works are characterized by the teaching of the *via moderna* upon this matter. Luther's later view that anyone attempting to do *quod in se est* sinned mortally remains notionally within this framework, while ultimately subverting its theological plausibility." McGrath, *Iustitia Dei*, 88–89. Cf. Luther, *Psalmenvorlesung*, in WA 4:262.4–5.

316. For an extensive study comparing Biel and Luther, see Grane, *Contra Gabrielem*.

317. On this point, see Maas, "Justification by Faith Alone," 517–18.

318. Grimm, "Introduction," in *LW* 31:6.

319. To qualify, in other, later writings Luther did take issue with Lombard, for example, critical of Lombard's seven sacraments. However, Luther's reaction in *Disputation of against Scholastic Theology* is against Ockham and Biel.

320. McGrath also adds to the nuance when he observes the difference between the Swiss Reformation

Luther and the Reformers no doubt reacted against Scholasticism, but as we have seen, their real target was not the high medieval Scholasticism of Anselm or Thomas but the late medieval Scholasticism that shifted in radical ways. "In later generations, particularly among the sixteenth-century Reformers, a *decayed* Scholastic theology would be criticized *for lacking contact with the patristic heritage.*"[321] Emero Stiegman's choice word—*decayed*—should be underlined. He did not apply "decayed" to high medieval Scholasticism, or at least not to its core, which was no doubt in touch with its patristic (catholic) inheritance. We must conclude that the Reformation was not so much a reaction to Scholasticism wholesale, but to this "decayed" Scholasticism exhibited in figures like Scotus, Ockham, and Biel, who strayed from patristic commitments (like Augustine's doctrine of grace). As chapter 4 revealed, core Scholastics like Thomas Aquinas aimed at the very least to be faithful to the patristic consensus (both in theology proper and in Augustinian soteriology). As far as the Reformers considered themselves "catholic," they were also "Scholastic" in this sense: they shared a common commitment to Christian orthodoxy and a basic Augustinian theology of grace like the best of the Scholastics. Although they did not always realize it, the Reformers' fiery rhetoric against Scholasticism was truly aimed at radical abuses of Scholasticism, the "decayed" version. Not the real thing.

---

and the German Reformation. Both reacted to late medieval Scholastics, but for different reasons and within different contexts. On the other hand, Luther reacted to Ockham and Biel as he studied and lectured in the university setting. Within the halls of academia, Luther came face-to-face with Biel's theological intellect. On the other hand, Zwingli and Zurich, at least early on, were not so much concerned with a theological reform as a moral one. Therefore, Scholasticism—an intellectual and theological enterprise—was simply irrelevant. "The Swiss reformers could afford to ridicule scholasticism, for it posed no threat to them—but Luther had to engage with it directly." McGrath, *Reformation Thought*, 63.

321. Stiegman, "Bernard of Clairvaux, William of St. Thierry, the Victorines," 131.

6

FROM REBIRTH TO ABERRATION

The Reformation and Renaissance Humanism

Once I bought an edition of Homer in order to become a Greek.
—Martin Luther to Eobanus Hessus

I f the Reformation owed an unwitting debt to Scholasticism, perhaps not in whole but at least in part, then it owed an equal debt to humanism.

Martin Luther was the first to admit as much. In 1523 some Germans said Luther's theology would lead to a decline in learning. But "I myself am convinced that without the knowledge of the [humanistic] studies, pure theology can by no means exist," said Luther in response. The Christian who believes in God's providential activity in ancient civilizations should expect nothing less. "I realize there has never been a great revelation of God's Word unless God has first prepared the way by the rise and flourishing of languages and learning, as though these were forerunners, a sort of [John] the Baptist."[1]

Luther's unembarrassed debt to humanism demonstrates how complex the sixteenth century could be; the Reformation itself was not monolithic and neither were the movements that made it possible. However, humanism's influence is difficult to exaggerate. Therefore, this chapter will be but a brief entryway into its main contours, its diverse representatives, and its appropriation for the sake of the Reformation. Meanwhile, the shadow of Scholasticism will trail closely behind as we explore its conflicting but compatible relationship to humanism, a story not often told.[2]

REBIRTH: RENAISSANCE HUMANISM

The Renaissance was one of the most exhilarating eras of Western history, an animation captured by the slogan *Christianismus renascens*—"Christianity being born again." Historians debate when this elating era started and when it faded away, but its broad outline can be traced from AD 1300 to 1600. Although the

---

1. *LW* 49:34.
2. Except for Erasmus, all primary sources from Renaissance humanism in this chapter originate from Kenneth Bartlett, ed., *The Civilization of the Italian Renaissance: A Sourcebook.*

Renaissance spread across Northern Europe, Italy was the maternal source of its vitality.[3]

Yet the Renaissance was diverse. The years 1300 to 1600 gave birth to different children, some Scholastics, some humanists.[4] Since chapters 3–4 drew attention to the former, this chapter will focus on the latter, although the two cannot be described without reference to one another. Both Scholastics and humanists were indebted to the early and high medieval eras before them even if they each provided their own critique.

The Return to Classical Antiquity and the Pursuit of Eloquence

"By humanism we mean merely the general tendency of the age to attach the greatest importance to classical studies, and to consider classical antiquity as the common standard and model by which to guide all cultural activities."[5] Paul Kristeller's definition of humanism captures its essence: a return to classical antiquity with full confidence that its ancient perspective contained the seeds by which present society could be reborn. "They believed that classical antiquity was in most respects a perfect age; that it was followed by a long period of decline, the Dark or Middle Ages; and that it was the task and destiny of their own age to accomplish a rebirth or renaissance of classical antiquity, or of its learning, arts, and sciences."[6]

If classical antiquity contained the remedy, then dedication to the retrieval of classical sources—Greek and Roman—was essential. *Ad fontes*—back to the source or fountainhead—became the theme song of Renaissance humanism.[7] On the surface, humanists were characterized by a renewed, energetic attention to the texts of classical antiquity, sacred and otherwise. As humanists took root in Florence, Italy—one of the centers for Renaissance thought—scholars devoted themselves to the recovery of classical voices, from Cicero to Virgil. Yet beneath the surface resided a deeper commitment. The retrieval of ancient texts was not the destiny but the pathway to a particular terminus: (1) the perfection of eloquence for (2) the sake of cultural and educational renewal.

---

3. To qualify further, the Renaissance's heartbeat could be heard in Italy, but even its spirit stemmed from France at points, and France was an epicenter for medieval thought. See Kristeller, *Renaissance Thought*, 92–97.

4. It may be tempting to consider humanism synonymous with the Renaissance, but Paul Kristeller warned against that assumption: humanism "did not represent the sum total of learning in the Italian Renaissance." Kristeller, 111.

5. Kristeller, 95. As a student at an Italian university during the fifteenth century, for example, one might hear the term *humanista* used in colloquial conversations. But *humanista* did not mean what moderns mean when they use the term *humanism*—a word whose origins are very recent. As Kristeller explained, "The new term *humanism* reflects the modern and false conception that Renaissance humanism was a basically new philosophical movement. . . . The old term *humanista*, on the other hand, reflects the more modest, but correct, contemporary view that the humanists were the teachers and representatives of a certain branch of learning which at that time was expanding and in vogue" (111).

6. "The humanists themselves thus helped to shape the concept of the Renaissance." Kristeller, 124.

7. In French, *renaissance* means to be born again.

First, *eloquence*. Few names embody the pristine brilliance of eloquence like Cicero, so naturally enough he occupied the minds of the best humanists in countless ways. "Above all, Cicero's rhetorical works provided the theory, and his orations, letters, and dialogues the concrete models for the main branches of prose literature, whereas the structure of his well-cadenced sentences was imitated in all kinds of literary compositions." When Cicero's eloquence was coupled with his love for ideas, the result was nothing less than intellectual and moral acumen. For "the synthesis of philosophy and rhetoric in his work provided the humanists with a favorite ideal, namely the combination of eloquence and wisdom."[8]

For example, consider the Italian humanist Lorenzo Valla (1406–57), introduced later in this chapter. Lorenzo, who originated from Rome, not only wrote notes on the New Testament that influenced Erasmus's 1516 Greek text, but he wrote *The Glory of the Latin Language*, which students all over Europe read to understand why cultural revival must stem from the eloquence of the Latin tongue. Valla looked at the state of education in his day and lamented its poor condition: "Sorrow hinders and torments me, and forces me to weep as I contemplate the state which eloquence had once attained and the condition into which it has now fallen." Why had eloquence dissipated? Valla listed many reasons, two of which were the neglect of classical literature (and all the wisdom it contained) and with it the pitiful state of the Latin language itself. "Students of philosophy have not possessed, nor do they possess, the works of the ancient philosophers; nor do rhetoricians have the orators; nor lawyers the jurisconsults; nor teachers the known works of the ancients, as if after the Roman Empire had fallen, it would not be fitting to speak or utter in the Roman fashion, and the glory of Latinity was allowed to decay in rust and mould."[9]

Valla was convinced that the Latin language was superior, a vocabulary spanning disciplines—from law to theology, from oratory to science—connecting the modern scholar with the best expression of human nature from the past. The Latin language contains a certain persuasiveness that is effectual; Valla even called it a *sacramental power* that spans culture and class to sprinkle its blessings everywhere. "The Roman dominion, the peoples and nations long ago threw off as unwelcome burden; the language of Rome they have thought sweeter than any nectar, more splendid than any silk, more precious than any gold or gems, and they have embraced it as if it were a god sent from Paradise." Therefore, said Valla, great "is the sacramental power of the Latin language, truly great in its divinity, which has been preserved these many centuries with religious and

---

8. Kristeller, 21. And again, "Hence I am inclined to consider the humanists," said Kristeller, "not as philosophers with a curious lack of philosophical ideas and a curious fancy for eloquence and for classical studies, but rather as professional rhetoricians with a new, classicist ideal of culture, who tried to assert the importance of their field of learning and to impose their standards upon the other fields of learning and of science, including philosophy" (19).

9. Valla, *The Glory of the Latin Language*, 81; cf. full text: *De elegantiis linguae latinae*.

holy awe, by strangers, by barbarians, by enemies, so that we Romans should not grieve but rejoice, and the whole listening earth should glory."[10]

If the Latin tongue does possess a sacramental power, then its recovery is the key to society's rebirth and renewal. As Valla promised, "We have lost Rome, we have lost authority, we have lost dominion, not by our own fault but by that of the times, yet we reign still, by this one splendid sovereignty, in a great part of the world. Ours is Italy, ours Gaul, ours Spain, Germany, Pannonia, Dalmatia, Illyricum, and many other lands. For wherever the Roman tongue holds sway, there is the Roman Empire."[11]

Second, *renewal*. For a humanist like Valla, ancient texts were not mere artifacts for historical intrigue but retrieved for the purpose of educational and cultural renewal. They were read from a spirit of sacred interpretation since these ancient texts embodied the type of rhetorical eloquence that is a rich soil for cultural revitalization, even rebirth. By "eloquence" Renaissance humanists did not mean a superficial desire to impress but ventured to draw out the true nature of the human person. The Creator made man and woman to create and communicate through various mediums, namely, the arts. From rhetoric to art, from music to letters, the human person is designed to convey truth, goodness, and beauty, imitating his Maker, the one who is truth, goodness, and beauty. And no era in civilization exemplified this purpose so well as the classical era. By recovering its methods, the humanists could restore society to a culture altogether reborn. With that aim, humanists were fixated on humanity. They were not unaware of divinity, but in contrast to the monks in the monasteries the humanists did not depart from society but sought its rejuvenation, from science to education, from politics to poetry.

Renaissance humanists gravitated to certain provinces in society. The university, for example, was an obvious destination for those with humanist aspirations, since education was ground zero for influencing the next generation in classical thought. But humanists were by no means limited to the lectern. Besides teachers, humanists were also secretaries to notable, even powerful members of society or nobility. In these occupations, humanists were specialists in the art of writing letters, for instance. For monumental public addresses, humanists were considered a necessity, skilled in the art of rhetoric. Like Cicero, they were trained in the craft of oration.[12] It was no accident, then, that those Reformers who learned the skills of the humanist became some of the most persuasive preachers.

Humanists were known for their imitation of classical literary and rhetorical methods, but they were also known for their translations and critical editions

---

10. Valla, 81.

11. Valla, 81.

12. "It was the novel contribution of the humanists to add the firm belief that in order to write and to speak well it was necessary to study and to imitate the ancients. Thus we can understand why classical studies in the Renaissance were rarely, if ever, separated from the literary and practical aim of the rhetorician to write and to speak well." Kristeller, *Renaissance Thought*, 13. Kristeller also listed poetry and history (11).

of classical texts, especially their commentaries on those texts. Earlier medieval thinkers were not unfamiliar with classical texts, but humanists were determined to translate, print, and then embody the classical style, and at times the classical outlook on the world. That objective motivated humanist students to learn Greek so that they could translate its literature into Latin either for the first time or for the purpose of a superior text. That objective also motivated humanists to dedicate their minds to the discipline of textual criticism and the history and science of linguistics (philology). Humanists made the Scriptures available in the original languages and produced some of the best critical editions of the church fathers, which benefitted the Reformation's retrieval of ancient texts.

A Philosophy or a Cultural, Literary Movement of Rebirth?

This interpretation of Renaissance humanism resists those who have tried to reduce the humanist movement to a certain political or even philosophical position. On one hand, the humanist movement did involve a renewed interest in the political structures of Rome's republic. The correlation, for example, between Florence's republic and the Roman republic was anything but accidental. Also, humanists exhibited an animated reeducation in Greek philosophy, Plato most of all.[13] *Ad fontes* was a license to read and retrieve a Platonic or Aristotelian outlook on its own warrant rather than depend on late medieval assumptions, some accurate but others less so.[14] And since the classical tradition was the source of the type of eloquence that leads to wisdom, a return to the sources meant a return to classical literature in all its political and philosophical variety.

On the other hand, to press any of these interests and emphases—political or philosophical—to the center as if they were *the* commitment or organizing theme of the humanist movement is to risk misinterpretation. "Thus I should like to understand Renaissance humanism," said Kristeller, "as a broad cultural and literary movement, which in its substance was not philosophical, but had important philosophical implications and consequences."[15] Therefore, "Renaissance humanism was not as such a philosophical tendency or system, but rather a cultural and educational program which emphasized and developed an important but limited area of studies."[16] Renaissance humanism, in other words, may affect philosophy—and certainly its representatives embodied certain philosophies, even divergent philosophies—but the movement itself was not a philosophical position or program per se. The closest the humanist movement came to a whole system of philosophy occurred when its representatives touched on the subject of morality (see Erasmus's *philosophi Christi* below). Nevertheless,

---

13. On the spread of Neo-Platonism among humanists, see Bartlett, *A Short History of the Italian Renaissance*, 209–24.

14. For five reasons why Renaissance humanism first caught on, see McGrath, *Reformation Thought*, 36–37. McGrath warns against resting too much weight on the word *humanism* since this was not a word used by Renaissance representatives but is a word of more recent use.

15. Kristeller, *Renaissance Thought*, 102 (cf. 22).

16. Kristeller, 10.

even then their opinions on ethics were not intended as a proposal for a full-scale moral philosophy or theological system.[17]

Pushing aside central motif theories, the historian should recognize how diverse the Renaissance could be. A political, philosophical, or religious viewpoint was not represented by all and sometimes not even by most. The Renaissance, therefore, was not so much a viewpoint as a mindset. Humanists were "concerned with *how ideas were obtained and expressed*, rather than with *the actual substance of those ideas.*" The humanist movement, explains McGrath, was not "an ideological program" but instead a "cultural program, which appealed to classical antiquity as a model of eloquence."[18]

Humanism versus Scholasticism? Renaissance Platonism versus Medieval Aristotelianism?

If humanism was not so much ideological but cultural, then the relationship between humanism and Scholasticism is not as incompatible as some have said.

For example, an older interpretation—which said Renaissance humanists sided with Plato over against Aristotle (the Scholastic choice)—is more of a caricature than an accurate portrayal. Granted, as a generalization, streams of Renaissance humanism committed to a renewed interest in Plato, and at points certain humanists were critical of the Scholastic method, which relied on Aristotelian vocabulary or structure. However, that renewed interest in Plato by no means precluded Aristotle and the philosopher's ongoing influence. Humanists considered the Greek corpus essential reading for the student committed to classical learning, which explains why many humanists not only provided fresh translations of Aristotle from Greek to Latin but lectured from translations as well.[19]

Kristeller was not misguided when he reacted against the anti-Aristotelian interpretation of past historians. In his opinion, claiming Renaissance humanists were anti-Aristotelian is a claim too "often exaggerated or misunderstood," and one blind to the reasons for the criticism itself. To be precise, the humanist critique was "neither unified nor effective."[20] Not all humanists were critical, and those that were critical were not always unified in their reasons why. Nor was the criticism itself effective since the criticism had more to do with methodological dissatisfaction than philosophy itself. Kristeller listed three specific critiques certain humanists leveled against the Scholastics: (1) bad (Latin) style,

---

17. Kristeller did qualify this way: "The *studia humanitatis* includes one philosophical discipline, that is, morals, but it excludes by definition such fields as logic, natural philosophy, and metaphysics, as well as mathematics and astronomy, medicine, law, and theology." Kristeller, 10.

18. For this reason, McGrath calls humanism an "attitude." McGrath, *Reformation Thought*, 39. Examples of nailing the Renaissance to a particular position include Baron, *The Crisis of the Early Italian Renaissance*, and Burckhardt, *The Civilization of the Renaissance*.

19. Kristeller, *Renaissance Thought*, 24–25, 38–39.

20. Furthermore, it is irresponsible to exaggerate anti-Aristotelianism, because the reuse of Aristotle was only a recent phenomenon. In other words, an interpretation that says the humanists were "overthrowing a tradition of many centuries" is seriously misguided. Kristeller, 43.

(2) ignorance of classical sources, and (3) preoccupation with supposedly unimportant questions.[21]

Even if all these criticisms were legitimate (a claim that is now questioned by historians), humanists who lobbed these criticisms "failed to make positive contributions to the philosophical and scientific disciplines with which the Scholastics were concerned."[22] On that count, the Scholastics had the upper hand. Regardless, the historian should not create too wide a dichotomy, as if Scholastics and humanists were two different philosophies or theologies. Their squabble had more to do with "departmental rivalry" and the "battle of the arts" than anything. "Renaissance Platonism, which many historians have been inclined to oppose to medieval Aristotelianism, was not as persistently anti-Aristotelian as we might expect."[23]

In sum, one of the tragedies of modern interpretation is the misinformed caricature of the Middle Ages as the Dark Ages.[24] That assumption also rests on an exaggeration: the humanists were anti-Scholastic. However, the Renaissance relationship between Scholastics and humanists was far more nuanced and much more complicated. As a result, Reformers were not necessarily one or the other, as if to be pro-humanist was to be anti-Scholastic. A Reformer like Peter Martyr Vermigli, for example, was indebted to humanism and Scholasticism; he did not consider the two antithetical to one another but complementary. Over against the caricature, therefore, Frank James III concludes, "Thus, in virtually all Protestant theological exposition, there was a fundamental continuity between humanism and scholasticism."[25] Perhaps James's claim should be nuanced a little since some Reformers vocalized and exemplified that continuity more than others. Nevertheless, his point is a needed correction against the common tendency to overplay the differences between humanism and Scholasticism only to assume the Reformers embodied a contrast instead of a continuity. The Reformers were planted in the soil of *both* humanism and Scholasticism, and they borrowed the tools of both as far as they served the cause of the Reformation.

RENAISSANCE HUMANISM IN ITALY

Why did humanism experience success on such a broad stage—across Northern Europe? To answer that question, compare humanism to Scholasticism. The Schoolmen were university men. Their domain of influence was the classroom and the treatises they produced for the intellectually privileged. However,

---

21. Kristeller, 43 (cf. 101).

22. Kristeller, 43.

23. "The anti-Aristotelian revolution which marks the beginning of the modern period in the physical sciences and in philosophy had some of its roots and forerunners in the Renaissance period, but did not actually occur until later." Kristeller, 46.

24. That label—the Dark Ages—may apply to the physical survival of medieval people (e.g., the black plague), but its application to their intellectual thought is unfair.

25. See James, "Peter Martyr Vermigli, 71.

humanism was far more widespread, penetrating not only the university but liberal arts wherever they were practiced in society.

In addition, the two movements took different forms. Humanism criticized Scholasticism for its occupation with technical questions via long treatises in the style of a systematic presentation. Meanwhile, humanism prized eloquence, far more concerned with the beauty of its prose and the persuasiveness of its rhetoric. "In an age in which rhetoric and dialectic were seen as mutually incompatible, the superior appeal of the former virtually guaranteed the decline of the latter."[26]

These differences may seem small—matters of method more than philosophy or theology. Yet such differences explain in part the reason for humanism's spread across Europe. However, before its European influence can be observed, its source deserves recognition. Renaissance humanism came to life in Italian cities, Florence and Milan in particular, though certainly Venice as well. Out of these cities and others were born classical scholars of a unique caliber.

Petrarch

For example, one of the first and most talented humanists was the poet Francesco Petrarca, or Petrarch (1304–74).[27] Born to Florentine parents, Petrarch first opened his eyes in a household that was far from affluent, situated in the town of Arezzo. Why was Petrarch born in Arezzo instead of Florence? "They had been expelled from their native city," Petrarch recounted, by the Black Guelphs one year before. Their expulsion was not the first but occurred not long after the medieval poet Dante himself was banished.[28] But the young Petrarch did not remain in Arezzo; his parents moved from one place to another, from Incisa to Pisa to Farther Gaul and eventually to Avignon. Petrarch was but a youth when the papacy moved to Avignon in 1309.[29] Later in life, Petrarch expressed his distaste for Avignon, a "disgusting city ... which I heartily abhorred," at least in contrast to the ancient history percolating in a city like Rome.[30] Petrarch remembered his boyhood on "the windy banks of the river Rhone," although he lingered in other towns like Carpentras, where he learned "grammar, logic and rhetoric."[31] Looking back on that opportunity, he considered himself fortunate since many others were not as fortunate to receive an education.

Petrarch immersed himself in civil law during his university days at Montpellier and later at Bologna, but he gave up on law when he did not have to submit to his parents' vision for his future any longer. He had great respect for law and found himself mesmerized by its Roman heritage, but he could not

26. McGrath, *Reformation Thought*, 62.
27. The details of his career are found in Bartlett, ed., *Civilization of the Italian Renaissance*, 25–26.
28. Petrarch, *Letter to Posterity*, 28.
29. See chapter 7 on why the papacy moved to Avignon.
30. Petrarch, *Letter to Posterity*, 29.
31. Petrarch, *Letter to Posterity*, 28–29.

stomach the practice because its use (misuse?) by its practitioners betrayed his high esteem for the law itself. "My reason was that, although the dignity of the law, which is doubtless very great, and especially the numerous references it contains to Roman antiquity, did not fail to delight me, I felt it to be habitually degraded by those who practice it. It went against me painfully to acquire an art which I would not practice dishonestly, and could hardly hope to exercise otherwise."[32]

Petrarch was only twenty-two years old when he quit and retreated to Avignon, where he found a steady occupation in the church, a scenario uncanny in its surface similarity to young Martin Luther a century later in Germany.[33] However, unlike Luther he was not set on holiness but let himself indulge in his lust for women. By his own admission, he was "carried away by the fire of youth," and later in life he regretted his indulgence.[34]

All along, Petrarch's real interest was not law; he was arrested by a growing admiration for classical antiquity and its Latin corpus. This interest rose to the surface when he was sent as a novice cleric to see the Holy City in Rome. Although Petrarch was there mostly for religious responsibilities, his head turned whenever he saw the surviving architecture of the Roman Empire. Inspired by classical literature, Petrarch came back from Rome determined to dedicate himself to writing poetry in the vein of the classical poets. His sonnets spoke of enduring love, love that Petrarch knew firsthand.[35] His poetry was so moving that he was summoned back to Rome to receive an honor unprecedented in his day. "While leading a leisurely existence . . . I received, remarkable as it may seem, upon one and the same day [1 September 1340], letters both from the Senate at Rome and the Chancellor of the University of Paris, pressing me to appear in Rome and Paris, respectively, to receive the poet's crown of laurel." What was Petrarch's reaction? "In my youthful elation I convinced myself that I was quite worthy of this honor; the recognition came from eminent judges, and I accepted their verdict rather than that of my own better judgment."[36]

Petrarch acknowledged his youthful pride and honestly lamented over his youthful indulgences. Petrarch contrasted his twenties and thirties with a crisis that occurred as he approached midlife. "As I approached the age of forty, while my powers were unimpaired and my passions were still strong, I not only abruptly threw off my bad habits, but even the very recollection of them, as if I had never looked upon a woman. This I mention as among the greatest of my blessings, and I render thanks to God, who freed me, while still sound

---

32. Petrarch, *Letter to Posterity*, 29.

33. For Petrarch's relationship with the Colonnesi family, a relationship so critical to his livelihood, see Petrarch, *Letter to Posterity*, 29.

34. Eventually Petrarch had children out of wedlock as a result. See Petrarch, *Letter to Posterity*, 27.

35. On Petrarch's love for Laura, a beautiful woman if there ever was one, see Bartlett, *Civilization of the Italian Renaissance*, 25.

36. Petrarch, *Letter to Posterity*, 30.

and vigorous from a disgusting slavery which had always been hateful to me."[37] Petrarch's spiritual crisis and conversion bears striking similarities to Augustine's garden experience as recorded in *Confessions*. Although Petrarch's early career as a priest was scandalous, much like Augustine he was overcome by conviction, a conviction that drove him to the same God as Augustine.

In that light, it is not surprising that Petrarch considered Augustine the greatest of the church fathers and his book *Confessions* the supreme Christian classic. In his work titled *The Ascent of Mount Ventoux*, Petrarch reflected on his love for nature as he ascended the colossal mountain to reach its transcendent peak. The reflection is humanist to the core, implanting value in humanity's engagement with the natural world as the means to spiritual elevation. At one point, "I finally sat down in a valley and transferred my winged thoughts from things corporeal to the immaterial."[38] Then came a scary thought:

> Thus I turned over the last ten years in my mind, and then, fixing my anxious gaze on the future, I asked myself, "If, perchance, thou shouldst prolong this uncertain life of thine for yet two lusters, and shouldst make an advance toward virtue proportionate to the distance to which thou hast departed from thine original infatuation during the past two years, since the new longing first encountered the old, couldst thou, on reaching thy fortieth year, face death, if not with complete assurance, at least with hopefulness, calmly dismissing from thy thoughts the residuum of life as it faded into old age?"[39]

Such a distressing question was met by further conviction when Petrarch looked at the mountain regions around him, opened Augustine, only to discover the wisdom he had overlooked for so long:

> While I was thus dividing my thoughts, now turning my attention to some terrestrial object that lay before me, now raising my soul, as I had done my body, to higher places, it occurred to me to look into my copy of St. Augustine's *Confessions*. ... I opened the compact little volume ... [and] where I first fixed my eyes it was written: "And men go about to wonder at the heights of the mountains, and the mighty waves of the sea, and the wide sweep of rivers, and the circuit of the ocean, and the revolution of the stars, but themselves they consider not." I was abashed, and ... I closed the book, angry with myself that I should still be admiring earthly things who might long ago have learned from even the pagan philosophers that nothing is wonderful but the soul, which, when great itself, finds nothing great outside itself. ... What I had there read I believed to be addressed to me and to no other, remembering that St. Augustine had once suspected

37. Petrarch, *Letter to Posterity*, 27.
38. Petrarch, *Ascent of Mount Ventoux*, in *Civilization of the Italian Renaissance*, 31.
39. Petrarch, *Ascent of Mount Ventoux*, 32.

the same thing in his own case, when, on opening the book of the Apostle, as he himself tells us, the first words that he saw there were, "Not in rioting and drunkenness, not in chambering and wantonness, not in strife and envying. But put ye on the Lord Jesus Christ, and make not provision for the flesh, to fulfill the lusts thereof."[40]

Petrarch's transformation is no doubt indebted to Augustine and the Scriptures, both of which led him to abandon the lusts of the flesh for the bliss of the spirit. Yet that transformation was not antithetical with his humanist interests but complementary. In his story, Petrarch mentioned how even the "pagan philosophers" understood that "nothing is wonderful but the soul." Since the context is Augustine's *Confessions*, Petrarch may have had in mind Plato and the Platonist philosophers. Following Augustine, Petrarch became an advocate for Plato's philosophy, which he considered a buttress to his humanist inclinations. The humanist in Petrarch valued the goodness of creation and believed humankind was the pinnacle of God's artwork. Yet the goodness of creation led Petrarch to turn his attention to the essence of human nature, namely, the soul. By doing so, his own soul was released from the shackles of sin to contemplate the goodness of his Creator. That move was both Platonic and Augustinian and for Petrarch entirely Christian.

Petrarch, however, considered medieval Scholasticism a barrier to that vision. As mentioned, Kristeller listed three reasons Renaissance humanists criticized Scholasticism—inferior Latin, neglect of classical antiquity, and obsession with irrelevant, speculative questions. Petrarch voiced these three criticisms of Scholasticism.[41] And, as his *The Ascent of Mount Ventoux* spelled out, Petrarch considered both the rhetorical style and the spiritual focus of an Augustine superior to the Scholastics. The Scholastics would have been shocked to hear this contrast considering their own commitment to Augustine's theology and spirituality.

Gemistos Plethon, Marsilio Ficino, and the Platonic Academy

Petrarch was not the only one who turned against Aristotelian Scholasticism and favored Platonist Augustinianism, as manifested in Gemistos Plethon (1355–1450) and his book *On the Difference between Plato and Aristotle*. Plethon, too, considered Platonism and Christianity compatible, and no one embodied that synthesis more than Augustine. Plethon was succeeded by Marsilio Ficino (1433–99) whose patron was Lorenzo de' Medici (1449–92). The Medici family gained a reputation for funding some of the most impressive humanists of the fifteenth century, from Pico della Mirandola to Michelangelo himself. With Medici's support, Ficino started an academy at his patron's villa in Careggi,

---

40. Petrarch, *Ascent of Mount Ventoux*, 33.
41. See Bartlett, *Civilization of the Italian Renaissance*, 26.

an academy that carried on Plethon's dedication to Plato's thought but also Plato's heirs, philosophers such as Plotinus, for example.

Ficino and his Platonic Academy (1462) were instrumental to the synthesis between Neoplatonism and Christianity during the Italian Renaissance. Ficino's book *Platonic Theology* (1474) demonstrated that Florentine Neoplatonists could harmonize Christianity and Greek philosophy in a way that did not hinder but advanced the pursuit of truth.[42] (Ironically, as long as the pursuit of truth—wherever it can be found—was primary, the Italian Renaissance humanists had more in common with medieval Scholastics than they knew, even if they disagreed on sources and style.) Or consider Ficino's *Commentary on Plato's Symposium on Love*, which described the soul's beauty and immortality in both scriptural and platonic terms. Diotima addressed Socrates, asking,

> But what is it that I urge you to love in the soul? The beauty of the soul. The beauty of bodies is a light; the beauty of the soul is also a light. The light of the soul is truth, which is the only thing which your friend Plato seems to ask of God in his prayers:
>
> > Grant to me, O God, he says, that my soul may become beautiful, and that those things which pertain to the body may not impair the beauty of the soul, and that I may think only the wise man rich.
>
> In this prayer Plato says that the beauty of the soul consists in truth and wisdom, and that it is given to men by God. Truth, which is given to us by God single and uniform, through its various effects acquires the names of various virtues.[43]

After defining these virtues—both intellectual and moral—Ficino left his readers with an imperative: "Seek first the single truth of the moral virtues, the most beautiful light of the soul." Within these moral virtues the "beauty of the soul" resides. Here Ficino's Neoplatonism connected to his Christianity since "the perfectly simple light of the One itself is infinite beauty."[44] For Ficino, the One who is perfect light and infinite beauty is none other than God. "Thus the light and beauty of God, which is utterly pure and free of all other things, may be called without the slightest question, infinite beauty." If he is infinite beauty, then the soul's beauty finds its culmination when it loves this God without reserve. "But infinite beauty also requires immense love. Therefore I beg you, O Socrates, to love other things with a certain moderation and limit, but to love God with an infinite love, and let there be no moderation in divine love."[45]

---

42. "Indeed, Christian religion was seen as perfectly compatible with the thought of the Platonists and formed a part of the belief in the unity of all truth." Bartlett, *Civilization of the Italian Renaissance*, 96.

43. Ficino, *Commentary on Plato's Symposium on Love*, 101.

44. Ficino, 101.

45. Ficino, 102. To see the humanist vision for the ascent of the soul through moral virtues, consult Giovanni Pico della Mirandola's *Oration on the Dignity of Man*, 104–8.

OPPOSITION: SAVONAROLA

Italian humanism had its critics. Girolamo Savonarola (1452–98), for example, was hostile toward Ficino and his program. Savonarola started in the Dominican order and, like other Dominicans, took preaching to be his calling. But Savonarola put a fiery edge on his preaching, one with a political verve as well. Not only did he strive to take down Medici's influence in the Florentine Republic, but he also attempted to expunge Ficino's classical program. Surely Jerusalem will only be corrupted by Athens, a mentality that led Savonarola to extinguish classical texts wherever they were found. To his credit, Savonarola did not discriminate: he not only decried the influence of Medici in politics and Ficino in education, but the papacy in religion. According to Savonarola, Pope Alexander VI was corrupt, as were most popes of the Renaissance era. Not only was Savonarola excommunicated, but when his political clout was undermined by the incoming French, the protester was burned at the stake in Florence just on the eve of the Reformation in 1498.

For further context to Savonarola's political and religious reform, see Bartlett, ed., *The Civilization of the Italian Renaissance*, 220.

In sum, many a Florentine Neoplatonist considered Greek philosophy and Christianity compatible, and many were even convinced the former was a pathway to the latter. As Giovanni Pico della Mirandola once said, using Jacob's ladder as an illustration, if we climb the ladder of moral philosophy, "we shall be made perfect with the felicity of theology." Therefore, "let us bathe in moral philosophy as if in a living river."[46]

Northern Europe: Variegated Humanists and Scholastic Reception

As Renaissance humanism spread, it transcended geographical and cultural boundaries. While it thrived in Italy (especially Florence), its spirit also entranced France, Switzerland, and England, as well as Germany and Spain.[47] Sometimes the spread of Italian humanism was direct, moving from Italy to Northern Europe. Marsilio Ficino was a mentor to the French humanist Jacques Lefevre d'Étaples (ca. 1460–1536), for example. Ficino's Platonic Academy also received the English humanist John Colete (1467–1519), who came to Florence after his studies at Oxford. When he left the Platonic Academy in 1496 and returned to Oxford, Colet mimicked the anti-Scholastic spirit of his Italian mentors, though within the first decade of the sixteenth century, Colet also turned his criticisms toward the church for its credulous trust in the visible at the neglect of the invisible, the spiritual.

---

46. Mirandol, *Oration on the Dignity of Man*, 108.

47. Its pervasiveness across Europe also meant it transcended religious conflict, imbibed by Italian and French Catholics to be sure, but inhaled just the same albeit in various forms by first- and second-generation Reformers on the Continent.

Yet sometimes the influence of Italian humanism on Northern Europe was more indirect, through literary publications. The Italian humanist Lorenzo Valla, for instance, had a major influence on a Dutch humanist like Erasmus due to Valla's notes on the text of the New Testament, an influence that aided Erasmus in his publication of the Greek New Testament.

As humanism spread, many of its core emphases were retained, although its appropriation sometimes changed depending on the priorities of humanists in any specific country. Some humanists like Erasmus envisioned a transcending universal humanism so attached to classical culture that it became detached from nationalist commitments. Yet others, especially in Germany, were more concerned with how humanism might elevate nationalism in their country.[48] Some humanists in Italy could carry notable disdain for Scholasticism, as could humanists in northern Europe like Erasmus. However, humanists in Spain welcomed Scholasticism.

While other examples of diversity between Italian and northern European humanism could be listed, that last one deserves attention for its inimitability. In Spain the worlds of humanism and Scholasticism did not collide like they did in Italy and France. One major reason why concerns the influence of Francisco Ximènez de Cisneros (1436–1517), a Franciscan who rose in prominence during the 1490s as priest to Queen Isabella and archbishop of Toledo. Cisneros possessed considerable affection for Scholastics like Thomas Aquinas and saw no conflict between his Thomism and humanism whatsoever. One reason why: many of the Spanish humanists were, like other humanists across Europe, lovers of Augustine. But a close comparison of Augustine and Thomas Aquinas reveals the influence of the former on the latter. In fact, as chapter 4 conveyed, Thomas considered himself Augustinian in many of his convictions. The Spanish humanists, therefore, saw more continuity than discontinuity between Augustine and Thomas, or even Scholasticism in general.

As a result, Neo-Thomism became the great interest of Spanish universities in the fourteenth and early fifteenth centuries, lecturers and students alike exploring both classical literature and Thomas's *Summa*. They were merely following the example of the archbishop. Cisneros set apart humanists at the University of Alcala (which Cisneros himself established at the turn of the sixteenth century) to the Complutensian Polyglot Bible, perhaps a pinnacle example of what the humanist program can produce when devoted to the ancient languages. Yet Cisneros also implemented the study of Thomas in the classrooms of his university. Unlike other Europeans, humanist endeavors and Scholastic ambitions were not antithetical but complementary in the minds of many Spanish.[49]

---

48. For humanists with nationalist desires, consult those in Germany (Rudolf Agricola, Sebastian Brant, Conrad Celtis, Jacob Wimpfeling, Willibald Pirckheimer, Johannes Reuchlin, Crotus Rubeanus, Ulrich von Hutten, et al.).

49. Needham, *Two Thousand Years of Christ's Power*, 3:36–37.

However, one of the most famous humanists, Erasmus, did not mute his animosity toward Scholasticism.

ERASMUS OF ROTTERDAM

Northern European humanism did not begin and end with the Dutch scholar Erasmus (1466–1536). But the story of humanism is incomplete without Erasmus, one of its greatest advocates and most impressive talents.

Portrait of Erasmus of Rotterdam,
Quentin Massys, 1517
Public Domain

Erasmus had a hard childhood.[50] At only thirteen, he lost his mother to the plague. Erasmus was a young student in Deventer (Netherlands) at the time, a school that prided itself on some of its most impressive graduates, spiritualists like Thomas à Kempis and Nicholas of Cusa. The plague that took his mother then took his classmates, but somehow Erasmus survived. To escape the grip of the plague, Erasmus left Deventer and was sent to a different school in 's-Hertogenbosch. This new school, the Brethren of the Common Life, had a lasting influence on Erasmus because of its serious focus on Christian godliness. The Brethren of the Common Life criticized the type of religious conformity that masked itself in intellectual pride. Instead, they emphasized the necessity of genuine, heartfelt conviction, a type of piety indebted no doubt to the medieval school of the modern devotion. Some speculate whether Erasmus's *philosophia Christi* grew out of this monastic experience with the Brethren of the Common Life.[51] At the very least, Erasmus's interest in humanism sprouted during these formative years as the young thinker started writing what would later become his published works.[52]

Yet Erasmus's humanism always grew within the soil of his religious commitments. When Erasmus came under the supervision of the bishop of Cambrai, Henry of Bergen, the budding humanist was ordained as a priest in 1492. Nevertheless, Erasmus never did take up the life of a monk for good. Grateful as he was for the Brethren, he had aspirations for humanist scholarship that could not be contained. In 1495 those aspirations started to materialize when

---

50. The details of Erasmus's life have been chronicled by many: see Levi, "Introduction," xi-lvi; Bainton, *Erasmus of Christendom.*

51. Erasmus "took the term *philosophia Christi* from [Rudolf] Agricola." Levi, "Introduction," xxxviii.

52. Note his work *Anti-Barbari,* for example.

Erasmus traveled to Paris, where he met other like-minded humanists. During his stay in Paris, Erasmus continued to write, producing both his *Colloquies* and his *Adages*. Erasmus also developed key connections, like his friendship with William Blount Lord Mountjoy.

In Erasmus's day a humanist required a patron; otherwise, it was almost impossible to devote oneself to intense, consuming study of classical literature and languages. Lord Mountjoy became the patron Erasmus needed to free him up to pursue his publications. Patrons were also key because of their networks; they were capable of sharing their connections with those they sponsored. Lord Mountjoy, for instance, introduced Erasmus to life in Oxford, England, starting in 1499, where he first met other humanists who eventually became his closest colleagues—English humanists such as John Colet and Thomas More. In time these friendships also gave Erasmus the opportunity to practice writing letters, an art essential to humanism. Modern scholarship now recognizes that Erasmus was one of the greatest men of letters, each one displaying his humanist spirit. These humanists introduced Erasmus to Platonism, one of the standout marks of Italian humanism that had made its way into northern European humanist circles. As will be seen, Erasmus utilized the Platonist worldview to make sense of the Pauline emphases on the spiritual (as opposed to the flesh), the latter of which he first encountered in the experiential piety of the Brethren of the Common Life.

Erasmus's Debt to Italian Humanist Lorenzo Valla

The year 1499 and the years that followed were critical for Erasmus and his future career. At the start of the next year, Erasmus left Oxford for Paris to publish his *Adages*, but he did not stay long. Erasmus traveled across Europe, desperate to keep himself safe from the plague, but he also took advantage of his travels to immerse himself in the writings of classical and patristic literature. From 1501 to 1504 Erasmus stayed in Holland. The timing was providential: he read for the humanist Lorenzo Valla, including his annotations on the text of the New Testament, and in 1505 Erasmus published Valla's notes. Over a decade later, when Erasmus published his Greek New Testament, these notes were instrumental to questioning the Vulgate's Latin.[53] The significance of Valla and his scholarship cannot be overemphasized. Apart from Valla's study of the New Testament, Erasmus may not have turned into the Erasmus so many recognize today.[54]

At the start of the fifteenth century, Lorenzo Valla was born and bred on Italian humanism. As a young, budding humanist, he could be found in the court of Alfonso I. Valla knew Italian humanists who criticized the pope and his cardinals. Criticism was not unprecedented, but Valla gave credence to their criticisms when he made the discovery of the millennium—that the famous

---

53. Valla wrote others works that influenced Erasmus as well, such as *The Glory of the Latin Language*. See Gragg, *Latin Writings of the Italian Humanists*; cf. Bartlett, *Civilization of the Italian Renaissance*, 80–82.

54. Battles and Hugo, "Introduction," 28.

Donation of Constantine was a forgery. The Donation of Constantine said Rome and the entire Western Empire belonged to the pope. The document reported that Constantine had turned over the authority of his empire to the papacy without reservation. On this basis, the popes ever since exercised their authority over ecclesiastical and political domains, commanding militaries and waging wars. However, Lorenzo Valla examined the document and proved that it was not authentic. The discovery discredited the papacy overnight and was a major embarrassment for an ecclesiastical empire that rested so much of its authority on the claims of the document. In 1440 Valla wrote *On the False Donation of Constantine*, and with humanist verve he said the following:

> I understand that the ears of men have been waiting for a long time to hear with what crime I am about to charge the Roman Pontiffs. Surely it is a most serious crime, of either lackadaisical ignorance or enormous greed, which is a form of idolatry, or the vain will to power, which is always accompanied by cruelty. In fact, for several centuries now either the Popes have not understood that the donation of Constantine is a forgery and a fabrication, or they have invented it themselves, else, as followers treading in the footsteps of their predecessors' deceit, they have defended it as being true, even while knowing it was false. Thus they have disgraced the dignity of the Pontificate and the memory of the early Popes, dishonored the Christian religion and caused general confusion with their massacres, destruction, and shameful actions. They say that theirs are the city of Rome, the Kingdom of Sicily and Naples, the whole of Italy, Gaul, Spain, the lands of the Germans and Britons, and, finally, all of the West. And all these things, purportedly are contained in the document describing the donation. Are these lands then all yours, oh Supreme Pontiff? Do you intend to recover all of them? Do you plan to strip all the kings and princes in the West of their cities or compel them to pay annual taxes to you? On the contrary, I deem it to be more just if the rulers are allowed to deprive you of all the dominion you hold, since, as I shall demonstrate, that donation, from which the Popes claim their rights derive, was unknown either to Pope Sylvester or to the Emperor Constantine.[55]

The tide was turning, and budding humanists like Erasmus eventually joined the chorus with sarcastic tracts that exposed corruption in the church. But first Erasmus needed to establish himself with a contribution that presented his vision for renewal.

Philosophi Christi, Christian Platonism, and Allegory

To his surprise, Erasmus's most popular work was a book he published in 1503 called *Handbook [Enchiridion] of the Christian Soldier*, a book that outlined

---

55. Valla, *The Principal Arguments from the Falsely-Believed and Forged Donation of Constantine*, 206–7.

his program for Christian renewal.[56] The *Enchiridion* advances what Erasmus called the philosophy of Christ, a pious pursuit of ethical fidelity, the kind exemplified by Christ himself. Erasmus believed Christianity and the Christian life are, in essence, about imitating Christ. To emulate Christ, the Christian must battle against the flesh (which brings death) and follow instead the spirit (which breathes life).

Erasmus's contrast between flesh and spirit is the key to understanding his marriage between Christianity and ancient, classical thought. On one hand, the battle between flesh and spirit is a Pauline emphasis, and Erasmus was astute to point that out. That Pauline emphasis is one reason why Erasmus encouraged the Christian to return to the Scriptures for guidance. For "there is no attack of the enemy so violent, that is, no temptation so formidable, that an eager study of the Scriptures will not easily beat it off."[57]

On the other hand, Erasmus coupled the Pauline emphasis with logic from ancient Greek philosophy.[58] Those enslaved by the flesh are like those still stuck in Plato's cave, groping around in the darkness, unable to see that the shadows on the cave's wall are not the real thing but copies of the real thing in the world outside the cave. "The crowd consists of those who in that Platonic cave, chained to their passions, admire as the truest things what are really empty images of things." The way out of the cave, the way to be free from the passions of the flesh, is nothing less than the morality of Christ or the "rule of Christ."[59] The Christian Platonism of Augustine is a prime example. He was lost in the darkness of lust, but when he put on Christ, he left the pleasures of the flesh behind and entered the light.[60]

Erasmus made a habit of coupling Platonism with the church fathers—a move not hard to substantiate since fathers in the East and West critically appropriated Platonism (see chapter 5). Augustine was not the only example. Origen also loomed large in Erasmus's estimation. Turning to Origen's commentary on Romans, Erasmus appreciated how Origen connected the spirit to divinity. "The spirit represents in us the likeness of the divine nature." If true, then the "Spirit renders us gods," but the flesh renders us animals. The dichotomy is discernible: "If, renouncing the flesh, it [the soul] conducts itself toward the parts of the spirit, it will likewise become spiritual. But if it once abandons itself to the desires of the flesh, it will degenerate likewise into the body."[61]

With ancient voices like Plato, Virgil, and Horace on one shoulder, and ancient fathers like Jerome, Origen, and Augustine on the other shoulder, Erasmus put forward twenty-two rules, each of which in their own way advocate

---

56. Although some wonder whether the *Enchiridion* was published in 1504 instead.

57. Erasmus, *Enchiridion*, 303.

58. Erasmus was adamant that the Platonists were the way forward because they "approach as closely as possible the prophetic and Gospel pattern." Erasmus, *Enchiridion*, 305.

59. Erasmus, *Enchiridion*, 350.

60. Erasmus, *Enchiridion*, 352.

61. Erasmus, *Enchiridion*, 319.

for the law of Christ. For Erasmus, Christianity was about loving Christ and living for Christ. As his fourth rule stated, "Set before you Christ as the only goal of your whole life, to whom alone you dedicate all zeal, all efforts, all leisure and business. . . . Let it [your eye] gaze toward Christ alone, your sole and highest good, so that you may love nothing, be in awe of nothing, seeking after nothing, other than Christ himself, or for Christ's sake."[62]

With this goal in mind, a goal that presupposed the contrast between flesh and spirit, Erasmus issued a strong warning against the "visible world" (in contrast to the "intelligible world").[63] Two implications follow: (1) Erasmus was irritated with literal interpretations of the Bible, and (2) Erasmus was disgusted with superstitious, external ceremonies. Consider each.

First, Erasmus was impatient with those "theologians" (he named Duns Scotus as an example) who majored on the literal reading of Scripture but had no place for the allegorical. That is death. Without the allegorical, the "mystery" is lost and with it the "spiritual." Paul knew this, and so did the best patristic interpreters. "Now the apostle Paul opened certain fountains of allegory after Christ. Origen follows him. . . . But our theologians either almost despise allegory or actually treat it coldly, for they are either equal or superior to the ancients in the sharpness of their disputation."[64] That is a colossal mistake, for the allegorical component of the text takes the Christian beyond the historical setting to its spiritual significance. Erasmus advocated the following allegiance:

> From the interpreters of Holy Scripture choose those especially who depart as much as possible from the literal sense. Of this sort, after Paul, among the first are Origen, Ambrose, Jerome, Augustine. For I see the modern theologians too freely and with a certain captious subtlety drinking in the letter, rather than plucking out the mysteries and giving their attention (as if Paul had not spoken the truth) to the fact that our law is spiritual. . . . To such an extent has Duns Scotus brought confidence to them that, without ever having read the Holy Scriptures, they nevertheless think themselves to be absolute theologians.[65]

For Erasmus, a literalistic hermeneutic, when treated as sufficient, leads to a cold letter, a letter that kills. But if the reader follows the ancients, he will be "animated in spirit" rather than "trained in contention" like moderns. For the allegorical takes the reader to Christ and his gospel where life can be found.[66]

Second, Erasmus's emphasis on spirit over letter, allegory as opposed to merely literal interpretation, also motivated his admonishment toward overreliance on externals. Erasmus rebuked monks and their monasteries for a "monastic piety"

---

62. Erasmus, *Enchiridion*, 328.
63. Consider his fifth rule. Erasmus, *Enchiridion*, 332.
64. He blamed this mistake on their bent toward Aristotle instead of Plato. Erasmus, *Enchiridion*, 334.
65. Erasmus, *Enchiridion*, 305.
66. Erasmus, *Enchiridion*, 306.

that "grows cold, languishes, disappears on every side for no other reason than that the monks grow old and gray in the letter, and do not escape to the spiritual understanding of the Scriptures." As a result, they failed to "hear Christ in the Gospel proclaiming, 'The flesh profits nothing; it is the spirit that makes alive.'"[67]

Consider relics as an example. Erasmus did not think relics were intrinsically wrong. But he did believe they had been misappropriated. "You gaze in dumb amazement at the tunic or sweat cloth reputedly Christ's, yet half asleep you read the utterances of Christ?" You believe it to be much more important that you possess a small piece of the cross in your house. Yet this latter is nothing in comparison with bearing the mystery of the cross fixed in your breast."[68] Erasmus worried that the visible was calling Christians—ironically enough—away from Christ rather than toward Christ. Ceremonies, indulgences, and relics alike only create superstition.[69] True Christianity is not about what is seen but what is unseen, not about externals but what lies within the heart. Christianity concerns the spiritual life.[70]

Statements like these created no little stir. While the papacy depended on endless ceremonies for advancement in spirituality, Erasmus claimed renovation was not dependent on the system. The Christian may go to a priest for confession and penance, but he did not have to. Instead, heart change could occur right away when the Christian prayed straight to God. By claiming the Christian can go directly to God and need not depend on the clergy, Erasmus was also reorienting the source of Christian authority. Erasmus located Christianity's driving force in the churchgoer's spiritual devotion, not in the authority of the priest. Consequently, the path to renewal was not from the top down but from the bottom up. For that to happen, however, the laity needed access to the Scriptures in their most accurate form. Problem was, the Latin text was littered with translation mistakes, mistakes that created and cultivated the clerical system counterproductive to the renewal of the laity. It was a vicious circle, and *ad fontes* was the only way to break out.[71]

Moral versus Theological Reform: Erasmus, Luther, and Tyndale

Erasmus's *Enchiridion* approximates a Protestant spirituality because of its Christ-centered focus, a focus not foreign to the church fathers Erasmus appropriated. The book influenced many Reformers as they wrestled with the compatibility of their Augustinian theology and Erasmian spirituality. Nonetheless, the *Enchiridion* should not be confused with the program of the Reformation, whatever similarities exist. The reason is plain enough: the gospel and the grace it effects are missing. That may be an alarming claim; after all, Erasmus made the New

---

67. Erasmus, *Enchiridion*, 306.
68. Erasmus, *Enchiridion*, 338.
69. He went so far as to call it the new Judaism! See Erasmus, *Enchiridion*, 340.
70. Erasmus, *Enchiridion*, 341.
71. "Scripture should and must be made available to all, in order that all may return *ad fontes*, to drink of the fresh and living waters of the Christian faith, rather than the stagnant ponds of late medieval religion." McGrath, *Reformation Thought*, 48.

Testament his guide in his quest for Christian piety. Nevertheless, Christology—the type of Christology that led Luther not merely to *moralistic* changes but *theological* renovations—is absent. Erasmus's "punches were pulled," said David Daniell. "The activity of Christ in the Gospels, his special work of salvation so strongly detailed there and in the Epistles of Paul, is largely missing. Christologically, where Luther thunders, Erasmus makes a sweet sound: what to Tyndale was an impregnable stronghold feels in the *Enchiridion* like a summer pavilion."[72]

The Erasmus-Luther contrast exposes the absence of an evangelical conviction. Yet a contrast with Tyndale, an equally dedicated student of the languages, reveals the same. While Erasmus limited himself to the Greek and Latin, Tyndale took a step further by translating the Greek into the vernacular. Why take such a risk that could end in death? Erasmus did not take the risk. Tyndale did because he was convinced that translating the Scriptures into the vernacular was synonymous with making the evangelical view of grace accessible in the vernacular. Erasmus may have been discontent with abuses in the church of Rome, but he was not so discontent with the church's theology to put his own life on the line like Tyndale. Erasmus may have inspired other humanist endeavors, but Tyndale inspired a reformation. The difference was between *philosophia Christi* and *solus Christus*.[73]

Another major difference surfaces as well. Erasmus's *Enchiridion* possesses a subtle moralistic snark, which is ironic since the point of the book is to help the Christian soldier cultivate the morality of Christ. *Enchiridion* is a humanist piece of art, but it is coated by an elitist tone of preeminence, as if the humanist considers theology and its emphatic emphases irrelevant at best and embarrassing at worst.[74]

One could object that Erasmus did not say so in so many words. True. However, the spirit of the book coupled by what Erasmus did say in the 1520s adds incredible support to such a claim. For good reason, Erasmus's hero was Jerome, the translator critical of Augustine's anti-Pelagian rhetoric at points, while Luther's hero was Augustine, the theologian of grace. As chapter 8 will explain, this difference between Erasmus the humanist and Luther the theologian will become painfully conspicuous in their debate over the bondage of the will. Luther is characterized by a weighty theological urgency that is lacking in Erasmus, in part because the humanist did not interpret the state of theology at a crisis point as did Luther. Of course, Luther was not the only one. Again, a comparison of Erasmus and Tyndale communicates something similar: Tyndale was "ferociously single-minded." For the English Reformer, "the immediate access of

---

72. Daniell, *William Tyndale*, 69.
73. Daniell, 69.
74. "Not only is there no fully realized Christ or Devil in Erasmus's book for the Christian knight: there is a touch of irony about it all, with a feeling of the writer cultivating a faintly superior ambiguity: as if to be dogmatic, for example, about the full theology of the work of Christ was to be rather distasteful, below the best, elite, humanist heights." Daniell, 69.

the soul to God without intermediary, is far too important for hints of faintly ironic superiority [Erasmus]."[75]

Erasmus's Disdain for Scholastics, Monks, and Ecclesiastical Corruption

After his stay in Holland from 1501 to 1504, Erasmus traveled to Paris once again, only to make his way to England in 1505. Erasmus went hard to work translating Lucian (published 1506), a translation that occupied Erasmus for the next half a decade. In 1505 Erasmus did not translate Lucian alone, but he teamed up with Thomas More, who was becoming a close colleague of Erasmus. It is no accident that Erasmus wrote his *Praise of Folly*, one of his most biting satires, after he read and first set his mind to translating Lucian.[76] Erasmus had been deeply influenced by the king of satire himself. Lucian was a master at sarcasm, using comedy to expose foolishness and mock superstition. Erasmus was not the only one; More was influenced by Lucian just the same, as is plain in More's *Utopia*.

However, before Erasmus wrote *Praise of Folly*, he transitioned from England to Italy, where he lodged from 1506 to 1509. Those years were a turning point in his career. He received his doctorate in theology, which he started in Paris and was then awarded in Turin, Italy. The question now remained: Could Erasmus rise in the ranks of the Roman church? The longer Erasmus stayed, the more jaded he became toward the papacy. His disenchantment stemmed from several factors: Pope Julius II's involvement in warfare, the clergy's avarice manifested by taxation of the underprivileged, and a general inattention to the laity, among other failings.[77] Although Erasmus could have stayed in Italy and pursued a clerical promotion, his discouragement motivated his return to England, liberating him to write a sharp critique of the corruptions he resented. All this left a bitter taste in the mouth of Erasmus, who first came to Italy anticipating transformation due to the influence of the Italian Renaissance, only to discover corruption and superstition. This was not the Italy he read about from other humanists. The pope's religion had advanced in externals (politics, finances, etc.), but where was its spiritual effect on the hearts of the people? Erasmus's experience was not all that different from Luther's when the young German visited Rome.

When Erasmus arrived on English soil, where he stayed planted from 1509 to 1511, he went to his friend Thomas More and started writing *Praise of Folly*.

---

75. Daniell, 69. "Did Erasmus seriously believe that a successful, vigorous, amoral, independent arms trader [who inspired the writing of the book] might by some chance engineered by his pious wife settle down and study a rambling, rather disorganised Latin monologue on virtue, illuminated by reference to the best classical-humanist texts and the earlier Fathers, and as a result solemnly leave his mistress and his energetic ways for his wife's extreme piety? Even that assumes that the man could read and understand Latin" (70). Again, Daniell put his finger on the nerve: while a Luther or a Tyndale was primarily concerned with reaching the common person with the evangelical gospel and its grace, Erasmus was stuck within a humanist paradigm, with its "faintly superior ambiguity" that had little ability to effect change in the common Christian.

76. Erasmus was not alone. More wrote *Utopia*, which also utilized Lucian's technique to tear down the type of society built by the fool.

77. Levi, "Introduction," in *Praise of Folly*, xliv.

Taking a page from Lucian, Erasmus mocked each corner of the medieval world—Scholasticism, monasteries, papacy—and without mercy. The humanist learned Scholasticism from his teachers and watched his peers as they embraced its methods at the University of Paris. As they considered deep questions about God and the cosmos, Erasmus grew impatient.[78] For good reason, interpreters often say that Erasmus gave birth to the egg Luther hatched. However, the danger in such a saying is overlooking the obvious: Erasmus was no friend to theology—cynical in his disdain for dialectical reasoning, trumpeting rhetoric instead (to be exact: *theologia rhetorica*).[79] Not until 1525, when Luther and Erasmus battled over the bondage of the will, did the public recognize the latter was no sympathizer with the Reformation. Yet a close reading of his *Praise of Folly* manifests early signs of severe incompatibility between him and the Reformation. Granted, Erasmus's direct target was Scholasticism, not the Reformation, but Erasmus's disdain for Scholasticism revealed his secondary bias against the Reformation's continued use of the Scholastic method and its classical metaphysic. As will become evident, Erasmus cared far more about imitating Christ than deciphering theological debates over Christ.

In *Praise of Folly* Erasmus's distrust toward the Schoolmen exhibits itself in several satirical roasts. The Schoolmen "interpret hidden mysteries to suit themselves" he said, such as "how the world was created and designed; through what channels the stain of sin filtered down to posterity; by what means, in what measure, and how long Christ was formed in the Virgin's womb.... What was the exact moment of divine generation? Are there several filiations in Christ? Is it a possible proposition that God the Father could hate his Son? Could God have taken on the form of a woman, a devil, a donkey, a gourd, or a flint-stone?"[80] Erasmus called these "subtle refinements of subtleties" and "tortuous obscurities," and although he listed a litany of Scholastic schools that he held responsible, he blamed the Scotists in particular, those late medieval Scholastics.[81]

Erasmus aimed to expose the silliness of these Scholastic questions when he compared their interests and methods with those of the apostles. For example, consider the Eucharist. "The apostles consecrated the Eucharist with due piety, but had they been questioned about the *terminus a quo* and the *terminus ad quem*, about transubstantiation, and how the same body can be in different places ... they wouldn't, in my opinion have shown the same subtlety in their reply as the Scotists do in their dissertations and definitions."[82] Or consider

---

78. McGrath, *Reformation Thought*, 59.
79. Rummel, "The theology of Erasmus," 33; Trinkaus, *The Scope of Renaissance Humanism*.
80. Erasmus, *Praise of Folly*, 86–87.
81. He listed the "realists, nominalists, Thomists, Albertists, Ockhamists and Scotists" as the main sects. Erasmus, *Praise of Folly*, 88. However, Erasmus had a special vitriol for Scotus. In all kinds of ways, he referred to Scotus: the "reincarnation of Scotus himself" (100); "call on the spirit of Scotus" (116); etc. He also aimed at Scotus (in Erasmus, *Enchiridion*, 305–6), and said Scotus trained his disciples in contention, whereas the ancients were far more concerned with the soul's piety. In the mind of Erasmus, the ancients possessed the spirit that makes alive, while Scotus advocated the letter that kills.
82. Erasmus, *Praise of Folly*, 90.

Mary: "The apostles knew personally the mother of Jesus, but which of them proved how she had been kept immaculate from Adam's sin with the logic our theologians display?" Or consider baptism. "The apostles baptized wherever they went, yet nowhere did they teach the formal, material, efficient, and final cause of baptism, nor did they ever mention the delible and indelible marks of the sacraments." Erasmus, in other words, thought the focus, interests, and methods of New Testament Christians could not be more different than Scotist-like Scholastics. While the former cared about the spiritual state of sinners, the latter only cared about fine discussions of metaphysics. While the former cared about Jesus, the latter were more interested in Aristotle. After all, "Who *could* understand all this unless he has frittered away thirty-six whole years over the physics and metaphysics of Aristotle and Scotus?"[83]

In view of chapter 4's correction of caricatures, it should be plain that Erasmus's depiction of Scholasticism paints with too broad a brush. Erasmus was also inaccurate in his depiction of Scholastic motives, and he misrepresented the Scholastic attention to the biblical text. However, Erasmus could be persuasive in his day as he condemned the "Scotist spirit" and the "subtleties of the schoolmen" and mocked the "pigheaded Ockhamists."[84] Erasmus's contrast between the apostles and pagan philosophers made his rhetoric sound persuasive. According to Erasmus, the two had nothing to do with each other; in fact, the "apostles certainly refuted pagan philosophers." To mix the two is to corrupt the holy with the unholy. "Others too think it a damnable form of sacrilege and the worst sort of impiety for anyone to speak of matters so holy, which call for reverence rather than explanation, with a profane tongue, or to argue with the pagan subtlety of the heathen, presume to offer definitions, and pollute the majesty of divine theology with words and sentiments which are so trivial and even squalid."[85] *Reverence rather than explanation*—that summarizes Erasmus's approach to theology, and in 1525 it also motivated Erasmus to turn his wrath from Scholasticism toward Luther, who violated this boundary. For Erasmus, Christianity was about imitating Christ; doctrinal discussions and debates only got in the way of that holy goal. That explains why Erasmus never joined Luther's Reformation. The point deserves repeated emphasis: Luther was not merely advocating moral reform as forerunners before him, but a theological reform that hinged on doctrinal clarity and renewal.[86]

The Scholastics were not by any means the only targets in *Praise of Folly*. Among many others, monks and monasteries also came under humanist attack. Again, the reason why had to do with Erasmus's view of Christianity. The Christian religion is concerned not with external rituals but with the internal condition of the soul. Erasmus, therefore, had no patience for the show of

83. Erasmus, *Praise of Folly*, 91.
84. Erasmus, *Praise of Folly*, 91, 93.
85. Erasmus, *Praise of Folly*, 93.
86. Cameron, "Reconsidering Early-Reformation and Catholic-Reform Impulses," 15.

monks: "When they bray like donkeys in church, repeating by rote the psalms they haven't understood, they imagine they are charming the ears of their heavenly audience with infinite delight."[87] Erasmus had no stomach for their hypocrisy: they "shrink from the touch of money as if it were a deadly poison, but are less restrained when it comes to wine or contact with women.... They aren't interested in being like Christ but in being unlike each other."[88] Others consider their own merits and swell up with pride and self-righteousness. "Most of them rely so much on their ceremonies and petty man-made traditions that they suppose heaven alone will hardly be enough to reward merit such as theirs." Erasmus even labeled them the "new race of Jews," which was a reference to the Judaizers of the New Testament who relied on works of the law for their right standing with God.[89] Jesus does not recognize them, said Erasmus, for they fail to fulfill the greatest commandment he gave: love for God and for one's neighbor. Erasmus reserved this same biting criticism toward externals and self-righteousness when he turned to the pomp of the papacy and its priests.[90]

The irony of *Praise of Folly* is seen in its conclusion: despite Erasmus's condemnation of the Scholastics for mixing apostolic teaching with pagan philosophy, Erasmus himself ended with an extensive appropriation of Platonism for the sake of his definition of Christian spirituality. With Plato, Erasmus appealed to the metaphor of the cave to argue that there must be something more beyond the sensible world, something ultimate, absolute, and spiritual transcending the fleshly confines of this present existence, something that draws man "towards what is eternal, invisible, and spiritual."[91] It is this belief that separates the godly from the fool.

> In the same way, the common herd of men feels admiration only for the things of the body and believes that these alone exist, whereas the pious scorn whatever concerns the body and are wholly uplifted towards the contemplation of invisible things. The ordinary man gives first place to wealth, the second to bodily comforts, and leaves the last to the soul—which anyway most people believe doesn't exist because it is invisible to the eye. By contrast, the pious direct their entire endeavour towards God, who is absolute purity, and after him towards what is closest to him, the soul.[92]

Plato was right all along.[93]

87. Erasmus, *Praise of Folly*, 96.
88. Erasmus, *Praise of Folly*, 97.
89. Erasmus, *Praise of Folly*, 98.
90. Erasmus, *Praise of Folly*, 110–11.
91. Erasmus, *Praise of Folly*, 132. When Erasmus described what life in heaven will be like, he said, the "spirit will itself be absorbed by the supreme Mind," resulting in an "eternal bliss" that "far exceeds all pleasures of the body," and the spiritual will "surpass the physical, the invisible the visible" (133).
92. Erasmus, *Praise of Folly*, 129.
93. To be technical, Erasmus was more nuanced: "Christians *come very near* to agreeing with the Platonists that the soul is stifled and bound down by the fetters of the body, which by its gross matter prevents the soul from being able to contemplate and enjoy things as they truly are." Erasmus, *Praise of Folly*, 128.

Erasmus's retrieval of Plato demonstrates that sixteenth-century rhetoric should not be taken in the most literalistic fashion. A humanist or a Reformer might have condemned a Greek philosopher one minute only to rely on them the next (and sometimes without even acknowledging their debt). Like every century before, the sixteenth century was indebted to the common notions of non-Christian philosophy—they, too, were a footnote to Plato. Despite heated rhetoric, the real question was not whether humanists and Reformers were favorable to Greek philosophers but *which* philosopher they found most complimentary to the biblical witness. For Erasmus, like many other humanists, that philosopher was Plato, which explains his rejection of Scholasticism's reliance on Aristotle.

Novum Instrumentum Omne

In 1514 Erasmus landed in Holland once again, but this time he stayed until 1521, though not without intermittent trips back to England. The longevity of his stay was key to the production of his most important humanist contribution: the Greek New Testament.

To appreciate Renaissance humanism is to appreciate its dedication to translation. Humanists put a spotlight on the Greek language, implementing the study of Greek classics into the university curriculum and printing editions of Greek classics across Europe. Yet humanists went beyond the Greek to Latin, the academic language of the day. Due to their knowledge of Greek, humanists were able to translate works of classic literature from Greek into Latin. "Almost the whole of Greek poetry, oratory, historiography, theology, and non-Aristotelian philosophy was thus translated for the first time, whereas the medieval translations of Aristotle and of Greek scientific writers were replaced by new humanistic translations. These Latin translations of the Renaissance were the basis for most of the vernacular translations of the Greek classics, and they were much more widely read than were the original Greek texts."[94]

The humanist expertise in both Greek and Latin was the stage on which Erasmus reevaluated the Vulgate's Latin and found it wanting, only to produce a Greek text of the New Testament that exposed various errors in translation. With the help of Lorenzo Valla's critical commentary on the text, Erasmus put his mind to providing a Greek text that could result in clarity, even though he did not have all the manuscripts he needed (which showed later on).[95]

In 1516 Erasmus's text was published in Basel, which gave many the opportunity to compare the Greek to the Vulgate's Latin. The differences were blatant. For example, the Vulgate translated Jesus' command as "Do penance" (Matt. 4:17), a command Rome took seriously, building an entire penance system to ensure works of satisfaction were met. But Erasmus's *Novum Instrumentum omne* read

---

94. Kristeller, *Renaissance Thought*, 97.
95. For Erasmus's dependence on the notes of Lorenzo Valla, see McGrath, *Reformation Thought*, 48.

very differently: Jesus merely said, "Repent." In other words, Jesus did not have in mind works of penance to merit favor but an internal conviction of the heart. With the arrival of the kingdom, Jesus told the people to enter into a mindset of repentance. Many other discrepancies were exposed, and with each one not only the penance system but the sacramental system itself was called into question.[96]

With these discrepancies in plain view, many now wondered whether Rome's religious system rested on shaky ground. The result of that curiosity, especially once taken up by later Reformers, was shattering. If the church had based its penance system and its seven sacraments on mistranslations, what else could be wrong? Had the gospel itself, at least the gospel according to the papacy, been miscommunicated? Some thought so. For example, after reading the New Testament in Greek, Thomas Linacre in England made a shocking admission, "Either this is not the gospel, or we are not Christians."[97]

To clarify, Erasmus was no Reformer; in fact, the Reformation had not yet begun when Erasmus's edition was printed. However, his *Novum Instrumentum omne* did build on his previous criticisms in both *Enchiridion* and *Praise of Folly*. With that momentum his humanist learning now led him to textual discoveries that inevitably threw into question the legitimacy of major religious beliefs and practices, some even foundational for the papacy. For that reason, when the Reformation did erupt, the Reformers were indebted to humanist scholarship like Erasmus, even if these humanists never finally converted to the cause of the Reformation. *Ad fontes* became their calling as well, leading them not only to revisit the Scriptures but even the writings of the church fathers. To their advantage, Erasmus not only provided a Greek text but also equipped scholarship with new, more accurate editions of the patristic corpus, from Jerome to Augustine.

Erasmus among the Humanists

Despite Erasmus's success, the leading humanist did have his detractors, some within humanism itself, others from corners of the Reformation (the latter will be considered later in this chapter). Consider differences between Erasmus and other humanists. While Erasmus and other northern European humanists agreed on the basic commitments of the Renaissance, they disagreed on implementation and global outlook. In Germany and Switzerland, for example, humanism was an opportunity to secure, preserve, and promote local ethnicity, language, and cultural values. "Where Erasmus would have preferred to concentrate upon *eliminating* nationalist ideas and values, the Swiss humanists Glarean, Myconius, and Xylotecus saw themselves as having a sacred duty to defend Swiss national identity and culture by literary means."[98]

By means of Renaissance tools—such as the publication of literature—humanists could pass down the nationalism they thought worth perpetuating.

---

96. For a more elaborate list of discrepancies, see McGrath, 49–50.
97. Quoted in McGrath, 49.
98. McGrath, 47.

Erasmus strongly disagreed with such an ethnocentric use of humanism. As a citizen of the world, the humanist should altogether transcend nationalism and subordinate his cultural commitments to cosmopolitan ideals. This debate was present in politics, law, the arts, and especially language. Instead of clinging to the German language, for example, Erasmus advocated a universal use of classical Latin.

How different from Luther, who did not devote himself to the education of the laity in the Latin tongue but committed himself to the translation of the Bible into German. Reform should be embedded within the German tongue, said Luther. While Erasmus was not against translations in the vernacular—at points he was vocal in his support—nevertheless, his humanist outlook craved a worldwide dedication to Latin above all other languages.[99]

In the end, Erasmus was far more occupied with correcting abuses in the church than inaugurating theological reform. His primary concerns were moral and social, not doctrinal reform.[100]

PICO DELLA MIRANDOLA'S DEFENSE OF FIRST PRINCIPLES ON REFORMATION EVE

On the eve of the Reformation, Scholasticism's contribution was not always appreciated. Certain humanists, like Hermolao Barbaro did not hesitate to voice stark criticisms. However, other humanists, like philosopher Giovanni Pico della Mirandola (1463–94), defended Scholasticism, reminding his colleagues that apart from Scholasticism the humanist enterprise—with its premium on the mind—had no foundation on which to stand. Barbaro concluded that Scholastics were obsessive in their meticulous exploration of divine mysteries. But Pico responded: any movement that takes truth seriously is necessarily precise. The real danger, said Pico, is a type of movement that becomes indifferent to the deep things of God, to the laborious pursuit of wisdom, and to the absolute necessity of first principles in theology.[101]

Pico worried that the caricatures of Barbaro might lead others to forget that Scholastics like Thomas Aquinas went to great lengths to wed reason to revelation. Granted, the Scholastics entertained hypothetical questions, but for those following in the trail of Thomas, the seemingly endless exploration of questions stemmed from a Christian commitment: the pilgrimage for understanding begins and ends with faith.[102]

While Barbaro measured a doctrine's importance by its usefulness, and the pastor or scholar's effectiveness by the persuasiveness of his rhetoric, Pico

---

99. Ciceronian Latin to be exact. McGrath, 47.

100. Rummel, "The theology of Erasmus," 37.

101. "Pico considered the real danger to be not that men would go too far in the investigation of first principles, as the critics of scholasticism charged, but that they might lose interest in first principles altogether." Ozment, *Age of Reform*, 80.

102. For Pico's view, see *CR*, 9:678–86; cf. Ozment, *Age of Reform*, 80–81.

believed rhetoric would only have a lasting effect if its practitioner was grounded in the pursuit of wisdom first and foremost. "They sin who tear asunder eloquence and wisdom, but what is all eloquence without understanding?" asked Pico. "We can live without language, although not well, but we cannot live at all without the mind. He who is untouched by good letters may not be humane, but he who is destitute of philosophy is no longer a man."[103]

Pico demonstrated that humanism was variegated. Some like Erasmus unleashed vitriolic disdain toward Scholasticism, while others like Mirandola expressed gratitude, recognizing academic and pastoral debt to Scholasticism's best minds.

THE REFORMATION, A DEVELOPMENT *WITHIN* THE RENAISSANCE?

Was the Renaissance a separate movement and phenomenon than the Reformation, or were the Reformers part of the Renaissance? The answer to this question is not easily answered. Real differences exist between the motives, aspirations, and goals of Renaissance humanism and the Reformation. However, it is artificial to segregate the Reformation from the Renaissance altogether for two reasons, the first historical and the second biographical.

First, the Reformation was born out of a Renaissance environment and was affected by its methods and productivity, both in direct and indirect ways. It is reasonable to ask whether the Reformation was even possible apart from the prior advances of the Renaissance. Rather than labeling the Reformation a "new epoch different from, and in a sense opposed to, the Renaissance" it is better to "consider the Reformation as an important development *within* the broader historical period which . . . we continue to call . . . the Renaissance."[104]

As mentioned, Kristeller did not assume the Renaissance was synonymous with humanism but considered the Renaissance era a big enough umbrella for both Scholastic and humanist figureheads. The Reformation developed under that same Renaissance canopy and as a result was influenced by Scholasticism and humanism alike. If more nuance is needed to avoid caricatures of the Reformation and Scholasticism (e.g., the oppositional narrative), then the same can be said of the Reformation and humanism. As chapter 4 pointed out, the Reformers took issue with certain aspects of Scholastic discourse and theology and certain high and late medieval Scholastics, but were also born into the Scholastic system and indebted to it in legions of ways. Likewise with Renaissance humanism: the Reformation was distinct from humanism, but the Reformation

---

103. *CR*, 9:686; cf. Ozment, *Age of Reform*, 81.

104. Kristeller, *Renaissance Thought*, 70. Part of the misconception (that considers the Reformation a new, even opposing epoch) may be due to a misguided definition of the Renaissance that confuses Renaissance methods with religious belief(s). Kristeller proposed otherwise: "I am convinced that humanism was in its core neither religious nor antireligious, but a literary and scholarly orientation that could be and, in many cases, was pursued without any explicit discourse on religious topics by individuals who otherwise might be fervent or nominal members of one of the Christian churches" (74–75).

should also be situated within the context of humanism since it benefited from its countless literary endeavors and sought to model its methods and values.

Second, some Reformers were trained as humanists and even explored humanist ambitions prior to their careers as Reformers. Others were not. For the latter, that does not mean they were unaffected by humanism. Few Reformers if any could claim they operated within a cultural or ecclesiastical context sanitized from the effects of humanism. Ready access to the Greek text of Erasmus, fresh translations of classical texts, renewed attention to inner spirituality and ecclesiastical renovation—these and many other factors were advantageous to the advent of the Reformation.

Nevertheless, if the question of correlation asks whether the Reformation is strictly a child of humanism, then the answer is more negative. For not all Reformers were trained as humanists first. Luther, for example, rose out of Scholastic soil, which explains his early engagements with late medievals like Biel. However, other Reformers were trained in the humanist spirit and were glad practitioners of its methods; even entire territories embraced the humanist spirit.

For example, Switzerland welcomed northern European humanism, as corroborated by the University of Vienna and some of its leading scholars, from Konrad Celtis to Joachim von Watt (aka Vadian), at the turn of the sixteenth century. Vienna was a microcosm of humanism across Swiss universities, such as Basel, for example.[105] Graduates embodied humanist ideals as they entered faculties and sometimes even pulpits. Huldrych Zwingli, for instance, studied at Vienna first and Basel second, finishing at the latter by 1506. That explains, if only in part, why Zwingli's early years in Zurich had more of a humanist flavor than an evangelical one. For Eastern Swiss humanism did not concern itself primarily with dogma. That choice was convictional. The problem, as they perceived it, was not the corruption of theology but morality.[106] Influenced by humanism's ethical focus, Zwingli entered Zurich set on a moral reform. However, Zwingli's reform did not take on a doctrinal agenda until he turned an Augustinian corner.[107]

Zwingli was anything but unique.[108] Consider two Reformers: Calvin and Vermigli.

The Humanism of Calvin and Vermigli

Like Zwingli, Calvin was influenced by humanism, but not in the same way or with the same results. The eloquence of Calvin's rhetoric, both in the pulpit

105. On Basel, see McGrath, *Reformation Thought*, 44.

106. "For its leading representatives–Vadian, Xylotectus, Beatus Rhenanus, Glarean, and Myconius–Christianity was primarily a way of life, rather than a set of doctrines." McGrath, 44.

107. McGrath does not believe Zwingli was influenced by Augustine until the 1520s, and he does not mark Zwingli's turn from moralistic humanism to evangelical reformation until 1523 or at the latest, 1525. McGrath, 44.

108. Luther could also be examined. See Rosin, "Humanism, Luther, and the Wittenberg Reformation," 91–104.

and in his *Institutes*, must be credited to his personal talents (the same cannot be said of every other Reformer on the continent). Likewise, Calvin's linguistic attention to the text, as exemplified in his commentaries, is remarkable and should be attributed to his intuitive literary judgment. Yet Calvin's skill was born out of a context, cultivated early in his career by the tools of French humanism, specifically its influence over the legal profession.[109] To post-Enlightenment practitioners, the combination of jurisprudence and philology may appear worlds apart. Yet these two became bedfellows due to a shift in the study of law, a shift that occurred on the eve of Calvin's own educational experience.

For example, certain lecturers at universities such as Orléans and Bourges, both of which Calvin attended, no longer exhibited unquestioned dependence on legal commentaries but adopted a more critical analysis involving the reception of classical legal texts.[110] Roman law became a deep well from which to draw, but the *method* of retrieving its fresh water could no longer be limited to the (distorted) readings of default interpreters.[111] A renewed engagement with the text according to its original intention and surrounding classical literary background was now the goal.

This new proposal was controversial, and the man responsible was Guillaume Budé. His sympathizers—not only French but Spanish—criticized default commentaries for misreading classical legal texts and leading others to do the same. Yet just as shocking was Budé's boldness: he was a trained lawyer, and yet he utilized the methods of humanist philology. In other words, Budé was the bridge at the intersection of jurisprudence and philology.[112] Budé himself modeled integration, incorporating both classical literature and philosophy into his study of law, and at times he even published on classical literature and linguistics as an end in and of itself.

None of this was lost on Calvin when he transitioned in 1529 from Orléans to Bourges to continue his study of law.[113] "He was a student of Roman Law, indeed,

109. A full study cannot be conducted here, but see Breen, *Calvin*, and McGrath, *Reformation Thought*, 45.

110. For this story, see McGrath, 445; Battles and Hugo, "Introduction," 19–20.

111. The *Glossa Magna* of Accursius was one text that came under fire.

112. "It was a courageous thing which Budé had done, since most of his associates at court were lawyers who had been trained in the tradition of the medieval glossators and post-glossators, whereas he had approached the text of the Pandects not (as the glossators had done) from a purely pragmatic point of view, so as to make the Roman statutes somehow fit into the actual conditions of feudal France, but first and foremost as a philologian. That is to say, he had tried first of all to establish the best possible text from the best manuscripts he could obtain, and then he had set out to explain the Latin terms in their own peculiar historical setting, making long digressions where necessary, in order to elucidate the meaning of one important term. In other words, Budé had introduced into the field of French jurisprudence that method of scientific philological exposition of which Lorenzo Valla had been the first advocate and exponent in modern Europe. Henceforth it was no longer queer for a jurist to be an ardent reader of the classics, or for a humanist man of letters to evince a lively interest in the text-books of Roman Law." Battles and Hugo, "Introduction," 19–20.

113. At Bourges Calvin was caught in the middle of a rivalry. On one side was the Frenchman de l'Estoile; on the other side was the Italian Andrea Alciati. The two had profound disagreements on method, specifically on how ancient sources should be utilized for contemporary law. The debate was complex, but l'Estoile represented a medieval approach that shied away from the historical context of texts to focus instead on specific words and their usages. Alciati judged l'Estoile's method too narrow; instead, ancient texts were to

but like many of his contemporaries he was hankering after a more academic, a more humanistic, a more literary and historical approach to the subject."[114] Calvin's peers also grew discontent with those faculty "still seeing Roman Law through medieval spectacles." Why not "have Roman Law presented to them as something specifically Roman, as the product of ancient Roman history, and thinking, and institutions."[115] Furthermore, while the humanist turn to classical antiquity through the medium of the law affected Calvin, its influence motivated him to pursue humanist interests more widely as well. By doing so, Calvin was merely following the lead of Budé, who not only wrote in the field of Roman law but also wrote on the broader contributions of classical antiquity.[116]

For example, toward the conclusion of his law studies at Bourges, Calvin exhibited his humanist interests by writing a commentary on Seneca's *De Clementia*, later published in 1532.[117] The timing was not ideal; Calvin's father was dying. Still, Calvin dedicated himself to one of the most ambitious projects he could have chosen, resolved to distinguish himself as a budding humanist scholar. It was a bold move because the project's very existence challenged the paramount humanist scholar of the day, Erasmus, who had already devoted himself to Seneca's writings (1529).[118]

---

be treated more holistically, regardless of whether the interpreter could make sense of inconsistencies. Alciati, however, did not help himself when he insulted the French in the process. In 1531 one of Calvin's peers, Nicolas Duchemin, wrote a treatise (*Antapologia adversus Aurelii Albucci*) defending l'Estoile and asked Calvin to write the preface. Calvin agreed, but Calvin did not write the preface in a style that threw full support behind l'Estoile; instead, Calvin positioned himself as arbitrator between the two parties. It is possible that Calvin appreciated Alciati's Italian humanism and careful attention to historical context. But Calvin was a Frenchman first, and his preface sympathized most with l'Estoile, even if Calvin's style was his subtle way of resisting peer conformity. Gordon, *Calvin*, 21. Gordon believes Calvin's style in his preface reveal's "Calvin's intellectual independence... an unwillingness to submit to the intellectual agenda of another." But as for Calvin's support of de l'Estoile, Gordon believes more was going on than first meets the eye: "De l'Estoile's significance for Calvin went beyond the mere scholarly; he represented the Gallic church and its proud tradition of independence from Rome. Calvin the humanist was also Calvin the Frenchman." At the same time, Calvin the humanist was no doubt indebted to Alciati, who taught Calvin "how the exposition of Roman laws might be enlivened by means of the '*deliciae humanarum literarum*,' that is to say, by illustrative passages taken from the grammarians, the antiquarians, the historians, the poets, the philosophers and the orators of Greece and Rome." Battles and Hugo, "Introduction," 24. Aside from the debate itself, Calvin's preface conveys a young lawyer in training who was a humanist at heart, comfortable in the world of classic literature as he dialogued with a spectrum of ancient voices with skill.

114. Battles and Hugo, "Introduction," 21.

115. "They were all patriotic Frenchman to a man, but as students they were primarily interested in the culture and institutions of the ancients." Battles and Hugo, 22.

116. Battles and Hugo, 22, 27.

117. Some ask, why was a student of law writing in the humanist track? Calvin admired Roman law, but he did not desire the life of a practitioner. Instead, as Calvin himself said later in his life, he was intrigued by the quiet life. Like Erasmus, Calvin could envision himself as a man of letters; Calvin could see his future editing, translating, and writing on the best of classical antiquity. His training up to that point gave him the knowledge to pursue that intrigue as well and left a lacuna not yet filled. Battles and Hugo also speculated whether Calvin did not want to become like his father, always wrapped up in financial and legal concerns. See Battles and Hugo, 15–16.

118. Calvin did not find the financial support he expected from the de Hangest family, and his dedicatory letter reveals the little praise they received as a result. On what this reveals about Calvin, see Gordon, *Calvin*, 23.

Calvin's commentary received no response from the academic world, which must have stung Calvin's humanist ambitions and might explain in part why the young talent turned from humanist endeavors to the study of theology. Despite its lack of sales, the commentary spoke volumes about the young humanist and the skills that would soon serve him in the reformation of the church.[119] A few examples must suffice.

The commentary was not just a historical window into the Roman Stoic philosopher. Seneca was instrumental in the retrieval of classical methods and virtues that sixteenth-century humanism valued. As to rhetoric and writing, Seneca exemplified a fastidiousness and persuasiveness that humanism prized. As to values, Seneca pleaded with Nero to resist tyranny and become a leader who wooed the people, which featured Seneca's own preoccupation with the necessity of justice and mercy, morality and clemency. As to sources, Seneca engaged those sources both ancient and wise, beginning with Plato and Aristotle, resourcing the wisdom of the past for the present rather than relying on one's own ingenuity and novelty.

Each one of these skills and priorities was absorbed by Calvin like a sponge, including his retrieval of the classical Christian tradition and its Augustinianism for the sake of his doctrine of grace, his theological articulation of the law both in justification and the Christian life, his logistical and synthetic harmonization of classical sources in his *Institutes of the Christian Religion*, his exegetical and linguistic precision present throughout his *Commentaries*, and his juristic mediations in political and ecclesiastical crises. To some degree, Calvin's humanist training can be credited for his later success as a Reformer. Without the skills Calvin gained as a student in diverse humanist and legal traditions, he may never have been the orator and writer known today. In the words of Calvin scholar Bruce Gordon,

> Calvin's rigorous legal training left its imprint on every aspect of his life. It sharpened his mind to interpret texts and form precise arguments based on humanist methods; it provided him with a thorough grasp of subjects, ranging from marriage and property to crime. He was taught to frame legislation, write constitutions and offer legal opinions, all of which would loom large in his Genevan career. But the legacy was also intellectual. It was from the law that he would draw some of his most fundamental theological concepts, such as the Holy Spirit as "witness," the nature of "justification," God as "legislator" and "judge," and Christ as the "perpetual advocate." The philosophical and historical methods drawn from both de l'Estoile and Alciati would become the foundations of his biblical commentaries as he revolutionized the art of interpreting Scripture.[120]

---

119. Historians disagree on the nature of humanism's influence: "Some would limit Calvin's humanism to his use of its methodology, while others would include his acceptance of some of its substantive views of human nature and history." Lindberg, *European Reformations*, 251. Both, in my estimation, are legitimate when properly outlined.

120. Gordon, *Calvin*, 22 (cf. 28). The connections I've noted are but the beginning; see 24–29. And, as chapter 14 will insinuate, this humanist legal training paid no little dividends when Calvin was entrusted with the reform of Geneva's judicial system. Also see Partee, *Calvin and Classical Philosophy*, 2–26.

The connection between Calvin's legal and humanist background and his future as a theologian and a churchman cannot be overemphasized.

For example, Seneca's focal point throughout was clemency, the virtue of all virtues, the bedrock of individual dignity but also the cornerstone of society's stability.[121] Without clemency, said Calvin, cruelty reigns, "which is nothing else than harshness of mind in exacting punishments."[122] Clemency is an indispensable attribute of the state since without it those in authority turn into tyrants. Clemency ensures they govern with justice, passing down judgments "in accordance with what is fair and good."[123] Seneca's concern to elevate clemency to protect society's welfare stemmed from the same program that defined Plato, Aristotle, and Cicero, among others. In other words, it was a classical conviction that Seneca heralded. Many years later, Calvin embodied this same priority, not as a statesman but as a churchman eager to establish peace and structure in Geneva.[124]

Calvin's humanist skills prepared the way for his future as a Reformer. However, it is premature to read evangelical motives back into Calvin's commentary on Seneca. Calvin's aspirations were more political. As Carter Lindberg observes, "This commentary, contrary to some suggestions, is not a source for Calvin's move toward the Reformation or a plea for religious toleration but rather an expression of his response to the volatile political context of the early Reformation in France confronted by royal absolutism. As a young lawyer Calvin is proposing the 'golden mean' of clemency between tyranny and revolt."[125]

Calvin's political aspirations, however, did not preclude the influence of French evangelicalism. He wrestled with his religious identity in the early 1530s as well. At Bourges Calvin became close friends with Melchior Wolmar, who studied Greek with Calvin and must have known about Calvin's interests in Seneca. Yet Wolmar was a Lutheran, a dangerous religious allegiance in France at the time. For the past decade, Luther's writings had been condemned by the Sorbonne. "The fear of schism inspired men with a distrust of all novelties, however good in themselves."[126] Still, the condemning voice of the Sorbonne did not stop conversions to the evangelical point of view. And although Calvin had hesitations, he did listen to his friend Wolmar, as well as to other friends and some extended family, as they articulated the logic of the evangelical conviction and why it even followed from humanist methods.

---

121. Calvin, *De Clementia*, 1.19.

122. Calvin, 2.4.

123. Calvin, 2.7.

124. Battles and Hugo, "Introduction," 129. However, Calvin's legal training did not impose categories on Scripture and theology that were otherwise not there. In Calvin's mind, the forensic focus—with a doctrine like justification for example—is Scripture's *own* emphasis. Calvin drew his theological concepts from Scripture's legally charged narrative and didactic content, which confirms Gordon's insightful observation,. Calvin's training in the law was instrumental and essential, like new lenses that opened Calvin's eyes to their existence in the midst of a late medieval context where such categories were either missed or misunderstood.

125. "As such, this commentary is a clue both to his later address to Francis I that prefaces the *Institutes* and to his perennial concern for order in the course of reform." Lindberg, *European Reformations*, 251.

126. Battles and Hugo, "Introduction," 17.

In the early 1530s, young John Calvin considered the risk French evangelicals took for the sake of their biblical and theological commitments. Even if Calvin, who described his younger self as timid, worked up the nerve to come out and commit himself to French reformation, a plethora of grave questions nagged him. For example, "Would it not be a colossal mistake, nay worse even, an unforgivable error against the one holy Catholic Church in which he had been baptized and reared?"[127] Calvin had to be convinced that the evangelical cause did not betray but preserved the true meaning of the one, holy, catholic, and apostolic church.[128]

Calvin has served as a case study, but he was not unique. Many others, such as Peter Martyr Vermigli, were influenced not only by Scholasticism but humanism as well.[129] Classical thought pervaded various pockets of the Reformation across Europe due to the spread of humanism. The radicals of the sixteenth century decried the influence of pagan voices (see chapter 13), but most of the Reformers valued the classical heritage due to a shared, patristic, and medieval presupposition: they recognized the validity of general revelation and common grace, persuaded that the Christian not only could but should sit at the feet of the specialist, whether that specialist be a believer or not. The humanist in each Reformer gave them an appreciation for truth and its coherency wherever it could be found. Yet the Reformers went further: the greatest minds of classical antiquity prepared the way for supernatural revelation and its most spectacular manifestation, that is, the incarnation of Jesus Christ.

Calvin's *Institutes of the Christian Religion* are a prime example. "Budé's literary output points to his conviction not merely that the classical heritage, including its legal institutions and codes, was laden with importance for the present, but also that the study of antiquity was a proper preparation for the gospel of Jesus Christ. Calvin would adopt a similar approach in the great 1559 edition of the *Institutes of the Christian Religion*, allowing Cicero to guide the reader from the natural religion of antiquity toward the superior gospel of Jesus Christ."[130] Supernatural revelation was a prerequisite to know the gospel, but humanist-trained Reformers like Calvin did not consider this gospel antithetical to natural revelation and natural theology. Instead, natural theology was like John the Baptist, preparing the way for Christ and his kingdom. Within its proper parameter, Athens has much to do with Jerusalem.

As the young Calvin transitioned from a career in humanism to a career in theology, he did not consider this shift a departure from the humanist spirit but an instrumental even if indirect medium for its implementation. "When Calvin

---

127. Battles and Hugo, 19. Yet Lutheranism was not the only target; humanism came under suspicion as well. The middle to late 1520s are littered with publications by French authors attacking humanism, and even specific humanists like Erasmus. For a list, see Battles and Hugo, 17.

128. Eventually Calvin came to the conclusion that he "could be in favor of all these things (e.g., Lefèvre d'Estaples' *evangélisme*), and yet remain a faithful son of the Church." Battles and Hugo, 16.

129. James, "Peter Martyr Vermigli," 71.

130. McGrath, *Reformation Thought*, 45.

read the Bible, he did so, not only in company with his contemporaries and the Christian traditions that formed them, but also in an inescapable dialogue with the ancient philosophers of Athens and Rome," says Steinmetz. And as he refined his own theology, "Calvin found that lively conversation with ancient philosophers remained an inescapable part of his theological task."[131] In that way, Calvin and other Reformers like Vermigli did not pioneer a new path so much as they followed an old one, mimicking the voice of the Alexandrian tradition that believed God primed the pump for Christ by his providential provision of Greek antiquity.[132] For Calvin, God's providence in antiquity was a gift; Calvin interpreted those who neglected or rejected that gift as ungrateful, even radical. "After all, baptism is a renunciation of sin, not a wholesale repudiation of culture."[133]

FROM RENAISSANCE TO REFORMATION
A Lifeline to the Church Catholic

The case of Calvin demonstrates how much a Reformer could benefit from humanism and even embody its spirit and methodology. Yet Calvin is but one among many. Before the Geneva Reformer, the Zurich Reformer, Ulrich Zwingli, so quoted classical philosophy and literature—from Plato and Aristotle to Cicero and Homer—that Bruce Gordon says the "world of antiquity was his playground.... He had been shaped by Erasmus' belief that the classical world could be baptized into the Christian."[134] Zwingli believed the Greeks, for example, understood virtue and its indispensability to happiness, especially for the good ordering and flourishing of society, which concerned a magisterial Reformer like Zwingli.

Benefiting from humanism, however, was only possible because humanist ideas made their way into Reformation territories. Renaissance humanism and its ideas made their way into northern European countries through publications and correspondence (humanists prided themselves on the art of writing letters), but also through firsthand education whenever a northern European scholar decided to study at the great universities of Italy only to return with the humanist fever.[135]

The humanist retrieval of ancient texts, as well as its sacred spirit of interpretation, contributed to the rise of the Reformation in many ways, whether intentional or not. The retrieval of ancient texts by means of the original languages, for example, opened a whole new world to the Reformers. To begin with, the Reformers did not have to trust the translations and interpretations of the Bible by the late medieval church. By dedicating themselves to Hebrew and Greek,

---

131. Steinmetz, *Calvin in Context,* 235.

132. "According to Clement [of Alexandria] there are so many elements of truth discernible in Greek philosophy that it may be considered to have been, under the guidance of God, a preparation for the Gospel among the heathen. Philosophy was the rain sent by God to drench the field from which Faith was eventually to sprout forth." Battles and Hugo, "Introduction," 47.

133. "In his view Christians have a moral duty to engage secular learning at its best." Calvin was not uncritical, but he did look for those more likely to contain the truth (e.g., Aristotelians) than those who strayed too far from it (e.g., Epicureans). Steinmetz, *Calvin in Context,* 245.

134. Gordon, *Zwingli,* 9 (cf. 23–24).

135. McGrath, *Reformation Thought,* 42.

they now had immediate access to the Scriptures. Now they could formulate their own evaluations, even create their own translations.

Moreover, the call—back to the fountainhead—also invited the Reformers to retrieve the wealth of patristic writings, from both East and West, as well as early and high medieval works of commentary and theology. The well of patristic and medieval thought was not only a source from which to draw spiritual water, but a shovel by which to dig their way back to the grace of the gospel they believed the late medieval papacy had misconstrued. *Ad fontes* "was more than a slogan: it was a lifeline to those who despaired of the state of the late medieval church."[136] As chapter 8 will reveal, Martin Luther is a prime example. Erasmus's Greek New Testament gave Luther an opportunity to return to the text afresh and consider whether the soteriology he imbibed was indeed scriptural. Yet Luther's breakthrough discovery of *justificatio sola fide* was due not only to his renewed reading of Paul's epistles and the Psalms, but also to his study of the corpus of Augustine. It is not an overstatement to say that Augustine's doctrine of grace set Luther free. *Ad fontes* was the key that unlocked that discovery. Whether Luther knew it or not, humanists like Erasmus played no little role in resurrecting fresh translations of Augustine.

However, for the Reformers the benefit of humanism was not a retrieval of sources for the sake of the sources themselves. Rather, these sources were a lifeline to the church catholic. Over against the "heretic" Reformers, the papacy claimed it represented the one, holy, catholic, and apostolic church. By recovering more accurate translations of the Scriptures and by reading the Fathers and Scholastics for themselves, the Reformers discovered that the gospel they preached was anything but novel. On second glance, it was quite ancient. Although it outraged papal theologians, the Reformers claimed to be the true heirs of Augustinianism. If *ad fontes* was the channel by which humanists could reach an eloquence capable of renewing civilization, *ad fontes* was the avenue by which the Reformers could *retrieve the church catholic and claim it as their own.* Both saw renewal as the goal, but for the Reformers the renewal was not merely in morality but theology, not merely in ethics but dogmatics.

That claim assumes, however, that not every humanist joined the Reformation. No humanist so famously exemplified eventual but decisive resistance to the evangelical movement as one of its finest talents, Erasmus.

Initial Synonymity, Progressive Diversion

In the early years of the Reformation, many assumed Erasmus either was or would soon join the Reformation. That assumption was reasonable in the late 1510s and early 1520s.

On the surface, humanism and evangelical reform appeared congruous if not synonymous. The reasons for the association are many. In method they both

---

136. McGrath, 41.

were concerned with retrieval. They both called on the laity to retrieve Scripture and the church fathers afresh—*ad fontes*. In ethics, they both were impatient with the corruption of the clergy and papacy, and called the church to renewal.[137] Therefore, when colleagues first heard Luther speak, they sometimes missed his motives and assumed Luther was a new, bold advocate of humanist principles. Some like Martin Bucer were first attracted to Luther based on that misconception. Others like Zwingli even started reform out of moralistic endeavors, not necessarily doctrinal ambitions.[138]

The synonymity between northern European humanism and the Reformation seemed logical from a literary perspective as well. For example, while the young Luther grew irritated over the abuse of indulgences, Erasmus went public with his own disgust with papal corruption in his book *Julius Excluded from Heaven*. If Erasmus used satire in his prior books—such as *Praise of Folly*—this latest publication had fun at the expense of the pope himself, Julius II (1503–13), although according to the humanist, Julius deserved the ridicule. In the book, as Julius approaches the gates of heaven, he is stopped by the apostle Peter.

> **Julius:** What the devil's going on here? Doors won't open, eh? Looks as if the lock's been changed, or at least tampered with.
>
> **Julius's guardian spirit:** You'd better check and see that you didn't bring the wrong key with you. You don't open this door, you know, with the same key that opens your money-box!
>
> **Julius:** I'm getting fed up. I'll pound on the door. Hey! Hey! Someone open this door at once! . . .
>
> **Peter:** Well, it's a good thing we have a gate like iron! Otherwise this fellow (whoever he is) would have broken the doors down. Some giant or tyrant, a wrecker of cities, must have arrived. But eternal God, what a sewer I smell here! I won't open the doors directly; I'll just peep through the bars of the window and see what monster this is. . . .
>
> **Julius:** I've had enough of all this talk. Unless you obey me right this minute, I will hurl even against *you* the thunderbolt of excommunication, with which I once terrified the mightiest kings and entire kingdoms! Behold the Bull I've already drawn up for the purpose. . . .
>
> **Peter:** Perhaps you did once terrify some people with this hot air, but up here it doesn't mean a thing. Here you have to operate with truth. This citadel is won by good deeds, not evil words.[139]

---

137. For an elaboration on all of these areas and others, see McGrath, 54–57.

138. McGrath believes the marginalization of theology is plain in Zwingli's early years (e.g., the 1519 Leipzig Disputation). In the 1520s, however, Zwingli changed and considered the problem through a theological lens. McGrath, 54.

139. Quoted in Needham, *Two Thousand Years of Christ's Power*, 3:63.

The dialogue explains Erasmus's disdain.

Although Erasmus was smart enough to leave his real name off the book's title page, it was obvious to everyone who had read his prior satires who the author must be. On the surface, Erasmus and Luther seemed to wear the same glove of protest. But on closer look, differences emerge. The humanist's irritation with the pope and papacy was mostly for moral reasons, but Luther not only took issue with corruption in the church but with its late medieval beliefs, some soteriological, some epistemological.

In short time, the gulf between the humanism of Erasmus and evangelical reform became conspicuous, as much as the latter benefited from the tools of the former. Granted, in method they both heralded retrieval but with divergent allegiances and with different purposes. While a humanist like Erasmus looked to Jerome and his translation work as a model, a Reformer like Luther was occupied with Augustine and his doctrine of grace. The reason: humanism and the Reformation had divergent goals. For the Reformers, Augustine had exegetical and doctrinal insights into sin and salvation that opened their eyes to Rome's faults, faults with enormous consequences for justification and eternal life.

As for ethics, humanists like Erasmus believed the answer to ecclesiastical corruption was the *philosophia Christi*. Imitate Christ and moral standards will return to the halls of the sanctuary. Erasmus desired inner, spiritual renewal. *But the Reformers considered that imperative—imitate Christ—misleading apart from justification by grace alone through faith alone in Christ alone.* Apart from a new righteous status, imitating Christ was a fool's errand, keeping the sinner captive to a meritorious system that could only lead to failure and divine judgment. Certainly, ethical reform was essential, but it was consequential to that primary concern, which was doctrinal. The solution was not *imitatio Christi*. How could it be, when all of humanity is guilty and corrupt in Adam, resulting not only in condemnation but a spiritual inability? As Luther pointed out to Erasmus in his *Bondage of the Will*, what good does it do to tell the ungodly to imitate Christ when the sinner's nature itself is polluted by sin? The solution, therefore, must not be an imperative but an indicative, not something internal but external, namely, Christ and his imputed righteousness.

Erasmus was a window into that corner of humanism that desired a reform in morality, even one that was rooted in the laity, but nonetheless parted ways with evangelicals who desired reform in theology.[140] As much as humanism depended

---

140. It is a caricature to say that humanists were hostile to theology. It is far more accurate to say instead that doctrine was not their primary concern nor, in their minds, the solution to the problem. McGrath (*Reformation Thought*, 55–56) lists several test cases (Scholastic theology, Scripture, patristics, education, and rhetoric) that exhibit the different "attitudes" toward each by humanists and Reformers. Consider Scholastic theology. Both humanists and the Reformers voiced criticisms toward segments of Scholasticism. However, their motives were not the same by any means. Humanists disliked the Scholastic method of argumentation, which could be analytical and systematic, even dense in its intricacies. To the humanist, the Scholastics lacked style. Rhetorical eloquence was missing, they said. They also dismissed Scholasticism because they could not comprehend (or sympathize) with its theological and philosophical debates. In the estimation of the humanist, the Scholastic lacked rhetorical eloquence due to the incomprehensibility of its ideas and meticulous form of

on religion for its context and flourishment, it prided itself on its transcendence of religious debate. That is plain in the simple fact that both Catholics and Protestants used humanist tools to advance their ideas. The values of humanism could be advantageous to either side, even wielded for one side against the other. Again, consider Erasmus. On one hand, Erasmus could be critical of moral laxity in the Catholic Church (see his *Praise of Folly*) and advocate translation reform based on his Greek New Testament, a bold move when the established church considered the Vulgate authoritative. On the other hand, Erasmus could rebuke the Reformers for refusing to submit themselves to the judgments of the papacy. He could even discriminate against evangelical theology, calling into question its departure from assumed religious beliefs and practices, admonishing Luther and his protest against the papacy's authority and system of soteriology.

When did humanist and evangelical differences become apparent? That question is difficult to answer because it assumes humanism was monolithic, which it was not. While Erasmus resisted the Reformation, others like Philip Melanchthon did not but remained equally committed to the tools of humanism as they were to the theology of reform. That diversity has led some historians to ponder whether a generational gap existed between older humanists (Erasmus) and younger humanists (Melanchthon, Zwingli, Calvin).[141] Regardless of the reason, a divide did emerge between some humanists (Erasmus) and other humanists who committed to the Reformation, though exactly when may be debated. The year 1525, however, may be a definitive mark of departure. The debate between Luther and Erasmus over the bondage of the will (see chapter 8) dispelled any synonymity between humanism and the Reformation. While the debate concerned the ability or inability of the sinner, it exposed the differences mentioned above. Erasmus was famous as a humanist for his translations of the Fathers, Augustine included. Not only humanists but Reformers used these critical editions to understand the theologian so responsible for Christian theology. However, Erasmus's own theological conclusions were at odds with Augustine. In his debate with Luther over the bondage of the will, Luther's position was far more Augustinian. Erasmus's confidence in human ability stood in stark contrast with Augustine's doctrine of original sin.[142] The irony was not lost on humanists and Reformers alike: the method of the humanists—*ad fontes*—resulted in the

---

communication. However, the Reformers criticized certain Scholastics (not all, despite McGrath's generalizing language) for an entirely different reason: theology. The barrier was not style but doctrine. The hurdle was not the lack of eloquence but biblical support. This showed when both groups had to evaluate the Christian tradition. What serves as the criteria? "The humanists were not prepared to use such an explicitly theological criterion in evaluating the relative merits of the Fathers, thus heightening the tension between these two movements" (56). Likewise with Scripture. "For the humanists, the authority of Scripture rested in its eloquence, simplicity, and antiquity." But the Reformers, given their commitment to *sola scriptura*, had a more theological rationale. While the humanists "regarded Scripture primarily as a source of moral guidance," the Reformers said the Scripture was "primarily . . . a record of God's gracious promises of salvation to those who believed" (55).

141. I am indebted to Nick Needham for this observation.
142. On Erasmus's bent toward Jerome instead of Augustine, see Kristeller, *Renaissance Thought*, 84.

excavation of not only texts but a theology they could not agree with. On this account at least, the Reformers believed their method of retrieval and the theology retrieved (Augustinianism) were perfectly compatible.

At the same time, the divide between humanists and Reformers should not be overplayed. For many humanists did commit to the evangelical program, some early, others late. This divergence within humanism reveals the movement's own diversity: Erasmus was a shining light of humanism, but other humanists shined bright as well, even if their radiance displayed a different color, either by way of their nationalist outlook or by way of their religious commitments.

Nevertheless, such diversity in the ranks of humanism was impossible to hide with each passing year due to the evolving conflict with the papacy. Humanist and Reformer alike had to decide whether the conflict with Rome justified protest and if so, what kind and to what extent. That bristling dilemma is the subject of the next chapter.

THE ECCLESIASTICAL WATERSHED

Conciliarism, Curialism, and the Papacy
on the Eve of the Reformation

> *In the first case Tradition was seen as the instrumental vehicle of*
> *Scripture which brings the contents of Holy Scripture to life in a constant*
> *dialogue between the doctors of Scripture and the Church; in the second*
> *case Tradition was seen as the authoritative vehicle of divine truth,*
> *embedded in Scripture but overflowing in extrascriptural apostolic tradi-*
> *tion handed down through episcopal succession.*
>
> —Heiko Oberman, *Forerunners of the Reformation*

Histories of the Reformation have sometimes assumed that one major difference between the Reformers and their medieval predecessors was an allegiance to Scripture's authority by the Reformers and an allegiance to tradition's authority by their medieval predecessors. That contrast, however, is far too simplistic to be credible. As chapter 13 will reveal, such a contrast confuses the Reformers with the radicals of the sixteenth century, the latter jettisoning tradition. No less than Rome, the Reformers stood for a tradition and were adamant they stood *within* the catholic tradition. Their conflict with the papacy was not a choice between Scripture and tradition, but a conflict between their view of tradition and the papacy's view of tradition.

Heiko Oberman led the way in correcting this simplistic view—Scripture versus tradition—by observing a variety of views of tradition in the medieval era. Two types of "tradition" emerge, and his definition of each could not be more important for framing the Reformation.

Tradition 1 (T1)

The sole authority of Holy Scripture is upheld as canon, or standard, of revealed truth in such a way that Scripture is not contrasted with Tradition. Scripture, it is argued, can be understood only within the Church and has been understood within the Church by the great doctors specifically committed to the task of interpretation of Scripture and especially endowed with the gift of understanding this unique source of truth. The history of obedient interpretation is the Tradition of the Church.

Tradition 2 (T2)

It is argued that the Apostles did not commit everything to writing, usually on the grounds that the scriptural authors reported what Christ said and did during His lifetime but not what Christ taught His disciples in the period between the resurrection and the ascension. During these forty days an oral Tradition originated which is to be regarded as a complement to Holy Scripture, handed down to the Church of later times as a second source of revelation.[1]

For T1 the inspired teachings of Holy Scripture were handed down, so that the church catholic (universal) grew from adolescence to maturity. Guided by the Spirit's illumination and providence, tradition became the carrier of Scripture's rule of faith—*regula fidei*. By means of faithful perpetuation, tradition continually resurrected the teachings of Scripture so church fathers so devoted to its pages could provide the church with an orthodox interpretation free from the misjudgments of heresy. As a result, tradition served the church by developing a theology that kept the church faithful to its Savior. In that sense, tradition became a ministerial authority. Tradition 2, by contrast, considered tradition a magisterial authority, even an additional channel of divine revelation itself. An extra tradition with content just as apostolic as Scripture but nonetheless kept external to Scripture became the infallible property of Peter's successors.[2]

As will become apparent in chapter 7, the Reformers advocated for T1 while some of their papal counterparts defended T2, also called the two-source theory, a theory that culminated at the Council of Trent (although interpretations of Trent are not without controversy; see chapter 17).[3] A close examination of the medieval era also reveals that even among those who held to T2, disagreement emerged over the possession of authority. In other words, who within this tradition could claim ultimate authority: council or pope? Conciliarists answered for the latter while curialists defended the former, and the debate between these parties grew fierce as both sides struggled for primacy in the two centuries that preceded the Reformation. On the eve of the Reformation, the curialists gained prominence, which motivated forerunners and Reformers alike to petition for a council, though their petitions were met with resistance.

To understand the Reformation's reaction to claims for papal supremacy, this chapter will introduce the evolution of papal supremacy while also paying attention to its conciliarist resisters, especially on the precipice of the sixteenth century.

---

1. Oberman, "Introduction," 54, emphasis added.
2. Oberman, "Introduction," 55. Cf. George, *Reading Scripture with the Reformers*, 32.
3. More recently Josef Rupert Geiselmann has challenged this interpretation in an attempt to read Trent as closer to the Reformation view. However, see Oberman's response: Oberman, "Introduction," 53.

DEBATE OVER ORIGINS

A previous generation of impressive historians such as Heiko Oberman and
G. H. Tavard traced the origins of T2 to the canon lawyers of the twelfth century, convinced by certain quotations that T2 was articulated by Ivo of Chartres
and Gratian of Bologna.[4] However, after a thorough examination of canonists
between AD 1150 and 1250, Brian Tierney has challenged the Oberman-Tavard
thesis with some success and argued instead that T2 was alien to the mindset
and methodology of twelfth-century canonists. They considered the creeds, for
example, key to "define various tenets of Christian doctrine with absolute fidelity." However, these creeds were "not considered to be a body of revealed truth
supplementary to sacred Scripture." The "dilemma" of later generations that set
Scripture and tradition apart from one another (or even in opposition to one
another) was "indeed hardly imaginable."[5] According to Tierney, the twelfth-
century canonists followed the lead of the patristics. "In this view Scripture
recorded divine truth once and for all and the living voice of the church, guided
by the Holy Spirit, interpreted that truth and proclaimed it anew to each succeeding generation."[6] Even when debate did erupt in the fourteenth century,
many canonists continued to teach T1, the view assumed by their forebears back
in the twelfth century.[7]

How, then, should the canonists' high view of the papacy be reconciled with
their T1 position? Although the medieval canonists did not consider tradition a second source of divine revelation, they did elevate the pope above other
ecclesiastical powers. For the canonists, the pope was head of Christ's church,
his vicar on earth, until the Lord's return. Following Augustine's interpretation of Matthew 16:19, the keys of the kingdom were given to Peter because
Peter was the church's "symbol."[8] While the apostles governed by means of holy

---

4. For his association of T2 with the twelfth century, see Oberman, *Harvest of Medieval Theology*, 369–72.
Also see Tavard, *Holy Writ or Holy Church*. Oberman even entertained the possibility that early signs of T2
were visible in Basil the Great (ca. 330–370) and Augustine. Oberman, "Introduction," 55. However, Oberman
did qualify, "For them [medieval doctors] theology is the science of Holy Scripture. . . . Holy Scripture is understood as the authoritative source—the standard for judging the interpretation of later commentators" (55–56).
In addition, Oberman did preclude T2 from the Early Middle Ages: "Tradition I and Tradition II cannot be
clearly separated for the simple reason that those who *de facto* hold Tradition II continue to declare themselves
for the material sufficiency of Holy Scripture" (59).
5. Tierney, *Origins of Papal Infallibility 1150–1350*, 16, 17. Tierney takes issue as well with the *reason*
Oberman and Tavard both gave for the twelfth-century canonist supposed embrace of T2. "One asserts that
the canonists favored a 'two-sources theory' of divine revelation because of their excessive regard for ancient
tradition, the other that they favored this same theory because of an excessive regard for the innovative powers
of the pope. In fact neither assertion is correct. Canonistic teaching throughout the twelfth and thirteenth
centuries was entirely consistent with the doctrines commonly taught by the theologians of that age—that
sacred Scripture contained implicitly or explicitly all the revealed truths of Christian faith and that papal
power was wholly subordinate to Scriptural revelation where matters of faith were concerned" (18).
6. Creeds "could be called in the twelfth century a 'summary' of the contents of Scripture." Tierney,
Origins of Papal Infallibility 1150–1350, 16.
7. Tierney, *Origins of Papal Infallibility 1150–1350*, 18. For a more extensive treatment, see Tierney,
Foundations of the Conciliar Theory.
8. *Figura ecclesiae.* Tierney, *Origins of Papal Infallibility 1150–1350*, 32.

orders, Peter and his successors possessed jurisdiction, a superior administrative authority to resolve theological and ecclesiastical disagreements. Nevertheless, the canonists did not assume that such jurisdiction meant the pope was infallible or that his decrees were irreformable. He may be head of the church, but only the church universal is guaranteed perpetual fidelity by God's grace.[9]

Consider two examples: Huguccio and Johannes Teutonicus. Neither one interpreted Luke 22:32 as a text teaching papal infallibility. Prior to Peter's betrayal, Jesus told Peter that he had prayed for him so that his faith would not fail in the end, but even after his betrayal Peter would be restored. Jesus said he had prayed that Peter's faith might not fail. Jesus was not referring to Peter's inability to err (the entire context speaks to Peter's fallibility), but instead to the impossibility of final apostasy. Furthermore, both Huguccio and Teutonicus asked whether Peter himself was in view or whether Peter represented the whole church. Teutonicus answered, "*That your faith shall not fail*, that is the faith of the church, which is your faith, for the church has never failed because it existed even at the Lord's death at least in the Blessed Virgin. The church can be small; it cannot be nothing."[10] The promise of Jesus is directed to the church; there will always be a remnant that cannot be snuffed out, an elect people whom God preserves from apostasy. Huguccio made this point by contrasting the fallibility of the pope with that of the faithful: "For although the Roman pope has sometimes erred this does not mean that the Roman church has, which is understood to be not he alone but all the faithful, for the church is the aggregate of the faithful; if it does not exist at Rome it exists in the regions of Gaul or wherever the faithful are." Huguccio returned to Jesus' words and concluded, "The church can indeed cease to be but this will never happen for it was said to Peter, and in the person of Peter to the universal church, 'that your faith shall not fail.'"[11]

Tierney's careful presentation of canonist voices should guard the historian from setting a Reformation adherence to scriptural authority over against a medieval allegiance to tradition. The medieval period is far too variegated for such a broad-brush contrast, especially since many a medieval theologian did not ascribe to a two-source theory but upheld the primacy of the Scriptures. The historian has a far better chance of observing T1 and T2 in opposition to one another by turning to the *late* Middle Ages, starting with the fourteenth century. As this chapter will explore, by the fourteenth century the difference between T1 and T2 became conspicuous with papal bulls and theologians like John Brevicoxa and his *A Treatise on Faith, the Church, the Roman Pontiff, and*

---

9. For more on the distinction between the power to govern (holy orders) and the power of jurisdiction, see Tierney, *Origins of Papal Infallibility 1150–1350*, 32. On the canonists and the absence of an irreformability doctrine, see 53–57.

10. Teutonicus, *Summa Cantabrigiensis* 0.5.17, fol. 8va, *ad Dist.* 21 *ante* c. 1; quoted in Tierney, *Origins of Papal Infallibility 1150–1350*, 36.

11. Huguccio, *Summa ad* 24 q. 1 c. 9, MS Vat. Lat. 2280, fol. 251 vb; quoted in Tierney, *Origins of Papal Infallibility 1150–1350*, 37.

the General Council (ca. 1375). That did not mean, however, that Brevicoxa was an advocate for papal supremacy; even among those who affirmed T2 in the fourteenth century many were conciliarists instead of curialists.[12] The evolving and escalating struggle between curialism and conciliarism in the thirteenth and fourteenth centuries once again is a reminder that as T2 emerged, its advocates disagreed on the type of authority that should govern this revelatory tradition.

FROM BONAVENTURE TO PIETRO OLIVI

The absence of papal infallibility and T2 in the twelfth century canonists influenced the outlook of the next century as well. Even a Franciscan like Bonaventure (ca. 1221–74), one of the most vocal advocates for papal jurisdiction, was attuned to the same nuance seen in canonists like Huguccio and Teutonicus. Careful attention to his advocacy for the papacy reveals that infallibility was missing from his affirmation of papal power. The pope may have been superior in his adjudications, but only the church universal was free from failure.[13] Recognizing the absence of papal infallibility should not have precluded Bonaventure from setting the stage for change in the fourteenth century. Although Bonaventure did not advocate for papal infallibility, his adamant advocacy for papal sovereignty did prove congenial to later advocates of papal infallibility. Nevertheless, reading infallibility back into a thirteenth-century figure like Bonaventure is anachronistic.

However, after Bonaventure came a Franciscan who was, by best estimation, the first to teach papal infallibility *explicitly*: Pietro Olivi (ca. 1248–98).[14] Olivi lived in strife-ridden times for a Franciscan. The order was divided: on one side stood the Spirituals who were adamant that true godliness required a return to Francis's original intention for the order—the vow of poverty and with it the surrender of personal property. Olivi was dedicated to this traditional viewpoint of his order's founder. However, others—named the Community—were far more liberal in their interpretation of their founder's commitments, less concerned with the daily discipline of personal poverty than the reallocation of property for the sake of the papacy.[15]

Olivi celebrated a victory when Nicholas III released a bull in 1279 labeled *Exiit*, which said in no uncertain terms that poverty should be practiced by both the individual and the community. The "renunciation of property in all things, in this fashion, not merely individually but also in common for the sake of God,

---

12. Also, even when conciliarism was articulated in the twelfth century, the canonists did not establish a "systematic theory of conciliarism as an ideal system of church government." Tierney, *Origins of Papal Infallibility 1150–1350*, 49.

13. Tierney, *Origins of Papal Infallibility 1150–1350*, 58–92.

14. Tierney points out that many interpreters have misjudged Olivi because they assume papal infallibility was already custom and therefore fail to see the novel contribution Olivi makes. See Tierney, *Origins of Papal Infallibility 1150–1350*, 93–130.

15. Tierney, *Origins of Papal Infallibility 1150–1350*, 97.

is meritorious and holy and that Christ, showing the way of perfection, taught this by word and confirmed it by example." More telling, for the purposes of this chapter, was the way Francis received this rule of poverty according to *Exiit*. "This is the way of religious life ... descending from the Father of lights, handed on by his Son to the apostles by word and example, and finally inspired in blessed Francis and his followers by the Holy Spirit."[16] Here was a bold claim: Francis had received a special revelation from God.

The year after *Exiit*, Olivi started to attract considerable attention when he then put forward a novel position for papal infallibility. Anyone, said Olivi, who "is not permitted to err is to be followed as an unerring rule. But God has given this authority to the Roman pontiff." According to Olivi's logic, God would not instruct the Roman pontiff to discern debates over the faith when the Roman pontiff is prone to err. "It is impossible for God to give to any one the full authority to decide about doubts concerning the faith and divine law with this condition, that He would permit him to err."[17] The motive behind his advocacy for papal infallibility was connected to his spiritual commitment to Franciscan poverty: if past papal decrees were not infallible then future popes could depart from Franciscan poverty if they pleased. Papal infallibility was necessary to secure forever the vow of poverty. The pope must not only be submitted to as judge over all, but he must be submitted to as an infallible judge over all, his decrees fixed for future posterity. Future posterity not only included laity and clergy, but future popes as well. Should they try to divert from a prior papal decree, like *Exiit*, they would forfeit the validity of their papacy and invite ecclesiastical discipline. While papal infallibility might appear to increase a pope's power, the long view of history tells a different story: papal infallibility restricts the liberality of future pontiffs and keeps them accountable to their catholic heritage. "Olivi wanted to diminish the capacity of future occupants of the Roman see to injure the church so he insisted on the infallibility—and consequent irreformability—of doctrinal decisions already established by preceding popes."[18]

Olivi's position was not only novel but clouded by his own mixed legacy. Were repeated heresy accusations due to his theology or his view of poverty or both?[19] Regardless of the answer, after Olivi's death his writings were burned, and his views were denounced. His novel position was overshadowed until another generation picked it up again for altogether different reasons.

---

16. *Liber Sextus*, ed. E. Friedberg, in *Corpus Iuris Canonici*, 2 (Leipzig, 1879), Sect. 5.7.3, col. 1110; cf. Tierney, *Origins of Papal Infallibility 1150–1350*, 98.

17. Maccarrone, "Una questione inedita dell'Olivi sull'infallibilità del papa," 328; cf. Tierney, *Origins of Papal Infallibility 1150–1350*, 116. To see Olivi's broader argument for papal supremacy, consult his treatise *Quaestiones de perfectione evangelica* (ca. 1280).

18. Tierney, *Origins of Papal Infallibility 1150–1350*, 129.

19. For a detailed account of the aftermath and heresy charges, see Tierney, *Origins of Papal Infallibility 1150–1350*, 100–101.

HENRY OF GHENT AND DUNS SCOTUS

Pietro Olivi died around AD 1298, and due to the fierce opposition he received both during and after his lifetime, his novel position of papal infallibility had an uncertain future. That uncertainty could have been due to a variety of reasons: Olivi's own controversial legacy, the recognition that past popes had erred, or the unwillingness to circumscribe present papal sovereignty by the infallible decrees of past popes.[20] Regardless of the reasons, from 1280 to 1320 a variety of voices entered the broader conversation over Scripture and its relationship to tradition but shelved Olivi's specific proposal for papal infallibility.

For example, in the thirteenth century, Henry of Ghent entertained a question in his *Summa Quaestionum* that was previously unfathomable: Is there a divergence between Scripture and tradition? Why was such a question asked in the first place?[21] In Henry's day the debate over Franciscan poverty continued. Some asked whether the revelation that Francis received could be contrary to Scripture. If so, should the Christian assume that Scripture and tradition are always compatible? While those in favor of Franciscan poverty said Scripture and tradition were compatible, those seeking to dismantle the original Franciscan vision said the rule of Francis was inconsistent with, even contrary to Scripture. That was no small claim since Francis was considered a saint.[22]

Henry did not approve of tradition as a subsequent and additional source of divine revelation. He did believe the Christian should follow both the Fathers and the Scriptures, and he also believed that God intended the former to expound and elaborate on the latter. "Just as the apostles expounded the Scriptures not expounded by Christ on the model of those that he did expound," said Henry, "so too down to the end of the world Catholic doctors should expound those that Christ and the apostles did not expound on the model of those that they did expound—nor should they be content with old expositions." Henry had a high view of the Fathers, persuaded they were charged with teaching in areas that Scripture did not address. As the apostle John said, there were many things Jesus intended to say to his listeners, but they could not handle them at the time. Therefore, the Spirit of truth was required to lead his church into further truth (John 16:12–13). Although Henry did not propose further revelation, nevertheless, the Fathers were charged with filling out what was lacking in knowledge.

---

20. Tierney offers several educated guesses why: "Perhaps they sensed that the idea of infallibility, with its necessary corollary of irreformability, was incompatible with the theories of papal sovereignty which they were propounding. Probably they had no wish to consecrate as infallible all the decrees of earlier popes that were to be found in Gratian's Decretum, . . . In any case, at the beginning of the fourteenth century, no one doubted that some popes of the past had indeed erred in faith and, to most thinkers, this still seemed to preclude the possibility of developing any theory of papal infallibility." Tierney, *Origins of Papal Infallibility 1150–1350*, 131.

21. Henry of Ghent, *Summa Quaestionum*, supra p. 65 n. 1; cf. Tierney, *Origins of Papal Infallibility 1150–1350*, 133.

22. Tierney, *Origins of Papal Infallibility 1150–1350*, 133.

However, should there be a conflict between the Scriptures and the church—and here Henry has more recent tradition in view than the patristic heritage—then the Scriptures should be prioritized. Henry criticized the church of his day, convinced it had strayed, as evident in the missteps of recent popes and their decrees.[23] Nevertheless, Henry was confident that even if the church—led astray by these papal mistakes—did stray, God would always preserve a remnant as the true church, however small that remnant might be. In such a circumstance, the Scriptures should be followed, not the papacy, a point Henry belabored in his *Quodlibeta*.[24]

As mentioned, in prior centuries patristic and medieval theologians taught what Oberman labeled Tradition 1. They did not divide Scripture and tradition apart but considered tradition the "instrumental vehicle of Scripture" which alone is sacred revelation. However, in the fourteenth century the divide between Scripture and tradition widened. Some considered Henry dangerous due to his pessimistic eschatological outlook coupled with his quick determination to ascribe error to the papacy. Some considered Henry a threat since Henry believed the theologian has the prerogative to dissect and expose the papacy's misjudgments.

Henry's conflict with the papacy expressed a subtle widening between Scripture and tradition, a widening that assumed the two may diverge from one another. That assumption was new. In past centuries, many patristic and medieval theologians also considered Scripture the highest and final authority. Yet they did not, like Henry, entertain whether Scripture and tradition might be incompatible; indeed, the question was unfathomable. As Oberman's definition of Tradition 1 explains, "In the first case Tradition was seen as the instrumental vehicle of Scripture which brings the contents of Holy Scripture to life in a constant dialogue between the doctors of Scripture and the Church."[25] Ironically, in his attempt to elevate Scripture, Henry introduced a new wedge between Scripture and tradition, even if that divide was still primitive in form.[26]

If Henry prized church doctors—like himself—as judges of the papacy, Duns Scotus turned to a general council for the same purpose. Historians are uncertain whether Scotus adopted a Tradition 1 or 2 viewpoint; statements by Scotus can be marshaled in both directions. His deep commitment to the universal church, however, is apparent, and his strong advocacy for its primacy has led some historians to interpret Scotus in the lane of T2. For example, when Scotus wrestled with the logical consistency of a doctrine like transubstantiation, he concluded that even if the Scriptures do not explain the doctrine, the church

23. Tierney, *Origins of Papal Infallibility 1150–1350*, 139.
24. *Quodlibeta Magistri Henrici Goethals a Gandavo*, 1 (Paris, 1518), Quodl, 5. Q. 36, fol. 212r; cf. Tierney, *Origins of Papal Infallibility 1150–1350*, 137–40.
25. Oberman, "Introduction," 55.
26. Tierney thinks Henry may be the first to do so in such radical terms. See Tierney, *Origins of Papal Infallibility 1150–1350*, 140.

does. "I hold this principally on account of the authority of the church which does not err in faith and morals."[27] Or as Scotus said in one of his lectures, "The church holds and teaches many things *which the apostles did not hand down* but which the church has ordained at the command of the Holy Spirit."[28]

Did Scotus mean church teaching ordained by the Spirit was new revelation, or did he mean church teaching was additional revelation? The answer to that question is debated. Regardless, Scotus did convey his deep conviction in the authority of the church catholic. Based on this authority, said Scotus, the church can depose a pope in grave error since the church represents the faithful across time. If the church must take disciplinary action, it can channel the authority of the universal church in the assembly of a general council. For its bishops do not represent themselves alone but all the faithful, a representation far more catholic than a single pope.[29]

However, a new wind blew into the courtyard of church and council in the fourteenth century. That new wind was papal supremacy.

UNAM SANCTAM AND PAPAL SUPREMACY

In the years prior to the Fourth Lateran Council (1215), Pope Innocent asserted himself as the vicar of Christ on earth, a title that in no uncertain terms elevated the pope to a level of supremacy that even encompassed secular jurisdiction. That papal claim created endless tension between popes and Holy Roman emperors, even after Innocent died in 1216.

The effect was variegated. For example, the papacy vied for control in Germany, a control Frederick II (1210–50) resisted to his dying breath. Subdued, Germany no longer presented a united front against foreign authority. Germany splintered as a result, and power shifted from the emperor to princes across German territories.[30] As chapters 10–11 will explain, these princes became instrumental to the Reformation, protecting Martin Luther from the emperor and the papacy alike.

However, France did maintain its independence. Furthermore, France gained the upper hand on the papacy for the good part of the fourteenth century. King Philip the Fair (1285–1314) believed he was sovereign, which only challenged Pope Boniface VIII (1294–1303) and his claims to supremacy. Like Innocent before him, Boniface stretched his papal power over the political province. The secular realm, not merely the spiritual realm, must recognize the pope as Christ's representative on earth, said Boniface.

---

27. Duns Scotus, *Reportata parisiensia*, 4, d. 11 q. 3 n. 13, in *Opera* (Vivès), 24, p. 120 (Rosato, p. 239); cf. Tierney, *Origins of Papal Infallibility 1150–1350*, 143.
28. *Reportatio examinate* 1, d. 11 n. 18 (Rosato, loc. cit.); cf. Tierney, *Origins of Papal Infallibility 1150–1350*, 141.
29. Tierney points to the year 1300 in particular and concludes that "other scholars were emphasizing the authority of general councils in the church precisely in order to limit the centralized power that was commonly attributed to the popes." Tierney, *Origins of Papal Infallibility 1150–1350*, 154.
30. Needham, *Two Thousand Years of Christ's Power*, 2:403.

However, Philip took advantage of ecclesiastical assets to benefit his army. Philip taxed the clergy in France and then used the funds to strengthen his army. The stronger Philip's army the more likely his defeat of England. Taking a page from Innocent, Boniface threatened excommunication when Philip IV persisted. But unlike Innocent, Boniface could not overcome the political shrewdness of Philip or the strength of his military. For example, Philip retaliated by shutting down the channel between France and Rome that disseminated gold and silver, generating a recession in Rome that threatened their survival. Boniface had no choice but to relent.

The power struggle continued to escalate with each passing conflict as both Philip and Boniface claimed supremacy.[31] Then in 1302 Boniface sanctioned the bull *Unam Sanctam*, articulating papal supremacy in a way that was far more explicit than the Fourth Lateran Council. The bull reiterated the Fourth Lateran Council's statement on the exclusivity of salvation in the Catholic Church by comparing the church to Noah's ark. The pope was like Noah, the "helmsman and captain; outside which all things on earth, we read, were destroyed." Like the ark, "outside this church there is neither salvation nor remission of sins." As for the pope, he held the keys to the ark. "Of this one and only church there is one body and one head—not two heads, like a monster—namely Christ, and Christ's vicar is Peter, and Peter's successor. . . . Therefore, if the Greeks or others say that they were not committed to Peter and his successors, they necessarily confess that they are not of Christ's sheep, for the Lord says in John, 'There is one fold and one shepherd.'"[32]

What was the extent of the pope's domain? The pope's dominion extended from the church outward, across every country, every state, every territory. In practice, that meant that the pope not only had the right to bear the spiritual sword (the Scriptures) but the political sword (for bloodshed) as well. "And we learn from the words of the gospel that in this church and in her power are two swords, the spiritual and the temporal. . . . Both are in the power of the church, the spiritual sword and the material. But the latter is to be used for the church, the former by her; the former by the priest, the latter by kings and captains but at the will and by the permission of the priest." Which sword then is subject to the other? "The one sword, then, should be under the other, and temporal authority subject to spiritual. . . . We must clearly recognize that the spiritual power without doubt is superior to temporal, in worth and nobility, and this all the more, since spiritual things are clearly superior to temporal matters. For it is proven to be true that spiritual power must establish and judge earthly power, if it be not good."[33]

In the High Middle Ages, the distinction between the two swords assumed

---

31. The conflict that immediately precipitated the bull, *Unam sanctam*, was the imprisonment of the pope's legate, Bernard of Saisset, and the accusation of treason.

32. *CCFCT* 1:746.

33. *CCFCT* 1:746–47.

two separate entities: the spiritual and the temporal. The state wielded the material sword, the church wielded the spiritual sword. But in the mind of a pope like Boniface, the state swung its sword out of a responsibility, even in obedience *to the pope and the church*. Temporal authorities should bear the sword to punish those who dissent from church doctrine and practice. Heresy was condemned by the papacy, and the punishment was meted out by the state. A spiritual misstep could cost a heretic his livelihood and even his life.

Boniface did not claim absolute sovereignty merely because he believed Scripture justified papal supremacy. Boniface believed his supreme authority as pope was God-given, divinely appointed. "For this authority, although given to a man and exercised by a man, is not human, but rather divine, given at God's mouth to Peter and established on a rock for him and his successors in him whom he confessed, the Lord saying to Peter himself, 'Whatsoever you shall bind,' etc." Since the pope's authority was divine in origin, to resist the pope was to resist God himself and place oneself outside the hope of redemption. "Whoever therefore resists this power thus ordained of God, resists the ordinance of God. . . . Furthermore, we declare, state, define, and pronounce that it is altogether necessary to salvation for every human creature to be subject to the Roman pontiff."[34]

Did Philip heed the pope's claim to papal supremacy? No, he claimed instead that Boniface should be held accountable to a church council, one that recruited both East and West to decide whether Boniface should remain in Peter's chair. Boniface was outraged: how dare Philip and Parliament and the French challenge papal supremacy with an ecumenical council! Yet Boniface was no match for Philip. He pulled out his excommunication card, and Philip unsheathed his sword, capturing Boniface at last. By then, however, Boniface was fragile and died not long after.

Boniface made bold theological claims to papal supremacy, but the conflict diminished papal power against the bulwark of a united foreign front. "Nationalism as a political and anti-papal force had arrived on the European scene."[35] Philip had not only challenged the pope, but in the years ahead managed to put a French pope on Peter's throne to do his bidding. That pope was none other than Gascon Clement V (1305–14).

CLEMENT V AND THE AVIGNON CAPTIVITY

Clement V's acquiesce to Philip was already a defeat for the papacy. In the eyes of critics, Philip himself might as well have been the pope. Furthermore, Clement changed the papacy's future trajectory when he relocated the papacy from Rome to Avignon, where it remained from 1309 to 1377.

A more significant statement could not have been made; a more disheartening

---

34. *CCFCT* 1:746–47.
35. Needham, *Two Thousand Years of Christ's Power*, 2:405.

defeat could not have been accomplished. Past popes considered themselves the true successors of Peter. Innocent had even announced himself as the very vicar of Christ on earth. The papacy *must* reside in Rome, where Christ appointed Peter as the first bishop of the church. Now that the papacy had been relocated to French jurisdiction and restructured with French popes and cardinals, all was lost. The papacy had entered a period of captivity, an Avignon captivity comparable to the Babylonian captivity experienced by Israel in the Old Testament. It was not a coincidence that Martin Luther used this phrase—Babylonian captivity—to describe the corruption of the papacy of Rome, a slander that cut deep into the Roman ego, exposing a deeper captivity, a spiritual captivity, one that no state lines could control (see chapter 8).

The Avignon captivity marked the downfall of papal popularity and power during the fourteenth century. During the captivity the papacy became the target of severe criticism. The reasons were many: First, so many popes were French that critics considered the papacy the handmaid of French governance. Other countries struggled to submit themselves to the authority of the papacy when that ecclesiastical authority felt governed by the national agenda of the French. As the English engaged in the Hundred Years' War with France, this tension became palpable.[36]

Second, the papacy practiced simony. For the right price, most offices could be bought. Critics joked but were quite serious when they laughed and said, "All things are for sale in Avignon." From benefices small and great to legal cases, the papacy had its fingers in every monetary purse. The papacy evolved—"From a body enjoying a considerable degree of local autonomy it was transformed into a highly centralized and absolutistic organization increasingly subject to the will of the pope."[37]

During this Avignon era, the question of papal authority and even infallibility came under debate once more.[38] For example, in his 1324 work *Defender of Peace*, Marsilius of Padua questioned the infallibility of the Church of Rome, the pope included. As for ultimate authority, Marsilius threw into doubt the divine right of the pope and proposed instead that ecumenical councils, governed by Scripture, should represent the people. In that same vein, Marsilius also challenged the pope's jurisdiction, over against the claims of Boniface, for example. The pope and clergy stretched beyond their office when they interfered with the affairs of secular rulers and governments. For Marsilius, society was a divine construct, which means God positioned the secular authorities to oversee and even decide on matters in the church from councils to clergy. For these reasons, some historians label Marsilius a Protestant Reformer before there ever was such a thing.[39]

---

36. Spinka, "Conciliarism as Ecclesiastical Reform," 91.
37. Spinka, "Conciliarism as Ecclesiastical Reform," 92.
38. We will examine Marsilius and Ockham, but also noteworthy is John of Paris and Michael de Cesena. See Spinka, "Conciliarism as Ecclesiastical Reform," 93.
39. Needham, *Two Thousand Years of Christ's Power*, 2:407.

POPE JOHN XXII, WILLIAM OF OCKHAM, AND THE UNIVERSAL CHURCH

In the 1320s, the debate over Franciscan poverty continued, but this time Francis's rule met a ready challenger in Pope John XXII. Almost a decade into his papacy John XXII rejected *Exiit*, the 1279 bull of Nicholas III in support of Franciscan poverty. The reaction was as innovative as it was fierce, since the argument used against Pope John XXII was papal infallibility. What right did John XXII have to revoke an established papal bull? The question (objection) assumed past papal decrees might be infallible and if infallible then irreformable.[40] Since Olivi, suspicion hovered like a dark cloud over papal infallibility. But Pope John XXII's bold disregard now motivated his opponents to resurrect the doctrine even though it lacked significant precedent. "What the Roman pontiffs have once defined in faith and morals with the key of knowledge stands so immutably that it is not permitted to a successor to revoke it."[41] In 1324 Pope John XXII defended himself by pointing out the obvious—papal infallibility had no official historical heritage. Condemning its unorthodoxy in his own bull, *Quia quorundam*, John then proceeded to discredit papal infallibility because it undermined papal sovereignty, binding the present pope to decisions and decrees of the past that may or may not be relevant or even right.[42]

The Franciscans replied with fire of their own, accusing the pope of heresy for revoking a decree that concerned faith and morals. John questioned their verdict; his bull was not so specific to revoke a decree in both faith and morals. Instead, John was revoking the rule of poverty, which was not necessarily a matter of "faith" and was nowhere taught in Scripture.[43] Implied in John's reply was his appeal to Scripture as if it were the single supreme source of divine revelation and therefore the principal authority in the matter, which did not satisfy his Franciscan critics, who elevated the tradition of the papacy as an additional source of revelation with equal authority to Scripture in their attempt to defend papal infallibility. "The whole theology of 'ecclesiastical fideism' that had dominated Franciscan theology since the days of Bonaventure, the belief that the church was a second source of divine revelation, supplementary to Scripture, was alien to Pope John. He had no sympathy with such a system and perhaps little understanding of it. He had been brought up in the canonist tradition that saw Scripture as the unique source of Christian faith."[44]

---

40. Tierney, *Origins of Papal Infallibility 1150–1350*, 171. Also see Tierney, *Crisis of Church and State 1050–1300*.

41. These are Pope John XXII's words describing the claim of his opponents. *Extrav. Ioann. XXII*, Tit. 14, c. 5, col. 1231; cf. Tierney, *Origins of Papal Infallibility 1150–1350*, 186.

42. For his argument, see *Quodlibeta Joannis Bachonis Anglici* (Venice, 1527), fol. 63v; cf. Tierney, *Origins of Papal Infallibility 1150–1350*, 188–89.

43. Tierney, *Origins of Papal Infallibility 1150–1350*, 191–92. Tierney highlights the irony of the back-and-forth debate: "Not only did the pope's opponents rather than the pope himself advance the doctrine of infallibility. Further, that doctrine had been created by Pietro Olivi; and the men who gave it a new currency were not Olivi's followers in the Franciscan order but their most bitter [*sic*] enemies, the Michaelists" (189).

44. Tierney, *Origins of Papal Infallibility 1150–1350*, 193.

One Franciscan, William of Ockham, managed to condemn Pope John XXII while advocating for a somewhat novel if not paradoxical viewpoint. Ockham's ecclesiology is infamous for its lack of systematic clarity, which has led interpreters to opposite conclusions.[45] However, Ockham was perspicuous when he reached the conclusion that Pope John XXII was a heretic. By the time Ockham reached this conclusion, he was already in the middle of controversy. As chapter 5 explained, Ockham's rejection of universals, his skepticism toward natural theology, as well as his separation of faith and reason all brought him into conflict with his own order, the Franciscans. Ockham was, in short, departing from the classical Christian tradition before him, from Augustine to Anselm to Thomas Aquinas, challenging major facets of classical realism. In 1323 Ockham was in England when he was summoned to give an account for his controversial positions before his order. When his opponents took Ockham's deviance a step up the ecclesiastical ladder and reported to the papacy, Ockham was summoned to Avignon.

From 1324 to 1328, Ockham had to convince the papacy he was not a heretic. During that time, Ockham was approached by Michael of Cesena, who was disturbed over Pope John XXII's denial of Franciscan poverty just prior to Ockham's arrival in Avignon. The Franciscans prided themselves on their apostolic model: they disowned all possessions to follow Lady Poverty (see chapter 2). Pope John XXII decided the vow was disagreeable. How could the Franciscans disavow poverty and all possessions yet claim others were obligated to lend their land and possessions for Franciscan use? The Franciscans claimed their model was apostolic, but such a practice is absent from Scripture and ancient tradition alike.

Ockham was outraged and concluded that he was one of the few left in the church who remained faithful to catholic orthodoxy. He put on himself the responsibility to alert the rest of the church: the vicar of Christ was leading the sheep into apostasy.[46] Since John was a heretic in Ockham's estimation, he was not truly pope at all. Ockham's high view of the papacy was relevant to his pronouncement that the pope was a heretic. Assuming a two-source theory of Scripture and tradition, the papal decrees of the past were true, certain, and immutable, an infallible channel of revelation complementary to Scripture. In short, the papal decrees were irreformable. John was a heretic because he believed he could rescind prior papal decrees. To make matters worse, the pope thought he could annul not only papal decrees that addressed the morality of the church but even those decrees that addressed the beliefs of the church. However, since Pope John never actually said such a thing in so many words, Ockham had to prove his case by putting together John's statements with what those statements implied.

---

45. Ockham's works on ecclesiology include: *Epistola ad Fratres Minores; Dialogus; Opus nonaginta dierum; Contra Iohannes; Contra Benedictum.* In 1343 Ockham's *Dialogue* shocked a patriarchal society and church when he proposed that not only men, but women, too, should be able to participate in a general council. See Spinka, "Conciliarism as Ecclesiastical Reform," 94. For an exposition of Ockham's ecclesiology, see Tierney, *Origins of Papal Infallibility 1150–1350*, 205–37.

46. Tierney, *Origins of Papal Infallibility 1150–1350*, 210.

Ockham was not bothered by the tension between his irreformable doctrine and his present claim that the pope was fallible. Ockham made a distinction that relieved the tension: "Whatever (John) defined with the key of knowledge, *while he was supreme pontiff*, should not be called into question. But what he defined against the definitions of the Roman pontiffs was not defined through the key of knowledge but through heretical depravity."[47] For Ockham, Scripture did not err. Nor did the church universal. However, as Pope John XXII exemplified, a pope can err. "No pope is the rule of Christian faith for he can err and be stained with heresy," said Ockham.[48] Was Ockham the Luther of the fourteenth century? Far from it, considering his two-source presupposition. Although he might sound like a forerunner, the context of such statements manifests Ockham's T2 position. For example, when Ockham arrived at certain doctrines of the faith—like transubstantiation—he wrestled with their logical validity. Nevertheless, he decided that even if such doctrines were neither logical nor present in the Scriptures, at some point they were revealed to the church and therefore must be believed. Otherwise the Christian was not a true catholic.[49]

However, Ockham was no average conciliarist, either. On one hand, Ockham did elevate the authority of a council above the pope. On the other hand, Ockham said a council can err. Therefore, Ockham was not comfortable admitting that a council can epitomize the universal church. The universal church alone is incapable of error or apostasy.[50] If the universal church is the only entity where impeccable assurance is found, then any and every individual Christian can judge the credibility of the pope. It follows, then, that even if the whole papacy and all its councils stand against the individual, that one individual who is left may be the universal church while the rest go to hell. In summary, Ockham deconstructed the historic, institutional church. For Ockham, "no dissent from the generally accepted faith could be answered by an appeal to the authority of the institutional church. In Ockham's ecclesiology, the individual dissenter might well constitute the one true church."[51]

Ockham was not blind to where the logic of his argument must lead: the elect may be, in the end, a minuscule remnant. Hypothetically, the elect may be Ockham and Ockham alone. Critics of Ockham point out the contradictory

---

47. *Opus nonaginta dierum*, 844; cf. Tierney, *Origins of Papal Infallibility 1150–1350*, 215.

48. "If different supreme pontiffs are shown to have contrary opinions on anything pertaining to orthodox faith, recourse is to be had to sacred Scripture and the doctrine or assertion of the universal church.... Sacred Scripture and the doctrine of the universal church which cannot err, this is our rule of faith." *Tractatus contra Ioannem, Opera politica*, 3, p. 72; cf. Tierney, *Origins of Papal Infallibility 1150–1350*, 218.

49. Both Oberman and Tierney pushed back against older interpretations of Ockham that attempted to interpret Ockham as a forerunner of the Reformation. See Oberman, *The Harvest of Medieval Theology*, 361–82; Tierney, *Origins of Papal Infallibility 1150–1350*, 220–24.

50. Ockham, *Dialogus*, in M. Goldast, *Monarchia S. Romani imperii* 2 (Frankfurt, 1614), 494–98; cf. Tierney, *Origins of Papal Infallibility 1150–1350*, 231–32.

51. "Quite consistently Ockham maintained (in the *Breviloquium*) that every individual Catholic had the right and duty of judging the orthodoxy of papal pronouncements by the light of his own knowledge of the faith." Tierney, *Origins of Papal Infallibility 1150–1350*, 232–33.

nature of his logic: "He wanted the institutional church to crush error while denying that any church institution could certainly define the truth. He offers us only dogma without order, anarchy without freedom, subjectivism without tolerance."[52] And yet Ockham's argument stemmed from a T2 framework, one that matured in the centuries after Ockham and eventually found full expression at Trent over against Reformers like Luther.[53]

PAPAL INFALLIBILITY: FROM GUIDO TERRENI TO VATICAN COUNCIL I

Despite the attention papal infallibility received by the heated controversy over Pope John XII, Franciscan fire aimed at securing past papal decrees like *Exiit*. However, a strategic move originated from Guido Terreni, who advanced the argument for papal infallibility by not only focusing on how papal infallibility could secure the past but also buttress the power of the pope in the present. By doing so, Terreni connected the pope to the church universal, disallowing opponents to appeal to the church universal over against the pope. For example, Terreni wrote, "It is to be said of the supreme pontiff that although in himself he can err as a single person, nevertheless the Holy Spirit does not permit him to define anything contrary to the faith of the church for the sake of the community of the faithful and the universal church, for whose faith the Lord prayed" (*Quaestio*, 28).

Terreni claimed that Thomas Aquinas was a defender of papal infallibility, but historians like Tierney have demonstrated that claim is not supported by evidence. Regardless, with Terreni's well-rounded apologetic for papal infallibility, the church was now set on a trajectory that reached its pinnacle when the First Vatican Council decreed papal infallibility to be official church dogma on July 18, 1870:

> Therefore faithfully adhering to the tradition received from the beginning of the Christian faith . . . we teach and define that it is a dogma divinely revealed: that the Roman Pontiff, when he speaks *ex cathedra*, that is, when in discharge of the office of Pastor and Doctor of all Christians, by virtue of his supreme Apostolic authority he defines a doctrine regarding faith or morals to be held by the Universal Church, by the divine assistance promised to him in blessed Peter, is possessed of that infallibility with which the divine Redeemer willed that His Church should be endowed for defining doctrine regarding faith or morals: and that therefore such definitions of the Roman Pontiff are irreformable of themselves, and not from the consent of the Church. (C. Butler, *The Vatican Council*, 295; cf. Tierney, *Origins of Papal Infallibility 1150–1350*, 1, 245–49.)

---

52. Tierney, *Origins of Papal Infallibility 1150–1350*, 236. "Ockham showed how a belief in the infallibility of the pope and the church (the true pope and the true church of course) could just as logically lead to a position of radical dissent. Ockham began by insisting on the unity in faith of the church. He ended by justifying the most radical sectarianism" (237).

53. Oberman, *The Harvest of Medieval Theology*, 361–82. Tierney goes so far to channel the two-source

Historians debate whether Ockham's ecclesiology was the outcome of his nominalist metaphysic and epistemology (see chapter 5). Denis Janz argued that various strands of Ockhamists were born out of his theology. For some, Ockham's rejection of universals resulted in a church whose mediating power was in name only. The "distinction between God's absolute and ordained power seemed to relativize the mediatorial role of the church and its sacraments. These were, after all, contingent: the Church mediated God's grace not because of its intrinsic nature but because of God's free decision." However, other Ockhamists attempted a less radical conclusion: "Even if they saw the church as a strictly historical institution, [they] emphasized God's eternal and unalterable commitment to grant his grace through it."[54] The latter did not stake their flag against the pope himself whose office they retained, so much as voice their insistence that the papacy should not be synonymous with the church itself.[55] However, other historians have been less enthusiastic to draw such a connection between Ockham's nominalism and ecclesiology.[56] Either way, the elevation of the laity by Ockham is likely driven by a different paradigm (and different motives) than the Reformation's priesthood of believers. And from one uncommon perspective, the Protestant notion of priesthood could be far more realist than nominalist since every believer *participates* in the priesthood of Christ.

Ockham's opposition to Pope John XXII did not end well for the late medieval Scholastic. His reaction was ironic: Ockham was already in Avignon because his opponents claimed he was a heretic. Then Ockham decided during his stay to declare the pope himself a heretic. The year he did so, 1328, Ockham fled for his life. He found refuge in Munich, Germany, thanks to Ludwig of Bavaria, but that did not stop the pope from excommunicating Ockham that same year.

THE GREAT SCHISM AND THE CAMPAIGN FOR CONCILIARISM

In 1377, after almost seventy years of French control, the papacy finally celebrated its homecoming in Rome with Pope Gregory XI. But Gregory died in 1378, and the papacy was plagued by international and sometimes internal competition and conflict. Division reached new heights, marking the start of the Great Schism (1378–1417), a seemingly endless conflict between rival popes.

The Italian pope Urban VI (1378–89) vied against the French pope Clement VII (1378–94), with each claiming to be the rightful successor of Peter and each excommunicating the other. In part, the cardinals were to blame: intimidated by the Italians, they decided to choose Urban but later changed their minds and chose Clement instead in September 1378. Now the church had two competing

---

theory through Ockham as if Ockham is the launching pad for Pierre d'Ailly, Jean Gerson, Gabriel Biel, and then Trent. *Origins of Papal Infallibility 1150–1350*, 220, 270.

54. Janz, "Late medieval theology," 12–13.

55. Janz gives diverse examples, from Gabriel Biel to the Council of Constance, Pierre d'Ailly, and Jean Gerson. Janz, "Late medieval theology," 13.

56. E.g., Tierney, *Origins of Papal Infallibility 1150–1350*, 205–237.

popes, one in Rome, one in Avignon, neither one about to back down. To cement the division, both popes recruited international allies, dividing up all of Europe.[57] The complexity of the conflict was only magnified by Urban's and Clement's successors.

Prior popes had prided themselves on the unity of the church, claiming there was but one universal church with one supreme head. But any prior romance with catholic church unity was now dispelled. So, too, were prior dreams of universal papal jurisdiction over secular authorities. The division now marked entire countries off for one side or the other and gave kings and rulers the upper hand to dictate the papacy on their terms, rather than vice versa. Even the church took part.

For example, referring to *the* church became problematic; depending on the country, the church might identify itself as independent from the church in Rome, as seen when the French or Gallican Church denied the papacy any authority except in the domain of theology at the turn of the fifteenth century.[58] "Gallicanism can be conveniently described as medieval 'de Gaullism' which emphasizes the independence of the French Church from the Roman Church and conceives of the two as equal partners in the Church Universal. Religiously it represents a point of view opposed to ultramontanism which looks for authority and spiritual guidance to 'the other side of the mountains,' that is, south of the Alps to Italy, to Rome." The effects, however, were not only religious but political. "Politically it will not concede to either Italy or Germany the succession of the Roman Empire but presses its own political privileges and inheritance." Gallicanism, concluded Oberman, become a "natural breeding ground for conciliarism which emphasizes the Council as the highest authority in the Church and opposes curialism in its doctrine of papal supremacy."[59]

In sum, the type of papal power and supremacy envisioned by Innocent and Boniface was inconceivable at the moment. Yet the most significant damage was spiritual: a divided papacy characterized by anathemas all around lost its salvific authority, no longer trusted as the fountain of salvation. Roman Catholics in the twentieth century noted the collateral damage. For example, Joseph Ratzinger, later to become Pope Benedict XVI, observed, "For nearly half a century, the Church was split into two or three obediences that excommunicated one another, so that every Catholic lived under excommunication by one pope or another, and, in the last analysis, no one could say with certainty which of the contenders had right on his side. The Church no longer offered certainty of salvation; she had become questionable in her whole objective form—the true Church, the true pledge of salvation, had to be sought outside the institution."[60]

57. England and its allies supported Urban while Scotland, Spain, Portugal, Savoy, and some German territories supported Clement. See Spinka, "Conciliarism as Ecclesiastical Reform," 93.
58. See the *Subtraction of Obedience* (1398); the *Liberties of the Gallican Church* (1407).
59. Oberman, *Forerunners of the Reformation*, 61.
60. Ratzinger, *Principles of Catholic Theology*, 196.

However, those known as conciliarists believed unity could be restored but could only return through the authority of a council, not a pope(s). The conciliarists distinguished between the Catholic Church and the Roman Church. The former was superior, representing the body of believers across time (the universal church), while the latter was subordinate, representing the pope and cardinals of the day. The Catholic Church gathered at councils from which the authority of the pope and cardinals stemmed. Derivative in authority, the pope and cardinals could err, and when they did err it was the responsibility of the Catholic Church to correct them by virtue of an infallible council. In canon law, the phrase "unless he deviates from the faith," was included so that if the pope did transgress the doctrines or practices or spirit of the Catholic Church, he could be disciplined.[61] According to the conciliarists, even cardinals participated in such a disciplinary measure, claiming the right to call a council if they believed the pope was leading the church astray.

The conciliar concept was not new. As mentioned, in the first half of the fourteenth century Marsilius had made similar statements, as did late medieval Scholastics like William of Ockham. Now, as the fifteenth century approached, new voices were needed to address an evolving context. One such voice was the French theologian John Brevicoxa, who was no stranger to the work of William of Ockham. Brevicoxa was not as well known in his own day as his colleagues at the Parisian College of Navarre or the University of Paris. However, as historians look back on the fourteenth century and discern signs of conciliarism, Brevicoxa rises above others for his nuanced advocacy. His view of councils and the papacy are apparent as far back as his student days at Navarre.

Brevicoxa wrote a work called *A Treatise on Faith, the Church, the Roman Pontiff, and the General Council* (1375), distinguishing between T1 and T2. In the words of Brevicoxa, T1 refers to "only those truths which have authority from Divine Scripture, that is, which can be plainly deduced from Scripture, ought to be counted among Catholic truths." By contrast, T2 means "many truths not found in Sacred Scripture, nor necessarily deducible from its contents alone, ought to be assented to as a condition for salvation."[62] According to T2, the nature of the church substantiates those truths otherwise not deducible from Scripture but nonetheless required for salvation (Brevicoxa assumed the validity of "implicit faith" as well).[63] "The Universal Church cannot err," and therefore T2 is "more probable."[64] Brevicoxa was not a forerunner of *sola scriptura* or T1, but he did have conciliarism running through his veins. Infallibility

---

61. In Latin: *nisi deprehendatur a fide devius*. Cf. George, *Reading Scripture with the Reformers*, 102–36.

62. Brevicoxa, *A Treatise on Faith, the Church, the Roman Pontiff, and the General Council*, 71.

63. Implicit faith means that "he who holds all things contained in Scripture or taught by the Universal Church to be true and sane, and does not adhere stubbornly to anything contrary to Catholic truth, has a complete and uncorrupted faith and, according to this definition, ought to be counted as a Catholic." Brevicoxa, 84.

64. Brevicoxa, 72.

was affirmed, but Brevicoxa located infallibility in the church universal, not in a single office such as the pope's.[65]

Many conciliarists were born out of the University of Paris. In his feud with the French pope Clement VII over the rightful claim to the papal throne, Urban VI did whatever he could to undermine the success of German theologians at the University of Paris, including Conrad of Gelnhausen (d. 1390) and Henry of Langenstein (d. 1397).[66] Like Ockham, these German theologians advocated for the *via concilli*, the way of the council. Conrad of Gelnhausen, for example, wrote *A Short Letter* (1379) directed at the French king Charles V of France and the Roman king Wenceslas IV, appealing to a general council. When his letter was ignored, Conrad then wrote a second one, *A Letter of Concord* (1380).[67] Even though the two letters were unsuccessful in producing a council, they are evidence of the growing case for conciliarism as the fifteenth century approached.

The next year the case for the *via concilli* pushed forward when Conrad of Gelnhausen and Henry of Langenstein galvanized the University of Paris to go public with a statement advocating conciliarism (1381). The same year the University of Paris made its proposal, Henry published *A Letter on Behalf of a Council of Peace*.[68] The letter was bold, calling out simony and avarice in the church, shaming those sowing seeds of schism. "Religion is in exile, apostasy rules supreme," said Henry.[69] Nevertheless, Henry also believed this apostasy was an opportunity for restoration, even reformation. However, reformation that results in concord will only happen if a council intervenes. Henry spent much of his letter answering the most typical objections to the intervention of a council. He gave special credibility to historical precedence as he answered these objections.

For example, when "the emperor Constantine wished to exalt the Church by a grant of temporal privileges, etc., he held a universal assembly of the imperial court. Thus, a fortiori, a universal convocation must be held for the spiritual good of the Church." Likewise, when Augustine strained to settle the Pelagian controversy and put heresy to bed, Augustine believed a council was the only hope. "'Against this heresy' (namely, the Pelagian), he writes, 'there was at first much discussion; then, as the ultimate resource, it was referred to the episcopal councils.'"[70] Henry followed Augustine's lead when he added, "The pope is able to err in passing judg-

---

65. Oberman identified a "Gallican trend" in the thought of Brevicoxa, one that "becomes even more discernible when he agrees with the 'unanimous witness of all scholastics' that the Universal Church, in contrast to the Roman Church, cannot err (col. 893)." Oberman, *Forerunners of the Reformation*, 61.

66. For the context, see Spinka, "Conciliarism as Ecclesiastical Reform," 94.

67. Spinka, "Conciliarism as Ecclesiastical Reform," 94.

68. "The section dealing with the *via concilli* is obviously dependent upon Conrad of Gelnhausen; but the latter's work was similarly used by Peter d'Ailly, who incorporated almost all of chapters 16–19 into his *Tractatus super reformation ecclesiae* (A Treatise on the Reformation of the Church); and John Gerson, whose verbatim transcript (save one section) of it was published by the Council of Constance. It was likewise used on the same occasion by Dietrich of Niem." Spinka, "Conciliarism as Ecclesiastical Reform," 95.

69. Henry of Langenstein, *A Letter on Behalf of a Council of Peace* (1381), in *Advocates of Reform*, 108.

70. Henry was quoting *De gratia et libero arbitrio*. Henry of Langenstein, *A Letter on Behalf of a Council of Peace* (1381), 117.

ment," but the "Universal Church ... is not able to err" and therefore is "superior to the college of cardinals and the pope because he does not have this prerogative."[71] Conciliar superiority is indebted to two factors: (1) the guidance of the Holy Spirit and (2) the "never-failing Head" of the church, Christ Jesus.[72]

Did these bold advocacies for conciliarism work? They did not, but back-fired instead. Clement VII tightened his grip on the university until the German theologians were pressured out, leaving Paris for Vienna, where Henry of Langenstein started a university in the conciliarist vein.[73] With the exit of Henry of Langenstein and the German theologians, the baton for conciliarism in Paris needed fresh advocates but ones just as persistent. Two of Ockham's theological heirs rose to the challenge.

The first was Peter d'Ailly (ca. 1350/51–1420), chancellor at Paris University, and the second was his successor, John Gerson (1363–1429). Gerson wrote *A Tractate on the Unity of the Church* (1409), which prioritized Christ as the head of the church. Gerson put forward many scenarios that not only permitted but demanded disobedience to the pope, even insurrection. For example, should the pope be responsible for either schism or heresy, it was the duty of the church to convene without him and, potentially, to consider inflicting the severest pun-ishment. "It would be permissible to hold a general council against his will; and finally, to force him to abdicate, or, if he resisted, to deprive him of all honor and rank, and even his life."[74] *Papa fluit, papatus stabilis est.* "The pope passes, the papacy remains."[75]

The conciliarists of the fifteenth century did face unique challenges. They had to advance their position within a different political and ecclesiastical con-text than conciliarists before them. "Ockham and Marsilius had put their anti-papal ideas forward on behalf of the Holy Roman Empire in its political conflict with the papacy. D'Ailly, Gerson, and Cusa gave conciliarism a fresh cutting edge by propagating it in the name of the Church, at a time when (due to the Schism) there was no effective papacy."[76] To their own detriment, the conciliarists made a series of decisions that guaranteed their downfall, and these decisions had much to do with the resolution to the Great Schism itself.

---

71. Henry of Langenstein, 118–19.

72. Henry of Langenstein, 127–32.

73. Spinka, "Conciliarism as Ecclesiastical Reform," 96. Other advocates of conciliarism in Germany that deserve mention include Dietrich of Niem (d. 1418) and Nicholas of Cusa (1401–64). For example, consult Dietrich's *Ways of Uniting and Reforming the Church (1410)*, 149–74.

74. "In a word, all these and similar actions are permissible according to the immutable divine and natural law, because against this truth no law or constitution of a mere man ought to be made without fresh authoriza-tion from God, except to be condemned as intolerable error." Gerson, *On the Unity of the Church (1409)*, 146.

75. Spinka, "Conciliarism as Ecclesiastical Reform," 100.

76. Needham, *Two Thousand Years of Christ's Power*, 2:410. The conciliarists "claimed that the plenitude potestatis, 'fulness of power,' resided only in God, not in any individual man, not even in the pope. The con-ciliarists advocated one pope, one undivided church, and a program of moral reform modeled on the example of the early church" (George, *Theology of the Reformers*, 33). The conciliarist-curialist debate can also be found in the Netherlands during the latter half of the fifteenth century. See, e.g., *Letter from Jacob Hoeck and Wessel Gansfort*, 93–120.

THE RESOLUTION TO SCHISM AND THE
TRIUMPH OF CURIALISM

In 1409, the same year Gerson's *De unitate* was published, the conciliarist Council of Pisa in Italy convened in an attempt to conclude the schism.[77] The cardinals decided they had the right as a council to elect a pope that would supersede Gregory XII in Rome and Benedict XIII in Avignon. In other words, by taking matters into their own hands, they did not listen to Gerson, who said that universal support should accompany the establishment of a new pope. The council chose Alexander V as the alternative replacement, but the cardinals failed to anticipate immediate disregard of the council from both sides as each side still stayed loyal to their preexisting pope. Rather than solving the problem of a divided papacy, the council now convoluted the problem by introducing yet another pope. The failure of their election matched the short tenure of Alexander V's service (1409–10). By the next year, a successor was found, John XXIII (1410–15), and the tripartite contention continued.

From 1414 to 1418 the Council of Constance in Switzerland attempted to succeed where Pisa had failed. Whereas Pisa was called by cardinals, Constance was called by the Holy Roman emperor. Sigismund was forceful in ways the cardinals were not, managing to eliminate all three popes through his political astuteness. John XXIII agreed to abdicate on one condition: the other popes also had to abdicate.[78] With the abdication of all three, now a new pope could be elected, Martin V (1417–31), without warring competition from the previous popes and their allies. The plan worked. Martin V was elected by the end of 1417, successfully terminating the schism that had divided the church for decades on end.

Did conciliarism win in the end? Constance issued a decree, *Sacrosancta* (1415), parading the supremacy of the church council over papal supremacy, claiming such authority came from Christ in heaven and demanded the subservience of any pope.[79] However, what appeared to be a victory for conciliarism proved to be a serendipitous opportunity for curialism, the supremacy of the papacy over a council. For the pope elected, Martin V, rejected conciliarism, and his successor, Eugenius IV (1431–47), fostered the same animosity toward conciliarism. For example, Eugenius proceeded in an arduous battle with the Council of Basel. But the fatal flaw of the conciliarists was their decision to depose Eugenius. They returned to the tactics they used at Pisa but did not learn from them. True, they succeeded in electing a papal substitute, Felix V (1439–49), but like Pisa, they were perceived as creating more problems than solutions, resurrecting the Great Schism Constance had overcome by once again introducing competing popes. Public opinion turned on the conciliarists, and they lost

---

77. For the events that led to Pisa, see Spinka, "Conciliarism as Ecclesiastical Reform," 94–99.

78. However, the abdications did not proceed as Sigismund anticipated. See Spinka, "Conciliarism as Ecclesiastical Reform," 102–3.

79. Cameron, *European Reformation*, 54.

the confidence they needed to thrive against curialism moving forward. Like salt in the wound, some of the most notable conciliarists flipped, joining the curialists instead.

By 1449 defeat was inevitable, and the latter half of the fifteenth century was marked by the rise of papal power, supremacy, and claims to infallibility. In 1460, for example, Pope Pius II issued a bull called *Execrabilis*, promising to excommunicate all those who dared appeal to a future council rather than the pope. The bull, observed Oberman, "struck at the heart of conciliarism . . . [and] thus declared—with more vigor than Pope Martin V before—null and void the two famous decrees of Constance: *Sacrosancta* (the superiority of the council over the pope—April 6, 1415) and *Frequens* (at least once every ten years a council as highest court of appeal—October 9, 1417)."[80] For example, the bull reads,

> A horrible and in earlier times unheard-of abuse has sprung up in our period. Some men, imbued with a spirit of rebellion and moved not with a desire for sound decisions but rather with a desire to escape the punishment for sin, suppose that they can appeal from the pope, vicar of Jesus Christ . . . to a future council. How harmful this is to the Christian republic as well as contrary to canon law anyone who is not ignorant of the law can understand. . . . Desirous, therefore, of banishing this deadly poison from the Church of Christ, and concerned with the salvation of the sheep committed to us and the protection of the sheepfold of our Savior from all causes of scandal; with the counsel and with the assent drawn from our venerable Fathers of the Holy Roman Church, all the cardinals and prelates and all those who interpret divine and human law in accordance with the curia, and being fully informed, we condemn appeals of this kind, reject them as erroneous and abominable, declare them to be completely null and void.[81]

The bull concludes by threatening excommunication and the wrath of God to anyone who violates this command.

At the start of the sixteenth century, just before the Reformation's genesis, Pope Julius II ensured that the Fifth Lateran Council (1512–17) consisted of cardinals in support of papal supremacy. However, the sixteenth century also heard renewed calls for conciliarism. One of the most vocal was John Major (or Mair), who served at universities such as Paris, Glasgow, and St. Andrews. In his 1529 book, *A Disputation on the Authority of a Council*, the subtitle raised the perennial question: *Is the Pope Subject to Brotherly Correction by a General Council?* Major answered in the affirmative. A council, said Major, represents the universal church; therefore, if the pope is above a council, he is above the universal church itself. That simply cannot be since he has the same spiritual accountability as every other Christian under the reign of Christ. "For the

---

80. Oberman, *Forerunners of the Reformation*, 213–14.
81. Pope Pius II, "Execrabilis," 238–39.

Roman pontiff is our brother; he has the same Father in heaven as we have; and he says the Lord's Prayer just as we do; and, like other pilgrims, is a man beset with weakness. Every Christian is our brother. Therefore we can reprove him and at times we are bound to do so."[82]

Major's argument is a sophisticated synthesis of Scripture, the Fathers, and Aristotle. For example, Major appeals to Matthew 18:15–19, where Jesus presents the process of church discipline. Where does Jesus locate final authority? When all else fails, "Tell it to the church," he says. But Jesus gave the keys of the kingdom to Peter, did he not? "The keys were not given to Peter except in the name of the Church and for her sake," Major countered. Quoting Aristotle, Major explained Jesus' logic: "Therefore they were given previously to the church, 'because the cause of an attribute's inherence in a subject always itself inheres in the subject more firmly than that attribute.'"[83] When Jesus said whatever is bound on earth is bound in heaven, he was not speaking to Peter alone. As Augustine said, "If this was said only to Peter, it gives no ground for action to the Church. But if this is also the case in the Church, then that which is bound on earth shall also be bound in heaven. . . . Peter in receiving the keys represented the holy Church."[84]

Did Major's case for conciliarism influence the Reformers? When Major lectured at the University of Paris, he built on the Gallican church before him to galvanize conciliarists until the university itself went public with its support for a council. Major's efforts caught Martin Luther's attention in Wittenberg, giving Luther confidence in his own appeal to a council in 1518, an appeal that looked similar to the one drafted in Paris.[85] That same year, Major left Paris for Glasgow only to leave Glasgow for St. Andrews in 1522. Some believe John Knox was one of Major's students at St. Andrews University. If so, Major's influence might explain some of Knox's labors in Scottish ecclesiastical and civil reform.[86]

FORERUNNERS OF REFORM

Medieval historian Heiko Oberman warned against ascribing T2 to the medieval era at large since many medieval theologians did not show explicit signs of a two-source theory. The early medieval era does not show a patent, clean split between T1 and T2. However, T2 did disclose itself in the canon lawyers as the medieval era progressed. Nevertheless, even when the late medieval period arrived, those protesting abuses in the church, from John Wyclif to Jan Hus, did not do so outside a tradition. "Fourteenth- and fifteenth-century theologians such as John Wyclif, Jan Hus, and Wessel Gansfort do not defend Scripture

---

82. Major, *A Disputation on the Authority of a Council*, 176.
83. Major was quoting Aristotle's *Posterior Analytics*. Major, 177. Later Major appealed to Acts 15 as well to point out that even though Peter was present, the decision belonged to the Jerusalem elders (p. 179).
84. Major was quoting Augustine's *Decretum*. Major, 177–78.
85. Spinka, "Conciliarism as Ecclesiastical Reform," 105.
86. Spinka, "Conciliarism as Ecclesiastical Reform," 104.

against Tradition, but they pose Tradition I against Tradition II."[87] In their minds they were opposing corrupt innovations within the tradition of their day, calling people back to an earlier, even purer tradition in conformity with the sacred Scriptures. In this sense, they can be called *forerunners*.

Wyclif and Lollards

When the unity of the Catholic Church was dissolving in the fourteenth century, a protester in England spoke up. His name was John Wyclif (ca. 1328/30–84), and he was unafraid to expose publicly the papal corruption and clerical pollution he grew to hate.[88] Wyclif had a platform at the University of Oxford from which to make his complaints heard. Since Edward III (1327–77) despised and resisted the pope's claim over England, he did not shut Wyclif up. Instead, he listened, asked for Wyclif's counsel, and even echoed Wyclif's arguments, especially his claim that God had appointed the state to mandate, even discipline the church when it strayed from Christian faith and practice.[89] Wyclif's favor in the eyes of Edward III, as well as his favor with Edward's successor Richard II, worked to his advantage on no few occasions when others in England, as well as Pope Gregory XI (1370–78) in Rome, resented Wyclif's critical words and conspired to bring him to an end. Wyclif not only won favor with kings but with nobility and the common citizens of England who equally resented the clergy's privileges and abuses.

Wyclif lived long enough to see the church divided by the Great Schism and was not ignorant of papal claims to supremacy. Wyclif believed such claims were an affront to Scripture, which is the church's final and only infallible authority.[90] Yet Wyclif also recognized that few English people had the opportunity to read the Bible in the vernacular. Wyclif lamented this literary vacancy and labored to translate the Scriptures, working from the Vulgate to the English language. Christian truth was not the privilege of the clergy but should be disseminated among the laity no matter how ordinary or uneducated they might be.[91] Furthermore, with the primacy of the Scriptures in view, Wyclif believed the preaching of the Scriptures should be the central focus of the church. Both for his translating work and his elevation of the Scriptures, historians have labeled Wyclif a forerunner of the Reformation, its morning star.[92]

If Wyclif foreshadowed the Reformation's call to *sola scriptura*, he also foreshadowed the Reformation's call to *sola gratia*. The Reformers were heirs of

---

87. Oberman, "Introduction," in *Forerunners of the Reformation*, 59.

88. For a fuller account of Wyclif, consult Evans, *John Wyclif*.

89. "This idea appealed to the English nobility, who were only too eager to seize the vast wealth and property of the English Church." Needham, *Two Thousand Years of Christ's Power*, 2:414.

90. See Wyclif's book *The Truth of Holy Scripture*.

91. And if the layperson could not read the Scriptures, and many could not, at least they could hear them read. Wyclif's translation project was continued by John Purvey (1353–1428), who refined Wyclif's posthumous translation of 1384 with one of his own in 1396. See Needham, *Two Thousand Years of Christ's Power*, 2:416, 418. For a summary of Wyclif's thought, see 415–20.

92. Among other Protestant-like emphases, such as the right of a minister to marry.

Augustine, intentionally retrieving his theology of grace. Yet so was Wyclif who learned from one of the greatest Augustinians of his day, Thomas Bradwardine (ca. 1290–1349). Wyclif embodied their appeal to Scripture's emphasis on predestination and argued that the sinner is chosen by God on the basis of divine grace alone, not human merit.

Wyclif's predestinarian teaching had significant implications for his view of the church. If God chooses his elect by grace, then the true body of Christ is not decided by external, ritual conformity but is recognized by the inward disposition of the heart, namely, faith and repentance. As the author of their faith, Christ is the true head of the church. The pope may stand over the external manifestation of the church in Rome, for example, but the people of God are an invisible assembly, made up of true believers—past, present, and future. In time, Wyclif even condemned the pope, identifying him as the Antichrist on earth, a tone not all that different from Luther in the sixteenth century.

Wyclif's ecclesiological reform depended, then, on the purification of the pastoral office. Sometime before or during 1378, Wyclif released *On the Pastoral Office*, laying out the biblical qualifications of a bishop. While these qualifications may have been standard in Paul's letter to Timothy, for example, they were absent among many clergy, lamented Wyclif. The sins of the clergy were numerous. For instance, they were greedy for gain, a gain that was not spiritual but temporal. They took advantage of the generosity of their people—often through the giving of alms, tithes, and offerings—so that they could become wealthy. Worse still, they acquired wealth by threatening spiritual penalties. "Prelates say in effect today, 'Despoil your poor sheep and simple ones of so much money, else I will thoroughly excommunicate you and I will suspend them from entering the church and from divine service.'"[93] They "love shameful gain of temporal goods more than their own soul's salvation."[94]

What these clergy did with the alms of their people was egregious as well: they funded extravagant banquets and paid for prostitutes. "Where, I ask, could be the conscience of such a pastor but rather more truly of a ravisher, not fearing to seize the tithes of his poor parishioners in order to wallow with such a prostitute in lust, and with this to set himself up as worthy to exercise any pastoral office for the salvation of his own soul or of the souls of his subjects? Surely such a one seems to be not only a rapacious wolf but even a strangler of his simple sheep for salvation both of body and of soul."[95] Such hypocrisy was nothing short of manipulative. Consider the friars, for example, who were renowned for their preaching. They talked as if preaching was their priority, but they preached for selfish, greedy motives, not for the sake of the gospel. "It is certain that such preaching of the friars in hope of temporal gain is in the sight of God notorious

---

93. Wyclif, *Pastoral Office*, 37.
94. Wyclif, *Pastoral Office*, 38.
95. Wyclif, *Pastoral Office*, 45.

simony."[96] In truth, their "every solicitude is not to propagate the words of the gospel, useful to the salvation of the souls of the subjects, but jesting, lying frauds, through which they are able more easily to despoil the people."[97] They did not proclaim the Scriptures but were more interested in entertaining the people with anecdotes and stories of their own.[98]

Wyclif issued a clear call to reform the status of pastor. Two things are required: "the holiness of the pastor and the wholesomeness of his teaching." As for the pastor's holiness, Wyclif said the pastor should be so committed to Christian virtues that "he would rather desert every kind of human intercourse, all the temporal things of this world, even mortal life itself, before he would sinfully depart from the truth of Christ." If not, then he should not be a pastor because he does not "have the likeness of Christ whereby he might lay down his soul for the sheep, and teach them faithfully."[99] Teaching them faithfully—that is the second requirement. Not only is the pastor to "shine with sanctity in his own person," but he "ought to be resplendent with righteousness of doctrine before his sheep." If he is not both, then "his preaching would be useless." For Wyclif, righteousness in life and righteousness in doctrine were inseparable. If the former went, the latter suffered. "Therefore the first condition of the pastor is to cleanse his own spring, that it may not infect the Word of God."[100]

With these two kinds of pastoral righteousness in place, Wyclif said the pastor's office is threefold:

1. To feed his sheep spiritually on the Word of God, that through pastures ever green they may be initiated into the blessedness of heaven.
2. To purge wisely the sheep of disease, that they may not infect themselves and others as well.
3. To defend his sheep from ravening wolves, both sensible and insensible.[101]

To accomplish this threefold office, the continual priority of the pastor must be "sowing the Word of God among his sheep." Sowing, however, is not merely preaching. The sower's "manner of life" must match his teaching. If it does, then his preaching may be "made efficacious." A preacher who lives according to what he preaches is far more effective than mere preaching alone. For the "life of a good pastor is of necessity a mirror to be imitated by his flock."[102]

Wyclif's emphasis on the indivisibility of preaching and pastoral fidelity

96. "The Antichrist is afraid that such ludicrous falsehoods and heresies concerning spiritual support, which have been spread abroad by the friars, will be publicly exposed, and they will not have as much booty from the Church as they are wont." Wyclif, *Pastoral Office*, 52.

97. Wyclif, *Pastoral Office*, 53.

98. Wyclif, *On the Eucharist*, in Spinka, *Advocates of Reform*, 73 n. 69.

99. Wyclif, *On the Eucharist*, 32–33.

100. Wyclif, *On the Eucharist*, 48.

101. Wyclif, *On the Eucharist*, 48.

102. Wyclif, *On the Eucharist*, 48.

serves to further classify Wyclif as a forerunner of the Reformation. The Reformers not only intended to reform the church according to sound doctrine, but they also understood that the office of the pastor must reflect such doctrinal instruction. As chapters 14–15 will reveal, Reformers like Martin Bucer and John Calvin instituted a company of pastors who were trained in the fundamentals of theology, a theology they believed was potent enough to be exemplified by the pastor as a model to the congregation. The pastor's portrayal of Reformation theology in his daily life and ministry was paradigmatic for his sheep. This model, first promoted by Wyclif then promulgated by the Reformers, closed the gap Rome had erected between clergy and laity. No longer could priests, curates, or friars preach one way and live another. The Word had to be implemented in their lives; otherwise the Reformation had no legitimate claim to the priesthood of all believers.[103]

Wyclif may have started off with the support of the king and the nobility, but he lost that support at the end of his life when he moved beyond criticisms of the papacy itself to an attack on the doctrine of transubstantiation with his 1380 book, *On the Eucharist*. "Transubstantiation is the passage of one substance according to its entirety into another, with the whole multitude of accidents remaining, so that neither matter nor substantial form which were in the bread and wine remain after consecration, but all material or formal substance which was in them is destroyed," said Wyclif. "The body of Christ succeeds through conversion under the same accidents, and thus there is no annihilation of any substance, both because of the conversion of the entire substance into a better one, and also because the accidents that were previously in the bread and wine remain."[104] If transubstantiation is true, then even "a hog, a dog, or a mouse can eat our Lord, because they can eat the body of Christ, that is, God." But their "assumption is false," responded Wyclif, since "beasts can eat the consecrated host, but it is the bare sacrament and not the body or blood of Christ."[105] When churchgoers see the host on the altar, they should not assume that "it is itself the body of Christ, but that the body of Christ is *sacramentally concealed in it*."[106] The host is the sign, but it is not the reality itself. "The host co-existed with the body of Christ, becoming Christ's body *sacramentaliter* (sacramentally)."[107]

Wyclif was not naive; he understood that he was moving against the grain. He surveyed a variety of opinions, from Thomas Aquinas to Duns Scotus to Berengarius, and concluded that Berengarius's view matched with "the Holy Synod." For example, Berengarius confessed, "I believe that the bread and wine

---

103. *The Power of the Pope* (1379).

104. Wyclif, *On the Eucharist*, 73. Wyclif would spend considerable time and space challenging the assumption that no annihilation occurs in transubstantiation. "For every accident must have a subject," said Wyclif (cf. 75–77).

105. For example, if "a lion devours a man, it does not also devour his soul; yet his soul is present in every part of his body." Wyclif, *On the Eucharist*, 61.

106. Emphasis added. Wyclif, *On the Eucharist*, 62.

107. Scase, "Lollardy," 17.

which are placed upon the altar are, after consecration, not only a sacrament but also the true body and blood of our Lord Jesus Christ, perceivable by the sense not only sacramentally but in truth grasped and broken by the hands of the priests and crushed by the teeth of the faithful."[108] By contrast, Wyclif believed he had the support of Augustine, who said we do not eat and drink in a carnal sense, but only in a spiritual sense. The "doctor [was] clear" when he said "not that an unworthy person visibly presses the *body* of Christ with his teeth, but that he visibly presses the *sacrament* of the body and blood of Christ with his teeth. For that sacrament ought especially to be distinguished from the body of Christ which is the matter of the sacrament thereof."[109] Here is the difference: "In carnal eating that which is eaten changes into nourishment for the eater when it is taken in by his members. But in spiritual eating it is otherwise. When one eats the body of Christ spiritually, one is thereby incorporated into the members of the Church, and thus into Christ." Which one is superior then? "The act of spiritual eating then exceeds mere carnal eating."[110]

Wyclif believed that read in the right way, the works of certain church fathers not only advanced a view of the sacrament that differed from the church of his day, but an alternative hermeneutic altogether. Rather than insisting on a literalistic reading of Jesus' words ("This is my body"), the interpreter should follow a figurative reading. The bread, for example, "is not really the body of Christ, but the efficacious sign thereof."[111] A figurative reading is customary across the testaments. For example, in 1 Corinthians 10:4, the apostle Paul said Israel was led out of Egypt into the wilderness and drank from the rock, yet this rock was Christ. In other words, the "rock mystically figured Christ."[112] Likewise, when Christ said, "This cup is the new covenant in my blood" (1 Cor. 11:25), he intended his words to convey a figurative sense.[113] Again, recruiting Augustine to his side, Wyclif said Christ speaks "figuratively or in a trope" so that the "bread is signified by the pronoun 'this,'"—*this* is my body.[114] What is signified exactly? Union with Christ. The host, in other words, "signifies, among other things, the union of Christ with the Church," concluded Wyclif.[115] For that reason, Jesus' words may be figurative but not in a meaningless sense. Wyclif may have denied that the consecrated bread is "identical with the body of Christ," but he believed

---

108. *Decretum*, pars 3, dist. 2, c. 42, 1, 1328–39. Cited in Wyclif, *On the Eucharist*, 67. Wyclif would set Peter Lombard, the master of *The Sentences*, over against Thomas Aquinas and Ambrose, claiming Lombard believed Jesus' words were a figure of speech and the host was a sign (see p. 79).

109. Wyclif, *On the Eucharist*, 66, emphasis added. For Augustine, see PL 35:1614.

110. Wyclif, *On the Eucharist*, 66–67.

111. Wyclif, *On the Eucharist*, 70.

112. Wyclif, *On the Eucharist*, 72.

113. For "the new testament figures the wine in the cup just as the blood of the bullock was the sign of confirmation of the old testament. . . . Thus it is seen that the saints of the primitive Church and their sons after them figuratively understood through the bread the wine and the body and blood of Christ." Wyclif, *On the Eucharist*, 72 (cf. 86).

114. Wyclif, *On the Eucharist*, 83. And again, "They fail to distinguish between the figure and the thing figured, and to heed the figurative meaning" (88).

115. Wyclif, *On the Eucharist*, 85.

nonetheless that the bread is an "efficacious sign" of the body of Christ and all its benefits for his bride, the church.[116]

Wyclif's case may have been a remonstrance, but it was a well-informed protest. By the end, Wyclif summoned not only Scripture but reason and the saints, claiming all three of these stood by his side over against Rome.[117] His claim to possess threefold support—Scripture, reason, and the Fathers—was bold in the face of Rome. Yet Wyclif was convinced of this: "The Fathers of the Church never truly believed that that bread was numerically identical with Christ's body."[118] For Wyclif, then, the debate was between the "primitive Church" and the "modern Church," and Wycliff claimed the former.[119] Furthermore, Wyclif was persuaded the stakes could not be elevated higher. For as long as transubstantiation continued to be adopted by the church, the church risked idolatry. "At the very least, an accident would be mostly falsely worshiped as a sacred sign in lieu of substance, and would impose upon God the responsibility of being the author of falsehood."[120]

In 1382 Wyclif stood before the archbishop of Canterbury, William Courtenay, and confessed, "I know that the sacrament of the altar is God's very body in the form of bread, but it is God's body in another manner than it is in heaven." In heaven Christ's body retains its material nature but can only be in the sacrament by a miracle and even then he cannot be in the bread "in the form of a man." How, then, should the Christian think of the bread and wine? "But as a man tends to disregard the nature of an image, [that is] whether it be of oak or ash, and sets his thought on him whom the image depicts, so much more should a man disregard the nature of the bread, but think upon Christ, for his body is the same bread that is the sacrament of the altar, and with all the purity, all the devotion, and all the love that God has granted him, should he worship Christ."[121] These criticisms moved Wyclif into the category of heretic, a condemnation pronounced in the next century by the Council of Constance, which responded to Wyclif on the subject of the Eucharist. Years later Wyclif was exhumed, burned, and thrown into the river.

Wyclif died in 1384, but his beliefs carried on, enduring all the way to the advent of the Reformation. Those Lollards, followers of Wyclif, who survived persecution, resorted to underground meetings, though they were not so much a codified movement as a persecuted and scattered resistance.[122] They joined the Reformation in England, all the more reason to consider Wyclif and his follow-

---

116. Wyclif, *On the Eucharist*, 87.
117. "The Church would not be burdened by such unusual novelty unless either faith in Scripture or lively reasoning or effective witness of the saints requires this, but each of these three is lacking in the aforesaid error concerning the sacrament of the altar." Wyclif, *On the Eucharist*, 82.
118. Wyclif, *On the Eucharist*, 88.
119. Wyclif, *On the Eucharist*, 73.
120. Wyclif, *On the Eucharist*, 82.
121. *CCFCT* 1:783.
122. Scase, "Lollardy," 21.

ers forerunners of the Reformation. Although Wyclif fell out of favor with the English nobility at the end of his life, later Lollards rose up within Parliament itself. In 1395 they wrote *The Twelve Conclusions*, protesting many of the same Catholic beliefs and practices as Wyclif. The Lollards begin *The Twelve Conclusions* by calling for the "reformation of the holy Church of England" since it had "been blind and leprous for many years because of the doing of arrogant prelates borne up by the curried favors of the religious, who have become a great and onerous burden to the people here in England."

The Lollards criticized the Church of England for listening to her "step-mother the great Church of Rome," a stepmother that introduced a priesthood defined by "rites" nowhere found in Scripture and "sodomy," which only corrupted a church that should be holy.[123] The Lollards also took aim at transubstantiation by claiming it was the sign of false religion. The "feigned miracle of the sacrament of bread induces all men but a few to idolatry because they believe that God's body, which never leaves heaven, should, by virtue of the priest's words, be closed essentially in a little piece of bread that they show to the people."[124]

If the "miracle of the sacrament" is no miracle at all but idolatry, then all those "exorcisms and blessings" the priest pronounced over altars, vestments, holy water, and so on are in truth nothing more than "necromancy." Targeting "Brother Thomas [Aquinas]" and *Corpus Christi,* the Lollards concluded, "by such exorcisms creatures are said to be endowed with a higher virtue than they are by nature, and we have seen nothing of change in any such creature that is so charmed unless moved by false belief, which is the principal trait of the devil's craft."[125]

The Lollards also condemned the institution of almshouses with their prayers for the dead or the damned. The "gift of temporal good bestowed on the priesthood and houses of alms is the principal cause of private prayer, which is not far from simony." These special prayers "made for men damned to everlasting pain is very displeasing to God." So, too, are "pilgrimages, prayers, and offerings made to blind crosses and to deaf images of wood and stone," which can be nothing else but "idolatry." The Christian should not give alms for these images, but should instead give to the "men who are needy, for they are the image of God in more likeness than wood or stone."[126]

The Lollards's ninth conclusion, written more than a hundred years prior to Luther's Ninety-Five Theses, targeted the priesthood and pope himself.

They [priests] say that they are God's representatives to judge every sin, to pardon and to cleanse whomsoever they please. They say that they have the keys of heaven

123. *CCFCT* 1:786.
124. *CCFCT* 1:787.
125. *CCFCT* 1:787.
126. *CCFCT* 1:788.

and of hell, they may curse and bless, bind and loose, at their will, in so much that for a bushel of wheat or twelve pence a year they will sell the blessing of heaven with charter and close warrant sealed with the common seal. This conclusion is so notorious that it needs no other proof. It is a corollary that the pope of Rome, who pretends to be the treasurer of the holy church, having the worthy jewel of Christ's passion in his keeping, together with the merits of all saints in heaven, whereby he grants pretended indulgences from penalty and guilt—is a treasurer almost devoid of charity, in that he can set free all that are prisoners in hell at his will, and cause that they should never come there.[127]

For several years, Lollards in Parliament appeared to make progress and Lollards all over England multiplied in size. But Henry IV (1399–1413) put an end to whatever progress was achieved, legalizing the execution of heretics, a practice his successor, Henry V (1413–22) continued by burning Lollards at the stake. The flames of the stake stamped out Lollard influence among Parliament and the nobility. However, Lollards could still be found among the laity, even though they did not enjoy religious liberty. Meeting in each other's homes was the secret to their survival, especially in big cities with eyes everywhere.

Hus, the Hussites, and the Holy Mother Church

Wyclif was an Englishman, but his ideas spread across Europe and were even absorbed by other forerunners of the Reformation. Consider Bohemia or what is today called the Czech Republic, home to the Prague preacher Jan Hus (ca. 1370/72–1415). Hus was no stranger to the ideas of Wyclif, and neither were Bohemians.[128] Bohemian students at the University of Oxford read Wyclif's writings and then took them back to their homeland. So, when Hus reincarnated Wyclif's views within his Bohemian context, they were well received. Yet Hus's support transcended the university and stemmed from a king and nobility that took pride in their Slavic heritage. Fearful they might lose their heritage to the Germans of the Holy Roman Empire, the university ousted Germans in 1409.[129]

Hus did not echo Wyclif's every conviction. For example, Hus did not protest transubstantiation. Nevertheless, he did protest indulgences beginning in 1411, a protest that foreshadowed Luther's Ninety-Five Theses. The timing was not ideal since Hus faced potential wrath from multiple popes during the Great Schism (1378–1417). Pope John XXIII took the most offense since he relied on the profit of indulgences to fund his war with Pope Gregory XII. To save his indulgence campaign, John XXIII labeled Hus a heretic and excommunicated him.

---

127. *CCFCT* 1:789.
128. Hus was not only influenced by Wyclif but also Jerome of Prague (ca. 1370–1416).
129. Peter of Mladoňovic, *End of the Saintly and Reverend Master John Hus*, 10. There was also a political connection since the Bohemian king's sister, Anne of Luxembourg was married to England's King Richard II. Needham, *Two Thousand Years of Christ's Power*, 2:421.

Hostility to indulgences was a betrayal of the church itself.[130] When Hus refused to stand trial in Rome, Pope John XXIII excommunicated the Czech Reformer.

As Hus looked at the church and became convinced corruption was originating from within, he had to explain how this church could still be the bride of Christ. With that goal in mind, Hus turned to the creeds to confess that the church is holy and universal, as well as apostolic and catholic. Hus had no hesitation referring to her as the holy mother church.[131] But how could the church be one? It was one, said Hus, but not in the way that Rome thought. In an Augustinian vein, Hus wrote the following in his 1413 book, *On the Church,*

> The unity of the Catholic Church consists in the bond of predestination, since her individual members are united by predestination. . . . Predestination is the key since not everyone who is *in* the Church is *of* the Church. "It is one thing to be of the Church, another thing to be in the Church. Clearly it does not follow that all living persons who are in the Church are of the Church. . . . For just as excrements proceed from food and the solid members of the body but are not identified with them, so the refuse of the Church, the reprobate, proceed from the Church, but are not of it and are not real parts, since no true members of the Church can permanently fall away from it, because the bond of predestination binding them to the Church never fails, as Paul said to the Corinthians.[132]

Hus identified four types of pilgrims:

1. Some are in the church in name and in reality, as are predestined Catholics obedient to Christ.
2. Some are neither in name nor reality in the church, as are reprobate pagans.
3. Others are in the church in name only, as are, for example, reprobate hypocrites.
4. Still others are in the church in reality and, although they appear to be in name outside it, are predestined Christians, as are those who are seen to be condemned by the satraps of the Antichrist before the church.[133]

These categories foreshadow the Reformation's own doctrine of the church. As Reformers were excommunicated by Rome, they revisited their ecclesiology to explain how to identify true membership in the church catholic. Rome looked to externals, but the Reformers believed internals were the determining factors. Likewise with forerunners such as Hus. "Neither status nor human prerogatives

---

130. Pope John "threatened to place Prague under an interdict" as well. "To save the city, Hus retired from Prague into southern Bohemia, protected by friendly Bohemian nobles." Needham, *Two Thousand Years of Christ's Power,* 2:422.
131. Hus, *On the Church,* 218–19.
132. Hus, *On the Church,* 219.
133. Hus, *On the Church,* 219–20.

can make anyone a member of the holy, universal Church," said Hus, "but only divine predestination can, as it does for everyone who steadfastly follows Christ in love." Once again turning to Augustine, Hus defined what he meant by predestination: "According to Augustine, predestination is the election by the divine will through grace; or, as it is usually said, 'predestination is the preparation for grace in the present and for glory in the future.'"[134]

The move was strategic, especially for someone like Hus who would in time be captured and burned under the condemnation of the church. Hus grounded true membership in the electing grace of God rather than the external righteousness of man. The former is permanent, the latter is temporary. "The one is the grace of predestination, from which the preordained can never ultimately fall away. The other grace is according to present righteousness which is present today and gone tomorrow, effective today but failing tomorrow."[135]

Hus did not deny that those who are truly predestined, those who do have "their roots in grace," can and sometimes are "temporarily deprived of the flow of grace." Take Peter, for example, who confessed Jesus to be the Christ yet was rebuked as if he were Satan himself for denying Jesus the path to crucifixion. Like Peter, we "can be righteous due to the grace of predestination and unrighteous due to an insurmountable sin"; nevertheless, those who are recipients of predestined grace "cannot fall away." They are, after all, under the "bond of predestination."[136] There is, in other words, a difference between a Judas and a Peter. However, until the last judgment the elect and reprobate coexist in the church, as Jesus' many parables reveal. Until then, the two sides are not necessarily discernible. For "we cannot without revelation clearly discern the true members of the mystical body of Christ so long as they are still in the course of their earthly pilgrimage."[137] Utilizing medieval, Scholastic distinctions, Hus concluded,

> In a true sense the Church is the Church of the predestined. In a nominal sense the Church is the congregation of the reprobate, although it is plainly an error on the part of those still on their pilgrimage to reckon the reprobate in the holy Mother Church. Thus many are, according to worldly reputation, heads or members of the Church, even though according to the foreknowledge of God they are members of the devil, those who for a time believed but later fell away, or those who now and always have been faithful.[138]

Hus then asked the pivotal question based on the Augustinian doctrine of predestination: Is Rome the one, holy, and apostolic church? What about the pope?

---

134. Hus, *On the Church*, 220; quoting Augustine, *De Predestinatione Sanctorum*, PL 44, col. 959ff.
135. Hus, *On the Church*, 221.
136. Hus, *On the Church*, 223.
137. Hus, *On the Church*, 228.
138. "In this way therefore, many can be said to be of the Church nominally according to present righteousness but not truly according to predestination to glory. Hus, *On the Church*, 229.

Appealing to canon law and the patristic witness, Hus concluded that Rome is still the true church. For "there is no other Church than the Roman Church. Therefore the Roman Church is the holy, universal Church."[139] But Hus denied this status to the pope. "But the Church thus understood cannot be said to be a pope with his cardinals and his household, because they all come and go."[140] More than that, "the pope can err." "Therefore, neither the pope nor his household can be that Church which cannot err."[141]

The pope's claim that he was head of the church put the pope in competition with Christ himself. For Christ alone is the head of his church, said Hus. The pope is "not the head nor are the cardinals the entire body of the holy, Catholic, and universal Church. For Christ alone is the head of that Church and all predestined together form the body, and each alone is a member of that body, because the bride of Christ is united with him."[142] Hus was no curialist, but it may not be accurate to label him a conciliarist either since he opposed not only the "one highest prelate" but the "gathered prelates." Yet Hus "does not pit Scripture against Tradition but rather, as the upholder of Tradition I, he argues on grounds of Scripture and its doctoral exposition against the extrascriptural tradition of the authority of canon law."[143] And yet, as a constant practitioner of retrieval, summoning the tradition's authority to buttress his polemic, Hus was no biblicist either. "Scripture was never alone."[144]

In 1413 Hus published *On Simony*.[145] Simony was a derogatory label named after Simon the sorcerer who tried to buy the power of the Holy Spirit from the apostles (Acts 8:9–25). The title of Hus's work was an accusation: the church was corrupt, buying and selling the spiritual for earthly gain. Hus used the word *svatokupectui* (Czech), a word that exposed the church for "trafficking in holy things."[146] Yet simony does not apply only to the one who sells holy things; simony applies just as well to the one who buys holy things.

Simony was not restricted to one segment of the church. Hus believed simony was pervasive, infecting the bloodstream like a cancer. Not only popes and cardinals but monks and laity participated in simony in countless ways. For example, consider the following, all of which could be sold for a price and purchased:

---

139. Hus, *On the Church*, 230.

140. Hus, *On the Church*, 233.

141. Hus, *On the Church*, 233. Was Hus a Donatist? Oberman believed Wyclif may have been, but he labeled Hus a Semi-Donatist (see 210–11).

142. Hus, *On the Church*, 236 (cf. 229).

143. For that reason, Oberman said that it is "therefore not his doctrine of predestination, prominent as it is in his work *On the Church*, but his understanding of the relation of Scripture and Tradition which gives the revolutionary edge to this chief work of Hus." Oberman, *Forerunners of the Reformation*, 211.

144. Fudge, "Hussite theology and the law of God," 25.

145. Hus, *On Simony* (1413), 196–278.

146. Hus, *On Simony*, 201. Elsewhere Hus defined simony as follows: "Those who sell spiritual power or the gift of the Holy Spirit for money or other valuables, or for improper services—sometimes openly, at other times secretly—or express willingness to pay for what they desire.... Therefore, all those who buy or sell the gifts of God, either for money or for some other consideration, or knowingly aid in such traffic, are called simoniacs, or in Czech *svatokupci*" (209).

- singing Mass
- administering the sacraments
- preaching a sermon
- hearing a confession
- granting absolution
- baptism
- confirmation
- extreme unction
- burial of the dead
- ordination of clergy
- consecration of deacons
- consecration of a church or chapel
- consecration of an altar, chalice, or a cope
- appointment to a benefice, parish, or bishopric
- administering holy oil[147]

Many a priest, said Hus, "refuses to receive confession unless the sick person first leave a legacy to the parish."[148] Hus exposed those priests who not only squandered funds on prostitutes but paid for permission to retain a mistress. "The apostles of Christ decreed that anyone who committed fornication after baptism could not become a priest; and that if a priest committed fornication, he was to be deprived of priesthood. But the vicars of the apostles—the bishops— themselves commit fornication, and do not forbid it to others! Like father, like son. The son gives, and the father receives, money so that the son can have a mistress."[149]

Hus, appealing to Augustine's definition of heresy, was convinced that "simoniacs" were heretical since "heresy is a stubborn adherence to an error contrary to the Holy Scriptures."[150] Heresy, according to Hus, has three types: (1) apostasy: the rejection of the law of God; (2) blasphemy: the defamation of the divine faith; and (3) simony: the heresy of overthrowing the divine order.[151] All three are an affront to the Trinity: "God the Father is contemned by apostasy, for he rules mightily by a pure and immaculate law; he also has provided a bride of Christ which is the congregation of all the elect; God the Son, who is the Wisdom of God is contemned by the second heresy—blasphemy; and God the Holy Spirit, who in his supreme goodness wisely and humbly governs God's house, is contemned by the accursed simony which is contrary to his order."[152]

Hus also called simony a "spiritual leprosy" because it is "difficult to be

---

147. These examples come from Hus, *On Simony*, 225. I have tried to preserve some of Hus's wording.
148. Hus, *On Simony*, 245.
149. Hus, *On Simony*, 253.
150. Hus, *On Simony*, 196.
151. Hus's words. Hus, *On Simony*, 201.
152. Hus, *On Simony*, 201.

driven out from the soul save by God's special miracle."[153] Hus believed simony is a matter of the heart, occurring whenever a "corrupt will consents to such an exchange." Like adultery, simony is "first a mortal sin in the soul, and afterward in deed."[154] That was no small point for Hus since he thought simony was, at its root, a distortion of divine grace. Christ said, "Freely you have received; freely give" (Matt. 10:8 NIV). "The apostles received freely, without bribery, without unworthy subservience, or material favor; therefore, they likewise gave freely, without such bribery. But since now clergy do not receive freely, they likewise do not give freely, neither absolution, nor ordination, nor extreme unction, nor other spiritual things."[155] In other words, salvation is a matter of grace, but the clergy had turned salvation into a matter of works. Since they no longer "received freely," no longer did they give their ministry freely either. Simony is not only a moral corruption within the church, but a sign of theological corruption, the death of *sola gratia*.

Hus also questioned the purses of the clergy, calling the pope himself a simoniac, perhaps Hus's more threatening accusation. The pope claimed to be "lord of all the world," but "there is only one Lord of all the world who cannot sin."[156] By elevating himself—allowing others to flatter him with the title "most holy father"—the pope revealed his hypocrisy. "For what avails it that a man be called holy when in the sight of God he is damned? What avails it to the Antichrist that he exalts himself above God when Christ shall hurl him into hell?"[157] Hus could be so bold to imply the pope was damned because Hus believed the pope had committed simony in three ways:

1. The pope desires the papal dignity on account of emoluments and worldly esteem.... For if he does not follow Christ and Peter in his manner of life more than others, he should be called the apostolic adversary rather than the apostolic successor.
2. The pope's simony consists in the various regulations contrary to the law of God which the pope promulgates in order to secure material gain, even though not openly, but in such a manner that it could be interpreted as against the law of God.
3. The pope's simony involves the "appointment of bishops and priests for money."[158]

This last proof was personal for Hus. In 1402 the pope appointed Nicholas Puchník archbishop of Prague. The pope's decision was influenced by the 3,300

153. Hus, *On Simony*, 101.
154. Hus, *On Simony*, 202.
155. Hus, *On Simony*, 203.
156. Hus, *On Simony*, 211.
157. Hus, *On Simony*, 212.
158. Hus, *On Simony*, 213.

gulden Nicholas planned to place in the pope's pocket once confirmed.[159] Hus saw this exchange of monies for church offices as hard evidence of papal greed and corruption. To make matters worse, the pope's pockets were lined at the expense of his people. "For there may be a pope so avaricious that he may retain the incomes of all deceased bishops and other priests, and leave the people shepherdless. Thus he himself would not labor, nor would he appoint others to labor, unless it were such as would seek gain for their own purses but not the salvation of souls and the glory of our Savior Jesus Christ."[160] In his Ninety-Five Theses, Luther echoed Hus by questioning the pope's priorities.

Also typological of Luther, Hus identified the consequences of simony for the heart of the laity. By selling a state of spirituality, often through indulgences, the papacy gives the impression that remorse and repentance are unnecessary. "In regard to the granting of indulgences for money, Saint Peter shows, by his refusal to sell to Simon the power of laying on of hands on men that they might thus receive the gift of the Holy Spirit, that such indulgences are improper," Hus lamented. "But now the priests, because of their avarice, vie with one another in a race to buy indulgence, and the people, wishing to rid themselves of their sins by a payment of money, do not repent rightly. Thus both sides are deceived: the priests in selling and the people in buying."[161] Likewise, the priest cheated the system as well: he could easily "farm indulgences" and make a quick profit, extinguishing true pastoral motive, neglecting his "episcopal duties."[162] Some even took the profit for themselves, giving it to their friends instead of to the poor.

Furthermore, simony fosters a substandard priesthood. If an office can be sold and purchased, then spiritual qualifications are secondary or perhaps irrelevant altogether. Hus laid the blame on monks since they favored their relatives even though they were "unfit to minister to God's people."[163] Some were so reckless they "waste[d] alms" on parties, on "drinking bouts with their friends," and "some of them squander[ed] on dogs and bitches!" Hus appealed to Saint Bernard, the monk who mourned how other monks guzzled liquor with the alms of the people. Unfortunately, concluded Hus, if Bernard were to reappear in Bohemia, he would discover that nothing had changed.[164] There is a brotherhood, but its members "eat, drink, and guzzle to surfeit," yet they "do not remember the poor and fail to attend Masses at home; and returning from the fraternal revels, these 'brethren' take several days to grow sober!"[165] By contrast, Hus proposed a different brotherhood: "Since all faithful Christians have such a good Brother and gracious Father [as Christ], they love each other according to his commandment, and have the same spiritual food, his holy body, and the same

159. He died beforehand. On the debt's absorption by his successor, see Hus, *On Simony*, 213 n. 56.
160. Hus, *On Simony*, 216.
161. Hus, *On Simony*, 221.
162. Hus, *On Simony*, 221, 223.
163. Hus, *On Simony*, 237.
164. Hus, *On Simony*, 238.
165. Hus, *On Simony*, 241. See p. 251 where Hus said they squandered funds on prostitutes.

drink, his holy blood. They all are clad in the same robe—love—and live in the same house—holy Church. They all share in common good works, so that each participates in them in accordance with his Father's pleasure. That is called the communion of saints."[166]

What, then, was Hus's solution to simony in the papacy, the priesthood, and the monastery? First, Hus summoned a higher authority: "Papal power is limited by God's law, the law of nature, and the pronouncements of saints which are grounded in God's Word."[167] Second, Hus called on the temporal authorities to rid Christ's vineyard of this wild boar. Ironically, this would be the same language used to excommunicate Luther. But in Hus's day, the wild boar destroying the vineyard was the simoniacs. Although these papal simoniacs claimed kings and lords had no right to rule over them, Hus called on the secular authorities to exercise their God-given power over priests and pope alike and banish simony once for all.[168] One century later, Reformers across Europe made the same appeal.

Three years after Hus's initial assault on indulgences, the Council of Constance convened (1414) and summoned Hus to appear.[169] As mentioned, Constance was the attempt of key conciliarists to triumph over certain curialists. Over against papal claims to absolute supremacy, the conciliarists appealed to the authority of church councils. With no end to the Great Schism in view, Constance ended the schism in its choice of a new pope, communicating to the world that the authority of a council, not a pope, could settle the divide. Although Hus was far more sympathetic with councils than popes—with a council there was at least the possibility of a fair hearing—this council (Constance) was hostile to Hus's attack on church doctrine and practices. The emperor, Sigismund, promised Hus that if he came to the council he would not be harmed. Hus knew it was a risk, especially since he had already been excommunicated, but he took the risk anyway.

The risk cost him his life. The council had no intention of protecting Hus. The council's only intention was to capture Hus, condemn the heretic, and burn him at the stake, which is exactly what they did in 1415 after a period of brutal imprisonment.[170] But not before they dragged Hus through a humiliating trial. Sigismund sent Wenceslas of Dubá and John of Chlum, among other bishops, to Constance where Hus was imprisoned in the Brothers Minor. On July 5 Hus was summoned, and Lord John told the prisoner to recant. Hus responded, "Lord John, be sure that if I knew that I had written or preached anything erroneous

---

166. Hus, *On Simony*, 241.

167. Hus, *On Simony*, 218.

168. Hus, *On Simony*, 273, 275.

169. Hus's "theology was unacceptable even to the conciliarist reformers like John Gerson who controlled the Council." For the details of Hus's trial that follow, see Needham, *Two Thousand Years of Christ's Power*, 2:423.

170. Oberman believed Hus's condemnation was not ultimately due to his views on the visible-invisible church, but "probably due to his opposition to the authority of extrascriptural canon law," which the conciliarists could not tolerate. Oberman, *Forerunners of the Reformation*, 212.

against the law and against the holy mother Church, I would desire humbly to recant it—God is my witness! I have every desire to be shown better and more relevant Scripture than those that I have written and taught. And if they were shown me, I am ready most willingly to recant."[171] Hus appealed to his continuity with the church catholic (mother church), but the council interpreted Hus's reply as arrogance, a reckless temerity, as if he knew better than the council itself.

The next day, Hus stood before the council again, but his fate was already sealed due to his refusal to recant the day before. At the start, priestly vestments, sacerdotal garments, and the chasuble for Mass were placed before Hus, and the council proceeded to unfrock him, a most humiliating discrimination for a minister. One of the bishops from Lodi also preached a sermon against heresy, reminding the council that its duty is to protect the church against schism caused by heretics. Next, several articles were read, each article reporting Hus's teaching. However, the articles did not accurately represent Hus or his teaching. When Hus interjected, Pierre d'Ailly, the cardinal of Cambrai, said, "Be silent now; it were better that you reply later to all of them together."[172] Yet with each additional article, Hus begged to be heard since each one falsely represented him, creating a cumulative case against him. The articles were extreme as well. For example, one of them claimed Hus taught that he was the fourth person of the Trinity. Hus could not stay quiet: "Be it far from me, a miserable wretch, that I should want to name myself the fourth person of the Godhead, for that has never entered my heart; but I unswervingly assert that the Father, the Son, and the Holy Spirit are one God, one essence, and a trinity of persons."[173]

Another article claimed that when Hus was excommunicated, he "bore it contumaciously" as if he were a schismatic in spirit. Hus again defended himself, this time revealing his true motives and past pleas: "I did not bear it contumaciously, but having appealed, I preached and celebrated the mass. But although I have twice sent procurators to the Roman curia, advancing reasons for not appearing personally, I was never able to obtain a hearing: instead, some of my procurators were incarcerated and others were ill-treated. . . . Above all, I even came to this Council freely, having the safe-conduct of the lord king here present, desiring to show my innocence and to give account of my faith."[174] Hus went on to clarify, "I have never been obstinate, and am not now. But I have ever desired, and to this day I desire, more relevant instruction from the Scriptures."

Each time Hus tried to respond, the council forbade him from doing so. They proceeded to present Hus's books before the council, condemning each one as heretical and worthy of burning. Hus asked the council to show from Scripture why each one was erroneous. Hus also asked how the council could condemn certain books written in Czech and other languages, books the council had not

---

171. Quotes from Peter of Mladoňovic's account: *End of the Saintly and Reverend Master John Hus*, 11.
172. Peter of Mladoňovic, 11.
173. Peter of Mladoňovic, 12.
174. Quoted in Peter of Mladoňovic, 12.

and could not have read. Hus prayed for all to hear, "Lord Jesus Christ, I implore Thee, forgive all my enemies for Thy great mercy's sake; and Thou knowest that they have falsely accused me and have produced false witnesses and have concocted false articles against me!"[175]

Hearing his prayer, the bishops dressed Hus in the vestments preparing to unfrock him as a Judas. Weeping, Hus made a declaration that foreshadowed Luther at the Diet of Worms:

> Behold, these bishops exhort me to recant and abjure. But I fear to do so, lest I be a liar in the sight of the Lord, and also lest I offend my own conscience and the truth of God. For I have never held these articles that are falsely witnessed against me, but rather have written, taught, and preached their opposite; and also lest I offend the multitude to whom I have preached and others who faithfully preach the Word of God.[176]

In the estimation of his opponents, Hus's words only confirmed him to be the heretic they said he was. "We see now how obdurate he is in his wickedness and obstinate in heresy."[177] So they unfrocked him before the assembly. Yet Hus turned the tables on the bishops, interpreting the unfrocking as a parallel to the garments Herod placed on Christ. Jesus, too, was unfrocked of his kingly robe and mocked by the religious leaders of his day.

Hus at Council of Constance
Public Domain

---

175. Quoted in Peter of Mladoňovic, 12.
176. Quoted in Peter of Mladoňovic, 13.
177. Quoted in Peter of Mladoňovic, 13.

Hus's comparison did not keep the bishops from mocking him further. They placed a paper crown with three devils on his head and condemned him, saying, "We commit your soul to the devil!"[178] Next, they handed Hus over to the authorities for execution while his books were gathered and burned in a nearby cemetery. Hus was tied to a stake and wood and straw stacked around his body all the way up to his neck. Just before the fire was lit, Hoppe of Poppenheim gave Hus one last chance to recant, to which he responded, "God is my witness that those things that are falsely ascribed to me and of which the false witnesses accuse me, I have never taught or preached. But that the principal intention of my preaching and of all my other acts or writings was solely that I might turn men from sin. And in that truth of the Gospel that I wrote, taught, and preached in accordance with the sayings and expositions of the holy doctors, I am willing gladly to die today."[179]

When a heretic was burned, the church usually worried that zealous followers would interpret execution as martyrdom. Sometimes pieces of the martyr's clothes or even parts of his body were taken from the ashes and kept as relics. To prohibit the proliferation of relics, those who burned Hus in the fire then took what was left of his body and destroyed it. The head of Hus, for example, was clubbed and charred. The heart of Hus was impaled, torn into pieces, and scorched. They labored until Hus was nothing but ash, ash to be discarded into the river Rhine.[180]

Constance may have ended Hus's life, but his martyrdom only galvanized Hus's supporters back in Bohemia. The emperor tried to squash the Hussites once more by burning Jerome of Prague the next year, but Jerome went to the flames in the same spirit as his master, which only further animated Hussites in Bohemia. The king of Bohemia was Emperor Sigismund's brother, Wenceslas. When Sigismund's brother died (1419), the Holy Roman emperor himself had the right to sit on the Bohemian throne. The people of Bohemia rose in protest and armed themselves, ready to fight against the emperor if necessary—after all, this was the same emperor who had betrayed and burned Hus at the stake.

Pope Martin V drafted his crusaders to help Sigismund defeat the Bohemian Hussites, but to their surprise they were defeated again and again, forcing them, after nearly a decade and a half, to compromise. The Hussite Wars (1420–34) were a humiliating moment for the Catholic crusaders, but especially for the Catholic Church, an indication that their jurisdiction could be resisted despite claims to supremacy over the temporal authorities of Europe.

The Hussites, however, were not of one voice. When a negotiated document consisting of four articles was put forward by the Council of Basel, civil war inundated the Hussite camp.[181] The Utraquists (or Calixtines) approved the

---

178. Quoted in Peter of Mladoňovic, 13.
179. Quoted in Peter of Mladoňovic, 14.
180. Quoted in Peter of Mladoňovic, 14.
181. In 1420 *The Four Articles of Prague* tried to oppose Sigismund but also unite the Utraquists and

articles, articles that certified the Hussites could receive both bread and wine and preach the Scriptures. The label Utraquists was taken from the Latin phrase *sub utraque specie*, meaning "under each kind." The church taught that Christ was "fully received under one kind, and that therefore reception in both kinds was unnecessary."[182] The clergy, therefore, only distributed the bread, not the cup. The Utraquists countered that Christ was present *under each kind*, and the laity should receive both bread and cup.

The Utraquists were willing to negotiate with the Catholic Church because they were determined to stay within the Catholic Church but reform it according to Hussite convictions—one measure of reform being the reception of both wine and bread. Not so for the Taborites. These Hussites believed the Catholic Church, especially with its unwavering commitment to doctrines like transubstantiation, was a lost cause, even a devilish cause. The only answer was to overcome the Catholics in warfare (the Taborite generals were among the best in Europe) and establish their own property, church, and Bohemian society. Civil war erupted as a result of this impasse, and despite the superior skills of the Taborite generals, the Taborites were defeated in 1434 because the Catholic army joined arms with the Utraquist army on the battlefield in a striking irony.[183]

That did not mean, however, that Hussites and Catholics after 1434 put aside their differences. The Hussites continued within the Catholic Church but nonetheless remained dissatisfied until Hussite measures were taken. In that sense, the Hussites were forerunners of the Reformation, and it is little surprise they were in support of the Reformation when it arrived by the next century. The Reformers even returned the support. For example, in 1535 Luther wrote the preface to *The Bohemian Confession*.[184] In the 1510s, Luther thought the Bohemians were heretics, but he changed his mind at the start of his own evangelical reform.[185] "Without being aware of it, I have until now taught and held the whole doctrine of Jan Hus," said Luther when he first encountered *De ecclesia* by Hus. "In short, we are all Hussites without knowing it. Even Paul and Augustine are really Hussites."[186] A decade and a half later, Luther was willing to back Bohemian reform. This proved uncharacteristic for Luther. For *The Bohemian Confession* was not an exact alignment with the Lutheran view of the Lord's Supper. Nevertheless, Luther embodied an amicable, even ecumenical spirit, believing the Bohemians did affirm the true, real presence of Christ. "In his conciliatory posture, Luther even seems to echo the spirit of Martin Bucer

---

Taborites. See "Four Articles of Prague, 1420," 1:793–95. These four articles were later used to create *The Basel Compacts* (1434–37). Sigismund finally approved *The Basel Compacts*.

182. Bray, ed., *Documents of the English Reformation*, 227.

183. To further understand the differences between the Taborites and Utraquists, as well as the history of the Taborites after their defeat in 1434, see Needham, *Two Thousand Years of Christ's Power*, 425–26.

184. Luther recounts his pilgrimage from Rome to the Reformation: "Preface by Doctor Martin Luther," in *CCFCT* 1:799–801.

185. *LW* 31.217; *WA* 1:608.28–35; cf. Wernisch, "Luther and Medieval Reform Movements, Particularly the Hussites," 63.

186. *WABr* 2:42. A letter from Luther to Georg Spalatin. Quoted in *CCFCT* 1:796.

when he says of the differences between Lutheran and Brethren views: 'das man nicht umb wort und rede zancken sol' [one should not argue about words and phrases]. . . . Perhaps it was his early admiration of Hus that led Luther to trust the spiritual descendants of the reformer."[187]

To clarify, Hus and Luther did have differences that defined their reforms. Hus was more aligned with Augustine and Aquinas than Luther on justification, and Hus's reforming measures were more concerned with moral reform by the law than theological reform by justification *sola fide*.[188] Still, Hus's martyrdom prepared the way for Martin Luther, like the prophet John the Baptist preparing the way for Christ. The Reformer that first ignited reform in Germany was forced to wrestle with similar ecclesiastical tensions that motivated Hus's reform. Luther even adopted Hus's rhetorical tactics, naming pope and papacy Antichrist. Hus was martyred by "Satan's council," said Luther. But now, with Hus's insight, Luther could not be quiet either, especially since he considered the last days at hand.[189] But would Luther suffer the same fate as Hus? Or would Luther somehow—in a most miraculous feat—cheat the stake to carry forward reforming measures in the church that Hus never had the chance to implement?

---

187. "Long after Luther's death, in 1575, the Brethren adopted a new confession. . . . On the nature of the eucharist, however, they admitted a more Phillippist view and subsequently moved closer to Calvinism in their doctrine and practices, including an emphasis on discipline as a mark of the church." Pelikan and Hotchkiss, "Introduction," in *CCFCT* 1:797 (quoting *WA* 38:78).

188. Fudge, "Hussite theology and the law of God," 22, 25.

189. *WA* 53:167–71; cf. Wernisch, "Luther and Medieval Reform Movements, Particularly the Hussites," 66.

Part 2

THE GENESIS OF
REFORMATION

*There is a clear and present danger that the devil may take away from us
the pure doctrine of faith and may substitute for it the doctrines of works
and of human traditions. It is very necessary, therefore, that this doctrine of
faith be continually read and heard in public. . . . This doctrine can never
be discussed and taught enough. If it is lost and perishes, the whole knowledge of truth, life, and salvation is lost and perishes at the same time. But
if it flourishes, everything good flourishes—religion, true worship, the glory
of God, and the right knowledge of all things and of all social conditions.*

—Martin Luther

*All that was noble and good about the word "Catholic" found an echo in
him. Despite his estrangement from Rome, Luther remained a Catholic
all his life, and his liturgical views and productions are evidence of this
continuing Catholicity.*

—Jaroslav Pelikan

*But he [Luther] acknowledged that there were important issues on which
they did not disagree at all. The medieval Catholic Church did not need to
be recalled, corrected, and reformed on every point of doctrine. In merciful
providence of God, the Catholic Church had provided on some issues a
constant witness to the truth. On such issues the Lutheran laity needed
to be formed in the Christian faith as it had traditionally been taught.*

—David Steinmetz

8

MARTIN LUTHER AS A
LATE MEDIEVAL MAN

Luther's Augustinianism,
the Via Moderna, *and the Papacy*

I teach that people should put their trust in nothing but Jesus Christ
alone, not in their prayers, merits, or their own good deeds.

—Martin Luther

He was god and devil, saint and monster.

—David Daniell

Hans Luther was a man of no little ambition.[1] Martin Luther once said that when his father was a young man, he was but "a poor miner" and his mother "carried all her wood home on her back." They worked hard, and their work ethic left an impression on their son. "It was in this way that they brought us up."[2] The hard worked paid off, and Hans built a profitable business in the mining industry. Yet, like many fathers, Hans dreamed that his son, Martin, would pursue a far more lucrative career, one with social status. Hans believed a career in law was the answer. To pursue a career in law, young Martin needed an education, and Hans took the initiative to ensure that his son received that education. In a century without the technology of modern transportation, where a young student attended university depended in large part on where that student was born and raised.

Martin was born in Eisleben, Germany, but he was raised as a boy and then as an adolescent in Mansfeld, ten miles from where he was born. In the sixteenth century, transportation depended on one's two feet. Walking from town to town was the surest way to get around.[3] If the family owned a horse, maybe even two, then

---

1. My narrative of Luther in this chapter and the chapters that follow is indebted to many different Luther historians, including Hendrix, *Martin Luther*; Brecht, *Martin Luther*, 3 vols.; Oberman, *Luther*; Rupp, *Luther's Progress to the Diet of Worms*; MacCulloch, *The Reformation*; Cameron, *The European Reformation*.

2. *Table Talk*, in *LW* 54:178.

3. Of course, everything depended on health. Life expectancy was no more than forty if one survived childhood.

one's horizons widened. But either way, the average sixteenth-century European saw very little beyond his or her place of birth. That was true for Martin Luther, who traveled to Rome once but spent most of his life within a connected network of German territories in Electoral Saxony, mindful of those who could ensure his safety. Martin Luther heard reports of Turks and newly discovered lands across the ocean, like the Americas, but that is all they were, reports. Martin never visited such places, which makes his enduring influence all the more extraordinary.

In the spring of 1501, Martin Luther, who could not have been more than seventeen years old, traveled for two whole days to Erfurt. To become a student at the university that summer, Martin needed to register. Erfurt was called the Rome of the North because it was home to legions of Catholic institutions. Despite its reputation as the Rome of the North, Erfurt was anything but a holy city. For example, students learned on arrival that Erfurt was home to numerous whorehouses.[4] Luther acknowledged this much later in life, though there is no reason to believe Luther indulged like other students he knew.

Hans sent his son to Erfurt because this university was the ticket to his son's future prosperous legal profession. What kind of education did young Martin Luther receive? Luther is forever remembered by historians as the Reformer, the man who ignited, albeit unintentionally, the German Reformation. However, to understand what instigated Luther's reform, Luther's identity as a medieval man cannot be overlooked. Like every other student, Luther was a late medieval person, and the university he attended was a late medieval institution. In the late medieval era, most institutions were indebted to the realism of Aristotle (see chapter 4). Universities majored on logic, ethics, and metaphysics. Psychology and physics were in focus as well. These disciplines, and Aristotle's approach to these disciplines, were the bedrock to learning Catholic theology.[5] To understand the miracle of the incarnation or the transubstantiation at the altar, an education in participation might help, though many priests never received one.

Furthermore, a new movement had been birthed by the time Luther entered university at Erfurt: Renaissance humanism (see chapter 8). The century prior to Luther's arrival at university, humanism had made inroads into university curriculum across Europe. Its influence was seen in the diversity of subjects offered, from logic to ethics, from grammar to rhetoric. Mathematics and geometry were options as well. As a lute player himself, Luther may have appreciated the emphasis on music. Luther, to one degree or another, was trained in the spirit of humanism. Like other Reformers, humanism, especially its emphasis on grammar and rhetoric, and its retrieval of classical texts, influenced Luther's Reformation whether he knew it or not. That influence became conspicuous years later when Luther applied his linguistic skills to writing a new translation of the Bible in the vernacular.

In 1502 Luther finished his bachelor of arts, and in 1505 he took his exams for

---

4. Hendrix, *Martin Luther*, 29.
5. Hendrix, 30–31.

the master of arts.[6] His scores reveal precociousness: Luther received the second highest mark in his class. As was custom, Luther was now invited into the world of teaching, which included not only lectures but disputations, both of which Luther engaged in and led. His participation left a deep, permanent mark. In time Luther became a churchman, but from the start he was a professor at heart. Over his lifetime, his lectures and disputations not only provoked the Reformation but continued to fuel and sustain the Reformation well into his later years.

However, Luther's path to law, which now appeared imminent, diverged. At university Luther's college was Heaven's Gate. That is where Luther rose early in the morning to perform his academic duties. But blocks away, within walking distance, was the Augustinian monastery. It was not, by any means, the only monastery young males might consider, but it was close to Luther and had gained a reputation for strict, holy living. Later, reflecting on this monastery, Luther said its strictness was appealing, even alluring.[7] Luther's change of heart, from law to the monastery, is often attributed to the storm incident, as if this change was as unexpected as Paul's conversion on the road to Damascus. But that is unlikely. Judging by his reaction, Luther contemplated a religious calling prior to the storm incident recounted below, concerned as he was to live a life of holiness. As Luther came and went from Heaven's Gate, he no doubt saw the monastery or even its members enter and exit, and he heard of its reputation within the university. But a change so drastic and radical could only infuriate his father, who was investing so much into Luther's legal future.

Nevertheless, Luther defied his father's wishes beginning July 2, 1505. Luther was traveling from Mansfeld back to Erfurt when a terrifying storm erupted over his head but miles before reaching his destination. Lightning flashed and thunder cracked, causing Luther to fear for his life. In a moment of utter terror and desperation, he cried out to Saint Anne, the patron saint of miners, and vowed that if God spare his life, he would become a monk. Although Luther did not have to keep such a vow, he chose to. Why? Most likely Luther was not as scared of physical death as he was of the uncertainty of salvation and the judgment that awaited him in life after death.[8]

Was this the first time Luther had encountered the gates of death and cried out to a saint in fear? It was not. A few years prior to the storm crisis, Luther was traveling back home and cut his leg on his sword by accident. His artery was slit

---

6. Historians do not always agree on the dates. For example, Hillerbrand, *Division of Christendom*, 30, dated Luther's baccalaureate to 1503.

7. Brecht, *Martin Luther*, 1:51–106.

8. Did Luther have to keep this vow? Hillerbrand said, "Vows made under such duress did not have to be kept." Consider this: "Any spiritual counselor would have assured Luther that he could be relieved of the obligation." So why did Luther keep his vow? "That he nonetheless fulfilled his vow suggests that there were other reasons. In later years Luther gave his decision a spiritual meaning. He had entered the monastery, so he stated, in order to obtain 'my salvation,' and one may well see this as the fundamental cause. Spiritual concerns triggered Luther's decision, and they converged with—perhaps overshadowed—the mistaken pursuit of law. In his later years, Luther clearly saw his decision as fundamentally flawed; in the monastery, so he observed, 'I should have killed myself with vigils and prayers.'" Hillerbrand, *Division of Christendom*, 30. Cf. *WA* 38:143.

open and his leg gushed blood. Luther was fortunate to have a friend with him who ran at least half a mile to fetch a doctor. Luther tried to stop the bleeding by applying pressure, but then his leg became swollen, as if it was going to burst. Luther thought he was going to die, so he cried out, "Mary, help!" "I would have died," Luther later said, "with my trust in Mary."[9]

When Luther's friends heard that he was resolved to enter the monastery, they tried to persuade him against it. But Luther's mind was made up, which made his father furious. Hans had purchased Luther's law books. Now Luther was dispensing with law altogether, giving his books to friends pursuing the career his father intended for him. To make matters worse, Hans was unprepared for this news; his son had never communicated his change in career, which was as inconsiderate as it was disrespectful.

Two weeks after the storm, on July 17, 1505, Luther walked into the Augustinian monastery.[10]

A LATE MEDIEVAL MAN: LUTHER AND THE *VIA MODERNA*

Not just anyone and everyone could join the Augustinians. There were standards, as well as a process to ensure commitment and stability. First, Luther had to answer questions about his intent, his motivation, before he was extended further entrance. Second, he was granted admission only after he made a public confession. He spread his body across the floor, petitioning his hearers for grace and mercy. Satisfied with Luther's confession, they granted him a one-year probation (*novitiate*). At that point, his physical appearance had to be changed, starting with his hair, which the Augustinians shaved down to the scalp, leaving only a circle on the top with his bald head coming through the middle. The distinguished haircut was paired with a woolen, hooded gown with a leather belt at the waist. As Luther was clipped and clothed, like a sheep preparing to meet his shepherd, he was handed a Bible, and the other brothers joined in a hymn that praised Saint Augustine himself for this novice's zeal. Had Luther read Augustine prior to that hymn? Maybe not. But Augustine, in the years that followed, became a central catalyst in Luther's evolving paradigm—some might say he became the central catalyst.

If Luther survived the *novitiate*, if his commitment to the monastery prevailed after such a probation, then more serious steps were inaugurated. The rigor of the monastery was not to be underestimated. Seven times a day he joined the others in singing the liturgy, a liturgy encrusted by the psalter. When he was not chanting the liturgy, he was at Mass, studying, or doing chores. Not even mealtimes were wasted: he ate in silence while reading and digesting a sacred text.[11] A year passed and he was still standing, ready to continue, determined to devote his life to God. Passing probation, Luther was rewarded with a private

---

9. *Table Talk*, in *LW* 54:15. Theodore G. Tappert dated this incident to April 16, 1503.
10. I.e., the house of observant Augustinian Eremites. Cameron, *European Reformation*, 114.
11. Hendrix, *Martin Luther*, 35.

room so that he could pray in solitude. Awarded his own copy of the rule of the Augustinian order, he found his quiet cell an ideal place for concentrated study.

Luther's formal studies in theology were just beginning. To become a priest, Luther was required to complete a postgraduate degree in theology. Preparation for priesthood was not segregated from the university. The monastery was a place for pious concentration within the university for students of divinity. University faculty were also teachers in the monastery. One of Luther's professors and teachers was Johann Nathin who studied in Tübingen, most likely hearing the lectures of the late medieval theologian Gabriel Biel firsthand. An adherent of Biel's theology, Nathin assigned Biel's dogmatics to Luther, as well as his commentary on the canon of the Mass. Biel's work had a dual effect: it introduced Luther to myriad patristic and medieval thinkers, but its most significant effect was the substantial dose of Biel's theology Luther swallowed.[12] However, the closer Luther came to 1517, the more he separated himself from Biel, until the divorce was as final as it was flagrant.

To review (see chapter 5), two schools of thought vied for disciples in the late medieval period. One was the *via moderna*, the modern way, a school of thought that boasted fourteenth-century representatives like William of Ockham, Robert Holcot, and Pierre d'Ailly.[13] The *via moderna* was known and criticized for its anthropological optimism. Should people do their very best, that which lies within, then God will accept them into heaven. By contrast, the *schola Augustiniana moderna*, believed that people were in such a state of sinfulness and bondage that God's grace was necessary from the start. This school was represented by Thomas Bradwardine (ca. 1290–1349) and Gregory of Rimini (ca. 1300–1358) among others.

These two schools of thought debated with one another, and sometimes the debate was fierce. For example, Bradwardine was convinced the *via moderna* was a reincarnation of Pelagianism, as is plain in the title of his 1344 book, *The Cause of God against Pelagius*.[14] Bradwardine was not merely addressing the historical heresy of Pelagianism back in the days of Augustine but applying the label to his contemporaries in the school of the *via moderna*, especially Robert Holcot. Bradwardine wrote the book while chancellor of Saint Paul's in London. He admitted that he used to be a Pelagian while at Oxford. But his eyes were opened to the necessity and sovereignty of divine grace in the book of Romans, especially chapter 9, which has much to say about God's unconditioned choice of his elect.

He was not alone: Gregory of Rimini took an Augustinian view of sin and grace across the channel in Paris. Hailing from the order of the Hermits of Saint Augustine, Gregory took strides to resurrect the writings and theology of Augustine in his own day, especially Augustine's teaching on predestination and the total gratuity of grace. To some extent, Rimini influenced Luther too, or at least Luther's opponents identified him with Rimini's view. For example, Luther

---

12. See *WATR* 3, 564 (no. 3722); cf. Hendrix, *Martin Luther*, 36.
13. For an analysis of Holcot, e.g., consider Slotemaker and Witt, *Robert Holcot*.
14. For an analysis of his argument and its context, see Leff, *Bradwardine and the Pelagians*.

once wrote to Frederick the Wise about his debate with Johann Eck (1519) and said, "In debating with me he [Eck] rejected Gregory of Rimini as one who alone supported my opinion against all theologians."[15]

To understand Luther's departure from the *via moderna* at the start of his evangelical pilgrimage, a brief review of Biel's soteriology is in order.[16]

GABRIEL BIEL

Gabriel Biel was born around 1418 or 1420, after the major representatives of the *via moderna*, but indebted to each of them, especially the nominalist philosopher William of Ockham. Biel died in 1495, just on the eve of Luther's theological and personal breakthrough. For this reason, Biel was one of the few remaining Scholastics before the advent of the Reformation. Although dead, his thought carried on into the sixteenth century. Biel influenced Luther's professor, John Nathin, but he also influenced many of Luther's future Roman opponents, such as Johann Eck. Although he is not named, threads of Biel's theology might even be located within the Council of Trent (1545–63), Rome's official response and condemnation of the Reformers.

Biel's view of salvation appeared simultaneously grace-filled and man-centered, a paradox some praised but others dammed. "God has established the rule [covenant] that whoever turns to him and does what he can will receive forgiveness of sins from God. God infuses assisting grace into such a man, who is thus taken back into friendship with God."[17] As demonstrated in chapter 5, this rule or covenant was central to Biel, the reason why Biel believed his view began with grace. Since Biel's God possesses radical, voluntarist freedom, this God can make a covenant with humankind: whoever does what is within him, God will reward with an infused, assisting grace. Whoever does his best, God will forgive, irrespective of the real value of the man's works.

For Biel, this covenant is voluntary on God's part, meaning he didn't have to create a covenant but he chose to in order to help sinners. But it is also voluntarist, meaning God does not reward the sinner's works according to their intrinsic merit; if he did, grace would never come. Instead, God makes a pact, a covenant, that if one does his or her best, regardless of whether his or her works meet God's bar (which they don't), God will respond with assisting grace. Prior medieval thinkers argued that God rewards according to the inherent value of one's works. If he does not, then his justice is not just and his character is compromised. Biel disagreed: God is God, so he can do what he wants, rewarding a person's best works even if they do not add up.

A gifted preacher, Biel knew he needed an illustration to communicate the idea of the covenant to churchgoers. Imagine that there is a king, a "most lenient king who shows so much mercy to his people that he publishes a decree saying

---

15. *LW* 31:322.
16. For the full treatment of Biel, review chapter 5.
17. Biel, "Circumcision of the Lord," 173.

that he will embrace with his favor any of his enemies who desire his friendship," but there is a condition: "provided they mend their ways for the present and the future." Should they fix themselves up, the king will welcome them in and put a golden ring on their finger, even if the person's works are not perfect. He can do that because he is the king. "The king gives to such a man by way of delegation of his royal authority such a position that every work done to the honor of the king, regardless of where performed or how large or small it is, shall be rewarded by the king above and beyond its value."[18] How gracious of the king, how gracious of God. Our works don't add up, but if we try our hardest, God will reward them above and beyond their worth simply by divine fiat, irrespective of true value.

Furthermore, as part of the reward, God will give to anyone who does their best grace to then do even more works so that one's sins are forgiven. Biel returned to his illustration to explain, "And to give him extra strength to perform this kind of meritorious work precious and powerful stones are inserted in the ring to encourage him who wears it, so that his body does not fail him when he needs it but increases in ability to gain further rewards the more the body is exercised and accustomed to resist every adverse force."[19]

What Biel was proposing had a certain logic or order to it: First, a voluntarist God wills a covenant, promising to reward above and beyond the intrinsic value of one's work. Second, the condition of that covenant is this: one must do one's best, looking to what lies within one's powers. Third, if that condition is met, then God will infuse grace into the sinner so that they have more strength to perform more meritorious works to achieve the remission of their sins. This order differed considerably from those Scholastics who came before, prior to the *via moderna*. For example, consider Thomas Aquinas (ca. 1225–74), who died not long before William of Ockham, one of Biel's theological forefathers in the *via moderna*. Unlike Ockham and Biel, Thomas did not put off grace, as if one first had to do one's best to receive grace. Thomas had a far more pessimistic, far more Augustinian view of man and his sinful nature, believing man could not do his best or what lies within because what lies within is tainted and bound by original sin. Grace has to come first. For Thomas, first God infuses a habit of grace within. Second, the sinner cooperates and is made righteous. Third, the sinner receives the remission of his sins. Thomas spelled out this order himself: "The first is the infusion of grace; the second, the free-will's movement towards God; the third, the free-will's movement towards sin; the fourth, the remission of sin."[20] Point is, grace is prevenient. "God infuses a habitual gift into the soul of certain forms or supernatural qualities into those whom he moves to seek after supernatural and eternal good, that they may be thus moved by him to seek it sweetly and readily." Grace is, then, a real "gift," albeit a "certain quality" that is infused into a person.[21]

---

18. Biel, 173.
19. Biel, 173.
20. *ST* 1a2ae. 113, 8; cf. 1a2ae. 113, 7. Also consult Ozment, *Age of Reform*, 233.
21. *ST*, 1a2ae. 110, 2.

Although Luther rarely interacted with Thomas, there is reason to believe Luther's journey was not all that different from Thomas's. The young Thomas also wrote a commentary on Peter Lombard's *Sentences*, a tradition that continued into Luther's day and one he would emulate. At that time, Thomas was quite man-centered (by his own admission later, he was even Semi-Pelagian), believing man had to do what lies within him to merit grace. But as he started writing his magnum opus, his *Summa Theologiae* and his *Summa Contra Gentiles*, Thomas realized he had it all backward: grace came first.[22] On that point, Thomas and the Reformers had much in common. But the primacy of grace was anathema to Biel. God may be liberal in the covenant, agreeing to give "so much for so little," but if the sinner is to get grace, the sinner must first perform his or her best works.

Biel assumed the sinner is not so sinful that he cannot do his best, a clear departure from Augustine. Biel looked at the sinner and concluded that he had considerable power within, the free will to pull himself up and offer his best to God. While God may set up the entire arrangement through his covenant, man not only must act first, but man can act first, performing his best to inaugurate the covenant blessings promised. Libertarian free will has not been so damaged by the fall that it has lost its power to merit grace and the remission of sins. Wounded, yes, and perhaps more inclined to evil than good, but by no means so disabled it relies on grace to come first.

If man's will is merely impeded, then all that is needed is a strengthening of his will. That is where grace comes into the picture. Imagine a bird, said Biel, that has a stone tied around it, weighing it down. The bird can "scarcely fly away." But what if the bird does its best to flap its wings and begin to fly? Then grace comes along, not to lift the burden off the bird, but to strengthen the bird's wings so it has less trouble flying. If "this bird's wings were strengthened, then we would say that the impediment to flight had been lessened, although the weight of the stone had not been lessened."[23] So, too, with us. If we do our best, God infuses grace into our wings. That way we can do more good works, but this time more easily. "And thus grace weakens the remaining power of sin, not—as many doctors say—because it forgives or wipes out sins, but because it strengthens human power."[24] Biel did not believe he succumbed to Pelagianism because such grace was a gift from God himself, the same God who first, and so graciously, initiated the covenant in the first place.

Nevertheless, like Pelagius before him, Biel's concern was pastoral at its core. In view of the covenant, the churchgoer yet to receive grace is motivated to do his best or what lies within him so that he does receive grace. The churchgoer who has done his best to receive grace is motivated to do greater works to merit the remission of his sins. "By this grace we are able to remain without difficulty in

---

22. Oberman, *Forerunners of the Reformation*, 130; McGrath, *Iustitia Dei*, 110–11; Janz, *Luther on Thomas Aquinas*, 359.

23. Biel, "Circumcision of the Lord," 172.

24. Biel, 171.

His friendship, and to grow continually through good works. On such a foundation we can easily overcome the onslaughts of the devil, the world, and flesh, and gain a great reward in store for us."[25]

Luther may have first encountered the *via moderna* during his student days at the University of Erfurt. Jodocus Trutfetter and Bartholomaeus Arnoldi were instructors at Erfurt whom Luther may very well have known and possibly listened to at some point. "The Amplonian College," observed Oberman, "which may have been Luther's residence hall for several years, was expressly instructed to teach according to the modern way, 'secundum modernos.'"[26] Yet Johann von Paltz and Johann Nathin may have been more influential.[27] As mentioned in chapter 5, historians have good reason to believe Nathin was one of Gabriel Biel's students and eventually a colleague. Nathin assigned Biel's writings to Luther for sympathetic study, and as early as 1506 or 1507 Luther was reading Biel's commentary on the canon of the Mass. A few years later in 1509 and 1510, Luther was reading and commenting on Lombard's *Sentences* but not without echoing the type of criticisms leveled by Ockham and Biel before him.[28] Also, as indicated in chapter 8, when Luther started lecturing on the Psalms (1513–15) he sounded not all that different from Biel, saying, "The doctors rightly say that, *when people do their best*, God infallibly gives grace. This cannot be understood as meaning that this preparation for grace is *de condigno* [meritorious], as they are incomparable, but it can be regarded as *de congruo* on account of this promise of God and the covenant (*pactum*) of mercy."[29] However, by 1515 or 1516, Luther showed signs of resistance.[30]

Biel's emphasis on doing one's best to receive grace could not have helped Luther's ongoing anxieties back in the monastery over his right standing with God. Biel swore that God would not go back on his word despite the fact that he could do anything to the contrary. God would come through with grace since he bound himself to such a promise in his covenant. Since Biel had asserted a voluntarist view of God, Biel had to reassure his listeners of God's faithfulness. But what if Biel was wrong? What if God's voluntarist, libertarian freedom did mean he might not come through and infuse grace once we had done our best? Anyway, could one ever know if he had done his best? If grace came only to those who proved themselves, could anyone have total assurance he would reach salvation in the end?

Luther found no answer that comforted him, no solution that calmed his troubled soul. No matter how hard he worked, no matter how many works he performed, these questions nagged at him like a thousand needles in the scalp,

---

25. Biel, 173.
26. Oberman, *Luther,* 116.
27. Bagchi, "Sic Et Non: Luther and Scholasticism," 4; Urban, "Die 'via moderna' an der Universität Erfurt am Vorabend der Reformation," 311–30; Oberman, *Luther,* 114–15.
28. For Luther's criticism of *habitus,* see *WA* 9:28–94. Cf. Bagchi, "Sic Et Non: Luther and Scholasticism," 5.
29. *WA* 4:262.4–7 (cf. 3:288.37–289.4), emphasis added. Cf. McGrath, *Iustitia Dei,* 116; *LW* 11:396.
30. Bagchi points out, "As late as 1520, long after Luther had decisively rejected Scholastic theology, he continued to describe himself as an Ockhamist, a modern, or a terminist, and to speak of the Venerable Inceptor himself as a logician of the highest ability." Bagchi, "Sic Et Non: Luther and Scholasticism," 5. Cf. *WA* 6:195.3–6; 6:600.10–12; *WATR* 2:516, l. 6; *WA* 38:160.3; 39.1:420.27; 30.2:300.10 (*LW* 34:27).

giving him an existential albeit spiritual migraine. As Luther understood it, one not only had to do one's best, but one's best had to be sincere, characterized by *super omnia*, the type of love that loves God out of uncorrupted purity and devotion. Luther searched the inner recesses of his soul, and every time he mustered love for God, he knew within it was impure. No matter how hard Luther worked to love God, it fell short and could never be his best. God remained Luther's Judge. Whatever love Luther mustered turned quickly into hate. The angst that came next was unbearable.[31]

LUTHER PERFORMS HIS FIRST MASS

Luther did not enter the monastery for the typical reasons. He did not enter its quarters out of an ambition for tranquil devotion without distraction. Nor did he commit to its rules to obtain the opportunity to pursue theological research. His decision was not motivated, as it was for some, by a tiresome longing to escape the world either. While he no doubt enjoyed all these benefits, Luther's motive was Godward. "It was fear for his salvation that had driven him." As Oberman insists, Luther "was driven by his desire to find a merciful God."[32] Upon entry, the conversation for a new candidate went as follows:

> Prior: What do you seek here?
> Luther: The gracious God and your mercy.
> Prior: Lord, save Thy servant . . . grant him Thy mercy. . . . so that he
>   shall deserve to achieve eternal life through our Lord Jesus Christ.[33]

In that same spirit of inauguration, Luther later acknowledged his motives during this time: "In the monastery I did not think about women, money, or possessions; instead my heart trembled and fidgeted about whether God would bestow His grace on me."[34]

As he pursued that fearful goal, however, Luther lived out the anxiety that Biel's late medieval soteriology cultivated.[35] Later in life, Luther reflected on his days in the monastery and shared the anxiety that plagued him due to his failure to find favor with a holy and righteous God no matter how many works of penance he performed. "I almost fasted myself to death, for again and again I went for three days without taking a drop of water or a morsel of food. I was very serious about it. I really crucified the Lord Christ. I wasn't simply an observer but helped to carry him and pierce [his hands and feet]. God forgive me for it, for

---

31. To qualify, the *via moderna* contributed to Luther's angst while wrestling with its nominalist, voluntarist God in the monastery. However, it is likely a step too far to assume the nominalism and voluntarism of the *via moderna* is what drove Luther into the monastery in the first place. Oberman, *Luther*, 123.

32. Oberman, *Luther*, 127.

33. Oberman, *Luther*, 128.

34. *WA* 47:590.6–10; cf. Oberman, *Luther*, 128.

35. Others have drawn the connection between Biel's *via moderna* soteriology and Luther's anxiety: e.g., Kolb, *Martin Luther*, 32.

I have confessed it openly! This is the truth: the most pious monk is the worst scoundrel. He denies that Christ is the mediator and high priest and turns him into a judge."[36]

Fasting was not Luther's only instrument of punishment. Through a relentless, exhausting, and vigorous schedule of pious acts, Luther attempted to win favor with God to somehow receive the grace needed to grant him peace of mind. "I chose twenty-one saints and prayed to three every day when I celebrated mass; thus I completed the number of every week. I prayed especially to the Blessed Virgin, who with her womanly heart would compassionately appease her Son. Ah, if the article on justification hadn't fallen, the brotherhoods, pilgrimages, masses, invocation of saints, etc., would have found no place in the church. If it falls again (which may God prevent!) these idols will return."[37] Christ was Luther's Judge, not Savior. And although Luther spent every waking moment trying to appease this wrathful Judge, he found no relief. "If ever a monk came to heaven through monkery, it should have been I," Luther said.[38] If Luther had not discovered in time that monkery was not the path to heaven, he might have killed not only his soul but his body in the process.

In 1507 Luther tasted the fruit of his hard but anxious labor: that spring Luther was ordained. Today, in many low church denominations, ordination is no longer a rite of passage or a commission into the ministry, ignored and relegated as an ancient relic of an outdated ecclesiastical era. Or if it is performed, it is casual, a mere formality, one that may or may not be necessary for pastoral ministry. But in the sixteenth century, ordination was a significant moment, a benchmark in Luther's journey. It was nothing less than Luther's entryway into the priesthood itself. The vows he took were binding and the responsibility now on Luther's shoulders was sacred.

The sanctity of Luther's calling took public form the next month when he performed his first Mass. Luther was a nervous wreck. "When I was about to hold my first mass my father sent twenty gulden for food and came with twenty persons, all of whom he put up. Somebody said to him, 'You must have a good friend here that you should come to visit him with such a large company.'" But there was a deeper, far more theological explanation for Luther's anxiety, and it had to do with his heavenly Father. "When at length I stood before the altar and was to consecrate, I was so terrified by the words *aeterno vivo vero Deo* [to Thee, the eternal, living, and true God] that I thought of running away from the altar." *Terrified* is the key word: "So terrified was I by those words! Already I had forebodings that something was wrong, but God didn't give me an understanding of this until later." Later in life, Luther confessed he did not respect his father but "boldly ignored" him, so "sure of my own righteousness."[39]

36. *LW* 54:340.
37. *LW* 54:340.
38. *WATR* 1:502. Cf. Hillerbrand, *Division of Christendom*, 38.
39. *LW* 54:156.

HAS ANYTHING GOOD EVER COME OUT OF WITTENBERG?

Historians have often marveled that such an international movement like the Reformation originated in Wittenberg. In comparison to other towns and cities, Wittenberg was nothing special. Just off the Elbe River, Wittenberg consisted of hardworking gatherers and hunters. The town was not affluent, conspicuous to any visitor who walked into Wittenberg on dirty streets and into buildings in need of repair. Wittenberg also had little to brag about in the religious and academic domains. Like other towns, Wittenberg had its monasteries; but unlike other places, Wittenberg had a mere two: the Augustinians and the Franciscans. If anything stood out, it was the castle church, the proud handiwork of the elector Frederick. The castle church housed the elector's relics—thousands of them—which he had purchased from across Europe and brought back to Wittenberg. Wittenberg was also home to a university, but like the castle church, the university was new, founded in 1502. The university was barely a decade old by the time Luther became a professor in 1512.

Whether Frederick's castle church or the university itself, anything spectacular in Wittenberg was new, hardly comparable to the ancient cathedrals and castles that stood tall in other European towns. Wittenberg, like Nazareth, was the last place in the world anyone expected change to come.

With such doubt in play, haunting Luther so that he could barely perform Mass, Luther must not have been encouraged by his father's words that day: "Let us hope that your vow was not an illusion." Then Hans reminded his religious son that he had violated the fifth commandment: "Have you not heard that parents are to be obeyed?"[40] In another account, Luther said he responded to his father, explaining how he was "so frightened by a storm that he was compelled to become a monk," but his father replied, "Just so it wasn't a phantom you saw!" Hans then told his son to leave the priesthood and go "get married."[41]

One day Luther would marry, yet not to escape the faith but to prove its true character over against the pope.

THE PASTORAL GUIDANCE OF AN AUGUSTINIAN: STAUPITZ

After ordination, Luther received an invitation to become a one-year lecturer in philosophy at the University of Wittenberg. Apparently Luther had a growing reputation as a budding scholar. In 1508 Luther left Erfurt for Wittenberg, where he lectured on Aristotle's *Ethics*. Afterward (1509) Luther returned to Erfurt to lecture on the Scriptures as well as Peter Lombard's *Sentences*.

Luther could have studied and lectured on Lombard's *Sentences* in one year; other students took this expedient approach to their education. Not Luther.

---

40. *LW* 48:322; *WA* 8, 574. Cf. Hendrix, *Martin Luther*, 38.
41. *LW* 54:109; cf. 54:354.

This early in his career, he exhibited a trait that would mark him for the rest of his life: painstaking meticulousness. Whether it was a work of theology, a commentary on the Bible, or the Scriptures themselves, Luther was thorough. He intended to examine not only Lombard—comparing various editions of *The Sentences*—but also the catholic tradition that preceded Lombard, contrasting Lombard's theology with the Fathers, Augustine in particular.

For two years, not just one, Luther lectured on *The Sentences*. Three times per week he not only commented on Lombard but shared his insights into the patristic tradition from Augustine to Anselm. Luther also compared medieval commentaries on Lombard's *Sentences*, from Bonaventure to Duns Scotus, from William of Ockham to Gabriel Biel, sifting out their differences as well as their common consensus. Much later in life Luther the Reformer reflected on his early lectures and praised many of them, though not without his typical wit. "Peter Lombard was adequate as a theologian; none has been his equal. He read Hilary, Augustine, Ambrose, Gregory, and also all the councils. He was a great man. If he had by chance come upon the Bible he would no doubt have been the greatest."[42] At the time of his lectures, however, Luther was not so critical of Lombard, who proved a second gateway—Biel being the first—into the patristic world.

Others noted Luther's excelling scholarship, including John Staupitz at the University of Wittenberg. Staupitz first drew Luther to Wittenberg back in 1508 for a short stint on Aristotle's *Ethics*. By 1511 Staupitz was determined to bring Luther on as a permanent member of the faculty. Staupitz was an old friend of Frederick the Wise, elector of Saxony, who recruited Staupitz to come and help the new university, which was born just at the turn of the century. Not long after Staupitz's arrival, Frederick knew he had made the right decision; Staupitz was a success. Staupitz not only became vicar general of the Augustinians but professor of theology at the University of Wittenberg. Besides his lecturing responsibilities, Staupitz oversaw some thirty plus cloisters (also known as Reformed Congregations). With Frederick's support, Staupitz was determined to turn the university into the theological center for the Augustinian cloisters. But the responsibilities of both positions were legion; Staupitz decided he needed to devote his attention to the cloisters alone. Who could succeed him as professor? While there were many bright minds in nearby Erfurt, Staupitz was set on Luther.

Luther had already lectured on Lombard's *Sentences*, which qualified him for a master of theology and an opportunity to teach. His professors were insistent Luther stay in Erfurt to complete his doctorate, but Staupitz contested that advice, telling Luther he must come to Wittenberg instead. Luther resisted for over a dozen reasons, but when Frederick agreed to pay for a portion of Luther's education, Luther agreed. Staupitz also persuaded Luther's close friend John Lang to come as well, which was a major improvement to Wittenberg since Lang

42. *LW* 54:26. Cf. Hendrix, *Martin Luther*, 38-39.

was a blossoming Greek scholar. The university had positioned itself in the years prior as a center for humanist scholarship and brought in faculty to reflect such interests, Staupitz being one of them. Now, with Lang and Luther, the institution had a growing number of humanists to rival the faculty of Erfurt.

Did Luther's soteriological anxieties rescind by the time he arrived in Wittenberg? They did not. But Luther did have Staupitz to mentor him, and Staupitz, about twenty years older than Luther, knew something of Augustine's theology of grace and had many years of pastoral experience to draw from.

Luther scholarship in the twentieth century was characterized by continual debate over Staupitz's influence on Luther. There is no question Staupitz affected Luther; although Luther's evangelical convictions eventually led to disagreement with Staupitz, Luther never moved from his admission that he owed everything to Staupitz.[43] The years prior to 1512 were formative; after 1512, and the closer Luther approached 1524, Luther developed his own evangelical position. The question under debate is what *type* of influence Staupitz exercised over young Luther. Behind these debates is a desire to understand what tradition(s) informed the young Luther. Polarizing theories have been proposed. Did Staupitz counter the *via moderna* by channeling an Augustinian Thomism? Or perhaps the theology of Gregory of Rimini, the *via Gregorii*? Although that was possible, David Steinmetz shared conventional wisdom by paying attention to the type of mentor Luther received in Staupitz. Luther, full of angst, first received relief from Staupitz in the confessional. From there forward, however academic Staupitz involvement may have been at points, the mentor's main area of influence was *pastoral*.[44] Luther was plagued with guilt; Staupitz was Luther's pastoral balm, reassuring the despondent young man of God's love and mercy.

The type of pastoral counsel Staupitz provided Luther was so priceless that historians have praised Staupitz as the unwitting father of the Reformation. Consider, for example, that period when Luther kept returning to the confessional plagued by every single sin, no matter how small. Luther was not met with a dismissive Staupitz—"Stop being petty and ridiculous, Luther!" Nor was Luther met by a Staupitz that intensified the system of fear Luther inhabited—"Yes, you should be plagued by guilt; until you've really done your best you will not receive the love of God." Rather, Luther was met by an Augustinian pastor, one who reminded the young man that God's love came first, as did his divine mercy. Staupitz's approach, in other words, flew in the face of Luther's *via moderna* academic training precisely because Staupitz's point of view was so Augustinian. As Steinmetz explains, Staupitz may have been educated himself on various patristic and medieval traditions, but his pastoral encounters were quite simple: he presented what he believed Scripture said, and what Scripture said seemed best represented by Augustine.

43. *WATR* 1.173 (February or March 1532).
44. Steinmetz, *Luther and Staupitz*, 30–31. For a survey and critique of the various theories, see 4–27.

NOT CONTRITE ENOUGH: LUTHER'S AFFLICTED CONSCIENCE

Some have doubted whether Luther was motivated by his angst before a holy God. Certainly, other factors contributed to Luther's transformation. And by the time Luther posted his Ninety-Five Theses, he was motivated by the abuses he witnessed, not so much by his own anxiety. Nevertheless, when Luther entered the monastery, an afflicted conscience did plague him. Luther himself wrote, "When I was a monk, I tried with all diligence to live according to the Rule, and I used to be contrite, to confess and number off my sins, and often repeated my confession, and sedulously performed my allotted penance. And yet my conscience could never give me certainty, but I always doubted and said, 'You did not perform that correctly. You were not contrite enough. You left that out of your confession.' The more I tried to remedy an uncertain, weak and afflicted conscience with the traditions of men, the more each day found it more uncertain, weaker, more troubled" (WA 40.ii.414.15). That testimony has led Gordon Rupp to call Luther "Mr. Fearing" (*Luther's Progress to the Diet of Worms*, 26).

Practically, that meant Staupitz had to get tough with Luther, although it was a tough *love* he used to slap Luther into a theology of trust as opposed to distrust in God's promises. Staupitz recognized that Luther's insanity was fueled by mulish unbelief, not piety as Luther supposed. Steinmetz's profound evaluation captured Staupitz's pastoral brilliance:

When Luther tried to confess faults that were not sins, Staupitz accused him of parading toy sins before God and of confusing social indiscretions with moral transgressions. When Luther was inclined to mope and indulge in a morbid introspection of his conscience, Staupitz set him to work studying for his theological doctorate. The study of theology might make clear to Luther that while God is merciful to real sinners, imaginary sinners remain trapped in illusions spun out of their own fears. Staupitz was convinced that soft handling would never teach Luther the difference between real sin and entirely unjustified feelings of guilt. Luther had to learn that it was not a sign of great piety to distrust the mercy of God but of stupid, obstinate, and wholly unnecessary unbelief. Clinging to God's "No" when one should celebrate God's "Yes" in the gospel was the worst kind of unbelief.[45]

---

45. "The worst thing a pastor could do with a scrupulous penitent was cater to him, nurse along his neurotic guilt, protect him from confrontation with the fact that his refusal to believe in God's mercy was a dangerous and potentially fatal sin. If our thoughts condemn us, our thoughts are not Christ. Our anger with God is not the same thing as God's anger with us. There is, of course, such a thing as the wrath of God and it is to be feared. But the wrath of God never falls on even the weakest penitent who clings simply to the cross of Christ." Steinmetz, *Luther and Staupitz*, 32–33.

ROME AND THE SANTA SCALA

Either in 1510 or in 1511 Staupitz sent Luther to Rome to settle a dispute among the Augustinians. The journey was rigorous. Luther climbed the Alps and must have been exhausted by the time he reached Rome. He then spent a month trying but failing to bring about peace. When Luther explored the city, he grew disturbed by the priesthood's prosaic approach to Mass at the altar of St. Sebastian. They either lacked respect, knowledge, or care for the ritual—and sometimes all three. "Priests appeared to him to be ignorant and corrupt functionaries who scorned the pious, profanely raced through their obligatory Masses, and blasphemously hurried Luther through those he celebrated" (Marty, *Martin Luther*, 13). Besides Masses, like many a pilgrim Luther visited and venerated relics to reduce time in purgatory for his parents. Unfortunately, his parents were still alive. If only they were dead and could sin no more, Luther's efforts might be more effective. As Luther said, "For I would have loved to deliver them from purgatory with my masses and other special works and prayers" (*WA* 31/1:226.11–17; cf. Oberman, *Luther*, 147). Luther even bowed to his knees to climb the steps Jesus walked when he ascended into the presence of Pilate. Transported from Jerusalem, the Santa Scala was filled with other pilgrims saying prayers. Luther was hopeful his ascent might liberate at least his grandfather from purgatory. When Luther reached the top, however, he exhaled and said, "Who knows whether this is really true?" Oberman warns against interpreting Luther's doubt through the lens of modernity, as if Luther became a skeptic in that moment and threw off the chains of tradition.

Present day Roman Catholics ascending the sanctuary of holy
stairs for a plenary indulgence. Santa Scala, Rome.
Matthew Barrett

Rather, Luther's doubt "arose from the conviction that God would not allow Himself to be pinned down in this way" (*Luther*, 147). Luther feared the Lord, but he did not sense that same fear in the priests who said Mass in Rome. Luther said his first Mass trembling; they said Mass with a juvenile grin. Luther left nauseated by the cheap grace he encountered.

As mentioned, interpreters have likely read too much into Staupitz, as if Staupitz's main channel of influence on Luther was academic when in fact it was pastoral. Nevertheless, Staupitz's pastoral counsel to Luther was theological. While debates persist over who Staupitz was indebted to most, the Augustinian flavor of Staupitz's approach seems undeniable. Contrary to what Luther had been taught from the writings of Biel, divine love comes first. Only then can confession and penance be properly understood. If Luther believed, as Biel taught, that divine love and the justification it brings are conditioned on doing one's best, Luther would never have escaped the crushing burden of his own inability and its condemnation. Staupitz "warned Luther of the danger of trusting in one's own natural moral energies, even though Luther had learned that it was precisely by relying on those same natural powers that one could merit the favor of God."[46]

In that light, when Staupitz recommended that Luther pursue his doctorate, he was not trying merely to keep Luther's anxious mind busy, nor was Staupitz dismissing Luther's spiritual crisis for that which really matters: academics. Staupitz, like Augustine before him, believed theology was the answer to Luther's spiritual crisis. However, Staupitz understood it had to be the right theology; an erroneous theology could have disastrous pastoral consequences. Luther was exhibit A.

Was Staupitz successful? The rest of Luther's story proves his mentor did succeed. For this reason, Staupitz may have saved the Reformation before it started. Perhaps there is justification for labeling Staupitz a forerunner after all.[47]

ROMANS AND THE RIGHTEOUSNESS OF GOD

When Luther returned from Rome, the university was ready to award Luther a doctorate in theology. It was customary for another faculty member to step forward on behalf of the candidate. In the fall of 1512, Andreas Bodenstein von Karlstadt announced he intended to sponsor Luther. Over the course of two days, Luther's achievements were celebrated by his colleagues in a formal ceremony. In the castle church, he took an oath, swearing allegiance to the sacred Scriptures. He also promised to reject all those heresies denounced by the Catholic Church. He took the vow with great seriousness, so that later, in his

---

46. "He taught Luther that penance begins with the love of God, even though Luther had been given to understand that the love of God is the final step in a process of self-discipline and the assumption of rigorous responsibility for one's status in the presence of God." Steinmetz, *Luther and Staupitz*, 33.

47. Steinmetz, *Luther and Staupitz*, 144–45.

reforming years, he reminded his opponents of his oath to uphold the Scriptures and all that they taught.

When Luther was appointed professor in biblical studies, he inaugurated his tenure with lectures on the Psalms. Remember, in the monastery, the liturgy memorized and chanted incorporated the entire psalter.[48] Its canon was not foreign to Luther. Yet Luther had never lectured on the Psalms, which required studious preparation, not only consulting the Hebrew but the history of interpretation. Day after day Luther not only studied the psalter but many commentaries, including the *glossa ordinaria*, the established commentary, a compilation of patristic and medieval commentary set side by side with the text itself, allowing Luther to move back and forth between the two. By the fall of 1513, Luther was ready and delivered his insights to a growing class of students, a class far larger than prior years at the university.

After the Psalms, Luther pursued other books, including Romans (1515–16), Galatians (1516–17), and Hebrews (1517–18). As Luther lectured on the Scriptures, his debt to Augustine became more and more visible. Tension even formed between Luther and Karlstadt over Luther's interpretation of Augustine. Karlstadt then read *De Spiritu et Littera* by Augustine with every intention of challenging this new colleague, who not only offered a different understanding of Paul but Augustine. In time Karlstadt could not shake the validity of Luther's argument.[49]

Luther also wrote theses for students to defend at disputations, as well as exams for those students finishing their masters of arts in theology. In the Scholastic education system, the questions posed to students set the agenda for a disputation. If the disputation involved a candidate for the doctorate, then the question would likely be one that stemmed from Lombard's *Sentences*. However, in special cases a school might choose a question of their own, which set the agenda for a quodlibetal disputation (see chapter 8). Whatever the disputation, the structure was organized: one student spoke, another student replied, followed by a back-and-forth exchange in an attempt to answer the questions in play. After the students had their try, the teacher had the last word, not only answering the question but assessing the answers given by the students. The goal of this Scholastic practice was clarity on the greatest ideas of the Christian faith.[50]

On top of these academic responsibilities, Luther had innumerable monastic obligations. In a letter to Lang, Luther vented, explaining how overwhelmed he was. Not only did he have enough letters to answer for two secretaries, not only was he scheduled to preach regularly at the monastery and at the city church, but he was expected to supervise eleven different cloisters. "Plus: I am warden of the fish pond at Leitzkau." Luther was so busy with religious duties he barely had enough time and energy to celebrate Mass. "Besides," Luther complained, "I have

---

48. Hendrix, *Martin Luther*, 48–49.
49. Hillerbrand, *Division of Christendom*, 31; Hendrix, *Martin Luther*, 53.
50. Steinmetz, "Scholastic Calvin," 21.

my own struggles with the flesh, the world, and the devil. See what a lazy man I am!"[51]

Important as these many responsibilities may have been, it was Luther's lectures on Romans, accompanied by his preparation of theses for disputation, that proved transformative for Luther. The timing was impeccable: as Luther encountered Romans, he also read Augustine's anti-Pelagian writings.[52] Nathin and the faculty at Erfurt were loyal to the covenant, voluntarist soteriology of Ockham and Biel. But as Luther studied Biel's *Collectorium* on Lombard's *Sentences*, contrasted with his reading of Augustine's *On the Spirit and the Letter*, only capitalized by his study of Romans, his eyes were opened to the total gratuity of God's righteousness, which could not be reconciled with Biel's program.[53] Often labeled Luther's "tower experience," Luther recalled how he felt altogether born again after wrestling with Romans 1:17:

> Though I lived as a monk without reproach, I felt that I was a sinner before God with an extremely disturbed conscience. I could not believe that he was placated by my satisfaction. I did not love, yes, I hated the righteous God who punishes sinners, and secretly, if not blasphemously, certainly murmuring greatly, I was angry with God, and said, "As if, indeed, it is not enough, that miserable sinners, eternally lost through original sin, are crushed by every kind of calamity by the law of the decalogue, without having God add pain to pain by the gospel and also by the gospel threatening us with his righteousness and wrath!" Thus I raged with a fierce and troubled conscience. Nevertheless, I beat importunately upon Paul at that place, most ardently desiring to know what St. Paul wanted.
>
> At last, by the mercy of God, meditating day and night, I gave heed to the context of the words, namely, "In it the righteousness of God is revealed, as it is written, 'He who through faith is righteous shall live.'" There I began to understand that the righteousness of God is that by which the righteous lives by the gift of God, namely by faith. And this is the meaning: the righteousness of God is revealed by the gospel, namely, the passive righteousness with which merciful God justifies us by faith, as it is written, "He who through faith is righteous shall live." Here I felt that I was altogether born again and had entered paradise itself through open gates. . . .
>
> And I extolled my sweetest word with a love as great as the hatred with which I had before hated the word "righteousness of God." Thus that place in Paul was for me truly the gate to paradise. Later I read Augustine's *The Spirit and the Letter*, where contrary to hope I found that he, too, interpreted God's righteousness in

---

51. *LW* 48:27–28. Cf. Hendrix, *Martin Luther*, 44–46.

52. Herrmann, "Luther's Absorption of Medieval Biblical Interpretation," 79.

53. For Luther's annotations on Biel's *Collectorium*, see *WA* 1:145–51. On Luther's reading of Augustine, see *WABr* 1:70, lines 8–16, no. 27. Cf. Bagchi, "Sic Et Non," 7. Cameron claims, however, that even as early as Luther's lectures on the Psalms (1513–15) there were signs of discontentment with the *via moderna*. Cameron, *European Reformation*, 116.

a similar way, as the righteousness with which God clothes us when he justifies us. Although this was heretofore said imperfectly and he did not explain all things concerning imputation clearly, it nevertheless was pleasing that God's righteousness with which we are justified was taught. Armed more fully with these thoughts, I began a second time to interpret the Psalter. And the work would have grown into a large commentary, if I had not again been compelled to leave the work begun, because Emperor Charles V in the following year convened the diet of Worms.[54]

The text is an example of catholicity in the Reformation. First, Reformers like Luther did not consider a right reading of the Scriptures antithetical to a right reading of tradition, as Luther's mention of Augustine demonstrates. Second, even with the doctrine of justification, they did not consider themselves breaking *in toto* from the tradition. Luther did not think Augustine took him as far as a forensic account of imputation, as indebted as Augustine was to the paradigm of infused grace. Nonetheless, Luther credited Augustine with his discovery because Augustine at least understood Paul to mean a righteousness that is a gift (much in contrast to the *via moderna* soteriology of Ockham and Biel). Augustine was not an enemy but an ally, and so were any others who followed his interpretation. For these reasons, Luther later groaned how his training prior to 1509 gave him Scotus but not Augustine.[55]

Scholars debate when this tower experience occurred.[56] Did it occur right after Luther returned from Rome, the same year he received his doctorate (1512)? Or did it occur sometime before or during his lectures on the book of Romans (1515–16)? Or did it occur later, perhaps in the aftermath of the Ninety-Five Theses (1517) and his lectures on Hebrews (1518), closer to the Diet of Worms (1521)? Luther's own recollection could be inaccurate at points and it is possible (even likely) that Luther's breakthrough did not occur all at once but was a process with marked development from 1513–1519.[57] Luther may have been using the rhetorical method of past Christians as he gave the impression of an instantaneous discovery. Augustine, for example, recounted his conversion experience in the garden. He heard a child singing, "Pick up and read," so he opened the Scriptures, and his eyes were opened. Luther may have been positioning himself in that same stream. However sudden that experience may have been for Luther, nevertheless, there are reasons to believe many other circumstances and influences contributed to this breakthrough throughout those critical years. Rome was not built in a day; neither was the Reformation.

---

54. *LW* 34:336–38. To see Luther's negative reaction to the *via moderna*, consult *WA* 56:502.32–503.5 (*LW* 25:497); 56.274.14 (*LW* 25:261). Cf. Bagchi, "Sic Et Non," 6; Hendrix, *Martin Luther*, 51.

55. *WABr* 1:70, 19–21; cf. Oberman, *Luther*, 161.

56. It has been called his "tower experience" because some have claimed Luther had this epiphany in the monastery's tower.

57. Oberman, *Luther*, 165.

Whenever the tower experience occurred, Luther experienced a paradigm shift. In his own mind, Paul had opened his eyes to justification by faith. For the first time, Luther no longer hated God. Christ was no longer a judge that Luther could not appease. Instead, Christ was his Savior; by giving himself over to death, God could offer forgiveness free of charge. By faith in Christ alone, the ungodly are pardoned from all guilt, receiving every assurance they no longer stand under divine condemnation. The righteousness of God, which haunted Luther for so long, was now good news. Righteousness was a gift received by faith alone (hence Luther called it a passive righteousness). Upon faith in Christ the righteousness of Christ is reckoned to the believer. In Christ God justifies the ungodly.

And yet, Luther's renewed vision of justification also showed signs of debt to the scholastic and monastic traditions that preceded him. Rather than dispensing altogether with their understanding of ascent, Luther critically appropriated the patristic and medieval doctrine of ascent to capture the Christian life and its telos, the beatific vision. As articulated in his interpretation of Jacob's ladder in Genesis 28, Christians ascend to heaven, but they do so only because Christ has descended first in his humiliation. His incarnation, therefore, is the ladder that drops from heaven. Once the sinner is justified in Christ, he is led by the Word and Spirit up the ladder to enjoy communion with God. Satan schemes day and night, mustering all his power to knock the Christian off the ladder of Christ.[58] Calvin's description of Jacob's ladder sounds similar because the Reformers are appropriating the medieval doctrine of ascent but refining its use now that ascent itself is absent of justifying merit.

When his former professors heard about Luther's criticisms of Biel—students tend to talk—those in Erfurt were not pleased with Luther's decision to depart from the late medieval theology on which he was bred.[59] Even Karlstadt reacted against Luther. However, when Karlstadt consulted Augustine, he, too, was persuaded that Biel was mistaken, and with newfound illumination, Karlstadt took decisive initiative to ensure that the students were taught Augustine's theology in the semesters ahead. First Luther, now Karlstadt—both were discovering that to be truly catholic, truly orthodox in fact, they needed to move past the innovations of the *via moderna* and reconsider their catholic heritage without such a filter.

At the time, Luther described his breakthrough as something "new." But new to whom? Luther himself conceded his debt to Augustine. While Luther protested "Scholastics," Luther did not appear to have read the span of medieval theology. Could it be that Luther had in view a certain strand of late medieval Scholastics? Reformation historian Heiko Oberman answered in the affirmative. Despite Luther's hyperbole—as if his "new" discovery contradicted all the

---

58. Oberman gives a similar summary of Luther's (Jacob's) ladder: *Luther,* 167. Cf. *WA* 43:582.
59. *WABr* 1:65–66. Cf. Hendrix, *Martin Luther,* 50–51.

ancient doctors, patristic and medieval—Oberman showed at great length that a certain Scholastic was in view, namely, Biel.[60]

That insight would become undeniable when Luther's disputation against Scholastic theology targeted Scotus, Ockham, and Biel—not all Scholastic theology.[61]

LUTHER'S BREAK WITH THE *VIA MODERNA*

On a fall day in September 1517, Franz Günther, a student of Martin Luther, rose to defend a set of theses. If successful, Günther would be awarded his bachelor's degree. As was custom, theses were prepared by one's professor, in this case Martin Luther. In most cases, the student graduated, and the theses were nothing more than another exam to pass on the way to earning a degree. But this time was different. These theses revealed a decisive shift in Martin Luther's thinking, and a public one at that. Luther took aim at the late medieval Scholastics, and with rapid fire brought down the very foundation on which his theological world up to that point had been built.

The main Scholastic theologian Luther targeted in these theses was none other than Gabriel Biel himself.[62] Prior to 1517 there were distress signals. Back in 1513, when Luther was lecturing on the Psalms, Luther was more or less still sympathetic with Biel. "The doctors rightly say that, when people do their best, God infallibly gives grace. This cannot be understood as meaning that this preparation for grace is *de condigno* [meritorious], as they are incomparable, but it can be regarded as *de congruo* on account of this promise of God and the covenant (*pactum*) of mercy."[63] Here is a clear retrieval of Biel's voluntarist concept of the covenant. At the same time, doing one's best, or doing what lies within, was not disconnected from a certain understanding of righteousness for Luther. "Righteousness (*iustitia*) is thus said to be rendering to each what is due to them. Yet equity is prior to righteousness, and is its prerequisite. Equity identifies merit; righteousness renders rewards. Thus the Lord judged the world 'in equity' (that is, wishing all to be saved), and judges 'in righteousness' (because

---

60. Although a Scholastic like Lombard was not far from Luther's mind. For example, he wrote to Johann Lang on May 18, 1517, the following update: "Our theology and St Augustine proceed apace and are dominant in our university, by the grace of God. Aristotle declines steadily and is heading for total oblivion. All object to hearing lectures on the text-books of the Sentences, and no one can expect an audience who does not advance this theology—that is, the Bible or St. Augustine, or some other doctor with ecclesiastical authority." *WABr* 1:98–99, no. 41.

61. See Oberman, *Harvest of Medieval Theology*. Hillerbrand raised the issue as well: "As far as Luther was concerned, his discovery was new, dramatically new, indeed, 'contrary to the opinion of all the doctors.' Unfortunately, there was more exuberance than accuracy in Luther's reflection. Was it really so dramatically 'contrary to the opinion of all the doctors'? Had Luther not read widely enough in medieval theology? Had he misunderstood the 'doctors,' or had his Catholic protagonists misunderstood them? These are the perplexing scholarly questions hovering over Luther's spiritual maturing and thereby over the early Reformation." Hillerbrand, *Division of Christendom*, 39. Hillerbrand pointed not only to Oberman but to H. Denifle, *Die abendländischen Schriftausleger. . . .*

62. For a more extensive look at Luther's reaction to Biel in his *Disputation*, see Grane, *Contra Gabrielem*.

63. *WA* 4:262.4–7; cf. 3:288.37–289.4. Cf. McGrath, *Iustitia Dei*, 116; *LW* 11:396.

God renders to each their reward)."[64] Sometime between 1515 and 1516, Luther's breakthrough resulted in a paradigm shift, a redefinition of the "righteousness" of God. That paradigm shift also resulted in a total rejection of the *via moderna* scheme Luther was taught as a student, so that by 1517 Luther turned hostile against Biel, concluding that the last of the Scholastics was in complete conflict with the apostle Paul, as well as Augustine himself. Although Luther did not know it, earlier Scholastics might have agreed with Luther in his disgust for Biel.

Luther began his *Disputation against Scholastic Theology* in a way that would have made Bradwardine proud: a full-scale condemnation of Pelagianism. In doing so, Luther set himself over against Biel as a replay of the debate between Augustine and Pelagius. At the start, Luther attacked the main issue: the depravity of mankind. Appealing to texts like Matthew 7:17–18, Luther argued that sinners cannot do their best because there has been something fundamentally wrong with human nature ever since Adam and Eve ate of the Tree of the Knowledge of Good and Evil. The sinner is, by nature, a "bad tree," and for that reason the sinner "can only will and do evil."[65] Doing one's best to merit grace is a nonstarter because there is no best to begin with. The problem of salvation is not solved by behavior modification but by a complete renovation of the sinful nature. The sinner "can only will and do evil," said Luther, because the sinner's corrupt choices stem from a corrupt nature. Free will is a myth. Captivity is the reality. "It is false to state that man's inclination is free to choose between either of two opposites. Indeed, the inclination is not free, but captive."[66] In "opposition to Scotus and Gabriel," said Luther, it "is false to state that the will can by nature conform to the correct precept."[67] Conformity is an impossibility when the sinner is in bondage to a sinful nature, his inclination captive and therefore desiring only that which is ungodly.

Grace, then, cannot be after the fact, a reward merited by doing one's best. No, grace is absolutely necessary from the start. Without it, the sinner is hopeless. "As a matter of fact," said Luther, again countering Scotus and Biel, "without the grace of God the will produces an act that is perverse and evil."[68] Due to the sinful nature of Adam, the will is "innately and inevitably evil and corrupt" and "is not free to strive toward whatever is declared good," a point that also runs "in opposition to Scotus and Gabriel."[69] Corrupt and polluted, "it is impossible" for the sinner "to love God."[70]

The paradox of it all is not lost on Luther. On one hand, the will is in bondage, captive and enslaved, incapable of doing its best to merit grace. On the other

---

64. *WA* 55.1:70.9–11; cf. 4:262.4–5.
65. *LW* 31:9 (thesis 4).
66. *LW* 31:9 (thesis 5).
67. *LW* 31:9 (thesis 6).
68. *LW* 31:9 (thesis 7).
69. *LW* 31:9 (theses 9, 10). Luther qualified that the will is not "by nature evil," or "essentially evil," as the Manichaeans said. Rather, the will is in bondage to evil due to the sinful nature of Adam. Cf. 31:9 (thesis 8).
70. *LW* 31:10 (thesis 16).

hand, this bondage is a *willful* bondage. It's not as if the sinner wants grace, but God won't give it. It's not as if the sinner desires God, but God refuses. Rather, the captivity that prohibits willful cooperation is a desired captivity. Luther, a wordsmith with the German language, said it this way: "Man is by nature unable to want God to be God."[71] Biel thought he could motivate the sinner to *want* God. But Luther corrected him: as long as man's nature remains corrupt, he will never want God. "To love God above all things by nature is a fictitious term, a chimera, as it were."[72]

If the sinner is to regain friendship with God, which is what Biel was after, then the sinner must depend on God himself to initiate and institute that friendship by his grace. If the sinner relies on his own nature to create such a friendship, as Biel taught, it will never happen, for no sinner wants such a friendship in the first place, nor can he since his nature is predisposed to corruption. "An act of friendship is done, not according to nature, but according to prevenient grace. This in opposition to Gabriel."[73]

Where, though, does divine grace originate from if it is not in response to man doing his best? Luther's answer approaches what today is labeled *sola gratia*, grace alone. If man doing that "which is in" him is the cause of grace for Biel, man has nothing to do with grace at all for Luther. Grace is not conditioned on man's will, but its origin is from eternity: "The best and infallible preparation for grace and the sole disposition toward grace is the eternal election and predestination of God."[74] God's will, not man's, deserves the credit for the sinner's turn toward Christ.

Here is also the beginning of Luther's famous contrast between law and grace. Luther spent twenty theses on the difference between the two, which he believed Biel confused. The law commands and demands obedience. It is our "taskmaster."[75] But sinners cannot fulfill the law, nor do they want to. "What the law wants, the will never wants," said Luther. [76] "Condemned are all those who do the works of the law." [77] How cruel, then, for Ockham and Biel to dangle grace in front of the sinner, as if he can have it if only he obeys. He cannot. It is an impossibility. Grace will never come. The law cannot save us, but only condemns us. "Law and will are two implacable foes without the grace of God."[78] But with the grace of God, everything changes. "The grace of God, however, makes justice abound through Jesus Christ because it causes one to be pleased with the law."[79]

---

71. *LW* 31:10 (thesis 17).
72. *LW* 31:10 (thesis 18).
73. *LW* 31:10 (thesis 20). Thesis 21: "No act is done according to nature that is not an act of concupiscence against God." In thesis 23, Luther said, "Nor is it true that an act of concupiscence can be set aright by the virtue of hope. This in opposition to Gabriel."
74. *LW* 31:11 (thesis 29).
75. *LW* 31:14 (thesis 73).
76. *LW* 31:14 (thesis 72).
77. *LW* 31:14 (thesis 79).
78. *LW* 31:14 (thesis 71).
79. *LW* 31:14 (thesis 75).

Grace "is not given so that good deeds might be induced more frequently and readily, but because without it no act of love is performed," and again, this is in "opposition to Gabriel."[80]

Luther's *Disputation against Scholastic Theology* may have been the beginning of his future Reformation, but it was the end of his affair with Biel and the *via moderna*. That does not mean Luther had reached his mature understanding of justification yet. Luther had abandoned Biel for Augustine, but in the months and years after his *Disputation*, Luther was also convicted that justification itself is not only by grace alone but is also a forensic, legal concept. The sinner is not *made* righteous but *declared* righteous. Such a declaration is made by God not on the basis of works, not even faith-motivated or inspired works. Rather, God declares the sinner "not guilty" but "righteous" in his sight on account of another's righteousness, an alien righteousness that has been reckoned to the sinner's account. That righteousness is none other than the righteousness of Christ. Christ's righteousness is not infused, as if justification is a process of moral transformation, one that incorporates and depends on one's good merits. Rather, Christ's righteousness is imputed at the moment of faith in Christ.

It is difficult to identify the exact point Luther arrived at his forensic understanding of justification, and with it, imputation.[81] Some believe Luther darted in this direction sometime between 1518 and 1521. Luther's lectures on Hebrews in 1518 may still show signs of a medieval view of justification, even if slight. The ungodly are righteous "not because they are, but because they have begun to be and should become people of this kind by making constant progress."[82] If remnants remained, Luther had taken fire at the *via moderna*, returned to an Augustinian understanding of *sola gratia*, but was still in process until he reached a forensic view of justification.

By 1521, however, there were clear indicators that Luther's view had changed. As Luther scholar Korey Maas points out, Luther's definition of grace transitioned from "an inherent quality or substance by which one is prepared to become righteous" to "favor of God."[83] Could it be that the addition of Philip Melanchthon to the Wittenberg's faculty (1518) had something to do with it?

---

80. *LW* 31:14 (thesis 91).

81. To be clear, Luther *did* arrive at imputation. The failure to recognize Luther's progression into the 1520s has led the New Finnish interpretation of Luther to impose the Reformer's pre-1520 soteriology onto his mature justification theology. By consequence, they interpret Luther's doctrine of justification as comparable to a type of Eastern deification (*theosis*). In the New Finnish school, justification occurs through God's essential righteousness deifying a person. Posed is a false dichotomy as well, as if Luther is either teaching participation or forensic justification. See Braatan and Jenson, *Union with Christ*; and Mannermaa, *Christ Present in Faith*. For a critique of the New Finnish interpretation, see Horton, *Covenant and Salvation*, 127–260; Kolb and Arand, *Genius of Luther's Theology*; Trueman, "Is the Finnish Line a New Beginning?," 231–44; Forde, *Christ Present in Faith*, 55–56.

82. *LW* 29:139.

83. Maas, "Justification by Faith Alone," 520. Cf. *LW* 32:227. Cameron concurs when he says that by 1521 Luther ceased using the analogy of a disease cured by a medicine. Cameron thinks a shift to forensic language could be as early as 1518–19 since Luther then spoke of a twofold righteousness. He also marks 1519 as the year Luther began making a clear distinction between justification and sanctification. *European Reformation*, 117, 148.

Maybe. Melanchthon's *Loci Communes* define grace in forensic categories, not as some quality within but as God's favor toward us in his Son. Luther did not hide his approval and appreciation for Melanchthon's *Loci Communes* on numerous occasions, both in his writings and at the Luther table.[84] Luther also appeared dependent on Melanchthon's exegesis of passages like Hebrews 11, redefining faith in legal categories.

Regardless of when the shift occurred, the more Luther lectured and preached on books of the Bible, the more his new view of justification rose to the surface. Nowhere does its mature articulation radiate with greater brightness than in Luther's 1535 lectures on Galatians. Even then, almost twenty years later, Luther had not forgotten how contrary his forensic view of justification was to the *via moderna*. "But this most excellent righteousness, the righteousness of faith, which God imputes to us through Christ without works, is neither political nor ceremonial nor legal nor work-righteousness but is quite the opposite; it is a merely passive righteousness, while all the others, listed above, are active. For here we work nothing, render nothing to God; we only receive and permit someone else to work in us, namely, God. Therefore it is appropriate to call the righteousness of faith or Christian righteousness 'passive.'"[85] This passive righteousness is the key, said Luther, to a conscience no longer tormented but at peace.

> Therefore the afflicted conscience has no remedy against despair and eternal death except to take hold of the promise of grace offered in Christ, that is, this righteousness of faith, this passive or Christian righteousness, which says with confidence: "I do not seek active righteousness. I ought to have and perform it; but I declare that even if I did have it and perform it, I cannot trust in it or stand up before the judgment of God on the basis of it. Thus I put myself beyond all active righteousness, all righteousness of my own or of the divine Law, and I embrace only that passive righteousness which is the righteousness of grace, mercy, and the forgiveness of sins." In other words, this is the righteousness of Christ and of the Holy Spirit, which we do not perform but receive, which we do not have but accept, when God the Father grants it to us through Jesus Christ.[86]

It is but a false hope to think "that doing all that one is able to do"—again, Luther quoted Biel precisely—"Can remove the obstacles to grace."[87] Despite what the "philosophers" imagine, we "are not masters of our actions, from beginning to end, but servants."[88]

Historians will continue to speculate and debate exactly when Luther's shift

---

84. Maas, "Justification by Faith Alone," 521. Cf. Melanchthon, *Loci Communes Theologici* (1521), 87. To understand Melanchthon's influence on Luther further, see Hendrix, *Martin Luther*, 76

85. *LW* 26:5.

86. *LW* 26:5–6.

87. *LW* 31:11 (thesis 33).

88. *LW* 31:11 (thesis 39).

occurred to his mature doctrine of justification and imputation. The year 1517, nevertheless, does represent clear shifts in two directions: (1) Luther's break with the *via moderna* for Augustinianism and (2) Luther's inability to keep quiet on that ecclesiastical practice among the masses that he believed was undermining reliance on grace's primacy, namely, indulgences.

PENANCE AND PLENARY INDULGENCE

In the late medieval church, the structure of salvation hinged on a nuanced definition of sin. The *guilt* from sin, due to Christ's atonement, could be absolved by the priest at confession. Nevertheless, the *penalty* for sin remained and demanded payment. If the temporal punishment for sin was not fully satisfied in this life, it had to be paid for in the next life. Before entering heaven, the sinner still stained by sin's penalty must suffer the temporal punishment that remains in purgatory. In the present life, only the super saints—Mary, the apostles, the saints—go straight to heaven.

How did a sinner pay such a penalty in this life? The answer is found in the system of penance, or as it was called, the sacrament of penance, also labeled the second plank of salvation (see chapter 3). Baptism, the first plank, was a one-time event that washed away the original sin every person inherited from Adam. The waters of baptism are powerful, so powerful they washed away not only the *culpa* (guilt) but the *poena* (punishment) of sin. Some believed that if someone died immediately after baptism, before they had the chance to sin again, they went straight to heaven. That belief led some to postpone baptism.

What can be done about those sins committed after baptism? Post-baptismal sins had to be addressed by the second plank, the sacrament of penance, which, unlike baptism, can and must be repeated over the course of a lifetime. First, the sinner should be contrite, experiencing genuine remorse for wrongdoing. Second, the sinner must go to a priest and confess sin out of remorse. Upon confession the priest may pronounce an absolution, acquitting the sinner from guilt. However, the temporal punishment and penalty of sin remain. Third, the priest assigns works of satisfaction to pay for that penalty. Perhaps fasting from food. Perhaps saying a certain number of prayers to Mary and the saints. Perhaps giving alms to the poor in the community. Or perhaps paying homage to relics, such as the bones of the saints, a piece of Christ's cross, or a corner cut from Mary's veil. If ambitious, the sinner might visit a shrine in a nearby town, or, best of all, take a pilgrimage to Rome itself, the home of relics. Not just any work of satisfaction was assigned; usually, the difficulty of the work matched the gravity of the sin.

By the sixteenth century, indulgences became a key facet to the penance process. An indulgence is one type of work of satisfaction. The word *indulgence* referred to a relaxation of the penalty for sin, either in part or in full, the latter known as a plenary indulgence.[89] Acquiring an indulgence was significant;

---

89. Cameron dates the plenary indulgence back to 1476. *European Reformation*, 87.

it meant the temporal penalty for sin was reduced (relaxed). Years in purgatory were decreased, although no one knew for certain just how many years a sinner had to suffer in purgatory. The power for such a relaxation came from heaven itself, drawn from the treasury of merit. This treasure chest was filled with the superabundant works of Jesus, Mary, and the saints. They were so holy that whatever good merit they performed but did not need was hidden away in the treasury of merit. If someone acquired an indulgence slip, then works of merit in that treasury were transferred, reducing the debt the sinner otherwise had to pay in this life and in purgatory. This description of penance, purgatory, and indulgences represents the mature process by Luther's day. However, the penance process evolved over centuries, and new facets were added or adapted according to their meaning, application, and significance. Consider, for example, the history of indulgences.

Indulgences did not suddenly surface in the sixteenth century but can be traced as far back as the twelfth century. In an effort to reclaim Jerusalem, that most holy of cities, Pope Urban II issued a plenary indulgence in 1095 to all those who enlisted in the Crusade. Fighting Muslims was an intimidating prospect, even if the holy land was at stake. But many enlisted, motivated by the promise from the pope himself that the penalty for all their sins was paid. That was not the only motive, however. Soldiers also "looked on their venture as an imitation of the self-sacrifice of the religious, even as an approximation of their higher spiritual perfection."[90] While monks exited society for ascetical self-denial in the wilderness, soldiers entered the battlefields, believing their sacrifice also imaged the suffering Savior.

A little over a hundred years later (1300), Pope Boniface VIII announced a plenary indulgence to anyone and everyone who embarked on a pilgrimage to Rome. Snagging an Old Testament concept, Boniface labeled this opportunity a *jubilee* indulgence, one that would not be offered for another twenty-five years. The proliferation of indulgences did not mean, however, that the pope and his theologians had thought through the theological rationale of the practice in all its complexity. Pope and people alike assumed it was the right of Peter's successor since he had inherited the keys Jesus promised in Matthew 16:18–19. Nevertheless, not until the fourteenth century was a more formal explanation provided, identifying the source for such indulgences. When the year of jubilee returned midcentury (AD 1350), Pope Clement VI explained that an indulgence drew from the treasury of merit, accessing all the surplus merit left behind by Jesus, his mother, and the saints.

Indulgences evolved further at the end of the fifteenth century, just on the eve of the Reformation. In 1476 Pope Sixtus IV drew the connection between an indulgence and purgatory. Now, for the first time, not only could an indulgence be acquired for one's own soul, but the souls of the dead suffering in the fires of

---

90. Ozment, *Age of Reform*, 86. Cf. Tentler, *Sin and Confession on the Eve of the Reformation*.

purgatory. Nevertheless, ambiguity remained. Such an indulgence was unprecedented in many ways. Some thought Pope Sixtus was petitioning God himself for this incredible indulgence. Others thought Pope Sixtus simply had authority over purgatory by the authority of his office. And yet Pope Sixtus was not all that different from prior popes, motivated by financial gain, eager to fund a crusade so crucial to triumphing over the Turks. He was successful: after several campaigns, around half a million guilders were exchanged for indulgences.[91]

At the turn of the sixteenth century, Pope Julius II was motivated by the same Turkish threat. He, too, needed the finances necessary to keep the Ottoman Empire at bay. But Julius had an additional motive: like King David he desired to build God his own basilica. St. Peter's Basilica would be the pride of not only Rome but the world, drawing all the faithful to the heart of the papacy.[92]

POPE LEO X AND ALBERT OF BRANDENBURG

One campaign after another, however, left the people's purses dry. Nevertheless, Pope Leo X was determined to finish what Julius had started. To make it happen, however, Leo needed an extraordinary offer, a plenary indulgence that promised more than ever before. He also needed an indulgence that was extensive in reach, drawing from the finances of the German people. A genius plan was concocted behind closed doors, a negotiation the obscure German theologian, Martin Luther, did not know about. Leo called on Archbishop Albert of Brandenburg to run the campaign in territories like Mainz and Magdeburg. The choice of Albert was not coincidental: Albert had taken out a major loan from the Fugger banking family in Augsburg (with some interest too). Albert had become archbishop of Magdeburg in 1513, and that same year he acquired the administration of Halberstadt. In 1514 he also became archbishop of Mainz. However, canon law said the acquisition of more than one ecclesiastical office was prohibited. An exception could be made but only by papal dispensation.[93] That, too, was acquired by Albert but at the high price of 24,000 ducats.[94]

Naturally, for Albert the sale of indulgences was the ideal opportunity to pay back his loan in the years 1516 and 1517. As long as Albert put his energy into

---

91. On the specifics, see Hendrix, *Martin Luther*, 56–57.

92. Hillerbrand, *Division of Christendom*, 34.

93. Canon law prohibited someone so young from acquiring these offices, but these were "purely administrative arrangements; those involved, from the curia on down, would have reacted with genuine dismay if chided that such arrangements would effect the cure of souls." Hillerbrand observed how alluring these political-ecclesiastical offices could be: "For Albert there was the prospect of substantial income from his new archbishopric and the splendor of his powerful political stature. The archbishop of Mainze also served as imperial chancellor, who presided over the meetings of the electors, cast the last vote in an imperial election, and crowned the emperor. Intoxicating stuff for the youthful Albert." Hillerbrand, 35.

94. "In this instance fee and *pallium* tax, ordinarily paid by the new archbishop's dioceses, were covered by the Augsburg banking house of the Fuggers (at an exorbitant interest rate) and by Albert's brother, Elector Joachim I of Brandenburg, whose political importance as German elector explains at once why Albert won out over the other candidates for the Mainz position. Moreover, since the archbishop of Mainz was one of the seven German electors, the papacy could rest assured that it had two of the electors on its side when a new emperor was to be elected." Hillerbrand, 35.

the indulgence campaign, Leo agreed Albert got a cut, up to half the proceeds. Indulgences may have been marketed as a spiritual matter of life and death, but the men behind them, one a pope, the other an archbishop, were savvy businessmen. Albert was not the only one to benefit. By virtue of this arrangement, the pope not only continued to fund St. Peter's, but with Albert in office he extended his arm further into the territories of the German people, increasing his ecclesiastical and political power.[95]

Yet the prospect of selling indulgences to the German people was no guarantee for success. The German people had seen indulgence campaigns come through their lands before, and they did not appreciate giving their money for a project in Rome, not Germany. Later, when Luther reacted with theses against the abuse of indulgences, he put pressure on this nerve. The German people asked, "Why does not the pope, whose wealth is today greater than the wealth of the richest Crassus, build this one basilica of St. Peter with his own money, rather than with the money of poor believers?"[96] The theological principle in Luther's protest could not be separated from the political agenda, which is one reason why Luther resonated with the German masses.

Albrecht added yet another barrier when he failed to ask a German prince to spread the word about Leo's indulgence and instead asked the German Observant Franciscans. That was a terrible decision. The Franciscans had no stomach for the opulence of Rome at the expense of German labor. Rejected, Albert turned to the Dominicans and found a candidate in John Tetzel. Even still, Tetzel could not just enter into any territory in Germany. For example, Electoral Saxony was off limits not because Frederick despised indulgences and the relics that accompanied them. Frederick had his own, proud collection of relics and was not about to compete with an incoming preacher commissioned by Rome. That would be bad for business, turning attention away from the relics he worked hard to establish, diverting funds to Rome rather than keeping them within German hands.

WHEN THE COIN IN THE COFFER RINGS, THE SOUL FROM PURGATORY SPRINGS

The relic collection of Frederick was impressive. In preparation for All Saints' Day, November 1, Frederick had a catalog printed listing the relics for viewing. The catalog, called *The Wittenberg Book of Holies*, made bold claims. For example, the catalog said Frederick possessed genuine pieces from the cross on which Christ died. The catalog also said Frederick had a piece of the stone that was rolled in front of Christ's grave and a piece of the stone Christ stood on when he ascended to his Father. In total Frederick's collection came to 5,005 pieces, filling eight rooms. How much time in purgatory was relinquished if venerated?

---

95. Hillerbrand, 35; Hendrix, *Martin Luther*, 58–59.
96. *LW* 31:26 (thesis 86).

"An indulgence of one hundred days for each piece."[97] If a persevering soul visited the entire collection, almost two million years were subtracted—1,900,000 to be exact.

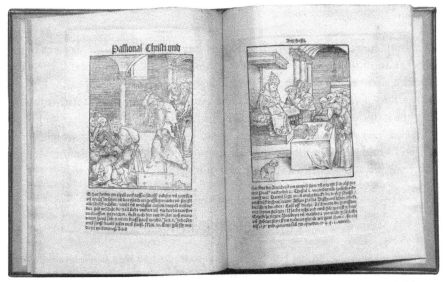

Passional Christi und Antichristi, Lucas Cranach the Elder's first woodcut, 1521
Public Domain

With such a collection retrieved from the holy land, is it any wonder why Frederick did not want Tetzel entering Saxony? Nevertheless, Tetzel could get close, setting up his indulgence campaign in nearby Jüterbog, but twenty-four miles from Wittenberg. The message Tetzel preached was as fiery as it was threatening, and it laid the guilt trip on thick:

> You should know that all who confess and in penance put alms into the coffer according to the counsel of the confessor, will obtain complete remission of all their sins.
>
> ... Why are you then standing there? Run for the salvation of your souls! Be as careful and concerned for the salvation of your souls as you are for your temporal goods, which you seek both day and night.
>
> ... Don't you hear the voices of your wailing dead parents and others who say, "Have mercy upon me, have mercy upon me, because we are in severe punishment and pain. From this you could redeem us with small alms and yet you do not want to do so." Open your ears as the father says to the son and the mother to the daughter.... "We have created you, fed you, cared for you, and left you our

temporal goods. Why then are you so cruel and harsh that you do not want to save us, though it only takes a little? You let us lie in flames so that we only slowly come to the promised glory." You may have letters which let you have, once in life and in the hour of death ... full remission of the punishment which belongs to sin.[98]

The complete remission of all their sins? Language like this seems to exaggerate what an indulgence could do. At the same time, Tetzel had been instructed to make such an offer. Albert himself wrote up a manual called *Summary Instruction for Indulgence Preachers*. The *Instruction* starts by confirming that the pope is, indeed, offering a "complete indulgence" for "the complete remission of all sins." And "through such forgiveness of sin the punishment which one is obliged to undergo in purgatory on account of the offense of the divine Majesty is all remitted and the pain of purgatory is altogether done away with."[99]

LUTHER ON INDULGENCES

Once they acquire indulgence letters, the poor souls believe they can be sure of their salvation. . . . Good God! Souls that are instructed thus under your care are being sent to their death, and it will be harder and harder for you to account for all this. Therefore I could keep quiet no longer.
　　—Luther to Archbishop Albert of Mainz, October 31, 1517 (*WA* 1, 111; *LW* 48, 46)

In the *Instruction*, indulgence preachers were told that those showing up to purchase an indulgence slip should be sorry for their sins. But this condition is so nuanced—a sinner must merely intend to confess sins at some point—that it is easy to see how it was overlooked in the event of preaching, especially when pressure was on to hook the sale. The manual reads, "Everyone who is contrite in heart and has confessed with his mouth—or at least has the intention of confessing at a suitable time—shall visit the designated seven churches in which the papal coat of arms is displayed and pray in each church five devout Lord's Prayers, and five Hail Mary's in honor of the five wounds of our Lord Jesus Christ."[100] What an indulgence meant in the technical minds of monks and theologians was not necessarily what it meant on the street. As evident with Tetzel, the guilt-laden sermons of indulgence preachers placed far more emphasis on acquiring the indulgence than on being contrite. Luther saw firsthand how churchgoers contracted the indulgence fever and assumed they need not confess their sins or even be contrite at all to spring themselves or a loved one from purgatory.

---

98. Tetzel, "A Sermon [1517]," 20–21.
99. Albert of Brandenburg, "Summary Instruction for Indulgence Preachers," 15.
100. Albert of Brandenburg, 15.

FREDERICK'S RELIC COLLECTION

What kind of relics did Frederick present in his collection? Here are just a few relics that concern Christ:

One piece of the stone on which Jesus stood while weeping over Jerusalem.

One piece of the stone from which Christ got on the donkey.

Two pieces of the ground where the Lord Christ was arrested.

Five pieces of the table on which the Lord Christ held the Last Supper with his disciples.

One piece of the bread of which Christ ate with his disciples during the Last Supper.

One piece of the land which was bought for the thirty pieces of silver for which Christ was betrayed.

One piece of the Holy Land.

Three pieces of the stone where the Lord sweated blood.

One piece of the stone sprinkled with the blood of Christ. . . .

One piece of the cloth with which the Lord wiped his disciples' feet.

One piece of the robe of Christ.

One piece of his purple robe.

Three pieces of the white robe in which the Lord was ridiculed by Herod.

Three pieces of the cloth with which our Lord's holy eyes were blindfolded.

One piece of the beard of the Lord Jesus.

One piece of the wax of the candles which touched the sudarium of Christ.

One piece of the wedge with which the cross of Christ was held in place.

Three pieces of the stone on which the cross stood.

Three pieces of the place where the cross of Christ was found.

Twelve pieces of the pillar where the Lord Christ was scourged and flogged.

One piece of the rope with which Jesus was tied.

Three pieces of the rod with which the Lord Jesus was scourged.

Three pieces of the whip with which the Lord was flogged.

One piece of the stone upon which the Lord Jesus sat when he was crowned.

One piece of the stone which was crushed while the Lord carried the cross.

One piece of the sponge with which the Lord was given vinegar and gall.

Two pieces of the crown of the Lord Jesus.

Eight complete thorns of the crown of the Lord Jesus.

One large piece of one nail which was driven through the hands or feet of the Lord Jesus.

A thorn which wounded the holy head of the Lord Jesus.

(Frederick the Wise, Elector of Saxony, *The Wittenberg Book of Holies*, in *The Protestant Reformation*, ed. Hans. J. Hillerbrand, 22–23.)

As a result, the sacrament of penance was emptied of its power, perhaps even its urgency, thought Luther. Luther grew to resent such a "relaxation or 'indulgence' of penitential obligation."[101]

To be accurate, the *Instruction* may have encouraged buyers to be contrite before purchasing an indulgence for themselves. However, such contrition was not compulsory when purchasing an indulgence for the dead in purgatory. It was "not necessary that the persons who place their contributions in the chest for the dead should be contrite in heart and have orally confessed, since this grace is based simply on the state of grace in which the dead departed, and on the contribution of the living, as is evident from the text of the bull."[102] Indulgences—or to be more accurate, their abuse—galvanized Luther, motivating him to write ninety-five theses that questioned the motives of the authorities who encouraged them.

NINETY-FIVE THESES

Some picture Luther as a raging mad protester, eager to charge the gates of Rome and bring down the church. That caricature is far from the truth. Luther was not attempting to divide the church, let alone bring Rome crashing down. His intent was to reform from within, as a son of the mother church. We see that intent when Luther said at the start of his theses that he was presenting them for public discussion but out "of love and zeal for truth and the desire to bring it to light."[103] Luther's theses exhibited zeal, even serious consternation, but behind his bold discontent was a deeper motive—love—love for God and love for his church.

Furthermore, the writing and posting of theses was anything but novel. It was not the first time Luther had written up theses for debate. Nor was Luther alone in this practice. In the past, many of his colleagues, including Karlstadt, had done the same. It is likely Luther was imitating the examples of many who came before him. That is not to downplay Luther's irritation, but in all likelihood, Luther only intended to invite an academic dispute, not a revolt among the masses.

Historians also wonder whether Luther posted the theses himself. Some are doubtful, while others are not.[104] In 2007 a note was discovered with the handwriting of George Rörer, an assistant to Luther, claiming Luther himself posted his theses on the castle church door. Also, George Major said in one of his letters that he was a young man when he saw Luther post the theses.[105] If correct, it appears Luther himself ensured his theses were visible to all those who came to view Frederick's relic collection, though it is doubtful Luther had the fanfare portrayed in popular literature. If Luther posted them at all, no one marched

101. Hendrix, *Luther and the Papacy*, 24.
102. Hendrix, *Luther and the Papacy*, 18.
103. *LW* 31:25.
104. Pettegree makes a case for Luther posting the theses himself. Pettegree, *Brand Luther*, 71.
105. Hendrix, *Martin Luther*, 61.

behind him on his way to the castle church, nor did a large crowd gather to witness the event.

Whether or not Luther posted the theses, it is certain Luther sent the theses to Archbishop Albert since he presided over Tetzel's indulgence preaching. Luther also sent the theses to many of his friends. That move is revealing. Some wonder whether Luther's aim all along was not academic disputation but public, pastoral clarification, and one as significant as salvation itself.[106] His theses, with their pastoral angle, may indicate as much.

LEGENDS FROM THE UNDERWORLD

Legend says that Pope Severinus in the seventh century and Pope Paschal I in the ninth century wished to stay in purgatory even longer than required. Why would they wish that on themselves? According to legend, these popes believed that they would be elevated to a higher state of glory once they were released from purgatory into paradise. Luther responded to this legend in thesis 29: "Who knows whether all souls in purgatory wish to be redeemed, since we have exceptions in St. Severinus and St. Paschal, as related in a legend." Luther questioned the overconfidence of many in his day who believed souls flew out of purgatory at the sound of money in the chest.

Luther's first thesis challenged Rome's interpretation of Matthew 4:17. "When our Lord and Master Jesus Christ said, 'Repent' [Matt. 4:17], he willed the entire life of believers to be one of repentance." "Repent" in Latin is *poenitentiam agite*, and in German *tut Busse*. Judging by the Vulgate, many assumed Jesus was commanding the sinner to "do penance."[107] But Luther preferred the alternative translation, "repent," unwilling to read Rome's entire penance system, indulgences included, into a simple command to turn from sin. "This word cannot be understood as referring to the sacrament of penance, that is, confession and satisfaction, as administered by the clergy."[108] Rather, it means "solely inner repentance." Perhaps speaking from personal experiences, Luther warned against "repentance" that has no external fruit: "such inner repentance is worthless unless it produces various outward modifications of the flesh."[109]

When Luther addressed sin, he still assumed Rome's distinction between the

---

106. "One suspects that Luther's real intent was not so much an internal university disputation at Wittenberg. The extant copies of the theses give no indication of time or place of the proposed disputation, making it rather impossible for outsiders (assuming they wished to participate) to know when and where to present themselves in Wittenberg. By all odds, an actual disputation at Wittenberg was a secondary concern; Luther's letter to Albert and his sending copies of the theses to friends clearly suggests that he wanted to fire a shot across the bow about a practice that in his judgment endangered the souls of simple believers." Hillerbrand, *Division of Christendom*, 33.

107. *LW* 31:25 n. 3.

108. *LW* 31:25 (thesis 2).

109. *LW* 31:25 (thesis 3).

guilt of sin and the penalty of sin, believing that the latter remains "until our entrance into the kingdom of heaven."[110] Luther discouraged appealing to the pope, as if the pope could somehow rid Christians of the penalty of sin. "The pope neither desires nor is able to remit any penalties except those imposed by his own authority or that of the canons." And again, "The pope cannot remit any guilt, except by declaring and showing that it has been remitted by God; or, to be sure, by remitting guilt in cases reserved to his judgment."[111]

Furthermore, the sinner should not think he can find remission of his guilt if he is not truly repentant. "God remits guilt to no one unless at the same time he humbles him in all things and makes him submissive to his vicar, the priest."[112] In 1517 Luther had yet to jettison Rome's view of the priesthood. But he was irritated with priests, especially those who abused the concept of purgatory. "Those priests act ignorantly and wickedly who, in the case of the dying, reserve canonical penalties for purgatory."[113] It used to be the case, said Luther, that "penalties were imposed, not after, but before absolution, as tests of true contrition."[114] Not anymore. That worried Luther to no end; perhaps he talked to churchgoers who assumed that once they were absolved the penalties were nothing.

As to purgatory, Luther was convinced it was approached in all the wrong ways. The preachers of purgatory—like Tetzel—used fear to convey purgatory's purpose. But fear is not the goal, nor should it be the driving factor. "It seems as though for the souls in purgatory fear should necessarily decrease and love increase."[115] They are not "outside the state of merit" as if they are "unable to grow in love."[116] Plus, these preachers of purgatory misled buyers of indulgences. When the pope granted a "plenary remission of all penalties," he "[did] not actually mean 'all penalties,' but only those imposed by himself."[117] "Thus those indulgence preachers are in error who say that a man is absolved from every penalty and saved by papal indulgences."[118] Luther was convinced that people everywhere were misinformed, even misled. "For this reason most people are necessarily deceived by that indiscriminate and high-sounding promise of release from penalty."[119]

Luther also claimed that those purgatory preachers, like Tetzel, were proclaiming lies when they promised immediate release from purgatory at the

---

110. *LW* 31:26 (thesis 4).
111. *LW* 31:26 (theses 5, 6).
112. *LW* 31:26 (thesis 7).
113. *LW* 31:26 (thesis 10).
114. *LW* 31:26 (thesis 12).
115. *LW* 31:27 (thesis 17).
116. *LW* 31:27 (thesis 18).
117. *LW* 31:27 (thesis 20).
118. *LW* 31:27 (thesis 21). The next two theses elaborate: "22. As a matter of fact, the pope remits to souls in purgatory no penalty which, according to canon law, they should have paid in this life." "23. If remission of all penalties whatsoever could be granted to anyone at all, certainly it would be granted only to the most perfect, that is, to very few."
119. *LW* 31:27 (thesis 24).

purchase of an indulgence slip. "They preach only human doctrines who say that as soon as the money clinks into the money chest, the soul flies out of purgatory."[120] As the money chest increased, "greed and avarice" increased all the more.[121] Luther reminded Christians that if they could not even be sure that their own repentance was genuine, how then could they be certain the penalty for all their sins was remitted by indulgences? "No one is sure of the integrity of his own contrition, much less of having received plenary remission."[122]

Satire of Indulgences, Matthias
Gerung's woodcut, 1536
INTERFOTO/Alamy Stock Photo

Considering the thesis that follows, Luther might well have flipped the indulgence tables upside down himself: "Those who believe that they can be certain of their salvation because they have indulgence letters will be eternally damned, together with their teachers."[123] Luther's strong language—damnation!—conveyed his disgust. Sinners rushed to the indulgence tables under the impression that if they had enough money to purchase the slip, then they would escape

---

120. *LW* 31:27–28 (thesis 27).
121. *LW* 31:28 (thesis 28).
122. *LW* 31:28 (thesis 30).
123. *LW* 31:28 (thesis 32).

purgatory, regardless of whether they were repentant.[124] Some even said that an indulgence could "absolve a man even if he had . . . violated the mother of God" herself! "Madness!" cried Luther.[125] What a total abuse of the penance system, as if satisfaction for the temporal punishment for one's sins was for sale irrespective of genuine confession, irrespective of what sins one had committed. "They who teach that contrition is not necessary on the part of those who intend to buy souls out of purgatory or to buy confessional privileges preach unchristian doctrine."[126] Luther objected with such vehemence because he was convinced cheap grace was offered at the expense of the heart's sanctification.[127]

Then Luther put forward a thesis that must have infuriated preachers like Tetzel: "Any truly repentant Christian has a right to full remission of penalty and guilt, even without indulgence letters."[128] Preachers of "papal indulgences" who refused to exercise "caution" gave the laity the impression that other "good works of love" were less important. They were not, replied Luther.[129] He who "lends to the needy does a better deed than he who buys indulgences."[130] And like that, Luther undermined the entire system of indulgences, throwing in question the motivation of those selling them, as well as their salvific value.

Did Luther have an accurate understanding of the pope and his involvement in the indulgence affair? Luther gave the pope the benefit of the doubt. As if the pope would put a stop to the selling and buying of indulgences if he only knew how such indulgences were abused. If "the pope knew the exactions of the indulgence preachers, he would rather that the basilica of St. Peter were burned to ashes than built up with the skin, flesh, and bones of his sheep."[131] Little did Luther realize how wrong he was.

At this point in Luther's journey, he did not reject the authority of the pope altogether but merely clarified papal authority, which he feared had been misappropriated by others. Luther brought down the pope's authority to the level of the common bishop: "That power which the pope has in general over purgatory corresponds to the power which any bishop or curate has in a particular way in his own diocese or parish."[132] Luther even raised questions about the keys: "The

124. *LW* 31:28 (thesis 31).
125. *LW* 31:32 (thesis 75).
126. *LW* 31:28 (thesis 35).
127. Also see *WA* 2:13–14. Cf. Yeago, "The Catholic Luther," 24, who makes the argument that Luther's concern about cheap grace was the primary issue in his protestation, not "the need to comfort the anxious conscience." I do not believe, however, we must choose between the two.
128. *LW* 31:28 (thesis 36). "Thesis 37: Any true Christian, whether living or dead, participates in all the blessings of Christ and the church; and this is granted him by God, even without indulgence letters."
129. *LW* 31:29 (thesis 41).
130. *LW* 31:29 (thesis 43).
131. *LW* 31:30 (thesis 50). In theses 82–89, Luther listed many objections that the laity threw at the pope (e.g., Why doesn't he empty all of purgatory out of holy love if he has the power?), but still seemed to think that if the pope knew what the laity were thinking and how their concerns muddied the pope's reputation, he would have removed indulgences.
132. *LW* 31:27 (thesis 25).

pope does very well when he grants remission to souls in purgatory, not by the power of the keys, which he does not have, but by way of intercession for them."[133]

The Ninety-Five Theses reveal that Luther was still a novice in his quest for reform. Beliefs he later abandoned were still present. Nevertheless, the heart of his concerns was present and proved explosive in the right hands.

TO THE FLAMES

The reactions to Luther's theses were varied. Luther sent his theses to Albert of Mainz, alerting the archbishop what abuses were being carried out in his name.[134] Luther was optimistic, if not ignorant, assuming Albert would hear about Tetzel and correct the abuses, which only confirms that Luther was unaware that Albert supported indulgences and the rhetoric the preachers used. Summarizing many of the "false fables" fed to the people, Luther left Albert with a question: Are indulgences more important than the gospel? "Christ nowhere commanded to preach indulgences, but emphatically insisted on the preaching of the gospel." The bishop who disagreed, Luther warned, was in "great danger."[135]

At first Luther's concern was, more or less, handled from within. Albert sent the theses to academics at the University of Mainz, asking for their critique. Next, Albert sent the theses to Pope Leo. Albert wanted a formal investigation, one that could determine whether Luther was a heretic as Albert suspected. His doing so is what brought Luther into tension with Rome. If Albert had ignored the theses and never forwarded them to Leo, it is likely they would have gone unaddressed. But once the theses landed in the hands of Leo, the curia became involved and pursued Luther. Pope Leo had every intention of resolving the conflict within Luther's own context, asking the vicar of the Augustinian order to discuss the theses with Luther.

Others reacted with far less patience. Tetzel was boisterous in his agitation. He, with the help of a professor in Brandenburg, wrote theses in response, inviting debate. How did Luther respond? With pen and pulpit. For example, Luther preached a sermon on indulgences and grace, both clarifying his intent in the Ninety-Five Theses but also giving his own evaluation of Tetzel's theses. More important was the medium: a sermon. Luther's theses were academic in style, difficult for the average churchgoer to understand, since they required theological knowledge. They were also in Latin. Few on their way to venerate relics could even read them. By contrast, a sermon was accessible, accommodating those who may or may not have read Luther's theses, theses then published in the vernacular. Luther put forward twenty articles in his sermon, far more consumable than his Ninety-Five Theses. When Tetzel read the sermon and these twenty articles,

---

133. *LW* 31:27 (thesis 26).

134. "Luther's theses sought to blackmail Albert, plain and simple, with the threat to go public with such an instance of theological perversion." Hillerbrand, *Division of Christendom*, 36.

135. Luther, "Letter to Archbishop Albert of Mainz. [1517]," 26.

he said Luther should be tied to the stake and consumed by the flames like every other heretic.[136] More theses followed, this time accusing Luther of questioning the pope's authority.

Others did not respond with the same vehemence as Tetzel, but they did reply with just as much conviction. Unlike Tetzel, who was more of a preacher than a theologian, Silvester Prierias was Luther's intellectual match, one of the first appointed to investigate Luther's theology. Prierias was a Dominican friar in Rome as well as the curia's chief theologian. Like Tetzel, he, too, accused Luther of challenging papal authority. "He who does not accept the doctrine of the Church of Rome and pontiff of Rome as an infallible rule of faith, from which the Holy Scriptures, too, draw their strength and authority, is a heretic," Prierias wrote in *A Dialogue against Martin Luther's Presumptuous Theses Concerning the Power of the Pope* (1518).[137] Luther's initial conflict concerned faith and grace, but his dispute with Prierias surfaced another source of conflict: authority. Who has final authority to decide on these matters? Papal infallibility as official dogma was still over two centuries to come; nevertheless, it was unofficially presupposed by some of Luther's nemeses, as hinted at in Prierias's reaction to Luther. Prierias even positioned the papacy as an additional *revelatory* authority. The three fountains of revelation included (1) Scripture, (2) written/unwritten tradition, and (3) papal doctrine.[138]

In some sense Prierias's reaction surprised Luther. As Luther explained in his sermon on indulgences and grace, he did not write his Ninety-Five Theses to question papal authority or insult the pope himself.[139] Instead, Luther was appealing to the pope as if he were an informant, opening the pope's eyes to the corruption within his church. Again, Luther's intent was to reform the church from within, as a good catholic, not destroy it or tear it down, let alone start another church altogether. But it was not long until Luther discovered that the pope was not on his side. Soon Luther had to come face-to-face with an undeniable and irreconcilable, even foundational difference: unlike his Roman interlocutors, he could not position the Scriptures in a subordinate stance to the papacy.

---

136. Hendrix, *Martin Luther*, 64–65.

137. Quoted in Oberman, *Luther*, 193. Hillerbrand noted that Prieria's book is marked by a "certain superficiality of approach and an unwillingness to engage Luther seriously" but nevertheless a real ability to identify the deeper issues at play, such as papal authority. Hillerbrand, *Division of Christendom*, 41. Also see Hendrix, *Martin Luther*, 65, 66.

138. Bagchi labels this the "hard-liners" position. Although Prierias's position was shared by Pighi, Cochlaeus, and Eck, the "majority of Catholic theologians did not, however, go this far" ("Catholic theologians of the period before Trent," 224).

139. However, Hillerbrand may have been right that "Luther had hurled a fundamental challenge to the church to mend its ways." Some, like Erasmus, sensed the challenge right away. In a letter to Thomas More in England, Erasmus wrote, "I am sending you theses concerning the vices of the papacy." *EE*, letter 785, 3:239. Hillerbrand commented, "Unlike his humanist confreres, he [Luther] did not focus on clerical shortcomings or practical abuses. While clad in the evasive format of propositions for an academic debate, the truth of which was yet to be ascertained, Luther's theses argued that the eternal salvation of the faithful was in jeopardy because the church had come to misrepresent the authentic teaching of the gospel. That was the 'vice of the papacy' of which Erasmus spoke, and that made the stakes very high." Hillerbrand, 36–37.

LUTHER'S THEOLOGY OF THE CROSS: HEIDELBERG

In 1518 Pope Leo X attempted to handle Luther by means of the Reformer's own superiors. Leo commissioned Gabriel della Volta (Venetus), general of the Augustinian Eremite, who in turn communicated with Johann von Staupitz. Luther's mentor had to convey to his disciple the seriousness of the situation with the hope that Luther might be censored.

In April the Augustinians' general chapter met in Heidelberg, and Luther was summoned to attend. Luther went and Leonhard Beier accompanied him. No official reprimand or censure was issued, but Staupitz by means of Beier did request that Luther present his position on sin and grace. At Heidelberg, Luther reiterated some of the same points he made the year before, such as his belief that the will is passive and cannot obtain grace but can only do evil, and that one is not righteous by works but through faith. Two theses, however, stand out, representing an advance in Luther's thought:

> 19. The person does not deserve to be called a theologian who looks upon the invisible things of God as though they were clearly perceptible in those things which have actually happened [Rom. 1:20].
>
> 20. He deserves to be called a theologian, however, who comprehends the visible and manifest things of God seen through suffering and the cross.[140]

Luther contrasted the theologian of glory with the theologian of the cross. The theologian of glory is presumptuous; he assumes he can comprehend the incomprehensible God and therefore climb up to God by virtue of his own reason, by means of his works. Here lies Luther's motive for saying that reason is the devil's whore. Luther was not opposed to reason (and philosophy), which he considered instrumental to exegesis, theology, and pastoral ministry.[141] He was opposed to the abuse of reason in the hands of a theologian of glory, a reason so bald and brash to think it could save itself.[142]

By contrast, the theologian of the cross is humble; he respects God's incomprehensibility and is content to turn to God's works. And what greater work than the gospel? At the cross, God has accommodated himself to the ungodly by his Son's sacrifice. Rather than pressing into the inner life of a holy God apart from the mediation of a Savior, the theologian of the cross looks to Calvary because God has made himself known by his work of redemption.[143] While the

---

140. Consult *LW* 31:37–70.

141. Kolb clarifies that Luther "appreciated Aristotle's works when used for specific purposes." However, Luther criticized Aristotle when the latter "defined humanity in terms of human performance of proper acts" (*Martin Luther,* 34). Kolb gives a litany of examples for both. Also consult Lohse, *Martin Luther's Theology,* 196–205.

142. Marty, *Martin Luther,* 177. On reason's abuse, consult *LW* 40:174–75; 51:374; 76:39; cf. Haines, *Martin Luther and the Rule of Faith,* 3–5.

143. Turning to 1 Cor. 1:21–24, Luther says the same in *LW* 26:28–29. To clarify, "Luther does not reduce God's revelation to the cross . . . but he does make it the fundamental criterion for the theology of the

theologian of glory presumes that God finds the sinner already lovely, the theologian of the cross assumes no one is lovely until God makes him so. As he says in thesis 28, "The love of God does not find, but creates, that which is pleasing to it." By contrast, "The love of man comes into being through that which is pleasing to it."[144] In the hands of the theologian of the cross, reason is no whore, but a "beautiful, marvelous instrument and tool of God," even the "greatest, inestimable gift of God."[145]

The theses represent a further break with late medieval Scholastics like Scotus, Ockham, and Biel. To be clear, they did not necessarily mean Luther was breaking with *all* of medieval Scholasticism, which was diverse (see chapters 3–5). His reference to a theology of glory once again struck at the *via moderna*, which clung to works—doing one's best—as if the sinner could do his best and climb his way up into God's favor to be rewarded with justification and forgiveness. Luther believed a theology of glory would always result in Semi-Pelagianism at best and Pelagianism at worst.[146]

What was the outcome of the Heidelberg Disputation? Those twice Luther's age were resistant. Those still early in their career sympathized, and some were convinced. Martin Bucer, the future Reformer of Strasbourg, was one of them. In a letter to Beatus Rhenanus just after the disputation, Bucer praised Luther for his knowledge not only of Scripture but of the patristics, proof Luther was in touch with his catholic heritage.[147] Luther did not know it at the time, but the Heidelberg Disputation was a key stepping-stone solidifying the survival of the Reformation in its early years. As young theologians like Bucer came into contact with Luther's theology, they were transformed in their thinking and took steps to spread Luther's message across Germany.

However, on Luther's journey back home, he discovered that many if not most in Erfurt were disappointed with his conclusions; they found Luther's methods to be strange. The professors at the university, for example, were not enthusiastic about Luther's appeal to the church fathers rather than late medieval Scholastics like Scotus, Ockham, or Biel.[148] This disparity divided the Erfurt school from the Wittenberg school, only adding to a tension already present between these competing faculties. Despite the lack of reception in Erfurt, Luther pressed on, lecturing on the epistle to the Hebrews that summer.

---

gospel, in light of which God's revelation as a whole must be understood." Trueman, *Luther on the Christian Life*, 63.

144. *LW* 31:41.

145. *LW* 75:290.

146. On Luther's theology of the cross, see Forde, *On Being a Theologian of the Cross*, 69–102; and McGrath, *Luther's Theology of the Cross*, 202–14.

147. Martin Bucer to Beatus Rhenanus, May 1, 1518, 1, 61; Luther's Correspondence 1, 82. Cf. Hendrix, *Martin Luther*, 70.

148. *WABr* 1:173; *LW* 48:61–62; Luther to Trutvetter, May 9, 1518, in *WABr* 1:170. Cf. Hendrix, *Martin Luther*, 71.

"I CHERISH AND FOLLOW THE CHURCH IN
ALL THINGS": AUGSBURG (1518)

By the summer of 1518, controversy escalated. Whatever lack of urgency Leo
may have first exhibited quickly dissipated. Even before Luther became aware
of how much trouble he was in, the pope and his theologians were at work to
hold Luther accountable. By August Leo issued the *admonitio caritativa*, giving
Luther sixty days to report to Rome.[149] This summons may have been called a
loving admonition, but it was more like a final warning, even a threat, admonishing Luther that if he did not appear in Rome, he could be condemned as a
heretic. Pope Leo X ordered Cajetan to detain Luther in Germany and bring
him back to Rome himself.[150] The pope was even so bold as to write to Frederick
the Wise and insist that this son of perdition be arrested and sent to Rome.

Frederick was not so easily intimidated. He understood he had leverage that
the pope could not afford to ignore. The elector's motives for resisting the pope
were not so much theological as political. For example, Frederick did not appreciate the Roman see inserting itself into the affairs of the German people, especially when it affected their money purses. As papal legate in Germany, Thomas
Cajetan (Thomas Cardinal de Vio) appeared at the diet in Augsburg to ensure
that funds flowed to the papacy by virtue of a new tax. These funds were supposed to be used in the papacy's efforts to counter the threat of the Turks. The
estates were not so easily persuaded. The papacy had already sucked German
funds in the name of all their former priorities. A new tax was just the latest
endeavor to strip the estates of their financial liberty and fortitude. Rome's insistence that a German named Martin Luther be handed over for interrogation (or
worse) smacked of further interference. In addition, could Frederick trust Rome
to treat his professor with clemency? Probably not. They considered him a heretic, and he had yet to step foot in Rome. Frederick may not have held Luther's
theological positions as early as 1518 or 1519, but he did value a judicial system
built on the rigor of a fair trial.[151]

On not a few occasions, Frederick's political mediation spared Luther and
is one major reason why the Reformation succeeded when past attempts at
reform failed.[152] Augsburg was an early example. Frederick was not going to send

---

149. The admonition was motivated by Prieria's report back to Rome. Hillerbrand, *Division of
Christendom*, 41.

150. "Promptly, toward the end of that month, the head of the Saxon province of the Augustinian Order
and Thomas Cardinal Cajetan, papal legate in Germany, were instructed to have Luther apprehended as a
notorious heretic." Hillerbrand, 41.

151. Other issues were at play as well: the Estates "called attention to . . . the appointment of foreigners to
ecclesiastical positions in Germany and the increasing financial burdens imposed by the church on the common people." As for Frederick, he "had strongly opposed the notion of a 'Turkish' tax, which he saw as an ill-
disguised scheme to funnel moneys [*sic*] to Rome, and he had also not taken kindly to Emperor Maximilian's
active lobbying for his nephew Charles as his imperial successor. There was, in short, an independent streak in
Frederick, who was not likely to hand Luther over to the Roman judiciary." Hillerbrand, 42.

152. More details on what follows can be found in Hendrix, *Martin Luther*, 72–73.

Luther to Rome, but he did agree to an exchange between Luther and Cajetan in Augsburg on German soil. Frederick had the advantage for several reasons. The emperor Maximilian needed to appease the pope if Charles I of Spain, the emperor's grandson, had a chance to reign after him (Maximilian was in poor health and needed to secure his successor soon). So Maximilian agreed to let a papal representative put Luther to the test. If Luther was found guilty of heresy, Maximilian would support the verdict. However, Maximilian could not do without Frederick's support either, nor could the Roman curia if they wanted to retain their hand in the selection of the next emperor. Apart from the German princes, Charles I might not be successor at all. Frederick, therefore, was untouchable, both emperor and pope unable to force his hand without compromising other political interests. For these reasons, Rome was off the table; the meeting had to take place somewhere in German territory, and Augsburg was the ideal location.

That October Luther was destined for Augsburg to face off with one of Rome's most challenging cardinals, the Dominican theologian Cajetan. The pope insisted that the meeting between Cajetan and Luther not turn into a disputation. Luther was to recant. Nothing less. If Luther did not, he must be arrested and taken to Rome. But again, Frederick interceded, and the emperor promised Luther no harm.[153]

Despite the pope's wishes, debate did ensue in Augsburg, especially around the 1343 papal bull called *Extravagante*, also known as *Unigenitus*, issued by Clement VI. Luther was accused of violating this papal bull in his Ninety-Five Theses. In his *Proceedings at Augsburg*, Luther recounted the accusation brought against him by Cajetan: "After he [Cajetan] had stated that he did not wish to argue with me, but to settle the matter peacefully and in a fatherly fashion, he proposed that I do three things which, he said, had been demanded by the pope: first, that I come to my senses and retract my errors; second, that I promise to abstain from them in the future; and third, that I abstain from doing anything which might disturb the church." Luther responded by asking Cajetan to explain where he had erred. "Then he referred to the *Extravagante* of Clement VI, which begins with the word *Unigenitus*, because in Thesis 58 I had asserted contrary to it that the merits of Christ did not constitute the treasury of merits of indulgences." That thesis reads, '58. Nor are they [indulgences] the merits of Christ and the saints, for, even without the pope, the latter always work grace for the inner man, and the cross, death, and hell for the outer man.'"[154]

---

153. Hendrix notes the irony on the meeting location: the house of the Fugger banking family. "Luther must have realized the irony: the family had lent Albert of Mainz money to pay Rome for his cardinal's hat. Albert in turn was paying the Fuggers back with money earned from selling the St. Peter's indulgence that Luther criticized. Now Luther was forced to defend himself against heresy in the very house where the loan to Albert originated." Hendrix, *Martin Luther*, 73.

154. *LW* 31:30; cf. 31:281.

CLARIFYING *SOLA SCRIPTURA*

The reason Luther could claim Scripture as the final authority was only because Luther believed Scripture was breathed out by God and therefore without error. *Sola scriptura*, according to Luther, presupposed Scripture's divine origin and infallible, inerrant nature. On that basis, Luther compared Scripture to Rome's innovative beliefs and concluded that only the former is without contradictions and flaws. In 1521 he wrote his *The Misuse of the Mass* and said that the Fathers must always be "weighed and judged according to the Scripture," but Rome makes the "word of men . . . equal to the Word of God." Luther concluded, "The saints could err . . . but the Scriptures cannot err" (*LW* 36:136–37; cf. *LW* 32:11–12).

That does not mean, however, that Luther disowned the Fathers or believed they and their councils were without authority. He often appealed to them as authoritative and labored his entire life at the prospect of a general council. *Sola scriptura* was not, as perceived in popular narratives, a battle between Scripture and tradition, as if the Reformers were against tradition. They were not. Rather, the Reformation and Rome was a battle between two different conceptions of tradition. Rome elevated tradition to a second source of revelation, sometimes even a superior source. Luther and the Reformers, by contrast, believed tradition was an authority, but a ministerial authority, subservient to Scripture, its magisterial authority. For Luther *sola scriptura* "did not mean that he believed that the Holy Spirit communicates only through reading the biblical texts," clarifies Robert Kolb. "What the Holy Spirit delivered to the church in Scripture informs and does its work through the tradition of the church and through contemporary use in the oral, other written, and sacramental forms of the biblical message" (*Martin Luther*, 49). In the estimation of the Reformers, *sola scriptura* was not a novel belief but a patristic doctrine.

However, Cajetan underestimated Luther: "Then he demanded that I retract and confidently pursued the matter, sure of victory; for he was certain and secure in assuming that I had not seen the *Extravagante*, probably relying upon the fact that not all editions of the canon law contain it."[155]

Cajetan confronted other theses as well: "He reproached me for having taught in the explanation of Thesis 7 that a person taking the sacrament had to have faith or he would take it to his own damnation, for he wished to have this judged a new and erroneous doctrine." The error was located in Luther's bold claim that a believer could have assurance of salvation. In Cajetan's estimation, "every person going to the sacrament was uncertain whether or not he would receive grace."[156]

Luther also did not appreciate how smug Cajetan came off. "By his boldness he made it appear as though I had been defeated, especially since the Italians

155. *LW* 31:261.
156. *LW* 31:261.

and others of his companions smiled and, according to their custom, even giggled aloud."[157] Luther had become the heretical clown, as if he was less of a theologian than Cajetan, another ignorant and unprepared German. But their giggling stopped when Luther unveiled his full knowledge of the bull: "I then answered that I had carefully examined not only this *Extravagante* of Clement, but also the other one of Sixtus IV which emulated and was similar to it. . . . The *Extravagante* did not impress me as being truthful or authoritative for many reasons, but especially because it distorts the Holy Scriptures and audaciously twists the words . . . into a meaning which they do not have in their context, in fact into a contrary meaning." As for thesis 7 in his Ninety-Five Theses, Luther reasserted that such a thesis followed the Scriptures, which "are to be preferred to the bull in every case."[158]

Luther's elevation of the Scriptures over a bull issued by the pope became a major focal point in the debate. Cajetan "began to extol the authority of the pope, stating that it is above church councils, Scripture, and the entire church." Luther did not play along. "I denied that the pope was superior to the council and Scripture."[159] Here was the dividing line, and no matter what other issues the debate turned its attention to, somehow the conflict always came back to the matter of authority.

For example, consider another focal point, the treasury of merit, which *Extravagante* supported but Luther found wanting. The bull "maintains that the merits of the saints constitute a treasure, despite the fact that the entire Scripture states that God rewards far beyond all our worth" (cf. Rom. 8:18).[160] Luther believed Augustine was in his corner. Appealing to Augustine's *Confessions*, Luther concluded that "the saints are saved, not by their merits, but alone by the mercy of God, as I have stated more fully in my *Explanations*."[161] Rome will respond that the treasury of merit was "committed to Peter," but there is "nothing either in the gospel or any part of the Bible" to suggest such a belief.[162] Luther did not find appeals to the pope convincing: "For the pope is not above but under the word of God" (cf. Gal. 1:8).[163]

Or consider Luther's defense of justification by faith. Cajetan reacted against thesis 7, where Luther "stated that no one can be justified except by faith." "Thus it is clearly necessary that a man must believe with firm faith that he is justified and in no way doubt that he will obtain grace. For if he doubts and is uncertain, he is not justified but rejects grace." But Cajetan considered "this theology new and erroneous."[164]

---

157. *LW* 31:262.
158. *LW* 31:262.
159. *LW* 31:262.
160. *LW* 31:266.
161. *LW* 31:266.
162. *LW* 31:267.
163. *LW* 31:266–67.
164. *LW* 31:270.

By the end of the disputation, Cajetan issued a warning: he "insisted that I retract, threatening me with the punishments which had been recommended to him, and said that if I did not retract I should leave him and stay out of his sight."[165] But Luther refused. As he reflected on the standoff, Luther became annoyed: "It has long been believed that whatever the Roman church says, damns, or wants, all people must eventually say, damn, or want, and that no other reason need be given than that the Apostolic See and the Roman church hold that opinion. Therefore, since the sacred Scriptures are abandoned and the traditions and words of men are accepted, it happens that the church of Christ is not nourished by its own measure of wheat, that is, by the word of Christ, but is usually misled by the indiscretion and rash will of an unlearned flatterer."[166]

The church of Christ is not nourished—ecclesiology was at the heart of Luther's refusal to recant. From this point forward, Luther saw Rome as Babylon and his own reform as the *recovery of the church*. "There are also those who brazenly state in public that the pope cannot err and is above Scripture. If these monstrous claims were admitted, Scripture would perish and consequently the church also, and nothing would remain in the church but the word of man. These flatterers actually seek to arouse hatred for the church, then its ruin and destruction." Luther did not consider himself a rebel but a faithful son of the mother church, attempting to recover her true catholicity against the papacy's innovations. "For this reason, my reader, I declare before you that *I cherish and follow the church in all things*. I resist only those who in the name of the Roman church strive to erect a Babylon for us and wish that whatever occurs to them . . . be accepted as the interpretation of the Roman church, as if Holy Scripture no longer existed, according to which (as Augustine says) we must judge all things, and against which the Roman church certainly never teaches or acts."[167] Luther historians have sometimes assumed that by 1518 Luther was breaking with the church, but Luther's words should correct that misinterpretation. Luther may have been turning away from the papacy, but in doing so he was turning *toward* the church *catholic* and its Great Tradition.[168]

After Cajetan insisted Luther recant and Luther refused, an uncertain silence followed. Cajetan told Luther to get out of his sight and never return unless he was ready to recant. That instilled some fear in Luther, now worried he might be held in contempt for insubordination. Not wanting to appear more rebellious than he already did, Luther waited. At first Cajetan recruited Staupitz to talk to Luther and induce him into revocation.[169] That was not going to happen. But Luther remained present nonetheless. Yet day after day there was only silence.

---

165. *LW* 31:275.

166. "We have come to this in our great misfortune that these people begin to force us to renounce the Christian faith and deny Holy Scripture." *LW* 31:276.

167. *LW* 31:285, emphasis added.

168. Yeago, "The Catholic Luther," 29.

169. *LW* 31:277. "Luther, realizing his acute danger, quickly drafted an appeal to 'a not-well-informed pope so that he be better informed,' in which he explained that ill health, poverty, and the threat of sword and

Staupitz had reason to believe Luther was about to be arrested, so he released Luther from the vow he made in the Augustinian monastery and left. Released from a vow that required Luther to submit to silence should his superiors judge him unruly, Luther was now free to speak his mind at his own peril. Luther persisted to get in touch with Cajetan by letter but had no success. Interpreting the silence as ominous, Luther took the opportunity to leave while he still had the chance.[170]

Fleeing Augsburg left a mark on Luther, who now expected to be hunted down and killed. He returned to Wittenberg but was ready to flee as soon as he heard the footsteps of Rome. Nevertheless, that fear did not extinguish Luther's boldness. In his debate with Cajetan, Luther said he denied the pope was superior not only to Scripture but to councils. Now back in Wittenberg, Luther put to print his official appeal to a general council. If Luther had not convinced Rome he was a dangerous heretic, this appeal certainly did.[171]

A PLEDGE TO BE A FAITHFUL CATHOLIC: LEIPZIG (1519)

Unable to draw Luther to Rome, the pope took measures to force Luther's hand. For example, a papal bull (*Cum Postquam*) was published by Leo in November 1518, which declared the pope had the right and power to issue indulgences. With such an official stance made public, Luther's prior as well as ongoing opposition was now considered an unequivocal threat to the official teaching of the church, making Luther a prime candidate for excommunication.

However, Leo depended on Frederick's support. At the start of the new year, 1519, Maximilian died. Leo did not want Charles I as emperor but desired an emperor who hailed from the land of the papacy. Frederick's vote was necessary for such expediency. In an effort to manipulate Frederick, Leo announced that Frederick was one of Rome's most faithful constituents. As a reward, Frederick was given the Golden Rose.[172] Frederick, however, was not so easily bought.

While presenting the Golden Rose to Frederick, Karl von Miltitz also met with Luther. After the Augsburg debacle, as well as Luther's appeal to a general council (no little threat to papal authority), one might think Luther was finished with the church. Not so. Luther still hoped for reform from within the catholic church. With a nudge from Miltitz, Luther wrote the pope and expressed his willingness to reach a resolution by means of academic discussion—Miltitz's idea. And if the pope pulled back his papal theologians, Luther promised to be content and return to his duties, refraining from polemical publishing. Although

---

poison had made his journey to Rome impossible. He volunteered not to write anything against Scripture, the Fathers, and canon law, and then fled." Hillerbrand, *Division of Christendom*, 44.

170. *LW* 31:277.

171. "Though such appeals had been condemned in the fifteenth century, Luther's move had recent precedents, for example, an appeal of the faculty of the University of Paris in the spring of 1517. Indeed, at points Luther followed the Parisian document almost word for word." Hillerbrand, *Division of Christendom*, 45.

172. On the politics, see Hendrix, *Martin Luther*, 77. Papal indulgences were also gifted, so that Frederick could use them to the advantage of his castle church. See Hillerbrand, 45.

the letter was met by silence, it was "an indication that Luther wanted to remain a *faithful Catholic*."[173] The pope would have to excommunicate him to terminate the Reformer's undying dedication to remain catholic. Luther was not the rebel so many make him out to be.

Luther was prepared to keep his promise. But the pope and his theologians were not willing to pledge the same, which became apparent in the summer of 1519. John Eck, a priest and professor, as well as a talented rhetorician in the heat of debate, was anything but silent, going on the offensive to refute the new Wittenberg theology. Two years prior, the two of them exchanged cordial letters, but their correspondence came to an abrupt halt when Eck wrote his comments, or *Obelisks*, a merciless refutation of Luther's Ninety-Five Theses, which only prodded Luther to respond with a work of his own: *Asterisks* (1518).

Luther was not the only one who came under Eck's fire. So, too, did Karlstadt.[174] So much so that Eck challenged Karlstadt to a disputation in Leipzig. But Luther was to participate as well; he was, in the end, Eck's prized target. With great anticipation, in June 1519 an audience grew in Leipzig as large as the hype that preceded the disputation, although Eck was right to expect a majority to favor him instead of Karlstadt and Luther.

As mentioned, Luther had promised to refrain from addressing indulgences as long as his opponents did not either. That was wishful thinking. Eck had every intention to bring up indulgences, as apparent in a set of theses he sent ahead of the disputation itself. Yet one of the theses did address the supremacy of the pope as well. These theses released Luther from his promise. In preparation for Leipzig, Luther wrote a response of his own, and, like Eck, he intended to treat not only indulgences but the authority of the papacy as well.

The first week the debate was between Eck and Karlstadt over the freedom of the will and the nature of justifying grace. While Karlstadt was accurate in his representation of Luther's theology, he was no match for the rhetorical abilities of Eck in the moment of debate. During the second and third weeks the debate was between Eck and Luther on issues such as the primacy of the pope, penance, purgatory, the power of a priest to grant absolution, and indulgences.[175]

Whether Luther knew it at the time is uncertain, but the Leipzig debate was one of the most pivotal moments in the escalating conflict. Eck forced Luther to vocalize whether Scripture had primacy over the papacy. This was a strategic move on Eck's part. While many before Luther had voiced criticisms of the papacy, Eck pushed Luther further, forcing the Wittenberg theologian to voice Scripture's superiority and not merely over popes but councils as well. Eck's strategy was genius in its execution. To force Luther's hand, Eck identified

---

173. Hillerbrand, 46, emphasis added. The pledge is sometimes called the Altenburg agreement.

174. In 1518 Karlstadt (or Carlstadt) wrote 379 theses (which turned into 405 eventually). When Eck responded, Karlstadt wrote more theses. "With each round the tone became more bitter and vehement." Hillerbrand, 40.

175. *LW* 31:320–22.

Luther with two heretics: John Wyclif and Jan Hus (on both, see chapter 8). Hus was burned at the stake as a heretic by the Council of Constance for denying that Peter was head of the Roman Church, among other "heresies." The mere mention of Hus sent shivers up the spines of listeners, especially at a place like the University of Leipzig, which was founded by opponents of the Hussite movement.[176]

When the disputation took a break, Luther decided he should refresh his knowledge of Hus for himself.[177] Afterward, Luther admitted he agreed with Hus after all. That sent shock waves once more because an agreement with Hus was the same as an accusation, an accusation that a council like Constance did err. When Eck succeeded in drawing that admission out of Luther's mouth, Duke George failed to contain himself and said, "Das walt die Sucht." In other words, "I'll be damned!"[178] He then walked out. Eck responded by calling Luther a heathen, one of the worst labels a sixteenth-century churchman could receive.

Eck had put Luther in jeopardy. Now the divide between the Reformation and Rome was naked, exposed for all to see. Unfortunately, the nuance of Luther's words was lost in the shock and awe—the hysteria—of the moment. Luther was not rejecting the authority of councils. Nor was he denying that many councils were in fact without error. As Luther's own work on councils reveals, he was a glad and loyal subscriber to orthodox creeds and submitted himself to their councils. Luther did not say councils erred *de fide*, that is, in theological issues and matters of faith. Rather, Luther only intended to say that councils are not without error in all matters (including practical matters) they address.[179]

Luther infuriated Eck when he concluded with Hus that a mere layman with the Scriptures in hand has more authority and credibility than the Roman pontiff himself without the Scriptures. Luther also protested that the pope and the church should not, indeed cannot, establish new, novel articles of faith, like indulgences and purgatory, which Luther said lacked scriptural and creedal warrant. They were novel, out of step with the church catholic that Luther intended to defend. Assuming Scripture derived its authority from the pope, Eck was now

---

176. Hillerbrand observed why the introduction of Hus was inflammatory in Leipzig: "This elicited deep anxiety among those who heard it, for the University of Leipzig had an intimate connection with the Hussite movement: it had been founded, roughly a century before, by German emigrants who had left the University of Prague in opposition to Hussitism." Hillerbrand, *Division of Christendom*, 47.

177. "Despite his claims never to have read anything by Hus before 1519, Luther showed at Leipzig in that year that he had read something of the Acts of the Council of Constance and had remembered passages from Hus's book *On the Church* not contained in the condemnatory decrees of that Council, though they may well have been recorded in other anti-Hussite writings. . . . Although he was taught that Hus was a heretic to be avoided, there were nevertheless influences in his early life which gave him a proclivity for the Czech Reformer that made itself more prominent as his thought progressed." Pelikan, *Obedient Rebels*, 109.

178. Translated by Hillerbrand, *Division of Christendom*, 47.

179. "In fact, of course, Luther had used rather careful language when he challenged the authority of councils. Astutely, he had tempered his rejection of councils with the qualification that councils have erred in 'matters not *de fide*,' not concerning faith and doctrine. Luther had meant to argue that councils should not be understood as having been infallible in absolutely everything they promulgated. But his important qualification got lost in the shuffle." Hillerbrand, 48.

convinced that Luther had solidified his own fate. And he was right, whether Luther knew it or not.

Many years later, sometime between 1530 and 1540, an artist (unknown) created a woodcut of Luther and Hus. In the middle of the woodcut, Christ hangs crucified on his cross. Around the cross a flock of sheep, representing the church, gather and baa, looking up at Christ. On either side of the cross are Luther and Hus, each holding open the Bible. The woodcut not only connects the two Reformers but positions each of them as shepherds of God's flock, in contrast to Rome who led the sheep astray.[180] The connection between Hus and Luther stuck, and the general populace understood, through woodcuts like this, that God was preserving his church through the centuries; it was not lost despite abuse and corruption.

THE GERMAN NOBILITY

Other factors were at work, besides Luther, to throw into question Rome's credibility. For example, the humanist, Ulrich von Hutten, exposed the *Donation of Constantine* as a fake (see chapter 6). This medieval document claimed that Constantine handed Pope Sylvester imperial power. The document was then used by popes to justify the extension of their rule in civil affairs. When Ulrich heard of Luther, he believed he had an ally and told Luther he could protect him (other knights made the same offer). Luther declined, but at least he knew he was not alone. The Christian German nobility were sympathetic with Luther and might be persuaded. Luther's fate need not depend on the pope; the German people could offer him support.

The Leipzig experience was incredibly frustrating to Luther, who called the debate a tragedy.[181] There were many reasons why. One was the crowd, who did everything in their power to put Luther and Karlstadt at a disadvantage. On the day the Wittenbergers arrived, the papal decree on indulgences from the year before, *Inhibition*, had been posted to the doors of all the churches, an attempt to void the debate before it started.[182] Next, they met with Karlstadt alone, trying to persuade him to conduct the debate without stenographers. That way Eck's "loud shouting and impressive delivery" might win the debate, not its written record.[183] Then they disputed what judges were to be selected to approve the written record of the debate. During the debate, the crowd started clamoring and shouting when Karlstadt quoted from books to show that Eck's view was

---

180. Unknown artist, *Luther and Hus as Good Shepherds*, ca. 1530–40, in *Renaissance and Reformation*, 110–11.

181. *LW* 31:320–25.

182. *LW* 31:319.

183. *LW* 31:319.

contrary to the church fathers. With enough uproar, books were banished, a clear advantage for Eck once more. Throughout their stay, Luther and Karlstadt felt as welcomed as Israel in Babylon. "The citizens of Leipzig neither greeted nor called on us but treated us as though we were their bitterest enemies." Not Eck. "Eck, however, they followed around town, clung to, banqueted, entertained, and finally presented with a robe and added a chamois-hair gown. They also rode horseback with him. In short, they did whatever they could to insult us."[184]

Another reason Leipzig proved a great tragedy had to do with Eck himself, whom Luther believed was full of deception and trickery, a relentless nuisance. During the third week, Luther anticipated a lengthy debate over indulgences. It never happened, at least not how Luther had hoped. The "debate over indulgences fell completely flat, for Eck agreed with me in nearly all respects, and his former defense of indulgences came to appear like mockery and derision, whereas I had hoped that this would be the main topic of the debate."[185] Over the last three days, during Eck's debate with Karlstadt, "virtually nothing was treated in the manner which it deserved," and Eck was so "pleased with himself" that he celebrated his victory in advance, as if he "rule[d] the roost."[186] Luther felt disrespected, as did Karlstadt. Even after the debate, the conflict perpetuated further. Luther was asked to preach in the chapel castle, but Eck, with the support of the university faculty, went on a mission to preach four sermons to Luther's one in the surrounding churches. The town of Leipzig made sure Eck always had the last word.[187]

Even after Leipzig, Eck traveled from church to church celebrating his triumph over Luther and his followers. Eck especially capitalized on Luther's association with the heretic Hus, a tactic that could be very persuasive. The association was not far-fetched either. By the end of the year, Luther, like Hus before him, said that both the bread and the wine should be offered to the laity.[188] Luther also read Hus for himself, and by the start of 1520, Luther reached a conclusion: "Up to now I have taught and held all the teachings of John Hus. Staupitz has taught them equally unawares. In short we are all Hussites without knowing it. Even Paul and Augustine were in reality Hussites."[189]

Luther left Leipzig alive but feeling hopeless his reform might make any difference. Nevertheless, he did not despair but persisted, believing that he must not leave the church but reform it; otherwise, it would never return to sound doctrine. "The worse it [the church] gets, the faster we should run and cling to it; tearing oneself away or spurning it will not make it better."[190] Furthermore,

---

184. *LW* 31:323.
185. *LW* 31:322.
186. *LW* 31:323.
187. *LW* 31:324.
188. See Wurm, "Johannes Eck und die Disputation von Leipzig 1519," 104, 106; *WABr* 2:42; *LW* 48:153. Cf. Hendrix, *Martin Luther*, 84.
189. *WABr* 2:42; *LW* 48:153. Cf. Hendrix, *Martin Luther*, 84.
190. *WA* 2:72; Clement 1, 153. Cf. Hendrix, *Martin Luther*, 83.

although Leipzig proved discouraging, another avenue looked promising: what if Luther took to the printers, even more than before, and reached the hearts of the German laity at large?[191]

THE SACRAMENTS OF PENANCE AND BAPTISM

In 1519 Luther took to the printers as his mind was drawn to the sacraments of penance, baptism, and the Eucharist.[192] The sacrament of penance was indispensable for Luther in 1519 because the sinner needs forgiveness. Yet forgiveness in the sacrament takes two forms:

1. *Forgiveness of punishment (earthly indulgence):* "does away with works and efforts of satisfaction that have been imposed and thus reconciles a person outwardly with the Christian Church."
2. *Forgiveness of guilt (heavenly indulgence):* "does away with the heart's fear and timidity before God; it makes the conscience glad and joyful within and reconciles man with God."[193]

Out of the two, guilt is more serious because God alone can grant such a remission that is necessary for salvation itself. For Luther, forgiveness of guilt is the wellspring of true happiness. A "joyful confidence overcomes him that God has forgiven him his sins forever."[194] Therefore, if Luther must choose between the two types of forgiveness, the choice is easy: the forgiveness of guilt. Since the sinner cannot be saved "without a joyful conscience and a glad heart toward God," Luther would rather "buy no indulgences at all, than to forget this forgiveness of guilt or omit to practice it first and foremost every day." Yet rather than running to Rome to buy indulgences, a vain hope in Luther's estimation, the sinner should sprint to God for "peace of heart." Luther may have been drawing from personal experience when he said that running after indulgences will only destroy the body and mind alike. Everything is backwards: the sinner does not do works to receive forgiveness, but he receives forgiveness so that he does good works. "For works do not drive out sin, but the driving out of sin leads to good works. For good works must be done with joyful heart and good conscience toward God, that is, out of the forgiveness of guilt."[195] If reversed, the sinner's *anfechtung* will result in nothing but terror before the sacrament. However, the sacrament is meant to appease the fury of *anfechtung* by relieving the conscience with forgiveness, producing comfort rather than despair.[196]

---

191. "I heard daily that many people belittle my poverty and say I produce only little pamphlets and sermons in German for the uneducated laity. That does not bother me. I will be satisfied if I work my whole life for the improvement of one layperson." *WA* 6, 203.
192. *LW* 35:3–74.
193. *LW* 35:9.
194. *LW* 35:9.
195. *LW* 35:10.
196. *LW* 35:11.

If absolution from the priest precedes works, so that the grace of forgiveness produces peace, then faith must accompany the sacrament of penance, believing that such absolution will indeed produce comfort. "Everything, then, depends on this faith, which alone makes the sacraments accomplish that which they signify, and everything that the priest says come true. For as you believe, so it is done for you."[197] While contrition is key, the sinner must *believe* that his guilt is remitted and such belief has a certain desperation to it: "You must cast yourself upon the grace of God, hear his sufficiently sure word in the sacrament, accept it in free and joyful faith, and never doubt that you have come to grace—not by your own merits or contrition but by his gracious and divine mercy, which promises, offers, and grants you full and free forgiveness of sins in order that in the face of all the assaults [*anfechtung*] of sin, conscience, and the devil, you thus learn to glory and trust not in yourself or your own actions, but in the grace and mercy of your dear Father in heaven."[198]

Penance consisted of three parts:

1. contrition
2. confession (accompanied by absolution)
3. satisfaction

However, Luther clarified that three parts also make penance a sacrament that is effective:

1. the word of God or absolution
2. faith which trusts in the word of God or absolution
3. peace, the forgiveness of sins[199]

As long as faith is present, the former three (contrition, confession, and satisfaction) are "less weighty," meaning there is "no danger of there being too little or too much." Luther used to obsess over the perfection of those three—contrition, confession, and satisfaction—and was tormented by the imperfection of his performance. But in 1519 the primacy of trust in God's Word and grace offered relief: "For the faith of the sacrament makes all the crooked straight and fills up all the uneven ground. So no one who has this sacramental faith can err, whether in contrition, confession, or satisfaction, and even if he does err, it does him no harm."[200]

Luther's emphasis on God's Word, faith, and peace of conscience did not mean the priest was no longer instrumental. God's good news is delivered daily

---

197. "Without this faith all absolution and all sacraments are in vain and indeed do more harm than good." *LW* 35:11.
198. *LW* 35:15. And again, "Whoever believes, to him everything is helpful, nothing is harmful. Whoever does not believe, to him everything is harmful, nothing is helpful" (22).
199. *LW* 35:19.
200. *LW* 35:20.

through the priest, who is a trumpet of free forgiveness to anyone with faith in Christ. However, Luther's view matured from 1519 forward so that the foundation of forgiveness was not the priestly office itself but the promise of God's Word in the gospel.[201] All those who came to the priest to confess and receive absolution could leave confident they were forgiven if their faith resided in the gospel and its power to remit sins. In Luther's experience, however, Rome used penance to rob the Christian of assurance. Luther extended penance (and absolution in particular) as a gift instead, one that blessed the believer with assurance.

As Luther taught on the "keys" in the decade that followed, this purpose became even more conspicuous in his definition of the church. Christ's disciples unlocked heaven with the keys, keys that rattle with forgiveness and therefore sound jubilation, not terror to those united to Christ. If the priest is not at hand, one Christian may offer absolution to another Christian—such was the potency of Luther's priesthood of believers.[202] For such a priesthood was not the property of the priest's office, as if he controls sacramental grace itself or can create faith within (something only God can do). Rather, God confers the power of his gospel and its forgiveness through the office of the priest so that when the priest absolves the sinner it is "as true as if God had spoken it, whether it is grasped by faith or not."[203] Priesthood, therefore, was both vertical and horizontal. Priesthood was vertical since all united to Christ were priests—priesthood was not the monopoly of the office itself. And yet, priesthood was horizontal, meaning God does not call everyone to the *vocation* of a priest, an office reserved for those he summons to distribute his written, oral, and sacramental word. "That is why all Christians share the same power, but not the right to exercise it in the public sphere."[204]

In 1519 *The Holy and Blessed Sacrament of Baptism* also made its appearance, as Luther defined baptism according to (1) the sign, (2) the significance of the sign, and (3) faith. Parents should bring their children to the priest where he submerges—Luther believed in immersion—the child under the waters, which serve as the sign itself. The submersion itself "signifies that the old man and the sinful birth of the flesh and blood are to be wholly drowned by the grace of God."[205] When the child is lifted up out of the baptismal water—*aus der Taufe gehoben*—"A new man, born in grace, comes forth and rises." As Paul said, by the "washing of regeneration" (Titus 3:5), the child is "born again and made new."[206] Or as Jesus told Nicodemus, "Unless you are born again of *water* and the Spirit (of grace), you may not enter into the kingdom of heaven" (John 3:5). For Luther, baptism regenerates. Luther uses the biblical language of new creation as well

---

201. *LW* 35:13–22; cf. Kolb, *Martin Luther*, 134.
202. *LW* 35:22. Cf. Kolb, *Martin Luther*, 133–134; *WA* 47:297.36–298.14; *LW* 6:128; 8:183; 40:353–59.
203. *LW* 35:22.
204. Kolb, *Martin Luther*, 159. The vertical-horizontal distinction is Kolb's (158), though he is reliant on Althaus, *Theology*, 323–32; Lohse, *Theology*, 286–97; Vajta, *Luther on Worship*, 109–21.
205. *LW* 35:29.
206. *LW* 35:30.

to capture the new life baptism produces, though this language appears in his writings after 1528.[207]

However, baptism is only the beginning. Although baptism is a one-time event, its effect is ongoing and continual. True, "sins are drowned in baptism, and in place of sin, righteousness comes forth," but the significance of baptism "is not fulfilled completely in this life." Not until the Last Day will baptism's significance—that is, the thing signified—reach its culmination. That which is signified—death and new life—is inaugurated with baptism but does not reach its finality until glorification. Until then, the "whole life is nothing else than a spiritual baptism which does not cease till death, and he who is baptized is condemned to die."[208]

Since baptism is a regenerate act, it cannot be a subjective event centered on the believer's faith, which could only return baptism to the legalism of the *via moderna*. Since baptism is regenerative, it is a supernatural achievement by God himself. Since the Holy Spirit raises the child from spiritual death to life in the waters, baptism is a covenant that ensures no little consolation.[209] "This blessed sacrament of baptism helps you because in it God allies himself with you and becomes one with you in a gracious covenant of comfort."[210] Luther's language—he becomes one with you—means baptism unites the child to Christ.

That union has a two-sided effect. First, in baptism itself God slays the sinful nature. Second, he pledges to slay the sinful nature from that day forward, preparing the believer for death and resurrection.[211] Consider Augustine's description of baptism and Luther's interpretation of Augustine:

Augustine: Sin is altogether forgiven in baptism; not in such a manner that it is no longer present, but in such a manner that it is not imputed.

Luther's interpretation of Augustine: It is as if he were to say, "Sin remains in our flesh even until death and works without ceasing. But so long as we do not give our consent to it or desire to remain in it, sin is so overruled by our baptism that it does not condemn us and is not harmful to us. Rather it is daily being more and more destroyed in us until our death."[212]

Therefore, on the foundation of God's pledge "there is no greater comfort on earth than baptism."[213] When Luther experienced *Anfechtungen*, he threw this

---

207. Kolb also observes how Luther does not use the word *sign* as much in the 1530s because the Anabaptists used the word to convey mere symbolism. Kolb, *Martin Luther*, 136, 139; cf. *WA* 46:175.1–2.

208. *LW* 35:30.

209. Luther is conservative about his use of "covenant," says Kolb, due to the *via moderna's* misuse of the concept, but he does use it with baptism. Kolb, *Martin Luther*, 140.

210. *LW* 35:33.

211. *LW* 35:33–35.

212. *LW* 35:34–35.

213. *LW* 35:34.

dart at Satan: I have been baptized. The word of God's promise in baptism will not return void should the believer cling to it by faith. When Satan presses in with an onslaught of doubt, nothing provides so much comfort than clinging to baptism.

The mention of faith might sound conflicting since Luther advocated for baptismal regeneration, but Luther himself saw no tension. If water is the sign, and death and new life the thing signified, then faith is what latches hold of the thing signified. Faith not only believes in what baptism signifies, but faith trusts that baptism "establishes a covenant between us and God to the effect that we will fight against sin and slay it, even to our dying breath, while he for his part will be merciful to us, deal graciously with us, and—because we are not sinless in this life until purified by death—not judge us with severity."[214] Luther believed baptism was powerful, effecting new life, but baptism power did not produce total perfection in life. Faith is necessary—the ground for all comfort as Luther called it. In other words, Luther believed the Spirit was the agent of baptism, but Luther conditioned baptism's fulfillment and ongoing transformation in the life of the believer on faith and its fight against sin. For "if anyone has fallen into sin, he should all the more remember his baptism, how God has here made a covenant with him to forgive all his sins, *if only he will fight against them even until death*."[215] Otherwise, God will not forgive their sins.[216] The Nicene Creed was right, concludes Luther. "*I believe* [credo] in the Holy Spirit . . . [in] one baptism for the remission of sins." That which is signified in baptism, therefore, is grasped by faith. "Believe, and you have it. Doubt, and you are lost. . . . Thus everything depends on faith."[217]

The next year, Luther's *The Babylonian Captivity of the Church* reiterated the points outlined in *The Holy and Blessed Sacrament of Baptism* but this time with the sharp vehemency of a polemical edge. Rome had stolen the covenantal comfort baptism provides and replaced it with anxiety by turning the sacrament of faith into a sacrament of works.[218] Luther denied that the sacraments contained a "power efficacious for justification." Baptism does not justify, said Luther, "but it is faith in that word of promise to which baptism is added."[219] Or to use that common saying handed down to Luther, "Not the sacrament, but the faith of the sacrament, justifies."

Luther blamed Peter Lombard and his *Sentences*. Rather than drawing the

---

214. *LW* 35:35.

215. *LW* 35:37.

216. "He will not count sin against us if only we keep striving against it with many trials. . . . To them who do this not, God will not forgive their sins. For they do not live according to their baptism and covenant, and they hinder the work of God and of their baptism which has been begun." *LW* 35:37.

217. "So we find that through sin baptism is indeed hindered in its work, in the forgiveness and the slaying of sin. Yet only by lack of faith in its operation is baptism canceled out. Faith, in turn, removes the hindrance to the operation of baptism." *LW* 35:38. At the end, Luther warns against presumption that takes advantage of God's grace.

218. *LW* 36:42.

219. *LW* 36:66.

believer's attention to the word promised in the sign, Lombard fixated on the sign itself turning it into a work. Here lies the captivity of the sacraments, Luther warned: "Pay heed more to the word than to the sign, more to faith than to the work or use of the sign." For the sacraments are not "fulfilled when they are taking place, but when they are being believed."[220]

If faith is the fulfilment of that which baptism signifies, then the papacy has committed a most grievous error by distracting the church with other ceremonies that depend on merit. Rather than resting in the word of promise contained within baptism, the papacy says, "one must reach heaven by another way, as if baptism had now become entirely useless."[221] Worse yet, the pope has imposed these ceremonies on the church, making laws that require works. Luther labeled this imposition an oppression of the gospel, nothing less than the papal tyranny of the Antichrist.[222]

From where then will freedom come?

A LITERARY FIRESTORM (1520)

After Leipzig Luther wrote with fury, as if every book was his last. He might have felt that way too; Luther often thought he was not destined to die. It was a matter of time before his body was licked up by the flames of the papacy. Luther also wrote with a hustle because he was a man of no little conviction. With each new revelation, Luther's quill moved with expediency. And now that Eck had cornered Luther, exposing the subsidiary issue of biblical authority, Luther was liberated, emboldened even, and ready to call on the church and the German people to arrive at the same convictions as him.

After Luther's tussle with Eck in the summer of 1519, Luther produced a literary firestorm, publishing dozens of tracts and books that fanned the flames of his reform. Luther's genius was his target audience: he did not limit himself to the academy or to Latin prose like some of his Roman opponents; he appealed to laypeople in their own vernacular. With the help of local printers, Luther wrote not only larger works, but especially pamphlets that could be quickly and easily digested by the average German Christian. His approach was a success; hundreds of thousands of copies of his works were published in 1519 alone.[223] In 1520 three works proved instrumental to Luther's conflict with Rome.

To the Christian Nobility of the German Nation

To the Christian Nobility of the German Nation was pivotal to the success of the Reformation because Luther invoked the authority of the state (the German nobility, or as Luther called them, the "temporal power") over the authority of

---

220. "This faith justifies, and fulfils that which baptism signifies." *LW* 36:66.
221. *LW* 36:69.
222. *LW* 36:70–73.
223. Hendrix estimates over a quarter million. On Luther's printer, Melchior Lotter, see Hendrix, *Martin Luther*, 81–82.

the Roman Church (the "spiritual power"). Rome had erected three walls that appeared impenetrable:

1. When pressed by the temporal power they have made decrees and declared that the temporal power had no jurisdiction over them, but that, on the contrary, the spiritual power is above the temporal.
2. When the attempt is made to reprove them [Rome] with the Scriptures, they raise the objection that only the pope may interpret the Scriptures.
3. If threatened with a council, their story is that no one may summon a council but the pope.[224]

Like Joshua, Luther sounded the trumpets until the "walls of Jericho were overthrown."[225]

First Wall

As to the first wall, Rome assumed that the spiritual power (clergy) can be preeminent over the temporal authority (laity), an assumption that created no little tension in the Middle Ages between the power of the papacy and the jurisdiction of the ruler or magistrate. However, Luther flipped Rome's assumption upside down: the temporal power is over the spiritual power, not vice versa. The temporal authorities "bear the sword and rod in their hand"—as Paul set forth in Romans 12 and 1 Corinthians 12, as well as Peter in 1 Peter 2—"To punish the wicked and protect the good." Should the church turn wicked, which Luther was convinced had already occurred, then the temporal power has every right to punish and reform the spiritual power. "I say therefore that since the temporal power is ordained of God to punish the wicked and protect the good, it should be left free to perform its office in the whole body of Christendom without restriction and without respect to persons, whether it affects pope, bishops, priests, monks, nuns or anyone else."[226]

Granting the magistrate such a right to intervene in the affairs of the church may sound peculiar to modern ears. In modern society, civil authorities may be entirely secular in outlook, operating within a post-Christendom cultural framework. But a secular authority—at least in the modern sense—was a category without a frame of reference in the sixteenth century. However, in the sixteenth century Christianity rivaled opposing religions (Judaism, Islam). Nevertheless, when Luther gave his trust to the temporal authorities, he did so with every reason to believe they would take action *for* the church. The only question was whether the authorities were for a reforming church or a Roman church. In Luther's immediate context, the former became more and more of a reality with every advance of the Reformation. Luther's language revealed his

---

224. *LW* 44:126.
225. *LW* 44:127.
226. *LW* 44:130.

optimism: "The temporal *Christian* authority ought to exercise its office without hindrance," even if the pope himself turned corrupt and needed to be corrected or excommunicated.[227] Luther was not calling for insurrection or revolution, which he detested. He was calling for reform, but a reform that should be governed by temporal powers.

Rome resisted such correction because it was intolerable that a sacred authority as high as the pope himself could be reprimanded, let alone deposed by a civil ruler who, apart from the law, was but a peasant or townsman and certainly only a layman. Rome believed that when a candidate was inducted into priesthood, he could never lose such a right or return to the laity. That belief contributed to the wide divide between clergy and laity in the late medieval age: clergy had a higher, even holier spiritual status. When Luther, driven by scriptural language, said all who have faith are priests, he closed the gap between clergy and laity. No longer was one spiritual and the other earthly, as if the former possessed a greater status than the latter. In Christ all God's people are priests comprising a royal priesthood. Could Luther's early lectures on the book of Hebrews be having their full effect as Luther appealed to the priesthood of believers?[228]

The priesthood of all believers did not lead Luther to an extreme, as if no office of priest should remain.[229] Luther was no radical. He believed in the equality of all believers, not the identity of all believers, as *To the Christian Nobility* makes clear. While every Christian has the same status in Christ, only some Christians are called by God to exercise the office of priest. Everyone who is baptized and justified *sola fide* is a priest in God's sight; nevertheless, God has ordained an office to ensure order in his church and pastoral care. As Luther explained, "Therefore, a priest in Christendom is nothing else but an office-holder. As long as he holds office he takes precedence; where he is deposed, he is a peasant or a townsman like anybody else. Indeed, a priest is never a priest when he is deposed."[230] There is, then, "no true, basic difference between laymen and priests, princes and bishops, between religious and secular, except for the sake of office and work, but not for the sake of status. . . . Christ does not have two different bodies, one temporal, and the other spiritual. There is but one Head and one body."[231]

Luther presented a hypothetical: suppose a group of laymen are stranded in the desert, and to ensure their spiritual growth in the gospel, they ordain a priest

---

227. *LW* 44:131.

228. Hebrews highlights the priesthood of Christ, but for Luther the believer has been united to Christ; therefore, he, too, is a priest. Baptism is the medium by which consecration is inaugurated. He wrote, "We are all consecrated priests through baptism . . . whoever comes out of the water of baptism can boast that he is already a consecrated priest, bishop, and pope." *WA* 6:407–8; *LW* 44:127–29. Cf. Cameron, *European Reformation*, 176.

229. Luther was not the only one to defend the priesthood of believers, but with nuance to avoid radical conclusions. The Reformed tradition, for instance, used the language of the "communion of saints." Consult Lord's Day 21 (Question 55) of the Heidelberg Catechism for example.

230. *LW* 44:129.

231. *LW* 44:129–30.

from among their own midst. That priest performs all the duties a priest should perform (baptism, Mass, absolution, etc.). Rome refuses to admit this man is a priest since he is not chosen and confirmed by the pope and his bishops. Not Luther. "Such a man would be as truly a priest as though he had been ordained by all the bishops and popes in the world." As it turned out, Luther's hypothetical was anything but imaginary. "St. Augustine, Ambrose, and Cyprian each became [a bishop in this way]."[232]

If the gulf between clergy and laity is not as wide as Rome says, then temporal authorities—who are also laymen—can act to correct not only a priest but even the pope himself. "Inasmuch as the temporal power has become a member of the Christian body it is a spiritual estate, even though its work is physical. Therefore, its work should extend without hindrance to all the members of the whole body to punish and use force whenever guilt deserves or necessity demands, without regard to whether the culprit is pope, bishop, or priest."[233] Luther was speaking to matters of discipline. However, Luther also believed the temporal powers could play a positive role. Since the laity—who may carry temporal power—make up the same body of Christ as the clergy, they are in their right to call a council. Such an argument worked in Luther's favor: he was calling on the German nobility to summon a general council, like the emperors of the patristic era, a council that could decide in favor of the Reformation.

Luther's Two Kingdoms

Luther tore down Rome's first wall and the wide divide between temporal and spiritual powers, a divide that prioritized the latter over the former. In return, Luther erected a substitute framework. Across his lifetime, Luther proposed two kingdoms, a spiritual kingdom governed by Word and Spirit and a worldly kingdom governed by the sword.[234] To be clear, both kingdoms are God's kingdoms. He rules each, but he does so in different ways.[235]

God governs his spiritual kingdom by the gospel (the Word) and the righteousness of its King, Christ Jesus. In the spiritual kingdom, every Christian has equal status in Christ, whether clergy or laity. Yet God has appointed ministers to administer his Word for the salvation and sanctification of his church.

God governs his worldly kingdom by means of his natural law, which not

---

232. *LW* 44:128.

233. "That is why guilty priests, when they are handed over to secular law, are first deprived of their priestly dignities. It would not be right unless the secular sword previously had had authority over these priests by divine right." *LW* 44:131–32.

234. Luther's treatment of these two kingdoms is evident in his *To the Christian Nobility of the German Nation*, but it is especially plain in his *Temporal Authority: To What Extent It Should Be Obeyed*, in *LW* 45:75–130.

235. Reinhold Niebuhr was critical of Luther's two kingdoms, convinced they led to withdrawal and passivity. Steinmetz responded, "A man who numbered among his personal enemies half a dozen heads of state . . . and who could wring concessions out of the most seasoned diplomat cannot, I think, be dismissed as a political 'quietist' or 'defeatist.'" Steinmetz, "Luther and the Two Kingdoms," 113. See Niebuhr, *The Nature and Destiny of Man*, 185–97.

only includes his moral law but the wisdom and reason he has implanted within humankind. In his worldly kingdom, God pursues the righteousness of society, the justice that should define humanity. However, sin has corrupted human society, requiring God to maintain justice and detain wickedness by means of the sword and civil magistrate.

The two kingdoms complement each other, but they must be differentiated from each other. Otherwise, the responsibilities of ministers and magistrates, church and city, Spirit and sword will be confused and consequently jeopardized. For example, if an evangelical church desires to eradicate images from its premises, they should first seek the approval of the civil government since an estate is affected. However, the government does not have an intrinsic right to dictate, decide, or disseminate the gospel. That responsibility belongs to the clergy alone since God has entrusted to them the state of the soul.[236]

To keep both—complementarity and differentiation—Luther believed the doctrine of justification must inform both kingdoms. In the spiritual kingdom, the gospel is proclaimed with all its promises in Christ, and those who receive it by faith alone are clothed in the righteousness of Christ. For that reason, no one in the spiritual kingdom can boast over another; each is an equal heir of the riches God has provided in his Son.

The Christian is justified by faith alone, and yet such faith is never alone but is always producing fruit. Set free from the bondage of sin and the condemnation of the law, the believer is now liberated to love his neighbor, not to be reconciled with God but only because he has been reconciled with God.[237] Although the believer is not justified by works of love, works of love fall from the tree of justification in abundance, the inevitable fruit of new life in Christ. These works of love not only define life together in the church, but they should also be marked by an external focus: love for others in society at large. Set free, the Christian is now ready to serve and become everyman's servant.

Such a mindset—servant of all—puts the Christian's role in the worldly kingdom in proper perspective. The Christian exists in both kingdoms and is accountable to both authorities, both to ministers within the spiritual kingdom and to magistrates within the worldly kingdom.[238] Since the Christian is not only a member of the spiritual kingdom but also a citizen of the worldly kingdom, he is to submit himself to the authority of the magistrate, even if that authority does not rule with righteousness as he should. Revolution and anarchy were reprehensible to Luther.

---

236. Tuininga, *Calvin's Political Theology and the Public Engagement of the Church*, 33–34.

237. "Luther does not reject good works except as the basis for justification. On the contrary, Luther wishes to stress as much as possible the importance of good works in the life of faith. Christ does not free men and women from good works but from false opinions concerning them.... They do not perform good works in order to be justified but because they already are." Steinmetz, "Luther and the Two Kingdoms," 119.

238. At points Luther used "two kingdoms" or *Zwei-Reiche-Lehre*, but he also transitioned to a more specific distinction: "two governments" or *Zwei-Regimente-Lehre*. See Steinmetz, "Luther and the Two Kingdoms," 115.

That conviction—subservience to civil authority—applies to the clergy just the same. Luther warned his German colleagues to learn from Rome's mistake: Rome confused the two kingdoms, granting pope and papacy rights that belonged to the worldly kingdom alone. In essence, Rome transgressed the limits of its jurisdiction, as if it should rule over temporal authorities or even become the temporal authority. Luther now aimed to repair the damage caused by Rome but with a better paradigm, a two-kingdoms paradigm that assigned responsibilities to each kingdom and prohibited the church from clamoring for civil power not its own.[239]

Did Luther live up to his own standard, keeping the two kingdoms distinct? Both in his own day and ever since, that question has been debated. As will be seen, the Peasants' Revolt, the chaos of Anabaptism, and the ongoing battle with Rome for the church all posed a test: could the Reformer stay true to his two-kingdom distinction not just in theory but in practice? Luther continued to warn civil powers against ecclesiastical intrusion, yet he also expected the government to protect and push forward a Reformation church and even punish detractors. Luther did not believe he was inconsistent: these groups (and others) advocated for beliefs and practices that not only threatened the spirituality of the church but invited chaos into society itself (see chapter 13).[240] Yet since no system, no official ecclesiastical polity was established by Luther, the relationship between temporal authorities and the church remained ambiguous at points, even somewhat fluid. "Luther's two kingdoms doctrine notwithstanding, the form that the Reformation ultimately took in Lutheran territories looked a lot like the caesaropapism that had been advocated in the thirteenth century by Marsilius of Padua, which in Protestant circles came to be known as Erastianism."[241]

Furthermore, a two-kingdoms distinction did not necessarily guarantee uniformity between Reformers on the type of civil government that should define the worldly kingdom. Even when Reformers did agree on a two-kingdom paradigm (e.g., compare Luther to Calvin in chapter 15), they did not always agree on the political structure of that worldly kingdom. Luther's interaction with the German nobility depended on a type of monarchial governance. Luther did not believe God prescribed one and only one type of civil polity; nonetheless, Luther believed some form of monarchy was best.[242] Yet other Reformers like Calvin were convinced tyranny could be the only outcome since power in one individual—whether a prince, king, or queen—was far too centralized.[243]

---

239. In the above treatment, I depend on Luther's *To the German Nobility* and have chosen to incorporate Steinmetz at points. However, many fine treatments of this topic can be found in other histories. Although I do not engage McGrath, he has a superb survey on the various Reformers and their views of government, from Luther to Calvin and everyone in between. See McGrath, *Reformation Thought*, 207–21.

240. Chapters 12–13 explain the reasoning behind putting Anabaptists to death, Anabaptists whose deviance was considered a threat to society's order and structure.

241. Tuininga, *Calvin's Political Theology and the Public Engagement of the Church*, 41. For a chronology of Luther's evolving opinions, especially his writings and controversies in the 1530s, see pp. 36–40.

242. Steinmetz, "Luther and the Two Kingdoms," 123–25.

243. Alternatives were embraced instead. For example, Strasbourg was governed by a city council.

In addition, although many Reformers did assert a two-kingdom structure, some did not, criticizing Luther's paradigm. For example, Zwingli's *corpus christianum* treated city and church as one, blurring the lines until one kingdom was the goal. In Zurich's Christian commonwealth the city and the church were as impossible to separate as the body and the soul.[244] Such indivisibility presupposed Zwingli's hermeneutic, which assumed the pastor is like the prophet in Israel and the magistrate is like the king of Israel (except Zurich was governed by an aristocracy, much in contrast to Luther's penchant for monarchy).[245] That inseparable relationship between minister and magistrate meant the governing authorities were an outpost under the umbrella of the church itself. The lines between citizen and Christian were indistinct; sometimes city and church were referred to as if the two were synonymous. That put the church in the position to influence, even manage civil affairs, which Zwingli capitalized on with expediency (see chapter 12). In return, Zwingli expected the magistrate to punish anyone who violated Zurich's theology with imprisonment, banishment, or even the death sentence (e.g., Anabaptists). Of course, control could go both ways, as the magistrate considered affairs in the church their jurisdiction as well. Zwingli's political reform resulted in his own death and motivated Zurich to reconsider Zwingli's paradigm, a decision that ultimately led to the primacy of the magistrate over the church in future decades.

In the late 1520s, the Lutherans criticized Zwingli for collapsing the worldly kingdom into the spiritual kingdom.[246] Zwingli replied by attacking the Lutherans, first accusing them of ignoring Scriptures that supported a council's administration of the church, and then accusing the Lutherans of assuming the separation approach of the radical Reformers.[247] Zwingli's association of Lutherans with radicals was not accurate, but it was a tactic that could create incredible fright in those who believed the accusation. Chapters 12 and 14–15 will explore further tensions as the political theology of Heinrich Bullinger, Martin Bucer, and John Calvin are examined, but the late 1520s debate between Lutherans and Zwinglians demonstrates that Luther's destruction of the papacy's first wall could be celebrated even while heated debate followed on what kind of wall should be erected in its place.

Second and Third Walls

Rome's second wall was a source of no little frustration for Luther. Whenever Scripture was used against the pope and his curia, they responded with the claim that the pope alone could interpret Scripture. "The Romanists want to be the

---

244. Consult Zwingli's "Divine and Human Righteousness," 2:1–41.
245. The aristocracy model faced challenges of its own: power was not centralized in one individual (monarchy), but it was still circumscribed to a select group of society and, when abused, invited accusations of oligarchy. McGrath, *Reformation Thought*, 215–18.
246. See Potter, "Church and State, 1528," 108–24.
247. For an overview of the debate, see Tuininga, *Calvin's Political Theology and the Public Engagement of the Church*, 44–45.

only masters of Holy Scripture.... They assume the sole authority for themselves, and, quite unashamed, they play about with words before our very eyes, trying to persuade us that the pope cannot err in matters of faith, regardless of whether he is righteous or wicked."[248] Against this wall, Luther wielded a two sided-hammer, not only appealing to Scripture as the only inerrant authority, but also enlisting the priesthood of believers once more: "If we are all priests... and all have one faith, one gospel, one sacrament, why should we not also have the power to test and judge what is right or wrong in matters of faith?"[249] Again Luther enlisted Old Testament imagery, but this time with his eminent, sharp wit: "If God spoke then through an ass against a prophet, why should he not be able even now to speak through a righteous man against the pope?" (Num. 22).[250]

As to Rome's third wall, they "have no basis in Scripture for their claim that the pope alone has the right to call or confirm a council."[251] As precedent had it, temporal authorities often called councils. "Even the Council of Nicaea, the most famous of all councils, was neither called nor confirmed by the bishop of Rome, but by the emperor Constantine... and yet these councils were the most Christian of all. But if the pope alone has the right to convene councils, then these councils would all have been heretical."[252]

If the church was as corrupt as Luther said, what matters should a council have addressed, assuming Luther got his way? The second half of *To the German Nobility* was concerned with the specifics: Luther called for the abolition of countless Roman practices, such as the kissing of the pope's feet, making vows such as the vow of celibacy, which prohibited clergy from marriage, saying masses on behalf of the dead in purgatory, erecting forest chapels for pilgrimages, misusing Aristotle's teachings in universities, entering the priesthood for financial livelihood, and so on.[253]

Most pertinent to the German nobility, however, was Rome's manipulation of German funds in the name of salvation, such as the selling of indulgences. If the German nobility did not sever itself from Rome, the papacy would take and take until the German people had nothing left, not even the clothes on their backs. "Above all, we should drive out of German territory the papal legates with their faculties, which they sell to us for large sums of money. This traffic is nothing but skullduggery." Luther even called this trafficking demonic. "They assert that the pope has authority to do this. It is the devil who tells them to say these things. They sell us doctrine so satanic, and take money for it, that they are teaching us sin and leading us to hell."[254] Luther then introduced a charge that

---

248. *LW* 44:133.
249. *LW* 44:135.
250. *LW* 44:136.
251. *LW* 44:136.
252. *LW* 44:137.
253. Luther wrote much on the subject of monastic vows, such as *The Judgment of Martin Luther on Monastic Vows* (1521), in *LW* 44:245–400.
254. *LW* 44:193.

he would resort to throughout his fight with Rome: Antichrist. "If there were no other base trickery to prove that the pope is the true Antichrist, this one would be enough to prove it. Hear this, O pope, not of all men the holiest but of all men the most sinful! O that God from heaven would soon destroy your throne and sink it in the abyss of hell!"[255]

Had Luther gone too far in his rhetoric? Perhaps. But the mountain of opposition demanded the most extreme rhetoric. "I have attacked many things too severely. But how else ought I to do it?" he said. Yes, human authorities would judge him, but Luther was far more concerned with the Divine Judge himself. "I would rather have the wrath of the world upon me than the wrath of God. The world can do no more to me than take my life."[256] And so the world tried. Whether Luther could evade its brutality remained to be seen.

Did Luther's rhetoric prove effective? The book sold out at once, thousands and thousands of copies circulating Germany, and a second printing in quick demand.[257] However, one consequence affected Luther personally. Just a week and a half after Luther's book was published, Staupitz told Luther he could no longer be vicar general of the Reformed Congregations. Excommunication was imminent; if Staupitz did continue, Rome would demand he surrender Luther over at once, which Staupitz knew he could not do in good conscience. But this way, Staupitz relieved himself of the dilemma and removed Luther from any immediate danger on his account.[258]

The Babylon Captivity of the Church

To the Christian Nobility of the German Nation was an attack on Rome's three walls, but in the minds of many Germans, Luther not only created cracks in these walls but brought the walls tumbling down in heaps. Now Rome was unprotected, vulnerable to a further attack. This time Luther went deep into the Roman fortress, straight for the jugular: the sacraments.

According to Rome, a sacrament channeled grace from God to his people. The grace communicated may be invisible to the eye, but the eye could rest on something visible, namely, the sign itself. A sacrament, said Duns Scotus, is "a physical sign, instituted by God, which efficaciously signifies the grace of God, or the gracious action of God."[259] Seven sacraments buttressed the church and the salvation only Rome could offer (see chapter 3). These included (1) baptism, (2) Mass, (3) penance, (4) confirmation, (5) marriage, (6) ordination, and (7) extreme unction.

In *The Babylonian Captivity of the Church*, Luther charged at all seven, and

---

255. *LW* 44:193.

256. *LW* 44:217.

257. Hendrix says the first printing was four thousand copies. Hendrix, *Martin Luther*, 92.

258. See Hendrix, *Martin Luther*, 93, who highlights Luther's undying gratitude: "It is not right for me to forget you or to be ungrateful, for it was through you that the light of the gospel began to shine out of darkness into our hearts." *WABr* 3:155–56; *LW* 49:48.

259. McGrath, *Reformation Thought*, 163.

the Mass above all. Luther denied that there should be seven sacraments; there are but three—baptism, penance, and the bread. "All three have been subjected to a miserable captivity by the Roman curia, and the church has been robbed of all her liberty."[260] Just as Israel was taken into captivity by the Babylonians, so, too, the church had been taken into bondage by the Roman papacy.

In time Luther even erased penance from the number of sacraments, reducing the list to two. On what grounds did Luther deny sacramental legitimacy to penance? If Duns Scotus was right that a sacrament is a physical sign, then penance cannot qualify. For unlike the waters of baptism and the bread and wine at the table, penance has no corresponding physical sign.

Luther did not merely protest the number of sacraments. He envisioned a redefinition of the sacraments altogether. In his estimation, they had been taken captive and misrepresented. Consider the Mass, for example, which Luther said had not one, not two, but three captivities of its own. First, when the bread and wine were presented at the altar, the cup was withheld from the laity. Second, when the elements were offered, Rome claimed a transubstantiation took place, as if, by the power of the priest's command, the elements turned into the body and blood of Christ while their external appearance (their "accidents" or accidental qualities) looked the same. Third, Rome treated this ritual as if a sacrifice occurred.

Should the Cup Be Withheld from the Laity? Luther and Cyprian

A little over one hundred years before Luther wrote his *Babylonian Captivity*, the Council of Constance met and burned the forerunner of the Reformation, Jan Hus, at the stake. They sent Hus to the flames in part because he challenged the church's decision to keep the wine from the laity.[261] Now Luther challenged the decision once more. Rome called him a heretic for doing so, but Luther called Rome the real heretic. They, not Luther, had violated the Scriptures, which never withhold Christ from his bride. "Rise up then, you popish flatterers, one and all! Get busy and defend yourselves against the charges of impiety, tyranny, and *lèse-majesté* and of the crime of slandering your brethren. You decry as heretics those who refuse to contravene such plain and powerful words of Scripture in order to acknowledge the mere dreams of your brains!" Luther always knew how to lob an insult. But the insult cut deeper still when he then concluded that it was not the Hussites (Bohemians) who were "heretics and schismatics" since they "take their stand upon the Gospels." Instead, it is "the Romans who are the heretics and godless schismatics, for you presume upon your figments alone against the clear Scriptures of God."[262] Luther's doctrine of *sola scriptura* proved the deciding factor.

---

260. *LW* 36:18.
261. Over a decade later that all changed, and Hussites, or Bohemians as they were called, now had the right to give the laity the cup. See the Council of Basel. *LW* 36:27, n. 55.
262. *LW* 36:24.

Woodcut, Holy Communion in both kinds (Wittenberg, Luther Museum)
Public Domain

That did not mean Luther failed to invoke the authority of tradition. Luther exposed Rome further when he demonstrated that Rome did not have the church fathers on its side as it thought. Exhibiting his knowledge of the patristics, Luther made much of Cyprian, "who alone is strong enough to refute all the Romanists." Cyprian's *On the Lapsed* makes no secret of its posture: "to administer both kinds [bread and wine] to the laity, even to children, indeed, to give the body of the Lord into their hands."[263] How could the Fathers do otherwise when Christ raised the cup and said it was his blood poured out for many for the forgiveness of sins? Were the laity not included? If not, said Luther, then the "sign as such is incomparably less than the thing signified." But Rome esteemed the "sign[s] more than the things they signify."[264] Rome violated not only the Scriptures but the testimony of the church catholic.

---

263. *LW* 36:25–26.
264. *LW* 36:23.

Transubstantiation, a True Catholic Doctrine?

Luther challenged Rome not only for withholding the cup but also for her belief that a transubstantiation occurs. In 1215 Innocent II and the Fourth Lateran Council pronounced transubstantiation to be official church teaching. But again, Luther believed that ancient, catholic tradition was not on Rome's side. Luther was not convinced transubstantiation was taught by the majority of church fathers or by theologians during the Early Middle Ages. Before the Fourth Lateran Council, "the church kept the true faith for more than twelve hundred years, during which time the holy fathers never, at any time or place, mentioned this transubstantiation (a monstrous word and a monstrous idea), until the pseudo philosophy of Aristotle began to make its inroads into the church in these last three hundred years."[265]

Mass of St Gregory
Public Domain

265. *LW* 36:31.

Luther's jab at pseudo-Aristotle is not to be overlooked. Aristotle was not a Christian, but that did not mean his philosophical categories as presented in his *Metaphysics* were anti-Christian either. As chapter 4 revealed, many of Aristotle's categories—like causation—made good sense out of the material world and even pointed to divinity beyond this world. Nevertheless, some medieval theologians (though not all) *abused* Aristotle's distinction between "substance" and "accidents" for the sake of their interpretation of the Lord's Supper.[266] The substance of the bread and wine was truly changed, transformed, and transubstantiated into the body and blood of Christ, but the accidents—the appearance—looked the same. To reiterate, Rome's use of Aristotle was an *abuse* of Aristotelian categories. As Trueman explains, "Luther's criticism of Aristotelianism at this point is misplaced. Aristotle would have regarded the idea of something having the substance of one thing and the unrelated accidents of another as being incoherent."[267] Yet Luther failed to understand Rome was misusing Aristotle, which explains why Luther blamed the philosopher.

One further correction deserves attention: Luther did not reject transubstantiation because Rome held to the presence of Christ's substance. He rejected transubstantiation because Rome did not retain the substance well enough. Luther's problem "is the absence of the substance of bread and wine . . . rather than the presence of Christ."[268] In other words, by transubstantiating the body and blood of Christ *into* the bread and wine, Christ's real presence was short-circuited. In response, Luther turned philosopher himself: "Why could not Christ include his body in the substance of the bread just as well as in the accidents? In red-hot iron, for instance, the two substances, fire and iron, are so mingled that every part is both iron and fire. Why is it not even more possible that the body of Christ be contained in every part of the substance of the bread?"[269] They "pretend that a new substance is created by God for those accidents on the altar," as if accidents can be "present without substance." By contrast, Luther believed "Christ's body and blood are truly contained there" but refused to speculate as to "what contains them."[270] Luther was happy to be ignorant. He was not troubled if "philosophy cannot fathom this" since the "Holy Spirit is greater than Aristotle."[271]

Luther did not follow his own advice. When he attempted to explain how divinity and humanity operated within the one person of Christ, Luther did return to Lady Philosophy for help: "In order for the divine nature to dwell in him bodily [Col. 2:9], it is not necessary for the human nature to be transubstantiated and the divine nature contained under the accidents of the human nature. Both natures are simply there in their entirety." And in "like manner, it is

---

266. Theologians argue that Aristotle would not have agreed with the use of his distinction. See Van Asselt, *Introduction to Reformed Scholasticism*, 26–44.

267. Trueman, *Luther on the Christian Life*, 148 n. 34; cf. *LW* 36:28–35.

268. Trueman, *Luther on the Christian Life*, 148.

269. *LW* 36:32.

270. *LW* 36:32.

271. *LW* 36:34.

not necessary in the sacrament that the bread and wine be transubstantiated and that Christ be contained under their accidents in order that the real body and real blood may be present."[272]

In 1520 Luther had yet to reveal, at least in all its maturity, his alternative to transubstantiation (see chapter 10), but as his appeal to Christology conveyed, the seeds were present. Nevertheless, he did not conceal in the slightest his opposition to Rome's doctrine of the Eucharist, and the Reformation that followed in Luther's trail would in due time define itself by that same hostility, even if other Reformers came to disagree with Luther over what the supper did signify.[273]

Is Christ Sacrificed on the Altar?

Every priest verbalized "the canon of the mass," that instance in the liturgy when certain words were said in Latin to enact the miracle of transubstantiation: "We humbly beseech Thee, most merciful Father, through Jesus Christ, Thy Son, our Lord, that Thou wilt deign to be pleased with and bless these gifts, these presents, these holy unspotted sacrifices, which we offer Thee especially for Thy holy universal Christian Church."[274] That phrase "unspotted sacrifices" is loaded with meaning. "It is the common belief," said Luther, "that the mass is a sacrifice, which is offered to God."[275] Other phrases spoken throughout the liturgy implied the same, such as "this offering" and "the sacrifice of the altar."[276]

Rome also believed the sacrament was an *opus operatum*. The "mass is effective simply by virtue of the act having been performed," irrespective of the beneficiary's faith.[277] The priest also recited the canon of the Mass quietly and in Latin, both of which made it nearly impossible for the laity to hear.[278] The priest's own words had the power to usher Christ down from the heavenlies for this sacrifice. And many priests did so in a service embedded with elaborate rituals, or what Luther called "the glamor of the ceremonies" and a "multitude of pompous forms."[279]

It was this third captivity that convinced Luther that Rome had misunderstood the effects of the gospel itself. The Mass is a "covenant," "testament," or "promise," said Luther. A promise of what? A promise "of the forgiveness of sins made to us by God." That promise "has been confirmed by the death of the Son of God."[280] In the Mass, then, the promise (word/covenant/testament) is made visible in the sign (sacrament), extended to the recipient who eats and drinks.[281]

---

272. *LW* 36:35.
273. E.g., the English Reformers were martyred not so much for their belief in *sola scriptura* or *sola fide*, or even for their opposition to the papacy, but for their rejection of transubstantiation. See chapter 16.
274. Luther's translation. *Abomination of the Secret Mass*, in *LW* 36:314; referenced in *LW* 36:51.
275. *LW* 36:51.
276. *LW* 36:51.
277. *LW* 36:47.
278. *LW* 36:41.
279. *LW* 36:52.
280. *LW* 36:38.
281. "So in the mass also, the foremost promise of all, he adds as a memorial sign of such a great promise his

If the Mass is a gospel promise, then "access to it is to be gained, not with any works, or powers, or merits of one's own, but by faith alone." *Sola fide* is instrumental. "For where there is the Word of the promising God, there must necessarily be the faith of the accepting man. It is plain therefore, that the beginning of our salvation is a faith which clings to the Word of the promising God, who, without any effort on our part, in free and unmerited mercy takes the initiative and offers us the word of his promise."[282] Therefore, the only right way to approach Mass is with humility: the recipient is an unworthy sinner and should come to the table with the same attitude of a beggar in the presence of his lord. This should be the church's mindset: "I know that I am receiving more than a worthless one like me deserves; indeed, I have deserved the very opposite. But I claim what I claim by the right of a bequest and of another's goodness."[283]

Some in Rome claimed that such unworthiness was reason enough to withhold the cup from the laity.[284] *No!* Luther shouted back. That is the exact reason the laity need the meal, and not just in part but in whole. Plus, how arrogant can we be, how insulting to Christ have we become? "If to him it was not an unworthy thing to bequeath so great a sum to an unworthy person, why should I refuse to accept it because of my unworthiness? Indeed, it is for this very reason that I cherish all the more his unmerited gift—because I am unworthy!"[285] Luther was after consistency in his application of *sola fide*. If we are justified by faith *alone*, then we cannot treat the Mass as if it is a work itself, daring to contribute our own merits so that we are deemed worthy. Consider an illustration:

> What heir will imagine that he is doing his departed father a kindness by accepting the terms of the will and the inheritance it bequeaths to him? What godless audacity is it, therefore, when we who are to receive the testament of God come as those who would perform a good work for him! . . . When we ought to be grateful for benefits received, we come arrogantly to give that which we ought to take. With unheard-of perversity we mock the mercy of the giver by giving as a work the thing we receive as a gift, so that the testator, instead of being a dispenser of his own goods, becomes the recipient of ours. Woe to such sacrilege![286]

---

own body and his own blood in the bread and wine, when he says: 'Do this in remembrance of me' [Luke 22:19; 1 Cor. 11:24–25]." *LW* 36:44.

282. *LW* 36:38–39.

283. *LW* 36:46.

284. *LW* 36:31. They also said that the laity might be tempted to worship the elements and commit idolatry. Luther responded, "How ridiculous! The laymen have never become familiar with their fine-spun philosophy of substance and accidents, and could not grasp it if it were taught to them. Besides, there is the same danger in the accidents which remain and which they see, as in the case of the substance which they do not see. If they do not worship the accidents, but the Christ hidden under them, why should they worship the [substance of the] bread, which they do not see?" (36:32).

285. *LW* 36:46.

286. *LW* 36:48.

Here is the heart of the problem: Rome reversed the intended design of the Mass by turning recipients into givers—givers of their good works. Even the Mass itself becomes a good work. "They all imagine that they are offering up Christ himself to God the Father as an all-sufficient sacrifice, and performing a good work for all those whom they intend to benefit, for they put their trust in the work which the mass accomplishes."[287] But sinners are unworthy recipients, benefactors of God's undeserved grace, and benefactors *alone*. Should sinners turn the Mass into a sacrifice, they turn their attention to themselves and what they can give, but the Mass is supposed to be all about the promise God gives, promises his children receive through simple trust in him.[288]

At the most fundamental level, never does the gospel "sanction the idea that the mass is a sacrifice" to begin with.[289] Christ is not sacrificed on the altar, but his gospel promise is signified in the sacrament. Anyone and everyone can be the recipient of this promise by faith. And with bold confidence too. "For, since the word of divine promise in this sacrament sets forth the forgiveness of sins, let every one draw near fearlessly, whoever he may be, who is troubled by his sins, whether by remorse or by temptation. For this testament of Christ is the one remedy against sins, past, present and future, if you but cling to it with unwavering faith and believe that what the words of the testament declare is freely granted to you." The outcome could not be more applicable to the Christian life: "For faith alone means peace of conscience, while unbelief means only distress of conscience."[290] Any other view "shall lose the whole gospel and all its comfort."[291]

The Freedom of a Christian

Luther's third tract was *The Freedom of a Christian*. If the first two books were polemical, this third book was collegial, an amicable attempt to give the people a presentation of his newfound beliefs and how those beliefs should influence the Christian life. In a word, the book was devotional. How did such a conciliatory work sprout from the soil of Luther's otherwise critical tone? In part, credit should be given to Karl Miltitz, the peacemaker, who repeatedly arranged meetings between Luther and others he knew Luther would respect, including Johann von Staupitz, in order to persuade Luther to write to Leo X himself. The plan was not for Luther to criticize Leo but to reassure the pope that his concerns from the start were a matter of right doctrine and reform, not personal

---

287. *LW* 36:50.

288. "Therefore, just as distributing a testament or accepting a promise differs diametrically from offering a sacrifice, so it is a contradiction in terms to call the mass a sacrifice, for the former is something that we receive and the latter is something that we give." *LW* 36:52.

289. *LW* 36:54.

290. *LW* 36:57.

291. *LW* 36:51. "Now the mass is part of the gospel; indeed, it is the sum and substance of it. For what is the whole gospel but the good tidings of the forgiveness of sins? Whatever can be said about forgiveness of sins and the mercy of God in the broadest and richest sense is all briefly comprehended in the word of this testament" (36:56).

assaults. Luther complied. In the letter, he defended himself by recounting his own defense of the pope in the past. "I have called you a Daniel in Babylon . . . against your defamer Sylvester" [Prierias].[292] When Luther did go on the attack, he did so in reaction to the "ungodliness" of his opponents, like Christ when he "called his opponents 'a brood of vipers.'" But as for Leo, "I have never thought ill of you personally," said Luther.

Nevertheless, while Luther was willing to "yield to any man whatsoever"— Leo included—he had "neither the power nor the will to deny the Word of God."[293] Therefore his convictions remain. So, too, his opposition. For the corruption of the Roman curia was conspicuous: "I have despised your see, the Roman curia, which, however, neither you nor anyone else can deny is more corrupt than Babylon or Sodom ever was, and which, as far as I can see, is characterized by a completely depraved, hopeless, and notorious godlessness." Leo sat "as a lamb in the midst of wolves" and "like Daniel in the midst of lions"; he was Ezekiel: "You live among scorpions." "How can you alone oppose these monsters?" They were, in Luther's estimation, entirely hopeless: "The Roman Curia is already lost, for God's wrath has relentlessly fallen upon it. It detests church councils, it fears a reformation, it cannot allay its own corruption. . . . The Roman Curia does not deserve to have you or men like you, but it should have Satan himself as pope, for he now actually rules in that Babylon more than you do."[294]

For Luther, the pope was one thing, the curia another. But the pope, whether Luther knew it or not, did not assume such a dichotomy. The curia was an apple from the tree. Did Luther really believe accusations at one did not reflect or transfer to the other? Regardless, Luther intended his letter as a plea to Leo. Luther informed the pope that his curia erred by exalting itself high "above a council and the church universal," ascribing to itself alone "the right of interpreting Scripture," but Leo would not have disagreed with the authority and supremacy his curia attributed to him.[295]

Luther sent the letter along with a copy of *The Freedom of a Christian*, a book that "contains the whole of Christian life in brief form."[296] Despite Luther's strong words in his letter to Leo, the book itself is a short, positive presentation of the Christian life in its essentials, one of Luther's most accessible and influential works to this day. Luther wrote it to "make the way smoother for the unlearned."[297]

Luther began at the center. One thing is necessary for the Christian life: "the

---

292. *LW* 31:334. Despite his mention of Prierias and Cajetan, Luther's letter attacked Eck more than anyone, convinced as Luther was that Eck was the real enemy of the pope and all that was Christian. See 31:339–41.

293. *LW* 31:335.

294. *LW* 31:336–37.

295. *LW* 31:342.

296. *LW* 31:343.

297. *LW* 31:344.

most holy Word of God, the gospel of Christ." Without it there "is no help at all for the soul." But the Christian has the Word of God; he has everything and lacks nothing.[298] Unfortunately, there is a gospel famine, said Luther. To make matters worse, posers prevail: there are many different gospels that claim to be authentic but are not. Turning to Romans, Luther identified the true gospel: "The Word is the gospel of God concerning his Son, who was made flesh, suffered, rose from the dead, and was glorified through the Spirit who sanctifies."

How does one receive all the benefits of this gospel? Luther's answer: by faith alone. "Faith alone is the saving and efficacious use of the Word of God." For that reason, it is sufficient: the "soul needs only the Word of God for its life and righteousness, so it is justified by faith alone and not any works."[299] Since no one is righteous, justification must be through faith alone, grounded as it is not in ourselves but in the righteousness of another: Christ. Luther became an evangelist: "When you have learned this [that you are not righteous] you will know that you need Christ, who suffered and rose again for you so that, if you believe in him, you may through this faith become a new man in so far as your sins are forgiven and you are justified by the merits of another, namely, of Christ alone."[300]

Here is that Reformation *sola* that differentiated Luther from Rome: *solus Christus*, Christ alone. An exchange occurs, one entirely dependent on the sinless, sacrificial Mediator: "Christ is full of grace, life, and salvation. The soul is full of sins, death, and damnation. Now let faith come between them and sins, death, and damnation will be Christ's, while grace, life, and salvation will be the soul's." That exchange results in an ineffable union, a union described in Scripture by the marriage metaphor: "For if Christ is a bridegroom, he must take upon himself the things which are his bride's and bestow upon her the things that are his. . . . Her sins cannot now destroy her, since they are laid upon Christ and swallowed up by him. And she has the righteousness in Christ, her husband, of which she may boast as of her own and which she can confidently display alongside her sins in the face of death and hell and say, 'If I have sinned, yet my Christ, in whom I believe, has not sinned, and all his is mine and all mine is his.'"[301] While Luther may not have used more contemporary phrases like "imputed righteousness," that is what he was after, what he so vividly described by means of the union metaphor.

If the sinner is not justified by works, does that mean works are superfluous? Not at all. While works cannot justify, they do sanctify. Works "themselves do not justify him before God, but he does the works out of spontaneous love in obedience to God and considers nothing except the approval of God, whom he would most scrupulously obey in all things."[302] Prior to Christ, the sinner's

---

298. *LW* 31:345.
299. *LW* 31:346.
300. *LW* 31:347.
301. *LW* 31:351–52.
302. *LW* 31:359.

works held him captive to sin, condemning him for transgressing the perfect law of God. But now that Christ's righteousness belongs to the believer, now that justification depends not on works but on the works of the Mediator, the works the believer performs are a sign of liberty. He is not in bondage, but free, liberated to love God and neighbor, not out of anxiety to somehow earn God's favor, but out of joy, knowing that God's favor rests on him entirely apart from himself.[303]

Such a paradox, such a dialectic drove Rome mad. But Luther found it emancipating. Justified by grace alone through faith alone in Christ alone, Luther could now do good works with a pure heart, confident and assured of salvation in Christ, rather than a heart distressed by its inability to merit right standing with God. The Christian, then, is governed by what appears, to some at least, to be a blatant contradiction:

> A Christian is a perfectly free lord of all, subject to none.
> A Christian is a perfectly dutiful servant of all, subject to all.[304]

On one hand, the Christian is free, and insofar "as he is free he does no works." After all, he is justified through faith alone. On the other hand, the Christian is free to work, imitating the humility of Christ, becoming a "servant" in all he does, so that insofar "as he is a servant he does all kinds of works."[305] Put together, on the basis of union with Christ, the believer is then free to imitate Christ. And since suffering is the way of Christ, the Christian's imitation is manifested in the humility of a servant.[306]

If that did not drive Rome mad enough, Luther went further, confessing not only that the sinner is free from works and freed to do works, but counting the believer a *priest* in the service of Christ. For Christ is the Great High Priest, interceding for his bride first by his sacrificial death but also by his ongoing heavenly reign. As those who have been united to this Priest, believers become little priests, so that his church is an entire priesthood of believers (1 Peter 2:9). "Hence all of us who believe in Christ are priests and kings in Christ." Therefore, concluded Luther, "Christ has made it possible for us, provided we believe in him, to be not only his brethren, co-heirs, and fellow-kings, but also his fellow-priests."[307] By empowering the believer with a priestly status and responsibility, Rome's polity was threatened. If every believer is a priest, then why must the Christian depend on a priest to absolve guilt, to assign penance, and to dispense grace through Mass? Can the believer not go directly to Christ and bypass the priest and all the saints, even Mary herself? Furthermore, if the believer has been

---

303. *LW* 31:355–59.
304. *LW* 31:344.
305. *LW* 31:358.
306. Trueman, *Luther on the Christian Life,* 73.
307. *LW* 31:354, 355.

united to Christ, then is not every believer a type of priest who then imitates his master whenever he intercedes on behalf of his brother or sister in Christ?[308]

As these questions demonstrate, *The Freedom of a Christian* may have been a positive, didactical treatise on the Christian life, but it carried within an explosive doctrine, one that made the foundational pillars of Rome shake.

A WILD BOAR RAVAGING GOD'S VINEYARD

Before Luther wrote his flurry of theological treatises in the fall of 1520, Pope Leo decided to take action, the severest and most serious action the pope could have taken: he issued a bull promising excommunication if Luther did not recant in sixty days and communicate his change of mind to Rome by an additional sixty days.

Eck's hand in the indictment was obvious. After Leipzig, Eck's reaction to Luther's epistemological claims was ferocious. Eck wasted no time; he traveled to Rome and handed off his latest publication on the authority and primacy of the pope and his papacy. Eck embarked on a quest to see Luther undone, calling Luther a heretic, insisting the pope pursue a trial. To his satisfaction, Eck was appointed with others to write up an indictment. The indictment identified and rejected forty-one statements by Luther and warned Luther that if he did not recant each one of them, then he would be excommunicated. With Pope Leo's approval, this indictment became official, published on June 15, 1520, as *Exsurge Domine*, "Arise, O Lord." Luther was described as a wild boar, destroying the vineyard of the Lord by his teachings. If he did not stop, the Lord himself would return to his vineyard and hunt Luther down by virtue of his earthly representative, the pope. As was custom, Luther's books were piled together and burned, a visible warning and ominous threat to the Reformer.[309]

The papal bull, however, did not entirely work in the papacy's favor. Released in the summer of 1520, the bull was rushed, which showed in its odd compilation of forty-one sentences attributed to Luther. However, these sentences did not always represent Luther with accuracy or focus on the most important issues under debate. Moreover, some of the bull's reasons for condemning Luther had not been officially resolved by the papacy itself, but diversity of opinions existed. How ironic: Luther was condemned by a bull for a host of matters, yet none of them were justification by faith alone, a reminder that in the eyes of the papacy Luther's opposition to other doctrines, especially transubstantiation, proved the breaking point.[310]

Luther did not receive the bull until the end of the year, as late as December, although the broad contours of its contents traveled almost right away. What did he think of it? The erratic focus of the bull's forty-one sentences was frustrating

---

308. On this last question, see Trueman, *Luther on the Christian Life*, 74.

309. To hear Luther's response to Rome forbidding his books, see *LW* 44: 221–29.

310. These points and many more are also made by Hillerbrand, "Martin Luther and the Bull Exsurge Domine," 109; Hillerbrand, *Division of Christendom*, 51.

if not infuriating. After all Luther had been through, after all Luther had written, the papacy still did not understand the essence of his protest or his vision for reform. Granted, the bull was released prior to Luther's publication of *The Babylonian Captivity of the Church*, but still Luther had published and said more than enough for the papacy to understand the heart of his differences. In addition, the bull did not add credibility to the German public's opinion. "Far from clarifying the controversy, the bull was bound to intensify the uncertainty among the theologians and the common people," said Hans Hillerbrand. Observers "were forced to conclude that the sloppiness of the bull was evidence of Luther's unfair treatment by the church."[311]

Luther's public response was as dramatic as Rome's bull was serious. Luther and his sympathizers met at the Chapel of the Holy Cross in Wittenberg, right at the spot where diseased rags from the deceased were burned to avoid contamination. On December 10, 1520, Luther displayed his resolve not to back down. He threw into the flames the pope's bull, as well as volumes of canon law and papal decretals.[312] As they burned in the flames, Luther said, "Because you have grieved the saints of the Lord, may eternal fire grieve you."[313] Now Luther's fate was sealed: excommunication was inevitable and death by execution was most probable. Luther's actions made a statement, one that was irrevocable, and all of Rome heard about it.

In his letter to Leo, the one attached to his *Freedom of a Christian*, Luther tried his hardest to separate the pope from his curia. But that letter was written before Luther received and burned Leo's bull. Now that excommunication was pending, Luther's rhetoric changed: *the pope is Antichrist.* Luther's bold charge was not novel, but he placed himself within a medieval stream that voiced the same.[314] Since Leo thinks he, as pope, does not derive his "existence, strength, and dignity from Scripture" but "Scripture from him," Luther believed he was justified in his accusation: the pope is the "man of lawlessness," leading "all the world to sin and hell."[315] The pope and his curia thought the same of Luther. The real question was, *who would be sent to hell first?*

In retellings of the Reformation, it is sometimes assumed Luther broke with Rome.[316] Luther was no bystander—he did take an irreversible, even

311. Hillerbrand, *Division of Christendom*, 51.

312. Luther outlined all the errors in the books he burned in thirty theses (or articles). See *LW* 31:385–95.

313. Quoted in Hillerbrand, *Division of Christendom*, 55, who also observed, "It was not so much the burning of the bull that was so offensive, although papal authority had been dramatically defied with this act, but the burning of copies of the decretals and canon law, the very foundation of societal and religious law and order. Quite profoundly Luther noted to Spalatin, 'the dice has been cast.' He had defied the church."

314. Kolb, *Martin Luther,* 90; cf. Hendrix, *Luther and the Papacy.*

315. The man of lawlessness is a reference to 2 Thessalonians 2. *LW* 31:392; cf. 32:3–100.

316. "People were drawn to him because his writings appeared to be theologically orthodox (at least they emphatically made that claim). They assumed that the church would come to realize his orthodoxy and spiritual concerns before long. Certainly until Luther's excommunication in 1521, support for Luther was not taken to entail defiance of the Roman Church. Luther—we do well to remember—outdid himself with expressions of loyalty to church and pope as late as 1520, for example, in his cover letter to Pope Leo in the treatise of Christian freedom." Hillerbrand, *Division of Christendom*, 88.

stubborn stance that stood counter to the papacy of his day. However, Luther protested from *within*, as one catholic to another. He did not break with Rome, but Rome did break with him, removing the Reformer from its body, handing him over to Satan and hell itself (nothing was more condemning than excommunication). On January 3, 1521, the pope issued a final bull, *Decet Pontificem* (It Is Fitting That the Pope), and Luther was denounced by the church.

It was now official; Luther was a heretic.

The label *heretic* was a damning one. For it not only conveyed misbelief but ungodliness, the type that is saturated in narcissism. In Lombard's *Sentences*, he quoted Augustine's definition of a heretic to this effect: "A heretic is one who, for the sake of some temporal advantage, and especially for the sake of his own glory and pre-eminence, either gives rise to, or follows, false or new opinions."[317] For the Fathers and Scholastics, theology was not divorced from spirituality. The road to unorthodoxy was paved by selfishness and stubbornness, vain glory at the expense of divine majesty. Was Luther a man out for himself, lobbying his false and novel opinions out of a sense of self-glory? The year 1521 was not the last year Luther heard that accusation.

Although the pope's excommunication was supposed to be the end of Luther, the Wittenberg professor was well protected as long as he stayed within German territory. Churches in his jurisdiction allied themselves with Luther and now looked to this heretic to decide how the church should look different moving forward.

CAPTIVE TO THE WORD OF GOD: WORMS (1521)

As instrumental as previous disputations may have been to Rome's confrontation of Martin Luther, the Diet of Worms escalated the conflict to an imperial stage. For unlike prior confrontations, now the emperor himself, Charles V, summoned Luther to give an answer for his writings.

At first Charles had moderate interest in dealing with Luther himself. Luther had been excommunicated by the church; that should have been the end of it as far as Charles was concerned. The church had already decided this heretic's fate. Furthermore, Charles was far more interested in his political affairs with Spain than theological squabbles within German territories, which were altogether another world to Charles, who did not even speak the language. However, Charles could not disregard his responsibilities as emperor in German lands, especially when the estates insisted he give Luther an honest and just hearing, unconvinced Luther had yet to receive one. Charles could not ignore their demands since his office as emperor was conditioned on the inability to condemn someone as an outlaw until that person had his day in court. Many other reasons for a diet weighed heavy on him. For example, those like Frederick already despised a foreign verdict from Rome deciding the fate of one of their own.

---

317. Augustine, *De utilitate credenda*, ch. 1 n. 1; Lombard, *Sentences* 4.14.1.

The estates were clear they were not about to follow the papacy's instructions to subdue Luther let alone hand him over for execution. Since Charles depended on the support of the estates, he had to listen. He could not afford a rebellion at the start of his reign, which might fracture his empire and diminish his power.[318]

At the same time, Charles had to consider how the other side might react. Summoning Luther to a diet might appease the estates, but it could also incur the wrath of the papacy, which Charles also did not want. The papal bull had already settled the matter, but opening the Luther case up once more conveyed a different message. According to the papacy, the secular authorities in other countries should carry out whatever punishment followed from the church's decision (especially in the case of excommunication), not reopen the case for further investigation or discussion.[319] Furthermore, why give the heretic a hearing at all? To do so might give the populace an opportunity to rise up—Luther was, after all, popular among the German people. But then again, if Charles denounced Luther without an official diet, that, too, might stir up the masses. Injustice might fuel a mob. Both options were risky, but Charles capitulated to the estates in the end. He was an emperor, and adjudicating the current division at least exhibited his leadership and reinforced his power not merely over his empire but over Christendom itself.[320]

That did not mean, however, that delegates agreed on whether Luther should appear at the diet. In January 1521 the delegates met but struggled to reach a consensus. The room grew tense, and Elector Joachim of Brandenburg and Elector Frederick went after each other, nearly exchanging punches.[321] In the end, they decided that Luther must appear and stand before Charles. That March Luther received notice.

Some thought Luther must be a fool to go. Jan Hus was promised safe passage to the Council of Constance only to be executed. Surely Luther's fate would be the same. But Frederick secured official letters from the emperor and his princes to guarantee Luther's safe passage to and from the diet. Nevertheless, Luther considered the possibility of death and trembled at the thought of his flesh burning. Yet Luther was a Christian with conviction. Should he not turn up now, his stance against Rome's moral and doctrinal corruption might lack integrity, even credibility. Luther decided he must pick up his cross and die if he must.[322]

---

318. For more on this context, see Hillerbrand, *Division of Christendom*, 56.

319. "The papal nuncio Aleander bluntly reminded the emperor and the estates that the church had spoken, that a condemned heretic could not receive a further hearing, and that it was the responsibility of the secular authorities to issue a mandate against Luther and his followers without delay. The emperor shared Aleander's sentiment for prompt action, but his chancellor Gattinara urged him not to proceed against Luther without consultation with the estates. Gattinara realized that the emperor could hardly afford a confrontation with the estates at the very beginning of his rule since he needed their support in the future." Hillerbrand, 56.

320. Even the papal nuncio came around: "Aleander realized that Luther's citation was in the best ecclesiastical interest: Luther's recantation might resolve the whole controversy, and if he did not recant, his condemnation by the diet would put the blame on the German rulers rather than on the Roman curia." Hillerbrand, 57.

321. Hendrix, *Martin Luther*, 100.

322. "We will come to Worms in spite of all the gates of hell." Or as Luther later said, "We will come to

Yet Luther considered how even Jesus, prior to the cross, was celebrated with cheers as he rode into Jerusalem on a donkey. When Luther stopped in Erfurt on his way to Worms, he called the jubilee entrance his Palm Sunday.[323] A parade of horsemen escorted Luther into the city, which proved necessary as the crowds pressed in, every person eager to get a glimpse at the man who dared to oppose pope and emperor. The next day, Sunday, Luther preached and condemned the corruption he had seen in the church, lamenting that few preachers of the true gospel were left.[324]

Luther became ill along the way, which Luther attributed to Satan, a tactic attempting to keep Luther from his cross. Nevertheless, he arrived in Worms at last, April 16, 1521. The population had doubled, and the requests for visitations with Luther were innumerable. These requests could not be met. Luther had little time; he was expected to appear the next day, the afternoon of April 17. Maneuvering the path to ensure he stood in the room that afternoon was no easy task. He later remembered how large the crowd was; some even climbed onto rooftops for the chance to see the Reformer. Luther had to be escorted through an alternative route.[325]

John Von der Ecken, not to be confused with the Eck at Leipzig, ran lead, questioning Luther. Ecken got right to the point, informing Luther that he was summoned by the emperor for two reasons: to acknowledge his publications and to retract every one of them. Luther was not summoned to debate the issues under controversy but to revoke or else face the emperor's judgment.

When faced with this direct ultimatum, Luther did not take it lightly. He acknowledged the large table with his books, but when asked if he would revoke his views, Luther was anything but flippant. He was not some hasty heretic. "Because this is a question of faith and the salvation of souls, and because it concerns the divine Word, which we are all bound to reverence, for there is nothing greater in heaven or on earth, it would be rash and at the same time dangerous for me to put forth anything without proper consideration.... For this reason I beseech your imperial majesty for time to think, in order to satisfactorily answer the question without violence to the divine Word and danger to my own soul."[326] Ecken did not think Luther deserved time to consider. Nevertheless, Luther was granted one day.

Luther returned the next afternoon, dressed in his monastic apparel, and this time he was ready. First, he addressed his books on the table, some in Latin, some in German. It was a sweeping demand to require him to revoke all these writings when they addressed diverse subjects. Luther divided his books into three

---

Worms even if there were as many devils ready to jump on me as there are tiles on the roofs." *WABr* 2:298. Cf. Hillerbrand, *Division of Christendom*, 58.

    323. *WABr* 2:296. Cf. Hendrix, *Martin Luther*, 102.

    324. Sermon at Erfurt on the Journey to Worms, April 7, 1521, in *WA* 7:810; *LW* 51:65. Cf. Hendrix, *Martin Luther*, 102.

    325. *LW* 32:106.

    326. *LW* 32:107.

categories: morals, attacks on the papacy, and private debates with specific individuals. To begin with, how could he disavow his books on morality? "Would not I, alone of all men, be condemning the very truth upon which friends and enemies equally agree, striving alone against the harmonious confession of all?" Never could he take back his attacks on the papacy, either on their "doctrines" or their "wicked examples." "If, therefore, I should have retracted these writings, I should have done nothing other than to have added strength to this [papal] tyranny and I should have opened not only windows but doors to such great godlessness. It would rage farther and more freely than ever it has dared up to this time."[327] Luther did confess that his private writings against "distinguished individuals" were "more violent than my religion or profession demands." But Luther never pretended to be a saint. Anyway, it "is not proper for me to retract these works, because by this retraction it would again happen that tyranny and godlessness would, with my patronage, rule and rage among the people of God more violently than ever before."[328] Regardless which work was in view, Luther challenged Ecken to identify where he erred. If he had erred, then he promised to be "quite ready to renounce every error, and I shall be the first to cast my books into the fire."[329]

Luther's response did not sit well with Ecken, who interpreted Luther's explanation as a "horned" reply, lacking lucidity and transparency. Ecken also used Luther's survey of his own works as an opportunity to classify Luther with the heretics of the past, both Hus and Wyclif. Their fate might just be Luther's as well: "[If you] continue to persist in your notorious errors and heresies, as you have begun to do, there is no doubt that all memory of you will be wiped out."[330]

Ecken questioned Luther's motives as well: Was Luther so proud to think he was the first one to read the Bible? "Do not, I intreat you, Martin, do not claim for yourself that you, I say, that you are the one and only man who has knowledge of the Bible, who has the true understanding of holy Scripture, to which understanding the most holy doctors toiling night and day in the exposition of Scripture, have attained through great labor and effort."[331]

In response, Ecken demanded a "simple" reply. Stop expecting debate, he told Luther. Face the matter head on and give an "answer sincerely and candidly, not ambiguously, not dialectically, whether or not you wish to recall and retract your books and the errors contained in them, which have been disseminated by you."[332]

Ecken asked for it, so a simple reply is what he then received in return, and one that displayed Luther's fixed resolve. The words Luther spoke next were not only clear but bold and have forever since been cemented in the minds of any heritage

327. *LW* 32:110.
328. *LW* 32:111.
329. *LW* 32:111.
330. *LW* 32:128.
331. *LW* 32:129.
332. *LW* 32:130.

that traces its origin back to the Reformation. "Since then your serene majesty and your lordships seek a simple answer, I will give it in this manner, neither horned nor toothed: Unless I am convinced by the testimony of the Scriptures or by clear reason (for I do not trust either in the pope or in councils alone, since it is well known that they have often erred and contradicted themselves), I am bound by the Scriptures I have quoted and my conscience is captive to the Word of God. I cannot and I will not retract anything, since it is neither safe nor right to go against conscience."[333] Luther's famous words were considered bold because he dared to utter them in front of company as distinguished as the emperor himself. Yet his words were also bold because he took his stance on the Scriptures over against the pope. The clash was one of authority, and not just authority but captivity. As Luther spoke these fatal words, there lay his book on the table in front of him, *The Babylonian Captivity of the Church*. The church was captive to its Roman Babylon, but Luther was captive only to the Word of God. From that perspective, Luther was most free, liberated from false teaching, free to obey his conscience, subject only to the gospel life the Word of God brings.

The days that followed involved further dialogue, but without success in persuading Luther to recant. Luther only reiterated his appeal to the final authority of the Scriptures. Again, that did not mean, as it did for future radicals that Luther had yet to encounter, an abandonment of tradition, but merely a right concept of tradition. For instance, to buttress his stance on biblical authority, at one point Luther invoked Augustine's authority. Augustine claimed that only those books in the canon hold truth so absolute, so perfect, so divinely inspired that they should be followed without question. All fathers of the church were to be followed as well, but only insofar as they adhered to the truth of the Scriptures.[334] *Sola scriptura* at Worms may have sounded shocking to his opponents, but Luther was saying nothing that church fathers before him had not said already.[335] *Sola scriptura* was a catholic doctrine, Luther insisted.

That is no small point since several modern theologians (see chapter 1) have attempted to read Luther's words at Worms as the stance of an Enlightenment man, an individual revolutionary protesting the received tradition of the church. To say, as Luther did, that he could not go against "conscience" or "clear reason" made Luther, so it is argued, a precursor to the Enlightenment, a movement that prided itself on the elevation of human reason over against the mindless adherence to ecclesiastical traditions. Unless a doctrine passed the test of reason, it was to be discarded. Others have gone so far as to blame Luther, as if his rugged autonomy unleashed modernity and all the secularism that followed. But that is

---

333. In the Latin text in which Luther's words are recorded, a German sentence is added: "I cannot do otherwise, here I stand, may God help me, Amen." It is possible Luther said these words, but some believe it apocryphal. *LW* 32:112,–13.

334. *LW* 32:118.

335. Consider Henry of Ghent, who came to the same conclusion in the thirteenth century, says George. George, *Reading Scripture with the Reformers*, 113.

to misread Luther in the most anachronistic of ways. Luther appealed to his conscience but only because his conscience was *captive to the Word of God*. Reason was ministerial for Luther, a tool to understand Scripture properly, which was Luther's magisterial authority. Luther was not setting the Scriptures and "clear reason" up as two competing authorities. Luther rather meant that the pope himself needed to persuade Luther with a logic that was as lucid as it was biblical. Neither Rome nor Luther could have envisioned a world in which reason stood on its own, autonomous from either the Scriptures or the theological perception of the world they both inhabited. Reason and the Scriptures are both from God and serve to embody his truth; to go against one is to go against the other.

By the next day, Charles had already decided against Luther. Although the estates wanted further deliberation, Charles had made up his mind that Luther was a heretic as Rome had said, an enemy of the church to whom Charles was most loyal. Nevertheless, the estates prevailed in convincing Charles that a fair investigation and trial must show Luther exactly where he had erred. But when they did, Luther budged not an inch. The papal nuncio Aleander tried to find a solution to the conflict that might appease both sides: the authorities would not hunt down Luther and punish him so long as Luther did not keep spreading his opinions. Neither side was persuaded. They thought Luther's beliefs were heretical, and Luther was not the type to settle for a life of silence.[336] No solution to the impasse was possible. Therefore, Charles moved forward with an edict, one that cemented a division in Christendom that has never been repaired.

CHARLES, EDICT, AND EMPIRE

After Worms, Charles published an official edict labeling Luther and anyone who helped him an *outlaw*. That edict, published about a month after Luther left Worms, put Luther in grave danger. Nevertheless, inside Electoral Saxony Luther was more or less safe thanks to the protective efforts of Frederick, who convinced Charles not to press the edict in his territory.[337] Perhaps it seemed to others advantageous for Charles to take swift action and arrest Luther. But such a hasty maneuver could have put Charles himself in a precarious position. An arrest or an execution might instigate insurrection by the German people or forfeit support from Frederick, elector of Saxony, and other German territories.

To understand Charles's predicament, consider the years 1509 to 1519. These years represent a shift in political power as new kings ascended their thrones across Europe: Henry VIII in England (1509), Francis I in France (1515), and Charles of Habsburg in Spain (1516). Out of the three, however, Charles became the next Holy Roman emperor (1519), which granted him an authority without parallel. "The election consolidated Charles's claims under various titles, to lands that today roughly comprise Germany, Holland, Belgium, Austria,

---

336. Hillerbrand, *Division of Christendom*, 61.
337. Hendrix, *Martin Luther*, 108.

Switzerland, the Czech Republic, Hungary, Slovakia, parts of Northern Italy, and eastern France."[338]

With such incomparable power and authority, Charles could have eliminated Luther in the aftermath of Worms. Yet he could not do so without further compromising his need for allies to buttress his fight against other threatening powers. First, Charles faced off with Francis I. In 1515 Francis had conquered the Duchy of Milan, stealing it away from the Holy Roman emperor.[339] Four years later, when Charles became Holy Roman emperor, Francis felt sandwiched between territories now loyal to the emperor. As Francis and Charles evolved into colossal rivals, the two rulers entered a spiral of warfare, Francis ever trying to hold on to Milan, losing then winning only to lose again throughout the early 1520s. Charles appeared to gain the upper hand time after time; the conflict was a perpetual threat to his empire, one he could not afford to lose.

Yet Francis was not the only threat Charles faced. Charles also had to square with the increasing invasion of the Turks due to the leadership of Sultan Suleiman the Magnificent. From 1521 to 1529, the Sultan marched across Europe, taking one territory at a time, striking fear into the hearts of Europeans, wondering whether all of Europe might become Muslim soon enough.[340] With the Turks on his left and Francis on his right, Charles could not afford to lose the support of German nobles, the elector Frederick of Saxony being one of the most important. To Charles's disadvantage, already he had managed to create resistance. The German nobles were their own masters. Each enjoyed a certain measure of freedom to govern the land and the people under their jurisdiction. The immense extent of Charles's power, therefore, was concerning. The last thing they wanted was an emperor bent on intrusion. "They resented him [Charles] and saw in the religious turmoil sparked by Luther's success a chance to reduce him to size."[341] In one sense, it did not matter whether the nobles decided for Luther or remained in the traditional church. They did not appreciate Charles dictating the terms, let alone controlling the destiny of a theologian under the jurisdiction of one of their very own, the elector of Saxony.

This tension continued into the 1530s until the German nobles joined together and formed the Smalcald League, creating a unified barrier against Charles, while helping advance the Reformation at the same time. Early in Luther's conflict with Rome, Luther had pleaded for a free council. Now the Smalcald League took up Luther's banner with Charles, insisting a council on their own German soil was the right way to enter into peace talks over the

---

338. O'Malley, *Trent*, 52.

339. "That triumph allowed him, as mentioned, to sign the Concordat of Bologna with Pope Leo X, which delivered into his hands the nomination of French bishops." O'Malley, 50.

340. "The fall of Constantinople in 1453 had opened the gates of Europe to the Turks. Hardly had Suleiman come to the throne in 1520 when he led his troops in a successful campaign against the Christian strongholds of Belgrade, Rhodes, and most of Hungary, so that by 1529 he arrived at the gates of Vienna itself." O'Malley, 53.

341. O'Malley, 52.

Reformation and its future. However, by the 1530s the case for a free council on their home turf was complicated by a Lutheran view of the papacy, church councils, and the church itself. These were significant enough ecclesiastical barriers to prohibit traditionalists from cooperating.[342]

Even though Charles hated what Luther stood for and could not disagree more with Luther's protest, nevertheless, Charles agreed with the German nobles that a council was the best way forward. After all, Charles was first and foremost concerned with preserving the unification of his own empire. If he retained a unified empire, his power not only remained undiminished, but he had the potential to increase his prominence. Internal conflict, especially war, could undermine both the unity and the supremacy of Charles all at once and leave him prey to foreign powers, whether they be the French or the Turks or the pope himself.[343]

Both the French and the papacy resented Charles's advocacy for a council. They recognized it for what it was: a maneuver to solidify Charles's power, and one that simultaneously gave the Reformation the hearing (and legitimacy) it wanted. That did not deter Charles, but the emperor spent the next two decades laboring to make this council a reality. To Charles's dismay, the council did finally meet at Trent starting in the 1540s, but it was not the council Charles originally envisioned, and it certainly was not the council German Protestants favored.

WHOSE EDICT, WHOSE HERETIC?

The emperor had condemned Luther as an outlaw in his May 25 edict. Still, controversy ensued over the legitimacy of the edict itself. For the diet had already concluded. Charles and Elector Joachim of Brandenburg released the edict, which said the counsel as well as the estates were in total support, including electors and rulers. That was not true. It could not be true since so many of them had departed before the edict was even released.

Mishandling the edict was a poor political maneuver on the part of Charles. Charles moved forward with the diet to appease the estates, but now he had decided on a verdict without the estates. He had unraveled the whole fabric of the diet. Yes, an edict was pronounced, but it was the edict of Charles, said many when they heard the news. It was not an edict reached by a "unanimous counsel," as Charles claimed. Some even questioned whether the edict was legitimate at all.[344]

The mishandling of the edict did not deter the confidence of Charles, however. In his mind, he had dealt with Luther, granted the estates the fair hearing they demanded, and appeased his Catholic conscience and constituency by

---

342. O'Malley, 53.
343. O'Malley, 55, goes so far to say Charles was pro-council because he believed even the heretic deserved to be heard and considered.
344. Hillerbrand, *Division of Christendom*, 61.

declaring the heretic an outlaw, further confirming the papacy's verdict. Charles wasted no time in leaving Worms for Spain, where his good name needed to be repaired.[345] His presence in Spain was reasonable enough, but his absence only erected yet another barrier to the edict's effectiveness. Distracted by real challenges to his name in Spain, Charles was not present to enforce the edict and silence Luther the outlaw.[346]

Furthermore, Charles had underestimated both Luther and his followers. They were not a group of individuals with like-minded ideas; they were on the cusp of turning into a movement in their own right.[347] By the time Charles realized he was not dealing with one passionate, obscure monk, it was too late. In time he came to curse the day he promised safe passage to the German Reformer who forever remained a thorn in the side of the emperor.

Amid the controversy over the legitimacy of the edict, Luther left Worms on April 26, 1521. The journey was fraught with risks. Luther and his guards were told they would never make it back alive. Sure enough, as Luther's party made their way through the Thuringian forest, two masked men on horseback stopped them in their tracks and took Luther. Had Luther's safe conduct guarantee been violated much like Hus? To the public, it appeared Luther had been kidnapped, and they now waited, expecting to hear the worst: Luther was executed. Albrecht Dürer's turmoil was shared by many: "O God, if Luther is dead, who will henceforth proclaim to us the holy Gospel?"[348]

But not all was as it seemed.

---

345. "After some difficult negotiations, a *Reichsregiment* had been installed to exercise a coordinating function in his absence; he had turned over the Austrian lands and the claims to Bohemia and Hungary to his brother Ferdinand; and he had disposed (on paper, that is) of the heretical menace.... Not surprisingly, he directed his attention to Spain, where his election to the imperial throne had been received with ill-concealed apprehension. The prospect of an absentee ruler and higher taxes, the latter a virtual prerequisite for Charles's exercise of the imperial office, was hardly calculated to arouse warm feelings. Moreover, the *comuneros* revolt, a rebellion of towns against the nobility had erupted in May 1520, and even though it was quickly suppressed, it underscored deep problems in Spain and the necessity of Charles's presence." Hillerbrand, 140.

346. On the succession of popes after Leo X, see Hillerbrand, 141.

347. "The issue was not, as Charles assumed, a single monk with heretical ideas, but a movement of increasingly widespread dimension." Hillerbrand, 73.

348. Quoted in Heidrich, *Albrecht Dürer's schriftlicher Nachlass*, 96. Cf. Hillerbrand, 72.

9

REFORMING THE REFORMATION

Liturgical Catholicity and Prospects for Renewal

> *I trust they [the peasants] will not steal my courage and joy. Their own god [the devil], and no one else, may believe their statement that they are not like Müntzer.*
>
> —Luther to John Rühel

> *In comparison with Luther's Bible, almost everything is just literature, that is, it is a thing that has not grown in Germany and has not grown, and is not growing into German hearts as the Bible had done.*
>
> —Friedrich Nietzsche

> *One little word shall fell him.*
>
> —Luther, "A Mighty Fortress Is Our God"

What looked like a kidnapping was in truth a rescue mission. Luther was taken by the two men, and instead of heading back to Wittenberg, they hid Luther away in the Wartburg fortress near Eisenach. The two men were commissioned by Frederick. Fresh out of Worms and doubtless to be declared an outlaw, his exile was now a necessity.[1] Luther was kidnapped, but it was the most amicable kidnapping in history, one to be expected, at least as long as the German Reformer had friends in high places.

THE WARTBURG (1521–22)

If Luther's pilgrimage to Worms was his Passion, the Wartburg was his Patmos.[2] Except for a few select individuals, no one knew where Luther was or how to get in touch with him. That was as it had to be. And it had to be that way for some time. To keep his identity hidden, Luther had to blend in. Wartburg, a castle built in the eleventh century, was the perfect hiding place. Wearing his Augustinian attire did not exactly exude an inconspicuous look. So Luther

---

1. *WABr* 2:305; *LW* 48:202. Cf. Hendrix, *Martin Luther*, 108–9.
2. *WABr* 2:347–49; *LW* 48:236. Cf. Hendrix, 110.

dressed as a knight instead and took the name Junker Jörg as an alias. Those who came across the knight, now adorned by a full beard, had heard rumors that he had noble blood. And yet the name Junker Jörg did not sound like any celebrity they knew.

Luther remained in exile for almost a year—May 4, 1521, to March 1, 1522.[3] He was no stranger to quiet seclusion or the spiritual tumult that accompanied confinement. Yet his time in Wartburg was different than his monastic life. This time he was an outlaw in the empire and an enemy of the church. Despite his breakthrough discovery, despite his courageous stand at Worms, Luther now retreated to four walls of lonely exile. Some days the confinement of those walls galvanized Luther to write and encourage the church out in the world. Some days those walls seemed to close in on Luther, suffocating him with questions, doubts, and insecurities. "My heart often trembled and pounded and reproached me," Luther said, reflecting on his year in hiding. Was he the reforming catholic he thought he was, or was he a heretic like the church thought? He asked himself, "Are you alone wise? Is everyone else in error? Have so many centuries been in ignorance? What if you have been wrong and dragged many with you into error and eternal damnation?"[4]

In hiding, solitary and secluded, Luther kept the line of communication open with his sympathizers back in Wittenberg now attempting to institute the reforms Luther had made possible. Spalatin was key, the main messenger between Luther and others. Luther corresponded with Philip Melanchthon in particular, and over the course of Luther's exile, his trust and reliance on his colleague only grew. Luther not only wrote letters to stay informed on progress, but as Christmas approached, Luther wrote postils to guide the church in its liturgy and instruct preachers on specific texts so that they in turn could teach their people about the incarnation of their Lord. Ministers untrained but nonetheless eager to spread Luther's contagious gospel could even enter their pulpits and read Luther's postils to the people, which had the incredible effect of spreading Luther's ideas in churches everywhere even though the author himself remained unseen.[5]

Not only did Luther write postils, but he also called on his training in the original languages to translate the New Testament into the vernacular. No longer could the German people rely on the Latin, which played to Rome's advantage due to mistakes in the Vulgate; the laity were not proficient in Latin anyway. The German people needed to hear the gospel in their native tongue, translated directly from the Greek. Using the 1519 edition of Erasmus's Greek

---

3. Luther did not step foot in Wittenberg, however, until March 6.

4. *WA* 8:421. Cf. Hillerbrand, *Division of Christendom*, 73.

5. The effect was impressive: "Luther's word echoed from a thousand pulpits and the mouths of clergy for decades, if not centuries, to come, in later years more for the sake of convenience than lack of training." Hillerbrand, *Division of Christendom*, 74. During his time in hiding, Luther also wrote theological works. For example, he responded to Jacobus Latomus (see his *A Lutheran Rejection of the Explanation of Latomus* in *LW* 32:133–260), defending his positions on biblical authority, original sin, and the Christian life.

New Testament, Luther set himself to this herculean task.[6] By the end of his exile, Luther had translated the New Testament.

The product, published in September 1522, was not a sole achievement. Luther was gifted at communicating the Scriptures in a way the German laity could understand. But he needed a colleague to refine the technicalities of his Greek-to-German translation, which is exactly what he found in the young mind of Melanchthon. In the decade ahead, not only Melanchthon but a team of Hebrew and Greek linguists joined Luther to translate the entire canon. Luther interpreted the project on a cosmic scale: "Satan tries his best to make me desert my valuable work and chase after matters of no substance."[7] But Satan failed: in 1534 the German people had a translation of the entire Scripture at last. Revisions followed, but at least the people could read the whole canon in the mother tongue.[8]

LUTHER, THE CANON, AND HERMENEUTICS

To be an authentic source of faith a biblical passage must "Christum treiben," "proclaim Christ." Luther insisted that not all Scripture did so: certainly not the Epistle of James (an "epistle of straw," Luther remarked, that is not worth much), certainly not the book of Revelation. Luther was also ambivalent about the Synoptic Gospels but spoke most highly of the Gospel of John, of Romans, Galatians, Ephesians, and 1 Peter. . . . Luther eased his blunt differentiation in later years to make sure that no one understood him to advocate a revision of the biblical canon. The Epistle of James, after all, was in the canon, and Luther never questioned the decision of the early church in this regard. He meant to call attention to the fact that not all of the Christian canon equally expressed the divine salvation history culminating in Jesus Christ.

—Hillerbrand, *The Division of Christendom*, 77

Yet the people not only had the Bible in their native tongue but had Luther's exegetical and theological thoughts on the Bible as well, a corpus that mimicked the patristics and their many commentaries. Luther included prefaces for each book of the Bible. He also included his notes on specific chapters and verses.[9] By today's standards, Luther had delivered a study Bible to the German people. Although this Bible was more expensive than Luther's New Testament, it sold well and could be seen in the hands of clergy and laity alike, thanks to the labor of German printers.

---

6. Luther did not rely on the Greek alone, but also found help from Erasmus's Latin translation as well as his annotations on the text. See Hendrix, *Martin Luther*, 126ff.

7. *WABr* 7:37. Cf. Hendrix, 240.

8. On their philosophy of translation, see *WA* 38:9–13; *LW* 35:209–16.

9. Hendrix, *Martin Luther*, 240, also notes the inclusion of over a hundred woodcuts as well as the Apocrypha. For specifics on what occurred within a session of translation, see 263.

As anticipated, Rome's response to Luther's translation was hostile. They not only questioned the legitimacy of the translation but challenged Luther's accuracy in specific chapters and books of the Bible. For example, Luther translated Romans 3:28 so that Paul said the "just shall live by faith alone." He added the word *alone*, and papal theologians believed Luther was forcing his theology on the text. In his defense, Luther said Thomas Aquinas did the same. Plus, the context of verse 28 supports the addition of the *sola* since Paul was determined to show justification apart from works.[10]

Despite Rome's critical reviews, Luther's translation project was a success. Its popularity grew, and that was due in part to Luther's way with words. Here was an example of what humanist scholarship could accomplish when tasked with reforming the church. Like so many of Luther's writing projects, the gospel itself was the driving motive, something that cannot be said of all Christian humanists (e.g., Erasmus). The Scriptures first opened Luther's eyes to the righteousness of Christ, a righteousness embraced by faith alone. By giving the German nation these same Scriptures, they might also see that these sacred writings are the garments that wrap the incarnate Christ and hold him out to a world in need of salvation.

BACK IN WITTENBERG

Back home, reform was implemented with expediency. Andreas Karlstadt took immediate and swift action. He attacked the established practice of clerical celibacy, an unscriptural belief if there ever was one, he said. Vows of celibacy were standard among monks and priests alike. But Karlstadt, and Melanchthon as well, proposed a radical alternative: priests should marry if they pleased; no one sins if a vow is broken. Hearing this liberating news, several priests broke their vows and married.

As early as August 1521, Luther took a noncommittal approach to the issue, only willing to support those who had made vows in their youth. But after Luther reflected further on his own experience, as well as the lack of biblical merits for the belief itself, he changed his mind. Vows should not be a law that burdens the Christian. In Christ the Christian is free. By November Luther decided that no one sins if a vow is broken to enjoy God's good gift of marriage and sex.[11]

Dispensing with vows was only the beginning. Karlstadt pushed for many other alterations in the church. If the gospel was for the ungodly, Mass should be said in German. If the Mass was not a recapitulation of the cross, but a promise guaranteeing forgiveness to all who have faith in Christ, then laity should receive

---

10. *WA* 30/2:636ff. Cf. Hillerbrand, *Division of Christendom*, 77. Notice that the Anglican Homilies did something similar; that maneuver was a regular one in patristic and medieval texts (esp. the *Glossa Ordinaria*). See Gatiss, *First Book of Homilies*.

11. Compare: *WABr* 2:370; *LW* 48:277, and *WABr* 2:403; *LW* 48:328. Cf. Hendrix, *Martin Luther*, 120–21; Hillerbrand, *Division of Christendom*, 74.

both elements, the bread and the wine. The church and the priest himself were committing a terrible evil by withholding the wine. In contrast to Karlstadt, Luther was not so black-and-white. Luther agreed that the laity should benefit from both elements. Nonetheless, Luther did not think the church should make or force the laity to take both.[12] To do so hurried reform before it was ready to be accepted and might even scar the consciences of the people so that they retreated to Rome.

Nonetheless, Luther encouraged his supporters, Melanchthon in particular, not to worry about whether the aftermath of new reforms evolved without flaw. "Be a sinner and sin boldly," Luther told Melanchthon. "No sin will separate us from the Lamb, even though we commit fornication and murder a thousand times a day."[13] Luther was not advocating a licentious lifestyle by virtue of the liberty the gospel instituted in the church. In the context of Luther's letter, the Reformer in exile was injecting his colleague with confidence, telling him not to hesitate out of fear for the future and what it might bring. Push on with reform, even if the outcome is messy, said Luther. They were taking the right action; God was pleased with their efforts to purify the church. Leave it to him to smooth out the rough edges that followed.

One day in early December 1521, a traveler stopped in Wittenberg and stayed at the house of Amsdorf hoping not to be seen. If anyone watched closely, they might have noticed several Wittenbergers coming and going, including Melanchthon. Luther had left the Wartburg and snuck into Wittenberg just for a short, secret visit. While Luther happened to be in town, a series of protests turned violent and persisted for days. Priests were intimidated right out of their churches, statutes and altars were demolished, and monks feared for their very lives.[14] Despite Luther's satisfaction with the ecclesiastical reforms so far, measures of violence concerned Luther. Not only was there talk about the public disturbances, some of which had the potential to be violent, but a general attitude of distrust toward the church surfaced in the process, manifesting an insatiable bitterness.

When Luther returned to the Wartburg, he took to writing again, his only medium of influence while in exile, and in little time at all sent off *A Sincere Admonition by Martin Luther to All Christians to Guard against Insurrection and Rebellion*. On one hand, Luther did not disagree with the people's outrage at Rome. He even hoped it might result in change: "I am not at all displeased to hear that the clergy are in such a state of fear and anxiety; perhaps they will come to their senses and moderate their mad tyranny."[15] Luther even invited the wrath of God to descend on the pope for his lies. Should the papists be dismissive and

---

12. *WABr* 2:372; *LW* 48:280. Cf. Hendrix, 121. Also see Luther's stance against private masses: *LW* 36:127–230.
13. *WABr* 2:372; *LW* 48:281–28. Cf. Hendrix, 121.
14. On the specifics, see Hendrix, 123; Hillerbrand, *Division of Christendom*, 79.
15. *LW* 45:58.

say, "O well, the Last Day is still a long way off," Luther reminded them that Jesus said it would happen "in the twinkling of an eye," and before they knew it, they would "lie in a heap at the bottom of hell-fire."[16]

Still, Luther refused to advocate violence. A trust in divine judgment can alone keep the church from picking up the sword. For the sword is only a temporary blow, while the sins of the papacy have eternal consequences. "Their wickedness is so horrible that no punishment is adequate except the wrath of God itself. . . . For this reason I have never yet let them persuade me to oppose those who threaten to use fist and flail."[17] More basic still, insurrection has no good practical outcome, nor should we forget that God himself forbids rebellion.[18] Insurrection is "most certainly a suggestion of the devil" since violence can only strengthen the papal regime.[19] Prayer and truth, however, are his enemies, so Luther encouraged the people to devote themselves to this double-edged sword instead.[20] Like Luther, they must use their mouths not their hands: "Get busy now; spread the holy gospel."[21] In doing so, they, along with Luther, followed the example of their Savior.

The speed of these reforms was too much for Frederick. The Wittenbergers wanted changes to occur, and fast, and they did not hesitate to put their proposal for social and ecclesiastical reform before Frederick that December. Frederick, however, wanted everything to slow down; he did not want Wittenberg in flames by Christmas. Karlstadt refused to listen. When he learned that his plans for instituting changes to the Mass would be opposed at the new year, he started early. On Christmas Day, Wittenbergers assembled in the castle church. Karlstadt not only commenced the Lord's Supper in German but gave both the bread and the wine to the laity, warning the people that they would sin if they did not take both. Then, by accident of course, a few wafers slipped out, falling to the ground. Had the Lord's real body been contaminated? No one presumed to touch the wafers, but in the spirit of the Reformation's rejection of transubstantiation, Karlstadt reached down, picked up the wafers, and moved on.[22]

Karlstadt was just getting started. The day after Christmas, he proposed to Anna von Mochau, and in January the two married. She was only sixteen years old, but the real scandal in the eyes of Rome was Karlstadt's abrogation of celibacy. Karlstadt was the first Wittenberg priest to break his vow of celibacy.[23] However, with the arrival of the new year, violence returned once more. Under the leadership of Gabriel Zwilling, statues of the saints were decapitated and

16. *LW* 45:61. For the stance of city councils on reforming measures, see Hillerbrand, *Division of Christendom*, 80, 89.

17. *LW* 45:61.

18. *LW* 45:62–63.

19. *LW* 45:63–64.

20. *LW* 45:67.

21. *LW* 45:68.

22. Hendrix, *Martin Luther*, 124; Hillerbrand, *Division of Christendom*, 79; Matry, *Martin Luther*, 79.

23. Hendrix, 125.

anything symbolic of Roman theology was thrown to the ground only to be engulfed in flames. In the spirit of iconoclasm, relics were wiped out. By the end of January, Wittenberg had officially committed to Reformation.

When Luther heard, he was determined to return. Frederick resisted, telling the Reformer that now was not the right time. But he could not convince Luther, who had already made up his mind, even if returning meant dying on a cross. Frederick wanted to boast of his relic collection? Well, now he would have a new relic—Luther nailed to a crucifix.[24] If Luther did not return, all chaos would erupt and the devil himself might win in the end. All that Luther had worked so hard to achieve could be lost overnight to impatient churchmen like Karlstadt and violent rebels like Zwilling.

LUTHER AND LITURGICAL CATHOLICITY

On March 6, 1522, Luther stepped foot in Wittenberg at last. The next Sunday, he took to the pulpit in the town church, embarking on the first of eight sermons (the Invocavit Sermons) designed to assist the church with reform but at the right pace and in the right way.[25] Luther did not even have to say a word as he entered the town church with all eyes on him. His attire said it all. He walked into the church dressed as a medieval Augustinian monk, the same attire he wore *before* his exile. He had not changed. "That is how the Wittenbergers had seen him preach all these years, and that is how he stood in front of them—as if he had never preached against monasticism, never argued against monastic vows, and as if he himself had not been the foremost agent of calling the reform."[26]

Luther's disapproval of Karlstadt's methods was insinuated in Luther's attire and his message. Luther refused to rush reform in externals with the same brute force. Nor would Luther make every issue a primary issue or every measure mandatory. Luther wanted change on a range of practices, from monastic vows to private confessions to the presence of statues of saints. But the church had been steeped in these beliefs and practices for hundreds of years. Discarding not only beliefs but visual representations of those beliefs was as scarring as tearing off one's own skin. Karlstadt's hurry left jagged scars hurting those weak in faith.[27] Surgery had to be careful and methodical. Luther's words resonated in part because they were pastoral; he did not want to lose the brother or sister still trying to mature. Luther was essentially holding out his hand and inviting the church to take one step at a time with the Reformer, slow and steady but bold nonetheless.

How could Luther institute reform if he left so much liberty in the hands of the people, allowing them time to change but only when they felt ready and willing? Luther had one answer: *words*. To be precise: the Word. Here was the secret

---

24. *WABr* 2:448; *LW* 48:387.
25. See *LW* 51. Cf. Hendrix, *Martin Luther*, 129.
26. Hillerbrand, *Division of Christendom*, 80.
27. *LW* 53:19.

to Luther's reform. Just as God had spoken through his Son to give his people the gospel, likewise Luther spoke the Word of God to the people of God and let the Spirit transform the heart. Through the Word preached and proclaimed, Satan would fall, if not all at once then one day at a time. The gospel, after all, was the battle ram that brought reform in the first place. "I opposed indulgences and all the papists, but never with force. I simply taught, preached, and wrote God's Word; otherwise I did nothing. And while I slept, or drank Wittenberg beer with my friends Philip and Amsdorf, the Word so greatly weakened the papacy that no prince or emperor ever inflicted such losses upon it. I did nothing; the Word did everything."[28] If the papacy falls, it will only fall as the gospel marches around its walls, not by means of demolition in mere externals. Therefore, the many disputes fixating the Wittenbergers were tertiary and should stay that way. God's Word proclaimed was the means for change.

Nevertheless, by the end of 1523, even Luther felt it was time to speed up the process of reform. Those with weak consciences had been given long enough; it was time to make the changes Luther intended all along. Serving both bread and wine was first on the list.[29] Churches in other German territories could decide for themselves. As for Wittenberg, this change was now implemented with permanent ramifications.[30]

Luther's reforms to the liturgy were not piecemeal, however, as if he nitpicked little alterations that dissatisfied him otherwise. No, Luther's vision for Christian service was holistic. Rome's emphasis fell on the reception of grace for the purpose of merit, which always left the worshiper burdened by the weight of his or her own inadequacy and need to do more to appease God. Transubstantiation, withholding the wine, prayers to the saints, penance, veneration of relics, vigils, private Masses, vows of celibacy, shrines—such a framework communicated an endless cycle of merit. Luther adjusted the paradigm when he announced that every Christian is justified through faith alone. The service had to be reconstructed so that the Christian could come to celebrate what Christ accomplished once and for all, and leave church assured of forgiveness and eternal life, both of which are received through faith in God's promises, as communicated through the preached Word, baptism, and Lord's Supper.[31]

Personally, Luther did not look back; these ecclesiastical reforms were the healthy and natural fruit of his Augustinian soteriology. But the shift was not so obvious to the people who may or may not have already internalized Luther's same intellectual and spiritual conversion. Luther spent his career, as did Melanchthon and other Wittenberg pastors and professors, implementing these

---

28. *LW* 51:77; cf. *WA* 10/3:5. For a thorough look at this theme, see Hillerbrand, *Division of Christendom*, 81; Kolb, *Martin Luther and the Enduring Word of God*.

29. *WA* 12:205–20; *LW* 53:15–40.

30. Luther also had little tolerance for those coming to church only on major holidays, assuming they could still take the elements. Luther required a confession of faith to take the Lord's Supper. See *WA* 12:215; *LW* 53: 32. Cf. Hendrix, *Martin Luther*, 138; *WA* 10:2, 375; *LW* 43:11–12.

31. For an excellent elaboration on Luther's paradigm shift, see Hendrix, *Martin Luther*, 138–39.

external changes until they took root in the hearts and minds of a German laity otherwise steeped in the spirituality of late medieval soteriology.

At the same time, however, Luther's reforms to the liturgy were a renewal of the church's ancient, catholic heritage. His *An Order of Mass and Communion for the Church at Wittenberg,* his *The Formula of the Mass,* and later on his *German Mass,* led the church forward by moving the church backward, returning to a liturgy Luther said aligned with the worship of the true catholic faith. If the historian buys into the tradition-versus-Scripture caricature, one might assume Luther instructed the German church to use nothing but the Bible. Yet Luther should not be confused with those who radicalized *sola scriptura,* transforming the formal principle into *nuda scriptura* (see chapter 13). For Luther, Scripture held primacy in the church, the swaddling clothes presenting Jesus and the gospel to the church. Yet that gospel had been beautifully expressed in all kinds of ways across the history of the church in its varied forms of liturgy. A catholic liturgical tradition had been passed down and embraced. Although Luther desired to rid the liturgy of papal innovations, he saw every reason to preserve all that was truly catholic in the received liturgy. "Loyalty to Scripture did not, therefore, produce liturgical radicalism in Luther's case."[32]

Liberated from a liturgical radicalism, Luther felt free to keep patristic and even medieval elements but provide the church with a truly catholic interpretation of those practices. Luther did not think he was inserting a meaning in a patristic and medieval practice that was never intended. Instead, he saw his fresh interpretation of the liturgy as a recovery of its true meaning, instrumental even, helping the church understand that the Reformation was not disconnected from its liturgical past but was its culmination. In other words, "the liturgy was one of the ways by which the church could symbolize and bear witness to . . . continuity." As Jaroslav Pelikan observed, "It was not his purpose, Luther explained at the beginning of his *Formula of the Mass,* to do away with the liturgy altogether, but to purge the existing liturgy of the abominations that had been added to it. But immediately thereafter, he hastened to print out that the 'additions of the early fathers' did not belong to this category, but were commendable and should be retained."[33]

With that mindset, Luther criticized radicals who removed liturgical traditions from their liturgy altogether, as if everything was a remnant of Roman idolatry. In contrast, Luther retained the *Gloria Patri,* the Apostles' Creed, the elevation of the bread, kneeling before the Lord's table, and other medieval church practices. And when Luther considered the flow of the liturgy as a whole, he kept monastic elements, such as *lectio, meditatio, oratio.* Eventually, he added a fourth: *tentatio.* Luther knew the Christian life was a struggle and tribulation,

---

32. The words of the *Gloria Patri* "were not indeed Scriptural in their exact words"; they "were in harmony with the message of Scripture." Pelikan, *Obedient Rebels,* 83.

33. Pelikan, *Obedient Rebels,* 86. Cf. *WA* 12, 206. Trueman says the same: Luther is "emphatic that it is not his intention to abolish liturgical worship but rather to correct it and purify it in light of his theological reforms." *Luther on the Christian Life,* 100. Cf. *LW,* 53:20.

sometimes with the devil himself. Therefore, *Anfechtung* must enter the liturgy like it does the Christian life.[34] As early as 1523 Luther's liturgy was "essentially a cleaned-up version of the traditional Mass, still in Latin except for the sermon and a few hymns."[35] And when German eventually replaced Latin, Luther insisted that such a change should not be a requirement. He feared such a strict regulation could resurrect the very legalism he worked so hard to bury.

Luther the churchman may have been the most visible proof of Luther the catholic. "All that was noble and good about the word 'Catholic' found an echo in him. Despite his estrangement from Rome, Luther remained a Catholic all his life, and his liturgical views and productions are evidence of this continuity Catholicity."[36]

STAB, SMITE, SLAY: THE PEASANTS' REVOLT (1525)

As irritating as Karlstadt proved to be, a thorn in Luther's side, he was nothing compared to the tens of thousands of German peasants set on revolt. In 1525 tension between peasants and their landlords was explosive.

The peasants worked the land, but the land itself and a majority of the produce it brought forth belonged to their lords. After a day in the dirt, the peasants went home to sleep in the dirt, each peasant family living in a clay hut. By the 1520s the peasants grew intolerant toward the heavy burden of additional taxation. They became disheartened by the "autocratic tendencies of their lords," which "marginalized the peasants in the country and the 'common man' in the towns."[37] In 1524 the conditions were unsustainable in the opinion of the peasants, and riots erupted. They wanted to be heard; better yet, they wanted a say in their future work and living conditions. No longer could they be sidelined; they demanded a seat at the community table.[38] The rebellion may have started small, but it grew large and spread across Germany when the average German citizen joined the cause against the affluent in society. As the movement evolved, the uprising was no longer confined to country peasants; urban peasants joined the revolution and eventually attracted the participation of nobility.

Did the peasants perceive their cause through a Lutheran lens? To a degree. For example, consider the *Twelve Articles of the Swabian Peasants*. The Christian Union addressed many issues of social unrest, but the underlining justification for their protest was an appeal to the authority of God's Word. Their demands were based on God's law, not man's. What did God's law prescribe? Man's law invented autocracy, but God's law prescribed freedom—freedom for everyone

---

34. *LW* 34:285–87; Kolb, *Martin Luther,* 49.

35. "It was not until October 29, 1525, that a full German Mass was celebrated in Wittenberg, and not until 1526 that the liturgy was published." Trueman, *Luther on the Christian Life,* 101.

36. Pelikan, 89. "As he [Luther] defended against his left-wing opponents the freedom to use such forms, so he defended against his Roman Catholic opponents the freedom to dispense with such forms" (91).

37. Hillerbrand, *Division of Christendom,* 143.

38. "Rioters in cities were those who felt deprived of participation in the affairs in their communities. The objective was, as for example in Rothenburg, to bring about a more participatory form of governance." Hillerbrand, 143.

made in God's image. In the church, freedom according to God's law meant that the people had a say in who would be their next minister, a point Luther sympathized with, at least in 1525. In society, freedom according to God's law meant that the people had a say in their work conditions and the equal distribution of revenue and resources.[39] The peasants had listened to Luther when he taught them that the plowboy with the Scriptures was better fortified than the pope himself. Now the common man was ready to apply Luther's principle not only in the church but all of society. If the priesthood of all believers demanded equality in the church, why not the world? Luther could not hide from such an extension of his ideas. His writings up to 1525, particularly *Open Letter to the Christian Nobility*, not only addressed matters of ecclesiology but conditions in wider society. "When the uprising did happen, the influence of Luther and the movement for reform was unmistakable."[40]

At first Luther sought to be diplomatic. He had read *The Twelve Articles* and decided to reply with his *Admonition to Peace* in the spring of 1525. Luther thought this little book could, on one hand, motivate the princes to be flexible, perhaps even soften some, so that they might consider what the peasants wanted. Luther even laid culpability for the current mess at the feet of the princes. As for the peasants, they must not pick up the sword, nor should they be under the impression that the gospel in any way justifies bloodshed or revolution. If anything, the gospel calls on Christians to respect and acquiesce to those God has put in charge. Luther had made a similar point in *To the Christian Nobility of the German Nation* when he advised laity to be subservient to the rulers over them.

Luther's *Admonition to Peace*, however, never even had the chance to effect peace. The peasants wasted no time in revolting, looting, setting castles and monasteries on fire, even spilling blood. Luther was infuriated. Any hope of compromise and concession was now lost. Whatever patience he had harbored was now liquidated. He penned one of his most acerbic tracts in response, *Against the Robbing and Murdering Hordes of Peasants* (1525). These "mad dogs" were doing nothing but "the devil's work."[41] "Fine Christians they are! I think there is not a devil left in hell; they have all gone into the peasants."[42] There was no guiltier verdict in Luther's vocabulary than association or identification with the devil himself. Luther did not think the association was too harsh but believed he was right for three reasons: the peasants broke their oath to remain obedient, started a rebellion that involved violence, and perhaps worst of all, cloaked this "sin with the gospel."[43] All three, said Luther, deserved death, death to soul and body alike, but the third was unforgivable; it was blasphemy itself.

Luther summoned the rulers of the land to act and to act now: "Stab smite,

---

39. Hillerbrand, 143.
40. Hillerbrand, 144.
41. *LW* 46:49.
42. *LW* 46:51–52.
43. *LW* 46:50.

slay." And if "you die in doing it, good for you!"[44] To do nothing was to be an accomplice. "If he is able to punish and does not do it—even though he would have had to kill someone or shed blood—he becomes guilty of all the murder and evil that these people commit." Not grace, but sword, said Luther.[45] And if you die trying to kill one of these rebellious peasants, fear not—you are a "true martyr in the eyes of God."[46]

By its conclusion, the Peasants' War resulted in mass carnage. Different numbers have been estimated, but something like eighty thousand may have died in battle.[47] One of them was none other than Müntzer himself (see chapter 13). At the Battle of Frankenhausen (May 1525), Müntzer and six thousand common folk strapped on whatever weapon they could manage and went out to fight against an army that was trained for warfare and much larger. While Catholics and Protestants did not agree on a range of matters, they did agree to unite their forces. Soldiers under both Duke George of Saxony and Count Philip of Hesse linked arms to fight against Müntzer and his rebel fighters. As expected, Müntzer lost. To discourage future rebellion, they cut off Müntzer's head and showcased it for others to see.

Across Germany the insurrection was snuffed out, dead bodies lay everywhere, and the outcry in Germany was so agonizing it felt unbearable. Luther failed to anticipate the uncontrollable backlash. Luther had summoned support for military action, but he had no control over the extent of retribution. Some on the battlefield had bloodlust, torturing their prisoners and killing them by the tens of thousands without mercy. With countless corpses rotting in the hot summer sun, Luther's commission now seemed cruel, even malicious, and his credibility was tarnished, as was the reputation of the Reformation as a whole. Even those typically on Luther's side cringed. As for the peasants, they no longer trusted Luther; he had betrayed them. They followed Luther's core ideas and took them to their logical end only to have the Reformer himself denounce them and condemn them to death.[48] Luther may have criticized medieval soteriology, but in many ways he remained a medieval man, a continuity conspicuous in his reluctance to break with a conservative feudalism.[49]

Could this be the last days? As blood flowed through fields and streets, not only Reformers like Luther but electors like Frederick of Saxony thought the end must be near.[50] The carnage was apocalyptic in proportion, and the devastation was so severe that recovery felt like an impossibility.[51]

---

44. *LW* 46:54.
45. *LW* 46:53.
46. *LW* 46:53.
47. Hendrix, *Martin Luther*, 156.
48. Despite the damage to Luther's name, the Reformer did not regret his previous writings. He wrote *An Open Letter on the Harsh Book against the Peasants* and further defended himself (*LW* 46:57–87).
49. Trueman, *Luther on the Christian Life*, 81.
50. Hillerbrand believed this eschatology was accompanied by a "ubiquitous sense of despondency." Hillerbrand, *Division of Christendom*, 155.
51. For Luther's interpretation, see *LW* 46:54. Also consult Hendrix, *Martin Luther*, 270–85, for Luther's understanding of the last days.

THE REFORMATION'S FIRST MARTYRS

Luther never imagined he would live long. He knew the fate of Hus, and on numerous occasions thought his own destiny was bound to be the same. Although an outlaw, Luther survived year after year, despite some of his most vitriolic attacks on Rome. However, others who followed Luther's lead were not so fortunate. Even the peasants, as far as they blamed Luther for their massacre, believed the fate of their dead in some sense stemmed from Luther's ideas.

As for religious Reformers, many suffered terrible persecution for following Luther's doctrines and practices and teaching their churches to do likewise. Consider the Augustinian friar, Henry of Zütphen. Henry hailed from Antwerp, Belgium, but he spent a season studying in Wittenberg. Influenced by Luther's theology, Henry returned home and began spreading the Reformation message. He was not alone. Having traveled the same path, Jacob Probst joined Henry on his mission to educate their fellow friars in Luther's doctrine. Many of the friars gave Luther's theology a warm reception; some became so fervent they found ways to spread Luther's thought despite opposition from Margaret of Savoy. Their message, however, was met by resistance when a group of them were captured and condemned in Brussels. The punishment: death. That was enough to pressure many of the friars to retract their allegiance to Luther. But not all. Two friars refused. Their stalwart commitment to the Reformation faith came at a cost: both of them were licked up by the flames in the summer of 1523.[52] Jan van Essen and Hendrik Vos were Protestantism's first martyrs.[53]

Henry of Zütphen and Jacob Probst, however, evaded the authorities and found their way back to Germany. Perhaps they intended to return to Wittenberg and meet up with Luther. On their way, they spread the Reformation message in Bremen. Henry's gift as a preacher was enjoyed by his listeners, and interest in his message grew from surrounding churches. When he was invited to preach outside Bremen at the parish at Meldorf in Dithmarschen by Pastor Nicolas Boye, Henry's friends warned him not to go. It was too dangerous; if the crowds and city officials found him, he could be executed. Henry went anyway, planning only to stay a short time. Sure enough, the warning proved prophetic. Not only peasants, but Dominicans, clergy, and civil leaders all turned on Henry. A drunken mob was recruited, and in the middle of the night Henry was kidnapped, dragged naked in the streets, beaten, stabbed, and finally thrown into the flames.[54] As he died, Henry recited the creed. On December 10, 1524, the Reformation lost another disciple to martyrdom. But many others across Europe were martyred as well: Caspar Tauber in Vienna, Georg Buchführer in Hungary, and still others in Prague.[55]

Luther learned about Henry from Jacob Probst, who was a household guest

---

52. For the full story, see Hendrix, 193.
53. *LW* 32:266.
54. *LW* 32:263.
55. See Luther's account of the whole affair: *LW* 32:266, 272–86.

and longtime friend reaching back to his time in Wittenberg.[56] Luther was so moved by Henry's sacrifice as well as by the need to provide assurance to those Protestants Henry left behind in Bremen that he wrote *The Burning of Brother Henry* (1525).[57] Luther wrote with gusto. Henry's blood "will drown the papacy and its god, the devil." Henry's martyrdom only certified further that he was teaching and preaching the right doctrine under the influence of the Spirit. Luther then associated these first martyrs with the early church's first martyrs. Luther had his proof: the Reformation's authentic catholicity was verified by the blood of its martyrs.[58]

THE CARDINAL ISSUE: LUTHER VERSUS ERASMUS (1525)

If the church, however, had any hope of renewing the core of its catholic heritage, Luther was convinced the people of God needed the Word of God most of all. When Luther went into hiding at Wartburg, he set himself to translating the New Testament from Greek into German and used Erasmus's text to do it. The Reformers did not hesitate to use the labor of humanists to advance their cause. Some Reformers were even trained as humanists prior to their evangelical conversion. But whether the relationship between humanism and the Reformation was formal or informal, the Reformers benefited from the humanists in countless ways. Humanism's call back to the original sources—*ad fontes*—affected education at large, the Reformation included (see chapter 6). The Reformers claimed Rome had misunderstood and even perverted the catholic faith. The only way forward was backward—back to the Fathers—but ultimately to the Scriptures themselves in their original languages.

That did not mean, however, that all humanists became Reformers (see chapter 6). In the case of Justus Jonas, that certainly was true, but the same cannot be said of Erasmus, perhaps the most famous and talented humanist of the sixteenth century. Erasmus, like Luther, believed there were real, serious problems in the papacy. Yet the two did not agree on the solution to these problems. In a letter to Justus Jonas, Erasmus wrote,

> You will ask me, dearest Jonas, why I spin this long complaint to you when it is already too late. For this reason: Although things have gone farther than they ought to have, we should be watchful in case it is possible to still this dreadful storm. We have a pope most merciful by nature, we have an emperor whose spirit is mild and forgiving. . . . If there are things we do not like in the men whose judgment governs human affairs, my view is that we must leave them to their Lord and Master. If their commands are just, it is reasonable to obey; if unjust, it is a good

---

56. See *WABr* 3:400–403; 4:313–14. Cf. Hendrix, *Martin Luther*, 194.

57. Luther also composed *A New Song*, which remembered the martyrdom of Vos and Van Essen. Hendrix, 193.

58. *LW* 32:266. For this reason, in his work against Hanswurst, Luther said suffering was proof the Lutherans were the true catholics. See *LW* 41:193–96.

man's duty to endure them, lest worst befall. If our generation cannot endure Christ in his fullness, it is something nonetheless to preach him as far as we may.[59]

Luther did not share the same mindset. When the pope's commands were just, they were reasonable to be obeyed. But Luther did not agree that the Christian should endure the pope's commands when they were unjust, especially when those same commands taught Christians to believe in a different Christ or way to salvation. Luther had taken a vow to teach God's Word; it was his obligation to say something when others did not. His concern was not merely individual; Luther had pastoral motivations, convinced Rome was leading the sheep astray. Erasmus, on the other hand, disagreed. Not only did he think Reformers like Luther were "raving maniacs," but if he had to choose between the "tyranny of those Pharisees" (Rome) and those "sordid oppressors" (Reformers), the choice was easy: he defaulted to the papacy every time.[60]

Another reason Erasmus and Luther diverged was methodological. For Erasmus, the Scriptures were a mystery. God does not intend everyone—let alone just anyone—to understand them. Many places in the Scriptures are unclear, leaving the reader and interpreter alike perplexed. Who are we to think we can understand what the Scriptures say about a doctrine as difficult and complicated as original sin, for example? Erasmus read Luther's writings on sin and salvation and was offended by Luther's confident arrogance in his interpretation of the Scriptures, as if the Scriptures were that clear. As Erasmus complained to Justus Jonas, Luther is "pouring it all out at once, making even cobblers aware of things which used to be discussed only amongst the learned, as mysteries and forbidden knowledge."[61] But for Luther, the Scriptures were lucid, at least in their main message and with regard to catholic doctrines of the faith like sin and salvation. The Holy Spirit is no skeptic, quipped Luther, especially with a doctrine as essential as original sin. Scripture is repetitive in its clear pronouncement against the will's ability to overcome depravity and merit justification. The meat of the nut—the depravity of human nature, the effect of original sin on the will, and the efficacy of grace—became the dividing line. "Indeed, as you should know," said Luther to Erasmus, "this is the cardinal issue between us, the point on which everything in this controversy turns."[62]

In the years that preceded the debate, Erasmus felt continual pressure to speak out either in favor of or against Luther and his Reformation. Even Luther himself wrote Erasmus in 1519 to persuade him to join his cause, but Erasmus insisted that he must not take sides. However, in time Erasmus became less and less sympathetic and more irritated with Luther's attacks on Rome. Eventually Erasmus

---

59. *WABr* 2:349; *LW* 48:236. Cf. Hendrix, *Martin Luther*, 120.
60. *CWE* 10:376–77. Cf. Hendrix, 169.
61. *EE* 4:487–93 (no. 1202).
62. *LW* 33:35. The following look at the controversy is brief, but for a more extensive look, see Kolb, *Bound Choice, Election, and Wittenberg Theological Method*; Gatiss, *Cornerstones of Salvation*, 15–42.

decided he must dissociate himself from Luther while simultaneously aiming not to harm the cause of reform the two of them desired.[63] Given his disagreement with Luther's views on grace and free will in *An Assertion of All the Articles of Martin Luther Condemned by the Latest Bull of Leo X* (1520), Erasmus believed that he had found the right opportunity to distance himself from Luther.[64] So in 1524 Erasmus published his diatribe *De libero arbitrio* (*The Freedom of the Will*), which argued that Luther's denial of free will and affirmation that all things happen by necessity contradicted the beliefs of the church in ages past. Luther responded to Erasmus with *De servo arbitrio* (*The Bondage of the Will*) in 1525, arguing from both Scripture and tradition that the will is enslaved and totally dependent on God's grace for liberation. Luther's argument was a lucid alignment with the Augustinian tradition.[65] As a result of these publications, Erasmus's stance toward the Reformer and Luther's perception of the humanist no longer remained a secret. Now all knew that Erasmus did not support Luther's Reformation or take his side against Rome.

The timing of the controversy, however, was unfortunate for Luther. Typically Luther was a quick responder to his debating partners, which usually gave Luther some momentum, writing in the heat and bustle of the controversy itself. But with Erasmus, Luther took a long time, sixteen months total. The year 1525, as seen already, was one of the most tumultuous years of Luther's life, and the demands on his time were enough to occupy four Reformers at once. For starters, he published *Against the Robbing and Murdering Hordes of Peasants*, attempting to respond to the social unrest that put the future of the Reformation in Germany in some jeopardy. He also lectured and wrote commentaries on many of the prophets and was determined to finish and publish the postils he had started years before, postils that were widely popular but needed to be expanded to cover the church calendar. It did not help that some of them were stolen, which forced Luther to rewrite them.[66] In this same year, Frederick died, and Luther, along with Melanchthon, spoke and preached at his funeral. Not long after, Luther and Katharina were married and embarked on their new life on a slim budget within the former Augustinian cloister, which was in much need of repair. Erasmus published his criticism of Luther toward the end of 1524, but Luther did not have the opportunity to devote real attention to it until the fall of 1525.[67] He tried many times before to start his reply, but it was just not possible. When Luther finally devoted himself to the task, he finished it in just

---

63. Watson, "Introduction," *LW* 33:8.

64. *WA* 7:94–151.

65. Melanchthon also opposed Erasmus, though his approach differed from Luther's. Melanchthon wielded Colossians 2:8 against Erasmus, for example, claiming Erasmus had a faulty understanding of philosophy from the start. For a chronology and outline of Melanchthon's polemic, see Wengert, *Human Freedom, Christian Righteousness*.

66. Hendrix, *Martin Luther*, 162. Cf. *WA* 17:1, xxxi; *WATR* 5:657 (no. 6429).

67. Erasmus offered a response to Luther's *Bondage of the Will* called *Hyperaspistes* (*Defense*).

three months. That was remarkable, considering the nature of his treatise, which was written in Latin, engaging fine theological points for an academic audience.[68]

Free Will, Contingency, and Necessity

The debate between Erasmus and Luther turned on the question of free will. For example, Erasmus said, "By free choice in this place we mean a power of the human will by which a man can apply himself to the things which lead to eternal salvation, or turn away from them."[69] Erasmus undoubtedly affirmed the will's power of contrary choice, and such a definition negated Luther's belief in necessity. It also makes man active and cooperative (or resistive) in the conversion process, since he is able to apply himself to salvation or turn away from it.

Erasmus's definition was untenable to Luther due to Luther's definition of contingency and necessity. In Luther's mind the "thunderbolt" argument that refutes free will as Erasmus understood it was God's immutable and eternal foreknowledge. To explain, "God foreknows nothing contingently" but instead "foresees and purposes and does all things by his immutable, eternal, and infallible will."[70] Therefore, if God foreknows nothing contingently, mankind cannot possess a freedom of contrary choice. For everything man does has been foreseen by God because all that man does has been willed by God and will occur according to his eternal decree.

Another way to make such a point is to say that God "foreknows necessarily," and therefore man cannot possess the ability to choose other than that which God necessarily foreknows and wills.[71] Luther made this point with blunt force: "If God foreknows a thing, that thing necessarily happens." Therefore, "there is no such thing as free choice."[72] Luther refused to divorce God's foreknowledge from God's willing of all things. The two are inseparable. "If he foreknows as he wills," said Luther, "then his will is eternal and unchanging (because his nature is so), and if he wills as he foreknows, then his knowledge is eternal and unchanging (because his nature is so)."[73] Luther anticipated the conclusion that must follow: "From this it follows irrefutably that everything we do, everything that happens, even if it seems to us to happen mutably and contingently, happens in fact nonetheless necessarily and immutably, if you have regard to the will of God. For the will of God is effectual and cannot be hindered, since it is the power of the divine nature itself."[74]

How, then, did Luther prefer to reconcile man's willful choices to God's

---

68. *WA* 3:653; *LW* 49:140. Cf. Hendrix, *Martin Luther*, 171. For a much fuller treatment than can be provided here, see Gerharde O. Forde, *The Captivation of the Will: Luther vs. Erasmus on Freedom and Bondage*, ed. Steven Paulson, Lutheran Quarterly Books (Grand Rapids: Eerdmans, 2005).

69. As quoted in *LW* 33:103.

70. *LW* 33:37.

71. *LW* 33:37. For Luther's extended discussion of foreknowledge and necessity, see *LW* 33:184–92.

72. *LW* 33:195.

73. *LW* 33:37.

74. *LW* 33:195, 37.

foreknowledge and decree? While Luther used the term *necessity*, he lamented that it was not ideal since it might wrongly convey a "kind of compulsion," which Luther flatly denied. To be clear, Luther rejected any view that would say, fatalistically, that God or man wills under compulsion rather than out of "pleasure or desire" (two words that, for Luther, described "true freedom").[75] By denying coercion, Luther in no way intended to deny that God's will is immutable and infallible. We should not miss Luther's contrast: while God's will remains immutable, our will remains mutable, and the former governs—even controls—the latter. As Boethius, a precursor to the Scholastics, poetically remarked, "Remaining fixed, Thou makest all things move." Certainly man's will is included: "Our will, especially when it is evil, cannot of itself do good."[76] In summary, God's will works by necessity but not by coercion. Luther's distinction had obvious implications for man's will: man's will is under divine necessity, though not under coercion. So he wills necessarily but not by force. As many scriptural passages confirm, "all things happen by necessity."[77]

Moreover, necessity is not only inevitable due to external factors (i.e., God, the world) but is also an effect due to something within us (i.e., nature's bondage to sin). Prior to God's converting power, man is bound and enslaved to sin and the devil. Salvation, therefore, "is beyond our own powers and devices, and depends on the work of God alone." If God is "not present and at work in us," Luther remarked, "everything we do is evil and we necessarily do what is of no avail for salvation." "For if it is not we, but only God, who works salvation in us, then before he works we can do nothing of saving significance, whether we wish to or not."[78] Man's bondage, in other words, demands a monergistic work of God within.

Luther clarified that such necessity is not the same thing as coercion. Here we get to the meat of the nut, for Luther articulated a freedom of inclination. Necessity, in other words, does not preclude desire but entails man's desire. Notice how carefully Luther worked to avoid compulsion. Luther could say man sins necessarily and not by compulsion precisely because such necessity is driven by inclination and desire, not coercion. Luther explained, "When a man is without the Spirit of God he does not do evil against his will, as if he were taken by the scruff of the neck and forced to it, like a thief or robber carried off against his will to punishment, but he does it of his own accord and with a ready will. And this readiness or will to act he cannot by his own powers omit, restrain,

---

75. *LW* 33:39.
76. *LW* 33:39.
77. *LW* 33:39, 60. Luther further aimed to establish his argument by appealing to Romans 9:18, 22 ("he hardens whomever he wills," and "God, desiring to show his wrath"), as well as Jesus' words in Matthew 22:14 ("Many are called, but few are chosen") and John 13:18 ("I know whom I have chosen"). Additionally, Scripture says that "all things stand or fall by the choice and authority of God, and all the earth should keep silence before the Lord [Hab. 2:20]" (*LW* 33:60). How can necessity, Luther asked, be removed from these passages? (Luther also appealed to Isaiah 46:10.)
78. *LW* 33:64.

or change, but he keeps on willing and being ready."[79] Luther only furthered his case for a freedom of inclination that is compatible with necessity when he explained how the Spirit works within the sinner. Prior to the Spirit, the will is in bondage, and yet it is a willful, desired bondage. However, when the Spirit works within the enslaved sinner, the "will is changed" and "gently breathed upon by the Spirit of God." Does such a work by the Spirit annihilate or coerce man's will since it is irresistible? By no means. The Spirit works on the will so that the will acts from "pure willingness and inclination and of its own accord, not from compulsion, so that it cannot be turned another way by any opposition, nor be overcome or compelled even by the gates of hell, but it goes on willing and delighting in and loving the good, just as before it willed and delighted in and loved evil."[80] Or in the words of the Augustinian tradition, grace perfects nature.

To reiterate Luther's point, the will is free not because it has a power of contrary choice but because it necessarily chooses that which it most desires, that which it finds itself inclined toward. Prior to the work of the Spirit, the will sins necessarily because it is enslaved to sin, and yet it is not a coerced bondage but one it desires more than anything else. However, when the Spirit comes upon God's elect, the will is transformed, given new desires. Again, necessity is very much at play, for the Spirit works effectually on the will.[81] Yet such efficacy is not coercion since the sinner's new inclinations now lead him to desire Christ more than anything else. In short, whereas before it necessarily desired evil, now it necessarily desires good, finding good to be its greatest delight.

The Enslavement of the Will

It should be apparent by now that Luther had no hesitation affirming the will's enslavement and the spiritual inability of the sinner in matters of salvation prior to the Spirit's work of new birth and conversion.

Such bondage, however, had multiple sources. Luther identified two: the devil and the world. Having in mind 2 Timothy 2:26, Luther demonstrated that every person is under the god of this world, captive to do his will. Does this captivity

---

79. *LW* 33:64.
80. *LW* 33:65.
81. When it comes to Luther's language of "absolute necessity," it should be qualified that Luther used this language, as this chapter demonstrates, in the context of his disputation with Erasmus. However, it does not appear that Luther leaned on such language in his writings after 1525. Later on (e.g., in his lectures on Genesis), Luther warned against misunderstanding his *De servo arbitrio*, though he never retracted what he wrote. In my personal correspondence with Luther scholar Robert Kolb, he noted that after 1525, Luther instead leaned on the promises given in the Word (oral and written) and in the sacraments to provide God's people with assurance, assurance that he sought to undergird by appealing to election in his *De servo arbitrio*. Perhaps this can be traced back to Luther's developing emphasis on law and gospel. While the law reveals that we are culpable for our own damnation, the gospel reveals that God receives the credit for our salvation. Luther did not try to sort out the tension between these twin truths logically; nevertheless, he believed they were each critical in pastoral care. Luther, therefore, preached law. He was aware that preaching predestination to damnation might have one of two unfortunate effect: (1) creating presumption or (2) libertinism among those who might venture to use election as an excuse or as creating despair in those who failed to hear the promise of the gospel. For Luther, therefore, predestination was meant to undergird the promise of the gospel.

477 Reforming the Reformation

to Satan involve necessity? Absolutely. "We cannot will anything but what he wills."[82] With Luke 11:18–21 in view, Luther taught that it takes a "Stronger One" (Christ) to overcome the devil, and Christ does just that through the Spirit. We are transferred from one slavery to another, though our slavery to Christ is actually a "royal freedom" that enables us to "readily will and do what he wills."[83]

Luther famously pictured the will situated between God and the devil like a beast of burden: "If God rides it, it wills and goes where God wills, as the psalm says: 'I am become as a beast [before thee] and I am always with thee.'" But if Satan rides it, "it wills and goes where Satan wills." One might think, then, that the will must only run to (or choose) whichever rider he pleases. Luther countered, "Nor can it [the will] choose to run to either of the two riders or to seek him out, but the riders themselves contend for the possession and control of it."[84]

Luther's Monergism

As insinuated already, the bondage of the will led Luther to a monergistic understanding of God's liberating grace. Consider Luther's appeal to 1 Peter 5:5. Luther believed that "God has assuredly promised his grace to the humble." But who are the humble? They are those "who lament and despair of themselves." Lest the reader think such repentance is not from God, Luther quickly qualified, "But no man can be thoroughly humbled until he knows that his salvation is utterly beyond his own powers, devices, endeavors, will, and works, and depends entirely on the choice, will, and work of another, namely, God alone." Luther went on to eliminate synergism, even synergism in the slightest: "For as long as he [man] is persuaded that he himself can do even the least thing toward his salvation, he retains some self-confidence and does not altogether despair of himself, and therefore he is not humbled before God, but presumes that there is—or at least hopes or desires that there may be—some place, time, and work for him, by which he may at length attain salvation." What, then, is the solution to man's plight? "When a man has no doubt that everything depends on the will of God, then he completely despairs of himself and chooses nothing for himself, but waits for God to work; then he has come close to grace, and can be saved."[85]

---

82. *LW* 33:65.

83. *LW* 33:65.

84. *LW* 33:65–66. In that light, Luther wished theologians would simply avoid the phrase *free will*. It is not helpful but adds enormous confusion (and is even dangerous, said Luther). Since "we do everything by necessity, and nothing by free choice," the phrase "free will" should be abandoned lest it give people the opposite impression, namely, that free choice is a "power that can turn itself freely in either direction, without being under anyone's influence or control" (*LW* 33:68). Nonetheless, Luther was reasonable when he said that the phrase *free will* refuses to disappear. So, he insisted, if it is to be used, then one must be sure it is used properly. If the term is used honestly, it would mean that free choice is applied to man only "with respect to what is beneath him and not what is above him," that is, matters concerning God, salvation, and damnation (*LW* 33:70). For readers in the twenty-first century, it should be obvious that Luther rejected outright what philosophers and theologians call *libertarian freedom*.

85. *LW* 33:61–62.

The first sign that man is on the right path is when he acknowledges that nothing can come from himself but that everything must come from God. Stated otherwise, man must come to grips with the fact that he is totally and absolutely dependent on God's grace and mercy and can do nothing, even in the slightest, to save himself: "Free choice without the grace of God is not free at all, but immutably the captive and slave of evil, since it cannot of itself turn to the good."[86] Luther recognized, however, how common it is for men to resist such a humiliating view of themselves. They condemn "this teaching of self-despair, wishing for something, however little, to be left for them to do themselves; so they remain secretly proud and enemies of the grace of God."[87]

To press Luther's monergism further, in contrast to Erasmus's synergism, consider Erasmus's definition once more: "By free choice in this place we mean a power of the human will by which a man can apply himself to the things which lead to eternal salvation, or turn away from them."[88] Commenting on Erasmus's definition, Luther elaborated on its meaning: "On the authority of Erasmus, then, free choice is a power of the will that is able of itself to will and unwill the word and work of God, by which it is led to those things which exceed both its grasp and its perception."[89] Luther went on to point out that if, for Erasmus, man can "will or unwill," then he can also "love and hate," which also means he can "in some small degree do the works of the law and believe the gospel."[90] What was Luther's critique? If this is how we define free will, then nothing in salvation is left to the grace of God and the power of the Holy Spirit. "This plainly means attributing divinity to free choice, since to will the law and the gospel, to unwill sin and to will death, belongs to divine power alone, as Paul says in more than one place."[91]

In contrast, Luther was convinced by an Augustinian reading of Scripture that the Spirit works within us without our help (i.e., monergism): "Before man is changed into a new creature of the Kingdom of the Spirit, he does nothing and attempts nothing to prepare himself for this renewal and this Kingdom."[92] Elsewhere, Luther equally guarded his readers from Semi-Pelagianism and Semi-Augustinianism. Contrary to Erasmus, he held that it is not as if man just needs a little of God's help, and then he can "prepare himself by morally good works for the divine favor." To the contrary, "if through the law sin abounds, how is it possible that a man should be able to prepare himself by moral works for the divine favor? How can works help when the law does not help?"[93]

---

86. *LW* 33:67.
87. *LW* 33:62.
88. As quoted in *LW* 33:103.
89. *LW* 33:106.
90. *LW* 33:106–7.
91. *LW* 33:107.
92. *LW* 33:243.
93. *LW* 33:219.

MELANCHTHON AND THE SYNERGISM CONTROVERSY

Luther once said that after a theologian reads the Bible, Philip Melanchthon's *Loci Communes* should be next. Not even the devil himself could shake a theologian fortified by Melanchthon (*LW* 54:439–440; 33:16). Such high praise did not mean, however, that Melanchthon always agreed with Luther. Operating from a monergistic standpoint in his debate with Erasmus, Luther said the will is enslaved to a corrupt nature and is completely dependent on the will of God for liberation. When Lutherans read Melanchthon's *Loci Communes*, some interpreted him as more sympathetic toward synergism. Melanchthon's view can be traced as follows:

- 1521 *Loci Communes:* Melanchthon disliked the phrase *free will*, affirmed original sin, and said God alone can convert man.
- 1530 *Augsburg Confession* and *Apology:* Melanchthon said human nature is corrupt and therefore the will is enslaved. Man is helpless apart from a spiritual rebirth.
- 1543 *Loci Communes:* While affirming the necessity of the Spirit to deliver man from his corruption, Melanchthon did not rule out the activity of the will to cooperate and even resist the Spirit. "But since the struggle is great and difficult, the will is not idle but assents weakly" (Melanchthon, *Loci Communes 1543*, 43).

In the last years of his life, Melanchthon also persisted in his effort to separate himself from Luther's doctrine of absolute necessity, as well as Calvin's affirmation of double predestination. However, his stance was met by opposition, and two sides formed in the 1560s and 1570s. "In the heat of the battle," says Robert Kolb, "the Philippists remained convinced that the Gnesio-Lutherans were Stoic and Manichaean in their insistence that the human will actively opposes God until the Holy Spirit overcomes that opposition, and the Gnesio-Lutherans could not lay aside their suspicions that the Philippist insistence on human integrity led to expressions that placed a controlling role in coming to faith into the powers of the will to make some move, be it ever so tiny, in God's direction" (*Bound Choice*, 287–88). How did the Formula of Concord fit into this heated debate? "The Formula of Concord produced a settlement that pleased most Gnesio-Lutherans, apart from Flacius's most devoted disciples, and also a majority of the Philippists." (288). Yet, at the same time, the Formula of Concord explicitly sided with Luther's stance on the bondage of the will.

How did other Reformers respond to Melanchthon's position? In the late 1530s, Calvin noticed Melanchthon's silence on predestination and free will, which Calvin pointed out, though graciously, in his 1539 *Commentary on Romans*. However, after the publication of Melanchthon's 1543 *Loci Communes*, it was impossible for Calvin to say nothing at all. Indeed, the timing was impeccable. Albert Pighius had written a book defending free will while simultaneously opposing Calvin's views. Pighius also censured Melanchthon for his departure from Luther and Calvin. With wit, when Calvin published his response to Pighius—*The Bondage and Liberation of the Will*—he dedicated the book to Melanchthon. Calvin "was taking a subtle dig at Melanchthon over his newly changed formulations"

(Graybill, *Evangelical Free Will*, 247), though it may also be the case that Calvin was attempting to bring Melanchthon into public support of his position.

In subsequent correspondence between the two, it became plain that Melanchthon did not agree with Calvin's distinction between a general and effectual call. For Melanchthon, only the former was viable. Melanchthon did believe it was the Holy Spirit who moved the human will to respond to the gospel call, but the success of the Spirit's call was contingent on man's will—even if it was a Spirit-enabled will—and this was enough to cause consternation for Calvin. While Calvin did not enter into open debate with Melanchthon like he did with Pighius, nevertheless, he did hint at his disapproval in his 1546 preface to the French edition of Melanchthon's *Loci Communes*, noting how Melanchthon had shifted his position on free will. Even so, the two avoided public debate since neither one of them desired to create an unnecessary barrier to further reformation. But after Melanchthon died in 1560, Calvin criticized Melanchthon's views from the pulpit. For Calvin, Melanchthon had misrepresented him and compromised the biblical view. For a thorough treatment of the Melanchthon controversy, see Barrett, ed. *Reformation Theology*, 451–510.

In summary, Luther would not grant even an inch to free will in man's new birth. To quote Luther, we must avoid the temptation to find a "middle way" that would concede even "a tiny bit" to free will.[94] It was all or nothing for Luther: "We must therefore go all out and completely deny free choice, referring everything to God; then there will be no contradictions in Scripture."[95] A stronger affirmation of divine monergism is difficult to imagine.

Law and Gospel

If Luther was right, objected Erasmus, then why did God give so many commands in the Scriptures? Do not these laws and imperatives imply ability on man's part? Does not *ought* mean *can*? Indeed, this was an argument Erasmus clung to in his defense of free will. However, Luther believed Erasmus had misunderstood the purpose of the law in reference to the unbeliever.

God's imperatives in no way are meant to imply that man has it within him to fulfill such commands. Instead, God is driving man to the law in order to reveal his impotence, as Paul asserted in Romans 3:20. "For human nature," said Luther, "is so blind that it does not know its own powers, or rather diseases, and so proud as to imagine that it knows and can do everything; and for this pride and blindness God has no readier remedy than the propounding of his law."[96] Far from proving man's freedom, biblical imperatives expose his corruption and captivity, not to mention his pride, contempt, and ignorance. Therefore, when one encounters precepts in the law, one must recognize that such precepts are not the same thing as promises. For example, God may command sinners, but

---

94. *LW* 33:245.
95. *LW* 33:245.
96. *LW* 33:121.

these commands by no means promise man that he will not sin or break God's precepts or that man even has it within his ability to fulfill such commands.

The same caution applies to divine invitations as well. For example, God said in Deuteronomy 30:15, 19, "I have set before you today life and good, death and evil.... Therefore choose life." Erasmus thought such verses as these proved his case. After all, God leaves it up to man, for man has the freedom to choose. But Luther disagreed. Passages like Deuteronomy 30 offer life, but God never said that man has the ability to choose life, nor did God guarantee he would bestow life. Certain conditions must be met, and while God sincerely places two paths in front of man (life and death), Scripture shows that unregenerate man chooses death over life every time. So the law only exposes man's inability to fulfil the divine precepts as long as he remains a child of Adam. However, the impossibility of fulfilling the law is not due to some inherent fault in God's commands. Rather, the failure to obey God's law is due to man's corruption in Adam and captivity to sin, the world, and the devil. Unless God sends the Spirit, this is the state in which man will remain.[97] As Luther succinctly put it, "Man perpetually and necessarily sins and errs until he is put right by the Spirit of God."[98]

At this point, Luther's distinction between law and gospel played a key role. When held up against the law, man's inability is apparent; hence the gospel shines bright as the sinner's only hope. As Luther said elsewhere, the gospel "knocks out the teeth of the Law, blunts its sting and all its weapons, and utterly disables it."[99] Should we reverse this biblical order between law and gospel, as Luther believed Erasmus did, we then turn law into gospel and gospel into law. Therefore, understanding the law *as* law is essential.[100]

It should not be missed that for Luther the law played a crucial role in preparing sinners for the gospel. The law makes "man's plight plain to him," breaking him down, confounding him by "self-knowledge, so as to prepare him for grace and send him to Christ that he may be saved."[101] Should the law show man his spiritual ability rather than his captivity, then the law would not lead to gospel and grace but would instead lead man right back to himself as the one who can will and achieve his own righteousness. But should the law expose man's captivity and depravity, man must depend entirely on what Christ has done for him and rely on the Spirit's gifts of new birth, faith, and repentance. For the Spirit alone is omnipotent enough to overcome man's rebellious nature and unite him to Christ, ensuring the sinner participates in the life of the Holy Spirit by grace alone.[102]

---

97. *LW* 33:126.

98. *LW* 33:177.

99. *LW* 26:161.

100. *LW* 33:127, 132–33.

101. *LW* 33:130–31. Luther also showed how the law and Satan differ in this respect: while Satan deceives man into thinking he is free (when really man is at Satan's mercy), Moses and the lawgiver use the law to show man that he is not free at all but bound and condemned.

102. One does not have to agree with Miikka Ruokanen's amendment to the Finnish school to appreciate his recovery of Luther's trinitarian emphasis *De servo arbitrio*. see Ruokanan, *Trinitarian Grace in Martin Luther's The Bondage of the Will.*

How significant was the debate with Erasmus in the estimation of Luther? Toward the end of his life, Luther reflected on this early debate and said all his works could be lost to the fire, but if his *Bondage of the Will* was preserved, then the meat of the Reformation would remain.[103] For Luther, *sola gratia* was at stake.

IMPLEMENTING REFORMATION (1526–30)

The years 1517 to 1524 represented Luther's ongoing protests against Rome's theology and abuses, but 1525 and the years that followed reveal a Luther resolved to turn his attention to the re-formation of the German church.

Although the clergy can be credited with advancing the Reformation, so, too, must civil authorities. Apart from the assistance and favor of temporal powers, the Reformation may have been snuffed out in its early stages. The Reformation was not merely a movement of the people but also a movement backed by those in political power.[104] Early on, Frederick protected Luther from his many opponents, but later on it was Elector John who sought the Reformation's public acceptance.[105] If John officially approved Luther's endeavors to reform the church, the Reformation would no longer be a movement merely defined by its anti-Roman polemic but a movement that truly implemented reform within a renewed catholic church.

To reiterate, Luther's intent was always to reform the church from within. Contrary to misconceptions of Luther the rebel, Luther was after evangelical, catholic renewal as an insider. His Ninety-Five Theses proposed such a reform, starting with the indulgence system, but was never accepted. Now, with Elector John, that initial proposal was possible, and on a much grander scale than Luther ever imagined back in 1517. As Luther matured in his own understanding of doctrine, so, too, did his view of reformation in the church. In 1525, on the anniversary of Luther's Ninety-Five Theses (October 31), Luther had sent Elector John his vision for reform in the church. In 1526 John was now prepared to stand behind Luther's proposal for renewal.[106] Luther's proposition was sweeping, a plan to change not only individual parishes, from their liturgy to their pulpits, but the university system as well.[107]

One significant roadblock stood in the way. To accomplish such a pervasive reform *within* the church each parish needed a Reformer, like Luther, to visit, pass an evaluation, and then set forward a plan for how reform should proceed.

---

103. Gatiss, *Cornerstones of Salvation*, 15–42.

104. Hendrix, *Martin Luther*, 172, goes so far as to say that prior to 1525 the Reformation was a "populist endeavor," one from the bottom up, but after 1525 it was from the top down. As a sweeping observation, Hendrix may be right, though I do not want to push this too far; as we have seen, even after 1525 much reform is to be credited to the populists.

105. Hendrix, 174–76.

106. Hendrix, 176.

107. On the specifics, see Hendrix, 176–77.

Luther admitted that the "parishes everywhere are in such miserable condition."[108] Someone needed to show up in the flesh to take an honest look at the pastor, his pulpit ministry, the liturgy, the finances, and what remnants of Rome remained. Approving such visitations, however, was not an easy decision. Remember, after Worms, not only Luther but anyone who backed his reforming efforts was considered an outlaw. Backing Luther put Elector John under the same condemnation. To make matters worse, the Diet of Speyer was set to meet the summer of 1526, and Speyer might impose Worms.

But the tables turned in Luther's favor at Speyer. The diet's major concern was financial. With the Turks on the move, troops were needed if Hungary and Austria were not to fall victim. But more troops meant more money. The Lutherans were in a position to give more money, but not if the emperor put a stop to their reformation endeavors and further condemned Luther and his ecclesiastical and political allies. Archduke Ferdinand decided that all territories sympathetic to the Lutherans could continue with their reforms. No punishment should be inflicted. Now Elector John could officially back Luther's measures.[109]

In the years that followed, Luther and other Reformers took immense steps to ensure the Reformation did not remain a matter of mere academics but an ecclesiastical endeavor with untold spiritual consequences. First, every parish needed to be evaluated and then assisted with changes. Luther knew ahead of time the results of such an evaluation because he was well aware of Rome's teachings and customs, as well as the long-lasting effects they had in the weekly rhythm of parish life. Although the Reformation was two decades in, remnants of late medieval beliefs and practices lingered and were hard to shake. Even if formal practices changed, altering the actual mindsets of the people took dedicated conditioning. A select group of Reformers visited and inspected each parish in Electoral Saxony; Luther was slotted as one of them. To guide the process, an *Instruction of the Visitors* set the contours in place for the course ahead.[110]

Second, Luther took up a rigorous preaching schedule. John Bugenhagen traveled to churches in other cities to implement the new changes, but the responsibilities of weekly preaching and instruction in the town church fell to Luther. Luther's pace was incredible: in one year he preached 180 times.[111]

Third, Luther took a page from medieval theology and practice and wrote catechisms. In the eleventh century, for example, a catechism was utilized by Bruno of Würzburg, a practice that continued in the centuries that followed.[112] Even prior to writing his own catechisms, Luther advocated that each pastor

---

108. *WABr* 3:595; *LW* 53:135. Cf. Hendrix, 176–77.

109. Hendrix, 177–78.

110. See *LW* 40:263–320. "Luther made it sound as if the *Instruction* were provisional; but neither he nor Elector John foresaw a return to the old order of papal bishops and parishes, celibate clergy, and the medieval mass. Compromise was out of the question." Hendrix, 195.

111. Hendrix, 195.

112. Trueman, *Luther on the Christian Life*, 109.

should catechize his people, including the children and youth, in five core components, many of which were present in medieval catechisms: (1) the Ten Commandments, (2) the Apostles' Creed, (3) the Lord's Prayer, (4) baptism, and (5) the Lord's Supper. The pastor might catechize his people according to this analogy of faith during a sermon or a specific lesson during the week.[113] In 1529 Luther published both small and large catechisms, the former designed to help the average Christian with no theological training so that he or she could learn each of the five components.[114] The goal was not only to memorize the Apostles' Creed or the Lord's Prayer, for example, but to understand its meaning and how to live in light of its resonance.

Fourth, and perhaps most important of all, Luther wrote hymns. His publications were pervasive, and his sermons were influential, but music was the medium through which the average German Christian imbibed the convictions of the Reformation. And Luther knew it. In his lifetime, Luther wrote more than thirty-five hymns, and many of them had been written prior to 1530. When churches in Wittenberg opened their *Achtliederbuch* around half of the hymns they sang were written by Luther himself.[115] Perhaps Luther's most famous hymn to this day is "A Mighty Fortress Is Our God." True to his theology, consistent with the interpretation of his times, Luther positioned the devil over against God but gave every believer the assurance that Christ was, is, and will be the victor.

PROTESTANTS EMERGE: THE PRINCE'S REFORMATION AND THE DIET OF SPEYER

As the chapter closed on the 1520s, the Reformation transitioned from its early days as a theological movement to a movement adopted or opposed by political powers. After the Peasants' War of 1525, rulers had to decide how to respond to the Reformation moving forward. In Germany rulers and their territories could be on either side, some Catholic, others evangelical. This diversity created no little tension, and those sympathetic to the evangelical movement discussed whether it was time to form an alliance in case papal armies moved to the offensive. What if, for example, they squashed another revolution only to use it as an excuse to eliminate evangelicals everywhere? Or what if they decided to enforce the Edict of Worms, which the evangelical territories had no intention of upholding? With these questions unanswered, evangelical rulers made plans, fortifying their ranks for potential warfare, while simultaneously becoming more vocal about their support for the Reformation.[116]

---

113. Sometimes placards were made to exhibit Luther's explanation of each of the five. Hendrix, 195.

114. *BC*, 345–480.

115. *Achtliederbuch* means "Book of Eight Hymns"; see Hendrix, 197.

116. This was a natural, uncontested move since "people in the sixteenth century understood religion not only as a private but also as a public matter," said Hillerbrand. This observation has led some historians to refer to a Prince's Reformation. "The term presupposes the propriety of certain parallel terms, such as 'Communal Reformation,' 'Peasant Reformation,' 'Urban Reformation,' in each instance indicating a particular characteristic of phases or stages of the movement of reform." Hillerbrand wondered if the Prince's Reformation

The Prince's Reformation, as it has been called, was possible in part because the emperor was absent from Germany. Occupied with his ongoing rivalry with Francis, Charles V could not be present to enforce his Edict of Worms. When Charles defeated Francis at the start of 1525 and Francis signed the Peace of Madrid at the start of 1526, Charles promised to turn his attention back to Germany. By signing the Peace of Madrid, both Charles and Francis agreed to suppress Lutherans. But Charles should have known better. Francis would never honor the Peace of Madrid, not as long as he had his freedom, which he did as soon as they released the prisoner king. Free and full of spite, Francis turned right around and created an alliance to prepare his retaliation.[117] Francis was so bent on conquering Charles that the French king linked arms with Muslims and asked the Ottoman Empire to assist him in his fight against the emperor.

The headache Francis and the Peace of Madrid created for Charles turned into a migraine when his hired troops abandoned post and marched from northern Italy to Rome. Frustrated by the emperor's lack of compensation, these German guerrillas planned to take over the sacred city and enjoy its wealth as their reward. The outcome was embarrassing for the pope. Not only was Rome easily defeated but Clement had to flee for his life, escaping by a tunnel to the Castel Sant'Angelo, only to be cornered by mercenaries. By 1527 the sacred city was unrecognizable.

What did the *sacco di Roma* have to do with the advance of the Reformation? Everything. First, it revealed Christendom was anything but a single, unified entity as Rome sometimes gave the impression. "The *sacco di Roma* turned into an important episode in the history of sixteenth-century Christianity because it demonstrated that the Christian house was divided."[118] Second, the chaos preoccupied Charles, giving Lutheran territories space to pursue the Reformation further and solidify their territories in the event of conflict. The emperor's absence failed to inspire Catholic estates in their suppression of Lutheran opponents.

By the time the Diet of Speyer convened, these unresolved issues set the diet up for failure. "Consequently, some Catholic estates decided not even to bother attending the diet that had been convened to meet at Speyer in June 1526."[119] The divide between Catholics and evangelicals continued unchanged: the former continued with Mass and the latter refused to conceal their convictions—*Verbum Dei Manet in Eternum* (The Word of God Remains Forever).[120] The evangelicals created additional alliances. Elector John of Saxony and Philip of Hesse strategized how they might combine troops in the event of an invasion. As word spread, other German estates added their support. These alliances opened

---

started in 1522, given the liturgical changes made by Elector Frederick of Saxony. Hillerbrand, *Division of Christendom*, 155.

117. "In May 1526 he formed the League of Cognac, which, also with papal concurrence, committed itself to breaking the Habsburg dominance of northern Italy." Hillerbrand, 156.

118. Hillerbrand, 157.

119. Hillerbrand, 157.

120. Isa. 40:8.

the door for theological and liturgical advances as well, allowing ministers to eliminate any remnants of Roman worship and Mass still at large.[121]

The year 1526 was inconclusive. The Diet of Speyer could not enforce the Edict of Worms, and a truce had to suffice, though the Catholics anticipated the truce would end as soon as Charles returned to Germany. Although the truce was not intended by the Catholics as a license to further Reformation, the German territories used it as a license nonetheless.[122] However, in 1529 Speyer reconvened, and this time the evangelicals were commanded to return to the Catholic Church or else. Ferdinand, speaking on behalf of Charles, was clear that the estates should no longer tolerate the evangelicals, especially since the emperor needed a united front against the Ottoman Empire. Evangelicals who persisted in protest were considered a public threat against the empire's advance on the Turks and had to be dealt with expediently. In years past, the threats of the emperor were extended from a distance, but this time the threat was imminent.

The seriousness of the threat, however, did not pressure evangelicals into cooperation but protest. That April the evangelicals read their protest to the assembly despite the fact that the Catholics had a majority at hand. While many events during the sixteenth century embodied the widening gulf between evangelicals and Catholics, the Speyer diet of 1529 revealed that the division was more or less permanent. The protest would not stop until either the protestors were eliminated or the Catholics conceded their reforms, both of which were impossible. Having read their statement, the evangelicals were now labeled *Protestants*. "The implication of the statement was that the medieval world, with its ideal of the *corpus christianum*, the one Christian body, had broken apart."[123]

The time had come: Protestants not only needed a protest but a protector, they not only needed a confession (at Augsburg) but a league (at Smalcald). Unfortunately, many questioned whether the Reformers could unite for such a cause when they were divided among themselves over a theological controversy as explosive as the Lord's Supper.

---

121. The details surrounding all these alliances are chronicled in Hillerbrand, *Division of Christendom*, 157.

122. Hillerbrand believed the evangelicals misinterpreted the truce and consequently "felt tricked or at least misunderstood." Hillerbrand, 158.

123. Hillerbrand, as the title of his book reveals, thought the Protestants were challenging the unity of the church. Hillerbrand, 161. That may be true on the political side since a refusal to conform to the emperor's demands necessitated the Protestant estates be prepared for war, which entailed a break. However, the Reformers did not necessarily attempt to break the unity of the church. They intended to reform the one church.

10

FROM UNION TO SCHISM

The Eucharist, the Turks, and the League

*I testify on my part that I regard Zwingli as un-Christian, with all his
teachings for he holds and teaches no part of the Christian faith rightly.
He is seven times worse than when he was a papist.*

—Martin Luther

According to Rome, a sacrament channeled grace from God to his people.
Grace was invisible to the eye of the laity. However, the sign was not
invisible, instead taking tangible form. From baptism to extreme unction, the
sacraments became ecclesiological signposts, marking the church's perceptible
distribution of divine mercy.

The Eucharist was one of the most important sacraments for clergy and laity.
As the priest performed the Latin Mass, everyone anticipated the moment of
transubstantiation, a sacred miracle performed by God through the priest. The
priest not only served the people but himself: by faith this good work of consecration contributed to his own favor with God. Rome believed that although
the bread and wine still looked and tasted like bread and wine (their accidents
appeared unchanged), nevertheless, these elements became the body and blood
of the Lord (the substance transformed).[1]

Rome missed the point of the sacraments, said Luther in response. Granted,
the sacraments were gifts from God, given for our good. God himself meets us
in our weakness in the Eucharist. However, the sacraments were signs and seals,
pledges and testaments to the promise of God to forgive our trespasses. The word
testament is most appropriate: the testament is ratified by the blood of Christ,
and upon his death its promises are ready-made to deliver all the benefits his
death has procured.[2] As a testament, the sacrament increases our faith, granting
us every assurance of our right standing with God on the basis of Christ's spilled
blood at Calvary. In the flow of the Reformation liturgy, the church hears the
gospel proclaimed, sees the gospel spread out on the table, and eats and drinks

---

1. McGrath, *Reformation Thought*, 164.
2. These testaments take visible, physical form, the Creator and Savior's way of accommodating the creature. On accommodation, see McGrath, 166.

its benefits by faith, confirming and cultivating all the promises now operative for those united to Christ. In the sacrament, said Luther, "a person is given a sure sign from God himself that he or she is united with Christ and the saints, and has all things in common with them, and that Christ's suffering and life are his own."[3]

As chapter 8 revealed, Luther's *Babylonian Captivity of the Church* was a fierce attack on the sacramental system as a whole, the papacy's view of the Eucharist included. However, Luther's dissatisfaction was not wholesale. "It is essential to appreciate that Luther did *not* criticize the underlying basic idea that the bread and wine became the body and blood of Christ," says Alistair McGrath. "Luther's objection was not to the idea of the 'real presence' as such, but to *one specific way of explaining that presence*. For Luther, God is not merely *behind* the sacraments: he is *in* them as well."[4] That qualification is significant, explaining why Luther became the target of so many Swiss criticisms, criticisms that occupied the latter half of the 1520s.

Luther was not the only one to challenge the papacy's sacramental system as a failure to be sacramental enough. Toward the conclusion of 1524, Karlstadt published a book opposing Rome's position as well.[5] However, Karlstadt went further than Luther, precluding the real presence of Christ in the elements altogether, which horrified Luther.[6] Since Karlstadt now lived in Strasbourg, he sought to persuade its churches and leaders to adopt his position. To decide their own viewpoint, those in Strasbourg wrote to Luther asking him to expand his position for consideration. Luther wrote back—*A Letter to the Christians at Strasburg in Opposition to the Fanatic Spirit*—and took aim at Karlstadt, whom Luther labeled a radical.[7]

Karlstadt erred by stripping the Lord's Supper down to the believer's remembrance of Christ. The supper, countered Luther, was much more. By taking the supper in faith, believers embrace God's promise to forgive their sins. Without the supper, believers are left with anxiety and uncertainty. By receiving the bread and wine, believers have every assurance they are pardoned. As important as the cross may be, the benefits Christ accomplished are applied by virtue of his real presence in the supper. The Eucharist is the medium through which believers receive Christ.

In 1524 Luther did not think the debate was so significant that it should divide one Reformer from another. By stirring up other cities to do the same, Karlstadt was displaying his fanatical spirit.[8] In the years ahead, however, Luther

---

3. *LW* 35:52. Cf. McGrath, 167.

4. McGrath, 172.

5. Karlstadt, *A Dialogue or Conversation concerning the Abominable and Idolatrous Misuse of the Most Honorable Sacrament of Jesus Christ.*

6. For a study of the controversy, see Burnett, *Karlstadt and the Origins of the Eucharistic Controversy*, 54–148.

7. See *LW* 40:61–72.

8. *LW* 40:61–72. Cf. Hendrix, *Martin Luther*, 160.

changed his mind on the significance of the debate as Ulrich Zwingli, the Reformer from Zurich, became Luther's main disputant.

"THIS *SIGNIFIES* MY BODY": ZWINGLI

Zwingli resurrected the polemic against transubstantiation (as cultivated in a Reformer like Karlstadt) with his treatise *On the Lord's Supper*. The work targets the papacy as well as some humanists and Lutherans. If papal theologians said the *crucified* Christ was present in the Eucharist, humanists like Erasmus said the *resurrected* Christ was present. Regardless, *On the Lord's Supper* was a sweeping strike against both positions that say Christ's human body is really or essentially present. Although the Lutheran view is addressed sporadically, Zwingli's aim was set against the apologetic for transubstantiation. Yet even in Zwingli's polemic, the discerning reader will notice Luther and Zwingli disagreed with the papacy for different reasons. To understand why, consider Zwingli's overall perspective on the supper, followed by a closer look at his exegesis.[9]

For Zwingli the supper was not all that different from celebrating a military victory. The battle is a historic event, either won or lost. Depending on the outcome there is either celebration or lament after battle. If a soldier is victorious, then he has every reason to commemorate his triumph. Zwingli used this illustration—one not far removed from his younger days as a chaplain—to explain what occurs when the supper is remembered.[10] *Remembered*—though Zwingli's position cannot be reduced to remembrance that word does serve as a point of emphasis for Zwingli. For the supper is a type of public memorial that honors what Jesus accomplished for his people. The bread and wine are symbols that help his church remember the cost of their redemption until he returns. The supper is not all that different from other symbols, such as a husband who wears a wedding ring as a symbol of his marriage. The husband might give his wedding ring to his wife while he is gone on a trip so that every time she looks at it she will remember him.[11] Right now, Christ is absent. He ascended to the right hand of the Father.[12] However, the supper (like the husband's ring) is a pledge, both a pledge of his benevolence toward his church and a pledge that he will come again. In the meantime, we eat the bread and drink the wine to remember what Christ did while on earth. In that sense, Zwingli was comfortable calling the supper a *commemoration*.

Jesus' ascension was critical to Zwingli's logic, logic that also appealed to the Apostles' Creed. As much as he navigated the intricacies of scriptural interpretation, examining one text after another to demonstrate the figural hermeneutic at

---

9. For a more extensive treatment, see Potter, *Zwingli*, 287–315.

10. Zwingli specifically referred to the Swiss victory over the Austrians (1388) for the illustration. See Zwingli, *On Baptism*; *CR* 91:217. Cf. McGrath, *Reformation Thought*, 175–76.

11. McGrath, 176.

12. Luther had his reply ready: "Christ's body is everywhere because the right hand of God is everywhere." *LW* 37:207; cf. 37:47, 55.

work in Christ's words, the treatise as a whole positioned Zwingli as a defender of the Apostles' Creed (and by default the Nicene Creed). According to the creed, "He ascended into heaven, and sitteth on the right hand of God the Father Almighty; from thence he shall come to judge the quick and the dead." Here was the linchpin of Zwingli's argument against the real, essential presence of Christ's body (crucified or resurrected). Zwingli believed his opponents were caught: "They must either abandon the false doctrine of the presence of the essential body of Christ in this sacrament, or else they must at once renounce these three articles, which God forbid that anyone should ever dream of doing."[13] The basis of Rome's and the humanists' violation of the creed was lucid enough: Christ's human nature is fixed to its heavenly domain, as it should be, until Christ returns in judgment.

Zwingli made a sharp distinction (though his Lutheran opponents said too sharp a distinction, a Nestorian divide) between the divine and human natures of Christ, concluding that the human nature ascended and remains in heaven while the divine nature enjoys ubiquity.

> According to his divine nature Christ never left the right hand of the Father.... He did not need to ascend up to heaven: for he is omnipresent.... The other nature is Christ's human nature. For our sakes he took this upon him in the pure body of Mary by the receiving and fructifying of the Holy Spirit, and he carried it truly in this present time. According to this nature he increased and grew both in wisdom and stature. According to it he suffered hunger and thirst and cold and heat and all other infirmities, sin only excepted. According to it he was lifted up on the cross, and with it he ascended up in heaven. This nature was a guest in heaven, for no flesh had ever previously ascended up into it.... Therefore in respect of his divine nature he did not need to ascend up into heaven although we are not at fault but speak quite rightly if we say: The Son of God ascended up into heaven, for he who ascended up is God. Strictly speaking, however, the Ascension is proper only to his human nature.[14]

The creed's affirmation of the bodily ascension of Christ, then, is the proof Zwingli thought he needed. For "if he has gone away, if he has left the world, if he is no longer with us, then either the Creed is unfaithful to the words of Christ, which is impossible, or else the body and blood of Christ cannot be present in the sacrament.... He sits at the right hand of the Father, he has left the world, he is no longer present with us.... It is impossible to maintain that his flesh and blood are present in the sacrament."[15]

---

13. Zwingli, *On the Lord's Supper*, 186.
14. Zwingli, *On the Lord's Supper*, 212–13. Zwingli advocated for a version of the *extra Calvinisticum* long before Calvin (see ch. 10).
15. Zwingli, *On the Lord's Supper*, 214–15.

LUTHER AND THE FAITH OF THE BAPTIZED INFANT

The controversy over the Lord's Supper occupied everyone's attention on the stage of the Reformation. However, Luther's evolution over infant baptism should not be overlooked. Luther was the herald of justification by faith alone, but is faith present in the baptism of an infant? In 1520 Luther turned to the parents and the church to say that their faith becomes the infant's faith. However, five years later Luther appeared to adjust his position: now he said the infant itself has faith, however passive that faith may be. The waters of baptism, then, stir up the faith of the infant.

See *WA* 6:538; *LW* 36:73; cf. Cameron, *The European Reformation*, 187.

With the creed in his right hand, Zwingli then turned to the Fathers in his left hand, summoning Jerome, Ambrose, and especially Augustine.[16] In Augustine's voice, Zwingli argued at length that Jesus did not intend in his many parables and teachings to use literalistic language, but he used metaphorical language to convey the points he was after. For example, in John 6 Jesus commanded his listeners to "feed" on him (6:48–59); by "feed" Jesus meant "believe" (6:35), as the context reveals with its emphasis on faith. Those who feed/believe will be filled with life eternal, said Jesus. When Augustine explained this passage, he "did not mean: He who believes on him feeds physically on his flesh and blood, for already Augustine has shown that the partaking which is needed is to believe in him." What Augustine meant was this: "When you come to this thanksgiving you need neither teeth to press the body of Christ nor stomach to receive that which you have chewed, for if you believe in him you have already partaken of him." So when "you partake of the two elements of bread and wine, all that you do is to confess publicly that you believe in the Lord Jesus Christ."[17]

For Zwingli, then, a "sacrament is the sign of a holy thing." The bread, for example, is a "symbol of the body of Christ who was put to death for our sakes." Therefore, the "sign and the thing signified cannot be one and the same." This is the great sin of an essential, real presence: the sign and the signified are collapsed, even confused with one another. But for Zwingli the "sacrament of the body of Christ cannot be the body itself."[18] Zwingli said that in Zurich his people had no issue with the words of Christ—"This is my body." Yet the Zurich church did explain what these words mean, pointing to the interpretation of the early church to show Christ's figural intention: "This *signifies* my body."[19]

---

16. E.g., Zwingli, *On the Lord's Supper*, 231–32. Zwingli also appealed to Berengarius of Tours in the eleventh century and Gratian in the twelfth century, both of whom entered into conflict with the papacy over their resistance to an essential presence position (see 193, 197).

17. Zwingli, *On the Lord's Supper*, 198.

18. Zwingli, *On the Lord's Supper*, 188.

19. Zwingli, *On the Lord's Supper*, 235; cf. 225.

Zwingli rested much of his exegetical case on the word *signify*. Several years before he published *On the Lord's Supper*, Zwingli was most likely influenced by the research of the late medieval thinker Wessel Gansfort (ca. 1419–89) as mediated through the more recent anti-Roman polemics of Cornelius Hoen.[20] "This *is* my body" should read "This *signifies* (*significat*) my body." Jesus is not speaking in a literalistic fashion, but his language is intentionally figurative. And if Jesus' language is figurative—Zwingli used the patristic and Greek term *tropos*—then real presence misses the message of the Last Supper. According to Zwingli (and Oecolampadius as well), the bread and wine are nothing special; they have no intrinsic worth or value. They only mean something by association. Again, consider the illustration of a ring. By itself, the ring is nothing, merely metal, but when the ring is put in a chapel, all of a sudden it means something. The ring hasn't changed at all, but the context has. Likewise, nothing occurs in the bread and the wine. However, when the bread and the wine are taken from the kitchen cupboard and placed in the church, all of a sudden they mean something. They are now associated with Christ and serve as aids, helping us to remember and commemorate what Jesus has accomplished until he returns.[21]

Zwingli's writings on the supper were often wrapped in a polemical context. Yet Zwingli's efforts to refute Luther's real presence position in the years ahead did not mean Zwingli's outlook aligned with diverse radicals from Karlstadt to various Anabaptists in Zurich. Zwingli did believe in a spiritual presence, observed G. R. Potter. "It was for the believer only that Christ was really present, spiritually, not physically, but assuredly present—*dum fides adest homini, habet deum praesentem*. It was therefore perfectly reasonable to describe the symbolical bread as the body of the Lord."[22] As will be discussed soon enough, Zwingli's realism may have galvanized his interpretation. In one sense, he could affirm the real presence but only if interpreted as a spiritual presence of Christ within the believer eating the bread. "The bread in the communion was an outward and visible sign of an inward and spiritual grace, but no more. There was a substantial real presence of Christ when the elements were distributed, but in the hearts of the faithful only. Christ was spiritually present, but that was no miracle."[23] When Zwingli and Luther met at Marburg, Zwingli's wording appeared prom-

---

20. How did Luther discover the research of Gansfort? In 1509, observes McGrath, "a change of personnel at a small library in the Lowlands took place, necessitating the cataloguing of its holdings. The work was entrusted to Cornelius Hoen, who discovered that the library contained a significant collection of the writings of the noted humanist Wessel Gansfort (c. 1420–89). One of these was entitled *On the Sacrament of the Eucharist*. Although Gansfort did not actually deny the doctrine of transubstantiation, he developed the idea of a spiritual communion between Christ and the believer. Hoen, apparently attracted to this idea, reworked it into a radical critique of the doctrine of transubstantiation, which he wrote up in the form of a letter. It seems that this letter found its way to Luther at some point in 1521.... By 1523 the letter had reached Zurich, where it was read by Zwingli." McGrath goes on to credit Hoen with Zwingli's use of the ring illustration as well. McGrath, *Reformation Thought*, 176–77.

21. McGrath, 179.

22. Potter, *Zwingli*, 304; cf. *Z* 5, 553, 586.

23. Potter, *Zwingli*, 212–313; cf. *Z* 5, 200.

ising at first, signaling an approval of Christ's presence (a point to which we will return), but in the end proved a disappointment to Luther. For as soon as Luther pressured Zwingli to confess Christ as really present, Zwingli qualified that such presence inheres *within the people* who eat and drink.[24] The presence is not concrete in the Eucharist itself. Zwingli's application of classical realism differed from Luther's.

Rome and Lutherans alike took issue with Zwingli's hermeneutic and his Christology. Yet Zwingli stated over and over again in his defense that he was practicing the patristic method of interpreting Scripture according to Scripture (the analogy of Scripture), which he did not believe either Rome, Erasmus, or the Lutherans had practiced with true balance.[25]

HOC EST CORPUS MEUM: LUTHER AND
THE SACRAMENTAL UNION

In contrast to Zwingli, Luther believed Christ was bodily present in the Lord's Supper and the believer participates in a real, bodily eating of Christ at the table.[26] Luther's argument for a real presence, however, should not be confused with the medieval notion of local presence (*praesentia localis*). The concept of *consubstantiatio* may have been entertained at least by late medieval theologians like Duns Scotus and William of Ockham, but it "implies only a presence with and not a union of Christ and the sacramental elements."[27] Luther said far more, advancing *unio sacramentalis*, sacramental unity, a phrase that best captures Luther's position, in contrast to consubstantiation, a word absent from Luther's vocabulary.[28] Luther intended a "real but illocal presence of Christ's body and blood that is grounded in the omnipresence of Christ's person, and therefore a supernatural and sacramental, rather than a local, union with the visible elements of the sacrament."[29] Luther would not have been satisfied with the way Ockham wielded his voluntarism and nominalism at the table.

Due to the union of the two natures in the one person of Christ, Luther said the humanity of Christ may be as omnipresent as the divinity of Christ. Therefore, Luther concluded that the body of Christ is really, bodily present with, under, and around the elements to ensure a sacramental union occurs. As Luther later said, "Under the bread is Christ's body."[30] Likewise the cup.

---

24. Potter, *Zwingli*, 328–39.
25. E.g., Zwingli, *On the Lord's Supper*, 223.
26. The bodily eating did not preclude a spiritual eating, an emphasis in both the early and later Luther, including Marburg Colloquy. Lohse, *Martin Luther's Theology*, 310; cf. *LW* 23:116, 128; 37:85, 93.
27. In consubstantiation, "the body and blood of Christ become substantially present together with the substance of the bread and the wine" and "indicates the presence of Christ's body according to a unique sacramental mode of presence that is proper to Christ's body as such, and it is therefore a local presence." *Consubstantiatio* is similar to *impanatio* (impanation). Muller, *Dictionary*, consubstantiation, s.v.
28. For this language, see *LW* 37:299–301; cf. Lohse, *Martin Luther's Theology*, 309. Lohse also observes that "consubstantiation" was not used until the 1550s by Luther's Reformed opponents.
29. Muller, *Dictionary*, s.v.
30. And "in the bread is Christ's body." *LW* 37:166; cf. 37:65.

A LITERARY FEAST

Like his other debates, Luther's output on the Lord's Supper was prolific. He wrote almost a book a year on the topic. That sounds like Luther was obsessed with the topic, but Luther's opponents wrote more than twice as many books. Luther's books include these:

The Blessed Sacrament of the Holy and True Body of Christ (1519)
A Treatise on the New Testament, That Is, the Holy Mass (1520)
The Misuse of the Mass (1521)
Receiving Both Kinds in the Sacrament (1522)
The Adoration of the Sacrament (1523)
The Abomination of the Secret Mass (1525)
Against the Heavenly Prophets (1525)
The Sacrament of the Body and Blood of Christ—against the Fanatics (1526)
That These Words of Christ, "This Is My Body," Etc., Still Stand Firm against the Fanatics (1527)
Confession Concerning Christ's Supper (1528)

"'This cup is the new testament in my blood,' cannot be a trope, because the expression 'in my blood' has the same meaning as 'through' or 'with' my blood."[31] The bread and cup are no mere signs.

In 1527 the Frankfurt spring fair released books on both sides of the debate. Zwingli published two books: one in Latin called *Friendly Exposition of the Eucharist Affair, to Martin Luther,* and a second, more accessible book in German called *Friendly Rejoinder and Rebuttal to the Sermon of the Eminent Martin Luther against the Fanatics.*[32]

Zwingli felt Luther was turning a secondary issue into a primary issue, forfeiting the united front of the Reformation in the process. Despite his previous tone with Karlstadt, Luther disagreed; the supper was a gospel issue. If Christ's body is not really present, then how is the church supposed to receive the whole Christ and all the assurance of salvation he brings? The meal becomes more about the recipient than the Giver. The Mass is "something the Christian does (remember Christ; express faith and solidarity with the church in a public fashion) rather than something Christ does for the Christian."[33] Plus, he resented Zwingli's haughty tone.[34] The rhetoric on both sides grew sharp, and with each passing month hatred for each other escalated.

---

31. *LW* 37:336.
32. See *CR* 92, 562ff. and *CR* 92, 771ff.; *St. L.* 20, 1104ff.
33. Trueman, *Luther on the Christian Life,* 150.
34. See the letter Zwingli sent to Luther with his two books: *WABr* 4:184ff. Also see the letter Zwingli sent to Andreas Osiander: *CR* 96, 129–30. Cf. *LW* 37:154.

Another round of attacks followed the Frankfurt fair instigated by the publication of Luther's latest book, *That These Words of Christ, "This Is My Body," Etc., Still Stand Firm against the Fanatics (1527)*. The title was an insult, designed to instigate further animosity from the Swiss.[35] Further attacks on Luther followed, but the timing was not convenient for the Wittenberg Reformer. Luther was bombarded by familial, academic, and pastoral responsibilities. Nevertheless, by the end of 1527, Luther was determined to reply one last time. By next year's Frankfurt spring fair, his last stand emerged: *Confession Concerning Christ's Supper* (1528).[36]

Throughout, Luther devoted himself to answering many of the exegetical challenges Zwingli posed. Luther struggled to take Zwingli and Oecolampadius's method of interpretation seriously: *Who can believe Christ means, when he holds up the bread, that "This signifies my body"?*[37] Luther demanded they "prove to us out of Scripture that the word 'is' means the same as 'represents' in the Supper."[38] Luther examined the many biblical examples Zwingli and Oecolampadius appealed to (e.g., Christ is the vine, the Lamb) but concluded that none of them "produce a sound argument for making a metaphor out of the 'is'" at the last Supper.[39]

Luther was also concerned to present a christological case for the Lord's Supper. Zwingli and Oecolampadius charged Luther with a "contradiction that Christ's body is in heaven and in the Supper."[40] They feared Luther violated the hypostatic union, transferring divine attributes (like omnipresence) to his human nature. "They raise a hue and cry against us, saying that we mingle the two natures into one essence."[41] Luther was not moved by this accusation since anything that is true of one nature is true of the *person* of the Son. "Although, so to speak, the one part (namely, the divinity) does not suffer, nevertheless the person, who is God, suffers in the other part (namely, in the humanity). . . . Thus we should ascribe to the whole person whatever pertains to one part of the person, because both parts constitute one person."[42]

COMMUNICATIO IDIOMATUM

A common assumption says Luther was an innovator, rejecting medieval Christology before him, all to support his view of Christ's presence in the Eucharist. Luther taught that attributes of the divine nature were directly communicated (*communicatio idiomatum*) to the human nature, so the argument

---

35. See *CR* 92, 805ff.; *St. L.* 20, 1122ff. Cf. *LW* 37:154.

36. Although, consult his 1544 book, *Brief Confession on the Holy Sacrament*, in *WA* 54:141ff.

37. *LW* 37:168.

38. *LW* 37:170.

39. *LW* 37:175. E.g., "For Christ is not a likeness of the vine, but on the contrary the vine is a likeness of Christ" (37:253).

40. *LW* 37:203.

41. *LW* 37:212.

42. *LW* 37:210, 211.

goes. However, Johannes Brenz, one of Luther's colleagues, was the true source of such a Christology.[43] Brenz was not the only one. In *On the Two Natures in Christ* Martin Chemnitz identified three *genera*:

1. *Genus idiomaticum*: The characteristics peculiar to either of the natures were the characteristics of the entire person of Christ.
2. *Genus apotelesmaticum*: In his redemptive actions each nature within Christ performed what is peculiar to itself, with the participation of the other.
3. *Genus maiestaticum*: Christ's divine nature shares with his human nature all his divine characteristics for common possession, use, and designation within the one person of Christ.[44]

The third—*genus maiestaticum*—was as essential as it was controversial in explaining the logic of the Lutheran supper, but it was repugnant to the Reformed position. If the divine nature communicates its divine presence with the human nature, as if from one nature into the other, then Christ's body and blood can be really present in the bread and wine everywhere and in every place it is celebrated.

Such a Christology created debate between Brenz and, most notably, Peter Martyr Vermigli.[45] Brenz's position also invited critique from other reformed theologians, such as Heinrich Bullinger and Theodore Beza. In a well-spoken statement, Beza identified the major divide: "You wish that the flesh of Christ is adorned with all the properties of the divinity; we wish to unite it to the divine essence of the Son, so that one and the same thing [viz., the person] is essentially God and man."[46] If the Reformed conceived of a *communicatio idiomatum*, a communication of divine or human attributes had to be predicated to the *person* of the Son. A communication of divine attributes to the human *nature* of Jesus, said Reformed theologians, confused the natures, threatening the integrity of the human nature. In their estimation, Lutherans like Brenz had violated the Definition of Chalcedon, misusing it to their advantage.

However, if Brenz's position is not forced on Luther, then Luther's reliance on

---

43. Brenz's "position is thus quite different from Luther's, and attempts . . . to foist on Luther Brenz's view that the hypostatic union requires the human nature's participation in divine attributes are pure eisegesis." Cross, *Communicatio Idiomatum*, 35.

44. Kolb, "Confessional Lutheran theology," 78. Kolb thinks nominalism influenced Chemnitz's position. For all three categories, also see Muller, *Dictionary,* communicatio idiomatum, s.v.

45. E.g., Brenz, *Recognitio propheticae . . .* ; Vermigli, *Dialogus de utraque in Christo natura.* For a survey of the debate, see Cross, 142–57. Much disagreement persists as to Vermigli's position, but McLelland argues that Vermigli "was closest to both Cranmer and Bullinger, the Zurich *antistes* who made common ground with Calvin in the 1549 *Consensus Tigurinus*" ("Translator's Introduction," xxv).

46. Beza, *Ad Domini Joannis Brentii argumenta. . . .* Cf. Cross, 153–57, who says at the conclusion of his treatment of Beza, "Overall, there is little here that could not have been asserted by Melanchthon or Calvin; and barring Beza's claim about the impossibility of non-spatial bodily presence, nothing that could not have been asserted by Ockham or Biel, or Aquinas or Scotus" (157). That cannot be said of Brenz, however.

a more Scholastic Christology becomes apparent. Furthermore, it may explain in part why Luther was convinced he could deny Zwingli's accusation that he taught some form of Monophysitism, as if he mingled the natures into one essence. "Rather," said Luther, "we merge the two distinct natures into one single person."[47] Zwingli, however, transgressed Chalcedonian Christology, Luther protested. To deny Christ's real presence is to divorce the two natures from one another, creating instead two persons, which is the heresy of Nestorianism.[48] Luther had no doubt he was more orthodox: "Our faith maintains that Christ is God and man, and the two natures are one person, so that this person may not be divided in two; therefore, he can surely show himself in a corporeal, circumscribed manner at whatever place he will, as he did after the resurrection and will do on the Last Day."[49] Luther concluded that "if you can say, 'Here is God,' then you must also say, 'Christ the man is present too.'"[50] *The man*—that is the key qualifier, distinguishing Luther's view. For "wherever you place God for me," said Luther, "you must also place the humanity for me." If not, then the person is divided, like "Master Jack" who "takes off his coat and lays it aside when he goes to bed."[51]

THE PRINCE OF HELL'S POISON

Out of Luther's many accusations, one was incomparable and unforgivable from the Swiss point of view. On one hand, Luther had no respect for the exegetical, theological, or philosophical reasoning of Zwingli and Oecolampadius, which Luther called "flimsy" and "false." "If a boy came up with that kind of syllogism in school, he would receive a good whipping; should a master of the sophists do it, he would be called an ass."[52]

On the other hand, Luther lobbed more than insults—he questioned Zwingli's Christian identity. Like other disputes, Luther identified the teacher of his opponents as none other than the devil himself.[53] Zwingli and Oecolampadius did not know it, but they were the devil's puppets. Luther could sniff the devil all over them: "So must the devil always seal his wisdom with

---

47. *LW* 37:210, 212. Cross provides elaborative insight into Zwingli and Luther's logic: "Luther's understanding of bodily omnipresence was ... wholly Scholastic and Medieval. But Zwingli did not interpret it that way. Zwingli argued that omnipresence entails infinity. Since he rejected the view that Christ's human nature was infinite, he reasoned that Christ's body was not omnipresent. Luther's Medieval understanding of the nature of body allowed him simply to reject the inference from omnipresence to infinity. But ... later Lutherans accepted the consequence, and instead of rejecting infinity accepted the contrapositive of Zwingli's argument: since the body is omnipresent, it is infinite and thus can be characterized by a divine attribute—in some sense or other to be specified." Cross, 85.

48. *LW* 37:210 (for context see 22–213).

49. *LW* 37:218.

50. *LW* 37:218.

51. *LW* 37:210, 219.

52. *LW* 37:179.

53. *LW* 37:167; cf. 37:170, 171, 188, 269. This devilish association became so common in Luther's writings against Zwingli and company that in their responses to Luther they tallied up the innumerable times he made such an accusation to help readers see through the rhetoric. See *WA* 26:401 nn. 3–4; cf. *LW* 37:269 n. 171.

his own dung, and leave his stench behind, so that one may be aware that he has been present."[54] But then came the worst insult of all: "Whoever will take a warning let him beware of Zwingli and shun his books as the prince of hell's poison. For the man is completely perverted and has entirely lost Christ. . . . I regard Zwingli as un-Christian . . . seven times worse than when he was a papist."[55]

How could Luther make such a statement of a fellow Reformer? Christ's bodily presence was no tertiary doctrine for Luther. To eat Christ is to receive forgiveness of sins. Only a real presence can sustain and nourish the believer's trust in the crucified and resurrected Christ until the last day. If Christ is not bodily present, the good news of Jesus Christ is not appropriated in the Lord's Supper. Therefore, to deny Luther's view of the supper was to deny Christ himself. To oppose the real presence of Christ in the sacrament is to oppose the gospel itself. And to settle for a "spiritual or figurative" participation instead of a "physical participation" is to miss the Savior and his sacrifice altogether.[56] The metaphysics of a real participation was not merely a point of philosophy for Luther but necessary first principle on which the Lord's Supper depended and with it, the gospel.

Those who rush to paint every wall in Luther's theological house with a nominalist brush will fumble Luther's Eucharist Christology. True, Luther did emphasize the sign, what it signifies, and faith itself—especially in the early years of 1519–1520. Yet after 1523, in the heat of controversy, Luther elaborated and accentuated his doctrine of real presence, which fortified his belief in a bodily participation based on 1 Corinthians 10:16.[57] Nominalism may have influenced diverse corners of Luther's thought, but at the table Luther embodied one possible application of realism that ensured Christ inheres in the bread and the wine. Otherwise, Luther could not have advocated a *sacramental* unity at the table for the forgiveness of sins. Furthermore, in Luther's mind his interpretation *and* application of Jesus' words personified catholicity. From start to finish Luther not only retained a *sacramentum* but an *exemplum*. The sacrament, in other words, was the paradigm for discipleship, a "formula originating with Augustine." According to Lohse, "Even the relation to the church universal and its fellowship was viewed in the context of his doctrine of the Supper."[58]

THE MARBURG COLLOQUY (1529)

Now that Luther had declared Zwingli un-Christian, all hope of a united Reformation front was lost. Except one politician still held out hope. Back in

---

54. *LW* 37:179. "What purpose could it serve for me to handle all this devil's dung?" (285).
55. *LW* 37:206, 231.
56. *LW* 37:355, 357, 359.
57. Lohse does not believe Luther's Eucharist theology changed, but Luther added an "accent," especially after his conflict with Karlstadt (*Martin Luther's Theology*, 307; cf. *LW* 40:181).
58. Lohse, *Martin Luther's Theology*, 313.

1526, the First Diet of Speyer convened, and relationships were built between rulers and Reformers. Churches sympathetic to the Reformation were officially permitted to proceed with their intended reforms. After the diet, talks about a potential federation were entertained as well, confident that a federation could bring Reformers together and present a united front over against Rome and radicals. The Strasbourg Reformer Wolfgang Capito and Landgrave Philip of Hesse were two of the talking heads, although Zwingli was included as well. The federation, if pulled off, was not to be merely ecclesiastical but political. Philip of Hesse hoped it could give territories sympathetic or committed to the Reformation some stability, especially since Rome occupied so many territories already. To even entertain such an idea, however, there had to be common ground, *theological* territory that the Reformers could agree on. The elephant in the room was the Lord's Supper. Was it possible to put Zwingli and Luther in the same room and have them walk out arm in arm? Philip was determined to make it happen. He approached Luther with the proposal in 1527.

Luther declined. His books were written; his mind was made up. Zwingli was wrong, very wrong, and Luther had nothing more to say. The year 1528 was a deadlock. Yet Philip was no jellyfish; he had backbone, and his political ideals motivated him to keep on. He was so close; Zwingli, Capito, and Bucer had all agreed.[59] He only had to persuade Luther, the Reformer who was single-handedly capable of stopping or advancing Reformation progress. Zwingli believed he and Luther could disagree but nevertheless retain friendship and cooperation. The Christian faith, and the Reformation cause, was far bigger than their interpretation of the Lord's Supper. Although the supper was not unimportant, the debate over Christ's presence was secondary to the gospel itself. Whether Luther felt the same way or was at least willing to come halfway for the sake of a united front was not likely, however.

IN THE MARBURG CASTLE

What representatives appeared in the Marburg castle? The Swiss included Zwingli, Rudolph Collin, Ulrich Funk, Oecolampadius, Rudolph Frey, Caspar Heido, Martin Bucer, and Jacob Sturm.

Those from Wittenberg included Luther, Melanchthon, Justus Jonas, Caspar Cruciger, George Rörer, and Veit Dietrich.

Other Lutherans from southern Germany came, too, but were late: Osiander, Brenz, and Stephan Agricola.

---

59. *WA* 26:247.

In 1529 the Second Diet of Speyer met under Archduke Ferdinand.[60] Rome was not passive but active in its determination to shut down Reformation influence. While the first diet of 1526 permitted reforms, this second diet put a stop to them and insisted the church must return to its beliefs and practices prior to the first advances of Luther or the Diet of Worms.

Philip of Hesse, along with many other princes, protested but with no success. As a consequence, those with Reformation commitments were labeled "Protestants." Now more than ever Philip knew a federation was needed. Conveniently, Philip Melanchthon had attended the diet, allowing Philip of Hesse to approach Melanchthon with an idea: What if a colloquy was convened, one that brought Reformers together for alliance and confederation? Could Melanchthon persuade Luther?

At the time, Europe was divided over the Lord's Supper, many in southwest Germany leaning in the direction of Zwingli rather than Luther. However, if the two sides could be brought together, the union promised not only theological but political fortification. Such a union required compromise and compliance, the two sides putting away differences in order to join forces to stand tall against Charles, a risky endeavor if there ever was one.[61]

When Melanchthon took the idea back to Luther, Luther was resistant. He told Elector John not to take the bait either. Philip, however, knew politics; he got John's attention and tried to persuade him that the idea was the key to survival. Eventually, Luther agreed, although he remained skeptical that such a meeting could be successful; it might move both sides to dig their heels in deeper. But Philip believed the risk was worth it.

Luther approached the colloquy with demands. He wanted the other side to arrive at the colloquy already willing to yield to his views. If they showed up only to insist on their view, nothing good would come of it. But Luther himself admitted that he was not as flexible: "That I cannot yield after their arguments have been presented, I know as certainly as I know they are in error."[62] This letter to Philip should have been a forecast predicting how the colloquy might end. But again, Philip was determined.

Another indication was hidden within the *Schwabach Articles*. In the spirit of alliance, Elector John decided that a set of articles could help, a document around which to unite.[63] And who better than Luther to write up the articles? However, when the Lord's Supper was addressed, Luther put forward his position without qualification, which automatically put the other positions in a state of conflict.

---

60. Ferdinand "blamed the evangelical princes for the Turkish victory in Hungary that resulted in the death of his brother-in-law, King Louis, and allowed Suleyman to threaten Vienna." Hendrix, *Martin Luther*, 204.

61. Hendrix, 205–6.

62. *S-J* 2:484; *WABr* 5, 101–2.

63. Hendrix, *Martin Luther*, 205.

At the end of September, both the Swiss and Wittenberg representatives arrived in Marburg for a colloquy to start on Saturday morning, October 2, and to continue into Sunday evening. Philip of Hesse hosted both sides in his castle, and a modest audience came to watch. Before the two sides met for all to hear, Philip decided it was best they meet the day before in private to discuss rules of engagement and remind the Reformers of the goal of the meeting in the first place. Philip anticipated that the two sides might at least recognize what they had in common over the Lord's Supper so that the colloquy that followed moved toward unity, not division.

Despite Philip's commendable efforts at ecumenical dialogue, the colloquy turned into a debate. Both sides assumed Scripture was in their corner, and both sides appealed to the church fathers. Augustine, for example, was quoted by everyone, although Oecolampadius and Zwingli appealed to the church fathers more than Luther. Most catastrophic of all was this presupposition both parties brought to the table: they both insisted the burden of proof was the responsibility of the other side.

At the heart of the debate was a disagreement over hermeneutics. Before Luther started speaking, he picked up a piece of chalk and wrote Jesus' words on the table: *Hoc est corpus meum,* "This is my body." He then covered the words with velvet fabric only to throw it off at a pivotal moment in the debate when he most wanted to stress Jesus' words.[64] Jesus meant what he said. He also meant what he commanded: "If he should command me to eat dung, I would do it."[65] The debate hinged, then, on these words. "Do justice to that text!" demanded Luther.[66]

Zwingli and Oecolampadius sat at the table staring at the words in chalk, but neither of them was persuaded by Luther's dramatic argument. Their reason why had much to do with biblical interpretation. To understand one text, the interpreter must read other texts. Scripture must interpret Scripture, they replied.[67] When Scripture is considered as a whole, it teaches us that Jesus often used and assumed figurative expressions to communicate a truth. We do not need a passage that says "This is the figure of my body" since other texts assume Jesus does not speak in a literalistic fashion. In John 6:54–56, for example, Jesus commanded his disciples to eat his flesh and drink his blood to receive eternal life, but Jesus did not intend his disciples to take a bite out of his arm or put a cup to his veins. When Jesus said, "This *is* my body," the "is" could only mean "signifies."[68] Jesus did not refer, then, to a "bodily eating" in the supper.[69] That would

---

64. Hendrix, 207. Cf. *LW* 38:64, 67.
65. *LW* 38:19 (cf. 52).
66. *LW* 38:17.
67. *LW* 38:20.
68. *LW* 38:22. Zwingli and Oecolampadius appealed to a number of passages, texts that "prohibit a literal understanding."
69. *LW* 38:20.

contradict our own identity: "The soul is spirit; the soul does not eat flesh, but spirit eats spirit."[70]

Luther believed Zwingli and Oecolampadius forced unbiblical restrictions on an omnipresent Christ. "Christ is in the sacrament substantially," but Oecolampadius "does not want to allow that he is in heaven in the same way as he is in the bread," said Luther.[71] In response to Luther's "idea that the body of Christ is everywhere"—which raised the question, is Christ's humanity infinite?—Zwingli concluded that the "body of Christ is in one place, nor can it be in many places."[72] When Christ bodily ascended to heaven, that is where his body remained. Luther chided at such logic. "We must not search out what is in heaven in the same way as we investigate what is on earth. Christ is not in the Lord's Supper as if he were in one place. . . . God can cause his body not to be in one place, to be in one place and not to be in one place."[73] So, too, with the incarnate Son. His body can be both in heaven and in the supper. If not, then no "sacramental union" occurs, and the word of the gospel does not inhere through its sacramental form.[74] This point was not lost on Zwingli, who returned Sunday morning and pressed the issue further by reminding Luther that the body of Christ "is finite" and that "it must therefore be in a certain place."[75]

Many have ventured to explain the philosophical and theological rationale behind Zwingli's assertions, assertions that not only distinguish Zwingli from Lutheranism but other Reformed theologians. For example, in his expansive study of Zwingli, historian W. Peter Stephens suggests that Luther moved from Word-to-Spirit whereas Zwingli reversed the order to Spirit-then-Word, as if the Word is contingent upon the Spirit. If so, then a "Platonist opposition" could be at play "between outward and inward, so that what is outward cannot affect what is inward." Yet Stephens does not think Platonism is the only factor. Augustinianism may also be an influence, with its "stress on the sovereignty of God, which does not allow that word and sacraments can convey the Spirit, for this would put the gift of the Spirit in the power of those who preach the Word and celebrate the sacraments."[76] Other historians like Robert Kolb also believe a Platonist or realist presupposition set the parameters of Zwingli's position. "Zwingli's humanist training at Vienna and Basel had reinforced his 'Realist' conviction that 'the finite cannot convey the infinite.' Therefore, he concluded that the bread and wine of the sacrament can only represent, not convey,

70. *LW* 38:21.
71. *LW* 38:30.
72. *LW* 38:31.
73. *LW* 38:32.
74. Luther uses the language of sacramental union across his corpus and it appears in the Wittenberg Concord: "with the bread and wine the body and blood of Christ are truly and essentially present, distributed, and received. . . . through the sacramental union the bread is the body of Christ." *CR* 3: 75–81; cf. Kolb, *Martin Luther*, 148–49.
75. *LW* 38:32.
76. Stephens, "The theology of Zwingli," 97.

Christ's body and blood."[77] If a realist impression did influence Zwingli (and Oecolampadius), possibly by means of humanist sympathies (see chapter 6), then the irony is palpable.

The secularization thesis blames the Reformation for modernity, as if the Reformers were the carriers of the nominalist virus. But as chapter 1 advised, such an explanation is simplistic since realism's influence cannot be denied either. Furthermore, the irony thickens since critics display the transubstantiation of Rome as the true heir of realism. And yet, a form of realism may also explain a position like Zwingli's on the opposite side of the spectrum. Perhaps realism is not as monolithic as critics suppose, but it is far more elastic in its variegated manifestations across *loci*, especially the nature of Christ's presence in the supper.

Regardless of the rationale, at Marburg Zwingli did not budge in locating the body of Christ in heaven rather than on earth. As the debate progressed into Sunday afternoon, it was obvious that the dispute was not just theological; personality and rhetoric had their place as well. Even halfway through the first day, tempers started to fly. Throughout the debate, Zwingli kept pleading with Luther, "Please do not be angry about this!" But Luther believed he had cause to be angry: Zwingli "was speaking spitefully."[78] When Zwingli refused to leave John 6, asking Luther to explain it, Luther threw an insult: "Your logic is very poor; it is the kind of logic for which a schoolboy is caned and sent to the corner."[79] Zwingli returned with an insult of his own: "This passage is going to break your neck." But Luther quipped back, "Don't boast too much. Necks do not break that easily here. You are in Hesse, not in Switzerland."[80] Luther insulted Zwingli's homeland; he could not have lobbed a more hurtful insult. The debate had moved beyond exegesis and theology to national pride and disrespect. By the end of the debate, Zwingli and Oecolampadius's pleas for friendship instead of anger and spite fell on deaf ears.

Zwingli wept.

How did Luther respond? "Pray that you may come to a right understanding of this matter." Oecolampadius was not afraid to demand Luther do the same: "You, too, should pray for this, for you have the same need."[81]

Meanwhile, Zwingli's tears continued.

By Sunday evening, it was apparent that agreement could not be reached. Still, Philip of Hesse refused defeat. On Monday he asked Luther to write articles that the two sides could agree to, despite their inability to agree on Christ's presence. Luther complied, though he was solidified in his disagreement with Zwingli and Oecolampadius and expected nothing less from them either. Nevertheless,

---

77. Kolb, *Martin Luther,* 143; cf. Bolliger, *Infiniti contemplatio.*
78. *LW* 38:25.
79. *LW* 38:25.
80. *LW* 38:26.
81. *LW* 38:36.

Philip gained a small victory when Zwingli and his camp read the articles and said they were willing to sign them.

They agreed on so much: the Trinity of the Nicene Creed, the hypostatic union, original sin, justification by faith alone, preaching the gospel, baptism, and good works. They even agreed Rome's view of the supper was wrong. But they could not agree on the presence of Christ. The last article read as follows:

> Fifteenth, we all believe and hold concerning the Supper of our dear Lord Jesus Christ that both kinds should be used according to the institution by Christ; [also that the Mass is not a work with which one can secure grace for someone else, whether he is dead or alive;] also that the Sacrament of the Altar is a sacrament of the true body and blood of Jesus Christ and that the spiritual partaking of the same body and blood is especially necessary for every Christian. Similarly, that the use of the sacrament, like the word, has been given and ordained by God Almighty in order that weak consciences may thereby be excited to faith by the Holy Spirit *And although at this time, we have not reached an agreement as to whether the true body and blood of Christ are bodily present in the bread and wine, nevertheless, each side should show Christian love to the other side insofar as conscience will permit,* and both sides should diligently pray to Almighty God that through his Spirit he might confirm us in the right understanding. Amen.

Martin Luther
Justus Jonas
Philip Melanchthon
Andreas Osiander
Stephen Agricola
John Brenz
John Oecolampadius
Huldrych Zwingli
Martin Bucer
Caspar Heido[82]

If Philip had asked Zwingli and his camp to write the fifteen articles, they would have read otherwise, even on those subjects of agreement. When Zwingli's theology is considered, it is uncertain he aligned with the articles Luther wrote in all their detail. Nevertheless, Zwingli and company signed the articles for the sake of unity. After all, Zwingli was one of the original talking heads who wanted, along with Philip, some type of united front or federation in the first place. Despite his conflict with Luther, a conflict that was as personal as it was theological, Zwingli put his name to the document, as did Luther. Although article 15 acknowledged their conflict, it was written in a conciliar tone that

---

82. *LW* 38:88–89. The sentence in brackets is added in the Zurich edition.

encouraged cooperation, at least as far as "conscience will permit." Philip did not get the unanimity he dreamed about, but at least he had fifteen articles to present to the public.

Was it enough to muster a united front against the Reformation's many enemies? Philip left Marburg convinced it was. An alliance had been sufficiently formed, an imperfect alliance but an alliance nonetheless.

THE TURKISH THREAT

The struggle to achieve agreement was not the only pressing issue faced by Reformation territories. As the Reformers debated the presence of Christ in the Lord's Supper, the Ottoman Turks continued their conquest. As the Ottoman Turks advanced, the German people had urgent questions about the threat they posed to Western civilization as they knew it.

In 1453 the Turks marched on Constantinople and won. Over half a century later, the Turks were advancing still. Suleiman the Magnificent commanded the Turkish army to begin a conquest of Hungary. In 1521 Belgrade was overcome. In the years that followed, the Turks seemed irrepressible, attaining one victory after another. Who was to stop the Turks from claiming all of Europe? To complicate matters further, not everyone agreed on how to respond. Some said war was the only way. Others were convinced that popular stereotypes had misrepresented the Turks. They believed nonresistance was the answer.[83]

People wanted to know Luther's opinion as well. A decade earlier, Luther was asked whether a soldier could be saved, whether someone who wielded the sword could also be a Christian.[84] Now they wanted to know whether the sword should be used to fight off the Muslims and, if so, by whom. Luther had no reservations about the emperor fighting off the Turks. He did warn, however, that the name of Christ should not be the banner in such a war. In contrast to Rome, Luther was set against the idea of a crusade.

Those who had a recent memory did wonder if Luther was contradicting his earlier advice. A decade earlier Luther had said that "to fight against the Turk is the same as resisting God, who visits our sin upon us with this rod."[85] Context did play a factor in Luther's earlier advice. At that time, Luther was opposing the popes of the past who "used the Turkish war as a cover for their game and robbed Germany of money by means of indulgences."[86] The real issue, the driving motive, was this: "They undertook to fight against the Turk in the name

---

83. As Luther complained, "Some actually want the Turk to come and rule because they think our German people are wild and uncivilized—indeed, that they are half-devil and half-man." There are some "stupid preachers among us Germans (as I am sorry to hear) who are making the people believe that we ought not and must not fight against the Turks." *LW* 46:161.

84. Also see Luther, *Temporal Authority: To What Extent It Should Be Obeyed* (1523); *LW* 45:75–130.

85. *LW* 31:91–92.

86. *LW* 46:164. "Think of all the heartbreak and misery that have been caused by the *cruciata*, by the indulgences, and by crusade taxes. With these Christians have been stirred up to take the sword and fight the Turk when they ought to have been fighting the devil and unbelief with the word and with prayer" (46:186).

of Christ, and taught and incited men to do this, as though our people were an army of Christians against the Turks, who were enemies of Christ. This is absolutely contrary to Christ's doctrine and name. . . . This is the greatest of all sins and is one that no Turk commits, for Christ's name is used for sin and shame and thus dishonored."[87]

Luther's advice, then, was to pay attention to the office and the calling God had given to each person. He said that if you were the emperor and under God's command, then your office and calling were to protect the nation from any threat—the Turks included—that might compromise the safety of civilization. That calling, however, was a civil duty, not a Christian one; therefore, no emperor or soldier should crusade against the Turks in the name of Jesus.[88] As for bishops and priests, their calling and office resided in a different domain: the church. Therefore, any bishop who tried to join the emperor with a crusading motive was to be sent away. "If I were emperor, king, or prince and were in a campaign against the Turk, I would exhort my bishops and priests to stay at home and attend to the duties of their office, praying, fasting, saying mass, preaching, and caring for the poor, as not only Holy Scripture, but their own canon law teaches and requires." What if they disobeyed? Use force, said Luther, to send them away and attend to their true calling. "It would be less harmful to have three devils in the army than one disobedient, apostate bishop who had given up his office and assumed the office of another."[89] If Luther were called to be a soldier and saw a priest on the battlefield waving the banner of the cross, what would he do? "[I should] run as though the devil were chasing me," said Luther.[90] For "the church ought not to strive or fight with the sword."[91] Likewise, the "emperor is not the head of Christendom or defender of the gospel or the faith."[92] Both the church and emperor fight, but the former with prayer and petition, the latter with bronze and bow.

And there is much to pray against. Luther instructed Christians on the differences between Christianity and Islam, comparing Muhammad to Jesus, and the Qur'an to the Bible. As to the civil authorities, Luther had instruction to give as well: he warned them not to underestimate the power of the Turkish sword; it was sharper than any they had seen before. Luther felt the need to say this because he worried his fellow Germans took too much pride in his country's past victories.[93] Luther had nothing but rebuke and admonishment: stop persecuting the gospel he preached and start focusing on the real threat—the Turk.[94]

The Turkish threat was imminent, and Europeans needed expedient reassur-

---

87. *LW* 46:165.
88. *LW* 46:188–89.
89. *LW* 46:167, 168.
90. *LW* 46:168. Even if the pope himself picked up the sword, he should be treated like he was a Turk himself (46:198).
91. *LW* 46:168; cf. 46:185.
92. *LW* 46:185.
93. *LW* 46:202.
94. *LW* 46:204.

ance that they were not as vulnerable as other territories more easily conquered. As the Turkish armies marched closer, they arrived at Vienna in the fall of 1529. Their sheer size was intimidating, but the soldiers defending Vienna held their ground and overcame.

The next year, Charles was on the lookout to solidify resistance to the Turks. By amalgamating support in Germany, Charles might establish a bulwark the Turks could not penetrate. However, Germany was ground zero for the Reformation, and a number of princes and their territories were sympathetic if not committed to Luther's cause. He called for an imperial diet to meet in Augsburg in 1530, giving the German princes and theologians the opportunity to present their beliefs.

DEFENDING REFORMATION CATHOLICITY: MELANCHTHON AND THE DIET OF AUGSBURG

Although Charles remained committed to the religion of the papacy, nevertheless, he desired concord in his empire and craved a resolution to the seemingly impassable division. That gave the estates hope. Elector John of Saxony, for example, now believed Augsburg might be the solution, especially if the emperor was willing at least to listen and consider the Lutheran faith. The estates needed someone who could articulate core Protestant beliefs but without the aggressive polemic that could forfeit concord. Philip Melanchthon was the natural choice.

However, the task was most difficult since it was unlikely any document could meet the emperor's expectations. John, elector of Saxony, tested the waters and found them choppy when he presented the emperor with the *Schwabach Articles*, only to receive the emperor's scorn. The estates were off to a bad start as soon as they stepped into Augsburg. The elector despaired to himself, doubtful anything good could come out of Augsburg.[95]

Yet Melanchthon was not without support. Many of Luther's best and brightest colleagues traveled to Augsburg with the elector of Saxony, dropping Luther off at the Coburg castle on the way for safekeeping. Ever since the Diet of Worms, Luther was an outlaw, banned from the empire. Entering Augsburg could result in his arrest and execution. Nevertheless, Luther stayed close enough at the castle of Coburg to correspond with Philip Melanchthon, receiving updates on any progress and giving instruction on negotiations.

The presence of the German Reformers was not insignificant.[96] The summer of 1530 was an opportunity for all gathered at the diet to hear the gospel and the doctrines that not only set them apart from the papacy but, they hoped, might even define (and reform) the church of the future. Many if not most of Luther's writings had a polemical tone to them. But a confession, especially one they hoped the emperor might cooperate with, could not have as many sharp rhetorical edges.

---

95. Hillerbrand observed that John almost didn't attend for these reasons. Hillerbrand, *Division of Christendom*, 162.

96. Others included Justus Jonas, Georg Spalatin, Johann Agricola, et al.

CREEDS AND CATHOLICITY (1538)

Melanchthon was not alone in his defense of the Reformation's catholic fidelity. In 1538 Luther wrote *The Three Symbols or Creeds of the Christian Faith* out of a similar concern. Luther argued that the Reformation churches were part of the "real Christian Church," over against Rome, "that false arrogant church" (*LW* 34:201). Luther appealed to the Apostles' Creed and the Athanasian Creed, the latter a symbol credited to Augustine and Ambrose. He spent considerable space appealing to Hebrews 1:3, where Christ is said to be the brilliance of the Father's glory and the image of his divine substance. Sounding much like the church fathers, Luther asserted the eternal generation of the Son: "Christ arose out of the Father's divine nature from eternity and is his substantial image, *substantialis imago, non artificialis aut facta vel create*, which has the Father's divine nature wholly and completely in itself, and of which nature *is* itself, not made or created out of something else, just as the divine substance itself is not made or created out of something else" (*LW* 34:221). Believing the Son to be begotten from the Father from all eternity, Luther petitioned the Nicene Creed, which he said was "sung in the mass every Sunday" (34:228). Luther showed that his churches were not a rebellion so much as a reform, returning the church to its Christian roots.

That did not mean the German evangelicals compromised, but they were cognizant of this opportune moment, striving to balance conviction in belief with a conciliatory tone. The product was inspirational to the German church, both at the time and for centuries to come.

When Melanchthon and the others arrived in Augsburg, Johann Eck had just published *Four Hundred Four Propositions*, a compilation of quotes not only from Luther but from other "heretical" groups, like the Swiss (Zwinglians) and certain radical sects (Anabaptists). By putting them all in the same book, Eck made Luther and his disciples look like just another group of schismatic heretics. Eck even traced the Anabaptist cause to Luther himself. Eck's compilation drove home an accusation: the German theologians were pushing novel doctrines.[97] To counter the caricature and to distinguish the Reformation from radicals, Melanchthon gave the *Augsburg Confession* a strong emphasis on catholicity.[98]

Consider several examples. Augsburg's first article is on God, and the first sentence references the Council of Nicaea in its affirmation of key tenets of classical Christian theism, especially divine simplicity and the undivided nature the persons of the Trinity have in common.[99] When the confession moves from the Trinity to the Son of God, it echoes and quotes the Apostles' Creed at length.[100] Likewise, when the confession articulates original sin, it reveals a

---

97. On Eck and the charge of novelty, see Kolb and Wengert, *Book of Concord*, 28.
98. Melanchthon drew on a variety of sources; cf. Kolb and Wengert, 28.
99. *Augsburg Confession* 1.
100. *Augsburg Confession* 3.

conspicuous debt to Thomas Aquinas's definition, which describes the loss of original righteousness in Augustinian overtones.[101] Or consider its articles on the church. Contrary to Rome's accusations, the confession located the Reformers *within* the one, true church: "at all times there must be and remain one holy, Christian church. It is the assembly of all believers among whom the gospel is purely preached and the holy sacraments are administered according to the gospel."[102] Insinuated was the Reformation claim that their churches had retrieved the true gospel and the right administration of baptism and the supper, which confirmed the Reformers' own belief that from the beginning they were not intending to divide but renew the church.

With each article, the confession not only put forward its affirmations but its denials. Yet those condemnations were not merely directed at Rome; many of them were directed at the "Anabaptists." At the time, the Wittenbergers collapsed diverse radicals into this one category. That may appear historically inaccurate, but that misses their main concern, which was not to spell out the differences between variegated sects but to separate *themselves* from *all* sects. They were on the side of orthodox Christianity; these sects were not. Rome had failed to make that distinction, but the confession was sure to correct it. For example, on the preaching office the confession said, "Condemned are the Anabaptists and others who teach that we obtain the Holy Spirit without the external word of the gospel through our own preparation, thoughts, and works."[103] By the end of part 1, the confession concluded that it had only taught that which was "clearly grounded in Holy Scripture" and had taught nothing that was "against nor contrary to the universal Christian church" or the "writings of the Fathers."[104]

Later, the confession presented the Wittenbergers' definition of repentance: "True repentance is nothing else than to have contrition and sorrow, or terror about sin, and yet at the same time to believe in the gospel and absolution that sin is forgiven and grace is obtained through Christ." While faith "comforts the heart and puts it at peace," nevertheless, "improvement should also follow" and there should be "fruits of repentance." That definition sounded innocent enough, but in truth it was a sharp dividing line, separating the Wittenbergers from Anabaptist Spiritualists like Hans Denck and Caspar Schwenckfeld, who both taught forms of Christian perfection. "Rejected here," said the confession, "are those who teach that whoever has once become righteous cannot fall

---

101. Compare article 2 to *ST* 1a2ae. 82, 3. "Here the confession appropriated a definition of original sin derived from Aquinas, who had based it upon certain formulations of Augustine. Sin consisted negatively of 'a lack of original righteousness' and positively of 'concupiscence.'" Pelikan, *Obedient Rebels*, 46.

102. *Augsburg Confession* 8. That is not to say, however, that the Reformers thought (as did some radicals) that the sacraments were invalid if administered by Rome. The "sacraments—even though administered by unrighteous priests—are efficacious all the same. . . . Condemned, therefore, are the Donatists and all others who hold a different view" (8).

103. *Augsburg Confession* 5. Kolb and Wengert think "others" may insinuate late medievals like Gabriel Biel.

104. *Augsburg Confession*, conclusion of pt. 1.

again."[105] So, too, the confession's article on the last judgment rejected those "Anabaptists"—Hans Denck, Melchior, and others—who taught "that the devils and condemned human beings will not suffer eternal torture and torment." The confession also condemns those—like Thomas Müntzer—who thought that "righteous people alone will possess a secular kingdom and will annihilate all the ungodly."[106]

Even the latter part of the confession, which was more concerned with ecclesiastical offices and the ethics of Christian living, was deeply concerned with catholicity. When the confession made its case for marriage among the clergy, it appealed to the "writings of the Fathers" to show how "it was customary in the Christian church of ancient times for priests and deacons to have wives."[107] The confession followed Scripture's lead in its "high esteem" for marriage, but it also looked to Fathers such as Cyprian, who "advised that women who do not keep the vow of chastity should get married."[108]

Likewise, when the Wittenbergers distinguished their view of the Mass from Rome, they claimed official church teaching was on their side. They denied that the Mass involved a sacrifice and instead defined the Mass as communion. "Thus, the Mass remains among us in its proper use, as it was observed formerly in the church."[109] The confession then quoted from the Nicene canons only to conclude that no "novelty has been introduced that did not exist in the church in days of old. . . . Therefore this way of celebrating Mass should, in all fairness, not be condemned as heretical or unchristian."[110]

This stress on catholicity was no minute notation. The first years of the Reformation trumpeted *sola scriptura* without having to worry yet about implementing the formal principal in the practical life of the church. Two instigators motivated the Reformers to explain, however, what kind of scriptural heritage the Reformers descended from. One was Rome herself; she claimed the Reformation beliefs were novel, out of sync with the church catholic. The second was the radical wing; biblicist sects the Reformers disassociated from also appealed to the Bible and sometimes with a total disregard for the church catholic. Over against both, the Reformers labored to demonstrate that the doctrines they claimed as biblical were none other than the same doctrines taught by Christian orthodoxy for the last millennia and a half. The Reformers taught nothing novel but embodied a tradition true to the apostolic heritage and its

---

105. *Augsburg Confession* 12.

106. *Augsburg Confession* 17.

107. *Augsburg Confession* 23. Kolb and Wengert note, "Originally, priests were not permitted to marry a second time; then they could not marry after their priestly vows; and since the fourth century they had to refrain from marital relations altogether. However, it was not until the end of the eleventh century that the requirement of celibacy was generally enforced by Pope Gregory VII. At that time most priests in Germany were still married" (64 n. 134).

108. *Augsburg Confession* 23.

109. *Augsburg Confession* 24.

110. *Augsburg Confession* 24. Many other examples exist: e.g., see art. 26, where appeal is made to ancient Fathers for liberty on church ceremonies.

HANS DENCK ATTACKS MARTIN LUTHER

Hans Denck has been labeled a forerunner of the Spiritualist tradition, which should be distinguished from other religious radical traditions (see chapter 2 and the Spiritualist tradition). The Spiritualists agreed with the Anabaptists that the church had been corrupted by the papacy across history. But unlike the Anabaptists, the Spiritualists were pessimistic about collective appeals to a restoration of one pure Anabaptist church. If restoration was possible, the individual Christian might experience restoration by the Spirit. Spiritualists dismissed the simplistic literalism (or biblicist hermeneutic) of many Anabaptists, especially those who used the text to justify their apocalyptic agendas. The Spiritualists criticized reading doctrines and making apocalyptic forecasts right off the pages of Scripture. The Scriptures, after all, were written by human authors. Needed, instead, is the Holy Spirit. Without the Spirit, the Scriptures are useless. That is why the *Augsburg Confession* condemned those who said "we obtain the Holy Spirit without the external word."

Hans Denck (ca. 1495/1500–1527) was a forerunner of the Spiritualist tradition that blossomed with Franck and Schwenckfeld. Denck studied at the University of Ingolstadt and became a schoolmaster in Regensburg. As Luther's ideas made their way to Denck, Denck converted to the Lutheran cause. Denck also studied in Basel, and some historians think Denck might even have studied under Erasmus for a short time. He certainly sat under Oecolampadius. Afterward Denck traveled to Nuremberg in 1523 and was set to be a leading Reformer. However, the next year Denck changed his mind about Lutheranism after Hans Hut stayed with him overnight and introduced Denck to the radical mindset and its critique of Luther. Not long after, the city council discovered Denck's criticisms of externals, the sacraments in particular. Discounting infant baptism as a channel for grace, Denck emphasized the inner baptism of the Spirit instead. While Denck may have favored the Anabaptist position, nonetheless, he still criticized all appeals (Anabaptist included) to an external rite for undermining the inner work of the Spirit. The Lord's Supper fell under the same rubric: the bread and wine are not necessary; what truly matters is the inner bread, namely, righteous living by faith.

Denck eventually made his way to Augsburg, where he was rebaptized in 1526. In Augsburg Denck also opposed other Lutheran doctrines, for example, attacking Luther's *Bondage of the Will*. Siding with Erasmus, Denck defended free will in salvation, accentuating the individual in the reception of the Spirit and the pursuit of righteous living. Furthermore, objected Denck, if the will is enslaved, then God is the author of evil instead of man.

Also in 1526, Denck was confronted by Urbanus Rhegius and summoned to a disputation, but Denck fled to Strasbourg. In Strasbourg Denck entered into fierce debate with Martin Bucer, who grew frustrated at the radical's ambiguity when questioned about his theology. Bucer's frustration says something; out of all the Reformers, Bucer was one of the most generous in his interpretations of others, attempting to achieve unity if possible. But not with Denck. At the request of Bucer, the magistrates expelled Denck from Strasbourg. Sojourning from one city to the next, Denck fell victim to the plague in Basel, dying young in 1527 before his potential as an up-and-coming radical could be reached.

patristic and medieval heirs. Pelikan's assessment of the *Augsburg Confession* could be applied to the Reformation as a whole: the Reformers "refused to be identified with those movements, past [Donatism] and present [Anabaptism], which accepted the identification between Roman and Catholic and then proceeded to reject both. Rather, the *Augsburg Confession* sought to root its protest against Rome in the Catholic tradition."[111] In short, Augsburg represented a *catholic* argument over against a *Roman* church. Put otherwise, the papacy was Roman but not catholic (see chapter 17).

THE HEIDELBERG CATECHISM

Due to the Peace of Augsburg (1555), both Lutherans and Roman Catholics were free to worship without penalty. However, that agreement did not include the Reformed wing of the Reformation. Nevertheless, the University of Heidelberg started entertaining Reformed influence at the end of the 1550s. Controversy ignited when Reformed and Lutheran Protestants clashed over Christ's presence at the Lord's Table, and in 1560 Elector Frederick III attempted to resolve that tension by using the Scholastic method of disputation. The Reformed disputants were persuasive enough to throw into question the *Augsburg Confession*'s interpretation of the Lord's Supper. Even Frederick himself was influenced by their argument, and in 1562 he summoned the university's faculty—including Caspar Olevianus (1536–87) and Zacharius Ursinus (1534–83)—to write a catechism. The Heidelberg Catechism (1563) was then used to teach the laity the Reformed faith. The catechism not only served children but adults as well, and even proved a theological guardrail for the Reformed preacher. Yet most of all, the Heidelberg Catechism served as a medium for Reformed catholicity as churches rallied around the catechism when they encountered Roman Catholic and Lutheran opposition.

For the history of the catechism, see Bierma, ed., *An Introduction to the Heidelberg Catechism*.

With that bold claim, the *Augsburg Confession* became one of the most mature confessions of the German Reformation. For the confession not only put forward key distinctives—*sola fide*, for example—but it did so within a patristic tradition that Rome said she alone could claim. The effect was foundational to the survival of the Reformation: the Germans were no mere protestors, but they were retrieving the true, catholic heritage Rome had either distorted or abandoned by means of the church's innovations. Luther's polemical books had unquestioned value, kickstarting a reformation. But the *Augsburg Confession* gave the German churches a fortification, not one they had to invent but one that predated Rome, rooted as it was in the earliest orthodox creeds. If Luther's

---

111. Pelikan, *Obedient Rebels*, 45.

tracts and treatises were dynamite, exploding layers of ecclesiastical and doctrinal novelties, the *Augsburg Confession* was the first layer of a new foundation. Ironically, that foundation was laid on top of an old foundation, an apostolic and patristic foundation that Rome claimed was hers alone. For that reason, Augsburg was only the beginning of a long confessional era.[112]

As for the father of the German Reformation himself, he could not have been more pleased. Luther said of the confession, "There is nothing that might be improved or changed." No small words coming from Luther, who acknowledged he was not the type to be "soft and subtle."[113] But whether the *Augsburg Confession* was destined to be a conciliatory success remained to be seen.[114] In June 1530, tension developed between Charles and the estates. The emperor prohibited Protestant preaching in Augsburg, which set off Margrave George of Brandenburg. Before the emperor himself, the preacher declared his allegiance to the proclamation of the Word even if it meant death, which only further inspired the Protestants to abstain from *Corpus Christi* later that day (June 15). George, however, may have overreacted. As forceful and intimidating as Charles could be, he did come to Augsburg ready to listen and achieve a resolution, not to put anyone to death.[115] That intention was apparent in the words of the emperor at the start of the diet (June 21). Charles, after all, needed allies against the Turks and peace within his own imperial German household.[116]

The *Augsburg Confession* was signed on June 23, 1530, by representatives of numerous Lutheran territories, which was fitting since the document had political ramifications. Two days later the *Confession* was read before the emperor in German.[117] Some say Charles fell asleep during the two-hour reading. It is possible, especially since German was not his native tongue.[118] The Catholics, however, folded their arms, standing against the pressure to present a Catholic confession. They represented the church; they were not heretics. Therefore, they did not have to defend their position—that burden belonged to the Protestant estates. After the presentation of the *Augsburg Confession*, the Lutherans waited for the emperor's response.[119] If the emperor was at all open to the Lutheran

---

112. *CCFCT* 2:205.

113. *WABr*, 5:319.

114. When the Augsburg Confession was republished in 1540, Melanchthon made a change: rather than saying Christ is truly present (*vere adsint*) in the bread and wine he said Christ is truly presented (*vere exhibeantur*). The Smalcald League abided by this change when the Augsburg Confession was presented at the Colloquy of Worms (1540). Kusukawa, "Melanchthon," 65.

115. "The emperor, taken aback by such determination, reportedly retorted in broken German, 'Lieber Fürst, nicht Köpfe ab' (Dear ruler, no heads chopped off)." Hillerbrand, *Division of Christendom*, 163.

116. The concern for religious peace, said Hillerbrand, was primary for Charles at the diet. Hillerbrand, 163.

117. On the specific territories and cities, see Hendrix, *Martin Luther*, 218; Hillerbrand, 164.

118. Hendrix, 218, says the "loud reading may have sounded like a droning in the background."

119. They were not the only ones to present; others sent their belief statements. For example, Zwingli sent his *Ratio fidei* (see chapters 10, 12), which was far more polemical than Melanchthon's confession, not only attacking Rome but the Lutherans. Also, Wolfgang Capito, Jakob Sturm, and Martin Bucer presented their *Confessio Tetrapolitana*, but the *Tetrapolitana* was not well received since it attempted too many concessions all around and was not as well argued as Melanchthon's confession. Those from Strasbourg could not

Confession, which itself was a high hope, that did not mean he would accept it in its entirety. In that event, negotiation was inevitable.

Melanchthon was willing to concede on certain issues to achieve unity. Luther was not.[120] Despite his lofty praise, when Luther received the *Augsburg Confession*, he was not satisfied with everything. Luther was delighted with the *Augsburg Confession*'s articulation of doctrine. However, Luther saw no polemical edge, no direct refutation and condemnation of the papacy and its beliefs and practices. Here was the difference between Luther and Melanchthon: Luther was determined to stand his ground, with zero concessions, no matter what the fallout or consequence, regardless of whether threats and death itself should put an end to the Lutheran churches. But Melanchthon was more diplomatic, attempting to achieve unity even if it was unlikely. For Melanchthon, negotiations might deter use of the sword. If sufficient agreement could be reached, the Reformation might have a chance at survival as well.

A group of Roman theologians, including Johann Eck of Ingolstadt, who had challenged Luther back in 1519 at Leipzig, responded with a *Confutation* at the start of August, which Charles immediately concluded was triumphant. The *Confutation* was lucid in its rejection of the *Confession* and its doctrines. In the weeks ahead, negotiations ensued. The Catholics and Lutherans appeared to find common ground on a number of theological issues. Nevertheless, the Catholics refused to abandon those many practices (e.g., vows, clerical celibacy) that the *Confession* considered in need of correction. "Doctrines were discussable because they were concepts that mattered mainly to theologians; but religious practices were not negotiable because they gave access to the presence and power of the divine, and that access was the reason religion existed."[121] Such stratagem worked to the advantage of the Catholics more than the Protestants. "This strategy fit harmoniously with that of the papal legate, Lorenzo Campeggio, to grant minor concessions to the Protestants and thereby prevent the convening of a general council."[122] In time Luther became convinced that the whole affair was destined to result in failure. The Reformers should disengage lest too much be conceded to their opponents. Luther wrote to his colleagues and told them to abandon the diet altogether.[123] Melanchthon ignored Luther, pressing forward and negotiating with Lorenzo Campeggio.[124]

---

bring themselves to sign Melanchthon's confession due to differences over the Lord's Supper. Nevertheless, some cities in southern Germany did sign it, including Lindau, Strasbourg, Constance, and Memmingen. See *Tetrapolitan Confession, 1530*, 2:220–48.

120. *WABr* 5:405–6; *LW* 49:328, 330. Cf. Hendrix, *Martin Luther*, 218.

121. Hendrix, 221.

122. Hillerbrand, *Division of Christendom*, 165.

123. See *WABr* 5:405–8, 479–80; cf. *LW* 34:6–7; 49:345–47.

124. "Melanchthon secretly approached the papal legate Campeggio with the proposition that in return for the Communion cup and priestly marriage, concessions would be possible in the other contested issues—a proposal that, once it became public, caused considerable consternation on the part of the Protestants. The curia responded with a categorical no to these maneuverings." Hillerbrand, *Division of Christendom*, 165.

MELANCHTHON CULTIVATES REFORMATION

Not all Reformers were like Luther. If they were, the Reformation may have quickly burst into flames and died out. Luther's personality galvanized a bold protest that was needed in the early years of opposition. But other personalities, like Melanchthon's, stabilized the Reformation until it slowly grew and matured, and was strong enough to persist through various trials. That task required Melanchthon's more subdued, peaceful disposition, which allowed him to navigate tricky diplomatic conversations not only with other Reformers across Europe but civil rulers. Luther knew as much. In one of his letters, he acknowledged how he and Melanchthon complemented one another: "For this I was born: to fight and take the field against mobs and devils. Therefore many of my books are stormy and war-like. I must pull out the stumps and roots, hack away at thorns and thistles, drain the swamps. I am the coarse woodsman who must blaze a new trail. But Master Philip comes neatly and quietly behind me, cultivates and plants, sows and waters with joy, according to the gifts that God has richly given him" (*WA* 30:2, 68–69).

In the end, Charles reached a conclusion that did not reflect the patient negotiations between Protestants and Catholics. That September the emperor sided once more with the *Confutation* in his draft of the recess. Charles told the world that the German Reformers had been trounced. Anxiety spread like a plague when Charles announced that the Reformers and their sympathizers had until April 15, 1531, to conform to the *Confutation* or else. The draft did mention Reformation apprehensions, as if they would be further considered by a future council. However, the draft condemned Reformation convictions nonetheless.[125] As for the church across German territories, the emperor's draft demanded they return to the theology and liturgy the papacy practiced, including the Mass, before the Reformation began.[126]

Did the emperor expect the Protestants to agree and submit to these demands? If so, he was wide of the mark. When Melanchthon got his hands on a copy of the *Confutation* that October, he wrote an *Apology* that defended the *Augsburg Confession*. But it was too late. For the Imperial Edict of Augsburg was more or less decided, and the Protestants were not the victors in the eyes of the emperor.

At the start of the diet, some on both sides hoped for peace and reconciliation, or at least anticipated that cooperation was attainable.[127] By consequence, Augsburg was no simple or sharp divergence between Protestants and Catholics.

---

125. Although Protestants were not about to submit, they did reluctantly agree that if the Turks invaded they would not merely stand by but aid the emperor. See Hillerbrand, 166.

126. There were other demands too: the draft "prohibited future evangelical publications, insisted on the reestablishment of monasteries and convents that had been dissolved," for example. Hillerbrand, 166.

127. Even at the start of the *Augsburg Confession*, it reads, "Thus, the matters at issue between the parties may be presented in writing on both sides; they may be negotiated charitably and amicably; and these same differences may be so explained as to unite us in one, true religion, since we are all enlisted under one Christ and should confess Christ." *Augsburg Confession*, preface (32).

EXHORTATION TO ALL CLERGY

Melanchthon was the chief author of the *Augsburg Confession*, but Luther also published a brief book in June 1530 that landed in the hands of those at the diet. *Exhortation to All Clergy Assembled at Augsburg* was not an attempt at concession—Luther was not one to concede on doctrines central to the Reformation. Rather, Luther attempted to persuade bishops at Augsburg to commit to the evangelical movement. He revisited the Roman beliefs that first motivated his initial call to reform:

> 1. They sold the indulgence as the divine grace which forgives sin. Thereby Christ's blood and death were denied and blasphemed together with the Holy Spirit and the gospel.
> 2. They falsely sold souls out of purgatory through it, to the great shame of the Divine Majesty, but it brought in lots of money.
> 3. They thereby put the pope in heaven as a god who could command the angels to carry to heaven the souls of pilgrims who died on their trip to Rome.
> 4. The gospel, which is, after all, the only true indulgence, had to keep silence in the churches in deference to the indulgence. . . .
> 11. They finally exalted indulgence so high that they taught if someone had even slept with the mother of God, through indulgence it would be forgiven.
> 12. They taught that when the penny rang in the money box, the soul rose to heaven.
> 13. One need have neither contrition nor sorrow to receive the indulgence. It was enough that one now deposit the money. (*LW* 34:16–17)

As Luther looked back at the state of the church, he recounted how "no one knew how to preach even the gospel" in any way except Rome's emphasis on works of merit. Luther's *Exhortation* systematically addressed each area of corruption in the Roman Church, leaving the bishops at Augsburg with a question no one but Luther dared to ask: "Who, then, is the church?" Luther's answer struck at the heart of the Reformation: "The right church must surely be the one which holds to God's Word and suffers for it, as we do, praise God. . . ." As for Rome, "you are the devil's church!" (*LW* 34:21, 39).

Within both camps were mediators eager to reach a compromise, meaning the distance between the two camps was not as wide as others said.[128] At first the initial remarks of Charles inspired Protestant optimism—he planned to listen and take Protestant concerns into consideration. But his final decision was less amicable and certainly not as flexible as the Protestants hoped. Charles had no lasting patience with the Reformation cause. Now was his chance to show

---

128. Hillerbrand said there were not only "hawks" but "doves," the later mediators trying to bridge that gap. In part, the divergent opinions within each camp also concerned a disagreement over what was at stake, theology or practice. Was it enough to reform in practice, or did theological changes have to be made? Hillerbrand, *Division of Christendom*, 167.

the German Protestants their true fate: concession or termination. "The recess should be seen as the emperor's definitive turn against the movement of reform, nine years after he had first sought to do so at Worms."[129] In that spirit, the final edict that November reinstated the verdict of Worms. Luther remained an outlaw; his churches remained complicit. Protestants now waited to see if the pope would come through on a council, though it seemed unlikely the outcome would be any different than Augsburg. Furthermore, calling a council required the pope and papacy to submit to conciliar authority, at least to some degree. That, too, appeared dubious. "The fear of conciliarism ran deep in papal bones."[130]

The condemning conclusion to the diet left a nasty, bitter taste in the mouths of the German Reformers, forcing them to prepare for the worst. However, they also understood that the emperor's bark might hurt more than his bite. For as long as Charles depended on Protestant funds to keep the Turks at bay, he could not implement his verdict to the degree he desired. In addition, historians do wonder to what degree Charles's final decision was influenced by the Roman curia. At the start of the diet, Charles appeared open to cooperation for the sake of concord; unity or something close to it could only buttress his political endeavors across Europe. However, the Roman curia had a significant say in the diet. Was Charles's decisive conclusion capitulating to the curia's most vocal opponents of the Reformation? Whatever the answer, one thing was clear: "Augsburg revealed an ambiguous situation, more hopeful than some had dreamed, more discouraging than others had feared."[131]

THE SMALCALD LEAGUE AND LUTHER'S DEFENSE OF ARMS

After the verdict of the Imperial Diet of Augsburg, Philip of Hesse believed an alliance of Reformation territories was needed more than ever. Should the emperor decide to attack Reformation territories, a defense must prepare, or else they could lose everything. Princes must join arms to ensure the survival of their people. Landgrave Philip of Hesse and the Saxon elector considered whether forming a league could guard their people from attack. But would princes agree to join? Even the act of forming a league was considered defiance and might invite the emperor's wrath.

Several hurdles had to be jumped before a league was formed. For one, it was no secret that territories disagreed over the meaning of Christ's presence in the supper. Some sided with Luther; others were sympathetic with Zwingli. Also, in the past Luther prohibited Christians from picking up the sword against the emperor. The insubordination of the Peasants' Revolt was exhibit A. Would Luther now encourage just the opposite to save the Reformation?

In October 1530, Elector John summoned Luther to Torgau to sense whether Luther would lend his support. That October Luther also wrote his *Warning to*

---

129. Hillerbrand, 166.
130. Hillerbrand, 167.
131. Hillerbrand, 168.

His Dear German People, although it was not published until April 1531. Luther nuanced his position: although committed to Romans 13, when civil authorities defy God, it is permissible for princes to disobey and defend their people.[132] In short, Luther gave the German people permission not to roll over but to defend themselves and fight back. In the past, Luther advocated civil disobedience—he himself refused to recant when Rome insisted he do so.[133] But civil disobedience can be passive and receptive; it need not be aggressive, let alone violent. Luther knew the difference between receiving harm due to incompliance and actively taking up arms. In the past, Luther exemplified the former, but he was now open to the latter, however much he resented being put in such a position.[134] The German people were not to sit back and become victims of the grave; if attacked they were forced—yes, *forced*—to go to war. Luther's rhetoric was far less aggressive than his advice prior to the Peasants' War. And he admitted as much:

> It is not fitting for me, a preacher, vested with the spiritual office, to wage war or to counsel war or incite it, but rather to dissuade from war and to direct to peace, as I have done until now with all diligence. All the world must bear witness to this. However, our enemies do not want to have peace, but war. If war should come now, I will surely hold my pen in check and keep silent and not intervene as I did in the last uprising [Peasants' Revolt, 1525]. I will let matters take their course, even though not a bishop, priest, or monk survives and I myself also perish. . . .
>
> Furthermore, if war breaks out—which God forbid—I will not reprove those who defend themselves against the murderous and bloodthirsty papists, nor let anyone else rebuke them as being seditious, but I will accept their action and let it pass as self-defense. . . . It is in truth no insurrection to rise against them and defend oneself.[135]

Was Luther contradicting himself, or was he having to adapt to the fast-paced, ever-evolving political complexity the church now faced? Perhaps only he himself could give the answer. Regardless, he hated what the future threatened and reassured his people that they were not radicals, like those at Münzer. Rather, they were oppressed, forced to defend their right to adhere to a different gospel, the true gospel. When all was said and done, Rome had no right to blame the Lutherans; they pursued peace, but Rome threw peace back in their faces.

---

132. *LW* 47:11–55. Around the same time, Luther's *Commentary on the Alleged Imperial Edit* (*LW* 34:67–104) was also published.

133. *LW* 47:6. See also see Luther's *Temporal Authority: To What Extent It Should Be Obeyed*, in *LW* 45:75–130.

134. *LW* 47:6.

135. *LW* 47:18–19. At the end of his letter, Luther went above and beyond to make sure he was not blamed for the bloodbath in the future: "I do not wish to incite or spur anyone to war or rebellion or even self-defense, but solely to peace. But if the papists—our devil—refuse to keep the peace and, impenitently raging against the Holy Spirit with their persistent abominations, insist on war, and thereby get their heads bloodied or even perish, I want to witness publicly here that this was not my doing, nor did I give any cause for it. It is they who want to have it that way. May their blood be on their heads! I am exonerated: I have done my duty faithfully" (55).

Our "conscience is clear," concluded Luther. True, he said, we may "go to our death together," but they will "go to hell in the name of all devils," while Luther and the Germans with him would go "to heaven in the name of God."[136]

By the last day of the year, 1530, a league was formed in Smalcald, and by the following February, a variety of territories across Germany signed their names pledging support to one another. If the emperor attacked, an alliance of armies awaited him.[137] The league's ongoing existence was primarily defensive for that reason. While the representatives agreed on this common cause, nevertheless, the years ahead demonstrated they differed on myriad other political and theological matters. But as long as the league could keep those differences subordinate to the main cause, a sturdy wall of protection remained for the next decade, one that the papacy and the emperor alike could not easily overcome.

April 15, 1531—that ominous deadline by which the Protestants had to conform—came and went, and Charles did nothing. Nor could he. Six months had gone by since he set that date back in Augsburg, six months of political maneuvers that complicated any sort of attack on the Protestants. The pope had not advanced a general council either. The league now stood as a tall barrier, posing a military challenge. As for the Turks, they were still an imminent threat of invasion, so that Charles remained dependent on German funds for support. By 1532 the emperor was not destined to enforce the edict of Augsburg.

THE PEACE OF NUREMBERG

The Turkish threat was real in 1532. Some estimate the Turkish army consisted of more than three hundred thousand soldiers.[138] The Ottoman Empire was both a serious terror and a providential savior to the Reformation. The Turks posed a threat because of their religious beliefs, which were contrary to Christianity and its gospel. The writings of the Reformers against the Turks, therefore, were just as polemically charged as their writings against the papacy. At the same time, the historian must wonder if the Reformation would have survived at all without the threat of the Ottoman Empire. The ever-present worry that the Turks might invade kept the emperor from extinguishing the Protestants as Worms, Speyer, and Augsburg threatened.[139]

---

136. *LW* 47:13–15.

137. Luther wrote that next January, "If princes as princes are permitted to resist the emperor, let it be a matter of their judgment and their conscience. Such a resistance is certainly not permitted to a Christian, who has died to the world." *WABr* 6:17. Navigating the implications of Luther's position was not so easy. All territories present at Augsburg joined Philip's alliance except Nuremberg, who appealed to Luther's prior convictions. When Nuremberg was told that Luther now supported the use of the sword, Luther had to explain himself. Hendrix captures the tension in Luther's reply: "Luther was caught where he never wanted to be: watching his theology used as evidence by both sides in a political quarrel. By saying Christians were dead to the world but princes could act as princes, he was attempting to keep theology from being compromised by politics. It was a noble purpose but, as it turned out, a hopeless endeavor." Hendrix, *Martin Luther*, 225.

138. Hendrix, 234.

139. On this love-hate relationship with the Ottoman Empire, see Hillerbrand, *Division of Christendom*, 172–73.

As the Turks advanced, Charles had to take an honest look at his defense. He continued to despise the Reformers in Germany and the division they not only created with other German Catholic estates but also provoked across Europe through their writing and preaching. Nevertheless, the emperor could not afford to lose the support of German Protestant rulers. Now, with the Turkish threat looming on the horizon, the emperor reopened the Catholic-Lutheran dialogue once more, this time with real intentions to reach a resolution. With the Diet of Regensburg in motion, why not take the opportunity to host peace talks at the same time? Perhaps Charles could recruit the aid of Protestant estates yet.

The representatives who signed the *Augsburg Confession* attended. Except Strasbourg. Martin Bucer and Luther did not align on the Lord's Supper, so Bucer did not sign the *Augsburg Confession*. However, circumstances had changed by 1532. With the worrisome possibility of an imminent Turkish invasion, the emperor might alleviate or at least suspend the edict of Augsburg and all the harm it promised. With such a prospect, Bucer no longer withheld his name from the *Augsburg Confession*.

The Protestant estates were shrewd. They knew Charles needed them if he had any chance of fighting off the Ottoman Empire. So they leveraged this threat to obtain their own religious freedom. Their strategy worked. Charles promised not to harm the Protestant estates, and the estates pledged financial support in view of the Turkish threat. That compromise also meant Charles would endure the Protestant estates until the Protestant-Catholic dispute was addressed at a future general council. At last this agreement was finalized in Nuremberg, and the emperor swore not to inflict the punishments first threatened at Augsburg. The Peace of Nuremberg was now official.[140] Charles's plans to inflict the threats of Augsburg did not disappear forever; they would resurface when circumstances changed. But at least the princes and Reformers had time to further their Reformation without fear of war.

Reaching that agreement did not, however, put Charles at peace with Catholic estates. They did not appreciate or agree with the leniency Charles showed the Protestant estates. Toleration of Protestant princes also meant toleration of Protestant beliefs. The Catholic estates, therefore, were eager for a general council, one that could settle the dispute once and for all. The Catholic estates also did not appreciate the contradictory nature of 1532. Augsburg had not been rescinded; its demands remained in effect. Yet the Protestants had gained religious liberty (at least in the meantime) due to Regensburg. The Catholic estates hoped this opacity could be resolved by a general council, one that might reconsider Augsburg and follow through on its threats.[141] In their evaluation, Charles had been played for a fool. The Catholic estates were not worried about a Turkish threat, which became evident at the Diet of Regensburg when they

---

140. All these details are chronicled in Hendrix, *Martin Luther*, 234. As at Augsburg, Luther was not present.

141. Hillerbrand, *Division of Christendom*, 173.

refused to pledge their purses. Charles, in their estimation, had been leveraged on the basis of an illusion.[142]

After the Peace of Nuremberg, Charles moved his military to Vienna. The Turks were expected to invade Vienna anytime. Like the crusaders of old, Charles was convinced that if he died in battle, his sacrifice would merit him entrance into eternal life and his name would go down in history as a brave defender of the empire and the Christian faith. If he was not defeated in battle, then he had the victory he came for, securing the peace of his empire.[143] To his disappointment, the Turks never made it as far as Vienna.[144] Charles now made his way to Italy, and the world waited on Pope Clement VII to decide on a general council to resolve the Protestant dilemma. As chapter 17 will reveal, Charles thought he had persuaded Clement to move forward, but the pope's real intentions were not so transparent.

Protestants across Europe continued to multiply. As new territories converted, they, too, desired protection under the Peace of Nuremberg. Rome voiced its disapproval. Nuremberg applied to those already Protestant in 1532; territories turning Protestant after 1532 could not claim Nuremberg's security. Catholics were insistent that newly converted territories should not be exempt from prosecution by the Supreme Court. That did not stop Protestants, however. They continued to claim territories and fight for church-related properties, properties the state had no right to control or keep from them.[145]

As for German churches, the 1530s and 1540s were ripe for further ecclesiastical maturity. That maturity, Luther learned, did not mean moving past first things—such as the gospel, justification, and assurance—but a return to first things to prepare for the future. For the future, as Luther knew all too well from the past, was uncertain, full of surprises. The only certainty the Christian possessed had lived and died and was resurrected. The only assurance the church could claim was the living Word.

As papal and imperial pressure tempted the church to return to Rome, that message became relevant once more.

---

142. There were other reasons the Catholic majority were unfavorable toward Charles at Regensburg. See, for example, the conflict between Charles and Ferdinand. Hillerbrand, 171.

143. "Should I be defeated, I will leave a noble name behind me in the world and enter into paradise; should I be victorious, I will not only have merit before God but will only sure restore the ancient boundaries of the empire and obtain immortal glory." Quoted by Hillerbrand, 173.

144. They were successfully challenged in Güns (western Hungary).

145. Hillerbrand explained the legal issue of "the status of church property that had been confiscated by reforming territories and cities and was used as the material basis for the support of churches, schools, and charities. The Protestants argued that the issue of ecclesiastical property was a religious issue over which the court had no jurisdiction." Hillerbrand, *Division of Christendom*, 184.

11

PROTAGONISTS AND PROTESTANTS

Defining the Center of Reform

It behooves a preacher to know the world better than I did when I was a monk. Back then I thought the world was so upright that people would rush forward as soon as they heard the gospel. What happened, however, was the contrary.

—Martin Luther

The law says, "do this," and it is never done. Grace says, "believe in this," and everything is already done."

—Heidelberg Disputation

THE *WITTENBERG CONCORD* AND THE *SMALCALD ARTICLES*

In 1534 Rome welcomed a new pope—Alessandro Farnese, Pope Paul III. Pope Paul III was serious about washing the church clean of any exploitations in order to conduct a council that overcame division between Rome and the Reformers. But the Reformers and the Smalcald League desired a council that was free, one uncontrolled by the papacy or its agenda. That required meeting on German soil instead of Italian territory, which did not seem probable.

Nevertheless, Pope Paul III did commission envoys to visit with Protestant representatives, and in 1535 one even met with Luther himself. Luther did not want rumors to spread that he was a joke, some old clown, so he went to his barber for a shave. Although Luther looked young again, with just as much energy as when he first began, the outcome was as old as Luther's original debates. Peter Paul Vergerio, the envoy, concluded that Luther was a rebel, a heretic, pretentious for opposing papal authority.[1] That accusation was yesterday's news.

But developments had multiplied since Worms. In 1535 and 1536, the Smalcald League was growing larger and posed a barrier to imperial and Roman animosity. Nevertheless, division among the Reformers remained over the Lord's Supper, a division that was geographically visible. Despite his past resistance to sympathizers of Zwingli, Luther did not like to see territories divided. Committed as he was

---

1. *WATR* 5, 633–35 (no. 6384). Cf. Hendrix, *Martin Luther*, 245–46.

to his convictions, even Luther desired to see the Reformation he started come together as one voice. In a surprising turn of events, Luther himself expressed his readiness to revisit talks on the Lord's Supper. Philip of Hesse was delighted. Perhaps disunity was not the final word after all.

Philip Melanchthon and Martin Bucer were the first to meet, and both departed full of optimism. Melanchthon must have been all the more optimistic when the document he and Bucer had labored over proved agreeable to Luther back in Wittenberg. What some Reformers saw as a weakness (Bucer's willingness to compromise), others took as a strength (Bucer's unique ability to bring Reformers together).[2] But would the Reformers in south Germany be as amenable? Luther was unsure, but Bucer was determined to win them over.[3]

In May 1536 Bucer and Capito met with Melanchthon and Luther in Wittenberg to revisit a negotiation.[4] Luther insisted that Bucer and Capito adopt his view of the Lord's Supper for talks to continue. Despite Bucer's progress persuading those in the south, Luther wanted confirmation. What better confirmation than acceptance of his position and a promise to adopt it as their own? But when the position of the churches in the south was represented the following day, Luther was satisfied, and Melanchthon went to work drafting a statement that both sides could stand behind.[5]

By the end of May, the *Wittenberg Concord*—the product proudly completed by Philip Melanchthon and Martin Bucer—was agreed upon and signed. After the unhappy ending at Marburg, few could have anticipated that years later Luther himself would have initiated and then signed such a negotiated document, even though the document signed was more or less Lutheran in its stance. Bullinger and the Swiss were not without their criticisms, but winning territories in southern Germany was worth it in the eyes of Melanchthon and Bucer. The advantages included the recruitment of theological allies and the political fortification of the Smalcald League itself.[6]

United, the Lutherans now stood tall. The only question left was whether they could agree to join a council called by the pope and hosted in papal territory. The pope did move forward with his plans for a council in Mantua, Italy, in the summer of 1536, but Mantua was doomed from the start (see chapter 11). Neither the French nor the Smalcald League were likely to attend a council in northern Italy.[7] Regardless, the Lutheran territories needed to prepare themselves

---

2. Some say Bucer compromised—how else could he achieve the *Wittenberg Concord*? Others believe Bucer was far more amenable to the Lutheran position *as articulated by Philip Melanchthon*, which goes a little ways in explaining the success of the concord. Hillerbrand, *Division of Christendom*, 184.

3. *WABr* 7:109–10; 157–58; *WA* 38, 330. Cf. Hendrix, *Martin Luther*, 248 (see p. 249 on the early meetings that took place between Bucer, Capito, and Melanchthon in Eisenach, as well as the curious absence of Luther).

4. This was not the first time Bucer and Luther met and discussed the Lord's Supper; they did so when Luther stayed at the Coburg castle during the imperial diet of Augsburg (1530).

5. Hendrix, *Martin Luther*, 250, observes that the south Germans did agree to sign the *Augsburg Confession* and the *Apology*.

6. Hillerbrand, *Division of Christendom*, 185.

7. "In June 1536 Pope Paul III convened a council to meet in Mantua, in northern Italy. King Francis

in the event of a council that did meet their requirements. Elector John Frederick asked Luther if he would outline topics that needed discussion at a council. The product was the *Smalcald Articles*, articles that gave Luther the rare opportunity to put down his most essential beliefs in systematic fashion. Luther's priority of the Word was among them: "We must hold firmly to the conviction that God gives no one his Spirit or grace except through or with the external Word."[8] As Luther considered the future of the church, he envisioned an assembly whose preaching, worship, and sacraments all revolved around a Word exterior to the people themselves. Left to themselves, the people could only be crushed by the weight of the law and their inability to fulfill its commands. Outside of themselves, however, the gospel of Jesus Christ penetrated their condemnation with a promise so that by faith they received grace upon grace.[9]

However, since these articles criticized the pope and papacy, their future use was doubtful. Although the elector did not mind the articles, others knew these articles did not set the right tone for peace negotiations.[10] Melanchthon most likely anticipated this problem, which is why he signed his name but with a qualifying statement expressing his hope that the gospel would be accepted by the pope so that concord followed. If so, then the Lutherans would acknowledge the pope's authority over the bishops under his care in Rome.[11]

The *Smalcald Articles* were never activated and applied. When the Smalcald League met at the start of 1537, Melanchthon told Philip it was wise to keep the *Smalcald Articles* quiet, otherwise controversy might ignite, dividing representatives on doctrines like the Lord's Supper. The league also made the formal decision not to travel to Italy to participate in the pope's council.[12] The Lutherans had asked for a council for years, but a council in the pope's own territory, on his terms, run by his cardinals and bishops? That sounded more like an invitation to excommunication than negotiation.

In the years ahead, Charles changed tactics. As much as he desired a general council that could find a solution to the religious divide, he took to colloquies as an alternative, if not experimental solution.[13] From 1540 to 1542, for example, colloquies met in Hagenau, Worms, and Regensburg. At the start of these colloquies, a scandal made news, a scandal that at first seemed small due to its secrecy

---

I of France promptly refused to allow the French bishops to attend (Mantua was situated in the emperor's territory), and the League of Schmalkald likewise declined to send representatives, but because the council never settled down to business, these refusals made little difference." Hillerbrand, 185.

8. Article 8.3 (*LW* 31:41).

9. Trueman, *Luther on the Christian Life*, 91. For a full treatment of Luther's priority of the Word, see Kolb, *Martin Luther and the Enduring Word of God*, 17–238; Thompson, *A Sure Ground on Which to Stand*, 47–288. For Luther's method of interpreting the Word, see Wengert, *Reading the Bible with Martin Luther*.

10. Hendrix, *Martin Luther*, 251, wonders if the elector "may have ordered the *Smalcald Articles* because he needed a personal declaration of Luther's theology in case disputes arose among his colleagues after Luther died." Luther was, more and more, experiencing health problems.

11. The *Smalcald Articles* (1537), 326. Cf. Hendrix, 256.

12. Hendrix, 252 (see 258–59 on the repeated postponements of this council).

13. For the sake of space, I am skipping the history of the Peace of Frankfurt (April 19, 1539), but see Hillerbrand, *Division of Christendom*, 186.

but then grew large, calling into question the moral integrity of the colloquies. Landgrave Philip of Hesse entered a political marriage with the daughter of George, Duke of Saxony. However, Philip and Christina's marriage was plagued by the landgrave's affairs with other women. If he had a second wife, Philip wondered, perhaps his persistent need for other women might resolve itself. His sister offered one of her own servants, Margarete von der Saale, but Philip figured he should consult with Luther himself. Luther wrote back that exceptions were permissible in circumstances like Philip's. Following the lead of the Old Testament patriarchs, Philip could marry another woman as long as this bigamous arrangement was not proclaimed from rooftops. This advice not only stemmed from Luther but many of his colleagues in Wittenberg, which made Philip even more confident he was reasonable to move forward with the marriage in March 1540.[14] Luther was naive to think the public, and especially his Catholic nemeses, would not find out. When they did, not only was Philip attacked but also Luther and the Reformation as a whole, a deep stab to its credibility.

The scandal also had major political ramifications, both for Philip and for the league. Bigamy was illegal, punishable by death. Granted, Charles had to be senseless to put Philip to death, unless he wanted to incite a war. Nonetheless, Philip was now at the emperor's mercy. When the two met in private during the summer of 1541, Philip requested pardon, the only way he could keep intact his political future. But the pardon came at an enormous cost. Philip gave Charles the keys to the kingdom: to receive pardon, Philip and the league could not recruit military support from remote territories. Furthermore, the Duke of Cleves had to be excluded from the league. The worst part of this arrangement was not what was said but what was insinuated. The pardon was only valid in times of peace. Should war erupt, the pardon was void. That statement by Charles was ominous. Was the emperor planning on attacking the league?[15]

PORTRAITS AND PROTAGONISTS

In a narrative describing the political machinations of emperor, pope, and princes in the sixteenth century, artwork might seem irrelevant and tangential. But nothing could be further from the truth. As each side attempted to maneuver for political advantage, art increasingly became a crucial medium of persuasion and propaganda.[16] Art even became warfare. In a single painting, the Reformation could either be justified or demonized, and viewers were put in a position to decide whether they were persuaded or not.

On the side of the Reformation, few mastered the art of persuasion—or perhaps we should say, the persuasion of art—like Lucas Cranach the Elder and

---

14. For the correspondence and the scandal's full details, see Hillerbrand, 188; Rockwell, *Die Doppeleche des Landgrafen Philipp von Hessen.* The permission to continue with bigamy was not limited to Wittenberg but was advised by Martin Bucer as well (see Greschat, *Martin Bucer,* 161).

15. Hillerbrand, 188.

16. Art historians have observed that there was a steady rise in Reformation and Catholic art that corresponded to the founding of the Smalcald League. Roth, "Reformation and Polemics," 95.

Lucas Cranach the Younger. Cranach the Elder was a master at portraits. When a person viewed one of Cranach the Elder's portraits, that person immediately knew whether the subject was Luther or Melanchthon.[17] But Cranach the Elder's woodcuts were equally as significant because each of them told a story. Each story pictured the battle between the Reformers and Rome but also so much more: a cosmic battle between God and the devil in the last days.

Cranach the Elder also portrayed the Reformation movement as favored by God, while portraying Rome as God's enemy deserving his eternal wrath. For example, in 1530 Cranach the Elder illustrated Israel crossing the Red Sea. Just as Moses leads God's people to safety, Israel turns to witness Pharaoh's army drown in the waters, waters that God brought crashing down on their heads. Rome was identified with the Egyptians, always resisting and fighting against true religion, while the Reformers were identified with Israel, trusting God's grace to deliver them.[18] By picturing life and death, Israel and Egypt, Cranach the Elder captured two sides: those for God and those against him.

Lucas the Younger did the same. Consider two 1546 woodcuts. The first is a 1546 woodcut called the *Difference between the True Religion of Christ and the False Idolatrous Teaching of the Antichrist.* . . . Cranach the Younger erected a large pillar right down the middle to separate two different outcomes. On the left-hand side of the pillar, Luther and the Reformers go about their ministry: a baby is baptized, the wine and bread are both distributed—to males and females alike, and Luther stands in the pulpit with the Word of God open, preaching as not only his congregation but a German prince listens. Above all of Luther's ministry, the Trinity looks down from heaven with approval. The Father looks to the Son, who is also pictured as a slain lamb, and the Spirit hovers over Luther as he preaches. Meanwhile, Luther points upward at the lamb, showing his people the way to reconciliation.

On the right-hand side, however, no grace is to be found. Back-to-back with Luther, on the other side of the pillar, is a chubby monk, but instead of the Spirit, this monk has a demon blowing air into his ear. And instead of pointing upward, the monk points to a table behind the congregation that offers indulgences next to bags of money, exposing the greed of Rome. Nearby, Rome's other sacraments are illustrated, and God stands over them with his arm outstretched, witnessing the many abuses below.[19]

---

17. Consider Cranach's 1532 portrait of Martin Luther as well as his portrait of Melanchthon the same year; cf. *Renaissance and Reformation*, 94. Others, like Heinrich Aldegrever, completed portraits in 1536 of Bernd Knipperdolling and Jan van Leiden, two leaders of the Münster movement. When defeated, Knipperdolling was tortured to death and Van Leiden's body was hung from the tower of the Lambertikirche (see 98–99).

18. Lucas Cranach the Elder, *The Pharaoh's Hosts Engulfed in the Red Sea, 1530*, 100–101.

19. Lucas Cranach the Younger and Pancratius Kempff, *Difference between the True Religion of Christ and the False Idolatrous Teaching of the Antichrist in Its Principal Features / Protestantism and Catholicism, 1546*, 103. Using a pillar was not uncommon; Georg Pencz did the same; see his "Protestant and Catholic Preaching, Broadsheet, 1529," 102. Others used different objects. Peter Gottlandt's "Law and Grace: Allegory of Redemption, 1552," 102, uses a tree, withered on one side where Moses holds the Law, but lush on the other side where John the Baptist points upward to the cross.

Difference between the True Religion of Christ and the False Idolatrous Teaching of the Antichrist, Woodcut by Lucas the Younger, 1546
Public Domain

The second woodcut is called *The False and the True Church*, also finished in 1546. In the middle, Luther is elevated in the pulpit with the Scripture open in front of him. With one hand, he points to the cross where Jesus hangs crucified. Below is the church kneeling to receive both the bread and wine at the altar as a lamb carrying a cross trots back and forth. With his other hand, Luther points to popes, cardinals, monks, and demons who are engulfed in the flames of hell, which is portrayed as the giant mouth of a monster. The message is clear: the viewer is to choose between life and death, blessedness and judgment, heaven and hell. Rome's destiny is never in doubt.[20]

Rome, too, had its own artistic ammunition. Hans Brosamer's 1529 woodcut was included in Johannes Cochlaeus's work *Seven Heads of Martin Luther*. According to the book of Revelation, a seven-headed beast will emerge during the Apocalypse. In this woodcut, Luther is the beast.[21] The Reformers repaid the compliment. Sometime between 1530 and 1543, an artist (unknown) designed a woodcut of the seven-headed beast, yet this time it was not Luther but the pope himself. The different heads represent various minions of the pope, including monks, cardinals, bishops, and others, all seven lying on top of a chest of indulgence monies, and with a demon rising out of the rear. On top of the chest is a large cross, but instead of "Jesus of Nazareth, King of the Jews" (INRI), it reads, "For money a sack / full of indulgences."[22]

20. Lucas Cranach the Younger, *The False and True Church, c. 1546*, 106.
21. Hans Brosamer, *Seven-Headed Martin Luther, c. 1529*, 108.
22. Unknown Artist, *The Seven-Headed Pope Animal, c. 1530–43*, 109.

Woodcut by Lucas the Younger, 1546, *The False and the True Church*
Public Domain

Or consider Lucas Cranach the Elder's first woodcut, *Passional of Christ and the Antichrist*, dating as early as 1521. The pope was identified with the Antichrist himself. In contrast to Jesus, who clears the temple with his whip, cleansing God's house, the pope is pictured back-to-back with Jesus but above a table of money, handing out indulgence slips.[23] Two years later, Lucas Cranach the Elder designed two more woodcuts that have ever since been remembered: one a monk's calf and the other a papal ass, each with all kinds of strange and horrific disfigurements.[24] These physical irregularities were not considered fanciful. In the sixteenth century, abnormalities could be interpreted as divine disfavor or demonic dominion. When beastly looking animals were discovered both in Rome and in Saxony, Luther and Melanchthon alike interpreted them as signs from God that the pope and his papacy had demonic origins and destinies.[25]

Nor was it uncommon to see the pope pictured as the servant of the devil himself, the ultimate accusation and insult. In Matthias Gerung's 1536 woodcut *Satire of Indulgences*, Satan is pictured as a grotesque mythic-like monster. He sits on top of an indulgence slip with a foot inside a bucket containing the church's holy water. The devil's mouth is stretched wide open, and inside is a table around which monks and nuns have a meal. Nearby, the pope, holding the keys of the kingdom, flies through the air and is carried by a little demon to the table of

23. Lucas Cranach the Elder, *Passional of Christ and the Antichrist*, 110.
24. Workshop of Lucas Cranach the Elder, *Monk's Calf, 1523*, and *Papal Ass, 1523*, 110, 112–13.
25. See in Estep, *Renaissance and Reformation*, 113.

monks and nuns inside Satan's mouth.[26] Some, like Melchior Lorch, went so far as to picture the pope as the incarnation of Satan, defecating in purgatory as he vomits creatures out of his mouth.[27]

Polemicist artwork did not die with Luther and the Reformers. In 1617, for example, one artist (unknown) created a woodcut to celebrate the one-hundred-year anniversary of Luther's Ninety-Five Theses. Luther is writing his theses on the church door with a giant quill. Toward the end of the quill is a lion (Pope Leo) whose head has been impaled on the quill. Next to the lion is the pope again, this time in the flesh. But as the quill punctures the lion's head, it extends further and smacks the pope's tiara off so that it falls to the ground, a gesture of his defeat by the Word.[28]

Innumerable woodcuts and paintings could be described, but these examples demonstrate how instrumental artwork could be to winning or losing the battle for sixteenth-century catholicity. While emperor, princes, and popes waged a verbal war over politics, ecclesiology, and theology, artists were recruited for both sides. Their woodcuts were no mere descriptive artifacts, but historical propaganda that described a spiritual, even cosmic warfare between good and evil, God and the devil.

THE DOCTRINE ON WHICH THE CHURCH STANDS OR FALLS

If the Reformation and Rome was a battle of cosmic proportions, then the future of the church hung in the balance. In the minds of the Reformers, few doctrines determined whether the church was tottering than justification. In the last decade of Luther's life, the Reformer revisited his first love, *sola fide*. But by the mid-1530s, Luther had a major advantage in comparison to his younger self: he now had years of polemical experience, and with such experience came a certain maturity in his articulation of the doctrine.

In 1535 Luther's lectures on Galatians were published, a large tome that served as a commentary on chapters 1 through 4.[29] Unlike other books of the Bible, Galatians had a special place in Luther's heart. One might go so far as to say that the Pauline epistle was at the core of Luther's reforming worldview, though not to the exclusion of other biblical books. Luther once said, "The Epistle to the Galatians is my epistle, to which I am betrothed. It is my Katie von Bora."[30] In his brief comments preceding his lectures on Galatians, the reason why becomes plain.

We have taken it upon ourselves in the Lord's name to lecture on this Epistle of Paul to the Galatians once more. This is not because we want to teach something

---

26. Matthias Gerung, *Satire of Indulgences, before 1536*, 114.
27. Melchior Lorch, *The Pope as Wild Man, after 1545*, 1115.
28. Unknown Artist, *Broadsheet for the Centenary of the Reformation, 1617*, 107.
29. These lectures were originally given in 1531.
30. *LW* 26:ix.

new or unknown, for by the grace of God Paul is now very well known to you. But it is because, as I often warn you, there is a clear and present danger that the devil may take away from us the pure doctrine of faith and may substitute for it the doctrines of works and of human traditions. It is very necessary, therefore, that this doctrine of faith be continually read and heard in public. No matter how well known it may be or how carefully learned, the devil, our adversary, who prowls around and seeks to devour us (1 Peter 5:8), is not dead. Our flesh also goes on living. Besides, temptations of every sort attack and oppress us on every side. Therefore this doctrine can never be discussed and taught enough. If it is lost and perishes, the whole knowledge of truth, life, and salvation is lost and perishes at the same time. But if it flourishes, everything good flourishes—religion, true worship, the glory of God, and the right knowledge of all things and of all social conditions.[31]

Luther believed he had an ally in Paul. Like Luther with Rome, Paul fought off the Judaizers who imposed works on the Gentiles. Luther also felt an affinity to Paul because this was the same apostle who rebuked the Galatians for being so easily deceived, quickly abandoning the gospel. When Luther wrote his lectures and certainly by the time they were published, he, too, worried Protestants might return to Rome under papal and imperial pressure.

At the start of his lectures, Luther built the core of his Reformation message like a master architect. No sinner will be saved by works of the law. "For although the Law is the best of all things in the world, it still cannot bring peace to a terrified conscience but makes it even sadder and drives it to despair. For by the Law sin becomes exceedingly sinful (Rom. 7:13)."[32] What, then, is the hope of the ungodly? Hope is not found within. Hope is found without, in someone else: Christ.

Therefore the afflicted conscience has no remedy against despair and eternal death except to take hold of the promise of grace offered in Christ, that is, this righteousness of faith, this passive or Christian righteousness, which says with confidence: "I do not seek active righteousness. I ought to have and perform it; but I declare that even if I did have it and perform it, I cannot trust in it or stand up before the judgment of God on the basis of it. Thus I put myself beyond all active righteousness, all righteousness of my own or of the divine Law, and I embrace only that passive righteousness which is the righteousness of grace, mercy, and the forgiveness of sins." In other words, this is the righteousness of Christ and of the Holy Spirit, which we do not perform but receive, which we do not have but accept, when God the Father grants it to us through Jesus Christ.[33]

---

31. *LW* 26:3.
32. *LW* 26:5.
33. *LW* 26:5–6.

Luther's distinction between active and passive righteousness is key. Active righteousness is that which we attempt to achieve; it is a fool's errand before a God so holy and impeccable. The outcome of this righteousness is damning—condemnation by the law. But a passive righteousness is different; it is a righteousness external to ourselves, one given to us as a gift. It is none other than the righteousness of Christ.

How is such righteousness reckoned to the sinner's account? By faith and by faith alone. Luther was describing the doctrine of imputation. In contrast to Rome, Luther affirmed "the righteousness of faith, which God imputes to us through Christ without works," and this righteousness "is neither political nor ceremonial nor legal nor work-righteousness but is quite the opposite; it is a merely passive righteousness, while all the others, listed above, are active." It is passive because the sinner does nothing but receive.[34] As Luther would explain in his lectures on Galatians, not only is this righteousness passive, but it is forensic too. Justification, and more specifically imputation, is not a moral renewal within, a life-long, sanitated transformation. Rather, justification is a verdict. God declares the ungodly not guilty but righteous in his sight. He can do so only because Christ's perfect record of obedience is credited to the sinner's account. The sinner's penalty has been paid by the suffering of Christ, and the believer is counted legally righteous on the basis of the obedience of Christ.[35] Luther's doctrine of imputed righteousness stood on the foundation of the active and passive obedience (or righteousness) of Christ, a distinction the Reformed tradition knew as well.

For Luther, this great, happy, marvelous exchange—sin imputed to Christ, his righteousness imputed to the believer—is the Christian's greatest source of comfort.[36] It is the reason Luther himself did not despair. Luther, with pastoral confidence, invited every believer to say with him, "Although I am a sinner according to the Law, judged by the righteousness of the Law, nevertheless I do not despair. I do not die, because Christ lives who is my righteousness and my eternal and heavenly life. In that righteousness and life I have no sin, conscience, and death. I am indeed a sinner according to the present life and its righteousness as a son of Adam where the Law accuses me, death reigns and devours me. But above this life I have another righteousness, another life, which is Christ, the Son of God, who does not know sin and death but is righteousness and eternal life."[37]

---

34. *LW* 26:4–5.

35. Note Luther's emphasis on the penal and substitutionary nature of the atonement: *LW* 26:277–83.

36. *LW* 26:5.

37. *LW* 26:9. Luther taught Christians to answer the accusations of the Law in this way: "Law, you want to ascend into the realm of conscience and rule there. You want to denounce its sin and take away the joy of my heart, which I have through faith in Christ. You want to plunge me into despair, in order that I may perish. You are exceeding your jurisdiction. Stay within your limits, and exercise your dominion over the flesh. You shall not touch my conscience. For I am baptized; and through the Gospel I have been called to a fellowship of righteousness and eternal life, to the kingdom of Christ, in which my conscience is at peace, where there

In the face of hell itself, the sinner can look the devil in the eye and say with absolute certainty that the law's accusation is futile; in Christ righteousness is guaranteed, and everlasting blessedness with it. Luther was convinced that he had what every pastor needed. In the ministry of the church, the consciences of Christians will be tempted to doubt their justification. But fear not, said Luther. The pastor can, indeed he must, "console them, and take them from the Law to grace, from active righteousness to passive righteousness, in short, from Moses to Christ."[38]

Had Luther left the halls of catholicity to propose an exchange that was novel, as if the doctrine on which the church stands or falls (as much later disciples called it) is founded on an innovation? Luther thought his happy exchange was as ancient as the church itself. Even in the second century, the Fathers imitated the apostle Paul. The *Epistle to Diognetus*, for example, used the language of a "sweet exchange" and confessed that the "lawlessness of many might be hidden in the one righteous man, while the righteousness of one might justify many lawless men."[39] Against Rome's claim that the imputation doctrine departed from the teaching of the church, Luther could claim it was purely catholic.

Such confidence, however, did not spell the death of good works. Quite the opposite, assurance grounded in the imputation of Christ's righteousness is the driving force behind every Christian's piety: "When I have this righteousness within me, I descend from heaven like the rain that makes the earth fertile. That is, I come forth into another kingdom, and I perform good works whenever the opportunity arises. If I am a minister of the Word, I preach, I comfort the saddened, I administer the sacraments. If I am a father, I rule my household and family, I train my children in piety and honesty."[40]

Luther's distinction between active and passive righteousness acted as the hinge of his justification theology. For Luther, the Reformation depended on the antithesis between law and gospel. "For if the doctrine of justification is lost, the whole of Christian doctrine is lost."[41] The 1529 painting by Lucas Cranach the Elder called *Law and Gospel* pictured this antithesis to perfection.

---

is no Law but only the forgiveness of sins, peace, quiet, happiness, salvation, and eternal life. Do not disturb me in these matters. In my conscience not the Law will reign, that hard tyrant and cruel disciplinarian, but Christ, the Son of God, the King of peace and righteousness, the sweet Savior and Mediator. He will preserve my conscience happy and peaceful in the sound and pure doctrine of the Gospel and in the knowledge of this passive righteousness" (26:11). Luther said something similar to instructors (26:10).

38. *LW* 26:10.

39. *Epistle to Diognetus*, 5. Cf. Brian Arnold's translation in *Justification in the Second Century*, 90. Arnold makes a thorough case for the presence of justification by faith in Clement of Rome, Ignatius of Antioch, Justin Martyr, and others over against the claims of Torrance, *The Doctrine of Grace in the Apostolic Fathers*. Others have made a similar claim: e.g., Pelikan, *Development of Christian Doctrine*, 65.

40. *LW* 26:11. Luther spelled out the implications for civil and ecclesiastical relations with the empire and Rome: "In short, whoever knows for sure that Christ is his righteousness not only cheerfully and gladly works in his calling but also submits himself for the sake of love to magistrates, also to their wicked laws, and to everything else in this present life—even, if need be, to burden and danger. For he knows that God wants this and that this obedience pleases him" (12).

41. *LW* 26:9.

Law and Gospel, Painting by Lucas Cranach the Elder, 1529
Public Domain

A tall tree divides the middle of the painting. On one side, the tree is without leaves, withered and dying. Below, Adam and Even disobey the command of God not to eat from the Tree of the Knowledge of Good and Evil. Next to the first couple, Israel is encamped. Men and women lay prostrate on the ground, and a bronze snake is wrapped around a pole. In Numbers 21 God sent a plague on Israel for their sin; only by looking up at the serpent on the pole were the people healed. Below these scenes, toward the front of the painting, stands Moses, holding and pointing at the Ten Commandments. Next to him is Everyman, naked and running, chased by the devil, who is pictured as a hideous monster, and death, who is a skeleton with a spear. Christ hovers over the entire scene with a sword, ready to judge. The message is clear: man cannot obey or keep the law, and the consequence is death and condemnation.[42]

However, the other side of the painting is a message of hope: life and justification are given to those who trust in the crucified and risen Christ. Unlike his Reformed contemporaries, Luther did not detest and destroy art in the church as a violation of the second commandment. Rather, he welcomed the visible portrayal of the incarnate Son because he was a theologian of the cross, convinced God remains hidden unless he accommodates himself to our weak faith through the weakness of the flesh itself.[43] To display that paradox, Cranach the elder

---

42. To clarify, Luther did not equate law with the Old Testament and gospel with the New Testament, but he saw law and gospel in both testaments. Kolb, *Martin Luther*, 47.

43. See Trueman's comparison of Luther's approach to images with the Heidelberg Catechism: *Luther on*

pictures John the Baptist pointing everyman to the cross where Christ hangs crucified. Below the cross is the Lamb of God, who takes away the sin of the world, standing triumphant over Satan and death underneath. Behind the cross is the tomb of Jesus, with the stone rolled away and Christ ascending into the sky, his payment for sin and defeat of Satan confirmed.[44]

The contrast Cranach the Elder portrayed captures the nucleus of Luther's experience and discovery. In the Augustinian monastery, Luther was crushed by the law and its demands, which he could not meet. He feared Christ as Judge. Then he discovered the righteousness of God, not a judging righteousness but the righteousness of Christ given to the ungodly at no cost. Now that he knew Christ as Savior, Luther was altogether liberated, free from works and free to perform works as fruit from the tree of grace.

However, not every Reformer appreciated Luther's understanding of the law and gospel.

LAW GONE LAX? JOHN AGRICOLA AND THE ANTINOMIAN CONTROVERSY

After the publication of his Galatians lectures, Luther continued to defend imputation with fervency. In 1536, for example, Luther entered a disputation on the topic, putting forward numerous theses over against late medieval Scholastics, challenging their definitions of original sin, congruous and condign merit, as well as their conception of faith and love.[45]

The next year proved most challenging. By the 1530s, Luther was used to opposition from Rome, but now he encountered opposition from one of his own. Luther's close and longtime friend, John Agricola, challenged the father of the German Reformation. Agricola was at Marburg. He joined Luther from southern Germany and signed the *Marburg Articles*. But as Luther aged, close friendships became vulnerable. Sometimes the issue was methodological, like Karlstadt's rush to institute reform by force. Other times it was theological, like Luther's dispute with Agricola. Regardless of the underlying reason, the outcome was almost always political.

Luther and Agricola's friendship took a turn for the worse when the two Reformers could not agree over the role and necessity of the law. From its inception, the Reformation oscillated on key doctrines like *sola gratia*, *sola fide*, and *solus Christus*. But these Reformation distinctives also incited charges of antinomianism from papal headquarters, charges Luther was quick to respond to early on in his career, as is plain in books like *A Treatise on Good Works* (1520).[46]

the Christian Life, 138. Luther defined God's hiddenness in three ways: Kolb, *Martin Luther*, 57; Ozment, *Homo Spiritualis*, 130–81.

44. Lucas Cranach the Elder, *Law and Gospel, 1529*, in *Renaissance and Reformation*, 52. Compare to a similarly themed painting: Lucas Cranach the Younger, *Epitaph of Duke John Frederick and His Family, 1555*, in *Renaissance and Reformation*, 53.

45. *LW* 26:145–96.

46. *LW* 44:15–114.

Luther spent much of his career clarifying that (1) passive righteousness bears fruit in active righteousness, and (2) the whole of the Christian life is a faith defined by repentance, a point Luther retrieved from Bernard of Clairvaux and Jacques Lefèvre.[47]

Luther was not the only one eager to counter misconceptions. As early as 1523 Melanchthon's said in his gloss on the Ten Commandments: "Where there is no fear, there can be no faith. For faith should comfort the terrified heart, so that it firmly holds that God has forgiven sin for the sake of Christ."[48] And in 1534 Melanchthon added a third use of the law to explain the place of good works. The law (1) restrains wickedness ensuring civil concord and (2) convicts the sinner of his evil before a holy God, but the law also (3) instructs the Christian in the way of obedience. The Decalogue, therefore, is relevant since "obedience is required" of the Christian. "The divine law, written in the minds of human beings, teach[es] that God must be obeyed; moreover, the gospel requires obedience toward God."[49] In summary, the "law coerces (first use); the law terrifies (second use); the law requires obedience (third use)."[50] When Melanchthon wrote instructions for pastors—a manual published in 1528 and used by visiting clergy to help them evaluate the conditions of parish churches—he told them to make sure the law was still preached from the pulpit.[51] Melanchthon worried that churchgoers indulged immorality in the name of Reformation doctrine. All gospel, no law. All forgiveness, no repentance.[52]

Some, however, did not appreciate Melanchthon's emphasis on the law. As far back as 1527, John Agricola gave the opposite instruction, which put his close friendship with Melanchthon in jeopardy. Preachers need not preach the law for sinners to turn from sin to Christ. Just preach grace and the Jesus who offers it. That is the preacher's starting point. Law comes later, after faith has formed. Even then, it should not be the Mosaic law, but the apostolic law. The former had papal connotations and provoked Agricola's disdain.

Agricola believed, furthermore, that he was being faithful to Luther's theology. He was first converted to the Reformation after sitting under Luther's lectures in 1517, when he heard Luther teach that the sinner, by faith alone in a merciful Christ, can be forgiven. From that point forward, he faithfully supported Luther through his many disputations, diets, and debates. He even signed the *Smalcald Articles*. As for his debate with Melanchthon, he was merely

---

47. Kolb, *Martin Luther*, 69, who has in view *WA* 1:233.10–11; 3:29.9–30.8; 4:403.27–407.17; 468.1–5.

48. *SM* 5.1:64. An extensive treatment of the debate between Melanchthon and Agricola cannot be detailed here, but see Wengert, *Law and Gospel*, who explains the role of *poenitentia* in the controversy.

49. *Scholia* 1534, XCIII.v.

50. Weingert, *Law and Gospel*, 199. Weingert argues that Melanchthon was neither "caving in to his opponents" or "abandoning Luther's theology" (195). Weingert does not think Luther taught the third use of the law. However, Trueman believes the idea is present in Luther's writings after 1525 even if the label is absent (*Luther on the Christian Life*, 172.

51. *Instructions for the Visitors of Parish Pastors in Electoral Saxony*. See *LW* 40:263–320.

52. *LW* 40:274; 47:101.

preserving Luther's pure message, guarding it from a law that could only compromise the gratuity of grace.

The conflict between Melanchthon and Agricola required Luther to intercede. But eventually Luther's patience with Agricola's persistence wore out. For instance, in 1537 Luther asked Agricola to fill in for him while he traveled to Smalcald. When Agricola stepped into Luther's pulpit, his position on the law surfaced in no time. He also published sermons and theses attacking both Melanchthon's and Luther's understandings of the law. Luther looked the other way for business outside Wittenberg, and Agricola stabbed Luther in the back—in the pulpit of all places. Nevertheless, the two reconciled. But that summer Agricola was at it again, this time publishing more theses. A second knife in Luther's back.

Now that the debate was out, Luther could not put it back in.[53] At the end of 1537 and well into 1538, Luther arranged three different disputations. Agricola did not show for the first and third disputations. Whenever reconciliation appeared possible, the scab of controversy was ripped off once more until it scarred both sides and healing seemed impossible. The dispute grew political as well. Agricola came to Wittenberg in 1536 when he and Luther were on friendly terms. With Luther's help, Agricola might rise to the rank of professor, although it was ambiguous whether the position was Agricola's to begin with. As years went by and controversy followed, Agricola now feared all was lost.

Agricola sought to mend the mess at the end of 1538, even agreeing that he would recant if Luther wrote out what he had to say. So Luther did. It read, "Master John Eisleben[54] wishes to withdraw what he taught or wrote against the law or the Ten Commandments and to stand with us here in Wittenberg, as the *Confession* and the *Apology* did before the emperor at Augsburg; and if he should later depart from this or teach otherwise, it will be worthless and will stand condemned."[55] Luther did not write this recantation and hand it to Agricola. Instead, he placed the recantation within his own refutation of Agricola, *Against the Antinomians*. He said these "new spirits"—Luther's label for the antinomians— "Dared to expel the law of God or the Ten Commandments from the church and to assign them to city hall."[56] Luther saw the antinomians for what they really were: just another one of the devil's tactics. First it was the pope, then Münzer, then Karlstadt, then the Anabaptists, then Servetus and Campanus, and now the antinomians.[57] Yet unlike Luther's early controversies, the year was 1539 and Luther was a seasoned polemicist. He was not blind to that great extinguisher of gospel light but could see that sneaky devil coming a mile away.[58]

---

53. The debate has been labeled the Antinomian controversy, a label designed to highlight Agricola's opposition to the law.

54. Like Luther, Agricola was from Eisleben.

55. *LW* 47:108–9.

56. *LW* 47:107.

57. *LW* 47:116.

58. *LW* 47:117.

This time the devil's tactic was a clever one: persuade one of Luther's own friends to work "secretly behind [his] back" and misrepresent the Reformation, as if Luther's catechisms, confessions, and books did not teach the church and families alike to learn God's law.[59] Next, so emphasize the gospel and its grace that repentance is no longer rooted in the law itself. Luther, turning to Paul's letter to the Romans, reminded Christians that without the law there is no conviction of sin. Without the law, the ungodly will never grieve over their transgressions and repent. Without the law, the world will never understand their need for a wrath-bearing substitute. Without the law, sinners will never rejoice that Christ has fulfilled God's commands on their behalf. No law, no gospel. The antinomians say gospel and then law, grace and then wrath. They have the reality backward; it is the reverse.[60]

Everything came to a head in 1540. Whether they agreed with his views or not, there were other faculty at the University of Wittenberg who supported Agricola climbing the institutional ladder. Luther resisted, now totally and unequivocally opposed.[61] If Agricola rose in the ranks, his antinomianism would rise with him. Who, then, could stop the spread of this plague once Agricola was deep in the university system? The whole affair was frozen until an investigation could determine what was best; in the meantime, Agricola was not to leave. He did anyway, refusing to wait for the verdict, and took a preaching position in Brandenburg near Berlin.[62]

In the end, the friendships between Agricola and Melanchthon and Luther never healed. Agricola was not just opposing the law; he was opposing Melanchthon, one of Luther's closest and most trusted colleagues and fellow Reformers. And if that was not enough, he opposed Luther himself, challenging the doctrine so central to the Reformation's genesis and survival.

THE REGENSBURG COLLOQUY: JUSTIFICATION AND DOUBLE RIGHTEOUSNESS

The Protestant doctrine of justification was established in Luther's mind and irreconcilable with the papacy's position on the same doctrine. In the late 1530s and early 1540s, however, other Reformers sensed movement on the other side of the Tiber and grew curious about whether some form of conciliation could be achieved. Although the conciliating efforts of each colloquy are worthy of attention, Regensburg is memorable for the unprecedented agreement reached on the doctrine of justification, even if the outcome did not result in the concord both sides envisioned.

In 1540 and 1541, select theologians on each side of the divide gathered

---

59. *LW* 47:109.
60. *LW* 47:109–14.
61. *WA* 51:429ff; *LW* 37:105.
62. Did Agricola ever recant? He did, although it appears to be a version written by Melanchthon instead of Luther. *LW* 37:106.

first in Hagenau, then in Worms, and finally in Regensburg. Martin Luther did not participate, but Philip Melanchthon did. John Calvin was not chosen, but Martin Bucer was selected along with Johann Pistorius. Their counterparts were formidable, including Johann Eck, Luther's early nemesis, as well as Johann Gropper and Julius Pflug.[63] Achieving agreement over a doctrine as central to the Reformation as justification proved a colossal task. Theoretically, such an achievement appeared in reach since the papacy had yet to put forward its official teaching on justification (which changed once Trent convened). That did not mean, however, that opinions were not solidified beforehand. Eck, for example, had no hesitancy putting forward what he believed was the unquestionable view of the church. Furthermore, Eck came to Regensburg already prejudiced against the colloquy. His colleagues worried that Eck's disinterest in real negotiation could undermine their efforts to discuss justification with the Reformers, a worry that only escalated existing suspicions Eck harbored toward his colleagues. Coupled with Eck's fierce polemical style, compromise seemed unlikely to either side.[64]

The final version of article 5 begins with a strong affirmation of man's "slavery to sin."[65] Acknowledging that all are "born children of wrath" and cannot be "set free from slavery to sin, except by Christ the one mediator," the article then introduces the "prevenient movement of the Holy Spirit, by which their mind and will are moved to hate sin." Article 5 appeals not only to the Scriptures but also to Augustine to establish the condition of repentance for justification. Naturally, the focus on repentance is shared by attention to faith. "Next, man's mind is moved toward God by the Holy Spirit through Christ and this movement is through faith." By this faith, the sinner has every "certainty" and "confidence" that he is a recipient of God's promises in Christ. "By this faith, he is lifted up to God by the Holy Spirit and so he receives the Holy Spirit, remission of sins, imputation of righteousness and countless other gifts." Article 5 later specifies that the imputation of righteousness is none other than the imputation of *Christ's* righteousness.

However, when article 5 says faith believes that Christ's righteousness is imputed, it also says this faith receives the promise of "love." The mention of "love" brings article 5 into contact with controversy. Is the believer justified by faith *and* love, as if love is a category that includes works, albeit works of charity? Or is love mentioned merely as the natural and necessary outcome of justifying faith? From another angle, is love infused as if justification involves an inward, moral transformation? Or is the infusion of love the fruit of Christ's imputed righteousness? The full context of article 5.4 deserves consideration:

---

63. For the background that follows, see Lane, *Regensburg Article 5 on Justification*, 13–32.

64. On the difficult if not impossible relationships between Eck and his colleagues at Regensburg, see Lane, 17–18.

65. For the text, see *ARC* 6:52–54; *MBDS* 9/1:397–401; *ADRG* 3/1:288–95. However, Lane has provided an updated text with Latin and English in *Regensburg Article 5 on Justification*, 329–33, which I will use.

(1) So it is a reliable and sound doctrine that the sinner is justified by living and effectual faith, for through it we are pleasing and acceptable to God on account of Christ. (2) And living faith is what we call the movement of the Holy Spirit, by which those who truly repent of their old life are lifted up to God and truly appropriate the mercy promised in Christ, so that they now truly recognize that they have received the remission of sins and reconciliation on account of the merits of Christ, through the free goodness of God. . . . (3) But this happens to no one unless also at the same time love is infused which heals the will so that the healed will may begin to fulfill the law, just as Saint Augustine said. (4) So living faith is that which both appropriates mercy in Christ, believing that the righteousness which is in Christ is freely imputed to it, and at the same time receives the promise of the Holy Spirit and love. (5) Therefore the faith that truly justifies is that faith which is effectual through love [Gal 5:6]. (6) Nevertheless it remains true, that it is by this faith that we are justified (i.e. accepted and reconciled to God) inasmuch as it appropriates the mercy and righteousness which is imputed to us on account of Christ and his merit, not on account of the worthiness or perfection of the righteousness communicated to us in Christ.

If the previous mention of "love" and an "effectual faith" raised questions among Protestants, so, too, did the mention of "inherent" righteousness in article 5.5.

Although the one who is justified receives righteousness and through Christ also has inherent [righteousness], as the apostle says: "you are washed, you are sanctified, you are justified, etc." [1 Cor 6:11] (which is why the holy fathers made use of [the term] "to be justified" even to mean "to receive inherent righteousness"), nevertheless, the faithful soul depends not on this, but only on the righteousness of Christ given to us as a gift, without which there is and can be no righteousness at all. (2) And thus by faith in Christ we are justified or reckoned to be righteous, that is we are accepted through his merits and not on account of our own worthiness or works. (3) And on account of the righteousness inherent in us we are said to be righteous, because the works which we perform are righteous, according to the saying of John: "whoever does what is right is righteous" [1 John 3:7].

Anthony Lane is wise to encourage the contemporary interpreter of Regensburg to consider hermeneutics when reading article 5. The historian should not only read to determine what it says concerning the doctrine of justification but must also consider how the article as a whole seeks to satisfy the "concerns" situated behind both a Protestant and Roman doctrine of justification.[66] On one hand, article 5 underlines categories like *sola fide* and the imputed righteousness of Christ to safeguard the Protestant concern for a totally gratuitous justification. On the other hand, article 5 inserts categories like "living faith" and "effectual

---

66. Lane, *Regensburg Article 5 on Justification*, 275–76.

faith" and "love" to meet the Roman concern for a justification that does not produce antinomianism. The latter concern is evident in the closing paragraphs of article 5, which promise not only assurance but a justification that does not lead to "idle" Christian living, a life without works.[67] "Now those who say, 'we are justified by faith alone,' should at the same time teach the doctrine of repentance, of the fear of God, of the judgment of God and of good works, so that all the chief points of the preaching may remain firm."[68]

In a remarkable feat, both sides signed off on article 5, and their agreement gave both sides hope for the future. Yet that hope was dashed in little time both for internal and external reasons. Internally, each debater signed article 5 of Regensburg, but agreement around other *loci* was not so easily won. For example, when the debaters turned to the subject of transubstantiation, little flexibility was possible or even desirable from either side. The Fourth Lateran Council (1215) had already inserted transubstantiation into the official teaching of the church. To modify or abandon this doctrine was unthinkable not only to Eck but also to the other theologians.[69]

External factors contributed as well. Although agreement at Regensburg was cause for celebration, Wittenberg and Rome alike criticized the achievement. Martin Luther despised the *Regensburg Book*, convinced it compromised the evangelical doctrine of justification, and concluded that the devil himself was at work at the colloquy in secret.[70] The Reformer said article 5 was patchwork, an attempt to sow together two otherwise incongruous garments of justification. If justification is by faith and love, even if it is a faith that works through love, then justification cannot be *sola fide*.[71] Faith formed by love (*fides caritate formata*) and faith effectual through love (*fides efficax per caritatem*) compromised the Lutheran doctrine of justification, Luther concluded. Article 5 "is too weak and will cause much more disagreement and disunity than has hitherto occurred."[72] Luther also became inimical toward those Protestants, such as Martin Bucer, whom he believed compromised justification at Regensburg. Bucer's full support for Regensburg was offensive to Luther, an unforgivable sin.[73] While Luther's reaction may seem extreme, from Luther's perspective his anger was appropriate.

---

67. "Therefore, although the inheritance of eternal life is due to the regenerate on account of the promise, as soon as they are reborn in Christ, nevertheless God also renders a reward to good works, not according to the substance of the works, nor because they come from us, but to the extent that they are performed in faith and proceed from the Holy Spirit, who dwells in us, free choice concurring as a partial agent" (art. 5.8).

68. Art. 5.10.

69. Lane, *Regensburg Article 5 on Justification*, 30.

70. *WABr* 9:486. Cf. Lane, 38.

71. Luther also believed article 5's reference to Galatians 5:6 was misguided since the context does not speak of Christian living but how one is right with God. In other words, Paul was concerned about justification, not sanctification. See Luther and Bugenhagen to Johann Friedrich (10/11 May) in *WABr* 9:406–9; *ADRG* 3/1:169–72. Cf. Lane, 36.

72. *WABr* 9:461–62; *ADRG* 3/2:557. Cf. Lane, 37. Lane questions whether Luther understood Regensburg with accuracy and treated article 5 in a spirit of fairness (188).

73. *WABr* 9:590; *WATR* 5:166 (no. 5461). Cf. Lane, 43.

Luther had offered his own life on the altar of an evangelical doctrine of justification; in a single colloquy Bucer threatened to undermine that sacrifice.

Melanchthon shared Luther's dissatisfaction, although he did sign his name to Regensburg. "Those who love this [clarity in speech] will flee ambiguous statements, of which there are many in this [Regensburg] book, which contains a number of passages manifestly in conflict with the doctrines of our churches."[74] Melanchthon neither appreciated the debates, which he found frustrating, nor the wording in article 5, which he found ambiguous. Although Melanchthon agreed to article 5 and did not consider it at odds with the *Augsburg Confession* or his *Apology*, his optimism waned not long after Regensburg. He concluded that "many things are obscure and some even offensive to us" in article 5.[75] Despite the specifics of article 5, Melanchthon was not satisfied, wanting clarification on a host of statements that he feared could be read in a more Roman direction.[76]

Although John Calvin was not one of the debaters, he did attend and give counsel. At the start of the colloquy, Calvin was anything but optimistic. However, when Calvin saw the willingness to accept Protestant terms (e.g., imputation) by the Roman theologians, he changed his mind. He wrote to William Farel, "You will be astonished, I am sure, that our opponents have yielded so much. . . . Our friends have thus retained also the substance of the true doctrine, so that nothing can be comprehended within it which is not to be found in our writings." Calvin admitted that Farel would read it and still crave a "clearer exposition," which Calvin himself said he desired as well. "However, if you consider with what kind of men we have to agree upon this doctrine, you will acknowledge that much has been accomplished."[77]

Rome's response also proved to be yet another barrier to Regensburg's future. Eck, for starters, gave the impression that Regensburg taught his view of justification, as if article 5 supported an infused righteousness and condemned justification *sola fide*.[78] Eck's report was not exactly accurate, and it only served to accentuate Luther's worst fears and Melanchthon's concerns over ambiguity in the text. Eck's one-sided interpretation was puzzling since his Roman colleagues did not interpret article 5 the same way. Nor did Eck hide his total contempt for Regensburg, calling it "stupid" and full of "errors and defects."[79] Did Eck promulgate such a report to save face, lest he look like he compromised the substance of a Roman view of justification? Most likely. At the very least, it explains why Eck turned right around and wrote his own treatise criticizing Regensburg.[80]

---

74. *CR* 4:668; *MBW* T10:516. Cf. Lane, 42.

75. *CR* 4:417; *ADRG* 3/2:541; *MBW* T10:307. Cf. Lane, 40.

76. Melanchthon to Luther (May 19) in *CR* 4:303; *WABr* 9:414; *ADRG* 3/1:213; *MBW* T10:200. For the many places Melanchthon expressed his opinion and concerns over ambiguity, see Lane, 40–41.

77. *CTS* 4:260. Cf. Lane, 38.

78. *ADRG* 3/2:520–26, at 520. Cf. Lane, 44.

79. *CR* 4:459–60; *ADRG* 3/2:567; *ARC* 3:387. Cf. Lane, 48.

80. Lane offers this explanation in *Regensburg Article 5 on Justification*, 44. For Eck's *Responsum*, see Dittrich, "Miscellanea Ratisbonesia," 12–19; *ADRG* 3/2:574–83.

Eck's fears were not unrealistic. In 1541, immediately after Regensburg, Rome did not react with sympathy toward those Catholics at Regensburg who shielded and then promoted article 5. They were accused of selling out to the Reformation, regardless of whether such an accusation had real validity.[81] Then, in 1542, the pope released a bull that galvanized the Inquisition and started an intense investigation into those Roman theologians in support of Regensburg.[82] Contarini died before the Inquisition could interrogate him, but Morone did not have such luck and was incarcerated under suspicion of heresy. "The Italian hand that had joined hands with the German Reformation was to be cut off with the sword. What many had considered an acceptable Catholic position had now become heresy."[83] The Council of Trent's verdict on justification only confirmed the curia's stance against Regensburg.

In the end, Regensburg failed to unite both sides. Whether Luther was accurate in his interpretation of article 5 may be debated, but his fear that Regensburg could only result in further division was not unfounded. The debate over justification at Regensburg produced four camps: (1) Protestants against Regensburg, (2) Protestants for Regensburg, (3) Catholics against Regensburg, and (4) Catholics for Regensburg.[84] Even among those camps that supported Regensburg, a chief concern still prevailed: a desire for further clarity. However, the curia's turn against Regensburg and its sympathizers as well as Trent's official position on justification meant that such desire was wishful thinking. Even if Calvin was right that article 5 contained the substance of evangelical doctrine, Regensburg had failed to repair the breach.

With both Catholics and Protestants rejecting Regensburg, Charles's attempt to solve the divide with colloquies appeared a lost cause. Charles, among others, punted to a future general council of the church. However, behind closed doors Charles played the politician, reassuring both Protestants and Catholics they each could have their way.[85] That was impossible; Charles must have known it. Yet speaking out of both sides of his mouth bought the emperor time until he could figure out his next move.

Whatever that move might have been, the emperor's attention was diverted by war once more. France, always the thorn in Charles's side, was on the move once again, this time more determined than before to triumph over the emperor. With allies by his side, King Francis targeted the Low Countries, but victory was not his to win. He underestimated what allies might assist Charles, from

---

81. Contarini, for example, came under severe attack. See *Regesten*, 346–47. Cf. Lane, 47.

82. The papal bull was *Licet ab initio*.

83. Lane, 58.

84. "The situation turned hopelessly chaotic, because there were actually four factions: the hard-lined Catholics and Protestants and the conciliatory theologians on both sides. The specter of a permanent division among Catholics, Protestants, and those who accepted mediation hung over the diet and indicated that anything less than an enthusiastic and full agreement was bound to be unsatisfactory." Hillerbrand, *Division of Christendom*, 189–90.

85. On the specifics, see Hillerbrand, 190.

Holland to England.[86] In the past, war kept Charles from suppressing the Protestant estates, distracting the emperor with more pressing military matters. This time around the Treaty of Venlo in 1543, which symbolized the conquest of Charles, served to rally Catholics to his side, including Catholics in Germany. Charles had tasted the sweetness of brute power and now wondered whether a military victory over the league might secure religious cooperation in a far more expedient fashion than endless debates and negotiations at colloquies.[87] Should he stand on Protestant necks, surely they would have to attend a general council led by the pope and his curia.

LUTHER AND THE JEWS

If any word was reiterated by Luther across his lifetime, it was the word *gospel*. Luther's relentless adherence to the gospel defined the church throughout Germany. Christ crucified for the justification of the ungodly was preached from pulpits, taught in catechisms, and illustrated in woodcuts. As German Christians came to the table, they feasted on Christ and his benefits in the bread and the wine. What a shock it is, then, to discover that Luther, at the end of his life, held deep-rooted hatred for the Jews, the people Luther's Christ came to save in the first place.

Early on, the young Luther had a posture toward the Jews that appeared full of patience. In 1523, for example, he released *That Jesus Christ Was Born a Jew* and advised the use of persuasion, not force, and recommended kindness rather than insults. He also shamed Rome for its mistreatment of the Jews, scolding Rome for its lack of Christian charity toward God's people.[88] With the Reformation just underway, perhaps Luther was also a bit optimistic. The gospel could not be thwarted by all-powerful Rome; what could stand in its way as it was taken to the world afresh? Surely if people just heard it, they would have the same experience as Luther. Although Luther had expressed concern over the Jews in his early lectures on the Bible, in the 1520s he at least appeared tolerant toward the Jews.[89]

Yet twenty years later, Luther's rhetoric changed and became fierce.[90] In 1543 Luther published *On the Jews and Their Lies*, one of his most aggressive, vitriolic polemics against any group.[91] The Jewish people were skewered. Even Luther's closest friends blushed when they read Luther's words.[92] Why such a change in tone? Was Luther disenchanted with his prior anticipation at Jewish conversion?

---

86. Maria of Holland was sister to Charles. On the turn of events, which involved Charles's victory over the Duke of Cleves, see Hillerbrand's treatment of the Treaty of Venlo (September 6, 1543). Hillerbrand, 190.

87. Hillerbrand identified Regensburg in particular as the straw that broke the emperor's back: "The failure of the negotiations at Regensburg convinced him that no theological compromise was possible. Because the Protestants were recalcitrant, only force remained, and that was how Charles prepared to solve the religious problem in Germany." Hillerbrand, 191.

88. *LW* 45:195–230.

89. On the evolution of his rhetoric, see *LW* 47:123–26.

90. Although, Hendrix does not believe Luther's attitude ever changed. Hendrix, *Martin Luther*, 264.

91. Also consult Luther's 1537 work, *Against the Sabbatarians*, in *LW* 47:57–98.

92. For examples, see *LW* 47:123.

Was he enraged by Jewish apologetics against Christian doctrine? Was Luther becoming more disgruntled than usual due to his unrelenting illnesses? Or was this antagonism inside Luther all along, hidden but not revealed?[93] There may be a measure of truth to any number of explanations. It was 1543, and by then a multitude of motives may have escalated until their cumulative effect finally resulted in a volcanic eruption.

Regardless of the reason or motive behind his rhetoric, Luther did tell his readers at the start that he received a "treatise in which a Jew engages in dialogue with a Christian," and the Jew "dares to pervert the scriptural passages which we cite in testimony to our faith, concerning our Lord Christ and Mary his mother, and to interpreter them quite differently." Luther was furious: "With this argument he thinks he can destroy the basis of our faith."[94] As a result, some of Luther's most vehement rhetoric followed in an effort to discredit this Jewish line of thought.

Why had the Jews suffered desolation ever since their temple was destroyed, nearly 1,468 years and counting? There was only one answer: the wrath of God. What else could explain such a long rebellion? "Therefore this work of wrath is proof that the Jews, surely rejected by God, are no longer his people, and neither is he any longer their God."[95] But what if the Jews accepted Christ rather than rejecting him? They won't, Luther retorted. He used to hold out hope, but he now saw why that was foolish. "From their youth they have been so nurtured with venom and rancor against our Lord that there is no hope until they reach the point where their misery finally makes them pliable and they are forced to confess that the Messiah has come, and that he is our Jesus. Until such a time it is much too early, yes, it is useless to argue with them about how God is triune, how he became man, and how Mary is the mother of God." Should the Christian not try? "No human reason nor any human heart will ever grant these things, much less the embittered, venomous, blind heart of the Jews.... What God cannot reform with such cruel blows, we will be unable to change with words and works."[96]

Luther did let on to yet another reason for his attack: he could not stand the *theological* arrogance in the Jews. They boast, he said, in their bloodline, circumcision, and law, full of "pride, usury, conceit, and curses against us Gentiles."[97] All the while, they are the ones who murdered the Messiah. Luther was especially infuriated by those Jews who called Jesus "a whore's son, saying that his mother Mary was a whore," because she "conceived him in adultery with a blacksmith."[98] Luther returned to the Old Testament to show how Israel was a "defiled bride,

---

93. For an overview of each theory, consult Franklin Sherman's survey in *LW* 47:125–27. Also note the influence of Urban Rhegius; see Hendrix, *Martin Luther*, 265–66.

94. *LW* 47:137.

95. *LW* 47:139.

96. *LW* 47:139.

97. *LW* 47:167.

98. *LW* 47:257.

yes, an incorrigible whore and an evil slut with whom God ever had to wrangle, scuffle, and fight."[99] Luther was unconvinced they had changed since.

With his mind made up, Luther issued a startling announcement, even a command: lords and princes everywhere must rid their societies of the "devilish Jews." We cannot "convert the Jews," so a "sharp mercy" is the only resort left.[100] Luther advised a seven-step plan:

1. To set fire to their synagogues or schools and to bury and cover with dirt whatever will not burn, so that no man will ever again see a stone or cinder of them.... All who are able toss in sulphur and pitch; it would be good if someone could also throw in some hellfire.[101]
2. I advise that their houses also be razed and destroyed.
3. I advise that all their prayer books and Talmudic writings, in which such idolatry, lies, cursing, and blasphemy are taught, be taken from them.
4. I advise that their rabbis be forbidden to teach henceforth on pain of loss of life and limb.
5. I advise that safe-conduct on the highways be abolished completely for the Jews.
6. I advise that usury be prohibited to them, and that all cash and treasure of silver and gold be taken from them and put aside for safekeeping.
7. I recommend putting a flail, an ax, a hoe, a spade, a distaff, or a spindle into the hands of young, strong Jews and Jewesses....[102]

As for pastors who have Jews living in their towns and cities, they must insist their lords and princes put all seven into action.

Luther's language was as sharp and pointed against the Jews as it was against the pope and his papacy, as well as the Turks—like most opponents, the Jews were also on the devil's team.[103] Further, Luther's argument was just as theological against the Jews as it was against the pope and his papacy, as well as the Turks; he spent no little time proving Old Testament prophecy must be fulfilled in Jesus.[104] However, Luther's attack on the Jews was different: in his dashed hopes at Jewish conversion (assuming that was at least one of his main motives), he shifted from a theological polemic to a racial one. He also masked the latter in the name of the former. It is one thing to express disappointment that a people has rejected Christ, but it is another thing to then insult them in the harshest of terms. How could Luther justify such vile words of hate with his indiscriminate offer of the gospel? On this chilling note, Luther concluded his long diatribe

---

99. *LW* 47:166.
100. *LW* 47:268.
101. *LW* 47:268, 285.
102. *LW* 47:268–72.
103. E.g., *LW* 47:137, 257, 275–78.
104. *LW* 47:176ff.

against the Jews: "My essay, I hope, will furnish a Christian (who in any case has no desire to become a Jew) with enough material not only to defend himself against the blind, venomous Jews, but also to become the foe of the Jews' malice, lying, and cursing, and to understand not only that their belief is false but that they are surely possessed by all the devils."[105]

Was Luther's polemic against the Jews limited to a Protestant predisposition? No, Catholics also had a long and violent history of anti-Semitism. For example, the Fourth Lateran Council (1215) instigated segregation for unconverted Jews. Anti-Semitism prevailed in England and France as well, where Jews were expelled at the start of the thirteenth and fourteenth centuries and on the eve of the fifteenth century. Rather than expel Jews, Spain decided to kill them toward the end of the fourteenth century, and almost one hundred years later attempted to chase every last Jew out of the country. Germany was no exception. In 1349 Catholics in Strasbourg herded the Jewish community to the cemetery where they were burned and buried. What caused such hatred? Unlike Catholics, Jews had no prohibition against extending loans, and as a result the Jewish community became affluent. Sometimes Catholics were even indebted to Jews.[106]

But economics was not the only factor, even if it may have been a major one. Others hated the Jews for their rejection of Jesus as Messiah. Luther lived almost two centuries after these international outbreaks of anti-Semitism, but his motive also appeared religious. Yet even if the start of Jewish persecution was religious, Luther's infamous rhetoric turned his stance against the Jews into something more, something with potential cultural, economic, political, and racial consequences. While Luther limited himself to the pen, Jews living in Europe had to be worried that the state might use the sword once again if Luther's words were taken seriously.

BENEFICIUM, NON DOMINIUM: LUTHER'S FINAL ATTACK ON "THE INSTITUTION OF THE DEVIL"

As Luther's days came to an end, the Reformer engaged in one last major conflict with the papacy. This last battle seemed fitting in a way: the Reformation erupted when Luther wrote theses to debate papal practices like indulgences; now the Reformation's fate hung in the balance as the papacy assembled for a council set to condemn the Reformation Luther started.

In the 1540s, Charles continued to face enemies on two fronts: the Turks and the French.[107] Charles needed allies, so he reached out to princes from Germany at the Diet of Speyer (1544). In an attempt to gain their support, Charles prom-

---

105. *LW* 47:305–6.

106. Needham, *Two Thousand Years of Christ's Power*, 2:332–33. Needham also chronicles some of the "stories" that fostered hatred for Jews, stories that claimed "Jews kidnapped and murdered Christian babies, and practiced religious rituals in which they treated the wafer of holy communion with blasphemous mockery and contempt."

107. What follows is detailed in *LW* 41:259–61.

ised to pull back the ongoing political and ecclesiastical penalties and attacks on German Protestants, and he even said a future diet in Germany was a possibility.[108]

Pope Paul III was livid at these concessions and further infuriated that the emperor was meddling in his ecclesiastical jurisdiction. What infuriated the pope most, however, was the way Charles sidelined the papacy as if irrelevant. Furthermore, talk of a future diet without his approval undermined his papal power and posed a threat. Since the start of his protest, Luther asked for a free council, but such conciliarism was interpreted as a threat to the papacy. Now the emperor threatened the same papal establishment due to his need for political backing.

The pope wrote two briefs in response, calling for retraction of these concessions. But Pope Paul's briefs were marked "Return to sender" due to complications in delivery. Charles pushed ahead and negotiated with Francis I. Without the pope, they decided a council could meet in the city of Trent. To his unending annoyance, the pope had to comply, and he wrote two additional briefs saying he would.

By the new year, copies landed on Luther's desk. The Council of Trent was set to assemble on March 25, 1545. Luther was determined to have his response published at the same time. *Against the Roman Papacy Founded by the Devil* (1545) was perhaps Luther's most insulting attack on Rome.[109] Luther could not have thought worse of Pope Paul III, whom Luther addressed throughout as "the Most Hellish Father."[110] Luther was simply returning the compliment; the papacy had insulted Luther just the same. As for Luther's motive, the Reformer was convinced the association with the devil was true.

Luther's reasons were many, but chief among them was the pope's tyranny and total control. The German people desired a free, Christian council, one that did not need the pope's permission, nor one that was controlled by the pope's political or theological agenda. But the pope "would rather let himself be torn to pieces and would rather become Turkish or devilish" before he allowed such a council to meet.[111]

The irony was striking. Ever since Luther's early conflict with Rome, the papacy and its theologians appealed to the Council of Constance (1415) to associate Luther with Hus, the heretic who was burned at the stake. And yet that same council elected the next pope. At the time, three different popes vied for power—John XXIII, Gregory XII, and Benedict XIII. But the council chose a fourth individual, Martin V, instead. Constance was evidence against the pope's claims to ultimate power. A "council is superior to the pope, not the pope to the council." A council has the "power to judge, sentence, punish, elect, or depose the pope," not vice versa. "Ow, ouch, oh!" Luther retorted.[112]

---

108. *LW* 41:259.

109. But Luther was not the only one to write against the pope and papacy. Years earlier Melanchthon wrote *Treatise on the Power and Primacy of the Pope*, 329–44.

110. *LW* 41:263.

111. *LW* 41:265; cf. 41:269.

112. *LW* 41:265–266. Luther also felt the pope was insincere. He claimed he was for a "Christian" council, but a Christian council would consult the gospel and Holy Scripture. What he wanted was a papal council, one in which he could advance the cause of purgatory, indulgences, the Holy Virgin, the Mass as sacrifice, simony,

Pope Paul III wrote in his briefs to Charles, "You should know that it is not your prerogative to choose who shall be in the council, for that is the prerogative of our jurisdiction."[113] Luther feared the pope was about to embarrass himself. "Oh, dearest little ass-pope, don't dance around. . . . For the ice is very solidly frozen this year because there was no wind—you might fall and break a leg. If a fart should escape you while you were falling, the whole world would laugh at you and say, 'Ugh, the devil! How the ass-pope has befouled himself!'" Luther warned the "Hellish Father" to consider the "danger beforehand."[114] But the slip up appeared inevitable: the pope claimed only that he had the right and power to call a council and appoint those in the council. The pope needed a class on church history, said Luther. For the earliest ecumenical church councils—Nicaea, Constantinople, Ephesus, and Chalcedon—were called by emperors, not popes or bishops. The pope needed a better filter on his mouth as well, said Luther. But which mouth? "The one from which the farts come? (You can keep that yourself!) Or the one into which the good Corsican wine flows? (Let a dog shit into that!)."[115]

Luther's constant obsession with flatulence and excrement may appear elementary—after all, when the pope talked, Luther said the "farter in Rome" speaks, the "ass-pope fart" has said, and "pope fart-ass" commands.[116] At the same time, Luther turned to this grotesque insult for a reason: the pope's theology and methodology were foul, and not just foul but debasing to those in the church. The pope not only wanted total control over a council but had passed law after law controlling every aspect of life, both Christian and civilian. "Whoever drinks milk on Friday, Saturday, on the eve of the Apostles' Day or of my saints' days, which I have made, is guilty of a deadly sin and eternal damnation; except that I am not bound to observe this. Whoever eats butter, cheese, or eggs on those same days is guilty of a deadly sin and hell."[117] Such a heavy, legalistic burden weighed down the people of God. It also assumed the pope had supreme authority, as if he had the power to bind and loose like God himself. Imitating the pope, Luther played along: "Whoever does not worship my fart is guilty of a deadly sin and hell, for he does not acknowledge that I have the authority to bind and command everything."[118]

Binding and loosing—that was the real issue Luther was after. By the end of Luther's life, the core issues had not changed. He came full circle, back to the debate over authority. The pope thought he was Peter's successor, and since Peter was called the rock on which Christ promised to build his church, the pope and his papal line of succession were the key to the church and the kingdom of

and much, much more. But these, said Luther, were "un-Christian, heretical views"; they were not worthy of the name Christian. *LW* 41:271–72.
113. *LW* 41:280.
114. *LW* 41:280.
115. *LW* 41:281.
116. *LW* 41:336, 335.
117. *LW* 41:336.
118. *LW* 41:337.

God. In Luther's mind, however, such exegesis of Matthew 16 stunk as badly as the pope's monopoly of power. Peter is not the rock; the rock is Christ. Peter is but the man of the rock, the one who recognized the rock for what he is: the Messiah, the Savior.[119] Luther paraphrased Jesus to say, "On this rock, that is, on me, Christ, I will build all of my Christendom, just as you and the other disciples are built on it through my Father in heaven, who revealed it to you."[120] So that "whoever believes in Christ is built on this rock and will attain salvation, even against all the gates of hell."[121]

Luther stripped the "Hellish Father" of his keys. Paul III, and the popes before him, manipulated their office: the "power to bind and loose sin was not given to the apostles and saints for their sovereignty over the church, but solely for the good and use of sinners."[122] The power to bind and loose is "not a worldly power with which the bishops wish to boast and rule over the churches (it is grace, not power), but is a spiritual power given for the good and salvation of sinners, so that they might seek and find these things through the bishops and churches as often as they need them."[123] Here was the key difference between Rome and Wittenberg: *beneficium, non dominium,* grace, not power.

The Last Judgment, by Lucas Cranach the Elder, oil on wood panel, c.1525/30
IanDagnall Computing/Alamy Stock Photo

119. *LW* 41:314–415.
120. *LW* 41:314.
121. *LW* 41:315.
122. *LW* 41:316.
123. *LW* 41:316.

Claiming as it did to be Christ's presence on earth, the papacy remained the "very image of the devil" as long as power was in their eyes.[124] When would Rome learn that Christ humbled himself to bring grace instead? Luther was unconvinced Rome ever would. She remained the institution of the devil. By contrast, Luther called all Reformers and their churches to retrieve the true spirit of the apostles and confess, "I believe in one holy, Christian church." That confession does not mean what Rome thinks. For "wherever there is a church, anywhere in the whole world, it still has no other gospel and Scripture, no other baptism and communion, no other faith and Spirit, no other Christ and God, no other Lord's Prayer and prayer, no other hope and eternal life than we have here in our church in Wittenberg."[125] With those words Luther threw off the yoke of Rome, liberating the German church with the confident assurance that their bishops were no less equal.

And yet, even at the end of his life, Luther remained a medieval man marked by the theology and spirituality of the Middle Ages. His last trumpet blast, much like his early trumpet blasts, associated the papacy with the devil. Even in his most vicious separation from the papacy, Luther embodied the medieval fixation on the influence of the demonic, the devil never failing to mark Luther's polemic, however redirected its target.[126]

RIGHTEOUS IN CHRIST TO THE END

When a sixteenth-century Christian neared those final moments in this world, the priest would enter the room for a last confession. Even to the bitter end, the sacraments were there to transfer the Christian from this life into purgatory.

Luther had protested such innovations all his life, but at the moment of death would he sober up and return to the seven sacraments for the sake of his soul? Luther remained a committed Protestant to the end. When he died, he made only one confession: his faith was in Jesus alone.[127] And yet, the style in which he died—what some called the *Ars Moriendi*, the art of dying—followed medieval custom.[128] Following the protocol of the Middle Ages, Justus Jonas asked whether Luther still stood by his teachings. Luther answered yes, a final, definitive confession by which the Reformer aligned himself with the church universal.[129] The young Luther was tormented by his sin and Satan. He hated the God he was taught and felt nothing but death and condemnation under the burden of his guilt. But in his dying moments, Luther believed he had never been so free as then. Liberated by the mercy of Christ, Luther was confident that his sins were pardoned, and he was counted righteous in Christ. Now he was ready to die in Christ so that in death he might live.

---

124. *LW* 41:323.
125. *LW* 41:358.
126. Trueman, *Luther on the Christian Life*, 81.
127. "Dying without agony was the sign of a good death, which demonstrated that the person was right with God." Hendrix, *Martin Luther*, 284.
128. Luther had preached on the topic as well: *A Sermon on Preparing to Die* (*LW* 42:99–117).
129. Oberman, *Luther*, 3.

Part 3

THE FORMATION OF
REFORMED CATHOLICITY

For we teach not a single jot which we have not learned from the sacred Scriptures. Nor do we make a single assertion for which we have not the authority of the first doctors of the Church . . . those ancient Fathers who drew more purely from the fountainhead.

—Ulrich Zwingli, *An Exposition of the Faith*

Despite its polemic against the Roman church, the theological structures which emerged in the Swiss Reformation stood firmly on the traditional teaching of the church. This was achieved through a deliberate appropriation of the early church and a good deal of the medieval church. The Swiss reformers' theology was grounded in a sense of historical continuity.

—Bruce Gordon, *The Swiss Reformation*

12

THE RENEWAL OF A CATHOLIC HERITAGE

The Reformation among the Swiss

So ought the blind heretics who have lost the holy faith fall into the dark abyss of all heresy so that your lords can easily see what a false and devilish faith these hardened men teach, who are full of contradictions.

—Johann Eck, letter to Swiss confederates

Zwingli inherited from medieval Christianity a powerful sense of orthodoxy and utter intolerance of heresy.

—Bruce Gordon, *Zwingli*

Historians have sometimes cast Ulrich Zwingli as a secondary Reformer in comparison to Martin Luther and the German Reformation. When positioned as a predecessor to the explosion of Reformed churches and their leading theologians, Zwingli is still subordinated. History, however, tells a different story.[1] Zwingli came to his evangelical convictions apart from Luther and deserves the original title *Reformer* as much as any first-generation evangelical. Furthermore, second-generation Reformers owed Zwingli an inestimable debt because Zwingli, whatever his faults and failures, pushed the Reformation through, giving birth to the Reformed Church not only in Zurich but across Swiss territories and beyond. Whether a Reformed tradition existed at all was in large part due to Zwingli, and for that reason he deserves to be called the father of the Reformed Church. More so, the "shape and cadence of Reformed Christianity came from Zurich," says Bruce Gordon. Zwingli "was the artist, while his successor Heinrich Bullinger and Calvin in Geneva were the craftsmen."[2] "Artist" may be a bold title, but nevertheless an appropriate one since Zwingli not only reclaimed the best of the classical and catholic heritage but put those traditions to work with creative application to his own Swiss context to the point of originality.

---

1. Gordon, *Zwingli*, 6.
2. Gordon, *Zwingli*, 7.

SERMONS IN THE BENEDICTINE HOUSE

As in most territories at the start of the sixteenth century, the people of Zurich were embedded within the papacy's ecclesiastical mindset. That changed in a short period of time due in large part to Ulrich Zwingli. Prior to his career as a Reformer, Zwingli immersed himself in humanist *and* Scholastic methods. He appreciated the diversity humanism had to offer, from its reclamation of classic literature and languages to its love for rhetoric and theater to its philosophical (Platonic) foundation for Christian theology. As Zwingli turned his interests to church life, his humanistic mind followed. Indebted to Erasmus, he learned not only Latin but Hebrew and Greek; he studied not only classical literature but patristic classics; and he refined his rhetoric so that his words in the pulpit carried a certain persuasion.[3] During his time in Basel and Glarus, Zwingli also soaked up the teachings of the Scriptures, the church fathers, and the medieval Scholastics. His library grew large, filled with books by authors ranging from Peter Lombard to Thomas Aquinas.[4] He was also familiar with the philosophy of Duns Scotus and was anything but ignorant of the *via moderna* in the days of Ockham and Biel.

ZWINGLI, ERASMUS, AND DEBATE OVER RETRIEVAL

Zwingli's debt to Erasmus is hard to overstate. In the 1520s, however, Zwingli and Erasmus parted ways. Both scholars recovered classical resources but for divergent reasons. Erasmus retrieved classical resources for the sake of his humanist endeavors. Zwingli retrieved classical resources for the sake of advancing his Reformation program. Erasmus disputed Luther in the 1520s over the bondage of the will. While Erasmus did not enter the same type of public debate with Zwingli, nonetheless he resented the way Zwingli used classical resources for reform. The divide was painful for Zwingli because his mentor in humanism became his critic in reform.

In 1516, only one year prior to Luther's posting of his Ninety-Five Theses in Germany, Zwingli could be heard preaching sermons in the Benedictine house. Zwingli's reputation in Einsiedeln spread when pilgrims from Zurich heard Zwingli's preaching, preaching that was not only doctrinal but political. The pulpit, for Zwingli, was not merely an opportunity for scriptural exposition but application in the realm of municipal life. For example, Zwingli had no tolerance for the bribes that pervaded Swiss business. Zwingli made his opinion heard,

---

3. He changed his name to Huldrych, meaning "rich in grace." On humanism's influence on Zwingli, see Gordon, *Swiss Reformation*, 49. For the details of Zwingli's career and an overview of his theology, see Potter, *Zwingli*.

4. Gordon, *Zwingli*, 33.

but what Zwingli called "bribes" others called "gifts" and did not appreciate Zwingli condemning a current of exchange longstanding in the Swiss economy.[5]

During the years 1516 and 1518, a change in perspective occurred, however incomplete and immature. Zwingli later reflected on this period and claimed he learned to preach the gospel by studying both John and Paul but with the help of Augustine.[6] As a student, Zwingli had been taught the theology of the late medieval Scholastics, but the tools of humanism gave Zwingli the ability to go back further to the first several centuries of the church. As Zwingli spent many hours working through the corpus of Augustine, at some point (though it is difficult to know exactly when) Zwingli saw a stark contrast between Augustine's soteriological framework and the late medieval Schoolmen on which Zwingli was born and bred (e.g., Scotus, Ockham, Biel). Zwingli's investment in Augustine was only encouraged by Martin Luther, whose works Zwingli read with a sympathetic eye, even if Zwingli eventually came to his conclusions independent of the Wittenberg Reformer.[7]

LECTIO CONTINUA: ZWINGLI AND JOHN CHRYSOSTOM

By the end of 1518, Zwingli became the people's priest—*Leutpriester*. In the Grossmünster church at the start of 1519, Zwingli's method of preaching took a page from John Chrysostom. Previously, Zwingli preached from whatever scriptural passages were listed in that Sunday's lectionary. But when Zwingli adopted the *lectio continua* style, he exposited his way through entire books of the Bible, such as the Gospel of Matthew.[8] Although his sermons took their agenda from the text, Zwingli's preaching retained its polemical and political edge.

For example, Zwingli was not afraid to confront the greedy ambitions of those in church office. Nor was he shy to stir up popular dissatisfaction with the mercenary service and foreign wars that made the magistrates wealthy. The tension between the feudal establishment and the rural community only escalated.[9] Throughout his short lifetime, Zwingli compared the mercenary service

---

5. Zwingli "articulated unequivocal opposition to both the French alliance and to pensions and mercenary service. Not all, however, within the city shared these opinions, and there were influential men who sought to block his appointment as *Leutpriester*. . . . Money and gifts were part of the political discourse, and the line between legitimate practice and bribery was hotly debated. Thus for many Zwingli's preaching seemed extreme and intemperate." Gordon, *Swiss Reformation*, 50. To understand the mercenary service in light of the Swiss Confederation, see Gordon, *Zwingli*, 18–22.

6. Zwingli dated the change to as early as 1516. *Z* 5:713.2–714.1; Zwingli, *Selected Writings*, 2:344. Cf. Gordon, *Zwingli*, 40.

7. "Before anyone among us had heard the name of Luther, I had begun in 1516 to preach the Gospel of Christ. When I entered the pulpit, I did not preach the words from the Gospel lesson appointed for the mass that morning, but rather from the biblical text alone." *Z* 2:144.32–145.4. Cf. Gordon, *Zwingli*, 41.

8. Gordon, *Swiss Reformation*, 51. Cf. *Z* 1:286.11–14; *Latin Works*, 1:239.

9. "Unsurprisingly, the mercenary service and war loomed large in Zwingli's sermons of 1520–21, and he compared the French and papal agents who recruited in the villages to the devil beguiling Eve in the Garden of Eden. In contrast to these corrupt servants of worldly princes, he opined, stood the virtuous Swiss youth descended from their heroic forefathers who had fought to free the Confederation from feudal lords. In taking on the mercenary system Zwingli was directing his words against the establishment: the wealth brought in by

to prostitution with foreigners and, like a prophet of old, predicted God's coming wrath.[10]

Had Zurich committed itself to the Reformation by 1520? No. Zwingli's preaching showed strong signs of evangelical influence and included critique of certain papal doctrines, like the intercession of the saints. Even still, the magistrates continued to pursue cooperation with the papacy. The magistrates may have tolerated or even entertained Zwingli's evangelical emphases, but they remained suspicious of Lutheran rhetoric, although it is unlikely the magistrates understood Reformation theology.[11] Zwingli understood reform could work only if he gained the support of the magistrates, which might explain in part why Zwingli's rhetoric between 1519 and 1520 was not as overt in its criticism of the papacy as his rhetoric in later years.

Nevertheless, small tremors were noticeable: in 1520 Zwingli decided to part with the papacy's pension, and the Grossmünster even dropped the *Ave Maria* from its liturgy.[12] The climate changed further in 1521: on the heels of its conflict with France, Zurich decided it would no longer outsource troops to foreign territories. At the start of 1522, Zurich troops in the command of the papacy were told to return home. When soldiers walked back into their Zurich homes unpaid by the pope, goodwill toward the papacy waned. With the advent of Lent in 1522 Zwingli's evangelical sympathies and anti-papal rhetoric could now take concrete form and find a ready hearing.

THE SAUSAGE AFFAIR

For sixteenth-century Catholics, Lent took on strong Roman overtones. Every good Catholic fasted, and the church instituted numerous laws instructing Christians what foods to refrain from, meat being one of them. Within Rome's system, obeying these restrictions became yet another means to meriting favor with God by faith. Naturally, disobeying such restrictions was a statement in favor of an evangelical theology.

When Zwingli attended a dinner party at Christoph Froschauer's house in 1522, a dinner that revolved around a plateful of Zurich sausages, he was fully aware this meal was an opportunity to declare Christian freedom. Zwingli

---

the mercenary service was staggering. . . . The magistrates found themselves in an awkward position; the flow of pensions into the city, and into their pockets, was making the rural population restive, and this made the civic rulers jittery." Gordon, *Swiss Reformation*, 52–53.

10. Gordon, *Zwingli*, 25, 83.

11. "The preaching mandates of the early 1520s did not signal the willingness of the magistrates to accept the Reformation; they were rather naive attempts to separate Gospel preaching from the heretical 'Lutheran' doctrines. The theologically illiterate magistrates were caught between the evangelical preachers and their supporters in the guilds, on the one hand, and influential opponents of the Reformation, both internal and external on the other." Even when reforming measures were taken, either ecclesiastical or social, they were moderate, and no one would have considered these measures as anything less than "properly Catholic." Gordon, *Swiss Reformation*, 52–53.

12. Gordon thinks *Exsurge domine* was also a tipping point, pushing Zwingli to view the papacy as a threat. Gordon, *Zwingli*, 54–55. For the larger story that follows concerning Zurich's split with the papacy over its soldiers, see 61–62.

himself did not eat a sausage. His self-restraint, however, was not due to some principled hesitancy. Rather, Zwingli had already so inflamed preexisting tensions over Christian freedom that eating sausages might invite an opportunity for formal investigation and castigation. Nevertheless, Zwingli was present to encourage others, and that was sufficient to send a message concerning his own stance in favor of evangelical freedom. Like other Reformers, Zwingli was adamant in the pulpit that submitting to Lent's restrictions returned Christians to slavery under the law. Yet those who have trusted in Christ alone have been set free, liberated to love one another with full assurance of their right standing with God.[13] More to the point, Rome had no scriptural grounds to prohibit meat during Lent.

The incident created conflict between the magistrates and the bishops. While the bishops were ready to punish Zwingli, they were prohibited by the magistrates, who took the opportunity to make it crystal clear to the bishops where disciplinary authority resides. "Thus a key to Zwingli's early success was the degree to which he was protected by the city's determination not to tolerate any encroachments upon its control of the church. The city's response to the incident, delivered on 9 April, was to condemn the breaking of the fast, but also to ask the bishops of Constance to consider whether fasting was consonant with scripture."[14] The sausage affair was a sign that support for Zwingli's flavor of evangelical reform was on the rise, however incremental those evangelical instincts may have been.

CLERICAL CELIBACY

The same year as the sausage controversy, Zwingli initiated further conflict when he targeted clerical celibacy. Zwingli was convinced that the requirement of celibacy was not only a rule unsupported from Scripture, but a rule that was impossible to keep for all too many priests. Insisting on lifelong abstinence from a woman forced men to choose between the priesthood or marriage, and when they chose the former, it was but a matter of time before they broke their vow and secretly slept with a woman.

Zwingli was speaking from personal experience. Prior to Grossmünster, Zwingli succumbed to temptation and spent the night with a woman. In the sixteenth century, however, the laity came to expect such behavior from priests. Nevertheless, Zwingli's admission of the affair created a storm cloud of scandal. In the end, the authorities did not follow through on any formal disciplinary measures, and Zwingli moved forward, penitent and resolved not to fall prey to temptation again (though the stench from the scandal never dissipated

---

13. Zwingli put his position to paper in *Concerning the Choice and Freedom of Food*. On Zwingli's sermon and pamphlet on the topic, as well as the protesting activities of others (Erasmus) during Lent, see Gordon, *Swiss Reformation*, 54; Gordon, *Zwingli*, 64. Zwingli's argument echoes Luther's *The Freedom of the Christian*. Hillerbrand, *Division of Christendom*, 97.

14. Gordon, *Swiss Reformation*, 54–55.

altogether and was sometimes resurrected in polemics by his nemeses).[15] Zwingli
may have been hypocritical to speak to the issue of celibacy after only a short
passage of time since his own moral failing. From Zwingli's perspective, however,
his sexual sin gave him just the vantage point and incentive needed to oppose
clerical celibacy. He now recognized, from his own failing, celibacy's biblical
indefensibility and its practical implausibility. The controversy was inflamed
further when news leaked out that Zwingli had already married, breaking rank
with clerical celibacy.[16] Zwingli married the widowed Anna Reinhart out of
love and a desire for marital friendship, yet once discovered, the secret marriage
inevitably became a theological and political statement.

DIVINE SIMPLICITY, THE *IMAGO DEI*,
AND THE PERSPICUITY OF SCRIPTURE

Behind each of these controversies were deeper, permeating theological
issues, such as biblical authority and perspicuity. When bishops in the Swiss
Confederation heard Zwingli's sermons or read Zwingli's belief statement, they
grew irritated that the preacher was so ready to disregard traditional practices
because they lacked scriptural backing.[17] These were practices the church herself had instituted, and since the church held *the* authoritative interpretation of
Scripture, these practices were beyond scrutiny. If the Christian shifted away
from the church, or the papacy in particular, as the clear interpreter of whatever
ambiguities surrounded the sacred text, then no certainty remained. One person's interpretation was just as legitimate as another.

Zwingli disagreed: Scripture was not chock-full of ambiguities that could be
settled only by the clear interpretation of the papacy. Scripture itself was perspicuous, as he argued in his 1522 sermon *The Clarity and Certainty of the Bible*.
Zwingli's defense of scriptural perspicuity does not presuppose, however, the
typical approach of other Protestants in the sixteenth century. Few theologians
in the history of the church take the *imago Dei* as their starting point for their
doctrine of Scripture. In that sense, Zwingli's logic was original. He began in the
beginning, quoting Genesis 1. When God said, "Let us make man in our image,
after our likeness," Zwingli followed the patristics and said that the plurality of
the speaker was none other than allusion to the Trinitarian persons. That was no
minuscule detail for Zwingli, whose theology was classical, presupposing a patristic understanding of God's attributes and the Trinitarian persons. By adhering
to the catholic understanding of God—*catholic* meaning orthodox—Zwingli set
in place guardrails that would keep him from unorthodox interpretations.

---

15. Gordon, *Swiss Reformation*, 50. Zwingli slept with the "barber's daughter in Einsiedeln, but his candor
in facing up to the matter (not to mention his putting all the blame on the woman) resolved the complication."
Hillerbrand, *Division of Christendom*, 95.

16. The public ceremony later occurred in 1524. Gordon, *Swiss Reformation*, 55. See Zwingli's work
against clerical celibacy titled *First and Last Explanation*.

17. Zwingli presented his beliefs in the 1522 work *Apologeticus Archeteles*, and Bishop Hugo von
Hohenlandenburg of Constance responded. Gordon, *Swiss Reformation*, 56.

For example, if man is made in the image of God, is the image material or spiritual? Zwingli immediately concluded the image could not be the body of man. For God, says Scripture, does not have a body; he is without form. If he did have form, then he no longer was a God of absolute simplicity, a God without parts. Composed and compounded by parts, he no longer could be immutable and eternal, impassible and infinite. In short, a God made up of parts would be a God who could fall apart. "Now if we are made in the divine image in respect of the body, then that means that God has a body composed of different members and that our body is a copy of his. But if we grant that, then it follows that God is a being which has been constituted and may finally be dissolved."[18] Like catholic orthodoxy before him, Zwingli recognized that such a God—a God who is not simple but compounded by parts—is "non-Christian, heretical, and blasphemous."[19]

Zwingli, always an astute historian, recognized as well that such a heretical view of God was taught by Melitus and the anthropomorphites "who rashly presumed to say God has human form."[20] They did not know how to interpret the text but concluded that the assignment of physical parts to God—hands, feet, face, eyes, mouth, ears—was literal, forgetting that the biblical authors were using anthropomorphic vocabulary to say something about God's knowledge, providence, and omnipotence.

A better way is an Augustinian approach, said Zwingli. The *imago Dei* is not a reference to the body, but to the soul or mind.[21] Zwingli retrieved Augustine's *De Trinitate*, in which the church father distinguished between intellect, will, and memory to identify how the image reflects the one God who is triune. "The opinion of Augustine and the early doctors is that the three faculties of intellect, will and memory, which are distinct and yet constitute the one soul, are a similitude of the one God in respect of the existence and the trinity of the Persons. This I do not dispute, so long as we are not led astray by the three faculties and imagine that in God as in us there is a conflict of will."[22]

Augustine would not have disputed Zwingli's careful qualification either; he, too, labored to protect the simplicity of the divine essence and will, even acknowledging the analogical use of intellect, memory, and will. Zwingli followed in this Augustinian vein. For if God is composed of parts, then the triune God's unity is no more. Complexity is inserted into divinity, God no longer having one will and one essence from which the three persons subsist. That would annihilate the catholic, orthodox Trinity of the Scriptures.

---

18. Zwingli, *Of the Clarity and Certainty or Power of the Word of God*, 59.
19. Zwingli, *Of the Clarity and Certainty or Power of the Word of God*, 59–60.
20. Zwingli, *Of the Clarity and Certainty or Power of the Word of God*, 60.
21. Although Zwingli, still very much in the patristic spirit, appealed to mystery to qualify how far our scriptural reasoning on the matter can go: "The exact form of that likeness it is not for us to know except that the soul is the substance upon which that likeness is particularly stamped." Zwingli, *Of the Clarity and Certainty or Power of the Word of God*, 60.
22. Zwingli, *Of the Clarity and Certainty or Power of the Word of God*, 61.

We must remember that in God there is no duality or contradiction as there is in us; for the desire of the flesh which we also call our will strives against the will of the mind and spirit, as St. Paul teaches in Romans 7. Now we have never seen God as he is in himself. Therefore we can never know in what respect our soul is like him in its substance and essence. For the soul does not even know itself in its substance and essence. And in the last analysis we can only conclude that the activities and faculties of the soul, will, intellect and memory are merely the signs of that essential likeness which we shall never see until we see God as he is in himself, and ourselves in him.[23]

If the *imago Dei* is not corporeal in its reflection but spiritual, and even then, analogical lest the simplicity of God be compromised, then something intrinsic to the soul must be the key to *imago Dei*. Again, Zwingli said Augustine had the answer: within the soul is an "awareness of the divine likeness" and a "looking to God and to the words of God which is a sure sign of the divine relationship, image and similitude within us."[24] Such a "thirst after God" is true of humankind across all time, everyman desiring that eternal bliss and blessedness his Maker can alone give. Adam's fall and human depravity do not extinguish the image and its chief characteristic—humankind's innate longing after eternal bliss. Even in a fallen world, this intrinsic awareness of deity and eternity breaks through: "For if they do not see the need of eternal blessedness, at least they have the fear of eternal loss. For every human spirit looks forward to eternal joy and fears eternal loss, desiring like all else to return to its first beginning.... The desire for salvation is present within us by nature, not the nature of the flesh and its lusts, but the likeness which God the masterworkman has impressed upon us."[25]

The image's innate longing after its Creator is instrumental to Zwingli's theology of the Word. For nothing can satisfy the wrestling soul but God's Word. If inward man, said Zwingli, "delights in the law of God because it is created in the divine image in order to have fellowship with him, it follows necessarily that there is no law or word which will give greater delight to the inward man than the Word of God."

---

23. He then quoted 1 Corinthians 13 and 1 John 3. Zwingli, *Of the Clarity and Certainty or Power of the Word of God*, 61.

24. Zwingli, *Of the Clarity and Certainty or Power of the Word of God*, 61. In two other places Zwingli defined this image: "So too it is in the case of man, for he has this in common with God, not merely that he is rational, but that he looks to God and to the words of God, thus signifying that by nature he is more closely related, more nearly akin to God, far more like God, all of which undoubtedly derives from the fact that he is created in the divine image" (62). And again, "we are made in the image of God and that that image is implanted within us in order that it may enjoy the closest possible relationship with its maker and creator" (65).

25. Zwingli, *Of the Clarity and Certainty or Power of the Word of God*, 62–63. Zwingli approached Genesis 2 and concluded that when God breathed the breath of life into Adam, he was implanting a longing for life eternal (see 64).

That is, God is the bridegroom and husband of the soul. He wills that it should remain inviolate, for he cannot allow any other to be loved—that is, to be as highly esteemed and precious—as he is. Nor does he will that the soul should seek comfort anywhere but in him, or allow any other word to minister comfort but his Word. For in the same way it is the husband's will that the wife should cleave only to him, lavishing all her care upon him and seeking no other comfort but that which he can give. . . . So then we have come to the point where, from the fact that we are the image of God, we may see that there is nothing which can give greater joy or assurance or comfort to the soul than the Word of its creator and maker.[26]

If the image finds its true identity and purpose in the pursuit of this greater joy, assurance, and comfort, which the Word of the Creator alone can provide, then how critical it is to establish the clarity and infallibility of this Word. For Zwingli, without it the *imago Dei* was superfluous, and reform was a farce.

In turn, the clarity and infallibility of this Word depends on divine omnipotence. One should not forget the significance of creation *ex nihilo*. At creation the "Word of God is so sure and strong that if God wills, all things are done the moment that he speaks his Word."[27] The power of God's Word continues across the story of the Old Testament; whenever God speaks, his will is done. But the ultimate proof of the Word's power is seen in the gospel itself. The word of promise spoken through the prophets has come true in none other than *the Word* himself, Christ Jesus. "The whole teaching of the Gospel is a sure demonstration that what God has promised will certainly be performed. For the Gospel is now an accomplished fact: the One who was promised to the patriarchs, and to the whole race, has now been given to us, and in him we have the assurance of all our hope, as Simeon said in Luke 2."[28]

RETRIEVING AND REFORMING THE CONTEMPLATIVE LIFE

The power and efficacy of this creative Word has no little effect on the existential reception and understanding of the Scriptures by the human interpreter. "When the Word of God shines on the human understanding, it enlightens it in such a way that it understands and confesses the Word and knows the certainty of it."[29] Such a shining is none other than the supernatural work of the Holy Spirit. Here is the dividing line between a Reformer like Zwingli and late medieval and papal mentalities.

For example, consider this question: How does one know the way to salvation? The Carthusian answers, "Enter our order, and you will assuredly be saved, for it is the most rigorous." The Benedictine answers, "Salvation is easiest in our order, for it

---

26. Zwingli, *Of the Clarity and Certainty or Power of the Word of God*, 68.
27. Zwingli, *Of the Clarity and Certainty or Power of the Word of God*, 68.
28. Zwingli, *Of the Clarity and Certainty or Power of the Word of God*, 72.
29. Zwingli, *Of the Clarity and Certainty or Power of the Word of God*, 75.

is the most ancient." The Dominican answers, "In our order salvation is certain, for it was given from heaven by our Lady." The Franciscan answers, "Our order is the greatest and most famous of all." The pope answers, "It is easiest with an indulgence." Why is it, asked Zwingli, that nobody turns to Christ, whom John called the light of the world (John 8:12)? "You fool, you go to God simply that he may distinguish between men, and you do not ask him to show you that way of salvation which is pleasing to him and which he himself regards as sure and certain. Note that you are merely asking God to confirm something which men have told you."[30]

Zwingli was frustrated with the monastic orders that boasted they knew the way to salvation, while all along they neglected *the Way*, Christ, and the light he brings to humble readers of the Scriptures by his Spirit, a light that leaves every one of them with clarity and certainty in the power of the gospel. These orders claimed the contemplative life, but it was the Reformers "who [led] the contemplative life."[31] *True contemplative living has its source in the gospel.* For the gospel of Jesus Christ, that evangelical doctrine at the nucleus of the Reformation cause, is the means by which the sinner knows God and has every assurance he has been saved by God. The gospel, said Zwingli, is "all that God has revealed to man in order that he may instruct him and give him a sure knowledge of his will."[32]

This gospel which sheds clarity and certainty has been inscripturated as well. The church is not left an orphan; the Holy Spirit inspired the human authors of Scripture to ensure the gospel took on permanent witness for the salvation of the people of God.[33] Scripture's *theopneuston* (2 Tim. 3:16) identity, said Zwingli, means the Scriptures cannot be approached like any other book: "We should hold the Word of God in the highest possible esteem—meaning by the Word of God only that which comes from the Spirit of God—and we should give to it a trust which we cannot give to any other word. For the Word of God is certain and can never fail. It is clear and will never leave us in darkness." Zwingli's memorable words of assurance are followed with pastoral confidence that he did not believe Rome could contest: the Word of God "teaches its own truth. It arises and irradiates the soul of man with full salvation and grace. It gives the soul sure comfort in God."[34]

Zwingli did recognize, however, that in practice Christian certainty is not so easily attained. Although Christians know their confidence is grounded on nothing less than the Word and the Spirit's internal witness, nevertheless, confusion and chaos reign because so many priests wield the Scriptures like an ax, chopping down the interpretations of others only to manipulate the Scriptures to justify their own agendas.[35] Zwingli's answer was personal, reflecting on his

---

30. Zwingli, *Of the Clarity and Certainty or Power of the Word of God*, 84.

31. Zwingli included Mary as well: "The orders may rest in their foolish and arrogant boasting; it is we who are the true sons of Mary Magdalene and who lead the contemplative life." Zwingli, *Of the Clarity and Certainty or Power of the Word of God*, 84.

32. Zwingli, *Of the Clarity and Certainty or Power of the Word of God*, 86.

33. Zwingli, *Of the Clarity and Certainty or Power of the Word of God*, 93.

34. Zwingli, *Of the Clarity and Certainty or Power of the Word of God*, 93.

35. Zwingli used many examples. For instance, "They quote 1 Peter 2: *regale sacerdotium:* a royal

own conversion to the Reformation. He, too, was confused by the varied and sometimes contradictory teachings of philosophers and theologians until he surrendered himself to be "led by Word and Spirit." He said, "Then I began to ask God for light and the Scriptures became far clearer to me—even though I read nothing else—than if I had studied many commentators and expositors."[36] Zwingli's point is this: if the Christian desires certainty, then he must go to the source, God himself. For until God becomes the Christian's teacher, he will never find the assurance he is seeking.

It may be tempting to read Zwingli as an anti-intellectualist, a narrow biblicist in the stream of the radical Reformation. Certainly, Zwingli did have strong words targeting the "whole philosophical system" that he thought perverted salvation.[37] However, Zwingli was no radical; he called on the authority of fathers like Hilary, for example, to support his appeal to Word and Spirit. Furthermore, trained in classical learning as he was, Zwingli targeted only those philosophies that led astray, not the discipline of medieval philosophy itself, which Zwingli depended on throughout his writings. Zwingli's aim, in context, was far more fundamental: the Christian's ultimate basis for certainty and clarity must be Word and Spirit. In that sense, the Christian is taught by God—*theodidacti*—when his eyes are first opened to the benevolence of Christ in the gospel.[38]

Zwingli's passionate point is not a rant on philosophical education—which he helped establish in Zurich—but a Luther-like plea for a theology of the cross over against a theology of glory. Appealing to 1 Corinthians 2, Zwingli was intent on distinguishing between the natural and the spiritual man, claiming that no clear and certain knowledge of the gospel will descend on God's people if they look within rather than without.[39] Zwingli was persuaded that the papacy, with all its priestly misinterpretations of Scripture, had succumbed to a hermeneutic of the natural man.[40]

FROM PRIEST TO PREACHER: THE DISPUTATION OVER AUTHORITY

By October 1522, the council in Zurich recognized that Zwingli had departed from Rome, who now considered Zwingli one of the worst heretics among the Reformers. No longer was it permissible for Zwingli to continue as a priest. That did not mean, however, that the Zurich council dismissed Zwingli. He was no longer a priest, but the council decided he should continue as a preacher, and

---

priesthood. And with the sword they now force Peter: what he meant was that the clergy can be temporal princes and wield secular authority. That is what the axe can do. But Peter's real meaning was that the Lord Jesus Christ has called all Christians to kingly honour and to the priesthood, so that they do not need a sacrificing priest to offer on their behalf, for they are all priests, offering spiritual gifts, that is, dedicating themselves wholly to God." Zwingli, *Of the Clarity and Certainty or Power of the Word of God*, 88.

36. Zwingli, *Of the Clarity and Certainty or Power of the Word of God*, 91.
37. Zwingli, *Of the Clarity and Certainty or Power of the Word of God*, 89.
38. Zwingli, *Of the Clarity and Certainty or Power of the Word of God*, 89.
39. Zwingli, *Of the Clarity and Certainty or Power of the Word of God*, 91.
40. Zwingli, *Of the Clarity and Certainty or Power of the Word of God*, 92–94, and Zwingli's twelve rules for determining whether a priest's teaching was pure.

an office was created for this purpose. Zwingli knew, however, that he needed to persuade those in political power to side with his evangelical reform; otherwise his cause could not last.

Despite Zwingli's alliance with the Reformation, Zurich had yet to make the same decisive break with Rome. Yet Zurich could not walk the line of neutrality forever. If the heretic was to continue as one of Zurich's preachers, then the magistrates had to give an account and either defend him or discard him, or face the accusation of negligence, one of the more serious charges that could be leveled against a magistrate.[41] For these reasons, Zurich's back was against a wall, called to give an account by the Confederate diet at Baden in 1523. To determine their own stance, Zurich called a disputation, summoning representatives from surrounding Swiss cities, including Zwingli's nemesis from Constance.[42] Johannes Fabri from Constance was chosen as the comparable disputant for Zwingli.

But again, the issue that rose to the surface more than any other was *authority*. Zwingli petitioned the six hundred people in attendance. Since they had the ultimate authority of the Scriptures in hand, they had every right to act as the church in their evaluation of the debate. Zwingli's opponents disagreed, throwing into question the disputation itself in favor of a general council.[43]

Zwingli prepared sixty-seven articles for the disputation on January 29, 1523.[44] The articles begin by summarizing the gospel to establish Christ as the head of the church, a move that countered Rome's elevation of the pope. Then Zwingli moved one by one through each belief and practice that cannot bind the conscience of the Christian, including papal supremacy, the Mass, the intercession of the saints, pilgrimages, vows, purgatory, and more. For example, consider Zwingli's condemnation of the Mass as a sacrifice:

18. That Christ, who offered himself up once and for all, is in eternity a perpetual sacrifice in payment of the sins of all believers, from which it follows that the

---

41. "Zurich's political orientation was still towards the papacy, although the city had little need of Rome and was not inclined to send troops to Italy." Gordon, *Swiss Reformation*, 56–7.

42. Hillerbrand explained all the pressuring factors: "On the face of things, the Zurich council should have implemented official policy as promulgated by church and empire rather than act as if such policy did not exist. The explanation for the decision of the Zurich city council (not only in Zurich, but in other centers of reform as well) is found in the convergence of several factors: the desire of the council to reign in the traditional role of the church in the community; the impact of the new evangelical message; the judgment that order and calm in the community called for accommodating the advocates of reform; and the sentiment that the decisions of church and state concerning reform were not final and definitive." Hillerbrand concluded, "The call for a disputation implied that the Zurich city council saw itself as arbiter in matters of religion. If the church at large did not convene a council to resolve the controversy, so the argument ran, then the Christian community in Zurich was at liberty to proceed on its own to ponder the issues and arrive at proper conclusions." Hillerbrand, *Division of Christendom*, 98.

43. Gordon, *Swiss Reformation*, 58.

44. Zwingli, *Sixty-Seven Articles*, 2:209–14. For Erhard Hegenwald's narration of the disputation, see *CR* 93/1:114–68. The articles were published in July 1523 as the *Exposition of the Sixty-Seven Articles*. Years later Zwingli then published *A Commentary on True and False Religion* as well, which outlined some of the same concerns against the papacy.

mass is not a sacrifice but a recollection of the sacrifice and an assurance of the redemption which Christ has manifested to us.[45]

Zwingli chose to devote ten articles to the magistrates, establishing their authority and the required subservience of their subjects. That authority, however, is not limited to the civil realm but extends to the church. For example, consider article thirty-five:

> 35. The temporal power, however, does have power and confirmation in the doctrine and work of Christ.[46]

A REFORM BUILT ON MEDIEVAL FOUNDATIONS OF CHURCH ORDER

Since the aggressiveness of Zwingli's methods were met with equal urgency, one might assume Zwingli cast off the shackles of anything medieval to form a whole new ecclesiology. Bruce Gordon warns against that assumption by shining light on the ways Zwingli's reformation depended on medieval ecclesiology, however radical his purification.

> Zwingli's Zurich was an admixture of innovation and conservation. The Reformation in Zurich, as across Europe, was built on the medieval foundations of church order, retaining the ideal that each community was focused on the parochial church and served by a cleric. It was not a liberation from a dark past. The Zurich that Zwingli entered in December 1518 was filled with processions, relics, interceding saints and the body of Christ in the hands of priests. His reformation eviscerated the Catholic doctrines and practices, and priests became pastors; but the laity still made their way to the local church to be baptized, confirmed, married and then, eventually, buried. The Reformed emphasis on the link between moral rectitude and true belief had deep roots in the medieval world, as did the violent proscription of deviant behavior—all that polluted the communal body had to be excised. (*Zwingli*, 5; cf. 110)

Furthermore, Zwingli's view of the magistrates also reflected medieval influence. If Zwingli was like an Old Testament prophet, the magistrates were like Old Testament kings, and the church was like Old Testament Israel. Zwingli not only preached the Scriptures from the pulpit but used the pulpit to address civic concerns, from the economy to foreign wars. Since he expected the church to follow the orders of the magistrate for life in the church, Zwingli's polity had much in common with the medieval church and its canon law (*Zwingli*, 195–96). Other Reformers did not always agree with Zwingli, fighting for the rights of the preachers, rather than the magistrates, to excommunicate.

---

45. Zwingli, *Sixty-Seven Articles*, 2:210.
46. Zwingli, *Sixty-Seven Articles*, 2:212.

In later articles, Zwingli articulated his expectation that these magistrates would govern according to the will of God (if they did not then they forfeit their authority). As long as they did so, their power ensured Christianity was practiced. Zwingli anticipated the magistrates would establish the Protestant religion by mandate if they committed to the Reformation.

By the end of the disputation, the council decided that the gospel should continue to be preached by all clergy in Zurich. The announcement was strategic since the papacy could not object to the gospel preached. The announcement itself was vague enough to permit evangelical preachers and their theology without overt endorsement from the council.[47] The council also announced that Zwingli should stay. The heretic's vindication was critical for the future of the Reformation in Zurich, as well as other Swiss territories. However, the fact that the magistrates had made the final decision in the matter proved just as essential. For if evangelical reform had any chance for success in Zurich, it had to be sanctioned by the authorities. If not, Swiss evangelicalism might remain a small, underground movement with little lasting effect. *Here is the paradox of Zwingli's reform, a reform rooted in the people but controlled by the magistrates.*[48]

ICONOCLASM AND THE ABOLITION OF THE MASS

In the mind of Zwingli, the first disputation of 1523 was a step in the right direction, a movement toward reform. But further reform remained, including the reform of images. Zwingli and Leo Jud, among many others, decried images from the pulpit. As others echoed this sentiment, they equated images with idols, convinced Rome had dunked the laity in idolatry by commending the veneration of saints through relics, statues, icons, and more. Furthermore, as long as the Mass continued as the modus operandi in the church, the minds and hearts of the people were content to stay embedded within Rome's penance system.

Those preachers following Zwingli's lead were in a predicament, ministering within a visual and liturgical environment that was antithetical to the reform they advocated from the pulpit. Spotting that awkward predicament, Zwingli published his *Short Christian Introduction*, which attempted to reeducate for the sake of encompassing reform in the church.[49]

In October 1523 a second disputation was scheduled, but this time the focus was not Christian freedom during Lent or clerical celibacy, but the rising tide of iconoclasm that continued to decimate Zurich churches. Swiss Reformers agreed on the formal principle, but applying *sola scriptura* in the context of a late medieval church was far more difficult and no less divisive. A diversity of opinions existed. Some advocated total purgation; the walls of an evangelical church

---

47. Hillerbrand, *Division of Christendom*, 99.

48. "He was prepared to stir the people to pressure the council into accepting his position, but he would not accept any notion of reform from below." Gordon, *Swiss Reformation*, 62. Gordon believes this first disputation was the birth of the Reformed church (cf. *Zwingli*, 92).

49. Zwingli, *Short Christian Instruction*, in *Huldrych Zwingli Writings*, 2:43–76.

should display nothing but white paint. Anything less violated the second commandment. Others were more nuanced, believing some images were overtly idolatrous but others were not. Still other Reformers were convinced that images were appropriate in the service, inspiration for the soul's devotion and instruction.

The papacy interpreted iconoclasm as confirmation that the Reformation was indeed schismatic. In the patristic and medieval church, heresy was typically inseparable from immoral behavior, and destroying a sacred place like the church only confirmed the papacy's heretical accusations. By contrast, evangelical iconoclasts associated images with the veneration and the temptation to idolatry. Zwingli's stance was both firm and staggered. Zwingli was a true believer in the removal of all images. Yet even in his zeal he cautioned against rushing into demolition. Removing images was pointless if the hearts of the people had not changed first. Before there was a renovation in externals, there needed to be a spiritual renovation; otherwise the people would look reformed on the outside but remain committed to Rome on the inside. Ironically, Zwingli sounded a lot like his archnemesis on the Lord's Supper, Martin Luther, who made the same point after he returned to Wittenberg and witnessed Karlstadt's rush into reform.[50]

This range of opinions motivated the magistrates to land somewhere in the middle, protecting images financed by the church but permitting the removal of images funded by specific individuals.[51] That mediating approach did not sit well with those determined to wash idolatry off the walls once and for all. By the end of 1523, their discontent was loud and clear. In the months ahead, iconoclasm only escalated. People assembled, marched their way into churches, and then dragged all kinds of icons into the streets for destruction. At one point, a figure of Christ sitting on a donkey was hurled into a lake, and parishioners cheered as the wooden mule drowned.[52] How violent were these iconoclastic raids? "Apart from the pillaging of religious houses by Vikings," says Gordon, "the Western Church had never witnessed such intentional destruction of the fabric of worship and devotion."[53]

These demonstrations put the council in a hard position. They sympathized with the theological motivations driving iconoclasm, but rioting and pillaging were inexcusable and intolerable. Nevertheless, the pressure had become so unbearable that images were removed entirely in 1524, although demolition and refurnishing was conducted according to the council's guidelines to avoid further populace outburst.[54]

---

50. However, Zwingli and Luther did not necessarily see eye to eye on the presence of images in the church.

51. Gordon, *Swiss Reformation*, 63.

52. Gordon, *Swiss Reformation*, 63.

53. Gordon, *Zwingli*, 118.

54. Gordon, *Swiss Reformation*, 64. Gordon notes that Zwingli's reforming measures were interpreted in different ways. For example, "Many who had heard Zwingli and his colleagues preach had interpreted the evangelical message as a validation of their aspirations for local autonomy. The hopes included the cessation of payment of tithes to overlords and the election of ministers to serve in the community. . . . The confluence of the desire for control over communal affairs with the teaching of the evangelical faith benefited both, but there was no automatic connection between the two ideals" (65).

If 1523 marked the establishment of evangelical preaching and 1524 marked the destruction of Catholic images, then 1525 marked the next and perhaps most ambitious step in Zwingli's reform: the abolition of the Roman Mass. Zwingli preached against the Mass, appealing to Scripture but also to tradition.[55] Nevertheless, terminating the Mass was one thing; however, establishing its substitute was altogether another challenge. Zwingli and Leo Jud, among others, went to work creating a liturgy stripped of transubstantiation and the penance system. However, Zwingli and Jud did not discard the medieval Mass *in toto*. Prayers to Mary and the saints were dismissed, but the preacher's petition for Christ's intercession remained essential. Penance was absent but not corporate confession lest the people miss an assurance of pardon from the gospel promise. The laity did not kneel before the Eucharist expecting transubstantiation to occur, but they still kneeled to receive the Lord's Supper, listening to Zwingli's words of consecration.[56] Zwingli and Jud's approach to the Mass reveals the meaning of reform: a purification of abuses but a retrieval of those components both apostolic and catholic.

The Zurich council was favorable toward Zwingli and Jud, and they were determined to strike a balance between Rome on the right and more radical Reformers on the left, radicals increasingly dissatisfied with the pace of Zwingli's reforming efforts. As with iconoclasm, the council once again controlled the speed at which liturgical reform took place, ensuring changes did not spin off into a more radical agenda.[57]

Determining the success of Zwingli's ecclesiastical reforms was relative to Zurich. Zwingli's abolition of the Mass further distinguished Zurich from Rome. However, other Swiss states were not necessarily persuaded by Zwingli or comfortable departing from Rome. The year 1525 revealed both Zwingli's success as a Reformer of Zurich and the challenge to move beyond Zurich to reform the Swiss church at large. That challenge always seemed just out of reach for Zwingli.[58] Zwingli's limited regional success became patent when nine states adopted resolutions that emerged from the diet at Baden, resolutions that condemned Zwingli as a heretic and reaffirmed their allegiance to Rome.

JOHANNES ECK VERSUS JOHANNES OECOLAMPADIUS

In 1526 the disputation at Baden proved a threat to Zwingli's reform when one of Rome's most aggressive theologians challenged Zwingli to a one-on-one debate. Johannes Eck of Ingolstadt had confronted Luther in 1519 at Leipzig, cornering Luther until he admitted Scripture was the church's final infallible authority. Now he took aim at Zwingli, recognizing the following the Reformer had

---

55. In 1524 Jerome Emser and Johann Eck both had attacked Zwingli's claim that the Mass was an innovation. Gordon, *Zwingli*, 122; Schreiner, *Are You Alone Wise?*, 177.

56. E.g., Zwingli, *Subsidiary Essay on the Eucharist*, in *Writings* 2:187–231; Gordon, *Zwingli*, 137–38. The establishment of the liturgy should be credited most of all to Leo Jud.

57. Gordon, *Swiss Reformation*, 68; Gordon, *Zwingli*, 134–38. Gordon observes that the council's concern over radicalism was motivated in part by what they saw in Germany: the Peasants' War.

58. Gordon, *Swiss Reformation*, 71. For the story of Baden that follows but in greater detail, see 69–71.

attracted with his writings. With Zwingli's hand in the abolition of the Mass, Eck intended to critique Zwingli's view of the Lord's Supper, pitting it against other Reformers like Luther but also exposing it as a novelty that could not align with the teachings of the church fathers. Previous disputations in Zurich worked to the advantage of Zwingli; a new disputation had to occur outside of Zwingli's territory. Baden was chosen, which did not sit well with Zwingli, knowing full well his own life could be in danger if he agreed to travel outside of Zurich. So, Zwingli declined. His life was not harmed as a result, but the same could not be said of his reputation. The papacy painted Zwingli a coward, and Eck proceeded without mercy, condemning Zwingli as the prince of all heretics.

Nor was Zwingli's evangelical cause helped by Johannes Oecolampadius and Berchtold Haller, the two evangelicals who replaced Zwingli in Baden. Oecolampadius was one of the most impressive Reformation scholars of the sixteenth century. As a young monk, Oecolampadius was influenced by the writings of Martin Luther and in time wrote his own defense of *sola fide*. In the years ahead, he devoted himself to the study of the patristics as well and labored to publish a new edition of the church fathers. His skills in the languages must be credited to the influence of Erasmus. In Oecolampadius the best of humanism and the classical tradition converged to form one of the most respected Swiss intellectuals. Oecolampadius's humanist background, patristic scholarship, and appreciation for Luther meant he had much in common with Zwingli, to whom he wrote often. Oecolampadius had also formed friendships with many other Reformers, including Philip Melanchthon and Wolfgang Capito.

Oecolampadius was no doubt skilled in biblical scholarship, and his insights into the text informed an accurate message from the pulpit, but he had a soft voice that could barely be heard without straining one's ears. In a century yet to benefit from modern technology, this proved a fatal flaw. Since services could be as noisy as taverns, a weak voice was a curse, forever sentencing the preacher to a ministry of ineffective pulpit communication.

Not only one's voice but one's personality in the pulpit was instrumental to the success of reform, as is plain in the ministries of Zwingli, Luther, and Calvin. Although his evangelical scholarship did contribute in significant ways toward Berne's adoption of the Reformation in the late 1520s, nevertheless, Oecolampadius did not possess a persona equivalent to other Reformers, a persona so crucial to commanding attention in a disputation.

As a result, one of Rome's most decorated theologians mastered Oecolampadius in the heat of debate.[59] Furthermore, the disputation did not turn out to be a disputation. The Catholics controlled and orchestrated the disputation from start to finish, giving Oecolampadius little opportunity to respond to Eck. Oecolampadius was declared the loser by the end of the disputation, and Eck was celebrated as the clear winner.

---

59. Backus, "The Disputations of Baden, 1526 and Berne, 1528," 1–78; Gordon, *Swiss Reformation*, 104.

REFORMING BODY AND SOUL ACCORDING
TO CLASSICAL EDUCATION

The Reformation was first and foremost a reformation of the church. However, the Reformers also contributed to the reformation of education. In 1523, for example, Zwingli wrote a short essay called *Of the Education of Youth*. The Minster school was strategic, a training ground for students, some of whom might one day become pastors. In his essay, Zwingli put forward a program grounded in classical literature, indebted to the Renaissance. The student was to learn Latin, Hebrew, and Greek—all of which Zwingli called "gifts of the Holy Ghost" to humanity—but Latin was to have primacy since it was the language of medieval theology. The student also learned the art of rhetoric from the ancients, as well as the importance of virtue for the formation of character, which can also be retrieved from classical education.

Unfortunately, Zwingli did not give much attention to the sciences, mentioning math but warning students not to give the subject too much time. In the sixteenth century, math and science had yet to rise to prominence like they would in the modern world where technological inventions changed society. Zwingli also issued a warning about war. Few Reformers knew the battlefield like Zwingli, yet he dispelled any romantic notions of the battlefield. Death is a terrible thing. "A Christian should avoid the weapons of war as far as the security and peace of the state allow." Yet war may be necessary for self-defense. If a student is required to learn the art of war, "he must see to it that his only purpose is to protect his own country and those whom God approves" (113). Zwingli himself followed this line of recommendation to his own death on the battlefield.

Zwingli's educational paradigm, however, was not all work and no play. Zwingli recommended social gatherings so that girls and boys might become acquainted with one another and pursue marriage. Zwingli also advocated for Swiss sports, knowing how important it was for youth to spend their energy and train their bodies. But he did not care for swimming. Today swimming is a luxury, but in the sixteenth century swimming was associated with the river, which could be a dangerous place if the swimmer was not experienced and fit.

Although Zwingli devoted his attention to a Renaissance method of education, his primary concern was Christian education. Part 1 of his essay is entirely devoted to the importance of the gospel. Yet Zwingli did not turn Pelagian at this point, as if education itself is sufficient. Zwingli recognized that without the Spirit of God, the Word will accomplish nothing in the hearts of children and young adults. "Therefore it is necessary not merely to instill faith into the young by the pure words which proceed from the mouth of God, but to pray that he who alone can give faith will illuminate by his Spirit those whom we instruct in his Word" (104). With the priority of the gospel in view, out of the three parts that compose his essay, Zwingli spent all of part 1 presenting the gospel.

Moreover, Zwingli's gospel is grounded in a classical view of God, one indebted to the Scriptures as interpreted by the church catholic. Echoing the church fathers and Scholastics before him, Zwingli connected theology proper to the conversion of the student and that student's work ethic. "For God is . . . a perfect and immutable force which moves all things and itself remains unmoved. And as such, he will never allow the heart which he has drawn to himself to be unmoved or static. This statement has to be confirmed, not by proofs but by practice. For only believers know and experience the fact that Christ will not let his people be idle. They alone know how joyful and pleasant a thing it is to engage in his serve." Evidently Zwingli saw no conflict with retrieving Aristotle's Unmoved Mover within biblical and catholic categories (the church fathers and Scholastics adopted the same vocabulary), only to identify this perfect being as the very source of studious productivity (rather than laxity). Often Calvin is credited with a predestination that motivates a Reformed work ethic, but Zwingli made his own contribution as well. He concluded, "Therefore those who have rightly understood the mystery of the Gospel will exert themselves to live rightly. As far as possible, then, we should learn the Gospel with all exactness and diligence" (107–8).

The Catholics appeared to achieve another victory when Zwingli and Luther could not reach a reconciliation over the meaning of Christ's presence in the Lord's Supper. Catholics like Eck had already promised that exiting Rome could only result in schism and divisiveness. Without the one true interpretation of Scripture the Catholic Church provided, a multitude of vying interpretations would inevitably follow, splintering the evangelical church. *Sola scriptura*, in the minds of Catholics, was a dangerous doctrine, one that could only compromise the unity of the church, a unity that Christ commanded and expected.

THE PROPHEZEI AND THE *LECTORIUM*

Zwingli's reform was not merely a deconstruction of the church; it was an attempt to reconstruct the church according to the Scriptures. From iconoclasm to the abolition of the Mass, he tore down those ecclesiastical edifices that, in his estimation, cultivated idolatry. Now he had the responsibility of erecting pillars that instituted true worship. Zwingli, like other Reformers, was convinced that such an architectural project was possible but only if the Scriptures served as the blueprint.

If the Scriptures were the blueprint, then the minister was appointed by God as the architect. In view of Zwingli's reform, a different title may be more appropriate: the minister as prophet. Zwingli took his cue from the Old Testament and recast the evangelical preacher in prophetic garb. In that spirit, he was instrumental in the founding of the Prophezei in 1525. The Prophezei was the link between academic study of the Scriptures and their application in the church. The focus was the Old Testament Scriptures, and the Prophezei centered around the Hebrew text and its translation into the sixteenth-century vernacular. The Prophezei met each day as its instructors showcased their exegesis of a particular text, speaking in Latin but commenting on the Hebrew.[60]

In the sixteenth century, ministers educated in the original languages and

---

60. Gordon, *Swiss Reformation*, 232.

instructed in humanist methods were not readily available. The clergy reflected the condition of the laity. In a rural church, farmers walked through the doors and depended on what they could see and hear since they could not typically read. In urban churches, literacy rates were higher, but there was still no guarantee that a minister was addressing a church that, as a whole, could read the Scriptures for themselves. Therefore, educating ministers was foundational to the success of the Reformation. Each corner of the Reformation understood that in order for evangelical theology to infiltrate an otherwise Catholic clergy, education had to be the starting point.

For that reason, Zwingli treated the Prophezei with great seriousness. His hope was ambitious but simple: the generation of evangelical ministers after him would be in a much better position to implement Reformation worship. In that vein, the Prophezei was arduous but rewarding. The Prophezei met Monday through Thursday first thing in the morning. After filing into the Grossmünster, participants heard an opening prayer and encountered the following process:

1. Kaspar Megander read from the Latin (Vulgate).
2. Jakob Ceporin then read the Hebrew text and translated it into Greek and Latin, giving a full explanation of its philological import.
3. Zwingli then read the text from the Septuagint (Greek) and translated it into Latin, giving a theological explication.
4. Finally, Leo Jud gathered the fruits of the morning's learning in a sermon, which he would deliver in German to the wider community. Jud was the public face of the Prophezei.[61]

The process from philological to doctrinal to ecclesiastical was strategic: the Prophezei started in Latin but ended in German, demonstrating how a minister can move from academic study to pastoral care. Retaining Latin conformed to medieval academic integrity, and introducing German added an accessibility the Reformers prized for the laity.

The *Prophezei* sessions were restricted to the Old Testament. However, Zwingli did not intend the *Prophezei* to monopolize educational reform; in the afternoons Oswald Myconius was invited to lecture on the New Testament, and Zwingli was known to join him.[62]

The fruit of the *Prophezei* was abundant, producing many works of biblical scholarship. While Zwingli is often caricatured as a philosopher, he was in truth one of the most impressive biblical scholars of the Reformation.[63]

---

61. Gordon, *Swiss Reformation*, 233; Gordon, *Zwingli*, 142–43.

62. In time, other instructors joined the Prophezei, including Konrad Pellikan. Gordon, *Swiss Reformation*, 233. Gordon identifies three "streams" of education reform: "the *lectiones publicae* (*Prophezei*), principally taught by Zwingli and Pellikan; the Arts faculty, where Collin and Ammann taught Latin, dialectic, and rhetoric; and the Fraumünster lectures of Myconius and Zwingli." Gordon, *Swiss Reformation*, 234.

63. This caricature can be traced back to the Lutherans: "In Lutheran polemic Zwingli was frequently branded a 'mere philosopher' who had an insufficient grasp of scripture. There was a certain irony in this

FEAST FOR THE EYES: THE 1531 ZURICH BIBLE

The Zurich Bible was one of the greatest triumphs of the Reformation. Unfortunately, it is often lost to history, and other Bibles, such as Luther's German Bible or the Geneva Bible, receive attention instead. The Zurich Bible was the product of Swiss biblical scholarship, a translation produced by Zwingli, Leo Jud, and others who participated in the Prophezei morning sessions. The Zurich Bible was indebted to the translation work of Luther's German Bible. However, the Zurich scholars made many contributions of their own: adjusting the translation to reflect Zwingli's theological distinctives, adding summaries to help the reader understand the message of each book and chapter of the Bible, including appendices to solidify Swiss confessionalism, inserting hundreds of woodcuts to help the average Swiss Christian better picture events in the biblical story, interweaving maps so that the reader could pinpoint key cities, and so on. Because of these features, Bruce Gordon calls the 1531 Zurich Bible a "feast for the eyes." "The technical and artistic quality of the Bible were the visible expression of the humanist scholarship now residing in Zurich" (Gordon, *The Swiss Reformation*, 243).

Whether Luther or Zwingli's translations are in view, their purpose was different from that of the humanists. The latter translated for scholarship's sake, but the Reformers for the gospel's sake (see Cameron, *The European Reformation*, 168).

For example, he took his exegesis of the Old Testament for the Prophezei and used those insights, as well as any insights gained from the process, to translate the text for the Zurich Bible (1531), write his own commentaries, and prepare his own sermons for the church.

After Zwingli's death, the Prophezei was handed on to his successor, Heinrich Bullinger, who advanced Zurich's educational reform by also preparing potential professors with the introduction of the *Lectorium*. Young students sat at the feet of learned professors—Konrad Pellikan, Theodore Bibliander, Johann Jakob Ammann, and eventually Konrad Gesner—taking copious notes each day to understand Scripture, theology, philosophy, history, and rhetoric.[64] By virtue of Bullinger, Zurich joined other Reformation territories, such as Geneva and Lausanne, as a training ground for evangelical scholarship.

Whether Zwingli's Prophezei or Calvin's company of pastors is in view (see chapters 12, 15), both examples push against the popular interpretation of Reformation preaching that says *sola scriptura* means anyone and everyone can

---

pejorative tag, for in his student days Zwingli was called the 'Philosopher' on account of his fondness for Aristotle. His careful scholarship in the preparation of the 1531 Bible revealed that not only was his theology not simply drawn from philosophical texts, but that Zwingli was among the most skilled biblical exegetes of his generation." Gordon, *Swiss Reformation*, 242.

64. On what Bullinger learned from Beza's Geneva Academy, on the financial backing of the *Lectorium*, as well as its influence on Berne and Kaspar Megander, see Gordon, *Swiss Reformation*, 235–37.

simply open, understand, and apply the Scriptures. Despite their emphasis on the authority and clarity of Scripture, the Reformers did apply "filters." Consider three:

1. Scripture revealed itself *by* the Spirit, but *through* the Word.
2. Preaching the Word was the common, not the individual, property of Christians.
3. The vast didactic output of the reforming writers themselves ... was consciously intended to prepare, orient, and, one might say, prejudice the believer before laypeople tackled the text of Scripture themselves.[65]

The third point is significant, explaining why the Reformers first instructed believers by way of a catechism before they immersed them in the deep waters of the Bible.[66]

The Reformers would not recognize the modern impulse to keep doctrine at bay until the Scriptures are understood. Doctrine was *instrumental* to a right interpretation of the Scriptures. Unlike the radicals, the Reformers did not so stress the individual that their preaching became the property of the self-appointed prophet, nor did the Reformers assume the average churchgoer could understand without the help of the expert.

ANABAPTIST INNOVATORS: SECTARIAN BETRAYALS OF CATHOLICITY

Both in Zurich and across Europe, the Reformation emphasis on the preached Word was a major step toward reform under the banner of *sola scriptura*. However, adherence to the formal principle and the priority of exposition in the pulpit was no guarantee of unanimity in exegesis. Few conflicts brought to light the plurality of interpretations like Zwingli's never-ending irritation with the Anabaptists.

In 1523 Anabaptism came into focus, attracting new disciples with its vocal polemic. Anabaptists looked different in each locale, but in Zurich Anabaptists were both appreciative and critical of the Reformation. They were appreciative since they agreed with the Reformers' criticisms of Rome but critical because they did not believe the Reformers had reformed the church to a sufficient degree.

The Anabaptists Zwingli encountered made the New Testament (not so much the Old Testament) their sacred manual.[67] With the New Testament's emphasis on *sola fide*, the Anabaptists concluded that faith must precede baptism. Only those who have trusted in Christ can be baptized in the name of Christ. Those who are members of Christ's bride, the church, are the same individuals who have placed their faith in Christ, the Savior. Infants, therefore, cannot and should not be the beneficiaries of baptism. The Anabaptists stressed

---

65. Cameron, *European Reformation*, 170.
66. Cameron notes that they studied the catechism for years first. Cameron, 171.
67. Konrad Grebel (1498–1526), Felix Manz (1498–1527), et al. See ch. 13.

those New Testament texts where the recipients of baptism are the same persons who have submitted themselves to the apostles' command to repent.

Early on Zwingli was somewhat sympathetic to the Anabaptist argument. He appreciated their exegetical rigor, the attention they paid to the New Testament in particular, and (especially) their emphasis on *sola fide*, even flirting with the idea of faith as a prerequisite to entrance into the waters and the family of God. Zwingli conceded as much in his later polemics: "For some time I myself was deceived by the error and I thought it better not to baptize children until they came to years of discretion."[68] But by 1524 Zwingli had made up his mind against the Anabaptist argument as well as the Anabaptist movement. For Anabaptism quickly distinguished itself as a seditious sect, one that depended on the Reformation's critique of Rome but nonetheless departed from the Reformation and sometimes even turned to revolution. Some Swiss Anabaptists were in conversation with Thomas Müntzer, influenced not only by his theology but by his methods.[69]

The presence of Anabaptists in Zurich posed a face-off, for Anabaptists did not consider their convictions negotiable but essential to Christianity as they defined it. Prohibiting their views and practices only motivated them to assert their beliefs all the more, leading to rebaptism at the start of 1525. Rebaptism—the literal meaning of anabaptism—was required of anyone who desired to become a member of their church. Since most Christians in the sixteenth century were baptized as infants, anyone who wanted to leave Rome or Protestantism had to be rebaptized to enter the Anabaptist community. The requirement was radical in the eyes of both Rome and Protestantism. Even the Reformers, who disagreed with the penance soteriology behind Rome's sacraments, still welcomed converts to the evangelical church and considered their prior baptisms legitimate.

For example, Martin Bucer said in his *Of the Holy Catholic Church*, "Today we do not acknowledge the upstart Romish church of the pope (we are not speaking now of the old apostolic Church) to be the true Church of Christ, but we do not rebaptize those who were baptized by priests imbrued with popish corruption, for we know that they are baptized with the baptism of Christ's Church and not of the pope, in the name of the Holy Trinity, to the articles of the catholic faith, not to the errors and superstitions and papistical impieties."[70] The Reformers did not fall prey to the Donatist conception of the church during the patristic era. As Bucer clarified, "We confess that today the unworthiness of the minister

---

68. He qualified, however, to what extent he was sympathetic: "But I was not so dogmatically of this opinion as to take the course of many today, who although they are far too young and inexperienced in the matter argue and rashly assert that infant baptism derives from the papacy or the devil or something equally nonsensical I am always pleased when I see strength and constancy in a Christian, but a senseless fury in which there is neither the love nor discipline of Christian decorum can give pleasure only to those who are violent and rebellious." Zwingli, *Of Baptism*, 139.

69. See *DCR* 210. Cf. Bromiley, "Introduction," 119 n. 2.

70. Bucer, *Of the Holy Catholic Church*, 304.

cannot derogate at all from the service of God. Similarly we do not refuse the Lord's Prayer or the Apostles' Creed or finally the canonical Scriptures themselves simply because the Romish church also uses them, for that church does not have them of itself, but received them from the true Church of God. Hence we use them in common with it, not for the Romish church's sake, but we use them because they came from the true Church of Christ."[71]

Bucer and other Reformers believed in the catholicity of the church, even in eras when abuses prevailed. They distinguished between the apostolic continuation of the church through its sacred texts (Scripture and creeds) and sacraments and the modern corruption of the church through papal abuses. For that reason, their ecclesiology flexed, understanding as they did that God's true church is always present, even if it be muddied by wayward shepherds. The Reformers explained this tension by virtue of their ecclesiological distinction: the visible and invisible church. In the visible church, both true grain and weeds grow side by side, the former preserved by sacred texts and sacraments. Nevertheless, God knows who belongs to him. His elect on earth and his elect in heaven comprise his invisible church.

By contrast, the Anabaptists collapsed the distinction, said Zwingli. The visible church is the invisible church. More radical yet, the true church is the Anabaptists alone. While the true church had been extinguished since the time of the apostles, the Anabaptists had resurrected the true church. Only those within their assembly were members of God's true body. As helpful as the Reformers may be to the destruction of papal doctrines and practices, nevertheless, the Reformers remain outside the true church as long as they resist rebaptism. As Zwingli reported, "They say: We are the Church, and those who do not belong to our Church are not Christians. The Church was founded by us: before us there was no Church."[72] That deserves repeating: not only Rome, but also Protestants believed such an Anabaptist exclusivism was radical. To Zwingli, such sectarianism was a sure sign of an autonomous individualism that betrayed the catholicity the Reformers aimed to cultivate in their church. "That is always the way with sectarians who separate themselves on their own authority."[73] Imagine the Reformers' frustration: after laboring with little success to persuade Rome that they were not innovators, let alone heretics, the Anabaptists claimed to be the true Reformers and the only representatives of God's true church, discarding every infant baptism as illegitimate. For Rome in particular, that claim could not be more offensive since baptism was not a mere sign but a conduit of grace, washing away original sin.

Zwingli's sympathies with the Anabaptists also waned because some Anabaptists he encountered connected rebaptism with Christian perfectionism, which only narrowed Anabaptist exclusivism that much more. The "Anabaptists

---

71. Bucer, *Of the Holy Catholic Church*, 304.
72. Zwingli, *Of Baptism*, 158.
73. Zwingli, *Of Baptism*, 158.

claim," said Zwingli, "that only those who know that they can live without sin ought to receive the sign of baptism."[74] To Zwingli and other Reformers, such a demand sounded like works righteousness all over again. The Anabaptists "[brought] back the hypocrisy of legal righteousness" that the Reformers had labored to extinguish from churches influenced by Rome.[75] All the more reason for impatience on the part of the Reformers.

THE NEW LEGALISM? ANABAPTISM AND ZWINGLI'S COVENANT THEOLOGY

The rise of the Anabaptist sect could not be ignored in Zurich. At the start of 1525, the Anabaptists vocalized their determination, started rebaptizing followers, and remained unpersuaded by the Reformers even after a disputation by that March. The result: Zurich officials ordered the arrest of Anabaptists, but even physical restraint proved ineffectual since the Anabaptists escaped from prison that April. As the conflict continued to escalate, the Zurich authorities concluded that the Anabaptist sect's persistence revealed their heresy, and so they took the fiercest step that November—execution. Any Anabaptist who was arrested and refused to recant was drowned in the river.[76] Zwingli was no silent observer but supported the decision, saying, "Whoever will be baptized hereafter will be submerged permanently."[77] In the opinion of the Anabaptists, Zwingli watching Anabaptists drown was like Saul holding men's cloaks as they stoned Stephen.

Zwingli also took to the printing press to squash the sect. First, he set out to distinguish himself from the Anabaptist sect in his *Commentary on True and False Religion* by affirming the ongoing pursuit of piety in the Christian life as opposed to the triumphant perfectionism of the radicals. Zwingli soon wrote yet another response called *Of Baptism* (May 1525), in which he paid special attention to the nature of the sacrament itself.[78] Zwingli took aim at Rome's definition of a sacrament. For Rome a sacrament is something "that has power to take away sin and to make us holy." But for Zwingli that definition perverts a sacrament's true meaning since Christ alone (*solus Christus*) "can take away the sins of us Christians and make us holy." Rather, a sacrament is a "covenant sign or pledge" alone. Do not confuse the sign, said Zwingli, with that which the sign signifies.[79]

Zwingli acknowledged that many church fathers "ascribed to the water a power which it does not have."[80] That assumption, in Zwingli's estimation,

---

74. Zwingli, *Of Baptism*, 139.

75. Zwingli, *Of Baptism*, 139.

76. Bromiley, "Introduction," 120.

77. Zwingli to Vadian, March 7, 1526, *Z* 8:542. Cf. Gordon, *Zwingli*, 191.

78. For the responses of Grebel and Hubmaier, as well as Zwingli's counter-response *Refutation of the Tricks of the Catabaptists* in 1531, see Bromiley, "Introduction," 121.

79. Zwingli, *Of Baptism*, 131.

80. Zwingli, *Of Baptism*, 130. "The Fathers were in error in this matter of water-baptism because they thought that the water itself effects cleansing and salvation. In such circumstances error was inevitable, and one result was that they did not find the true foundation for infant baptism, for they grounded it in part upon the external baptism of water. But it is clear that the external baptism of water cannot effect spiritual

undermined the material principle of the Reformation and forgot that Christ came and "abolished external things, so that we are not to hope in them or to look to them for justification." In contrast, "we are not to ascribe cleansing to the external things" like water. To do so is a failure to understand the progression from old to new covenant. "For if in the Old Testament they were only carnal and outward, not being able to cleanse us or to give us peace or to assure the conscience, how much less are they able to accomplish anything in Christ, in whom it is the Spirit alone that quickeneth."[81] Furthermore, Zwingli saw no evidence that the Scriptures unite baptism and conversion. "Christ himself did not connect salvation with baptism: it is always by faith alone."[82]

Zwingli also took aim at the Anabaptists by qualifying the relationship between faith and baptism. The Anabaptists connected faith and the assurance of faith to the sacrament of baptism. Faith was the prerequisite, and baptism itself was, at least in part, a sign of the believer's faith. But Zwingli countered by focusing on the word *covenant*. He said, like circumcision in the Old Testament, "baptism in the New Testament is a covenant sign." That means baptism "does not justify the one who is baptized, nor does it confirm his faith, for it is not possible for an external thing to confirm faith."[83] The Anabaptists assumed baptism could not be applied to infants since the whole point of baptism was to "confirm faith," and of course, "infants are not able to believe" in the first place.[84] In response, Zwingli was determined to oppose the Anabaptist notion that baptism confirms faith, so he removed faith from the sign of baptism altogether, which served to support his case for infant baptism. "For faith does not proceed from external things. It proceeds only from the God who draws us. Therefore it cannot be grounded in any external thing."[85]

Furthermore, Zwingli asked the Anabaptists whether "it is lawful to administer baptism before faith is made perfect or not, and the same in the case of knowledge."[86] Zwingli engaged Anabaptists who connected baptism to perfection. For "the Anabaptists do hold that they live without sin. This is proved by what they and some others write and teach concerning the *perseverantia justorum*, or perseverance of saints. In this they are committed absolutely to the view that they can and do live without sin."[87] Zwingli played along: "Clearly, then, baptism cannot bind us in such a way that we must not accept it unless we know that we can live without sin: for if that be the case, baptism was instituted in vain, for not one of us can claim to do that before God."

cleansing. Hence water-baptism is nothing but an external ceremony, that is, an outward sign that we are incorporated and engrafted into the Lord Jesus Christ and pledged to live to him and to follow him" (156).

81. Zwingli, *Of Baptism*, 130.
82. Zwingli, *Of Baptism*, 131.
83. "Circumcision did not confirm the faith of Abraham. It was a covenant sign between God and the seed of Abraham." Zwingli, *Of Baptism*, 138.
84. Zwingli, *Of Baptism*, 139.
85. Zwingli, *Of Baptism*, 139.
86. Zwingli, *Of Baptism*, 146.
87. Zwingli, *Of Baptism*, 140.

ANABAPTISTS, SOUL SLEEP, AND INSURRECTION

In his *Exposition of the Faith*, Zwingli insisted that the Reformation was not a movement that betrayed the church. Zwingli put the blame on the Anabaptists instead, who advocated erroneous (sometimes even heretical doctrines) like soul sleep—the belief that the soul after death experiences no heavenly, intermediate state with Christ but is asleep until the resurrection. Soul sleep is an impossibility since the believer's afterlife is dependent on the life of the eternal God. And "if God does not sleep, then it is no more possible for the soul to sleep than for the air not to be clear and transparent when the sun arises on the earth." In contrast to those "foolish and presumptuous" Anabaptists, the Reformers believed that as soon as believers "depart the body the faithful fly away to God, joining themselves to God and enjoying eternal felicity" (275).

Zwingli was convinced these Anabaptists were out for deception. "O king . . . [their] trade is the enticement of old women by grandiose speeches on divine things, by which they procure for themselves both a livelihood and also considerable monetary gifts." They proceed each day to "scan new errors like weeds amongst the good seed of God." But worst of all, they "ascribe their heresies to us." And not just heresies, but revolution against temporal authorities. Zwingli granted that many of them originated from the Reformation movement, but he quoted the apostle John in his defense: "They have gone out from us because they were not of us" (276).

Zwingli interpreted the Anabaptist conflict with the Reformers as a replay of old friction between the church fathers and their heretical nemeses. They were like the Valentians whom Irenaeus opposed; they were of the same spirit as the Eunomians whom Gregory of Nazianzus condemned. Setting himself and the Reformers on the side of the orthodox, Zwingli pleaded with the king not to confuse the Anabaptist revolt against magistrates with the Reformation, a magisterial movement. Do "not believe any rumours of this type concerning us, that is, concerning preachers of the Gospel in the cities of the Christian Civic Alliance" (277).

What confusion the Anabaptists created: the Reformers entered a city with the gospel and sought to reform a city under the administration of the magistrates. Then the "Anabaptist pest" emerged, eating away at the harvest the Reformers labored to cultivate, until nothing was left. "We have seen whole cities and townships which had begun to receive the Gospel well but were then infected and hindered by this pest and could make no further headway, both spiritual and civic affairs being wholly neglected in the resultant confusion" (277). Already the Reformers must protect their seed from the birds of Rome; now they must also worry about the Anabaptists planting weeds from within.

To set the Reformers apart, Zwingli confirmed the Reformation's support of government over against those who defied it. "Far from undermining authority, most pious king, or advocating its dissolution, as we are accused of doing, we teach that authority is necessary to the completeness of the body of the Church" (266). Zwingli so labored to demonstrate the Reformation's allegiance to the magistrates that he concluded, "There can be no Church without government," a government that God, by his wise providence, has established for the protection of his church (268; cf. 278–279).

In contrast, "baptism is a covenant sign which indicates that all those who receive it are willing to amend their lives and to follow Christ. In short, it is an initiation to new life."[88] To Zwingli's original question—whether baptism could be administered before faith was perfected—he answered, "If they say: Baptism must not be administered before faith is made perfect, my reply is this, that we should all remain unbaptized, for faith is constantly developing."[89] Zwingli's point was persuasive for many in Zurich: the Anabaptists had an overrealized eschatology.

Zwingli proposed that baptism be defined as "a mark or pledge by which those who receive it are dedicated to God."[90] Or to be more Pauline, "baptism is an initiatory sign which introduces or pledges us to Christ, that in him we may be new men and live a new life." Yet even in this definition, Zwingli elaborated in a way that the Anabaptists could only have concluded further buttressed their position: "Immersion in the water signifies death, that as Christ was dead and buried, so we, too, die to the world. Reemergence from the water signifies the resurrection of Christ, that as he rose again to die no more, we too have a new life in Christ, and can never die, but have passed from death unto life (John 5)."[91]

At last, Zwingli may have been thankful for the ways Anabaptists exposed Rome's belief that baptism cleanses the recipient from sin, a cleansing apart from which a child is damned. "Water-baptism cannot contribute in any way to the washing away of sin," said Zwingli and Anabaptists alike.[92] Nevertheless, the Anabaptist alternative was dangerous. Zwingli pleaded with Swiss churches everywhere, "Go and live the best possible Christian life, as the grace of God permits, but leave off rebaptizing: for obviously by rebaptizing you form a sect." For not only is there "no basis for rebaptization in the Word of God," but the "only outcome of rebaptism is a constraint which provokes opposition, as was always the case under the monastic system."[93] Zwingli compared the Anabaptist practice to the monastic system because both, as far as he was concerned, turned baptism into a new legalism. "The monks used to talk like that. . . . And now the devil is leading us back to the same evil ways. We disclosed his stratagems and revealed the hypocrisy of the monks. And now he is trying a new trick—he is using the light itself to bring us back to darkness. . . . Note well that this is nothing other than monkery, separatism, sectarianism, a new legalism."[94]

In the sixteenth-century, theology was anything but apolitical. Rebaptism was not merely an article on a doctrinal statement; it was a gunshot announcing

---

88. "Baptism is therefore an initiatory sign, *ceremonii*, or Greek *teleta*." Zwingli, *Of Baptism*, 141.

89. Zwingli, *Of Baptism*, 141.

90. Zwingli, *Of Baptism*, 146. Earlier he was more specific: "Baptism is a sign which pledges us to the Lord Jesus Christ" (131).

91. Zwingli, *Of Baptism*, 151. "Necessarily, then, water-baptism is an initiatory sign, pledging us to a new life, and engrafting us into Christ" (152).

92. Zwingli, *Of Baptism*, 153.

93. Zwingli, *Of Baptism*, 152.

94. Zwingli, *Of Baptism*, 157.

ecclesiastical rebellion, possibly even revolution. For the Anabaptist sect not only proposed a new way into the church, one that failed to conform to the apostolic heritage, but a new church altogether, said Zwingli. Just as egregious, they moved forward without the recommendation or approval of the magistrates. In the eyes of the Reformers, the Anabaptists might as well have waved a flag in the air that read "Sectarians." As Zwingli explained, "The root of the trouble is that the Anabaptists will not recognize any Christians except themselves or any Church except their own. And that is always the way with sectarians who separate themselves on their own authority."[95] And they "have made innovations in our midst without saying a word to anyone, not to speak of their public preaching in the congregation, to which they have no lawful calling."[96]

Rebaptism, new legalism, unsanctioned ecclesiology—these are some of the most unsettling reasons Zwingli labeled the Anabaptists *innovators*, a damning label in the sixteenth century if there ever was one. Zwingli pleaded with Swiss churches everywhere to avoid the Anabaptist sect and their innovations like a plague.[97] Rome may have perverted the sacrament of baptism, but the Anabaptists took it away altogether, and with it the church catholic.[98]

INNOVATIONS OF HIS OWN? ZWINGLI, ORIGINAL SIN, AND THE PAGAN SAINT

Throughout Zwingli's short career, he labored to demonstrate, often over against the Anabaptists, that he stood on the shoulders of the early church; his heritage was an apostolic one. In 1526, however, Zwingli himself was confronted for his doctrine of original sin, which some said was unsound, departing from the Augustinian heritage. Word got out and the rumor spread that Zwingli was not as catholic as he had claimed.

By August 1526, Zwingli responded with his *Declaration . . . regarding Original Sin*, acknowledging at the start that Urbanus Rhegius, whom Zwingli called "preacher of the gospel at Augsburg," was "not the only one who thinks that I hold and write an unusual doctrine with regard to the pollution of human descent."[99] Early on Rhegius converted to the Reformation cause and in 1520 took up a post at Augsburg as cathedral preacher.

Many before Zwingli and many after Zwingli, especially in the Reformed tradition that followed, believed that original sin involved not only the inheritance of a corrupt, polluted nature but a guilty status. When Adam sinned, his guilt and pollution were transferred to his posterity (although various theories were put forward from the fourth to fifteenth centuries explaining how exactly Adam's guilt and corruption were transferred to his posterity). Original sin was

95. Zwingli, *Of Baptism*, 158.
96. Zwingli, *Of Baptism*, 159.
97. Zwingli, *Of Baptism*, 159.
98. Zwingli, *Of Baptism*, 131.
99. Zwingli, *Declaration . . . regarding Original Sin*, 2.

universal in scope; no human being escaped its clutches. Original sin was also present from birth—not a result of an actual sin but a status and condition every infant is born into. For Augustine, infants were damned due to their original sin until their original sin found its remedy. And for many fathers of the church, infant baptism was essential, washing away original sin.

As noted in *Of Baptism*, Zwingli had no patience for a baptism whose waters cleansed the recipient of original sin. That did not raise alarm, at least not with every corner of the Reformation, since the Reformers stood to reform Rome's sacramentalism even if their opinions on baptism and original sin differed from one another.[100] Nevertheless, what did raise alarm was Zwingli's definition of original sin and its theological as well as practical repercussions. Zwingli did not describe original sin as a status but only as a condition. Original sin does not have to do with the guilt of Adam's sin but only with the sinful nature we receive from Adam. "For things which come from nature cannot be put down as crimes or guilt." Original sin, then, could be relabeled as an *original contamination* since it is a "disease, not a sin, because sin implies guilt, and guilt comes from a transgression or trespass on the part of the one who designedly perpetrates a deed."[101]

Zwingli's rejection of original guilt conflicted with the convictions of many Reformed theologians in the sixteenth and seventeenth centuries who assumed original guilt in their affirmation of Christ's imputed righteousness. In Zwingli's opinion, however, he had not gone the way of Pelagianism or Semi-Pelagianism. Although he rejected original guilt, he still affirmed original pollution, and this pollution was crippling, pervading the inclinations of the unregenerate so that their disposition was anything but Godward. As Zwingli himself said, "Our nature was vitiated in our first parent, so that it is constantly sinning through excessive self-love, and if God should leave it to itself, could mediate nothing sincere and generous, any more than runaway slaves. This propensity to sin, therefore, from self-love is 'original sin'; the propensity is not properly sin, but is a sort of source of and disposition to it."[102]

But even if humanity only receives Adam's corrupt nature, does not such a pollution lead to and result in damnation anyway? True, said Zwingli, it could. However, the corrupt nature inherited from Adam is merely hypothetical, at least in this sense: Christ's death on the cross has remedied original disease; he is the healing medicine to our inherited infliction. Thus, whatever would be the damning effects of this original disease, Christ has nullified.

Original sin damns, to be sure, so far as its force and nature are concerned, *but a very present remedy saves and supports, and it has been applied not too late but just*

---

100. For example, compare Luther's doctrine of baptism and original sin with Zwingli's.
101. Zwingli, *Declaration . . . regarding Original Sin*, 5; cf. 6.
102. Zwingli, *Declaration . . . regarding Original Sin*, 9. Zwingli believed self-love is the essence of sin. His interpretation of the fall places self-love in the hearts of Adam and Eve, the reason why they disobeyed. So, too, with all Adam's posterity (see 10–11).

in time. We are all going to destruction through original *disease*, but we are on the way to restoration to safety through the remedy which God has discovered against the disease.... All are damned by it [original disease], but that, since a remedy has been found which restores every thing, they are wrong who rashly damn all men.... But the everlasting death, for which He found no remedy... *He remedied with His own Son.*[103]

Are any of Adam's children, then, born into a condition of contamination? Zwingli thought not, or at least if man's birth is cursed by contamination, it never actually harms (damns?) Adam's posterity.

Our birth is, to be sure, contaminated by inclination to sin, but the contamination harmeth not, for its poison has been taken from it through Christ. And in Christ are not only the parents whom Divine Mercy has brought into the light and grace of faith, but also their children, no less than those who were born of Abraham according to the promise. For the faith is the same and the testament or covenant the same as far as the inner man is concerned. For those men of old leaned upon the mercy of God through the promise of Christ just as much as we do now that He has appeared. *He, therefore, by His blood so thoroughly atoned for whatever could damn that there is nothing left that can exercise tyranny over us—not the flesh, nor the law, nor the Devil, the Prince of this World.*[104]

Why is Zwingli so motivated to define original sin as a disease, defect, or condition over against any notion of inherited guilt?[105] If original sin involves guilt, then infants stand condemned before God prior to any actions of their own. That is a harsh belief, one without scriptural justification, said Zwingli. "For what could be said more briefly and plainly than that original sin is not sin but disease, and that the children of Christians are not condemned to eternal punishment on account of that disease?"[106]

Zwingli's logic was twofold: election and covenant. It is ironic that Zwingli was resistant to the Augustinian belief that infants stand condemned due to original sin unless cleansed by the waters of baptism, because Zwingli's own remedy—predestination—was quite Augustinian.[107] "The bliss of everlasting life and the pain of everlasting death are altogether matters of free election or rejec-

---

103. Zwingli, *Declaration ... regarding Original Sin*, 15, 16–17. Elsewhere: "the original defect is removed only by the blood of Christ and cannot be removed by the washing of baptism" (6).

104. Zwingli, *Declaration ... regarding Original Sin*, 30.

105. Zwingli, *Declaration ... regarding Original Sin*, 6.

106. Zwingli, *Declaration ... regarding Original Sin*, 3.

107. Throughout his work on original sin, Zwingli expressed a love-hate relationship with the Fathers. On one hand, he said their utterances were "dark and involved" and "based upon human rather than celestial teaching" when they taught that the waters of baptism wash away original sin. Zwingli, *Declaration ... regarding Original Sin*, 30. On the other hand, he claimed Augustine and the Fathers whenever he positioned himself against the Anabaptists and Rome. In fact, Zwingli would claim the patristics across his writings, indebted to their arguments, exegetical and theological, at every turn (see 29).

tion by the divine will. Therefore, all who have ever discussed this question seem to have drawn the lines rather incautiously in damning all infants or all grown persons who have not been circumcised or washed with the water of baptism." Zwingli believed he was more faithful to the Reformation by grounding the salvation of the infant not in some external sign or work, but in the predetermining mercy of God. "For what else is Paul after, in Romans from the ninth to the twelfth chapter, than to show that blessedness cometh to those elected of God, *not to those who do this or that?*... Since, therefore, everlasting life belongs to those who have been elected to it by God, why do we form rash judgments about any, since God's election is hidden from us?... Why do we in our indiscretion damn those who have not been marked with the external sign?"[108]

At the same time, Zwingli did not divorce the matter of infant salvation from the sign of baptism altogether. For the sign is a *covenant* sign, marking off children for the promise of the covenant God first made with Abraham. Consider Genesis 17:7: "I will establish my covenant between me and thee and thy seed after thee in their generations, for an everlasting covenant, to be a God unto thee and to thy seed after thee" (KJV).[109] The token of the covenant with Abraham was circumcision, but now the token is baptism. "Therefore, the infants were included in the covenant, for the token was given to them, that it might be an indication that they were just as much in the covenant as Abraham. Therefore, also, our children are included in the covenant just as much as they were, for we are sons of the promise."[110] Still, Zwingli's turn to the covenant sign circles back to his doctrine of predestination. The covenant does not entail that the infant is saved by the holiness of his or her parent; such a mentality falls back into works righteousness. Rather, the covenant sign points away from ourselves to God's electing choice. "I am not tying up the immunity of infants from original sin with the holiness of their parents but with that of God who elects, just as among the ancients children had immunity from it, not on account of the special holiness of the lump or dough, though they were partakers in the testament, but in the consequence of the goodness of God who elects and calls."[111]

---

108. Zwingli spent considerable space demonstrating that God can and does write his law on the heart; therefore, someone may have the law written on their heart even if they are never baptized. Zwingli, *Declaration . . . regarding Original Sin*, 11.

109. Zwingli commented, "If, therefore, He promises that He will be a God to Abraham's seed, that seed cannot have been damned because of original guilt, and He is speaking of the seed born to him according to the promise." Zwingli, *Declaration . . . regarding Original Sin*, 21.

110. Zwingli, *Declaration . . . regarding Original Sin*, 21. "Original sin cannot damn the children of Christians, because although sin would, to be sure, damn according to the law, it cannot damn on account of the remedy provided by Christ, especially it cannot damn those who are included in the covenant which was concluded with Abraham" (23). Ironically, Zwingli believed the Anabaptists and Rome committed the same error. The Anabaptists "do not look to the free election of God, but think salvation is bound up with symbols as the pontifical party does" (21–22).

111. Zwingli, *Declaration . . . regarding Original Sin*, 22. Zwingli went on to address whether there is an age of innocence: "This point must not be passed over, either, that whether our children only or those of the heathen also, if that view should prevail, are altogether restored in nature through Christ as far as the original pollution is concerned they are in the state of innocence as long as they are too young to know the law, as I have

What about infants outside the church, those born to pagan parents? At first Zwingli expressed uncertainty either way, but an uncertainty that nevertheless leaned toward salvation. "I am sure about the children of Christians, that they are not damned by original sin; as to those of others I am less sure, though to confess frankly, the view that I have taught seems to me the more probable one, that we have no right to pronounce rashly about the children even of Gentiles and those who do the works of the law according to the law written in their hearts by the finger of God."[112] As Zwingli then labored to explain his reasoning, he utilized a universal reading of Romans 5 to conclude with much confidence that "those born outside of the church are cleansed of original pollution."[113]

Zwingli's apology for infants outside the church does raise a question, a question that may have been ahead of his time but nonetheless a question he addressed with brevity. If Christ's death nullifies the contamination of original sin, will all be saved or, at the very least, can the pagan seeker who never hears the name of Christ be saved? Zwingli's answer to the former was no, but his answer to the latter was yes. He answered no to universalism because other parts of Scripture contradict such an interpretation of Romans 5.[114] Yet he was far more open to the possibility of salvation among the unevangelized. While he made no mention of this possibility in his work on original sin, he did entertain the possibility in his *Exposition of the Faith*. God is, after all, sovereign, without limitations to his omnipotence. God's everlasting, eternal nature led Zwingli to say that pagan seekers of transcendence will be in heaven. Not only are Abel and Enoch with the Lord, but Hercules and Socrates. "In short there has not lived a single good man, there has not been a single pious heart or believing soul from the beginning of the world to the end, which you will not see there in the presence of God."[115] Zwingli did not explain how such an extensive inclusivism is reconciled with his commitment to *solus Christus*, but the interpreter may assume a wide mercy is motivated by the boundless love of predestination in the mind of Zwingli. Yet many of the Reformers, just as committed to an Augustinian doctrine of predestination, did not feel compelled to follow Zwingli's logic.

THE (AUGUSTINIAN) REFORMATION IN BERNE

Despite the setback of Baden and Marburg, the start of 1528 marked a turn of events in favor of evangelicals influenced by Zwingli in Berne. In the early 1520s,

---

unhesitatingly maintained, relying for support upon the authority of Paul to the Romans, 4:15, 'For where no law is, there is no transgression'" (25).

112. Zwingli, *Declaration . . . regarding Original Sin*, 19.

113. At the end of the day, Zwingli believed Augustinianism was far more excusable than the position of Rome: "But if any one shall say in regard to these also that it is more probable that the children of the heathen are saved through Christ than that they are damned, certainly he will diminish the work of Christ less than those who damn those born within the Church, if they die without the washing of baptism, and he will have more basis and authority for his view in the Scriptures than those who deny this." Zwingli, *Declaration . . . regarding Original Sin*, 23.

114. Zwingli, *Declaration . . . regarding Original Sin*, 23.

115. Zwingli, *Exposition of the Faith*, 276.

evangelical preachers were set on moving Berne in the direction of reform.[116] Despite Roman opposition, the magistrates commissioned its preachers to keep proclaiming the Scriptures and the gospel, though the magistrates did not express a formal commitment to the Reformation, nor did they abrogate the Mass or the use of images. In the middle of the 1520s, the magistrates were presented with a crossroads as the Five Inner States petitioned Berne to declare itself for the church of Rome. If they did, Zurich would be isolated all the more for its evangelical persuasion. Whatever should become of Berne, the magistrates were determined to be the deciders, not the Five Inner States, not Zurich, not even Berne's own preachers or the populace. Nevertheless, it was impossible not to notice that those in the city were enthusiastic for evangelical reform, while those in rural regions were not.[117]

In January 1528, the magistrates called a disputation and welcomed representatives across Europe, from the Confederation to Charles V himself, although many repudiated the invitation. Major representatives of the Reformation flocked to Berne, from Martin Bucer to Heinrich Bullinger, from Wolfgang Capito to Johannes Oecolampadius. And, of course, Zwingli made an appearance as well and may even have been involved as an adviser to the theses drafted.[118] Haller and company were far more experienced this time, drafting ten propositions, some of which showed signs of Zwingli's influence. These ten theses occupied both sides for three weeks.

The theses first establish Christ as the "only head" of the church, which is "born of the word of God" rather than vice versa (thesis 1).[119] As for "ecclesiastical commandments," they are only as binding as far as they are "based on and commanded by God's word" (thesis 2). The middle theses then turn to soteriology. Those at Berne echoing the convictions of Zwingli identified themselves as Augustinians. As they interpreted Scripture, they did so through an Augustinian hermeneutic, so that it was apparent that their Catholic counterparts were not merely opposing Zwingli or Haller or others, but the doctor of grace himself.[120] With an Augustinian spirit, thesis 3 credits salvation entirely to Christ and removes the individual's merit as the basis for right standing with God.[121] The rest of the theses position themselves over against Rome. Thesis 5, for example, attacks the Mass as a "blasphemy against the most holy sacrifice, passion, and death of Christ" and labels the Mass, "on account of its abuses, an abomination before God." After thesis 6 recognizes Christ alone as Mediator, the remaining

---

116. E.g., Georg Brunner and Sebastian Meyer.

117. Gordon, *Swiss Reformation*, 105.

118. *CCFCT* 2:215.

119. All theses come from *Ten Theses of Bern*, 2:217.

120. On Augustinianism at Berne, see Backus, "Disputations," 98; Gordon, *Swiss Reformation*, 107.

121. "Christ is our only wisdom, righteousness, redemption, and payment for the sins of the whole world. Hence it is a denial of Christ when we acknowledge another merit for salvation and satisfaction for sin" (thesis 3).

theses warn against purgatory, vigils, requiems, the veneration of images, bans against matrimony, and all innovations that betray the one, holy, catholic, and apostolic church.[122]

At the end of the three weeks, a vote was taken, announcing the evangelicals as the victors, leading Berne to mandate the Reformation faith moving forward. Images were discarded, the Mass was abolished, and discipline was enforced by the magistrates. One year later, due to the reforming efforts of Oecolampadius, the Reformation was implemented in Basel as well.

WAR OR PEACE?

The mercenary service proved a thorn in Zwingli's reform from start to finish and one he could not shake off. Money talks, and the profit accumulated from the mercenary service took precedence over any noise by Swiss Reformers. "At every level of society, from the magistrates whose pockets were lined with French money to the rural youth hungry for adventure and wealth, the allurements of mercenary service beguiled, silencing the censorious sermons of the evangelical preachers."[123] The financial benefits of the mercenary service, coupled with a centuries old proclivity to stay with Rome, all but guaranteed Swiss evangelicals would remain the minority. Nor was the minority report helped by an ongoing suspicion toward Zurich and sense of security and time-tested unity within the confines of the Confederation.[124] While Zwingli's ideas may have influenced Zurich, Berne, and Basel, other territories remained fixed in their resistance, unpersuaded by Zwingli's proposal to reconfigure the Confederation not merely as a political entity but as a political entity with Zurich as its head and Reformation theology as its governing priority.[125]

Zwingli, however, was not one to settle. In his mind, war was necessary to ensure the Swiss Reformation's adoption and controlling power.[126] Zwingli had plans, plans for Zurich to form substantial enough alliances to guarantee a military victory over the Catholic Five Inner States and their ally, Austria.

---

122. See theses 7–9. Thesis 10 warns against sexual immorality.

123. Gordon, *Swiss Reformation*, 119.

124. "An intense distrust of Zurich, a desire to maintain the Confederation as it was, and a sense of solidarity with the original Confederates were joined with a flat rejection of the evangelical faith." Gordon, *Swiss Reformation*, 121.

125. Gordon warns, "We should not be tempted into thinking that Zwingli stood at the front of a unified movement. During the 1520s Zwingli had real political power in Zurich, and in the lands over which Zurich exercised influence, but nowhere else.... What Zwingli demanded of the Swiss in the late 1520s was a change of mentality and historical purpose; for just over two hundred years the Confederates had understood their connectedness in terms of defense and the maintenance of peace. Zwingli sought to redefine the Confederation as a religious body, held together by a common adherence to the Gospel in opposition to the Roman church. Instead of governance through mutual consent, he envisaged a Confederation led by Zurich, and he was highly successful in redirecting Zurich's age-old hegemonic aspirations to serve the spread of the Reformation. The collapse of the Swiss Reformation between 1529 and 1531 is a tale of fatal political compromises and bloodlust. It is surprising that the Confederation survived at all." Gordon, *Swiss Reformation*, 122.

126. See Zwingli's *Plan for a Military Campaign* (ca. 1527).

Tension grew between both sides, and when an evangelical was burned at the stake, war became inevitable.[127] By the middle of 1529, thousands of soldiers faced off at Kappel. Yet they remained unengaged when both sides agreed to the First Peace of Kappel in June, acquiescent to respect the right to worship as a Protestant in Protestant territory and as a Catholic in Catholic territory.[128] The Swiss Confederation continued to be a coalition of territories united by Swiss culture but divided by religious allegiances.[129]

Zwingli was greatly disappointed by the outcome. Like most, he revolted at the idea of bloodshed. He had seen his fair share in 1515 as a young chaplain at the Battle of Marignano. Watching his fellow Swiss brothers bleed to death on the battlefield was a horrific memory, one that forever scarred him. For this reason, Zwingli could not tolerate Swiss dependence on the mercenary service, no matter how profitable it could be.[130] Nevertheless, Zwingli believed war in the late 1520s and early 1530s was justified. Although Zwingli disagreed with medieval views of soteriology, like many other Reformers, Zwingli was indebted to numerous other components of Scholastic theology (see chapter 12). Zwingli appreciated, for example, Thomas Aquinas and the way Thomas approached ethics and just war theory. War was to be avoided unless there was a just reason that substantiated its necessity. In the mind of Zwingli, the cause of the Reformation was a justifiable reason for war.[131]

However, Zwingli's magistrates did not agree; nor did all fellow Swiss Reformers. From the perspective of the magistrates, peace was preferable to bloodshed, especially if it meant preserving the Confederation. Even if Zwingli could convince Zurich, there was another barrier: persuading other Swiss territories. Berne, always the competitor with Zurich, would rather preserve the peace with Swiss Catholics to safeguard the Confederation than dismantle the Confederation in an effort to coerce religious conformity, an effort that had no guarantee of success.[132]

As Zwingli's advocacy for arms on the war front fell flat, another front presented him with an opportunity: the Diet of Augsburg (1530). Philipp of Hesse was optimistic that Reformers might form a united front before Charles V (see chapter 10).

---

127. Jakob Kaiser (May 1529). Burned in Schwyz.

128. As for the Mandated Territories, each village was to vote. For details, see Gordon, *Swiss Reformation*, 125; Gordon, *Zwingli*, 218ff.

129. Gordon, *Swiss Reformation*, 126. The "Swiss Confederation was not a state but a collection of semi-autonomous lands bound together by alliances, language, culture, and history" (1).

130. Gordon, *Swiss Reformation*, 125.

131. Zwingli's "theology had always worked through the dialectical relation of opposites: the Reformation had come to a point where Christian freedom would have to be won by military coercion." Gordon, *Swiss Reformation*, 127.

132. Zwingli might have recruited the military aid of France, but France was disinterested in the Catholic-Protestant debates that plagued the Confederation. On the northern territories, see Gordon, *Swiss Reformation*, 128.

HEIR OF TRUE CATHOLIC ORTHODOXY:
CLASSICAL METAPHYSICS AND REFORMED SOTERIOLOGY

Although Zwingli did not attend the Diet of Augsburg in person, he attempted to make his presence known by writing a confession called *An Account [or Reckoning] of the Faith*. Zwingli's account was revealing: he provided an original, systematic summary of his beliefs, capturing the essence of his reform in Zurich; however, his clarity created strong reactions from everyone who did not hold his convictions.

For example, consider not just the content of Zwingli's *Account* but its method and movement from start to finish. He opened on a creedal note, singing the tune of catholicity in order to situate his entire program within the apostolic and patristic tradition. As he began with the perfections of God and moved into an orthodox articulation of the Trinity and the incarnation, Zwingli was explicit in his allegiance to the Apostles' Creed, the Nicene Creed, and the Athanasian Creed.[133] Furthermore, the structure of these creeds, especially the Apostles' Creed, frames Zwingli's own presentation, including his affirmation of the visible and invisible church.[134]

Despite Zwingli's overt claim to catholicity, his own views mark him off from other Reformers. He continued his idiosyncratic position on original sin articulated back in 1526.[135] And, as expected, his articulation of the "holy Eucharist" set him over against the Lutherans. For "the true body of Christ is present *by the contemplation of faith*. . . . But that the body of Christ in essence and really, *i.e.*, the natural body itself, is either present in the supper or masticated with our mouth and teeth, as the Papists or some [the Lutherans] who look back to the fleshpots of Egypt assert, we not only deny, but constantly maintain to be an error, contrary to the Word of God."[136]

Even here, however, Zwingli did not think of his position as a detour from the church catholic. Zwingli appealed to Augustine, specifically his *Homilies on the Gospel of John*, to differentiate between the omnipresence of Christ's divinity and the restricted location of Christ's humanity at the right hand of the Father.[137] That distinction invited the charge that Zwingli had divided the one person of Christ, but Zwingli believed he had only preserved the Chalcedonian command not to confuse the two natures of Christ.[138] Whether he was correct or not, other Reformers would judge themselves more faithful to Chalcedon.

Regardless, Zwingli's intention was relentless in its claim on orthodoxy, which even entered his polemics as he attacked Luther for not only undermining

133. Zwingli, *Account of the Faith*, 36. Also consult *CCFCT* 2:249–71, as well as Bromiley, *Zwingli and Bullinger*, 239–82.
134. Zwingli, *Account of the Faith*, 44–45.
135. Zwingli, *Account of the Faith*, 40–43.
136. Zwingli, *Account of the Faith*, 49, 50–51.
137. Zwingli, *Account of the Faith*, 49.
138. Zwingli belabored this point in *Exposition of the Faith*, 251.

solus Christus but misappropriating Irenaeus and *Against Heresies*.[139] Ultimately, Zwingli punted his case to Oecolampadius, whom he said had refuted Melanchthon's interpretation of the church fathers.[140] Notwithstanding Zwingli's attempt to situate himself within the apostolic heritage and present himself as the true evangelical and catholic path forward, his position and polemic provoked both Rome and Reformers alike. When Melanchthon read the *Account*, for example, he said to Luther in a letter that Melanchthon was insane for doubling down on his view of the Eucharist; Luther's response in a letter to Justus Jonas was just as rancorous.[141]

The *Account* was not publicly read at the Diet of Augsburg, but it was privately read and considered, evidenced by John Eck who thrashed Zwingli's *Account* in July 1530.[142] Nevertheless, it was, to Zwingli's credit, one of his finest and most lucid articulations of *his* reformation program. And, despite disagreement, the *Account* did put forward a concept of "covenant" theology that became prominent in Reformed thought in the generations after Zwingli.[143]

In 1531 Zwingli wrote another articulation of his evangelical faith, this time titled *An Exposition of the Faith*, posthumously published in 1536 by Heinrich Bullinger. Bullinger may have published the *Exposition* as a sort of tribute and also to convey that now he was carrying Zwingli's baton. Zwingli was gone, but his reformation voice could not be silenced. Bullinger released the *Exposition* alongside the *First Helvetic Confession*, and together these two served such a strategy.

In many ways, Zwingli's *Exposition* is a summary of his beliefs over the whole course of his short life.[144] As a Reformation report, the *Exposition* reiterates those evangelical beliefs that first shaped the 1520s in Zurich but also in Germany. The *Exposition* carries a polemical edge as Zwingli also aimed at the soteriology of Rome once more.[145] None of this was surprising by the 1530s. However, what is often overlooked in the *Exposition* is the bridge Zwingli erected between two terms: his *classical theology* and his *Reformed soteriology*. First, Zwingli's *Exposition* is a salient manifesto of his allegiance to classical Christianity. For Zwingli was attempting to persuade the king—Zwingli's *Exposition* is dedicated to the king of France—that the Reformation was not a novel, heretical movement, but the heir of true orthodoxy, over against Rome who had betrayed the catholic heritage. For example, Zwingli began with theology proper. While many Reformation documents turn their first attention to soteriological matters,

---

139. Zwingli, *Account of the Faith*, 53.
140. Zwingli also enlisted numerous church fathers and Scholastics to support specific exegetical conclusions, including Ambrose, Augustine, Peter Lombard, and Gratian. Zwingli, *Account of the Faith*, 54–56.
141. For Melanchthon, see *CR* 2:193 (no. 781); for Luther, see *WABr* 5, no. 1657. Cf. *CCFCT* 2:250.
142. See Eck, *Refutation of the Articles of Zwingli*, 62–104. For Zwingli's reply to Eck, see his *Letter of Huldreich Zwingli to the Most Illustrious Princes of Germany Assembled at Augsburg, regarding the Insults of Eck*, 105–27.
143. On Zwingli and covenant, see Gordon, *Swiss Reformation*, 228.
144. For background, see Bromiley's "Introduction" to *Exposition of the Faith*," 239–44.
145. Zwingli, *Exposition of the Faith*, 248–49, 254, 268–72.

Zwingli took a page from the patristics and began by confessing a Trinitarian classical theism. Borrowing the framework of the Apostles' Creed (and possibly the Nicene Creed), Zwingli distinguished between the Creator and the creature. "God alone is uncreated, for only one thing can be uncreated."[146] As uncreated, he and he alone is the eternal, infinite Being. On that basis, Zwingli believed the Christian faith should follow the Creed: "I believe in God the Father Almighty, Maker of heaven and earth," which is the church's "infallible faith because it rests upon the one and only God." Zwingli's creedal retrieval was strategic, the foundation on which he would then build his faith. "Only the eternal and infinite and uncreated God is the basis of faith."[147]

In the vein of Nicaea, Zwingli then established that this eternal, infinite, and uncreated God is none other than Father, Son, and Holy Ghost. Zwingli used Nicene vocabulary: "The three are all one, one essence, one *ousia* or existence, one power and might, one knowledge and providence, one goodness and loving kindness." In other words, there "are three names or persons, but each and all are one and the self-same God."[148] Zwingli's emphasis on divine simplicity is arresting. In the pro-Nicene tradition, the persons are not individual centers of consciousness and will, a later innovation of modern social Trinitarianism. Rather, the essence has three modes of subsistence, each person a subsisting relation of the one, indivisible, undivided essence. Zwingli may not have used this exact language, but his articulation sounds close to the Athanasian Creed, certifying that no matter what divine attributes are described—power, knowledge, goodness, love—they must be essential properties.[149]

PROFESSION OF FAITH AND THE ONE, HOLY, CATHOLIC, APOSTOLIC CHURCH

Zwingli saw no conflict between his reformed convictions and his adherence to the "one, holy, catholic, that is, universal Church." He was persuaded that the Reformation church was a continuation and fulfillment of this one, holy, catholic, and apostolic church.

Like other Reformers, Zwingli distinguished between the invisible and the visible church. The invisible church consists of the elect "concealed from the eyes of men" and "known only to God and to themselves." The visible church, however, is "not the Roman pontiff and others who bear the mitre, but all who make profession of faith in Christ the whole world over" (*Exposition of the Faith*, 265).

---

146. Zwingli, *Exposition of the Faith*, 246.
147. Zwingli, *Exposition of the Faith*, 247.
148. Zwingli, *Exposition of the Faith*, 249.
149. Presupposing simplicity, Zwingli could say, for example, that there are not three powers, but one power.

Second, when Zwingli did transition to his articulation of these essential properties, he still did so within the framework of classical theism, a move most consequential for Zwingli's evangelical soteriology. By establishing classical attributes like immutability and impassibility, Zwingli was now in a position to assert God's "irrevocable justice." In Zwingli's estimation, only an impassible, immutable righteousness can then substantiate Christ's sacrifice for sin, a sacrifice Zwingli called a propitiation, satisfying once for all the wrath of God against the ungodly.[150] Once more, Zwingli presupposed divine simplicity: "Justice and mercy were conjoined, the one furnishing the sacrifice, the other accepting it as a sacrifice for all sin."[151]

Consider another example: Zwingli warned against worshiping Mary, turning her into a second mediator. Nevertheless, he clarified (for the king's sake, no doubt) that evangelicals did not disrespect Mary. She is the Virgin, the Mother of God, *theotokos*, as the church fathers called her, a qualification that could have made Cyril of Alexandria grin.[152] Or consider another example: the Apostles' Creed. When he approached that line in the Creed—"He descended into hell"—Zwingli was affirmative. He believed the Fathers meant to use "this expression periphrastically, to signify the reality of his death—for to be numbered amongst those who have descended into hell means to have died—and also to make it clear that the power of his atonement penetrates even to the underworld."[153] And when Zwingli followed this descent with Christ's ascent in the resurrection, his appeal was to the "holy Father" who "said that the body of Christ nourishes us to the resurrection."[154]

Zwingli's argument may not be original, but his marriage of classical metaphysics and evangelical soteriology had a prophetic ring, anticipating the advent of Reformed Orthodoxy after his premature death. On that score, Zwingli's *Exposition* adds a contribution that defined the Reformed Church for centuries to come.

A PROPHET SLAIN ON THE KING'S BATTLEFIELD

Even before he arrived in Zurich, the young Zwingli did not hide his pacifism. Protesting against the mercenary service, the name Zwingli became synonymous with opposition to sending Swiss soldiers to fight wars in other countries. Furthermore, the young Zwingli was on guard against attempts to rope the church into the political conflicts of magistrates. However, in 1524 Zwingli started to soften toward the use of the sword. The Edict of Worms haunted Reformers, placing a target on their back as heretics to be punished. When the diet at Regensburg decided to put that threat into action, Zwingli's pacifist

---

150. Zwingli, *Exposition of the Faith*, 250.
151. Zwingli, *Exposition of the Faith*, 250.
152. Zwingli, *Exposition of the Faith*, 247.
153. Like the Fathers, Zwingli believed Christ's descent is supported by 1 Peter 3:19–20. Zwingli, *Exposition of the Faith*, 252.
154. Zwingli, *Exposition of the Faith*, 253.

commitment began to fade into his past.[155] Furthermore, when the Five States became hostile, the Zurich Reformer started to ask himself not *if* but *when* the church should support the use of the sword to protect and secure the future of evangelical reform. Zwingli's change in perspective was the beginning of the end, ultimately explaining why a preacher like Zwingli took to the battlefield.

Zwingli's battle plans had been thwarted by the First Peace of Kappel (1529). However, as Charles V flexed his political muscles, Zwingli believed the battlefield was inevitable. The diet at Augsburg did not end well for Protestants, and the recess of 1530 gave Protestants one option: return to the Roman Church. Although German territories felt the fear that resulted from that threat most, Swiss Protestants were not immune. If the Catholic cantons decided to fight, would the Protestants align with one another? To Zwingli's disappointment, Zurich would be alone on the battlefield. Berne was certainly not going to help, and other states in the Confederation were not jumping at the prospect of war either, as the 1531 diet in Zurich made clear.[156] Zwingli issued a clarion call to war, but no one budged, although they did agree to cut off food and other supplies from the Catholic cantons to apply pressure in hopes of conformity.[157] That pressure did not push the Catholics to conform but fight.

Unlike others in Swiss states, Zwingli placed little confidence in the Confederation in this sense: the Confederation should not tolerate Catholic and Protestant territories, but the Confederation itself should be evangelical. For Zwingli this conviction was not the belief of a power-hungry preacher who had turned politician. The Confederation possessed a God-given responsibility to protect and prosper the evangelical faith. He filtered Zurich through an Old Testament hermeneutic. Israel bore the sword to rid idolatry and advance true worship, a responsibility pursued by the king under the accountability of God's prophet.[158] Zwingli was that prophet, commissioned by God himself to speak with authority to earthly rulers and sovereigns, discontent until those with the sword wielded their weapons for the evangelical cause. However, the sword wielded had increasingly been put back in its sheath. Even Zurich, who was most likely to follow Zwingli into war, did not have the military strength necessary to win. Zwingli had to face the conflict of his competing commitments: previously he had preached against the mercenary service, its revenue, and the military strength it provided. As a result, Zurich had neither the finances, the weaponry, or the military training needed to fight against the Catholics.[159] Furthermore, the people had been told so many times during the 1520s to gird for battle that the war cry no longer motivated the patriotic.[160]

---

155. Gordon labels the young Zwingli an Erasmian pacifist. Gordon, *Zwingli*, 115.
156. Gordon, *Swiss Reformation*, 130.
157. Hillerbrand, *Division of Christendom*, 175.
158. On the Reformer as prophet, see Gordon, *Swiss Reformation*, 140.
159. Gordon, *Swiss Reformation*, 131.
160. "No fewer than twenty-one military mobilizations had occurred in Zurich between 1524 and 1531,

To make matters worse, Zwingli did not exactly have the spirit of the Zurich people behind him. Those in the country showed little enthusiasm for the preacher's political preoccupations, while those in the city could not, in good conscience, tolerate a blockade that cut off the food supply to their Catholic neighbors.[161] Nevertheless, despite rural indifference and urban resistance, Zwingli and the magistrates remained undeterred. Catholics in the Confederation were not about to stand by and watch their people starve. By October 1531, war was inescapable.

The fight was a mismatch if there ever was one. Not only were Zurich soldiers grossly outnumbered at Kappel, but they were children compared to the experienced Catholic fighters. The result: slaughter. Zwingli was found among the dead with a sword in his hand. When the Catholics discovered Zwingli's body, they recreated the trial they had always wanted, declaring Zwingli not only guilty of treason but heresy. They cut off his head, quartered his body, and then lit his body on fire. Zwingli's supporters back home tried to vindicate the Reformer by claiming the flames, hot as they were, could not turn Zwingli's heart into ash. This was a desperate attempt to read the events through the lens of Providence, as a sign of God's favor as opposed to God's wrath. But with victory in their hands, and the head of Zwingli himself severed, the Catholics had little trouble persuading others that God had finally revealed the identity of his true people. In the sixteenth century, victory was a sign of God's favor, defeat a sign of his judgment. "The Battle of Kappel offered eloquent proof that in the sixteenth century war could also be the final reasoning of theologians, or, to vary Clausewitz's famous definition, the 'continuation of theological controversy by other means.'"[162] Other Reformers did not agree with the Catholic interpretation, but they did agree that divine providence was sending a message. Luther rejoiced at the news of Zwingli's death, concluding that God had finally punished Zwingli for his erroneous theology of the Lord's Supper.[163]

In the weeks and months that followed, it became clear that the Catholic cantons had won before the war had even begun. Zurich's immediate defeat and Zwingli's postmortem trial and burning were an embarrassment; Zurich was humiliated by a war many of its people did not want in the first place but were pressured from the pulpit to engage. The war was so devastating that many wondered whether the Confederation could continue. But the Confederation found a way: the Second Peace of Kappel. In view of their recent victories, the Catholics

---

and—like the shepherd boy in Aesop's fable—they were not taken seriously in the end." Hillerbrand, *Division of Christendom*, 175.

161. Concerning the former: "What did the farmers along Lake Zurich care about alliances with Hesse or Strasbourg, or the rights of the abbot of St Gall, or whether the Gospel was preached in some Mandated Territory? The call to arms issued by the Zurich council in late summer 1531 fell on deaf ears as most inhabitants of Zurich's rural territories prepared themselves for the harvest." Gordon, *Swiss Reformation*, 132.

162. Hillerbrand, *Division of Christendom*, 176.

163. For the details of the war, see Gordon, *Swiss Reformation*, 132–33, 140 (for Luther's reaction, see 174); Hillerbrand, *Division of Christendom*, 175.

now had the upper hand, ensuring that the Second Peace recognized the veracity and prosperity of the victors' religion. God's providence on the battlefield had made that much perspicuous.

Nevertheless, for the Confederation to work, spanning Swiss territories, its representatives had to let go of Zwingli's dream of a religiously motivated governance. Each Swiss state was permitted to worship according to its own convictions.[164] But the damage had been done; evangelical territories now faced the seemingly insurmountable challenge of recovering from war. That challenge not only involved overcoming the burden of financial restitution, but finding new preachers with a new paradigm, a paradigm that did not use the pulpit for political maneuver. A new leader was needed, one who could recover the confidence of the magistrates and restore the integrity of the Swiss evangelical pulpit.

THE RISE OF HEINRICH BULLINGER

The new leader was Heinrich Bullinger, a young minister from Strasbourg passionate about shepherding the people according to the Scriptures rather than establishing a political program from the pulpit.[165] Bullinger was a child of the Reformation, reading not only humanists but all the major Reformers as well. Bullinger spent the 1520s trying on his newfound evangelical commitments within Kappel's Cistercian monastery. Unlike those of other Reformers, Bullinger's teachings were met with interest.[166]

When Bullinger became head pastor in Zurich, he was only twenty-seven years old. How could a pastor so young lead a church that had been through so much? Bullinger, however, was wise beyond his youth. Although still in his twenties, he was no stranger to the past decade's disputations. Not only had he observed Zurich's transformation, but the new pastor had learned from Zwingli while he was still alive. Thus began almost four and a half decades in the Zurich pastorate, establishing one of the most enduring Reformed pulpits of the sixteenth century.[167]

Bullinger's achievements over the course of four decades were legion. Not only was he prolific in sermon and book alike, but he guaranteed the survival of the Swiss pastorate due to his instrumental role in the Zurich academy. However, one of his greatest achievements came as early as the pastorate itself: Bullinger found a way to help the church survive defeat at Kappel. If Zwingli drove the Zurich church to a near-death experience on the battlefield, Bullinger revived the church by resurrecting its original purpose, the preaching of the evangelical faith. No longer were ministers to mix their responsibilities within the sphere of

---

164. "The Second Peace of Kappel was an attempt to hold the Confederation together, and little more than that: it enshrined no principles of religious toleration or acceptance." Gordon, *Swiss Reformation*, 135.

165. The Bernese looked to Wolfgang Capito.

166. Hillerbrand, *Division of Christendom*, 176. For Bullinger's contribution, see Bruce Gordon and Emidio Campi, *Architect of Reformation*.

167. Hillerbrand, 177.

national and international politics, even warfare. That shift in mindset did place the magistrate in a position of power over the church.[168] Whether that was for better or worse can be debated, but one thing is clear: repositioning the church's focus did grant Bullinger longevity otherwise absent in Zwingli.

As the church turned its attention from politics to ecclesiology, Bullinger led the way in the formation of a Zurich liturgy, one of his most monumental successes. Following the patristics, Zwingli centralized the sermon in the service. That focus continued with Bullinger, but a certain liturgy cemented as well, one that structured the whole service on the gospel and its catholicity. In the 1520s, Zwingli had reformed the liturgy and placed a notable emphasis on the biblical concept of covenant. Each Sunday the liturgy reminded the people that they, like Israel, had entered into a covenant with the Lord. By means of this covenant, the Lord had redeemed them. Rescued, they now needed to turn to their Lord's stipulations to learn what life in the covenant looked like. The concept of covenant in the liturgy was no passing pragmatic endeavor. For Bullinger, covenant theology was central to his interpretation of the Bible and his theological paradigm for the church, as is plain in his 1534 book, *Concerning the Unique and Eternal Covenant or Testament of God.*[169]

By the latter half of the 1530s, Bullinger consolidated the liturgy's format to ensure its adoption throughout the Confederation. A typical evangelical Swiss service started with a minister instructing the people to examine themselves, removing all presumption lest they fail to humble themselves in worship. Next, the people joined hands with the church catholic, reciting the Creed, confessing the faith once for all delivered to the saints. After the Creed, the people were encouraged to confess their sins to the Lord, acknowledging their iniquity and need for forgiveness. Afterward the minister assured the people that they were forgiven, thanks to the blood of Christ. Absolution was followed by prayer, and prayer was followed by a Scripture reading, most likely on the passion of Christ. By positioning the church within the finished and sufficient work of Christ, the people of God were now prepared to be admonished from the Word of God. After his exposition of the text, the minister offered a Communion prayer, followed by a recitation of the Lord's Prayer. After the meaning of the Lord's Supper was explained and the people were admonished once more, Communion was administered, accompanied by the singing of psalms. A blessing concluded the service.[170]

Bullinger's contribution was not limited to the liturgy, however—he also made strides to heal the breach Zwingli created. That task demanded patience and endurance.

---

168. Hillerbrand, 177.

169. Reformed Orthodox theologians utilized Bullinger's work for the sake of covenant theology. Hillerbrand, *Division of Christendom*, 177.

170. This order is from Gordon, *Swiss Reformation*, 248. Gordon notes that psalms were not sung in Zurich or Berne. Bullinger didn't condemn singing, but others felt strongly against it.

REPAIRING THE LUTHERAN BREACH?
THE *FIRST HELVETIC CONFESSION*

During the 1530s, Bullinger was occupied with simply recovering from the rupture left by Zwingli. In time Bullinger rose to prominence as a leading Swiss Reformer, but until then he worked to reconcile Swiss and German tension over the Lord's Supper. Martin Bucer traveled around Europe armed with such a mission. At the end of 1535, for example, progress was made. Representatives from Zurich (such as Leo Jud) met in Aarau with representatives from Basel (such as Oswald Myconius), and before they left, they produced five articles on the Lord's Supper that not only found favor with Bullinger but even earned an examination by Luther himself and without his usual wrath in response.[171]

The next year, Reformers traveled to Basel from all over to attend the first council of Swiss Reformed churches, hoping to produce a confessional statement that not only clarified the Swiss Reformed faith but served to close the gap of hostility between Swiss and German Reformers. Oswald Myconius, Heinrich Bullinger, Martin Bucer, Wolfgang Capito, Simon Grynaeus of Basel, Leo Jud (or Juda) of Zurich, Caspar Megander of Berne, and others all contributed in different ways to the *First Helvetic Confession* (1536).

PETER MARTYR VERMIGLI COMES TO ZURICH (1556)

In the late 1550s, Zurich took a step in the direction of Geneva. The Reformed scholar Peter Martyr Vermigli moved to Zurich to teach Old Testament. Vermigli's presence proved a true test; after all, Vermigli held Calvin's view of predestination while others in Zurich did not, including Bullinger himself. Theodor Bibliander stood up to Vermigli, but Zurich surprised the watching Reformed world when they decided to back Vermigli (Gordon, *Swiss Reformation*, 176–77).

The confession was short, merely twenty-eight concise articles. Although the confession did not necessarily compromise the Zwinglian position, it did flex to accommodate a Lutheran interpretation. Bucer and Capito should be credited for such elasticity since they made room for Luther himself. For example, article 22 says the Lord's Supper "truly offers his body and blood, that is, himself, to his own," even if Christ's body and blood are not "naturally united with the bread and wine or . . . are spatially enclosed within them."[172] Although Luther exhibited no hostility against the *First Helvetic Confession*, the confession was not destined to be the document that united Lutherans and the Swiss Reformed.[173] However, those Swiss territories, typically those still utilizing the German

---

171. Gordon, *Swiss Reformation*, 147.
172. *First Helvetic Confession* 2:289 (art. 22).
173. "The Latin version in particular expresses the understanding of the eucharist in terms more

language, were eager for a united front should the opportunity for a general council present itself. The confession became a source of confidence for such conciliar hope.

In the years ahead, Luther continued to lob belligerent attacks against the Swiss, and by the 1540s, Bullinger grew disenchanted with him, maddened by the Reformer's infamous vitriol to his fellow evangelicals. By 1545 Bullinger expressed his own critique of the Wittenberg Reformer in his *True Confession*, shaming Luther for his inability to love a fellow evangelical like Zwingli despite disagreement. By contrast, Bullinger claimed he was serious about evangelical unity; Luther was not and deserved rebuke no matter what his accomplishments.[174]

REFORMED CATHOLICITY: *OF THE HOLY CATHOLIC CHURCH*

If Calvin is remembered for his *Institutes*, then Bullinger may be remembered for his *Decades*.[175] Bullinger's *Decades* consisted of sermons he preached, published from 1549 to 1551. Motivated to rebuild a unity on the sure foundation of theology, Bullinger used the medium of preaching to solidify the Reformed Church as a lifeline to the church universal. The fifth decade (1551) is relevant because Bullinger asked his Reformed church to consider a singular question: *Is the Reformation a departure from the one, holy, catholic, and apostolic church—as Rome claimed—or is the Reformation a proper albeit evangelical renewal of the one, holy, catholic, and apostolic church?* To answer that question, Bullinger was driven to define the church and its marks.

The church, *ecclesia* in Greek or *ein Gemeind* in German, is the "congregation, communion, or assembly" of those whom God has "called together" or "called forth."[176] In other words, the "Church is the whole company and multitude of the faithful, as it is partly in heaven and partly remains still upon earth: and as it agrees plainly in unity of faith or true doctrine and in the lawful partaking of the sacraments: for it is not divided, but united and joined together as it were in one house and fellowship."[177]

In Bullinger's definition, he assumed the church is not restricted to this world but transcends the here and now, which explains why the Apostles' Creed says the church is catholic. "This Church is usually called catholic, that is to say, universal. For it sends out its branches into all places of the wide world, in all times and all ages; and it comprehends generally all the faithful the whole world over."[178]

The catholicity of the church, however, requires two distinctions to explain

---

conciliatory to the Lutheran view, calling the bread and wine 'symbols by which the true communication of his body and blood is exhibited [*exhibeatur*]' (article 22)." Pelikan and Hotchkiss, "Introduction," *CCFCT* 2:280.

174. Bullinger was responding to Luther's harsh words concerning the Zurich Bible. Gordon, *Swiss Reformation*, 174.

175. Since his sermons were organized by tens, his work was called *Decades*.

176. Bullinger, *Of the Holy Catholic Church*, 288–89.

177. Bullinger, 289.

178. Bullinger, 289. And again, "The universal Church consists of all individual churches throughout the whole earth, and of all the visible parts and members of them" (293).

how the church can be so extensive when Satan and sin prevail so often in this present world. Bullinger distinguished between the church triumphant and militant. On one hand, the "Church *triumphant* is the great company of holy spirits in heaven, triumphing because of the victory which has now been won against the world, and sin and the devil, and enjoying the vision of God, in which there consists the fulness of all kinds of joy and pleasure, and concerning which they set forth God's glory and praise his goodness for ever." On the other hand, the "Church *militant* is a congregation of men upon earth, professing the name and religion of Christ, and still fighting in the world against the devil, sin, the flesh and the world, in the camp and tents and under the banner of our Lord Christ."[179]

Bullinger also distinguished between the inward, invisible church and the external, visible church. The *invisible* church is "the elect bride of Christ, known only to God, who alone knows who are his." In other words, "It is this Church especially which we confess when we say as we are instructed in the Apostles' Creed: 'I believe in the holy Catholic Church, the Communion of Saints.'"[180] By contrast, the *visible* church is mixed. Not "even the wicked and hypocrites . . . are excluded and put out of the Church," as seen in the New Testament with individuals like Judas.[181]

Or consider the distinction from an alternative angle: the visible church is marked by the Word, sacraments, and public confession of faith, while the invisible church is secret, not judged by sight but known only to God. Bullinger elaborated:

> The visible and outward Church is that which is outwardly known by men and to be a Church, by hearing God's Word, and partaking of his sacraments, and by public confession of their faith. The invisible and inward is so called, not because the men are invisible, but because it cannot be seen with the eye of man, but appears before the eyes of God, who are the true and unfeigned believers. For the true believers are the true and lively members of this inward Church, which I earlier called the Church militant in its stricter sense: but the other and visible Church comprises both good and bad, and has to be taken in a wider sense.[182]

This distinction is found in the parable of the weeds (Matt. 13:24–43).[183] The kingdom of heaven is like the farmer who sows seed in his field so that he will reap a harvest of wheat. But at night his enemy sneaks in and sows weeds too. When the wheat begins to sprout, so do the weeds. Yet Jesus cautioned against pulling up the weeds lest the wheat be pulled out in the process. Instead, both

---

179. Bullinger, 290, 291, emphasis added. Bullinger cited Scripture at length to support this distinction, especially the book of Revelation and Paul's epistles.

180. Bullinger, 291–92.

181. Bullinger, 292.

182. Bullinger, 299.

183. Bullinger, 296.

grow together until the time of harvest arrives. Then the weeds will be pulled and burned while the wheat is collected for the barn. But how will we know true wheat from weeds, the churchgoer might ask, when both grow side by side? Relying on the apostle Paul, Bullinger answered: "It is the disposition of the true members of Christ never to forsake Christ and his Church, but to continue and also to prosper and increase daily more and more." Should someone in the church break off and depart from the way of Christ, then we know. We can say with John, "They went out from us, but they were none of us.... If they had been of us they had still tarried with us."[184]

The distinction should be an encouragement to the people of God, even a comfort. For even in the worst of days, when it appears the light of the church is all but extinguished either due to persecution or corruption, the Christian can rest assured that God is at work across the world to preserve his true body. The "catholic Church of God has continued with us from age to age from the very first, and at this very time it is dispersed throughout the whole world, both visibly and invisibly; and the Lord's people and God's house shall remain upon the earth to the world's end."[185] Hell itself, as Jesus said, shall not prevail.

Bullinger also turned his attention to a pressing polemic: with the conflict between Rome and the Reformation, what marks a true church? Bullinger answered with two marks: "the sincere preaching of the Word of God, and the lawful partaking of the sacraments of Christ."[186] Both are essential, and both reassure an assembly that they belong to Christ. Granted, hypocrites may be in the church practicing both. They may be "sanctified visibly," but in truth "these things do not properly belong to them" since they "are without faith and due obedience."[187]

However, Bullinger warned that mere proclamation is insufficient: "It is not enough to brag about the Word of God or about Scripture unless we also embrace and retain and uphold the true sense and that which agrees with the articles of the faith."[188] Bullinger was holding the preacher accountable to the rule of Scripture as well as the rule of faith. Consider the fourth-century controversy over Arianism. The Arians preached the Scriptures, but their preaching corrupted the true meaning of the text and violated the rule of faith by subordinating the Son to the Father. "That church denied our Lord Jesus Christ to be of one substance with God the Father, which the sense of Scripture and the orthodox faith both affirmed and urged as one of the principal points of our faith. Hence it did not allege the sincere and pure Word of God, however much it boasted of it, but an adulterated word, thrusting in and defending its own heretical opinion instead of the true and perfect meaning of Holy Scripture."

---

184. Bullinger, 298.
185. Bullinger, 293.
186. Bullinger, 300.
187. Bullinger, 301.
188. Bullinger, 302.

The consequence for ecclesiology must not be overlooked. "Therefore it did not have the true mark of the Church and it was not the true Church of God."[189] In other words, if a church betrays an orthodox hermeneutic, they cannot be a true church no matter how often they preach the Scriptures. Likewise with the sacraments. It is insufficient for a church to be marked by the sacraments. To be a true church, they must institute the sacraments in conformity to Christ's own teaching: "For unless they are used orderly and lawfully, in the order in which the Lord himself instituted them, they are not marks or signs of the Church of God."[190]

Bullinger also advanced three "inward marks"—the "fellowship of God's Spirit, a sincere faith, and twofold charity." The difference between the two marks of the church—proclamation and sacraments—and these three inward marks is this: proclamation and sacraments are outward, distributed to all who enter the church in faith, but fellowship, faith, and love are inward because they "belong specially to the godly alone" and for that reason can be titled "peculiar gifts."[191] For Bullinger, these three were the key to unity, both christological and ecclesiological concord. By these three marks, believers are "united and knit together, first to their head Christ, and then to all members of the body ecclesiastical."[192] For example, consider faith. Faith "joins us to our head Christ, yet it also knits us to all Christ's members upon earth."[193] As Paul told the church, there is but one faith, one Spirit, one head (Christ), and therefore one body (Eph. 4:5).

These three marks, however, do deserve qualification. Although they may be unique to the elect, nevertheless, they are not divorced from two encompassing marks that fall on everyone: proclamation and sacrament. Faith may be the mark of a true believer, but faith comes only by hearing, and hearing only happens through the Word of God preached. The church, therefore, must not forget its source nor "how it is planted, propagated and preserved."[194] Christ uses the two broad marks—preaching and sacraments—to build up his church, creating fellowship, faith, and love in his elect.

What did these marks mean, then, for the church of Rome who, in the opinion of the Reformers, did not practice preaching or the sacraments in a way that fostered pure worship? To escalate the tension, the pope claimed apostolic succession that traced his lineage back to the one true church. To answer, Bullinger first tackled papal succession. He affirmed the apostolicity of the church: the apostles built the church on the foundation of Christ, and Christ's bride will be preserved to the very end. Bullinger also used the title *orthodox* because this apostolic church is of "sound judgment, opinion and faith." Apostolic and

---

189. Bullinger, 303.
190. Bullinger, 303.
191. Bullinger, 304.
192. Bullinger, 305.
193. Bullinger, 306.
194. Bullinger, 307.

orthodox, the church is necessary for faith. "For without the Church there is no true faith, nor perfect doctrine concerning true virtue and felicity." Bullinger, like Calvin, was quite comfortable calling the church "mother."[195]

Yet Bullinger did not assume that Rome had the sole right or the exclusive credibility to claim such apostolicity or orthodoxy: "By their continual succession of bishops who do not teach the Word of God sincerely or execute the office and duty of pastors, these men do not prove any more than if they were to set before the eyes of the world a company of idols."[196] Bullinger struck at the lineage of recent popes as well: "For who dare deny that many, indeed the majority of bishops of Rome since Gregory the Great were idols and wolves and devourers like those described by the prophet Zechariah?"[197] Bullinger could not make a more threatening accusation. Essentially, he was denying pure catholicity to those popes who betrayed the church with their idolatry.

By contrast, Bullinger desired to set a different standard for apostolicity: *true succession is not a matter of papal lineage but true doctrine and piety.* "The apostles themselves would not allow any to be counted their true followers and successors but those who walked uprightly in the doctrine and way of Christ."[198] The way to identify the true successors of the apostles is not a matter of externals but internals. Bullinger built on those "inward marks" to jettison Rome's definition of apostolic succession and substitute a spiritual one. As long as the papacy forsook truth, he said, "they have fallen from the faith and doctrine of the apostles," and their "derivation and apostolic succession does not in any way help them." He concluded "that of itself the continual succession of bishops does not prove anything, but on the contrary that succession which lacks the purity of evangelical and apostolic doctrine is not valid."

Evangelical—that was Bullinger's hinge category. Apostolicity—and with it, catholicity—was a matter of gospel fidelity. While Rome detested Bullinger's definition of apostolicity, Bullinger told his people they were on sure footing, for the church fathers, Tertullian in particular, defined succession the same way as Bullinger. "Tertullian, although he greatly esteems (and rightly) the continual succession of pastors in the Church, yet he requires it to be approved by the sincerity of apostolic doctrine; indeed, he accepts as apostolic churches those churches which are instructed with pure doctrine and yet cannot make any reckoning of a succession of bishops."[199] Like Tertullian before him, notice how Bullinger appreciated the succession of pastors in the church. He was no radical Reformer who had jettisoned any and all notions of succession, as if the church ceased to exist after the early apostolic era. But he also believed that the

---

195. Bullinger, 309.
196. Bullinger, 310.
197. Bullinger, 310.
198. Bullinger, 311.
199. Bullinger, 311. Bullinger went on to quote from *Of the Prescription of Heretics.*

true measure of a pastor's succession is the purity of his doctrine. "The apostolic sword is the Word of God."[200]

Bullinger's bold renewal of evangelical apostolicity did, like Luther's before him, bring into orbit the formal principle of the Reformation: *sola scriptura*. For if the papacy had miscalculated the true meaning of apostolicity, then the papacy had been in error. But could the church err? That was Bullinger's final question. His answer was as careful as it was nuanced, following through on his distinction between the church invisible and visible, triumphant and militant. "Now, therefore, if we understand by the Church the blessed spirits in heaven, the Church can never error. But if we understand the wicked or hypocrites joined and mingled with the good, and the wicked alone, they do not do anything else but err, but they are joined unto the good and faithful and follow them; they either err or do not err. For the Church of the good and the faithful on earth both errs and does not err."[201] Bullinger did believe in an infallible church, but that church is in the heavenlies, consisting of God's elect across time. He said that until God's kingdom is achieved on earth as it is in heaven, the church must be on guard against an overrealized eschatology, as if the church on earth is incapable of error. Until the eschaton, the church on earth consists of wheat and tares.[202]

In sixteenth-century debates, this question of error is a trigger to a deeper issue: *authority*. Over against papal supremacy, Bullinger identified Christ as the head of the church. His Word is the instrument by which he governs his people. "Therefore the Church is said to err when a part of it has lost the Word of God and errs. . . . The true Church is grounded upon Jesus Christ and governed by his Word alone."[203] Showing no little awareness of the medieval debates between curialists and conciliarists, Bullinger appealed to Augustine's commentary on John's gospel to argue that absolute power belongs to Christ since he is the continual "head, king and bishop of the Church for ever."[204] The church does possess power and authority, but it is always derivative and therefore both limited and accountable to its source.[205] That put Rome in a position of guilt.

---

200. Bullinger, 314.

201. Bullinger, 314. Always the pastor, Bullinger also explained types of errors and what encouragement the Christian has in Christ: "There are some errors in doctrine and faith, and some in life and conduct. . . . And God for his mercy's sake always purges in his saints all dregs and infirmities as long as they live in this world, the elect being continually renewed and defiled" (315).

202. Matt. 13:24–30.

203. Bullinger, *Of the Holy Catholic Church*, 316, 317. Bullinger did qualify: "And it does not err wholly or altogether, for certain remnants (by the grace of God) are reserved, by whom the truth can flourish against and be spread abroad again in every place." What determines whether the church has fallen into error? Doctrine. "Therefore that holy Church erred in so far as it did not continue steadfastly in true doctrine, and it did not err in so far as it did not depart from the truth delivered by the apostles."

204. Bullinger, 320. John Gerson, for example, "has defined ecclesiastical authority as a 'power supernaturally and spiritually given of the Lord to his disciples and their lawful successors unto the end of the world, for the edification of the church militant according to the laws of the Gospel for the obtaining of eternal felicity'" (317).

205. Bullinger identified the limits: "The ordaining of the ministers of the Church, doctrine and the discerning between doctrines, and finally, the ordering of ecclesiastical matters." Bullinger, 321.

For the whole point of power is to edify, not destroy. That "power which tends to the hindrance and destruction of the Church is a devilish tyranny, and not an ecclesiastical power which proceeds from God."[206] In summary, "canonical truth teaches us that Christ himself holds and exercises absolute or full power of the Church" and that "he has given ministerial power to the Church, which executes it for the most part by ministers, and religiously executes it according to the rule of God's Word."[207]

Bullinger had identified the formal difference between the Reformation and Rome: Christ, not the pope, exercises absolute authority, but he does so *through* the shepherds of his sheep by virtue of their distribution of the gospel. That meant that the pastor's authority—even the pope's authority—was ministerial by nature. The Reformers, in other words, saw themselves as servants of the Word, prophets even, always drawing attention away from themselves to the God they proclaimed and his saving grace. Bullinger could not say the same of the pope and his cardinals.[208]

Bullinger's *Of the Holy Catholic Church* is sometimes overlooked in histories of the Reformation, the same histories that see the Reformation as a new and quite modern movement breaking with the past. However, this text captures the heartbeat of sixteenth-century reform, which located its identity within the church catholic and claimed its protest was a renewal of sacred doctrine rather than a departure. In the words of Bruce Gordon, Bullinger possessed a "passionate belief in the catholicity of the Reformed church." And by "this he meant that the *Reformed churches of the sixteenth century stood in direct theological continuity with the apostolic church and the Fathers of the early church.*" Bold as that claim may be, such continuity meant the Reformers saw themselves as sixteenth-century church fathers. Their debates with Rome were reincarnations of ancient debates. "Bullinger saw himself as a latter-day Church Father struggling against heresy, as Augustine had against the Donatists and Pelagians. Bullinger had a profound belief in the historical continuity of the church; he was by no means an opponent of tradition." For Bullinger the struggle with Rome was not only soteriological but ecclesiological, a test to determine which view of the church was congruous with the past. "The great enemy was not the Roman Catholic church, whom he freely admitted was full of fellow Christians, but the papacy, which he readily identified with Antichrist."[209]

---

206. Bullinger, 321.

207. Bullinger, 324.

208. Despite Bullinger's polemic, he did not go so far as to discount baptism by Roman priests. See Bullinger, 304.

209. Gordon, *Swiss Reformation*, 183. Gordon does not believe this continuity eliminated the medieval church either. "Despite its polemic against the Roman church, the theological structures which emerged in the Swiss Reformation stood firmly on the traditional teaching of the church. Certain of the Church Fathers, such as Augustine, Chrysostom, and Cyprian, were taken as authoritative voices when their views were found sympathetic (when not they were ignored as 'secondary authorities'), whilst medieval Scholasticism, often *sotto*

REFORMED CATHOLIC:
FROM BULLINGER TO WILLIAM PERKINS

Bullinger's case for catholicity was not the last Reformed defense of continuity. His efforts, along with the other Reformers, set the stage for the post-Reformation Reformed Church that followed in the next century. On that foundation, William Perkins (1558–1602) could label English Protestantism a "Reformed Catholic" church, an identity that was stamped on many of his students at Cambridge, from Richard Sibbes to William Ames.

The full title of Perkins's book says everything, manifesting his belief that the Church of Rome has betrayed catholic principles that the Reformed Church has preserved: *A Reformed Catholic or a Declaration Showing How Near We May Come to the Present Church of Rome in Sundry Points of Religion, and Wherein We Must Forever Depart from Them, with an Advertisement to All Favorers of the Roman Religion, Showing That the Said Religion Is against the Catholic Principles and Grounds of the Catechism* (1598). At the start, Perkins turned the table on Rome: Rome had accused Protestants of schism and heresy, but Perkins said Rome was the true schismatic.[210]

When Perkins confronted Rome's deviation from the Scriptures and the apostolic tradition, the entire treatise was limited to only two loci: soteriology and ecclesiology. Why did Perkins not address countless other doctrinal domains? Perkins confined himself to soteriology and ecclesiology because Protestants and Roman Catholics otherwise affirmed a common heritage. That is, Perkins believed Protestants and Roman Catholics alike were orthodox in other areas, such as the doctrine of God and Christology, which explains why Perkins and many others like him (e.g., John Owen and Richard Baxter) could appeal to creeds, church fathers, and even medieval Scholastics (like Thomas Aquinas) with equal claim to their theology.

If Bullinger's *Of the Holy Catholic Church* established a hermeneutical foundation for Reformed catholicity, exemplifying how the Reformers believed their own movement should be interpreted, then Perkins's *A Reformed Catholic* is proof of its continued legacy, a bridge leading to the seventeenth century's solidification of Reformed catholicity across Europe. Catholicity, in other words, not only transferred across generations but countries. The constancy of catholicity was not circumscribed to any one Reformer or territory because the concept itself was intrinsic to the Reformation's identity, located at its core.

---

voce, continued to exert considerable influence. Zwingli and the Swiss followed Luther in proclaiming something bold and new in their vision of *sola fide*, but the subsequent theology which they derived from this principle owed a great deal to tradition. From the 1528 Disputation of Berne onwards the Swiss reformers set about replacing the medieval Catholic church and its systems of authority with their own edifice, which reflected their own understanding of authority and tradition. This was achieved through a deliberate appropriation of the early church and a good deal of the medieval church. The Swiss reformers' theology was grounded in a sense of historical continuity and purpose" (186).

210. Perkins, *Reformed Catholic*, in *Works* 7:12.

THE *SECOND HELVETIC CONFESSION*:
CLAIMING THE HOLY CATHOLIC CHURCH

Prior to the 1560s, the Lord's Supper was a dividing line. Not only did a variety of Reformed camps disagree with Luther, but they also disagreed with one another. Zurich and Geneva, just to name two, were at odds with each other. And churches and evangelicals across Germany watched, trying to decide which side was right. Bullinger managed to move beyond this impasse, to a degree at least, by writing the *Second Helvetic Confession* (1566), a masterful improvement on the *First Helvetic Confession*.

Bullinger's ambitions were expansive: he hoped his doctrinal summary might lead churches across Swiss territories into a common confession. And he succeeded; Protestants across Switzerland embraced his confession. But the appeal of the confession reached beyond Swiss states, making inroads into Germany, France, Scotland, Poland, England, the Netherlands, and Hungary.[211] For these reasons, Gordon calls Bullinger's confession the "greatest theological work to emerge out of the Swiss Reformation," no little praise considering the colossal disagreements that stood in the way of a united Reformed front.[212] On the heels of the Council of Trent, such unity among the Swiss cantons was critical to survival.

The confession was so successful because it managed to commit itself to Protestant distinctives and at the same utilized conciliatory language on the Lord's Supper that permitted otherwise disagreeable camps to unite.[213] For example, when Bullinger addressed the controversial issue of Christ's presence at the Lord's Table, he both affirmed that "the body of Christ is in heaven at the right hand of the Father" while also qualifying, "Yet the Lord is not absent from his church when she celebrates the supper." Although Christ's body "is absent from us in heaven," nevertheless, Christ is "present with us, not corporeally, but spiritually, by his vivifying operation," said Bullinger. "Whence it follows that we do not have the supper without Christ, and yet at the same time have an unbloody and mystical supper, as it was universally called by antiquity."[214]

Bullinger's reference to the universal consensus of antiquity should not be overlooked. His stress on catholicity was apparent in his *Of the Holy Catholic Church*, but with the *Second Helvetic Confession* he influenced churches across Europe to recognize and embrace such catholicity as a collective Protestant network. In chapter 17 of the *Second Helvetic Confession*, Bullinger called on this network to claim its rights as citizens of the one commonwealth, namely, the church universal. The Protestants were, in other words, members of the "holy

---

211. Rudolph Gwalther was tasked with making an apology for the *Second Helvetic Confession* in other Swiss states. Gordon, *Swiss Reformation*, 182–83.

212. Gordon, *Swiss Reformation*, 182.

213. Hillerbrand observed how Bullinger pulled language from the *Consensus Tigurinus* (see chapter 10 of this book) to do so. Hillerbrand, *Division of Christendom*, 178.

214. *Second Helvetic Confession*, 2:513 (ch. 21, art. 10).

catholic church, the communion of saints"—citing the words of the Creed. "We, therefore, call this church catholic because it is universal, scattered through all parts of the world, and extended unto all times, and is not limited to any times or places." Rome, however, had narrowed such catholicity in a way that could not be legitimate. The confession did not "approve of the Roman clergy, who have recently passed off only the Roman Church as catholic."[215]

Protestants, wherever they were found, linked arms with the church universal, and Bullinger did not think they needed to be members of the Roman Church to qualify for such benefits. Should Rome object that the Protestant churches were plagued with division, Bullinger reminded Rome that they should not overlook the many sects and contentions that paved Rome's history. Besides, Rome was blind if they thought division precluded catholicity. Did not Paul oppose Peter? Did not Barnabas abandon Paul? Did the church gather in Acts 15 because they were at peace? God sustains and remains present with his church even through times of intense disagreement. "For thus it pleases God to use the dissensions that arise in the church to the glory of his name, to illustrate the truth, and in order that those who are in the right might be manifest."[216] Bullinger insinuated that the Swiss were in the right, and when the storm of controversy settled, the legitimacy of their catholicity would reveal itself. Therefore, when Bullinger affirmed that slogan—"There is no salvation outside the church"—he did not consider Protestants outside but inside the church, Swiss evangelicals being a true source of salvation.[217]

While Bullinger planted his Reformation flag in the soil of the holy catholic church, radical Reformers all over Europe defied Rome and Reformers alike by claiming their perception of catholicity did not exist. Rather than claiming continuity with the patristic and medieval church, tracing God's architectural fingerprints across time, the radicals offered a different interpretation of history, the Reformation included. By aligning themselves with the apostles alone, the radicals interpreted history through the lens of discontinuity, severing themselves from even the most celebrated fathers of the faith.

---

215. Bullinger went on to distinguish between the church militant and triumphant, and also acknowledged particular churches on earth, yet he was clear that all of these are unified in the catholic, universal church. *Second Helvetic Confession*, 2:492 (ch. 17).

216. *Second Helvetic Confession*, 2:494 (ch. 17, art. 10).

217. *Second Helvetic Confession*, 2:495 (ch. 17, art. 13).

13

ABANDONING CATHOLICITY FOR PRIMITIVE CHRISTIANITY

Radicals and Revolutionaries

We are baptized because we are regenerated by faith in God's word,
since regeneration is not the result of baptism, but baptism is the result
of regeneration.

—Menno Simons

No baptism, no church.

—Balthasar Hubmaier

Foolish Ambrose, Augustine, Jerome, Gregory—of whom not even one
knew the Lord, so help me God, nor was sent by God to teach. But rather
all were the apostles of Antichrist.

—Sebastian Franck

And this is always the way with sectarians who separate themselves on
their own authority. It is what the papacy itself did, claiming to be the true
Church without either the approval or the consent of genuine churches.

—Ulrich Zwingli, *Of Baptism*

SPIRIT AND SWORD: MÜNTZER AND THE ZWICKAU PROPHETS

The same year Luther appeared at Worms and was taken into hiding at the
Wartburg, a group of "fanatics"—as both Rome and Luther called them—
created unrest. Their fearless leader was Thomas Müntzer, previously a student
in Wittenberg.[1] Since Müntzer ministered to a church in Zwickau, his supporters became known as the Zwickau prophets.[2] The unrest stemmed from
Müntzer's conviction that Luther's reforming measures fell short.

Müntzer faced constant opposition, for both his methods and his beliefs.

---

1. Others included Marcus Stübner, Martin Cellarius, and Nicholas Storch. Followers were diverse, some
laity, others students, still others professors or pastors themselves.
2. Three men appeared in Wittenberg at the end of 1521. They intended to talk to Luther, but Luther

He did not stay in Zwickau long due to conflict with the church and state alike. In 1521 he was forced to leave. He then traveled to Prague, where he stayed until 1523. His layover in Prague was instrumental to a radical reading of history: after studying the first and second centuries of the church, he reached the conclusion that the church had lost its way ever since. In short, the church disappeared after the apostles. After nearly a millennium and a half of darkness, God was now calling Müntzer to return the church back to its apostolic roots and start a new apostolic church. Müntzer had to act fast, too, because God was about to bring the world to an end. The last days had arrived. Judgment day was at hand.

First, Müntzer needed to rally all those truly saved—God's elect. Second, this Christian army of God's elect then had to wipe out all the nonelect, which included both Rome and Reformers alike, Luther included. After his enlightenment in Prague, Müntzer was ready to embark on a religious cleansing—a holy genocide—of everyone who was not part of his assembled league. In his mind, however, he was saving the true church.[3]

Müntzer and the Zwickau prophets also spoke with a self-recognized *prophetic* authority. Influenced by certain medieval spiritualists, they claimed that the Holy Spirit spoke to them with direct and infallible revelation. The message they received from the Spirit trumped not only the church but the Bible itself. The Bible was no longer the final, infallible, and sufficient authority for faith and practice. "The Bible means nothing. It is Bible—Booble—Babel," they retorted. "You yourself must hear the voice of God and experience the work of God in you and feel how much your talents weigh."[4] By locating authority in the Spirit-moved individual rather than the Spirit-inspired text, Müntzer and his prophets departed from Wittenbergers like Luther.

Müntzer's emphasis on the Spirit also illuminated his confident criticism of Luther's forensic notion of justification. *Sola fide* in the alien and imputed righteousness of Christ was disturbing. What good is a change in legal standing when the believer remains ungodly within? Luther's justification was a fiction, a cheap grace with no power to produce change. In its place, Müntzer proposed a daily, Spirit-empowered crucifixion of sin. Faith must be transformative, an experiential obedience to Christ.[5]

Not only did Müntzer and the elect claim to possess the Spirit, but this Spirit also told them to pick up the sword. Like Moses and Joshua in the Old Testament, the Zwickau prophets had received a divine commission to conquer God's enemies to eradicate idolatry from the land. Violence was the way forward, and when the time came, they must not look back but take the kingdom by force. As God's elect, Müntzer and his men could not fail.

---

was in hiding so that they spoke with Melanchthon instead. Even as early as December 1521, Melanchthon recognized the radical ideas of these visitors.

3. Hendrix, *Martin Luther*, 149.

4. Quoted in *LW* 40:50.

5. Packull, "An introduction to Anabaptist theology," 206.

In the spring of 1523, Müntzer traveled to Allstedt, where he became a pastor and reconfigured the liturgy to reflect his beliefs.[6] Frederick did not know about this election. If he had known, then he might have prohibited it right away. For once Müntzer had attained a position of power—his influence grew, and rumors of revolution spread fast.

Destruction ensued: images, shrines, and all the rest were thrown to the ground and burned by mobs. Not only churches but monasteries were destroyed. Müntzer exhibited no reserve in his call to arms. It mattered not whether it was the pope, the emperor, or a Reformer like Luther—anyone and everyone in the way of his cleansing must be executed. Bloodshed was the path to purification.

As early as the fall of 1523, Luther told Spalatin how troubled he was by Müntzer's program. When attempts to meet with Müntzer in person proved no remedy, it was only a matter of time before Luther advised the civil authorities to take action.[7] The next year, 1524, Frederick the Wise's brother, Duke John, asked Müntzer to deliver a sermon in his own Allstedt castle. Electoral officials were invited to come and listen to Müntzer themselves and make their own evaluation. Even prior to this invitation Duke John was favorable to the religious radicals.[8] His son, however, was not, but agreed with the Reformers and their criticisms.

Müntzer did not disappoint. His theology of history and his apocalyptic interpretation of the present were put on full display that July. Müntzer set the tone from the start by lamenting Christendom's disintegration. The devil himself had infiltrated the heart of Christendom. How long had such corruption been in effect? Nearly the church's entire existence. The "church since its beginning has become in all places dilapidated, until the present time," Müntzer lamented.[9] By contrast, he planned to return his followers to the primitive church, or what he called "real, pure Christianity" during the days of Jesus and his apostles.[10]

Although Müntzer grieved the corruption of Christendom for the preceding fourteen hundred years, nevertheless, he was not surprised. He gave an extended commentary on biblical history, concluding that the prophets of the Old Testament predicted such a time would one day come.[11] The sure sign that God's judgment had descended to punish Christendom for its pollution was the conquest of the Turks and the mocking of the Jews.[12]

---

6. St. John's parish.

7. Müntzer was asked to come to Wittenberg by Duke John Frederick. This was Luther's idea, as he was hoping that Müntzer could be questioned. But Müntzer was not about to enter Luther's home territory. Instead, Müntzer and Frederick met in Allstedt. Müntzer, however, did not change his tactics or beliefs but used the meeting to showcase them (Hendrix, *Martin Luther*, 149).

8. George Williams and Angel Mergal say Duke John was influenced by Wolfgang Stein, Jacob Strauss, and Karlstadt. See Williams and Mergal, *Spiritual and Anabaptist Writers*, 47.

9. Müntzer, *Sermon before the Princes*, 50–51.

10. Müntzer, *Sermon before the Princes*, 50.

11. Müntzer, *Sermon before the Princes*, 51.

12. Müntzer, *Sermon before the Princes*, 52–53.

THE SPIRIT OF LUTHER

Luther contrasted his humble obedience to Scripture with the radical appeal to some secret revelation from the Spirit. "At Worms I had to appear before the Emperor and the whole realm, though I already knew well that my safe-conduct was worthless, and all kinds of strange wiles and deceit were directed at me. Weak and poor though I was there, yet this was the disposition of my heart: If I had known that as many devils as there were tiles on the roofs at Worms took aim at me, I would still have entered the city on horseback, and this, even though I had never heard of a heavenly voice, or of God's talents and works or of the Allstedt spirit." Luther's point was that the Lord did not work through lofty words or direct prophecy but by a "word-consuming spirit." Luther, like Paul, did not speak with boasting and bragging but with fear and trembling ("Letter to the Princes of Saxony," in *LW* 40:53).

Nevertheless, Müntzer was anything but hopeless, for God's revelation had not ceased and the Holy Spirit was active. He turned to the book of Daniel and concluded that the Holy Spirit would reveal God's will in the last days. Müntzer was confident the advent of the eschaton was immanent since many in his day received revelations from the Spirit. "It is true, and [I] know it to be true, that the Spirit of God is revealing to many elect, pious persons a decisive, inevitable, imminent reformation [accompanied] by great anguish, and it must be carried out to completion. Defend oneself against it as one may, the prophecy of Daniel remains unweakened, even if no one believes it, as also Paul says to the Romans (ch. 3:3)."[13]

Who would interpret these new revelations as the end drew near and God's true people (the religious radicals) took action? Müntzer believed he was the one God had appointed for this task. "For the pitiable corruption of holy Christendom has become so great that at the present time no tongue can tell it all. Therefore a new Daniel must arise and interpret for you your vision and this [prophet], as Moses teaches (Deut. 20:2), must go in front of the army." The new Daniel was none other than Müntzer himself. "He must reconcile the anger of the princes and the enraged people. For if you will rightly experience the corruption of Christendom and the deception of the false clerics and the vicious reprobates, you will become so enraged at them that no one can think it through."[14]

By the end of his sermon, Müntzer summoned the electoral officials not to hesitate in sacrificing everything for the sake of Müntzer's mission: "Therefore, you cherished fathers of Saxony, you must hazard all for the sake of the gospel.... Be but daring!"[15] Reinstate the commands of Moses who instructed God's

---

13. Müntzer, *Sermon before the Princes*, 62.
14. Müntzer, *Sermon before the Princes*, 65.
15. Müntzer, *Sermon before the Princes*, 67, 70.

people to "Break down their altars, smash up their images and burn them up, that I be not angry with you."[16]

THAT REBELLIOUS SPIRIT—*SCHWÄRMER*

Luther detested Müntzer's interpretation of history. In 1524 Luther wrote a letter to the princes of Saxony "concerning the rebellious spirit," *Schwärmer*, as he called it in German. He petitioned the authorities to act and to act swiftly lest revolt erupted. But on what grounds should the princes have listened to him?

To begin with, the princes had to be sure not to overlook Satan's schemes. When the Word of God blossoms as it did at Worms, Satan tries to crush it. But when the Word prevails, he must turn to other methods, subtler methods, drawing from individuals from within. They are the most dangerous threat if turned, like a cancer inside the body eating away at its host. Is this not what happened in Allstedt? Satan "thrust forth false prophets and erring spirits, filling the world with heretics and sects" until mobs were formed and ready to unleash violence.[17]

Luther saw through their cunning devices: they claimed to have the Holy Spirit, yet they had not the Spirit of Christ, who refused to call down his angels but suffered instead. For all their talk about the Spirit, their violent methods that wreaked havoc resembled not one of the Spirit's fruits—not love, patience, gentleness, or kindness, and certainly not peace. Violence "may gain fame and honor" but it does not "win any soul's salvation." The latter is what defined the ministry of Jesus. By his gospel, Jesus won people's hearts. So, too, did Luther. If he had resorted to violence at Worms like the Zwickau prophets, "hearts in all the world would still be in captivity." He said that by not resorting to force, "I have done more damage to the pope than a mighty king could do." The Zwickau prophets, however, were superficial: they wanted "badly to do something bigger and better," and when they were "not able to do it," when they could not "free souls," they instead "attack[ed] wood and stone." Behold! Luther shouted, this was "the wonderfully new work of the lofty spirit."[18]

From the beginning, Luther sought to reform the church from within, but these Zwickau prophets declared themselves kings and popes. They claimed to abide by the rule of the Spirit, but they were accountable to no one. They justified their rights from the Old Testament, but Israel "was not a self-appointed mob." Nor was the church situated in the same context. "We are not commanded to imitate all the various deeds, else we should have to be circumcised and follow all Jewish customs." If the church was a direct comparison of Israel, she would have to put every non-Christian to death.[19] But that was not the role of the church. Use of the sword belonged to the prince instead. To the prince, Luther wrote, "Your

16. "These words Christ has not abrogated, but rather he wishes to fulfill them for us (Matt. 5:17)." Müntzer, *Sermon before the Princes*, 67.
17. *LW* 40:49.
18. *LW* 40:58.
19. *LW* 40:59.

obligation and duty to maintain order requires you to guard against such mischief and to prevent rebellion." Preserving the peace and punishing evildoers were responsibilities Paul attributed to governing authorities (Rom. 13:4). "Therefore your Grace should not sleep nor be idle."[20] How would the princes know the difference between a true Reformer and a radical? Easy, "they are not Christians who want to go beyond the Word and to use violence, but are not ready to suffer much else, even if they boast of being full and overfull with the holy spirit."[21]

Not long after Luther's letter was published, the princes planned to come down with full force on Müntzer, but Müntzer got away. He escaped to Mühlhausen next, except this time his power multiplied with his following. The entire city was, so it seemed, under his command. Luther was convinced Müntzer's revolt could not last, not even if he fled from city to city. It was but a matter of time until Müntzer met the same fate as the godless he purged from Christendom.

DEVOURING THE SPIRIT FEATHERS AND ALL: KARLSTADT'S DISSENT FROM LUTHER

When Luther wrote to the princes of Saxony, charging them to take action against the Zwickau prophets, he was inclined to associate Karlstadt with this rebellious movement. Karlstadt swore the association was illegitimate, but whether Luther believed him was another matter.

Karlstadt swore he declined to join Müntzer when asked. In July 1524, Müntzer approached Karlstadt in an attempt to recruit him to his cause. If he was successful, Karlstadt might bring with him many other sympathetic territories, bolstering Müntzer's band of soldiers. But Karlstadt said no; he did not believe bloodshed was the answer.[22]

However, Luther looked at Karlstadt's impatience with the speed of reform, as well as Karlstadt's proclivities to an overemphasis on the Spirit, and concluded that Karlstadt, even if not as extreme as Müntzer, was still born from the same spirit. Karlstadt wanted reformation, but unlike Luther, who used the spoken word, Karlstadt was willing, and sometimes all too eager, to make his reform mandatory for the people. Karlstadt denied formal association with Müntzer, but in Luther's eyes it did not help Karlstadt's case that both Karlstadt and Müntzer wrote treatises against him in 1524 with similar if not identical criticisms. Müntzer's was titled *An Obligatory Defense and Reply to the Spiritless Soft-Living Flesh at Wittenberg*. That title summed up Müntzer's and Karlstadt's dissatisfaction, even if the latter did not adopt Müntzer's apocalyptic methods.

But methodology was not the only difference between Luther and Karlstadt. The two disagreed on how to interpret and apply the law of Moses—especially the Ten Commandments, which condemned idols—and what action should be

---

20. *LW* 40:51.
21. *LW* 40:59.
22. Müntzer, *Briefwechsel*, 2:285–92 (nos. 84, 86). Hendrix, *Martin Luther*, 149, has investigated Karlstadt's writings and reports that only twice in all his writings did he condone the use of violent measures.

taken (or not taken) against images in the churches.[23] Karlstadt counseled others that images must be destroyed, for the laity was tempted to worship them. Even a mural depicting a scene from the Bible or a crucifix symbolizing Christ's sacrifice should not be preserved. Images in the late medieval era were designed to be visual, even powerful guides to heaven. Karlstadt disagreed: "It cannot therefore be true that images are the textbooks of laypersons." The laity "are unable to learn their salvation from them" and risk relocating where true salvation terminates: on the ears, not the eyes. "How can you save laypersons when you ascribe to images the power which God alone gave to His word alone?"[24] Karlstadt was a fiery preacher, his messages full of conviction and obligation. The laity walked away from his sermons heavy with burden, convinced that if they did not take a stand against images, they were persisting in sin. Iconoclasm, according to Karlstadt, was no tertiary matter either.

As a result, mobs and riots erupted when Karlstadt bypassed the channels of authority and went straight to action. Once Luther did attempt to reason with Karlstadt. In August 1524, Luther talked with Karlstadt in Jena, but the conversation was futile. Karlstadt complained that Luther had misrepresented him by assuming he was part of Müntzer's party, as if he, too, was advocating bloodshed, a point Luther conceded. Then Karlstadt attacked Luther's theology, including his understanding of the gospel, which Luther did not take kindly. Luther later concluded that Karlstadt did in fact embody the same radical mind-set of Müntzer.[25]

That same year, Karlstadt was kicked out of Saxony, and he journeyed as far south as Basel, where he took up his cause once more. This time his tongue lashed out against Luther himself. Karlstadt wrote with vengeance, not only opposing images but infant baptism and Luther's view of the Lord's Supper. Now there was no hiding the fission within the Reformation's own camp. Luther did not see Karlstadt as if he was on the side of the Reformation; he was no true Reformer at all. "Doctor Andreas Karlstadt has deserted us, and on top of that has become our worst enemy," said Luther.[26] Why did Luther come to such a fatal conclusion? Karlstadt demanded the demolition of images lest idolatry prevail; to do otherwise was sin. But from Luther's perspective, Karlstadt had burdened, even enslaved, the Christian conscience to a new law, a new *works righteousness*—as if one's choice to break or not break images made them either "upright or a sinner."[27]

---

23. The debate between Luther and Karlstadt was, at its root, about hermeneutics. Karlstadt appealed to the law of Moses, believing images to be a violation of the second commandment. Luther countered that the law of Moses does not apply to Gentile Christians like it did to Israel. See *LW* 40:92ff.

24. *CRR* 8:107; cf. *RCS* 5:138.

25. *WABr* 3, 346; *WABr* 3, 353. Cf. Hendrix, *Martin Luther*, 150.

26. *LW* 40:79.

27. *LW* 40:82. Luther elaborated later, "For although the matter of images is a minor, external thing, when one seeks to burden the conscience with sin through it, as through the law of God, it becomes the most important of all. For it destroys faith, profanes the blood of Christ, blasphemes the gospel, and sets all that Christ has won for us at nought, so that this Karlstadtian abomination is no less effective in destroying the kingdom of Christ and a good conscience, than the papacy has become with its prohibitions regarding food and marriage,

LUTHER AND THE DEVIL

Modern readers will find it jarring that Luther almost always attributed his conflicts to the devil and associated his enemies with the devil. But Luther did not live in the modern world, which finds the supernatural unbelievable. The devil was as real as God for sixteenth-century Catholics and Protestants alike. The only question was what side the devil was on. Luther interpreted his era as a war between God and the devil playing itself out on the world stage, and Luther was caught somewhere in between. As for his Roman opponents, they were pedaling the devil's theology. As for the peasants in revolt, their unrest and fatalities were but another opportunity for the devil to block the gospel from influencing German society.

In that sense, Karlstadt was worse than the papacy itself, creating a new legalism, the very thing Luther had protested with his life.[28] True Christians were apparently only those who became iconoclasts.

This was not the way of the Spirit, Luther replied. The Spirit's way is the gospel and faith, not the smashing of images. Karlstadt had "devoured the Holy Spirit feathers and all."[29] Furthermore, Karlstadt had violated Christian freedom by making images a matter of primary significance. They were not. Whether or not images remained was a trivial concern. To say otherwise was to be used by the devil himself. He loves to "spruce up such minor matters, thereby drawing the attention of the people so that the truly important matters are neglected." Luther had no doubt the devil was using Karlstadt for such a purpose.

Furthermore, Luther was determined his methods matched each controversy's level of importance. He petitioned Paul's letters to the Corinthians: matters of food and clothing were not to bind the Christian's conscience. Luther, too, hoped some images might be relinquished, but to rip the artifact out of the church was all backwards. First, one must tear images out of the heart. Only then will it matter if the eye cannot see them anymore.[30] Luther was drumming the heartbeat of the Reformation: true, evangelical, catholic reform had to occur within, by hearing with faith, not merely by means of the visible eye. The latter was the way of Rome. Ironically, Karlstadt was not radical enough. For all his talk about abolishing remnants of Rome, he still operated according to the same old Roman assumption, as if the eye is what mattered most. *No!* shouted Luther. The ear is where reform penetrates. *The organ of faith is the ear.*[31] That did not

---

and all else that was free and without sin. For eating and drinking are also minor, external things. Yet to ensure the conscience with laws in these matters is death for the soul" (40:90).

28. *LW* 40:85, 90.

29. *LW* 40:83; cf. 40:82.

30. *LW* 40:84.

31. Sure, Karlstadt made the church *look* reformed, but the heart remained stuck on works as ever before:

mean Luther was in favor of images, but such renovation had to be accomplished in the right way: with the approval of the authorities, not with mobs modeling a "factious, violent, and fanatical spirit."[32]

Luther's debate with Karlstadt left uncertainty in the air. Luther had challenged emperor and pope, but if his reformation was challenged by those from within, would his supporters remain united?

CONRAD GREBEL, SIMON STUMPF, AND FREE WILL BAPTISM

Many of the radicals whom the Reformers opposed originated from within their own camps, and that painful truth was inescapable.[33] Early on Luther never could have known that one of his own colleagues, Karlstadt, would in time become one of his most obstinate critics. Likewise, Zwingli could not have predicted that Conrad Grebel, one of his own converts and most zealous advocates during the early 1520s, would turn on him and help start the Anabaptist movement in Zurich. In fact, Grebel's break with Zwingli was even indebted to Karlstadt's literary influence.

The split between Zwingli and Grebel was born during the Second Zurich Disputation of 1523. Zwingli criticized images in churches that fostered veneration of saints and Mary and protested the Mass, giving his critique of transubstantiation. But how and when these remnants of the Roman Church should be dealt with became an in-house debate. Zwingli made his case for reform and left the matter to the magistrates, believing that the best reform was one sanctioned by the lords of Zurich. It was not until 1524 that icons were eliminated and 1525 that the Mass was abrogated (see chapter 8).

Zwingli's strategy was met with disgust. He defaulted to the lords, but Simon Stumpf defaulted to the Holy Spirit: "Master Ulrich! You do not have the power to reserve judgment to my lords, for judgment has already been given: The Spirit of God decides. If my lords were to arrive at some decision contrary to the judgment of God, I would implore Christ for the guidance of his spirit and would teach and act in opposition."[34]

The root cause of dissent was freedom. Zwingli's strategy summoned the magistrates to commit to the Reformation. He called on the state to enforce evangelical beliefs and practices. Grebel loathed such petitioning. Pastors should not entreat the state to sponsor reform. That maneuver might result in an evangelical church and even a reforming society, but only at the expense of

---

"He only smashes them in pieces outwardly, while he permits idols to remain in the heart and sets up others alongside them, namely false confidence and pride in works." *LW* 40:85.

32. *LW* 40:85. Later, in 1528, Luther wrote, "Images, bells, eucharistic vestments, church ornaments, altar lights, and the like I regard as things indifferent. Anyone who wishes may omit them. Images or pictures taken from the Scriptures and from good histories, however, I consider very useful yet indifferent and optional. I have no sympathy with the iconoclasts." *LW* 37:371.

33. Not all did, however. We will examine their diversity in what follows, but for an extensive treatment, see Williams, *Radical Reformation*.

34. Cited in Lindberg, *European Reformations*, 212.

the church's liberty. The state would surely govern if not control reform in the church.[35] The difference between Zwingli and Grebel came down to the latter's insistence on a free church.

Yet freedom was not the only dividing difference. So, too, was expediency, or Zwingli's lack thereof. Zwingli's reform was not only dependent on the magistrates but was slow moving. Stumpf's appeal to the Holy Spirit not only revealed the locus of authority for the radicals but the pace at which they expected (demanded) reform to operate. For Zwingli, once he achieved approval from the lords, the preaching of the Scriptures could have its effect. Zwingli was not so naive as to assume the people's hearts could be won overnight. Proclamation that produced real transformation took time. How fast the church made changes needed to match the maturity of the people being changed; otherwise reform could only remain superficial, a reformation merely in externals.

Again, Grebel grew frustrated with Zwingli's pace of reform, so frustrated that he no longer believed Zwingli a reliable leader. Zwingli's failure to destroy every remnant of papal practice and with expediency only verified Grebel's suspicion: Zwingli had become a false prophet. He was now part of the problem, not the solution. He was no longer a true advocate of reformation but a sellout, willing to concede key components of reform to appease the agenda of his lords.[36]

The 1520s proved devastating for these dissenters, as Zwingli was further solidified as the Reformer to lead the way moving forward.[37] Dissenters had lost; worse still, none of their preachers were allowed to preach without permission first, and if any of their infants were not baptized in a week's time, they would be banished from Zurich.[38] Rather than subduing the dissenters, these restrictions inflamed their cause. George Blaurock (or Cajakob) baptized Grebel, marking the first rebaptism. Others followed Grebel's lead, and a community of Anabaptists became official. Next, Grebel jettisoned the Mass and gave his followers both bread and wine at the table.[39]

Several characteristics of these early baptisms deserve attention so that they are not confused with modern baptistic methods and movements. First, the initial baptisms in Zurich were unlike modern adult baptisms. With these first baptisms at least, believers were not immersed in water (although immersion came

---

35. To clarify, "Zwingli did not believe that the council had jurisdiction over doctrinal matters, but it was responsible for maintaining the peace and guarding consciences. Thus for Zwingli the practical implementation of the new church order was a matter for the magistrates." Lindberg, 212.

36. Lindberg, 212.

37. Historians provide different dates, some say 1524 and others 1525. The discrepancy could be due to an older form of dating.

38. "All those who have hitherto left their children unbaptized shall have them baptized within the next eight days. And anyone who refuses to do this shall, with wife and child and possessions, leave our lord's city, jurisdiction, and domain, and never return, or await what happens to him." Harder *Sources of Swiss Anabaptism*, 333.

39. "The emphasis in these early rebaptisms was not on the human capability to believe but rather on that to repent. 'Rebaptism had taken the place of the sacrament of penance, long debased by the indulgence traffic, while the eucharistic elements were becoming the sacramental cement, giving coherence to the brotherhood of would-be saints' (Williams, 1992: 218)." Lindberg, *European Reformations*, 214.

soon enough with the movement).[40] Grebel was baptized by affusion instead. At this point, the focus was not so much on the mode of baptism as the recipient.

Second, no little emphasis fell on the believer's free will and free choice. For the magisterial Reformers, the sacramental focus was Godward: Christ's presence in the supper; God's covenant sealed through the water. Consider Luther, for example. At first glance, Luther's affirmation of infant baptism—an ancient practice traced back to the early church—might appear inconsistent with his crusade for *sola fide*. How can an infant be baptized when faith is absent? Does this incongruity not undermine justification by faith alone? Such objections, however, miss the point, said Luther. *Sola fide* is designed to draw attention away from ourselves to the grace of Christ. Fixating on faith as a prerequisite of baptism turns our attention inward, on whether the candidate for baptism is good enough.

Furthermore, even when justification was considered, Luther did not believe faith grounded justification, which might turn faith into a new kind of works righteousness. Instead, the ungodly are justified on the basis of Christ and his salvific work. By grace, God grants unbelievers faith so that they will trust in Christ alone for redemption. If faith is a gift, then infant baptism is entirely appropriate. For the waters of baptism convey the gracious nature of justification.[41]

Also, in baptism the Word and waters meet, so that if faith is absent, faith itself may be created. For Luther, baptism could produce faith in the infant through the Word. When the priest speaks the gospel to the infant, the infant is hearing the words of Christ himself. And Scripture is clear that God's Word will not return void but is effective, producing faith and its fruit. Baptism, therefore, serves multiple purposes, washing away sin, bestowing faith itself, and then strengthening faith in preparation for glory.[42]

In contrast to Luther, the early Anabaptists gave prominence to the believer's faith and voluntary choice, both in baptism and the Lord's Supper. Baptism did not regenerate or create faith. It was the consequence of regeneration and faith, the believer's outward testimony to his or her faith in Christ, and thus qualified the believer to enter into the community of the church. The issue was ecclesiological: baptizing infants introduced unregenerate members into the church, forfeiting a believer's church. Similarly, regarding the Lord's Supper, the individual exercising faith was qualified to approach the table. By eating and drinking, the believer not only remembered what Christ had accomplished but expressed his personal commitment to Christ and his bride.[43] This emphasis on the indi-

---

40. Although Pearse does qualify, "Baptism by immersion was to take place the following month, when Grebel baptized Wolfgang Ulimann, an ex-monk, stark naked in the River Rhine—an action which required a higher degree of discipleship in February than it might have done at another time of the year." Pearse, *Great Restoration*, 50.

41. "In a paradoxical way, infant baptism is totally consistent with the doctrine of justification by faith, because it emphasizes that faith is not something we can achieve, but something which is given to us graciously." McGrath, *Reformation Thought*, 174.

42. See Luther, *Larger Catechism*, pt. 4 (456–67). Cf. McGrath, *Reformation Thought*, 174.

43. For sample quotations from Anabaptists to this effect, see McGrath, 184.

vidual's faith was most unsettling for the state-sponsored church. "If it became a matter of personal choice as to who was, or was not, part of the official church, then the chief moral, social and political 'handle' on ordinary people's lives … would have gone, and with it any possibility of stable social order."[44]

Third, unlike denominational disagreements over baptism in the modern era, in the sixteenth century rebaptism was a capital offense punishable by death, a retribution that originated in the patristic era and continued to be practiced in the medieval period only to be reaffirmed by Protestant and papal territories alike.[45] The ultimate reason was not the nature of baptism itself but what rebaptism represented: a rebellion against the state and its church. Rebaptism was no mere theological disagreement; it was sedition. And the Anabaptists were not ignorant—their subversion of the state and its church was intentional in every way. They counted the cost before they embarked on their revolution, more or less officially inaugurated with the baptism of Grebel.[46]

WE JUST BELIEVE THE BIBLE: BIBLICISTS AND SPIRITUALISTS IN ST. GALL

Anabaptism was contagious, spreading to numerable other Swiss and German areas. And as it spread, its celebration sometimes turned into chaos. For example, east of Zurich, Anabaptism caught on in St. Gall. Here Grebel had useful connections—his brother-in-law was mayor, and one of his baptized converts, Wolfgang Ulimann, was hard at work spreading Anabaptist teaching. When Grebel arrived in Gall, he baptized many, although the city council was reluctant and some suspicious. Nevertheless, "despite his proclamation of believer's baptism he had not yet arrived at a clear view of a believer's church separated from the world. … No attempt was made to organize the newly baptized into gathered churches."[47]

However, among those baptized was a group that took their newfound zeal in a biblicist direction, interpreting the words of Scripture in a literalistic fashion.[48] They read Jesus' words that unless they became like children they could not enter the kingdom of heaven, so they resorted to talking and acting like children. They read Paul's words that the letter kills, so they burned their copies of the Scriptures.

---

44. Pearse, *Great Restoration*, 48.

45. Lindberg traces the capital offense of rebaptism back to "the days of Roman law under the emperors Theodosius and Justinian." He then points to the "Theodosian code of 412," which was "directed against the Donatists of North Africa, who rebaptized their recruits from the Catholic church." As for its continuance during the medieval era, Lindberg pinpoints the Cathari's persecution under the Inquisition. Concerning its embrace by the Diet of Speyer, Lindberg observes that although "Speyer may be called the moment of the birth of Protestantism, it ought not to be forgotten that it was also the moment of death for Anabaptism." Lindberg, *European Reformations*, 215. Cf. Wohlfeil and Goertz, *Gewissensfreiheit als Bedingung der Neuzeit*, 25.

46. Yet rebaptism was not the only crime they committed nor the only threat they posed. As the Anabaptist movement multiplied in members and spread from one Zurich canton parish to another, other acts of rebellion became just as prominent. For example, rural Anabaptists refused to pay tithes, convinced the tithe was a means for the state to maintain control over the parishes. Lindberg, 213–14.

47. Pearse, *Great Restoration*, 51.

48. See chapter 1 for a definition of *biblicism*.

Others read Paul's instructions to the Corinthians concerning speaking in tongues and started experimenting in glossolalia.[49] Still others so emphasized the Spirit that they justified immorality and self-harming behavior in the name of new revelation. "There was sexual immorality, presumably on the usual rationale . . . that acts of the flesh do not matter, since the disposition of the spirit alone counts with God. . . . One man was even (at his own request) beheaded by his brother, it apparently having been revealed to him that this was the will of God."[50]

When reports of radicalization reached Reformers like Zwingli, his initial worry that Anabaptism could lead to extremism was confirmed, even if these excesses did not represent all or even most Anabaptist leaders. St. Gall was now a weapon used against the Anabaptist, showcasing what could happen when the individual's subjective choice became primary and ecclesiastical and political governance was removed. To the Roman Church, these radicals were the natural product of a biblicist hermeneutic that prided itself on the individual's interpretation over against that of the church.

THE ANABAPTIST THREAT AGAINST ZURICH'S COMMONWEALTH

In September 1524, Grebel became all the more a threat when he and his followers expressed their agreement with Thomas Müntzer in two letters. Grebel agreed with Müntzer that a free church was the way forward and praised Müntzer for leading the way. Over against the magisterial Reformers, Müntzer was the true, pure model of a Reformer, refusing to capitulate to the state and its sponsored church. At the end of the second letter (really a postscript), Grebel and his cast of characters signed their names as if they were joining Müntzer in his fight against the Reformers:

Conrad Grebel, Andrew Castleberg, Felix Mantz, Henry Aberli, Johannes Pannicellus, John Ockenfuss, John Hujuff, the countryman of Halle, thy brethren, *and seven new young Müntzers against Luther.*[51]

Grebel showed great sympathy with Müntzer. For example, Grebel reflected an interpretation of history common among religious radicals. He began by blaming "our forebears" who "fell away from the one true God and from the one true, common, divine Word," settling for a "superficial faith" that persists in "ritualistic and anti-Christian customs of baptism and the Lord's Supper." These forebears turned to the "word of the pope and of the antipapal preachers [the Reformers]," which is "not equal to the divine Word nor in harmony with it." Grebel was convinced the church had been corrupt in every age since the time of Christ, but the church in his age was the most perverse yet. "In respecting

49. These examples are listed in Pearse, 51–52; Williams, *Radical Reformation*, 228.
50. Pearse, 52.
51. Grebel, "Letters to Thomas Müntzer," 85.

persons and in manifold seduction there is grosser and more pernicious error now than ever has been since the beginning of the world." Who was to blame most of all? The Reformers. "In the same error we too lingered as long as we heard and read only the evangelical preachers who are to blame for all this, in punishment for our sins." However, Grebel and his followers saw through the idolatry of the Reformers and came to the light: "But after we took Scripture in hand too, and consulted it on many points, we have been instructed somewhat and have discovered the great and harmful error of the shepherds, of ours too, namely, that we do not daily beseech God earnestly with constant groaning to be brought out of this destruction of all godly life and out of human abominations, to attain to the true faith and divine practice." The Reformers convoluted the Scriptures with human traditions; here lay the root problem. "The cause of all this is false forbearance, the hiding of the divine Word, and the mixing of it with the human."[52]

Yet Grebel was not without critique of Müntzer, wondering whether the radical was radical enough. Grebel and his followers were biblicists at the core, so while they agreed with Müntzer they were also concerned that his application of reform might not apply a literal interpretation of the Bible as extensively as they desired. (That accusation was ironic since it was Grebel's original criticism of the Reformers, one that he now applied against his own kind.) For example, consider the liturgy. "We understand and have seen that thou hast translated the Mass into German and hast introduced new German hymns. That cannot be for the good, since we find nothing taught in the New Testament about singing, no example of it." Grebel and company followed a biblicist hermeneutic by contrast: "Whatever we are not taught by clear passages or examples must be regarded as forbidden." While Luther permitted practices if they were not contrary to Scripture or condemned by Scripture, Grebel condemned anything that was not prescribed by Scripture, a far more limiting allowance for what could and could not pass for Christian worship and practice.

To illustrate his point, Grebel not only condemned the "evangelical preachers" for turning the Lord's Supper into a "veritable idol" but also condemned anything more than a recitation of Scripture's exact words. The pastor was to read the text of Scripture, "no more, no less."[53] Should singing accompany the Lord's Supper? Absolutely not. For the pastor must "act in all things only according to the Word."

Grebel also took issue with Müntzer and his potential use of violence. For "the gospel and its adherents are not to be protected by the sword, nor are they thus to protect themselves" but should lay down their lives as "sheep among wolves, sheep for the slaughter." Grebel, too, was filled with apocalyptic anticipation, but he did not believe the Christian was called to usher in the end by

---

52. Grebel, "Letters to Thomas Müntzer," 74. Another edition of the letter can be found in *CTM*, 121–32.
53. Grebel, 76.

his own might. Rather, the end would surface on the blood of the saints. "True Christian believers . . . must be baptized in anguish and affliction, tribulation, persecution, suffering, and death; they must be tried with fire, and must reach the fatherland of eternal rest, not by killing their bodily, but by mortifying their spiritual enemies. Neither do they use worldly sword or war, since all killing has ceased with them—unless, indeed, we would still be of the old law."[54]

The conclusion of Grebel's letter is confrontational but sanguine. He asked Müntzer whether he and Karlstadt "are of one mind." Grebel answered his own question: "We hope and believe it."[55] Grebel even encouraged Müntzer and Karlstadt to write back as one voice. Grebel's request demonstrated that early on religious radicals did not necessarily think of themselves and others as separate movements. As time expanded and some turned to violence while others remained pacifists, that self-awareness evolved. Hard and fast distinctions between radicals and their movements became far more concrete. But Grebel's early letters should caution against strict application of neat, tidy categories, lest the variegated evolution of the radical movement(s) be lost in the process. While some interpreters may be eager to separate someone like Grebel from someone like Müntzer and the Peasants' War, such a separation was not present in Grebel's own mind, at least not this early.

DEATH BY DROWNING

Authorities responded to the Anabaptist movement of 1524–26 in different ways. Consider Zurich to start. At first rulers gave repeated warnings. Then they imprisoned Anabaptists who persisted. In some cases, they even tortured Anabaptists in prison. Others were released but banished from Zurich. Yet the ultimate measure of the suppression arrived when Zurich announced that Anabaptism was punishable by death. The second Diet of Speyer reached the same verdict in 1529, placing a black mark on Anabaptism across the Holy Roman Empire. In 1526 the major Anabaptist figureheads—Grebel, Blaurock, and Mantz—reinvigorated their attack on Zwingli and the church, resulting in a series of imprisonments, prison breaks, reimprisonments, and eventually banishment or execution.

Although the plague took Grebel's life in 1526, the magistrates ended Mantz's life by drowning on January 5, 1527, in the river Limmat. The method of execution sent an unambiguous message to other dissenters. Zurich was not alone either; neighboring areas assisted in the capture of Anabaptists and transferred them back to Zurich for punishment. Blaurock was beaten and tortured but then released and banished since he was not a citizen. He persisted with recruiting converts in Austrian Tyrol and was burned at the stake in 1529.[56]

---

54. Grebel, 80.
55. Grebel, 82.
56. Pearse, *Great Restoration*, 55.

WERE SEVENTEENTH-CENTURY BAPTISTS
THE HEIRS OF ANABAPTISTS?

Although both Baptists and Anabaptists affirm a believer's baptism, the seventeenth-century Baptists considered themselves children of the magisterial Reformers instead. The "case for indirect Anabaptist influence through the separatists carries little weight," says historian David Bebbington in *Baptists through the Centuries* (40). For example, the Anabaptists "were the source of most of the mature convictions of John Smyth, but not his creation of the first Baptist church" (38). General Baptists like Thomas Helwys were influenced by Anabaptist soteriology, but Helwys's turn to believer's baptism itself was not derivative. General Baptists were even insistent at times that they had nothing to do with heretical Anabaptist beliefs (Melchiorite Christology) or revolutionary practices (Münster). And when the Particular Baptists in London drew up a confession in 1677, they did not turn to Anabaptist documents, but they took their wording from the Savoy Declaration, with exceptions like baptism. They were not unaware that the Savoy had itself taken its wording from the *Westminster Confession*. Both the 1677 and 1689 versions are unambiguous in their debt to the Reformed tradition.

The Anabaptists, however, interpreted Mantz's drowning as a martyrdom and other executions as signs that they must be the true church—for the early church experienced the same fate at the hands of the Romans. The Anabaptists remembered the words of Grebel in his letter to Thomas Müntzer: we "must be baptized into anxiety and dereliction, tribulation, persecution, suffering and dying, must be tried in the fire and find the fatherland of eternal rest."[57]

MICHAEL SATTLER, THE *SCHLEITHEIM ARTICLES*, AND RADICAL SEPARATION

Grebel, Blaurock, and Mantz fought for the Anabaptist vision in Zwingli's Zurich, but other notable Anabaptists spread the vision across Europe.

Consider, for example, Michael Sattler (ca. 1490–1527). A German-born Benedictine monk turned Anabaptist, Sattler was an itinerant Anabaptist preacher, itinerant not by choice but more often by force as he was never able to stay long in any one city due to his Anabaptist convictions. For a time, Sattler lived in Zurich until the authorities banned him from the city. His stay in Strasbourg was more successful since Strasbourg had a reputation for religious toleration.[58] Strasbourg's tolerance may be credited to its politicians, but its theologians also deserve credit, especially Wolfgang Capito, who cringed at religious persecution whatever the form. While in Strasbourg, Sattler engaged

---

57. *CTMC*, 121–32. Cf. Lindberg, *European Reformations*, 213.
58. Pearse claims Strasbourg was "the most religiously tolerant city in Europe." Pearse, 56.

Martin Bucer and Wolfgang Capito, although Sattler could not persuade them of his view on baptism. Nevertheless, his engagement with the two Strasbourg Reformers may have afforded Sattler the opportunity to further consider whether his view of baptism should more precisely define the type of church he envisioned and distinguish this church from the Reformation church, which was sponsored by the state. If only believers should be baptized, then church membership should also be conditioned on faith, a conviction Sattler then implemented in his own church plant.[59]

In 1527 a group of Swiss Brethren met, and Sattler was the one to lead them in the formation of the *Schleitheim Articles*, the first of the Anabaptist confessions.[60] The Anabaptists at Schleitheim turned separation into a primary concern.[61] They warned against "false brothers and sisters" who served "their father, the devil." And they gave a radical command: "Separate yourselves from them, for they are perverted." So important was separation that when the Anabaptists introduced the articles, they listed "separation from abomination" as an article of the faith.[62] Who were those who had committed abomination? All those who practiced infant baptism, which was "the greatest and first abomination of the pope."[63]

Separation, however, was not merely an external factor but was implemented from within the Anabaptist camp as well. If an Anabaptist gave in to sin's temptation, they would be confronted twice and then "publicly admonished before the entire congregation" and banned from the Lord's Table.[64] If there was union, then union could come only by means of separation. "We have been united concerning the separation that shall take place from the evil and the wickedness which the devil has planted in the world, simply in this; that we have no fellowship with them, and do not run with them in the confusion of their abominations." In their defense, the Anabaptists considered themselves to be in the light and others to be in the darkness, and light and darkness can have as much to do with one another as "God's temple and idols, Christ and Belial."[65]

On that basis the Anabaptists introduced their practice of shunning: "From all this we should learn that everything which has not been united with our God

---

59. "Believers' baptism could not possibly coexist with a state-supported church; it demanded a congregation restricted to committed believers only. He began preaching this message in the Black Forest area around the town of Horb, where he was successful in planting an Anabaptist church." Pearse, 56.

60. At least according to Sebastian Franck. *Schleitheim Confession* 2:696–703.

61. For a detailed chronicle of political ethics preceding Schleitheim, see Stayer, *Anabaptist and the Sword*. Stayer observes diversity, noting the progression from early radicals using the sword but second generation Swiss Brethren receding towards pacifism. Cf. Packull, "An introduction to Anabaptist theology," 215.

62. *Schleitheim Confession* 2:697.

63. *Schleitheim Confession* 2:697 (art. 1). "Separatism is the *Confession*'s constant motif. . . . The authors at Schleitheim strove to make clear that their Reformation was neither a Reformation from 'above' dependent on magisterial authority nor a Reformation from 'below' assisted by revolutionary powers. They sought a third way. Their reform program was no longer focused on the expurgation of existing Christendom, but rather on radical separation from the world." Lindberg, *European Reformations*, 61, 218.

64. *Schleitheim Confession* 2:698 (art. 3).

65. *Schleitheim Confession* 2:698 (art. 4).

in Christ is nothing but an abomination which we should shun." Who exactly should be shunned? "By this are meant all popish and re-popish works and idolatry, gatherings, church attendance, winehouses, guarantees and commitments of unbelief, and other things of the kind. . . . From all this we shall be separated and have no part with such, for they are nothing but abominations."[66]

Separation, for radical Reformers, was a hallmark that relished a church in conflict with the world. Such a hallmark deserves underlining because it distinguished the radicals from the magisterial Reformers. For the radicals, the world was stained, contaminated, and satanic. Contact with the world put the Christian in jeopardy, compromising faithfulness and purity. Therefore they cultivated a mindset that said, "We alone are the elect," and then expected, even counted on the world to oppose them. At times they wore this opposition—from Christian magistrates and pastors alike—as a badge of honor, as proof even that they were on the side of the angels while everyone else was on the side of the devil. They were with Christ, everyone else was Antichrist.

The *Schleitheim Confession* added to separation an equally committed pacifism. According to the Anabaptism mindset, pacifism was instrumental to separation. Since Christians were by definition to be separated from all those enslaved to abominations, so, too, Christians must not pollute themselves by picking up a worldly weapon. The Anabaptists, therefore, should not use the sword to fight a spiritual battle. Nor should Anabaptists become magistrates. Christ denied the opportunity to become king. Instead, he followed the path to the cross. So, too, should his followers, which is why Christ "himself further forbids the violence of the sword."[67]

Why did authorities across Europe consider Sattler such a threat when he advocated nonviolence? The answer explains why the Austrian tribunal decided to put Sattler to death. When Sattler was arrested, he was accused of many ecclesial violations: denying Christ's presence in the Lord's Supper, rejecting pedobaptism, disrespect toward the Virgin Mary and the saints, refusing to take oaths, embracing pacifism, and more. However, Sattler's particular expression of pacifism was especially threatening. The Austrians were facing the real threat of Turkish invasion and warfare. Sattler's advice? Do not fight the Turks when they invade. To kill a Turk is to break the fifth commandment. However, if murder was permitted, then Sattler would not bother trying to kill Turks when others lived who were far more deserving of execution: Christians![68] For the Austrians, and many other territories across Europe, the Anabaptists claimed to be pacifists; however, their hostility to Christendom could create a violent uprising and revolution. The Austrian prediction was corroborated at Münster only six years after Sattler was executed.

---

66. *Schleitheim Confession* 2:698–99 (art. 5).
67. Appeal is made to John 6:15; Matthew 20:25; Romans 8:30; and 1 Peter 2:21. *Schleitheim Confession* 2:700 (art. 6).
68. Williams and Mergal, *Spiritual and Anabaptist Writers*, 141; Lindberg, *European Reformations*, 220.

Sattler's death was brutal, so brutal that Capito wrote to the Horb council after the fact, shaming them, though without aligning himself with Sattler's theology. First, they cut out Sattler's tongue, or at least part of it. Then they dragged him behind a wagon until his flesh was scraped off. Next, they carved up his body with burning tongs. Last, they burned Sattler at the stake until finally dead. After Sattler was burned, some of his followers were beheaded and his wife was tossed in the river Neckar and drowned.[69]

HANS HUT AND BALTHASAR HUBMAIER

Sattler's threatening version of pacifism was not the only model among sixteenth-century radicals. For example, Grebel and company flattered Müntzer and were forthright in their enthusiasm and support. Nevertheless, their biblicism led them to express some critique of Müntzer's liturgy. Their eschatology also took them in a different direction than Müntzer, advocating pacificism rather than militancy. The same can be said of Sattler's *Schleitheim Articles*. However, other Anabaptists were far more inclined to apocalyptic warfare, some even joining Müntzer.

Hubmaier and the Jews

Balthasar Hubmaier (d. 1528) may be the most educated of the religious radicals. Hubmaier was a student at Freiburg as well as the University of Ingolstadt, and at both he learned from one of Luther's most impressive nemeses, Johannes Eck. With doctorate in hand, Regensburg Cathedral found a ready chaplain and preacher in Hubmaier, who gained immediate popularity due to his anti-Semitic messages.[70] Luther's anti-Semitism at the end of his life is often the target of criticism today, but Hubmaier's anti-Semitism had far more immediate consequences. By 1519 the council was convinced that the Jews were the avaricious menaces to society and anti-Christian blasphemers Hubmaier said they were, oppressing the rest of society under its affluence and religious convictions. The outcome: banishment from the city. Segregation was not good enough; the Jews had to be driven out of town. So they were, like dirty, unwanted rodents.

Hubmaier's prejudice, however convincing to his listeners, distorted reality. The Jewish people were in an impossible sociopolitical situation. Already the Jews had been segregated to a section of the city and precluded from entering the rest of society, which of course made employment a near impossibility. However, the Jewish community gained affluence because many of them entered the one profession not off limits: usury. The late medieval church condemned this profession and prohibited Christians from entering the world of usury. And yet the economy could only suffer without it. The standard by which Jews were judged

---

69. Apparently, the Countess of Zollern pleaded with Sattler's wife, asking her to reject her beliefs and save her life, but she would not, following her husband's lead to the death. See Pearse, *Great Restoration*, 59.

70. See Pearse, 67–68; Oberman, *Roots of Anti-Semitism*, 77–84.

was unjust: society barred them from other professions only to resent them for prospering at the one profession the rest of society needed.[71] The resentment and ill treatment became so fierce, in part due to Hubmaier's preaching, that when the city banished the Jews once and for all, they also tore down their Jewish synagogue and replaced it with a church of their own.[72]

Hubmaier's Double Conversion and Political Theology

From Regensburg Hubmaier traveled to Waldshut. Even though Hubmaier continued his priestly duties, subtle indications of disenchantment started to show until he was converted to the Reformation in 1522 and 1523. What drove Hubmaier toward the evangelical faith? Luther. He read Luther's works and was persuaded that he had believed in many false doctrines. Zwingli also influenced Hubmaier, so much so that Hubmaier took a trip to Zurich to hear and learn from the Reformer himself. Back in Waldshut Hubmaier began implementing Reformation principles, but unlike his success in persuading the city council of Regensburg, now that he was pedaling evangelical teaching to the people, the authorities in Waldshut did not follow Hubmaier's lead. Hubmaier hoped he might talk the authorities of Waldshut into adopting the Reformation much like Zwingli had done in Zurich, but that was a false hope. The authorities turned against him, but Hubmaier had the support of many in the town, enough to keep the authorities at bay.

Not long after his conversion to Luther's and Zwingli's ideas, however, Hubmaier decided Luther's and Zwingli's reforms were insufficient, still marked by remnants of Rome like infant baptism. In the mid-1520s the Anabaptist Wilhelm Reublin came to Waldshut and baptized Hubmaier, only for Hubmaier to turn around and baptize hundreds of converts himself. Hubmaier now gained a considerable following. That same year he found disciples in the peasants who were in support of the Peasants' War (1524–25) just underway, right around the corner from Waldshut. The peasant army entered talks with Waldshut to find out whether the town might lend their support. Hubmaier and the rest of the town had to consider the philosophy and strategy of Thomas Müntzer. The timing, for Hubmaier, could not have been better. "Hubmaier had created, in effect, an evangelical state employing—almost enforcing—believers' baptism, and allied with the local peasant rebels. For him, radical reformation suited his role as champion of the people; as with his anti-Semitic campaign in Regensburg, it had become a part of the struggle for a more egalitarian society." A shift

---

71. "Medieval hypocrisy, however, then blamed the Jews for performing an economically necessary function which had, effectively, been forced upon them." Pearse, 68.

72. "When I was a preacher in Regensburg, I saw the great oppression that the population suffered from the Jews.... Then I said to the people from the pulpit, that they ought not to suffer in this wise for the future." This statement by Hubmaier was made in Zurich in 1526. Pearse mentions it to demonstrate that although Hubmaier did not continue his anti-Semitic preaching in later years, he never showed signs of remorse, not even after his conversion to Anabaptism. Pearse, 69.

occurred away from a traditionalist mindset that defaulted to the individual's faith-infused, voluntary choice.[73]

Hubmaier's newfound enthusiasm for a believers' church did not entail, as it did for other Anabaptists, an ecclesial separation from the state. Whether it be a remaining influence from his Zurich days or some other influence, Hubmaier still retained the idea that the church could and should be endorsed by the magistrates. "Grebel and his circle had, for a short time, vaguely thought something of the kind; it had quickly become clear to them though that state support *meant* an all-embracing church (as a way of running society), and that conversely to call for a believers' church was to demand the destruction of precisely that monolith."[74] But in 1524 Hubmaier had acquired an Anabaptist approach to the sacraments without embracing an Anabaptist separation from society. Nevertheless, he did campaign for a freedom of religious belief and practice that discouraged magistrates from harsh measures against dissidents, as is plain in his 1524 book, *On Heretics and Those Who Burn Them.*

Whatever Hubmaier might have turned Waldshut into, history will never know. By the end of 1524, Waldshut was monopolized by an anti-Protestant, anti-Anabaptist army, forcing Hubmaier to run for his life. Hubmaier made the unfortunate decision of seeking asylum in Zurich. In 1525 Hubmaier faced a series of arrests and torture. He recanted his views, then picked them up again, only to recant again after further torture. Hubmaier's final recantation, which he read to the public, may have kept him from execution by drowning or burning at the stake. The authorities were appeased, and Hubmaier was banished from the city.[75] Hubmaier then traveled in secret to Nikolsburg, Moravia, where he found a far more supportive audience in 1526. Unlike in Waldshut, however, Hubmaier persuaded the authorities this time of his Anabaptist ways. The pump may have been primed by the church there, which had already opened itself up to Reformation ideas. Hubmaier only had to persuade them that Anabaptist ideas were the logical next step.[76]

Hubmaier's Modified *Via Moderna* and Anabaptism's Voluntary Association

Hubmaier, however, did not always see eye to eye with other Anabaptists. For example, Hubmaier learned that some Anabaptists observed the debate between Luther and Erasmus over the bondage of the will and sided with Luther.

---

73. "Priestcraft, clericalism and ritual were to be brought to an emphatic end and, in baptism, each was to have the opportunity to declare for themselves their faith in the promises of God." Pearse, 70.

74. Pearse, 70.

75. Pearse, 71.

76. "Nikolsburg, like the rest of Moravia, was a city with a fair amount of autonomy from the imperial authorities. So when its German-speaking congregation turned evangelical under the influence of its pastor, Oswald Glaidt, the local rulers, Lord Leonhard and Lord Hans von Liechtenstein, did not fear immediate retribution from the Habsburgs. The lords already governed over Catholics and several varieties of Hussites." Pearse, 71.

Hubmaier grew agitated; not only did he disagree with Luther on infant baptism, but he also believed Luther destroyed the freedom of the will.

In 1527 Hubmaier wrote two small books on the subject, taking aim at Luther: *On the Freedom of the Will* and *The Second Booklet on Human Free Will*.[77] The book surfaced an irony: on the question of baptism, Hubmaier departed from the consensus of the church, past and present. Yet on the subject of the will, it was Luther who departed from the *via moderna* of the late medieval period with its novel soteriology, while Hubmaier continued to embody some of the *via moderna*'s most basic instincts.[78] Luther learned a *via moderna* soteriology from his university educators; Hubmaier did as well but at different universities (Freiburg and Ingolstadt). However, Hubmaier was far more read in Scholasticism than Luther. He not only studied Scholastics in the *via moderna* but Scholastics in the High Middle Ages who were far more Augustinian, such as Thomas Aquinas. In contrast, Luther only learned Thomas through the misrepresentation of Gabriel Biel (see chapter 5).[79]

In his treatment of free will, Hubmaier exposited an anthropology that retained a modified version of the *via moderna*, whether he knew it or not. Here, too, is an irony: Hubmaier had strong words for Rome, yet his defense of free will is indebted to his old teacher, Eck, who modified the *via moderna* before him.[80] Hubmaier was unique in that he wedded Scholastic distinctions to a body, spirit, and soul argument that was not common in other Anabaptists.[81] On one hand, Hubmaier did not sound all that different from Luther on the doctrine of original sin. "After our first father, Adam, through disobedience, had transgressed the command of God, he lost this freedom for himself and all of his descendants. . . . all must bear the guilt of their forefather, so the flesh, by the fall of Adam, lost its goodness and freedom irrevocably, and became utterly nought and helpless, even unto death. It can do nothing except sin, strive against God, and hate his commands."[82] On this score, Hubmaier is a noted improvement from Gabriel Biel and William of Ockham.

On the other hand, Hubmaier significantly modified such inability by his understanding of the "spirit." Although the soul and body were "maimed in will" by Adam's sin, nevertheless, the will of the "spirit" was not maimed but remained "utterly upright and intact before, during and after the Fall," since it never consented to eating the fruit in the garden. "But it was forced against its will, as a prisoner in the body, to participate in the eating." Therefore, the body and the soul may be under the influence of the devil but the spirit remains

---

77. See Hubmaier, *Schriften*, 379–431.

78. Steinmetz, *Luther in Context*, 60.

79. To compare the educations of Luther and Hubmaier, see Steinmetz, 60.

80. Steinmetz thought Eck adjusted Biel's version of the *via moderna* to align with the "Old Franciscan theological tradition" as represented in figures like Bonaventure. Steinmetz, 67.

81. See Hubmaier's discussion of *voluntas ordinate* and *voluntas revelata*, for example. Hubmaier, "On Free Will," 132–34.

82. Hubmaier, "On Free Will," 119.

"whole and safe in the day of judgment."[83] Said otherwise, "Both flesh and soul are devastated and sorely wounded. Only the spirit has maintained its inherited righteousness, in which it was first created."[84]

Carving out a part of man not completely swallowed up by the fall mattered for Hubmaier, allowing him a resolution that can still incorporate man's active participation and cooperation (much in contrast to Luther, who saw the sinner as totally passive and spiritually dead until the Spirit creates new life within). Since the soul and body are wounded but the will of the spirit remains righteous, the Holy Spirit merely illuminates and enlightens through the gospel until man's will consents and cooperates so that the Spirit can subsequently act to regenerate. As Hubmaier said, "Enlightened through the Holy Spirit ... the soul now again comes to know what is good and what is evil. It has recovered its lost freedom. It can now freely and willingly be obedient to the spirit and can will and choose the good, just as well as though it were in paradise."[85] Free will has been given to humankind, the gospel has been offered; now God waits on sinners to decide their fate. That is the arrangement he has made in his covenant, according to his ordained will. "The God of Hubmaier no less than the God of Biel is a God who manifests fidelity to his covenant."[86] Yet the covenant is conditioned on a person's choice for its success. As Hubmaier says, God may have "created you without your aid, but he will not save you without your aid."[87] Hubmaier may not have been a Pelagian, but at this point he had left Augustinianism behind and not looked back.

Hubmaier did place Christ at the center of this covenant condition. Without his merits, freedom is an impossibility. By his merits, however, humankind is given a universal grace by which to decide whether they will accept or reject further, subsequent acts of grace that produce new birth. Hubmaier gave the example of a wedding. Like the father of the bride, God summons everyone to the celebration. "God gives power and capacity to all men in so far as they themselves desire it. ... Free choice is restored to them to come, and a new birth, a new beginning of the creaturely, as man had been originally in paradise, save for the flesh."[88] *So far as they themselves desire it*—Hubmaier conditioned God's regenerate gift on what lies within man. Free will is restored, he said, but the decision lies with man whether he will cooperate with God's drawing effort or resist. God "wills and draws all men unto salvation. Yet choice is still left to man," qualified

83. Hubmaier, "On Free Will," 120.
84. Hubmaier, "On Free Will," 124.
85. Hubmaier, "On Free Will," 124.
86. "While God has taken the initiative in establishing the structure in which human beings may be saved, his act of regenerating sinners is itself a response to the human act of fulfilling the condition of the covenant." What then did Hubmaier do with Romans 9? "Hubmaier does not deny that God could deal with human beings in such an arbitrary fashion [according to his hidden, absolute will], but he clearly regards it as a hypothetical possibility which God has chosen not to actualize." Steinmetz, *Luther in Context*, 69.
87. Hubmaier, "On Free Will," 125.
88. Hubmaier, "On Free Will," 129.

Hubmaier.[89] In that vein, Hubmaier was in lockstep with Gabriel Biel and the *via moderna* (see chapter 5).[90]

Hubmaier's synergistic view of free will was not disconnected from his Anabaptist vision for ecclesiology. Consider the following syllogism:

1. Church membership is a free-will, voluntary decision conditioned on believer's baptism.
2. Baptism requires a regenerate heart, which itself is conditioned on a free-will decision.
3. Therefore, baptism can be administered only to believers.

That ecclesiological logic, which depends from start to finish on the freedom of the will, precluded infant baptism for Hubmaier. As Steinmetz explained, "Since free human decision is essential as preparation for regeneration, and regeneration is essential as a precondition for the reception of baptism, it follows that baptism cannot be administered to infants."[91] To deny the freedom of the will as a precondition for regeneration, baptism, and church membership as Luther had was a threat to Hubmaier's Anabaptist ecclesiology. "Affirm freedom of the will, and the Anabaptist vision of redemption can be affirmed with it. Deny freedom of the will (as Luther has done), and the Anabaptist position becomes impossible to maintain. The two stand or fall together for Hubmaier."[92] In similar fashion, Hubmaier's stress on free will also buttressed his apocalyptic vision with its sharp, inflexible contrast between the holiness of the church and the corruption of the world. "The Church does not embrace the whole community but is rather a society of men and women baptized as adults and living in conscious tension with the world."[93] By absorbing the society (infants included) within its ecclesiastical territory, the magisterial Reformers had polluted the church.

Hubmaier and Hans Hut

Hubmaier attracted many different converts to Anabaptism, some local, others foreign, some merely lay converts, others present and future Anabaptist leads. One was Hans Hut. Early on, Hut was a supporter of Müntzer, printing and distributing Müntzer's writings. Although Hut did not fight like the others, he did join Müntzer at the Battle of Frankenhausen. Hut was captured and imprisoned, but since he never fought alongside Müntzer, he was set free. From the perspective of his captors, Hut's release was a misjudgment. Hut turned right around and encouraged those in Bibra to pick up their swords and fight with the same bravado as Müntzer.

---

89. Hubmaier, "On Free Will," 135.
90. "In Hubmaier's theology as in Biel's, sinners cannot plead that they could not come to God. They can only admit that they did not come." Steinmetz, *Luther in Context*, 70.
91. Steinmetz, 70.
92. Steinmetz, 70.
93. Steinmetz, 70.

Hut had embraced an apocalyptic view of history like Müntzer, believing the end of the world was near and it was only a matter of time before the true church was called upon by God to put the wicked (those not rebaptized) to death. The Anabaptists must be patient and wait for the appointed time, however, rather than turning to violence too soon. But in Hut's mind, the time was near.[94] By the time Hut landed in Nikolsburg in 1527, however, Hut's enchantment with Müntzer had waned. Hut did not ditch his apocalyptic vision, but he did conclude that Müntzer's revolution was premature and narcissistic. Yes, God would call on his true church (Anabaptists) to fight and put to death the ungodly, but until then they should not resort to such violent measures.[95]

Hubmaier and Hut did not always see eye to eye. As mentioned, Hubmaier was in favor of an Anabaptist church, but one endorsed by Christian magistrates. Hut, much like the mature Grebel, believed that a state-supported church was a fool's errand; separation was the only way. To separate, the church should live in a communal lifestyle, distributing all possessions in equal measure, restoring the church to its primitive roots in the book of Acts. Unlike Müntzer, however, Hut did not believe this redistribution of possessions should be forced on Anabaptists who disagreed.[96] When Hut spoke up in support of those who opposed Hubmaier's state-endorsed Anabaptism, Hut was arrested by the magistrates. He hatched a prison break in Nikolsburg but was caught in late 1527 in Augsburg, where he died in prison from a fire.[97]

Hubmaier enjoyed support from the magistrates in his dispute with Hut, but not even Hubmaier could rely on unconditional assistance from the magistrates. In 1527 the Lords von Liechtenstein came under enormous pressure from Frederick of Austria to hand Hubmaier over. Frederick knew Hubmaier's ideas were influential, not only in Moravia but across the German landscape. He relied on the support of Protestant magistrates in his war with the Turks, so he could not imprison and execute them. However, Protestants would not protest if religious radicals were shut up and annihilated instead. That summer the Lords von Liechtenstein capitulated to the pressure of Ferdinand, who finally got his Hubmaier. In 1528 Hubmaier was tortured in Vienna.

---

94. "For him, the advance of the Ottoman Turks into Christendom, reaching ever closer to Vienna, was a judgment of God and a sign of the end—a concept which struck a chord with the jittery population of central Europe. Those who repented would face persecution and suffering, but true Christians would eventually slay the godless and rule the earth with Christ. In the interim, no violence was to be used, but believers' baptism was the sign without which destruction at the hands of the saints would be certain." Pearse, *Great Restoration*, 67.

95. How would Hut know when the time had come? "The Turks were being used as an instrument of God's judgment upon an apostate Christendom, and the saints would eventually rise to take the Kingdom by force. In the meantime, the godly should be pacifist. G. H. Williams describes this as 'apocalyptically oriented pacifism (or suspended bellicosity).'" Pearse, 71. Cf. Williams, *Radical Reformation*, 269.

96. Or as Pearse says, "Unlike the proto-socialism of Müntzer's peasants (so beloved by the twentieth-century East German government), the sharing of goods was to be restricted to the microcosm of the voluntary community of committed believers, not imposed on all and sundry by all-wise social visionaries." Nevertheless, Pearse still calls Hut's approach "communism." Pearse, 73.

97. I am passing over many other rising figures in the aftermath of Hut's death, such as Jakob Hutter (ca. 1502–36), but see Pearse, 74–78.

Unwilling to recant as before, Hubmaier was burned at the stake. Three days later they drowned his wife.[98]

BAPTISM, BIBLICISM, AND BLOODSHED: MÜNSTER (1533–35)

The execution of Hubmaier sent a message that created no little fear. However, executions did not always terminate the multiplication of radicals. Anabaptism did not die with Grebel, Blaurock, and Mantz, nor was it extinguished with Sattler, but lived on in its disciples. Luther's Reformation demonstrated that ideas could travel, both directly through disciples crossing borders or indirectly through the propagation of ideas by means of the printing press. So, too, with smaller figures and movements like the Anabaptists. Anabaptism was not restricted to its local victories and defeats, but Anabaptists spread across the continent reaching into the Netherlands.

Melchior Hoffman and the Melchiorites

Unlike more educated Reformers, who had studied in a particular monastery or university, the father of Dutch Anabaptism, Melchior Hoffman (ca. 1495–1543), was a working-class man who traded furs for a living.[99] Originating from southwest Germany, Hoffman was a Lutheran, preaching in one city until he was expelled and forced to preach in another, which happened often and became customary. From 1523 to 1529, Hoffman developed several distinctives that set his movement on a revolutionary, even apocalyptic trajectory. Some of these distinctives were typical for Lutheran polemics, such as Hoffman's remonstrance against the Mass.[100] However, other distinctives took on a more aggressive, eschatological agenda. He protested images and icons, but in a way that motivated mobs to destroy churches; he encouraged pastors to seek the gift of prophecy and share prophecies with their congregations; he announced God's coming wrath on all who resisted reform; and he undermined the authority of magistrates by advising parishes wherever he went to appoint their own pastors.[101] With each expulsion, Hoffman became a larger and larger target for civil authorities.

After numerous expulsions, Hoffman made his way to Strasbourg, where he was influenced by Anabaptist beliefs. Turning against Luther's belief in the bondage of the will, Hoffman instead emphasized free will in salvation. He so majored on the individual's libertarian free will that believer's baptism became the logical next step. Such logic was not uncommon. Sacramentarians who sided with Zwingli over against Luther on the Lord's Supper were predisposed to abandon infant baptism. For "if communion was indeed a human act, rather than a divine one, then baptism must be too," says Pearse. "Communion was

---

98. Pearse, 72–73.
99. I am indebted to Lindberg, *European Reformations*, 221–25, for this section.
100. However, by 1529 Hoffman's views on the Eucharist were Zwinglian to one degree or another. His days as a Lutheran were numbered. Pearse, *Great Restoration*, 80.
101. Pearse, 79.

an act of worship and a calling to mind by the participants of Christ's sacrifice for sin, not an infusion of grace; for only faith in Christ's sacrifice could call forth grace." Likewise with baptism: "In the same way, baptism was a plea before God for a good conscience on the part of the one being baptized, and a pledge of obedience, marking that person off as dead to self and alive to Christ. Like communion, it was not a *means* of grace but rather a sign that, through faith in Christ's death, grace had already been received."[102] Hoffman had already shown signs of his sacramentarian spirit; therefore the transition to believer's baptism was natural, and in April 1530 Hoffman was rebaptized.

Through the advent of new prophecies, Hoffman also claimed to be the new Elijah sent by God to establish the new Jerusalem promised in the book of Revelation. Revelation from God identifying the new Jerusalem was a major advantage, allowing Hoffman to make his way to the holy city and call on all its residents to be rebaptized in preparation for Christ's return. With Christ's second coming now imminent, judgment was sure to fall on the unrepentant and unholy.

Hoffman traveled in the Netherlands where he had wild success raising up a new generation of Dutch Anabaptists. Some were executed, but many others lived to spread Hoffman's ideas. Despite his success in the Netherlands from 1530 to 1533, Hoffman returned to Strasbourg. A new prophecy was all abuzz: if Hoffman submitted himself to imprisonment, then Jesus himself would return in the year 1533, enter Strasbourg (the new Jerusalem), and enact his earthly reign. Hoffman decided the prophecy was right on target.

When Hoffman first entered prison, he wrote *Concerning the Pure Fear of God* (1533), claiming that prior to Christ's return his true church (the Anabaptists) would reign over the earth. What would happen to everyone else? Everyone outside the true church would be put to death. Hoffman's vision from God was inspiring, spreading all over the Netherlands, creating great anticipation for this promised apocalypse and final victory ushering in the Messiah's second advent.

But 1533 came and went, and Jesus never returned. Hoffman spent the next ten years rotting away in prison. Then another new prophet realized that the location of the new Jerusalem was not Strasbourg but Münster, a city just on the edge of the Netherlands in Westphalia. This new prophet was Jan Mathijs.

From Jan Mathijs to Jan of Leiden

Hoffman's instrumental role in the early birth of Anabaptism should not be overlooked. Pearse warns that some modern Anabaptist heirs find Hoffman the apocalyptic visionary an embarrassment, especially in view of the Münster bloodshed that came next. Therefore, they downplay Hoffman's significance. "Given that Hoffman is the vital link between the original Swiss and South-German Anabaptism and the later Dutch/North-German Mennonites, this

---

102. Pearse, 83.

is a strange omission."[103] At the same time, too much blame for bloodshed at Münster should not be assigned to Hoffman since Jan Mathijs did birth his campaign over against Hoffman's authority.[104]

Jan Mathijs had an advantage that Hoffman did not: the two years prior to Mathijs's revolution in Münster, an evangelical-turned-Anabaptist, Bernhard Rothmann, had prepared the way and turned Münster into a magnet for persecuted Anabaptists from all over. By the middle of 1533, Melchiorites were a major portion of the population. The radicals in the city became so powerful that they climbed their way into the town council by virtue of the 1534 elections. After the election results were in, Mathijs posed an ultimatum to the people of Münster. God had appointed him to annihilate the ungodly from the earth. Anyone who did not join the Anabaptists must be put to death. When one of his own advised a more merciful policy, Mathijs said God had spoken to him once more and instructed Mathijs to banish the ungodly from the city instead.

Over the next month and a half, Mathijs attempted to construct a city and a church according to the book of Acts, one in which all possessions were confiscated for the grand goal of sharing all things in common, just as the first Christians did. Such communalism found its origins in the Anabaptist ecclesiological approach as a whole. They believed the church was lost in the dark ages of patristic and medieval thought but was now restored in the Anabaptist elect. They alone knew the secret to restoring the primitive church of the first-century Christians. In short, Anabaptist communalism was grounded in the Anabaptist interpretation of history. However, Mathijs's vision was not merely communalism but a form of communism. Goods were taken from citizens and handed over to the government to be redistributed as they saw fit. Nevertheless, the people were told that such communism was the will of God, modeled for them in the book of Acts.[105]

When Mathijs was killed in battle, Jan of Leiden took his place and directed Münster into a brave new world of antinomian, Spirit-led, apocalyptic ethics.[106] To begin with, Jan of Leiden increased his authority. He was not just another prophet in the vein of Hoffman or Mathijs; he was the king of righteousness himself. He was chosen by God to establish the new Jerusalem on earth.

---

103. Pearse, 94. Pearse does give reasons why Hoffman may not be to blame for the events that transpired next at Münster.

104. Hoffman's apocalyptic prophecies were structured by his biblicist hermeneutic: "From his prison cell, he called for the temporary suspension of believers' baptism, citing by way of justification the book of Ezra. The enemies of the children of Israel had wanted to stop them 'restoring the walls and repairing the foundations' (4:12) of Jerusalem, an enterprise analogous to the restoration of the church in which the Melchiorites were now engaged. And so (4:24) 'the work on the house of God in Jerusalem came to a standstill until the second year of the reign of Darius King of Persia'; believers' baptism, Hofmann decreed, should be suspended for two years." Jan Mathijs challenged this suspension. Pearse, 83–84.

105. Pearse, 89.

106. "Mathijs himself was killed when he led a sortie against the army assembled by the bishop besieging the city. It seems that he had received a vision that God would make him invulnerable to the weapons of the godless. Williams ([*The Radical Reformation*], 567) suggests that his successor 'may have encouraged him in this fatuous expectation.'" Lindberg, *European Reformations*, 222.

What was this long-awaited Zion supposed to look like? Jan of Leiden continued Mathijs's communalism but eclipsed any distinction between church and state, justifying his command to execute all sinners. "Sinners were identified by their blasphemy, seditious language, disobedience to parents and masters, adultery, lewd conduct, backbiting, spreading scandal, and complaining!"[107]

Furthermore, in the name of communalism he turned Münster into a polygamous society, putting to death anyone who protested his new vision of marriage. Sharing all things in common included wives.[108] If the community were to have a chance of reaching a population of 144,000—the number of God's elect in the book of Revelation—then polygamy was the answer. Polygamy was also the natural outcome of biblical manhood and womanhood. Restricting a man to one wife only encouraged the woman to be head of her husband.[109] Despite Jan of Leiden's apologetic for polygamy, Lindberg observes the underlining motive: "In political perspective, what Jan was doing was ensuring control over the majority of the population [who were women]."[110]

How did the women respond? With resistance. They, too, desired the advent of Christ and were all for populating the New Zion, but they did not want to become the sexual property of one man along with a group of other women. "Those women who dissented from the new rule of polygamy were imprisoned. Jan himself beheaded and trampled the body of one of his wives in the marketplace in front of the rest of them. That seems to have quieted their murmurings."[111]

Jan of Leiden's vision for an earthly Zion was squelched in the summer of 1535. The writing was on the wall when the residents began starving to death. Overwhelmed and outnumbered by a Catholic-Protestant invading army, the blood of the Anabaptists ran through the streets of Münster like a river for several days. As for Jan of Leiden and those leaders not killed in battle, they were tortured, executed, and placed in cages hung in front of a church—a smelly, bloody visual of each carcass to warn society what happens to radicals.

Defeat at Müntzer was heard around the European world, which put Anabaptists in other territories in grave danger. Reports of Rothmann and Jan of Leiden's radical communalism spread fast, and whatever credibility Anabaptists still mustered up to that point was lost. Prior to 1535, civil authorities across Europe already worried that the Anabaptist worldview could turn violent, immoral, and apocalyptic. Münster was all their worst nightmares come true. Any lingering toleration for Anabaptists disappeared overnight. Dissenters and separatists needed a new approach moving forward if they wanted to survive the calamities of Münster and avoid guilt by association.

---

107. Lindberg, 222–23.

108. There were more women than men in the city, in part because some men who were banished from the city left their wives behind!

109. "Rothmann added that sexual dependence upon one woman lets her lead a man about 'like a bear on a rope.'" Lindberg, *European Reformations*, 223. Cf. Zuck, ed., *Christianity and Revolution*, 101.

110. Lindberg, 223.

111. Lindberg, 223.

After Münster: David Joris and the Batenburgers

After the bloodshed at Münster, Anabaptists were in disarray, fleeing to various parts of the continent. In 1536 a group of them decided to come together at Bocholt for a convention and regroup. Unity was difficult to achieve when those present had serious disagreements with one another. On one side were the Melchiorites and Obbenites; on the other side were the Batenburgers, disciples of Jan van Batenburg. The Batenburgers were zealous for more violence. Their ideals were similar to the social structures and ethics seen at Münster (e.g., communism and polygamy) and their methods involved the same aggressive approach (e.g., killing the ungodly), but the Batenburgers were even more spiteful in the aftermath of Münster. They even turned against other Anabaptists like David Joris.

Also present at the convention were Anabaptists who somehow managed to escape death at Münster, although many of these individuals were less inclined, after seeing the outcome at Münster, to press on with violent means. Nevertheless, they retained their apocalyptic hopes, confident Jesus' return was sooner rather than later. The Obbenites, however, did not share such an apocalyptic mentality.

With so much disagreement, how could any consensus be reached? David Joris proposed a way forward. Many present believed God's kingdom would come by means of the sword. Yet, in the wake of Münster, most agreed they should hold off on violent methods. Perhaps those at Münster jumped the gun, thinking they could usher in the millennium when the time had not yet come. Nevertheless, once they knew for certain when the thousand-year reign of Christ was at hand, then the use of the sword could be revisited.

Despite the delay of the apocalypse, David Joris still came to the conclusion that he was one of the end-time prophets promised in the book of Revelation. The law came through Moses, the good news came through Christ, but the Spirit came through Joris.[112] The years ahead demonstrated, however, that the future was bleak for all groups present at the convention. Not all radicals adopted Joris's apocalypticism. Menno Simons is an example of an outlier.

MENNO SIMONS

Menno Simons (1496–1561) was no stranger to the Münsterites. His own brother may have been caught up in the Münsterites' excitement, which likely led to his death. But unlike the Münsterites, Menno believed he could preserve a separatist, dissenting mindset without the excesses of a Jan of Leiden.

Menno Simons started his religious journey in Frisia with the Franciscans, only to be appointed an assistant priest in 1524. During his ministry in Pingjum, Menno started questioning transubstantiation. Whenever he assisted in the

---

112. Pearse, 98. For a more extensive account of the aftermath of Münster, see Pearse, 96–99. How did Joris convince the Batenburgers to cooperate? Pearse (98–99) and Waite wonder whether the allowance of polygamy could have been the reason. See Waite, *Anabaptist Writings of David Joris, 1535–1543*, 66.

performance of the Mass, he wondered if the bread and wine were truly trans-figured into the body and blood of Christ. Based on his study of the Scriptures and Luther's works on the sacraments, Menno could no longer believe in tran-substantiation. That was not the only doctrine Menno abandoned. Menno was sympathetic to Reformers like Luther, Bucer, and Bullinger on *loci* like *sola fide*. But when Menno examined their doctrine of infant baptism and found no explicit teaching on the subject in Scripture, he rejected the practice, a move that permanently separated him from the magisterial Reformers.

After his conversion to Anabaptism, did Menno retain remnants of a monastic spirituality, the type he absorbed within the Franciscan framework? Some have entertained an affirmative answer. Both Menno and medieval monasticism were characterized by withdrawal from the world, communalism, pacifism, some vari-ation of asceticism, and suffering. However, discontinuity must also be acknowl-edged: "although the monastic movement shared a common life and a common goal, each monk was primarily concerned for his own salvation. The Mennonite and Hutterite Anabaptist advance beyond medieval religious asceticism and individualism consisted in developing a covenanted community of families that claimed to be *the church* itself, outside of which there is no salvation."[113]

Nevertheless, one element of continuity between Menno and monasticism was retained, namely, nonviolence. Menno persuaded some under his care of Anabaptism, but he did not agree when they expressed sympathies with Münster and entertained violent methods to effect change. Menno may have jettisoned his papal heritage, but in 1535 he had yet to go public. That did not stop him, however, from expressing his disapproval of the Münsterites. Menno was deeply disturbed by their violent methods and in 1535 responded with a book, *The Blasphemy of John of Leiden*. Menno called out their leader for claiming that he was the new David and condemned his use of violence to advance God's king-dom.[114] Jan of Leiden, said Menno, had conflated the kingdom of this world with the kingdom of Christ, which explains his misuse of the sword. The move was pure arrogance; Jan of Leiden had robbed Christ of his throne and placed himself there instead as if he had the prerogative to usher in the judgment of the last days.

Menno's outrage at these abuses did not mean that he was not moved by their zeal and sacrifice, however misdirected and misinformed. For example, when Menno learned that so many had died putting their plan into action in Bolsward, his brother included, he could remain in the traditional church no longer. Granted, he did not agree with violent methods used by radical resisters, but he did marvel at their courage to stand for their beliefs, and such courage exposed his fearful hesitancy to be public about his own. "I saw that these zeal-ous children, although in error, willingly gave their lives and their estates for

113. Lindberg, *European Reformations*, 224–25.
114. See *OOT*, 619–31; *Complete Works* 2:425–40. Cf. Wenger, ed., *Complete Writings of Menno Simons*, 33–50.

their doctrine and faith. And I was one of those who had disclosed to some of them the abominations of the papal system. But I myself was continuing in my comfortable life and acknowledged abominations simply in order that I might enjoy physical comfort and escape the cross of Christ." To Menno, his official, public conversion to Anabaptism, which is often dated around the start of 1536, was an unambiguous call to pick up his cross and follow Jesus. The blood of his brothers tormented him, a deep and piercing witness against his silence. After much anguish, Menno broke down and finally committed himself, knowing death could be his end. "Then I, without constraint, of a sudden, renounced all my worldly reputation, name and fame, my unchristian abominations, my masses, my infant baptism, and my easy life, and I willingly submitted to distress and poverty under the heavy cross of Christ."[115]

Menno's fears of persecution were not unfounded. Rarely could Menno rest, always on the lookout for his captors, moving across the Netherlands to ensure his evasion. Those out to capture Menno did not necessarily distinguish him from other radicals, especially those who were militant, such as the Münsterites.[116] That led Menno to explain and clarify what Dutch Anabaptists believed (see his *Foundation of Christian Doctrine* in 1539, for example) not only for the sake of his persecutors but also for the sake of novice Anabaptists.[117] From 1539 forward, Menno had to write numerous books, each attempting to clear up misunderstanding, each time hoping persecution might cease. When Menno defended his rejection of infant baptism in 1539, which earned him the label heretic, he also pleaded for religious toleration. From Menno's point of view, believer's baptism did not undermine but undergirded Reformation doctrines such as *sola fide* and *sola gratia*. By highlighting the necessity of a regenerate heart, Menno was convinced he was countering the true heresy: the papacy's sacramental theology encased by its works-based system of penance.[118] When Menno defended his emphasis on holiness in the Christian life in 1541, which invited the charge of legalism, he again pleaded for the cessation of persecution.[119] This pattern continued across his writings.

---

115. Wenger, ed., *Complete Writings of Menno Simons*, 670–71. Menno was ordained in 1537, most likely by Obbe Philips. However, Philips grew disillusioned with the Anabaptist movement and eventually "retreated to a kind of evangelical spiritualism: there was no one true church, even if the Anabaptists did give closest expression to the truth; Scripture was not necessarily to be understood literally; if the old church of Rome was corrupt, attempts to start again from scratch led only to deception; each person should follow Christ in his own heart and not be too harsh on his neighbors who might think, or act, differently." Pearse, *Great Restoration*, 104. Cf. Williams and Mergal, eds., *Spiritual and Anabaptist Writers*, 222–25.

116. Yet others like Polish Reformed theologian Johannes à Lasco "pleaded with the Countess Anna to find more creative ways than burning to suppress the growth of Menno's people, an action that counts as humanitarian in the sixteenth-century context." Pearse, *Great Restoration*, 105.

117. For Menno's *Foundation of Christian Doctrine*, see *OOT* 1–70; *Complete Works* 1:11–102. Cf. Wenger, ed., *Complete Writings of Menno Simons*, 105–226.

118. See his 1539 book *Christian Baptism* in *OOT* 393–433; *Complete Works* 2:189–231. Cf. Wenger, ed., *Complete Writings of Menno Simons*, 229–87.

119. *OOT* 1–70; *Complete Works* 1:11–102. Cf. Wenger, ed., *Complete Writings of Menno Simons*, 105–226.

The Ban and Second-Degree Separation

In many ways, Menno reflected the beliefs and practices of other Anabaptists.[120] Yet he also adopted beliefs and implemented those beliefs in ways that put him in tension with other Anabaptists. Consider two examples. First, Menno's writings and ministry were marked by his strict advocacy of the ban and second-degree separation.[121] On this score, Menno teamed up with Dirk Philips. Philips had gained quite the reputation for his bold refutation of Bernhard Rothmann's Münster-like methods.[122] Over against Rothmann's apocalyptic, theocratic vision, Philips emphasized the spirituality of the church, a church preserved not by sword but by faith and discipleship. Philips, echoing an Anabaptist distinctive, argued that the church had been lost, thanks to the long history of the papacy; nevertheless, the church had now been found thanks to the Anabaptists. This true, pure church could be identified by baptism of believers and its separation from the world, as well as its ban on those who compromise true Anabaptist theology and practice.[123] That line of logic was captured at the Bern Colloquium in 1538. The Reformed said God had preserved his church although it needed reform to experience renewal; the Swiss Brethren said the church was entirely polluted and had to be born all over again as it was at Pentecost.[124]

The ban became a hallmark of Philips and Menno's Anabaptism, so much so that Menno fixated on the ban's implementation the last decade or more of his life. As mentioned, separation from the world was a key identity mark of certain Anabaptists, a mere outcome of a more fundamental commitment: Anabaptism was the restoration of the one true and pure church. Therefore, the ban was a disciplinary measure that served to safeguard the purity of the people, keeping at bay even their own disciples if they had dissented in some disapproving way. The ban was extensive in scope as well. If someone was banned, the Anabaptists must shun not only that person but everyone who disrespected the ban and continued to associate with the banned individual. Second degree separation of this kind could be socially lethal, cutting off not just an individual but an entire group if that group in any way continued contact with the banned individual.[125] However, not all Dutch and German Anabaptists were as strict as Philips and Menno in their application of the ban. When they refused to conform, Menno

---

120. Historians debate the influence of Melchiorite theology on Menno. Abraham Friesen denies any influence, but Packull and others argue that the historical evidence does admit influence. See Packull, "An Introduction to Anabaptist Theology," 198.

121. E.g., consult *Clear Account of Excommunication* (1540), in *OOT* 337–50; 473–78; *Complete Works* 2:121–37; 2:276–81. Cf. Wenger, ed., *Complete Writings of Menno Simons*, 457–85.

122. Philips took on Rothmann's *Restitution of True and Sound Christian Teaching* (1534).

123. "So concerned was he, however, to minimize any millenarian implications of the restorationist ideal that he all but severed the biblical connection between this restitution and the second coming of Christ; the former was to take place 'until his return,' rather than as a sign of the imminence of that return." Pearse, *Great Restoration*, 107. Cf. Dyck, Keeney, and Beachy, *Writings of Dirk Philips*, 54–55, 341–47.

124. Packull, "An introduction to Anabaptist theology," 208.

125. Second degree separation was advocated by Leonard Bouwens in North Holland in particular, leading his group to separate even further. Pearse, *Great Restoration*, 108–9.

wrote to admonish them for their laxity, accusing them of disobedience, as if those who did not hold his strict position had compromised holiness itself.

Menno Simons versus Johannes à Lasco: Biblicism's Defiance of Chalcedonian Christology

Second, Menno advocated a Christology out of sync with the Chalcedonian fathers, a Christology that invited charges of unorthodoxy. He did defend the doctrine of the Trinity when another Anabaptist named Adam Pastor adopted what appears to be Arianism. When Pastor did not retract his denial of Jesus' eternal deity, Menno and Dirk Philips excommunicated him in 1547. Three years later, Menno wrote *Confession of the Triune God* (1550) and defended the divinity of the Son.[126] However, his emphasis on the divinity of Christ, coupled with a type of biblicism that neglected the philosophical insights of a Chalcedonian Christology, led him to reject a traditional conception of the humanity of Christ. The controversy occurred in the 1540s when the Polish Reformer Johannes à Lasco was ministering in East Friesland and grew concerned with the number of Anabaptists in the land. Since Lasco was one of the most patient and tolerant of the Reformers, he did not push for the execution of Anabaptists but instead invited dialogue and debate. For that purpose, Menno joined Lasco at the start of 1544 to discuss Anabaptist theology. Lasco discovered a feature of Menno's Christology that was not adopted by other Anabaptists: Menno denied that Jesus was from Mary's flesh.

Menno was motivated by his worry over a Nestorian Christ, a Christ whose two natures are so divided that they produce two persons, a divine person and a human person. In an effort to protect the unity of Christ's person, Menno stressed a conception that was credited to the Holy Spirit. As for Mary, she was a mere vessel. Or as Menno said in his book *Brief Confession on the Incarnation* (1544), Christ "did not become flesh *of* Mary, but *in* Mary."[127] He must be born *of* but not *in* Mary. If he became the flesh of Mary, then he would have been contaminated by her sinful nature. Menno's Christology was not unrelated to his ecclesiology, however. If the Son, pure in heaven, came down and assumed flesh, then how can the church be united to him without contracting his imperfection? Such a Christology could only infect a church called to separation, a church set apart from the pleasures of the flesh.[128]

When Lasco read Menno's words (of Mary, not in Mary), he published his *Defensio* (1545) in reply, confronting Menno for his unorthodox Christology. A decade after his *Brief Confession of the Incarnation*, Menno wrote a follow-up

---

126. *OOT* 383–91; *Complete Works* 2:179–88. Cf. Wenger, ed., *Complete Writings of Menno Simons*, 489–98.

127. Wenger, ed., *Complete Writings of Menno Simons*, 432, emphasis added (for the entire work, see 422–54). Cf. *OOT* 517–42; *Complete Works* 2:325–50.

128. Packull, "An introduction to Anabaptist theology," 208. Cf. Voolstra, *Menno Simons*.

work digging his heels in further, which led his own colleagues and future Mennonites to reject their founding father's Christology.[129]

A Mixed Legacy

Menno spent a good part of the 1540s and 1550s trying to defend but also encourage the Anabaptists or "Mennonites" influenced by him. Both Friesland and Charles V made it their mission to find, arrest, and imprison Menno. The hunt for Menno during the last decade and a half before his death transitioned from the Netherlands to North Germany. Yet the chase for Menno never extinguished his persistent words of comfort to his persecuted Anabaptist brethren. Menno continued to petition magistrates for tolerance and console those who received none.[130]

In summary, like every sixteenth-century dissenter, Menno's legacy is a mixed one. On one hand, his success at making disciples—the man had a gift for evangelicalism—and spreading Anabaptist theology was one reason why the Anabaptists had any chance of surviving in the aftermath of Münster. He was no revolutionary pioneer like earlier Anabaptists, but his formation of Anabaptist thought was far more systematic, serving to stabilize Anabaptist thinking moving forward. Menno taught his disciples how to pastor and sustain their congregations in a way that did not default to revolutionary violence and apocalyptic predictions but focused instead on Anabaptist first principles. On the other hand, his biblicism resulted in unorthodox Christology. Although he did not join the apocalyptic violence around him, his outlook was still apocalyptic—every Reformer's outlook was apocalyptic, for that matter. However, historians and theologians alike have wondered whether Menno's negative outlook (e.g., the church past and present committed apostasy, and nothing but debauchery can be found in humanity) served to move Menno toward a biblicism that disregarded the riches of patristic and medieval theology.[131] If so, his christological deviance is no doubt indebted to a biblicism that looked only at Bible passages and failed to consider the theological arguments of the church catholic or its long history of christological hermeneutics. Menno failed to read the Bible with the church catholic.

Additionally, Menno's legacy is mixed due to his application of the separatist principle. He went harder than most on this point, applying a strict ban that even required husbands to shun their wives if they discovered sin or came to the

---

129. The 1554 work is called *Incarnation of Our Lord*. See *OOT* 351–82; *Complete Works* 2:139–77. Cf. Wenger, ed., *Complete Writings of Menno Simons*, 785–834. Lasco was not the only one to debate Menno. Consider Menno's debate with Martin de Cleyne in 1554 in Wismar over the incarnation and other Anabaptist issues. From 1556 to 1558 the two engaged in a literary exchange as well. E.g., see Menno's longest book, *Reply to Martin Micron*, in *OOT* 543–98; *Complete Works* 2:351–401. Cf. Wenger, ed., *Complete Writings of Menno Simons*, 838–913.

130. See the following works: *Confession of the Distressed Christians* (1552); *Pathetic Supplication to All Magistrates* (1552); *Reply to False Accusations* (1552); *Cross of the Saints* (ca. 1554); and *Reply to Gellius Faber* (1554).

131. For an example of Menno's "apostasy" outlook, see *Why I Do Not Cease Teaching and Writing* (1539), in *OOT*, 435–55; *Complete Works* 2:233–55. Cf. Wenger, ed., *Complete Writings of Menno Simons*, 292–320.

conclusion that they were not sufficiently converted to the Anabaptist cause. This led Menno's most loyal colleagues and disciples in a legalistic direction that most of the Anabaptist tradition could not follow. Ironically, Menno even found himself in conflict with his own disciples, having to ban them when they disagreed with his Christology. His ecclesiology and Christology collided and formed a vicious circle. Perhaps Menno never did escape the disciplinary logic of the magisterial Reformers as he assumed.

Still, the following Menno created is indisputable. In the centuries that followed, Mennonites not only multiplied across Europe but pressed into Russia and North America. Menno's pacifism was a relief to those in grief over the bloodshed of the sixteenth century. Despite Menno's disagreements with the Reformers, Menno and his disciples were characterized by an evangelistic compassion rare in sixteenth-century polemics and politics. When Zwinglians were forced out of London in 1553, it was the Mennonites of Wismar who extended open arms.[132] It is nearly impossible to think of any other group in the sixteenth century who could display such love to a tradition that executed their Anabaptist brothers and sisters.

Why then did Protestant magistrates and Reformers alike consider these Anabaptists such a serious threat not only to the church but to society when so many of them were pacifists?

WHY WERE ANABAPTIST PACIFISTS CONSIDERED A THREAT? REFORMATION VERSUS REVOLUTION

If Anabaptists are caricatured as nothing more than advocates for a different view of baptism, then Zwingli and Zurich appear tribal, overreacting to any who questioned the status quo, as well as tyrannical, punishing all who challenged the authorities. But the Anabaptist worldview and the tension that worldview posed was far more complicated and serious. Nonconformity was never merely theological. Dissidence was, or at least could be, seditious. Luther, Zwingli, and Calvin may have started a reformation, but the Anabaptists represented a revolution in the estimation of the Reformers. The two were not to be confused. Otherwise, the Reformers feared the credibility of their catholicity could be severely compromised. If they were perceived as insubordinate schismatics, let alone revolutionaries breaking rank to establish a new church, their claim to renew the one, holy, catholic, and apostolic church could only be mute. The success of their claims to catholicity—and with it, orthodoxy—hinged on separating themselves from radicals. The Reformation's suppression of Anabaptists was severe, but in the estimation of Reformers such suppression was proof the Reformers were faithful heirs of the church catholic.

In Zurich the success of the Reformation depended in large part on the support and sanction of the civil authorities. Modern societies foster religious

---

132. "One of the ships arrived at Wismar on December 21 but froze fast in the ice some distance from the shore. The Mennonites of Wismar went to the aid of the refugees, taking to them bread and wine for their refreshment." Ve Wenger, ed., *Complete Writings of Menno Simons*, 836.

pluralism, and freedom is impinged if one religious group oppresses the others in an attempt to monopolize control of society. In the sixteenth century, however, freedom was enjoyed only when the magistrates decided in favor of one's religious convictions. Clemency and unity were acquired when the magistrates stood behind the Protestant church, fortifying its legitimacy and securing its longevity over against the threat of papal conquest. In the eyes of the Reformers, Anabaptists appeared to assist Rome by disrupting and even compromising the uniformity and security previously established by the magistrates and celebrated by the church. "Fearful of possible aggression from the Catholic cantons, Zurich and other reformed cantons believed that only a community united in religion could defend itself and maintain its freedom. Thus, in so far as the Anabaptists hindered this union they were seen as abetting the Counter-Reformation."[133]

The Anabaptists further abetted Rome by virtue of an exclusivist ecclesiology. The Reformers recognized that the one, holy, catholic, and apostolic church was already present even if not yet perfected. "Other Reformers such as Luther and Calvin agreed that there was but one catholic (i.e., universal) church with one creed. They understood that the visible church is coextensive with the local community wherein the people must live and worship in harmony."[134] The Anabaptists, by contrast, grew discontent with this mixed community on earth, so desiring its perfected state, a state in which only true believers make up the visible church, that they pressed for perfection in the present, the here and now, rather than the eschaton. "The Anabaptists initially shared this vision [of the Reformers] but could not actualize it," says Lindberg. "It may be argued that the Anabaptist withdrawal from the larger society was a consequence of their failure to achieve a *corpus Christianum* in their own image. In other words, formally Zwingli and the Zurich radicals were both striving for a Christian commonwealth." That failure pushed Anabaptists to reconsider their target constituency: "Failing to convince the whole community, the Anabaptists turned to local congregations of voluntary members who regarded themselves as altogether set apart from the state."[135]

The difference, then, was not only ecclesiastical but eschatological, the Anabaptists attempting to materialize a church absent of unbelief and impurity. Naturally, baptism—that sacrament that marked entrance into the community— had to be limited to authentic believers, guaranteeing that the visible church remained pure. A state-sanctioned church, where pastors welcomed infants yet incapable of faith and adults who may or may not possess true faith but nonetheless signal their allegiance, was cancerous. To establish a purer community—one in which every member was evaluated before entrance and every member committed by voluntary conviction—the Anabaptists had to separate themselves.[136]

---

133. Lindberg, *European Reformations*, 202.

134. Lindberg, 201–2.

135. Lindberg adds one exception: "One of the rare exceptions was Waldshut in the Black Forest under the leadership of Hubmaier." Lindberg, 201–2.

136. Lindberg, 202.

But separation was seditious in the eyes of the state and its sponsored church, nothing less than rebellion. The spirit of this rebellion was visualized within Anabaptist ecclesiology: their church superseded the authority of the state. While the Reformers claimed to renew the existing church, the Anabaptists insisted their new church was the only true church. Yet this spirit of rebellion was not only ecclesiastical but political: the Anabaptists resisted measures that positioned the state to govern their churches, some of which were basic to late medieval citizenship, such as taking oaths, paying taxes or tithes, or serving in the army.

For example, consider the Anabaptists' rebellion against oaths. Swearing by one's word was a major building block of late medieval society, ensuring a community built on the foundation of trust, reciprocity, and accountability. If a dispute was taken to court, one of the first indications of guilt was perjury. By refusing to accompany one's word with an oath, the Anabaptists threatened not merely individual trust in society but the entire judicial system itself. "Without the public oath, indispensable in any court of justice, the ordinary daily administration of public life was in danger of breaking down. The refusal to render an oath was tantamount to political separatism."[137]

The Anabaptists' rebellion against the tithe was one of the most radical statements they could have made, sending a loud message concerning their ecclesial and political independence. The tithe was a major assistance to the state, enabling them to buttress churches under their dominion. "For Zwingli, the tithe was a key to the centralized territorial church which he wanted to reform but not to dissolve."[138] By resisting the tithe, the Anabaptists signaled their desire to dissolve the church, not reform it in the vein of Zwingli. For this reason, historians have labeled them *radicals* over against *magisterial Reformers*, who worked with the state.

How did the public view this blatant disregard for the established church? First, refusing to pay the tithe created resentment. The Anabaptists refused to contribute, yet meanwhile they benefited from society's structure just like everyone else paying the tithe. Who did they think they were to exempt themselves from a responsibility designed to benefit the rest of society and the church? The Anabaptists were biting the hand that fed them. And the exemption came across as selfish and sectarian.

Second, in the estimation of evangelicals, the Anabaptists' refusal to pay the tithe felt all too familiar, a return to the elitism of the Roman Church and clergy. "To some at least, this rejection of tithes and taxes appeared very similar to the Catholic church's unpopular insistence upon exemption from taxation and from civil law courts. Similarly, the Anabaptist insistence upon a church of true believers, and thus the instituting of excommunication and the ban, also led people to associate the Anabaptists with elements of Catholicism."[139]

---

137. For this reason, Lindberg calls oaths "the 'glue' that held society together." Lindberg, 203.
138. Lindberg, 204.
139. Lindberg, 204.

CLASSIFYING RADICALS

In his extensive study *The Radical Reformation*, George Huntston Williams separated radicals into three parties: Anabaptists, Spiritualists, and Evangelical Rationalists. Each of these three parties is diverse. For example, Anabaptists and Spiritualists contained followers who could be either pacifists or revolutionaries. The weakness of Williams's paradigm, however, is its inflexibility at points. For instance, the categories should not be strict since mystics and pietists could be found among both Anabaptist and Spiritualist parties. But the Evangelical Rationalists may have been the most distinct, given their constituency of anti-Trinitarians (e.g., Servetus, Sozzini).

More recent scholarship has made Williams's paradigm more flexible. For example, Carlos Eire expands the Anabaptist party to include a wider collective of pacifists, apocalyptic activists, and moderates. Rather than restricting Karlstadt or Müntzer to the Spiritualist party, he describes them as moderate and apocalyptic Anabaptists (*Reformations*, 255).

These categories serve the historian, but their fluidity is a reminder that during the sixteenth century, distinctives took time to surface. The continuity and discontinuity between these parties was not as evident as it may be in retrospect.

That association was ironic, too, since the Anabaptists took no little pride in their total separation from the papacy, even accusing the Reformers of retaining a papal mindset, failing to take reform to its logical end. But in the eyes of the public, the Anabaptists were the guilty party, retaining a papal mindset, albeit through revolutionary rather than traditional methods. The Anabaptists were leading society back to Rome, but this time a Rome of their own making, said evangelicals.

In summary, resistance to basic if not essential aspects of citizenship not only set the Anabaptist ecclesiology apart but designated a separate Anabaptist politic, even if it was primitive in its beginnings. Rebellion not only created a new church but a new government—a "state within a state."[140] The religious, sociopolitical unity that the evangelical church and society enjoyed—the fabric of the Christian commonwealth—was threatened. Dissenting with doctrinal differences that resulted in social and political divergence from the commonwealth could result in nothing less than an ecclesiastical *and* political faction.

SPIRITUALISTS

To call a group "radical" may appear judgmental by modern standards of tolerance, but that is exactly what the Reformers intended since they lived in a century where sectarian beliefs could lead to execution. In the estimation of the

---

140. Lindberg, *European Reformations*, 203.

magisterial Reformers, the radicals were extreme due to their hubristic monopoly of the Holy Spirit and biblicist hermeneutic.

The umbrella "radical Reformation" includes not only Anabaptists but Spiritualists as well, though the latter is a broad term under which a variety of individuals can be included. Nevertheless, the category is useful because it connects those individuals and movements that took an aggressive turn toward subjective religious experience in the name of the Spirit, sometimes over against the letter. The label identifies those thinkers and societies that protested and dispensed with externals of all kinds and gave highest authority to the internal consciousness of the Spirit. And this elevation of the individual's subjective experience could not have been more threatening—even detestable—to the Reformers.

As notable already, such a broad description could absorb everyone from Karlstadt to Münster. To one degree or another, many of the radicals discussed so far threw off external, formalized authority and prioritized the Spirit's internal testimony (and with Münster, personal revelation itself). Yet certain individuals did epitomize the Spiritualist label in a way that set them apart from other radicals.

At the core of their identity was a pessimistic ecclesiology. The Spiritualists and the Anabaptists alike agreed on the corruption of Christendom and the great need for internal transformation, a true spiritual change, rather than a merely external change in ritual. Yet the Spiritualists parted company with the Anabaptists because they "tended not to believe in the possibility of a restoration of the true church, or to consider such a project to be of any value even if it were possible."[141] Pearse elucidates the Spiritualist logic when he describes the Spiritualist reading of ecclesiastical history: "Convinced by the radicals' critique of the Middle Ages, and persuaded also of the inadequacy of the Reformers' attempts to settle Christendom on an improved basis, they [the Spiritualists] were nevertheless too deeply ingrained with Catholic notions of apostolic succession and historical continuity to allow that the Anabaptists had a right to establish churches of their own from scratch. If the church had fallen, it could not be restored except by a new dispensation."[142]

The "new dispensation," however, was not bracketed by the apocalyptic vision cast by biblicists at Münster. The Spiritualists cringed at such literalism. "The conflicting—and rapidly proliferating—expositions of Scripture on offer by various groups provided ample demonstration that a simplistic appeal to 'what the Bible says' was no solution to anything. This being so, the best option was to cultivate the inner spiritual life on the basis of minimal doctrinal affirmations, to share fellowship with all who were truly devout and to submit to nobody's insistence that theirs was the only true church."[143]

---

141. By consequence, "no lasting ecclesial movement was bequeathed by them to posterity." Pearse, *Great Restoration*, 153–54.

142. Pearse, 140.

143. Pearse, 140. Other differences could be mentioned as well. For example, Packull thinks the Anabaptists were voluntarists while the Spiritualists were realists in the tradition of Neoplatonism.

Caspar Schwenkfeld: Aristocratic Spirituality, Anti-Corporate Ecclesiology

Caspar Schwenkfeld (1489–1561) originated from Liegnitz, and nobility ran through his blood—lower Silesian nobility to be exact. Schwenkfeld was called upon by Duke Friedrich II of Liegnitz to be his special adviser. As will be seen, Schwenkfeld's noble background influenced his approach to the church and spirituality, and he tended to attract those with aristocratic connections like himself.[144]

Schwenkfeld was no stranger to Luther's Reformation but followed the trail of writings Luther left behind. Persuaded by Luther in 1518, Schwenkfeld was persistent in his attempt to convince his prince to adopt Reformation ideals. From 1519 to 1524, Schwenkfeld was unrelenting in his advocacy for reform. In an ironic twist, just when Schwenkfeld convinced his prince to commit to the Reformation, Schwenkfeld himself turned on Luther.

By 1526 Schwenkfeld could no longer stomach Luther's reliance on an external means of grace like the Lord's Supper. Granted, Luther had abandoned transubstantiation, but he had not gone far enough.[145] Despite Luther's emphasis on *sola fide* and *sola gratia*, he still chained divine grace to a real presence in the sacrament as if the bread and wine remained mediums of forgiveness. "Schwenkfeld became convinced that the Lutheran conviction of the forgiveness of sin communicated in, with, and under the Lord's Supper was the source of immorality and lack of religious fervor. After all, had not Judas also participated in the Lord's Supper?"[146]

Rather than depending on externals, Schwenkfeld advocated complete reliance on the internal. The believer must turn inward toward the renewing work of the Spirit rather than outward to the sacraments. For Schwenkfeld, even Scripture itself was not the believer's ultimate destination. (He detested the biblicism of the Anabaptists, which determined its outlook by means of its literalistic hermeneutic and sometimes apocalyptic obsession of reading between the textual lines.) For Scripture, too, is an external, a mere type, pointing to that which is real: the internal word implanted by means of a spiritual encounter with God. Therefore, the Christian's first stop is not necessarily the Scriptures, but his or her individual, existential experience of the Spirit within. Only then can externals be of assistance.

For these reasons, Schwenkfeld dismissed debates over the presence of Christ in the Lord's Supper. Discussions over the Supper should be put aside since they draw the believer's focus in the wrong direction. They teach the believer to depend on externals as if the visible sacrament can mediate invisible grace or the Spirit.

---

144. Pearse, 149.

145. "Since 1520, he expressly rejected the doctrine of transubstantiation, not because of its theological intent but because he saw in it a mere theory that should not have been made binding. In its theological content, Luther's view of the real presence was not so far removed from the doctrine of transubstantiation." Lohse, *Martin Luther's Theology*, 308.

146. Lindberg, *European Reformations*, 226.

AN ANSWER TO LUTHER'S MALEDICTION

Did Schwenkfeld ever meet Luther and voice his dissent in person? He did. First, he wrote to Luther in 1525, but then he traveled to Wittenberg, where Luther took time to talk to the Spiritualist. Luther was not encouraged by Schwenckfeld's opposition to real presence in the supper. He wrote to Schwenckfeld months later, telling him to quit spreading opposition to his views. Luther even warned Schwenckfeld that if his disciples were hunted down and executed for adopting these dissenting views, their blood would be on Schwenckfeld's hands. Schwenckfeld persisted anyway. Even as late as 1544, he wrote *An Answer to Luther's Malediction*, outlining seven points in critique of Luther.

1. Physical eating of Christ and his body in external things not only cannot be authenticated by any Scripture, but such assertion is wrong because thereby the Christians are bewildered in the knowledge of Christ and are led away from the simplicity that is in Christ, contrary to Paul (2 Cor. 11:3).
2. [Luther] claims that the minister of the church can truly give, present, and distribute the body and blood of Christ to the communicants, and not only the Lord Christ himself, but this is in direct opposition to the entire sixth chapter of John and the aforementioned words of the Lord when he (6:51) promises us a living bread which he (he himself) will give, and an incorruptible food which the Son of Man will give, who also alone is sealed thereunto by God the Father.
3. [Luther] teaches that the physical mouth, also of the godless communicant, eats the body of Christ physically, yea, that . . . all unbelievers even yet may eat and drink him without faith. . . . [But Luther] wants to make the body of our Lord Jesus Christ and the blood of the New Eternal Covenant common to the unworthy and godless men, contrary to all Scripture.
4. [Luther] does not let the teaching of Christ about his flesh, body, and blood and of the heavenly food and drink of eternal life, remain one and the same doctrine, but divides it into multiplicity and makes it repugnant to itself. . . .
5. Without Scripture and proof, I cannot agree with Dr. M. Luther when he writes and teaches that our Lord Christ placed the strength and power of his passion in the visible sacrament, that one shall fetch, seek, and find it there, and he who has a bad conscience because of sin shall fetch and seek there in the sacrament consolation, salvation, and forgiveness of sin, which also I do not consider right. For what is this other than crying out a new indulgence with the holy sacrament and establishing a false confidence thereby.
6. [Luther] writes that the revered sacrament imparts life, grace, and salvation, yea, that it is a fountain of life and salvation. . . . But what is this other than perverting the laudable institution of Christ, binding salvation to the work out of the *opus operatum*, and making an idol out of the sacrament? It is setting up thereby a false confidence and fornication of the souls, if one wants to place the sacrament, symbol, or sign on a par with Christ Jesus, the only giver of all grace and salvation, with great offense to his honor and glory. . . .

7. [Luther's view is] contrary to Paul's principle of probation (*Proba Pauli*) when he writes about the observance of the holy sacrament and about the feast or celebration of the Lord's Supper in a good, pious manner, and says (1 Cor. 11:27–29): Let a man examine himself and so let him eat of the bread and drink of the cup. . . .

(*An Answer to Luther's Malediction By Caspar Schwenckfeld*, 168–78.)

In addition, the entire Lutheran apologetic depended on a literalistic reading of the text, which Schwenkfeld believed missed the point of Jesus' words. "This is my body"—these words were designed to help the Christian turn inward where he or she trusts in Christ and feeds upon Christ.[147] Schwenkfeld practiced what he preached, ceasing to celebrate the Lord's Supper from 1526 forward. Schwenkfeld was open to the supper being reintroduced one day, but not until serious theological shifts were accomplished, primarily the transition away from external sacraments to the internal testimony and transformation of the Holy Spirit.

As for the church, Schwenkfeld's emphasis on the inward, spiritual experience of the individual motivated him to criticize a high church ecclesiology that depended on outward rituals. Faith within the individual is what mattered most, and where faith-filled, Spirit-endowed believers were to be found, there the mystical church was located. Since the church, for Schwenkfeld, was primarily an invisible entity, he did not advocate (as many Anabaptists did) for separatism. Nevertheless, he had little tolerance for a state-endorsed church, either; on that point he and the Anabaptists agreed.[148]

In the end, Schwenkfeld's noble blood did not work to his advantage once Archduke Ferdinand of Austria acquired dominion over Silesian nobility.[149] Ferdinand was overt in his allegiance to the Roman Church, and Schwenkfeld was wise to leave rather than stay, even though his exile turned him into a permanent wayfarer, spending more than three decades away from his homeland. As for Schwenkfeld's influence, his Spiritualist theology was as attractive among peasants and the common laity as it was among those with the privilege of education or even aristocratic lifestyles. His "strongest appeal was to the more prosperous urban merchant classes, who saw in his teachings an affirmation of high culture and Renaissance rationalism, along with a slightly esoteric spirituality."[150] His following, then, did not draw from the masses. Yet its inward focus—independent as it was from corporate ecclesiology, unstained as it was by apocalyptic, revolutionary agendas—explains its longevity well into the modern era.

---

147. Likewise with baptism: "Though he rejected infant baptism . . . he believed, in point of fact, that baptism was an unimportant outer work; what mattered was the baptism of the Holy Spirit." Pearse, *Great Restoration*, 151. Space prohibits me from exploring his Christology, but see p. 15 in Pearse's work for a summary.

148. Pearse, 151.

149. Ferdinand of Austria gained the crown of Bohemia in 1529, and Silesia fell under Bohemian jurisdiction. Lindberg, *European Reformations*, 227.

150. Pearse, *Great Restoration*, 153.

Sebastian Franck's Damnation of Tradition and Ecclesial History

Spiritualists had an effect on the German population as well. For example, Sebastian Franck (1499–1542), a priest in Augsburg, had been influenced by Luther's Reformation in the 1520s and even labored to advance its influence in Nuremberg. At some point, however, Franck grew critical of Luther, much like Schwenkfeld, resenting remnants of externals in Luther's theology and practice and his stress on *sola fide*. Although Franck preached justification by faith alone, he became discouraged when individuals used *sola fide* to justify their spiritual laziness or even their immorality. Franck rivaled Schwenkfeld's anti-Lutheran polemic, condemning externals as satanic, advising instead that the believer rely on the Spirit's internal witness. Since the magistrates refused to excommunicate the licentious in his congregation, Franck decided he could not advance his beliefs and decided to resign. "Christendom was hopelessly split into innumerable factions, and so now, shunning all external ceremonies and organized churches, he advocated Spiritualism."[151]

In 1531 Franck wrote an extensive letter to John Campanus, a follower of Luther until he was influenced by Melchior Hoffman. Campanus and Franck shared a similar outlook, as evident in the title of Campanus's book *Against All the World Since the Apostles*. In his letter, Franck outlined his distinctives, all of which were coated by a radical suspicion toward tradition and the preservation of the church. Unlike the Reformers who retrieved the tradition in an effort to renew the one, holy, catholic, and apostolic church, Franck concluded that the church had been lost since the days of Christ and his apostles. While many Anabaptists believed the church had been lost after the reign of Constantine in the fourth century, Franck was more radical still, believing the church was corrupted as soon as the apostles were succeeded. "I am thus quite certain that for fourteen hundred years now there has existed no gathered church nor any sacrament."[152] Disposing of all of church history, Franck's view of tradition could not be more extreme: "foolish Ambrose, Augustine, Jerome, Gregory—of whom not even one knew the Lord, so help me God, nor was sent by God to teach. But rather all were the apostles of Antichrist.... *There is not one of them ... who appears to have been a Christian.*"[153]

These "apostles of Antichrist" had corrupted the church and its sacraments by turning their attention to the Old Testament, with all its focus on external ceremonies, instead of the New Testament. From the Old Testament, the church fathers thought they "prove[d] [the legitimacy of] war, oath, government, power of magistracy, tithes, priesthood," and so on.[154] Their perversion of the church by

---

151. Pearse, 146. "Given that he held such drastic views, it comes as something of a relief that Franck ascribed to himself no quasi-messianic role in rescuing the true church from this grim scenario. His pretensions were scholarly and spiritual, not prophetic. There was to be no reconstruction or restoration in which Franck could play a starring part" (147).

152. Franck, "A Letter to John Campanus," 149.

153. Franck, 151, emphasis added.

154. Franck, 151.

means of externals led Franck to take severe measures: the indefinite abandonment of the Lord's Supper. Since "all things external has [*sic*] fallen into decay" and "the church is dispersed among the heathen, truly it is my opinion that no persons on earth can without a special call from God gather up the same and bring again its sacraments into use.... Therefore I have said that the outward ceremonies of the church ought not to be reestablished unless Christ himself command it, who has not spoken orally to us but to the apostles."[155]

A certain irony shows itself by the end of Franck's letter. Franck was convinced the church disappeared after the days of the apostles. Franck considered even the holiest of saints non-Christians, disposing with tradition and church history altogether. And yet he opened his arms to the heathen, exhibiting strong sympathies toward universalism. "Consider as thy brothers all Turks and heathen, wherever they be, who fear God and work righteousness, instructed by God and inwardly drawn by him, even though they have never heard of baptism, indeed, of Christ himself, neither of his story or Scripture, but only of his power through the inner Word perceived within and made fruitful.... And therefore I hold that just as there are many Adams who do not know there was one Adam, so also there are many Christians who have never heard Christ's name."[156] While an Augustine was damned, the righteous Turk was saved. For Franck, no contradiction was at work because the determining factor in salvation is the Spirit not the letter. An Augustine might talk about the letter (the Scriptures and Christ), but his trust in externals and his perversion of externals (like baptism and the supper) revealed he was without the Spirit. Meanwhile, the Turk or heathen who had never read the letter or heard of Christ showed by his zeal for divinity that the Spirit was at work within him.

Thus, the Spirit had priority over the Letter (Scripture) in every way. Franck even grew frustrated with John Campanus for trusting in the external Letter when he should have been trusting in the Spirit within. "I should wish, however, that thou wert not so addicted to the letter of Scripture, thus withdrawing thy heart from the teaching of the Spirit, and that thou wouldst not drive out the Spirit of God as though it were Satan, crowding him against his will into the script and making Scripture thy god." For Franck, Scripture was only good as a verification of the subjective, inward conscience of the believer. "Thou shouldst much rather interpret the Scripture as a confirmation of thy conscience, so that it testifies to the heart and not against it. Again, thou shouldst not believe and accept something [merely] reported by Scripture—and feel that the God in thy heart must yield to Scripture. It were better that Scripture should remain Antichrist's!"[157]

155. Franck, 153.
156. Franck, 156.
157. Franck, 159.

Franck was not all talk but followed his own hermeneutical advice. For example, when he described the Spaniard Michael Servetus and his rejection of the Trinity, Franck expressed agreement. Servetus did away with three persons of the Trinity and instead described God as Father who is the Spirit. "Now the Spaniard of whom the bearer of this letter, thy brother, will speak postulates in his little book a single Person of the Godhead, namely, the Father, whom he calls most truly *the* Spirit or most properly the Spirit and says that neither of the [other] two is a Person. The Roman Church postulates three Persons in once essence. I should rather agree with the Spaniard."[158]

In the name of this one God who is one person, namely Spirit, Franck advised Campanus to unlearn all that he had learned since childhood. He was to abandon all that the papists, Luther, and Zwingli had taught him. "For one will sooner make a good Christian out of a Turk than out of a bad Christian or a learned divine!"[159] Franck knew his advice would lead to the gallows, but persecution was a sure indication that he was part of the true church, not the Antichrist. And the true church would "remain scattered among the heathen until the end of the world."[160]

"The end of the world"—Franck was not using hyperbole. At the second coming of Christ, the church will be manifested for all to see. Until then, however, the church remains a spiritual entity. Franck resisted the radical tendency to usher in the eschaton by assembling a visible community with himself as its head. Likewise, he dismissed the Anabaptist biblicism that looked for apocalyptic revelations on the surface of the text. Instead, the church's history was a wasteland, and so it would remain.[161]

Franck spent the 1530s and early 1540s on the run for his Spiritualist writings until his death in 1542. Unlike Schwenkfeld's legacy, however, Franck did not leave behind a visible heritage of churches. How could he when he had spent his life shaming the church's existence and defying its visible representation?

Historians have been known to blame the Reformers for the individualism and subjectivism that surfaced with the advent of the Enlightenment. In truth, however, if any sixteenth-century group is to be blamed (a move that should be made with caution) guilt may be laid at the feet of the Spiritualists. As Lindberg observes, with the Spiritualists one encounters the "first contours of the modern subjectivity that was to shake traditional Christianity to its foundations in the Enlightenment of the eighteenth century."[162]

---

158. Franck, 159.

159. Franck, 160.

160. Franck, 150.

161. I have focused on Franck's letter to Campanus, but Franck wrote theological works of significant influence in his own day and beyond, such as his *Chronica, Zeitbuch und Geschichtsbibel*, in which he traced the history of the church, damning one age after another since the apostles.

162. Lindberg, *European Reformations*, 225. Lindberg believes Karlstadt and Münster were the parents from which the Spiritualist mindset was born.

ABANDONING RE-FORMED CHRISTENDOM
FOR PRIMITIVE CHRISTIANITY

The Reformers insisted that they were not abandoning the church catholic but renewing the church from within, based on a retrieval of its own patristic and medieval heritage over against late medieval innovations. However, that Reformation claim to catholicity also alienated radicals of all stripes and colors. That alienation was intentional; the Reformers refused to be confused with radicals. While the Reformers sought to reform the one church, the radicals decided to abandon the one church and were not shy in their partial and sometimes total rejection of its catholic tradition. As Pearse says, "The movement had abandoned the attempt to re-form Christendom, the medieval *corpus christianum*, and had instead explicitly adopted the separation from the world that had always been implicit in their programme." That program depended on a radical reading of history. "The Anabaptists were henceforth seeking to restore primitive Christianity as they understood it. . . . [They] identified the restoration of a true baptism and a true eucharist as key elements in the restoration of a true and pure church in preparation for Christ's second coming."[163]

While every group—including the cardinals who tried to reform Rome itself during the Counter-Reformation—sought a "renewal," the key question became, a renewal of *what*? The Reformers believed they were renewing Christendom itself, but the radicals spit on the history of Christendom and made the most extreme claim possible: to restore primitive Christianity, Christendom must be abandoned. That claim was both ecclesiastical and eschatological in consequences. The last days were at hand; God was calling his pure church—the radicals—to separate themselves from the world and restore the sacraments as understood in the pages of the New Testament while he brought down fire and sulfur on Sodom.

Applying that apocalyptic vision, however, was subjective and variegated, even chaotic. Separating themselves from the world as God's elect resulted in no external accountability. Separating themselves from heathen Reformers sounded pure until the radicals realized there were always other radicals who were just not radical enough. And severing themselves from the catholic heritage sounded like a recovery of primitive Christianity until the radicals discovered that they no longer possessed the guardrails of historic orthodoxy. Radicalism was exhilarating. It was also isolating. Pure Christianity could be lonely when few others were radical enough to enjoy it.

---

163. Pearse, *Great Restoration*, 62. This chapter is a brief treatment of a variegated movement. For a more extensive treatment, consult Brewer, ed., *T&T Clark Handbook of Anabaptism*.

14

CONSTRUCTING A
REFORMED CHURCH

The Reformation in Strasbourg and Geneva

[They] accuse us of apostatizing from the church and destroying its discipline and rule! . . . [But] the fellowship of the Christian church consists not in ceremonies and outward practices, but in true faith, in obedience to the pure gospel, and in the right use of the holy sacraments as the Lord has ordained them.

—Martin Bucer, *Concerning the True Care of Souls*

If the contest were to be determined by patristic authority, the tide of victory—to put it very modestly—would turn to our side.

—Calvin, *Institutes of the Christian Religion*

NO SECT, NO APOSTASY:
MARTIN BUCER AND PROTESTANT UNITY

Like many of the first-generation Reformers, when Martin Bucer (1491–1551) arrived in Strasbourg, he faced a colossal task: could he persuade the city to embrace the Reformation? Bucer did not settle for personal protection but pushed the evangelical cause until the city applied its principles to church and society alike. Bucer encountered enormous opposition from Thomas Murner, whom he debated over the Mass, as well as Conrad Treger over the authority of the papacy.[1] Treger provoked evangelical preachers when he called them heretics; monasteries became targets as angry mobs reacted to that fiery charge. The city council was forced to act when a mob captured Treger and demanded prosecution.

When the council then decided to consider the evangelical cause, they asked Bucer to write a statement. In a strategic move, Bucer positioned evangelical subservience to the rulers over against subordination to the papacy. Bucer's maneuver called on the council to exercise its authority in favor of sound

---

1. See Bucer's *On the Lord's Supper* and *Dispute with Conrad Treger*.

doctrine for the church rather than submitting itself to the pope, as if he should decide the future of the church in Strasbourg. Bucer understood that he must win the support of the civil authorities; otherwise, Strasbourg would never take a decided turn toward the Reformation. Strasbourg finally took a step forward in favor of the Reformation at the start of 1529 with a respite over the Roman Mass.[2] Bucer's years as a spokesman for the Reformation to Strasbourg were rewarded at last, and the Reformer's growing success meant he became a spokesman of Strasbourg for further reformation across the continent. If reform was possible in Strasbourg, it was possible in other territories as well. Bucer was proof.

Bucer's increasing notoriety as a Reformer cannot be limited to his success in persuading Strasbourg; he labored most of his life to persuade fellow Reformers to work together as well. As prior chapters have revealed, Bucer's name appeared everywhere, like wallpaper that adorned every room in the house of the Reformation. With each major disputation and diet, Bucer was often behind the scenes, attempting to convince both sides to accommodate each other. Some have concluded that Bucer was all too eager to compromise, but that interpretation misunderstands Bucer's motive and strategy. Bucer held to his theological convictions, and his own theology was defined by an emphasis on justification by faith alone as well as the Holy Spirit's presence to create living virtue in the life of individual Christians and the church. Bucer also had uncompromising convictions on specific *loci*—such as the Lord's Supper. However, Bucer did not believe the Reformers should allow secondary or tertiary matters to divide a Reformation already struggling to survive against the attacks of Rome and radicals alike.[3]

Therefore, Bucer could denounce the Mass in no uncertain terms but at the same time mediate between Reformers in debates over the Lord's Supper to achieve concord. He understood where battle lines should be drawn and was equally cognizant when an olive branch should be extended to further evangelical progress. Contrary to his critics, Bucer's strategy was not weak but bold. When Luther said Zwingli was not of the same Christian spirit, Bucer responded, "If you immediately condemn anyone who doesn't quite believe the same as you do as forsaken by Christ's Spirit, and consider anyone to be the enemy of truth who holds something false to be true, who, pray tell, can you still consider a brother?" Bucer, in other words, rebuked Luther for forgetting the priority of evangelical catholicity.[4] The Reformation was not a party of one.

---

2. Greschat, *Martin Bucer*, 62. To be technical, Strasbourg only suspended the Mass, but the writing was on the wall. To understand how the rise and expansion of territorial princes worked in favor of the Reformation, see pp. 87–88.

3. Greschat, 71–78.

4. *Enarrationes perpetuae in sacra quatuor Evangelia*, Strasbourg 1530, fol. A2ᵛ; *BCor* 4, p. 40, 7–11. See context for this comment in Greschat, 94.

PAPAL SUCCESSION REPLACED WITH PASTORAL CALL

Not only Bucer but other Reformers discerned a substitute for papal succession: the calling of a pastor. Yet contrary to the radicals, that calling was not a self-appointment on the basis of an individual experience of the Spirit. The call was internal, as the Holy Spirit confirmed the pastoral vocation on the heart, but it was also external, as the church recognized someone was suited for the pastorate. Differences in polity then came into play to determine how the person was suited for ministry. For example, in 1523 Luther revealed his hand with the title of his book *That a Christian Congregation . . . Has the Right and Power to Judge All Teaching, and to Call, Install and Remove Its Teachers*. However, historians believe the later Luther "reverted to more traditional views on patronage." Regardless of how the candidate was ordained and appointed (whether by congregation, clergy, or magistrates, or an involvement of all three), all Reformers had the different task of avoiding the extremes of Rome and radicals alike. For the "Church was neither a consecrated elite of clergy, nor a huddle of self-proclaimed 'godly'" (Cameron, *The European Reformation*, 178).

Yet behind that concrete admonition was a loving motive. Years later, after receiving Luther's unfair, sharp accusation that he was nothing more than a "slippery tactician and a wordy opportunist," Bucer replied with incredible patience, revealing that his true concern was the Reformation itself. "In any case, we must seek unity and love in our relationships with everyone—regardless of how they behave towards us."[5] And Luther often behaved badly. For good reason, then, one of Bucer's biographers labeled Bucer the "champion of Protestant unity."[6]

Bucer has been labeled many things—missionary, ecumenicist, biblical scholar. But he deserves one title above all: pastor of the Reformation. His pastoral care not only extended to laity but other pastors, even theologians. For example, when a young John Calvin limped into Strasbourg after he was expelled from his church in Geneva, Bucer's encouragement and mentorship was instrumental to Calvin's healing process and renewed vision for the church.

Bucer's pastoral ministry was not without trials of its own. He ministered in a context that was volatile. Rome pressed in, convinced that Reformers like Bucer were heretical for advocating the Lutheran doctrine of justification. Meanwhile, Bucer was criticized by Anabaptists who did not consider his church fruitful, bearing true marks of discipline toward its members, despite Bucer's constant emphasis on the Holy Spirit for the sake of discipleship. Bucer also had his share

---

5. *BDS* 4, p. 503, 20ff. The first quote is Greschat summarizing the accusation (*Martin Bucer*, 100). In the 1530s, Bucer's persistent mindset for concord did see success. For examples on the progress Bucer made in places like Wittenberg, see pp. 129–61.

6. Describing the outcome of 1536, Greschat wrote, "Bucer had made concessions to Luther without having betrayed his own theological standpoint—which can be described as that of an exhibitive real spiritual presence of Christ in the Lord's Supper. Bucer had thus neither simply acquiesced to Luther nor glossed over real differences." Greschat, 138.

of vexations with the city council, who exercised significant control over matters of discipline in the church. He labored for independence, convinced the church should exercise its own discipline. After all, Jesus gave the keys to the church, and spiritual correction should be the responsibility of the pastor.[7]

With these burdens on his back, Bucer wrote his own treatise on pastoral ministry in 1538 called *Concerning the True Care of Souls and Genuine Pastoral Ministry, and How the Latter Is to Be Ordered and Carried Out in the Church of Christ*. The subtitle summarized the book: *Here You Will Find the Essential Means Whereby We Can Escape from the Present So Deplorable and Pernicious State of Religious Schism and Division and Return to True Unity and Good Christian Order in the Churches*.[8] Bucer advocated for liberty from the tyranny of the papacy, but he also wrote his treatise to advocate for an evangelical church in which the people were genuine Christians, believers not merely absorbed under the jurisdiction of a Roman Church but lit up with faith and eager to pursue discipline in its widest sense: discipleship.

Bucer began his treatise with an apologetic for the Reformation against Rome's charge that the Reformers were schismatics and sectarians, destroying the church's unity and severing themselves from the church's body. In doing this, Rome had lobbed the most serious accusation: they "accuse us of apostatizing from the church and destroying its discipline and rule!"[9] Bucer could not believe the charge because, from his point of view, it was Rome that had departed from truth: "But when we turn to the truth we find that on the contrary it is they who have not only torn and disturbed the church of Christ and all true fellowship of the saints in Christ, but completely swallowed up and eradicated all understanding of the church and fellowship of believers in Christ."[10]

Bucer's claim was bold, but it was based on his definition of unity in the church. Rome conditioned unity on externals so that when the Reformers deviated, they were accused of schism. Bucer, by contrast, claimed that ecclesiastical unity was grounded in something far more spiritual: "For the fellowship of the Christian church consists not in ceremonies and outward practices, but in true faith, in obedience to the pure gospel, and in the right use of the holy sacraments

---

7. Toward the end of his life, Bucer published his *De Regno Christi* (On the Kingdom of Christ), which put forward discipline as a third mark of the church and proposed that the church must be autonomous in order to perform such discipline. Yet Bucer's *exact* understanding of the nexus between temporal authorities and ecclesiastical authorities is not always so easy to define. See Greschat, who explained why Bucer could be heard defending both temporal and ecclesiastical authorities, placing "extraordinary confidence in the civil authorities" for the Christianization of society (115; cf. 111, 117) but also defending ecclesiastical independence in discipline (217, 241–43). For a window into Bucer's view, see his books *On the Office of Government* (a republication of Augustine's letter to Boniface) and *Dialogues or Discussion*.

8. For the treatise, see no. 59 in *Bibliographia Bucerana*. Cf. Bornkamm, *Martin Bucers Bedeutung für die europaische Reformationsgeschichte*. See Wright, "Historical Introduction," ix–xxvi. For an examination of Bucer's pastoral mindset and ministry, see Wright, *Martin Bucer*; and Burnett, *The Yoke of Christ*. For Bucer's wider context and biography, see Eells, *Martin Bucer*; and Krieger and Lienhard, *Martin Bucer and Sixteenth Century Europe*.

9. Bucer, *Concerning the True Care of Souls*, xxxii.

10. Bucer, *Concerning the True Care of Souls*, xxxi.

as the Lord ordained them." In other words, the gospel and its proper induction in the marks of a true church—baptism and the Lord's Supper—outlines unity and its boundaries.

Bucer did not picture himself or the Lutherans as obstinate, nor as deviants bent on leaving the church or dividing the church. "We do not, therefore, wish to tear ourselves away from any authority in the church. But there is no authority or power in the church except that which is for its good." Bucer advised evangelicals that pope, cardinals, and bishops "claim[ed] for themselves a greater authority in the church," but when the Scriptures and ancient councils were consulted, a different picture of authority emerged. The ancient councils recognized that authority stemmed from a fear of God. It was this fear that Bucer said was lacking in the pope, cardinals, and bishops, and the same fear he was hoping to infuse in the hearts and minds of ministers. "Were we not to separate from these false and godless church leaders and choose true and faithful ministers, we would lose our fear of God, violate the Lord's command, and stain ourselves with the godlessness of the false ministers." The church catholic supported Bucer in this bold claim too: "This was recognized and written with great solemnity by the holy martyr and bishop Cyprian in his fourth epistle. Indeed, the ancient holy fathers agree with him, both in the decrees of the councils and in their own writings." Therefore, concluded Bucer, "no-one is in a position to accuse us in any way of being a sect which has apostatized from the church and its obedience."[11] In other words, Bucer and the Reformers were faithful adherents to the church catholic, not a sect formed out of schism and apostasy.

Bucer passed on this belief to John Calvin, and Calvin embedded such an apologetic in his own defense against Rome as well as his vision for the Reformed Church in the decades to come. The story of Calvin and his vision for the church in Geneva—a church that was accused of apostasy—must begin with Calvin's own journey into the evangelical church, a pilgrimage he never intended at the start.

CLASSICAL EDUCATION AND HUMANIST INFLUENCE

Unlike Luther, who was an open book, John Calvin said little about himself. The library of letters that has survived conveys the dynamics at play in his ecclesiastical relationships, especially how he perceived others. But as to the inner workings of Calvin's mind or the events that surrounded his early life prior to Geneva, little is said. Nevertheless, much is known about the era in which Calvin grew up, including the birth of evangelical ideas in France.

Born in 1509, Jean Cauvin was raised north of Paris in Noyon, France.[12] His father, Girard Cauvin, was a man who made many connections, the type that rewarded him with a variety of local opportunities. By virtue of a good

---

11. Bucer, *Concerning the True Care of Souls*, xxxv.
12. Latin Calvinus.

relationship with the de Hangest family, Girard made the most of his patronage benefits. The de Hangest family consisted of bishops, and Girard was granted a variety of positions with ties to the church.[13] Girard's determination gave young John Calvin the chance at an education. Thanks to the financial backing of the de Hangest family, Calvin traveled to Paris around 1523, where he enrolled at the Collège de la Marche. Girard intended the Collège de la Marche to be the start of Calvin's preparation for the priesthood. The training was rigorous; the school had a reputation for strict protocol, demanding standards, and relentless discipline.

Learning from someone like Maturin Cordier may have been the most significant experience during Calvin's time at the Collège de la Marche. Later in life, Calvin recognized that he had received a unique opportunity to study under Cordier—he even identified the opportunity as a kindness of God.[14] Cordier was patient with Calvin as the young man improved his Latin. Cordier also instilled in Calvin the methods of humanism. Calvin learned the art and craft of writing well. Yet education, even publishing, was not an end in itself; the humanist wrote for piety's sake. If the noble life was not the goal, all the Latin in the world was a waste.[15] Such a method—scholarship as a means to godliness—never left Calvin and one day became a major priority in his *Institutes of the Christian Religion*.

After the Collège de la Marche, Calvin became a student at the Collège de Montaigu where he was introduced to Scholastic authors and their works.[16] Some of the best and brightest minds came out of the Collège de Montaigu, from Erasmus the humanist to Ignatius Loyola, the father of the Jesuits, who may have been a student at the same time as Calvin or perhaps not long after Calvin had left.[17] A strong work ethic was instilled in each student. Calvin arose as early as 4:00 a.m. to begin a day of rigorous study and spirituality.

Had the ideas of Luther made their way into France by the time Calvin was a student? Yes, but they were not as influential in France as they were in Germany.[18] Jacques Lefèvre d'Etaples was the Reformer who was featured on the front page of the evangelical movement. Jacques Lefèvre d'Etaples (ca. 1455–1536) was baptized in humanism, and in Paris he gained renown for his knowledge of Aristotle. His commentary on Paul's epistles also spread his name throughout Europe (though his commentaries on the Gospels and the Psalms cannot be overlooked either). His commentary created interest due in part to its revealed

---

13. For details see Gordon, *Calvin*, 4–5.

14. See the dedication page of Calvin's commentary on 1 Thessalonians. *CO* 13:525–26. Cf. Gordon, *Calvin*, 6.

15. Cordier's twofold emphasis and approach is plain in his 1530 book, *A Little Book for the Amendment of Corrupt Phrases in Our Speech*. Later the paths of Cordier and Calvin crossed again under the heat of persecution. On Cordier's exile to Geneva, see Gordon, *Calvin*, 6.

16. Battles and Hugo, "Introduction," in Calvin's *Commentary on Seneca's De Clementia*, 24.

17. Note Erasmus's comments on the brutal conditions: *Erasmi Opera*, 426, I, *Colloquia*, 806ff. Cf. Gordon, *Calvin*, 7.

18. Gordon, *Calvin*, 12, observes that Luther's devotional writings carried more weight than his polemical writings.

evangelical sympathies.[19] In the 1520s, d'Etaples's combination of humanist scholarship and evangelical reform made him the leading figure and instrument of change in France, so much so that opposition became fierce.

The same year that Calvin became a student at the Collège de Montaigu (1523), the Sorbonne took action against French evangelicals. The writings of the German Reformers and d'Etaples were condemned. Translations of the Bible into French, as well as Hebrew and Greek editions, were also censured. These steps were but precursors to a much more oppressive persecution of French evangelicals yet to come. Ironically, the humanism so many in France embraced had cultivated a theology that threatened French Catholicism.[20]

Whether Calvin was influenced by evangelical ideas in 1523 is unclear, although he no doubt was aware of them due to his peers and possibly considered his own future identity in view of these contending ideas.[21] Humanism's developing and deep influence on Calvin in the early 1520s, however, is plain, and Calvin became an example of how fruitful a Reformed pastor could be in expository and literary productivity when immersed in the humanist tradition. As chapter 6 explored, the early influence of humanism is evident in Calvin's shift from theology to law. Why Calvin shifted to law has been a matter of speculation, but one external factor was Calvin's father and his decision to swing his son's future away from the priesthood. Perhaps Calvin's father became convinced that law provided a better financial prospect for his son's future.[22] Perhaps the change to law was due to the conflict between Calvin's father and the Noyon clergy.[23] Regardless of the reason, in 1528 Calvin acquired his master of arts degree at the age of eighteen, only to travel south of Paris to Orlèans, which boasted of its law experts and jurists, especially Pierre de l'Estoile, whom Calvin called "the Prince of French lawyers."[24]

According to Theodore Beza, Calvin's biographer and successor in Geneva, Calvin's peers in Orlèans said he became a workhorse. When others went to bed, Calvin stayed up reading and researching late into the night. He was not interested in dinner because he was more interested in continuing with his studies. In the mornings, he started his day by reflecting on all he had absorbed the night before, committing everything to memory. This work ethic never escaped him even when he became a well-established Reformer in Geneva. He would apply the same regimen he used with his legal studies to the Scriptures as he prepared sermons, wrote commentaries, drafted polemical treatises, and navigated the

---

19. The second edition also critiqued Erasmus's New Testament and won the support of many Frenchmen. Moreover, however much Luther appreciated Lefèvre d'Etaples, Luther was not convinced Lefèvre d'Etaples had adopted his view of justification. Cf. Gordon, *Calvin*, 13.

20. See Gordon, *Calvin*, 14–15, where he describes this tension in the rule of Francis and outlines the contribution of humanism.

21. Battles and Hugo, "Introduction," in Calvin's *Commentary on Seneca's De Clementia*, 18–19.

22. On the theories, see Gordon, *Calvin*, 18.

23. Lindberg, *European Reformations*, 250.

24. As quoted in Gordon, *Calvin*, 19.

complicated ecclesiastical and political affairs of his day. As time passed by, his body suffered as a result.[25]

In 1529 Calvin left Orléans for Bourges, where his training in law continued. Judging by his dedication to Greek and the classics during his time in Bourges, his study of law was most likely out of duty and allegiance to his father.[26] Yet his humanist interests became irrepressible when he wrote and later published a commentary on Seneca's *De Clementia* (Paris, 1532).[27] The commentary received little to no attention, but the whole project was prophetic, unveiling the skills necessary for this young humanist to become a leading light in the literary advocacy of a reformed church (see chapter 6).[28]

CALVIN'S CONVERSION

In May 1531, Calvin's father died from an illness that had plagued his body. By the end of his life in Noyon, he was not in good standing with the church. Girard and the cathedral chapter did not get along; so fierce was their dispute that he was excommunicated. In medieval Catholicism, prior to death a Christian needed to undergo various rituals, such as receiving a final blessing from the church, an absolution after confession, and Communion. Due to his expulsion, Girard received none of these while still alive, including last rites, which was one of the worst states in which a sinner could perish.[29]

Just prior to his father's death, Calvin moved to Paris with plans to continue his studies and scholarship at the Collège Royal where he could encounter the best in French humanism.[30] In time Calvin transitioned to the Collège of Fortet, but the advent of the plague precluded any future educational plans in Paris. Calvin decided to travel to Orléans for law, but historians know little about Calvin's studies or his relationships between 1531 and 1533, except that Calvin did receive his law degree in 1532.

Yet one revealing change has surfaced from around the year 1533 (some say 1554): Calvin's conversion.[31] Writing at the end of his career in his commentary

---

25. Beza, *Life of Calvin*, 20 (as quoted in Gordon, *Calvin*, 20).

26. "That Calvin's pursuit of law was largely a matter of filial obedience is evident in the fact that upon the death of his father Calvin returned to Paris to study humanism." Lindberg, *European Reformations*, 250–51.

27. Calvin did not find the financial support he expected from the de Hangest family, and his dedicatory letter reveals the little praise they received as a result. On what this reveals about Calvin, see Gordon, *Calvin*, 23.

28. Historians disagree on the nature of humanism's influence: "Some would limit Calvin's humanism to his use of its methodology, while others would include his acceptance of some of its substantive views of human nature and history." Lindberg, *European Reformations*, 251.

29. Thanks to his son, Charles, he did receive a posthumous absolution. See Gordon, *Calvin*, 31.

30. "In Bourges and Orléans he had been in the presence of greatness in the figures of de l'Estoile and Alciati, but Calvin wanted more—to dwell among the Olympian figures of French humanism." Gordon, *Calvin*, 31.

31. Calvin reflected on his conversion once to Cardinal Sadoleto in 1539 and then again in 1557, but this time in his commentary on the Psalms. See *CO* 31:13–35; and John C. Olin, *Reformation Debate: Sadoleto's Letter to the Genevans and Calvin's Reply*. Some see the two accounts as contradictory, but consult Gordon, *Calvin*, 33–35, who gives an alternative explanation. Gordon is indebted to Heiko A. Oberman, "Subita Conversio: The Conversion of John Calvin," in Oberman et al., *Reformiertes Erbe*, 281–91; Willem

on the Psalms (1557), Calvin said he was a wretched sinner, but then, to his own surprise, he was subdued by God himself. When he tasted the knowledge of true piety, he was inflamed with an intense desire to pursue evangelical godliness. Afterward even his studies took a back seat to his newfound pursuit of Christian holiness.

Calvin's "conversion" was a turn away from the papacy, which Calvin said he was addicted to early in life, and a turn toward evangelical belief and worship. However, it was not so much a transition of allegiance from the established church to a new church; such an interpretation is somewhat anachronistic since a French evangelical reformation was only in its incipient stages. Calvin's conversion was a shift away from Rome to the Scriptures, from papal authority to biblical authority. Of course, that shift did not occur in a vacuum but was accompanied by a growing allegiance to Christian tradition—from Augustine to Bernard.

In his conversion accounts, Calvin cast himself as a prophet of God in the making. His own conversion to the Scriptures and its gospel was paradigmatic for the church that was to soon follow his lead. Yet for all his focus on conversion, Calvin's real focus was on the miracle worker himself. Just as God had changed the heart of a sinner like Calvin, so, too, would he change the church he summoned his prophet to lead. Calvin was convinced of that.

PERSECUTION IN PARIS AND THE PLACARDS AFFAIR

Conversion to evangelical beliefs and practices was a precarious endeavor. In the years prior to Calvin's conversion, significant strides by French humanists had been made to recover a commitment to ancient languages like Hebrew and Greek, but the Sorbonne was not sympathetic and could even be hostile.[32] As for Francis I, he was unpredictable. While he was an advocate of the Renaissance, he did not back the evangelical cause. His motives were political instead; favor toward Protestant princes in Germany, for example, had more to do with his loathing of Charles V than with his religious convictions.[33]

It was a matter of time before Francis I turned against evangelicals in France. In Paris, for example, on All Saints' Day 1533 an address drew attention in the church of the Mathurins. Nicolas Cop was the speaker, and his message revealed his sympathies not only for humanism but for Martin Luther's theology, including the Reformer's contrast between law and gospel.[34] The evangelical flavor

---

Nijenhuis, "Calvin's 'Subita Conversio': Notes to a Hypothesis," in Nijenhuis, *Ecclesia Reformata: Studies on the Reformation*, 2:3–23.

32. For example, "In 1530 the Sorbonne had condemned the principle that the biblical languages were essential to the study of the scripture." Gordon, *Calvin*, 32.

33. For example, "Charles had been elected Holy Roman emperor in 1519 over Francis, continuing the dynastic ascendancy of the Habsburgs in the empire that was to end only in 1806. To undermine his hated Habsburg rival Francis supported the Schmalkaldic League of Protestant German princes and cities, formed in 1531 to defend the German reformation against anticipated attack by the emperor. Francis' dealing with the League was a clear case of the enemy of my enemy being my friend." Gordon, *Calvin*, 36.

34. "Academic Discourse Delivered by Nicolas Cop on Assuming the Rectorship of the University of Paris on 1 November 1533," in Calvin, *Institutes of the Christian Religion, 1536 Edition*, ed. and trans. Battles.

of the address, as well as its impressive rhetoric, has left historians to debate whether Calvin himself, as his successor Theodore Beza said, had a hand in its formation or even wrote the address himself.[35] The response to Cop's address by the university was hostile. The king's reaction was also inimical. Since Cop's sympathies for Luther were conspicuous in his address, the king assumed Cop and company were Lutherans. Cop fled the city right away. So, too, did Calvin, and most likely for similar reasons.[36]

THE CENTRALIZATION OF AUTHORITY IN FRANCE

Why was the survival of the evangelical movement so tenuous in France in contrast to German and Swiss evangelical territories? The answer, in part, concerns the location of authority. In the Holy Roman Empire, an evangelical might enjoy protection if a magistrate, elector, or prince favored his cause or the freedom to champion that cause. However, in France authority resided with the king. Authority was centralized in the monarchy of Francis I. "One king, one law, one faith!" French evangelicals posed a threat to the type of centralized authority Francis I envisioned. "It was not at all in the political, let alone religious, interest of the king, Francis I, to tolerate reform movements incompatible with his drive to create political and national unity" (Lindberg, *The European Reformations*, 253).

Calvin was fortunate to take refuge in southwest France. Louis du Tillet, a friend from their years together as students, took Calvin under his care. In nearby Nérac, the influential evangelical Jacques Lefèvre was active, and many surrounding churches reflected Lefèvre's theology and methods. Calvin did have the chance to meet with Lefèvre, and although it is uncertain what they discussed, the seasoned Lefèvre must have shared his experience—especially in the midst of so much persecution—with the young evangelical.[37] Also nearby were libraries where Calvin could continue his studies. During this short exile of 1533 and 1534, for instance, Calvin studied the church fathers whose works were housed in these libraries, Fathers who later served Calvin well when he defended the catholicity of the Reformation in Geneva over against its Roman opposition from men like Sadoleto.[38] So critical were the Fathers as proof of Calvin's case for catholicity that later in life he could quote them from memory.

By the fall of 1534, persecution back in Paris heated up once more, and this

---

35. See Gordon, *Calvin*, 37–38, who weighs the arguments for and against.

36. Lindberg believes there was yet another reason to assume Calvin was, by this time, making a clear shift toward the evangelical cause: "Calvin's conversion was publicly attested by his return to Noyon in May 1534 to surrender the ecclesiastical benefices he had held since he was twelve. Unlike many French reform-minded humanists who remained publicly in the Roman church, Calvin made a clean break." Lindberg, *European Reformations*, 252.

37. For details, see Beza, *Life of Calvin*, 16; Gordon, *Calvin*, 38.

38. Gordon, *Calvin*, 38.

time with vengeance due to the Placards Affair. Antoine Marcourt wrote and produced placards or tracts that condemned the Catholic Mass. Marcourt's evangelical commitments had received traction among the laity. On October 17, 1534, placards were distributed all over Paris. When Francis I woke up that morning, he was greeted by a placard on the door of his own room—and he was furious. Evangelicals found a way to disseminate their thought, which incensed the king. Furthermore, clearly the king's own court had been penetrated and was not safe. Francis's anger escalated further when a second round of placards appeared in January 1535. Evangelicals were hunted down and executed in the months that followed.[39] Francis used the opportunity to associate French patriotism with the Catholic religion, which did not bode well for the future of French evangelicalism.[40]

INCOGNITO

Did Calvin have a hand in the affair? Maybe not, but the persecution that followed did put him at risk by default, and he was forced to leave Paris yet again. He traveled back to Orléans, but to be safe Calvin adopted an alias (Martinus Lucianus) and joined his friend Louis du Tillet, and together they fled for Strasbourg. From Strasbourg Calvin journeyed all the way to Basel by the conclusion of 1534, now entering into Swiss territory.

Young Calvin's pilgrimages did not keep him from writing and publishing. For example, he set his aim on Michael Servetus and other like-minded Italians back in Paris. The Spanish humanist was a renaissance man, a doctor of medicine as well as a theologically minded scholar. However, the originality of Servetus's theology was not as well received as his advances in medicine. Servetus's theology was far more radical, even heretical, than anything the Reformers taught. For instance, Servetus taught everywhere he traveled that after death the soul does not go to heaven to be with Christ until the soul is reunited with the body in future resurrection. In the meantime, the soul sleeps, a belief condemned by the Fifth Lateran Council (1512–17).

Calvin wrote a book in opposition to this soul sleep doctrine called *Psychopannychia*, even though some of his friends, such as Wolfgang Capito, did not think the book should be published. To a Reformer from Strasbourg, Calvin's style of writing was far too polemical.[41] Calvin did, however, attempt to

39. Gordon makes two observations: (1) Those behind the placards were far more Zwinglian in their theology than Lutheran. (2) The placards distinguished two different reforming groups. "The circle around Marguerite of Navarre, men such as Gérard Roussel, continued to espouse an Erasmian ideal of reform from within the institution of the church. Fiercely opposed to this were those who rejected the Catholic church and its hierarchy and saw those who remained within it as traitors to the Gospel. The most prominent figure in this later group was Guillaume Farel, once a member of the Meaux Circle but now living in exile in the Swiss Confederation. Farel, Marcourt, and others had been radicalized by the persecution and oppression of the 1520s and early 1530s." Gordon, *Calvin*, 41–42.

40. "The heretics who had committed this despicable act were not France, he said. They were vile and had to be dealt with like a disease." Hillerbrand, *Division of Christendom*, 322.

41. Throughout the book, Calvin refuted the "Anabaptists," but Servetus was the prime target. Gordon, *Calvin*, 43. For Capito's letter, see Capito to Calvin, *CO* 10:45–46.

meet with Servetus to discuss the matter in person. That was a dangerous move on Calvin's part. He could be exposed and caught; he might be thrown into prison or worse. Nonetheless, in 1534 Calvin planned to meet Servetus anyway. He traveled from Saintonge to Paris, but Servetus never showed. Calvin departed in quiet and continued his plans to publish his book defending the immortality of the soul, refuting the Spaniard.[42] Despite this failed meeting, one day Calvin and Servetus would meet face-to-face under far more austere circumstances.

BASEL AND THE GENESIS OF CALVIN'S *INSTITUTES*

Did Calvin the pilgrim, an evangelical on the run, have any idea what he wanted out of his career, assuming he could find safe haven? He wanted a literary life for starters. And one with protection. But in light of the Placards Affair, that desire was not easy to fulfill. Basel was an option and quite a good one by the time Calvin arrived. It had a growing reputation for taking in a variety of humanists and evangelicals from other countries like France. Basel was in a position to do so since it had signed its name to the Protestant cause as early as 1529. That did not mean, however, that Basel was a beacon of unity. Rome considered Basel a sellout to Protestantism. Yet Basel did not approach reform like other cities, such as Zurich, for example. Basel did not intend to break its ties with the Holy Roman Empire, which created tension in the 1530s between Basel and Zwingli's Zurich (see chapter 12).[43]

Basel was home to both Reformers and humanists. In the 1520s and early 1530s, the major Reformer of Basel was Johannes Oecolampadius, and the city could boast it was home to Erasmus. Furthermore, Basel was home to some of the most ambitious and prestigious printing presses in all of Europe, producing not only Erasmus's *Adages* (1513) but his critical edition of patristic texts. Erasmus's work on the church fathers cannot be overemphasized; his editorial scholarship served as a bridge connecting humanists and Reformers alike to the world and theology of the church fathers.[44] Basel also was renowned for its translations of the Bible and Bible commentaries, and not just by Swiss but also French evangelicals such as Lefèvre d'Etaples.[45]

By the time Calvin arrived in Basel toward the end of 1534, he became the recipient of these and many other literary treasures. Moreover, since Basel was home to so many humanists and Reformers, Calvin had the opportunity to engage them directly, whether they be French, German, or Swiss. Many of

---

42. *CO* 5:165–232. However, *Psychopannychia's* importance lay not merely in its theology of the afterlife. The book speaks to the young Calvin's wider theological convictions.

43. Gordon, *Calvin*, 48, highlights some key differences between the two cities: "The ruling patrician class [in Basel] had kept a cool distance from both Zwingli and Zurich, who represented a fierce Swiss patriotism for which they had little taste. Unlike the other major Swiss cities of Zurich and Berne, Basel saw itself as close to the Holy Roman Empire, and it remained a free imperial city, meaning that its loyalty was to the emperor and that it was entitled to representation at imperial diets."

44. Calvin and Erasmus never crossed paths during Calvin's stay in Basel.

45. For an extensive survey of individuals, see Gordon, *Calvin*, 49–51.

these individuals—from an evangelical like Pierre Viret to a Hebrew scholar like Sebastian Münster—continued to correspond with Calvin long after he had left Basel. Some of them, however, would one day join Calvin's many nemeses, like Pierre Caroli, and turn against Calvin.[46]

Three key developments materialized while Calvin was in Basel. First, by 1534 and 1535, the debate over the Lord's Supper between the Lutherans and the Zwinglians had reached its summit, and theologians like Bucer and Melanchthon were straining to achieve a negotiated unity somehow. Doubtless, Calvin was an observer, reading and listening to each side of the debate, as well as the ongoing attempts to reach a compromise. This experience early in Calvin's career served him well in the decades to come since he would one day emerge with an explanation of the Lord's Supper that attempted to move beyond the deadlock. Also, Bucer's persistent efforts to negotiate unity were not lost on Calvin. "Like Bucer, Calvin came to believe that reconciliation was possible if the parties really wanted it. Martin Bucer, in his relentless pursuit of unity, became Calvin's model churchman, and the greatest influence on his formation as a minister and teacher."[47]

Second, Calvin became a public apologist for Bible translation. Over against Rome, which had a history of condemning translations in the vernacular, Calvin—much like Tyndale and Luther before him—saw the necessity of such a project, even if it was illegal. In that spirit, Calvin wrote two prefaces, one in Latin and the other in French, to the Serrières Bible, attributed to Calvin's cousin Pierre-Robert Olivétan.[48] Calvin argued that it was entirely Christian for God's Word to be put in the language of the people, ensuring that even the most common citizen could comprehend and embrace the gospel. To make such an argument, Calvin appealed to the church fathers. Not only did the Fathers translate the Bible so that those in their churches could read the Scriptures, but they, too, defended the same conviction, persuaded as they were that God himself intended his speech to be heard in all languages.[49]

Third, Basel provided Calvin with the opportunity to see through his first edition of his *Institutes of the Christian Religion*. Most likely Calvin started his *Institutes* in France. Between 1534 and 1535 he continued to perfect his *Institutes* in Basel.[50] The word *institute* should not be confused with an institution but has something more like "instruction" in view. Calvin's first edition of his *Institutes* was short, written to instruct the church in the core components of the Christian faith. He followed the pattern of a typical sixteenth-century catechism, teaching churchgoers according to the Apostles' Creed. Like other

46. Gordon, *Calvin*, 50.
47. Gordon, *Calvin*, 54.
48. On the quality of the translation and Calvin's opinion, see Gordon, *Calvin*, 55.
49. Gordon, *Calvin*, 55.
50. The evidence for this dating: "The last two parts of the *Institutes* argue most heavily in favour of this possibility, for here Calvin offered a vigorous defence of the evangelicals persecuted in the wake of the Placards Affair." Gordon, *Calvin*, 46.

catechisms, his *Institutes* focused on the purpose of the Ten Commandments and the sacraments, and also taught Christians how to pray (the Lord's Prayer). The *Institutes* were to be used as a manual, assisting every Christian with his or her beliefs and how to live according to those beliefs. Calvin was not merely concerned with Christian doctrine but Christian godliness, not only right belief but right practice.

The focus on right practice surfaces another motive. Calvin contrasted true worship and religion from false worship and religion. Without becoming overtly polemical, Calvin claimed that the evangelicals were the promoters of true worship over against idolatry. That was no small point since evangelicals in France were being persecuted even as Calvin wrote his *Institutes*. That was one reason why Calvin could no longer make his home in France.

To complicate matters further, evangelicals were sometimes associated with the Anabaptists. Guilt by association gave the French authorities the ammunition they needed to persecute French evangelicals. They were, so it was said, insurrectionists bent on rebellion. With such a misrepresentation for the sake of persecution, Calvin could not remain silent. He included at the start of his 1536 *Institutes* a letter to Francis I, making his apology for French evangelicals, correcting caricatures of insurrection, solidifying evangelicals as obedient citizens rather than political schismatics. Yes, evangelicals were after religious reform, but that did not mean they were radicals seeking societal revolution.[51] Calvin's training in law shined bright: the "letter is a defense attorney's masterpiece of vindication for French Protestantism, and clearly exhibited Calvin's leadership qualities to Protestants everywhere."[52] Additionally, Calvin argued that the evangelicals were not heretics, inventing some new doctrine as Rome claimed, but stood in continuity with the church catholic.[53]

Who influenced Calvin as he wrote his *Institutes*? After all, it was nothing short of impressive that a young man only twenty-five years old and lacking formal training in biblical studies and theology could draft such a well-articulated, theologically insightful, and historically minded expression of the Christian faith. In one sense, Calvin's genius should be credited to his own mind as well as the self-discipline he mastered. The combination of Calvin's training in law with his self-discipline to read the Fathers and the Bible, not to forget his skills in humanist literature and rhetoric (as the Seneca commentary revealed), all contributed to Calvin's lucid and profound articulation of the Christian religion. In another sense, Calvin had benefited from the writings of first-generation Reformers. Although he did not say so explicitly, Martin Luther's work had influenced him. Calvin's first edition of the *Institutes* mimics the overall structure and biblical and theological vision of Luther's small and

---

51. *CO* 31:23. To read an English translation of Calvin's 1536 edition, see John Calvin, *Institutes of the Christian Religion: 1536 Edition*.
52. Lindberg, *European Reformations*, 254.
53. Gordon, *Calvin*, 59.

large catechisms.[54] Moreover, Calvin's outline is uncanny in its resemblance to Peter Lombard's *Sentences*, yet another indication that Calvin was dependent on medieval Scholasticism (see chapter 3).

Furthermore, Calvin appeared to imitate the early Luther who appealed to the innocence of the pope. Rather than attacking Francis I, Calvin blamed those under his reign, informing Francis that they were polluting true religion. Calvin's rhetorical strategy reflected Seneca as well. Seneca made an apology to none other than Nero himself, only attributing fault to those under him who were undoing his kingdom. "Calvin had become Seneca, and Francis was his Nero."[55] Calvin hoped that if he utilized the same tools as Seneca, Francis might come to the aid of French evangelicals and relieve them of their oppression. If he was able to persuade Francis, Francis might turn from oppressing the evangelicals to establishing equity, the type of equity Seneca heralded when he advocated for fair laws and generous liberty.[56] Both in his preface and throughout, Calvin was mustering the tools of legal argument he had acquired during his training in law, but this time for the sake of the evangelical cause.[57]

The first edition of the *Institutes* released in 1536 and was well received. Although Calvin had already put himself forward as a theological scholar in *Psychopannychia*, and a polemical one at that, the *Institutes* established Calvin as a theologian *for the church*, one the church could look to for instruction in doctrine and piety, as well as guidance in the midst of the turbulent and unpredictable relations between church and temporal powers. In Calvin's mind, the 1536 edition of the *Institutes* truly was a first edition, which he intended to perfect and even enlarge, helping the church think through the Scriptures and their application in far more detail in the decades ahead.

THE PATH THROUGH GENEVA AND THE DISPUTATION OF LAUSANNE

Was Francis I persuaded by Calvin to accommodate French evangelicals? No. But he did relent for a temporary period for political reasons, permitting French evangelicals in exile to return under certain conditions. At war with Charles V, Francis I could not afford to alienate Protestant allies. Calvin did not know it at the time, but this amnesty afforded him some of his final opportunities to step foot on French soil.

In March 1536, Calvin returned to France. That was possible thanks to the Mandate of Coucy in 1535. After the Placards Affair, Francis may have wished to eliminate all French evangelicals. He executed those he believed were responsible for the Placards Affair. Nevertheless, he restrained himself so that he did not provoke the Smalcald League. Evangelicals imprisoned by Francis were set free

---

54. For Luther's influence on Calvin, see Lindberg, *European Reformations*, 254.
55. Gordon, *Calvin*, 58.
56. Gordon, *Calvin*, 61. Gordon notes the similarities here with Luther's *Freedom of a Christian*.
57. Gordon, *Calvin*, 60, believes Calvin put on his law hat against Rome as well.

when the king signed the mandate. As for French evangelicals who had fled the country, they were permitted to return. Whether Calvin realized it or not, this was a rare opportunity, one he would never have again once the window closed due to renewed suppression starting in 1539.

Calvin met with Renée, daughter of King Louis XII and a sympathizer with the Reformation cause. Renée could not be explicit about her faith, however, since her context was Catholic. But she could sneak in meetings with Reformers like Calvin if she was careful. Most likely, the meeting was arranged after Renée was inspired by Calvin's *Institutes*. All did not go as planned: during Calvin's visit the authorities discovered that Renée was hiding French Reformers in her own court at Ferrara.[58] Arrests followed. Was Calvin taken into custody? No one knows for sure. Either way, the French Reformers were released when Renée petitioned Francis I, her cousin.

Although Calvin's presence in the whole affair may be uncertain, the close call does reveal that Protestants were still not safe in France. France allowed Protestants across Europe to return to their mother country as long as they shortly thereafter returned to the mother church, Rome.[59] If not they then risked capture by the authorities. Calvin worked the system, visiting his family, but not for so long that he put himself in danger.

In 1536, Calvin, his half sister Marie, and his brother Antoine decided it was time to leave France. Calvin assisted his siblings, and the family left France for the very last time. His plan: head to Swiss territory where he could pursue his scholarly ambitions. But he could not take his usual course due to the ongoing conflict between Francis I and Charles V. Instead, Calvin was forced to take an alternate route through Lake Léman. When he feared for his safety, he often adopted an alias, though other Reformers discovered John Calvin was in town, including Guillaume Farel (1489–1565).

Farel had a history of starting reformations in Swiss cities, especially those with French evangelical refugees. The man's approach was direct and often militant. Consider, for example, Farel's reforming measures in Neuchâtel: he condemned Rome from pulpits, calling Rome's doctrines and practices out as nothing less than idolatry. His rhetoric was also iconoclastic in nature and on not a few occasions ignited the destruction of images in churches. His forceful success should not be credited to him alone; other evangelicals like Pierre Viret helped Farel, as did willing printers, enabling Farel to spread propaganda with expediency.[60] He also had the military support of Berne, which was just as important as he entered into Swiss cities with French-speaking Catholics on one side and French-speaking evangelicals on the other.[61] Today a statue of Farel

---

58. Gordon, *Calvin*, 63, notes that some of these individuals had a hand in the Placards Affair (1534).
59. See the Edict of Coucy (1535).
60. E.g., Pierre de Vingle. See Gordon, *Calvin*, 66.
61. Although Gordon, *Calvin*, 66, qualifies that the evangelicals were the minority.

stands tall in Neuchâtel, portraying a bold individual holding the Bible above his head for all to see.

When Farel came to Geneva in 1532, he implemented a similar strategy to turn Geneva into a Reformation city. Four years later, the Bernese were on the move, conquering and acquiring territories as they approached Lake Léman. Geneva did not have a large military; surrounded as they were by so many other cities, they needed the Bernese as allies, even if they were intent on retaining the independence of Geneva long term. Nevertheless, politics and religion did not always agree. Political power may have shifted to Reformed-minded powers like the Bernese, but the hearts of the French-speaking people across Switzerland still had an allegiance to Rome. In such cases, the Bernese could not rely on mere persuasion. Farel, with his imposing strategy, was just the right match.

However, Farel needed others to join his reforming efforts in Geneva, and who better than the up-and-coming author of the *Institutes*? During a July night in 1536, Calvin stayed at Lake Léman, and Farel found out and met with Calvin, telling him that if he did not stay and teach in Geneva, God would curse all his writings. In his Psalms commentary, Calvin reflected on that encounter, an encounter he considered providential. "Farel, who burned with an extraordinary zeal to advance the Gospel, immediately strained every nerve to detain me. And after having learned that my heart was set on devoting myself to private studies, for which I wished to keep myself free from other pursuits, and finding that he gained nothing by entreaties, he proceeded to utter a threat that God would curse my retirement, and the tranquility of the studies which I sought, if I should withdraw and refuse to give assistance, when the necessity was so urgent." Calvin's response revealed a total change in disposition. "I was so struck with fear by this threat that I desisted from the journey which I had undertaken. . . ." Although Calvin gave in and promised to be of service in Geneva, he did not intend to become a pastor. Calvin said, "[I was] mindful of my natural bashfulness and timidity," and therefore decided "I would not bring myself under any obligation to discharge any particular office."[62] Calvin knew himself all too well. His personality was a fit for the quiet life of a scholar, not the public life of a churchman, which is why he at first refused Farel's invitation. Nevertheless, Calvin acquiesced and agreed to stay, believing the voice that threatened to curse his plans was none other than God's.

Calvin's decision to stay in Geneva was a turning point. Despite his disposition, Calvin was content (eventually) to become a churchman. That did not mean he left behind his scholarly acumen. Quite the opposite: he used his skills for the sake of the church. Not long after committing to stay in Geneva, for example, he contributed to a disputation in Lausanne initiated by the Bernese in an attempt to win Swiss territories over to the Reformation. Still in his late

---

62. *CO* 31:23–25.

twenties, young Calvin advanced the Reformation argument by quoting from the church fathers to clarify and defend an evangelical (versus Roman) view of the Lord's Supper.[63] He was not reading from the Fathers when he did so either—by recollection alone he reached deep into his past studies of the Fathers to solicit the church catholic to his side.

The Bernese may have won the disputation and issued formal changes to renovate the look and practices of the church, but that formality did not mean that a heart change had occurred within the people.[64] They conformed on the outside, but that did not mean they had given themselves over in their convictions. If history had taught them anything, it was this: wait, and before long the Catholic Church will return.

THE ORGANIZATION OF A REFORMED CHURCH

The relationship between the Genevans and the Bernese was complicated. The Genevans had been liberated by the Bernese. The House of Savoy was sandwiched between Italy and France and had significant political control in Geneva thanks to Savoy's ruler, who acted as both prince and bishop.[65] The House of Savoy grew nervous when they worried Geneva might follow the lead of Lausanne, who aligned with Protestant Berne. They were right to be worried; in 1526 Genevans linked arms with Berne (as well as Fribourg), which then strengthened the growing Swiss Confederacy. Geneva then set itself to the task of reconfiguring its government. In time the Genevan government consisted of three branches: (1) the Small Council (Petit Counsel), (2) the Council of Two Hundred, and (3) the General Assembly. Out of these three the Small Council had significant authority over the church. Within the Small Council, four magistrates (syndics) could decide who should be appointed or disposed as a minister in a Genevan church.[66]

Savoy, however, was not going to lose Geneva without a fight. In 1530 Savoy and Geneva went to war, but Savoy could not overcome Geneva once Geneva's allies—Berne and Fribourg—entered the conflict. With the threat of Savoy dissipating, the question remained: Would Geneva tailor its religious life in the fold of Fribourg, committed as Fribourg was to the papacy, or would Geneva instead align with Protestant Berne? In the years that followed, a fierce inner conflict ensued.[67] At the head of the Protestant cause was Farel, and in 1535 and 1536 the Council of Two Hundred took official steps to institute Protestant beliefs and

---

63. Gordon, *Calvin*, 66–67, qualifies that the disputation was not really a debate that could go either way; the Bernese had the upper hand from the start.

64. Gordon, *Calvin*, 67–68, reports that only two hundred priests converted, and in Lausanne Catholic customs continued as before.

65. Lindberg believes the connection was so close that this prince-bishop was "little more than an extension of the House of Savoy." Lindberg, *European Reformations*, 255.

66. For an overview of each, see Gordon, *Calvin*, 69.

67. For example, consider the conflict between the bishop and the Deux Cents in 1534. Tuininga, *Calvin's Political Theology and the Public Engagement of the Church*, 63.

practices.[68] Clergy still allegiant to the papacy were exiled, the Mass was abrogated, and icons promoting superstition or cultivating idolatry were removed.

Nevertheless, the Genevans—thankful as they were for Bernese assistance—did not desire freedom from Savoy only to be enslaved by Berne. Geneva was suspicious of attempts to situate a new ruler as both prince and bishop, even if a Protestant one. Geneva was determined to dispose the prince-bishop model. By August 1536, Geneva acquired the independence it desired all along. Berne remained a key and no doubt influential ally, but Geneva was accountable to its own people for once.[69] Nevertheless, like Berne, Geneva decided for the Protestant Reformation and with its newfound independence had to determine how evangelical principles should be fostered in church and society.

However, outward conformity did not necessarily translate into inward conviction. Calvin knew not to confuse exterior cooperation with heartfelt devotion. Like other cities under the eye of the Bernese, Geneva conformed, but many of its twelve thousand plus inhabitants were anything but enthusiastic toward the evangelical faith. Calvin understood that lasting reform could only grow permanent roots if the Holy Spirit worked on the heart through the preaching and implementation of the Word.

Since Calvin had not committed to becoming a permanent minister who preached the Scriptures, he was content to begin with teaching. In the fall of 1536, Calvin taught Paul's letter to the Romans in Saint-Pierre. Although the cathedral was less than half a mile from Lake Geneva's natural beauty, the church was surrounded by urban life. Stemming from Lake Geneva, the River Rhône divided the city into two parts: the north was home to St. Gervais and the south home to St. Germain Madeleine and St. Pierre. City hall, the hospital, and the prison all circled St. Pierre.

If Calvin was attuned to initial impressions, then he may have noticed that he was not liked by the magistrates of Geneva. He was considered an outsider, a foreigner from France, someone unacquainted with their customs and values. Nevertheless, his biblical and theological skills were second to none, especially since the average Genevan had no ability to read the Bible in the original languages. In 1537 Calvin transitioned from only teaching small groups to preaching from the pulpit of St. Pierre.

However, Calvin was not as experienced as Farel in restructuring legislation and liturgy, at least not at first.[70] It made sense then for Farel to take the lead; he was, after all, seasoned in the art of removing remnants of Rome to make way for future reform. The church, for example, needed new articles that outlined aspects of ecclesiology, such as how church discipline should work, how Christians should approach the Lord's Supper, and what format the liturgy

---

68. On how Farel accomplished such a feat, see Gordon, *Calvin*, 69–70, and his discussion of the Eidguenots (Les enfants). Gordon engages de Jussie, *Short Chronicle*, 128.

69. Lindberg, *European Reformations*, 256.

70. Consider Farel's *Summaire* (1529) and *Manière et fasson*. Gordon, *Calvin*, 72.

should take. The result: the *Articles concerning the Organization of the Church* (1537). These articles were a joint effort by the pastors, but they were also a hall-mark of Farel's efforts.[71]

TO BE REFORMED: THE *GENEVA CONFESSION* AND *GENEVA CATECHISM*

If Farel governed the *Geneva Articles*, Calvin crafted the *Geneva Confession* (1536) and *Geneva Catechism* (1537). The confession was indebted in many ways to the first edition of Calvin's *Institutes*. The confession was brief—only twenty-one short articles, each only a paragraph long—and although it did begin with a statement about God, most of it was oriented toward the believer's comfort in the God who saves.[72] In other words, the confession was soteriological in focus, positioning itself as a teacher of Protestant principles.

The doctrine of justification, therefore, occupied immediate attention as the confession transitioned from man's condemnation to his desperate need for the intercession of Jesus. For "by his righteousness and innocence we have remission of our sins.... And so we ought always to look for our righteousness in Jesus Christ and not at all in ourselves, and rest in him, and be assured, attributing nothing to our works."[73] Calvin's christological bedrock—*solus Christus*—impeded Rome's accretions, from the intercession of the saints to the seven sacraments to the "idolatry" of the Mass as a "sacrifice for the redemption of souls."[74]

Calvin's polemical language in the confession conveyed his uncompromising stance against Rome. He called to account her "execrable blasphemies and super-stitions" (e.g., pilgrimages, monasteries, prohibition of marriage, confessions), and when he considered her ecclesiology, he questioned her allegiance. "Hence the churches governed by the ordinances of the pope are rather synagogues of the devil than Christian churches."[75]

As for the Geneva Catechism, its questions and answers paralleled the mate-rial in the confession. Calvin first published a French edition of his catechism in 1537, followed by a Latin edition in 1538, but when he was invited back to Geneva after banishment, he used his original work to launch a more elaborate catechism in 1541.[76] The original editions of Calvin's catechisms (1537/1538) were influential for his *Institutes*, both his second edition (1539) and his French edition (1541). The catechism—incorporating Protestant theology alongside

---

71. Gordon, *Calvin*, 72, makes a case for Farel as main author, depending on the work of Frans Pieter van Stam, "Die Genfer Artikel vom Januar 1537: Aus Calvins oder Farels Feder?" *Zwingliana* 27 (2000): 87–101. Gordon also believes the document reveals the different roles of Calvin and Farel: "Farel was the oppositional prophet, while Calvin tended towards the building of the church."

72. *CCFCT* 2:313–19.

73. *CCFCT* 2:314, 315 (art. 7, 9).

74. *CCFCT* 2:316–17 (art. 16).

75. *CCFCT* 2:317 (art. 17, 18).

76. *CCFCT* 2:320–63; cf. Hesselink, *Calvin's First Catechism*.

traditional elements, from the Apostles' Creed to the Ten Commandments—became instrumental in the life of the Genevans.

Calvin was a second-generation Reformer; nevertheless, his confession and catechism were born early in the development of Reformed confessionalism. Six years prior to Calvin's confession, the Lutherans established themselves with the *Augsburg Confession* (1530), and by 1577 the Formula of Concord formed its wider foundation. Early in the life of the Reformation, the Lutherans and their confessions were called *reformed*, a label that set them in contrast to Rome. However, as Zwingli, Bullinger, and Calvin wrote confessions that not only distinguished their churches from Rome but from the Lutherans (on the Lord's Supper, for example), these confessions were labeled *Reformed*.[77] The label, however, was not primarily polemical in nature. As Pelikan observed, "These confessions and churches were to be defined not negatively as 'non-Lutheran' but positively as 'Reformed in accordance with the word of God [*nach Gottes Wort reformiert*].'"[78]

Both Calvin's confession and catechism posed questions and provided answers that educated the laity but most importantly marked off their *Reformed* identity in distinction from Rome—*nach Gottes Wort reformiert*. As the Caroli affair demonstrated soon enough, that identity became the dividing line.

VIRET, FAREL, AND CALVIN, HERETICS? THE CAROLI AFFAIR

The authority of the Bernese had so far worked in favor of Farel and Calvin. That changed when the Bernes decided Pierre Caroli should be chief preacher in Lausanne. Caroli was not the man Farel and Calvin wanted. Farel wanted his student, Viret, instead. They did not trust Caroli; one minute he appeared dedicated to the Reformation, and the next he seemed to pedal backward to Rome. Farel and Calvin's suspicions were not unwarranted. As the new chief preacher, Caroli launched his ministry by permitting and even encouraging his congregation to pray for their deceased loved ones. Praying for the dead sounded like capitulation to Rome in the estimation of Viret, Farel, and Calvin, and it was not long before Viret responded with a rebuke.

But Caroli had a reaction of his own: Viret, Farel, and Calvin were closet Arians. After all, Calvin's *Institutes* said little to nothing about the Trinity. The accusation stuck just enough so that Viret, Farel, and Calvin had the burden of proving to the Bernese that they were orthodox, a burden heavy enough to occupy their attention in 1537 with numerous meetings and letters. Calvin's knowledge of the Scriptures and his familiarity with the church fathers came to his aid once more.

Calvin did not believe, however, that the issue with Caroli was merely theological. In his opinion, Caroli was lusting after fame, pushing the doctrinal boundaries

---

77. *CCFCT*, 205.
78. *CCFCT*, 205.

676 *The Formation of Reformed Catholicity*

of Protestantism to get noticed, lobbing heretical accusations to steal a following that otherwise belonged to Viret, Farel, and Calvin. To make matters worse, Caroli was arduous to talk with, losing his temper when the conversation turned disagreeable and incapable of cooperating to meet a resolution. Negotiation was out of the question; the only solution was to meet force with force.[79]

In the end, the Geneva ministers were not persuaded by Caroli's heresy accusation but concluded that Viret, Farel, and Calvin were faithful to orthodox Trinitarianism. That conclusion did not work in favor of Caroli; his days as chief preacher in Lausanne were over. Still, Caroli had unleashed a report that threw the orthodoxy of Viret, Farel, and especially Calvin into question, and in the weeks and months ahead these Reformers labored to no end to squash misrepresentation across Europe. The reputation of individuals like Calvin was not the only or even the main reason for correcting the damage Caroli had unleashed. More and more, Calvin (along with others) now represented Protestantism in Geneva. He was not just clearing his name but Geneva's name, lest it come under scrutiny from older brother Burne. The Caroli affair reveals the quick-moving pace of sixteenth-century doctrinal controversies, as well as the relational fluidity and fragility between Reformers. The Caroli affair also conveys just how reliant ministers were on their good standing with magistrates, either local or foreign. The need for Viret, Farel, and Calvin to explain themselves to the Bernese authorities demonstrated how contingent the church could be on civil powers.

That contingency manifested itself in the most painful way when Farel and Calvin were kicked out of Geneva just as their reforming program was preparing to take off.

EXPELLED FROM GENEVA: DISCIPLINE, AUTONOMY, AND TWO KINGDOMS

Calvin started his theological career on a polemical note with *Psychopannychia*. Then he transitioned to a didactic style with the *Institutes*, a manual for Protestants structured on the Creed, accessible due to its literary lucidity and catechetical purpose. At the start of 1537, Calvin returned to polemics with *Epistolae*

---

79. "Demonstrating a remarkable insensitivity to the nature of the Bernese church, which was under the firm control of the council, Calvin told Megander not to wait for the magistrates to act, but to take matters into his own hands." Gordon, *Calvin*, 73. Gordon believes the Caroli-Calvin affair was Calvin's attempt at character assassination, as seen in his letter to Kaspar Megander and Heinrich Bullinger concerning Caroli. Gordon may be right; at the same time, it is possible that Caroli did live up to his reputation, giving Viret, Farel, and Calvin plenty of ammunition. For the letter, see Calvin to Megander, February 1537, *CO* 10:85–87; Bonnet, 1:25, as well as Calvin's letter to Grynaeus, *CO* 10:106–9; Bonnet, 1:32. Regardless, the years ahead did reveal Calvin's struggle with pride. See Calvin's letter to Bucer, January 1538, *CO* 10:137–44; and Gordon, *Calvin*, 75–76, on Calvin's relationships with other Reformers. In 1539 Caroli sought reconciliation, and other Reformers were receptive. Calvin's temper flared; Caroli could not possibly be recalcitrant. Calvin also became bitter toward the Reformers who had embraced Caroli irrespective of Calvin's opinions. But even Farel thought Calvin had become too headstrong. Later Calvin admitted that he had sinned in his outrage, although he remained convinced the right approach to Caroli had not been taken. Gordon captured the struggle within Calvin "between his passions, over which he could lose control, and his intellect, of which he entertained few doubts" (91). Bucer was the one to calm Calvin down. For Calvin's apology, see Calvin to Farel, October 8, 1539, *CO* 10:396–400.

duae, originally a set of lectures that took aim and fired at anyone who was not bold enough to depart from Rome. Previously, Calvin came face-to-face with individuals who were Protestants but nevertheless had to navigate carefully either their ecclesiastical or political positions due to ties with Rome.[80] Calvin himself had to navigate the complications of a Protestant identity within Catholic territory prior to his pilgrimage to Geneva, even if he was not yet in a public office.

By 1537, however, Calvin was convinced Protestants must make a clean and total break with Rome. Not to do so was nothing short of compromise. Rome was a factory of idolatry, said Calvin; to stay under its wings could only pollute the Christian and the church. A refusal to leave could only be interpreted as an approval of Rome's wickedness. A refusal to leave, warned Calvin, is the sign of vain thinking, as if Rome could somehow still be reformed from within. Yet what made the *Epistolae duae* so piercing was its intimate nature. The *Epistolae* consisted of letters written in response to former friends. One was Duhemin and the other was Gérard Roussel. To the former, Calvin condemned Rome. To the latter, Calvin condemned Roussel himself for becoming a bishop.[81]

At the end of 1537 and the start of 1538, Farel and Calvin's vocal, polemical disposition worked against them. In Calvin's *Geneva Confession*, he said that all citizens should take an oath. Before they can take the Lord's Supper, they must take an oath of allegiance to the confession. Calvin was not merely concerned with theological fidelity, but he desired a mechanism by which he and Farel, as pastors, could exercise discipline in the church. The oath was a way to keep those not serious about their sin from violating the Lord's Table.[82]

Calvin and Farel were denied these petitions. Discipline, excommunication of dissenters in particular, was a power that belonged to the magistrates. Under the surface there may have been deeper reasons. For example, the magistrates were Genevans; Calvin and Farel were not. To submit themselves to an oath let alone an excommunication implemented by the authority of a foreign figure was unthinkable. Many other Genevans shared this sentiment. Additionally, the Genevan magistrates still had the bitter taste of Savoy's prince-bishop in their mouths.[83] Furthermore, Geneva may be independent of Berne, but conformity to Berne—where magistrates possessed such authority in ecclesiastical matters— was critical to Geneva's future compatibility and independence from Berne.[84]

---

80. Renée, the daughter of King Louis XII, is but one example.

81. For the letters, see *Johannes Calvini, Opera Selecta*, 1:290ff. Gordon adds, "Calvin's two letters were written as he was involved in the publication of the records of the Lausanne Disputation.... He had come to share Farel's assessment of the Navarrists, those around Queen Marguerite, as a spent force from which nothing could be expected. They had traded the faith for high office in the church, and this was beneath contempt." Gordon, *Calvin*, 78.

82. Other petitions were also made. For example, Calvin asked for regular celebration of the Lord's Supper but this, too, was denied. The council sided with a quarterly practice instead.

83. "The town had not gotten rid of a Catholic prince-bishop in order to replace him with Protestant ones!" Lindberg, *European Reformations*, 257.

84. "Calvin saw the crisis in terms of pastoral freedom; the Genevan authorities saw it in terms of independence from Bernese interference. 'It was in the interests of Geneva to appease and conform to Berne in as

Whatever the underlying motive(s), Farel and Calvin read the restriction as a threat to their pastoral authority and responsibility. They expected magistrates to support the Reformation cause and even punish opponents, but that did not give magistrates a license to impede pastoral authority on a matter as spiritual and ecclesial as excommunication.

Farel and Calvin were handicapped further when the elections in February 1538 positioned syndics intolerant toward the French pastors. The next month the conflict escalated when Farel and Calvin were prohibited from using leavened bread at the Lord's Table. Leavened or unleavened, the real issue for Farel and Calvin was authority and autonomy: as pastors they were at the mercy of the magistrates *in their own churches*. The lack of autonomy also involved the explosive tension over Bernese control. "When the council ordered the pastors to reintroduce Bernese practices with respect to the Lord's Supper, baptism, and feast days, Farel and Calvin preached sermons denouncing the council's actions, Calvin referring to it as a 'council of the devil.'"[85]

The conflict erupted on Easter Sunday. Farel and Calvin decided beforehand that the magistrates should not dictate their pastoral responsibilities. To send that message, on Sunday morning they both barred their congregations from approaching the table. And out of all Sundays of the year, it was Easter Sunday. Without swearing an oath to the confession, no one could approach the table. The message was received, but the magistrates sent a message of their own in return: Farel and Calvin were finished. They were to pack their belongings and leave Geneva post haste.[86]

The conflict revealed a major difference in political theology. Calvin's two-kingdoms doctrine was mentioned in his first edition of his *Institutes*, prior to coming to Geneva. He may not have handled the conflict with patience; Martin Bucer was inclined toward Calvin's political theology, but even he did not think Calvin reacted well. Regardless, Calvin was at a crisis point because his understanding of magistrate and minister did not match that of the authorities of Geneva. Although he assumed magistrates should endorse a Reformation church, the church itself, and its ministers in particular, possessed a God-ordained independence. "At the heart of the problem was Calvin's desire to establish a relatively autonomous church *distinct*—though *not separate*—from the commonwealth."[87]

Distinct but not separate—that balance was ideal but difficult to achieve in the sixteenth century. As Luther's struggles indicated (see chapters 9–11),

many ways as possible in order to guarantee Bernese military support and to remove or reduce possible points of conflict while maintaining a maximum amount of internal independence" (Naphy 1994: 26)." Lindberg, 257.

85. "The council responded by forbidding the pastors to preach on political matters and informing them that their continued ministry in Geneva would require them to conform to Berne's demands. Yet Calvin and Farel were insistent that the magistrates did not have the authority to dictate church practice." Tuininga, *Calvin's Political Theology and the Public Engagement of the Church*, 65.

86. For a more extensive account, see Gordon, *Calvin*, 70–80.

87. Tuininga, *Calvin's Political Theology and the Public Engagement of the Church*, 65.

introducing a two-kingdom political theology felt most consistent with Scripture. However, in the sixteenth century it took enormous ingenuity to pioneer a political-ecclesiastical system that preserved the independence of clerical authority and still garnered the support of the magistrates. Luther grew frustrated and never ceased admonishing the magistrates when he felt the ecclesiastical line was crossed. The same can be said of Calvin, even after 1555, when he finally achieved a formal arrangement.

CALVIN AT THE FEET OF MARTIN BUCER: STRASBOURG AND FRENCH REFUGEES

Exiled from Geneva, Calvin and Farel did not receive a favorable reputation in the Reformation territories they encountered next, such as Berne. Although the two Reformers told their side of the story, many perceived them to be divisive, stirring up schism and creating division within the Protestant church. Since the Protestant church was just beginning, divisiveness was a great sin, one that played into the hands of Roman opponents. Or at best, Farel and Calvin had rushed in headlong and headstrong. Even other Reformers, such as Heinrich Bullinger and Martin Bucer, for example, grew frustrated and took the opportunity to admonish Farel and Calvin.[88] Divisiveness then exile? While Farel had made a career out of such tactics, Calvin had not, and he now had to consider whether this was the type of career he wanted to pursue moving forward.

Calvin spent the summer of 1538 in Basel and Strasbourg writing letter after letter to other Reformers, attempting to resurrect his reputation and his intentions back in Geneva.[89] Farel left Calvin to minister in another church, and Bucer believed that was for the better. Farel and Calvin should not team up again going forward, said Bucer. That advice put Calvin in the awkward position of considering whether he had a future and, if so, where. As long as Farel did not follow, Bucer invited Calvin to Strasbourg. The exile from Geneva, the ongoing criticisms from other Reformers, and the uncertainty of his future all added up, and the sheer weight started to crush Calvin. Calvin was not the same person as before; his confidence was shaken, and he was exhausted, which affected not only his health but his mind.[90] Perhaps Calvin's pastoral career was destined to come to an abrupt, premature end.

Calvin was saved from such a fate by virtue of his location: Strasbourg. To be more precise, he was saved by his proximity to one of the sixteenth century's most accomplished churchmen, Martin Bucer. Despite whatever admonition Calvin received from Bucer, the Strasbourg Reformer was adamant Calvin not just do anything or go anywhere: "Don't think that you can leave the ministry even for a short time without offending God, if another ministry is offered you."[91]

---

88. *CO* 10:195.
89. *CO* 10:200; Bonnet, 1:45; *CO* 10:220–21; Bonnet, 1:48–49.
90. On Calvin's suffering pride and fluctuating emotional state during this time, see Gordon, *Calvin*, 84.
91. As quoted in Bouwsma, *John Calvin*, 21–22; and Lindberg, *European Reformations*, 258.

The ministry offered to Calvin was none other than Bucer's own ecclesiastical context. As with Farel, Calvin humbled himself under Bucer's prophet-like threat.

With no formal ministry experience, Calvin had crashed and burned in Geneva. Now he had a unique opportunity to watch Bucer conduct the church as if it were his symphony, while practicing his own ministry under Bucer's guidance. Bucer took the initiative, seeing the potential in Calvin but also the potential benefit Calvin could be to the church once the bruised exile was reinvigorated by his training and sent out to begin again.

Starting in the fall of 1538, Calvin began preaching, leading liturgy, and overseeing access to the table among the French refugees in Strasbourg, all under Bucer's vision. Calvin also lectured in the academy.[92] These years in pastoral ministry proved inestimable. Calvin developed not only pastoral instincts but the type of rigorous routine that later made him so productive. Most importantly, he developed these skills and habits under the more seasoned supervision of Bucer and a number of other experienced churchmen. Calvin was no longer an individual on a mission to reform but was grafted into the reforming movement, imbibing its technique for the sake of pastoral longevity. In time these mentors turned into friends. Yet none of them was as important as Bucer. The man became Calvin's spiritual father. Bucer lived life with Calvin, becoming his neighbor, answering Calvin's questions late into the night, all because Bucer believed Calvin possessed something that could be a gift to the church. Despite all of Calvin's prior failings and flaws, Bucer loved Calvin like a son.[93]

Ministering to a French refugee church in Strasbourg also gave Calvin an opportunity to, in some degree, try out his two-kingdom theology. His two-kingdom outlook was already articulated in brief when he wrote the 1536 edition of his *Institutes*. In 1537 and 1538, Geneva was not open to Calvin's vision for the relationship between minister and magistrate. However, Strasbourg afforded Calvin the opportunity to explore what it might look like. With the bitter taste of Geneva still lingering in his mouth, Calvin departed from the Swiss model—as seen, for example, in Zurich—which conflated temporal and spiritual authorities. In Strasbourg, Calvin returned to the Scriptures, all the more convinced the magistrate should not be positioned within the church, as if another office.[94]

---

92. "Now he was also able to implement the church discipline he had proposed in Geneva: in the French church, admission to communion was only for those who presented themselves to the ministers for examination. The question of discipline in Strasbourg was deeply divisive as Bucer struggled for the institution of a rigorous system independent of the magistrates in which the church would have a free hand in the use of excommunication. Although he failed, and discipline remained in the grip of the magistrates, the experience taught Calvin much about the delicate balances to be maintained in dealing with temporal authorities." Gordon, *Calvin*, 86.

93. Gordon, *Calvin*, 88–90, does a superb job of bringing Calvin's relationship with Bucer into the open. Gordon points to Farel's letter to Calvin as confirmation of Bucer's affection for Calvin: May 25, 1551, in Smith, "Some Old Unpublished Letters," 212.

94. To explore Calvin's exegesis, see Tuininga, *Calvin's Political Theology and the Public Engagement of the Church*, 66–68.

While in Strasbourg Calvin also decided on four types of offices that should define a Reformed polity. These four offices matured as they were situated within Calvin's fully operating ecclesiastical vision (one that later involved a Company of Pastors, an academy, and a consistory).

1. *Teacher/doctors:* an instructional role in the church, teaching theology to laymen but also to pastoral interns within the academy.
2. *Pastor:* a preaching position that involved exposition in the pulpit and oversight of the Lord's Supper. Pastors were chosen by the Company of Pastors.
3. *Elder:* a disciplinary role that involved reproving and rectifying the wayward; also a role that involved general supervision of the people of God, a cultivation of spiritual care.
4. *Deacon:* Calvin envisioned two types, procurators and hospitallers. The former looked out for the needs of the poor while the latter cared for the sick.

These four were not entirely original to Calvin. Bucer also outlined these offices. However, Calvin gave each a biblical and theological rational, a lacuna yet to be filled by a Reformer. Calvin's robust exegetical defense showed itself in 1540 when his Romans commentary was published, and his theological logic manifested itself when he elaborated on these offices in future editions of his *Institutes.*[95]

THE DIVIDE OVER UNITY: BUCER AND CALVIN'S ECUMENICAL DIFFERENCES

The years 1539 and 1540 were a hinge in the life of Calvin, granting his reputation new life. Calvin, whose name was synonymous with division back in Geneva, became a peacemaker, consumed with the possibility of unity between the Germans and the Swiss. He grew optimistic that unity over the Lord's Supper might just be possible. In 1539 he traveled all over, from the Leipzig Disputation to the Smalcald League. The latter put him in touch with Melanchthon in person, although the meeting may have been more important to Calvin than Melanchthon. In years past, Calvin did not have a positive impression of the German Reformers. That changed when he spent time with Melanchthon. Although Melanchthon did not respond with support when Calvin shared his approach to church discipline, and although Melanchthon was not persuaded to use Calvin's theses on the Lord's Supper for negotiations with the Swiss, nevertheless, Calvin found Melanchthon's cooperative disposition encouraging. With Melanchthon the Germans and Swiss might overcome the impasse. The next year, 1540, Calvin put his support behind Melanchthon's revision of the

---

95. Tuininga, 68–69.

Augsburg Confession.[96] With time, however, Calvin came to see that unity was slow going. With every step forward, there were two steps back, a reality that frustrated Calvin.

Calvin's ecumenical efforts with other Reformers were a real possibility, but Calvin did not have the same high opinion of Protestant negotiations with Rome. He became convinced that unity with Rome was an impossibility, a fool's errand. In the years 1539–40, Calvin's hatred for Rome grew by the day. Luther had read Calvin's response to Sadoleto and sent him a letter in 1539 telling him so, which encouraged Calvin. The next year Calvin traveled to Worms where he defended the evangelical doctrine of justification over against Roman apologists.[97]

Bucer, by contrast, took the opposite approach, negotiating with Roman theologians. He interpreted any sign of sympathy for the Reformation doctrine or its ecclesiastical reform as an opportunity for renewed unity. Calvin worried, and was all but convinced, that Bucer's approach could compromise key components of the Reformed faith. Furthermore, Calvin was not persuaded that Rome would shift as far as the evangelicals desired. Calvin favored unity, but a unity among Reformers, not a unity with Rome. The latter was a lost cause, and he grew fatigued at Bucer's optimism. Calvin had learned much at the feet of Bucer, but negotiating with Rome was not how Calvin intended to lead the church, he was sure of that. The colloquy at Regensburg at the start of the next year (1541) only confirmed Calvin's suspicions and convinced him all the more that unity with Rome was Counter-Reformational, a dead end.[98]

Strasbourg, and Bucer in particular, had resurrected Calvin after a humiliating and possibly career-ending exile. Strasbourg had repositioned Calvin, thrusting him onto the international stage with other Reformers, giving him the opportunity to regain respect. And, perhaps most importantly, Strasbourg had exposed Calvin's own struggles—his hot temper, for example—but always with a safety net (i.e., Martin Bucer) capable of catching Calvin if he fell. Bucer taught Calvin how to become a churchman who could survive the fires of ministry without losing his cool or his integrity. But now, disheartened by Strasbourg's ecumenical optimism, perhaps it was time for Calvin to move on.

THE EVOLUTION OF THE *INSTITUTES*

In retrospect, Calvin called his time in Strasbourg (1538–41)—short as it may have been—the best time of his life. It was certainly one of the most fruitful,

---

96. The *Augsburg Confession* was published in 1530, revised in 1540 by Melanchthon. Calvin added his signature to the Variata. Calvin's support toward the Germans continued in the summer of 1540 at Hagenau; see Gordon, *Calvin*, 99.

97. "Before leaving for Worms, Calvin had engaged in a disputation in Strasbourg with the dean of Passau cathedral, Ruprecht Mosheim, on the subject of justification. . . . When Calvin demolished Mosheim once more at Worms Melanchthon was duly impressed." Gordon, *Calvin*, 100.

98. See Lindberg, *European Reformations*, 258–59, 272–73, for Calvin's international and "catholic" endeavors.

both in terms of Calvin's growing reputation as an international ecumenicist and as a maturing theologian and biblical commentator.[99]

For example, the publishing success of the 1536 *Institutes* had put Calvin on the map. The accomplishment—considering how it matured in the decades to come—was promising considering Calvin never received the formal theological training in medieval theology like other Reformed luminaries like Peter Martyr Vermigli.[100] Despite the reception of the 1536 edition Calvin soon grew discontent with the structure of his *Institutes*. Also, Calvin had left out a host of doctrines that were essential to the Christian faith, from predestination to excommunication, yet another reason for dissatisfaction. The 1536 *Institutes* served an important purpose, catechizing Christians in the church. Yet as Calvin matured in his theological thinking, he looked to expand his *Institutes* as an introductory manual outlining doctrine for those training as pastors of the church. If done right, perhaps a second edition could assist pastors with the doctrinal conclusions they drew from Scripture.[101]

Calvin was not the first to attempt such a manual of the Christian religion, or multiple editions, each one attempting to improve on the last. In Wittenberg Philip Melanchthon had written his *Loci Communes* ("Common Places"). If Luther was the polemicist, taking apart Rome's defense one brick at a time, Melanchthon was the architect, rebuilding the church one doctrine at a time. When Calvin published his first edition of the *Institutes* (1536), Melanchthon published his second edition of his *Loci Communes*.[102] And by the time Calvin published his second edition of the *Institutes* (1539), he had learned a great deal from Melanchthon's example. The apostle Paul's theology of justification in Romans was central to Luther's reformation breakthrough, and its structure proved just as formative to Melanchthon's *Loci Communes*. Calvin followed suit.[103] Paul's treatment of sin, justification, the righteousness of Christ, the Holy Spirit, predestination, and the church all informed Calvin's restructuring of the *Institutes*.

Paul's pastoral mind was just as important to Calvin. Calvin was, more and more, becoming a churchman in Strasbourg, and the apostle Paul became a model to the maturing Calvin, along with Martin Bucer. Calvin's first Latin edition of his *Institutes* in 1536 was not written for scholars but as a catechetical guide for the common Christian without extensive familiarity with the Scriptures or its theology.[104] Its immediate success was due to many factors, but

---

99. Bucer, however, was not the only one Calvin learned from. Calvin also studied the humanist instincts of Jean Sturm (1507–89), "whose educational labors made Strasbourg one of the foremost educational centers in Europe," says Lindberg, *European Reformations*, 259.

100. Muller, *PRRD* 1:105.

101. On Calvin's reordering of the *Institutes*, see Muller, *Unaccommodated Calvin*, 104–28.

102. First ed., 1521.

103. Gordon, *Calvin*, 92, notes that Romans also influenced Calvin's *Letter to All Those Who Love Jesus Christ* (1535).

104. De Greef, *Writings of John Calvin*, 183. For the first edition, see John Calvin, *Institutes of the Christian Religion, 1536 Edition*.

one of them was its pedagogical format and style. The format was familiar to a sixteenth-century Christian, including those *loci* always treated in medieval works of theology, from the Apostles' Creed to the Lord's Prayer.[105] Calvin also presented an evangelical theology to complement his orthodoxy, from his interpretation of the sacraments to his theology of God's two kingdoms, all of which betrayed the papacy. His first edition showed clear signs of influence from first-generation Reformers, above all, Martin Luther.[106] The 1536 edition has the feel of a catechism, like a shepherd guiding his sheep through the Christian faith. Calvin's aim—as the title itself conveys—was to lead the church into a knowledge of God and his saving work so that they knew how to pursue Christian piety. With that purpose in view, the 1536 edition placed no little emphasis on the catholicity of the church, marked as it was by a "suprahistorical" emphasis that summoned God's elect across time.[107] In subsequent years (and editions) the catholicity of the evangelical church proved foundational since Rome continued to lob its accusation of schism.

If the 1536 edition was tailored to the Christian, the 1539 Latin edition adopted a more intellectual tone, directed as it was toward students, Calvin being their master instructor. Yet the major contours did not change—the way to salvation remained central, and the pursuit of piety was still forefront. However, the 1539 edition did expand the 1536 edition, with the addition of topics such as divine election and free will. He also incorporated a basic introduction to the knowledge of God, which continued to expand in subsequent editions as he developed his *duplex cognition Dei* (twofold knowledge of God).[108] As Barbara Pitkin says, "It was just as important to know God as creator as it was to know God as redeemer."[109] On that score, Pitkin ascertains that Calvin's definition of faith was not settled in 1539 but continued to evolve as Calvin followed through on the implications of his *duplex* for the mediation of Christ and the believer's union with Christ, as evidenced in his commentaries (especially Psalms and Romans).[110] Indeed, by the final edition of Calvin's *Institutes* the seeds of his thought had grown into full maturity.

Furthermore, in 1539 Calvin had something to say about baptism and covenant theology (as it later became labeled) as well. That is not surprising. Exiled

---

105. De Greef, 185.

106. Who influenced Calvin and to what extent has occupied a large corpus of literature, but see De Greef, *Writings of John Calvin*, 185. Besides Luther, De Greef identifies the following: Melanchthon, Bucer, and Zwingli.

107. Maruyama, *Calvin's Ecclesiology*, 2.

108. Muller, *PRRD* 1:104.

109. Pitkin, *What Pure Eyes Could See*, 4. Pitkin is pushing back against Dowey, Schützeichel, Doumergue, etc.

110. Pitkin, *What Pure Eyes Could See*, 5. Pitkin argues that faith, for Calvin, is knowledge, though not mere cognition (intellect) but enlightenment as illumination. Thus, "the knowledge that is faith as indicated in Calvin's definition from 1539, is 'sealed on our hearts' as well as 'revealed to our minds.' For Calvin, this illumination is effected by the Holy Spirit, which opens the subject's eyes to perceive the objectively clear revelation of God in the person and work of Christ, in the scriptures, and in creation" (6).

from Geneva, he now had firsthand knowledge of Strasbourg Anabaptists, so he made it a point to reflect on the scriptural covenants in defense of infant baptism. Strasbourg also allowed Calvin the opportunity to learn from Martin Bucer's pastoral ministry as well as Bucer's Pauline scholarship and theology, and signs of both are evident in the second edition of the *Institutes*.[111]

Many more editions followed.[112] If the 1536 edition represents the genesis of Calvin's *catholic* ecclesiology, that catholicity was further wielded in the 1543 edition to give a formidable response to the accusation of schism. So long as the Reformation was synonymous with a renewed vision for union with Christ, Rome could not sever the Reformers from the one, holy, catholic, and apostolic church of which Christ is its head.[113] And yet, as much as the 1543 edition marks the maturity of that catholicity, Calvin reveals a notable advance towards a *Reformed* ecclesiology as well.[114] Calvin could build on the foundation of his catholic ecclesiology to then erect a polity differentiated from Lutherans, Anabaptists, and the papacy. Calvin was convinced his ecclesiology improved upon the ecclesiology of first generation Reformers because his polity better incorporated the catholic heritage.[115] The phrase *reformed catholicity* captures Calvin's ecclesiastical development from his 1536 to 1543 editions. By his 1559 edition, however, Calvin also had to consider international challenges as the Reformation across Europe experienced some success but also intense persecution. If his 1536 edition exhibited catholicity and his 1543 edition a Reformed pedigree, then his 1559 edition was marked by a *Reformation* accent. On the bedrock of his reformed catholic ecclesiology, Calvin's final edition could define the "Reformation church as an eschatological reality and depicted it as two concurrent images: one, the church as the theater's noble 'orchestra'; and the other, 'the church under the cross' of the suffering Christ."[116] Complemented by his work on the Psalms and the book of Daniel, a "prophetic dimension" seasoned Calvin's tone of voice as the church embraced the life of a pilgrim, exiles unwelcome in this world but promised a homeland in the next.[117]

Other additions followed in subsequent editions of the *Institutes* besides ecclesiology. His 1550 Latin edition gave birth to a French translation in 1551 with a conspicuous addition on Christ's resurrection, for example.[118] Yet the

---

111. De Greef believes Bucer's 1536 commentary on Romans influenced Calvin on doctrines like election. De Greef also thinks Melanchthon influenced the general format of the 1539 *Institutes* because of his 1535 *Loci Communes*, also structured according to Romans. See De Greef, 186–87.

112. Standard editions include 1536, 1539, 1543 and 1545, 1550, and 1559.

113. Muller, "Foreword," xi–xii.

114. Maruyama makes an argument for three stratums or modes (catholic, reformed, reformation), but concludes that the 1543 edition is "the most important edition concerning his [Calvin's] ecclesiology" (*Calvin's Ecclesiology*, 2).

115. Maruyama, 8.

116. Maruyama, 2–3. To clarify, Reformation ecclesiology is "not a theological but a historical concept" (8).

117. Maruyama, 8.

118. The addition on the resurrection "resulted from correspondence between Calvin and Lelio Sozzini in 1549," and "supplementary material was finally included also in the Latin edition of 1559 (see *Institutes* 3.25.7–8)." De Greef, *Writings of John Calvin*, 188.

final Latin edition of Calvin's *Institutes* came in 1559. Why 1559? One reason: Calvin almost died. Thinking the end was near, Calvin made one last effort to edit his *Institutes*, sectioning his entire work into four books, the broad outline still mimicking the Apostles' Creed. His method and aims had not changed, but Calvin so expanded his *Institutes* that the project became a fresh contribution in 1559, incorporating a career full of controversies.[119]

How were Calvin's *Institutes* received? Reformation-minded pastors and churchgoers received them with enthusiasm.[120] From the first edition to the last, Calvin had a growing readership that looked to the mind of the Genevan pastor for theological guidance in perilous times. However, not everyone appreciated the success of Calvin's *Institutes*. For example, when Calvin's 1539 Latin edition made its way into French in 1541, France prohibited citizens from reading and owning the *Institutes*.[121]

In a concrete way, the *Institutes* gave Reformed churches hope. The *Institutes* were instructive, demonstrating Reformation theology from Scripture. Yet they also served to fortify Reformation theology from Rome's accusation of novelty and heresy—an accusation the French king was open to entertaining.

A REFORMED CATHOLIC PARADIGM

In a companion volume, I will venture to explore Calvin's theology in his 1559 *Institutes*.[122] For our purposes, we will merely observe how Calvin positioned his theology within a reformed catholic paradigm, a spirit patterned in variegated ways by Reformers all over Europe.

Calvin's Case for Catholicity: Address to Francis I

When Calvin first envisioned his *Institutes*, he did not intend to begin by addressing the king of France. Yet the hostility of the French toward evangelicals—the French "burn with rage," said Calvin—motivated the Reformer to defend his own countrymen and the legitimacy of their evangelical conversion.[123] They not only needed an advocate, but a theological lawyer skilled at exposing false misrepresentation. Who better than Calvin?

At the start of his address to Francis I, Calvin conveyed his frustration: French evangelicals had been caricatured as heretics and traitors. Their nemeses were so convincing that they had stirred up white-hot hatred toward evangelicals,

---

119. De Greef lists the most significant: "The conflict with the Lutherans, especially Joachim Westphal, over the Lord's Supper; the debate with Andreas Osiander about the image of God, the work of Christ, and justification; and the debate with Lelio Sozzini about the merits of Christ and the bodily resurrection from the dead. But Calvin also enlarged the material on certain topics like the fall of humanity into sin and the loss of free will." De Greef, 189.

120. On the reception of the *Institutes*, see Gordon, *John Calvin's Institutes of the Christian Religion*.

121. "Both the Latin and French editions were condemned in France, and an edict issued by the Parliament of Paris on July 1, 1542, ordered that anyone possessing the *Institutes* had to be reported." De Greef, *Writings of John Calvin*, 187.

122. Forthcoming from Zondervan Academic.

123. Calvin, *Institutes*, prefatory address, 1 (p. 9).

creating extreme prejudice both in society and among the nobility. French evangelicals now faced a choice: death or exile. One other option had gained some traction: continue in the church but in silence. Calvin had no patience for this third option.

Francis may have chosen to ignore Calvin and to let injustice triumph, but he should not have then expected prosperity in his kingdom. As Augustine said in his *City of God*, "When justice is taken away, what are kingdoms but a vast banditry?"[124] Francis, and any king for that matter, should have been occupied with that central concern: "how God's glory may be kept safe on earth, how God's truth may retain its place of honor, how Christ's Kingdom may be kept in good repair among us."[125] Permitting the slaughter of evangelicals neither protected God's glory nor honored his truth.

What false accusation frustrated Calvin the most? The charge of *novelty*. The French reported to their king the disturbing news of a "new" sect, one unconfirmed by miracles, one antithetical to the testimony of the church fathers, and one schismatic at its heart, threatening the peace and unity of church and government alike. In the eyes of the king, the French evangelicals were no different from Anabaptist schismatics and sectarians, pedaling new ideas.[126] The prejudiced charge of "novelty" distressed Calvin: "I do not at all doubt that it [the evangelical faith] is new to them ... [but there is] nothing new among us." French evangelicals taught no "new gospel" but an ancient one, the same one the church universal had always believed.[127]

Calvin was sickened by the clever attempt to set French evangelicals over against the catholic fathers. Besides contradicting Scripture, nothing was more damning than incongruity with the apostolic and patristic witness. "If the contest were to be determined by patristic authority, the tide of victory—to put it very modestly—would turn to our side."[128] Not only was the Roman Church mistaken in its accusation of novelty, but it was also guilty of perverting the patristic witness. Calvin said, "You might say that their only care is to gather dung amid gold."[129] Displaying an extensive grasp of the patristic corpus, Calvin outlined a dozen doctrines and practices exhibiting the Roman Church's violation of patristic theology and practice. Calvin called an army of fathers to his side, from Chrysostom to Cyprian, from Tertullian to Augustine, summoning

---

124. *City of God* 4.4 (*PL* 41.115; tr. *NPNF¹* 2.66); quoted in Calvin, *Institutes*, prefatory address, 3 (p. 11).

125. Calvin, *Institutes*, prefatory address, 2 (p. 11). This chapter and the next are brief, but see a full examination of Calvin's vision from François Wendel, *Calvin: Origins and Development of His Religious Thought*.

126. De Greef, *Writings of John Calvin*, 183.

127. Calvin, *Institutes*, prefatory address, 3 (pp. 15, 16). The Roman Church assured themselves they were the true church by past and present miracles, confirming God's favor. But Calvin countered by connecting such presumption to the Donatists. The Donatists wielded a "battering-ram": "that they were mighty in miracles." Calvin, however, sided with Augustine's response: "The Lord made us wary of these miracle workers when he predicted that false prophets with lying signs and prodigies would come to draw even the elect (if possible) into error [Matt. 24:24]" (3; p. 17).

128. Calvin, *Institutes*, prefatory address, 4 (p. 18).

129. Calvin, *Institutes*, prefatory address, 4 (p. 18).

their insights into the sacred Scriptures. "What is involved here for Calvin is the one, holy, catholic church, and he proceeds to outline its true form."[130]

The French evangelicals were also discredited because their ecclesiology lacked institutional credibility. They had no pontiff of Rome, no apostolic see, no institution for ordination, and so on. Their bishops did not preside over renowned cities, but the "form of the church" was "always apparent and observable." The evangelicals, in other words, were without institutional form and therefore lacked visible assurance. Yet Calvin reminded Francis of how "dangerous is their desire to have the form of the church judged by some sort of vain pomp."[131] Calvin proposed an alternative ecclesiology, one grounded in something deeper, something truly divine: "We, on the contrary, affirm that the church can exist without any visible appearance, and that its appearance is not contained within that outward magnificence which they foolishly admire." If the church was not primarily identified by outward appearance, then what? Calvin's answer goes to the heart of the Reformation. Christ's church should be identified by two marks: "the pure preaching of God's Word and the lawful administration of the sacraments."[132] In a turn of irony, Calvin asked who were the true schismatics if these two marks identified the location of the gospel and the church. "Now let them go and cling to this outward mask—making Christ and all the prophets of God schismatics; Satan's ministers, conversely, the organs of the Holy Spirit!"[133]

French evangelicals were also oppressed because their preacher, so their enemies claimed, created no little unrest in society; the evangelicals acted as revolutionaries, a crime (perhaps even treason) deserving death. For this reason, the king refused to distinguish French evangelicals from Anabaptists, but Calvin asked Francis to consider history, specifically the strategy of Satan across history. The deceiver makes men think the truth is a lie. Could he be implementing such a strategy even now, Calvin asked, persuading the king's advisers that evangelicals were betraying the truth and must be a sect?[134] Contrary to what the king had heard, evangelicals did not overthrow kingdoms but rather prayed for kingdoms, including Francis's kingdom. Evangelicals did not whisper sedition in the corners of allies but openly lived quiet and simple lives, desiring only equity. With the eloquence and logic of an experienced lawyer, Calvin concluded his case by appealing to the King of kings:

The wicked poison of our calumniators has, O King, in its many details, been sufficiently disclosed that you may not incline an ear credulous beyond measure

---

130. De Greef, *Writings of John Calvin*, 183.

131. Calvin, *Institutes*, prefatory address, 6 (p. 26).

132. Calvin, *Institutes*, prefatory address, 6 (p. 24).

133. Calvin, *Institutes*, prefatory address, 6 (p. 26).

134. "How great is the malice that would ascribe to the very word of God itself the odium either of seditions, which wicked and rebellious men stir up against it, or of sects, which impostors excite, both of them in opposition to its teaching!" Calvin, *Institutes*, prefatory address, 7 (p. 28).

to their slanders. . . . I have not tried to formulate a defense, but merely to dispose your mind to give a hearing to the actual presentation of our case. Your mind is now indeed turned away and estranged from us, even inflamed, I may add, against us; but we trust that we can regain your favor, if in a quiet, composed mood you will once read this our confession, which we intend in lieu of a defense before Your Majesty. . . .

May the Lord, the King of Kings, establish your throne in righteousness [cf. Prov. 25:5], and your dominion in equity, most illustrious King.[135]

In the Bloodstream

Calvin was forthright at the start of his *Institutes*, wearing his reformed catholicity like skin. However, across the scope of Calvin's *Institutes*, his reformed catholicity was more like blood in the body, flowing beneath the skin, inconspicuous but pumping the heart of his vision for Christianity.

In book 1, for example, Calvin established the Reformation by properly ordering the Word and the church. In contrast to Rome, the Word gives birth to the church, not vice versa. Yet was Calvin betraying the early church? Augustine did say, "I should not believe the gospel except as moved by the authority of the catholic church." However, Rome had misinterpreted the church father, said Calvin. "Augustine is not, therefore, teaching that the faith of godly men is founded on the authority of the church; nor does he hold the view that the certainty of the gospel depends upon it. He is simply teaching that there would be no certainty of the gospel for unbelievers to win them to Christ if the consensus of the church did not impel them."[136] Throughout Calvin's corpus, the Geneva Reformer reclaimed Augustine from Roman abuse and stood the church father upright once more to demonstrate that Protestants were no less catholic than their opponents.

Also in book 1, Calvin may not have treated the doctrine of God at length (as did others such as Zanchi and Vermigli), but when he did answer textual questions about God "relenting" or "repenting," Calvin's instinct was to utilize an argument original to classical theism. Calvin appealed to divine accommodation to preserve attributes like immutability, for example.[137] To speak of God lisping like a nurse was to assume analogical predication, regardless of whether Calvin mentioned Thomas Aquinas or not.[138] Likewise, when Calvin warned against

---

135. Calvin, *Institutes*, prefatory address, 8 (p. 31).

136. Calvin reminded his readers to pay attention to historical context: "Augustine was there concerned with the Manichees, who wished to be believed without controversy when they claimed, but did not demonstrate, that they themselves possessed the truth." And later: Augustine "only meant to indicate what we also confess as true: those who have not yet been illumined by the Spirit of God are rendered teachable by reverence for the church, so that they may persevere in learning faith in Christ from the gospel. Thus, he avers, the authority of the church is an introduction through which we are prepared for faith in the gospel." Calvin, *Institutes* 1.7.3.

137. E.g., *Institutes* 1.17.12–13.

138. *Institutes* 1.13.1. Cf. Zachman, "Calvin as Analogical Theologian," 162; Horton, *Justification*, 1:329. Swain warns against interpreting Calvin's sparse theology proper as a departure from the tradition and instead

venerating images, he turned to a pillar in classical theology—divine incomprehensibility—to counter Rome.[139]

Additionally, Calvin's treatment of divine providence is defined by its scriptural allegiance, but who can overlook its deep Augustinian debt as well?[140] That Augustinian influence shone bright when Calvin transitioned in book 2 to the bondage and liberation of the will. Calvin's 1559 edition was published on the heels of his debates over predestination, original sin, free will, and effectual calling with Albert Pighius (1490–1542) and Jerome Bolsec.[141] Calvin revealed his familiarity with the church fathers when he sided with Augustine over against Jerome and accused Ockham and the *via moderna* of betraying Augustine's doctrine of grace.[142] Not only Augustine but Hilary of Poitiers was petitioned as Calvin established the proper relation between law and gospel on which his covenant theology depended.[143]

Once book 2 has established the covenant of grace, the person and work of Christ come into view. If Calvin built a Christology, he did so on the foundation of the Definition of Chalcedon, unveiling his acquaintance with the church fathers. For example, consider the "extra" that has been attached to Calvin's name. By assuming a human nature to his person, the incarnate Christ experienced hunger, fatigue, and grief. However, the person of Christ was not imprisoned by that human nature.

> They thrust upon us as something absurd the fact that if the Word of God became flesh, then he was confined within the narrow prison of an earthly body. This is mere impudence! For even if the Word in his immeasurable essence united with the nature of man into one person, we do not imagine that he was confined therein. Here is something marvelous: the Son of God descended from heaven in such a way that, without leaving heaven, he willed to be borne in the virgin's womb, to go about the earth, and to hang upon the cross; yet he continuously filled the world even as he had done from the beginning![144]

By virtue of his divine nature, the person of Christ transcended the earthly realm. Since he was not circumscribed by his flesh, the Son could walk with his disciples all the while still upholding the universe as he had done since the

---

explains why the Reformers did not disagree with Rome on the doctrine of God and therefore devoted their attention to soteriology and ecclesiology instead. "Trinity in the Reformers," 227–39.

139. Calvin, *Institutes* 1.11.2, 7, 9–11. However, Calvin's appeal to the Son's aseity did create Trinitarian controversy. For a detailed discussion of Calvin's motives, opponents (Caroli, Courtois, Chaponneau), and Calvin's minority report position itself, see Ellis, *Calvin, Classical Trinitarianism, and the Aseity of the Son.*

140. Calvin, *Institutes* 1.14.22; 1.16.1–4, 9; 1.17.1–2.

141. Calvin, *Institutes* 2.1.1–9; 2.2.6–12, 27; 2.3.6–10; Calvin, *Bondage and Liberation of the Will*; Calvin, *Predestination Book against Bolsec.*

142. *Institutes* 2.2.7; 2.3.10; 2.7.1–7, 10–12, 14–16.

143. *Institutes* 2.7.9, 10, 12.

144. Calvin, *Institutes* 2.13.4.

beginning. Something persists, in other words, even beyond the flesh (*etiam extra carnem*). One can see why Calvin said this mystery is marvelous.

The *extra*, however, was not original to Calvin, despite the label *extra Calvinisticum*. First, the *extra* had roots in patristic discourse and could be titled instead the *extra Catholicum* or *Christianum*.[145] For example, in *On the Incarnation*, Athanasius wrote,

> For he was not enclosed in the body, nor was he in the body but not elsewhere. Nor while he moved that [body] was the universe left void of his activity and providence. But, what is most marvelous, being the Word, he was not contained by anyone, but rather himself contained everything. And, as being in all creation, he is in essence outside of everything by his own power, arranging everything and unfolding his own providence in everything to all things, and giving life to each thing and to all things together, containing the universe and not being contained, but being wholly, in every respect, in his own Father alone. So also, being in the human body, and himself giving it life, he properly gives life to the universe also, and was both in everything and outside of all.[146]

For human persons, who have souls, contemplating heaven does not in any way affect the cosmos, as if the sun moves at our command. However, Christ—the *Logos* of God—is not limited in that way. "For he was not bound to the body, but rather was himself wielding it, so that he was both in it and in everything, and was outside everything and at rest in the Father alone. And the most wonderful thing was that he both sojourned as a human being, and as the Word begot life in everything, and as Son was with the Father."[147] Calvin's vocabulary can almost be heard in the phrases of Athanasius, which is not accidental. Calvin was drawing on this patristic doctrine to establish an orthodox Christology within the Reformed church. If the *extra* is not original to Calvin but grounded in a patristic witness, then David Willis was correct to use the label "Calvin's Catholic Christology."[148]

Second, even before Calvin's mature but brief articulation of the *extra*, the concept was present in the thought of other Reformers. Before Zwingli's literary battle with Luther over the presence of Christ in the Lord's Supper, Zwingli published *On the Lord's Supper* (1526), and some components of the *extra* were present. Once Zwingli and Luther locked swords later that year, the seeds of the *extra* started growing into full form in Zwingli's *Friendly Exegesis* (1527).

---

145. Willis, *Calvin's Catholic Christology*, 60; Oberman, "'Extra' Dimension in the Theology of Calvin," 59; McGinnis, *The Son of God Beyond the Flesh*, 8.

146. Athanasius, *On the Incarnation*, 17.

147. Athanasius, 17.

148. Willis, *Calvin's Catholic Christology*. Many other recent studies support the patristic pedigree and its Reformed retrieval, including Oberman, "'Extra' Dimension in the Theology of Calvin," 234–58; McGinnis, *Son of God beyond the Flesh*; Gordon, *Holy One in Our Midst*; Drake, *Flesh of the Word*.

FOUR CONDITIONS OF THE *EXTRA*

In his study of the sixteenth century, K. J. Drake identifies four conditions of the *extra*:

1. Jesus Christ, the God-man, maintained an existence *extra carnem* during his earthly ministry.
2. After the ascension and session, the human body of Christ exists locally in heaven.
3. The presence of Christ to the Christian in the time between his first and second comings is according to his divinity, power, and the Holy Spirit.
4. The *communication idiomatum* within the hypostatic union terminates on the person of Christ, and therefore excludes a sharing of properties between the divine and human natures themselves.

For an in-depth overview of Zwingli, Marburg, *Consensus Tigurinus*, and Vermigli, consult Drake's *The Flesh of the Word*, 16–204.

The *extra* laced the arguments of Zwingli and Oecolampadius as they sought to refute Luther at the Marburg Colloquy as well (see chapter 10). Zwingli's *Fidei Ratio* and *Fidei Expositio* perpetuated his teaching on the *extra*, two works that influenced Bullinger after him (see chapter 12).

The influence of the *extra* on Bullinger influenced his interaction with Calvin, enabling the two to cooperate with one another in the *Consensus Tigurinus*. K. J. Drake observes how monumental such a maneuver became for the Reformed tradition's confessional stance moving forward. "Bullinger and Calvin *confessionalized* this emphasis [on the *extra*] in the *Consensus Tigurinus* (1549), drawing an enduring line between the Lutheran and Reformed traditions."[149] Or consider the Heidelberg Catechism. Question 47 asks whether Christ is present with his people to the end. Distinguishing between both natures, the catechism says Christ's human nature is no longer on earth. Nevertheless, he is not absent from us, either, due to his Godhead. Then the catechism asks whether such a belief—the "manhood is not wherever the Godhead is"—does harm to the hypostatic *union*, separating the two natures. Its answer turns to the *extra*: "Not at all; for since divinity is incomprehensible and everywhere present, it must follow that the divinity is indeed *beyond the bounds of the*

---

149. "This driving concern led to further elaboration and reflection on the relationship of Christ's human and divine natures, which emerged as a controversy in its own right after the *Consensus*. As the Reformed tradition developed, theologians incorporated more sophisticated arguments and Scholastic distinctions to support and elaborate the *extra*, including philosophical reflection on the infinite and the finite. Yet despite more numerous and intricate arguments for the *extra*, a basic continuation of theological intent exists from Zwingli to the beginning of Reformed orthodoxy to secure the place of Christ as the mediator between God and humanity within a Chalcedonian articulation of Christ's person." Drake, 12.

humanity which it has assumed, and is yet nonetheless ever in that humanity as well, and remains personally united to it."[150]

The *extra*, therefore, was not limited to Calvin nor original to Calvin but was appreciated by a variety of Reformers, first and second generation, and became a major factor in sixteenth-century debates.[151] The *extra* transcended Geneva and pervaded pockets of the Reformation across Europe because the concept itself was articulated and defended by the patristic and medieval traditions as a natural consequence of Chalcedonian Christology. In other words, the Reformed appeal to the *extra* aligned the Reformers with a *catholic* Christology, a move they acknowledged and embraced to further support their orthodoxy.

In books 2 and 3, Calvin's Reformed catholic vision continues to mature as he transitions to the application of redemption by the Holy Spirit. For Calvin not only had to articulate what participation looked like for a Reformed catholic—a *duplex gratia* or double grace—but he then had to explain how this new, soteric identity applied to the entire body of Christ and its mission in the world.

SCHOOLS OF THE SORBONNE

Calvin reacted against the "schools of the Sorbonne" in particular—the "mothers of all errors." As mentioned in chapter 4, when Calvin admonished "Scholastics," he often had "Sorbonne" in view. Calvin was dissatisfied with the Sorbonne because they advocated a justification not by faith alone but a justification by "formed faith." *Fides formata*, in contrast to *fides informata*, includes works motivated by love (3.15.7). Granted, the principal cause of justification is grace, but that grace does not preclude free will, a free will that performs works of merit. Although many advocated *fides formata*, Calvin laid the blame at the feet of "their Pythagoras," Peter Lombard, whom Calvin charged with misusing Augustine as well as the Scriptures, especially a text like Ephesians 2:10, which precludes works from faith in the most absolute terms (3.15.7). Later Calvin would respond as well to the Schoolmen (most likely Scotus and Ockham, whose view was picked up by Eck) who taught an "accepting grace." "For they mean that works, otherwise insufficient to obtain salvation in accordance with the covenant of the law, still, by God's acceptance of them, are advanced to a value adequate for this. But I say that those works, defiled as well with other transgressions as with their own spots, have no other value except that the Lord extends pardon to both, that is, to bestow free righteousness upon man"(3.17.15).

---

150. "The Heidelberg Catechism," Q. 48 (2:438). For context, see Bierma, *Theology of the Heidelberg Catechism*; and Bierma et al., *Introduction to the Heidelberg Catechism*.

151. Drake calls the *extra* the *crux* of sixteenth-century polemics and warns against what he calls the "Calvin-centric understanding," which assumes the *extra* is limited to or original with Calvin. See Drake, *Flesh of the Word*, 11.

For example, in book 3 Calvin reacted against William of Ockham's implicit faith since it is as impossible to separate faith and the Word as it is "the rays from the sun from which they come." The Word is like a "mirror in which faith may contemplate God."[152] And yet, as essential as knowledge may be, knowledge alone is insufficient. Conviction must be present, yet conviction involves certainty, meaning the believer is confident in the promises of God in Christ. Knowing God's will means knowing God's *benevolence* and *mercy*. For if the "sole pledge of his love is Christ" then faith is "a firm and certain knowledge of God's benevolence toward us, founded upon the truth of the freely given promise in Christ, both revealed to our minds and sealed upon our hearts through the Holy Spirit."[153] Such a firm and certain knowledge of God's benevolence involves assurance and confidence, not in oneself, of course, but in divine benevolence.[154] Such a faith extinguishes an "uneasy doubting" by rendering the "conscience calm and peaceful before God's judgment."[155] Calvin was not so naive as to think that faith cannot be "violently buffeted hither and thither; so in the thick darkness of temptations its light is snuffed out." But do not lose hope, Calvin said with pastoral care, for "whatever happens, it [faith] ceases not its earnest quest for God."[156] Calvin was proud to credit Bernard of Clairvaux with his Reformed understanding of faith, citing at length his *Fifth Sermon on the Dedication of a Church*, unembarrassed that the evangelical formulation stood within one major stream of the medieval church.[157]

At the same time, Calvin was astute enough in his observation of medieval theology's diversity and complexity to praise Bernard while criticizing Lombard. "For Lombard explains that justification is given to us through Christ in two ways. First, he says, Christ's death justifies us, while love is aroused through it in our hearts and makes us righteous. Second, because through the same love, sin is extinguished by which the devil held us captive, so that he no longer has the wherewithal to condemn us. You see how he views God's grace especially in justification, in so far as we are directed through the grace of the Holy Spirit to good works."[158] Cloaked as Lombard's doctrine of justification may be in the gracious dispensation of the Spirit, nevertheless, it is still a justification that depends on works in some way, even if those works be directed by grace itself. That assumes as well that justification is an extended process by which works of love make a person righteous.[159]

---

152. Calvin, *Institutes* 3.2.6. For a thorough study on Calvin and faith that examines the reformer's commentaries as well, see Pitkin, *What Pure Eyes Could See*.

153. Calvin, *Institutes* 3.2.7.

154. By firm and certain knowledge, Calvin was not referring to some rationalistic comprehensive, exhaustive knowledge attained by the senses (in the Enlightenment sense), but a knowledge that consists of assurance (3.2.14) and confidence (3.2.15).

155. Calvin, *Institutes* 3.2.15, 16.

156. Calvin, *Institutes* 3.2.24.

157. Calvin, *Institutes* 3.2.25.

158. Calvin, *Institutes* 3.11.15.

159. Much later Calvin would also take aim at Duns Scotus and "accepting grace" as well as "works of supererogation," which can be found in a variety of medievals, including Bonaventura and Aquinas. See Calvin, *Institutes* 3.14.11–12.

CALVIN, OSIANDER, AND UNION WITH CHRIST

In 1550 Andreas Osiander wrote *Disputation on Justification*, followed by his *Confession of the Only Mediator and of Justification by Faith* the next year, both of which created a heated response from Lutheran headquarters. Osiander's view was idiosyncratic, neither agreeing entirely with Rome nor with the Reformers. He said an "essential" righteousness was imparted. This essential righteousness originates from the divine nature of Christ alone. Therefore, Osiander believed, "we are substantially righteous in God by the infusion both of his [Christ's] essence and of his quality" (cf. *Institutes* 3.11.5). In response, Calvin said Osiander had not only distorted the doctrine of union with Christ, but he had compromised Christ's own divinity by mixing it with humanity. "He says that we are one with Christ. We agree. But we deny that Christ's essence is mixed with our own. . . . He throws in a mixture of substances by which God—transfusing himself into us, as it were—makes us part of himself. . . . We are not justified by the grace of the Mediator alone, nor is righteousness simply or completely offered to us in his person, but that we are made partakers in God's righteousness when God is united to us in essence" (3.11.5). If correct, then the redemption Christ secures is limited to his divinity and has little to do, if anything at all, with Christ's humanity. Calvin could not stand for this limitation since Scripture explicitly ties the righteousness Christ won to his humanity and humility. "For if we ask how we have been justified, Paul answers, 'By Christ's obedience' [Rom. 5:19]. But did he obey in any other way than when he took upon himself the form of a servant [Phil. 2:7]? From this we conclude that in his flesh, righteousness has been manifested to us" (3.11.9).

As for justification itself, an essential righteousness turns what should be forensic into something transformative instead (3.11.6). "Osiander laughs at those men who teach that 'to be justified' is a legal term; because we must actually be righteous. Also, he despises nothing more than that we are justified by free imputation." In summary, Osiander could not tolerate forensic notions. He could not accept a justification in which the ungodly are righteous in their legal standing but simultaneously are not righteous within their moral nature. "Osiander objects that it would be insulting to God and contrary to his nature that he should justify those who actually remain wicked" (3.11.11).

Calvin's response was the reply of not only an exegete but a theologian. He returned to the concept of double grace—*duplex gratia*—to remind his readers of twin truths. First, the legal and the transformative are not to be confused. The former is an instantaneous, definitive, legal declaration (justification) that guarantees eternal right standing with God, while the latter certifies an inward, moral reformation over the course of a lifetime (sanctification), incomplete until glorification. Apart from the forensic foundation, none of the relational and transformative benefits follow. Second, although it is right to distinguish the forensic and the transformative, the two cannot be divorced. The double grace remains indivisible. Justification is distinct from sanctification, but the former is the cause of the latter.

Unfortunately, some Calvin interpreters (T. F. Torrance and J. B. Torrance) have posed a false dichotomy between union with Christ and justification. However, Calvin's polemic against Osiander confirmed that the Genevan pastor's attention to union with Christ was never at the expense of a forensic understanding of justification. Participation and imputation were not divorced from one other, but the latter was a means to the former. By virtue of imputation, the Christian possesses the right standing of Christ and therefore participates in all his benefits. In the end, the debate between Calvin and Osiander was between two opposed understandings of participation. As J. Todd Billings explains, quoting Calvin's use of participation language, "As a catholic thinker, Calvin does not hesitate to say that created humanity finds its primal identity in union and communion with God, and continues to 'participate' in God by the *imago Dei*. United to Christ by the Spirit, believers are 'participants not only in all his benefits but also in himself (Christ).' [*Institutes* 3.2.24]. . . . Yet Calvin refuses to think that this vision of transformation in Christ renders God's declaration of believers as righteous superfluous or unnecessary. To the contrary, in Calvin's logic, if the Christian moral life is to overcome the moral calculus so deeply characteristic of human pursuits, there must be a recognition of God's pardon declared upon sinners who are in Christ" ("The Catholic Calvin," 132–33). Billings pushes back against those who divorce Calvin's notion of participation from the Fathers. Both appealed to participation to distinguish (not conflate) the Creator and the creature. In other words, Calvin (not Osiander) had the Fathers on his side whether he used the patristic language of participation for the *duplex gratia* or deification itself.

The late medieval schools, said Calvin, ran with Lombard, taking the church from "bad to worse until, in a headlong ruin, they have plunged into a sort of Pelagianism." By contrast, Augustine was the better guide, along with all those Scholastic theologians who clung to Augustine's definition of grace. The doctor of grace taught Calvin, and Luther before him, that justification must be free from man's works, *sola gratia* the only remedy against the threat of Pelagianism. Despite Calvin's colossal debt to Augustine, Calvin did say that Augustine faltered just at the finish line. "For even though he admirably deprives man of all credit for righteousness and transfers it to God's grace, he still subsumes grace under sanctification, by which we are reborn in newness of life through the Spirit."[160] Despite his apologetic for *sola gratia*, Augustine still assumed justification was a transformative process.

Calvin disagreed with Augustine and the Scholastics who described justification as an infusion rather than an imputation of righteousness. And yet Calvin appropriated their Aristotelian categories nonetheless. For example, Calvin utilized Aristotle's four cases—each of which were prominent in the methodology of Thomas Aquinas—but he did so to advance his Reformed take on Augustine's theology of faith.

1. *Efficient cause.* For Scripture everywhere proclaims that the efficient cause of our obtaining eternal life is the mercy of the Heavenly Father and his freely given love toward us.

---

160. Calvin, *Institutes* 3.11.15.

2. *Material cause.* Surely the material cause is Christ, with his obedience, through which he acquired righteousness for us.

3. *Formal or instrumental.* What shall we say is the formal or instrumental cause but faith [cf. Jn. 3:16]?

4. *Final cause.* As for the final cause, the apostle testifies that it consists both in the proof of divine justice and in the praise of God's goodness.[161]

Examples could be multiplied.[162] As book 3 continues, Calvin's treatment of sanctification draws from Bernard once again; his extensive articulation of prayer draws from the ecclesiology of Ambrose, and his description of predestination and election is indebted to Augustine and Bernard alike.[163] However subtle these examples may be across the *Institutes*, Calvin's Reformed catholicity became conspicuous with his turn toward ecclesiology.

One, Holy, Catholic, and Apostolic Church

Literature has been drawn more to Calvin's soteriology than his ecclesiology. But as Calvin's opening words to Francis demonstrate, his ecclesiology was definitive for his understanding of the Reformation, which might explain in part why book 4 is one of the most polemical sections of his *Institutes*. It also might explain why book 4 occupies such a large portion of his *Institutes*.

Calvin's entryway into the doctrine of the church cannot be severed from union with Christ. For it is "by the faith in the gospel that Christ becomes ours and we are made partakers of the salvation and eternal blessedness brought by him." However, those united to Christ do not always pursue fellowship with Christ as they should, which Calvin attributed to either ignorance or sloth, or both. Needed are "outward helps to beget and increase faith within us, and advance it to its goal," and it is God's kindness that provides these "aids" so that we are not left to "our weakness."[164]

Where are these "aids" to be found? The church. To guarantee that "the preaching of the gospel might flourish, he deposited this treasure in the church." Paul said that is why God has given his church pastors and teachers (Eph. 4:11), as well as sacraments (baptism, Lord's Supper). Calvin first introduced the

---

161. Calvin, *Institutes* 3.14.17 (cf. 3.15.6 for Calvin's critique of the "Sophists" [Duns Scotus?] who utilized the categories the wrong way). Calvin was drawing on Aristotle's *Physics* and *Metaphysics*. But also note the use of these causes in theology by Aquinas in his *Summa* (see chapter 4). Later Calvin introduced these causes once again, but this time identified faith *as the gift of the Spirit* to clarify its instrumentality. The "efficient cause of our salvation consists in God the Father's love; the material cause in God the Son's obedience; the instrumental cause in the Spirit's illumination, that is, faith; the final cause, in the glory of God's great generosity" (3.14.21). We are looking at Calvin's understanding of faith in his *Institutes*, but a similar study could explore his commentaries. See Pitkin, *What Pure Eyes Could See*.

162. Some historians have devoted themselves to detailing the depth of Calvin's Reformed catholicity (e.g., Lane, *John Calvin*).

163. *Institutes* 3.11.13–15 and 3.16.1; 3.19.4–5 (sanctification); 3.20.1–27 (prayer); and 3.21.1–4, 8; 3.23.4–5, 8, 11; 3.24.5 (predestination and election).

164. Calvin, *Institutes* 4.1.1.

concept of divine accommodation in his doctrine of revelation (book 1), only to implement it further in his doctrine of salvation (book 2). Now he returned to it once more, this time to emphasize how gracious God is—a Father with providential care—to give gifts to his people to strengthen them in their weakness. "God, therefore, in his wonderful providence accommodating himself to our capacity, has prescribed a way for us, though still far off, to draw near to him."[165]

Since these "aids" are located in the church, Calvin used maternal language, calling the church the "bosom" of God into which he gathers his children so that they are nourished like babes at the breast. Into this bosom God gathers infants so that "they may be guided by her motherly care until they mature and at least reach the goal of faith." Following the Fathers, Calvin did not hesitate to call the church our mother: "for those to whom he is Father the church may also be Mother."[166] Calvin certainly agreed with Cyprian (and Augustine), who said, "You cannot have God for your Father unless you have the church for your Mother."[167] That explains why Calvin put such high stock in the church, telling his readers that if they had hope, it was a hope conditioned on their union with Christ's body. "For no hope of future inheritance remains to us unless we have been united with all other members under Christ, our head."[168]

To describe and define the mother church, where did Calvin begin? With the Nicene Creed, specifically with its *credo*: we believe in the church.[169] Calvin said the creed has in view not merely the visible church, but the invisible church, a distinction Augustine embodied throughout his *City of God*. The *visible* church refers to the "whole multitude of men spread over the earth who profess to worship one God and Christ." How do they enter this church? "By baptism we are initiated into faith in him; by partaking in the Lord's Supper we attest our unity in true doctrine and love; in the Word of the Lord we have agreement, and for the preaching of the Word the ministry instituted by Christ is preserved." Is the visible church the elect only? No. "In this church are mingled many hypocrites who have nothing of Christ but the name and outward appearance." On the other hand, the *invisible* church refers to the church "actually in God's presence, into which no persons are received but those who are children of God by grace of adoption and true members of Christ by sanctification of the Holy Spirit."

---

165. Calvin, *Institutes* 4.1.1. Calvin would also use the concept of accommodation to explain the visible church: "because he [God] foresaw it to be of some value for us to know who were to be counted as his children, he has in this regard accommodated himself to our capacity. And, since assurance of faith was not necessary, he substituted for it a certain charitable judgment whereby we recognize as members of the church those who, by confession of faith, by example of life, and by partaking of the sacraments, profess the same God and Christ with us" (*Institutes* 4.1.4).

166. Calvin, *Institutes* 4.1.1.

167. *On the Unity of the Catholic Church* vi (*CSEL* 3.1.214; tr. LCC 5:127–28). As quoted in Calvin, *Institutes* 4.1.1 (n. 2). McNeil also noted that Augustine said the same.

168. Calvin, *Institutes* 4.1.2.

169. Calvin, however, was discontent with the addition of the preposition ("We believe *in* the church"). He appealed to the Fathers, specifically Cyprian and Augustine, to argue for "I believe the church." Calvin, *Institutes* 4.1.2.

For Calvin, the invisible church is not a mixture. "Then, indeed, the church includes not only the saints presently living on earth, but all the elect from the beginning of the world."[170]

Notice Calvin's strategy: his case for the invisible church depends on his doctrine of election, which he treated just prior. The elect who make up the invisible church are small—a "contemptible number are hidden in a huge multitude and a few grains of wheat are covered by a pile of chaff"—and as with election, Calvin left their identity to the secret knowledge of God.[171] Also as with eternal election, the invisible church is the Christian's great comfort; no matter how savage Satan's fury may be, raising up persecutors, the church not only survives but thrives. "Christ's blood," said Calvin, cannot "be made barren."[172]

If the church is invisible, then it is also *universal* or *catholic*. Calvin did not tolerate Rome's claim to monopolize the word *catholic*. The Reformers were the true "catholics," as his later polemic would stress. But for now, Calvin appealed to the apostle Paul to demonstrate that catholicity is an essential characteristic of the church. For God's elect are not only united to Christ—he is their one head—but they are also united to one another. Paul called the church Christ's body, each body part connected to another (Eph. 4:16; Rom. 12:5; et al.). Again, *comfort is the fruit of catholicity*: in times of great persecution, the church may look like it is lost, but in truth God preserves his remnant. Like the death of Christ, the death of God's elect can only produce more fruit.[173]

Does the creed's *credo* extend to what Calvin calls the outward church or the visible church? It does. If the church is the body of Christ, then our union not only with Christ but with one another should show "in brotherly agreement." Also, every member "should yield to the church the authority it deserves" for by doing so each Christian acts as if he or she is "one of the flock." Calvin was laying a foundation for the communion of saints, which referred to the saints "gathered into the society of Christ on the principle that whatever benefits God confers upon them, they should in turn share with one another."[174] The word

---

170. Calvin, *Institutes* 4.1.7.

171. Calvin also drew attention to the "inner call": *Institutes* 4.1.2. Later Calvin, with Augustinian flare, would turn to predestination once more when explaining the mixed nature of the visible church: "Therefore, according to God's secret predestination (as Augustine says), 'many sheep are without, and many wolves are within.' For he knows and has marked those who know neither him nor themselves. Of those who openly wear his badge, his eyes alone see the ones who are unfeignedly holy and will persevere to the very end [Matt. 24:13]—the ultimate point of salvation."

172. Calvin, *Institutes* 4.1.2.

173. "Although the melancholy desolation which confronts us on every side may cry that no remnant of the church is left, let us know that Christ's death is fruitful, and that God miraculously keeps his church in hiding places." Calvin, *Institutes* 4.1.2. Later Calvin quoted Augustine to say the church may lay in hiding for a time (4.2.3).

174. Calvin should not be interpreted through a socialist lens. For he said next, "This does not, however, rule out diversity of grace, inasmuch as we know the gifts of the Spirit are variously distributed. Nor is civil order disturbed, which allows each individual to own his private possessions, since it is necessary to keep peace among men that the ownership of property should be distinct and personal among them." Calvin, *Institutes* 4.1.3.

communion was a favorite for Calvin and for other Reformers as well. The concept conveys the "wealth of comfort" that belongs to every Christian within the society of Christ. Calvin's choice of language means the *invisible* church is a *spiritual* people. Their unity, he said, is not something you can see or touch but "belongs to the realm of faith." Again, Calvin returned to the concept of election: "For here we are not bidden to distinguish between reprobate and elect—that is for God alone, not for us, to do—but to establish with certainty in our hearts that all those who, by the kindness of God the Father, through the working of the Holy Spirit, have entered into fellowship with Christ, are set apart as God's property and personal possession; and that when we are of their number we share that great grace."[175]

As Calvin turned from the invisible to the visible church, he applied maternal language once more: "For there is no other way to enter into life unless this mother conceive us in her womb, give us birth, nourish us at her breast, and lastly, unless she keep us under her care and guidance." But "away from her bosom one cannot hope for any forgiveness of sins or any salvation." She is not only a mother, but a lifelong teacher as well. "Our weakness does not allow us to be dismissed from her school until we have been pupils all our lives."[176]

How she teaches her pupils motivated Calvin to identify specific marks that define this church. Calvin limited these marks to two: "the preaching of the Word and the observance of the sacraments"—the sacraments include baptism and the Lord's Supper for Calvin.[177] Both marks cultivate the gospel in the life of the church. When they are not neglected, the church carries an authority, so that its councils may admonish those who threaten its unity. Calvin treated apostasy with colossal gravity: "For the Lord esteems the communion of his church so highly that he counts as a traitor and apostate from Christianity anyone who arrogantly leaves any Christian society, provided it cherishes the true ministry of Word and sacraments. He so esteems the authority of the church that when it is violated he believes his own diminished."[178] That statement deserves emphasis. For Reformers like Calvin were often painted by Rome as insubordinate to ecclesiastical authority. Calvin agreed that "no one is permitted to spurn its [the church's] authority" or "resist its counsels" as long as the church itself is faithful to Word and sacrament.[179]

If the church is the keeper of truth, those who separate themselves are asking God to "hurl the whole thunderbolt of his wrath" against them. As long as Word and sacrament are administered according to the gospel, the church remains a church. "The pure ministry of the Word and pure mode of celebrating

---

175. Calvin, *Institutes* 4.1.3.
176. Calvin, *Institutes* 4.1.4. Calvin appealed to the prophets to make this case, specifically Joel, Ezekiel, and Isaiah, though also the Psalms.
177. Calvin, *Institutes* 4.1.10.
178. Calvin, *Institutes* 4.1.10.
179. Calvin, *Institutes* 4.1.10.

the sacraments are, as we say, sufficient pledge and guarantee that we may safely embrace as church any society in which both these marks exist." Whatever weaknesses endure must be tolerated as long as these marks persist: "we must not reject it so long as it retains them, even if it otherwise swarms with many faults."[180]

Separation was so intolerable to Calvin that he advised a Christian to endure faults that plague these two marks. The Christian must persevere since not all faults are equally egregious. If no room for tolerance remains, then a Christian will leave every church he encounters until few are left. By contrast, Calvin recommended honesty: "We must condone delusion in those matters which can go unknown without harm to the sum of religion and without loss of salvation." Calvin was fearful anyone would "renounce the communion of the church" or "disturb its peace and duly ordered discipline."[181]

Who might this be in the sixteenth-century Reformed Church? The Anabaptists, whom Calvin compared to the Cathari (Novatianists) of the third century and the Donatists beginning in the fourth century.[182] In Calvin's estimation, the Anabaptists were sectarians. Some of them believed the church had been lost since the days of the apostles since a church with significant faults could not be a true church. That explains why Calvin advocated tolerance instead of separation if a church erred in matters that were not absolutely first order.[183] Calvin acknowledged that some of them "sin[ned] more out of ill-advised zeal for righteousness than out of that insane pride." But either way, whenever they failed to see the church and its people matching their perfect ideal of gospel living, he wrote, "they immediately judge that no church exists in that place." With frustrated exclamation, Calvin concluded that the Anabaptists defaulted to "immoderate severity" when the "Lord require[d] kindness" instead.[184] Even when discipline was required, such admonishment was always to be accomplished in a spirit of unity. Calvin quoted Augustine to this effect: "The godly manner and measure of church discipline ought at all times to be concerned with the 'unity of the Spirit in the bond of peace' [Eph. 4:3]."[185] The Anabaptists failed to model "mutual forbearance" like Paul because of their overrealized eschatology, judging the Reformed Church illegitimate because it lacked something close to total perfection.

If the Anabaptists were premature in their ecclesiology, expecting the eschaton now, what type of holiness should Christians expect from the church

---

180. Calvin, *Institutes* 4.1.11.

181. Calvin, *Institutes* 4.1.12.

182. Calvin, *Institutes* 4.1.13.

183. "Such are: God is one; Christ is God and the Son of God; our salvation rests in God's mercy; and the like." *Institutes* 4.1.12.

184. "For where the Lord requires kindness, they neglect it and give themselves over completely to immoderate severity. Indeed, because they think no church exists where there are not perfect purity and integrity of life, they depart out of hatred of wickedness from the lawful church, while they fancy themselves turning aside from the faction of the wicked." Calvin, *Institutes* 4.1.13.

185. Calvin, *Institutes* 4.1.16.

instead? Paul said Christ "cleansed her by the washing of water with the word, so that he might present the church to himself in splendor, without spot or wrinkle or any such thing, that she might be holy and without blemish" (Eph. 5:26–27). At the same time, the Lord is still "daily at work in smoothing out wrinkles and cleansing spots." The church may have a righteous status, but its actual sanctification is incomplete until glorification. "The church is holy, then," said Calvin echoing Cyprian, "in the sense that it is daily advancing and is not yet perfect: it makes progress from day to day but has not yet reached its goal of holiness."[186]

Calvin's tolerance for a church with wrinkles did not mean, however, that he would tolerate the papacy's corruption. It is one thing to be on the pursuit for holiness but quite another thing to pervert that pursuit, claiming to be holy when steeped in idolatry. That charge sounds audacious, but Calvin believed he was justified. Consider the two marks: the preaching of the Word and the sacraments. "Instead of the ministry of the Word, a perverse government compounded of lies rules there, which partly extinguishes the pure light, partly chokes it. The foulest sacrilege has been introduced in place of the Lord's Supper. The worship of God has been deformed by a diverse and unbearable mass of superstitions." Formal beliefs fare no better. "Doctrine (apart from which Christianity cannot stand) has been entirely buried and driven out." All in all, "Public assemblies have become schools of idolatry and ungodliness."[187]

What nagged Calvin most, however, was the papacy's claim to *exclusivity*. Rome had departed from right doctrine and practice yet continued to claim Rome alone was the source of truth and piety. Worse still, Rome condemned anyone and everyone outside its household. "They indeed gloriously extol their church to us to make it seem that there is no other in the world. Thereupon, as if the matter were settled, they conclude that all who dare withdraw from the obedience with which they adorn the church are schismatics; that all who dare mutter against its doctrine are heretics." Calvin found the claim of heresy ludicrous.

To begin with, had the church across all the world gone mad except for Rome, the only pure remnant left? "I ask them why they do not mention Africa, Egypt, and all Asia." They responded by claiming they alone were Peter's true lineage. "They therefore revert to the point that they have the true church because from its beginning it has not been destitute of bishops, for one has followed another in unbroken succession." But what about the Greeks? asked Calvin. Should we really conclude that the entire Eastern Church is anathema, all because the Greeks withdrew "from the apostolic see"? Calvin believed in an unbroken line of succession, yet such catholicity was not determined by bishopric but gospel fidelity.

---

186. Calvin, *Institutes* 4.1.17. For Calvin's use of Cyprian, see 4.1.19.
187. Calvin, *Institutes* 4.2.2.

CALVIN, CYPRIAN, AND THE UNITY OF THE CHURCH

When Calvin replied to Rome's claim to absolute primacy and supreme power, he relied on Cyprian's *On the Unity of the Catholic Church*. For example, Cyprian wrote,

> The episcopate is one, a "whole" of which a part is held by each bishop. And the church is one, which is spread abroad far and wide into a multitude by an increase of fruitfulness. As there are many rays of the sun, but one light; and many branches of a tree, but one strong trunk grounded in its tenacious root; and since from one spring flow many streams, although a goodly number seem outpoured from their bounty and superabundance, still at the source unity abides undivided. . . . So also the church, bathed in the light of the Lord, extends its rays over the whole earth: yet there is one light diffused everywhere. Nor is the unity of the body severed; it spreads its branches through the whole earth; it pours forth its overflowing streams; yet there is one head and one source.

Calvin asked, "Where is the primacy of the Roman see, if the unbroken episcopate rests in Christ's hands alone, and each bishop holds his part of it? The aim of these citations is to inform the reader, by the way, that that principle which the Romanists take to be generally acknowledged and undoubted—of the unity of the hierarchy under an earthly head—was utterly unknown to the ancient fathers." That said, in one of his most extensive surveys of church history, Calvin traced the origins of the papacy but identified the ways the papacy persuaded the church of its primacy through forgeries (see *Institutes* 4.7, where he engages the history of papal authority described in Gratian's *Decretum*).

See Cyprian, *On the Unity of the Catholic Church* 3.5 (CSEL 3. 1. 212, tr. LCC 5. 125–28), as quoted in Calvin, *Institutes* 4.6.17.

"It therefore follows that this pretense of succession is vain unless their descendants conserve safe and uncorrupted the truth of Christ which they have received at their fathers' hands, and abide in it."[188] Since Rome had failed to preserve the Word, Calvin was so bold to compare the papacy to the Jewish people at the time of Jesus. They looked like the people of God on the outside but were death itself on the inside.[189]

Christ's measuring rod for catholicity, however, is not grounded on externals, like priesthoods. Instead, Christ established his church on the *teaching* of the prophets and the apostles. The way to identify who belongs to God is to look for those who hear (receive) the words of God, as Jesus said in John 8:47. The "church is Christ's kingdom," and Christ "reigns by his Word alone."[190]

---

188. Calvin, *Institutes* 4.2.2.
189. Calvin, *Institutes* 4.2.3.
190. Calvin, *Institutes* 4.2.4.

That assumes, of course, that Christ is the head of his kingdom, his church.[191] Appealing at length to Cyprian's *On the Unity of the Catholic Church*, Calvin turned the tables on Rome: "Heresies and schisms arise because men return not to the Source of truth, seek not the Head, keep not the teaching of the Heavenly Master."[192] Who might that be in the sixteenth century? Not the Reformers, but Rome itself, said Calvin. How ironic: "They treat us as persons guilty of schism and heresy because we preach a doctrine unlike theirs," and therefore "break the communion of the church."[193] But in truth, the "sole cause of our separation is that they could in no way bear the pure profession of truth."[194] Calvin, like Luther before him, was also quick to point out that Rome cast out the Reformers by excommunication. Yet in doing so, they might as well have expelled the catholic church itself.

Was all lost? Were the Anabaptists right that Rome's corruption of Word and sacrament had resulted in the total disappearance of the one, holy, catholic, and apostolic church? Calvin answered in the negative for several reasons. For instance, baptism is a sign of God's goodness and the church's preservation. Calvin may have used language that resembled Luther's condemning tone, calling the papacy a harlot or even Antichrist, but Calvin nonetheless trusted God's secret providence.[195] First, he was nuanced enough to recognize gradations of corruption, much like Israel in the Old Testament.[196] Second, he was far too predestinarian to doubt the "certainty and constancy of God's goodness" to preserve his elect. If one asked, "Where do signs of God's goodness remain?" Calvin would answer, "In baptism." Despite the serious decline in doctrinal fidelity, Calvin looked at the many baptisms in the medieval church and concluded that here, in this sacrament, we still find a "witness to this covenant" of God.[197] As long as baptism remains, the Christian can rest assured that God's church continues, even if Antichrist himself walks its aisles. Granted, the Roman pontiff (on whom Calvin laid primary blame) had built a "wicked and abominable kingdom" and had established "deadly doctrines, which are like poisoned drinks." "In them Christ lies hidden, half buried, the gospel overthrown, piety scattered, the worship of God nearly wiped out." Nevertheless, the church continued. The church may be "woefully dispersed and scattered," Calvin said, but by God's grace "some marks of the church remain," which not even the devil himself could destroy.[198] Calvin, therefore, did not think of himself as a heretic or schismatic

---

191. Calvin, *Institutes* 4.2.6.

192. Calvin, *Institutes* 4.2.6. Cf. Cyprian, *On the Unity of the Catholic Church* 5 (*PL* 4:501–2; *CSEL* 3.1.213–14; tr. *ANF* 5:423; LCC 5:127).

193. Calvin, *Institutes* 4.2.5. According to Calvin, Rome failed to observe how this communion was welded together. Calvin, following Augustine, identified two bonds: (1) "agreement in sound doctrine" and (2) "brotherly love." Heretics violate the former, schismatics the latter, he said.

194. Calvin, *Institutes* 4.2.6.

195. Calvin, *Institutes* 4.2.3, 10–11.

196. Calvin, *Institutes* 4.2.8.

197. Calvin, *Institutes* 4.2.11.

198. Calvin, *Institutes* 4.2.12.

but as a pastor pleading for fidelity, a pastor whose ministry was dedicated to reforming the one, holy, catholic, and apostolic church.

With the Reformed Church now positioned on the side of catholic fidelity, Calvin put forward a Reformed polity rooted in a patristic pedigree (with a particular sympathy to Cyprian), over against the papacy's polity in Rome.[199] And when Calvin reached for the Eucharist, he was convinced he was retrieving an Augustinian sacramentalism over against Rome's transubstantiation.[200] Historians even debate whether Calvin's sacramental theology was more Thomistic or Franciscan.[201]

Regardless, Calvin's mature theology in his 1559 *Institutes* was the fruit of decades of editions. When Calvin wrote the first edition of his *Institutes* and defended the catholicity of evangelicals in France to the king, he was still exiled from Geneva. As Geneva became a possibility once more, Calvin had to ask himself whether he could institute the type of evangelical catholicity he defended. The verdict awaits the next chapter.

---

199. E.g., Calvin, *Institutes* 4.2.3; 4.4.1,11; 4.6–8.
200. E.g., Calvin, *Institutes* 4.14.
201. Gerrish, *Grace and Gratitude*, 162–68.

15

FORTIFYING A REFORMED CHURCH

The Reformation in Geneva, Berne, and France

While there is no doubt that Calvin and his followers in Reformed orthodoxy were antagonistic to their Roman Catholic contemporaries, their theological vision was not formed by building a theology on wholly new grounds. Rather, the early Reformed tradition sought to be rooted in Scripture, the Church Fathers, and the best in medieval theology and method, as they perceived it. . . . [Calvin] was a recatholicizing influence for early Protestantism—an approach shared by many later Scholastics. . . . Compared to many Reformed theologians who dismiss central claims in premodern catholic theology, Calvin and the Reformed Scholastics were on the catholic side of the divide. Before sola scriptura became an excuse to marginalize pre-Reformation exegesis and theology, there was another way of being Reformed. Ironically, while that earlier way often presented polemics against their Roman Catholic contemporaries, it also drank from the same catholic stream that many in the Reformed tradition have now left in search of new waters.

—J. Todd Billings, "The Catholic Calvin"

CALVIN'S CROSS: RETURN TO GENEVA

One might assume the Geneva magistrates were quite pleased with Calvin's absence.[1] Yet life in Geneva after Calvin spiraled into endless rivalries. Geneva appeared vulnerable, attracting the attention of cardinals curious about whether the church might return to Rome, as seen with Cardinal Sadoleto (see chapter 1). Rome had predicted that a break with the church could only result in schism and chaos. On this precarious precipice, Calvin's defense of the Reformation's catholicity was just the antidote Geneva needed. His apologetic served to redeem his status in the eyes of the Genevan magistrates, helping them recognize Calvin's inestimable worth as a Reformer. Furthermore, Geneva had developed in other

---

1. For an elaboration of this section, see Gordon, *Calvin*, 124. On Calvin's influence across Europe, political implications and tensions, as well as church and state relations, see 124–28.

ways that created space for Calvin. When Calvin was first exiled from Geneva, a galvanized faction worked against him and continued after him. However, by the mid-1540s, that hostile opposition dispersed and dissolved, perhaps not entirely but nevertheless to a significant degree.[2]

Could Calvin possibly be interested in returning after the catastrophe of 1538? When Pierre Viret posed that question to Calvin, Calvin said he would rather be tortured in hell for all eternity than return to Geneva. Then he told Viret not to bring Geneva up again.[3] But Viret refused to listen. He kept pestering Calvin, knowing firsthand how much Geneva needed Calvin to return. So did Farel, but this time Calvin was not about to be intimidated by his fiery threats. Calvin was a prophet now as well.

Calvin's time in Strasbourg had taught him that Reformation did not begin or end with ecclesiastical and political drama in Geneva. Since Geneva he was given opportunities to converse with Reformers from all over Europe, and not only Protestants but Catholics as well. He had a seat at the table of Protestant-Catholic negotiations. Still, these dialogues did not leave him optimistic. In his estimation, Protestants needed to unify not with Rome but with one another. Returning to Geneva was appealing because it was an opportunity to establish what the Protestant church should look like in his own mind. But if Calvin returned, things had to be different the second time around. He could not spend years laboring for reform only to be opposed by the civil authorities again. Plus, he had been hurt and was convinced he was the victim in the immediate aftermath of his exile, as his reputation was dragged through the mud not only by the Genevans but also by the Swiss.[4]

Calvin had conditions. The magistrates had to flex and permit clergy to exercise church discipline.[5] If they could not relinquish some level of authority to the church and its ministers in matters of excommunication, Calvin was not interested. When Geneva appeared amicable and pliable, Calvin returned and proposed a fresh foundation for church order, namely, his *Ecclesiastical Ordinances* (1541), a legislation that displayed a lawyer turned theologian.[6]

---

2. Gordon, 121, 124.

3. "But it would be far preferable to perish for eternity than be tormented in that place. If you wish me well, my dear Viret, do not mention the subject!" *CO* 11:36; Bonnet, 1:162–64.

4. Gordon, *Calvin*, 122. Cf. *CO* 11:230–33; Bonnet, 1:258–62.

5. Calvin had other conditions too. For example, a catechism had to be set in place for educational reform. "For Calvin, recovering the ancient practice of catechesis was critical to preserve reformed Christianity in the future: 'The church of God will never preserve itself without a catechism,' he noted, 'for it is like the seed to keep the good grain from dying out, causing it to multiply from age to age.'" Manetsch, *Calvin's Company of Pastors*, 266, quoting Calvin to Edward Seymour, *CO* 13, cols. 71–72; *CTS* 5:191. To see the fruit of Calvin's condition, read his 1541 *Catechism of the Church of Geneva*.

6. Qualification: Calvin "was too good a reformer and lawyer to believe that the New Testament provided a legislative basis for church government. There was no pretense that the structures set up by the *Ecclesiastical Ordinances* of 1541 were found in the early church; Calvin was more concerned to demonstrate that they embodied its spirit." Gordon, *Calvin*, 126. To understand the judicial nature of these ordinances, see Lindberg, *European Reformations*, 261.

RELOCATING THE CONFESSIONAL TO THE LIVING ROOM

In the sixteenth century, the home of a Protestant pastor was not segregated from his ministry. Students came to a pastor's home to discuss theology over the dinner table. Fellow pastors or pastors of nearby churches visited to talk about urgent matters of church life. And church members came to be discipled by their pastor. When Calvin returned to Geneva, this time they were liberal with his salary, allowing him to host in his home, a home they also provided for him within a short distance from the cathedral of Saint-Pierre. Although Luther's vocation was not an exact parallel, Luther, too, modeled the home as a ministry. His *Table Talk* records countless conversations over dinner where the German Reformer answered questions both theological and practical.

Pastors not only embodied a Protestant ministry in their homes, but they also took the Protestant ministry to the homes of their people. For example, when Calvin returned to Geneva a second time, he implemented another catechism to teach children (and parents ignorant of theology), and he looked for a way to prepare families for Sunday morning. He substituted penance and the confessional with pastoral visitations. These visits were amicable and casual but always spiritual, allowing the minister to prepare the family for the Lord's Supper on Sunday, for example. In other words, these visits were a means to discipline, not corporate discipline (e.g., excommunication) but minor discipline in the form of discipleship. Scott Manetsch notes that these visitations were sanctioned in 1550 by the Small Council and permitted four times a year (Manetsch, *Calvin's Company of Pastors*, 281–82). As Herman Selderhuis says, the confessional "was not thrown out, but was relocated to the living room" (*John Calvin*, 88). The Reformers were not against auricular confession (e.g., Luther continued to defend the practice), but they were concerned with its context, namely, the penance system. Auricular confession created immediate relief but not necessarily a turn away from sin and an active pursuit of holiness. Calvin warned against an auricular confession that was a license to sin.

Relocation rather than annihilation is a reminder that even in soteriology and ecclesiology, the Reformers did not consider their reform a total break with the medieval past. They did not abandon the concepts of contrition and confession, however much they needed an alternative ecclesial context. Even penance was not eradicated but was reconfigured within the context of church discipline (e.g., Cameron, *The European Reformation*, 159).

Few could have imagined that the negotiation and approval of these ordinances was instrumental not only to the longevity of Calvin's reforming program in Geneva but to the success of the Reformed Church after Calvin.[7]

Calvin's *Ecclesiastical Ordinances* made several advances. To begin with, the four offices Calvin fortified in Strasbourg were put forward.[8] To review, pastors

---

7. To see the many effects, consult Benedict, *Christ's Churches Purely Reformed*; Naphy, *Calvin and the Consolidation of the Genevan Reformation*.

8. On each office, see Gordon, *Calvin*, 128; Lindberg, *European Reformations*, 262.

were charged with preaching the Scriptures, supervising the sacraments, and reproving the recalcitrant. Second, Calvin intended to establish an academy for the training of potential pastors by doctors, although that vision was not implemented for decades after his return to Geneva. Doctors devoted themselves to supervising the doctrinal fidelity of the church, both for those who led, like clergy, and for those who received, like laity. Third, elders oversaw discipleship, ensuring that those under their care remained holy and faithful. Unlike doctors and pastors, who underwent some formal training, elders were laymen. Yet their role was instrumental, reporting the wayward for discipline. Fourth, deacons assisted those with physical needs, both in the church and in society.[9]

As for ecclesiastical independence in matters of discipline, Calvin did gain ground, establishing the minister's involvement and independence, but not to the degree that he ultimately wanted. He desired a relationship between magistrate and minister that respected God's two kingdoms and asserted that ministers operate within the spiritual sphere, a sphere the magistrate should not confuse with the civil realm. In turn, the council expressed their own boundaries, warning against a consistory that tried to interfere with civil concerns. Despite these delineations, a notable but unspoken ambiguity remained: Who had the ultimate say in the case of excommunication, minister or council?[10]

If Calvin had any chance of removing this ambiguity, he needed to win over members of the consistory, the council, and the Company of Pastors to his vision of two kingdoms. To understand how Calvin triumphed in the end, a brief tour of the consistory and Company of Pastors will be enlightening.

THE CONSISTORY AND GENEVA'S DEFENSE AGAINST ROME

Among Calvin's conditions for return was the establishment of a consistory to oversee the daily, religious, and civic lives of the people. The consistory, which consisted of pastors and magistrates, was responsible for church discipline, both on a minor and major level. The Word was not only preached from the pulpit but applied to the daily lives of the people. Each pastor was responsible for discipling the laity so that the Word took root in the common life of the congregation in society. When a Christian strayed from the Word, he or she was summoned by the consistory and questioned, like in a courtroom. Sometimes the offense was minor but not unimportant, like slandering a refugee, a fellow Christian, or perhaps even a pastor. Other times the offense might be major, like a husband

---

9. "There is some controversy in recent scholarship over whether Calvin's idea for this double diaconate ('administering the affairs of the poor' and 'caring for the poor themselves') derived from his knowledge of already existing welfare institutions in Geneva or from his biblical theology. Whatever the source, it was clear to Calvin that appeal to Scripture was paramount for the development of that society which so impressed John Knox." Lindberg, *European Reformations*, 262.

10. Tuininga thinks the omission was on purpose. He also explains the unfortunate misunderstanding that resulted: "Because of the ambiguity of the *Ecclesiastical Ordinances* regarding the final authority over excommunication, many of the magistrates viewed the Consistory simply as a committee of the state, a judgment echoed by some recent historians but vigorously rejected by Calvin and his supporters." Tuininga, *Calvin's Political Theology and the Public Engagement of the Church*, 75.

having an affair or a Christian returning to the beliefs and practices of Rome. In severe circumstances, especially cases where the person in question was unrepentant or hostile, the consistory could begin the steps of discipline according to Matthew 18.

The consistory's goal was mediation for the sake of resolution and reconciliation. If an individual was not living a civil or Christian life, that person was summoned and questioned by the consistory. If the person was not penitent, the consistory might ban that person from enjoying civil benefits (e.g., marriage) or ecclesiastical privileges (e.g., Lord's Supper). The ban was not punishment for punishment's sake, but punishment with the goal of restoration. In severe cases, the consistory had the power to send a person before the city's Small Council. That was a serious matter since the Small Council had judicial authority to imprison or even execute someone if necessary. Did the citizens of Geneva appreciate the consistory? Not necessarily. "The consistory was essentially a court in Geneva, but as the ministers who sat on it were mostly French, it was the object of much Genevan resentment of foreigners in their city."[11]

Modern society may be inclined to evaluate the consistory as harsh and controlling, even overbearing and legalistic. At times the consistory could lean that way. However, understanding the motives behind the consistory can keep a modern interpreter from premature judgment and anachronistic dismissal or even hubris, pushing modern, progressive standards on an age occupied by entirely different contextual pressures and challenges. Consider a few motives surrounding the consistory.

First, on not a few occasions the Reformers were accused of novelty. To most in Rome the Reformers were innovators. Originality was often accompanied by heresy.[12] Therefore, to be accused of innovation was often equivalent to being charged with unorthodoxy. The Reformers were bent on demonstrating quite the reverse. To counter Rome's charge of novelty, Reformers like Calvin established an ecclesiastical structure that fostered pastoral credibility and authority. By virtue of the consistory, Calvin established a courtroom that created (sometimes demanded) respect and acted like a shield against Rome.

Second, the consistory safeguarded Calvin's reformation from accusations of immorality. Next to novelty, such an accusation was fatal. In the sixteenth century, heresy was not merely a doctrinal issue but a moral issue, implying at the very least impiety. In the modern era, doctrine and piety have been bifurcated, but in the sixteenth century they were attached. A major theological error was either due to impiety or at the very least led one into impiety. Rome had no shortage of such accusations against the Reformers. When Luther married a runaway nun, the papacy capitalized on the scandal: this was the type of moral

---

11. Gordon, *Calvin*, 134.
12. "In fact, from the early church to the early modern period, innovation was equivalent to heresy." Lindberg, *European Reformations*, 263.

laxity that resulted from justification by faith alone, they said. Antinomianism was a constant charge. Those types of accusations did not stop at Wittenberg but could be found across Europe.[13]

Calvin's Geneva was no exception. Therefore, the consistory was a way to guard the reputation of Geneva's reformation from moral turpitude and thereby protect the theological and pastoral credibility of a Reformed Church. The consistory ensured that no one had a pass on Geneva's moral code, not even doctors, pastors, or magistrates. Even members of one of Geneva's councils were accountable. No one stood above the morality enforced by the consistory, not even members of the consistory itself.

With each passing decade Geneva became a model of a Reformation city, any hint of impiety in the lives of the people only confirmed what Rome suspected. The consistory, then, served to monitor morality in Geneva, all but guaranteeing to onlookers like Rome that immorality was intolerable by Reformation standards. A moral standard, not merely a doctrinal one, was also critical to defending the credibility of Geneva's catholicity.

Third, the primary goal of the consistory was not retributive but restorative. Contemporary interpreters are easily drawn to cases of discipline over playing cards or dancing or punishments that involved public shaming—images of Nathaniel Hawthorne's *The Scarlet Letter* begin to surface in the minds of moderns. However overbearing some of those restrictions may have been, a more balanced interpreter will also recognize that the driving purpose of the consistory originated from a pastoral heart to help and serve. For example, if a husband was abusing his wife, the consistory stepped in to protect the woman. If a French refugee was treated with extreme prejudice, the consistory stepped in to make sure equality was practiced. Or if a pilgrim passing through lingered to stir up schism, the consistory stepped in to safeguard peace among God's people.

An ecclesiastical courtroom that enacts punishment may be difficult for moderns to swallow, but that difficulty may be due to an unfamiliarity with (and perhaps bias against) communitarian societies. Prior to the modern era, people did not live their lives as individuals but as members accountable to wider communities, both ecclesial and civic. The priority was not the individual but the group. While that priority may have resulted in some disadvantages for the individual, on the whole that priority actually served the individual, situating him or her within a coalition that cared, even if at points it appeared to care too much. That was the societal and ecclesiastical fabric behind Geneva's consistory. "In Geneva, contrary to our contemporary urban anonymity and anomie, 'there were real networks of caring' . . . Calvin strove to construct a consistory that would provide education in the Christian faith and a counseling service designed for reconciliation. 'Discipline to these early Genevans meant more than social

13. See chapters 9–11 and Luther's advice to Philip of Hesse on his marriage. Also see Lindberg's example of the cardinal surprised to discover that Geneva was so holy. Lindberg, 199–220.

control. It also meant social help.'"[14] For that reason alone, we should avoid the temptation to judge Geneva as if Calvin was its chief tyrant.

Calvin's critics and enemies could paint him as a brutish punisher of anyone who did not match his moral standards. While he certainly had his weaknesses—he did lose his temper with friends and enemies alike—the caricature fails to consider the context of the consistory. That context had everything to do with the *motives* behind church discipline. Whereas the papacy pronounced excommunications that damned a person to hell—the Reformers included—Calvin and the consistory believed the power of the keys lay elsewhere. Excommunication, for the Protestant, certainly put one in peril—Jesus himself said the person should be treated as a Gentile or tax collector if he or she refused to listen to the whole church (Matt. 18:17). However, the motive, the desire, the hope from start to finish was nothing less than *reconciliation*. Discipline was, at least, designed to be a means to love the wayward so that they returned to safe haven in Christ and did not forfeit the endless benefits of everlasting blessedness in Christ. That was Calvin's heart even if he failed to embody such a Christlike motive in every case. In that light, Protestant Geneva could not have been more different than Rome. For Calvin and the consistory, discipline stemmed from *pastoral care*.[15]

Without the consistory, could Calvin's reforming measures have been so effective and enduring? Probably not. Calvin had no shortage of nemeses, some external to Geneva but many internal as well. Yet the *Ecclesiastical Ordinances*, the consistory, as well as the formidable support of many within the Company of Pastors, acted as a bulwark against dissenting voices.

THE VENERABLE COMPANY OF PASTORS

The consistory provided a disciplinary mechanism for oversight of the laity. Yet reform had to start with the pastoral office itself, and Calvin needed a system to train future pastors. Prior to Calvin's return, Geneva was in a desperate state due to the poor abilities and training of its ministers. "Those who were regarded as the leaders of faith," Calvin lamented, "neither understood thy Word, nor greatly cared for it. They drove unhappy people to and fro with strange doctrines, and deluded them with I know not what follies." The people fared no better: "Among the people themselves, the highest veneration paid to thy Word was to revere it at a distance, as a thing inaccessible, and abstain from all investigation of it." The consequence was serious: "Owing to this supreme state of the pastors, and this stupidity of the people, every place was filled with pernicious errors, falsehoods, and superstition."[16]

---

14. Lindberg, 264; Kingdon, "Calvinist Discipline in the Old World and the New," 666, 679; Kingdon, "Geneva Consistory in the Time of Calvin," 34.

15. To see this difference in more detail, see Manetsch, *Calvin's Company of Pastors*, 188–220.

16. John Calvin and Jacopo Sadoleto, *Reformation Debate*, 82.

CALVIN AND PIERRE VIRET

Calvin is often set apart as the one who single-handedly reformed the church of Geneva, but Calvin was the first to confess his dependence on others. For example, when Calvin returned to Geneva, no one was more important to Calvin than Pierre Viret. He once wrote to Farel, "Should Viret be taken away from me I shall be utterly ruined and this church will be past recovery. . . . Let Viret remain with me" (*CO* 11:321–2; Bonnet, 1:282–4). Calvin then proceeded to turn over every stone in an attempt to prevent Viret from leaving, although he did not succeed.

Why did Calvin value Viret? For many reasons. Viret had exceptional people skills, a rare ability to appease the disgruntled and win over the skeptic (much in contrast to Farel). When Calvin was in exile, Geneva turned into a combustion chamber, but thanks to Viret enough peace was achieved to call Calvin back.

Viret was also a superb preacher, making Reformation truths accessible to the average evangelical. In short, the Genevans loved Viret. And Viret supported Calvin's theology and reforming vision. Yet Calvin saw more: Viret would stand by him when he walked through the valley of his enemies. (On this friendship, see Gordon, *Calvin*, 153–55.)

To change this sad trajectory, Calvin had to model an alternative, and his preaching served this purpose with exegetical excellence. When Calvin returned to Geneva in 1541, he did not reenter the pulpit and chide the people and the magistrates, however tempting that might have been. Instead, he opened his text to the exact verse where he had left off when he was exiled and began preaching again. Like Luther, Calvin was committed first and foremost to a reformation by means of the Word, a Word potent enough to heal any wounds still festering from exile. Calvin did not hesitate to speak his mind from the pulpit, addressing the political and ecclesial affairs of Geneva, but he drew the line at manipulating the pulpit for the preacher's agenda. The pulpit was a megaphone for the gospel and its power to save. Upon Calvin's return, he set his attention on that original mission, though this time with a bit more experience to implement the gospel in the Genevan church.

Calvin's preaching was complemented by his literary output. His commentaries taught others how to interpret the Scriptures, his sermons taught others how to preach the Scriptures, and his *Institutes* and *Catechism* taught others how to confess and apply the Scriptures.[17] By modeling biblical interpretation, Calvin's preaching, teaching, and writing served to reform the church so that the laity could understand and apply the Scriptures as taught by a capable clergy.[18]

---

17. For Calvin's biblical exegesis, see Pitkin, *Calvin, the Bible, and History*; Holder, *John Calvin in Context*.

18. Zachman, *John Calvin as Teacher, Pastor, and Theologian*, 12–13.

Calvin's leadership served as a model for pastors. Each Friday morning, pastors and doctors gathered to hear one of their own teach from the Scriptures, followed by feedback from another minister.[19] As a means to influence the direction of the Genevan church, this Company of Pastors was particularly important to Calvin, who was their mediator, overseeing the lectures and often responding with his own insights into the text. After the public lecture and response time, Calvin and the Company of Pastors met behind closed doors to deliberate over pastoral candidates, attempting to judge whether an individual was ready or not. Candidates were judged not only on the fidelity of their theology and their teaching capabilities but the credibility of their godliness.[20] If the candidate was approved by the Company of Pastors, that candidate was then presented to the council for final approval.[21]

Candidates were selected, however, according to a Protestant paradigm. They considered each candidate's calling to the ministry *under* the Word. That presupposition mattered because Calvin did not believe that the Word's authority and success depended on the minister; rather, the minister's authority and success relied on the Word. And that countered the papacy's ministerial training: "the celibate Catholic priests whose primary role was to hear confessions and perform the miracle of the Mass was replaced by the married Protestant pastor whose chief responsibility was to proclaim the Word of God through sermon and sacraments."[22] Christ is the head of his church, which he governs by his word through his ministers. To invert this hierarchy—as Rome had—was self-centered rather than Christ-centered. Since Calvin is often caricatured as the dictator of Geneva, his own words should be heard: "Christ does not call his ministers to the teaching office that they may subdue the Church and dominate it but that he may make use of their faithful labors to unite it to himself."[23]

A comparison of the 1536 and 1543 editions of Calvin's *Institutes* also reveals an effort on Calvin's part to underline the source of a minister's validation. As Manetsch observes, in 1536 Calvin said a qualified candidate receives confirmation when magistrates and ministers alike express approval. Yet Calvin's 1543 edition emphasized confirmation by the congregation and the ministers, leaving magistrates out. "Calvin appealed to the example of the early Christian church to show that it was the responsibility of the ministers—not the magistrates—to appoint candidates to the ministry, with the consent and approval of the people."[24]

---

19. Laity were welcome to attend and voice insight as well. Gordon, *Calvin*, 129.

20. Gordon, 130. Cf. Flaming, "Apostolic and Pastoral Office," 163.

21. On how Calvin's personality affected the Company of Pastors, see Gordon, *Calvin*, 129, who writes, "To his opponents he [Calvin] seemed severe and unrelenting, but among most of his colleagues he commanded respect, particularly as the majority had been appointed by him." Calvin not only represented the Company of Pastors to the Small Council in an "advisory capacity," but also appeared before the council to "defend his own actions" (130).

22. Manetsch, *Calvin's Company of Pastors*, 72.

23. Commentary on John 3:29 in *CNTC*, 4:81. Manetsch, *Calvin's Company of Pastors*, 73, cites this passage at length and also points out this is one reason Calvin changed the vocabulary of the ministry and stopped using *priest* and *clergy* and instead preferred *elder* and *messenger*, among other titles.

24. Manetsch adds that for Calvin this calling also involved both the internal call of the Spirit to the vocation of pastor and the external call of the church. Manetsch, 80.

THE INFLUENCE OF THE CHURCH FATHERS
ON CALVIN'S PREACHING

If a Reformer like Calvin was dedicated to catholicity, then the historian should find traces of the church fathers across his preaching. As seen in the last chapter, Calvin's *Institutes* are littered with patristic voices. His preaching is also influenced by church fathers, but not in the same, overt manner of citation. Instead, Calvin studied the church fathers to determine the best method of preaching and to retrieve their hermeneutical and expository insights. John Chrysostom, the golden mouth preacher, was one major influence on Calvin, who translated and edited Chrysostom's homilies. Unfortunately, Calvin never finished the project, and many French pastors never did receive Calvin's complete translation of the church father.

In the pulpit, Calvin practiced the *lectio continua* method, which sequentially transitioned through a text or an entire book of the Bible. Calvin was not the first to utilize this method; Luther and Melanchthon, but especially Zwingli and Bullinger, also preached successively through biblical books (see chapter 12).

In addition, Calvin was not afraid to learn from non-Christian sources of rhetoric—from Socrates to Cicero to the latest humanists of the sixteenth century. Calvin followed the example of Melanchthon, who looked to the rhetorical wisdom and methods of Aristotle to master the public message as a persuasive speech act.

On Calvin's preaching, see T. H. L. Parker, *Calvin's Preaching*, as well as Manetsch, *Calvin's Company of Pastors*, chapter 6.

Although the edit is minor, it reveals Calvin's concentrated effort to be more faithful to a two-kingdom theology, a theology that located candidacy in the church. Ministers chose and elected new ministers, a sacred circle that Calvin's *Ecclesiastical Ordinances* said the magistrates should not hijack, nor ministers manipulate to become politicians in the pulpit.

Furthermore, Calvin assumed that the church—laity and ministers alike—should and must be guided by the Holy Spirit, asking for wisdom to discern if and when a man was called to serve the church. Calvin's approach differed from two extremes: Rome and the radicals. While Rome looked to the episcopacy to administer the minister's authority, many radicals jettisoned the need for ecclesiastical approval (the church was corrupt anyway) and instead decided their candidacy for themselves. Calvin's model steered clear of both extremes by acknowledging the necessity of ministerial approval while also recognizing the involvement of the corporate body.[25]

The process for election and ordination was rigorous. It evolved during and after Calvin's lifetime, but its mature structure can be summarized in the following ten steps:

25. Manetsch, 81.

1. *Theological examination.* The candidate's biblical and systematic understanding of theology are evaluated. May involve a disputation.
2. *Character examination.* The candidate's godliness is evaluated.
3. *Preaching examination.* The candidate's expository skills are evaluated.
4. *Assess.* Company of Pastors assembles to assess and vote.
5. *Pastoral charge.* Delivered by moderator.
6. *Small Council's examination.* The elected candidate's perception of magistrates is evaluated.
7. *Announcement to congregation.* The candidate's name is shared with Geneva churches for consideration.
8. *Installment.* On the next Sunday, the congregation celebrates ordination.
9. *Oath.* The elected and ordained minister recites an oath of allegiance to pastoral duties.
10. *Company of Pastors.* The new minister now joins the Company of Pastors.[26]

Calvin discovered, however, that the success of the Company of Pastors might take time—lots of time—until a series of pastoral residents could come through the Company and start effecting change in Geneva and across Europe. Patience was not Calvin's strong suit; change did not happen as fast as he desired. When Calvin returned to Geneva, his opinion of the ministers was low: many of them were inadequate for the task. Calvin did not feel that he could trust them. Some even sensed his distrust and eventually turned into his enemies.[27] Nevertheless, in 1546 a new crop of ministers arrived in Geneva, Frenchmen in particular. Unlike the ministers Calvin inherited, these ministers were not only on board with Calvin's strategy for church renewal but far more capable in the pulpit.[28]

What Was It like to Preach in a Reformed Church?

The Company of Pastors did receive regular training in preaching due to the Geneva "Congregation," a gathering of ministers once every week to hear a sermon. The meeting was not restricted to ministers; anyone from Geneva's churches could attend as well and listen to the Scriptures exposited. At one point or another, every minister's opportunity came. After his sermon, the Company of Pastors gave their critique. Knowing that evaluation followed a sermon made even the best preachers nervous; however, the intention of the Congregation was

---

26. For an elaboration of each, see Manetsch, 85–87. Manetsch does qualify that for candidates already ordained, the process looked different; examinations were not required. Also, usually the Small Council approved the election of candidates by the Company of Pastors. However, knowledge of some civil indiscretion could surface and disqualify the candidate.

27. *CO* 11:311, 377. See, e.g., the case of Henri de la Mare in Gordon, *Calvin*, 131; Naphy, *Calvin and the Consolidation of the Genevan Reformation*, 59–70; Jenkins, *Calvin's Tormentors*.

28. Calvin had successfully pushed out dissenters, and now a united front stood by his side. However, the Genevans did not always share Calvin's enthusiasm, especially since the ministers Calvin pushed out were loved by the Genevans. As for these new ministers, they were Frenchmen, and affluent Frenchmen at that, which created a class divide between clergy and laity. Gordon, *Calvin*, 133; Naphy, *Calvin and the Consolidation of the Genevan Reformation*, 72–75.

not ridicule but encouragement and assistance, guiding pastors as they improved their knowledge of the Scriptures and refined their preaching ability. In the process, the average Genevan churchgoer benefited as well, learning the Scriptures alongside that day's teacher. This practice was also intended to unite ministers with one another as they confessed the same doctrine. Biblical study and theology were a corporate affair. "The fewer discussions of doctrine we have together, the greater the danger of pernicious opinions," said Calvin.[29]

Interior of the Temple de Paradis, Lyon 1564, by Jacqus Perisin (Circle of faith)
Public Domain

What was it like to preach in one of Geneva's churches? In a word: *christological*. Calvin, for example, ascended the pulpit and opened the Scriptures because in the Scriptures alone was the gospel to be found. Unlike the late medieval churchgoer who left the cathedral with penance to repay, the evangelical churchgoer left the cathedral with full assurance of forgiveness, clothed in the righteousness of Christ. The pulpit was prime real estate to convey this good news.

---

29. *CO* 13, col. 434. Cf. Manetsch, *Calvin's Company of Pastors*, 134.

CALVIN'S VISION FOR CLASSICAL EDUCATION: THE GENEVA ACADEMY (1559)

Calvin's life was devoted to preaching in the pulpit for the church and then lecturing on books of the Bible to train future pastors. Toward the end of his life, Calvin's dream for a humanist education finally came to fruition. Like Luther, Calvin understood the importance of formalized education grounded in the finest humanist training, one in which the students learned ancient languages, read the classical texts, resourced the tools of philosophy and theology, and retrieved the hermeneutical insights of the Fathers in their study of the Scriptures. In 1559 an academy was created in Geneva for this purpose. Such an academy was not original to Geneva; Lausanne had one as well, but it had fallen apart due to the incompatibility of Viret and Beza. The latter's exit from Lausanne worked in Geneva's favor. Calvin trusted Beza, who was not all that different in his skill set from Calvin. Beza was the ideal candidate to lead the Geneva Academy. With Beza at the helm, many who taught and studied at Lausanne transferred to Geneva, and in little time the Geneva Academy became an operational institution that served the churches of Geneva by preparing future ministers within the confessional confines of the church. Geneva had so progressed that it now housed a collection of books in a newly established library, giving students access not only to the works of Calvin but of other Reformers as well. The Academy proved a natural fit for Calvin; students flocked to his lectures to hear his exegetical insights on books of the Bible. But as important as Calvin may have been to the spirit of the Geneva Academy, it was Beza who led the school and turned it into a thriving institute.

On the Geneva Academy, see Gordon, *Calvin*, 299–300, 313.

But the pulpit was also much more. From the pulpit, the pastor taught his people not only *what to believe* from the Bible, but also *how to read* the Scriptures. Now that the Scriptures were making their way into the vernacular—no longer limited to educated, elite clergy but finding their way into the hands of the laity—the pastor had the opportunity to model biblical interpretation. And no one was more skilled at pulpit hermeneutics than Calvin.

The pulpit was also an opportunity for application. Calvin not only communicated what the Scriptures meant but how they should be implemented in the daily lives of the people. At times Calvin and other pastors took to the pulpit to address theological, social, or political problems they perceived in the congregation and the city. This was a bold move that was not always received well by the offenders the preacher targeted. On some occasions even violence erupted as a result. The pulpit proved one of the most effective ways to address a problem in the congregation, pinpointing the culprits so that others in the congregation were not led astray.

However, those who voiced severe admonishments from the pulpit were held accountable. Many of the preachers in Geneva, Calvin included, were reprimanded for insulting the Genevans. At times Calvin even had to mediate between the mob and his colleagues. Using the pulpit to make a statement was dangerous business, setting certain Genevan families off, provoking their hostility moving forward.[30] Nevertheless, Calvin considered the pulpit a prophetic ministry, one in which the prophet of God proclaimed the truth to the people of God, whether they liked it or not.[31]

In essence, the pulpit became the *epicenter* for the Reformed Church. The caricature of the medieval era as a church without a sermon is gross. The medieval church was familiar with preaching long before the Reformation. "By the late Middle Ages, the typical city dweller in Western Europe may have had the opportunity to hear as many as eight hundred sermons over the course of a lifetime."[32] Thanks to mendicant orders, papal courts, and city-sponsored pulpits, preachers could be heard across the span of the church calendar. With the priority of rhetoric during the Renaissance, many of these sermons became models of intellect and eloquence. However, this flurry of sermons in the late medieval era was exterior to the mundane ministry of the average church. "Ironically," says Manetsch, "even as sermons were becoming an ever more popular aspect of religious life in the fifteenth century, they were, for the most part, absent from the day-to-day ministry of the Catholic parish." The reason why is unsettling: "Parish priests and curates were not expected (and few were qualified) to preach." Calvin experienced this sad state of preaching *within* the church when he first came to Geneva and then again when he returned from exile. "As a general rule, preaching on the eve of the Reformation was occasional and performed by mendicants and other specialists—not by parish clergy."[33]

Not only Calvin, but Luther and Melanchthon in Germany, as well as Zwingli and Bullinger in Zurich, all helped change that custom. Parish clergy were no longer put aside for the real event: a special occasion to hear a mendicant preacher. Now the clergy themselves became the preachers, which entirely changed their perception of ministry. As they became the shepherds, the sheep looked to them on a weekly basis to receive spiritual food. The church member no longer left his or her church and traveled to a mendicant order to hear a Franciscan or Dominican preacher for a special occasion. The Word was brought near, within the pulpit of the church down the street. This change meant that the theology of the Reformation could spread fast; the evangelical message of free grace could put down roots everywhere.

---

30. For examples, see Gordon, *Calvin*, 139–43. Gordon observes, however, that it was not until after 1555 that Calvin rose to a position of unequaled influence.

31. Calvin did have his limits, however, as his friction with John Knox exemplified. See chapter 16.

32. Manetsch, *Calvin's Company of Pastors*, 147.

33. Manetsch, 147.

What Was It Like to Worship in a Reformed Church?
Calvin's Living Icons and Sacramental Catholicity

Historians have long said that if Rome relied on the eyes and nose, the Reformers petitioned the ears, although even this contrast must be qualified by Calvin's substitution of dead for living images (a point we will return to). The cathedrals—Saint-Gervais, La Madeleine, Saint Pierre—were renovated in countless ways to reflect an evangelical theology that oscillated between the Word made visible (baptism, Lord's Supper) and the Word proclaimed (pulpit).[34] Walls were no longer clothed with images but were painted white. New pulpits were built and positioned for the regular preaching of Scripture. The position of the pulpit—typically high above the congregation—conveyed the centrality of the Word of God for the people of God. Its elevation also communicated the priesthood of all believers. "The pulpit's location also bespoke the Reformers' theological conviction of the essential spiritual equality of ministers and lay-people. No longer did the altar separate the 'spiritual clergy' from the rest of the congregation."[35]

The oratorical focus of the service, however, was not unilateral. Not only did the pastor preach the Word, but the congregation responded to the Word with their own voices. The laity no longer kneeled before the bread and wine but stood to sing psalms, children included. It is hard to overstate the importance of singing psalms. Like Luther, Calvin understood that music was an indispensable avenue into his people's hearts. Music also revealed how corporate the worship could become. Rather than watching the priest perform the Mass, the people lifted their voices as one, a noise that confirmed the priesthood of all believers. Calvin witnessed and even enacted these priorities while in Strasbourg. Upon his return to Geneva, he carried over Strasbourg's doxological structure in the *Form of Prayers and Ecclesiastical Songs* (1542) and underscored the significance of his methods in his more polemical work, *On the Necessity of Reforming the Church* (1544).

Calvin believed that if preaching and singing alike revolved around the Word, then the Holy Spirit would work within so that the heart was convicted of sin and would turn to Christ in faith. By neglecting the Word, however, the people were prone to idolatry, as exhibited by Rome's liturgy. The Word, therefore, was instrumental to reforming worship, and in Calvin's Geneva it could be heard not only on the lips of the preacher but from the mouths of the congregation as well.[36]

Some interpreters have been critical of Calvin's methods, as if clearing the church of images, recentering the people around the pulpit, and incorporating

---

34. For an outline of the many changes, see Gordon, *Calvin*, 136–37, as well as Manetsch, *Calvin's Company of Pastors*, 32.

35. "Further, the proclamation of Scripture in the middle of the congregation was a potent symbol that Christ, the living Word, continued to speak and dwell among his people." Manetsch, *Calvin's Company of Pastors*, 33.

36. On the Word and Spirit, see Manetsch, 34–35. Manetsch cites Calvin's commentary on John (*CNTC* 4:99).

song saturated in the Scriptures represented Calvin's "personal austerity" or his "aversion to the material world." That portrait of Calvin and worship is not accurate, but more importantly it misses the point of Reformed worship. Calvin's modest approach "reflected his conviction that only through pure and simple worship might the beauty of the gospel shine forth resplendent."[37]

As mentioned, Calvin's emphasis on the oratory nature of worship must be qualified, otherwise the historian will miss the fullness of Calvin's participation ecclesiology. An older generation of scholars believed Calvin had little to no place for visible images and instead placed all his emphasis on hearing the Word. The renovation of cathedrals as well as the centrality of the preached Word are proof. However, that thesis has been challenged with some success as scholars have now demonstrated that when Calvin removed "dead images," he replaced them with "living icons."[38] In Calvin's own words, "When I ponder the intended use of churches, somehow or other it seems to me unworthy of their holiness for them to take on images other than those living and symbolical ones which the Lord has consecrated by his Word." What are these living and symbolic images? The washing with water in baptism and the eating of bread and the drinking of wine at the Lord's table. Occupied by these visible icons, though there are other ceremonies as well, "our eyes must be too intensely gripped and too sharply affected to seek other images forged by human ingenuity."[39] If Calvin is taken seriously, then the historian cannot say in a strict sense that Rome was sacramental (visible) while Calvin was proclamatory (oratory). The common caricature that Rome was realist while Calvin was nominalist will not do either. "Calvin always claimed that his theology was both evangelical and orthodoxy," Randall Zachman clarifies. His sacramental theology means Calvin should "claim his place as a member of the broader catholic tradition."[40]

Two observations follow. First, the living icons were so extensive that Calvin saw living icons across the landscape of Christianity *and* the cosmos. In other words, his entire outlook of the church and creation was *sacramental*.[41] In contrast to a symbol, which merely represents something real, a sacrament participates in that which is real (i.e., reality). In other words, an icon is sacramental because it signifies a present reality that truly inheres in the sacrament itself. Creation was a type of icon for Calvin, *the theater of God's glory*, because God was really present, as if those with eyes to see could watch the play that the divine

---

37. Manetsch, 36.
38. The old theses were advocated by Edward Dowey, David Willis, Thomas F. Torrance, Lucien Richard, Alexandre Ganoczy, Brian Gerrish, Dawn de Vries, William Bouwsma, and Bernard Cottret. Those who have challenged that thesis include Mary Potter Engel, Susan Schreiner, Philip Butin, Barbara Pitkin, T. H. L. Parker, Edward Dowey, Thomas Davis, and most of all, Randall Zachman. Sometimes both emphases can be seen in Carlos M.N. Eire. For a survey of this literature, see Zachman, *Image and Word in the Theology of John Calvin*, 1–7.
39. Calvin, *Institutes* 1.11.13.
40. Zachman, *Image and Word in the Theology of John Calvin*, 22.
41. To understand the difference between symbol and sacrament, see Boersma, *Heavenly Participation*, 22–23.

craftsman had written across nature. Furthermore, those with eyes to see find themselves written into this play. For whoever has been made in the image of God steps into the theater as the pinnacle of theater itself, a living icon of the playwriter's glory. Since creation is a theater of God's glory, Calvin mimicked the Greek theater when the play takes a sharp turn as a tragedy. Onto the stage enter other living icons, beginning with the law, a mirror that unveils the horror of Adam's first sin, a turn away from virtue to vice. Calvin even considered the history of Israel a living icon as she betrayed her liberator and enslaved herself to the nations, exchanging the glory of the eternal God for images resembling mortal man (Rom. 1:25). Though darkness covers the theater of icons, suddenly light penetrates with a new icon: Christ. If the law is a mirror unveiling sin, the gospel is a mirror in which the sinner beholds Christ. And who is Christ but the image of the invisible God, the firstborn of all creation. Those who have been redeemed by the image of the invisible God have his Spirit to conform them more and more into the image of Christ. That conformity will be complete when they *see* Christ (the beatific vision) and are made like Christ. As Calvin wrote in his commentary on 1 John 3:2, right now "we see through a glass, darkly" (1 Cor. 13:12), but when our image is renewed and the corruption of our flesh is stripped away, we shall behold him face to face. With a spiritual nature "we shall be partakers of the divine glory" and "endued with a heavenly and blessed immortality," exclaimed Calvin.[42]

The beatific vision, therefore, is the ultimate fulfillment of Calvin's sacramental pilgrimage because at last those renewed into the image of Christ will enjoy the fullness of their participation in Christ as partakers of the divine nature. Until then, God has given his church living icons to shed light along the way, such as baptism (the icon of the covenant), the sacred Scriptures (an icon of light for our path), the Lord's Supper (an icon of communion that nourishes faith as the Spirit raises the church into the heavenlies with Christ), and many other ceremonies in the church (the corporate icon of God's assembly). Each of these icons may be coated in an evangelical color, but Zachman has shown that underneath each of them is the substance of catholicity, both its patristic and medieval varieties.

Furthermore, the sacramental nature of these icons is accented by Calvin's Christian Platonism. Living icons like the sacraments are steps on the ladder of ascent so that with each step the church participates further in the life of the holy Trinity.[43] Beginning with his 1539 *Institutes* Calvin exhibited his debt to Plato because the Greek philosopher understood that the soul's *summum bonum*

---

42. Calvin does qualify himself. First, no man can see God and live (Exod. 33:20), which explains why Moses could only see God's "back." So, Calvin says that the "manner" is more by "effect" than "cause." Second, even seeing God will not evaporate his incomprehensibility: "the perfection of glory will not be so great in us, that our seeing will enable us to comprehend all that God is; for the distance between us and him will be even then very great" (*Commentaries on the First Epistle of John*, 206).

43. Zachman wonders whether signs of Platonism in Calvin are due to the humanist influence of Erasmus's *Enchridion* for example. Zachman, *Image and Word in the Theology of John Calvin*, 15.

is located in the one who is goodness itself. The same can be said about beauty: the soul perceives beauty across the landscape of the cosmos through the senses, which leads him to ascend to the vision of Beauty itself. Zachman is convinced that Calvin paraphrased Plato's *Phaedrus* on the basis of the following comments, one taken from the *Institutes* and the others from Calvin's commentaries:

> *Institutes*: "But how can the mind be aroused to taste the divine goodness without at the same time being wholly kindled to love God in return? For truly, that abundant sweetness which God has stored up for those who fear him cannot be known without at the same time powerfully moving us. And once anyone has been moved by it, it utterly ravishes him and draws him to itself."

> *Commentary on 1 John* (2:3): "Granted that Plato was groping in the darkness; but he denied that the beautiful which he imagined could be known without ravishing a man with the admiration of itself—this in *Phaedrus* and elsewhere."

> *Commentary on 1 Peter* (2:3): "Now, it must be the case that the grace of God draws us all to Himself and inflames us with love of Him by whom we obtain a real perception of it. If Plato affirms this of his Beautiful, of which he saw only a shadowy idea from afar off, this is much more true with regard to God."[44]

Calvin, of course, was insistent on a *critical* appropriation—*Christian* must always qualify *Platonism*. Thus Calvin appealed to God's grace as the reason for the church's ascent up the ladder of participation. As he emphasized elsewhere, the living icons themselves are necessary to accommodate the weakness of humanity, seen most of all when the Son of God assumes flesh. Nevertheless, Calvin remained unembarrassed in his debt to Plato, appropriating the philosopher's language of participation to emphasize the way living icons lead us further up and further in until the vision of God beautifies his people.

Calvin may have stripped the church of dead icons that led the church into idolatry, but he replaced them with living icons that ensured a sacramental tapestry, one in which the church participates in the goodness and beauty of God both now and in the eschaton. Seeing God now may occur through a glass darkly, but one day we will see God in the face of Christ. Living icons are sacramental means to that beatific reality.

CALVIN'S VICTORY

As mentioned, Calvin established his *Ecclesiastical Ordinances* in 1541, but who had ultimate say in matters of excommunication was left unanswered. As long as the question remained ambiguous, Calvin's two-kingdom vision for city and

---

44. *Institutes* 3.2.41 (cf. 1.5.2); Comm. I John 2:3; CO 55:311A; *CNTC* 5:245; Comm. 1 Peter 2:3; *CO* 55:233B; *CNTC* 12:258. Cf. Zachman, *Image and Word in the Theology of John Calvin*, 16–17.

church also remained unfulfilled. A tension followed like a black cloud ready to burst. Between 1546 and 1555 the cloud broke open, and a fierce storm of factions threatened to rip Geneva apart.

The storm thundered when irreconcilable tension between the consistory and the Favre family created an explosive atmosphere. The Favre family resented the consistory, which called the family to account for breaking Geneva's moral code, from sexual immorality to the disrespect of pastors during the Lord's Supper. The Favre family did not acknowledge the consistory's authority either. Although the Favre family did not get away with their transgressions, or their disrespect, their ongoing resistance set a pattern for future conflict.[45]

For instance, riots exploded when the parents were prohibited from using Catholic baby names. The city did not recognize these names, and the ministers denied these parents the right of infant baptism. Even though the city and church agreed on the prohibition, they could not agree on how to respond to the riots. The consistory demanded excommunication; the council gave an inflexible no in reply. In 1547 consistory and council were paralyzed by their disagreement on how to proceed.[46] The paralysis exposed the ambiguity in the *Ecclesiastical Ordinances.* Who had final authority, minister or magistrate, consistory or council? In Calvin's opinion—which he did not hesitate to vocalize from the pulpit—the council needed to step aside; excommunication was the rightful duty of the minister. The civil authorities not only failed to back the consistory, but they were interfering in an ecclesiastical domain.

Favor swung in Calvin's favor in the years ahead in part because Calvin's supporters multiplied due to the number of French refugees.[47] Coming from France, where the government persecuted them, many of these refugees took Calvin's side without hesitation. The last thing they wanted was a Genevan government intruding in the affairs of the church. However, in 1553 Calvin was seriously opposed by a member of the Favre family, Ami Perrin. Calvin not only faced Perrin's tactics but also the ambitions of his many followers who managed to work their way into high-level positions in Geneva. Now that they were a majority in Genevan government, they set their sights on the consistory. If they could take over the consistory, Calvin and his ministerial colleagues had little chance of regulating ecclesiastical discipline.[48]

The tension in the years 1553 to 1555 was impossible to suppress. Everything came to a head when the Small Council acted unilaterally in a disciplinary case. Philibert Berthelier was on the path to excommunication, but when he expressed sorrow the council gave Berthelier permission to return to church and participate in the Lord's Supper. This news outraged the consistory since their participation in the Berthelier case—clearly a case of ecclesiastical discipline—was

---

45. For example, consider the opposition of Ami Perrin, who married into the Favre family.
46. Tuininga, *Calvin's Political Theology and the Public Engagement of the Church*, 76.
47. On the *Bourse Francaise* in the late 1540s and early 1550s, see Tuininga, 77.
48. Tuininga, 77.

never even solicited. Calvin had returned to Geneva on the condition of ministerial say in matters of church discipline, and the consistory was established for that very purpose. The Berthelier case ignored everything Calvin had labored to achieve, as if Calvin had been returned to those nightmare years just before exile. "Calvin and the pastors were furious. In an echo of the confrontation of 1538, they declared that they could not tolerate this usurpation of the Consistory's spiritual power, and that they would accept death rather than serve Berthelier communion."[49] Although Berthelier never did take Communion—an act that might have resulted in a brawl at the Lord's Table—the consistory and the Council were now, once more, at odds with one another over the right to fence the table and excommunicate. Would the Small Council kick Calvin out again for refusing to let an undisciplined Genevan come to the table?

With almost ten years of unresolved tension and ambiguity over disciplinary authority, the councils of Geneva decided not to exile the pastor they had asked to return. Instead, they gave Calvin the opportunity to present a thorough case for his position. Calvin was now at an advantage; few in Geneva could match Calvin's exegetical and theological persuasiveness. Calvin proceeded to demonstrate that discipline was an ecclesiastical privilege alone. Excommunication was not the duty of a magistrate but a minister. Whenever the civil government interfered with church discipline, it confused God's two kingdoms, conflating the spiritual with the temporal, even allowing the temporal to swallow up the spiritual, as the Berthelier case demonstrated. Discipline, excommunication in particular, was a spiritual matter, pertaining to the regeneration and sanctification of the unrepentant.[50] In short, Calvin was advocating for the independence of the church from the state, a path that deviated from that of other Protestant territories, from Germany to Switzerland. If successful in his 1555 proposal, Calvin could become a pioneer for a new approach to city-state relations, one that protected the autonomy of the church, ensuring that the civil government buoyed the practice of Protestantism but nevertheless remained distinct from ecclesiastical authority.

The councils were convinced. That same year the change took effect. New elections took place that gave Calvin's followers a fresh opportunity to regain momentum and the power that came with it, which they did. The followers of Ami Perrin lost control, and seeing their defeat, they resorted to riots.[51]

---

49. "The Council, stunned, sought to avoid confrontation by advising Berthelier to refrain voluntarily from the Supper. The Petit Counseil and the Deux Cents then declared that the Petit Counseil had concurrent jurisdiction over church discipline with the Consistory and could overturn sentences of excommunication." Tuininga, 79.

50. Tuininga, 79–80.

51. The government also made positive changes that differentiated the two kingdoms. For example, "in 1560 the magistrates legislated an important symbolic shift in the makeup of the Consistory, declaring that from now on elders could be chosen from among the foreign born and that when the syndic presided over the Consistory, he was no longer to carry his official baton, the sign of his magisterial office." Also, in the early 1560s deacons were positioned less in the political sphere than in the ecclesiastical realm. Tuininga, 80.

The outcome: capital punishment. The civil government could not tolerate revolt let alone violence.

From 1555 to Calvin's death, the ambiguity was at least resolved even if difficult circumstances created tension from year to year. By consequence, Calvin experienced almost a decade of ecclesiastical autonomy, unprecedented in almost any Reformation territory with Protestant magistrates.[52] Moreover, Calvin's model gained international influence. As the Protestant population in France grew to 10 percent by the end of 1562, as Geneva continued to send ministerial reinforcements, up to half of the churches in France adopted some form of Calvin's two-kingdom position, as manifested in the distinction made between magistrate and minister at the Synod of Lyon (1563).[53]

TWO KINGDOMS

The 1540s and 1550s were also decades of literary elaboration on the two kingdoms. Calvin outlined the jurisdiction of the two kingdoms both in editions of his *Institutes* and in his sermons and commentaries.[54] God governs his temporal (earthly, secular, political, outward) kingdom by his common grace, as manifested through his divine providence over creation and his revelation of natural law. Due to the spread of wickedness, God has established civil government to restrain evil and establish justice and peace.

God governs his spiritual (heavenly, inward) kingdom by his special grace. The kingdom of Christ is not instituted by the sword but through the Spirit's use of the Word of God, resulting not only in spiritual regeneration but sanctification. While the temporal kingdom produces a civil righteousness, the church cultivates a spiritual righteousness. While the temporal kingdom holds its citizens accountable to the moral, natural law of God, the spiritual kingdom is defined by justified sinners, liberated from the slavery of sin to freely serve others in obedience to the law of love.

Although these two kingdoms must not be confused or conflated, nevertheless, they are not divorced from one another (as seen in the extreme abuses of two kingdoms among some radical Reformers). In this life, the Christian lives in both kingdoms. Therefore, the Christian submits to both authorities in each sphere, contributing to the preservation of justice in society while simultaneously

---

52. I do not mean to give the impression that Calvin alone was responsible for this decade of victory. Naphy has demonstrated that many other factors contributed to Calvin's success, including the support of French refugees who flooded into Geneva at the time. Naphy, *Calvin and the Consolidation of the Genevan Reformation*, 167–207.

53. What was Calvin's position on political resistance? "Though his ultimate goal was the establishment of the Reformed church by the French monarchy, Calvin never claimed that religion justified violent rebellion. It was in defense of the French King, according to the law of his realm, and under the authority of a prince of the blood that the Huguenots had just cause to fight." Naphy, 91 (see 85–91 for Calvin's involvement in the volatile French situation).

54. On Calvin's two kingdoms, see *Institutes* 4.20. For one of the best exhaustive treatments of Calvin's two kingdoms doctrine in his sermons and commentaries, see Tuininga, *Calvin's Political Theology and the Public Engagement of the Church*, 92–354.

cultivating the restoration of true godliness and spirituality in the church. The Christian respects the authority of the civil realm and its disciplinary use of the sword as well as the authority of the spiritual realm and the church's disciplinary use of the Word.

Calvin set in place a paradigm that would forever change the course of church-state relations not only in Geneva but across Europe and eventually America. This two-kingdoms paradigm stood in stark contrast to what came before: the late medieval papacy demanded supremacy over the temporal sphere. Since the pope was vicar of Christ on earth, he had the right to exercise authority over the magistrate. Politics was a spiritual sphere for Rome, one over which the pope had jurisdiction. Vatican City and the papal states were not merely focal points for the church of Rome, but they exercised their own political power, administering ecclesiastical and civil discipline. The polar opposite of Rome was the radical movement (see chapter 13), which on the whole advocated for total separation from the world, politics included. Just as they radicalized *sola scriptura*, so, too, they radicalized the two kingdoms. The divorce between the kingdoms was so severe that the Christian no longer lived in God's two kingdoms. The Christian's citizenship was only in the spiritual kingdom; serving the temporal kingdom in some civil office was forbidden. In between these two extremes, though far closer to Rome than the radicals, were the majority of Protestant territories, from Henry VIII's England to Zwingli's and Bullinger's Zurich. The magistrate(s)—whether in the form of a king or queen or in the form of a city council—had every right to establish, govern, and even control ecclesiastical affairs.

As for the German Reformation, Luther attempted to safeguard a two-kingdoms distinction even though he never created a formalized system to see it implemented, as is plain in the relationship between German princes and ministers. Here was precisely the point where Calvin's contribution exhibited acumen. The Geneva Reformer not only held to two kingdoms in theory, but by 1555 he succeeded in establishing an official system that operated within a two-kingdoms paradigm. While Calvin often receives most credit for his theological distinctives—from predestination to union with Christ to justification—one of his most lasting contributions is the ecclesiastical independence he achieved. That ministerial autonomy stems from his theology of the kingdoms. For in Calvin's mind, theology and practice could not be severed.

AMBITIONS FOR INTERNATIONAL ALLIANCE

The 1540s and 1550s introduced Calvin to a tension that he struggled with until the day he died, a tension between his pursuit of unity and the necessity of engaging in endless controversy. First, consider Calvin's ambitions for an alliance.

In 1543 and 1544, Protestants felt considerable pressure from Charles V. In September 1544, Charles V and Francis I signed the Peace of Crépy. Previously, Charles V needed the support of the Smalcald League in his conflict with

Francis, yet the representatives of the League continued to put forward certain conditions to ensure the safety of Reformation territories. Now that the conflict between Charles V and Francis I had been steadied, would the emperor turn against the Protestants?[55]

The Diet at Speyer

That was the question on the minds of many Protestants who met Charles at the Diet at Speyer (1544), fearful the emperor might squash them and put an end, once and for all, to the Reformation Luther had ignited. The Protestants, therefore, needed a united front, now more than ever. At Speyer, the Reformers needed somebody who could represent their cause, propose a council, and rally Reformers from various territories around Reformation theology.

Calvin rose to the occasion. History has not been kind to Calvin. He is often portrayed as both stubborn and divisive. However, a more balanced reading of Calvin recognizes that the Reformer labored for unity among the Reformers. His actions at Speyer are one example. *On the Necessity of Reforming the Church* (1544), presented to the diet, was Calvin's call to unity between the Reformers. The Reformers had been "accused of rash and impious innovation" by proposing change to the present state of the church, said Calvin, addressing Charles V. Calvin's response to this accusation was one of both shock and outrage: "What!"[56] To demonstrate that the papacy in Rome was the true innovator who had left the church diseased, Calvin then proceeded to critique the papacy's soteriology and ecclesiology in exhaustive detail. For example, against the papacy's claim to the saints and their works of supererogation, Calvin said the Reformers aligned with the catholic tradition as exemplified in Augustine, who said, "No martyr's blood has been shed for the remission of sins. This was the work of Christ alone, and in this work he has bestowed not a thing which we should imitate, but one we should gratefully receive."[57] For Calvin, the proof of *solus Christus* was not original to the Reformers "but rather that of the Church Catholic."[58] Calvin applied this same argument ad nauseam. When he took aim at the primacy of the pope, he rallied the Reformers to their apostolic and catholic heritage: "For both the writings of holy Fathers, the acts of Councils, and all history, make it plain that this height of power, which the Roman Pontiff has not possessed for about four hundred years, was attained gradually, or rather was either craftily crept into, or violently seized."[59]

However, a united front was difficult to achieve when division over the Lord's Supper continued to divide Protestants. As chapter 10 demonstrated, attempts

---

55. On the political context preceding the diet at Speyer, see Gordon, *Calvin*, 164.

56. Calvin, *Reforming the Church*, 125.

57. Calvin, *Reforming the Church*, 164; quoting from Augustine's *Tract. In Joan* 84.

58. Calvin, *Reforming the Church*, 163. Calvin took this same tactic with other doctrines (e.g., baptism and bishops).

59. Calvin, *Reforming the Church*, 218.

were made in the 1530s to bring Luther (and the Lutherans) and Zwingli (and the Swiss) together but ultimately proved unsuccessful. Even when Martin Bucer—the reputable peacemaker—attempted to intercede, he was dismissed and criticized.[60] By 1544 the division seemed insurmountable, unity an impossibility. As Calvin evaluated the debate upon his return to Geneva, he decided he was far more sympathetic with the Lutherans than the Zwinglians, even if, in the end, Calvin could not adopt Luther's view of ubiquity or the Christology it required.[61] Calvin also appreciated how Bucer and the Strasbourg theologians were at least attempting to engage Luther and the Lutherans.

Despite bad blood between the Lutherans and Zwinglians, Calvin tried to intercede. At first a certain optimism characterized Calvin, an optimism that might be attributed to his interaction with Melanchthon. In 1544 Luther released his *Short Confession*, yet another condemnation of the Swiss position. Luther was also clear that he had no patience for mediators in the debate. That would be reconciliation at the expense of the truth. Those words stung, hurting Melanchthon and making him wonder if he had much of a future next to Luther.[62] In a series of letters, Calvin became mediator of this international dispute. He wrote to Bullinger, imagining how upset Bullinger must be and how vitriolic Bullinger had become in a response to Luther's *Short Confession*. Calvin did not blame Bullinger if he was irate; Luther, after all, had many faults, and they had littered the debate over the last decade. Yet Calvin also reminded Bullinger that Luther was the father of the Reformation. "Often I declared that even if he [Luther] were to call me a devil, I should still nonetheless hold him in such honour that I would acknowledge him as an illustrious servant of God."[63] Nevertheless, Calvin sent letters to Melanchthon, asking him to talk to Luther when the timing was right and deliver Calvin's letter for Luther's consideration. Calvin petitioned Luther to add his support to the Protestants in France. But Melanchthon never showed Luther the letter. He knew Calvin's letter could provoke Luther to anger since Luther associated Calvin with Bullinger and Zwingli.[64]

---

60. See both Luther's and Zurich's responses to Bucer in Gordon, *Calvin*, 163, 165. My chronicling of these events follows Gordon.

61. Gordon, *Calvin*, 167. Cf. *CO* 11:23–26. Gordon believes that prior to Strasbourg, Calvin's view was more in line with Zwingli's view; as proof Gordon points to Calvin's 1536 *Institutes*.

62. Gordon, *Calvin*, 168. Bucer was also the target.

63. For the whole context, see *CO* 11:772–75; Bonnet, 1:405–10.

64. *CO* 12:7–12; Bonnet, 1:410–18. Gordon, *Calvin*, 170, sums up the outcome: "Once so elated by Luther's positive assessment of his response to Sadoleto, Calvin had been rejected by his hero." The debate continued in 1548 in Lausanne, but this time between Pierre Viret (who represented Calvin) and André Zébédée (who defended Zwingli's position). However, Calvin did make progress when he took initiative and traveled all the way to Zurich in 1548 to meet with Bullinger. That decision was instrumental; the two Reformers developed a friendship. As Calvin separated himself from Bucer, Bullinger became more and more willing to engage Calvin on an amicable basis, even interceding in the affairs of Berne and Lausanne (see 172–73).

Lifted into Heaven: The Holy Spirit and
Participation in the Lord's Supper

Throughout the 1540s, Calvin continued to develop his own position on the Lord's Supper that was neither Lutheran or Zwinglian, a position that reached a full elaboration by the last edition of his *Institutes of the Christian Religion*.

For Calvin, the Lord's Supper was a visible picture of the union between Christ and the Christian, a sacrament that seals the promises of the gospel on the Christian conscience. Our Father feeds his children, adopted into his family, at the table of his Son, nourishing and strengthening their faith.[65] When they eat by faith, they participate in Christ and all his benefits.[66] But how can Christ grow into one with them when his flesh is taken from them at his accession? Calvin's answer is the Holy Spirit. Christ's flesh "penetrates to us, so that it becomes our food," through the "secret power of the Holy Spirit." Calvin was not a proto-pantheist or panentheist ahead of modernity's curve. Rather, he was explaining *how* God effects (seals) what he promises in the sign itself. "Now, that sacred partaking of his flesh and blood, by which Christ pours his life into us, as if it penetrated into our bones and marrow, he also testifies and seals in the Supper—not by presenting a vain and empty sign, but by manifesting there the effectiveness of his Spirit to fulfill what he promises."[67] Participation in Christ occurs in the supper but only by means of the Spirit, who alone can apply that spiritual truth within the physical sign to those at the table.[68]

Calvin's emphasis on participation by the Spirit is instrumental to understanding why the Reformer rejected the three major explanations of Christ's presence. First, Calvin was frustrated with Rome because its advocacy of transubstantiation failed to consider the Spirit as the bond between Christ and the Christian. "The bond of this connection is therefore the Spirit of Christ, with whom we are joined in unity, and is like a channel through which all that Christ himself is and has is conveyed to us. . . . The Spirit alone causes us to possess Christ completely and have him dwelling in us."[69] Rome errs by "leaving nothing to the secret working of the Spirit, which unites Christ himself to us. . . . Christ does not seem present unless he comes down to us. As though, if he should lift us to himself, we should not just as much enjoy his presence!"[70]

Second, if Christ is not brought down to the table in some carnal or corporeal way, then he is not present through a *conversion* of bread into body, as Rome taught, nor is he present by *enclosing* his body in the bread, as the Lutherans

---

65. Calvin, *Institutes* 4.17.1; cf. 4.17.3.

66. Calvin, *Institutes* 4.17.2, 10–11.

67. Calvin indicated that the requirement is faith: "And truly he offers and shows the reality there signified to all who sit at that spiritual banquet, although it is received with benefit by believers alone, who accept such great generosity with true faith and gratefulness of heart." Calvin, *Institutes* 4.17.10; cf. 4.17.5.

68. Calvin said the nature of this spiritual truth includes three things: "the signification, the matter that depends upon it, and the power or effect that follows from both." Calvin, *Institutes* 4.17.11.

69. Calvin, *Institutes* 4.17.12.

70. Calvin, *Institutes* 4.17.31. In context Calvin may be aiming at Peter Lombard.

assume.[71] Instead, Calvin teaches a spiritual presence (*praesentia spiritualis*), meaning the "body and blood of Christ, now in heaven, are mediated to believers by the power of the Spirit."[72] As Calvin said, the Spirit elevates the believer into the heavenlies with Christ. If we "are lifted up to heaven with our eyes and minds, to seek Christ there in the glory of his Kingdom, as the symbols invite us to him in his wholeness, so under the symbol of bread we shall be fed by his body, under the symbol of wine we shall separately drink his blood, to enjoy him at last in his wholeness." Christ sits at the right hand of the Father, yet his kingdom is "neither bounded by location in space nor circumscribed by any limits." Christ "shows his presence in power and strength, is always among his own people, and breathes his life upon them, and lives in them unharmed, as if he were present in the body." How is this possible? Again, the Holy Spirit is the answer. Christ "feeds his people with his own body, the communion of which he bestows upon them by the power of his Spirit."[73] Zanchi said something similar in his *Confession of Christian Religion*: "both the union and the eating are made by the Spirite and by faith" so that Christ is present by means of a sacramental "participation," which is why Scripture calls those who eat "partakers."[74] The "sacraments are visible words" so that what is signified in the sign is "given with it." Such giving occurs because Christ is made "made present by the Holy ghost."[75] In summary, for Calvin and other Reformed theologians, the notion of a spiritual feeding can be interpreted as a sacramental union (*unio sacramentalis*) "between the sign and the thing signified" so that "Christ is truly and substantially (*substantialiter*) given," yet without compromising his local, bodily presence in heaven.[76]

Third, Calvin did use the word *symbol* to describe the Lord's Supper, but he was quick to qualify that he did not consider the bread and wine empty symbols (a strike at Zwingli). When the symbols are presented, "the truth of the thing signified is surely present there." Otherwise, God tricks his people, presenting the symbol but denying them true participation in what the symbol signifies. "But if it is true that a visible sign is given us to seal the gift of a thing invisible, when we have received the symbol of the body, let us no less surely trust that the body itself is also given to us."[77]

Calvin feared Zwingli's position placed too much emphasis on the subjective rather than the objective, on faith rather than God's grace. For example, Zwingli's successor, Heinrich Bullinger, criticized Calvin's position as too similar to Rome's. In Bullinger's opinion, Calvin fastened grace to the Eucharist.

---

71. Calvin appears to have used "conversion" when referring to transubstantiation and "enclosed" or "fasten" or "circumscribed" when referring to Lutheran ubiquity. Calvin, *Institutes* 4.17.18, 19.

72. Muller, *Dictionary,* sacramentum, s.v.

73. Calvin, *Institutes* 4.17.19.

74. Zanchi, *De religione christiana fides,* 16.14, 15.

75. Zanchi, *De religione christiana fides,* 16.17.

76. Muller, *Dictionary,* sacramentum, s.v.

77. Calvin, *Institutes* 4.17.10.

Calvin said in reply that Bullinger misunderstood faith's purpose. God's grace is "indeed tied to the sacraments, not temporally or spatially, but only 'insofar as one brings the vessel of faith to obtain what is there depicted.'"[78] Calvin thought Bullinger separated grace and faith too much. God does not offer the Eucharist hoping someone will believe, but he grants faith itself only to confirm that same faith in and through the Eucharist.[79] The Eucharist, said Calvin, "is an outward sign by which the Lord seals on our consciences the promises of his good will toward us in order to sustain the weakness of our faith; and we in turn attest our piety toward him in the presence of the Lord and of his angels and before men. . . . [It is a] testimony of divine grace toward us, confirmed by an outward sign, with mutual attestation of our piety toward him."[80]

At the core of Calvin's concern was the "finality, not the objectivity, of a sacrament: what it gives is not some mysterious power, but the increase of faith." As Gerrish observes, "This is, to be sure, a different understanding of sacramental efficacy from the Roman Catholic view, but it is not a collapse into subjectivity."[81]

What God promises by his word he seals through the sacrament by granting and confirming faith in his people.[82] On that basis, Calvin is speaking of *efficacy*, yet not an efficacy by virtue of the sacrament itself. Rather, the efficacy of the sacrament is due to the power of God's Word to deliver on its promises, which is why the Eucharist is called a "sign and seal," confirming that which it signifies.[83] Calvin's sacramental efficacy was a step too far for Bullinger, who alongside Zwingli considered the supper more like a ring, a token by which to remember Christ and all he accomplished so that the believer can seal his allegiance to his Savior much like a soldier to his commanding officer.[84]

Bullinger's discomfort and Calvin's comfort with describing the Eucharist as an instrumental means of grace not only reveals the divide between them but also conveys Calvin's continuity with the church catholic. Although Calvin took issue with the medieval doctrine of transubstantiation, he did not jettison the good with the bad. In many ways, Calvin's appeal to the instrumentality of the Eucharist is striking in its similarity to Thomas Aquinas's.[85] Calvin's language has led interpreters to ask, is Calvin more of a Thomist or a Scotist? "Whereas for Thomas a sacrament was an instrumental cause by which God, the principal cause or agent, imparted grace to the soul, Scotus could only understand a

---

78. Gerrish, *Grace and Gratitude*, 161; quoting Calvin, *Calvini responsio ad annotations Bullingeri* (1549), *CO* 7:701.

79. Gerrish, 161.

80. Calvin, *Institutes* 4.14.1.

81. Gerrish adds, "Grace is offered even to those who do not believe; therein lies the 'integrity' of the sacrament. Gerrish, *Grace and Gratitude*, 161.

82. Gerrish says that for Calvin this is the "primary use of a sacrament, to confirm faith." Gerrish, 162.

83. "The indispensable component in a sacramental action is not the sign but the word, which the sign confirms and seals." Gerrish, 161.

84. Gerrish, 164.

85. "To be sure, he [Calvin] insisted that the primary agency in the sacraments is God's. (Thomas Aquinas had said the same.)" Gerrish, 166. Cf. *ST* 3, Q. 62, a. 1.

sacrament as a sure sign that, by a concomitant divine act, grace was simultane-ously being imparted." For Calvin, "a sign is the guarantee of a *present* reality."[86] Participation in the supper is participation in the body of Christ. On that score, Calvin had far more in common with Thomas Aquinas than Duns Scotus.

To Calvin's credit, he paved an alternative to Lutherans and Zwinglians alike. Yet whether his view could unite the Reformed Church remained questionable.

Bucer Signed the Augsburg Interim

Despite Calvin's effort across the 1540s, the impasse over the Lord's Supper wrecked his dream of unity, a dream that seemed to dissolve with each pass-ing year.[87] The future of Protestantism looked bleak from 1545 to 1547. Not only did the Reformers fail to unite around the Lord's Supper, but in 1545 Rome came together at the Council of Trent, which could only have one outcome, namely, the condemnation of the Reformation.[88] Then, in 1547 the Protestants' worst nightmare came true: Charles gained control. Charles made one advance after another into southern Germany until the Smalcald League was defeated (see chapter 10). Johann Frederick was taken into custody, and Philip of Hesse waved the white flag of surrender. By summer no one stood in Charles's way.[89]

Was Rome pleased with Charles's victory? Rome did not mind seeing Protestants overcome, but Rome had serious concerns with Charles wielding unchallenged authority. Charles and Rome did not necessarily share the same agenda for the church moving forward. Although Charles had conquered Protestant princes, that did not mean he would erase Protestants off the map. Charles remained committed to the papacy's religion, but he also commissioned bishops to be creative and find a way to include Protestants.[90] The result was the Augsburg Interim at the start of 1548, a document committed to Rome's core faith and practices but one postured toward Protestants with the hope they might add their signatures.

Calvin, without hesitancy, stood against the Augsburg Interim as strongly as he stood against all compromise for the sake of reunion with Rome. So, when Martin Bucer signed the Augsburg Interim, Calvin was speechless. Bucer's sig-nature forced Calvin to distance himself from Bucer even more than before. Ironically, Bucer's capitulation resulted in a closer union between the Reformed in Geneva and the Swiss in Zurich.[91]

---

86. Gerrish, 168.

87. *Short Treatise on the Lord's Supper.* Also see *Institutes* in chapters 14–15, as well as Calvin's 145/46 commentary on 1 Corinthians.

88. In response to Trent, Calvin published *Acts of the Council of Trent with Antidote* in 1547, and Johannes Cochlaeus responded by condemning Calvin as a heretic. See chapter 17 of this book for Calvin's *Antidote.*

89. Gordon, *Calvin,* 176, highlights Calvin's view of divine providence. Calvin concluded that God had brought Charles V against the Protestants much like he summoned Nebuchadnezzar against Israel due to her unfaithfulness and compromise with idolatry.

90. Gordon, *Calvin,* 175.

91. Calvin, at the encouragement of Bullinger, wrote a condemning response to the Augsburg Interim.

The combination of the Council of Trent and the victory of Charles V appeared to be the death sentence of the Reformation. But in an ironic twist, such a colossal defeat brought Calvin and Bullinger closer together, strategizing how their two camps might unite to ensure the Reformation transitioned from Wittenberg to Geneva and Zurich.[92]

Consensus Tigurinus

Calvin deserves credit for his quest for unity. Calvin traveled year after year to Swiss and German territories, putting his own health at risk, to secure the unity no one before him was able to solidify. Still, unity required compromise to some degree. In May 1549, Calvin and Bullinger, along with other representatives of Geneva and Zurich, met and signed twenty-four articles called the *Consensus Tigurinus*. However, these articles did have a distinctively Zurich flavor to them, playing to Bullinger's interpretation of the supper, which made Calvin uncomfortable.[93] The *Consensus* required a compromise on Calvin's part for the sake of consolidating the Reformed party. With the Reformation at stake, especially in the wake of both Trent and Charles V's victory, unity was needed now more than ever.[94]

In that spirit, the Consensus was signed in 1549, but it was not published for public distribution until 1551. In the years in between, the document was passed around, which gave Calvin the opportunity to propose two more articles that pulled the *Consensus* back in the direction of Geneva yet still could be interpreted by the Swiss to their liking.[95] To Calvin's disappointment, the *Consensus* did not work; unity was not achieved. Calvin had accomplished the impossible: an alliance with Bullinger and Zurich. But Berne and Basel declined, the former due to ecclesiastical politics and the latter due to theological incompatibility.[96] The failed consensus was a crushing blow to Calvin and foreshadowed Geneva's increasing isolation. Calvin, perhaps more than anyone, labored for unity, but in the end consensus was elusive. Like the many attempts before it, the *Consensus Tigurinus* was a document that could not breach the impasse.[97]

RELENTLESS CONTROVERSY

Calvin's high hopes for unity came crashing down when the *Consensus Tigurinus* failed to bring international union between Reformers. The *Consensus* was only the start of his discouragement. Over the next decade, Calvin was plagued by one

---

92. Gordon, *Calvin*, 176, draws a sobering conclusion: "The game was over: the Lutheran church had been crushed and the Reformation had failed. It now fell to those who were left to continue, and this made unity among the Swiss churches all the more imperative."

93. Note the mediating article: *Calvini Opera* 7:693ff.; Hillerbrand, *Division of Christendom*, 178.

94. Gordon, *Calvin*, 179.

95. Gordon, *Calvin*, 179.

96. For the specifics, see Gordon, *Calvin*, 180.

97. But later Calvin defended the *Consensus*: see his debate with Westphal in Gordon, *Calvin*, ch. 14.

controversy after another.[98] The conflicts were so strenuous on Calvin during the 1550s that Calvin once remarked how he might be happy if he could die already, unsure he could bear the burden of debate and infighting much longer.[99] With each passing year, he had a target on his back that only seemed to increase in size. If he had died in the mid-1550s, his legacy may have been different than many know it today. However, the latter half of the 1550s and the start of the 1560s proved the difference. Calvin emerged from the fires of controversy and the flames of criticism to become a leading Reformer with a mounting audience not only in Geneva but across Europe.

Consider but two of Calvin's many controversies: Bolsec and Servetus.

Bolsec, Bullinger, and the Bernese Alliance

In the 1550s and early 1560s, Geneva was a hot spot for French refugees. English and Italian refugees found their way to Geneva, but French evangelicals fled to Geneva by the thousands. They stood out from the native Genevans in various ways. For example, they were usually wealthy, much in contrast to the Genevans, which only added to the existing cultural tension.[100] Also, while Calvin experienced opposition from segments of Geneva's society, he enjoyed notable ministerial support from French refugees, many of whom became ministers themselves after training in Geneva. These refugees were full of gratitude to the French Reformer for protecting them in Geneva. They marveled at the advancement of the Reformation in the city, a city that stood in such contrast to cities in France where evangelicals were persecuted.

Not every refugee supported Calvin or the vision for Geneva set by the Company of Pastors. On some occasions, refugees introduced ecclesiastical and theological schism. For example, in 1551 a French refugee by the name of Jérome-Hermés Bolsec opposed Calvin. Bolsec was a friar in Paris who turned evangelical, but unlike other friars, he had medical skills. He fled Paris, fearful his evangelical convictions could be the end of him, and practiced as a medical doctor not far from Geneva.

When Bolsec encountered Calvin's teaching on predestination, he reacted with vehemence at the idea that God chose some to salvation and others to damnation. Bolsec accused Calvin of turning God into the devil, making God the author of evil. Bolsec's opposition was alarming because he was intentionally stirring up unrest, which the civil magistrates considered a threat to the relative peace enjoyed between Genevan pastors and magistrates.[101] Bolsec also had a bad reputation with the Swiss; like Calvin, Zwingli, too, came under fire.

---

98. Gary W. Jenkins surveys Tillet, Caroli, Sadoleto, Servetus, Castellio, Baudouin, Bolsec, Wesphal, Radicals, and more in *Calvin's Tormentors*, 1–172.

99. Furthermore, Calvin was disappointed by allies who, in the end, did not support him, some of whom even turned against him.

100. Gordon, *Calvin*, 200.

101. Gordon, *Calvin*, 205, says Bolsec's accusations were "audacious and idiotic."

Bolsec was arrested and locked in prison. Geneva, after taking counsel from the Swiss, decided banishment for the mischief-maker was best. However, the Bolsec affair did create conflict between Calvin and Bullinger. In a series of private letters, it became clear that Bullinger did not hold Calvin's view. While Bullinger also desired to attribute election to the grace of God, he cringed at the thought of reprobation. Reprobation is a consequence of man's disbelief, not the determination of God's will. Bullinger's reaction to Bolsec provided the opportunity for the Zurich Reformer to reveal simultaneously his discontentment with Calvin's *Institutes* and with Zwingli's book on divine providence.[102]

Calvin and Bullinger both agreed it was best to keep their differences private to avoid further division between Geneva and Zurich. As for Bolsec, Zurich did not agree with how the Genevan magistrates had handled him; too unforgiving, they said. Calvin disagreed. The Zurich pastors had failed to consider what was at stake, namely, the grace of God. Furthermore, the Zurich ministers did not understand why Bolsec was such a threat: he was seditious, undermining unity in the church. Zurich was defending "a man who seditiously disturbed a peaceful church, who strove to divide us by deadly discord, who, without ever having received the slightest provocation, loaded us with all sorts of abuse, who publicly taunted us with representing God as a tyrannical governor," said Calvin in response. Calvin then put forward his definite conclusion: "To defend such a man, I say, is the extreme of absurdity."[103]

The alliance between Geneva and Zurich took a hit as a result of the Bolsec affair, but Calvin and Bullinger's friendship did survive these theological and ecclesiastical differences of opinion. Calvin initiated correspondence with Bullinger even after the Bolsec affair to express his devotion to Bullinger, a friendship Calvin intended to cultivate despite whatever disagreements they had.[104]

The Bolsec affair put a spotlight on international politics, exposing alliances as weak and untrustworthy. The dispute not only revealed theological and ecclesiastical differences between Geneva and the Swiss but demonstrated that the Swiss were not as willing to support the Genevans as Calvin had hoped. The *Consensus Tigurinus* may have been a formalized statement of cooperation, but in practice it was the maximum movement the Swiss were willing to take toward the Genevans. "For the Swiss the Consensus was a ceiling rather than a floor, and, as the Bolsec case revealed, they were not prepared to negotiate."[105]

Bolsec was banished, but his protest did not disappear.[106] In 1554 Bolsec became more antagonistic than before, calling Calvin Antichrist.[107] Those in

---

102. *CO* 14:214–15. Cf. Gordon, *Calvin*, 206–7; Venema, *Heinrich Bullinger*, 61–62.
103. *CO* 14:513–54; Bonnet, 2:214–15.
104. *CO* 14:513–14; Bonnet, 2:384–6. Cf. Gordon, *Calvin*, 208.
105. Gordon, *Calvin*, 209.
106. Others in Geneva also opposed Calvin: e.g., Jean Trolliet.
107. "Bolsec's revenge was to publish in 1577 a scurrilous biography of Calvin, accusing him among other things of sodomy, which continued to be an arsenal for anti-Calvinist polemics for the next two centuries." Lindberg, *European Reformations*, 266.

Bernese territories followed Bolsec's lead and labeled Calvin a heretic. They would rather invite Rome back into their churches than tolerate Calvin's doctrine of predestination. Despite these theological charges, an underlying motive drove these assaults: the Bernese were deeply outraged that the Genevans and Calvin were not submitting themselves to the Bernese.[108] After all, Berne oversaw Protestantism across a wide range of territories, some French, some German. Predestination was the proverbial straw that broke the camel's back, bringing to light the many ways Calvin and Geneva failed to adopt Bernese practices in the church.[109] When the Bernese realized that Calvin's books were influencing the Lausanne Academy through teachers like Viret and Theodore Beza, they prohibited Calvin's writings, threw them in a pile, and lit them on fire. The sixteenth-century Reformation started with Rome burning Protestant writings, but now Protestants were burning each other's writings.[110] The news was scandalous to hear back in Geneva. Nevertheless, Geneva continued to support Calvin.

Bolsec had charged Calvin with heresy, a charge that did not persuade the Genevans, but soon the Genevan magistrates had to confront a true case of heresy that intruded their own church.

Servetus and the Threat to Orthodoxy

In the sixteenth century, no accusation was so threatening as the charge of heresy. In the modern era, heresy more often than not is strictly a theological matter, though perhaps with professional or ecclesiastical implications. Not so in the sixteenth century. The charge of heresy implied far more. Heretics were considered immoral, advocates of unbiblical theology that stemmed from ungodliness. The heretic was considered perverse. Furthermore, the charge of heresy was a corporate matter.[111] To teach heresy was an act of schism, stirring up the church, even leading the church down the path of hell itself. Yet heresy not only defiled the purity of the church but the peace and fidelity of the city. Heresy was a civil matter as well, a capital crime, punishable by death.

Heresy was insufferable for yet another reason, one entirely relevant to the Reformation. Remember, Rome accused the Reformers of teaching heresy. They also accused the Reformers of planting a soil ripe for more radical groups (e.g., Anabaptists). The Reformers denied such charges and labored to show that they were consistent with the church catholic, from its creeds to its interpretation of Scripture. For that reason alone, it was imperative that the Reformers

108. Gordon, *Calvin*, 211, says, "The dispute was less about theology than about personality. It is unlikely that many of Berne's magistrates were familiar with Calvin's words. The Frenchman embodied resistance against their authority, and he had to be dealt with."

109. Gordon, *Calvin*, 211. Gordon lists many examples: liturgy, baptismal names, Lord's Supper, excommunication, and more.

110. Burning conveyed heresy: "Book burning was a powerful symbol of heresy. For most Protestants it conjured up the worst images of papal abuse and corruption, a very sign of the presence of antichrist, and for Protestants to burn the works of other Protestants was shockingly unthinkable." To hear Calvin's response, see *CO* 15:550–51; Bonnet, 3:176–81.

111. Gordon, *Calvin*, 218.

condemn and punish heresy with expediency whenever true heresy appeared in their midst. Otherwise, they conceded credibility to Rome's accusations.[112] The Reformation's catholicity, therefore, depended on the immediate discipline of heretics.

In 1531 a book rolled off the presses of Strasbourg called *Seven Books on the Errors of the Trinity*. The author was a Spaniard by the name of Michael Servetus (ca. 1511–53).[113] As the title indicates, Servetus was dead set against the catholic doctrine of the Trinity. Protestants and Rome had battled one another for the last decade and a half, but now they found themselves on the same side, defending Nicene Trinitarianism against a heretic. Even Martin Bucer, known for his pliability for the sake of ecumenical compromise, called on authorities across Europe to find Servetus and put him to death as a heretic. Bucer was not alone in his judgment. Charles V had the same opinion. According to *Constitutio criminalis Carolina*, Servetus was a heretic and, if captured, should be executed.[114] No territory, Protestant or Catholic, was exempt from that political and religious obligation.

The next year Servetus released another book: *Two Dialogues on the Trinity* (1532). According to Servetus, not only was the Trinity heresy, but the church, in affirming this doctrine, had abandoned true religion. Nevertheless, God had chosen Servetus to return Christianity to its true, primitive foundation, a foundation uncorrupted by later doctrinal accretions. Doing so, however, was difficult since both the Protestant church and the Roman Church would arrest and execute Servetus if discovered. Servetus, if he had any chance of survival, must be discrete, a skill he sometimes lacked. Whatever city Servetus entered, he knew he might have to flee as soon as the authorities discovered his real identity. He disguised himself by his other profession—medicine—so that no one grew curious, but in time his alias was exposed.[115] Nevertheless, for twenty years Servetus managed to evade prosecution.

Calvin became a fixation for Servetus because the Reformer stood against everything Servetus represented. Servetus decided in his own mind that he must do battle with the Reformed theologian. Rome was devilish, yet Calvin was just as deserving of his animosity. Calvin was Antichrist. No one could convince Servetus otherwise. He engaged Calvin by letter, and although Servetus did not use his real name, it was obvious to Calvin. However, when Calvin realized he could not change Servetus's mind, he stopped replying to him.[116] Servetus,

---

112. Gordon, *Calvin*, 224.

113. For a more detailed account of the Servetus affair, see Bainton, *Hunted Heretic.*

114. Lindberg, *European Reformations*, 269.

115. "In the annals of medicine he has a certain fame for being one of the first to discover the pulmonary circulation of the blood, a discovery perhaps prompted by his concern to show that the Holy Spirit entered the blood system through the nostrils. Respiration is inspiration; the soul is in the blood (Genesis 9:4; Leviticus 17:11)." Lindberg, 268.

116. Consult Calvin's reflections: *CO* 8:283; Bonnet, 3:417. Cf. Gordon, *Calvin*, 218. For an extensive treatment of the Servetus trial, see Bainton, *Hunted Heretic.*

however, did not take a clue but continued to write dozens and dozens of letters to Calvin.

Servetus's undoing started with the publication of his 1553 book, *On the Restoration of Christianity.* Servetus could not put his real name on the book for fear of his life. The book argued that many of the foundational beliefs of current Christianity should be rejected. He scorned the Creator-creature distinction, embracing a form of pantheism. He denied the orthodox doctrine of the Trinity, repudiating Jesus as the eternal Son of God, convinced that Protestants like Calvin taught tritheism. Servetus also detested the concept of predestination, taught by both Roman and Protestant theologians. And he had no patience for infant baptism. As for eschatology, the end of the world was at hand, sure to occur in the decades ahead. Servetus even entertained his own role as initiator of the last days.

Servetus then used his publication to engage Calvin by letter again, but this time Calvin replied and included a copy of his *Institutes.* Servetus did not receive Calvin's message well but bled his scrutiny all over Calvin's *Institutes.* When Servetus entered the French city of Vienne and set up shop as a medical doctor under an alias—his usual form of disguise—the Inquisition of Lyon, thanks to help from Calvin, identified and captured the heretic. Servetus was scheduled for execution but escaped custody first.[117]

Rather than lying low, Servetus did the unthinkable: he entered Geneva. Servetus said he was just passing through, but that was unlikely since he could have traveled a different way and chosen countless other cities, some less aware of the heretic's history and methods. More likely, Servetus went to Geneva on purpose, a suicide mission. The time had come for Servetus to take on Calvin in the flesh. Servetus was inaugurating the final events of the apocalypse. "His arrival in Geneva was a provocation shaped by an apocalyptic view that in the final days as the Four Horsemen rode across Europe he would confront the man he held responsible for turning the Reformation into a new Rome. Servetus had arrived to make his final stand. In Geneva he would give a full account of his views, and die a martyr."[118] Servetus not only decided to enter into Geneva, but he walked right into a church service. This was not just any service, however—he walked into the church where Calvin ascended the pulpit. He could not have been more obvious by his presence. In little time, Servetus was noticed and arrested.

What proceeded was not the mindless, illogical, angry pandemonium of some angry mob. Geneva had a law and a court procedure, one that they had followed in the past.[119] What was Calvin's involvement? The issue of discipline was an ongoing, controversial power struggle in Geneva, and in the 1550s the tension continued to resurface. The magistrates believed they had the right to excommunicate, a right that extended their civil arm in the affairs of the

---

117. Gordon, *Calvin,* 218.
118. Gordon, *Calvin,* 219.
119. Gordon, *Calvin,* 219.

church and subordinated Calvin under their power. Despite contemporary caricatures, therefore, the Genevan magistrates, not Calvin, controlled the trial of Servetus and the heretic's fate.[120] They asked for Calvin's opinion, but they were free to reject it since they, not Calvin, were the powers to whom Servetus had to answer.

The Genevan council did ask for Calvin's theological assessment to determine whether Servetus was indeed teaching heresy. In thirty-eight articles, Calvin and the other ministers outlined the many Christian doctrines Servetus rejected. These articles only inflamed Servetus's hatred for Calvin; Servetus said that Satan himself had possessed Calvin to write these articles.[121] Calvin also wrote letters to Swiss and French Protestants, asking for their opinion of Servetus but also for their support.[122] The council wrote letters of their own on several occasions, letters that enlisted Calvin's theological evaluation but ultimately transcended him to recruit the support of the Swiss in their own prosecution of Servetus.[123] In reply, the Swiss backed the Genevan council and some, such as Bullinger, were especially vocal, reminding Geneva that they had an opportunity—indeed, an obligation—to put a stop to Satan's advance on God's kingdom.

When the council decided the punishment for heresy, they rejected Calvin's advice. Calvin agreed that Servetus was a heretic, and one who had set himself up for the severest and most standard punishment: execution Yet Calvin asked them to show Servetus mercy in the manner of execution. Calvin pleaded that the execution be swift (by sword), but the Geneva magistrates rejected his plea. Servetus was to be burned at the stake. The magistrates said it was essential to show all Protestant territories, as well as Rome itself, that the Genevans did not and would not tolerate heresy nor show mercy to the worst offenders.

At the request of Servetus, Calvin visited him in prison. He blew up at Calvin, furious and full of spite. Calvin responded by recounting to Servetus how many times he had tried to deter him from heresy with no success. He had signed his own death sentence; he could have avoided this fate years earlier.[124] Still, he could change his mind. But again, he refused. At his execution they asked Servetus to turn from heresy, but he remained committed. As the flames climbed Servetus, he cried, "O Jesus, Son of the Eternal God, have pity on me!"[125] The prayer maintained Servetus's commitment to heresy; he refused to call *Jesus himself*

---

120. Gordon, *Calvin*, 219. Gordon concludes, "Servetus provided an opportunity for the magistrates to demonstrate their authority over Calvin, and that is perhaps why his request that the condemned man be put to the sword was rejected" (224).

121. In response, Calvin wrote *Brief Refutation*.

122. Gordon, *Calvin*, 220–24. Cf. Calvin's letters throughout the trial: *CO* 14:590; Bonnet, 3:417, 422, 427.

123. "All of the Swiss churches had responded with support, though there was no consensus on how Servetus should be punished.... All agreed that the form of punishment should be left to the Genevan council." Gordon, *Calvin*, 222. Cf. the Swiss letters: *CO* 8:808–23.

124. Gordon, *Calvin*, 223; Bainton, *Hunted Heretic*, 209–10.

125. Quoted in Gordon, *Calvin*, 223.

the eternal Son of God. Instead, Jesus was merely the Son of the eternal God. Servetus denied the Trinity and divinity of Christ to his death. That heretical confession only confirmed, in the eyes of the Genevan council, that they had made the right decision. They gave Rome no opportunity to accuse them of breaking with the catholicity of the church.

However, in the months and years that followed, Calvin's innumerable enemies, particularly those in Basel but also many in Italy, used the Servetus execution to attack Calvin's reputation. Three motives galvanized Calvin's enemies: "revulsion at the Servetus execution, rejection of the broader principle of punishing heretics, and hatred of his doctrine of predestination."[126] Some of these individuals were sympathetic with Servetus's theology; others were not but nonetheless jumped on the opportunity to make Calvin out to be the tyrant, spreading word that Calvin was the chief prosecutor of Servetus.[127] Such a misinterpretation has continued into the modern era even though it ignores the historical context, particularly the controlling power of the Genevan council. Calvin was not dictator, let alone the chief prosecutor. For most of his career, Calvin ministered with one hand tied behind his back, laboring with little success to push off the intruding magistrates even in ecclesiastical affairs.

Modern interpreters may be inclined to react to the Servetus trial by condemning Calvin. It is true Calvin participated in the trial by offering his evaluation of Servetus. However, condemnation of Calvin by modern sensibilities is anachronistic at best. The sixteenth century knew nothing of freedom of religion as conceived today. Additionally, targeting Calvin is unbalanced and shortsighted. He did nothing remarkable in the Servetus affair. Countless other Reformers and Roman cardinals did the same and for decades prior to the Servetus trial. Particular denunciation of Calvin is "curious," says Lindberg, "because Zurich had been drowning Anabaptists since the 1520s." Calvin's followers were not immune either. "At the very time Servetus was executed so were Calvin's followers in France. And in the decades after Servetus, the streets and fields of France would be soaked with Calvinist blood. The modern toleration of religious pluralism is anachronistic for the sixteenth century."[128] Modern judgment may still hold Calvin accountable for the part he did play in the Servetus trial, but only to the same extent as every other sixteenth-century European participated in the killings of Protestants and Catholics alike.

---

126. Gordon, *Calvin*, 229.
127. For these individuals, see Gordon, *Calvin*, 224–32. Calvin wrote a defense called *Defence of the Orthodox Faith against the Errors of Michel Servetus*. Sebastian Castellio (maybe with the help of David Joris) wrote a polemical response: *Concerning Heretics and Whether They Are to Be Persecuted* (1554). Cf. Gordon, *Calvin*, 229.
128. Lindberg, *European Reformations*, 270. Reflecting on Calvin's broader consolidation of authority, Lindberg goes so far as to hold up Calvin as a model of democracy: "What is remarkable is not his efforts to consolidate authority but that in this process he did not succumb to favoritism to win support. Neither prominent citizens nor his own family were allowed to be above the law. In this, Calvin provided a model of democratic equality under the law that modern states would do well to emulate" (271).

In the aftermath of the Servetus execution, one enemy after another came after Calvin. By 1555 Calvin was not only exhausted but depressed to the point that he wished death itself might take him away and relieve him of these relentless attacks. Calvin said he would rather be burned alive by the pope than keep enduring one stab in the back after another by his Protestant neighbors.[129]

Despite the turmoil of constant conflict, the Servetus affair did serve to solidify Calvin's authority in Geneva for the future. Although the magistrates were in full control of the Servetus trial, their consultation of Calvin demonstrated just how reliant they were on the Reformer. In 1555 Calvin finally achieved the type of ministerial authority he had pleaded for since his return to Geneva: "restrictive and disciplinary elements in the city were enhanced; the Consistory became more of an ecclesiastical court; and the ministers were now consulted on the choice of elders."[130]

ENGLISH EXILES IN GENEVA

Calvin's international influence may have started as early as the late 1540s, but it emerged and matured as Calvin aged in the 1550s and 1560s. That did not mean Calvin was *the* Reformer; many others were just as influential, some even more so. Reformers like Melanchthon and especially Bullinger had wide followings in their own territories but also across Europe. Calvin was not necessarily the most read Reformer in other countries either, but he did become part of a coalition of Reformers who were read more than any other reforming voices.[131] Calvin's influence spread in two ways: internally and externally. Internally, many across Europe traveled to Geneva to learn from Calvin. Externally, Calvin corresponded with ministers and sovereigns across Europe, counseling them on matters related to the Reformation. For a period of time, Calvin's internal and external influence even converged, as exemplified by his engagement with reform in England and Scotland (see chapter 16).

For example, in the 1530s hopes for cooperation between England and the Continental Reformers were high. Good will formed: Reformers on the Continent sent their promising young protégés to England for university studies, and conversations about a future alliance were ongoing. By the 1540s, however, the hoped-for alliance failed to materialize.[132] Nevertheless, when Edward VI rose to power in 1547, hope renewed. The next year Calvin corresponded with the Duke of Somerset, and Edward Seymour listened as Calvin advocated for reform in England. Calvin understood Seymour's position of influence. If persuaded, the duke might promote Calvin's measures to Edward VI.[133]

129. Schwarz, *Johannes Calvins Lebenswerk in seinen Briefen*, 2:118–19. Cf. Gordon, *Calvin*, 233.

130. Lindberg, *European Reformations*, 270.

131. Gordon, *Calvin*, 251 and 258, argues that the three most read across Europe were Calvin, Bullinger, and Melanchthon; Bullinger was especially popular in England.

132. By 1540 it was conspicuous that Henry's theological views did not align with the *Augsburg Confession*. On the failure of the alliance, see Gordon, *Calvin*, 252.

133. *CO* 13:77–90; Bonnet, 2:168–84. Cf. Gordon, *Calvin*, 253–55.

Although the duke responded with favor, his reign did not last; in 1549 his correspondence with Calvin took place from prison.[134]

Continental Reformers, such as Martin Bucer and Peter Martyr Vermigli, grew discouraged at the start of the 1550s as well. With Charles V closing in on Reformation territories, they took refuge in England at the invitation of Thomas Cranmer. However, as months and then years passed, they realized reform was not going to happen at the level of intensity or with the expediency that they believed it should. Bucer blamed Cranmer.[135]

Calvin, too, hoped for an alliance and corresponded with Cranmer, optimistic that Edward VI might favor the Protestant cause. Calvin had reason to be hopeful since a Reformer like Peter Martyr Vermigli at Oxford was already in conversation with Cranmer. And Calvin was committed to making his way to England immediately if Cranmer initiated a council to begin an alliance. But when Cranmer took those initial steps by writing to German and Swiss Reformers, Melanchthon and Bullinger said in reply that they could not make the trip to England. Here was the opportunity Calvin had visualized for years, but the lack of cooperation between Reformers stood in the way once more. The long history of infighting disallowed yet another international alliance. Calvin was disheartened to say the least and blamed the poor leadership of the Reformers, whom he said were more concerned with their sinful pursuits than the unity of the Protestant church.[136] But Calvin also laid some of the blame at the feet of Cranmer, as had Bucer. Calvin wrote to Cranmer, criticizing him for a lack of urgency as well as a lack of resolve to reform the Church of England, which still retained Roman distinctives.[137]

Whatever alliance might have materialized in England could not have lasted long anyway. With the premature death of Edward, Mary Tudor, instead of Lady Jane Grey, won the throne in 1553. Due to Mary's hostility, Protestants fled for their lives to the Continent. French and Dutch Protestants who had left their homeland for England now had to leave and find refuge in Lutheran territories. The tension was combustible since some of these exiles were Reformed in their doctrinal commitments, much in contrast to the Lutheran territories they entered. Because of their insistence on retaining Cranmer's liturgy, English Protestants also encountered tension when they fled. Calvin found himself

---

134. Calvin sent two of his works to Somerset in prison for encouragement. "Calvin's pastoral letter contained genuine compassion for Somerset; he saw the protector as the true voice of reform in a kingdom which had only half-heartedly embraced the Gospel." Gordon, *Calvin*, 255.

135. Bucer's history with ecumenical cooperation did not lend itself to credibility, and those back on the Continent assumed Bucer was part of the problem. "The archbishop, however, was quick to remind his guests of the hospitality which had been afforded them after Charles V's triumph in the empire, and drew their attention to the numerous compromises made by German evangelicals. This was a bitter truth, but it was harsher still for Bucer to learn, as he did from Calvin, that many of his fellow reformers on the continent believed that he was complicit in the compromises of the Edwardian church." Gordon, *Calvin*, 255–56.

136. *CO* 14:312–14; Bonnet, 2:330–33. Cf. Gordon, *Calvin*, 256–57.

137. Bonnet, 2:341–43. Cf. Gordon, *Calvin*, 257–58. Calvin expressed a similar sentiment toward Johannes à Lasco, who was ministering to exiles in England.

playing mediator between both sides, pleading for each side to be more amicable and flexible.[138]

A group of English exiles made their way to Geneva and formed a model ecclesiastical body to exiles scattered across the Continent. In part, their exemplary ecclesiology was indebted to the Geneva model Calvin had toiled to establish. The English exiles examined Calvin's polity, liturgy, confession, catechism, and preaching, and they built on that foundation as they established their exiled community in Geneva.[139]

The Geneva Bible

The English exiles also took advantage of the printing press in Geneva. The printing press was essential to Calvin's reform, allowing Calvin to put catechisms, confessions, and liturgies, as well as his own writings, into the hands of average churchgoers. The English exiles saw how advantageous the press could be to printing the Bible in their vernacular so that the English people could read the Scriptures unbiased by Roman Catholicism. The result: the Geneva Bible of 1560.[140]

William Whittingham headed the translation project, previously at All Souls College, Oxford, and then at Frankfurt when persecution heated up. Whittingham, who filled the shoes of John Knox in the English-speaking congregation in Geneva, became close with the Calvin family, marrying Idelette de Bure's sister.[141] Whittingham was so dedicated to translating the Geneva Bible that he stayed in Geneva for a year and a half even after his fellow Englishmen returned to England after the death of Queen Mary in 1558. When finished, the Bible was dedicated to Queen Elizabeth since God had tasked her with rebuilding England, much like Zerubbabel in the Old Testament was called by God to rebuild the temple after years in Babylonian captivity.[142]

Whittingham could not have completed the Geneva Bible with such precision without the ready library of manuscripts in Geneva. For example, Whittingham consulted an early New Testament manuscript called Codex Bezae, which Theodore Beza had acquired. He also had the advantage of consulting Beza's commentary (*Annotations*) on the codex.[143] Furthermore, Whittingham depended on Beza's 1556 Latin translation of the New Testament. However, out of the many resources at Whittingham's disposal, none compared to Tyndale's 1526 translation of the New Testament into English. Nevertheless,

---

138. Gordon, *Calvin*, 260–62. Cf. Calvin's rebuke of the English exiles and the resolution of a revised *Book of Common Prayer* in 1555: *CO* 15:393–94; Bonnet, 4:117–19. Also consult Calvin's mediation between John Knox and Richard Cox: *CO* 15:628–29.

139. See specifically the *Forme of Prayers and Book of Common Order*. Gordon, *Calvin*, 262.

140. For a history of the Geneva Bible, see M. Metzger, "The Geneva Bible of 1560," 339–52.

141. Catherine Jaquemayne.

142. The woodcut included Psalm 34:19 and Exodus 14:14 to encourage the Marian exiles that God would deliver them from their distress.

143. For Beza's imprint on the Geneva Bible, see Metzger, "The Influence of Codex Bezae upon the Geneva Bible of 1560," 72–77; Backus, *Reformed Roots of the English New Testament*.

Whittingham's team surpassed Tyndale in this sense: they completed a translation of the Bible, including the Old Testament, one that depended not only on the Latin Vulgate but the Hebrew.[144]

Several editorial decisions guaranteed the Geneva Bible's success in the general English population. They can be summed up in one word: *accommodation*. Calvin taught that God accommodated himself in his revelation for the sake of humanity's salvation. Whittingham and company applied this principle of accommodation to justify, over against Rome, the necessity of accessibility.[145] Both in aesthetics and in substance, the Bible was made easy to read for the average English Christian. The translators discarded the Gothic typeface and replaced it with a Roman typeface so that the reader was not distracted in the reading process. The translators and editors also put in italics words they added to help the reader understand the meaning of a sentence. Maps and illustrations were included so that the reader could visualize a biblical story or locate the land of Israel or the city of Jerusalem. The Geneva Bible was even printed in small quarto editions so that the average English consumer could afford a copy.

As for content, one of the greatest contributions of the Geneva Bible was the textual, exegetical, and theological annotations included in the margins. The Geneva Bible was the first full-scale study Bible for the English. Each book of the Bible included a preface so that the reader could identify the author and the message of the book. As the reader turned the page to read the book, the margins were filled with notes that explained difficult passages. As stated in the preface to the Geneva Bible, "Whereas certain places in the books of Moses, of the Kings and Ezekiel seemed so dark that by no description they could be made easy to the simple reader; we have so set them forth with figures and notes for the full declaration thereof that they . . . as it were by the eye may sufficiently know the true meaning of all such places."

Furthermore, marginal commentary also gave the translators and editors the opportunity to emphasize where Reformation theology derived from the biblical text. Justification by grace alone through faith alone, for example, is spotted in the commentary on Galatians. Predestination and election are pinpointed across the Gospel of John, Romans, and Ephesians.[146] And the pope is identified as Antichrist in the commentary on Revelation.

The finished text was an original contribution. The English people now had a Bible that was precise in its accuracy but without compromising accessibility.

144. Bruce, *English Bible*, 86.
145. McGrath, *In the Beginning*, 119–20. The observations concerning accessibility that follow are indebted to Metzger, "Geneva Bible of 1560," 343ff.; and Bruce, *English Bible*, 856–89.
146. Calvin's influence on the Geneva Bible is debated (along with the influence of Beza and Bullinger). See Danner, "Contribution of the Geneva Bible of 1560 to the English Protestant Tradition," 5–18; Danner, "Later English Calvinists and the Geneva Bible," 504; Hall, "Genevan Version of the English Bible," 124–49; Daniell, *English Bible*, 292, 305–9; Eadie, *English Bible* 2:8; Westcott, *General View of the History of the English Bible*, 93; Metzger, "Geneva Bible of 1560," 348; Backus, *Reformed Roots of the English New Testament*. However, there is no debate that subsequent editions of the Geneva Bible included Calvin's catechisms and questions and answers on predestination.

And although it faced opposition, not printed in England until 1575, the Geneva Bible was a lasting contribution.[147] From 1560 to 1611 no other translation compared to the Geneva Bible's multiplying editions. While Tyndale's New Testament underwent five editions, the Great Bible seven, and the Bishop's Bible twenty-two, the Geneva Bible numbered more than one hundred twenty.[148] "England was a Protestant nation, and the Geneva Bible was its sacred book."[149]

Even after the King James Version was published in 1611 the Geneva Bible continued to be perpetuated. Both its translation and its theology had a formidable influence on playwrights like William Shakespeare, statesmen like Oliver Cromwell, and Puritans like John Bunyan, as well as those who migrated all the way to America.[150]

Return to England?

The English exiles in Geneva contemplated returning to England in 1558 when Elizabeth became the new queen and Protestantism was no longer under threat. The hope of renewed reform was not lost on Calvin. Just as he had corresponded with Cranmer hoping that, with Edward VI's favor, Cranmer might take serious measures to reform the English church and permit an international alliance, so now Calvin renewed his correspondence but this time with William Cecil. Calvin was confident that Elizabeth's most trusted adviser could influence the queen in the direction of reformation. As before, time was of the essence; the same urgency Calvin had impressed on Cranmer he now stressed in his correspondence with Cecil.[151]

Once more, Calvin's hopes were dashed on the rocks of other Reformers. In years past, Calvin learned that his association with Farel could be costly due to Farel's fiery disposition and inclination to quick condemnation of others. He learned the same lesson with John Knox. The Scottish Reformer stayed in Geneva and was mentored by Calvin, but when Elizabeth rose to power, Knox wrote a scathing book that protested female rulers. Knox even encouraged subjects to rise up against a female sovereign (see chapter 16).[152]

147. Archbishop Parker refused to back the Geneva Bible until his death in 1575. Elizabeth was also predisposed to disfavor the Geneva Bible since Calvin and Knox were behind it. But the Geneva Bible was popular among the people nonetheless. See McGrath, *In the Beginning*, 124–29; and Robertson, *Makers of the English Bible*, 88–96. On the relationship between the Bishop's Bible and the Geneva Bible, see Danner, "Later English Calvinists and the Geneva Bible," 499.

148. Berry, "Introduction to the Facsimile Edition," 14.

149. McGrath, *In the Beginning*, 129. Cf. Jensen, "'Simply' Reading the Geneva Bible," 31; Betteridge, "The Bitter Notes," 44–47.

150. Martin, "Geneva Bible," 46–51; Metzger, "Geneva Bible of 1560," 346. Through the influence of John Knox, the Geneva Bible was also embraced in Scotland. On the many reasons why King James rejected the Geneva Bible, see McGrath, *In the Beginning*, 141–48; Metzger, "Geneva Bible of 1560," 346ff.; Daniell, *English Bible*, 299–352.

151. Calvin dedicated his Isaiah commentary to Elizabeth as well. For his letters to Cecil, consult *CO* 17:419; Bonnet, 4:15–17, 46–48. Cf. Gordon, *Calvin*, 263.

152. The book was called *First Blast of the Trumpet against the Monsterous [sic] Regiment of Women*. Knox was not the only one; Goodman also wrote a book: *How Superior Powers Ought to Be Obeyd [sic] of Their Subjects*. For Goodman's story, see Gordon, *Calvin*, 263–64.

Elizabeth was outraged and ultimately blamed Calvin. The door was slammed shut on Calvin's influence on the future monarch and her approach to the Protestant church. While Calvin's mentorship of Knox paid significant dividends in the future reform of Scotland, that same mentorship cost him an open line of communication to England's new monarch. Knox's blast proved irreparable, not only compromising Calvin's credibility with the new sovereign but inviting Elizabeth's suppression of any and all English Reformers who were associated with Geneva. On account of Knox, they all met Elizabeth's disfavor.

Nevertheless, Calvin and Bullinger remained the "continental patriarchs of the British Reformers," and Calvin continued to influence the English Reformers and their parishioners even after his time.[153] His stamp on the English was due to his ecclesiastical hospitality and pastoral mentorship during their greatest moment of exilic need and, by consequence, the adoption of Calvin's *Institutes* and commentaries in the English church.[154]

And yet, as perpetual as Calvin's imprint on the English may have been, Calvin's stamp on the French during the latter half of the 1550s was historic.

THE MISSION TO FRANCE: PERSECUTION AND HUGUENOT HOPE

The success or failure of the Reformation in France depended on the stance of those in political power, especially the king. The Reformers understood this, which is why Calvin and Zwingli alike devoted certain writings to Francis I.[155] As chapter 16 revealed, the Reformation's longevity in England ultimately relied on whether the king or queen was for or against evangelical principles. In the end, England moved in the evangelical direction. The same cannot be said of France. While Protestantism had its grip on the French people and even French nobility, it failed to find lasting solidarity due to its ultimate rejection by the king.

Of course, the story of the Reformation in France is far more complicated, a roller coaster of political and religious strife. At high points, evangelicals were optimistic their religion would prevail; at low points, all seemed lost. To understand these highs and lows, consider in brief the rise of reforming voices and their downfall at the hands of political leaders.

---

153. Gordon, *Calvin*, 266. Calvin did defend himself in a letter to Cecil, attempting to clarify his interaction with Knox, even setting himself apart from Knox's views. Despite this setback, Calvin did not give up; he commissioned Nicolas des Gallars to minister to the French church in England. However, later disputes within the French church in London, sometimes even involving Calvin, limited Calvin's influence. Ultimately, however, Calvin and his writings continued to be a significant source of influence on English Reformers, particularly those who took safe haven in Geneva during Mary's reign (see 264–65). "They remained committed to what they had been taught there [in Geneva] and never felt comfortable in the compromised world of the Elizabethan settlement. Many of these 'Genevans' kept themselves apart from the English churches in order to preserve discipline, preferring to attend the services of the Dutch and French churches in London with their Genevan-style discipline rather than their own parishes" (266).

154. Gordon, *Calvin*, 266.

155. "The Protestant program was to achieve the legal acceptance of evangelical worship in the land." Hillerbrand, *Division of Christendom*, 319.

Lutheran and Calvinist Origins

Historians debate whether the rise of Reformation thought in France was indebted to Luther. This question of origins is not unimportant because it is really a question about French evangelical identity. But the answer evades a strict yes or no. There are plain signs of reform prior to Luther, as is plain in the protests of figures such as Jacques Lefèvre d'Ètaples. Lefèvre trumpeted humanist methods, calling for a return to the sources and a reform of corrupt practices within the church on the basis of Scripture.[156] However, these calls to renaissance were not necessarily identical with the full-orbed theological program issued later on by Luther and Melanchthon or Zwingli and Bullinger.

For that reason, Hillerbrand said the answer depends on how "Reformation" is defined. If Reformation refers to an interest in removing corruption from the church, then French reform precedes the arrival of Luther's writings in France. But if Reformation means something more than a humanist program, if it entails a *theological* renewal of the church over against Rome, then the French Reformation is without a doubt indebted to the influence of Luther and his writings. "However much Lefèvre deviated from medieval Scholasticism or however close his biblical commentaries came to a view of justification embraced by the Reformers, he was not a Protestant arguing the *sola fide* or the *sola Scriptura*. A humanist, Lefèvre was critical of the church, but always its loyal son, a fact illustrated by his continued faithful allegiance to the church after the Lutheran controversy had begun to divide people."[157] Hillerbrand dates, therefore, the genesis of the French Reformation to the advent of Luther's writing in France.

Luther's writings were prohibited as early as 1521. Wherever French Lutherans were discovered, the authorities acted with urgency to snuff out any signs of Protestant influence.[158] Francis I was in support. Always the nemeses of Charles V, Francis needed allies, and the pope was one of them. Tolerance of French evangelicals could compromise that arrangement so the 1520s and 1530s were two long decades of oppression for French evangelicals. Due to immediate suppression by the king himself, it is unwise to assume French evangelicals formed a unified constituency. However, 1542 was a turning point in the direction of French evangelical solidarity. Calvin's *Institutes* made their way into the French tongue and "a phase of consolidation began, where clarity of what it meant to be Protestant became the overriding issue."[159] If French evangelicals grasped for an identity during the 1520s and 1530s, they found one in the 1540s under the umbrella of Calvinism.

---

156. Marguerite d'Angoulême was also put forward as an example by Hillerbrand. Hillerbrand, 320.
157. Hillerbrand, 320.
158. See the activities of the Parlement of Paris and the Sorbonne; Hillerbrand, 320.
159. Prior to 1542, argued Hillerbrand, "no cohesive 'movement of reform' existed." Hillerbrand, 322.

The Burning Chamber and the Nicomedians

France in the 1540s remained a dangerous home to Huguenots. King Francis I died in 1547 and was succeeded by Henry II, who not only was set against French evangelicals but also quite organized in his plan to suppress them. He created "the burning chamber" (*chambre ardente*) for example, a court in Paris (*parlement*) designed to prosecute heresy. Hundreds of evangelicals were arrested, found guilty of heresy, and sent to their death from 1547 to 1551.

To make matters worse, in 1551 Henry II made heresy hunting a sport even the lowest courts in the land could enjoy. If an evangelical was caught, he or she need not go all the way up the chain to the burning chamber to be tried and executed. King Henry II intended these executions to squash rather than inspire other evangelicals. To accomplish that goal, the executioner took a knife and carved out the tongue of the evangelical so that he or she could not say any last, inspirational words while going up in flames.[160] But the tactic did not always work; the sight of a man or woman laying down his or her life for the sake of French evangelicalism was still a testimony no fire could put out. Writers like Jean Crespin made sure evangelicals in Geneva heard the stories of these martyrs.[161]

Not all evangelicals were faithful to the point of a severed tongue and a flaming stake. Some caved under the fierce pressure and returned to the French Catholic Church. Calvin was never short of encouragement for those evangelicals willing to die for their faith, but he had no patience for those who attempted to stay evangelical while remaining incognito *within* the French Catholic Church. Calvin labeled them Nicodemites after Nicodemus, the religious leader who approached Jesus at night to avoid being seen by his colleagues (John 3). Calvin posed an ultimatum: either go with Rome or commit to the Reformation.

Those who heeded Calvin's warning had a choice: meet death or flee to foreign soil. Many chose the latter, leaving France to find refuge in cities like Geneva. By the 1550s Geneva was filled with French refugees. This put Geneva in a unique position to send French ministers back to their motherland when the time was right. And that time was 1555.

Geneva and Berne Commission French Evangelicals

In 1555 churches committed to Reformed theology started to sprout up across France. Calvin spurred French Christians in Geneva to consider whether God was calling them to return to France to cultivate Reformed doctrine and piety. Perhaps God had raised them up for such a time as this, to preserve his church in France when the authorities were intent on squashing the Reformation faith.

---

160. Atherstone, *Reformation*, 164. On the Edict of Chateaubriand, which enabled such persecution, see Hillerbrand, 323.

161. Crespin's book was titled *Livre des martyrs* (1554), "the French equivalent of John Foxe's *Book of Martyrs*." Atherstone, *Reformation*, 164.

That call was not to be taken lightly; if the past was any indicator of the future, then death stood on the other side of the border, if not for all, most definitely for some. Despite that danger, many French with noble bloodlines answered that call.[162] However, Geneva could not carry the burden of preparing these ministers alone. Berne also lent support, and some more seasoned Reformers even committed themselves to return to France as well.[163]

In the eyes of French authorities, Geneva appeared uninvolved and indifferent. Maintaining that image was critical; otherwise Geneva risked an attack from French troops. Despite an apathetic appearance, within Genevan headquarters Calvin could not have been more animated. This was a mission he deeply cared about as a Frenchman himself. Therefore, Calvin was involved with the training process from start to finish. The training of French ministers was thorough, not only preparing these missionaries in theology but educating them on context so that they were strategic and shrewd in the way they reentered French society.

However, changing the political climate was not easy. In 1557 Henry positioned himself as the God-ordained sustainer of orthodoxy and judge of heresy by virtue of the Edict of Compiègne. Nothing less than the death penalty was in store for anyone he considered a heretic. To help, the Inquisition arrived in France to capture and torture anyone suspicious. The goal was to eradicate the heresy altogether. Henry also had the help of the French. Mobs rounded up entire churches caught worshiping. These tactics also revealed how committed French evangelicals were to their religion. If torture, mobs, and the death penalty did not extinguish but galvanized churches to meet in hiding, could the evangelical movement actually be eliminated? Moving to underground assemblies disclosed how intense the suppression had become, but it also unveiled how organized French Protestants had become. Unlike the 1520s and 1530s, the 1540s did not involve the suppression of sporadic groups of Protestants; the king was now dealing with a sophisticated, hidden coalition of churches as determined to survive as he was to suppress their efforts.[164]

The underground churches were a success in part due to the unrelenting missionary effort that stemmed from Reformed territories. Five to six years after the major push to send these French ministers back, Calvin received reports that churches were growing by leaps and bounds. He was elated. The Genevans and Bernese could not produce ministers quickly enough to meet this exponential growth.[165] By 1559 their growth was so promising that a coalition of French

---

162. "Most came from noble, bourgeois and artisan classes; there were no peasants to be found among them. A few were former priests. Those of noble birth were of immense benefit to the movement with their ability to move in higher social circles and win converts." Gordon estimates that nearly a hundred ministers went back to France. Gordon, *Calvin*, 313.

163. E.g., Piere Viret. Since those training to return to France were influenced by Calvin, this created tension when they prepared in Bernese territories. Gordon, *Calvin*, 313.

164. Hillerbrand, *The Division of Christendom*, 324, uses the language of "network" to capture how well organized these churches became.

165. Some asked why Calvin himself did not return to France; for Calvin's response, see the preface to his Daniel commentary, which he dedicated to French evangelicals: *CO* 18:615–23. Cf. Gordon, *Calvin*, 319.

ministers gathered in Paris. The synod was a risk; if caught, some thirty churches could lose their ministers to the flames. Calvin was so encouraged, however, that he helped write a confession that this synod could rally behind.

Geneva, thanks to Calvin's missionary training, letters, and doctrinal counsel, became mission central: one hundred missionaries landed in France by the time Calvin died, and their influence was so ubiquitous that by 1562 around 10 percent of the population was evangelical; even some French nobility converted to the Reformation cause.[166] These French evangelicals who were Calvinist in theology and ecclesiology became known as Huguenots.

Huguenots: the Contest for Power between Guise and Bourbons

The Huguenots were diverse; some were common citizens of France while others were nobility, but either way they were alike in their sacrifice, zealous enough to lay down their lives if necessary to ensure the survival of their kind.

At the start of the 1560s, several developments created optimism within the hearts and minds of the Huguenots. Unexpectedly, in 1559 Henry's reign of terror ended one day when he was jousting. Although wearing the proper protective armor, a splinter managed to sneak its way in between and pierced his head. Henry died from the complications this random injury caused, and he was succeeded by the teenage boy king Francis II. But who should be his regency? Charles Cardinal Guise took immediate control, which invited protest from the Bourbons (who were typically Protestant). In protest they asked why control was seized by Guise rather than distributed to a council. The Bourbons' protest was both politically and religiously charged since Guise's Catholic commitment could only result in the pope's mediated control of France.[167]

The country watched, waiting to see if a revolution was next. That raised a question: Could a *Protestant* prince participate in a revolution, let alone start one? Basing their logic on Calvin's "right of resistance," the Bourbons said revolt was justified if the Guises seized control in a way that violated the French constitution. The Bourbons were motivated, for if they had control, then French evangelicals would no longer be persecuted, a world hard to imagine since they had been suppressed for over a decade. Their cause was not only political but religious; persecution of the true church could finally come to an end. With that goal in view, Calvin added his support.[168]

The year 1559 was yet another turning point. No longer did Huguenots have to cower in fear for their lives. They were willing to be martyrs, of course, but now they might take matters into their own hands if they did not believe their country's constitution was honored. Calvin and Beza both were hesitant to

---

166. See the examples of King Henri II's cousin, Jeanne d'Albret, queen of Navarre, as well as Louis de Bourbon, Prince of Condé, Antoine de Bourbon, king of Navarre, and the Châfamily. Atherstone, *Reformation*, 165. Cf. Holt, *French Wars of Religion*, 38.

167. See specifically Antoine of Navarre; Hillerbrand, *Division of Christendom*, 326.

168. On Calvin's views and the events that led him to support Antoine of Navarre, see Hillerbrand, 326.

advocate reactionary revolt and advised waiting on God to see how events might transpire next, but the Huguenots did not share this reluctance.[169] The Bourbons were led by Antoine of Navarre and his brother Condé, the more aggressive of the two. Condé rallied their constituency to hatch a plot. At the start of 1560, the plan was single-minded: defeat the Guises so that an assembly could properly guide king and country. But to do so, the royal court had to be conquered and controlled. The plan was ambitious but possible, that is, until the Duke of Guise discovered the plot and relocated the royal court to a fortress. The Bourbons lost the element of surprise and now faced the daunting prospect of penetrating the castle of Amboise.[170] Although that March the *it d'Abolition* of Amboise promised reprieve, the Bourbons attacked the castle, which proved every bit as daunting as they imagined. Defeated and humiliated, their bodies were impaled on the castle walls to send a message.[171] Although the attack was not conducted in the name of Protestantism per se, the collateral damage of the Bourbon defeat certainly affected Protestant progress by default.

What followed was a fight for Protestant religious freedom in France. A Frenchman could be a Protestant; that much was permitted. However, corporate gatherings were forbidden, a policy most intolerable to Huguenots. How could the church continue if it could not meet? This could not go on forever. While their nemeses were content with such a restriction and the suppression it maintained, there was no scenario in which Huguenots could comply. A council was desperately needed so that the Huguenots could find a new way forward between martyrdom on the right and revolt on the left. Some tried to pave a *via media*, such as Admiral Coligny. "He was the advocate of a new policy, neither the suffering and martyrdom advocated by Calvin nor the open insurrection and revolution proposed by Condé.... Coligny should be seen as the French counterpart of Thomas Cromwell, deeply Protestant and at the same time concerned about the proper synthesis of religion and the body politic."[172] In the end, all was vain in 1560. Cardinal Guise could not think of the Huguenots as anything but heretics, and so the persecution continued until Francis II's sudden death at the end of the year.

The Colloquy of Poissy and the Edict of St. Germain

The boy king Charles IX ascended the throne, and once again conflict erupted over who should be regent. Protestants prayed Antoine of Navarre

---

169. "Prior to 1559 the French Protestants tended to be martyrs; after 1559 they were rebels.... [Calvin] counseled, pleaded, warned. 'Let us pray to God that he might still the turbulent waves through his wonderful wisdom and goodness.' Beza asked his French coreligionists if they possessed the *certa vocation* (the certain vocation) that God had called them to do what they were doing. Yet the Genevan reformers failed to influence the course of events. The *Huguenots de religions* and the *Huguenots d'état* came together to pursue common action." Hillerbrand, 326.

170. Hillerbrand, 328.

171. "The Protestants had been uninvolved in the conspiracy, and even [Gaspard de] Coligny, by his presence at Amboise, had indicated his aloofness. Suspicion fell at once on Condé, who emphatically protested his innocence." Hillerbrand, 328.

172. Hillerbrand, 328–29.

might take initiative, but he stepped aside as Catherine de Medici, the new king's mother, took control of the regency. As queen regent she took a different approach to the Huguenot movement. With a bloodline to the papacy as Pope Clement VII's niece, she pursued dialogue between Huguenots and Catholics in an attempt to move the fierce divide beyond its impasse. For as long as they vied for power, she could never enjoy peace under her reign. She decided that a national French council might be the solution. She invited Reformed ministers to the Colloquy of Poissy (1561). Calvin did not attend but sent Theodore Beza to represent Geneva instead. That was a smart move since Beza was congenial, taking Poissy with utmost seriousness. Without compromising Reformed convictions, Beza pursued conciliar conversation. He did face one significant challenge: he had to resurrect the Reformed reputation by putting on display Protestant subservience as opposed to insurrection. Cardinal Guise was unpersuaded and remained hostile; Protestants were nothing more than heretics. The Catholics in attendance demanded nothing less than a return to Rome.[173]

Catherine could not have appreciated the Catholic rhetoric. Her reasons were not religious but political. Although Catholics attended Poissy, they did not all agree that the colloquy was legitimate. What right did the queen regent have to decide on matters of the church? Surely Trent should arbitrate instead. Like other European countries, France had to decide whether pope, council, or king possessed ultimate authority.[174]

Much like prior attempts to bring Catholics and French Protestants together, Poissy resulted in no such compromise or union between the two groups. However, Catherine de Medici's attempts at reconciliation and negotiation did have their benefits. For example, at the beginning of 1562, the Edict of St. Germain gave Huguenots the right to gather together for worship without fear of persecution.[175] That shift was colossal not only for Huguenots but for political-religious history. "The notion of only one recognized religion in the realm, so central to the medieval world, ended. No longer was it possible to speak of *une foi, une loi, un roi*, since two faiths were recognized. That the French crown was willing to suspect (at least temporarily) the notion of the *corpus christianum*, a society where church and state were one, was revolutionary."[176]

Such unprecedented freedom, which the catholic courts detested, left the Huguenots hopeful; perhaps persecution was over and a new era was about to begin, an era of peace and religious liberty. They could not have been more mistaken.

---

173. Hillerbrand, 331. Other Reformed luminaries besides Beza attended as well, including Peter Martyr Vermigli, who was now in England.

174. See the protest of Jesuit Diego Laynez, for example. Hillerbrand, 331.

175. The "Edict of St-Germain-en-Laye in January 1562 granted freedom of worship to the Huguenots for the first time, provided they meet outside towns, unarmed, by day and under supervision." Atherstone, *Reformation*, 166.

176. Atherstone, 333.

The French Wars of Religion and Saint Bartholomew's Day Massacre

Freedom was granted in January but compromised by March when the Duke of Guise—François—walked into a Huguenot church in Vassy and slaughtered the congregation, children and women included. The church was meeting in a barn, and although their meeting was in conformity with the toleration recently granted, the catholic duke put every one of them to death. Regardless of who instigated the conflict, the duke's soldiers killed an entire congregation of Huguenots who had no ability to defend themselves.[177]

Huguenots all over France were enraged. To this day, historians struggle with giving the Duke of Guise the benefit of the doubt. One month prior to the massacre at the barn, the duke had already given the command to capture and hang Protestants on trees. His general received this order *after* the January edict, exposing the duke's disregard for the new edict of toleration.[178] While the massacre at the barn may not have been premeditated, it certainly emerged out of a mindset already predisposed toward persecution.

But unlike years prior, French Protestants were no longer short on numbers. With help from French nobility, they retaliated. The Duke of Guise may have only slaughtered one congregation in a barn, but as a result the French Wars of Religion (1562–98) were born in a gush of bloodshed. One battle after another ensued with no end in sight. The long, agonizing story of violence will not be rehearsed here. However, a snapshot of 1563 and 1570 can serve as two fitting windows into nearly four decades of warfare.

At the start of 1563, just on the heels of ongoing battles between Catholics and Huguenots, the leaders on both sides were eliminated, either due to capture or assassination. For example, the Duke of Guise (François) was picked off by an assassin, and the Guises believed Admiral Gaspard de Coligny was behind the plot.[179] The timing was right for Catherine to attempt mollification and end the bloodshed. That March the Peace of Amboise guaranteed the Huguenots freedom from persecution if they did not participate in Catholic services. The Peace of Amboise, however, was not a solution that could last.

Fault may lie on both sides. While Catherine safeguarded the Huguenots from future persecution, the Huguenots could still only worship in houses. Furthermore, this freedom was not extensive across France. Some towns and cities persisted in their prohibitions against Huguenots. To organize a Huguenot service in Paris, for example, was dangerous. Also, the Peace of Amboise created suspicion. Huguenots could meet in the homes of nobility, but what about the average Huguenot in France? He or she may not have such privileged access to worship. "Both Calvin and Coligny (admiral of France and a moderate

---

177. He later claimed a Huguenot fired at him first, but the facts of the event escape historians. Atherstone, 333.

178. The order was specifically given to his governor in Dauphine (near Vienne). Atherstone, 333.

179. On the other hand, Condé was captured and incarcerated. For the battles surrounding these events, see Atherstone, 335.

Huguenot leader) voiced their protest against the Peace, since it discriminated against the common people."[180]

Nevertheless, the Huguenots are also to blame. The Peace of Amboise may not have been everything they desired, but Catherine did take a first step toward cease-fire. That initial step, however, was doomed to fail as long as the Huguenots entertained a mindset of revolution. In other words, they were not shy about their determination to pursue insurrection however possible. Their bent on rebellion left Catherine fatigued until she finally gave up hopes for permanent conciliation and joined the Catholic side of the fight.[181] At least the Catholics were not rebels, she thought.

Now consider the year 1572. Two years prior, a truce was achieved as King Charles IX and Admiral de Coligny (representing the Huguenots) agreed to the Treaty of St-Germain (1570). The treaty advanced Huguenots to a new level of religious freedom, which led them to a spirit of cooperation. But in 1571 tension was dynamite between Coligny and Catherine, the former attempting to persuade the king to go to war with Spain, the latter opposing war with Spain, fearing France might suffer defeat. In the eyes of Catherine, Coligny was a cancer. So she plotted his assassination with help from the Guises. The Guises thought revenge would be sweet. Finally, they could pay back Coligny for the assassination of Duke François.

However, the assassination was a failure; Coligny was shot, but he survived. Fearful the king might uncover the plot, Catherine made up a lie: she had discovered a conspiracy by the Huguenots to assassinate royalty. At the news of Coligny's injury, King Charles was distressed, fearful the peace accomplished with St-Germain would be dissolved. But now, with news of a conspiracy, he became infuriated and plotted with Catherine to take down the Huguenots.

The perfect opportunity to pounce on the Huguenots arrived shortly after a wedding in August 1572, a marriage match between both parties.[182] The Huguenots were unsuspecting, anticipating merely another occasion to mend bad blood and solidify their religious freedom.[183] To celebrate the marriage, the Huguenots traveled to the capital, but only days after the wedding they discovered they had been tricked. Coligny was killed first. It was no secret, either. His dead body was heaved out of his bedroom window. The assassination of Coligny was the signal; all over Paris Huguenots were surrounded and slaughtered by French Catholics on the infamous day that forever became known as the Saint Bartholomew's Day massacre.

That day was only the beginning. Massacres of Huguenots billowed one after

---

180. Atherstone, 335.

181. Atherstone, 336.

182. Historians debate whether the plot and massacre were as well planned as some think. Hillerbrand, for example, thinks the "massacre was unpremeditated and a spontaneous decision on the part of Catherine." Hillerbrand, *Division of Christendom*, 339.

183. The marriage was between Marguerite de Valois, the sister of King Charles IX, and Henri de Bourbon, the nephew of the Prince of Condè. Atherstone, *Reformation*, 168.

another across France like crashing waves on the seashore. Historians speculate over the number of casualties, some estimating tens of thousands. Those who survived fled the country. After ten years of warfare and the achievement of supposed peace, the Reformed Church was nearly wiped off the French map in a series of massacres, dismantling any trust Huguenots had toward Catherine, a trust already tottering but now eliminated. The future of Reformed Protestantism in France was bleak; that much was clear to the Huguenots who survived. And Roman Catholics across Europe celebrated, convinced that God was afoot annihilating the heretics.[184]

The Wars of Religion in France expose the unpredictability and vulnerability of the Reformation. First, the wars exposed underlying disagreements between Reformers and put French Protestants in the awkward position of taking sides. Calvin had to be seriously persuaded that responding with physical force was necessary, as opposed to fleeing the country or laying down one's life as a martyr. Not so with Reformers like Viret and Farel. The sword and iconoclasm were justified when French authorities turned wicked and hostile. These differences formed deep wounds between Reformers, wounds never finally healed.[185] Worse still, these differences forced French evangelicals to contravene the political passivity of the Geneva leader whose theology they otherwise embraced.

Second, the Wars of Religion unveiled not only religious but political motives. Hillerbrand's observation may be unsettling, but there is truth to it: "In France religion was only the veneer in those wars: men exploited the sacred in order to pursue the profane."[186] That may be a historical judgment, but it is one most difficult to deny. Religion was entangled in the conflict; Roman Catholics and Protestants stood opposed in each war. However, underneath the surface these wars may not have been driven primarily by religious convictions but political ambitions. That qualification may assist present interpreters from assuming religion necessarily results in bloodshed. The political stakes were high, which should deter modern interpreters from assuming the wars were merely

---

184. Henry IV (Henry of Navarre) concluded the Wars of Religion. He was a Protestant-turned-Catholic but for political advantages. With the Edict of Nantes in 1598, Henry granted the Huguenots religious freedom. However, the edict also told the future: Protestantism would never be the official religion. Hillerbrand explained: "The Edict of Nantes [1598] marked the end of the Reformation in France. As in the Peace of Augsburg of 1555, the notion of religious freedom was anchored in a document of state. As in the Edict of Saint-Germain, the Edict of Nantes repudiated the principle of the *corpus christianum*, and in so doing it departed from over a thousand years of European history, during which each man, woman, and child had been, by the fact of citizenship, a Christian of the kind prescribed by the sovereign. The Edict of Nantes ended this organic union of church and state, paralleling a development that had found legal expression in Augsburg in 1555 and that eventually encompassed all of Europe.... The Edict of Nantes safeguarded the Protestant accomplishments, yet disallowed what they so determinedly strove for: to convert the country to the new faith." Hillerbrand, *Division of Christendom*, 344.

185. "They [Viret, Farel] summoned the faithful to action, not, as Calvin did, to wait on God's providence.... It was the path of Farel and Viret that they [the French Protestants] would follow: violence and resistance together with prophetic righteousness." Gordon, *Calvin*, 324, 328. Viret and Calvin in particular had irresolvable differences that festered; these differences escalated in 1563 when Viret promoted congregationalism in France over against Geneva's consistory model (see 327).

186. Hillerbrand, *Division of Christendom*, 334.

motivated by religion. A more balanced interpretation defies the label "Wars of Religion" itself.

Throughout the duration of these conflicts, French evangelicals were indebted to Calvin's pastoral and theological writings, which were instrumental to their genesis as a consolidated movement. Yet whether the Reformed Church could survive outside of Geneva was questionable. Because of persecution, Geneva itself was transformed into a haven for exiles. As seen already, English Reformers fled to Geneva for refuge, and those who remained often met the flames. All hope seemed lost to the English hiding in the shadows of Geneva, but to their surprise the Reformation in England was far more resilient than anyone could have imagined. We now turn to that unpredictable story of survival, a story on which the Protestant identity depends to the present day.

16

AN APOLOGY FOR THE UNIVERSAL CHURCH

The Reformation in England and Scotland

Play the man, Master Ridley. For this day we shall light a candle which shall never fail in England.

—Hugh Latimer to Nicholas Ridley when burned at the stake

The Reformation is somewhat violent, because the adversaries be stubborn.

—John Knox

THE MOST GREEDY WOLF OF HELL

When King Henry VIII read Luther's *Babylonian Captivity of the Church*, he became incensed with the heretic. In response came Henry's *Assertio septem sacramentorum*, which defended the sacramental system against Luther's assault. By defending the seven sacraments, Henry was defending the papacy itself. Although Henry was strategic in his ambiguity over the precise type of authority the pope did or did not have, he was perfectly clear that the papacy and its sacramentalism was in the right and Luther was in the wrong.[1] Yet that is to put Henry's response in a soft light; the king was vicious in his attack, calling the Reformer a greedy wolf of hell, brainwashed by the devil himself to spew out nothing but dung.

Henry did not write the entire response but was assisted by a team of theologians. Nevertheless, Henry got the credit. To reward him Pope Leo X gave the king the title Defender of the Faith. Word spread, and Henry's book sold well, which made some Lutherans worry that the princes who supported Luther could distance themselves from the Reformer.[2] Luther, however, read Henry's response and was so nauseated by its unbiblical arguments that he vomited one of his most venomous replies in his book *Contra Henricum Regem Angliae*.

---

1. Daniell, *William Tyndale*, 252.
2. Daniell, 253.

To defend his king from Luther, in 1523 the English humanist, politician, and churchman Thomas More wrote one of the most malicious responses to Luther in Counter-Reformation history. In 1518 and 1519, More was not hostile to Luther but considered him one more heretical zealot in a long line of others protesting abuses in the church.[3] Like many others, More underestimated Luther and turned antagonistic toward him after the Reformer was excommunicated. More had a hand in Henry's response to Luther, but More's own response served to intensify anti-Lutheran polemic. More recommended leaving "this mad friarlet and privy-minded rascal with his ragings and ravings, with his filth and dung, shitting and beshitted."[4] Meanwhile Cuthbert Tunstall advanced his campaign against Luther, determined to keep Lutheranism out of England, burning Luther's works whenever and wherever they were found.

Between Henry and More, England was a hostile place to be a Lutheran sympathizer. Only someone absolutely convinced by Luther's doctrine of *sola fide* dared to defy king and bishop to put the message of Scripture into the language of the people.

WILLIAM TYNDALE

William Tyndale received his bachelor of arts degree in 1512 at Oxford and then his master of arts at Oxford's Magdalen Hall in 1515. If the University of Paris was the prized medieval university of Europe, Oxford took the baton in the late medieval era, boasting great philosophers like Scotus and Ockham (see chapter 5).[5] And yet we know little about Tyndale during his student days at Oxford except that he looked back on his experience and was critical of the theological education he received. For example, he resented the Oxford disputations, unconvinced interlocuters paid enough attention to the scriptural witness in the process.[6]

After Oxford Tyndale transitioned to Cambridge, a university secondary to Oxford at the time, which has caused some to puzzle over Tyndale's decision. The reason is unknown, although Tyndale may have considered this more subdued university an ideal setting for studying the biblical languages or even preparing for the priesthood. From Cambridge Tyndale spent time in Gloucestershire, the place of his birth, and he may even have preached the Scriptures from an evangelical viewpoint at this early but transitional juncture. It is possible Tyndale's lifelong interest in translating the Scriptures had been born by his Gloucestershire

---

3. See *Complete Works of St. Thomas More*, 8:269–70. Cf. Daniell, 254.

4. *Complete Works of St. Thomas More*, 5, 1. Others responded as well, including John Fisher who wrote *Assertionis Lutheranae confutation*. Luther attempted a kinder tract to persuade Henry when he thought Henry might be sympathetic to him, a belief built on false information. Luther discovered Henry's true opinion when the king wrote a response just as aggressive and condemning as the first. More also responded to Luther again with a letter of his own, though it is uncertain if Luther ever received More's letter. Daniell, 259–61.

5. Daniell, 27.

6. E.g., see PS, 206, 315. Although, Daniell does remind interpreters to keep the context of Tyndale's criticisms in view: "Perhaps it should be remembered that each of the references he made was in a polemical work." Daniell, 41.

days, but it is difficult to know for certain since Tyndale's decision to embark on such a dangerous enterprise seems neither instantaneous nor vocalized in Gloucestershire. If he did, he was smart enough to keep it a secret. Regardless, Erasmus's Greek New Testament had released by 1516, and the young Tyndale must have been eager to study it.

"I Defy the Pope"

The closer Tyndale came to the task of translating the Scriptures into the vernacular, the clearer he saw the gaping unfamiliarity with the Scriptures in the English church. In Tyndale's experience, few knew the basics—the Ten Commandments, the Lord's Prayer, the Apostles' Creed. He held the clergy responsible and ultimately blamed the papacy. When Tyndale did set his mind to translate the Scriptures, his anti-papalism galvanized his efforts: "I defy the Pope and all his laws," said Tyndale to a man who considered the pope's law superior to God's law. Tyndale went on, "If God spare my life ere many years, I will cause a boy that driveth the plough, shall know more of the Scriptures than thou dost."

After Gloucestershire Tyndale spent around a year in London. Not only did the depressing state of biblical knowledge continue to weigh heavy on him, but the unlikelihood of translating the Scriptures became apparent as well. Other European countries had the Bible in their vernacular, but not England. As papal legate beginning in 1518, cardinal Thomas Wolsey (c. 1474–1530) made sure of it. While many reasons could be entertained, one of the most immediate was the threat Luther posed. If Luther's views migrated into England, the English might throw off the church of Rome, and the schism that was occurring in German territories could plague Wolsey's church as well. Wolsey was infamous in the eyes of Reformers, a representation of the affluent and extravagant clericalism they detested. And in the eyes of Wolsey, the Reformers represented an anticlericalism that was reminiscent of Wycliff and Lollardy (see chapter 7). Not only did Luther's beliefs pose a threat, but so did his translation of the Bible into German, a translation that introduced to the common people Scriptures the Reformers believed were untainted by beliefs like purgatory or penance or the papacy itself.[7]

If printing the Scriptures in the vernacular had any chance at success, Tyndale had to leave England in 1524 and find a European hub that could safely support this illegal endeavor. Cologne was Tyndale's destination, but it is probable he stopped in a variety of other cities first. He may have stayed in Wittenberg up to a year, for example. If so, Tyndale could have benefited from Wittenberg theologians and their teaching. However, whether Tyndale met Luther remains uncertain. Foxe said he did: "At his first departing out of the realm, he took his journey into the further parts of Germany, as into Saxony, where he had conference with Luther and other learned men in those quarters."[8] That may be

7. Daniell, 92–94.
8. Foxe, *Foxe's Book of Martyrs*, 18.

an assumption on Foxe's part since little evidence suggests Tyndale and Luther talked to one another.

When Tyndale did touch the soil of Cologne, Peter Quentell worked with Tyndale to begin printing the gospel of Matthew in 1525.[9] Tyndale's full translation of the New Testament (1526) did not contain marginal notes, but his Cologne printing did. They are not filled with anti-papal venom but represent Tyndale's primary aim: assisting the reader in understanding the meaning of the text. That does not mean, however, that the notes are cleansed of Lutheran influence. Quite the contrary, many of the notes are indebted to Luther and his theology.[10] Something similar is true of the prologue. Here readers find Tyndale's first thoughts on his translation and his motivations. Again, missing from the prologue is an anti-papal agenda. Tyndale presented himself instead as a translator. Nevertheless, the prologue is not atheological by any means. As Tyndale explained, he had translated the Scriptures from Greek into English for the edification of the congregation. Their edification consisted in knowing Christ and his gospel. Eternal life was at stake for Tyndale. Therefore, the English translator dedicated much of his prologue to distinguishing between law and gospel, only to define and defend justification *sola fide*. Although Tyndale did not explicitly attack Rome, his convictions were evangelical to the core, encouraging the English church to embrace Lutheran soteriology. Once again, Tyndale was indebted to Luther, yet he adopted his own style and method, that of an Englishman explaining the gospel and the need for the Scriptures in a way that other Englishmen could appreciate. Tyndale's prologue was such a clear presentation of the gospel and grace that it became a book of its own in 1531—*The Pathway to Holy Scripture*.[11]

As for the translation itself, Tyndale showed signs of both dependence and originality. Tyndale looked at Luther's translation as well as at the Vulgate, and at points decided to follow Luther's linguistic logic. Yet Tyndale relied on the Greek as he decided how best to word the English, attempting to capture the spirit of the text through the intonation of the English language. The outcome was a translation of Matthew influenced by Luther but nonetheless original to Tyndale, marked by a stark perspicuity and English tempo that mastered the meaning of Jesus' words.[12]

Despite the promising start in the publishing house, printing came to an immediate halt when Tyndale discovered he was about to be arrested. John Dobneck (or Cochlaeus) was printing a work of his own and stopped in to check on its progress when he overheard a few drunk workers discussing Tyndale's

9. Tyndale did not labor to provide a text for Quentell's printing house alone but had the help of William Roye.

10. Daniell did the math, calculating that out of the ninety notes, thirty represent Tyndale. *William Tyndale*, 117–18.

11. Daniell devoted much space to distinguishing between Luther and Tyndale, recognizing the debt but also setting Tyndale apart as his own man. Daniell, 111–33.

12. Daniell, 111–15.

New Testament. Dobneck reported the news to Herman Rinck, who took the news to Henry VIII himself. Tyndale was shrewd enough to take his quarto sheets and flee to Worms without delay.[13]

1526—Tyndale's New Testament

At last, in 1526 Tyndale's entire New Testament was printed in Worms, thanks to Peter Schoeffer's press. Tyndale acknowledged to the reader that his translation was far from perfect, and revisions were necessary to improve the text in the years ahead. Yet he prayed his translation could be a first step, giving the English people the sacred Scriptures—and in them, the gospel itself—in their own language.[14]

Despite its shortcomings, the accomplishment was monumental for the English people in ways Tyndale had yet to realize. The reasons are innumerable. Tyndale produced the first English translation from the Greek text. Yet the significance of Tyndale's New Testament is not limited to a first endeavor; the translation itself was special, set apart from the Latin of the Vulgate and the German of Luther's Bible. To begin with, Tyndale translated the New Testament into an English prose that was clear to the average English Christian. Tyndale chose simple words that could not be misunderstood, not only to achieve a superior text but also to remove any ambiguity around the grace of the gospel. And yet the enduring clarity of the English text did not compromise the tempo of the text nor domesticate its beauty. Tyndale paid attention to the movement of the story and respected each book's genre by retaining its literary essence, whether narrative or epistle, whether parable or apocalypse. Moreover, Tyndale coupled clarity in mind with the affections.[15] His translation was not stiff for the sake of the cerebral. Instead, his translation stirred within the reader the same joy and sadness, faith and doubt, compassion and anger exhibited by the biblical characters. Reading Tyndale not only conveyed the story's meaning but left the reader feeling as if he was there, as if Jesus was speaking directly to him. Although the King James Bible rose to prominence one century later, its success was due in large part to Tyndale. Tyndale's wording is all over the Authorized Version, and to this day English translation remains indebted to the English Reformer.

Tyndale's contributions were many, but one had significant consequences—even polemical implications—for the future of the English Reformation: by working from the Greek, the accuracy of Tyndale's translation unveiled the Vulgate's mistakes and, more importantly, the ways Rome had misunderstood and misused the text for its beliefs and practices. As mentioned earlier, when Tyndale considered the Greek word *metanoeo*, for example, he became dissatisfied with "do penance." The Savior's use of *metanoeo* does not convey a system

---

13. Daniell, 110.

14. *Tyndale's New Testament*, 3–16.

15. To see these attributes, and examples demonstrating each of them, consult Daniell, *William Tyndale*, 134–51.

of works but heartfelt sorrow for sin, even a change in disposition, one that leads to forgiveness and faithfulness. A more accurate rendering, Tyndale decided, was the English word *repent*. Tyndale "cannot possibly have been unaware that those words in particular undercut the entire sacramental structure of the thousand-year Church throughout Europe, Asia, and north Africa," said Daniell. "It was the Greek New Testament that was doing the undercutting."[16] And the future English Reformation benefited from such a textual breakthrough with theological and ecclesiastical consequences yet to be determined.

Already English evangelicals faced persecution. With the release of Tyndale's New Testament, the persecution intensified. Both Wolsey and Tunstall preached against the evangelical religion and led burnings of evangelical books. Raids became a sure way to expose prohibited books and their readers. However, Tyndale was appalled when he learned that Tunstall not only burned theological books but the Bible itself. Tyndale understood they hated him and his beliefs, but even still, how could a Christian man take the Scriptures themselves—and in his own language—and set them on fire?[17]

The Wicked Mammon and *The Obedience of a Christian Man*

In 1522 Martin Luther delivered a sermon on Luke 16, the parable of the wicked manager. That sermon influenced Tyndale, and six years after the Wittenberg sermon Tyndale published a book on the same parable. The book was called *The Parable of the Wicked Mammon*. The year was 1528, a year when the English Reformer was keeping a low profile in Antwerp. The city was a hub for both humanist literature and evangelical tracts and treatises, printing legions more literature than England at the time. Antwerp was the ideal location for Tyndale to print a book that could put his life in jeopardy. Tyndale's book was so dangerous because it was a direct affirmation of Luther's doctrine of justification *sola fide* and by its conclusion an attack against the papacy as Antichrist.

The Parable of the Wicked Mammon, however, is an original work, not merely an elaborated take on Luther's sermon. Tyndale did defend the Lutheran doctrine, but he did so in his own way, exploring different Scriptures, even using his own illustrations. Tyndale made a sharp distinction between law and gospel: the law enslaves but the gospel sets free, the law puts to death but the gospel brings to life. Faith in one's own works is a pretense for condemnation; no man can obey the law with perfection but stands under its judgment as a transgressor. By contrast, faith must reside in the gospel of Jesus Christ. Trust in the promises of God alone can result in life everlasting. Righteousness is not granted on the basis of works but by faith. Faith alone can justify the wicked. Therefore, faith must precede good works. With justification by faith alone established, Tyndale could affirm the meaning and value of good works. Works do not justify the

---

16. For other examples of word differences, see Daniell, 148.
17. On the burning of Tyndale's New Testament, see Daniell, 190–94.

sinner but are a sign the sinner has been justified, the fruit of a new right standing with God. Whether fasting or alms, works for God and neighbor display the sincere faith within the believer. They assume, however, that the Holy Spirit has regenerated the believer already; otherwise, such works—the fruit of faith—are an impossibility. Again, Tyndale sounded a Reformation note by asserting the bondage of the will and the Spirit's omnipotence in the miracle of spiritual rebirth, emphases present in his prologue to Romans as well.[18]

Tyndale already violated English law by translating the New Testament into the English language. Now, with *The Parable of the Wicked Mammon*, Tyndale showed the English church what theological conclusions that New Testament should produce. Its publication provoked the wrath of Wolsey, who now took measures to find Tyndale (and other English evangelicals in hiding) and punish the heretic. Wolsey was not the only one; Tunstall joined the hunt as well, infuriated by Tyndale's influence on English evangelicals as his *Parable* secretly made its way into English homes.[19]

The Parable of the Wicked Mammon was published in May 1528, and by that fall Tyndale released a second and his most significant book, *The Obedience of a Christian Man*. Tyndale's *Parable* gave no apology for its direct affirmation of Lutheran doctrine. However, following Luther in the 1520s could only invite misrepresentation. For example, the Peasants' Revolt left a black smudge on Luther's reputation. Protestant theology had already been accused of innovation and heresy; now critics added rebellion to the list, which led Luther to respond with a harsh rebuke against the peasants and their violence (see chapters 8–11). Luther was infuriated that his name was associated with violence. In 1528 Tyndale faced a similar accusation: by introducing Lutheranism to England, Tyndale opened the door for revolution to follow. Such an argument misrepresented Tyndale and served as a scare tactic.[20]

Tyndale not only found the accusation maddening but ironic. If anyone was responsible for violence over the last several centuries, it was the papacy. How many popes, asked Tyndale, waved the flag of war, promising indulgences to those who enlisted to fight against the Turk? Tyndale's Protestantism, by contrast, had nothing to do with violence. To demonstrate that claim, Tyndale embarked on an extensive tour of Scripture to prove the Christian is called by God to civil subservience. He believed that God had put kings and magistrates in place to distribute and protect his justice. To rebel against the ruler was to rebel against God, inviting his judgment by means of a ruler who did not bear the sword in vain. Furthermore, the Christian could not blame his disobedience on a magistrate who was less than perfect. The Christian should not pursue vengeance but should expect persecution. Like his master, the Christian was to suffer under the hand of an evil ruler, waiting on God for deliverance.

18. *Tyndale's New Testament* (1534 edition), 207–224.
19. On their efforts, see Daniell, 170–73.
20. Daniell, 224.

Such persecution was reassurance that the Spirit was present and would sustain his people until God decided to remove the evil ruler from his throne.

What shocked and offended the papacy was Tyndale's bold claim that even the pope himself was required to obey magistrates put in place by God. If Christ himself could give to Caesar what is Caesar's, who was the pope to think he was the exception? Tyndale shamed the papacy for extending itself beyond its God-ordained boundaries, as if bishops had been put on earth to orchestrate war to the advantage of the church. God had given to bishops one sword only, the Word of God.

Tyndale dedicated much of his book to demonstrating that the papacy had failed to wield this spiritual sword, the Scriptures. Two years prior, in February 1526, a crowd gathered at St. Paul's to burn any writings by Luther that made their way into England.[21] The burning of books was accompanied by a sermon by Fisher himself that condemned the Reformation in no uncertain terms. In *The Obedience of a Christian Man* Tyndale steadied himself and took aim at Fisher's sermon, shooting down one argument after another until the bishop of Rochester and his treatment of the Scriptures looked pathetic, even grotesque, in the ways it twisted the text. Tyndale concluded with a Luther-like pronouncement: the Church of Rome was under the sway of Antichrist. If the church was to find its way back to sound doctrine, then it must return to the Scriptures and pursue reliable methods of interpretation, like the analogy of Scripture. Tyndale was persuaded that if the church allowed Scripture to interpret Scripture, then the church would create a much-needed hedge against superstitious beliefs and practices from creeping in.

Although Tyndale's book instigated the wrath of his opponents, Henry VIII reacted with pleasure. Introduced to the book by Anne Boleyn, Henry appreciated Tyndale's firm imperative to submit to the king. That message certainly fit with Henry's approach to the crown.[22] However, Henry may have read Tyndale through his own regal agenda, as if Tyndale advocated for the king's unconditional authority. Henry ignored Tyndale's warning that the king himself was subject to God's judgment if he sinned; Henry overlooked the part of the book that said God may replace a king if he was unjust.[23] Of course, Henry did not think of himself as unjust nor as a king who had committed sin, so perhaps Tyndale's words did not bother Henry at all.

Ekklesia: More, Tyndale, and Debate over Catholicity

Tyndale may have attracted the momentary (and fleeting) approval of Henry with *Obedience*, but in the following years he also attracted the relentless fury

---

21. For more on Fisher, see Daniell, 233–35.

22. For the confiscation of the book by Richard Sampson and Wolsey but its recovery by Anne Boleyn with the king's help, see Daniell, 244–47.

23. Daniell makes the astute observation that Tyndale valued natural law and considered even a non-Christian king accountable to natural law. Daniell, 242.

of Thomas More. In 1529 More published the first of his many verbose attacks on Tyndale with his book *Dialogue Concerning Heresies*. When Tyndale gave his *Answer* in 1531, More escalated his attack by publishing two replies, his *Confutation of Tyndale's Answer* (1532) and *Apology* (1533).

Here the reader was introduced to a different More than the humanist who wrote *Utopia*. With ferocity More turned a blind eye to ecclesiastical affluence in the sixteenth century and instead defended the church's infallibility with compulsive potency. Like an assassin, More made every effort to eliminate the Protestant program, which he considered heretical both in its formal and material principles. In one sense, the debate between Tyndale and More was a replay of Luther's debate with Eck. More found each component of the Reformation disagreeable, but his main contention was the doctrine of *sola scriptura*. More was offended by the arrogance of the doctrine because it taught that the church can err, the papacy included. Criticizing Tyndale's translation of the New Testament, More became insatiable in his irritation over the word *congregation*, Tyndale's choice word for *ecclesia*. More accused Tyndale of destabilizing the hierarchy of the papacy as if the New Testament understood the church as an assembly of believers. If elevated, Tyndale's ecclesiology could threaten papal supremacy and ecclesiastical hierarchy.

Furthermore, in the hands of the "congregation," the Bible need not depend on the only correct and infallible interpretation of the papacy. For both Tyndale and More, the issue was *catholicity*: Tyndale thought the whole assembly of believers (the universal church) had and still could interpret the Scriptures in a way that continued to be refined and reformed; More narrowed catholicity to Rome, locating biblical interpretation within the confines of a papal religion. The consequences for the canon followed naturally from both positions: Tyndale thought Scripture was the mother of the church; More considered Scripture the offspring of the church. To reverse this order, insisted More, was to betray orthodoxy itself, inverting the proper relationship between church and canon.[24]

As the debate was received by sixteenth-century readers, More did not appear to be the obvious winner in the eyes of the public. For example, whatever theological merits More's argument for ecclesiological infallibility may or may not have, he refused to acknowledge that the church of his day was crooked in any sense. He did not want to concede this point to Tyndale; however, even other humanists, like More's friend Erasmus, cut their teeth on the undeniable fact that abuses were prevalent in the church of Rome across Europe. Also, More's responses to Tyndale were so protracted and repetitious—"Unreadable" in the opinion of Daniell—that the reader was left with a negative impression:

---

24. "Theologically, his [More's] whole attack can be boiled down to his objection to Tyndale's translation of four or five words: Tyndale translating *ekklesia* as 'congregation,' and so on, was of course at root offensive because More had to defend the orthodox doctrine that the Church came first and Scripture followed." Daniell, 276.

More was frantic, so desperate to score points against his opponent, that he could not land his argument no matter how many words he used.[25]

From Pentateuch to Romans

Despite More's many polemical works, each attempting to silence Tyndale, the English Reformer wasted no time at all in producing a translation of the Pentateuch from Hebrew into English. More must have been fatigued after writing not one, not two, but three tomes against Tyndale only to see the English Reformer's translation of Moses appear in January 1530.

Latin was the religious language of the day, encompassing the church from all four corners of its liturgy. While elite humanists like Erasmus and dedicated Reformers like Melanchthon knew Greek, few knew Hebrew. How Tyndale learned Hebrew remains another mystery that is lost to history. Who he sought out as a teacher and where he camped while he studied the ancient language is perplexing. Yet wherever and whenever he learned Hebrew, Tyndale demonstrated his mastery of the language. In the days preceding his arrest, he displayed a knowledge of Hebrew that paralleled his understanding of Greek, a compliment that could not be paid to many others in Europe. As in his translation of the New Testament, Tyndale demonstrated a rare and priceless talent for converting Hebrew into English with extreme clarity. He discovered that Hebrew and English were compatible languages, allowing him to convey the power of the text into the vernacular, bringing to life the story of Israel and the commands of Yahweh.[26]

Tyndale's Pentateuch is remarkable, a pioneering accomplishment in translation. Yet the Christian presuppositions he expected his readers to bring to the text should not be overlooked, either. In contrast to modern approaches to the Scriptures, he thought of the canon as a unity, written by many human authors but human authors carried along by the Holy Spirit. The canon's one Divine Author, in other words, gave Tyndale the confidence to read and translate the Pentateuch as if Moses knew something of the gospel itself. For example, Tyndale wrote of Deuteronomy, "This is a book worthy to be read in day and night and never to be out of hands. For it is the most excellent of all the books of Moses. It is easy also and light and a very pure gospel that is to wete, a preaching of faith and love: deducing the love to God out of faith, and the love of a man's neighbour out of the love of God."[27] Tyndale never had to the opportunity to finish translating the Old Testament, and that remains one of the greatest tragedies of the Reformation. Nevertheless, his Pentateuch remains and deserves recognition as a lasting contribution to the success of the Reformation. The lasting

---

25. For these points and others, consult Daniell, 261–80. See p. 274 for Daniell's "unreadable" conclusion.

26. On the relationship between Hebrew and English, see Daniell, 288–90. Daniell argued as well that Tyndale depended on Luther's Old Testament at points—"A good translator uses any help he can find"—but the translation is Tyndale's own and showcases his unique gifts (291; cf. 308).

27. Quoted in Daniell, 288.

significance of the Pentateuch was preserved by other translations of the whole Bible. For example, in 1535 England was introduced to Miles Coverdale's Great Bible and in 1537 John Rogers (aka Thomas Matthew) published the Matthew's Bible.[28] Rogers's translation absorbed Tyndale's New Testament as well as Tyndale's translation of Moses. As a result, all English Bibles published after the Matthew's Bible channeled Tyndale's translation, indebted in countless ways to the Reformer's original work.

In 1534 Tyndale released a second edition of his New Testament. He included marginal notes, which gave him the opportunity to comment on the text itself. Some notes were polemical, directed at the papacy and its beliefs, but most of them were didactic. Tyndale also included numerous prologues for books of the Bible, assisting the reader with each book's message and theology. Some are short, others long. Out of them all, Romans is the hermeneutical key, "the principal and most excellent part of the new testament, and most pure evangelion, that is to say glad tidings and that we call gospel, and also a light and a way in unto the whole of scripture."[29] On that note, Tyndale and Luther sang the same tune. At the same time, Tyndale's broader theology may be distinguished by the English Reformer's emphasis on the Holy Spirit's perfecting power in sanctification through the law, which explains why some are more comfortable labeling Tyndale's program a *modification* of Lutheranism.[30]

The 1534 edition unveils not only Tyndale's continuity with the Reformation but also the Reformation's continuity with the church catholic. For example, in his prologue to Hebrews Tyndale was frustrated that some have questioned the epistle's inclusion in the canon. Offended at its warning passages, they concluded Hebrews was neither "catholic or godly." First, Tyndale justified these passages on the basis of corresponding warnings in the Gospels (the analogy of Scripture). Second, Tyndale defended these passages on the basis of catholic doctrine (the analogy of faith). A suspicious stance towards Hebrews is the product of reading the book in isolation, apart from the church universal. "Wherefore seeing no scripture is of private interpretation: but must be expounded according to the general articles of our faith and agreeable to other open and evident texts, and confirmed or compared to like sentences, why should we not understand these places with like reverence as we do the other, namely when all the remnant of the epistle is so godly and of so great learning?"[31] The young Tyndale did promise that if God spared his life, he would cause the plough boy to know the Scriptures better than the pope. And yet, as his 1534 edition reveals, Tyndale had no intention for his bold charge in defiance of the papacy to produce private

---

28. Coverdale most likely joined Tyndale in Hamburg in the late 1520s. If so, Tyndale translated the Pentateuch with Coverdale's help. "Though his [Coverdale's] knowledge of Greek and Hebrew was small, Coverdale's ability to digest recent translations in Latin, German and French would be useful." Daniell also believed Coverdale joined Tyndale in Antwerp in the mid-1530s as well. Daniell, 199.

29. *Tyndale's New Testament* (1534 edition), 207.

30. Trueman, "The Theology of the English Reformers," 164. Cf. Trueman, *Luther's Legacy.*

31. *Tyndale's New Testament* (1534 edition), 346.

interpretation. "Wherefore seeing no scripture is of private interpretation: but must be expounded according to the general articles of our faith," Tyndale warned his reader in his prologue to the epistle to the Hebrews.[32] Liberation from the papacy was not substituted with a captivity to the individual but the freedom to interpret the Scriptures *with the church catholic (universal)*, according to the analogy of faith.

Return to England?

Tyndale first left England because translating the Bible into the vernacular could prove fatal. By 1529 and 1530, however, the political climate was changing and, potentially, working in Tyndale's favor. Henry continued his pursuit of divorce, which put him in conflict with Rome. Although Henry was Defender of the Faith, his marital ambitions put him in serious tension with the church. In 1528 Tyndale's work *The Obedience of a Christian Man* met Henry's approval as the king mustered his sovereignty, though Henry may not have read the book until 1529. Then Tyndale wrote *The Practice of Prelates: Whether the King's Grace May Be Separated from His Queen because She Was His Brother's Wife*, a book that criticized prelates that helped the king arrange a divorce. Most everyone else attempted to justify the king's divorce, but Tyndale said he could not exchange biblical convictions for political expediency. Still, at the start of 1531 Henry entertained the idea of bringing the heretic back to England. Given Tyndale's position on the king's sovereignty over the church, perhaps the Reformer could advance Henry's agenda. Cromwell then took steps to contact Tyndale and persuade the exile to come back home. Tyndale knew better than to trust a promise of safe passage made to a heretic and decided not to return until the king legalized the translation of the Scriptures into English.[33]

Lord, Open the King of England's Eyes

If Tyndale's great talent was translating the testaments, then his great weakness had to be his trusting, gullible spirit. In 1535 Tyndale was betrayed. The Reformer was living in Antwerp with his wife, enjoying the hospitality of Thomas Poyntz. The home was a translator's haven, keeping Tyndale from his enemies; it was also a workshop that allowed the linguist to focus his energy on translating the rest of the Old Testament. The goal was spectacular in the eyes of English evangelicals: a complete English Bible. Yet this dream was cut short when Tyndale trusted Henry Phillips. Phillips appeared in Antwerp all of a sudden with every intention of gaining Tyndale's confidence, only to hand the Reformer over to the authorities. He was a Judas.

Yet unlike the Judas of the Bible, this Judas was paid by an employer who escaped identification. Many in Europe associated the name of Henry Phillips

---

32. *Tyndale's New Testament*, 346.
33. See the conversation between Stephen Vaughan and Tyndale in Daniell, 209–17.

with treason. Phillips returned this European hatred with animosity of his own, an aversion that was directed at England as well.[34] It is most difficult to determine who hired Phillips as a spy, although whoever hired Phillips did reside in London. Since Phillips had fallen from affluency, the offer to betray Tyndale must have been irresistible, just the financial lift he needed. And since Phillips was no friend to English evangelicals or German Lutherans, the betrayal did not bother his conscience.

Phillips did what any spy would do: he moved on Tyndale as if a friend, an ally, even a servant to the cause of translation. The relationship was curious, but Tyndale was persuaded that Phillips had good intentions and could help. A friend of Tyndale was a friend to the Reformer's closest companions. But in May 1535, Phillips hatched his real intentions, convincing Tyndale to join him for a meal. In waiting were soldiers who surprised the Reformer with an arrest.

Tyndale languished in prison for a year and a half and was stripped of his ordination into the priesthood and convicted as a heretic worthy of the death sentence.[35] In prison Tyndale continued to hold fast to his Lutheran beliefs and wrote a book on *sola fide*. Although the book has not been found, Tyndale's decision to write on justification as one of his last projects does convey his dedication to the Reformation. He was not merely a translator but a theological advocate for reform.

Tyndale's devotion was also exhibited when he shared his evangelical faith with one of his guards. As John Foxe recounted, "Such was the power of his doctrine and sincerity of his life, that during the time of his imprisonment (which endured a year and a half) it is said, he converted his keeper, his daughter, and other of his household."[36] Tyndale knew the New Testament, and Acts 16 may have come to mind as he recapitulated the incarceration of Paul and Silas as if his guard were the Philippian jailer himself.

Unlike Paul and Silas, however, Tyndale did not go free, but in October 1536 he walked to the stake. Tyndale received the mercy of strangulation first. His executioner fastened Tyndale to the post, and before he tightened the chain around Tyndale's neck, Tyndale spoke his final words to God for the crowd to hear. He prayed, "Lord, open the king of England's eyes."[37] After he was strangled, Tyndale's body went up in flames.

Tyndale's life can serve as a corrective to misguided interpretations of the Reformation. "Modern champions of the Catholic position like to support a view of the Reformation," observed Daniell, "that it was entirely a political

---

34. In addition, what politician in Antwerp would arrange such a conspiracy? To do so might risk upsetting an otherwise peaceful and profitable trade alliance with England. Furthermore, Antwerp was not exactly a hub of Protestant persecution but a budding printing center that depended to some extent on forbearance. Daniell, 261–62.

35. On the attempt of Antwerp English Merchants and Cromwell to intercede, see Daniell, 365–73.

36. Foxe, *Foxe's Book of Martyrs*, 20.

37. Foxe, *Foxe's Book of Martyrs*, 20.

imposition by a ruthless minority in power against both the traditions and the wishes of the pious lay people of England, with the claim that, if matters had not been interfered with, the Church in its reforming wisdom would have got round to issuing a vernacular Bible in its own time."[38] Regardless of whether the church would have "got round" to a vernacular Bible, the belief that the success of the English Reformation was merely a product of politics fails to consider men like Tyndale. His evangelical commitments came from the heart, moved by the Scriptures to support evangelical beliefs. Maintaining those convictions meant working *against* the political authorities even at the cost of his life. Later years did involve a top-down implementation (even imposition) of reform, but appeal to politics as the only or all-encompassing reason for the English Reformation is simplistic and fails to account for the deaths of English martyrs and the lasting influence they created.

ENGLISH MARTYRS

While Tyndale's linguistic gifts and contribution were nothing short of unique, his martyrdom was not. Due to the investigative efforts of John Fisher, Cuthbert Tunstall, and Thomas More, the 1520s and 1530s were a bloodbath. Many went to their deaths in ways far more gruesome than Tyndale.

Even before Tyndale's New Testament was published, Luther's books had secretly made their way into the hands of the English, and so had Erasmus's Greek edition of the New Testament. The effect was transformative. In Cambridge, for example, Thomas Bilney was converted to an evangelical view of salvation, and many others were, too, when they heard Bilney's testimony. Men like Thomas Arthur, Robert Barnes, John Lambert, and Hugh Latimer took a fresh look at the Scriptures and concluded that they had misunderstood the nature of justification and saving faith. The cost of the Reformation was counted, and these individuals, among many others, were convinced that evangelical doctrine was worth the price of persecution. Nevertheless, the persecution could be as fierce as it was fatal.

When Thomas More and John Stokesley rose to power in 1529 and 1530, English evangelicals were targeted, convinced as they both were that evangelicals were nothing less than heretics. In their minds, heresy had to be snuffed out in the church and in society. A sure sign of heresy was the translating or smuggling of Tyndale's Bible. As his New Testament made its appearance in England, More discovered that Thomas Hitton was responsible. Hitton might as well have translated the New Testament himself; he was charged with heresy for hiding Tyndale's text and sneaking it to ready readers across England. In 1530 England watched as its first Reformation martyr was sent to the flames. More, however, did not flinch; the flames that licked Hitton's skin were only a foretaste of the

---

38. Daniell countered the objections: "It was not the result of political imposition. It came from the discovery of the Word of God as originally written." Daniell, *William Tyndale*, 58.

flames More was about to experience in hell itself. More was merely the gate-keeper, God's prosecutor.[39]

Hitton was but the beginning of a continuous, and seemingly never-ending stream of martyrs. Men were sent to the flames not only for hiding Bibles but for hiding any type of evangelical book. Others were burned for refusing to confess Roman doctrines. Still others for iconoclasm.[40] The persecution grew so fierce that men were not only put to death for overt acts of resistance, but for quiet acts of evangelical devotion. More and Stokesley went on the offensive, seeking out evangelicals, even if it meant raiding their houses or quietly sneaking up on them as they read their Bibles or Reformation literature in the remote fields of the countryside.

Martyrdom was not a merciful death either. As evangelicals were burned at the stake, their screams rose as high as the smoke coming off their flesh. England was no stranger to cruel forms of execution. From the thirteenth century to the sixteenth century, they became experts in the art of torturing a man for treason. First, the guilty man was dragged behind a horse. Second, he was hanged, strangled within inches of his life. Third, he was hoisted upright so that his genitals could be carved up with a knife. As he bled out from his genitals, his stomach was sliced open and his intestines and organs ripped out. During this entire process, the man with the knife was careful to keep the guilty man alive. Finally, the man's heart was cut out and the rest of his body was quartered, including decapitation, so that his body parts could be hung across town as a visual reminder of the penalty for treason.[41]

WHITE HORSE INN

A group of English Reformers met near Queen's College (University of Cambridge) at a tavern called the White Horse Inn. They updated one another on the latest progress of the Reformation in the Holy Roman Empire, shared their opinions of Luther's writings, especially his doctrine of *sola fide*. Who were these English Reformers? They included Robert Barnes, Thomas Bilney, Hugh Latimer, John Frith, Miles Coverdale, Thomas Cranmer, Nicholas Ridley, and Matthew Parker. However, these Reformers and others were not necessarily at the White Horse Inn all at the same time. Some wonder whether William Tyndale could have participated as well, although there is little to no evidence suggesting his presence. Each of these English Reformers died as a martyr with the exception of Coverdale and Parker.

---

39. *Complete Works of St. Thomas More*, vol. 8, pt.1, p. 17. Cf. Atherstone, *Reformation*, 89.
40. For the history of iconoclasm in England, see Duffy, *Stripping of the Altars*.
41. Atherstone, *Reformation*, 101.

Henry VIII used this form of execution to silence those who spoke against him, sending a loud message that resistance to his political-religious decisions would not be tolerated. For example, when Henry divorced Catherine, the prophetess Elizabeth Barton and her followers protested. Their opposition continued as Henry elevated himself to a position of power over the church. Barton said her prophecy originated from God himself and the day of God's return was near, a day of judgment for Henry. In response, Henry hanged Barton, cut off her head, and fastened it to the London Bridge for all to see. That was a merciful death since she was a woman. However, her male supporters were hanged, drawn, and quartered.[42] Disobedience, even for religious reasons, was a matter of treason and punishable by the worst form of execution.

How did Henry rise to such a prominent position?

HENRY VIII'S PURSUIT OF A MALE HEIR

The volatile story of the Reformation in England cannot be severed from the erratic political and religious evolution of Henry VIII.[43] More often than not, religious tolerance or persecution depended on the political climate. That political climate could be a brewing storm or prevailing rainfall.

At the start of the Reformation, Henry created his own thunderstorm of protest against the German protester himself, Martin Luther. To review, when the German Reformer wrote *The Babylonian Captivity of the Church*, Henry responded with a book of his own called *Assertion of the Seven Sacraments* (1521). Henry was outraged that this German heretic had the audacity to oppose Rome's seven sacraments.[44] That same year was when Pope Leo X rewarded Henry with the title Defender of the Faith (*fidei defensor*).

Despite Henry's early theological compatibility with the pope, in time he rebelled against the pope himself, although for different reasons than Luther. His reasons had everything to do with a male heir, Henry's lifelong obsession. At the turn of the century, Catherine of Aragon married Arthur of England. If Arthur had lived long enough, he would have become king instead of his brother, Henry. Arthur's marriage to Catherine, like many marriages crossing borders, was entirely for political reasons. But Catherine and Arthur were not even married for half a year when death stole her husband away. The daughter of Ferdinand and Isabella of Spain was but a young woman still, and the alliance between England and Spain was still fresh, an alliance that served to keep the troops of France at bay.[45] The responsibility fell to Arthur's brother Henry to marry Catherine.

---

42. These executions occurred in 1534. Atherstone, 94; Haigh, *English Reformations*, 138.

43. For a more in-depth account, see Bernard, *King's Reformation*; Duffy, *Reformation Divided*; and Marshall, *Heretics and Believers*. But for an account of its aftermath, see MacCulloch, *Later Reformation in England, 1547–1603*.

44. At first Luther said there were three sacraments: penance, the Eucharist, and baptism. Later he eliminated penance.

45. Hillerbrand, *Division of Christendom*, 218.

However, canon law frowned upon such an arrangement. Marrying your brother's widow needed a special dispensation from the pope himself. On what grounds could such a dispensation be granted? If the marriage between Arthur and Catherine was not consummated, then the dispensation was justified. Catherine exonerated herself from violating canon law and claimed her right to the papal dispensation because, according to her own testimony, Arthur never did consummate the marriage to begin with. Whether her claim was fact or fiction may not matter in the end since her testimony was sufficient to permit her marriage to Arthur's brother in the summer of 1503.[46] In 1509 Henry became Henry VIII, the new king of England. Henry now expected more than ever that Catherine's womb give birth to the next king of England.

In the years ahead, Henry reached the conclusion that Catherine's womb was fruitful but flawed: although she bore six children, only one of them lived, and it was a girl. In 1516 Catherine of Aragon gave birth to Mary. A female as the surviving heir was problematic on multiple levels. Medieval England had a history of civil war over the controversial ascension of a queen to the throne, as exemplified with the War of Roses. Also, a female heir raised the real possibility of divine judgment. This question circled round and round in Henry's head until it haunted him: Was Catherine's inability to produce a male heir God's way of punishing Henry for marrying the wife of his deceased brother? Henry had to wonder, especially since the Old Testament law said as much, at least the way Henry interpreted it.[47] Other factors contributed to Henry's growing discontent and separation from Catherine. Perhaps most personal was Henry's infidelity itself: the king became infatuated with the young Anne Boleyn, and the two had an ongoing affair. Although Henry claimed other motives for annulment of his marriage—biblical reasons even—Henry's love for Anne Boleyn must have affected the urgency of his petition.[48]

In short time, Henry became convinced he was justified to dissolve the marriage, a marriage that was, after all, invalid from the start. In the summer of 1527, Henry told Catherine their marriage of eighteen years was illegitimate. Catherine was crushed. Convincing Pope Clement VII of his opinion, however, proved far more difficult than Henry anticipated. The reasons were legion. For example, Catherine's nephew was none other than Charles V. Clement was not about to provoke Charles—who actively condemned Henry's petition for annulment—especially since Charles had just gained the upper hand over Rome. But Clement had internal reservations as well, reservations both ecclesiastical and legal. How could he grant an annulment to the same man who had

---

46. She stood by her testimony throughout her life, especially when Henry threw his marriage to Catherine into question. Hillerbrand, 218.

47. See Lev. 20:21.

48. Hillerbrand asked whether Anne was the main reason, a question Reginald Pole answered in the affirmative. Historians debate whether that was the case or not. But at the very least, it seems undeniable Anne was a major influence. Hillerbrand, *Division of Christendom*, 219. See also Ives, *Life and Death of Anne Boleyn*.

previously petitioned the papacy for a special dispensation to justify the marriage at its inception? Surely this would reflect on Clement and the papacy, not to mention their use or potential misuse of canon law. Even if the pope could convince himself that Henry's petition was justifiable, he still faced the barrier of legality. No canon lawyer would approve Henry's attempt to counter what canon law itself had previously permitted by means of a special dispensation. "Henry's case was by no means unique—with generations of canonists exploring every aspect of marriage law, it hardly could be—so for the pope to acquiesce to Henry meant to go contrary to virtually unanimous legal opinion."[49] Then there was the papal dilemma: if Clement granted an annulment of the marriage his precursor approved, Clement might throw into question the authority of the papacy in its pronouncements.[50]

For all these reasons, the pope was slow to give Henry an answer. Meanwhile, Henry grew more impatient with every passing month. Attempts were made by many to find a remedy, and all but one led to the demise of its advocates. Consider papal legate Cardinal Wolsey, who used both his confidence and his clout. The chancellor's optimism was naive, not only misjudging the pope's stiff stalwartness but also Henry's volatile temperament when denied what he desired. "At Henry's behest Wolsey traveled to France to secure Francis I's support to free the pope from the fangs of Charles's troops. The strategy was that the pope's gratitude would induce him to honor Henry's request for the annulment. Wolsey failed in his mission, and this meant the king's displeasure—undoubtedly he was influenced by Anne Boleyn."[51] The end of Wolsey was now near. Henry's escalating vitriol for papal authority and Wolsey's allegiance to Rome as papal legate collided at last—Wolsey was accused of treason. In 1529 Wolsey was stripped of his office, and the following year Wolsey was taken to the Tower of London, but he died before his trial took place. Wolsey's sudden demise revealed that the king would have his annulment no matter what, turning his back on even his most dedicated subjects if they failed his expectations or aligned themselves with his growing cast of nemeses.[52]

49. "The problem was that Henry's desire for an annulment of his marriage ran counter to the consensus of a formidable array of canon lawyers who claimed that, given certain conditions, a dispensation to marry one's brother's widow might be issued and did not conflict with either natural or divine law." Hillerbrand, *Division of Christendom*, 220.

50. Hillerbrand, 220.

51. Wolsey "was indicted for violation of the fourteenth-century statutes of praemunire. Known by this Latin term, which simply means 'strengthen,' these statutes vaguely prohibited the English from acknowledging any foreign power." Hillerbrand, 221.

52. "The legal proceedings moved to London, presided over at Blackfriars by Cardinal Wolsey and Cardinal Campeggio (the pope's legate). Campeggio recommended that Katherine become a nun, which would leave Henry free to marry again, but she refused to go quietly and appealed formally to Rome. This lack of progress angered the king and hastened Wolsey's downfall in 1529. The cardinal was a ruined man and was forced to forfeit all his property to his royal master, including his palace at Hampton Court, but died the following year, thus cheating the executioner." As for Cromwell and his new advisers, "first, they argued that the pope had no authority to overrule the teaching of the Bible, and therefore the king's marriage was invalid. Second, they insisted that the pope had no authority in England and could not command the king. As a result,

Wolsey's successor, Thomas More, was committed to the papacy and its anti-Protestant polemic, which did not fare well for English evangelicals in the early 1530s. However, More's polemic cut both ways; his commitment to Rome

put him at odds with the king's agenda and sidelined More almost immediately upon coming into office. None of this worked to More's favor. Standing against the king's divorce was sure to fail, and persecuting Protestants could not last, considering the king's growing separation from pope and papacy. "Indeed, More continued in his relentless pursuit of Protestant heretics even when it was clear that the king's pursuit of his 'divorce' meant that Protestants were beginning to be seen as the king's allies."[53]

As it happened, the solution that satisfied the king was planted in Protestant soil. A man at Cambridge by the name of Thomas Cranmer asked a most pertinent (and Protestant) question: Why rely on the approval of the pope when Henry was justified to decide on the matter on biblical grounds? Cranmer caught the king's attention; he was singing the king's tune. Cranmer's insight did not merely concern Henry's marital future but opened Henry's eyes to the potential, independent sovereignty he might acquire over both the political and ecclesiastical realms.

Hans Holbein's painting of Henry VIII
Public Domain

HENRY'S SPRINT FOR ECCLESIASTICAL JURISDICTION

The years 1529 to 1532 were pivotal to Henry's newfound vision. Henry did not relent until he had acquired the power to limit the reach of the clergy.[54] Toward the end of 1529, Henry called on Parliament to restrict the clergy, but Parliament was resistant. Over the next two years, Henry turned to other tactics. He even accused the clergy of treason since they were allegiant to the pope in Rome instead of to England's king. Although signs of resistance were present,

---

Henry began to exercise greater control over the church. He rediscovered the medieval law of 'praemunire,' which forbade the pope interference in the appointment of clergy to benefices, and extracted a massive fine from convocation for their guilt.... Yet the clergy refused to submit themselves to lay interference and their resistance seemed to the king like treason." Atherstone, *Reformation*, 92–93. On the events that transpired between 1529 and 1530 leading to Wolsey's execution, see Hillerbrand, *Division of Christendom*, 221.

53. Hillerbrand, 222.

54. McGrath, *Reformation Theology*, 228–29.

Parliament began to acquiesce to Henry.[55] The year 1532 was a turning point: Henry won a decisive battle with the House of Commons. He confronted them, telling them no longer could their allegiance be split between king and pope. Henry then achieved veto power in the church. If Henry didn't favor a canon, for example, he could veto that canon. Henry was winning his supremacy, subordinating church to king by means of veto power. The clergy now had to petition the king for ecclesiastical changes. That was a step too far for Thomas More, committed as he was to papal authority. He stepped down right away.[56] The writing was on the wall, and he knew it.

Henry's rise to supremacy in these pivotal years was especially indebted to the political and ecclesiastical shrewdness of Thomas Cromwell. Geoffrey Elton and Hans Hillerbrand went so far as to say that Cromwell was the "preeminent figure of the 1530s" due to his "genius of mind and the singleness of purpose." His primacy was also due to timing: he "stepped into a vacuum: no all-powerful Wolsey was around, and More had relinquished the office of lord chancellor."[57] That vacuum was the perfect opportunity to position Henry as sovereign over the clergy.[58]

Yet Henry had to win this battle for supremacy on two fronts, one on his own soil and the other on Rome's turf. An attempt to achieve the latter occurred at the start of 1532 with the Conditional Restraint of Annates. Parliament passed this restraint to hit Rome where it hurt most: in the purse. "This prohibited the payment of annates, the first-year revenue of an ecclesiastical position, to Rome. Henry meant to tighten the financial screws and deprive the pope of his English revenue. The message was unambiguous: no annulment, no money."[59]

Also, in 1532 the archbishop of Canterbury died. William Warham's death was the perfect opportunity for Henry to secure a successor of his liking. Thomas Cranmer was ideal in part because Cranmer was in support of Henry's annulled marriage. In 1533 Cranmer took office as the new archbishop of Canterbury. In time the elevation of Cranmer proved instrumental to reformation in England since Cranmer was committed to evangelical principles. Cranmer's evangelical principles had a chance to make headway in England with Anne Boleyn since she was sympathetic to the Protestant cause. Anne read but hid an English translation of the Bible as well as William Tyndale's *Obedience of a Christian*. Furthermore, Anne was bold, willing to challenge Henry in

---

55. Hillerbrand said Henry even blackmailed the clergy. But in return the clergy blackmailed Henry. "The clergy were stunned but, quickly regaining their equilibrium at the convocations of Canterbury and York in January 1531, they undertook to deal with this preposterous situation by bribing the king. In return for their pardons, they offered substantial 'subsidies' . . . as grants to the king in gratitude for his defense of the faith. Henry graciously accepted and allowed the convocations to pay off the subsidies in five annual installments." Hillerbrand, *Division of Christendom*, 223.

56. The tug-of-war with Parliament was a complicated turn of events. See Hillerbrand, 225; Atherstone, *Reformation*, 93ff.

57. Quote is Hillerbrand, *Division of Christendom*, 225, but also supported by Elton, *Policy and Police*.

58. Note Hillerbrand's discussion of the medieval view; Hillerbrand, *Division of Christendom*, 225.

59. Hillerbrand, 224.

conversations over the Bible and theology, though without losing sight of her subservient position. When Henry finally achieved his goal—his marriage to Catherine annulled at last in May 1533—Anne succeeded Catherine the next month. Later that year, however, Anne's womb was no more inclined toward a male heir than Catherine's. She gave birth to a girl, Elizabeth.

ACT OF SUPREMACY

In 1534 Henry's break with Rome became permanent by virtue of several acts granting Henry unparalleled supremacy. The Act of Supremacy established the king as the supreme head of the church. "The claim to supreme headship included the right to teach doctrine and reform the Church, but not the right to preach, ordain or administer the sacraments and rites of the Church. This right was known as the *potestas ordinis* and was reserved to the clergy."[60] The title created no little controversy. In the patristic era, councils may have been issued and ratified by the emperor, but the bishops present debated and generated doctrine. To one degree or another, first generation Reformers on the Continent like Luther and second-generation Reformers like Calvin looked to princes and magistrates to support the Reformation, although they still expected a certain type of pastoral and ecclesiastical freedom and authority over their people. But Henry took secular involvement to another level. His claim to supreme headship encroached on the jurisdiction of ecclesiastical affairs.[61] Nevertheless, Henry's theologians lent their theological support for royal supremacy over the church, as is plain in Stephen Gardiner and Thomas Cranmer's public apologetic.

If the Act of Supremacy secured Henry's sovereignty, the Act of Treason threatened the death penalty to anyone who dared to commit this crime by refusing to acknowledge or follow Henry as supreme head.[62] These acts and others by Parliament now repositioned the English church under royal jurisdiction in the strongest terms.[63] The Act of Supremacy and the Act of Succession may have officially established the king, but these acts did not necessarily reflect the hearts of the English people, at least not all of them. Yet Henry made sure opponents were swiftly dealt with. In 1534 and 1535, Henry conducted a series of arrests and executions, thanks to the hunting efforts of Thomas Cromwell.

---

60. Bray, ed., *Documents of the English Reformation*, 97. Note the economic effects as well: "Parliament put an end to the financial payment of 'annates' or 'first-fruits' from English bishops to the pope, forbade appeals to the ecclesiastical courts in Rome, and gave the crown the right to appoint bishops. It stopped the ancient papal taxation of England, known as 'Peter's Pence,' and refused to acknowledge papal dispensations from canon law." Atherstone, *Reformation*, 93.

61. "Henry VIII maintained that he was doing no more than assert[ing] the ancient rights of the secular power, which the Papacy had usurped in the course of the centuries." Bray, ed., *Documents of the English Reformation*, 97. Hillerbrand observed how Henry's position must have sat at odds with Luther's view of secular authorities. Hillerbrand, *Division of Christendom*, 230.

62. There were uprisings against Henry. Consult the Pilgrimage of Grace and the years 1536–37; see Hillerbrand, *Division of Christendom*, 231.

63. Consider others, such as the Act of Succession; the Ecclesiastical Appointment Act; the Dispensation Act; and the Act of Submission of the Clergy. Hillerbrand, 229.

THE *ACT OF SUPREMACY* (1534)

Albeit the King's Majesty justly and rightfully is and oweth to be the Supreme Head of the Church of England, and so is recognized by the clergy of this realm in their Convocations, yet nevertheless for corroboration and confirmation thereof, and for increase of virtue in Christ's religion within this realm of England, and to repress and extirp all errors, heresies, and other enormities and abuses herefore used in the same; be it enacted by authority of this present Parliament, that the King our Sovereign Lord, his heirs and successors, kings of this realm, shall be taken, accepted, and reputed the only Supreme Head in earth of the Church of England, called *Anglicana Ecclesia*, and shall have and enjoy, annexed and united to the imperial crown of this realm, as well the style and title thereof, as all honours, dignities, pre-eminences, jurisdictions, privileges, authorities, immunities, profits, and commodities, to the said dignity of Supreme Head of the same Church belonging and appertaining; and that our said Sovereign Lord, his heirs and successors, kings of this realm, shall have full power and authority from time to time to visit, repress, redress, reform, order, correct, restrain, and amend all such errors, heresies, abuses, offences, contempts, and enormities, whatsoever they be, which by any manner spiritual authority or jurisdiction ought or may lawfully be reformed, repressed, ordered, redressed, corrected, restrained, or amended, most to the pleasure of Almighty God, the increase of virtue in Christ's religion, and for the conservation of the peace, unity and tranquility of this realm; any usage, custom, foreign laws, foreign authority, prescription, or any other thing or things to the contrary hereof notwithstanding.

Those captured were hanged, drawn, and quartered without delay. Monks and priests were not exempt but were publicly dissected like other traitors.[64] Henry's message was loud and clear: no one, no one at all, was an exception.

Not even those closest to Henry, such as John Fisher and Thomas More, were exempt. Committed as they were to pope and papacy, they could not, in good conscience, submit themselves to the Act of Supremacy. Assuming the doctrine of papal supremacy, the title supreme head belonged to the pope alone. Fisher and More decided they would rather be tortured by Henry in this life than be tortured by the devil himself in hell for all eternity. However, Fisher and More were shown mercy; they were not hanged, drawn, and quartered. Instead, they were escorted to the Tower of London where they were beheaded.[65] "The irony of More's trial was that he appealed to the same ultimate principle as did Luther at the Diet of Worms: the existence of an objective divine order, which was not subjective dissent, but the acknowledgment of the compelling truth of that order, which could not more be denied than that the sky was blue and the grass green."[66]

---

64. For examples, see Atherstone, *Reformation*, 94.
65. Atherstone, 96; Haigh, *English Reformations*, 118.
66. Hillerbrand, *Division of Christendom*, 229.

THE FATE OF HENRY'S WIVES

From 1536 to 1540, Henry permitted Cromwell to lead the way in the destruction of icons in churches and the obliteration of monasteries. These raids benefited the king, who kept a majority of the monastic funds.[67] This revenue was a bulwark: Spain and France, both committed Catholic territories, were growing hostile to Henry, so Henry used the funds to buttress his military. However, Anne Boleyn and Cromwell disagreed on how these monastic funds should be used. The two grew to hate each other, each attempting to oppose the good reputation or plans of the other in the eyes of Henry. To bring Anne down, Cromwell made up lies, telling Henry that she was sleeping with another man. The lies worked, and Anne was arrested, escorted to the Tower of London, and beheaded in 1536. To Henry the conspiracy against Anne was the perfect excuse to get rid of yet another wife who failed to produce a male heir to the throne. To evangelicals, however, Anne's death was a setback. She was not only in favor of evangelical reformation but was a major influence on Henry to pass policies that favored English evangelicals.

Eleven days after Anne was beheaded, Henry married Jane Seymour (ca. 1508–37), already pregnant with Henry's child. Now Henry could finally have his male heir. Where Henry's previous wives had failed, Seymour succeeded. She gave birth to a son, and they named him Edward. At last Henry's royal lineage was secure. Seymour, though, did not live to see her son reign. In the days and weeks after her labor, Seymour's health plummeted due to a bacterial infection. Henry got the son he wanted but lost the queen who gave him his long-awaited heir.

After Jane Seymour's death, Henry married Anne of Cleves (1540). He was talked into the marriage by Cromwell, who believed the union could create an alliance with the Smalcald League. But Henry needed some convincing to marry a woman who did not even speak the king's English. He approved her on the basis of a painting by Holbein, but when she appeared in person Henry said the portrait was inaccurate, even misleading. *How could anyone expect the king to consummate a marriage with this woman?* protested Henry. An annulment followed, and Henry was free once more to marry.

Thomas Cromwell eventually made atonement for this failed marriage with his own blood. Stephen Gardiner, among others, convinced Henry that the debacle was Cromwell's mistake. Under the surface lay Gardiner's real motives: he was terrified of an alliance with German Lutherans. Henry's embarrassment over Anne of Cleves was the perfect opportunity to take Cromwell down.[68]

---

67. "Some of the confiscated revenue was redirected toward educational or charitable foundations, but most found its way into the coffers of the king and his friends. This wholesale destruction of England's traditional religious landscape led to uprisings across the north of the country from Lincolnshire to Yorkshire in October 1536, the so-called 'Pilgrimage of Grace,' but the rebels were exterminated in vicious reprisals." Atherstone, *Reformation*, 98.

68. How Gardiner achieved this victory with the help of the Duke of Norfolk is outlined by Hillerbrand, *Division of Christendom*, 233.

Although Cromwell begged the king for mercy from the Tower of London, he received none. Henry was a king who was so full of self-confidence that he rarely if ever showed signs of regret. Yet Cromwell's execution was one of those rare regrets for Henry; it occasionally haunted him in later years. How did he justify executing someone so loyal (and effective) as Cromwell? Historians old and new have pointed out the irony of that dark day: not only Cromwell, but a cast of both Protestants and Catholics were executed as well. Their blood flowed as one, demonstrating that the king was committed only to a church and state of his own invention and liking, one that sided neither with the papacy in Rome or Protestants on the Continent.[69]

After the failed union between Henry and Anne of Cleves, the king married the young Catherine Howard in 1540. Henry's disgust with the appearance of Anne returned on his own head when Catherine decided the king was unattractive himself. By 1540 Henry was not just a large man, but to be accurate, quite obese. Catherine was not quiet about her disgust for Henry and mocked his eating habits, but it was her affair with another lover that resulted in her beheading. When she was caught, she was sent to the executioner in 1542 like Anne Boleyn before her—execution was a risk whenever someone married Henry. Despite her execution, the Howard family influence continued, so that during the last years of Henry's life, two factions fought for power. The Howard family was serious about returning the Church of England to Rome.

The year after Catherine was executed, Henry married Katherine Parr (1543). Unlike Henry's preceding wife, Katherine Parr was not the type of woman to commit adultery. Influenced by English Reformers, Parr did her best to influence Henry in an evangelical direction, or at the least, to pressure Henry to tolerate Protestants in England. By Henry's own admission, Parr was his intellectual equal, if not his superior, and the two of them often discussed and debated both politics and theology. When English Catholics discovered this, they conspired against her, but the king liked Parr too much to listen.

ENGLISH-LUTHERAN ALLIANCE: CATHOLICITY OVER INNOVATION

Did the 1530s provide any hope that Protestantism might be acceptable to Henry rather than merely tolerable? The Act of Supremacy in 1534 had been a turning point, one that removed the English people from papal jurisdiction and established Henry himself as the supreme authority. By consequence, antipapal and anti-Catholic literature found a ready audience. Henry did not discourage tracts written by English Protestants attacking the papacy. That did not mean he agreed with their evangelical theology, but he did use their Protestant polemics to further buttress his claim as supreme head. English Protestants soon discovered, to their great discouragement, that Henry could permit Protestant

---

69. Hillerbrand called it Henry's "ecclesiastical via media." Hillerbrand, 233.

propaganda one minute and persecute Protestants the next for the same theology he used to justify his claims to hegemony. As Hillerbrand has observed, "To propound theological notions in Henry's England after the 'king's great matter' had triggered the break with Rome was rather like walking a tightrope. The argument had to be both antipapal and pro-Catholic, a combination that required an exquisite measure of theological versatility."[70] Some, like Cranmer, demonstrated how versatile they could be, but others could not stomach what felt like a contradiction on the road to compromise.

Henry's bold move toward supremacy, however, left England vulnerable. In the event the papacy persuaded its many allies to attack England, Henry needed allies of his own. In 1535 he sent delegates to Wittenberg. If the English and the German Lutherans could agree to doctrinal articles, perhaps the Smalcald League would join in an alliance with Henry. The English delegates did not arrive empty-handed but were ready to talk, proposals in hand.[71] The Lutherans listened and were responsive, writing articles of their own—the *Christmas Articles* (1535). The articles were written by a team of Lutherans, but Philip Melanchthon may have been the chief author. If Henry and his English delegates could sign their names to the *Christmas Articles*, then an alliance could form. The Lutherans, including Luther himself, were even ready to grant Henry the title commander in chief. But a barrier emerged: the *Christmas Articles* had a prerequisite, namely, the adoption of the *Augsburg Confession* by the English. At first Henry agreed. However, when Henry executed his wife Anne Boleyn, the Lutherans shut down talks of an alliance.[72] The timing could not have been worse. Lutherans in Wittenberg had prepared a confessional document—the *Wittenberg Articles* (1536)—to establish the alliance and Lutheran theology in England.

The *Wittenberg Articles* are a window into the Lutheran mind at the time. They also are a window into the minds of the English delegates and the type of theology they were willing to endorse. The articles begin with an immediate affirmation of the three creeds: the Apostles' Creed, the Nicene Creed, and the Athanasian Creed. The Lutherans were not shy in their adherence to *sola scriptura*, but they decided to take the creeds as their launching pad. And for this reason: "We desire that these creeds be held and considered very holy, unchangeable and not subject to alteration *by any man's* addition, we hold that *the articles of faith* given in them are so necessary for the salvation of souls *that those who believe differently cannot be members of the Church*, but are complete idolaters." Yet the *Wittenberg Articles* were concerned not only with subscription but with

---

70. Hillerbrand, 227. "England steered a middle course between Henry's staunch Catholicism and his repudiation of the papacy and the Roman Church" (228).

71. English delegates included Edward Fox, Nicholas Heath, and Richard Barnes. Bray, ed., *Documents of the English Reformation*, 102.

72. Bray, 102.

the very method of the creeds: "We maintain that the very *form of words in those articles* should be retained most precisely, just as it is *in the creeds themselves*, and that there should never be any drawing back from the form of words."[73]

Naturally, the church fathers were summoned next as the *Wittenberg Articles* pronounced allegiance to the patristic doctrine of original sin: "We clearly and without any ambiguity hold, teach and defend what St Paul teaches, as St Augustine interprets and defends it against the Pelagians, as well as others who follow Augustine's teaching, like Anselm and Bonaventure; and we hold that Augustine's is the true understanding of original sin and that it was rightly approved by the councils." Rather than appealing to Scripture alone, the *Wittenberg Articles* insisted on interpretating Scripture through the lens of the Fathers. For example, in defining original sin, article 2 says, "We particularly approve the definition of Anselm, who says that original sin is a lack of that original righteousness which ought to be in (man)."[74]

Expected is the Lutheran emphasis (and antidote to original sin): Augustinian grace. Yet a deliberate, vigorous concentration on the works produced by a penitent faith followed as well. Luther responded to antinomian charges as early as 1520 in *A Treatise on Good Works*.[75] That charge never quite left the Lutheran mind, and although it was never mentioned in the *Wittenberg Articles*, the articles placed no little stress on the necessity of genuine contrition and repentance, as well as the renewal of life that manifests itself in all those justified by God's grace. By baptism, says article 3, the ungodly "*obtain remission of sins* and grace *if on coming to baptism they bring true penitence, confession of the articles of faith, assure themselves of the promise which is attached to baptism, and believe that by it they are truly granted remission of sins and justification on account of God.*"[76] As for penitence itself, "We confess and defend the consensus of the Catholic Church which holds, in accordance with the Scriptures, *that penitence is necessary for those who have lapsed after baptism. And that the lapsed who do not do penitence in this life will certainly be damned.*"[77] Yet unlike the late medieval view of penitence, the *Wittenberg Articles* believed penitence consisted of three parts:

---

73. "Therefore *we* unanimously *condemn* the heresies of the Valentinians, Manichaeans, Adoptionists, Arians and Macedonians, and all other heresies like them, *which the Church* long ago *condemned in the four holy councils of Nicaea, Constantinople, Ephesus and Chalcedon.*" "Wittenberg Articles, 1536," art. 1 (Bray, 103–4).

74. Bray, *Documents of the English Reformation*, 104. Article 2 confesses both the imputation of guilt and corruption from Adam. Whether they knew it at the time or not, affirming both guilt and corruption is a contrast with Zwingli. Zwingli would not have appreciated article 3 either, which says that "*through baptism, children obtain remission of sins and grace. . . . Because children are born with original sin, they need remission of that sin*, and it is forgiven in such a way that guilt is removed, but the matter of sin, viz. corruption of nature or concupiscence, still remains in this life, although it begins to be healed, because the Holy Spirit is efficacious in children as well and cleanses them in his own way" (105).

75. *LW* 44:15–114.

76. "Wittenberg Articles, 1536," art. 3 (Bray, 106).

77. "Wittenberg Articles, 1536," art. 4 (Bray, 107–9).

1. ***Contrition***—when a conscience which is convicted by God's Word recognizes its sin, truly realizes that God is angry with the sin, and is genuinely terror-stricken and grieves that it has sinned, i.e., is truly ashamed and realizes that it is unable to make any human works or merits stand up against God's wrath.[78]
2. ***Faith***—by which we believe that our sins are forgiven us by God and that we are justified and accounted righteous and become sons of God, not because of the worthiness of our contrition or of other works, but freely for Christ's sake.... Being justified by faith, we have peace with God.[79]
3. ***Newness of life or new obedience***—since the Holy Spirit is effective, he also creates new promptings in our hearts, which assent to God's law, viz. faith, the love of God, the fear of God, hatred of sin, the determination not to sin, and other good fruits.... Therefore justification, which comes about through faith in the manner described, is renewal and regeneration. This is the view both of Scripture and the Church fathers concerning the remission of sins and faith.[80]

Contrition and faith—these articles appealed to the Great Tradition, from Ambrose to Bernard, which concluded that they must remain conjoined. If not, grace would be cheapened, nothing more than a license to sin. But a contrite faith "cannot exist in those who in carnal security despise God's judgment, indulge in vile affections."[81] Without compromising *sola gratia* or *sola fide*, the *Wittenberg Articles* underlined the necessity of works as the fruit of a contrite and trusting faith: *"For although our acceptance into eternal life is conjoined with our justification,* i.e. with the remission of sins and reconciliation, and (although) good *works* are not a payment for eternal life, *nevertheless they are necessary for salvation,* because they are a debt which ought of necessity to follow reconciliation."[82]

In the articles that follow, the Wittenberg theologians encouraged private confession and absolution (Reformers in other territories also retained this practice even after their break with Rome) although within the Lutheran framework of Christ's sufficient sacrifice *(solus Christus)*.[83] The Wittenberg theologians are not departing from Luther but advocating Luther's own retention and love for private confession. "I will allow no man to take private confession away from me," said Luther in a sermon in 1522, "and I would not give it up for all the

---

78. "Wittenberg Articles, 1536," art. 4 (Bray, 107–8).

79. "Wittenberg Articles, 1536," art. 4 (Bray, 108).

80. The article goes on to quote Bernard at length. "Wittenberg Articles, 1536," art. 4 (Bray, 109).

81. "Wittenberg Articles, 1536," art. 4 (Bray, 110).

82. "Wittenberg Articles, 1536," art. 5 (Bray, 111). In the articles that follow, absolution is preserved on the basis of another retained distinction "between the remission of guilt and the remission of temporal punishment." And for this reason: "since God often punishes sin by present and temporal punishments, it is very worthwhile that it be taught in the Church that *we not only receive eternal life* when we do penitence, *but also that our penitence and good works merit the remission or mitigation of* temporal *punishments* and calamities" (p. 121).

83. "Wittenberg Articles, 1536," art. 7 (Bray, 119).

treasures in the world, since I know what comfort and strength it has given me." Luther considered private confession such a consolation because it relinquished the devil's power in the midst of the sinner's *Anfechtungen*. "No one knows what it can do for him except one who has struggled often and long with the devil. Yea, the devil would have slain me long ago, if the confession had not sustained me." With private confession, Luther retained a form of absolution as well, yet another defeater of Satan. "We must have many absolutions, so that we may strengthen our timid consciences and despairing hearts against the devil and against God."[84] For Luther, private confession should be paired with the public proclamation of the Word. When the gospel is preached, the hearer who has confessed his sins in private then receives the Word by faith and is absolved, enjoying an assurance Christ provides by his Spirit.[85]

When the *Wittenberg Articles* turned to the sacraments and the Mass, the strategy was decisively in favor of catholicity once more. The articles set the Fathers over against recent innovation, denying that the sacraments "confer grace by virtue of the mere performance of the rite (*ex opera operato*) without the good intention of the recipient, i.e., only on the basis of the work done, even though the recipient should have no faith." Rather, faith must be present to receive the benefits of God's promises.[86] *Ex opera operato* was "unknown to the ancient Church," and the Fathers "did not think that this rite performed for others merits remission of guilt and remission of punishment . . . but they thought that in the celebration of the sacrament their faith should be exercised and thanksgiving made." The advent of the private Mass was subsequent to many of the church fathers.[87] Likewise, the Fathers did not withhold one of the elements from the laity. This, too, was a novelty. As an examination of both Jerome and Gelasius reveal, the congregation was given both elements.[88]

When celibacy was addressed, the *Wittenberg Articles* continued to situate their Lutheran-English alliance within a catholic heritage—patristic and medieval—that exposed the novelty of papal doctrine. Both England and the Holy Roman Empire were set aflame with debates between evangelicals and papal theologians over sex, marriage, and the family. While the *Wittenberg Articles* did not hesitate to affirm 1 Corinthians 7:32–33—Paul's charge to remain celibate to serve Christ without practical obligations—the articles also did not hesitate to qualify that such a recommendation is not a command. Christ himself "bears witness that not all are suited to perpetual celibacy," and "therefore we hold that marriage ought not to be forbidden" nor should the

---

84. *LW* 51:99.

85. In contrast to Luther, Osiander rejected corporate confession. See *LW* 40:367; Trueman, *Luther on the Christian Life*, 107.

86. "Wittenberg Articles, 1536," art. 8 (Bray, 122). Echoing Augustine's debate with the Donatists, article 9 concludes, "Therefore we condemn those who say that one may not receive the Word and the sacraments from evil ministers, as if the Word and the sacraments were for that reason inefficacious and void" (123).

87. "Wittenberg Articles, 1536," arts. 12, 13 (Bray, 128, 129).

88. "Wittenberg Articles, 1536," art. 13 (Bray, 130). This article appeals to Gelasius's *Comperimus*.

church prohibit the "marriage of priests," a "purely human tradition" if there ever was one.[89] And not only a human tradition but an entirely novel one: "This new tradition, which forbids the marriage of priests and which dissolves marriages, did not arise from the councils, but only from the Roman bishops."[90] The "Church for a long time, not only in the east but also in the west, had priests who were married." The articles exposed an incongruity: the bishop of Rome was in error, while the "Greek churches" basked in the truth.[91]

The closing of the *Wittenberg Articles*, however, delivers a surprise to modern interpreters who assume all Reformers were captive to a narrow patriarchalism. First, the church was admonished: sound doctrine will never find a recovery if monasteries and universities do not prioritize the training of ministers. In contrast to some corners of the Reformation that sought to abolish monasteries, the articles employed the monasteries but for evangelical purposes. Monasteries were a thorn in the side of the evangelical cause because so many of them taught that "monastic vows merit the remission of sins and eternal life" and "constitute righteousness or Christian perfection." But if monasteries can be stripped of such a "superstition," they might be used for good.[92]

What might that good be? Appealing to Gregory of Nazianzus and Basil of Caesarea, the articles warn against choosing novices for a ministry that requires learned minds. The articles cite Ambrose and Augustine, both advocates for bishops immersed in doctrinal education.[93] The articles lament the way young boys and girls have been "pushed and shoved into the monasteries in order to make vows before the right age." What should happen instead? Those young people in such a bind should receive "permission to leave the monasteries" so that they can pursue godliness in another "state of life."[94]

Yet the Reformers did not merely look to resolve the current state of affairs; they dreamed of a future education different from the start. For example, "Communities in which girls may learn the arts and the Christian teaching of godliness may also exist, but girls who desire to marry ought not to be retained in cloisters, nor should they be burdened with vows."[95] The *Wittenberg Articles* not only outlined a renewed plan of education for young boys but for young girls as well. The articles could not conclude with a more revolutionary paradigm shift. University education "was soon implemented to a large extent for men," observes Gerald Bray, "but it is a tragedy that women were excluded for over 300 years,

---

89. "Wittenberg Articles, 1536," art. 14 (Bray, 131).
90. "Wittenberg Articles, 1536," art. 14 (Bray, 131).
91. "Wittenberg Articles, 1536," art. 14 (Bray, 132).
92. The articles take a similar approach to images, approving them for the illiterate but warning that they should not be abused: "For we teach that images are not to be worshipped, nor is to be thought that they have power, nor should people think that setting up images of God or of the saints is serving God, or that God is more gracious or does more than otherwise if he is invoked before such an image." "Wittenberg Articles, 1536," art. 17 (Bray, 139).
93. "Wittenberg Articles, 1536," art. 15 (Bray, 134).
94. "Wittenberg Articles, 1536," art. 15 (Bray, 136).
95. "Wittenberg Articles, 1536," art. 15 (Bray, 137).

and that by the time provision was made for them, education was becoming secularized." As for the education of women, these Reformers were pioneers. "Not until the 1970s would women be accepted for theological training on the same basis as men, even though Luther and the English delegates to Wittenberg had been prepared for it so many centuries ago!"[96]

The remarkable patristic spirit within these articles, combined with an evangelical elasticity regarding Christian freedom and education, leaves the historian curious about what might have transpired if the Lutheran-English alliance would have succeeded. Perhaps Henry's forthcoming persecution of English evangelicals could have been avoided given his commitment to a Lutheran inspired confessional document. Perhaps Henry himself might have prepared a more ambitious path to further reform, one that provided greater momentum for Edward before Mary dissolved the entire program overnight. These hypotheticals will never be answered. However, no speculation exists over Henry's tentative interest in the evangelical movement at the time. Henry opened a line of communication with the Lutherans almost entirely for political advantage. Even if Henry had followed through on the alliance, optimism may not have been in order.

The Lutherans originally intended for the English delegates to return to their homeland with the *Wittenberg Articles* in hand. Yet little to no evidence suggests that the articles exited the Continent, at least not as a whole.[97] Nevertheless, Lutheran influence on the English was still to come but had to wait until Edward ascended the throne.[98] For when the English delegates returned, Henry commissioned *The Ten Articles* (1536) instead, which reiterated Henry's supremacy and departed from evangelical convictions by its promotion of the penance system, among many other papal doctrines.[99]

For example, penance was defined according to its traditional late medieval formulation, including (1) contrition (sorrow and fear), (2) confession (to a priest, followed by his words of absolution), and (3) works of satisfaction (prayers, fastings, almsdeeds, restitution, etc.).[100] However, *The Ten Articles* also incorporated some slight evangelical convictions. For example, works of merit were excluded from justification, and the believer was told to place his trust in the merits of

96. Bray, ed., *Documents of the English Reformation*, 103.

97. The English edition appears to have disappeared altogether. The "German copy was not rediscovered until 1904." Bray, 102.

98. That does not mean, however, that Lutheranism had no effect prior to Edward. For example, Thomas Cranmer was influenced by Luther's theology, as is plain in *The Thirteen Articles, with Three Additional Articles, 1538*. These articles, lost but then rediscovered in the nineteenth century, were never finished and never acquired public authority. But as Bray observes, "The Thirteen Articles are the most clearly Lutheran document ever to be penned by an English churchman." Bray even credits the *Wittenberg Articles* with influencing Cranmer and *The Thirteen Articles*, although he attributes most credit to the *Augsburg Confession*. Bray, 161 (for the articles, see 162–94).

99. E.g., penance (art. 3), veneration of images (art. 6), cult of saints (arts. 7, 8), prayers for the dead (art. 10), quotations of Scripture in Latin. Also see Bray, 141.

100. *Ten Articles, 1536*, art. 3 (Bray, 146).

Christ alone.[101] In addition, the *Ten Articles* may have advocated praying for the dead, but purgatory was spurned as a doctrine of the pope.[102]

THE BLOODY WHIP WITH SIX STRINGS

Despite these flirtations with evangelical doctrine, any optimism for an evangelical renaissance was crushed in 1539 when Parliament, under pressure from Henry, released The Six Articles Act, or as Protestants called it with such great affection, the "bloody whip with six strings."

> First, that in the most blessed sacrament of the altar, by the strength and efficacy of Christ's mighty word (it being spoken by the priest), is present really, under the form of bread and wine, the natural body and blood of our Saviour Jesus Christ, conceived of the Virgin Mary; and that after the consecration there remaineth no substance of bread and wine, nor any other substance, but the substance of Christ, God and man.
>
> Secondly, that communion in both kinds is not necessary *ad salute*, by the law of God, to all persons; and that it is to be believed, and not doubted of, but that in the flesh, under the form of bread, is the very blood; and with the blood, under the form of wine, is the very flesh; as well apart, as though they were both together.
>
> Thirdly, that priests after the order of priesthood received, as afore, may not marry, by the law of God.
>
> Fourthly, that vows of chastity or widowhood, by man or woman made to God advisedly, ought to be observed by the law of God; and that it exempts them from other liberties of Christian people, which without that they might enjoy.
>
> Fifthly, that it is meet and necessary that private masses be continued and admitted in this the King's English Church and Congregation, as whereby good Christian people, ordering themselves accordingly, do receive both godly and goodly consolations and benefits; and it is agreeable also to God's law.
>
> Sixthly, that auricular confession is expedient and necessary to be retained and continue, used and frequented in the Church of God.[103]

Any prior concessions to the evangelical movement were erased; the articles were an unequivocal return to Roman doctrines. Henry grew impatient not only with his latest marriage but with signs of evangelical influence. Despite his departure from papal jurisdiction in England, Henry remained a staunch administrator of the established religious practice.

---

101. *Ten Articles, 1536*, art. 5 (Bray, 148).

102. *Ten Articles, 1536*, art. 10 (Bray, 151–52). Also consult *First Henrician Injunctions, 1536*, and *Second Henrician Injunctions, 1538*, which Thomas Cromwell wrote, designed to apply *The Ten Articles* to the laity (Bray, 153–56, 157–60).

103. "The Act of the Six Articles, 1539." Bray, 197.

Like the Act of Treason, the consequence for remonstrance was lethal.[104] Bishops, like Latimer of Worcester, read the six articles and resigned, recognizing that his evangelical beliefs stood in direct conflict with Henry's enforced vision. Latimer's decision may have been best since these six articles continued to set the agenda in England until Edward succeeded Henry on the throne in 1547.

That did not mean, however, that *gospelers*—as English Protestants were sometimes labeled—like Thomas Cranmer did not look for other avenues to influence England in an evangelical direction. Consider the Bible's translation into the vernacular and its evolving implementation within the life of the church.

CRANMER'S APPEAL TO THE CHURCH FATHERS FOR A VERNACULAR BIBLE

After the Act of Supremacy in 1534, evangelicals pushed for the institution of an English Bible.[105] Yet translators, such as Miles Coverdale, who completed a translation of the entire Scripture with the backing of Thomas Cromwell, were already at work. Since Coverdale did not know the biblical languages, his Great Bible (1536) relied to a great extent on Tyndale's and Luther's translations. John Rogers also attempted a translation, finalizing his Matthew Bible in 1537—"Matthew" because Rogers took the alias Thomas Matthew.[106]

When the Second Henrician Injunctions of 1538 required an English Bible in every church, the tragic timing was not lost on English evangelicals: Tyndale was burned at the stake in 1536 for translating the Bible into English, yet two years later Henry himself issued a Bible for the English people. That Bible has been called the Great Bible, but it did not appear in churches until the end of 1539. The printing was delayed by the Inquisition's opposition in Paris, and the project was forced to move to English soil, only to be delayed further by printers unprepared for the rise in demand.[107]

When a second edition was issued the next year, Thomas Cranmer included a preface, which encouraged and cultivated an alternative title, Cranmer's Bible. A preface can be forgettable, but Cranmer's was memorable. And it might as well be credited to John Chrysostom and Gregory of Nazianzus since Cranmer built his exhortation to the reader on the foundation of these two patristics. In the first half, Cranmer summarized a sermon by Chrysostom in which the golden

---

104. "Bishop Latimer of Worcester and Bishop Shaxton of Salisbury resigned their sees in protest." Atherstone, *Reformation*, 100.

105. "Within months of the final break with Rome, the Convocation of Canterbury petitioned the King to order 'that the Holy Scripture should be translated into the vulgar English tongue by certain good and learned men, to be nominated by his Majesty, and should be delivered to the people for their instruction.'" Quoted in Bray, ed., *Documents of the English Reformation*, 205.

106. "Given this situation, the King's advisers thought it best to use Coverdale, and gave him the authority to make a further revision of Matthew's Bible." Both translations stood on the shoulders of Tyndale's scholarship. Bray, 205.

107. "Once again there were difficulties, though this time it was because demand for the edition was such that supplies were soon exhausted!" Bray, 205.

mouth preacher gave an apology for reading the Scriptures. Cranmer's retrieval of Chrysostom was strategic, anticipating the excuses of the ordinary laymen that they had no time to read the Bible because they must work and provide for their families. Chrysostom's and Cranmer's response was as practical as it was enthusiastic: that is all the more reason why laymen need the Bible. Unlike the life of the monk secluded in the confines of the monastery, the normal, working life of the average Christian was filled with all kinds of trials and temptations.

> Thy wife provoketh thee to anger, thy child giveth thee occasion to take sorrow and pensiveness, thine enemies lieth in wait for thee, thy friend (as thou takest him) sometimes envieth thee, thy neighbor misreporteth thee, or pricketh quarrels against thee, thy mate or partner undermineth thee, thy lord judge or justice threateneth thee, poverty is painful unto thee, the loss of thy dear and well-beloved causeth thee to mourn; prosperity exalteth thee, adversity bringeth thee low.[108]

How much more does the average working-class citizen need the Bible? The Scriptures "have thy remedies and medicines at hand." The Scriptures "have salve for thy sores." And the Scriptures "have the armour or fortress against thine assaults."[109] Cranmer's words are beautiful news for the Christian. For the Scriptures not only help the doctor teach theology, but they heal the Christian in the church from the wounds inflicted by sin.

Cranmer, with Chrysostom, anticipated another objection: we are not educated people. Have we forgotten, Cranmer replied, to whom the Bible is written? Not only to kings and philosophers, but fisherman and shepherds. Cranmer and Chrysostom asked whether such an objection was more of an excuse for idleness. For if understanding is the barrier, then "read it again and again," and if understanding still does not shine through with her bright rays, then seek "counsel with some other that is better learned." Cranmer and Chrysostom believed the real issue was not understanding, in other words, but mindset. Approach the text with a "diligence and readiness," and the Holy Spirit will "illuminate thee."[110]

The second half of the preface was almost entirely an extended excerpt from one of Gregory of Nazianzus's theological orations. Cranmer and Gregory turned to the methodology of the Bible reader. Too many manipulate the Scriptures for their agendas because they do not approach the text with fear and trembling, remembering what they hold in their hands. "Wherefore I would advise you all, that cometh to the reading or hearing of this book, which is the Word of God, the most precious jewel, and most holy relic that remaineth upon earth, that ye bring with you the fear of God, and that ye do it with all due reverence, and use your knowledge thereof, not to vainglory of frivolous disputation, but to the honour of God, increase of virtue and edification both of yourselves

---

108. "Cranmer's Preface to the Great Bible, 1540" (Bray, 208).
109. "Cranmer's Preface to the Great Bible, 1540" (Bray, 208).
110. "Cranmer's Preface to the Great Bible, 1540" (Bray, 209).

and other."[111] According to Cranmer, rather than beginning with personal speculation, which could only end study of the text with unsettled fear, right-minded interpreters open the text out of a holy reverence and fear so that they might finish their studies with a speculation that honors the high knowledge of divine mysteries.[112] Only if the English people began with fear would they acquire knowledge by the illumination of the Spirit that would lead to true, lasting reform.[113]

Cranmer's Bible was a major success, one edition after another, only to be succeeded by the Geneva Bible of 1560.[114] Nonetheless, the 1540s countered Cranmer's advancements by accelerating the suppression of English reformation. Despite the Second Henrician Injunctions of 1538, which required an English Bible in every church, in 1543 Henry prohibited common folk from reading the Bible in English. Consequently, only the elite of society had the privilege. English evangelicals considered the new policy's title nothing short of contradictory: *Act for the Advancement of True Religion*. This same act also reinstituted a late medieval soteriology.[115] Whatever prior advancements for evangelical reform had been accomplished were now cut off at the knees.

Henry's suppression of biblical literacy among the common man can also be seen in the *King's Book* of 1543. Henry lamented that the Bible among the average Englishman had resulted in a "sinister understanding of Scripture, presumption, arrogancy, carnal liberty, and contention."[116] Tyndale had given his life to translating the Scriptures into the vernacular so that the Christian man, whatever his trade or skill may be, could hear the gospel for himself. Now Henry removed that right because he feared the Bible in the hands of the common man might produce the type of chaotic uprising he saw from time to time on the Continent. While Henry did communicate with ecclesiastical leaders, he decided the outcome as supreme head.

ENGLAND'S KING JOSIAH? EDWARD VI

The years 1546 and 1547 were tumultuous, leaving any Englishman uncertain what the future might look like. The Howard faction gained increasing control only to lose it and face the accusation of treason. Those loyal to Edward, son of Jane Seymour, were now optimistic that when Henry died the evangelical cause might be resurrected by Henry's only male heir.[117] Their hopes were fulfilled when Henry passed at the start of the new year, 1547. But Edward was only nine years old. Could a child lead the country back toward evangelical convictions?

---

111. "Cranmer's Preface to the Great Bible, 1540" (Bray, 211).
112. "Cranmer's Preface to the Great Bible, 1540" (Bray, 213).
113. "Cranmer's Preface to the Great Bible, 1540" (Bray, 214).
114. The final edition of Cranmer's Bible was its tenth edition of 1562, two years after the Geneva Bible. The next authorized Bible was not until 1611, the King James Version. Bray, ed., *Documents of the English Reformation*, 206.
115. See *The King's Book* (its official title: *A Necessary Doctrine and Erudition for Any Christian Man*).
116. Quoted in Hillerbrand, *Division of Christendom*, 233.
117. Atherstone, *Reformation*, 102–3.

In 1570 a painting was commissioned to portray the death of Henry VIII and the rise of Edward VI in 1547.[118] The unknown painter commemorated the triumph of the evangelical cause in England. On the far left, Henry lays in bed dying, pointing to his little boy, Edward, who is sitting on the throne. Little as Edward may be, dwarfed by the throne around him, he has the backing of an entire crew, including Duke John Dudley, Protector Lord Somerset, and Archbishop Thomas Cranmer, among others. Their victory over Roman influence is guaranteed. Above their heads is a painting depicting Protestants lighting on fire a pile of icons and relics. Directly below Henry's feet the pope lies unconscious, clobbered in the head by a Bible that has been translated into English.

Paintings like these portrayed the new hope for reformation. Henry VIII never did commit himself to the evangelical cause, and by the end of his life whatever gains Cranmer had achieved were either lost or perilous at best. But when Henry died at the start of 1547, the wind shifted in favor of the evangelical party.[119] Jane Seymour never had the chance to raise her son, Edward, but when the boy grew, he revealed his commitment to the evangelical cause, which moved Cranmer to draw the uncanny resemblance between Edward and Josiah, that Old Testament king responsible for summoning Israel to repentance. Like King Josiah, Edward resurrected the Word of God so that the people of God might return to true worship, said Cranmer.[120]

ERASTIANISM

The Sacrament Act was not the only act released by Parliament in 1547. The Election of Bishops Act ensured that the state governed the church and its bishops. The level of control was encompassing, which is why historians have identified this act as Erastian in nature. Thomas Erastus (1524–83) was a Swiss theologian who contended that the state should exercise control over the operations and elections of the church. However, "degrees of Erastianism" did exist. Nevertheless, the 1547 act "represents an extreme form" (Bray, ed., *Documents of the English Reformation*, 232).

Yet he also resurrected the sacrament. Henry died in January 1547, but by November of that year Parliament passed "An Act against Revilers, and for Receiving in Both Kinds," otherwise known as *The Sacrament Act*. As the title conveys, under Edward VI both the wine and the bread must now be distributed to the people. This act was a means of retrieval, recovering the practice of the church catholic. Receiving both wine and bread was a custom of the patristic

---

118. Reign: 1547–1553.
119. Edward's uncle, the Duke of Somerset, took advantage of the change in reign and used the Council of Regency as his own. On Somerset, see Hillerbrand, *Division of Christendom*, 238.
120. Cox, *Miscellaneous Writings of Thomas Cranmer*, 127. Cf. Atherstone, *Reformation*, 139.

and early medieval church alike, but it was rescinded so that the laity received only the bread at the altar, a position Jan Hus protested, as did the Utraquists (see chapter 7).[121]

CRANMER'S REFORMING MEASURES

With Edward as king, Cranmer acted as architect, erecting three pillars that could hold up the edifice of future reform: the recruitment of Continental Reformers, the publications of homilies, and the institution of a prayer book for a new liturgy.[122]

Recruitment of Continental Reformers

When Edward succeeded his father, a slew of evangelical ministers came out of the shadows to replace clergy with allegiance to the papacy. As they came out of exile, they were appointed to key ecclesiastical positions. Meanwhile, former clergy were imprisoned or forced to flee into exile.[123] These resurrected evangelicals included Nicholas Ridley, Hugh Latimer, Miles Coverdale, and John Hooper, among many others.

They were not all English, either. With Charles V's victory over the Smalcald League, many Reformers on the Continent left in exile, sometimes even fleeing for their lives. Cranmer took advantage of this opportunity and invited all kinds of Reformers to England to help with evangelical reform, including the Italian Reformer Peter Martyr Vermigli, appointed Regius Professor of Divinity at Oxford (1547–53), and the Strasbourg Reformer Martin Bucer, appointed Regius Professor of Divinity at Cambridge (1549–52). At one point, Cranmer also invited Wolfgang Musculus to England, which may have been a natural fit in the mind of Cranmer. Musculus (1497–1563), who had studied under Bucer, was developing in the eyes of the public as an established biblical and theological scholar. His rising status eventually became apparent with the publication of his *Loci communes sacrae theologiae* in 1560, a work that made its way into English churches.[124] Musculus was strategic because he did not draw a hard line on the Lord's Supper, committing neither to Luther or Zwingli. If Musculus came to London, he could help Cranmer with German evangelicals, but Musculus declined. He was not the energetic youth he once was and felt his elderly years of ministry might be better served in Swiss territories. [125]

---

121. "It had been the universal custom of the early Church, and continued into the Middle Ages in the West, but it gradually died out, possibly because of fear of plague." Bray, *Documents of the English Reformation*, 227. Note that the Edwardian Injunctions were instituted not long after Henry's death: July 31, 1547. "The injunctions consolidated the reforms made under Henry VIII and gave notice that further changes were in the offing" (217; cf. 218–26 for injunctions).

122. He intended a fourth pillar, the preconception of canon law, but as we will see, that goal was interrupted. What follows on Cranmer will be brief, but consider MacCulloch, *Thomas Cranmer*.

123. Examples of the latter include Stephen Gardiner, Cuthbert Tunstal, and Edmund Bonner.

124. Muller, "John Calvin and later Calvinism," 133.

125. Specifically, Berne. Gordon, *Swiss Reformation*, 177.

Cranmer's strategy—recruiting Reformers from foreign soil—was to enlist the best help he could to train the next generation of clergy in evangelical truth. In that spirit, he also had aspirations for an international council, one that could rival the Council of Trent and would summon theologians from across the Continent, from Philip Melanchthon to John Calvin. This dream was not easily materialized. While Calvin agreed, Melanchthon declined, and with Edward's untimely death in 1553, the council never became a reality.

Two Books of Homilies (1547, 1562) and the Church Fathers

Another factor that signaled the start of a new, evangelical trajectory was the writing of homilies. Two sets or books of sermons known as the *Book of Homilies* were constructed to teach evangelical doctrine. They were not merely recommended—every minister was required to read a homily to his people each week. Furthermore, the presence of the Scriptures was nonnegotiable. The homilies required all clergy to possess the New Testament.[126]

The authorship of these homilies was not specified, yet most agree that Cranmer was the author of the homily on salvation. Some conclude that he was light on justification, nowhere teaching the Lutheran and Reformed adherence to an active obedience to Christ.[127] According to this interpretation, Cranmer neglected the belief that Jesus' obedience to the law merited a flawless righteous status, which he imputes to all who discard their dependence on works and trust in his righteousness alone. Such interpretations of Cranmer overlook the diversities of theological methods, however, especially in the art of preaching. A concept can be present or even prevalent even if the technical vocabulary is not named.[128] For example, consider the following words from the homily:

> For all the good works that we can do be unperfect, and therefore not able to deserve our justification, but our justification doth come freely by the mere mercy of God, and of so great and free mercy that, whereas all the world was not able of their selves to pay any part towards their ransom, it pleased our heavenly Father, of his infinite mercy, without any our desert or deserving, to prepare for us the most precious jewels of Christ's body and blood whereby our ransom might be fully paid, the law fulfilled and his justice fully satisfied. So that Christ is now the righteousness of all them that truly do believe in him. He for them paid their ransom by his death. He for them fulfilled the law in his life. So that now in him and by him every true Christian man may be called a fulfiller of the law, forasmuch as that which their infirmity lacketh Christ's justice hath supplied.[129]

---

126. The homilies said clergy should have "the New Testament both in Latin and in English, together with the paraphrase upon the same of Erasmus." Gee and Hardy, *Documents*, 417–18. Cf. Hillerbrand, *Division of Christendom*, 240.

127. E.g., McGrath, *Reformation Thought*, 235.

128. Parker argued against those who see a mediating position advocated. Parker, "Introduction," 257.

129. "Sermon of the Salvation of Mankind ...," 3.1.

The prophet Isaiah and his description of the Suffering Servant sits in the background of the homily. Christ is the ransom, the substitute who satisfies divine judgment on behalf of the ungodly. Justice itself was propitiated. Furthermore, the homily puts the spotlight on Christ's obedience. Christ "fulfilled the law in his life." Therefore, "Christ is now the righteousness of all them that truly do believe in him." Here is the doctrine of imputation. By faith the believer is clothed in an alien righteousness. He is not justified by his own works but counted righteous in Christ. Cranmer may not have used the technical language of academic discussion and debate, but that is not surprising since he was writing in the vein of a sermon instead. Nevertheless, the concept is present, and Cranmer should not be distanced from the Lutherans or the Calvinists on such a central doctrine as justification and imputation. Moreover, Cranmer considered his affirmation of justification by faith alone a catholic doctrine. At a strategic point in the homily, Cranmer listed church father after church father, both from East and West, to ensure the church that their evangelical belief was well grounded in the church catholic, despite the claims of Rome.[130]

The implementation of the homilies was but the beginning of more ambitious action. Also in 1547 visitations were organized. These visits were inspections wherein Cranmer could tell if churches were making the required changes in custom. For those clergy resisting evangelical changes, these visitations were not welcome, but they did prove effective. From icons to the Mass itself, revisions were made until churches looked more Protestant. They even sounded more Protestant, with the sanctioned homilies read from pulpits. Still, the most conspicuous and controversial change involved the Mass. Cranmer was adamant: both the bread and the wine should be given to the laity. The *Acts against Revilers and for Receiving in Both Kinds* made sure of that.

Now that the distribution of the Mass was adjusted, the English people needed a new liturgy, one that captured the theology of the church and the hearts of the people, inspiring their devotion.

A New but Ancient Liturgy: The *Book of Common Prayer* (1549, 1552)

Cranmer understood, much like Luther, Bucer, and Calvin, that for Reformation theology to take root within the people of God, it not only had to be taught from the pulpit but ingrained within the liturgy the people recited, sang, and prayed each week. Cranmer wrote the *Book of Common Prayer* for that purpose.

In 1549 the Act of Uniformity was passed, instituting the *Book of Common Prayer* as the official and legal liturgy for the Church of England.[131] The Act of Uniformity threatened imprisonment to anyone who stood opposed.

---

130. "Sermon of the Salvation of Mankind . . . ," 3.2.
131. "Act of Uniformity, 1549" (Bray, 235–50).

INFLUENCES ON CRANMER: LASCO, VERMILGI, BUCER

Cranmer was not acting apart from other Reformation voices, but he was influenced by a variety of Reformers in his labor to create a Reformed English church. Some of the Reformers who influenced Cranmer included the Polish theologian Johannes à Lasco (1499–1560). Lasco was from the Continent, but he was appointed to lead London's Strangers' Church. Cranmer was also influenced by Peter Martyr Vermigli as well as Martin Bucer, both of whom he recruited. All of these Reformers eventually made their way to Cranmer's house, where they discussed doctrines like the Lord's Supper. In time they even convinced Cranmer that the Reformed view of the Lord's Supper was the way forward. Other Reformers also had a major influence on English evangelicals, such as Heinrich Bullinger (1504–75) in Zurich.

With official sanction, Cranmer's prayer book was opened in every church as the people learned a new liturgical format that eloquently drew from the text of Scripture but in the vernacular and with unmatched clarity and accessibility.[132]

In Cranmer's preface to the prayer book, he defended the evangelical principles that infused the liturgy, but he did so by appealing to the "ancient Fathers" over against those who pined after innovation. Here "you have an order for prayer and for the reading of the Holy Scripture much agreeable to the mind and purpose of the old Fathers."[133] Unfortunately, lamented Cranmer, there are some "so new-fangled that they would innovate all things and so despise the old that nothing can like them, but that is new." Cranmer was positioning his prayer book with the church catholic on one side and papal doctrines under the umbrella of novelty on the other side. "For in such a case they ought rather to have reverence unto them [patristic practices] for their antiquity, if they will declare themselves to be more studious of unity and concord than of innovations and new-fangledness, which . . . is always to be eschewed."[134]

The 1549 prayer book was marked by evangelical convictions. The Mass, for instance, was not referred to as a sacrifice, and elevation of the host was prohibited. Even feasts and festivals were given minimal attention. However, not everyone interpreted and applied the *Book of Common Prayer* through an evangelical lens. Some language in the 1549 prayer book did not unequivocally preclude a papal interpretation, which led those under the old Henrician regime to accommodate the prayer book to their agenda and others in the new Edward's regime to grow discontent with the current prayer book and even voice severe

---

132. "The only exception allowed was in the universities of Oxford and Cambridge, where England's intellectual elite were still allowed to pray in Latin." Atherstone, *Reformation*, 141. However, there was rebellion against the *Book of Common Prayer* in Devon and Cornwall. On the "Western Rebellion," see 143.

133. "Preface to the Book of Common Prayer, 1549" (Bray, 242).

134. "Preface to the Book of Common Prayer, 1549" (Bray, 244–45).

criticisms.[135] Criticism targeted the Eucharist since the prayer book was vague concerning the corporeal presence of God. In sum, although Cranmer's prayer book was flavored with evangelical ingredients, some said they could still taste Rome; they did not believe Cranmer had gone far enough in his reform of the liturgy.

In 1552 Cranmer published a second edition under the umbrella of the Second Act of Uniformity.[136] He had help too. Able theologians like Martin Bucer (now in England) and Englishmen like Nicholas Ridley joined Cranmer. Together they revised the liturgy until it expressed evangelical commitments that could not be twisted or manipulated, eliminating any language—for example, *Mass, altar, consecrate*—that sounded too papal.[137] Missing was any mention of venerating Mary and the saints or prayers for the dead. As for the Eucharist, transubstantiation was absent, and a far more Reformed view was present.[138]

Furthermore, the 1552 edition used liturgical language that clergy and laity alike could understand and share. If there is one rhetorical reason for the prayer book's influence, not just in the sixteenth century but up to the present day, it must be its rare combination of theology set to poetry, an attribute that can only be explained by Cranmer's rare gifting. If Calvin's *Institutes* became ingrained in the minds of the Genevans as well as the French for its turn of a phrase, Cranmer's prayer book was stitched on the hearts of the English people for its theological rhythm. However, whereas Calvin's *Institutes* had to be read by the studious Christian and therefore could be neglected, Cranmer's prayer book was heard each Sunday as the people gathered for worship. In that sense, the prayer book became more ingrained in the spiritual life of the people than any other book.

Not all evangelicals in England and abroad welcomed the prayer book. John Knox was vocal in his dissatisfaction and dissent. Even the revised prayer book did not go far enough in eliminating remnants of Rome. Knox told his followers not to kneel for the sacrament as the prayer book advised. Papists kneeled in their adoration of the elements transfigured into a real sacrifice, the body and blood of Christ himself. To accommodate, a Black Rubric was included in the printed prayer book that clarified that the Church of England was not advocating this type of adoration. Instead, the prayer book was merely encouraging a posture of humility and thanksgiving.[139]

---

135. The prayer book could be "ambiguous" and at times granted "concessions to traditionalists." Atherstone, *Reformation*, 144. The ultimate example was the imprisoned Stephen Gardiner, who manipulated the prayer book to endorse transubstantiation. Due to its ambiguity, others like John Hooper, Martin Bucer, and Vermigli all expressed criticisms, some harsher than others. Even after the revision of the prayer book (1552), John Knox still protested its language (145).

136. This was possible due to Dudley. On the fall of Somerset and the influence of Dudley, see Hillerbrand, *Division of Christendom*, 242.

137. For its sanction, see "Act of Uniformity, 1552" (Bray, 250–52).

138. For a study comparing the wording, see Atherstone, *Reformation*, 145; Hillerbrand, *Division of Christendom*, 242.

139. Not "adoration but gratitude," clarified Hillerbrand. Hillerbrand, *Division of Christendom*, 243.

Forty-Two Articles

Another pillar in Cranmer's evangelical reform was planned subscription to forty-two articles of faith—eventually reduced to thirty-nine (1571)—approved June 19, 1553. The homilies turned the attention of the church to the Scriptures, and the liturgy cultivated Reformation theology within the hearts of the people. Yet the *Forty-Two Articles* differentiated the English Reformation and its doctrinal commitments.

To begin with, Cranmer retrieved a patristic doctrine of God in two ways: (1) he confessed classical attributes of God, from his infinitude to his impassibility ("without body, parts or passions"),[140] and (2) he was explicit in his fidelity to Nicene Trinitarianism, and like other confessions in the Reformed wing of the Reformation, Cranmer did not hesitate to subscribe to the Nicene Creed, Athanasian Creed, and Apostles' Creed.[141]

On the heels of classical Christian theism, Cranmer then retrieved another patristic distinctive: an Augustinian doctrine of original sin and divine grace. Over against the Pelagians and the Anabaptists, Cranmer connected Adam's guilt and corruption to all his progeny and identified the pervasive consequences of condemnation, including the infection of human nature. With Calvinist overtones, Cranmer also precluded Semi-Pelagianism when he said that man's condition is so severe that he has no power to perform works of merit.[142] Necessary, then, is the supernatural, sovereign power of the Holy Spirit to "take away the stony heart" and implant instead a "heart of flesh." "And . . . those that have no will to good things, He makes them to will."[143] Cranmer sounded no different from Luther and Calvin, both of whom taught the inability of the sinner, throwing the unregenerate entirely upon the mercy of God for regeneration, a regeneration that is as pervasive as original sin, making new the human will.

With such a Godward focus in regeneration—a monergistic act of God—Cranmer turned to the fruit of this new life, namely, *faith*, and stated without equivocation that justification is by faith *alone*.[144] Cranmer was well aware of the late medieval context and made a point to impede any notion of a deserving, congruent grace or work of supererogation:

Article 12: "Works done before the grace of Christ, and the inspiration of His Spirit, are not pleasant to God; forasmuch as they spring not of faith in Jesus

---

140. "Forty-Two Articles of the Church of England (1552/53)," art. 1.

141. "Forty-Two Articles of the Church of England (1552/53)," arts. 2, 5, 7.

142. "Forty-Two Articles of the Church of England (1552/53)," art. 8 (2:4). The 1571 edition is more explicit in its denial of Semi-Pelagianism: "The condition of man after the fall of man is such that he cannot turn and prepare himself by his own natural strength and good works to faith and calling upon God" (art. 9. 10).

143. "Forty-Two Articles of the Church of England (1552/53)," art. 10.

144. Article 11 is brief in the 1553 edition, a simple affirmation of justification by faith alone. But the 1563 edition added the following to article 11: "We are accounted righteous before God only for the merit of our Lord and Saviour Jesus Christ by faith, and not for our own works or deservings" (art. 11). This addition adds an undeniable forensic emphasis that lends itself to the doctrine of the imputation of Christ's righteousness.

Christ: neither do they make men meet to receive grace, or (as the School authors say) deserve grace of congruity: but because they are not done as God has willed and commanded them to be done, we doubt not but they have the nature of sin."

Article 13: "Voluntary works beside, over, and above God's commandments which they call works of supererogation, cannot be taught without arrogancy, and iniquity. For by them men do declare, that they do not only render to God, as much as they are bound to do; but that they do more for His sake, than of bounden duty is required: whereas Christ says plainly: When you have done all that is commanded, say, 'We are unprofitable servants.'"[145]

Like other Reformers, however, Cranmer did not intend the denial of merit in justification to foster antinomianism. Good works cannot appease divine judgment or result in the remission of sin, but they are the inevitable and necessary fruit of justifying faith in the Christian life. The proper analogy is a tree, good works being the bounty, the evidence or harvest that springs forth from justification.

Ultimately, Cranmer's dual emphasis on regeneration and justification was grounded in eternity, ensuring the unconditionality and total generosity of God's love. "Predestination to life is the everlasting purpose of God, whereby (before the foundations of the world were laid) He has constantly decreed, by His own judgment, secret to us, to deliver from the curse and damnation those whom He has chosen out of mankind, and to bring them to everlasting salvation by Christ, as vessels made to honor."[146] Such a free, gracious predestination alone can substantiate the efficacy of God's calling and justification and be the source of the believer's sanctification into the image of Christ.[147] While works can never be the basis of election, works in the Christian life are only possible because of God's gracious choice. Predestination, then, is not a cold, scary, and disheartening doctrine, but one that gives assurance and comfort, motivating good works of love toward one's Savior and neighbor. "As the godly consideration of predestination and our election in Christ is full of sweet, pleasant, and unspeakable comfort to godly persons, and such as feel in themselves the working of the Spirit of Christ, mortifying the works of the flesh, and their earthly members, and drawing up their mind to high and heavenly things; as well because it does greatly establish and confirm their faith of eternal salvation, to be enjoyed through Christ, as because it does fervently kindle their love towards God."[148]

145. "Forty-Two Articles of the Church of England (1552/53)," art. 17. The reference in article 13 to "congruity" refers to the medieval distinction between merit *de congruo* (concerning what is appropriate) and merit *de condigno* (concerning what is wholly deserving). Sinners are capable of *de congruo* by nature. However, they are only capable of *de condigno* by God's grace. Packer and Beckwith, *Thirty-Nine Articles*, 10 n. 9.

146. "Forty-Two Articles of the Church of England (1552/53)," art. 17.

147. "Whereupon such as have so excellent a benefit of God given unto them, are called, according to God's purpose, by His Spirit working in due season: they through grace obey the calling: they are justified freely: they are made sons by adoption: they are made like the image of God's only-begotten Son, Jesus Christ: they walk religiously in good works: and at length, by God's mercy, they attain to everlasting felicity."

148. On that basis, a warning was issued: "So for curious and carnal persons, lacking the Spirit of Christ,

On that Augustinian-Calvinistic note, Cranmer detailed several other distinctives of an evangelical Reformation, including *sola scriptura*, a denial of purgatory, a denial of mandatory clerical celibacy, and a limitation of the sacraments to two (baptism and the Lord's Supper) instead of seven.[149] Cranmer's articulation of the sacraments was pivotal, directing the Church of England away from Anabaptist and Zwinglian camps. For example, baptism is "not only a sign of profession . . . but it is also a sign and seal of our new birth." Baptism's sealing nature means baptism serves an instrumental role in ecclesiology: "whereby, as by an instrument, they that receive baptism rightly are grafted into the church: the promises of forgiveness of sin, and our adoption to be sons of God, are visibly signed and sealed: faith is confirmed: and grace increased, by virtue of prayer unto God." In contrast to the Anabaptists, the "custom of the church to christen young children, is to be commended, and in any wise to be retained in the church."[150]

With Edward VI on the throne, Cranmer was at liberty to be explicit in his rejection of transubstantiation. To explain why transubstantiation was illegitimate, Cranmer reclaimed a Chalcedonian Christology and identified the ways such a Christology was violated if the substance of bread and wine was changed into the substance of Christ's body. The second half of Article 29 reads:

> Forasmuch as the truth of man's nature requires, that the body of one, and the self same man, cannot be at one time in various places, but must be in some one certain place: therefore, the body of Christ cannot be present at one time in various places. And because (as Holy Scripture teaches) Christ was taken up into heaven, and there will continue unto the end of the world; a faithful man ought not either to believe, or openly to confess the real and bodily presence (as they term it) of Christ's flesh and blood in the sacrament of the Lord's Supper.[151]

---

to have continually before their eyes the sentence of God's predestination, is a most dangerous downfall: whereby the devil may thrust them either into desperation or into a carelessness of most unclean living, no less perilous than desperation." "Forty-Two Articles of the Church of England (1552/53)," art. 17.

149. "Forty-Two Articles of the Church of England (1552/53)," arts. 21, 23, 26, 31. On the formal principle, article 6 (p. 3) says Scripture contains all things necessary to salvation. Anything not contained in Scripture cannot be required for salvation. Sufficiency, however, does not negate the necessity of councils or the authority of the church. Rather, as articles 20 and 21 (p. 7) explain, the church did have power to establish ceremonies. It also had authority in debates over controversies concerning the faith. Nevertheless, the church was never to decree or ordain anything that contradicted the Scriptures. Cranmer advocated that evangelical hermeneutic, Scripture interprets Scripture, which precluded the church from using one part of Scripture in a way that contradicted or abused another part of Scripture. The church, said Cranmer, is given a high responsibility as a "witness and a keeper of Holy Writ," but at the same time the church should not decree anything that runs against Holy Writ. Cranmer simultaneously endorsed the authority of the church and its councils but always subordinated them to the only infallible authority, Scripture. On the Lord's Supper, later editions also included the reception of both kinds (bread and cup) by the laity. See art. 30.

150. "Forty-Two Articles of the Church of England (1552/53)," art. 28.

151. "Forty-Two Articles of the Church of England (1552/53)," art. 29. Also consult his 1550 Preface to the Reader in *Defence of the True and Catholic Doctrine of the Supper of the Lord*.

Did Cranmer's language have polemical undertones for real presence as well? Possibly, but since the article never mentioned Lutheranism, Cranmer may have had only Rome in view. Also, later editions, although sounding Reformed, did accommodate the Lutherans.[152] "At the last minute Article 29 (in the 1571 revision) was omitted, because it was thought that it would offend Lutherans, their doctrine of real presence. By 1571 the prospect of union with the Lutheran churches had faded, and the Article was reinstated."[153] Nevertheless, the articles did retain a Lutheran polemic, though in the context of English politics. At the end of the *Forty-Two Articles*, Cranmer continued Henry's legacy in this sense: the king was still titled "supreme head in earth, next under Christ" and the "bishop of Rome [had] no jurisdiction in this realm of England."[154]

With the *Forty-Two Articles* in place, Cranmer's confidence was fortified. He was eager to make a further advance for reform with a fresh articulation of canon law in an evangelical key.[155] However, his plans came to a devastating halt when he received the news that Edward VI, the Protestant hope for reform, was dead.

LADY JANE GREY

Shock blew through England like a wind during a storm. The *Forty-Two Articles* arrived on June 19, 1553, and Edward died on July 6, not even one month later. Were Cranmer's reforms in vain, a mere striving after the wind?

When Edward died, evangelical preachers and professors alike became uncertain whether their return from exile was short lived. Controversy ensued over who was to be next on the throne. Henry's marriage to Catherine of Aragon did produce a daughter, Mary. Before he died, Henry did declare in his will that Mary was next in line after the reign of Edward. But the very thought of her as queen turned the stomachs of evangelicals across England. Mary was a staunch Roman Catholic, and if she became queen, the English Reformation had no future. She would return church and country back to papal doctrine and liturgy with urgency.

In a desperate attempt—led by Duke John Dudley—to cut off Mary as the next heir, Lady Jane Grey was announced as the next queen only four days

---

152. Article 28 reads, "Christ's body was given only in a "heavenly and spiritual manner." Bray, *Documents of the English Reformation* (270). Notice, too, the elaboration in a Chalcedonian key: "Christ ascending to heaven gave immortality to his body but did not take away its nature; according to the Scriptures it retains the reality of human nature in perpetuity, so that it must be in one definite place and not diffused in many, or all places at the same time. Therefore Christ has been taken up into heaven and will remain there until the end of the age, and will come from there, and not from elsewhere (as Augustine says) to judge the living and the dead, a faithful man ought not either to believe or openly to confess the real and bodily presence, as they term it, of Christ's flesh and blood, in the sacrament of the Lord's Supper." Article 28 concludes, "The body of Christ is given, taken and eaten in the supper only after an heavenly and spiritual manner; and the means whereby the body of Christ is received and eaten in the supper is faith."

153. Bray, 253.

154. "Forty-Two Articles of the Church of England (1552/53)," art. 36. Later editions would change the language to "queen."

155. The *Reformatio Legum Ecclesiasticarum*.

after Edward died. She was not as young as Edward when he became King, but at fifteen years old, she was not a seasoned politician either. In the eyes of English evangelicals, what mattered more than her inexperience was her allegiance to Protestantism. However, her bloodline did not put her as close to the throne as Mary, so when Mary announced herself as the real queen, Catholics across England rallied to her side. Jane's reign lasted but nine short days.[156] Mary became queen on July 19, 1553. Lady Grey's fate was all but sealed.

MARY AND THE HUNT FOR HERESY

Mary moved with speed, reversing what her predecessors had set in motion. As the daughter of Catherine of Aragon, she declared Henry's annulment invalid; she was the lawful child of Henry and Catherine and therefore the legal and only true queen of England.

As for religion itself, Mary renounced Henry and Edward's claims to supreme headship and opened the door once more to papal supremacy.[157] At first Mary portrayed herself as a queen open to Protestant toleration. She assumed that if she promised leniency, the English people would welcome their homecoming to the Catholic Church. But Mary underestimated the deep roots of Protestantism. When the people did not return to the Catholic faith in droves, her rhetoric changed course, and evangelical ministers fled to the Continent by the hundreds.[158] Catholic-minded ministers were released from prison, and evangelical ministers were thrown into prison, at least those that did not flee the country.

Also, Mary reversed ecclesiastical legislation conducted under both Henry and Edward. For instance, the Election of Bishops Act (1547), the Act of Uniformity (1549), and the Act to Take Away All Positive Laws against the Marriage of Priests (1549) were repealed.[159] As for the church's theology and liturgy, Mary took a battering ram to Cranmer's reform, returning the church to papal allegiance and Catholic practice. Under pressure, even some evangelical ministers recanted and returned to Rome. By the end of 1554, England and Rome were externally reconciled under Mary's wings, and the evangelical faith was considered heretical and thus liable to the full legal penalties that followed.

How did Mary accomplish such a shift in momentum in the short time between 1553 and 1556? To answer that question, consider Mary's strategic endeavors in those early years of her reign. In 1553 Mary and Prince Philip of Spain formed an alliance. Like his father, Charles V, Philip was a committed Catholic, yet not everyone in Parliament was in favor of the marriage since

---

156. On the privy council switching to support Mary, see Atherstone, *Reformation*, 147.

157. However, Mary retained her authority as Supreme Head of the Church. On Parliament's resistance and the debate over property, see Hillerbrand, *Division of Christendom*, 245. Hillerbrand wrote, "Even though Mary did not at all concede that Parliament had a legitimate voice in ecclesiastical affairs, Parliament had to be involved—after all, the separation from Rome had occurred through legal acts of Parliament, and so new acts of Parliament had to formalize the separation's repeal" (247).

158. Hillerbrand cited eight hundred Marian exiles. Hillerbrand, 245.

159. See "Marian Injunctions, 1554," 282–83.

Philip was not English. Despite their disapproval, they had little recourse to action against Mary. When Sir Thomas Wyatt raised up a small militia, hoping to overthrow Mary and establish Elizabeth as the new queen, Wyatt and his men were slaughtered.[160] Mary then accelerated her suppression of potential resisters, and in February 1554, Lady Jane Grey was beheaded.

After Grey was beheaded, Mary and Cardinal Reginald Pole worked together to reconcile the Church of England with Rome, and by the end of 1554 Pope Julius III declared England no longer estranged but a lost prodigal now returning home. The whole matter was personal for Pole, as it was for Mary. He never fared well under Henry and was charged with treason for siding with the papacy during the king's grab for supremacy.[161] But now that Mary, a devout Catholic, sat on the throne, Pole was welcomed back into England and recruited to assist Mary in her vision for Catholic conformity. By the end of her life, Mary had formally returned the church to its late medieval days, before Henry severed the English church from its papal mother.

The restoration, however, was merely external. Mary had repealed religious legislation under Edward but could not reverse the heartfelt religious commitments of the English people overnight. "She was mistaken when she took the wave of popular enthusiasm that greeted her succession to the throne as an endorsement of her Catholic faith."[162] The sheer number of evangelical leaders willing to lay down their lives for their faith exhibited a truth Mary refused to accept: outward change did not necessarily mean change had occurred within the souls of the people.

Regardless, Mary was determined to eradicate the evangelical faith. She found assistance from the hands of Cardinal Pole and Bishop Gardner, who helped her initiate an aggressive hunt for heresy. Mary was no longer interested in making arrests that resulted in long imprisonments of English evangelicals—she now intended to spill blood. At the start of 1555, Mary had her first kill: John Rogers (ca. 1500–1555). Rogers was educated at the University of Cambridge before he became a chaplain at Antwerp in Brabant. While a chaplain, he encountered William Tyndale and Miles Coverdale, and they influenced him toward evangelical convictions. Rogers converted to the Reformation, eventually studied in Wittenberg, and then moved back to England when Edward rose to power. Rogers became a reader of divinity in the Cathedral Church of Paul and dedicated himself to the regular preaching of the evangelical gospel message.

Like many others, Mary's succession of King Edward placed Rogers in a precarious position. First, Rogers was summoned before a council and then imprisoned at Newgate. On February 4, 1555, he was awakened with the news that he was to burn at the stake that day. Rogers was transported from Newgate to

---

160. Atherstone, *Reformation*, 147.
161. On the persecution of Pole's family and on Pole's fall and then rise under Mary, see Hillerbrand, *Division of Christendom*, 245.
162. Hillerbrand, 244.

Smithfield. Master Woodruff asked him if he wanted to recant, to which Rogers responded, "That which I have preached, I will seal with my blood."[163] Woodruff answered, "Thou art an heretic." But Rogers said in reply, "That shall be known at the Day of Judgment."[164] John Foxe, in his *Actes and Monuments*, described Rogers's impression on the people with a word that he believed captured the English martyrs as a whole: *constancy*.[165] When Rogers was burned at the stake, the constancy of his witness influenced those watching. He went to the flames believing that the gospel he had proclaimed was now to be confirmed in his own death.

The next day the same constancy was present once more, this time with John Hooper (ca. 1497–1555). When Henry issued his Six Articles Act, Hooper came under close scrutiny, pressuring him to flee England for Paris, France. When Hooper decided to return to England, yet again he came under questioning, this time fleeing to Basel and Zurich where he learned from Heinrich Bullinger. When King Edward ascended the throne, Hooper returned to England set on preaching the evangelical message over against the papacy. Hooper was appointed bishop of Gloucester as well as bishop of Worcester. He gained a reputation not only for his preaching, however, but also for his pastoral care, which may be due to the influence of Bullinger. When Mary became queen, Hooper had the opportunity to flee again, but he refused. His reason was pastoral: "Once I did flee and took me to my feet, but now, because I am called to this place and vocation, I am thoroughly persuaded to tarry, and to live and die with my sheep."[166] Hooper believed he was at liberty to flee before since he had only himself to care for, but now, with so many sheep watching him and looking to his lead, Hooper felt obligated to follow the example of Christ.

The decision to stay was fatal. At first Hooper was imprisoned for an indefinite period of time. The prison was so riddled with disease that Hooper suffered from infections. In 1555 he was transferred to Gloucester, and on February 9 he was taken to the stake. Although Hooper remained adamant in his resistance to the papacy, his martyrdom was marked by a vocal, voluntary subjection to the queen. As Hooper himself said, "For I come not hither as one enforced or compelled to die (for it is well known, I might have had my life with worldly gain) but as one willing to offer and give my life for the truth, rather than to consent to the wicked papistical religion of the Bishop of Rome, received and set forth by the magistrates in England, to God's high displeasure and dishonour: and I trust by God's grace tomorrow to die a faithful servant of God, and a true obedient subject to the queen."[167]

John Foxe reported that around seven thousand attended Hooper's burning,

---

163. Robinson, *Original Letters*, 1:105. Cf. Atherstone, *Reformation*, 149.
164. Foxe, *Foxe's Book of Martyrs*, 40.
165. Foxe, *Foxe's Book of Martyrs*, 40.
166. Foxe, *Foxe's Book of Martyrs*, 59.
167. As quoted in Foxe, *Foxe's Book of Martyrs*, 66.

although many were there for the market as well. The makeup of the crowd was not lost on Hooper: he would die a shepherd in front of his own sheep. "When I was appointed here to be their pastor, I preached unto them true and sincere doctrine, and that out of the word of God. Because I will not now accompt the same to be heresy and untruth, this kind of death is prepared for me."[168] The location was even within shouting distance from where Hooper used to preach. "When he came to the place appointed where he should die, smilingly he beheld the stake and preparation made for him, which as near unto the great elm tree over against the college of priests, where he was wont to preach."[169]

As Hooper prepared for death, he recited the creed and the Lord's Prayer, and begged his executioners to make his death quick. Hooper did not receive his wish. It was a cold, wet, and windy morning, the fire refusing cooperation. Every time the fire started to climb Hooper, it petered out. The pain was unbearable: "For God's love (good people) let me have more fire." Three times more wood was collected until the fire reached Hooper's torso. Even then, when the fire at last reacted with the gunpowder, the explosion was not fatal. Hooper prayed, "Lord Jesus have mercy upon me. Lord Jesus have mercy upon me. Lord Jesus receive my spirit."[170] But he continued to survive the flames until his mouth turned black and nothing was left but his gums. Hooper kept beating his chest until one of his arms burned, detached, and fell off his body into the flames. He suffered almost up to an hour until death came at last.

Rogers and Hooper were but the beginning of an avalanche of martyrs totaling almost three hundred. These evangelical martyrs were diverse: clergy and laity, rich and poor, men and women, sometimes even youth. And although Smithfield and Canterbury competed for the most martyrs, evangelicals were executed all over England.[171]

Although these executions stirred fear in the hearts of many, Mary underestimated the power of martyrdom and its lasting influence in the hearts of others. The church father Tertullian said that the blood of the martyrs is the seed of the church. When an evangelical was sent to the flames or the block, the faith and courage displayed by each martyr only galvanized others to stay faithful in the face of persecution. Although these executions continued from 1555 to 1558, even within the first year of persecution the martyrs themselves recognized that their own blood could fuel the evangelical mission not only for years but for decades and centuries to come.

For example, consider the martyrdoms of Hugh Latimer and Nicholas Ridley. In 1555 both men were taken to the stake to be burned back-to-back. When they met each other at the stake, Ridley ran to Latimer, "embraced, and kissed him,"

---

168. Foxe, *Foxe's Book of Martyrs*, 67.
169. Foxe, *Foxe's Book of Martyrs*, 67.
170. Foxe, *Foxe's Book of Martyrs*, 70.
171. "Approximately one in five were women, including teenage girls, pregnant mothers, and elderly widows." For a description of many of them, see Atherstone, *Reformation*, 150.

and then told Latimer, "Be of good heart brother, for God will either assuage the fury of the flame, or else strengthen us to abide it."[172] As Ridley and Latimer were prepared for the stake, "Doctor Smith" preached a sermon warning the people in attendance against sects such as the Lutherans, Oecolampadians, and Zwinglians, all of which cannot agree with each other anyway, having "diversities in opinions." Their road is the path to heresy, he preached, and Ridley and Latimer were an example of its destination. Doctor Smith then admonished the people to stay with "the old Church of Christ, and the Catholic faith."[173] The contrast was clear: Doctor Smith was on the side of the Catholic faith; Ridley and Latimer were heretics, deviating from the Catholic heritage.

Ridley and Latimer were given one last opportunity to recant. "Master Ridley, if you will revoke your erroneous opinions, and recant the same, you shall not only have liberty so to do, but also the benefit of a subject, that is, have your life."[174] According to Foxe, Ridley did not have to think about it: "So long as the breath is in my body, I will never deny my Lord Christ, and his known truth: God's will be done in me."[175]

The execution was brutal. After they were chained to the post, gunpowder was tied to their necks. Ridley's brother brought the gunpowder, which ensured both men's suffering ended as soon as the flame ignited the gunpowder. When the fire was kindled and lit, Latimer said to Ridley, "Be of good comfort Master Ridley, and play the man: we shall this day light such a candle by God's grace in England, as (I trust) shall never be put out."[176] But the flame on Ridley's side of the stake stayed low, burning his legs due to the wood beneath him. Ridley screamed in pain and jumped up and down alongside the post, yelling "I cannot burn" until his legs were consumed. He then pleaded with God, "Lord have mercy upon me," and "Let the fire come unto me; I cannot burn."[177] Finally, the flame ignited the gunpowder, the chain got loose, and Ridley's body fell at the feet of Latimer.

In 1556 Mary had the ultimate proof that the English Reformation could be squeezed out if she applied enough pressure. Under enormous strain, Thomas Cranmer recanted, and not just once but six different times as the threat of a brutal death haunted him. Cranmer was even pressured into anathematizing other Reformers. Mary now assumed she had the evangelical movement by the jugular, but she was mistaken. Despite Cranmer's recalcitrance, Mary still wanted blood payment and decided to burn him at the stake. Before he went to his death, Mary required him to make one final recantation as well as an attestation to Church of Rome that he now embraced, putting his allegiance in a statement to the public at University Church (Oxford).

---

172. Foxe, *Foxe's Book of Martyrs*, 152.
173. Foxe, *Foxe's Book of Martyrs*, 152.
174. Foxe, *Foxe's Book of Martyrs*, 153.
175. Foxe, *Foxe's Book of Martyrs*, 153.
176. Foxe, *Foxe's Book of Martyrs*, 154.
177. Foxe, *Foxe's Book of Martyrs*, 156.

NICHOLAS RIDLEY VERSUS DUNS SCOTUS

Before Ridley was burned at the stake, he was locked up in prison in Oxford. Awaiting his pending death, Ridley wrote *A Treatise Agaynst the Errour of Transubstantiation* (1554 or 1555). The title gives away Ridley's stance against the papacy's view of the supper, and the reader of Ridley will not be shocked to discover that Ridley petitioned the church to give the sacrament to laymen. His reason was christological, opposing the sharp separation between clergy and laity: "Did not Christ shed his blood as well for the lay godly man as for the godly priests?" (Ridley, *Treatise Agaynst the Errour of Transubstantiation*, in Parker, *English Reformers*, 307). Over against Duns Scotus, Ridley appealed to the church fathers to refute the papacy's position.

But the treatise is far more revealing for another reason: Ridley articulated a view of the Lord's Supper that did not quite match that of the Continental Reformers in vocabulary. He did not utilize the typical arguments the Continental Reformers used to refute the defense of transubstantiation. Instead, he returned to a distinction to differentiate his position from the papacy's: they taught that Christ's presence was manifested by the real, natural change of the substance of bread and wine into the substance of his body and blood. Ridley didn't deny Christ's presence, but he did say that Christ was present *by grace* instead. Consider the sun: "the sun, which in substance never removeth his place out of the heavens, is yet present here by his beams, light, and natural influence, where it shineth upon the earth." So, too, with Christ in the supper. "Very bread cannot be his body in very substance. . . . But bread, retaining still his own very natural substance, may be thus by grace, and in a sacramental signification, his body" (Ridley, 301).

Ridley said something to a similar effect in his 1555 Oxford Disputation when he listed a litany of fathers—Cyprian, Athanasius, Basil, Augustine, Chrysostom, and others—to confess that "there is not only a signification of Christ's body set forth by the sacrament, but also that therewith is given to the godly and faithful the grace of Christ's body, that is, the food of life and immortality" (Ridley, 314). When the papacy fixated on a substantial change and real presence instead of grace, they undermined the sufficiency and efficacy of Christ's finished work on the cross: "There is no such necessity to offer up any more sacrifice propitiatory for the quick and the dead, for Christ our Saviour did that fully and perfectly once for all." As the catholic fathers taught, "The blood of Christ is in the chalice indeed, but not in real presence, but by grace and in a sacrament" (Ridley, 320; cf. Parker, 294).

Also notable is Ridley's subtle allusion to classic, Nicene Trinitarianism. "As a sound Trinitarian, Ridley believed that the works of God toward his creatures are the activity of the whole Godhead—of the Father, the Son, and the Holy Spirit." Inseparable operations, as the pro-Nicene said, means that the external works of God are undivided. Yet Ridley, also in line with the pro-Nicene tradition, affirmed divine appropriations. While the three persons work inseparably (because they are inseparable by nature), nevertheless, a particular work of creation and salvation may be appropriated by a particular person of the Godhead in a way that corresponds to that person's eternal relation of origin. Ridley drew attention, then, to the Spirit and "believed that the work which Christ wrought for his people is effected in them by the creative activity of the Spirit. The Spirit works generally through creaturely media—the preaching of the gospel and the Sacraments. He converts them, not into the actual voice of God or into the substantial body and blood of Christ, but into the effectual media of God's voice and of the incarnate Christ" (Parker, *English Reformers*, 295).

To Mary's surprise, Cranmer went off script. He stood in front of the people a broken man but still with enough resolve to recant his recantation.

> And now I come to the great thing, that so much troubleth my conscience more than anything that ever I did or said in my whole life, and that is the setting abroad of a writing contrary to the truth: which now here I renounce and refuse as things written with my hand, contrary to the truth which I thought in my heart, and written for fear of death, and to save my life if it might be, and that is, all such bills and papers which I have written or signed with my hand since my degradation: wherein I have written many things untrue. And forasmuch as my hand offended, writing contrary to my heart, my hand shall first be punished therefore: for may I come to the fire, it shall be first burned.
>
> And as for the pope, I refuse him as Christ's enemy and Antichrist, with all his false doctrine.
>
> And as for the sacrament, I believe as I have taught in my book against the Bishop of Winchester, the which my book teacheth so true a doctrine of the sacrament, that it shall stand at the last day before the judgment of God, where the papistical doctrine contrary thereto, shall be ashamed to show her face.[178]

The authorities were shocked and looked around at each other in disbelief. Cranmer's recantation of his recantation exposed their methods: the authorities had previously beaten a recantation out of him that did not match his real convictions. Now that he had exposed them, willing to go to his death as a committed evangelical, the authorities had no move left. "Briefly, it was a world to see the doctors beguiled of so great an hope. I think there was never cruelty more notably or better in time deluded and deceived. For it is not to be doubted but they looked for a glorious victory, and a perpetual triumph by this man's retractation," commented John Foxe. In a last minute maneuver, Cranmer had robbed Mary and her men of that victory. The victory was now his no matter what they did to him.

Livid, they tried to drag Cranmer away before he could keep talking, but it was too late. The crowd had already heard Cranmer condemn the pope and his sacrament and reaffirm the Reformed faith. Outraged at this surprise, the friars took Cranmer to his death, saying, "What madness hath brought thee again

---

178. Foxe, *Foxe's Book of Martyrs*, 193.

into this error, by which thou wilt draw innumerable souls with thee into hell?"[179] When Cranmer was tied to the stake and the flames climbed closer, he put his hand in the fire, the one he used to sign his recantations, conveying to those watching that he condemned his prior weakness and now was ready to pay the ultimate price for his faith. Cranmer was burned on the same grounds as Latimer and Ridley.[180]

Two years later the flames of the stake continued to lick up evangelical martyrs. All of Europe heard, and it appeared as if no end was in sight. What they could not have anticipated, however, was a drastic change in Mary's health. Mary was a master at hiding her illness, but on November 17, 1558, the queen who had sent so many to their death met her own. That same day the archbishop of Canterbury, Cardinal Pole, who had fueled Mary's heresy hunting, died as well.[181] As Pole breathed his last, English evangelicals everywhere exhaled for the first time in years.[182]

Mary's legacy was one stained by the blood of English evangelicals, but in the end this method proved ineffective. Since Mary's reversal of evangelical reformation was from the top down and was coupled with her brutality against Protestants, her religious legislation did not finally penetrate the hearts of the English people in a lasting way. England had officially returned to Rome, but the recent memory of evangelical martyrs left those sympathetic to reform ready for a new way forward.[183]

With Mary in the grave, the question on the mind of English Reformers was a pressing one: Could the new sovereign return England to its Edwardian past, a past that had so much promise but was cut off from the start?

THE BIRTH OF THE ELIZABETHAN SETTLEMENT

When Henry was pursuing a divorce with Catherine, his sights were set on Anne Boleyn as his next wife. Elizabeth was Henry and Anne's daughter, and when Mary died Elizabeth was twenty-five years old. Although young Elizabeth succeeded Mary, she did so with Protestant proclivities. The new queen received a warm welcome, although the country's lack of opposition may not have been all for religious reasons. Mary not only unleashed a harsh whip against Protestants but aligned the English with the Spanish in her marriage to Philip II (1554). The year after they married, Mary's new husband ascended the throne of both Spain and the Netherlands.[184] Therefore, when Elizabeth succeeded Mary on

---

179. Foxe, *Foxe's Book of Martyrs*, 194.
180. Foxe, *Foxe's Book of Martyrs*, 195–96.
181. Historians believe Mary died from stomach cancer and Pole died from influenza. Atherstone, *Reformation*, 154.
182. Hillerbrand said Pole was accused of heresy due to his view of justification.
183. "Failure in her religious policy was the end, for even though the Catholic faith had been formally restored in England, the hearts of the people had not been won." Hillerbrand, *Division of Christendom*, 249–50.
184. On the events of 1555, see Hillerbrand, 261.

the English throne, many were relieved that they no longer had to worry about the political ambiguities of a foreign power and that power's Roman Catholic influence. That is not to say Catholicism disappeared when Elizabeth became queen; a constituency remained among the clergy. But as the turn of the century approached, Elizabeth's Protestantism—moderate as it may have been in the eyes of those who desired more expedient, radical reform—left less and less room for polemical Catholics.

Was Elizabeth's turn toward Protestantism a mere political maneuver, or was it motivated by the queen's own religious conviction?[185] Historians debate to what degree Elizabeth shared a personal Protestant proclivity. However, the stretch of Elizabeth's forty-five-year reign requires at least some personal commitment to the Protestant faith, even if it be politically logical. That is unsurprising since every king or queen after Henry ascended a throne that was by definition head of the church.

Regardless, Elizabeth was clear on her ambitions: the new queen did not intend to carry on the intolerant Catholic legacy of her half sister. However, barriers faced Elizabeth from the start that challenged plans to implement quick or major change. Two divided camps posed resistance. Many bishops in England had been appointed by Mary and were allegiant to the papacy. They despised Elizabeth and what she represented. Nevertheless, the House of Commons was populated by Protestant sympathizers, eager to see the country advance an evangelical program, both in clergy and in laity. However, those in favor of evangelical reform were not prepared to settle for compromise; they wanted a reform just as ambitious—if not more so—than in the days of Edward VI.

Elizabeth walked in between these opposite sides of the spectrum. She was Protestant in her basic orientation but adhered to a mediating method that did not banish Roman sympathizers, at least not initially. By virtue of Parliament, this "Elizabethan settlement" took form by 1559, the year both the Act of Supremacy and the Act of Uniformity were passed.[186] Both resurrected the legislation Edward VI had instituted—except Elizabeth did not take on the title "supreme head" because evangelicals believed such a title belonged to Christ alone. Instead, she settled for "supreme governor on earth," although the power granted to the queen by the Act of Supremacy was not all that different in practice.[187]

---

185. For example, Hillerbrand said the evidence is inconclusive. Hillerbrand, 250.

186. Also, the Elizabethan Injunctions, 1559. For all three, see Bray, *Documents of the English Reformation*, 284–312.

187. See arts. 37 and 39 on the meaning of the title. Bray calls the change a "change of form, but not of substance." Bray, 97. However, Hillerbrand believes the change in title reflects theological self-awareness: "Elizabeth was not the self-confident theologian her father had seen himself to be. She was a partner of Parliament, and her 'governorship' was indirect at best. The new title lacked the theological significance of the old, and, as it turned out, both the theory and the practice of Elizabeth's ecclesiastical rule were different." Hillerbrand, *Division of Christendom*, 253.

RECUSANTS

By 1572 opposition to the queen was met by the death penalty. *Recusare* means "to refuse" in Latin (Atherstone, *Reformation*, 171–72). Some Catholics called "recusants" refused to conform. These recusants were either incognito or protesting from exile; they counted on the country returning to Catholicism as soon as Elizabeth could be overthrown either by a foreign power or by a faction from within. The most galvanized movement against Elizabeth was the Northern Rebellion (1569). As these recusants marched south, the plan was to storm the Tutbury Castle in Staffordshire where Mary, Queen of Scots, was imprisoned. At her lead, they would then defeat Elizabeth's army and take England back, returning the country to Catholicism. Neither happened. Elizabeth outsmarted and outnumbered these northern rebels until they fled for their lives across foreign borders. Those captured were hanged, drawn, and quartered.

During the Northern Rebellion, Elizabeth was excommunicated by Pope Pius V. (See the 1570 bull: *Regnans in Excelsis—Ruling in the Highest.*) Elizabeth's military was not surprised to discover that the Italians had plans to assassinate their queen so that their Catholic allies in the Spanish Netherlands could march on England. Once victorious, Mary, Queen of Scots, and the Duke of Norfolk would reign in her place. But when these plans were exposed, Norfolk was beheaded and any dreams of an invasion were cut off as well.

Many, from parliament to John Knox, believed Elizabeth should execute Mary, but Elizabeth refused. "However, parliament made it 'high treason' for any English subject to be reconciled to the bishop of Rome" (Atherstone, *Reformation*, 174. Cf. Elton, *Tudor Constitution*, 430).

In total the acts served to satisfy those bent on returning to the days of Edward VI, but they did not appease those who desired more ambitious reform. The acts pitched a broad enough tent to encourage those bishops still allegiant to the papacy to conform to one degree or another.[188] The reaction? "Most Protestants accepted the apparent compromise, recognizing the difficult political situation at the beginning of the new reign, though many hoped for further reform later."[189]

Elizabeth took additional steps that served the evangelical cause. First, she reminded the people of how cruel and suffocating persecution was under Mary. The smell of burning flesh never relented and was still in the nostrils of most

---

188. "The 1559 Act enjoined a Settlement which was clearly Protestant, though somewhat less radical than that of 1552. A number of minor concessions were made to traditionalist sensibilities, in the hope that those of Catholic sympathies might be reconciled to the new order." Bray, *Documents of the English Reformation*, 294.

189. "In this they were to be disappointed, and as time went on a 'Puritan' party emerged to make the case for a more thorough and consistent Reformation. Elizabeth I consistently opposed their demands, and encouraged conformist theologians to develop an apologetic for the 1559 Settlement, calling it the middle way (*via media*) between Geneva and Rome." Bray, 294.

Englishmen, thanks to the graphic accounts of martyrdom described by John Foxe in his *Acts and Monuments of These Latter Perilous Days* (1563). Second, with the Act of Uniformity resurrected, Elizabeth reestablished Cranmer's *Book of Common Prayer.* The prayer book was not unaltered, however.[190] Some of its more polemical language against Rome was removed and its description of the Lord's Supper appeared to borrow from Continental Reformers—both Lutheran and Reformed—but without committing wholesale to either.[191] Third, Elizabeth not only warned against Roman tyranny but made strides to reaffirm and implement a broad evangelical theology. Thomas Cranmer's *Forty-Two Articles* had barely seen the light of day when Mary threw Cranmer to the flames. However, Elizabeth retrieved Cranmer's initiative and modified the number of articles to thirty-eight (1563) and eventually thirty-nine.

The Elizabethan settlement in comparison with Mary's conquest was as opposite as white and black. Nevertheless, the settlement did steer a moderate course, clearly evangelical in sympathy but preserving a significant amount of liberality in details beyond the broad contours of the prayer book and articles.[192] Matthew Parker proved himself indispensable to the practical implementation of Elizabeth's reforming but moderate measures. The archbishop of Canterbury survived Mary's onslaught by retreating to obscurity, waiting for his opportune time to resurface once Elizabeth was crowned queen. Parker pitched Elizabeth's reforming measures as a return to the universal church. The Church of England, in other words, was now experiencing true catholic renewal, claimed Parker, a renewal of early Christianity as confessed by the apostles and modeled by the church fathers.[193]

In 1570 the papacy retaliated with a bull that was anything but ambiguous: Elizabeth, the queen of England, was excommunicated. Pius V was not only condemning Elizabeth's religion but posing a political threat by pronouncing a religious verdict and declaring Elizabeth an illegitimate queen. In that vein, the bull could be interpreted as an open invitation to other countries—Spain and France—to align and attack.[194] Although that alliance never materialized in an invasion of England, the queen grew increasingly suspicious, intolerant with Catholics in her country (Jesuits in particular). The "word 'Jesuit' conjured up feelings of fear and dismay, and the official contention that the Jesuits were but the advance contingent of a Catholic invasion of England was widely accepted."[195]

---

190. "In the litany the priest's petition, 'From the tyranny of the Bishop of Rome and all his detestable enormities, Good Lord, deliver us,' was omitted, and the 'Black Rubric' also disappeared. The new edition added a rubric to Morning Prayer prescribing the use of vestments, and two years later the prayer book was amended by the addition of a number of saints' days and festivals." Hillerbrand, *Division of Christendom*, 253.

191. The words of administration, nonetheless, retained their Reformed distinctive, even if the *Book of Common Prayer* still drew on prior editions. I am indebted to Lee Gatiss for this observation.

192. Hillerbrand called this a "minimalist settlement." *Division of Christendom*, 253.

193. Hillerbrand, 254.

194. On *Regnans in Excelsis* (1570), see Hillerbrand, 264.

195. Hillerbrand, 264.

The year after Elizabeth's excommunication, the confessional articles of the Church of England were ratified, but this time an article was added, establishing thirty-nine articles in total. The year 1571 was monumental, representing an irreversible commitment to Protestantism. The reign of Mary gave every appearance that England and its church were committed to reunion with the papacy. But with Mary's fatal illness, history decided a different fate. England and its church were solidified within Protestantism.

England had been grafted back into the Protestant tree, but in the years ahead a storm surfaced on the horizon because clergy could not agree on the type of Protestantism that should follow. A certain constituency of English clergy grew discontent with the extent of Elizabeth's reforming measures. They were called Puritans because they desired a purer church, one free of even the slightest remnant of papal religion, both in internals and externals. As the sun set on the sixteenth century, some clergy came to grips with the sobering truth that reforming the Elizabethan settlement was unlikely. That realization planted the seeds of separation. Exploring these dashed hopes and the late sixteenth- and seventeenth-century Puritan critique of the Elizabethan settlement is beyond the scope of this project. Nevertheless, the initial intentions of English Reformers at the genesis of Elizabeth's reign can help identify how the English interpreted the Reformation. Consider two examples: John Jewel and John Foxe.

An Apology for Catholicity: John Jewel

If the renewal and retrieval of evangelical catholicity was indispensable to the Reformation cause, then there may be no better way to conclude the story of the English Reformation than with John Jewel and his *An Apologie of the Church of England* (1560–61). In Jewel's day, the Council of Trent had yet to finish, and some entertained the possibility of England returning to the mother church. Despite discontent with the pace of reform in Elizabethan England, Elizabeth did not drive the country back to the papacy. Still, England's recent history— from Edward to Mary—left the question open to those on the Continent who still hoped Protestantism might not prevail.

To remove any remaining papal optimism, William Cecil summoned John Jewel to write an apologetic on behalf of the Church of England. The *Apologie* is a work in patristic and medieval scholarship. It had to be since "they call us heretics."[196] By *they* Jewel was referring to the Council of Trent, which did not hesitate to damn the Reformers as schismatics and innovators. Therefore, he embarked on a survey of the Fathers and Scholastics to demonstrate the inaccuracy of Trent's charge.

First, Jewel retrieved patristic voices, starting with Augustine and Jerome, to show that the "Catholic fathers" proved their doctrines from the Scriptures over

---

196. Jewel, *An Apologie of the Church of England*, 17.

against heretics.[197] The English Reformers had ancient precedent for their appeal to the formal principle. Second, the Church of England was not only consistent with the "catholic fathers" in their final appeal to the Scriptures, but in their inclusion within the catholic church. Jewel wrote, "We believe that there is one Church of God, and that the same is not shut up (as in times past among the Jews) into some one corner or kingdom, but that it is catholic and universal and dispersed throughout the whole world." However, over against the papacy Jewel claimed, "Christ alone is the prince of this kingdom . . . Christ alone is the head of this body . . . Christ alone is the bridegroom of this spouse."[198]

Deacons, priests, and bishops—Jewel's threefold polity—may be commissioned by Christ to instruct his church, but no one person can claim "the whole superiority in this universal state." To do so would be to undermine the extensiveness of Christ's divine presence. "Christ is ever present to assist his Church, and needeth not any man to supply his room, as his only heir to all his substance." No "one mortal creature" could "comprehend or conceive in his mind the universal Church . . . and to govern them rightly and duly." As catholic fathers like Cyprian taught, "There is but one bishoprick, and that a piece thereof is perfectly and wholly holden of every particular bishop." Or as the Council of Nicaea concluded, "The Bishop of Rome hath no more jurisdiction over the Church of God, than the rest of the patriarchs, either of Alexandria or Antiochia, have."[199]

The bishop of Rome had misunderstood (even perverted) his office; as Augustine observed, he was not a bishop in order to receive honor but to serve, not to be hailed as preeminent but to benefit others. The pope "can no more be head of the whole Church, or a bishop over all, than he can be the bridegroom, the light, the salvation, and life of the Church: for these privileges and names belong only to Christ, and [can] be properly and only fit for him alone."[200] Jewel surveyed the patristic councils and concluded that "no bishop of Rome did ever suffer himself to be called by such a proud name and title before Phocas the Emperor's time," but we also know that the "Council of Carthage did circumspectly provide, that no bishop should be called either the highest bishop or chief priest."[201] The pope claimed an authority that could only be attributed to Christ. Although he said this was the position of the church catholic, he could not be more wrong, more out of step with the "old fathers." Worse still, the pope had granted himself "a presumptuous, a profane, a sacrilegious, and antichristian name." Jewel, sounding no different than Luther before him, concluded that the

---

197. Jewel, 18–19.
198. Jewel, 21.
199. Jewel, 22. Jewel also challenged the pope's own definition of his office. Again, relying on the Council of Nicaea, Jewel said, "And as for the Bishop of Rome, who now calleth all matters before himself alone, except he do his duty as he ought to do, except he administer the sacraments, except he instruct the people, except he warn them and teach them, we say that he ought not of right once to be called a bishop, or so much as an elder."
200. Jewel, 22.
201. Jewel, 22–23.

pope was "the king of pride ... Lucifer" because he "preferreth himself before his brethren; ... he hath forsaken the faith, and is the forerunner of Antichrist."[202]

Unleashing a caustic accusation, Jewel found the papacy's claims to the power of the keys, clerical celibacy, transubstantiation, and other doctrines lacking patristic support. Consider the sacraments, for example. Jewel, "together with Tertullian, Origen, Ambrose, Augustine, Jerome, Chrysostom, Basil, Dionysius, and other Catholic fathers," called the sacraments "figures, signs, marks or badges, prints, copies, forms, seals, signets, similitudes, patterns, representations, remembrances, and memories."[203] Yet Jewel did not believe the Fathers went so far as the papacy to teach transubstantiation. "We affirm that bread and wine are holy and heavenly mysteries of the body and blood of Christ, and that by them Christ himself being the true bread of eternal life, is so presently given unto us, as that by faith we verily receive his body and his blood." But that does not, then, mean that the bread and wine become a carnal flesh and blood, as if "the nature of bread and wine is clearly changed." For Jewel, the reason why was hermeneutical: "For that was not Christ's meaning that the wheaten bread should lay apart his own nature, and receive a certain new divinity; but that he might rather change us, and (to use Theophylactus' words) might transform us into his body."[204]

How could such a resistance to the bishop of Rome and the papacy's adherence to transubstantiation, among other beliefs, not result in a departure from the one, true, holy, and apostolic church? Jewel felt the weight of that charge and reported, "[How often they] slander us as heretics, and say that we have left the Church and fellowship of Christ. . . . In this point they triumph marvellously, that they be the Church . . . and that without it there is no hope of salvation." By contrast, Protestants were accused of being renegades, "plucked quite off from the body of Christ," having "forsaken the Catholic faith."[205] Evangelicals pedaled nothing but "novelty."[206]

Jewel could not disagree more. Outrageous as it may sound, the Church of England had better claim to the Catholic Church than the bishop of Rome himself. Protestantism was no more novel than the gospel itself. "As for our doctrine, it is so far off from new, that God, who is above all most ancient, and the Father of our Lord Jesus Christ, hath left the same unto us in the Gospel, in the prophets' and apostles' works, being monuments of greatest age. So that no man can now think our doctrine to be new, unless the same think either the prophets' faith, or the Gospel, or else Christ himself to be new."[207] Jewel's argument captures the essence of evangelical legitimacy, however much it provoked the papacy.

---

202. Jewel, 23.
203. Jewel, 26.
204. Jewel quoted extensively, citing Ambrose, Gelasius, Theodoret, Augustine, Origen, Cyril, the Council of Nicaea, Chrysostom, Cyprian, and others. Jewel, 28.
205. Jewel, 33.
206. Jewel, 33.
207. Jewel, 39.

Protestant credibility relies not on externals but is established by that most stable of spiritual realities: Christ and his gospel. On that foundation, Protestants have a heritage as ancient as the "primitive Church" and the "holy fathers."[208]

Granted, the Church of England (and the Reformation as a whole) might have departed from the papacy—though at the genesis of the Reformation it was not Luther who departed from the papacy but the papacy who excommunicated Luther. And yet, by departing from the papacy, the Church of England (and the Reformation as a whole) had stayed true to the primitive church and holy fathers. "But, say they, ye have been once of our fellowship, but now ye are become forsakers of your profession, and have departed from us. It is true we have departed from them, and for so doing we both give thanks to Almighty God, and greatly rejoice on our own behalf. But yet for all this, from the primitive Church, from the apostles, and from Christ, we have not departed." So, if they continue to "condemn us for heretics" and label us "schismatics," said Jewel, then we will ask in return: Who really departed from the commandments of Christ and his apostles?[209]

Jewel observed a certain irony in the debate: the papacy claimed to represent the one Catholic Church, and yet it had "forsaken the Greeks" in its schism with the East. How could it claim to be the one universal church when it had discarded and condemned the entire eastern half of Christendom? The Western papacy looked down on the Eastern church with a holy hypocrisy. The Eastern patristics had been excommunicated, but they had "neither private masses, nor mangled sacraments, nor purgatories, nor pardons." Neither did they pride themselves on papal elevation: "As for the titles of high bishops, and those glorious names, they esteem them so as, whosoever he were that would take upon him the same, and would be called either universal bishop, or the head of the universal Church, they make no doubt to call such a one both a passing proud man, a man that worketh despite against all the other bishops his brethren, and a plain heretic."[210]

All in all, the irony was thick: the papacy claimed that the Church of England had departed from the one, holy, catholic, and apostolic church, but in truth it was the papacy who had betrayed both the apostles and the ancient Fathers. "We allure the people to read and to hear God's Word; they drive people from it."[211] Who then was more consistent with the church catholic?

---

208. Jewel, 39.

209. Jewel, 45.

210. Jewel, 45. Jewel was not the only one who appealed to the East. Calvin did the same in his reply to Sadoleto (see chapter 1 of this book).

211. "Let them compare our churches and theirs together, and they shall see that themselves have most shamefully gone from the apostles, and we most justly have gone from them. For we, following the example of Christ, of the apostles, and the holy fathers, give the people the Holy Communion whole and perfect. But these men, contrary to all the fathers, to all the apostles, and contrary to Christ himself, do sever the sacraments, and pluck away the one part from the people, and that with the most notorious sacrilege, as Gelasius termeth it." Jewel, 46. Jewel gave notable attention in the concluding section on whether the pope could err: "For of very truth we have departed from him, whom we saw had blinded the whole world this many an hundred year; from

Christ's Universal Church: John Foxe and History Retold

Jewel claimed that the papacy, not the Reformers, had departed from the one, holy, catholic, and apostolic church, but Foxe added to this apologetic by reclaiming what he considered a right interpretation of history. The papacy painted themselves on the side of the historic church; in contrast, the Reformers were the innovators, the schismatics, the heretics. History itself had been marshaled against them. Protestants in England knew such a narrative firsthand. During Mary's reign, the church, they were told, had returned to the right side of history by returning to the one, true church. With Elizabeth, however, the English Reformers now had a renewed chance to reconsider history's interpretation. "Accused of innovating and novelty," said T. H. L. Parker, "the Reformers were driven back to a study of the past, which could alone disprove the charge."[212]

Consider, for example, John Foxe, who had survived Mary's bloodshed and set out to tell the story of those English Reformers martyred under her reign in his *Actes and Monuments of These Latter and Perilous Days, Touching Matters of the Church* (first published in Latin in 1559).[213] Foxe was no mere reporter collecting the stories of the dead, as the more common title *Foxe's Book of Martyrs* might suggest. He said he was reclaiming history. Granted, it was more than that (e.g., a "manifesto directed against brutal forms of punishment," a "pedigree of the Church of England") but certainly not less.[214] Over against the charge of historical novelty, the Reformers claimed historical continuity. But it took a historian like John Foxe to manifest such continuity within the framework of the English Reformation's recent and bloody history. "It was a belief common to the Reformers," observed Parker, "that they had on their side not only the Bible but also, on the major dogmas at issue, the Church fathers. It was not they who were the innovators; it was the Romanists."[215]

Reframing history, however, proved a challenge since the average Christian living in sixteenth-century England was tempted to consider his or her own era as historic and deviations as modern. In other words, many Englishmen could not imagine a world in which late medieval conceptions of church and dogma were the true innovation, a departure from the catholic. Across England, said Parker, the Reformers "had the stubborn conservatism of the countryman to contend against (and that meant the majority of Englishmen). Innovation covered anything that had not been done 'in my time or my father's time or my grandfather's time'—in other words since about 1490." The English Reformers

---

him, who too far presumptuously was wont to say he could not err, and, whatsoever he did, no mortal man had power to condemn him, neither kings, nor emperors, nor the whole clergy, nor yet all the people in the world together, no, and though he should carry away with him to hell a thousand souls" (57). Jewel also turned to councils of the past to define what marked a true council, building on the examples of past councils, patristic and medieval (see p. 53).

212. Parker, "Introduction," 61.
213. Also *Foxe's Book of Martyrs*.
214. Parker, "Introduction," 64.
215. Parker, 64.

818 *The Formation of Reformed Catholicity*

believed that reading of history ignored the grand innovations certain late medieval thinkers had introduced over against the catholic heritage of the church fathers and early and high medieval eras.

Why, then, was this reading of recent history so popular? The answer: innovations by late medieval thinkers over against the classical Christian heritage did not gain traction all at once but were gradual and progressive over time. "For the learned Reformers, however, 'modern' meant the Lateran Council of 1215. It was precisely this problem that Foxe had in mind. The 'ignorant folk' had been accustomed to *late* medieval Christianity. No one could point to a great upheaval when this brand of religion had come in, because it had very slowly evolved. They had been taught that this was Christianity and they could imagine no other sort."[216]

As chapters 5 and 8 demonstrated, Luther's own story verifies Parker's claim. Gabriel Biel's soteriology was taught in the university, and its mentality was assumed on a wider scale in the popular approach to spirituality and soteriology. Luther's assumed paradigm experienced shock when he considered whether Biel could be out of step with the Augustinian heritage. Whether evangelical sympathizers with Luther in England had the exact same educational experience did not matter. The papal presuppositions and their prevalent influence in the church were systemic, submersing themselves deep in the minds of faithful clergy and laity alike. Yet more important than the institution of the papacy's dogma was the widespread assumption that the bishop of Rome, his cardinals, and their beliefs were the continuous representation of the church universal. Nothing new.

Whether they knew it or not, said Foxe, the sixteenth-century English Christians—and Christians across the Continent as well—absorbed a specific view of history. Yet not just a view of history, an experience of history. Whatever they experienced when they approached the indulgence table, or the altar of the Eucharist, they assumed through it all that they were merely faithful adherents to the church catholic. Foxe, however, was determined to expose that historical misconception by claiming—like other Reformers on the Continent—Rome was the true innovator. But he did so in a unique way: he wrote a new history book. "The history books," commented Parker, "had themselves sprung from this [modern, late medieval] religion and naturally enough treated it as the true faith. Foxe knew that the first need was for Bibles; but he believed that the second need was for history books that would put a different slant on things."[217]

When Foxe set out his agenda before the queen, he was clear that context was the motivator: the English people have been kept in ignorance, but a new history will help them "discern the better between antiquity and novelty."[218] For Foxe and his time, history was instrumental to revealing who was truly in conformity with the gospel and its ancient pedigree of apologists.

---

218. Foxe quoted in Parker, 64.

For example, in his prefatory address "To the True and Faithful Congregation of Christ's Universal Church," Foxe chronicled one papal corruption after another—clerical celibacy, adoration of the sacraments, indulgences, transubstantiation, and more—and concluded they were "new nothings lately coined in the mint of Rome without any stamp of antiquity," which he then said his own, new history would expose.[219]

Foxe admitted that his readers would be tempted to default not to faith but to sight. Upon first impressions, the "Church of Rome" appears to have a rich heritage and, with it, a God-ordained authority. The English would look at her, "so visible and glorious in the eyes of the world, so shining in outward beauty, to bear such a port, to carry such a train and multitude, and to stand in such high authority," and suppose she must be "the only right Catholic mother."[220] That outlook was, however, nothing short of superficial. "For although the right Church of God be not so invisible in the world that none can see it, yet neither is it so visible again that every worldly eye may perceive it."[221] Foxe marshaled his historian outlook to trace the history of the world and showed how often those who claim to be Christ's church are hypocrites. Foxe reminded his Englishmen as well that on not a few occasions those oppressed turned out to be the true church. There is one and only one church, but its long heritage reveals that its true, spiritual members are not represented by Roman bishops but those "repressed by the tyranny of Roman bishops." Nevertheless, God never permitted his church to be "so oppressed" that the gospel itself was extinguished.[222]

Underneath Foxe's bold claim lay that Reformation affirmation of the invisible church, a doctrine clung to when the visible church appeared corrupt, a doctrine appealed to when English evangelicals needed a long view of history. The bishops of Rome claimed the English Reformers were innovators, schismatics, and heretics, but Foxe reversed the claim, "professing one Christ" and "one unity of doctrine," even if in times of oppression they must gather "into one ark of the true Church together."[223]

THE REFORMATION IN SCOTLAND

As the Reformation in England fought for survival during the reigns of Henry and Mary, only to find political stability in Edward and Elizabeth, Reformation ideas also experienced resistance and reception in Scotland.[224] In the 1520s, Luther's writings were smuggled into Scotland, finding a hungry readership.

---

219. Foxe, *To the True and Faithful Congregation of Christ's Universal Church*, 77.

220. Foxe, 77.

221. "For like as is the nature of truth, so is the proper condition of the true Church that commonly none seeth it, but such only as be the members and partakers thereof. And, therefore, they which require that God's holy Church should be evident and visible to the whole world, seem to define the great synagogue of the world, rather than the true spiritual Church of God." Foxe, 78.

222. Foxe, 85.

223. Foxe, 86.

224. For a more extensive survey of the Scottish Reformation, see Donaldson, *Scottish Reformation*.

Like other European countries, Scotland banned Luther's book in 1525, a ban that continued well into the 1530s as well. Parliament said they were heretical, and if caught reading or possessing one of Luther's books, a Scotsman could be prosecuted in the severest of ways. One year after Parliament prohibited Luther's writings, Pope Clement VII congratulated Scotland for exterminating the Lutheran heresy wherever it was found.

The Reformation was slow to get off the ground in Scotland, and Parliament's act against the Lutheran heresy was one reason why. Committing to the Lutheran heresy was a death sentence. But some were willing to take that risk, such as Patrick Hamilton, who studied in Wittenberg only to make his way back to Scotland determined to spread the Lutheran gospel with the Scottish. Hamilton used his studies in Wittenberg to introduce Reformation thought in Scotland. The theses he defended for his degree were published for an English readership and titled *Dyvers Frutful Gatheringes of Scrypture Concernying Fayth and Workes*. Hamilton's attempt to introduce the Lutheran reformation to Scotland was short-lived. In 1528 Hamilton was burned at the stake, and on his way he gave his garments to a young man by the name of John Knox and reminded him that these bitter flames were the gateway to life everlasting. The memory of Hamilton going to the flames with such resolve left an impression on Knox, which Knox recounted in his *History of the Reformation in Scotland*.[225]

Almost two decades later another Protestant by the name of George Wishart also met the flames (March 1, 1546).[226] Although he remained in Scotland for around ten years, he eventually left for England. The migration from Scotland to England was not uncommon. Those who converted to Lutheran beliefs hoped the English might be more tolerable. Such an exodus, however, meant that the evangelical movement in Scotland was almost imperceptible. However, England was not a tolerant home for Scottish evangelicals, as Wishart discovered on arrival. He was captured and pressured to recant his evangelical convictions. If he had not, he would have been martyred in England. Despite his recantation, Wishart was resilient, returning to Scotland to start afresh.

Around 1544 the renewed Scotsman became public about his evangelical faith. The timing was, once again, unfortunate for the longevity of Wishart's reformation. After the death of King James V in 1542, Cardinal Beaton and James, Earl of Arran, a Protestant sympathizer, contested for control. But by 1546 Beaton had the upper hand, and Wishart was incarcerated in Beaton's castle. This time Wishart refused to recant and was burned at the stake in St. Andrews. He was executed for his religious convictions. However, committing to Protestantism was also political, a decision to side with James, Earl of Arran, and by default with the English, with whom James desired a closer alliance.[227]

---

225. Knox, *History of the Reformation in Scotland*, 1:76–78. Knox was not alone; John Foxe also recounted Hamilton's martyrdom in his *Actes and Monuments*. Cf. Hillerbrand, *Division of Christendom*, 354ff.

226. Some speculate whether Wishart was present at Hamilton's martyrdom.

227. On the political contest between Beaton and James, as well as the surprise invasion of Beaton's castle

Although the Scots lost Hamilton and Wishart, in the years ahead they gained a longer evangelical ministry at the plow of John Knox (ca. 1513–72).

THE MAKING OF JOHN KNOX

Wishart's martyrdom left an indelible mark on Knox. Wishart had become a spiritual father to Knox, who in turn became Wishart's devoted follower. Wishart taught Knox core *loci* of Reformation theology, from *sola fide* to *sola scriptura*. Knowing Wishart owned a personal translation of the *First Helvetic Confession* (1536), a confession that influenced his sermons, Knox likely also became familiar with the evangelical beliefs in the confession.[228]

Among those evangelical contours, Wishart imparted to Knox his understanding of the invisible church. Wishart (and Knox after him) agreed with the medieval fathers that no salvation exists outside mother church. However, Wishart also believed that the invisible church may be small, even indiscernible in times of persecution. That explains why Wishart, like the prophets of old, could call out the visible church in Scotland for its corruptions and idolatry, all the while confident that he and his followers were God's elect, part of the church catholic.[229]

These theological contours and others were passed down to Knox, but so was Wishart's style of preaching. Wishart took up the methods of Old Testament prophets, first warning the nation that God's judgment was imminent, then predicting what the future held in store.[230] Such warnings and prophecies were delivered through a fiery, animated sermon designed not merely to teach the mind but also to move the affections.

The details surrounding Knox's turn from Rome to the Reformation remain abstruse. What is certain is that the transformation occurred once Knox was introduced to Wishart's preaching in 1545. By the following year, Knox appears to have been a devout follower of Wishart. In the weeks leading up to Wishart's arrest and martyrdom, Knox went public with his allegiance to Wishart, walking in front of the prophet carrying a large sword for dramatic effect.[231] Although Knox did not use the sword himself, spiritual warfare was a theme Knox returned to throughout his preaching career, even becoming a default metaphor framing his attacks against the devil's soldiers, whether papal or magisterial.[232]

Wishart was executed as a one-off—Beaton determined to make an example out of him—but his disciples assumed their own lives could be in danger.

---

and assassination of Beaton himself all after Whishart's death, see Hillerbrand, *Division of Christendom*, 355; Dawson, *John Knox*, 38–41.

228. Wishart translated the confession and had his own personal copy, although the confession itself was not yet widely circulated. Dawson, *John Knox*, 32.

229. Dawson, 28, 32–33.

230. On Wishart's prophecies and Knox's confidence that such prophecies were fulfilled, see Dawson, 35.

231. "These staged entrances to demonstrate the preacher's importance probably came easily to a man who grew adept at recreating dramatic scenes in words." Dawson, 29.

232. Dawson observes instances when Knox used the military metaphor to attack the Mass. Dawson, 30. Cf. Knox, *History*, 2:12.

If Cardinal Beaton wanted, he could come after Knox next. Beaton, however, met his own end in May 1546, not long after Wishart met his. Beaton had his enemies, both English and Scottish. Certain Scotsmen—Norman Leslie and Melville of Carnbee in particular—came together in a plot against Beaton. If they could take Beaton out, surely the English would come to their aid. Barely two months after the execution of Wishart, assassins crept into the St. Andrews castle and into Beaton's own room. After they stabbed Beaton, they proceeded to commandeer the St. Andrews castle.[233] They now controlled the castle, but they were shut in once Regent Arran heard the news and surrounded the castle with his troops. A long, tortuous battle ensued with no sign of a clear victor.

Where was Knox during the siege? Longniddry, East Lothian. Knox took on a position as a tutor. He must have been relieved to hear Beaton was dead, but that relief could not have lasted long once Knox discovered that John Hamilton took up the baton to hunt down Scottish evangelicals in the spring of 1547.[234] As a recognized follower of Wishart and his anti-papist polemic, Knox was an obvious target. The Reformer decided he and his students might find security within the walls of St. Andrews castle, however perilous the siege might be. Knox continued tutoring his students and providing a running commentary on the Scriptures in the chapel each day, not far from the same place Wishart had been executed. Although Knox was summoned to become a preacher in the castle, he declined. But when he was publicly pressured by Henry Balnaves and John Rough, he reconsidered and preached what may have been his first sermon.[235]

The decision to become a preacher came with no little turmoil. The young Knox inside the castle under siege was not yet the confident, seasoned Knox of decades later. He had doubts: The Holy Spirit used Wishart, but could the Spirit use him to preach the Word as well? Could Knox have the prophet-like authority embodied by his mentor Wishart?[236] In time Knox realized these early fears had little warrant, especially as his confidence in God's call increased. He never did acquire a degree, but his preaching exhibited a rhetorical persuasion few contemporaries could rival, perhaps surpassing Wishart himself. Knox, like a lot of Reformers, knew the Scriptures well, but he also knew how to preach the Scriptures in the pulpit in a style that was both convincing and inspiring. He was no quiet commentator on the Scriptures but a fiery preacher whose voice boomed fearful admonitions, and in a day without the technology of microphones.

Following Wishart's lead, Knox interpreted his call through the paradigm of Old Testament prophets. The Lord commissioned Ezekiel, saying, "I have made you a watchman for the house of Israel. Whenever you hear a word from

---

233. Fuller details are narrated by Dawson, *John Knox*, 39–40.

234. Hamilton was related to Regent Arran, his half brother.

235. Dawson concludes that Rough blackmailed Knox through public embarrassment. The call to preach was urgent; Rough was desperate for a preacher who could challenge Dean Annand's defense of papal doctrine at Holy Trinity, a preaching match that eventually turned into a more private disputation at St Leonard's College Yards Church. See *John Knox*, 42–50.

236. For Knox's own account, see his *History*, 1:104. Cf. Dawson, *John Knox*, 44.

my mouth, you shall give them a warning from me" (Ezek. 3:17). Like Ezekiel, Knox considered himself God's watchman, sent to an obstinate people. From the pulpit, Knox not only preached evangelical doctrine but decried papist beliefs as idolatrous and with no little bombast. On his deathbed, Knox defended the motives behind his staunch rhetoric: "I know that many have complained much and loudly . . . of my great severity; but God knows that my mind was always free from hatred to the persons of those against whom I denounced the heavy judgments of God. . . . Therefore, I profess before God and his holy angels, that I never made gain of the sacred word of God, that I never studied to please men, never indulged my own private passions or those of others, but faithfully distributed my talent entrusted to my care for the edification of the church over which I did watch."[237]

Despite his promising start, in the summer of 1547 Knox's preaching came to an abrupt conclusion when French galleys invaded and conquered the St. Andrews castle. The English never did come to the rescue, which allowed France's new king, Henry II, to capitalize on the English absence by commissioning Leon Strozzi to attack by sea. Knox was taken prisoner and forced to row *Our Lady, Notre Dame*, where his trust in God's providence was put to the test. Hope of deliverance seemed to vanish as quickly as Scottish soil.[238] Labor in the galleys was brutal, breaking down the slave's body with rowing, accompanied by the whip of a master, only to be nourished by ship food (bread, water, and some vegetables). Many a slave expected to die. Yet the hardships were not only physical but spiritual. Knox and the other prisoners were told to attend Mass, recite the *Salve Regina*, and kiss an image of the Virgin. All three evangelicals on board refused to participate, and Knox himself became so antagonistic that he threw the Virgin into the water, commanding her to save herself.[239] He encouraged his fellow prisoners to trust in God's deliverance instead. Even when ill and close to death, he believed God would return him to Scotland to preach once again.

CONFLICT WITH CRANMER: KNOX AND THE RADICAL WING

At last Knox found deliverance in the spring of 1549, thanks to the English and their negotiations with the French. What a bright day that must have been when Knox put his two feet on soil, no longer a slave but a free man. Except the soil was not Scottish but English, Berwick to be exact. The timing was ideal: Knox entered England under the reign of Edward VI and the leadership of Thomas Cranmer, both Protestants encouraging evangelical reform. In Berwick Knox had the freedom to engage a working-class ministry with his evangelical preaching. Yet such freedom did not mean Knox did not protest in his own way.

---

237. Cited in Hillerbrand, *Division of Christendom*, 364.
238. On the experience, see his prayers in Hillerbrand, 357.
239. A Scotsman is mentioned, but it's likely he was Knox. Knox, *History*, 1:108. Cf. Dawson, *John Knox*, 56.

The year Knox arrived in Berwick was the same year the first *Book of Common Prayer* was put into practice. For all its evangelical contours, Knox still took issue and decided at points in the liturgy not to use the book, the Lord's Supper marking one of those critical points.[240]

Knox did not stay at Berwick long; in the spring of 1550 he made his way to Newcastle, where he no doubt caught the attention of Cuthbert Tunstal by calling the Mass a wicked abomination, even idolatry itself.[241] Knox certainly knew how to combine "vehement passion" with his "talent for identifying an enemy," says Dawson.[242] That combination never faded but followed Knox his whole life through. His ministry in Newcastle revealed his location on the pendulum of Reformers: as much as he aligned with the center point of the Reformation, he demonstrated again and again that he was most comfortable swinging to the far-right edge. England, perhaps more than other countries influenced by the Reformation, exposed that tendency in Knox.[243] In a roomful of Reformers, he was always the one advocating for the most aggressive, inflexible strategy. Knox's outlook was "black and white"—anything else was blasphemy.[244] His intolerance for adiaphora revealed his estimation of himself: he was not so much a theologian as a prophet denouncing the Antichrist. And he draped his polemical posture in the regulative principle, accepting nothing unless it was commanded by Scripture. "No honoring knaweth God, nor will accept, without it have the express commandment of his awn Word" so that everything "addit to the religioun of God, without his own express commandment, is Idolatrie." [245]

Few instances demonstrate Knox's radical approach more than his confrontation with Thomas Cranmer over the *Second Book of Common Prayer*. Knox had considerable freedom to amend the *Book of Common Prayer* when he pastored in the north of England, but as he made his way south and entered London, he discovered that his freedom was unique. Compliance with the *Book of Common Prayer* was expected. This proved unacceptable to Knox, who took issue with kneeling at the Lord's Supper.

In the fall of 1552, Knox made his opinion known when he preached at Windsor Castle. The *Second Book of Common Prayer* had already been approved by Parliament; nevertheless, after Knox's critical sermon, the prayer book mysteriously stopped being printed.[246] Cranmer's response was a dagger in the heart of Knox, calling the Scotsman and his followers unquiet spirits only concerned with their own fancies. Knox was a troublemaker and at the worst time, just

---

240. Knox "wrote his own prayers for at least part of the communion service." Dawson, *John Knox*, 60. Cf. Knox, *Works*, 5:480.

241. Knox, *A Vindication of the Doctrine That the Sacrifice of Mass Is Idolatry*, 3:33–70.

242. Dawson, *John Knox*, 61.

243. Dawson calls Knox and his camp the "radical wing of the Edwardian Church." Dawson, 63.

244. Trueman, "The Theology of the English Reformers," 171.

245. Cited in Wright, "The Scottish Reformation," 179.

246. "As a result the Privy Council instructed the printer to halt production of the book until 'certain faults' could be corrected." Dawson, 73.

when the country was achieving unprecedented peace and Protestant prosperity. Cranmer was not only a shrewd ecclesiastical politician but a theologian as well, refuting Knox's case against kneeling, one argument at a time.[247] In the end, the council supported Cranmer, and Knox took a heavy blow to his reputation in England.

Knox did not take defeat well. Although he initially capitulated, writing to his previous churches, instructing them to kneel rather than sit, he did so with reluctance and bitterness. The Cranmer dustup had an effect on Knox as he considered his future in England. When he considered opportunities to pastor (e.g., Rochester, London), refusal became a habit.[248] Taking note of his conflict with Cranmer, Knox at least understood that conformity to the Church of England would be required. English evangelicals who patiently suffered through Henry's reign considered Edward VI and the reforms that followed at the hands of Cranmer a welcome and encouraging sign of improvement. Knox, however, focused his attention not on what was accomplished but instead on everything still to be done and anything that he considered lingering remnants of Rome. That focus left Knox discontent at the pace of reform, frustrated by what he could only consider a deficiency in commitment.

English evangelicals laboring to make changes were offended by Knox. While gradualism was a wise strategy in the eyes of many English evangelicals, Knox considered it a sin. His approach could not have been more disagreeable to English evangelicals. "If a nail needed driving home the Scot reached for a sledgehammer; if salt were needed to cleanse and scour, then he picked up a shovel."[249] When Mary Tudor rose to the throne in 1553 and returned the country to Catholicism, Knox interpreted her persecution of English Protestants—treasonous as it was in his eyes—as God's judgment against such evangelical gradualism, a drum he was happy to beat in his *A Faithful Admonishment*.

Whether God's judgment or not, English Protestants and foreigners alike had a decision to make: stay and face persecution or flee elsewhere. Since Knox had chosen the career of a roaming preacher, he did not feel the same sense of obligation to stay like some pastors. That did not stop Knox from exercising a pastoral tone of discipline when he discovered soon enough that church members in his past congregations were returning to the beliefs and practices of the papacy rather than facing punishment for their evangelical convictions. He wrote them stern letters, threatening them with the fires of hell itself should they

---

247. Both MacCulloch and Dawson argue that Cranmer dismantled Knox's argument. MacCulloch, *Cranmer*, 529; Dawson, *John Knox*, 73. The entire incident led to the insertion of the "Black Rubric" when the Prayer Book was printed toward the end of the year.

248. I will not dwell on Knox's ministry in Northumberland and the context surrounding Rochester and All Hallows in London; see Dawson, *John Knox*, 76–77.

249. Dawson, 79. See, for example, the conflict between William Cecil and Knox (77–79). Dawson also observes differences between Knox and Cranmer in their approach to medieval ecclesiology: "Cranmer had attempted a complete overhaul of medieval canon law to make it fit for its new Protestant purpose within the Church of England. Despite, or perhaps because of, his notarial background a new canon law never appealed to Knox" (79).

continue. His words were just as condemning toward those who tried to have both conformity to Mary's Catholicism in externals but allegiance to evangelical beliefs in secret.[250]

Although departing England may have been bitter for Knox, the Reformer never did abandon his great love for the English people and partly considered himself one of them, even if by accident. That may in part explain Knox's never-ending concern with England's "idolatry" and Knox's self-assigned prerogative to call out that idolatry wherever it be—the church or the magistrate—even though he was a Scotsman by birth.

A NEW CATHAR? SCHISM IN FRANKFURT

Knox's future was uncertain once Mary ascended the throne. He escaped to Europe for a time, visiting different Reformation outlets, from Calvin's Geneva to Bullinger's Zurich. Knox had questions, such as, could civil rebellion against Mary Tudor be justified since she was Catholic and female and her ascension to the throne was questionable? Not all Reformers Knox encountered were entirely comfortable answering questions like these. That was not unreasonable considering their unfamiliarity with Knox's intentions and the volatile situation not only in England but other countries as well. They certainly did not want their names attached to a rebel resistance group if Knox did decide to go revolutionary.[251]

Knox intended on staying in Geneva, but then he received an invitation in the fall of 1554 to pastor a congregation of English exiles in Frankfurt, a city off the River Main, north of Strasbourg. Pressured by Calvin, Knox agreed, although not without his own reservations. Not long after his arrival in Frankfurt, controversy plagued the congregation over the 1552 *Book of Common Prayer*. Knox continued his criticisms of the prayer book, this time accompanied by William Whittingham.

However, others who had been living in England when the prayer book was originally published disagreed. To revise the prayer book now was premature and could send a disheartening message to those in England still trying to stay faithful to the evangelical faith. Imagine how discouraging such news would be to Cranmer as he languished in his cell, awaiting torture and probably death. Could not the same news be a stab in the backs of Ridley or even Latimer?

This argument was put forward by men in Frankfurt such as John Bale, but Reformers and churches across the European scene sympathized with it as well, including Heinrich Bullinger as well as Peter Martyr Vermigli, who had fled England. Like all church splits, this one turned ugly as both sides lowered themselves to name-calling, Knox calling his opponents papists, for example (and everyone knew what Knox thought of papists). Beale returned the insult with

---

250. Dawson concludes that Knox took the return to Rome as a "personal blow" that conveyed he was a "miserable failure." The result: depression. Dawson, 84.

251. On the interaction between Knox and the Reformers, see Dawson, 86–87. Cf. Knox, *Works*, 3:221–26.

biting satire against the self-righteousness of Knox, labeling the Scotsman a new Cathar (Cathars were medieval separatists the church pronounced unorthodox; see chapter 7).[252]

Knox and Whittingham attempted to cut off their opposition by taking the first step toward recruiting an ally who could pressure the congregation at Frankfurt to acquiesce. Calvin was chosen, but his letter to the congregation was not entirely supportive. He rebuked both sides for creating and cultivating such severe disunity, especially in exile. Calvin learned about Knox's inflexible temperament and uncompromising demand for revision, and concluded that Knox and Whittingham were to blame for their harshness. But Bale and his supporters were also to blame for their unwillingness to consider revision where revision was necessary or even inevitable if Mary had never become queen.[253]

A painful series of committee meetings followed, each attempting to resolve the church split. However, when Richard Cox and his supporters landed in Frankfurt, Knox was defeated and quickly had to leave Frankfurt, especially when the charges escalated to treason, an offense punishable by death if one was found guilty. Although the Communion was a total defeat for Knox as he left Frankfurt, it did push him to envision a Reformed liturgy that could one day find a home in Scotland.[254]

Knox had created a host of enemies—not only Cox and Bale but Edmund Grindal and John Jewel as well. The Scotsman was considered a liability. His polemically charged rhetoric and his inflexible stance on the prayer book had all the potential of putting English evangelicals at risk for more serious persecution than necessary. Knox was also labeled a schismatic, a label lobbed by fellow evangelicals committed to reform. These charges stayed with Knox for the rest of his life as he struggled to trust other evangelicals, especially if they possessed politically embedded roles in ecclesiastical leadership.[255]

ITINERANCY IN SCOTLAND

Knox found a way to be subtle and slip into Scotland. Subtlety never did suit Knox; not long after arriving in his homeland, the Scotsman started preaching, and although he did not plan on a temporary itinerancy across Scotland, his presence naturally invited one. Knox continued his preaching against the "idolatry" of the Roman Mass, which was abrasive for Scottish evangelicals still wrestling with the implications of their newfound faith.[256] Still, Knox's preaching created a sizable following, and he became a coveted preacher across Scotland.

---

252. Dawson, *John Knox*, 96–97.

253. *CO* 15:2091. Dawson, *John Knox*, 92–96, outlines the debate in far more detail. Thanks to the Goodman papers, a window into this controversy and Knox's time in Frankfurt has been opened.

254. For the series of events that precipitated Knox's exile, including Knox's fiery sermons against the prayer book and Cox's position, see Dawson, *John Knox*, 100–108.

255. Dawson, 108.

256. "Most had come slowly to accept Protestant doctrines while remaining part of normal parish life within their Catholic country. Although they met for Bible-reading and prayers, Protestant sacraments were

If Knox was entertaining the possibility of staying in Scotland, then the Reformer was caught in a tension. A segment of the Frankfurt congregation that supported Knox moved to Geneva for a fresh start. This congregation of English exiles called Knox to be their pastor, alongside Christopher Goodman, a compatible pastor and one of Knox's closest friends. When the English exiles in Geneva summoned Knox to return and begin his tenure, he was torn between unanticipated success preaching in his homeland and a new ministry shepherding English exiles. Despite his influence in Scotland, no permanent position demanded that Knox stay. By contrast, the English exiles had been dedicated to Knox since controversy in Frankfurt, and in 1556 they were ready for Knox to lead them in Geneva.

Meanwhile, persecution intensified in England, and some English evangelicals apostatized. Not knowing when or if persecution might spread, the potential pressure of persecution created no little anxiety among English exiles across Europe. English evangelicals had fled their country to escape persecution; now they had to consider whether their faith could withstand torture and even death if persecution followed them. Although troubling, none of this surprised Knox. Of course the Antichrist was on the hunt, picking off anyone unprepared to fight against the devil's schemes, said Knox.[257] The exiles in Geneva showed signs of hope, characterized more by anticipation than fear. Nevertheless, they needed Knox to return to Geneva to guide them.

When Knox left Scotland for Geneva in 1556, a foreboding image warned him not to return: an effigy in his honor. Scottish Catholics in Edinburgh turned the burning of the effigy into a public affair. The message was ominous: if Knox came back to Scotland, his fate would be the same as that of his mentor Wishart. The portentous message, however, did not keep Knox from trying. He was not in Geneva long when he decided he must temporarily return to Scotland in 1557 and fortify the evangelical movement even if it meant burning at the stake.

Yet Scotland was not the only country dangerous for evangelicals. Knox was putting his life at risk by passing through France by way of Dieppe. In the summer of 1557, for example, the Edict of Compiègne threatened Huguenots; Henry II hung capital punishment over every Huguenot head should he catch them practicing the evangelical faith or contacting allies for support. In the fall of 1557, Knox decided it was time, and his congregation figured they might never see Knox again, which created an emotional goodbye for many who did not want to lose their pastor.

That fear was not unrealistic. In Rue St. Jacques, Huguenots were arrested, and during their incarceration, expecting death was near, they wrote an *Apology*.

not available and an underground church had not been organized.... Knox's tough anti-Nicodemite position gave Scottish Protestants a jolt." Dawson, 114.

257. Knox's "violent language" reveals his "holy hatred" for his Catholic enemies, says Dawson, interpreting his battle with them through an "apocalyptic framework." Dawson, 124.

Knox played a hand in the *Apology*'s publication by providing a commentary on the many patristic quotations and a preface that advocated freedom of worship on behalf of the Huguenots.[258] Persecution in 1557, however, was not limited to France; John Hamilton roamed Scotland, looking to squelch any signs of a Reformation spirit. Toward the beginning of 1558, Knox decided he should return to Geneva; the Reformer must have wondered whether he would see his brothers and sisters in Scotland again.

FIRST BLAST AGAINST THE MONSTROUS REGIMENT OF WOMEN

The ferocity of persecution only further motivated Knox to opposition, targeting the female rulers who led England and Scotland into Catholic "idolatry." Scotland was a country wrapped in political turmoil over Mary Stuart. She had Tudor blood running through her veins since her grandmother, Margaret Tudor, was sister to Henry VIII. Margaret was married to James IV of Scotland. Their son, James V (Stuart), also became king of Scotland. James V married Mary of Guise, and they had a daughter, Mary, Queen of Scots. However, just after Mary's birth, James died. With an infant queen, Scotland had to be governed by a regent. Mary of Guise became a regent who nurtured an alliance with France. In 1558 a political marriage was formed between her daughter, Mary Stuart, and the future king, Francis II.[259] That did not bode well for evangelicals in Scotland since French influence could only result in the permanent dominance of Catholicism, so they thought.[260]

That year, 1558, was the same year Knox published his most aggressive tract: *First Blast against the Monstrous Regiment of Women*.[261] Unlike Calvin, who wrote amicable letters to female rulers and saw Old Testament precedent for a female sovereign, Knox opposed female rulers with vitriolic intensity and relentless detestation.[262] It could not be God's will for a female to be in such a position

---

258. For the letter, see Knox, *Works*, 4:297–347. Cf. Dawson, *John Knox*, 132.

259. However, from the 1540s to the 1570s, the longstanding French connection with Scotland also became a channel for French Reformed influence as well. Lindberg makes a case for the French connection in particular: "The Scottish-French connection extended back to the thirteenth century and had been reaffirmed on the eve of the Reformation through the marriage of James V to Mary of Guise. The French crown employed Scottish mercenary archers. French monastic orders had daughter houses in Scotland. Scottish scholars taught in French universities. Knox himself was fluent in French, and preached in the Reformed churches in France. Also, the national church organization in France, in contrast to the city organization of Geneva, was more amenable to the Scottish situation. Finally, there is the circumstantial argument that the Scots confession and discipline bears close affinity to that of the French Huguenots." Lindberg, *European Reformations*, 331.

260. In past decades, Scotland was no safe haven for Protestants. Yet the Scottish nobility of the 1550s was far more interested in the opinions, strategies, and influence of England than France. Scottish nobility were now curious whether they could appropriate the evangelical message in Scotland to gain political advantage over Mary. Hillerbrand, *Division of Christendom*, 358.

261. Knox opened with these inflammatory words: "To promote a woman to bear rule, superiority, dominion or empire above any realm, nation or city is repugnant to nature, contumely to God, a thing most contrarious to His revealed will and approved ordinance, and finally it is the subversion of good order, of all equity and justice." Knox, *First Blast of the Trumpet*, 8.

262. E.g., see Calvin's letter to Cecil, January 28, 1559, *ZL* 2:34–36. Cf. Dawson, *John Knox*, 142.

of power over men. Also, these women—Mary Tudor in particular—were not Protestants but Catholic "idolaters" bent on destroying the Protestant elect.[263]

Knox began with an appeal to nature, an appeal he believed exposed the inferiority of the female, both in mind and in body. "Nature, I say, doth paint them [female] forth to be weak, frail, impatient, feeble, and foolish; and experience hath declared them to be inconstant, variable, cruel and lacking the spirit of counsel and regiment. . . . The law [of nature] doth moreover pronounce womankind to be most avaricious (which is a vice intolerable in those that should rule or minister justice)."[264]

Next Knox appealed to Scripture and concluded that Scripture "permitteth no woman to rule above man." A woman "in the seat of God" (government), reigning and ruling above men, is not only a "monster in nature," but a "thing most regnant to His will and ordinance."[265] For Knox, a woman ruler is not only unnatural but sinful. "I say that the erecting of a woman to that honour is not only to invert the order which God hath established, but also it is to defile, pollute and profane . . . the throne and seat of God which He hath sanctified and appointed for man only."[266] Politically, a woman ruler is traitorous; religiously, a woman ruler is idolatrous.[267] When Knox turned his disdain toward the queen of England, he concluded his *First Blast* by calling her "that horrible monster Jezebel of England," a reference to that Old Testament ruler who killed God's prophets and led God's people into idolatry (1 Kings 18).[268]

Knox's ongoing outcry against these "monstrous" women was poor tactics and even worse timing in the opinion of many other Reformers. As mentioned, the year 1558 happened to be the same year English Protestants finally found relief from Mary and her bloody persecutions due to the rise of Elizabeth to the English throne. The smell of flesh burning still lingered in the air, and the screams of fellow evangelicals scarred the memories of English Protestants. But Elizabeth was a new hope for the advancement of the Reformation in England. When she learned of Knox's attack on "monstrous women," she took serious offense at his acerbic remarks against female rulers. Her offense could only result in disfavor and distrust toward evangelicals who were in some way associated with Knox. When Calvin heard about the *First Blast*, he cringed. He was not alone in his reaction; John Foxe blushed as well. And John Foxe chided his friend

---

263. Female rulers who came under Knox's condemnation across his preaching career included Mary Tudor (England), Mary Stuart (France), and Mary of Guise (Scotland), Knox's "unholy trinity of Marys." Lindberg, *European Reformations*, 332.

264. Knox, *First Blast of the Trumpet*, 9, 11. Knox continued, saying such avarice makes women illogical and untrustworthy: "I might adduce histories proving some women to have died for sudden joy; some for unpacience to have murdered themselves . . . and some to have been so desirous of dominion that for the obtaining of the same they have murdered the children of their own sons. Yea, and some have killed with cruelty their own husbands and children" (11).

265. Knox, *First Blast of the Trumpet*, 14, 15.

266. Knox, *First Blast of the Trumpet*, 28.

267. Knox, *First Blast of the Trumpet*, 43.

268. Knox, *First Blast of the Trumpet*, 46.

for such a harsh polemic that lacked ecclesiastical sensitivity, especially after everything English Protestants had been through with Mary.[269]

Foxe's frustration with Knox reveals that not all Reformers across the Continent responded to female sovereigns the way Knox did. So why did Knox react the way he did? While many reasons could be listed, one of them is hermeneutical. Knox appealed to Paul, who told Timothy that women should not be pastors. However, that logic was not limited to the pastorate but extended to all of society, at least according to Knox. Under that assumption, an appeal to the Old Testament seemed entirely appropriate. A king like David, for example, not only was responsible for the spiritual state of his people but also wielded the sword for their protection. In his *First Blast*, Knox assumed there was little discontinuity between ancient Israel and a country like England, which led him to directly appeal to the Old Testament to discount female rulers.[270]

That hermeneutic also led Knox to ask whether a people under a tyrant could rebel. In Knox's estimation, a female ruler was by definition a tyrant, and if a tyrant was on the throne, then the people of God not only possessed the right but the responsibility to revolt. Some historians ask whether Knox may have been more aligned, on this point at least, with the radicals than the Reformers. "Echoing Thomas Müntzer and the Münsterites, Knox suggests that the religious duty to revolt is incumbent on all true Christians."[271] His radical spirit of rebellion was not merely targeted at consciences in England but transferred to Scotland as well. The Reformer was not only protesting but giving the Scottish a free conscience should they decide to revolt. They were not obligated, in the estimation of Knox, to be subservient to the queen if the queen was against the Reformation. Her hostility toward true religion—tyranny!—justified insurrection.[272] Needless to say, Knox was considered a serious threat.

The consequences were extensive. Under the purview of Queen Elizabeth, not only Knox and Goodman but all English exiles in Geneva now lived under opprobrium because of *First Blast*. To make matters worse, all of Geneva, especially John Calvin, now sat under Elizabeth's contempt since Geneva was responsible for printing the *First Blast* (with Calvin unaware). Worse still, all those congregations marked by Knox's fingerprints came under suspicion as well. The weight of these consequences eventually affected Knox when he stated the obvious: "My First Blast hath blowne from me all my friends in England."[273] Instead of repairing the breached relations broken with Reformers, Knox acted caught off guard, as if he did not understand why they were (or should be) upset

---

269. How did the manuscript get published in Geneva in the first place, then? "Being written in English, which Calvin could not read, the tract was able to slip through the normal checks." Dawson, *John Knox*, 145.

270. Doing so, however, put Knox in an awkward position: he had to somehow explain why there were female rulers from time to time (e.g., Deborah). Knox, *First Blast of the Trumpet*, 36–42.

271. Lindberg, *European Reformations*, 333. Although, Dawson did not think Knox went quite so far as to advocate revolution, at least in his *Letter to the Commonalty*. Dawson, *John Knox*, 160.

272. Hillerbrand, *Division of Christendom*, 358.

273. Knox, *Works* 6:14. Cf. Dawson, *John Knox*, 170.

with him. Then he dug his heels in deeper, cultivating his initial resistance, but this time to Elizabeth, who was Protestant.

In Knox's mind, *First Blast* was not intended to position himself as a seditious revolutionary, but Elizabeth could not help seeing him in any other light. Even when Knox wrote an apology to Elizabeth, she poured scorn all over it, unable to take it seriously.[274] The damage was irreparable.

IDOLATRY: ICONOCLASM IN PERTH, CRISIS IN EDINBURGH

The year preceding Knox's *First Blast* certainly primed the pump for an uprising. In 1557 churches came together—calling themselves the Congregations of Christ—and by means of a covenant swore to defend the evangelical church against oppression. That next year (1558), Walter Mill was burned at the stake, which infuriated Scottish Protestants and led to increased support of the covenant. [275] In 1559 Mary of Guise hardened in her pursuit of a French alliance and Catholic allegiance. She turned even more hostile toward Scottish Protestants by declaring them not only heretics but outlaws whom she had every right to execute.[276] If the situation was not already as ripe as it could be for civil war, Knox's sudden return to Scotland in 1559 gave the Scottish Protestants confidence to keep moving forward. Knox toured Scotland, preaching passionate sermons, reassuring Protestant congregations they were right to resist Catholic oppression.

His most significant sermon was delivered on May 11, 1559. The Scottish Reformers traveled to Stirling to meet with regent Mary of Guise, but Knox and a large following stayed in Perth. As they waited, he preached another one of his fiery sermons against the idolatry of the papists. The time for waiting was over, said Knox. Idolatry in the church could no longer be tolerated. With his sermon preached, the Scottish Reformation had begun. But unlike previous sermons, this one resulted in a violent iconoclastic riot. The chaos combusted in severe damage, all in the name of destroying idols. Everything that represented papal beliefs and practices was smashed and burned.[277] Notable is the link between religion and politics: even though iconoclasm raged in the name of destroying idolatry, political overtones were present as politicians with animosity toward France backed the Congregation of Christ.[278]

From this point forward, a battle had begun, and the Lords of the Congregation now had to prepare to fight. For the duration of the battles that ensued, Knox and his family lived in St. Andrews. Yet the Scotsman was anything but stationary. As army chaplain, Knox preached sermons before major battles to rally the troops, commanding them to put their faith in God, and if

---

274. For Knox's 1559 letter, see Knox, *Works* 6:47–51. Cf. Dawson, *John Knox*, 173.

275. Hillerbrand, *Division of Christendom*, 358.

276. The door opened between Mary and the French in April 1559 due to the Peace of Cateau-Cambrèsis. Hillerbrand, 359.

277. See, e.g., the iconoclasm at the Grey Friars. Hillerbrand, 359. For Knox's account, see his *History*, 1:163. For a reconciliation between Knox's different accounts, see Dawson, *John Knox*, 180–82.

278. Hillerbrand, *Division of Christendom*, 360.

their faith was sincere and sufficient, their God would fight for them and give them the victory. Knox was the prophet, the evangelical soldiers were Israel, and the French troops were the idolatrous nations who proved no match for Yahweh.

In the summer of 1559, the Protestants occupied Edinburgh, but they needed substantial support. They turned to Queen Elizabeth and warned her that if the Congregation was defeated in battle, England could be the next target. When peace negotiations were reached in Edinburgh, Elizabeth at least decided to lend monetary support. After the truce in Edinburgh, Protestants had to leave the city, but as soon as they heard French troops had landed in Scotland, the Protestants returned to Edinburgh with renewed vigor. The decision was devastating: the Protestants were defeated and humiliated. Knox rebuked the Congregation of Christ, as if the loss was due to a lack of faith, not a lack of numbers.[279] All seemed lost. Then, in January 1560, the English navy was spotted off the coast, and by April Elizabeth's army enforced its presence as well, both of which breathed new life into a Scottish Congregation that was fighting on death's door. The timing was impeccable.

In the summer of 1560, Mary of Guise died. Knox interpreted her illness and death as God's judgment, and he rejoiced that another blow had been delivered against Antichrist. Once again Knox's rhetoric polarized his colleagues. Although they were enemies of Mary of Guise, nevertheless, they respected the dying regent as Scotsmen.[280] With victory in hand, Knox preached to Parliament, calling the country to rebuild Scotland as Haggai rebuilt the temple, ridding the country of papal idolatry, establishing in its place a Reformed commonwealth.

The unexpected and pivotal support of England in the Congregation's darkest hour was the dawn of a new horizon. Knox had now ministered in both countries and, as a result of his own condemning tracts, may have wondered if he was a prophet of judgment only, never to see the evangelical cause triumph. Knox experienced not only the return of Protestantism in both countries but a renewed toleration and cooperation between them, one that not only kept France in check but also strengthened the rise of the Protestant religion after a long hour of Catholic persecution.

FROM CLEANSING TO BUILDING A REFORMED KIRK: JEWEL VERSUS KNOX

The Scottish church did not change overnight; many Scottish hearts were still loyal to the Catholic faith. Reformation may have been officially approved, but Knox believed several measures had to be taken to renovate the religious structure, from the liturgy to doctrine.

Tearing down "idolatry" required a fiery, obstinate disposition. However, reconstructing the church demanded a patient, careful strategy. Disagreement

---

279. Hillerbrand, 360–61.
280. For Knox's own words, see his *History*, 1:322, 329. Cf. Dawson, *John Knox*, 190.

emerged over what strategy was best. Knox's vision was the same totalizing approach as before: every visage of idolatry must be removed and an exact order of worship and discipline substituted. John Jewel wrote a letter to Peter Martyr Vermigli using satire to criticize the all-or-nothing inflexibility of Knox. Jewel, who ascended the list of Knox's nemeses back in Frankfurt, considered Knox's methods primitive. He compared the Scotsman and his disciples to the Scythians, those Greeks who drank themselves to death by refusing to dilute their strong wine. Knox did the same with his reforming methods, refusing to accommodate lest he dilute his own ideal of a church. "You have often heard of drinking like a Scythian; but this is churching it like a Scythian," laughed Jewel.[281]

Jewel's comment may have also stemmed from his shock over Knox's revolutionary methods. As Dawson observes, Jewel and the English "expressed the profound concerns of European social elites about any direct action taken by 'the people.'" The Jewel-Knox contrast exposed a major difference between English and Scottish reformations. In contrast to the genesis of the English Reformation, which hinged on the disposition of the king, the Scottish Reformation began as a rebellion by the people against the regent and her French ally. "Unlike Jewel he [Knox] did not highlight the role of the nobility, being horrified instead by the actions of ordinary Scots."[282] None of this bothered Knox like it did Jewel. The Scotsman had his victory, the English navy and army assisted, and the church that was cleansed from "idolatry" was now ready for reconstruction. With idolatry out, true worship could now be established, said Knox.

From 1560 forward, steps toward change were taken, from the *First Book of Discipline* (1560) to the writing of the Scots *Confession of Faith* (1560), to the eventual adoption of a presbyterian polity (late 1570s).[283] Every Reformed theologian believed in ecclesiastical discipline, but Knox made discipline a distinct mark of a perfect Reformed Kirk, as he called it. However, Knox's high aspirations for reforming discipline were suddenly vulnerable to extinction when he received startling and surprising news.

MARY, QUEEN OF SCOTS, AND THE REFORMATION'S DIVISION WITH KNOX

Scotland's fate took a dramatic step in a new direction when Francis died in December 1560, and in 1561 his widow, Mary Stuart, made her way back to Scotland.[284] Although a decisive shift had occurred due to the wars of the Congregation, Mary still posed a threat to Scottish Protestants like Knox.

---

281. *ZL* 1:39–40.

282. Dawson, *John Knox*, 193.

283. As far as a presbyterian polity was implemented, Knox channeled Calvin's legacy.

284. "When Francis died in 1560, the queen mother, Catherine de' Medici, did not want the rivalry of Mary whose relationship to the Duke of Guise and his brother, the powerful cardinal of Lorraine, gave her too much power. The Guises themselves were in favor of Mary *returning to Scotland* to take up her crown because they believed she could also claim the throne of England and thus restore Catholicism there." Lindberg, *European Reformations*, 331–32.

The Reformer feared the country would return to Catholicism under the queen, reducing all his ecclesiastical cleansings to a recent memory.

Fearing the worst, Knox immediately issued the alarm, warning that if Scotland returned to idolatry, they would break the sacred covenant with God. As was his habit, Knox drew a straight line, directly connecting Scotland with ancient Israel, as if no new era had dawned since Christ. Knox threatened the people with the same fate: as Israel abandoned Yahweh in the promised land and were sent into exile, so, too, God would punish Scotland for the same breach in covenant. Therefore, Knox took up his mantle as an Edinburgh minister, warning the people of the capital city against the temptation to apostatize under Mary's return.[285]

Despite Knox's initial fears, on a number of occasions Mary, Queen of Scots, invited Knox to discuss the religious state of the country with her and even offered Knox a position as a religious adviser at one point. Knox, the fiery prophet preaching doom for idolatry and divine judgment against apostasy, was impossible to pacify for the sake of political opportunity. Although he did his best to express obedience, he made several tactical mistakes: he sounded defensive when Mary raised questions over the *First Blast*, still proud and perplexed at its offense; and he did not resist polemical rhetoric but called the queen's church, Rome, a harlot, even insinuating that the queen was naive in her allegiance. Knox's worse offense came years later in 1563 when he heard rumors of a marriage alliance with Spain, and he took to the pulpit to preach against this rumor. Knox was summoned to Mary, and the sobbing queen became so upset that she shouted Knox out of the room. He remained unapologetic.[286]

Knox's staunch, stubborn posture against Mary, Queen of Scots, created division in his Protestant camp. While he stood against the queen even before she stepped foot on Scottish soil, many others were interested in forming ties with the queen, optimistic she could be influenced in the Protestant direction, especially if she remarried someone partial to the Protestant cause. To Knox, the matter was always an issue of warfare, the elect fighting against the Antichrist. For other Scotsmen, however, the circumstances were far more complex than before when a queen (e.g., Mary Tudor) or regent (Mary of Guise) posed an obvious threat. They listened to Calvin and Bullinger, for example, who advocated a posture of civil compliance for the sake of ecclesiastical liberty. Knox did not take disagreement well; those not with him were against him. Knox refused to listen, considered them compromisers, and treated them as if they were Judas himself. Dawson's evaluation is fair: "Locked into an incorrect analysis of the actual situation in Scotland, the pessimistic Knox was blinded to many of the real challenges of establishing the Reformed Kirk within the realm."[287]

---

285. E.g., Knox, *History*, 2:8–13, 122–25. Dawson even calls Knox's covenant outlook the "cornerstone" of his approach to the nation. Dawon, *John Knox*, 240.

286. For an elaborate chronicle of Knox's visits, see Dawson, *John Knox*, 214–15, 234–37.

287. Dawson, 219. Cf. 216–26 on Knox and his antagonism toward betrayal. For Knox's own discouragement over the disagreement, see *Works*, 6:131–32, 134.

Another issue also infuriated Knox in the years ahead: the queen permitted the Scottish church freedom to worship and even allowed a prohibition against the Mass, though Mary herself continued to practice her Catholicism in private. Imperfect as the setup may have been, Scottish Protestants were willing to cooperate if granted such liberties. To Knox, however, the agreement was a sign that the Scots were opening the door back up for the devil to reintroduce papal religion. His colleagues had compromised, plain and simple. That outlook put Knox in tension with the church, particularly among those who considered Knox's approach far more concerned with prophetic denunciation than pastoral care.

The division Knox created became so tense that in 1565 the council prohibited Knox from preaching when the queen came to the capital city. Although the occasions were rare, Knox got the message. The council supported him, but even they had to exercise caution to prohibit another rebel riot like the one Knox instigated when the Scottish Reformation first started. He was hurt; preaching at St Giles was his megaphone for prophetic warnings, but it was also his calling, a calling the council now needed to censure to avoid the calamity they thought Knox could create.[288] Such schism accompanied by rejection sent him into a spiral of dejection, and he extracted himself from major affairs in Edinburgh the following year, once again becoming a roaming Reformer set on an isolated path.

In 1566 the queen married her nephew, Henry Stuart, Lord Darnley. The match was calamitous. Darnley's inability to govern with responsibility was obvious, even disastrous, which created no little rift between him and Mary.[289] To add fuel to the fire, Darnley became suspicious that Mary was having an affair with her secretary, David Riccio. Darnley recruited some muscle and stabbed Riccio to death in Mary's chamber. Mary turned manic with anger. But what was she to do? The husband she now hated was the father of her soon-to-be born son, James. Nevertheless, Darnley had gone too far. When Mary and Darnley were staying in Kirk o' Field, she left for a bit, which just happened to be the same moment the house exploded. Somehow Darnley lived through the explosion, but his body was found later. Someone hunted Darnley down and put him in his grave.[290]

That someone was James, Earl of Bothwell, whom Mary then ran off with after her husband's mysterious murder. Only months later, the two lovers married (1567). Since Bothwell was Protestant, the ceremony was not Catholic. Mary's affair with Bothwell, the assassination of her husband, the Protestant ceremony—it was all too much to overlook.[291] Mary tasted like fish oil in the mouths of the English and Scottish alike, and Scotland decided to spit her out.

---

288. Dawson highlights the problem: "His violent rhetoric encouraged such aggression, though with little planning or forethought about the consequences.... Knox did not seem to be in control of what was happening among Protestant radicals in Edinburgh or to have any clear plan of action." *John Knox*, 243.

289. Lindberg, *European Reformations*, 333.

290. Lindberg, 333.

291. Lindberg, 333.

She was arrested and imprisoned, and her infant son, James, became the future of Scotland—James VI.

Mary was imprisoned in Loch Leven in 1567. However, she was shrewd enough not to wait for her fate at the hands of the Scotts. With help she escaped, and in 1568 she decided to take her chances in England after losing the Battle of Langside. The decision was risky since she was perceived as a rival to Elizabeth. Deciding what to do with Mary was not obvious either. "Restoration of Mary to her throne would alienate Scottish allies, but not to restore her would provide a focus for Catholic disaffection in England, as well as alienate other monarchs who regardless of religion did not wish to see people depose rulers."[292] Elizabeth decided Mary could stay in England but under guard and constant watch. Yet Mary confirmed Elizabeth's suspicions when a plot to assassinate Elizabeth was uncovered and traced back to Mary. In February of 1587, two decades after Mary escaped Loch Leven and pursued safe haven in England, the Queen of Scots was executed.[293]

Although Knox did not live to see Mary's execution, her departure from Scotland had left Knox overjoyed. At last Regent Moray and Parliament ensured support for the Scottish kirk. And at last Knox and the General Assembly could agree on that much. Yet when the archbishop, John Hamilton, successfully carried out a plot to assassinate Moray, the wrath of Knox returned, along with all fears and the personal discouragement they created in him. Knox never truly recovered his brief optimism.

FEARFUL AND POLARIZING TO THE END

To the bitter end, Knox remained fearful that Scotland would return to Catholicism at the hands of his own nemeses. The Saint Bartholomew's Day massacre of 1572 left a sick and dying Knox all the more pessimistic. The Huguenots had been slaughtered, and Catholicism was taking over once again—what reason did Knox have to trust the Reformation's survival in Scotland? Carried into the pulpit, Knox the prophet admonished his people against the devilish ways of Catholicism and charged them to remain God's faithful, however small.

Such a message, which fueled Knox's calling from start to finish, does present a conflict in his ecclesiology. He publicly advocated for an ecclesiastical commonwealth, one that should be extensive in its reach. In a sense, his constant attraction to controversy stemmed from his belief that church *and* country must be reformed by true religion, king and parliament alike, a reform that guaranteed discipline across the country. His polemic assumed, however, that there would

---

292. Lindberg, 333–34.
293. What explains Mary's failure? That question has been debated. But Hillerbrand offered an answer: "Her fatal error was that she overestimated her own abilities and underestimated the power of the nobility. Scotland could not be ruled autocratically, as she wanted, and that was her failure." Hillerbrand, *Division of Christendom*, 363.

always be a battle in which the elect must fight to stay faithful; he assumed this battle would reveal the true church. Knox looked out over current affairs and concluded the faithful were a small remnant, everyone else idolaters. "Although strongly committed to the concept of a national Church encompassing an entire political community, he constantly reverted to the language of the persecuted minority."[294]

When this apparent conflict was coupled with Knox's inflexible personality and unyielding defense of pure worship, Knox not only polarized his enemies but created schism within his own Protestant brotherhood. Yet alienating Catholic enemies and Protestant friends alike was not problematic to Knox; although discouraging to the Reformer, he expected nothing less since God called him to be his prophet, forecasting judgment however isolated it left him in the end. Until his dying breath, this prophetic calling was enfleshed within a seasoned trepidation that God's people would turn back to idolatry and break the covenant. With Antichrist always on the move to dismantle the Reformation, Knox never could transition from his prophetic warnings and rancorous judgments, which left some Reformers more inclined to call Knox a radical than a Reformer. Yet a not-so-distant day did arrive when concord was achieved, and it is hard to imagine such an achievement was possible apart from the uprooting denunciations of Knox, reproofs that resulted in a liturgy, confession, and form of discipline on which the Scottish kirk was built.

---

294. Dawson, *John Knox*, 316. Dawson thinks Knox reconciled these two emphases in *Letter to Tyrie*.

Part 4

COUNTER-RENEWAL

The Reformation, in spite of its substantial contribution to the history of doctrine and the shock it delivered to theology and the church in the sixteenth century, was not an attack upon the whole of medieval theology or upon Christian tradition. The Reformation assaulted a limited spectrum of doctrinal and practical abuses with the intention of reaffirming the values of the historical church catholic. Thus, the mainstream Reformers reconstructed the doctrines of justification and the sacraments and then modified their ideas of the ordo salutis and of the church accordingly; but they did not alter the doctrines of God, creation, providence, and Christ, and they maintained the Augustinian tradition concerning predestination, human nature and sin. The reform of individual doctrines, like justification and the sacraments, occurred within the bounds of a traditional, orthodox, and catholic system which, on the grand scale, remained substantively unaltered.

　　　　—Richard Muller, *Post-Reformation Reformed Dogmatics*

The Reformation is the legitimate offspring, the greatest act of the Catholic Church; and on this account of true catholic nature itself, in its genuine conception: whereas the Church of Rome, instead of following the divine conduct of history has continued to stick in the old law of commandments, the garb of childhood, like the Jewish hierarchy in the time of Christ, and thus by its fixation as Romanism has parted with the character of catholicity in exchange for that particularity.

　　　　—Philip Schaff, *The Principle of Protestantism*

17

ROMAN BUT CATHOLIC?

Counter-Reformation, Catholic
Renewal, and the Antidote

Unless by this Council or by some other means we place a limit on our
morals, unless we force our greedy desire for human things, the source of
evils, to yield to the love of divine things, it is all over with Christendom.
—Giles of Viterbo to Pope Julius II at the Fifth Lateran Council

You know, Sadoleto, and if you venture to deny I will make it palpable to
all that you knew, yet cunningly and craftily disguised the fact, not only that
our agreement with antiquity is far closer than yours, but that all we have
attempted has been to renew that ancient form of the church, which, at first
sullied by illiterate men of indifferent character, was afterward flagitiously
mangled and almost destroyed by the Roman Pontiff and his faction.
—John Calvin, *Reply to Sadoleto*

Seminal theologians such as Vermigli, Musculus, Zanchi, Turretin, and
Owen were soaked in Aquinas, and it is not exaggerating to say that the
intellectual culture of Continental and British Calvinism was more
Thomistic than most Counter-Reformation theologians.
—Michael Horton, *Justification*

Despite the attempt by Luther's opponents to portray the church as uniform, the church had given birth to a diversity of individuals who attempted to sound an alarm and jumpstart reform. But by the end of the century, not all of them proved as effective as Luther. Why did some sixteenth-century reforms not stick? The reasons are many. But one of the chief reasons may be this: the church continued to prize the spirituality and ethical ascent of the individual. "Luther hammered at theological reform and Roman Catholic Reformers hammered at ethical renewal."[1]

---

1. Lindberg, *European Reformations*, 336; Olin, *Catholic Reform*, 11; Evennett, *Spirit of the Counter-Reformation*, 41; O'Malley, *First Jesuits*, 278.

841

In short, Luther believed the primary reason for reform was theological: the gospel and its corollaries (for example, justification) were central issues under consideration, but the Roman Church was incapable of defining reform as anything other than moral revitalization. That moral transformation may have been desperate; it even may have been directed at the top, toward the papacy itself, but the reform was not first and foremost a reconsideration of its doctrinal core, complained Luther. Although there may have been some exceptions to Luther's generalization, the point's validity was confirmed by the Counter-Reformation, especially in individuals like Ignatius Loyola and in official assemblies like the Council of Trent. However, the story is incomplete if what occurred in the years before, during, and after Trent are defined as a countermovement alone. A fuller narrative demonstrates that Rome pursued renewal of its own, however different that renewal looked in comparison to the Reformation. Such a renewal was revealing: although Trent took a hard stance against the Reformers, some within the church did recognize the necessity of renewing the one, holy, catholic, and apostolic faith. Nevertheless, such a conception of renewal triggered further polemical debates with the Reformers, both Lutheran and Reformed. In the aftermath of Trent's official decrees, the Reformers had to decide whether their claims to catholicity still had credibility and, if so, why.

CHARLES V, CLEMENT VII, AND THE FIGHT FOR A FREE COUNCIL: 1520s

The last chapter established that Charles, in the aftermath of the Diet of Worms (1521), became the major voice over the next two decades for a free council. Despite his opposition to Lutheranism and his conflicted relations with the German nobles, a council afforded Charles the opportunity to retain and consolidate his authority and power over against foreign threat, both from Francis I and the Turks. A council also had the potential to further establish Charles's power over Europe. As emperor, Charles saw himself as political sovereign and religious guardian—whether his reach was a reality on the ground was an altogether different matter—which naturally created tension with the pope.[2] Ironically, the emperor and the Protestants were not all that dissimilar in their basic demand for a council. However, the motivations behind each party could not be more different. "The emperor wanted a council to address moral reform in the church in order to revitalize it and thereby diminish the appeal of the Protestant heretics."[3]

Charles spent the better half of the 1520s and 1530s waving his banner in favor of a council. However, Francis I was on to Charles, recognizing that a council would only strengthen Charles's empire and make his own advance a near impossibility. Constantine called the Council of Nicaea, which served as a clear declaration of his oversight and even his authority. A council called by Charles could do the same and more. Furthermore, France's own history reveals that

---

2. Hillerbrand, *Division of Christendom*, 275.

3. Hillerbrand, 275.

the proposal for a council was an explosive issue: "The Parlement of Paris, the University of Paris, and much of the French episcopacy rejected the Concordat of Bologna as illegitimately delivering to the king control over the church, an offense against the French church's traditional 'liberties.' They appealed for a council to redress their grievances. Francis saw a council, therefore, as possibly jeopardizing the control that the Concordat guaranteed him." In other words, "'The Most Christian King,' to give Francis his official title, saw the council as a danger, therefore, to his domestic interests as well as to his foreign."[4]

On principle, the pope was not favorable to a council either. With the rise and triumph of curialism, what pope desired to welcome back conciliarism? A council was a risk. Theoretically, it could work in favor of the pope, even serve to substantiate his authority. But the primacy of the pope might be undermined if a council decided the pope should be subservient to its authority. Additionally, pope and papacy had political reasons to resist Charles. For example, when Clement VII became pope, he signed a treaty with Francis I that served as a blockade against the emperor. The pope was well aware of the prior battles between Charles and Francis over Milan. What if Charles decided to advance further into papal states?[5]

Clement's fears were valid. In 1525 Francis lost to Charles once more, but this time he was captured. Thanks to Clement's intervention, no harm came to Francis, who was released. Charles must have regretted that decision when Clement and Francis turned right around and created the League of Cognac, an alliance that also recruited Henry VIII. The league was unsuccessful. Rome fell to the imperial army in 1527—the Sack of Rome—and Clement fled for his life. Two years later Francis lost to Charles once again (1529).[6]

At the end of 1529, Clement and Charles attempted to achieve clemency in Bologna, but every time Charles thought he might solidify a council, Clement found a way to procrastinate. Clement acted like he was listening but in his own mind had little intention to take the steps necessary to form a council. In the end, Clement was not persuaded that a council was necessary or advantageous to his political and religious agenda.

POPE PAUL III AND THE TROJAN HORSE

In 1534 Alessandro Farnese was elected the new pope: Paul III. Unlike Clement, however, Paul III was in favor of a council for many reasons, much to the relief of the emperor. At the very least, a council might achieve some measure of clemency between European rivalries (Charles and Francis) and serve as a bulwark against internal and external opposition (the Reformation and the Turks).[7]

Furthermore, Paul III was cognizant of corruption within his own papacy.

---

4. O'Malley, *Trent*, 55.

5. "He feared Charles V. The emperor, through his Spanish crown ruler of the Kingdom of Naples just south of Rome, had after his victory over Francis in 1522 established himself in the north in the Duchy of Milan, ominously close to both the Papal States and Florence." O'Malley, 56.

6. As for the fall of Rome, "Charles did not sanction the terrible sack that ensued, during which Clement barely escaped capture, but he afterward tried to take advantage of it to bring pressure on the pope." O'Malley, 57.

7. O'Malley, 60.

He asked Gasparo Contarini, Reginald Pole, and Giampietro Carafa to lead a commission to investigate foul practice within their own ranks. The intent was to reform the church and prepare the way for a future council. The report acknowledged and condemned the sins of past popes, especially simony. The report called these corruptions from the hands of past popes the Trojan horse, secretly letting in "many abuses" and "grave diseases," which then "rushed upon the church of God" and now afflicts her "almost to the despair of salvation."[8] Paul III formed the commission in 1536, and the report was completed in 1537 and labeled the *Counsel . . . concerning the Reform of the Church.* The report was supposed to be private, but soon enough the public read it. Deep financial misconduct had penetrated into the papacy, and the Lutherans were quick to spread the news.

> The report was leaked and used by the Lutherans as proof positive of the corruption of the papacy. Lutheran exploitation was surely a factor persuading Paul not to move, or to move with extreme caution, on its specific provisions, most of which dealt with dispensations from canon law in exchange for a consideration and with similar procedures that at least looked like simony and that had contributed so mightily to setting off the fury against the papacy.
>
> The sad fact was that fees ("compositions") for "graces" granted through the papal office known as the Datary were deeply resented throughout Europe and a source of grave scandal, yet they brought in so much money that their abolition or radical reform was for the popes unthinkable. The Datary alone, through fees and taxes for the granting of dispensations, indults, privileges, and benefices, brought in well over 1,000,000 ducats a year, about half of the Curia's total income. The Datary was, however, only one among the many glaring instances of such "grievances" against the Holy See. "Reform of the head" threatened to subvert major sources of revenue of the financial system in which the papacy operated.[9]

To Paul III's credit, he did not drag his feet like his predecessor, Clement VII. He recognized, for example, that priests were not present in parishes. The statistics were staggering:

> At issue was that scores of bishops had never set foot in their dioceses and that thousands of priests had never celebrated Mass in parishes in which they were the canonical incumbents. The root problem was that the legal and financial emoluments did not necessarily accrue to those who performed the actual tasks and bore the real responsibilities of a particular position. Thus bishops received the revenue from their dioceses while a substitute fulfilled their canonical obligations. In the diocese of Lincoln, England, some 247 priests of a total of 1,088 were absent during a 1518–1519 visitation.[10]

---

8. Text can be found in Olin, *Catholic Reformation*, 186–87 (for full text see 182–97); as quoted in O'Malley, 62.

9. Olin, *Catholic Reformation*, 186–87 (for full text see 182–97); as quoted in O'Malley, *Trent*, 62.

10. Hillerbrand, *Division of Christendom*, 274.

These ecclesiastical liberalities motivated Paul III to issue reforming measures, including the Society of Jesus led by its stalwart spiritualist Ignatius of Loyola.

THE VITALITY OF CATHOLIC SPIRITUALITY: IGNATIUS LOYOLA, CATHOLIC REFORM, AND THE COUNTER-REFORMATION

Protestant polemics have often portrayed the religion of Rome in the sixteenth century as lifeless, a period of darkness. However, a closer look tells a different story. In the aftermath of the initial Reformation, the Roman Church experienced a reform of its own, and one that was laced with spiritual vitality. In part, some credit must be given to the Reformation protest itself. Certainly, the crisis Luther created motivated quarters of the Roman Church to examine itself only then to galvanize itself to resolute devotion. But it is not accurate to grant Protestantism all the credit, as if Rome's reform movement of the sixteenth century was merely reactionary. Figures like Ignatius of Loyola may have been opponents of the Reformation; nonetheless, they experienced a renovation of their own making. However, unlike Luther's crisis, those like Ignatius experienced a crisis that led them to further commitment to the church. "Ignatius, rather like Luther, had experienced a spiritual crisis, but in contrast to the German Reformer, he had found the answer in the church."[11] In that light, one need not choose between Rome's reform and a Counter-Reformation. Without question, elements of opposition were present, whether in Ignatius or Trent, both of which went to some length to condemn the Protestant doctrines as heresy. At the same time, both Ignatius and Trent must not be interpreted only within the spotlight of polemics. The historical context reveals independent resolve to renew the Roman Church and pursue a rigorous spiritual enterprise.

On the eve of the Council of Trent, few individuals so influenced the future of the Roman Church like Ignatius Loyola (1491–1556), founder of the Jesuits. In 1521 Loyola was a young man engaged in the genesis of Habsburg-Valois warfare. Born with noble blood, the siege of Pamplona was Loyola's chance to live up to his Basque family heritage and rise from the ashes victorious. Instead, Loyola was almost killed when hit by a cannonball. As Loyola lay on the battlefield, blood covering his uniform, he discovered that his right leg was broken. After he endured the pain of having his broken leg reset, he discovered the doctor had done a poor job. If Loyola lived, he might be a cripple as a result, but if he had a chance to walk again, his leg had to be rebroken and reset. Loyola was determined to endure the pain for the sake of his future, but the

---

11. Hillerbrand, 282. Hence Hillerbrand would write, "Protestant propaganda argued that the Catholic Church was unwilling (or unable) to undertake needed reform in the late fifteenth and early sixteenth centuries. Nothing could be further from the truth. To be sure, the pursuit of reform in the fifteenth century was haphazard and sporadic.... However, the Fifth Lateran Council, convened by Pope Julius II under political pressure from Germany and in session from 1512 to 1517, dealt extensively with reform issues, proof positive that the church wanted to put its house in order, although there was disagreement and even lack of full understanding of what that exactly meant" (268).

pain escalated when Loyola realized the path to recovery involved sawing off his bone, which was sticking out of his flesh. Nevertheless, Loyola endured the surgery and recovered.

The near-death experience gave Loyola an opportunity to consider his future.

Triumph of Faith over Idolatry, by Jean-Baptiste Théodon. Chiesa del Gesù, Rome, Italy. Mary triumphs over the Reformation with her left foot crushing the head of the serpent. Under the serpent's head is a book by Martin Luther.
Matthew Barrett

Triumph of Religion Over Heresy (1695-99), by Pierre Legros
the Younger. Chiesa del Gesù, Rome, Italy.
Mary throws Jan Hus and Martin Luther out of heaven into hell, while an
angel tears out pages from a book, probably a book by Martin Luther.
Matthew Barrett

No longer did he have a future as a knight. With his original plan shattered, much like his leg, Loyola was forced to rethink his life, and he came to the conclusion that he should pursue a spiritual life—but not one confined to the secluded corners of a distant monastery; one devoted to action, a life on the spiritual battlefield of this world.[12]

Loyola wasted no time but committed himself the next year to serve the church. From now on he would fight for Christ and his bride. Unfortunately for Loyola, his excitement to begin was detained by a ravaging plague, forcing him to wait and retreat to a cave, where he spent time preparing himself for service by self-examination, repentance, meditation on Christ and him crucified, and a renewed resolve to follow Christ whatever the cost.

---

12. The details of Loyola's injury and redirection in life can be found in Lindberg, *European Reformations*, 346. Lindberg clarifies, "Military imagery has often been used to describe the self-understanding and mission of Loyola and his followers, but this is misleading if understood in a modern sense. The Jesuit Formula or 'rule' describes a member of the Society 'as a soldier of God beneath the banner of the cross,' but in medieval parlance *militare Deo* was a synonym for a member of a religious order."

Ignatius holds a book in his hand that reads, "To the greater glory of God. Constitution of the Society of Jesus." With his left foot he stands in triumph over Martin Luther and Luther's German Bible.

Matthew Barrett, St. Peters Basilica at the Vatican, Rome

In 1523 Loyola set his face like flint toward Jerusalem, the Holy City. Unlike monks in past centuries who spent their lives in caves or devoted themselves to monastic retreat among a community, he went into the world to make converts. Muslims were his target; he aimed to approach them with the gospel so they would convert to Christianity. Loyola was mature enough to recognize, however, that such a mission needed preparation. Rather than going from Manresa to Jerusalem, he stopped his journey short and detoured in Barcelona, where he became a student at the University of Alcalá and created a little following before moving on to Paris in 1528 to pursue his master's degree.[13] While in Paris his following increased and attracted budding missionaries, such as Francis Xavier. This group of devotees were now just as committed to evangelizing the Muslims as Loyola.

By 1537 Loyola and his colleagues decided the time was right to make their

---

13. "Ironically, he was here suspected of heresy and twice imprisoned by the Spanish Inquisition." Lindberg, 347.

way to Jerusalem, but this time he was blocked by war. As the Turks fought for victory over Venice, Loyola's plans were so stifled that he decided God must be calling him to stay. Despite his disappointment at a mission never fulfilled, he found encouragement from Pope Paul III, who was so impressed by Loyola's determination to reach the Muslims that he placed his stamp of approval on Loyola's community, and in 1540 The Society of Jesus received official backing from Pope Paul III. Given how difficult it was by the sixteenth century to acquire the pope's approval for a new order, the papal endorsement was a major honor.[14] The pope's support had no little effect on Loyola. Like past monastic orders, Loyola's Society of Jesus was marked by the typical vows, such as poverty. However, the order was also marked by an additional vow of allegiance to the pope and his papacy. Over against the conciliarism of the medieval era, Loyola's papal allegiance embodied a type of curialism and aided its triumph in the years ahead. Loyola's allegiance was so unconditional, so absolute, that he said in his *Spiritual Exercises* (1548) that if the pope called black "white" and white "black," he would believe him without question, without doubt.[15] However, Loyola's loyalty to hierarchy was not an end in itself. The Society of Jesus did not exist merely to serve as a bulwark for papal supremacy. Rather, Loyola saw adherence to papal hierarchy as a means to a much more significant end: mission to the world. Yes, he would obey the pope no matter what, but his obedience to the pope was for the sake of being sent by the pope to the lost. "In this sense the fourth vow intends to express apostolic ministry to the world to be facilitated by the papacy rather than vice versa. That is, the fourth vow is not 'to the pope' but about mission and ministry."[16]

Loyola also became a bulwark against the Protestant Reformation. He did not agree with Luther's assessment of the church. Luther believed the *theology* of the church had gone astray in the late medieval era, which motivated him to achieve doctrinal reform in the sixteenth-century church. Loyola disagreed: the problem was not theological but *spiritual*.[17] Convinced the Reformers were a threat to the pope and spiritual reform, Loyola and his Jesuits labored to counter the Reformation, working with magistrates to expel evangelicals from their cities.

But the Jesuit strategy was not all penal, as if their identity was motivated or formed only by their opposition to the Reformation. Ignatius and the Jesuits that followed pursued the revival of a Catholic spirituality even apart from their

---

14. There was precedent. For example, Pope Clement VII had sanctioned the Theatine order in 1524. And even before 1540 and the approval of the Society of Jesus, Pope Paul sanctioned the Regulars of St. Paul in 1535 and the Capuchins in 1536. See Hillerbrand, *Division of Christendom*, 283.

15. For his entire argument, see Loyola, *Spiritual Exercises*, 113–214.

16. Lindberg, *European Reformations*, 349.

17. Was Loyola driven primarily by an anti-Protestant mentality? No. It is true, Loyola should be credited with establishing a Counter-Reformation program, one that had influence on Trent as we will see. However, Loyola's primary motive was the spiritual transformation of the individual. However much Protestants interfered with that program—or challenged its spiritual head, the pope—Loyola countered. But even if the Protestant Reformation never launched, Loyola's mission would have been birthed. Lindberg, 345. Cf. O'Malley, *Trent*, 16–18, 321, 280.

Protestant nemeses.[18] This pursuit took many practical forms. For example, they established schools in Rome and elsewhere to educate the next generation, part of which included induction into the doctrines of the Roman Church.[19] Yet in the estimation of so many of their heirs, the Jesuits countered the Reformation with greatest efficiency when it took its doctrines and practices into the wider world. A defining hallmark was the spread of Jesuit missions across the world, even as far as South America.[20] In that vein, the Jesuits rivaled Calvin's missionary enterprise in Geneva.

FAILED CONCESSION: CAJETAN, THE ITALIAN EVANGELISTS, AND REGENSBURG

In the 1520s and 1530s a cluster of smaller, provincial councils met (Lyons in 1527, Sens in 1528, Bourges in 1528, Cologne in 1536, Mantua in 1537, and others), some to address reform in the parishes, others to respond to the rise of the Lutherans, some to address both at the same time.

The Council of Sens, for example, put forward a polemical response to the Reformation, laying down sixteen points at stake in the debate. Sens was thorough, rejecting the Reformation program as a whole, from theological issues like the bondage of the will and *sola fide*, to epistemological issues like *sola scriptura*, to ecclesiastical issues like reducing the sacraments from seven to two and the rejection of clerical celibacy, vows, pilgrimages, and icons.[21] Sens was so thorough that Trent, to one degree or another, stood on the shoulders of Sens, yet without addressing every controversy Sens felt obligated to engage.[22]

Sens had no interest in reconciliation or cooperation; doctrinal concession was out of the question. Yet not all opponents of Lutheranism were as fixed. One might assume Cajetan represented a staunch stance of opposition; after all, his 1518 confrontation with Luther was a stepping-stone to Luther's eventual excommunication. But over a decade later, Cajetan showed signs of cooperation

---

18. "Ignatius of Loyola would have walked his path even if the world had never heard of Luther and the other Reformers. He symbolizes indigenous Catholic vitality in the sixteenth century and illustrates how such vitality could be turned to combat the Protestant Reformation." Hillerbrand, *Division of Christendom*, 284. Hillerbrand explores other examples besides Ignatius, including Juan de la Cruz (John of the Cross), Teresa of Avila, and Carlo Borromeo (see pp. 254–87).

19. Lindberg, *European Reformations*, 350, goes so far as to say that the "Jesuits sought to extirpate heresy and *win Protestants back* to Rome by means of political influence and effective education." Emphasis added.

20. Lindberg, 350. Lindberg lists "India, Malaysia, Africa, Ethiopia, Brazil, Japan, and China. "By Loyola's death in 1556 the order included over 1,000 members, and by 1626 there were about 15,000 Jesuits throughout the world and some 440 colleges."

21. "Although the Council of Sens equated Luther's teaching with ancient heresies, it deserves credit for hitting on the justification issue as the crucial doctrinal point, which none of these other councils did. It also deserves credit for balancing what it said about Luther's teaching with an insistence that Pelagius erred in the opposite direction. The church, the council implied, steers a midway course, teaching that three things are required for salvation: faith, good works, and grace. Of these three grace is the first and most important— 'primo tamen et principaliter.'" O'Malley, *Trent*, 65–66. Cf. Mansi, *Sacrorum conciliorum nova et amplissima collectio*, 32:1151.

22. O'Malley, *Trent*, 66–67. Cf. Mansi, *Sacrorum conciliorum . . .*, 32:1095–1161; Farge, *Orthodoxy and Reform in Early Reformation France*, 241.

for the sake of reconciliation. He did not have to concede to the Reformation's every protest, but he did see no harm in conceding certain practices. As O'Malley explains, "In 1530, he drew up for Clement VII a remarkable memo in which he suggested allowing the laity to partake of the Eucharist cup and, more radical, allowing priests in Germany to marry. He believed, as did other cardinals, that the church should not require fasting or reception of the sacraments under pain of sin. He even went so far as to propose that for reunion no formal retraction should be required of Lutheran theologians, only that they profess to believe what the universal church has always believed, and of Lutheran princes only a private affirmation of belief, no public ceremony."[23]

Cajetan's openness to reunion was criticized by his colleagues. However, it is revealing nonetheless for a variety of reasons. First, Cajetan's basic condition for the Lutherans—ascription to the beliefs of the universal church across time—assumed he thought the Reformers shared this core facet of catholicity. Yet he assumed that the Lutherans could confess a catholicity just as robust as their opponents, and he thought such catholicity could (should?) be the requirement for reunion. Second, Cajetan was recognized as the major Thomistic expert of his day. That, too, is telling. However much he thought the Lutherans had drifted from the church of the day, is it possible he thought some Protestant beliefs and practices could be aligned with (or at least were not contrary to) either the patristic or medieval traditions?

Cajetan's willingness to enter talks with the Lutherans on Clement VII's behalf was not a lone voice in the wilderness. Even within Italy not all took on the same anti-Protestant disposition as Sens and eventually Trent. Some were even more sympathetic to the Reformers than Cajetan, not only desiring cooperation rather than condemnation but perhaps even concession on doctrine. They became known as *spirituali*. They were committed to the institution of the Roman Church and its practices but nevertheless desired reform, reform not only in morals but in doctrine. They appreciated the doctrinal insights of the Reformers and advocated for an incorporation of Reformation theology but within the institutional church. "Their ideas were rooted in pre-Reformation perspectives but also strengthened by Reformation debates. It is striking that at least for a time during the pontificate of Paul III, exponents of evangelism reached into the curia."[24] The *spirituali* were not only influenced by Luther but by Calvin in particular, specifically his *Institutes of the Christian Religion*. "Thus, had the *spirituali* movement carried the day, the Italian Catholic church might have become Calvinist."[25] That hypothetical is extraordinary to consider.

What Reformation doctrines did the *spirituali* appreciate most? Justification *sola fide*. Rediscovering the material principle of the Reformation led to the conversion of some Italians to the evangelical camp but still nothing comparable to

---

23. O'Malley, *Trent*, 67. Cf. Wicks, *Cajetan Responds*, 201–3.
24. An example of a *spirituali* is Gasparo Contarini (1483–1542). Lindberg, *European Reformations*, 340.
25. Lindberg, 340.

German or Swiss territories. Historians hypothesize why so few conversions.[26] As for the *spirituali*, Lindberg offers his theory: "The theology of the *spirituali* defies easy generalization, but it seems that, unlike their Protestant brethren, they could not or did not draw the logical conclusion that theological reform led to institutional reform. We are reminded here of the first sharp exchange of the Reformation between Luther and Prierias on the issue of the theology of grace alone and ecclesiastical authority. The *spirituali* somehow believed it was possible to ensure the former by strengthening the latter."[27] That created a problem: they could not commit themselves to join the Reformers, yet their sympathies with the Reformers put them under the scrutinous eye of their Catholic colleagues committed to extinguishing the Reformation once and for all.

The golden years of the *spirituali* were from 1512 into the 1560s. That wide span of decades demonstrates what potential the *spirituali* had if not overshadowed by the Counter-Reformation and its finality at Trent. During these years, representatives of the *spirituali* attempted to persuade other priests and cardinals from within, advocating peace talks with the Reformers and even negotiations over doctrinal controversy (for example, the Regensburg Colloquy of 1541). They even pushed for a council that might reconcile both sides or at least achieve cooperation. In the end, the council came, but Trent was the anti-council, the council to end all ecumenical councils between the two sides during the sixteenth century.

TRENT'S GENESIS

By the mid-1540s, a lot of Lutheran water had passed under the Roman bridge. The *Augsburg Confession* of 1530 solidified Lutheran theology, and the failed colloquy at Regensburg in 1541 provided little hope of future reunion.

But the Lutherans were not the only ones who made a conciliatory council between parties untenable. Many in the Roman Church and papacy were skeptical toward a council. What were the chances that a council could bring together Charles, the pope, and Francis? To his credit, Paul III had tried before to convoke a council. For example, in 1537 the pope had summoned all of Christendom to Mantua, but he met resistance both from within his own camp and from those outside.[28] Many whom Paul hoped would support him were in truth indifferent at best and cynical at worst. As for the Lutherans, the Smalcald League was clear that any council that was not free and within their own territory was a nonstarter. Francis did not warm to the council either, as he conveyed by his fresh act of war on Charles. Even the Duke of Mantua was an impediment. He "insisted that the pope provide a guard of five to six thousand men for the city—a demand

---

26. Historians debate why. Was it out of fear of persecution? Perhaps. But others believe the lack of conversion was due more to conviction, Italian Catholics not convinced in the end by Reformation theology. See Lindberg, 340; Gleason, "Sixteenth-Century Italian Spirituality and the Papacy," 305.

27. Lindberg, *European Reformations*, 341.

28. See Paul III's 1536 bull *Ad Dominici Gregis Curam*.

interpreted as the equivalent of a refusal to host the council. Not only would the cost to the papacy have been unsustainable over a lengthy meeting, but such a force of armed men would give every impression of a council held in bondage to a papal army."[29] As a result, the pope backpedaled, and nothing came to fruition in Mantua.

Nevertheless, Paul renewed his efforts in the 1540s. First, he needed a new location, one that no one could object to, or at least most everyone could agree with. The choice was most difficult because whatever country or territory he chose, the other parties felt at a disadvantage and would refuse to participate. However, if Paul could convince Charles of a location, then his support might be enough to initiate the council irrespective of whatever dissent remained. He chose Trent because technically it was within Charles's own territory. The Italians might complain at the distance they had to travel, but they could not object that Trent was outside Italian purview.[30]

Paul had three goals for the council. First, find a way to fend off the Turks lest the Muslims take over Europe once and for all. Second, bring civil authorities together (for example, Charles and Francis) so that the fighting would stop and they might consolidate their resources against the Turks. Third, address the schism created by the Reformation.[31] Now that the location was settled and the council's aims set in place, Paul was ready to summon Christendom once again.

Despite Paul's commendable advance on a council, the year of his summons (1542) evaded a council like years past.[32] In large part, the delay came back to Francis once more. Not only did he resent the council's location, believing the council only served to further consolidate Charles's power, but Francis sent his troops to war once more against Charles. When Paul then refused to back Charles in his war with Francis, Charles backed out of the arrangement previously made concerning the council. All of Paul's plans were ruined, the council itself was postponed, and Paul almost gave up for good, which discredited him almost to the point of no return.[33]

Just when all seemed lost, Charles defeated Francis in 1544, placing the king at the mercy of Charles and by consequence the pope. Now Francis had to agree to a council or else.[34] Paul could not believe it; his dream had finally

29. "It was, moreover, becoming ever clearer—to Paul, Charles, and to many others besides—that the Lutherans almost certainly would not come to a council convoked by the pope and held under his auspices. At this point Paul planned to attend the council in person. This meant that if a council were held—and Paul, though frustrated at the moment, was determined to make it happen—the Lutherans would be condemned in their absence, which would inevitably mean their armed resistance to the emperor's implementation of the council's decrees. The dreaded civil war!" O'Malley, *Trent*, 68.

30. "On the Italian side of the Alps (and therefore, though not ideal, acceptable to Paul), Trent was under Habsburg hegemony and therefore could be considered 'in German lands.'" O'Malley, 70.

31. O'Malley, 70.

32. See his bull *Initii Nostri Huius Pontificatus*.

33. Paul put the council on hold in 1543. On the distrust that brewed between Paul and Charles, as well as Paul's lack of credibility in the eyes of his critics, see O'Malley, *Trent*, 71.

34. Consult the Peace of Crépy.

materialized and through Charles of all people. Many still remained skeptical the council would go through and open (which explains some of its low attendance those first years). Massive preparation had to be made to prime Trent for the large intake of travelers. However, the Council of Trent finally convened on December 13, 1545.

The year 1545 was an ominous year for the Lutherans. Not only had Paul succeeded in summoning a council that would counter the Reformation, but Charles, on the heels of his victory over Francis, grew more powerful than ever. Not even the Smalcald League could stand in his way. And Charles knew it, so he attacked the Smalcald League next. The Protestants were not going to attend Trent anyway, so why postpone his advance on Lutheran territories? In addition, he no longer needed the support of the German nobles now that Francis was defeated. As a bonus, Charles was committed to the Roman Church, so triumph over the Protestants meant the advance of his religion.[35] Potential victory over the Protestants was all the pope needed to hear; Paul sent financial and military support to aid Charles in no time at all. Even still, the emperor's increase in political power did not sit well with the pope.

FIRST ASSEMBLY: 1545–47

Session 3 (February 1546) of the Council of Trent listed two purposes for convening: "the rooting out of heresy and the reform of conduct." The first is doctrinal and the second pastoral. At Trent, theologians played no small role in reaching theological conclusions. Theologians were sent by their representative political and ecclesiastical associations, and as it turned out, many of them hailed from mendicant orders.[36] When Trent needed to discuss (and at times debate) theology, Marcello Cervini was tasked with directing the council. The task was an overwhelming one, burdened with mediation between heated debates, responsible for pushing theologians to reach agreement for the council's sake.

Prior to Trent, many of the council's theologians had never read the Reformers. Unacquaintance was not always by choice. Many of them could not read Luther or Melanchthon in German unless their works were translated and distributed in Italy. Nevertheless, Trent afforded its theologians the opportunity to study the writings of the Reformers. "Although the theologians had been trained in dispassionate analysis of texts, they almost without exception read the Reformers with unsympathetic eyes."[37] By putting forward a theology decidedly against the Reformers, Trent was confident its council was following the councils of the Fathers, the Council of Nicaea in particular. The Fathers "were

---

35. O'Malley, *Trent*, 74.

36. "The theologians played therefore an indispensable role at Trent and were fully integrated into the council's functioning. They came to the council at the behest of their sovereigns, their bishops, or their religious orders, which means the pope had no say in choosing them except for those he sent in his own name." O'Malley, 85.

37. O'Malley, 85.

accustomed to make use of this shield [the Nicene Creed] against all heresies, and in some cases by this means alone they have drawn unbelievers to the faith, defeated heretics, and strengthened the faithful."[38] Those three ambitions were embedded in Trent's purpose as well.

As for the second objective, the reform of conduct, the legates at Trent were appointed for this very reason, rather than the theologians.[39] Reaching agreement on pastoral reform was no easy task, either. The president, Giovanni Maria Del Monte, was charged with directing the legates as they discussed how to reform abuses in the church.

The Gospel, Scripture, and Tradition

In session 4 (April 1546), Trent put forward its first decree and made a statement from the start by beginning with the gospel. For the Reformers claimed that Rome had distorted and in some cases abandoned the gospel of grace. Trent countered out of the gate: "The purity of the gospel, purged of all errors, may be preserved in the church." How the truths of this gospel are handed down raised some controversy among the theologians at Trent. Are the Scriptures sufficient to know the gospel and the way to salvation? Or are traditions also necessary? That was no easy question to answer for several reasons: first, the church depended on a host of *traditions* (plural), from apostolic to doctrinal to auricular; second, the church fathers and many Scholastics appeared to confess Scripture's sufficiency at least with matters of salvation.[40] Some theologians at Trent were adamant that whatever decision was made, Scripture must be elevated to an authority above all. "To put Scripture and traditions on the same level is impious," said Jacopo Nacchianti.[41] But many others were unpersuaded by Nacchianti.

The wording in Trent's first decree is somewhat ambiguous as a result. Tradition is left undefined and notably still fixed in the plural—*traditions*.

> The council clearly perceives that this truth and rule are contained in written books and in unwritten traditions which were received by the apostles from the mouth of Christ himself, or else have come down to us, handed on as it were from the apostles themselves at the inspiration of the Holy Spirit. Following the example of the orthodox fathers, the council accepts and venerates with a like feeling of piety and reverence all the books of both the Old and the New Testament, since the one God is the author of both, as well as the traditions concerning both faith and conduct, as either directly spoken by Christ or dictated by the Holy Spirit, which have been preserved in unbroken sequence in the Catholic Church.[42]

---

38. *Dogmatic Decrees of the Council of Trent, 1545–63*, session 3 (p. 821).
39. O'Malley, *Trent*, 85.
40. More on both of these points can be found in O'Malley, *Trent*, 93.
41. *CT* 1:45–46; 5:71–72. Quoted in O'Malley, 95.
42. *Dogmatic Decrees of the Council of Trent, 1545–63*, session 4, first decree.

Two media or channels of revelation in the first decree are present—Scripture and traditions. How the two correspond to one another, however, is left unaddressed. O'Malley claims that Trent did not mean to "suppress the view expressed by some of the council fathers about the 'sufficiency' of Scripture for salvation."[43] Even if O'Malley is correct, and he may be, it is unlikely that Trent defined *sufficiency* in the Protestant sense. Two reasons explain why: (1) even if Trent did not specify the relationship between Scripture and traditions, it did use language that bends in the direction of equality ("The council accepts and *venerates with a like* feeling of piety and reverence"),[44] and (2) the rest of the decrees do appear to counter the spirit of *sola Scriptura*, not by Trent's affirmation of tradition's indispensable instrumentality, which the Reformers also shared, but by its appeal to the church as an infallible interpreter (a point to revisit).

Trent also countered the Protestant translations of the Scriptures into the vernacular, doubling down on the Latin Vulgate as the only "authentic" translation for the church. The council "declares that the old well-known Latin Vulgate edition which has been tested in the church by long use over so many centuries should be kept as the authentic text in public readings, debates, sermons, and explanations; and no one is to dare or presume on any pretext to reject it."[45] But this conclusion was not reached without debate. Cardinal Madruzzo, for example, stood opposed to any use of the Scriptures in the vernacular, which put Madruzzo in direct conflict with Cardinal Pacheco. As O'Malley explains, Trent was in between the proverbial rock and a hard place: "In France and Spain (as well as England) such translations had long been forbidden. If the council advocated them, the episcopacy and probably the crown would countermand the decree. If it forbade them, Germany, Italy, Poland, and other places where they were allowed would react just as negatively but for the opposite reason." To complicate matters further, the "bishops and theologians at Trent, many of them Humanistically trained, knew very well that the Vulgate needed revision, but were its problems so serious as to prevent its use by the council in its deliberations and by the church at large?"[46] Pietro Bertano was bold enough to suggest the council resist mandating the Vulgate or claiming the Vulgate alone to be authentic. Liberty should be prized, allowing churches to decide

---

43. O'Malley, *Trent*, 97, warns against interpreting these "two media" or "two channels" as "sources." However, that interpretation has been challenged since "two channels" is supported by Robert Bellarmine, the *Catechismus Romanus* (1566), Vatican I (1869–70), the papal encyclical *Humani Generis*, and Pope John XXIII's *Ad Petri Cathedram*. Twentieth-century Roman Catholics (Karl Rahner, Hans Küng, Yves Congar, George Tavard, J. R. Geiselmann) argue that revelation is partly contained in Scripture and partly in tradition. Geiselmann, for example, pushes against a view that says there are two sources, Scripture and tradition ("Scripture, Tradition, and the Church," 39–72). O'Malley proposes one source of Revelation with two modes. Nevertheless, he does not think Trent is specific on the issue. But again, it is difficult to side with Geiselmann when many surrounding Trent and after Trent did consider Scripture and tradition two sources. To explore this debate further, see Barrett, *God's Word Alone*, 72 and 348–49, where I point out that the debate is sometimes driven by ecumenical motivations.

44. *Dogmatic Decrees of the Council of Trent, 1545–63*, session 4, first decree (p. 822).

45. *Dogmatic Decrees of the Council of Trent, 1545–63*, session 4, second decree (p. 823).

46. O'Malley, *Trent*, 94.

what is best.[47] Yet the council's final choice of language, either intentionally or unintentionally, did not consider Bertano's suggestion a real possibility, declaring the Vulgate alone to be "authentic."

With the authentic text decided, how, then, should the text be interpreted? The more pertinent question, however, was *who* possessed the authoritative interpretation of the text. Interpreting the Reformation as a turn to the individual, Trent sided with the church: "The council further decrees, in order to control those of unbalanced character, that no one, relying on his personal judgment in matters of faith and customs which are linked to the establishment of Christian doctrine, shall dare to interpret the Sacred Scriptures either by twisting its text to his individual meaning in opposition to that which has been and is held by Holy Mother Church, whose function is to pass judgment on the true meaning and interpretation of the Sacred Scriptures; or by giving it meanings contrary to the unanimous consent of the fathers."[48]

Trent also censored printers. The ubiquitous distribution of Reformation tracts by local printing presses was one reason the Reformation took off among the common laity. Trent, however, condemned printing and distribution unsanctioned by the church. The council "wishes to impose a restriction also on printers who [think] they have a right to do what they wish without restraint and without the permission of ecclesiastical superiors." Trent also condemned printing Bibles with marginalia commentaries and tracts or treatises where the author's name was hidden from the public or a false name was used.[49]

Original Sin

In session 5 (June 1546), Trent turned to the doctrine of original sin in preparation for introducing the doctrine of justification in session 6. Trent affirmed original sin; Adam's sin did not damage him alone but his progeny. Furthermore, Adam did not merely transmit the death of the body but the death of the soul. His sin does not continue by imitation (as the Pelagians said) but by propagation. Since original sin is not something merely external (mimicked) but internal (inhering within), it cannot be "removed by human and natural powers, or by any remedy other than the merit of the one Mediator, our Lord Jesus Christ, who has reconciled us to God in his own blood, being made our righteousness and sanctification and redemption."[50]

How then does the merit of Christ actually remove original sin within the believer? Baptism. Trent warned against anyone who "denies that the actual merit of Christ Jesus is applied to both adults and infants through the sacrament of baptism duly administered in the form of the church."[51] Over against

---

47. *CT* 1:82; quoted in O'Malley, *Trent*, 95.
48. *Dogmatic Decrees of the Council of Trent, 1545–63*, session 4, second decree (p. 823).
49. *Dogmatic Decrees of the Council of Trent, 1545–63*, session 4, second decree (p. 823).
50. *Dogmatic Decrees of the Council of Trent, 1545–63*, session 5.1–2 (p. 825).
51. *Dogmatic Decrees of the Council of Trent, 1545–63*, session 5.3 (p. 825).

the Anabaptists, Trent condemned anyone who said "that recently born babies should not be baptized even if they have been born to baptized parents."[52] The guilt of original sin is remitted "through the grace of our Lord Jesus Christ which is given in baptism." Nevertheless, not everything is removed by baptism. For "concupiscence or a tendency to sin remains."[53] How this tendency to sin is to be remedied brought Trent to the controversial question of justification.

Justification, Faith, and Love

In session 6 (January 1547), Trent never mentioned Luther or the Reformers, but they were in view when Trent spurred those who had "spread an erroneous doctrine about justification," an error that had resulted in the "loss of many souls" and done "damage to the unity of the church."[54] Yet rather than beginning with a refutation of the Lutheran and Reformed view of justification, Trent began with its own articulation.

However, the end product was not easily reached. Despite whatever appearances Trent might have portrayed toward uniformity, the process was littered with controversy. First, not all theologians had a polemical agenda against Luther and the Reformation view of justification, though many did. Augustinian theologians like Girolamo Seripando thought Luther's articulation of justification had truth to it. Seripando also proposed Trent take seriously Luther's experience in the monastery and his liberating discovery of a gracious God, rather than approaching justification solely from an academic perspective.[55] Cervini trusted Seripando to a degree and even called on Seripando to help write a fresh draft on justification (Seripando was not in favor of the original draft by any means). Seripando did so with optimism, even though the draft he wrote was succeeded by other drafts. Nevertheless, remnants of Seripando's draft can be seen even in the final product.[56]

Second, the tension at Trent became so thick at one point that theologians literally came to punches with each other. For example, Tommaso Sanfelice was sympathetic to Luther's *Bondage of the Will*. The bishop of La Cava believed the will was captive to sin, whereas Trent's final statement affirmed the will's weakness due to sin but ultimately allowed for spiritual ability. Sanfelice also used Luther-like language on justification, including *sola fide*.[57] Sanfelice's stance was mocked by Dionisio de Zanettini. Zanettini and Sanfelice came to words—even blows—over the matter. When Zanettini called Sanfelice a fool, Sanfelice threw Zanettini down by his beard. The wrestling match only incited Zanettini to spit out more insults.

---

52. And anyone who "says that they are indeed baptized for the remission of sins, but incur no trace of the original sin of Adam needing to be cleansed by the water of rebirth for them to obtain eternal life, with the necessary consequence that in their case there is being understood a form of baptism for the remission of sins which is not true, but false: let him be anathema." *Dogmatic Decrees of the Council of Trent, 1545–63*, session 5.4 (pp. 825–26).

53. *Dogmatic Decrees of the Council of Trent, 1545–63*, session 5.5 (p. 826).

54. *Dogmatic Decrees of the Council of Trent, 1545–63*, session 6 (pp. 826–27).

55. On Seripando, see O'Malley, *Trent*, 104, 109.

56. O'Malley, 111.

57. *CT* 5:294–96, 352–54. Cf. O'Malley, 109.

CANONS ON JUSTIFICATION

Some of Trent's most stark statements appear not in its "chapters" but in its "canons." For example, consider its Counter-Reformation spirit in the following canons concerning justification:

> 9. If anyone says that the sinner is justified by faith alone, meaning thereby that no other cooperation is required for him to obtain the grace of justification, and that in no sense is it necessary for him to make preparation and be disposed by a movement of his own will: let him be anathema.
>
> 20. If anyone says that a justified person, of whatever degree of perfection, is not bound to keep the commandments of God and of the church but only to believe, as if the gospel were simply a bare and unqualified promise of eternal life without the condition of observing the commandments: let him be anathema.
>
> 30. If anyone says that once the grace of justification has been received, the fault of any repentant sinner is forgiven and the debt of eternal punishment is wiped out, in such a way that no debt of temporal punishment remains to be discharged, either in this world or later on in purgatory, before entry to the kingdom of heaven can lie open: let him be anathema. (*Dogmatic Decrees of the Council of Trent, 1545–63*, canons concerning justification, pp. 836–89)

Later on, Sanfelice left Trent altogether. The sharp words of Zanettini and the assault of Sanfelice demonstrate just how tense debate could be over the doctrine of justification. In the end, though, Trent did not put forward a doctrine of justification that accommodated Luther or the Reformation.

Trent began its treatment of justification with grace, countering any accusations of Pelagianism from the start: "Actual justification in adults takes its origin from a predisposing grace of God through Jesus Christ" so that "those who have been turned away from God by sins are disposed by God's grace inciting and helping them, to turn towards their own justification by giving free assent to and cooperating with this same grace." Trent guarded itself from the heresy of Pelagianism by admitting a "predisposing grace." However, preparation for justification remains a synergistic operation, one in which man is helped by grace but must cooperate for future justification to take effect. The sinner is not "able, by his own free will and without God's grace, to move." But once predisposing grace is granted, the sinner's will becomes active, and his future justification depends on his cooperation. Although "God touches a person's heart through the light of the Holy Spirit, neither does that person do absolutely nothing in receiving that movement of grace, for he can also reject it."[58]

So far, all of this preparation, as Trent called it, precedes actual justification,

---

58. *Dogmatic Decrees of the Council of Trent, 1545–63*, session 6.5 (p. 828).

"which consists not only in the forgiveness of sins but also in the sanctification and renewal of the inward being by a willing acceptance of the grace and gifts whereby someone from being unjust becomes just, from being an enemy becomes a friend, so that he is an heir in hope of eternal life."[59] Trent diverged from Protestantism not only with its synergism, but also, and especially, by its definition of justification in legal *and* transformative categories. For the Reformers, justification is a forensic declaration by God that results in a change in status; it is not a moral transformation in nature, the "renewal of the inward being." The latter is the effect and fruit of the former, not vice versa. But Trent included both the forgiveness of sins and sanctification within justification, making justification not only a process (rather than an instantaneous declaration) but also a moral change from within. In other words, justification is how a person is *made* righteous.

If justification is not only forgiveness but inward renewal, then justification's "instrumental cause" must be "the sacrament of baptism," and the "formal cause" must be "the justness of God." However, by justness Trent did not mean that justness by which God himself is just. Instead, Trent meant that justness "by which he makes us just." When we are "endowed" with such a justness, we are "renewed in the spirit of our mind, and are not merely considered to be just but we are truly named and are just, each one of us receiving individually his own justness according to the measure which the Holy Spirit apportions to each one as he wills, and in view of each one's dispositions and cooperation."[60] Justification, then, is not only a renewal but a renewal *in degree*. The degree is determined by the human will. The Spirit measures according to the level of human cooperation.

Since justification is an inward renewal involving human cooperation, justification is not the passive reception of a legal righteousness by means of imputation (as it was for the Reformers). Rather, justification must involve an *infusion*—an infusion of faith, hope, and love. Trent's wording set the trajectory for all Roman Catholic articulations of justification moving forward: justification is not by faith alone, but by "faith working through love."[61] *Faith working through love*—here was the nucleus of Rome's position over against the Reformers. The inclusion of love in justification ensures that justification is not by means of a dead faith; for as James said, faith without works is dead, a point Trent was not shy to make.

Assurance?

Trent's denial of justification by faith alone had real, practical consequences for the Christian life. For example, Trent did not believe Christians could have assurance that their salvation is secure, at least not in the Protestant sense.

---

59. *Dogmatic Decrees of the Council of Trent, 1545–63*, session 6.7 (p. 829).
60. *Dogmatic Decrees of the Council of Trent, 1545–63*, session 6.7 (p. 830).
61. *Dogmatic Decrees of the Council of Trent, 1545–63*, session 6.7 (p. 830).

But though it is necessary to believe that sins are not forgiven, nor have they ever been forgiven, save freely by the divine mercy on account of Christ; nevertheless, it must not be said that anyone's sins are or have been forgiven simply because he has a proud assurance and certainty that they have been forgiven, and relies solely on that. For this empty and ungodly assurance may exist among heretics and schismatics, as indeed it does exist in our day, and is preached most controversially against the Catholic Church. Neither should it be declared that those who are truly justified must determine within themselves beyond the slightest hesitation that they are justified, and that no one is absolved from sin and justified except one who believes with certainty that he has been absolved and justified, and that absolution and justification are effected by this faith alone—as if one who does not believe this is casting doubts on God's promises and on the efficacy of the death and resurrection of Christ. For, just as no devout person ought to doubt the mercy of God, the merit of Christ, and the power and efficacy of the sacraments; so it is possible for anyone, while he regards himself and his own weakness and lack of dispositions, to be anxious and fearful about his own state of grace, since no one can know, by that assurance of faith which excludes all falsehood, that he has obtained the grace of God.[62]

Trent may have oversimplified and even caricatured the Reformation position on assurance. Nonetheless, Trent's reaction and denial of assurance substantiated itself as a Counter-Reformation declaration. For Luther the Christian could have full assurance since faith depends not on one's own merits but rests on the merits of Christ alone. In contrast to the *via moderna*, which considered faith itself a work and therefore decided assurance was pretentious on the basis of its nominalism, Luther considered assurance a sign of humility (see chapter 5). The believer is *not* trusting in himself but resting entirely upon the goodness of God and his trusty promises. As Melanchthon defined faith, it is "a sure and constant trust in God's goodwill toward us ... nothing else than trust in the divine mercy promised in Christ. ... this trust in the goodwill or mercy of God first calms our hearts and then inflames us to give thanks to God."[63] Calvin assumed the same posture in his *Institutes*, as did Vermigli in his treatise on *Predestination and Justification*, and so, too, Cranmer in his homily on salvation. In unison, the Reformers clung to such confidence because they believed faith was a gift.

Rome considered the Reformers arrogant. For if they knew their own weakness and lack of disposition toward grace, they would never make such a pretentious grab for assurance. In a twist of irony, the Reformers believed their celebration of assurance depended entirely on their sober acknowledgment of

---

62. *Dogmatic Decrees of the Council of Trent, 1545–63*, session 6.9 (p. 831). Later Trent said, "No one should yield to complacency in faith alone, thinking that by faith alone he has been established as an heir, and that he will obtain that inheritance even if he has not suffered with Christ so as to be glorified with him." Session 6.11 (p. 832).

63. Melanchthon, *MWA* 2.i.92, 115–16. Cameron demonstrates that the nominalism of the *via moderna* led them to believe assurance was arrogance (*European Reformation*, 145).

their own weakness and lack of disposition. As is plain in Luther's *Bondage of the Will*, the Reformers took a far more pessimistic view of man's inability than Rome. Yet since their justification in no way relied on anything in them—not even faith-wrought, grace-infused works—but entirely depended on Christ's righteousness, assurance was a sweet and most definite reality.

That explains, in part, why the Reformers could recommend the doctrine of election. The justified sinner's standing is entirely due to the grace of God, a grace that originates in eternity due to nothing but the pure gratuity of God's decree. Trent, on the other hand, warned against the "rash presumption" of predestination: "no one, so long as he remains in this present life, ought to presume about the hidden mystery of divine predestination as to hold for certain that he is unquestionably of the number of the predestined, as if it were true that one justified is either no longer capable of sin or, if he sins, may promise himself sure repentance. For, apart from a special revelation, it is impossible to know whom God has chosen for himself."[64]

Trent's reaction against assurance (and with it, the certainty of election) is consistent with its corollary belief that the grace of justification can be lost. The justified "grow and increase in that very justness they have received through the grace of Christ, by faith united to good works."[65] If they can increase, however, they can also decrease and even "fall away by sin from the grace of justification which they had received." [66] What sins lead one to fall away? Apostasy. Also, any and every mortal sin.[67]

If the grace of justification is forfeited, can it be regained? Yes, but only if a person makes a real effort to perform works of penance. Those who have fallen away "can again be justified when at God's prompting they have made the efforts through the sacrament of penance to recover, by the merit of Christ, the grace which was lost."[68] Penance is for the restitution of those who have sinned after baptism, which is why penance is called the "second plank." Penance, which involves contrition, absolution, and works of satisfaction, does not remit eternal punishment—baptism serves that purpose by washing away original guilt. But the penance process does—depending on the quality of works of satisfaction— diminish the extent of temporal punishment.[69] Justification for the Reformers,

---

64. *Dogmatic Decrees of the Council of Trent, 1545–63*, session 6.12 (p. 833).

65. *Dogmatic Decrees of the Council of Trent, 1545–63*, session 6.10 (p. 831).

66. *Dogmatic Decrees of the Council of Trent, 1545–63*, session 6.14 (p. 833).

67. Trent listed "fornication, adultery, wantonness, sodomy, theft, avarice, drunkenness, slander, plundering." Yet Trent qualified that grace, not faith, is lost by mortal sins. *Dogmatic Decrees of the Council of Trent, 1545–63*, session 6.14 (p. 834).

68. "For this kind of justification is a restoration of the fallen, which the holy fathers suitably call a second plank for the grace shattered in a storm. It was for the sake of those who fall into sin after baptism that Jesus Christ instituted the sacrament of penance." *Dogmatic Decrees of the Council of Trent, 1545–63*, session 6.14 (p. 834).

69. Trent then defined penance: "Hence it must be taught that the repentance of a Christian after a fall is very different from repentance at baptism: it includes not only ceasing from sins and detestation of them, or a humble and contrite heart, but also confession of them in the sacrament of penance, to be made at least in desire and in due season, absolution by a priest, and also satisfaction by fasting, almsgiving, prayers, and other devout exercises of the spiritual life; these take the place, not indeed of eternal punishment which is remitted together with the guilt either by the sacrament or the desire of the sacrament, but of temporal punishment

by contrast, is not something gained or lost, nor does it increase or diminish. Justification is an instantaneous declaration by God himself that the ungodly are no longer guilty but forever righteous in his sight on the basis of Christ's perfect merits on their behalf. Upon the first instance of faith, Christ's righteous status is imputed, reckoned to the ungodly. Moral transformation then follows yet not as a condition for justification (which is done, complete) but as justification's natural, consequential fruit.[70]

Who Is Closer to Thomas Aquinas, Trent or the Reformers? Debate over Nominalism

Historians and theologians debate how to interpret Trent. For example, some desire to position Trent's decree on justification as a *via media*, somewhere in between the nominalist voluntarism of a Franciscan like Ockham or a scholastic as late as Biel and the evangelical formulation of Luther and the Reformers. However, in a provocative essay, Heiko Oberman examined representatives at Trent and concluded that Trent was indebted to nominalism.

Oberman's claim rests in part on improving the translation of Trent. "If our interpretation is *e mente auctorum*, a true presentation of the mind of the fathers of Trent, the nominalistic doctrine of justification has substantially contributed to the final formulation of the decree, and the Franciscan interest in the *meritum de congruo* has been fully validated, taken into account and safeguarded."[71] Oberman argued that the verb *promereri* must be taken into consideration. Appealing to Andreas de Vega's influence at Trent, Oberman said Trent thought merit *de condigno* was excluded but "sinners are able to earn their justification *de congruo*."[72] Convinced, others like Michael Horton believe the responsibility for nominalism's perpetuation needs reconsideration. "Not the Reformation but Trent represents the triumph of nominalism." If Trent is far closer to the nominalist soteriology of Ockham and Biel, then the "Reformers actually stand closer to Aquinas than does Trent."[73] The Reformers took issue with Thomas at points, but in the grand sweep of soteriology, Thomas became an ally due to his Augustinianism in comparison to the nominalist voluntarism of Ockham and Biel, which the Reformers believed capitulated to semi-Pelagianism at best and Pelagianism at worst. Calvin and Peter Martyr Vermigli, for example, both concluded that Trent was merely a more modest proposal than Pelagius.[74]

---

which (as Scripture teaches) is not wholly discharged—as happens in baptism—by those who, lacking gratitude for the grace of God which they have received, have grieved the Holy Spirit and not feared to violate the temple of God." *Dogmatic Decrees of the Council of Trent, 1545–63*, session 6.14 (p. 834).

70. Trent, too, had something to say about the "fruit of justification," but in a very different sense. *Dogmatic Decrees of the Council of Trent, 1545–63*, session 6.16 (p. 835).

71. Oberman, "Tridentine Decree on Justification," 39.

72. Oberman, 53.

73. "To the extent that they conceived election and justification as conditional and contractual, Ockham and Biel proved Aquinas's conclusion that the idea of merit could be advanced without the blemish of Pelagianism only by anchoring it in unconditional election." Horton, *Justification*, 1:352.

74. Calvin, "Antidote to Trent," 3:108; Vermigli, *Locus on Justification*, 156. Cf. Horton, *Justification*, 1:338.

Reconsidering Trent's relationship to the nominalism of the late medieval *via moderna* may be controversial, but even if valid in the slightest, an ironic turn of events has occurred: the secularization narrative (chapter 1) that claims the Reformers were *the* carriers of nominalism into modernity lacks credibility. That lack of credibility multiplies when post-Trent and post-Reformation figures are considered (see chapter 4). Michael Horton does not speak for himself alone but builds on the scholarship of other historians when he concludes, "At a time when numerous leading theologians on the Roman Catholic side were explicitly committed to nominalism, not a single reformer or refiner of Reformed orthodoxy in the sixteenth and seventeenth centuries attempted to incorporate the ideas of Ockham or Biel, even those purged of their Pelagianizing theses." That claim could be pressed further still since the majority of Reformed Orthodox rejected the univocity theory of Scotus as well. They were convinced it could not be reconciled with their adherence to classical theism's metaphysic of participation, a metaphysic that also proved essential to their Protestant soteriology of participation. As mentioned in chapter 4, Richard Muller has demonstrated as much and his conclusion needs to be repeated: "Whatever one concludes concerning the implications of the univocity of being, the claim that the concept invested itself in Protestant theology cannot be sustained, nor indeed that early modern Protestant thought evidenced a 'shift' away from a 'metaphysics of participation.'"[75]

Therefore, the Reformed Orthodox concluded that Trent was not the road back to an Augustinian-Thomist theology but was a path to a more modern tradition that surfaced within late medieval theology. "The broad consensus of Reformed scholasticism was given to Aquinas's analogical view of participation over against Scotus and especially nominalist departures."[76] Persuaded that catholicity was on their side, the Reformed church concluded that Trent's condemnation of the Reformation was in fact a condemnation of the Augustinian-Thomist tradition, however unwitting that condemnation may have been.[77]

Despite the progress made by the council, in 1547 the assembly came to an abrupt stop. The reasons were complicated. As Charles advanced to a position of superiority over the Smalcald League, Pope Paul III grew nervous at the emperor's increasing political and religious power. He was caught in between two desires: the defeat of Protestants and his fear of a dominating emperor. At the start of 1547, the pope pulled his troops.[78] That January Charles discovered his military front diminished as a result. In March rumors of a plague spread. Before the rise of modern medicine, a plague had the power to wipe out entire towns within weeks. Epidemics created mass panic, and towns not yet affected by the plague

---

75. Muller, "Not Scotist," 146.

76. Horton, *Justification*, 1:332. Horton observes that even as early as Calvin the analogical-participatory fabric was woven into the Reformation's tapestry. See Zachman, "Calvin as Analogical Theologian," 162–87.

77. "Clearly, after Trent, not only was the Reformation interpretation condemned, but the Augustinian path was closed off for good." Horton, *Justification*, 1:350.

78. Hillerbrand, *Division of Christendom*, 277.

closed their gates, not letting anyone in or out, hoping to avoid the worst. While it was still too early to tell if the plague had come to Trent, many at the council were not willing to wait and see. Some at the council already resented meeting in Trent and were all too eager to leave for any excuse. Many also saw this as an opportunity to move the council out of Trent (imperial territory) to a city like Bologna (papal jurisdiction).[79] The quick mass exodus put the council on pause. As it turned out, the panic was premature; no epidemic ever swept through Trent. A handful of citizens suffered from typhus, and nothing more came of it. Little did the council know that wider political troubles had only just begun.

SECOND ASSEMBLY: 1551–52

From 1547 to 1549, a convoluted series of events surrounding diverse rivalries unraveled, making the future of Trent unpredictable. To begin with, Charles was outraged when he discovered that the council had moved from Trent to Bologna without warning. He had won a small victory by persuading pope Paul III that the council should meet in an imperial city. Now that the council had left Trent, the emperor had little influence or guarantee that he could appease German Protestants, or even the Roman Church in his German landscape for that matter.

Previously, Paul III was fearful that Charles might take advantage of a council hosted in his own jurisdiction. Now the tables had turned: Charles feared the pope might have the upper hand. Paul III's indifference to Charles's irritation was due in part to his impatience with German Protestants. Charles held out hope that he could either persuade or force them to attend the council, but by 1547 nothing indicated that the German Protestants planned on making an appearance.[80]

As angry as Charles had become at the news, he was determined to bring the council back to Trent. He received word that the council had moved to Bologna in March 1547. One month later Charles defeated the Smalcald League. With victory in his hands Charles petitioned the pope to change his mind and return the council to Trent. The Protestants had to attend now that Charles had won, or at least so he thought. But if the pope refused, what Protestant would listen to a council that was neither free nor on German soil? Charles was not certain even Roman churches and theologians in his German lands would either, not for theology's sake but on the principle of authority. Yet Paul III did not budge. How could he hand power back over to Charles, the very sovereign who most threatened not only his church but his papal states, especially now that he had acquired unprecedented power in the wake of his Smalcald victory?[81]

Paul III's power play, however, was not as effective as he had hoped, at least not

---

79. See O'Malley, *Trent*, 121–26, for the ways certain persons used rumors of plague to move the council out of Trent. Ironically, the maneuver undermined initial motivations for expediency, drawing out the council for over a decade and a half.

80. O'Malley, 128.

81. O'Malley, 129–30.

in terms of the council's accomplishments. The council transitioned to Bologna and started discussions over the Eucharist, penance, indulgences, purgatory, matrimony, and more. As was their custom, they evaluated Luther's writings and then turned to formulate their stance. But little did they know at the start that their work would amount to little as soon as the political atmosphere grew worse and eventually even changed. For example, on September 10 Paul III's son was murdered not far from where the council was meeting. Pierluigi Farnese's death only hardened the distrust between Paul III and Charles since the pope believed the emperor was somehow connected if not behind his son's stabbing. Could this conspiracy be the first of many more advances on the papal states?[82] Even if the emperor had nothing to do with the murder of Farnese, nevertheless, the pope's suspicions conveyed the emperor's extensive control. He was a threat, and he could not be ignored.

In the months that followed, Paul III and the council corresponded, discussing what conditions had to be met for the council to return to Trent. One deciding factor was the guarantee from Charles that German Protestants would attend the council and acquiesce to its conclusions. Charles believed he could grant such a bold guarantee since the Smalcald League had been defeated. A long string of debates, standoffs, and threats ensued between both parties and their representatives at the council. Still, Paul III entertained the possibility of returning to Trent and commanded that conversations cease in Bologna. By September 1549, few prelates had any patience left to remain in Bologna.[83] Then Paul III died. Who would take his place? More to the point, would the next pope pick up the council in Trent, or was the council lost to history, cursed before it ever found traction?

By the end of 1549, Giovanni Maria Del Monte was elected the next pope.[84] As Julius III he shared Paul III's suspicions toward the emperor's increasing political and ecclesiastical power. Julius was not as supportive of the council as his predecessor, yet the new pope did ignite the council once again in 1551 on one condition: Charles must twist the arms of the Lutherans to attend the council. But since Julius III agreed to reconvene the council at Trent, he made an enemy out of France's new king, Henry II, who detested any concession that empowered the already invincible emperor. Henry II retaliated by claiming he might start a council of his own but in France instead. In essence, Henry II was putting before Julius III the real possibility of schism.[85]

Also in 1551 a heated conflict erupted between Ottavio Farnese and Pope

---

82. O'Malley, 135. While the two sides grew fixed in their opposition to one another, France's new king, Henry II, complicated an already tender political scene (cf. 135–38).

83. For the debates that ensued between 1547 and 1549, see O'Malley, 137–38.

84. Hillerbrand said it was February 1550. Who was right? See Hillerbrand, *Division of Christendom*, 277.

85. "More than that, as early as the summer of 1550, he contemplated an alliance with England, Denmark, Sweden, Poland, the Lutheran princes of the empire, and, possibly, the Republic of Venice to open hostilities against Charles. Most shocking, in early 1551 the Most Christian King entered into a military alliance with the sultan, 'the infidel,' whose forces pressed on Charles's eastern frontier." O'Malley, *Trent*, 141–42.

Julius, the former recruiting the military support of the French. The result was war. Ironically, Julius had no choice but to look for an ally in the emperor himself.[86] Meanwhile, the Council of Trent had just started and many of its bishops now wondered how funding could continue moving forward when the pope was sending his finances to the warfront instead. When Henry II gained the upper hand in the war, Julius negotiated peace with France, and new life was breathed back into the Council of Trent, even if the conflict resulted in few French participants at the council.[87]

The doctrine on the docket was the Eucharist, but also penance, two doctrines that served to inflame Luther's initial protest. Also on the agenda: the participation of German Protestants, the long-anticipated plan of the emperor. The Protestants had conditions: they, too, wanted the right to vote, the ability to influence the direction of the council and its theology. Attached to such a condition was another: the pope must submit himself to the council and its conclusions. In the Protestant reasoning, if they could attain voting status and affect the council in a more Protestant direction, then the pope would have to accept the outcome since he was under the council's authority.

These conditions, however, were never going to be met. Charles was not against giving the Protestants time and attention in the council to put forward their case. But Julius III was less flexible, only willing for Protestants to come if they yielded to the council. A compromise was met: "Crescenzio, yielding to pressure from the imperial representatives, proposed that on January 24 a quasi-unofficial (*secreta*) General Congregation be held at which the Protestants could present their case."[88] The meeting did not go well since Trent had already decided on justification during Trent's first assembly, and the Protestants would never agree to it. Furthermore, both sides disagreed on the nature of the council itself; to the Protestants the Council of Trent was not a free council as long as the Protestants were treated as heretics and refused voting privileges.

Interpretations of the Reformation sometimes assume the divide with the papacy was merely over a handful of issues, as if reconciliation was possible if only those few core issues could be resolved. But a closer look at the divide reveals that the foundation itself was cracked. The divide was not an issue-by-issue problem, but the divergence of two totally irreconcilable models. As O'Malley conveys, "The episode makes absolutely clear that, thirty-five years after the outbreak of the Reformation, the problem was no longer disagreement over this or that doctrine. The Protestants had developed and appropriated an operational

---

86. On the origins of this war, see O'Malley, 142–43.

87. Later "Henry asserted that the pope, under pressure from the emperor, had broken the peace, which meant that he, the king, could not safely send prelates to the council. But more fundamentally, he could not do so because he regarded the meeting at Trent not as a general council but as a private assembly to promote the concerns of those for whom it had been convoked rather than the general interests of the church. For that reason the French church did not consider itself bound by any decisions the assembly might take." O'Malley, 144–45.

88. More Protestant conditions are listed as well in O'Malley, 155.

paradigm that was incompatible with the corresponding paradigm of the bishops and theologians at Trent."[89] At some point, Charles realized as much, which had to be sobering. He had tried for so long to make sure the council met on his soil and Protestants finally attended, only to discover he was laboring for a lost cause from the start. Who did he blame? He blamed the council and the pope, who had no intention of considering the Protestant proposal for reform with any seriousness.[90]

If any of the chapters and canons of 1551 manifested such incompatibility with the Reformers, it had to be the Eucharist and penance. In session 13 (October 1551), Trent doubled down on its affirmation of real, essential presence: Christ's body is "truly, really, and substantially contained in the propitious sacrament of the holy eucharist under the appearance of those things which are perceptive to the sense."[91] The mechanism—transubstantiation—is asserted without qualification: "By consecration of the bread and wine, there takes place the change of the whole substance of the bread into the substance of the body of Christ our Lord, and of the whole substance of the wine into the substance of his blood."[92]

Since the elements change into the substance of Christ's body, although without losing their appearance, every Christian should venerate the elements. Veneration was one reason the Reformers associated idolatry with the Mass. Yet if Christ himself was "truly, really, and substantially contained" at the altar, then veneration was entirely appropriate. Once a year "this sublime and venerable sacrament should be hailed with particular veneration and solemnity, and carried with reverence and honor in processions through streets and public places."[93] Trent responded to the accusation of idolatry by anathematizing anyone who said the Son was "not to be adored in the holy Sacrament of the eucharist by the worship of adoration."[94] For Trent, adoration was fitting since the issue was christological.

Trent's articulation and defense of transubstantiation was polemical in nature. Seripando presented Luther's points on the Eucharist beforehand. However, the council could not absorb Luther's criticisms since they could only hear them through the paradigm of their own penance system. That much is obvious in the way Luther's criticisms were presented, namely, as points abstracted from the Reformation program. Seripando's "procedure precluded a presentation of the

89. "There was no possibility that the council would or could accede to the Protestant demands, just as there was no possibility that the Protestants would or could yield to the council as it was in fact constituted." O'Malley, 156; cf. 249.

90. "From his viewpoint, therefore, the council had failed in the purposes for which he had insisted on its being convened and then reconvened. The final blow had been dealt to his 'great plan.' He let Toledo know that he saw suspension as inevitable but that he did not want the initiative to come from himself." O'Malley, 157.

91. *Dogmatic Decrees of the Council of Trent, 1545–63*, 13.1 (p. 843).

92. *Dogmatic Decrees of the Council of Trent, 1545–63*, 13.4 (p. 845).

93. *Dogmatic Decrees of the Council of Trent, 1545–63*, 13.5 (p. 845).

94. *Dogmatic Decrees of the Council of Trent, 1545–63*, canon 6 (p. 848). Also, canon 8 denies a mere spiritual presence, and canon 11 denies that faith alone is sufficient for preparation.

system or synthesis from which the points were lifted. It judged them by the standard of a different system/synthesis and thus perforce indicated their incompatibility with that standard."[95] Luther's criticisms of transubstantiation, extracted from the foundation of *solus Christus, sola gratia,* and *sola fide,* made little sense and appeared thin. O'Malley concludes that Trent's "proof texting" hermeneutic of Luther and the Reformers was one of the council's greatest, even "systemic weaknesses." Reading through the chapters and canons of Trent, the interpreter wonders whether the theologians and bishops did (or could) understand Luther's paradigm *in toto.* Trent was so ingrained within its own late medieval paradigm that interpreting Luther with accuracy was tainted from the start.[96]

In session 14 (November 1551), Trent confirmed the system of penance already in practice across Europe among the laity. Trent started with the underlying issue: authority. Did the church and its priests have the authority and power to "forgive and retain sins"? Yes, said Trent, since this authority and power were "communicated to the apostles and to their lawful successors," the church being the latter.[97]

The priest could then say with confidence, "I absolve you," when the penitent confessed his or her transgressions. In its broadest sense, the penance process includes contrition, confession, absolution, and satisfaction (see chapter 3). All three are required "for the full and complete forgiveness of sins." These three produce "a peace and serenity of conscience"; Trent condemned anyone (Luther?) who said that the "parts of penance are the fears which afflict conscience and faith."[98] Trent's definition of each step was informative:

1. **Contrition:** a grief and detestation of mind at the sin committed, together with the resolution not to sin in the future.[99]
2. **Confession:** complete confession of sins ... necessary by divine law for all who have fallen after baptism.[100]
   Absolution: forgiving sins by the power of the Holy Spirit conferred in ordination.[101]

---

95. O'Malley, *Trent,* 132–33.

96. O'Malley, 249. O'Malley does put some of the blame at Luther's feet since Luther's style of writing was hyperbolic by nature. Yet Trent's gifted linguists and rhetoricians should have known that too.

97. *Dogmatic Decrees of the Council of Trent, 1545–63,* 14.1 (p. 849).

98. *Dogmatic Decrees of the Council of Trent, 1545–63,* 14.3 (p. 851).

99. Trent clarified that contrition is necessary and cannot be bypassed: "Some make false accusations against Catholic writers, as if they have taught that the sacrament of penance confers grace without a good impulse on the part of its recipients, something which the church of God has never taught nor imagined." *Dogmatic Decrees of the Council of Trent, 1545–63,* 14.4 (pp. 851–52).

100. "Here it follows that all mortal sins that penitents are aware of after a careful self-examination have to be related in the confession, even if they are very private.... For venial sins, by which we are not cut off from the grace of God and into which we more frequently fall, although they may be admitted in confession ... can nevertheless be passed over in silence without fault and expiated by many other remedies." *Dogmatic Decrees of the Council of Trent, 1545–63,* 14.5 (p. 852).

101. Trent says mortal sin in the priest does not annul the absolution of the penitent. *Dogmatic Decrees of the Council of Trent, 1545–63,* 14.6 (p. 854).

3. ***Satisfaction:*** [works the priest imposes] aimed at protecting the new life and at being a remedy against weakness, [but also] for the atonement and punishment of past sins.[102]

Notable is Trent's sharp rebuke toward those (Protestants) who thought that the power to forgive belonged to all Christians and not priests and bishops alone. Trent countered the priesthood of believers, a hallmark of the Reformation, by restricting the "ministry of the keys" to the clergy.[103] Notable as well was Trent's pastoral motive regarding works of satisfaction. The priest assigned works of penance, not merely with an aim to protect the penitent from future wickedness but to punish the penitent so they could pay for past wickedness.

A DECADE OF DEADLOCK AND INQUISITION

Trent came to another abrupt stop in 1552. War once again was a barrier. Henry II of France had attacked Charles, but this time his military strategy was effective, infiltrating imperial territory. No longer did the pope think Trent was safe.

Those at Trent may have thought the council could still convene within the next year or two, but Trent did not reopen for another ten years as political rivalries continued to overcrowd the council's plans. Between 1552 and 1562, a slew of political and ecclesiastical changes occurred that changed the landscape of Europe: Charles abdicated, and his brother Philip II was handed the Low Countries as well as Spain, Milan, and Naples, while his brother Ferdinand took the lead over Habsburg territories; the Lutherans recovered thanks to the Peace of Augsburg (1555), and German nobles resurrected in power; Pope Julius III died (1555) and was followed by Pope Marcellus II (Marcello Cervini) and then Paul IV (Giampietro Caraffa); Spain and Pope Paul IV took up arms against each other; Elizabeth became queen of England, giving English evangelicals relief from Bloody Mary; and the decades old rivalry between the empire and the French finally halted with the Treaty of Cateau-Cambrésis (1559), thanks to the negotiated equity between Philip II and Henry II.[104]

Out of all these changes, Paul IV's papal reign (1555–59) had notable effects for the future of reform. Paul IV took up the mantle of the Counter-Reformation with energy and hostility. He not only detested the emperors and their cooperation with the Lutherans during the Peace of Augsburg but lit a fire under the Inquisition to silence Protestantism wherever it could be found.[105] The Roman Inquisition's origins can be traced back to the 1540s. Pope Paul III grew tired of Protestant resistance and increasingly believed that the differences between Protestants and papacy were irreconcilable. As the veins of both camps

---

102. *Dogmatic Decrees of the Council of Trent, 1545–63*, 14.8 (p. 856).
103. *Dogmatic Decrees of the Council of Trent, 1545–63*, 14.6 (p. 854).
104. O'Malley, *Trent*, 159–67.
105. O'Malley, 159.

hardened, Paul III reluctantly agreed to the formation of a Roman Inquisition in 1542 under the heavy influence and pressure of Caraffa, who first observed the Inquisition in Spain.[106] Under the headship of the pope and with the governance of Caraffa, the Roman Inquisition went to work, sounding the heresy bell whenever evangelicals were located and confiscating evangelical books. Caraffa's aim was directed at Lutherans, but he targeted Calvinists in particular. His zeal was so impetuous that Caraffa said he would not hesitate to torture and burn his own father if he even sniffed an evangelical spirit in him.[107] When Caraffa became Pope Paul IV, the Inquisition entered its most aggressive format.

The Inquisition's success, in part, can be attributed to its censorship of printed books it considered contrary to the Church of Rome. It did not matter whether these books were old patristic works or more recent Protestant works; anything and everything that stood against Rome, either in theology or ethics, had to be burned. The Inquisition's *Index of Prohibited Books*, first published in 1559 by Paul IV, was used to flag, confiscate, and keep from distribution a whole range of evangelical works.[108]

The Inquisition also took a hands-on approach to suppressing dissent, whether by means of imprisonment, torture, or even execution. In the decades prior to the Reformation, the Spanish Inquisition gained a reputation for its merciless measures against heretics, a no tolerance policy. However, the Inquisition's methods were not any more extreme than punishment inflicted by civil authorities. The Inquisition's true success came not so much with punishment itself as with the *threat* of punishment. Its *reputation* had far more to do with its success in marketing its threats and prohibitions than it did with punishment carried out against its victims.[109]

Contrary to caricatures, the Inquisition was not so much an angry, capricious firestorm as a measured prosecution modeling secrecy (so the accused could retain their reputation if proven innocent), as well as moderation in methods of infliction. At points the Inquisition was far more concerned with justice in its

106. "Paul III, fearing popular hostility, was less than enthusiastic about the idea, but reluctantly allowed Caraffa to introduce the Inquisition since moderate reform efforts were failing to curb the growth of Protestantism.... On 21 July 1542, with the bull *Licet ab initio*, Paul III formally sanctioned the Roman Inquisition and extended its authority to all Christendom. It was an effective instrument so long as the monarch cooperated with it." Lindberg, *European Reformations*, 344, 345. Cf. Tedeschi, *Prosecution of Heresy*, 10–11, 23. Humanists were not exempt either, not even its greatest architects, says Lindberg. "In marked departure from the reception of Erasmus in other countries, Italy rejected him as a 'Lutheran' heretic" (342). Lindberg also observes how the Inquisition was not restricted to religious control but was also used for social control. For example, in Spain the Inquisition was used against immigrants from France. However, by the 1530s the Inquisition had turned mostly to the suppression of evangelicals.

107. Lindberg, 344–45; Spitz, *Renaissance and Reformation Movements*, 477.

108. Historians debate just how oppressive or effective the index could be. Lindberg, *European Reformations*, 342. What is clear, however, is just how scandalous others considered the Inquisition. "Paul's *Index* was so extreme that it elicited from the Jesuit Peter Canisius, certainly not known for being soft on heresy, the cry that it was a scandal.... When Paul died that very year, pressure mounted from all sides for a mitigation of its stipulations, a phenomenon that affected deliberations at the reconvened council." O'Malley, *Trent*, 160.

109. Lindberg, *European Reformations*, 343.

treatment of prisoners than its surrounding societies where civil authorities cared little about a fair trial or the conditions of its inmates.[110] Unlike civil authorities, where accountability may be limited, the Inquisition had to work in conjunction with both the state and the papacy, even if the Inquisition at times possessed unrivaled authority.[111] If torture resulted in a recantation, the papacy might question the legitimacy of the changed mind. The Inquisition, then, could not run wild in its punitive strategies. Torture might be used to prime the pump, but its use had real limits.[112] Tearing someone apart limb by limb to draw out a confession might be effective but was hardly convincing in the end.

If any organization gave credence to the label *Counter-Reformation*, it was the Inquisition. Yet the Inquisition and the *Index of Prohibited Books* were but two examples displaying Paul IV's determination to root out Protestantism. At the same time, Paul IV's Counter-Reformation agenda did not incline him to reconvene Trent, since he interpreted Trent's past assemblies as soft on Protestantism and loose on papal oversight.[113] For a host of reasons, by the end of Paul IV's life and reign as pope, he was extremely unpopular among his own holy city. If he could hear the city that he governed while he drew his last breath, he might have heard riots in the streets, angry citizens setting the city on fire, and decapitations of statues bearing the pope's resemblance.[114]

The next pope, Pius IV (Giovanni Angelo de' Medici) was elected in 1559 and was Paul IV's opposite, relaxed on morality and liberal with papal doctrine and practice.[115] Yet Pius IV was shrewd enough to recognize potential schism on France's part when he saw it. The French reign passed from Henry II to Francis II and then to the boy king, Charles IX. Serendipitous in timing, Calvinism made inroads among the nobility through it all, and the Huguenots became a political faction impossible to suppress, especially as they recruited allies to their cause.[116] In a shocking turn of French history, the world watched

---

110. Compare, e.g., Spain's corrupt legal system to the Inquisition. See Lindberg, 343; Tedeschi, *Prosecution of Heresy*, 8.

111. "In 1478 the pope granted the Spanish sovereigns the right to set up and direct the Inquisition. Inquisitors had power over all religious orders and (after 1531) even over bishops." Lindberg, 344.

112. "Confessions obtained by torture were not considered valid until ratified by the defendant 24 hours later outside the torture chamber. The judicial torture itself customarily was suspension of the victim by a rope and pulley, with arms bound behind the back. Supposedly the maximum length of suspension was an hour." Lindberg, 344. Cf. Tedeschi, *Prosecution of Heresy*, 145; and Kamen, *Inquisition and Society in Spain in Sixteenth and Seventeenth Centuries*, 161–77.

113. "On January 20, 1556, soon after his election, Paul announced to the cardinals his intention of creating a new commission on reform.... Even if Paul had lived longer, the plan, ever more grandiose, almost certainly could not have succeeded. The failure of yet another 'papal reform commission' fueled the widespread conviction that the papacy could not and would not reform itself." O'Malley, *Trent*, 161.

114. On the violence of these riots, see O'Malley, 162.

115. He relaxed and sometimes even reversed many of Paul IV's Counter-Reformation efforts, from the *Index* to indulgences. See O'Malley, 163.

116. "The Huguenots, as they were known, threatened to form a military alliance not unlike the earlier Schmalkaldic League. They were most obviously different from the Lutherans in that they drew notoriety to themselves by uncompromising iconoclasm, which resulted in the desecration of churches, the smashing of altars and statues, and the burning of sacred paintings." O'Malley, 165.

to see if France might become Protestant. To turn the tide back to the Roman Church, in 1560 Pius IV began the process to reconvene the Council of Trent. Pius had an advantage that past popes did not: the empire was, at long last, not at war. Pius might just gain the support of Charles's two brothers (Philip II and Ferdinand I) and the king of France (Francis II) at the same time, which was previously inconceivable.[117]

Nevertheless, agreement on the type of council was evasive: Philip was in favor of Trent's continuation, but Francis and Ferdinand demanded a brand-new council as the only way to negotiate with both the Huguenots and the Lutherans. Toward the end of 1560, the pope passed a bull that was vague enough to inaugurate a council without being specific as to what kind. Behind the bull, however, was Pius's unspoken intention that this future council continue the legacy of Trent.[118]

THIRD ASSEMBLY: 1562–63

With no lingering indication that Protestants would have a hand in the council moving forward, the years 1562 and 1563 reflect an uncompromising commitment to the ecclesiastical practices of the Roman Church over against the Reformation. Trent confirmed its certified stance, from the sacrifice of the Mass to penance and purgatory. However, that did not mean the council was one in heart and mind. Far from it. Relentless debates and divisions plagued these two years as factions within the council could not agree, and the three powers— monarchs, bishops, and papacy—cultivated already existing suspicions toward one another. At points the way forward appeared indiscernible, and many anticipated that the pope would adjourn the council, although that papal temptation was met with serious opposition by monarchs like Philip II and Ferdinand.[119] While the history of division from 1562 to 1563 was a web of convolution to say the least, several key dividing lines can be identified, though these are in no way exhaustive.

First, these years drove a wedge between those loyal to the pope and his supremacy (called zealots or the *zelanti*), and those who defaulted to the prerogative of the council and its bishops (called the Reforming Party). With each ongoing or new disagreement, doctrinal or ecclesiastical, the rupture festered further, bringing to the surface the fundamental disparity: the extent of the pope's authority over the council. That irresolvable tension led to countless quibbles, some minor and others major.[120]

Second, bishops could not agree on the source of their power and authority. Some bishops argued that their power ultimately originated from the pope.

---

117. "In the Treaty of Cateau-Cambrésis, both Philip II and Henry II had agreed to support the convocation of a council." O'Malley, 166.

118. The bull: *Ad Ecclesiae Regimen*. O'Malley, 167.

119. E.g., see Ferdinand's letter to the pope: *CT* 13/2:292–300. Cf. O'Malley, 202.

120. O'Malley, 173.

The Council of Trent by Pasquale Cati
Public Domain

After all, he was the vicar of Christ on earth and therefore the one who appointed them as bishops. Others said that only God himself deserves such credit; ordination is a divine act of consecration that can be attributed to none other than God himself (they affirmed the *jus divinum*).[121] This debate may have been the most difficult to overcome at Trent as both sides were immovable.

Third, the bishops could not agree on whether the cup in the Lord's Supper should be given to the laity, nor could they decide if clerical celibacy should be mandated. Consider the former. During the period of the early church, the cup was granted to the laity, as certain bishops were eager to point out. However, that practice changed with time and the rise of the papacy for various reasons.[122] The impasse between the two sides was so strong that the debate had to be taken to the pope when no other solution could be mustered, which set off those bishops already resistant to papal authority over the council.[123]

---

121. Many Spaniards and Northern Italians sided for *jus divinum*, while many Italians became zealots. O'Malley, 179, 197.

122. See O'Malley, 190, for history of this evolution.

123. "It was a disappointment to the members of the imperial party, who pleaded for a decision from the council itself. In their eyes remanding the matter to the pope was an abrogation of responsibility on the part of the council and weakened its authority" (O'Malley, 195). Did clerical celibacy run along the same lines of impasse? Yes, to a degree. "They unanimously agreed on the spiritual superiority of celibacy to matrimony, but

FRENCH CONCILIARISTS AND PIUS IV

In June 1561 Catherine summoned an assembly at Poissy to appoint French representatives for Trent. She also had plans to discuss possible solutions to the internal conflict due to the rising challenge of Huguenots in the nobility, perhaps the most urgent matter on the table. Huguenots were not prohibited from Poissy since Catherine intended to negotiate. Nevertheless, Catherine's summons appeased pope and emperor as well, giving them the impression that France still intended to back Trent (O'Malley, *Trent*, 199). However, when all sides assembled the next month, the attempt at concessions between French Catholics and Huguenots was a failure. Worried that Philip II would have to step in, Catherine promised that bishops would be sent to the Council of Trent, a promise she did not keep and may not have intended to keep at all. After a second try at a colloquy at Château de Saint-Germain-en Laye (1562), only to meet failure once more, Catherine had to come through on her word to send bishops to Trent.

Eventually the French did arrive at Trent, which put Pope Pius IV back in Rome through turmoil. "Pius IV had convoked the council particularly out of concern for France, but he, like all the popes of the period, knew that official repudiation of the Pragmatic Sanction of Bourges did not at all mean that conciliarist sentiments were dead among French bishops and theologians. For the French the principles upon which the Council of Basel had functioned were the ideal. For the pope they were an abomination. Pius feared French participation in the council as much as he wanted it" (O'Malley, *Trent*, 199).

Despite these dividing lines, Trent did manage to draft doctrinal chapters and canons that reflected its basic commitments and addressed some (not all) areas of internal controversy with broad strokes.

In session 21 (July 1562), Trent said the laity were not bound to receive both the bread and the cup, an indirect although more voluntary way of retaining the late medieval practice of withholding the cup.[124] Over against critics who said that withholding the cup from the laity resulted in receiving Christ only in part, Trent replied that one only need receive one element to receive the whole Christ. They are not "cheated of any grace necessary for salvation."[125]

Luther protested the Mass as a sacrifice. Such language, he said, turned the Mass into a work itself. Instead of looking to Christ's sacrifice on the cross by

---

they held diverse opinions on whether celibacy was a church law or intrinsic to the priesthood, and therefore whether the pope could dispense from celibacy a priest already ordained" (228–29).

124. *Dogmatic Decrees of the Council of Trent, 1545–63*, 21.1 (p. 859). However, the next chapter (21.2) is far more assertive in defending the church's authority and power to withhold the cup: "Although from the beginning of Christian worship the use of both kinds was common, yet that custom was very widely changed in the course of time; and so Holy Mother Church, acknowledging her authority over the administration of the sacraments and influenced by good and serious reasons, has approved this custom of communicating in one form and has decreed this to be its rule, which is not to be condemned nor freely changed without the church's own authority" (p. 860).

125. *Dogmatic Decrees of the Council of Trent, 1545–63*, 21.3 (p. 860).

faith alone, one looked to the Mass, as if by receiving it a good work had now been performed.[126] Nevertheless, in session 22 (September 1562), Trent retained the vocabulary of "altar" when referring to the Lord's Table and "sacrifice" when referring to the Mass. "In this divine sacrifice which is performed in the mass, the very same Christ is contained and offered in bloodless manner who made a bloody sacrifice of himself once for all on the cross." Therefore, Trent felt justified to call the Mass a "propitiatory sacrifice" that appeased the Lord when one sinned. The only difference between the cross and the Mass was the "manner" of the offering itself. Furthermore, the sacrifice of the Mass was not only offered to make satisfaction for the living, but also for those in purgatory "not yet fully cleansed."[127]

In retellings of Trent, the council was sometimes said to have prohibited Mass in the vernacular. However, Trent never condemned such a practice. Rather, Trent explained why its predecessors did not think a vernacular liturgy was "advantageous" in all places at all times.[128] Trent only condemned those who said the Mass should be celebrated only in the vernacular.[129] Nevertheless, those at Trent and those immediately after Trent were not likely to switch from a Latin liturgy to the vernacular. "Latin was such a badge of identity for Catholics that it prevailed unquestioned."[130] Still, Trent never did put forward a specific liturgy that all churches everywhere were required to follow.

In session 23 (July 1563), Trent outlined and defended hierarchy in the church as well as apostolic succession. The "power" the apostles received from Christ was passed down to the subsequent priesthood, infused with apostolic power to "consecrate" the Mass and "remit or retain sins."[131] Scripture and tradition support the church's belief that "grace is conferred in sacred ordination," thereby substantiating holy orders as one of the seven sacraments.[132] Trent, therefore, had no patience for the Reformation belief in the priesthood of all believers, as if priests and people alike were "equally endowed with the same spiritual power." Rather than "openly overthrowing the church's hierarchy," said Trent, not only should the differences between clergy and laity be preserved but the hierarchy within the clergy itself. Bishops "are higher than priests and are able to confer the sacrament of confirmation, to ordain the ministers of the church ... whereas those of lower order have no power to perform any of these acts."[133] Additionally, ordination itself depended in no way on secular powers or the authority of the people.[134]

---

126. O'Malley, *Trent*, 189.

127. *Dogmatic Decrees of the Council of Trent, 1545–63*, 21.2 (p. 862).

128. *Dogmatic Decrees of the Council of Trent, 1545–63*, 21.8 (p. 864).

129. *Dogmatic Decrees of the Council of Trent, 1545–63*, canon 9 (p. 865).

130. It became a nonnegotiable issue, allegedly written in stone by the Council of Trent. O'Malley, *Trent*, 190.

131. *Dogmatic Decrees of the Council of Trent, 1545–63*, 23.1 (p. 865).

132. *Dogmatic Decrees of the Council of Trent, 1545–63*, 23. 3 (p. 866).

133. *Dogmatic Decrees of the Council of Trent, 1545–63*, 23.4 (p. 867).

134. Trent denied true ordination to anyone appointed by secular authorities *alone* and not by the church. *Dogmatic Decrees of the Council of Trent, 1545–63*, 23.4 (p. 867). "At this time in the history of the church

In session 24 (November 1563), marriage was confirmed as one of the seven sacraments, and in session 25 (December 1563), purgatory, the intercession of the saints, the veneration of their relics, and sacred images were all established as key tenants that aided and ensured the success of the penance process. To condemn the intercession of the saints and the veneration of their relics or icons—as the iconoclasts did—was to cut oneself off from the instruments the Holy Spirit used to increase devotion. However, Trent intended to reform its practitioners, warning them against "superstition" and those who aimed to "profit" from relics and icons. If an image was erected in a church or holy site, its placement had to receive the approval of a bishop first. Abuses had to be "rooted out," concluded Trent.[135]

THE REFORM OF THE PARISH

One of Trent's most significant contributions was its reform of parishes. From the start of the council, the absentee priest was considered egregious by many, an easy target of the Reformation. Although Trent did not make residency in one's parish an absolute, nevertheless, Trent did mandate that every priest cultivate and complete his duties to his people.[136] Moreover, priests were not to neglect preaching the Scriptures to their people. Preaching was to be a natural habit— even a principal duty—if a priest was resident and responsible, present in the life of his church to feed his flock the spiritual food they needed. In this mandate, Trent took on a pastoral tone, galvanizing pastors to be shepherds of their flocks. The mandate worked; in the years and decades after Trent, preaching became a primary focus, especially among the Jesuits.[137]

Did Trent ever meet the goal of its reforming members to reform the head of the church himself and his curia? The impossibility of reforming the head was due to the inner conflict of the council itself, bishops disagreeing as they did over conciliarism and curialism. In part, the impossibility of reforming the head was due to the pope's (or popes') own regulatory evasiveness. The pope remained at a distance (even physically), which gave the superficial impression that the council was free. However, the pope was involved by means of bishops loyal to his agenda, though some might say this involvement was a mechanism for control. Francisco de Córdoba said that there was not one but two councils at play. "One is the council at Trent, and the other the council in Rome with the pope [and the cardinals]. They are somehow at war with each other."[138] If Francisco de Córdoba was right, then conciliarists fought for a reforming vision they never

bishops were chosen principally in three ways: nomination by the pope, nomination by a sovereign (in France, Spain, Portugal, Poland, and Hungary), or election by a cathedral chapter. The canon did not directly challenge these modes." However, there were some, like de Guise, who held a minority position that advocated the people's choice. O'Malley, *Trent*, 211, 215.

135. *Dogmatic Decrees of the Council of Trent, 1545–63*, 25 (pp. 869–70).
136. O'Malley, *Trent*, 199.
137. O'Malley, 257–59. O'Malley is so bold as to call this revival the "golden age."
138. *CT* 13/2:275; cited in O'Malley, 201.

really began. "Reformers at the council wanted to put limits on how the papacy exercised its authority, and the issue of councils' superiority over it, though never formally debated at the council, threatened time and again to raise its ugly head." But the case for episcopal instead of papal authority never won out: "On the burning question of 'reform of the head,' the popes from Paul III to Pius IV did everything in their power to keep it out of the hands of the council."[139]

CATHOLIC SUBSTANCE OR SECT? ANTIDOTES

"No previous council had ever so often and so explicitly insisted on its teaching's continuity with the authentic Christian past," says John O'Malley in a transparent evaluation.[140] His point is well taken. When presented with the Reformation, Trent labeled the Reformers innovators, deviators from the unbroken continuity with the catholic past, and therefore heretics. Trent operated from their conviction that the church of Rome was on the side of continuity and the Reformers were not. In time the label "Roman Catholic" solidified that divide, positioning the Reformation outside the confines of true, catholic teaching.

However, history did not prove so easily polemicized. Rome's claims—and its reading of history—raised serious questions. Trent's stance on justification, for example, was not only anti-Lutheran, but it also, perhaps inadvertently at points, condemned swaths of past expressions on justification by major theologians of the church catholic. "At Trent, a part of the previous Catholic tradition, whose roots went back to Bernard of Clairvaux and Augustine, was anathematized," says Anthony Lane. "The council excluded what had previously been acceptable Catholic teaching on justification."[141]

In the estimation of the Reformers, therefore, the problem with the papacy was not merely a lack of ecclesiastical purity or spiritual vitality. Those committed to the papacy like Ignatius of Loyola misunderstood the real problem, which was *theological*. "In Luther's view," said David Steinmetz, "the late medieval Church suffered, not so much from a failure to implement its own traditional principles (as Ignatius thought), but from a misguided and uncritical commitment to the wrong principles."[142]

From that vantage point, the Reformers considered Trent final proof for their original claims: *Trent may be Roman, but it is not purely catholic.* For example, Martin Chemnitz wrote an extensive reply called *Examination of the Council of Trent.*[143] Chemnitz's reply was a double-edged sword. It embodied Luther's formal principle, which first sparked controversy, claiming Trent's theology

---

139. O'Malley, 270. A qualification deserves emphasis: Trent was not universal in its application. For example, some French territories were not inclined toward Trent. I owe this insight to Lee Gatiss.

140. O'Malley, 274. O'Malley may caricature the Reformers when he reduces their protest to the belief that the church had departed from the gospel early on. That may be the position of the radicals, but the Reformers had a far more nuanced view of history.

141. Lane, *Regensburg Article 5 on Justification*, 87.

142. Steinmetz, *Luther in Context*, 127.

143. Chemnitz, *Examination of the Council of Trent*, 4 vols.

did not accord with Scripture itself. This point is plain in John Calvin's reply as well—*Canons and Decrees of the Council of Trent, with the Antidote*. Calvin labored from his opening pages out of great frustration: Trent elevated its own soteriological and ecclesiastical claims above the Scriptures.

Yet the other sharp edge of the Reformation sword cut just as deep—maybe more so for the sixteenth-century defender of Trent. Chemnitz (and Calvin) evaluated Trent and concluded that Trent's claims did not match the church catholic. With a quotation from the Formula of Concord, Pelikan sharpened the point of this Reformation sword:

> By adopting this teaching and by anathematizing Luther's doctrine [*sola fide* and imputation], Trent seemed to Chemnitz to be condemning not only the Protestant principle of Luther's Reformation, but considerable portions of the *Catholic substance* it purported to defend. For the weight of the Catholic tradition supported justification by grace alone without human merit, particularly if "Catholic tradition" included, as it did for Chemnitz, not merely learned theology, but also "all prayers of the saints in which they ask to be instructed, illumined, and sanctified by God. By these prayers they acknowledge that they cannot have what they are asking for by their own natural powers." . . . Thus he [Chemnitz] demonstrated the *truly traditional and Catholic character of the Reformation doctrine*, implying that by closing the door to this doctrine Trent was making Rome a sect.[144]

Pelikan's words "Trent was making Rome a sect" are bold, but in the opinion of the Reformers never truer than in the aftermath of Trent. The Reformers —Lutheran, Reformed, and Anglican—positioned their churches *within* that "truly traditional and Catholic" stream of the past. As for the present, Rome, not the Reformers, was the sect that departed from catholic teaching and history. From that angle, which side stood in line most with authentic catholicity depended on two divergent interpretations of history, one Roman, the other Reformational.[145]

And for both sides, nothing less than *renewal* was at stake.

---

144. Pelikan, *Obedient Rebels*, 52–53; quoting Formula of Concord, Solid Declaration, 15, *Bek.* (*BC* 523).

145. To qualify, the Reformers still thought Roman churches were churches. "We by no means deny that the churches under his [the pope's] tyranny remain churches," said Calvin. The reformer was persuaded that these churches retained "traces of the church" nonetheless. However, the diamond has been buried in a rubble. "Christ lies hidden, half buried, the gospel overthrown, piety scattered, the worship of God nearly wiped out" (*Institutes* 4.2.1). "Nearly" wiped out—that qualifier keeps Calvin from rejecting these churches as true churches altogether. In summary, Billings observes that Calvin was "deeply and passionately anti-Roman Catholic." Nevertheless, since Calvin thought these churches retained traces of the church, Calvin attempted to re-catholicize them according to their true catholic heritage. Billings, "Catholic Calvin," 120.

CONCLUSION

The One, Holy, Catholic, and Apostolic Church

They allege that we have fallen away from the holy church and set up a new church. . . . But . . . we are the true ancient [catholic] church. . . . You have fallen away from us.

—Martin Luther, *Against Hanswurst*

Luther was a medieval man with a tongue as sharp as a knight's sword. Toward the end of his life, he sharpened his sword once more and wielded its blade to cut down that accusation he may have hated most of all: the Reformation was a deviant sect and innovative heresy, a clean break with the catholicity of the church.

The sting of that accusation leveled by Henry of Braunschweig (Wolfenbüttel) hurt more than ever by the end of Luther's life because the Reformer had spent his best years proving otherwise. Luther called the Duke a *Hanswurst*, which in German is equivalent to a clumsy carnival clown. In German carnival culture, the clown wore a fat sausage, which accentuated the silliness of the Hanswurst.[1] In 1541 Luther wrote against Henry's accusation, which Luther considered as ridiculous as a clown, but he wrote with all the seriousness of a man fighting for his life against the devil himself. Luther inflicted words like *whore*, *devil*, and *Antichrist* ad nauseum, making this polemical book one of his most vitriolic. Henry—and Rome itself—claimed that "we have fallen away from the holy church and set up a new church," but "we are the true church, for have come from the ancient church and have remained in it." In a moment of irony, Luther turned the charge around: "But you have fallen away from us and have become a new church opposed to us."[2]

To manifest his catholicity, Luther proposed ten reasons (proofs) why the Reformation aligns with the creed when it says, we believe in one, holy, catholic, and apostolic church. They included the sacrament of baptism, the sacrament of the altar, the right exercise of the keys, the purity of preaching, adherence to the

---

1. Gritsch, "Introduction," in *LW* 41:182.
2. *LW* 41:193, 194.

Apostles' Creed, devotion to the Lord's Prayer, obedience to temporal authorities, honoring marriage, suffering, and prayer and fasting. Consider baptism as a sacrament:

> Now baptism is not new, invented by us in our own day, but it is the same ancient baptism instituted by Christ, in which the apostles and the early church and all Christians have been baptized. If then we have the same baptism as the original, ancient (and, as the creed says, "catholic," that is, "universal") Christian church, and are baptized in it, then we belong to the same ancient universal church; and they like us, and we like them, are baptized with one baptism; and therefore there is no difference between us as to baptism.[3]

The apostle Paul assured the Ephesians that there is one body, one faith, and one baptism. The Reformation can claim that unity with that same body on the basis of its authentic confession and obedient baptism. "This is why the papists cannot truthfully call us a different or a new or a heretical church, since we are children of the ancient baptism, together with the apostles themselves and all of Christendom," Luther insisted.[4]

When Luther turned to his fifth proof for catholicity, he named the Apostles' Creed to locate the Reformation within the orthodoxy of its creedal tradition. The *sola scriptura* principle in no way stalled Luther's command, ordering the churches of the Reformation to believe, sing, and confess the creeds. In his debate with radicals, the young Luther said they swallowed the Spirit, feathers and all, by setting the Spirit against the Word. Now the old Luther issued the same warning but with the creeds in view: to believe in God is to believe that his Spirit did not breathe its last breath at Pentecost but guided his church into a true confession of the faith, handed down to the communion of the saints. "Hence we belong to the ancient church and are one with it. There is, therefore, in this matter also, no reason the papists should really call us heretics or a new church, for whoever believes as the ancient church did and holds things in common with it belongs to the ancient church."[5] The Reformers, Luther concluded, were by no means excluded from *communio sanctorum*—the Augustinian and medieval notion of God's elect.

If the churches of the Reformation are "the true, ancient church, one body and one communion of saints with the holy, universal, Christian church," then who is the true innovator and sect, betraying its catholic heritage? Luther gave Hanswurst a straight answer since Hanswurst handed Luther a blunt assault: the papacy in Rome.[6] And to demonstrate his bold claim, Luther recruited twelve

---

3. *LW* 41:195.

4. *LW* 41:195.

5. *LW* 41:196. For the same emphasis in Melanchthon, see *Loci communes theologici*, CR 21:342.

6. At first, Luther was insistent that the papists were the "new false church, which is in everything apostate, separated from the true, ancient church, thus becoming Satan's whore and synagogue" (*LW* 41:199). However,

doctrines of the papacy that collide with the church catholic (universal)—from indulgences to pilgrimages, from transubstantiation to the papacy's keys over the secular domain.[7] When Luther's proofs were stacked next to Rome's proofs, the Reformers was confident one was ancient and the other an ecclesiastical avant-garde.

No one was so insistent on the final authority of God's Word, and no one was so aggressive in his condemnation of the papacy as Luther. Luther never hid his advocacy for change. And yet, in Luther's own mind, his call for reform was not a summons to something modern. His vision for renewal was catholic. Debate may persist over the success of that vision, but no debate should exist over its self-professing identity. In Luther's own words, "Thus we have proved that we are the true, ancient church, one body and one communion of saints with the holy, universal, Christian church."[8]

If Protestants today desire fidelity to the history of their own genesis, then they should listen to one of the Reformation's heirs, Abraham Kuyper: "A church that is unwilling to be catholic is not a church, because Christ is the savior not of a nation, but of the world.... We cannot therefore, without being untrue to our own principle, abandon the honorable title of 'catholic' as though it were the special possession of the Roman Church."[9]

What defines a true adherence to Protestantism? To be Protestant is to be catholic. But not Roman.

---

later he nuanced his accusation and said, she was baptized as a child of God and "even lived some years like the ancient church" but then grew up and "forgot your Christian faith, baptism, and sacrament becoming... little whores" (41:208).

7. *LW* 41:199–205.

8. *LW* 41, 199.

9. "The Synod of Dort in 1618 intended to be as catholic as the Council of Trent." Abraham Kuyper, *On the Church*, trans. Harry Van Dyke, Nelson D. Kloosterman, Todd M. Rester, and Arjen Vreugdenhilin, ed. John Halsey Wood Jr. and Andrew M. McGinnis, in *Abraham Kuyper: Collected Works in Public Theology* (Bellingham, WA: Lexham, 2016), 386.

AFTERWORD

In 2017, in commemoration of the 500th anniversary of the Protestant Reformation, I was asked by the journal *Modern Age* to write an essay titled "What the Reformers Thought They Were Doing."[1] What did they consciously aim at? What motivated their labors and struggles? What made them tick? Hardly anyone nowadays studies the Reformation with such questions in mind. In the past half-century, social, economic, and political history have dominated the field. Important research has been done on "reforming from below" as groups formerly marginalized in much of Reformation historiography have come into the limelight—women, peasants, dissenters, Jews, and others. We have studied the Reformation of the cities, the Reformation of the refugees, the Reformation of "the common man," and so on. We have also looked at the Reformation through the lenses of our postmodern masters—Marx, Freud, Darwin, and Nietzsche. And who can deny that these recent historical strategies have yielded impressive insights and much information? We know much more now than we did when I first set out as a young scholar to study the Reformation, with Roland Bainton's *Here I Stand* in one hand and Calvin's *Institutes* in the other. We know more, but do we perhaps see less?

If we are to understand what the Reformers thought they were doing, we need a vigorous program of demythologization. In particular, three myths about the Reformation should be exploded.

(1) "The Reformation divided the church." This old chestnut is the starting point for many Reformation histories published since 2017. But the rupture of Western Christendom did not begin in the sixteenth century. There was the split between East and West in 1054, the Babylonian Captivity (1309–77), followed by the Western schism (1378–1417), Lollard dissent in England, Hussite wars in Bohemia, the Waldensians in France and Italy, the Alumbrados in Spain. Division of the church was not the outcome of the Reformation but rather its starting point.

(2) "Luther was the first modern man." Adolf von Harnack, the champion of German liberal Protestantism, gave voice to this myth when he wrote in

---

1. Timothy George, "What the Reformers Thought They Were Doing?" *Modern Age* (Fall 2017): 17–26.

1923: "The modern age began along with Luther's Reformation on 31 October 1517; it was inaugurated by the blows of the hammer on the doors of the castle church at Wittenberg."[2] In this vein, Luther becomes the forerunner of everything desirable in the modern world, from individualism and political freedom to pretzels and peanut butter, which, they say, go good with German beer. The shadow side of this myth is to blame everything negative in the modern world, everything from nationalism to Nazism, on the monk of Wittenberg.

(3) "The Reformation was a German event." This myth was not even true in the sixteenth century when the message of the Reformers spread across the entire continent of Europe, from Lisbon to Lithuania, far beyond the space between the Elbe and the Rhine. Today, in an era of globalism and decolonization, the faith of the Reformers is more fervently and faithfully articulated in the majority world south of the equator rather than it is in the staid, withering Christianities of old Europe and North America.

In this impressive, sweeping study, Matthew Barrett helps dispel these and other myths as he offers us a fresh, contextual telling of the Reformation story. By *context* here, he means more than the years just before and just after the central events of the sixteenth century, in other words the late Middles Ages and early modernity. The context of the Reformation, largely understood, is the entire history of the people of God through the ages. Originality and innovation were not the agenda of the Reformers. They had no desire to leave the true catholic church, much less to start a new one. What the Reformers aimed for was the renewal of the one, holy, catholic, and apostolic church on the basis of the Word of God. What the Reformers thought they were doing was calling this church back to its true scriptural and evangelical origins—*ad fontes*! What they thought they were doing was presenting anew the gospel of God's free, unfettered grace in life and work of Jesus Christ, a gospel of real grace for real sinners. As Luther put it, "God does not save people who are only fictitious sinners. Be a sinner and sin boldly, but believe and rejoice in Christ even more boldly, for he is victorious over sin, death, and the world."[3]

Timothy George

---

2. Adolf von Harnack, "Die Reformation und inhre Vorstellung," in *Erforschtes und Erlebtes* (Giessen, 1923), 110, quoted in Heinz Schilling, *Martin Luther: Rebel in an Age of Upheaval* (Oxford: Oxford University Press, 2017), 524.

3. *LW* 48. 281–82.

ACKNOWLEDGMENTS

This book has been one of the hardest books I have written and one of the most rewarding as well. I owe much gratitude to my many assistants who helped me find resources and worked with the great staff at the library of Midwestern Baptist Theological Seminary. Thank you Lance English, Brett Fredenberg, and Scott Meadows. Scott proved an able fact checker and Lance an invaluable mind for the bibliography. I must also thank past assistants who have since graduated from MBTS, including Timothy Gatewood.

This book is better because two reviewers spent considerable time offering feedback and critique. Nick Needham and Lee Gatiss are both insightful historians who helped refine my argument. They also encouraged the argument of this book considering their own teaching experience, noticing how often the Reformation is misunderstood to this day. I am also grateful to patristic historian John Peter Kenney for his review, which gave me a more acute understanding of Platonism's organic, revolutionary intersection with the Great Tradition. Matthew Levering's review was instrumental as well, encouraging me to pursue a more elaborate analysis of both Thomas Aquinas and Duns Scotus. I owe similar gratitude to historian David Sytsma for his comments.

As always, I am grateful to teach at Midwestern Baptist Theological Seminary under the leadership of Jason Allen. I have taught the Reformation seminar to PhD students since I came to MBTS six years ago, and some of those years I was blessed to coteach the seminar with Jason Duesing. I must thank the students in that seminar over the years for their probing papers and robust Socratic dialogue. I pray this tome is fruit from the tree we have watered. As for Charles Smith, his ingenuity makes MBTS the force it is today, but it was his gift of a Woozoo that kept me cool while I climbed the mountain of edits. Thank you, neighbor, for friendship . . . and fans. We love your family.

I have a supportive and talented editor at Zondervan, Ryan Pazdur. He is both patient and flexible, which allowed me to turn this book into a fresh contribution that I hope will help readers understand what it really means to be Protestant. In God's providence, Ryan recruited Jenny-Lyn de Klerk to give my manuscript a thorough review. When I found out I was overjoyed because Jenny-Lyn was a former PhD student of mine whose historical expertise and writing wisdom was well-known to me already. She applied that same eagle's eye to my manuscript and helped it sparkle when it felt dull. Thank you, Jenny-Lyn, for your labor over this book. There are many others on the Zondervan team I should thank, from Matthew Estel to Laura Weller. Laura inserted thousands of inquiries that ensured a more precise read. I am grateful to Crossway publishing for granting permission for me to adapt some of the material in the chapters I contributed to *Reformation Theology* and *The Doctrine on Which the Church Stands or Falls.*

I knew this book was sinking in when women at Emmaus Church in Kansas City said to me one day, "Your wife, Elizabeth, is an amazing woman. Over lunch she explained to us why we Protestants are not a sect. We too have a rich, ancient heritage in the one, holy, catholic, and apostolic church. We have a history we can be proud of just as much as anyone else!" Thank you, Elizabeth, for your encouragement, longsuffering, transparency, and persistent ear. I agree, you are an amazing woman. Lorelei, Charlie, Georgia, and Cassandra—you are always welcome in my study. And remember, you can never have too many books.

Last, I dedicate this book to Michael Haykin, who first instilled within me a love for the church fathers. He pursued me to support my scholarship when I was young and unproven. I have tried to model his humility and generosity with my own students ever since. I have learned from his example that a professor's legacy is not so much his publications as his students.

ABBREVIATIONS

ADRG	*Akten der deutschen Reichsreligionsgespräche im 16. Jahrhundert.* Edited by Klaus Ganzer and Karl-Heinz zur Mühlen. 3 vols. Göttingen: Vandenhoeck & Ruprecht, 2000–2007.
ANF	*The Ante-Nicene Fathers*
ARC	*Acta Reformationis Catholicae Ecclesiam Germaniae Concernentia Saeculi XVI.* Edited by Georg Pfeilschifter. 6 vols. Regensburg: F. Pustet, 1959–74.
ARG	*Archiv für Reformationsgeschichte*
ASD	*Opera Omnia Desiderii Erasmi Roterodami.* Amsterdam: North Holland. 1969–.
AWA	*Archiv zur Weimarer Ausgabe der Werke Martin Luthers*
BB	"Bibliographia Bucerana." In *Schriften des Vereins für Reformationsgeschichte.* Edited by Robert Stupperich et al. Gütersloh: Bertelsmann, 1952. Vol. 169, pp. 37–96.
BC	*The Book of Concord: The Confessions of the Evangelical Lutheran Church.* Translated by Theodore G. Tappert, Jaroslav Pelikan, Robert H. Fischer, and Arthur C. Piepkorn. Philadelphia: Fortress, 1959.
BCor	*Correspondence de Martin Bucer.* Edited by Jean Rott et al. 5 vols. to date. Leiden: Brill, 1979–.
BDS	*Martin Bucers Deutsche Schriften.* Edited by Robert Stupperich et al. Gütersloh: Gütersloher Verlagshaus 1960–. To date: vols. 1–5; 6/1, 6/2, 6/3; 7; 8; 9/1; 10; 11/1; 11/2; 17.
Bek.	*Die Bekenntnisschriften der evangelisch-lutherischen Kirche.* Edited by Irene Dingel. 2nd ed. Göttingen: Vandenhoeck & Ruprecht, 2014.
Beveridge, *Tracts and Treatises*	John Calvin, *Tracts and Treatises.* Translated by Henry Beveridge. 3 vols. Edinburgh: Calvin Translation Society, 1844–51.
BHR	*Bibliothèque d'humanisme et renaissance*
BOL	*Martini Buceri opera latina.* Edited by François Wendel et al. 7 vols. to date. Paris: Presses Universitaires de France; Leiden: Brill, 1954–.

Br A   *Luthers Werke für das christliche Haus.* Edited by George Buchwald et al. 4th ed. Leipzig: M. Heinsius Nachfolger Eger & Sievers, 1924.

Bonnet   *Letters of Jean Calvin.* Edited by Jules Bonnet. Translated by David Constable. 4 vols. Edinburgh: Constable, 1855–57.

CC   Kaspar Schatzgeyer, *Corpus Catholicorum.* Münster: Aschendorff, 1919ff.

CCCM   *Corpus Christianorum, Continuatio Mediaevalis.* Turnhout: Brepols, 1966–.

CCFCT   Jaroslav Pelikan and Valerie R. Hotchkiss, eds. *Creeds and Confessions of Faith in the Christian Tradition.* 3 volumes. New Haven, CT: Yale University Press, 2003.

CL   *Luthers Werke in Auswahl.* Edited by Otto Clemen. Bonn: De Gruyter 1912–33; Berlin: de Gruyter, 1955–56.

CNTC   *Calvin's New Testament Commentaries.* 12 vols. Edited by D. W. Torrance and T. F. Torrance. 12 vols. Grand Rapids: Eerdmans, 1959–72.

CO   *Ioannis Calvini Opera Quae Supersunt Omnia.* Edited by G. Baum, E. Cunitz, and E. Reuss. 59 vols. *Corpus Reformatorum*, vols. 29–87. Braunschweig: A. Schwetschke and Son (M. Bruhn), 1863–1900.

COR   *Ioannis Calvini, Opera Omnia denuo recognita et adnotatione critica instructa notisque illustrata.* Geneva: Droz, 1992ff.

COTC   *Calvin's Old Testament Commentaries.* 3 vols. Edited by D. W. Torrance and T. F. Torrance. Grand Rapids: Eerdmans, 1959–72.

CR   *Corpus Reformatorum. Philippi Melanchthonis Opera Quae Supersunt Omnia.* Edited by C. G. Bretschneider and H. E. Bindseil. Halle: Schwetschke, 1834–60.

CRR   *Classics of the Radical Reformation.* 12 vols. Waterloo, ON, and Scottsdale, PA: Herald, 1973–2018. Reprint, Walden, NY: Plough, 2019–.

CSEL   *Corpus Scriptorum Ecclesiasticorum Latinorum*

CT   *Concilium Tridentinum: Diariorum, Actorum, Epistularum, Tractatuum Nova Collectio, Edidit Societas Goerresiana.* Freiburg: Herder, 1901–76.

CTJ   *Calvin Theological Journal*

CTM   *The Collected Works of Thomas* Müntzer. Translated and edited by Peter Matheson. Edinburgh: T&T Clark, 1988.

CTS   *Selected Works of John Calvin: Tracts and Letters.* Edited by Henry Beveridge. Calvin Translation Society ed. 7 vols. Grand Rapids: Baker, 1983.

CTSOT&NT	John Calvin. *Calvin's Commentaries.* Calvin Translation Society ed. 46 vols. Grand Rapids: Baker, 1989.
CW	Menno Simon. *The Complete Works of Menno Simon.* Elkhart: John F. Funk and Brother, 1871.
CWE	*Collected Works of Erasmus.* Edited and translated by Charles Fantazzi. 89 vols. Toronto: University of Toronto, 1974—.
CWM	*The Yale Edition of the Complete Works of St Thomas More.* 21 vols. New Haven, CT, and London: Yale University Press, 1969–.
DCR	*Documents Illustrative of the Continental Reformation.* Edited by Beresford James Kidd. Ithaca, NY: Cornell University Library, 2009.
De Clementia	*Calvin's Commentary on Seneca's De Clementia.* Edited by John T. McNeill. Translated by Ford Lewis Battles. 2 vols. Philadelphia: Westminster, 1960.
DND	Girolamo Zanchi. *Opera omnia theologica.* Vol. 2, *De natura Dei seu de divinis attributis.*
DTC	*Dictionnaire de Théologie Catholique.* Edited by A. Vacant, E. Mangenot, et al. Paris: Letouzey & Ane, 1923–50.
DVRC	Martin Bucer. *De Vera Ecclesiarum in Doctrina, Ceremoniis, et Disciplina Reconciliatione et Compositione.* Strassburg: Wendel Rihel, 1542.
EE	*Erasmi Epistolae.* Edited by P. S. Allen and H. M. Allen. 12 vols. Oxford: Oxford University Press, 1906–58.
ETL	*Ephemerides Theologicae Lovanienses*
E var	*D. Martini Lutheri Opera latina varii argumenti ad Reformationis historiam imprimis pertinentia.* Edited by Heinrich Schmid. 7 vols. C. Heyderus et H. Zimmeri: Frankofurti ad M. et Erlangae, 1826–98.
EvT	*Evangelische Theologie*
Foxe	*The Acts and Monuments of John Foxe.* Edited by Josiah Pratt and John Soughton. 8 vols. London: The Religious Tract Society, 1877.
HBB	Heinrich Bullinger. *Briefwechsel.* Zurich: Theologischer Verlag, c. 1973–.
HBW	Heinrich Bullinger. *Werke.* Edited by Fritz Busser et al. Letters. Zurich, 1973–.
HTS	Harvard Theological Studies
Institutes	John Calvin. *Institutes of the Christian Religion.* Edited by John T. McNeill. Translated by Ford Lewis Battles. 2 vols. Philadelphia: Westminster, 1960.
Latin Works	Ulrich Zwingli. *The Latin Works and the Correspondences of Huldreich Zwingli.* Edited by Samuel Macauley Jackson.

Translated by Henry Preble, Walter Lichenstein, and Lawrence A. McLouth. 3 vols. New York: Putnam, 1912–29.

LC43   Philip Melanchthon. *Loci Communes 1543*. Translated by J. A. O. Preus. St. Louis: Concordia, 1992.

LCC   Library of Christian Classics. Edited by John T. McNeill and Henry P. van Dusen. Philadelphia: Westminster John Knox, 1953–.

LCC 22   John Calvin. *Calvin: Theological Treatises*. Edited by J. K. S. Reid, Library of Christian Classics. Vol. 22. London: SCM; Philadelphia: Westminster, 1954.

LE   *The Precious and Sacred Writings of Martin Luther*. Edited by John Nicholas Lenker. Minneapolis: Lutherans in All Lands, 1904–9.

L&P   *Letters and Papers, Foreign and Domestic, of the Reign of Henry VIII*. Edited by J. S. Brewer, J. Dairdner, R. H. Brodie, et al. 21 vols. London: Longman, Green, Longman, & Roberts, 1862–1932.

LT43   Philip Melanchthon. *Loci Theologici Recens Recogniti*. Wittenberg: Peter Seitz, 1543.

Luther   *Luther: Zeitschrift der Luther-Gesellschaft*. Göttingen: Vandenhoeck & Ruprecht, 1987.

LW   American Edition of *Luther's Works*. Edited by Jaroslav Pelikan and Helmut T. Lehmann. 55 vols. Philadelphia: Fortress, and St. Louis: Concordia, 1957–.

LWZ   *The Latin Works of Huldreich Zwingli*. Translated and edited by S. M. Jackson et al. 3 vols. New York: G. P. Putnam's Sons, 1912; Philadelphia: Heidelberg Press, 1922, 1929.

MA   Martin Luther. *Ausgewählte Werke*. Edited by H. H. Borcherdt and George Merz. 3rd ed. Munich: Vandenhoeck & Ruprecht, 1948–.

MBB   Martin Bucer. *Martin Bucers Deutsche Schriften (1491–1551)–Bibliographie*. Edited by H. Pils, S. Ruderer, and P. Schaffrodt. Gutersloh: Gütersloher Verlagshaus, 2005.

MBDS   Martin Bucer. *Martin Bucers Deutsche Schriften*. Gutersloh: Gütersloher Verlagshaus / Mohn, 1960ff.

MBW   Philip Melanchthon. *Melanchthons Briefwechsel*. Edited by Heinz Scheible. 14 vols. Stuttgart–Bad Cannstatt: Frommann-Holzboog, 1977–.

MBW T   Philip Melanchthon. *Melanchthons Briefwechsel: Texte*. Edited by C. Mundhenk, H. Scheible, R. Wetzel, et al. 14 vols. Stuttgart–Bad Cannstatt, Frommann-Holzboog, 1991–.

ML-LDS Martin Luther. *Martin Luther Lateinisch-Deutsche*
Studienausgabe: Die Kirche und ihre Ämter. Edited by
W. Harle et al. 3 vols. Leipzig 2006–9.

MO *Philippi Melanthonis Opera Quae Supersunt Omnia.* 28 vols.
Corpus Reformatorum 1–28. Edited by C. G. Bretschneider.
1834–60. Reprint, New York: Johnson, 1963.

MWA *Melanchthons Werke in Auswahl.* Edited R. Stupperich et al.
7 vols. Gütersloh: 1951–83.

NPNF1 *A Select Library of Nicene and Post-Nicene Fathers of the*
Christian Church. Edited by Philip Schaff and Henry Wace.
28 vols. in 2 series. 1886–89. Peabody: Hendrickson, 1994.

OER *Oxford Encyclopedia of the Reformation.* Edited by Hans J.
Hillerbrand. Oxford: Oxford University Press, 1996.

OOT Menno Simons. *Opera Omnia Theologica.* Amsterdam:
Joannes van Veen, 1681.

Opera Huldreich Zwingli. *Huldreich Zwingli's Werke.* Edited by
Johannes Schulthess, and Melchior Schuler. 5 vols. Zurich:
F. Schulthess, 1828–35.

OS *Ioannis Calvini Opera Selecta.* Edited by Peter Barth
and Wilhelm Niesel. 5 vols. Munich: Kaiser, 1926–68
(1st–3rd eds.).

OX Duns Scotus. *Opus Oxoniense.* Edited by Mariano
Fernández García, O.F.M. 12 volumes. Quaracchi:
Typographia Collegii Sancti Bonaventurae, 1912 and 1914.

PE *Works of Martin Luther.* 6 vols. Philadelphia: Muhlenberg,
1915–43.

PG Patrologia, Series Graeca. Edited by Jacques-Paul Migne.
162 vols. Paris, 1857–86.

PL Patrologia, Series Latina. Edited by Jacques-Paul Migne.
217 vols. Paris, 1844–64.

PMA L. M. de Rijk. *La philosophie au moyen âge.* Leiden: Brill,
1985. Translation of *Middeleeuwse wijsbegeerte. Tradite en*
vernieuwing. Assen: Van Gorcum, 1977.

ProEccl *Pro Ecclesia*

PS William Tyndale. *Doctrinal Treatises and Introductions*
(1848); *Expositions* and Notes with *The Practice of Prelates*
(1849); *Answer to Sir Thomas More's Dialogue* (1850).
Edited by Henry Walter. Cambridge: The Parker Society.

RCS Timothy George, ed. *Reformation Commentary on*
Scripture. Downers Grove, IL: InterVarsity Press, 2012–.

Regesten Gasparo Contarini. *Regesten und briefe.* Edited by
Franz Dittrich. Braunsberg: von Huye's Buchhandlung
(Emil Bender), 1881.

RG   H. Bullinger, *Reformationsgeschichte.* 3 vols. Edited by
     J. J. Hottinger and H. H. Vogelin. Frauenfeld, 1838–40.

Romans   John Calvin. *The Epistles of Paul the Apostle to the Romans
         and to the Thessalonians.* Translated by Ross McKenzie.
         Edinburgh: Oliver & Boyd, 1960.

S   *Huldreich Zwinglis Werke.* Edited by Melchior Schuler and
    J. Schulhess. 8 vols. Zurich: PUB, 1828–42.

Selected Writings   *Selected Writings of Huldrych Zwingli.* Translated by
                    E. J. Furcha 2 vols. Alisson Park, PA: Pickwick, 1984.

Sentences   Peter Lombard, *The Sentences.* Translated by Giulio Silano.
            4 vols. Toronto, ON: Pontifical Institute of Mediaeval
            Studies, 2010.

SCG   *Summa Contra Gentiles.* 5 vols. Notre Dame, IN: University
      of Notre Dame Press, 1975.

Scheel, *Dokumente*   *Martin Luther. Dokumente zur Luthers Entwicklung.*
                      Edited by O. Scheel. 2nd ed. Tübingen: Mohr Siebeck 1929.

Scholia 1534   Philip Melanchthon. *Scholia in Epistolam Pauli ad Colossenses
               iterum ab authore recognita.* Wittenberg: J. Klug, 1534.

Scripta Anglicana   *Martini Buceri Scripta Anglicana Fere Omnia.* Edited by
                    Conrad Hubert. Basel: Petrus Perna, 1577.

SM   Philip Melanchthon. Supplementa *Melanchthoniana.* 4 vols.
     Leipzig: Rudolph Haupt, 1910–26.

ST   Thomas Aquinas. *Summa Theologiae.* 61 vols. London:
     Blackfriars, 1964. Reissued with Cambridge: Cambridge
     University Press, 2006.

StA   Martin Luther. *Martin Luther Studienausgabe.* Edited
      by Hans-Ulrich Delius et al. 6 vols. Berlin: Evangelische
      Verlagsanstalt, 1979–99.

St. L.   Martin Luther. *D. Martin Luthers sämmtliche Schriften.*
         Edited by J. G. Walch. Rev. ed. 23 vols. St. Louis: Concordia,
         1880–1910.

S-J   Martin Luther. *Luther's Correspondence and Other
      Contemporary Letters.* Edited by Preserved Smith and
      Charles Jacobs. 2 vols. Philadelphia: Lutheran Publication
      Society, 1913, 1918.

SJT   *Scottish Journal of Theology*

TFC   The Fathers of the Church: A New Translation. Edited
      by Ludwig Schopp. 154 vols. Washington, DC: Catholic
      University of America Press, 1947–.

WA   Martin Luther. *D. Martin Luthers Werke.* Kritische
     Gesamtausgabe. 73 vols. Weimar: Böhlau, 1883–2009.

WABr   Martin Luther. *D. Martin Luthers Werke.* Briefwechsel.
       18 vols. Weimar: Böhlau, 1930–85.

WATR Martin Luther. *D. Martin Luthers Werke*. Tischreden.
6 vols. Weimar: Böhlau, 1912–21.

WADB Martin Luther. *D. Martin Luthers Werke*. Deutsche Bibel.
12 vols. Weimar, Böhlau, 1906–61.

Works John Knox. *The Works of John Knox*. Edited by David
Laing. 6 vols. Edinburgh: Bannatyne Club, 1846–64.

Z *Huldreich Zwinglis sämtliche Werke*. In *Corpus
Reformatorum*, 88–. Edited by Emil Egli et al. Berlin,
Schwettschke, and Zurich, Theologischer Verlag, 1905–.

ZL *The Zurich Letters, Comprising the Correspondence of
Several English Bishops and Others, With Some of the
Helvetian Reformers, During the Early Part of the Reign
of Queen Elizabeth*. Translated and edited by Hastings
Robinson. First and Second Series. Cambridge: Parker
Society, 1842–45.

Zwingli Schriften *Huldrych Zwingli Schriften*. Edited by Thomas
Brunnschweiler and Samuel Lutz. 4 vols. Zurich:
Theologischer Verlag, 1995.

BIBLIOGRAPHY

Chapter 1. The Catholicity of the Reformation

Adams, Marilyn McCord. *Some Later Medieval Theories of the Eucharist*. New York: Oxford University Press, 2010.

———. *What Sort of Human Nature? Medieval Philosophy and the Systematics of Christology*. Milwaukee: Marquette University Press, 1999.

Allen, Michael, and Scott Swain. *Reformed Catholicity: The Promise of Retrieval for Theology and Biblical Interpretation*. Grand Rapids: Baker, 2015.

Benedict of Nursia. *The Rule of Benedict*. Milton Keynes: Penguin / Random House UK, 2008.

Billings, J. Todd. *Calvin, Participation, and the Gift: The Activity of Believers in Union with Christ*. Oxford: Oxford University Press, 2008.

Billings, J. Todd. "The Catholic Calvin." *Pro Ecclesia* 20 (2011): 120–34.

Boersma, Hans. *Five Things Theologians Wish Biblical Scholars Knew*. Downers Grove, IL: InterVarsity Press, 2021.

———. *Heavenly Participation: The Weaving of a Sacramental Tapestry*. Grand Rapids: Eerdmans, 2011.

———. *Nouvelle Théologie and Sacramental Ontology: A Return to Mystery*. Oxford: Oxford University Press, 2012.

Braaten, Carl E., and Robert Jensen. *The Catholicity of the Reformation*. Grand Rapids: Eerdmans, 1996.

Calvin, John. "Reply to Sadoleto." In *A Reformation Debate*, edited by John C. Olin, 49–94. Grand Rapids: Baker, 1996.

Cameron, Euan. *The European Reformation*. 2nd ed. Oxford: Oxford University Press, 2012.

———. "Reconsidering Early-Reformation and Catholic-Reform Impulses." In *Multiple Reformations?*, edited by Jan Stievermann and Randall C. Zachman, 3–16. Tübingen: Mohr Siebeck, 2018.

Canlis, Julie. *Calvin's Ladder: A Spiritual Theology of Ascent and Ascension*. Grand Rapids: Eerdmans, 2010.

Cary, Phillip. *The Meaning of Protestant Theology*. Grand Rapids: Baker, 2019.

Chemnitz, Martin. *Examination of the Council of Trent*. Edited by Fred Kramer. 4 vols. St. Louis: Concordia, 1971.

Clark, R. Scott. *Recovering the Reformed Confession: Our Theology, Piety, and Practice*. Phillipsburg, NJ: P&R, 2008.

Collins, Kenneth J., and Jerry L. Walls. *Roman but Not Catholic: What Remains at Stake 500 Years after the Reformation*. Grand Rapids: Baker Academic, 2017.

Cooper, Jordan. *Prolegomena: A Defense of the Scholastic Method*. A Contemporary Protestant Scholastic Theology. Ithaca: Just and Sinner, 2020.

Cross, Richard. *Duns Scotus*. New York: Oxford University Press, 1999.

Denifle, Heinrich. *Luther et le Luthéranisme: étude faite d'après les sources*. Vol. 3. Paris: Auguste Picard, 1916. Reprint, London: Forgotten Books, 2018.

Dieter, Theodor. "Luther as Late Medieval Theologian: His Positive and Negative Use of Nominalism and Realism." In *The Oxford Handbook of Martin Luther's Theology*, edited by Robert Kolb, Irene Dingel, and L'ubomír Batka, 31–48. Oxford: Oxford University Press, 2014.

Dupré, Louis. *Passage to Modernity: An Essay on the Hermeneutics of Nature and Culture*. New Haven, CT: Yale University Press, 1993.

———. *The Enlightenment and the Intellectual Foundations of Modern Culture*. New Haven, CT: Yale University Press, 2005.

Farthing, John L. *Thomas Aquinas and Gabriel Biel: Interpretations of St. Thomas Aquinas in German Nominalism on the Eve of the Reformation*. Durham, NC: Duke University Press, 1988.

Fesko, John V. *Beyond Calvin: Union with Christ and Justification in Early Modern Reformed Theology (1517–1700)*. Göttingen: Vandenhoeck & Ruprecht, 2012.

Funkenstein, Amos. *Theology and the Scientific Imagination: From the Middle Ages to the Seventeenth Century*. 2nd ed. Princeton: Princeton University Press, 2008.

Gatiss, Lee. *Cornerstones of Salvation*. Welwyn Garden City, UK: Evangelical Press, 2017.

———, ed. *The First Book of Homilies: The Church of England's Official Sermons in Modern English*. London: Lost Coin, 2021.

Gordon, Bruce. *Calvin*. New Haven, CT: Yale University Press, 2009.

Gregory, Brad S. *The Unintended Reformation: How a Religious Revolution Secularized Society*. Cambridge, MA: Belknap, 2015.

Greschat, Martin. *Martin Bucer: A Reformer and His Times*. Translated by Stephen E. Buckwalter. Louisville: Westminster John Knox, 2014.

Grummett, David. *Henri de Lubac and the Shaping of Modern Theology: A Reader*. San Francisco: Ignatius, 2020.

Hamm, Berndt, and Michael Welker. *Die Reformation, Potentiale der Freiheit*. Tübingen: Mohr Siebeck, 2008.

Harnack, Adolf von. *History of Dogma*. 7 vols. Translated by Neil Buchanan. New York: Dover, 1961.

Hegel, Georg Wilhelm Friedrich. *Lectures on the Philosophy of History: Introduction*. Translated by H. B. Nisbet. Cambridge: Cambridge University Press, 1975.

Hendrix, Scott H. *Martin Luther: Visionary Reformer*. New Haven, CT: Yale University Press, 2015.

Horan, Daniel P. *Postmodernity and Univocity: A Critical Account of Radical Orthodoxy and John Duns Scotus*. Minneapolis: Fortress, 2014.

Horton, Michael. *Justification*. 2 vols. Grand Rapids: Zondervan, 2018.

Janz, Denis R. *Luther and Late Medieval Thomism: A Study in Theological Anthropology*. Waterloo: Wilfrid Laurier University Press, 1983.

———. *Luther on Thomas Aquinas: The Angelic Doctor in the Thought of the Reformer*. Stuttgart: Steiner, 1989.

Legge, Dominic. *The Trinitarian Christology of St Thomas Aquinas*. Oxford: Oxford University Press, 2017.

Leithart, Peter. *The End of Protestantism: Pursuing Unity in a Fragmented Church*. Grand Rapids: Baker, 2016.

Leppin, Volker. "Luther's Transformation of Medieval Thought." In *The Oxford Handbook of Martin Luther's Theology*, edited by Robert Kolb, Irene Dingel, and L'ubomír Batka, 115–24. Oxford: Oxford University Press, 2014.

————. *Martin Luther: A Late Medieval Life*. Grand Rapids: Baker, 2017.

Luther, Martin. *Dokumente zur Luthers Entwicklung*. Edited by O. Scheel. 2nd ed. Tübingen: Mohr Siebeck, 1929.

McGrath, Alistair. *Christianity's Dangerous Idea: The Protestant Revolution—A History from the Sixteenth Century to the Twenty-First*. New York: HarperOne, 2007.

————. *Historical Theology: An Introduction to the History of Christian Thought*. 2nd ed. Malden, MA: Wiley-Blackwell, 2013.

————. *Reformation Thought: An Introduction*. 4th ed. Oxford: Wiley-Blackwell, 2012.

Milbank, John. "Alternative Protestantism." In *Creation, Covenant and Participation: Radical Orthodoxy and the Reformed Tradition*, edited by James K.A. Smith and James H. Olthius, 25–41. Grand Rapids: Baker Academic, 2005.

————. "Only Theology Overcomes Metaphysics." *New Blackfriars* 76 (1995): 325–43.

————. *Theology and Social Theory: Beyond Secular Reason*. Oxford: Blackwell, 1990, 2006.

————. *Being Reconciled: Ontology and Pardon*. New York: Routledge, 2003.

Milbank, John, Catherine Pickstock, and Graham Ward, eds. *Radical Orthodoxy: A New Theology*. New York: Routledge, 1999.

Milbank, John, and Simon Oliver, eds. *Radical Orthodoxy Reader*. New York: Routledge, 2009.

Meyendorff, John. *Catholicity and the Church*. Crestwood, NY: St Vladimir's Seminary Press, 1983.

Muller, Richard. *Calvin and the Reformed Tradition: On the Work of Christ and the Order of Salvation*. Grand Rapids: Baker Academic, 2012.

————. "Not Scotist: Understandings of Being, Univocity, and Analogy in Early-Modern Reformed Thought." *Reformation & Renaissance Review*. 14, no. 2 (2012): 127–150.

————. "Scholasticism in Calvin: a Question of Relation and Disjunction." In *Calvinus Sincerioris ReligionisVindex: Calvin as Protector of the Purer Religion*, ed. Wilhelm H. Neuser and Brian Armstrong, 247–65. Kirksville, MO: Sixteenth Century Journal Publishers, 1997.

————. "The Problem of Protestant Scholasticism: A Review and Definition." In *Reformation and Scholasticism: An Ecumenical Enterprise*, edited by Willem J. van Asselt and Eef Dekker, 45–64. Grand Rapids: Baker, 2001.

————. *Unaccommodated Calvin: Studies in the Foundation of a Theological Tradition*. Oxford: Oxford University Press, 2000.

Oberman, Heiko. "Headwaters of the Reformation: *Initia Lutheri—Initia Reformationis*." In *Luther and the Dawn of the Modern Era*, edited by H. A. Oberman, 40–88. Leiden, 1974.

The Harvest of Medieval Theology: Gabriel Biel and Late Medieval Nominalism. Rev. ed. Grand Rapids: Baker, 2000.

Ozment, Steven E. ed. *The Reformation in Medieval Perspective*. Chicago: Quadrangle, 1971.

————. *Age of Reform, 1250–1550: An Intellectual and Religious History of Late Medieval and Reformation Europe*. New Haven, CT: Yale University Press, 1980, 2020.

Parker, T. H. L. "Introduction." In *English Reformers*, ed. T. H. L. Parker, xv–xxii. Louisville: Westminster John Knox, 1966.

Pelikan, Jaroslav. *Obedient Rebels: Catholic Substance and Protestant Principle in Luther's Reformation*. New York: Harper and Row, 1964.

Pickstock, Catherine. *After Writing: On the Liturgical Consummation of Philosophy*. Oxford: Blackwell, 1998.

Rupp, Gordon. *The Righteousness of God: Luther Studies*. London: Hodder & Stoughton, 1953.

Ryrie, Alec. *Protestants: The Faith That Made the Modern World*. New York: Viking, 2017.

Saak, Eric Leland. *Creating Augustine: Interpreting Augustine and Augustinianism in the Later Middle Ages*. Oxford: Oxford University Press, 2012.

————. *Luther and the Reformation of the Later Middle Ages*. Cambridge: Cambridge University Press, 2017.

Sadoleto, Jacopo. *A Reformation Debate: Sadoleto's Letter to the Genevans and Calvin's Reply*. Edited by John C. Olin. Grand Rapids: Baker, 1966.

Schaff, Philip, and John W. Nevin. *The Principle of Protestantism*. Eugene, OR: Wipf & Stock, 2004.

Schleiermacher, Friedrich. *The Christian Faith*. Edited by H. R. Macintosh and J. S. Stewart. London: T&T Clark, 2004.

Steinmetz, David C. *Luther and Staupitz: An Essay in the Intellectual Origins of the Protestant Reformation*. Monographs in Medieval and Renaissance Studies 4. Durham, NC: Duke University Press, 1980.

————. *Luther in Context*. 2nd ed. Grand Rapids: Baker, 2002.

Taylor, Charles. *A Secular Age*. Cambridge, MA: Harvard University Press, 2007.

Tillich, Paul. *The Protestant Era*. Translated and edited by James L. Adams. Chicago: University of Chicago Press, 1948.

Torrell, Jean-Pierre. *Saint Thomas Aquinas*. Vol. 2, *Spiritual Master*. Translated by Robert Royal. Washington, DC: Catholic University of America Press, 2003.

Troeltsch, Ernst. *Protestantism and Progress: The Significance of Protestantism or the Rise of the Modern World*. Philadelphia: Fortress, 1912.

Vanhoozer, Kevin J. *Biblical Authority after Babel: Retrieving the Solas in the Spirit of Mere Protestant Christianity*. Grand Rapids: Brazos, 2016.

Ward, Graham. "The Church as the Erotic Community." In *Sacramental Presence in a Postmodern Context*, edited by L. Boeve and L. Leijssen, 167–204. Louvain: Peeters, 2001.

————. *Cities of God*. London: Routledge, 2001.

Wilken, Robert Louis. *The Spirit of Early Christian Thought*. New Haven, CT: Yale University Press, 2003.

White, Thomas Joseph, eds. *The Analogy of Being: Invention of the Antichrist or the Wisdom of God?* Grand Rapids: Eerdmans, 2011.

Wuellner, Bernard. *Dictionary of Scholastic Philosophy*. Richmond, NH: Loreto, 2013.

Zachman, Randall C. "The Birth of Protestantism? Or the Reemergence of the Catholic Church? How Its Participants Understood the Evangelical Reformation." In *Multiple Reformations?*, edited by Jan Stievermann and Randall C. Zachman, 17–30. Tübingen: Mohr Siebeck, 2018.

PART 1: THE REFORMATION'S CATHOLIC CONTEXT
General Studies on the Middle Ages

Backman, Clifford R. *The Worlds of Medieval Europe*. Oxford: Oxford University Press, 2009.

Bartlett, Robert. *The Natural and the Supernatural in the Middle Ages*. Cambridge: Cambridge University Press, 2008.

Bornstein, Daniel E., ed. *Medieval Christianity*. Vol. 4 of *A People's History of Christianity*. Minneapolis: Fortress, 2006.

Bredero, Adriaan H. *Christendom and Christianity in the Middle Ages: The Relations between Religion, Church and Society*. Grand Rapids: Eerdmans, 1994.

Cameron, Euan. *Enchanted Europe: Superstition, Reason, and Religion, 1250–1750*. Oxford: Oxford University Press, 2010.

Colish, Marcia L. *The Medieval Foundations of the Western Intellectual Tradition, 400–1400*. New Haven, CT: Yale University Press, 1997.

Constable, Giles. *The Reformation of the Twelfth Century*. Cambridge: Cambridge University Press, 1998.

Copleston, Frederick C. *A History of Philosophy.* 11 vols. New York: Continuum, 1946–86.

Evans, G. R. *The Medieval Theologians: An Introduction to Theology in the Medieval Period.* Oxford: Blackwell, 2008.

———. *Philosophy and Theology in the Middle Ages.* London: Routledge, 1994.

———. *The Roots of the Reformation.* 2nd ed. Grand Rapids: IVP Academic, 2012.

Gilson, Étienne H. *God and Philosophy.* New Haven, CT: Yale University Press, 1941.

———. *History of Christian Philosophy in the Middle Ages.* Washington, DC: Catholic University of America Press, 2019.

———. *The Spirit of Medieval Philosophy.* Notre Dame, IN: University of Notre Dame Press, 1991.

Gow, Andrew Colin. *Studies in Medieval and Reformation Thought.* Leiden: Brill, 1966.

Grundmann, Herbert. *Religious Movements in the Middle Ages.* Translated by Steven Rowan. Notre Dame, IN: University of Notre Dame Press, 1996.

Hamilton, Bernard. *Religion in the Medieval West.* Oxford: Oxford University Press, 2003.

Hamilton, Sarah. *The Practice of Penance, 900–1500.* Woodbridge, Suffolk: Boydell, 2001.

Hamm, Berndt. *The Reformation of Faith in the Context of Late Medieval Theology and Piety.* Edited by Robert J. Bast. Leiden: Brill, 2004.

Keen, M. H. *England in the Later Middle Ages.* London: Routledge, 2003.

Knowles, David. *The Evolution of Medieval Thought.* Edited by D. E. Luscombe. New York: Addison-Wesley Longman, 1989.

Lawrence, C. H. *Medieval Monasticism: Forms of Religious Life in Western Europe in the Middle Ages.* 3rd ed. New York: Routledge, 2015.

Leff, Gordon. *Heresy in the Later Middle Ages.* 2 vols. Manchester: Manchester University Press, 1967.

———. *Medieval Thought St. Augustine to Ockham.* Chicago: Quadrangle, 1959.

Logan, F. Donald. *A History of the Church in the Middle Ages.* London: Routledge, 2002.

Maag, Karin, and John D. Witvliet, eds. *Worship in Medieval and Early Modern Europe: Change and Continuity in Religious Practice.* Notre Dame, IN: University of Notre Dame Press, 2004.

Marenbon, John. *Later Medieval Philosophy (1150–1350).* London: Routledge, 1994.

McGrade, A. S., ed. *The Cambridge Companion to Medieval Philosophy.* Cambridge: Cambridge University Press, 2003.

McGrath, Alister. *Christianity's Dangerous Idea: The Protestant Revolution—A History from the Sixteenth Century to the Twenty-First.* New York: HarperOne, 2007.

———. *Historical Theology: An Introduction to the History of Christian Thought.* 2nd ed. Malden, MA: Wiley-Blackwell, 2013.

———. *The Intellectual Origins of the European Reformation.* Malden, MA: Blackwell, 1987.

Needham, Nick. *Two Thousand Years of Christ's Power.* 4 vols. Fearn, Ross-Shire: Mentor, 2016.

Oakley, Francis. *The Western Church in the Later Middle Ages.* Ithaca, NY: Cornell University Press, 1985.

Oberman, Heiko A. *The Dawn of the Reformation: Essays in Late Medieval and Early Reformation Thought.* Grand Rapids: Eerdmans, 1992.

Oliver, Simon. "The Eucharist before Nature and Culture." *Modern Theology* 15, no. 3 (1999): 331–53.

Ozment, Steven. *The Age of Reform, 1250–1550: An Intellectual and Religious History of Late Medieval and Reformation Europe.* New Haven, CT: Yale University Press, 1980.

Pasnau, Robert, ed. *The Cambridge History of Medieval Philosophy.* 2 vols. Cambridge: Cambridge University Press, 2015.

Pelikan, Jaroslav. *Development of Christian Doctrine: Some Historical Prolegomena.* New Haven, CT: Yale University Press, 1969.

———. *The Growth of Medieval Theology (600–1300)*. Vol. 3 of *The Christian Tradition*. Chicago: University of Chicago Press, 1980.

Pelikan, Jaroslav, and Valerie R. Hotchkiss, eds. *Creeds and Confessions of Faith in the Christian Tradition*. 3 vols. New Haven, CT: Yale University Press, 2003.

Phillips, J. R. S. *The Medieval Expansion of Europe*. 2nd ed. Oxford: Oxford University Press, 1998.

Schaff, Philip. *History of the Christian Church*. 8 vols. Peabody, MA: Hendrickson, 2006.

Southern, R. W. *Western Society and the Church in the Middle Ages*. New York: Penguin, 1990.

Van Asselt, Willem J. *Introduction to Reformed Scholasticism*. Grand Rapids: Reformation Heritage, 2011.

Vauchez, A. *Laity in the Middle Ages: Religious Beliefs and Devotional Practices*. Edited by D. J. Bornstein. Notre Dame, IN: University of Notre Dame Press, 1997.

Chapter 2. Spiritual Ascent and Mystical Dissent: The Reformation and Monasticism

Primary Sources

Benedict of Nursia. *The Rule of Benedict*. Milton Keynes: Penguin / Random House UK, 2008.

Bernard of Clairvaux. *Bernard of Clairvaux: Selected Works*. New York: Paulist, 1987.

———. *On Grace and Free Choice*. Translated by Daniel O'Donovan. Kalamazoo, MI: Cistercian, 1988.

———. *On Loving God*. Translated by Emero Stiegman. Kalamazoo, MI: Cistercian, 1995.

———. *Sancti Bernardi Opera*. Edited by Jean Leclercq, C. H. Talbot, and Henri Rochais. 8 vols. Rome: Editiones Cistercienses, 1957.

———. *Sermons on the Song of Songs*. 4 vols. Kalamazoo, MI: Cistercian, 1971–80.

Bonaventure. *Commentary on the Sentences* as *Opera Omnia of S. Bonaventure. Tome I. Commentaries on the First Book of the Sentences. On the One and Triune God*. Translated by Alexis Bugnolo. Westminster, MA: Franciscan Archive, 2014.

———. *The Journey of the Mind to God*. Edited by Stephen F. Brown. Translated by Philotheus Boehner. Indianapolis: Hackett, 1986.

———. *Opera Omnia*. Florence: Ad Claras Aquas (Quaracchi), 1882–1902.

———. *The Works of St. Bonaventure*. Edited by Robert Karris. Franciscan Institute. New York: St. Bonaventure University, n.d.

Eckhart, Meister. *Meister Eckhart: Die deutschen und lateinischen Werke harausgegeben im Auftrag der deutschen Forschungsgemeinschaft*. Stuttgart/Berlin: Kohlhammer, 1936–.

———. *Meister Eckhart: The Essential Sermons, Commentaries, Treatises, and Defense*. Edited by Bernard McGinn and Edmund College. New York: Paulist, 1981.

———. *Meiser Eckhart: Teacher and Preacher*. Edited by Bernard McGinn. New York: Paulist, 1986.

———. *Meister Eckhart. Werke* 1. *Predigten*. Edited by Niklaus Largier. Frankfurt: Deutscher Klassiker, 1993.

Thomas à Kempis. *The Imitation of Christ*. Edited and translated by Joseph N. Tylenda. New York: Random House, 1998.

Secondary Sources

Blommestijn, Hein, Charles Caspers, and Rijcklof Hofman. *Spirituality Renewed: Studies on Significant Representatives of the Modern Devotion*. Leuven: Peeters, 2003.

Cullen, Christopher. *Bonaventure*. Oxford: Oxford University Press, 2016.

Hackett, Jeremiah, ed. *A Companion to Meister Eckhart*. Leiden: Brill, 2012.

Hammond, Jay, Wayne Hellmann, and Jared Goff, eds. *A Companion to Bonaventure*. Leiden: Brill, 2013.

Knowles, David. *Christian Monasticism*. Oxford: Oxford University Press, 2002.

McGinn, Bernard. *The Growth of Mysticism: Gregory the Great through the Twelfth Century*. Vol. 2, *The Presence of God: A History of Western Christian Mysticism*. New York: Crossroad, 1994.

———. *The Harvest of Mysticism in Medieval Germany*. Vol. 4, *The Presence of God: A History of Christian Mysticism*. New York: Herder/Crossroad, 2005.

———. *The Mystical Thought of Meister Eckhart: The Man from Whom God Hid Nothing*. New York: Herder & Herder, 2001.

McGuire, Brian P., ed. *A Companion to Bernard of Clairvaux*. Leiden: Brill, 2011.

Snoek, Godefridus J. C. *Medieval Piety from Relics to the Eucharist*. Leiden: Brill, 1995.

Stiegman, Emero. "Bernard of Clairvaux, William of St. Thierry, the Victorines." In *Medieval Theologians*, edited by G. R. Evans, 129–55. Oxford: Blackwell, 2001.

Turner, Denys. *The Darkness of God: Negativity in Christian Mysticism*. Cambridge: Cambridge University Press, 1995.

Van Engen, John. *Sisters and Brothers of the Common Life: The Devotio Moderna and the World of the Later Middle Ages*. Philadelphia: University of Pennsylvania Press, 2008.

Chapter 3. Faith Seeking Understanding: The Advent of Scholasticism
Primary Sources

Abelard, Peter. *Commentary on the Epistle to the Romans*. Fathers of the Church. Mediaeval Continuation Series. Vol. 12. Washington, DC: Catholic University of America Press, 2011.

———. *Peter Abelard: Ethical Writings*. Indianapolis: Hackett, 1995.

———. *Theologia Christiana*. Corpus Christianorum: Continuatio Mediaevalis. Vol. 12. Turnhout: Brepols, 1969.

———. *Theologia Scholarium* and *Theologia Summi Boni*. Corpus Christianorum: Continuatio Mediaevalis. Vol. 13. Turnhout: Brepols, 1987.

Anselm of Canterbury. *Anselm of Canterbury*. Edited by Jasper Hopkins. 4 vols. Lewiston, NY: Mellen, 1974–76.

———. *The Major Works*. Edited by G. R. Evans and Brian Davies. Oxford: Oxford University Press, 2008.

———. *S. Anselmi Cantuarensis Archiepiscopi Opera Omnia*. Edited by F. S. Schmitt. 6 vols. Edinburgh: T&T Clark, 1946–61.

Lombard, Peter. *Magistri Petri Lombardi Sententiae in I libris distinctae*. Edited by Ignatius Brady. 2 vols. Spicilegium Bonaventurianum 4 and 5. Grottaferrata, Italy: Ad Claras Aquas, 1971, 1981.

———. *The Sentences*. Translated by Giulio Silano. 4 vols. Toronto: Pontifical Institute of Mediaeval Studies, 2007.

Secondary Sources

Armstrong, Chris R. *Medieval Wisdom for Modern Christians: Finding Authentic Faith in a Forgotten Age with C.S. Lewis*. Grand Rapids: Brazos, 2016.

Baxter, Jason. *The Medieval Mind of C.S. Lewis: How Great Books Shaped a Great Mind*. Downers Grove, IL: InterVarsity Press, 2022.

Colish, Marcia. *Peter Lombard*. 2 vols. Leiden: Brill, 1994.

Coolman, Boyd Taylor. *The Theology of Hugh of St. Victor: An Interpretation*. Cambridge: Cambridge University Press, 2010.

Davies, Brian, and Brian Leftow, eds. *The Cambridge Companion to Anselm*. Cambridge: Cambridge University Press, 2006.

Evans, G. R. *Anselm*. New York: Continuum, 2005.

Leclercq, Jean. *The Love of Learning and the Desire for God: A Study of Monastic Culture.* New York: Fordham University Press, 1982.

Luscombe, David. *The School of Peter Abelard.* Cambridge: Cambridge University Press, 1970.

Marenbon, John. *The Philosophy of Peter Abelard.* Cambridge: Cambridge University Press, 1997.

Pieper, Josef. *Scholasticism: Personalities and Problems of Medieval Philosophy.* South Bend, IN: St. Augustine's, 2001.

Robertson, Duncan. *Lectio Divina: The Medieval Experience of Reading.* Collegeville, MN: Liturgical, 2011.

Rosemann, Philipp. *Peter Lombard.* Oxford: Oxford University Press 2004.

Southern, R. W. *Saint Anselm: A Portrait in a Landscape.* Cambridge: Cambridge University Press, 2004.

Swanson, Jenny. "The *Glossa Ordinaria.*" In *Medieval Theologians,* edited by G. R. Evans, 156–67. Oxford: Blackwell, 2001.

Visser, Sandra, and Thomas Williams, eds. *Anselm of Canterbury.* Oxford: Oxford University Press, 2008.

Williams, Thomas. *Anselm of Canterbury.* Oxford: Oxford University Press, 2021.

Chapter 4. Thomas Aquinas as a "Sounder Scholastic": The Reformation's Critical Retrieval of Scholasticism
Primary Sources

Aquinas, Thomas. *An Exposition of the* On the Hebdomads *of Boethius.* Translated by Janice L. Schultz and Edward A. Synan. Washington: Catholic University of America Press, 2001.

———. *Catena Aurea: Commentary on the Four Gospels Collected Out of the Works of the Fathers.* Edited by John Henry Newman. 5 vols. Boonville, NY: Preserving Christian Publications, 2009.

———. *Commentary on the Letter of Saint Paul to the Romans.* Edited by Fabian R. Larcher, John Mortensen, and Enrique Alarcón. Lander, WY: Aquinas Institute, 2012.

———. *Expositio in Omnes Sancti Pauli Epistolas.* In *Sancti Thomae Aquinatis Doctoris Angelici Ordinis Praedicatorum Opera Omnia* 13. Parma, 1872.

———. *Sancti Thomae Aquinatis Doctoris Angelici Opera Omnia,* I–XXV. Parma: Petrus Fiaccadorus, 1852–73. Reprint, New York: Musurgia, 1948–50.

———. *Summa Contra Gentiles.* 4 vols. Notre Dame, IN: University of Notre Dame Press, 2009.

———. *Summa Theologiae.* 61 vols. London: Blackfriars, 1964. Reissued with Cambridge: Cambridge University Press, 2006.

———. *Summa Theologiae.* 5 vols. Fathers of the English Dominican Province. New York: Benziger, 1947. Reprint, Westminster, MD: Christian Classics, 1981.

———. *The Power of God.* Translated by Richard J. Regan. Oxford: Oxford University Press, 2012.

———. *Thomas Aquinas's Quodlibetal Questions.* Translated by Brian Davies and Turner Nevitt. Oxford: Oxford University Press, 2020.

Aristotle. *The Complete Works of Aristotle.* Princeton, NJ: Princeton University Press, 1995.

Augustine. *City of God.* London: Penguin, 2003.

Boethius. *The Consolation of Philosophy.* London: Penguin, 2003.

Bucer, Martin. *Metaphrases et Enarrationes Perpetuae Epistolarum d. Pauli Apostoli. Tomus Primus continens Metaphrasim et Enarrationem in Epistolam ad Romanos.* Strasbourg: Wendelin Rihel, 1536.

Budiman, K. "A Protestant Doctrine of Nature and Grace as Illustrated by Jerome Zanchi's Appropriation of Thomas Aquinas." PhD diss., Baylor University, 2011.

Bullinger, Heinrich. *In Sanctissimam Pauli ad Romanos Epistolam.* Zurich: Christophor Froschouer, 1533.

Calvin, Jean. *Commentaires sur l'épître aux Romains*. In *Commentaires de Jehan Calvin sur le Nouveau Testament*. Paris: Librairie de Ch. Meyrueis, 1855.

Dorsch, Johann Georg. *Thomas Aquinas, Dictus Doctor Angelicus, Exhibitus Confessor Veritatis Evangelicae Augustana Confessione Repetitae*. Frankfurt am Main: J. W. Ammonius, 1656.

Gregory the Great. *The Letters of Gregory the Great*. Translated by John R. C. Martyn. Medieval Sources in Translation 40. Toronto: Pontifical Institute of Medieval Studies, 2004.

Junius, Franciscus. *A Treatise on True Theology: With the Life of Franciscus Junius*. Translated by D. C. Noe. Grand Rapids: Reformation Heritage, 2014.

Melanchthon, Philip. *Commentarii in Epistolam Pauli ad Romanos*. Wittenberg: Clug, 1532.

Musculus, Wolfgang. *In Epistolam Apostoli Pauli ad Romanos*. Basel: Hervagius, 1555.

Oecolampadius, Johannes. *In Epistolam b. Pauli Apost. Ad Rhomanos Adnotationes*. Basel: Cratander, 1525.

Owen, John. *The Works of John Owen*. 16 vols. Edinburgh: Banner of Truth, 2000.

Vermigli, Peter Martyr. *Defensio doctrine veteris et apostolicae de sacrosancto Eucharistiae sacramento*. Basel, 1581.

———. *Dialogue on the Two Natures of Christ*. Kirksville, MO: Northeast Missouri State University, 1994. Reprint, Moscow, ID: Davenant, 2018.

———. *In epistolam S. Pauli apostoli ad Romanos*. Basel: Petrus Perna, 1558.

———. *In Primum Librum Mosis, qui vulgo Genesis dictur, commentarii*. Zurich: Froschouer, 1569.

———. *In selectissimam D. Pauli priorem ad Corinthios epistolam*. Zurich: Froschouer, 1551.

———. *Loci Communes*. London: Vautrollerius, 1583.

———. *On Free Will and the Law*. Vol. 2 of *a New Translation of the Loci Communes (1576)*. Translated and edited by Joseph A. Tipton. Moscow, ID: Davenant, 2021.

———. *On Original Sin*. Vol. 1 of *a New Translation of the Loci Communes (1576)*. Translated by Kirk Summers. Moscow, ID: Davenant, 2019.

———. *The Oxford Treatise and Disputation on the Eucharist*. Kirksville, MO: Northeast Missouri State University, 2000. Reprint, Moscow, ID: Davenant, 2018.

———. *The Peter Martyr Library*. Edited by John Patrick Donnelly and Joseph C. McLelland. 9 vols. Sixteenth Century Essays and Studies. Kirksville, MO: Sixteenth Century Journal Publishers, 1994–.

———. *The Peter Martyr Reader*. Edited by John Patrick Donnelly, Frank A. James III, and Joseph C. McLelland. Kirksville, MO: Truman State University Press, 1999.

———. *Philosophical Works: On the Relation of Philosophy to Theology*. Translated and edited by J. C. McLelland. Kirksville, MO: Truman State University Press, 1996.

———. *Philosophical Works*. Kirksville, MO: Northeast Missouri State University, 1996. Reprint, Moscow, ID: Davenant, 2018.

———. *Predestination and Justification*. Kirksville, MO: Northeast Missouri State University, 2003. Reprint, Moscow, ID: Davenant, 2018.

Vissner, Arnoud S. Q. *Reading Augustine in the Reformation: The Flexibility of Intellectual Authority in Europe, 1500–1620*. New York: Oxford University Press, 2011.

Whitaker, William. *Disputatio de Sacra Scriptura, contra huius temporis papistas, inprimis Robertum Bellarminum iesuitam, Pontificium in Collegio Roman & Thomam Stapletonum*. Cambridge: Thomasius, 1588.

———. *A Disputation on Holy Scripture, against the Papists, Especially Bellarmine and Stapleton*. Translated by William Fitzgerald. Cambridge: Cambridge University Press, 1849.

———. *Opera Theologica*. 2 vols. Geneva: Crispin, 1610.

Zanchi, Jerome (Girolamo). *De Naturali Ascultatione, seu de principiis.* Strasbourg: Wendelin Rihel, 1554.

———. *Omnium operum theologicorum.* 8 vols. Geneva: Gamonetus, 1675.

———. *On the Law in General.* Translated by J. J. Veenstra. Grand Rapids: CLP Academic, 2012.

———. *Opera theologica.* Geneva, 1605.

———. *Operum theologicorum . . . Tomus Primus (-Octauus) [OT].* Geneva: Crespin, 1617–19.

———. *Praefatio in Fortnaus Crellus. Introductio in Logicam Aristotelis ordine Aristotelico conscripta.* Neustadt: Harnisch, 1581.

———. *De religione Christiana fides—Confession of Christian Religion.* Edited by Luca Baschera and Christian Moser. Leiden: Brill, 2007.

Zwingli, Huldrych. *In Evangelicam Historiam de Domino nostro Iesu Christo, per Matthaeum, Marcum, Lucam, et Ioannem conscriptam, Epistolasque aliquot Pauli, Annotationes D. Huldrychi Zwinglii per Leonem Iudae exceptae et aeditae.* Zurich: Froschouer, 1539.

Secondary Sources

Anderson, Marvin W. *Peter Martyr Vermigli, a Reformer in Exile (1542–1562).* Bibliotheca Humaniastica et Reformatorica 10. Nieuwkoop: De Graaf, 1975.

Armstrong, Brian G. *Calvinism and the Amyraut Heresy: Protestant Scholasticism and umanism in Seventeenth-Century France.* Madison: University of Wisconsin Press, 1969.

Aspray, Silvianne. *Metaphysics in the Reformation: The Case of Peter Martyr Vermigli.* Oxford: Oxford University Press, 2021.

Ballor, Jordan J. "Deformation and Reformation: Thomas Aquinas and the Rise of Protestant Scholasticism." In *Aquinas among the Protestants,* edited by Manfred Svenson and David VanDrunen, 27–48. Oxford: Blackwell, 2018.

———. "In the Footsteps of the Thomists: An Analysis of Thomism in the Junius-Arminius Correspondence." In *Beyond Dordt and* De Auxiliis: *The Dynamics of Protestant and Catholic Soteriology in the Sixteenth and Seventeenth Centuries,* edited by J. J. Ballor, M. T. Gaetano, and D. S. Sytsma, 127–47. Leiden: Brill, 2019.

Barth, Karl. *Natural Theology: Comprising Nature and Grace by Professor Dr. Emil Brunner and the Reply No! by Dr. Karl Barth.* London: Bles, 1946. Reprint, Eugene, OR: Wipf & Stock, 2002.

———. *The Knowledge of God and the Service of God According to the Teaching of the Reformation.* The Gifford Lectures, 1937–38. Translated by J. L. M. Haire and Ian Henderson. London: Hodder and Stoughton, 1938.

Bauerschmidt, Frederick Christian. *Thomas Aquinas: Faith, Reason, and Following Christ.* Christian Theology in Context. Oxford: Oxford University Press, 2015.

Carter, Craig A. *Interpreting Scripture with the Great Tradition: Recovering the Genius of Premodern Exegesis.* Grand Rapids: Baker, 2018.

Chenu, M. D. *Toward Understanding Saint Thomas.* Translated by A.-M. Landry and D. Hughes. Chicago: Regnery, 1964.

Chesterton, G. K. *Saint Thomas Aquinas.* New York: Image/Doubleday, 2001.

Cleveland, Christopher. *Thomism in John Owen.* Burlington, VT: Ashgate, 2013.

Davies, Brian. *Thomas Aquinas: Contemporary Philosophical Perspectives.* Oxford: Oxford University Press, 2002.

———. *Thomas Aquinas's* Summa Contra Gentiles: *A Guide and Commentary.* Oxford: Oxford University Press, 2016.

———. *The Thought of Thomas Aquinas.* Oxford: Clarendon, 2009.

Davies, Brian, and Eleonore Stump, eds. *The Oxford Handbook of Aquinas*. New York: Oxford University Press, 2012.

De Lubac, Henri. *Medieval Exegesis*. 3 vols. Grand Rapids: Eerdmans, 1998, 2000, 2009.

Donnelly, John Patrick. *Calvinism and Scholasticism in Vermigli's Doctrine of Man and Grace*. Studies in Medieval and Reformation Thought 18. Leiden: Brill, 1976.

———. "Calvinist Thomism." *Viator* 7 (1976): 441–55.

Dooyeweerd, Herman. *In the Twilight of Western Thought*. Grand Rapids: Paideia, 2012.

———. *Reformation and Scholasticism in Philosophy*. Vol. 1, *The Greek Prelude*. Edited by D.F.M. Strauss. Translated by Ray Togtmann. In *The Collected Works of Herman Dooyeweerd*. Series A. Vol. 5. Grand Rapids: Paideia, 2012.

Dorner, I. A. *History of the Development of the Doctrine of the Person of Christ*. Edinburgh: T&T Clark, 1880–1897.

Dowey, Edward A. *The Knowledge of God in Calvin's Theology*. New York: Columbia University Press, 1952.

Elders, Leo J. *The Philosophical Theology of St. Thomas Aquinas*. Leiden: Brill, 1990.

Elders, Leo J. *The Metaphysics of Being of St. Thomas Aquinas in a Historical Perspective*. Leiden: Brill, 1993.

Emery, Gilles. *The Trinitarian Theology of St Thomas Aquinas*. Oxford: Oxford University Press, 2010.

Farthing, John L. *Thomas Aquinas and Gabriel Biel: Interpretations of St. Thomas Aquinas in German Nominalism on the Eve of the Reformation*. Durham, NC: Duke University Press, 1988.

Frame, John. *A History of Western Philosophy and Theology*. Phillipsburg, NJ: P&R, 2015.

Gilson, Étienne. *History of Christian Philosophy in the Middle Ages*. Washington, DC: Catholic University of America Press, 2019.

———. *The Christian Philosophy of St. Thomas Aquinas*. Translated by L. K. Shook. Notre Dame, IN: University of Notre Dame Press, 1994.

———. *The Spirit of Mediaeval Philosophy*. Notre Dame, IN: University of Notre Dame Press, 1991.

———. *Thomism: The Philosophy of Thomas Aquinas*. Translated by Laurence K. Shook and Armand Maurer. 6th ed. Toronto: Pontifical Institute of Medieval Studies, 2002.

———. *Thomist Realism and The Critique of Knowledge*. San Francisco, CA: Ignatius, 2012.

Gründler, Otto. "Thomism and Calvinism in the Theology of Girolamo Zanchi (1516–1590)." PhD diss., Princeton Theological Seminary, 1961.

Haga, Joar. *Was There a Lutheran Metaphysics? The Interpretation of Communicatio Idiomatum in Early Modern Lutheranism*. Göttingen: Vandenhoeck & Ruprecht, 2012.

Haines, David. *Natural Theology: A Biblical and Historical Introduction and Defense*. Moscow, ID: Davenant Press, 2021.

Hall, Basil. "Calvin Against the Calvinists." In *John Calvin*, edited by G.E. Duffield, 19–37. Grand Rapids: Eerdmans, 1966.

Healy, Nicholas. *Thomas Aquinas: Theologian of the Christian Life*. Burlington, VT: Ashgate, 2003.

Helmer, Christine, ed. *The Medieval Luther*. Tübingen: Mohr Siebeck, 2020.

James, Frank A., III, *Peter Martyr Vermigli and Predestination: The Augustinian Inheritance of an Italian Reformer*. New York: Oxford University Press, 1998.

Janz, Denis R. "Late Medieval Theology." In *The Cambridge Companion to Reformation Theology*, edited by David Bagchi and David C. Steinmetz, 7–14. Cambridge: Cambridge University Press, 2004.

———. *Luther and Late Medieval Thomism: A Study in Theological Anthropology*. Waterloo, ON: Wilfrid Laurier University Press, 1983.

Jenkins, John I. *Knowledge and Faith in Thomas Aquinas.* Cambridge: Cambridge University Press, 1997.

Jordan, Mark D. *The Alleged Aristotelianism of Thomas Aquinas.* Toronto: Pontifical Institute of Medieval Studies, 1992.

Kaister, Christopher B. "Calvin's Understanding of Aristotelian Natural Philosophy: Its Extent and Possible Origins." In *Calviniana: Ideas and Influence of Jean Calvin,* edited by Robert V. Schnucker, 77–92. Sixteenth Century Essays and Studies 10. Kirksville, MO: Sixteenth Century Journal Publishers, 1988.

Kendall, R. T. *Calvin and English Calvinism to 1649.* New York: Oxford University Press, 1978.

Kingdon, Robert M. *The Political Thought of Peter Martyr Vermigli: Selected Texts and Commentary.* Geneva: Droz, 1980.

Kretzmann, Norman, and Eleonore Stump, eds. *The Cambridge Companion to Aquinas.* Cambridge: Cambridge University Press, 1993.

Lang, August. "Reformation and Natural Law." In *Calvin and the Reformation.* Translated by J. Gresham Machen. New York: Revell, 1927.

LaValee, A. A. "Calvin's Criticism of Scholastic Theology." PhD diss., Harvard University, 1967.

Leijssen, L. "Martin Bucer und Thomas von Aquin." *ETL* 55 (1979): 266–96.

Leinsle, Ulrich G. *Introduction to Scholastic Theology.* Translated by Michael J. Miller. Washington, DC: Catholic University of America Press, 1995.

Levering, Matthew. *Proofs of God: Classical Arguments from Tertullian to Barth.* Grand Rapids: Baker Academic, 2016.

Levering, Matthew, and Marcus Plested, eds. *The Oxford Handbook of the Reception of Aquinas.* Oxford: Oxford University Press, 2021.

Luy, David. *Dominus Mortis: Martin Luther on the Incorruptibility of God in Christ.* Minneapolis: Fortress Press, 2014.

———. "The Sixteenth-Century Reception of Thomas Aquinas by Luther and Lutheran Reformers." In *The Oxford Handbook of the Reception of Aquinas,* edited by Matthew Levering and Marcus Plested, 105–20. Oxford: Oxford University Press, 2021.

McCoster, Philip, and Denys Turner, eds. *The Cambridge Companion to the Summa Theologiae.* Cambridge: Cambridge University Press, 2016.

McInerny, Ralph. *Praeambula Fidei: Thomism and the God of the Philosophers.* Washington, DC: Catholic University of America Press, 2006.

McNair, Philip. *Peter Martyr in Italy.* New York: Oxford University Press, 1967.

Muller, Richard A. *Post-Reformation Reformed Dogmatics: The Rise and Development of Reformed Orthodoxy, ca. 1520 to ca. 1725.* 4 vols. Grand Rapids: Baker, 2003.

———. "Reading Aquinas from a Reformed Perspective: A Review Essay." *CTJ* 53, no. 2 (2018): 255–88.

———. "Scholasticism in Calvin: A Question of Relation and Disjunction." In *Calvinus Sincerioris ReligionisVindex: Calvin as Protector of the Purer Religion,* edited by Wilhelm H. Neuser and Brian Armstrong, 247–65. Kirksville, MO: Sixteenth Century Journal Publishers, 1997.

Muller, Richard A., and John L. Thompson, eds. *Biblical Interpretation in the Era of the Reformation.* Grand Rapids: Eerdmans, 1996.

O'Meara, Thomas F. *Thomas Aquinas: Theologian.* Notre Dame: University of Notre Dame Press, 1997.

Parker, T. H. *The Doctrine of the Knowledge of God: A Study in Calvin's Theology.* Rev. ed. Grand Rapids: Eerdmans, 1959.

Patterson, R. L. *The Conception of God in the Philosophy of Aquinas.* London: Allen & Unwin, 1933.

Phelan, G. B. *Saint Thomas on Analogy*. Milwaukee: Marquette University Press, 1941.

Raith, Charles II. *Aquinas and Calvin on Romans: God's Justification and Our Participation*. New York: Oxford University Press, 2014.

———. "Calvin and Aquinas Reconsidered." In *Beyond Dordt and De Auxiliis: The Dynamics of Protestant and Catholic Soteriology in the Sixteenth and Seventeenth Centuries*, edited by J. J. Ballor, M. T. Gaetano, and D. S. Sytsma, 19–34. Leiden: Brill, 2019.

———. "Calvin's Critique of Merit, and Why Aquinas (Mostly) Agrees." *ProEccl* 20, no. 2 (2011): 135–66.

Regan, Richard J. *A Philosophical Primer on the Summa Theologica*. Steubenville, OH: Franciscan University Press, 2018.

Rehnman, Sebastian. *Divine Discourse: The Theological Methodology of John Owen*. Grand Rapids: Baker, 2002.

Rogers, Jack B., and Donald K. McKim. *The Authority and Interpretation of the Bible: An Historical Approach*. San Francisco: Harper and Row, 1979.

Saak, Eric Leland. *Luther and the Reformation of the Later Middle Ages*. Cambridge: Cambridge University Press, 2017.

Schlosser, Friedrich Christoph. *Leben des Theodor de Beza und des Peter Martyr Vermigli*. Heidelberg, 1809.

Schreiner, Susan E. *Theater of His Glory: Nature and the Natural Order in the Thought of John Calvin*. Studies in Historical Theology 3. Durham, NC: Labyrinth, 1991.

Stanglin, Keith. *The Letter and the Spirit of Biblical Interpretation: From the Early Church to Modern Practice*. Grand Rapids: Baker Academic, 2018.

Steinmetz, David C. *Calvin in Context*. 2nd ed. Oxford: Oxford University Press, 2010.

Steinmetz, David. "The Superiority of Pre-Critical Exegesis." *Theology Today* 37, no. 1 (1980): 27–38.

Stump, Eleonore, and Thomas Joseph White, eds. *The New Cambridge Companion to Aquinas*. Cambridge: Cambridge University Press, 2022.

Svensson, Manfred. "Aristotelian Practical Philosophy from Melanchthon to Eisenhart: Protestant Commentaries on the Nicomachean Ethics 1529–1682." *Reformation & Renaissance Review* 21, no. 3 (2019): 218–38.

Svensson, Manfred, and David VanDrunen, eds. *Aquinas among the Protestants*. Hoboken, NJ: Wiley Blackwell, 2018.

Sytsma, David S. "Sixteenth-Century Reformed Reception of Aquinas." In *The Oxford Handbook of the Reception of Aquinas*, edited by Matthew Levering and Marcus Plested, 121–43. Oxford: Oxford University Press, 2021.

———. "Thomas Aquinas and Reformed Biblical Interpretation: The Contribution of William Whitaker." In *Aquinas among the Protestants*, edited by M. Svennson and D. VanDrunen, 49–74. Hoboken, NJ: Wiley-Blackwell, 2018.

———. "Vermigli Replicating Aquinas: An Overlooked Continuity in the Doctrine of Predestination." *Reformation & Renaissance Review* 20, no. 2 (2018): 155–67.

TeVelde, Rudi A. *Aquinas on God: The "Divine Science" of the Summa Theologiae*. Burlington, VT: Ashgate, 2006.

Torrell, Jean-Pierre. *Aquinas's* Summa: *Background, Structure, and Reception*. Translated by Benedict M. Guevin. Washington, DC: Catholic University of America Press, 2005.

Trueman, Carl R. *Grace Alone: Salvation as a Gift of God*. Five Solas. Edited by Matthew Barrett. Grand Rapids: Zondervan, 2017.

———. *John Owen: Reformed Catholic, Renaissance Man*. Burlington: Ashgate, 2007.

———. *The Claims of Truth: John Owen's Trinitarian Theology.* Carlisle: Paternoster, 1998.

———. "The Reception of Thomas Aquinas in Seventeenth-Century Reformed Orthodoxy and Anglicanism." In *The Oxford Handbook of the Reception of Aquinas*, edited by Matthew Levering and Marcus Plested, 207–20. Oxford: Oxford University Press, 2021.

Trueman, Carl R., and R. Scott Clark, eds. *Protestant Scholasticism: Essays in Reassessment.* Bletchley, UK: Paternoster, 2007.

Van Asselt, Willem J. *Introduction to Reformed Scholasticism.* Grand Rapids: Reformation Heritage, 2011.

———. "Protestant Scholasticism: Some Methodological Considerations in the Study of Its Development." *Dutch Review of Church History* 81, no. 3 (2001): 265–74.

Van Asselt, Willem J., and E. Dekker. *Reformation and Scholasticism.* Grand Rapids: Baker, 2001.

Van Asselt, Willem J., with T. Theo J. Pleizier, Pieter L. Rouwendal, and Maarten Wisse. *Introduction to Reformed Scholasticism.* Translated by Albert Gootjes. Grand Rapids: Reformation Heritage, 2011.

VanDrunnen, David. "Medieval Natural Law and the Reformation: A Comparison of Aquinas and Calvin." *American Catholic Philosophical Quarterly* 80, no. 1 (2006): 77–98.

Van Nieuwenhove, Rik. *An Introduction to Medieval Theology.* 2nd ed. Cambridge: Cambridge University Press, 2022.

———, ed. *The Theology of Thomas Aquinas.* Notre Dame, IN: University of Notre Dame Press, 2005.

———. *Thomas Aquinas and Contemplation.* Oxford: Oxford University Press, 2021.

Van Nieuwenhove, Rik, and Joseph Wawrykow. *The Theology of Thomas Aquinas.* Notre Dame, IN: University of Notre Dame Press, 2005.

Van't Spijker, W. "Early Reformation and Scholasticism." *Dutch Review of Church History* 81, no. 3 (2001): 290–305.

Van Til, Cornelius. *Defense of the Faith.* 3rd ed. Phillipsburg, NJ: P&R, 1966.

———. *Common Grace and the Gospel.* Phillipsburg, NJ: P&R, 1971.

Vos, Antoine. "Scholasticism and Reformation." In *Reformation and Scholasticism: An Ecumenical Enterprise*, edited by Willem J. van Asselt and Eef Dekker, 99–119. Grand Rapids: Baker Academic, 2001.

Vos, Arvin. *Aquinas, Calvin, and Contemporary Protestant Thought: A Critique of Protestant Views on the Thought of Thomas Aquinas.* Grand Rapids: Eerdmans, 1985.

Weber, Otto. *Foundations for Dogmatics.* 2 vol. Translated by Darrell Guder. Grand Rapids: Eerdmans, 1983.

Weinandy, Thomas, Daniel A. Keating, and John P. Yocum, eds. *Aquinas on Scripture: An Introduction to His Biblical Commentaries.* London: T&T Clark, 2005.

Weisheipl, James A. *Friar Thomas D'Aquino: His Life, Thought, and Work.* Garden City, NJ: Doubleday, 1974.

White, Graham. *Luther as Nominalist: A Study in the Logical Methods Used in Martin Luther's Disputations in the Light of their Medieval Background.* Luther-Agricola Society, 1994.

Wippel, John F. *Medieval Reactions to the Encounter Between Faith and Reason.* Milwaukee, WI: Marquette University Press, 1995.

———. *Metaphysical Themes in Thomas Aquinas II.* Washington, DC: Catholic University of America Press, 2007.

———. "Thomas Aquinas and the Condemnation of 1277." *The Modern Schoolman* LXXII (1995): 233–72.

———. *The Metaphysical Thought of Thomas Aquinas: From Finite Being to Uncreated Being.* Monographs of the Society for Medieval and Renaissance Philosophy 1. Washington, DC: The Catholic University of America Press, 2000.

Wisse, Maarten, Marcel Sarot, and Willemien Otten, eds. *Scholasticism Reformed: Essays in Honour of Willem J. van Asselt*. Leiden: Brill, 2010.

Zachman, Randall C. "The Birth of Protestantism? Or the Reemergence of the Catholic Church? How Its Participants Understood the Evangelical Reformation." In *Multiple Reformations?*, edited by Jan Stievermann and Randall C. Zachman, 17–30. Tübingen: Mohr Siebeck, 2018.

Zuidema, J. *Peter Martyr Vermigli (1499–1562) and the Outward Instruments of Divine Grace*. Göttingen: Vanderhoeck & Ruprecht, 2008.

Chapter 5. Provocation for Reformation: The *Via Moderna*, Nominalism, and the Late Medieval Departure from Thomistic Augustinianism

Primary Sources

Aristotle. *The Complete Works of Aristotle*. Edited by Jonathan Barnes. Princeton, NJ: Princeton University Press, 1984.

Biel, Gabriel. *Canonis misse expositio*, I–V. Edited by Heiko Oberman and William J. Courtenay. Wiesbaden: Franz Steiner, 1963–76.

———. *Collectorium circa quatuor libros Sententiarum*, I, II, III, IV-1, IV-2. Edited by Wilfredus Werbeck and Udo Hofmann. Tübingen: Mohr Siebeck, 1973–84.

———. *Epithome et collectorium ex Occamo circa quatuor Sententiarum libros*. Tübingen: 1501. Reprint, Frankfurt/Main: Minerva, 1965.

———. *Gabrielis Biel Canonis misse expositio*. Edited by Heiko A. Oberman and W. J. Courtenay. 4 vols. Wiesbaden, 1963–67.

Dillon, John. *The Middle Platonists: 80 B.C. to A.D. 220*. Ithaca, NY: Cornell University Press, 1996.

Dillon, John, and Lloyd P. Gerson. *Neoplatonic Philosophy: Introductory Readings*. Indianapolis: Hackett, 2004.

Henry of Ghent. *Summae quaestionum*. Paris, 1520.

———. *Quodlibeta Magistri Henrici Goethals a Gandavo Doctoris Solemnis*. Edited by I. Badius. 2 vols. Louvain: Bibliothéque SJ, 1961.

———. *Summae quaestionum ordinariarum*. St. Bonaventure, NY: Franciscan Institute, 1953.

Ockham, William. *Ockham: Philosophical Writings*. Edited by Philotheus Boehner. Edinburgh: Nelson, 1957. Reprint, Indianapolis: Hackett, 1977.

———. *Opus nonaginta dierum*. In J. G. Sikes et al., eds., *Guillelmi de Ockham opera politica*. 3 vols. Manchester: Manchester University Press, 1940–56.

———. *Opera plurima*. Bologna: Benedict Hector of Bologna, 1496.

———. *Opera plurima*. Lyon, 1494–96. Reprint, London: Gregg, 1962.

———. *Opera Philosophica et Theologica*. 17 vols. New York: Franciscan Institute, 1967–88.

———. *On the Power of Emperors and Popes*. Edited by Annabel S. Brett. Bristol: Thoemmes, 1998.

———. *Predestination, God's Foreknowledge, and Future Contingents*. Translated by Marilyn McCord Adams and Norman Kretzmann. Indianapolis: Hackett, 1983.

———. *Quodlibetal Questions*. Edited by Alfred J. Freddoso and Francis E. Kelley. New Haven, CT: Yale University Press, 1991.

Plato. *Complete Works*. Edited by John M. Cooper. Indianapolis: Hackett, 1997.

Plotinus. *The Enneads*. Edited by Lloyd P. Gerson. Cambridge: Cambridge University Press, 2018.

Scotus, Duns. *Philosophical Writings*. Edited by Allan B. Wolter. Edinburgh: Nelson, 1962.

———. *God and Creatures: The Quodlibetal Questions*. Translated and edited by Felix Alluntis and Allan B. Wolter. Princeton and London: Princeton University Press, 1975.

———. *The Examined Report of the Paris Lecture. Reportatio I-A*. Edited by Allan B. Wolter and Oleg Bychkov. 2 vols. New York: Franciscan Institute, 2004, 2008.

————. *The Examined Report of the Paris Lecture. Reportatio IV-A.* Edited by Oleg Bychkov and R. Trent Pomplun. New York: Franciscan Institute, 2016.

————. *Man's Natural Knowledge of God.* In *The Review of Metaphysics* 1, no. 2 (1947): 3–36.

————. *Opera Omnia.* Edited by C. Balic et al. Vatican City: Typis Polyglottis Vaticanis, 1950–.

————. *Opera Omnia.* Lugduni: Laurentius Durand, 1639. Reprint, Hildesheim: Olms, 1968.

————. *Opus Oxoniense.* Edited by Mariano Fernández García, OFM. 12 vol. Quaracchi: Typographia Collegii Sancti Bonaventurae, 1912 and 1914.

————. *Questions on the Metaphysics of Aristotle.* Edited by Girard Etzkorn and Allan Wolter. 2 vols. St. Bonaventure, NY: Franciscan Institute, 1997–98.

————. *Quaestiones in Metaphysicam.* Translated by Girard J. Eizkorn and Allan B. Wolter, OFM. Vols 1–2. St. Bonaventure, NY: Franciscan Institute, 1997–98.

————. *Quaestiones Super Libros Metaphysicorum Aristotelis.* In *Opera Philosophica*, edited by Girard Etzkorn et al. 5 vols. St. Bonaventure, NY: Franciscan Institute, 1997–2006.

Wallis, R. T. *Neoplatonism.* 2nd ed. Indianapolis: Hackett, 2004.

Secondary Sources

Adams, Marilyn McCord. *William of Ockham.* 2 vols. Notre Dame, IN: University of Notre Dame Press, 1987.

————. "Ockham on Will, Nature, and Morality." In *The Cambridge Companion to Ockham*, edited by Paul Vincent Space, 245–72. Cambridge: Cambridge University Press, 2006.

Balthasar, Hans Urs von. *The Glory of the Lord.* Vol. 5. San Francisco: Ignatius, 1991.

Bavinck, Herman. "Calvin and Common Grace." *The Princeton Theological Review* 7, no. 3 (1909): 437–65.

Cary, Phillip. *Inner Grace: Augustine in the Traditions of Plato and Paul.* Oxford: Oxford University Press, 2008.

————. *Augustine's Invention of the Inner Self: The Legacy of a Christian Platonist.* Oxford: Oxford University Press, 2003.

Chung, Miyon. "Faith, Merit, and Justification: Luther's Exodus from Ochamism *En Route* to Reformation." *Torch Trinity Journal* 6 (2003): 210–40.

Courtenay, William J. *Ockham and Ockhamism: Studies in the Dissemination and Impact of His Thought.* Leiden: Brill, 2008.

Cross, Richard. *Duns Scotus.* Oxford: Oxford University Press, 1999.

————. *The Metaphysics of the Incarnation: From Aquinas to Scotus.* New York: Oxford University Press, 2002.

————. "'Where Angels Fear to Tread': Duns Scotus and Radical Orthodoxy." *Antonianum* 76 (2001): 7–41.

Davison, Andrew. *Participation in God: A Study in Christian Doctrine and Metaphysics.* Cambridge: Cambridge University Press, 2019.

————. *The Love of Wisdom: An Introduction to Philosophy for Theologians.* London: SCM, 2013.

Freddoso, Alfred J. "Ockham on Faith and Reason." In *The Cambridge Companion to Ockham*, edited by Paul Vincent Space, 326–49. Cambridge: Cambridge University Press, 2006.

Gerson, Lloyd P. *Aristotle and Other Platonists.* Ithaca, NY: Cornell University Press, 2017.

————. *From Plato to Platonism.* Ithaca, NY: Cornell University Press, 2013.

————. *Platonism and Naturalism: The Possibility of Philosophy.* Ithaca, NY: Cornell University Press, 2020.

Gillespi, Michael Allen. *The Theological Origins of Modernity.* Chicago: The University of Chicago Press, 2008.

Gilson, Étienne. *John Duns Scotus: Introduction to His Fundamental Positions*. Translated by James G. Colbert. London: T&T Clark, 2020.

———. *History of Christian Philosophy in the Middle Ages*. New York: Random House, 1955. Reprint, Washington, DC: Catholic University of America Press, 2019.

———. *Thomist Realism and the Critique of Knowledge*. Translated by Mark A. Wauck. San Francisco: Ignatius, 1930, 1983.

Hall, Andrew. "Natural Theology in the Middle Ages." In *The Oxford Handbook of Natural Theology*, edited by Russell Re Manning, 57–74. Oxford: Oxford University Press, 2015.

Hampton, Alexander J. B., and John Peter Kenney, eds. *Christian Platonism: A History*. Cambridge: Cambridge University Press, 2021.

Harnack, Adolf von. *History of Dogma*. 7 vols. Translated by Neil Buchanan. New York: Dover, 1961.

Horan, Daniel P. *Postmodernity and Univocity: A Critical Account of Radical Orthodoxy and John Duns Scotus*. Minneapolis: Fortress, 2014.

Hyman, Arthur, and James Walsh, eds. *Philosophy in the Middle Ages: The Christian, Islamic and Jewish Traditions*. Indianapolis: Hackett, 1973.

Ingham, Mary. *Scotus for Dunces: An Introduction to the Subtle Doctor*. New York: Franciscan Institute, 2003.

Janz, Denis R. *Luther and Late Medieval Thomism: A Study in Theological Anthropology*. Waterloo: Wilfrid Laurier University Press, 1983.

Kenney, John Peter. "Augustine and the Platonists." In *Augustine and Tradition: Influences, Contexts, Legacy*, ed. David G. Hunter and Jonathan P. Yates, 127–52. Grand Rapids: Eerdmans, 2023.

King, Peter. "Duns Scotus on Metaphysics." In *The Cambridge Companion to Duns Scotus*, edited by Thomas Williams, 15–68. Cambridge: Cambridge University Press, 2003.

Leff, Gordon. *Bradwardine and the Pelagians*. Cambridge: Cambridge University Press, 1957.

———. *Gregory of Rimini: Tradition and innovation in Fourteenth Century Thought*. Manchester: Manchester University Press, 1961.

———. *Medieval Thought: St. Augustine to Ockham*. Baltimore: Penguin, 1958.

———. *William of Ockham: The Metamorphosis of Scholastic Discourse*. Manchester: Manchester University Press, 1975.

Levy, Ian Christopher. *Introducing Medieval Biblical Interpretation: The Senses of Scripture in Premodern Exegesis*. Grand Rapids: Baker Academic, 2018.

Lilla, Salvatore R. C. "The Neoplatonic Hypostases and the Christian Trinity." In *Studies in Plato and the Platonic Tradition*, edited by Mark Joyal, 127–89. Aldershot: Ashgate, 1997.

Lortz, Joseph. *Die Reformation in Deutschland*. 2 vols. Freiburg i.Br., 1941; English translation, New York: Herder, 1968.

———. *The Reformation in Germany*. 2 vols. Translated by Ronald Walls. London: Darton, Ronald, and Todd, 1968.

Mann, William E. "Duns Scotus on Natural and Supernatural Knowledge of God." In *The Cambridge Companion to Duns Scotus*, edited by Thomas Williams, 238–62. Cambridge: Cambridge University Press, 2003.

Markos, Louis. *From Plato to Christ: How Platonic Thought Shaped the Christian Faith*. Downers Grove, IL: InterVarsity Press, 2021.

Maurer, Armand. *The Philosophy of William of Ockham in the Light of Its Principles*. Toronto: Pontifical Institute of Medieval Studies, 1996.

Morello, Sebastian. *The World as God's Icon: Creator and Creation in the Platonic Thought of Thomas Aquinas*. Brooklyn, NY: Angelico, 2020.

Noone, Timothy B. "Universals and Individuation." In *The Cambridge Companion to Duns Scotus*, edited by Thomas Williams, 100–128. Cambridge: Cambridge University Press, 2003.

Oberman, Heiko. *The Harvest of Medieval Theology: Gabriel Biel and Late Medieval Nominalism*. Rev. ed. Grand Rapids: Baker, 2000.

———. *Werden und Wertung der Reformation*. Mohr: Tübingen, 1977.

Osborne, Thomas. "Faith, Philosophy, and the Nominalist Background to Luther's Defense of the Real Presence." *Journal of the History of Ideas* 63, no. 1 (2002): 63–82.

Ramos, Alice M. *Beauty and the Good: Recovering the Classical Tradition from Plato to Duns Scotus*. Washington, DC: Catholic University of America Press, 2020.

Ross, James F., and Todd Bates. "Duns Scotus and Natural Theology." In *The Cambridge Companion to Duns Scotus*, edited by Thomas Williams, 193–237. Cambridge: Cambridge University Press, 2003.

Shircel, Cyril. *The Univocity of the Concept of Being in the Philosophy of John Duns Scotus*. Washington, DC: Catholic University of America Press, 1942.

Slotemaker, John T., and Jeffrey C. Witt. *Robert Holcot*. Great Medieval Thinkers. Oxford: Oxford University Press, 2016.

Steinmetz, David C. *Misericordia Dei: The Theology of Johannes von Staupitz in Its Late Medieval Setting*. Studies in Medieval and Reformation Thought 4. Leiden: Brill, 1968.

Sweetman, Robert. "Univocity, Analogy, and the Mystery of Being according to John Duns Scotus." In *Radical Orthodoxy and the Reformed Tradition: Creation, Covenant, and Participation*, edited by James K. A. Smith and James H. Olthuis, 73–87. Grand Rapids: Baker Academic, 2005.

Spade, Paul Vincent. "Ockham's Nominalist Metaphysics: Some Main Themes." In *The Cambridge Companion to Ockham*, ed. Paul Vincent Space, 100–117. Cambridge: Cambridge University Press, 2006.

Tyson, Paul G. *Returning to Reality: Christian Platonism for Our Times*. Eugene, OR: Cascade, 2014.

White, Thomas Joseph. *The Trinity*. Washington, DC: Catholic University of America Press, 2022.

Wilken, Robert Louis. *The Spirit of Early Christian Thought: Seeking the Face of God*. New Haven, CT: Yale University Press, 2003.

Williams, Thomas. *The Cambridge Companion to Duns Scotus*. Cambridge: Cambridge University Press, 2006.

———. "The Doctrine of Univocity is True and Salutary." *Modern Theology* 21 (2005): 575–85.

———. "A Most Methodical Lover? On Scotus's Arbitrary Creator." *Journal of the History of Philosophy* 38 (2000): 169–202.

———. "Reason, Morality and Voluntarism in Duns Scotus: A Pseudo-Problem Dissolved." *Modern Schoolmen* 74 (1997): 73–94.

Wippel, John. "The Condemnation of 1270 and 1277 at Paris." *Journal of Medieval and Renaissance Studies* 7 (1977): 169–201.

Wolter, Allan. "Native Freedom of the Will as a Key to the Ethics of Scotus." In *The Philosophical Theology of John Duns Scotus*, edited by Marilyn McCord Adams, 148–62. Ithaca, NY: Cornell University Press, 1990.

Wood, Rega. "Ockham's Repudiation of Pelagianism." In *The Cambridge Companion to Ockham*, edited by Paul Vincent Space, 350–74. Cambridge: Cambridge University Press, 2006.

Vos, Antonie. *The Theology of John Duns Scotus*. Leiden: Brill, 2018.

Chapter 6. From Rebirth to Aberration:
The Reformation and Renaissance Humanism
Primary Sources

Bartlett, Kenneth R., ed. *The Civilization of the Italian Renaissance: A Sourcebook*. 2nd ed. Toronto: University of Toronto Press, 2011.

Erasmus, Desiderius. *Ausgewahlte Schriften.* Vol. 4, *De Libero Arbitrio & Hyperastistes Diatribae.* Edited by W. Lesowsky. Darmstadt 1969.

———. *Desiderii Erasmi Opera Omnia.* Edited by J. Leclerc. Leiden, 1703–6.

———. *Opera Omnia Desiderii Erasmi Roterodami.* Amsterdam, 1982.

———. *Praise of Folly.* London: Penguin, 1971.

———. *The Collected Works of Erasmus.* Toronto, 1988.

———. *The Enchiridion.* In *Advocates of Reform, from Wyclif to Erasmus*, edited by Matthew Spinka, 295–379. LCC 14. Philadelphia: Westminster, 1953.

Secondary Sources

Augustijn, Cornelius. *Erasmus: His Life, Works, and Influence.* Translated by J. C. Grayson. Toronto: University of Toronto Press, 1991.

Backus, I. "Erasmus and the Spirituality of the Early Church." In *Erasmus' Vision of the Church*, edited by Hilmar M. Pabel, 95–114. Kirksville, MO: Sixteenth Century Journal Publishers, 1995.

Becker, Reinhard P., ed. *German Humanism and the Reformation.* New York: Continuum, 1982.

Bejczy, Istvan. *Erasmus and the Middle Ages: The Historical Consciousness of a Christian Humanist.* Leiden: Brill, 2001.

Blum, Paul Richard, ed. *Philosophers of the Renaissance.* Washington, DC: Catholic University of America Press, 2010.

Bouwsma, William J. *The Waning of the Renaissance.* New Haven, CT: Yale University Press, 2000.

Boyle, Marjorie O'Rourke. *Erasmus on Language and Method in Theology.* Toronto: University of Toronto Press, 1977.

Copenhaver, Brian P., and Charles B. Schmitt. *Renaissance Philosophy.* Oxford: Oxford University Press, 1992.

Edelheit, Amos. *Ficino, Pico and Savonarola: The Evolution of Humanist Theology, 1461–1498.* Leiden: Brill, 2008.

Fiel, Arthur. *Origins of the Platonic Academy of Florence.* Princeton, NJ: Princeton University Press, 1988.

Goodman, Anthony, and Angus MacKay, eds. *The Impact of Humanism on Western Europe during the Renaissance.* London: Routledge, 1990.

Halkin, Leon. *Erasmus: A Critical Biography.* New York: Blackwell, 1993.

Hankins, James, ed. *The Cambridge Companion to Renaissance Philosophy.* Cambridge: Cambridge University Press, 2007.

Hankins, James, and Ada Palmer. *The Recovery of Ancient Philosophy in the Renaissance: A Brief Guide.* Florence: Olschki, 2008.

Hoffmann, Manfred. *Rhetoric and Theology: The Hermeneutic of Erasmus.* Toronto: University of Toronto Press, 1994.

Holt, Mack P., ed. *Renaissance and Reformation France, 1500–1648.* Oxford: Oxford University Press, 2002.

Huizinga, Johan. *Erasmus and the Age of Reformation.* New York: Harper, 1957.

Hyma, Albert. *Christian Renaissance: A History of the Devotio Moderna.* North Haven, CT: Archon, 1965.

Kekewich, Lucille, ed. *The Impact of Humanism.* New Haven, CT: Yale University Press, 2000.

Kristeller, Paul Oskar. *Eight Philosophers of the Italian Renaissance.* Redwood City, CA: Stanford University Press, 1964.

———. *Renaissance Thought: The Classic, Scholastic and Humanistic Strains.* Rev. ed. New York: Harper and Row, 1961.

Lee, Alexander. *Petrarch and St. Augustine: Classical Scholarship, Christian Theology, and the Origins of the Renaissance in Italy.* Leiden: Brill, 2012.

Mahoney, Edward P., ed. *Philosophy and Humanism: Renaissance Essays in Honor of Paul Oskar Kristeller.* Leiden: Brill, 1976.

Monfasani, John. *Greeks and Latins in Renaissance Italy: Studies on Humanism and Philosophy in the 15th Century.* Farnham, UK: Ashgate, 2004.

Najemy, John. *Italy in the Age of the Renaissance: 1300–1500.* Short Oxford History of Italy. Oxford: Oxford University Press, 2005.

Nauert, Charles G., Jr. *Humanism and the Culture of Renaissance Europe.* 2nd ed. Cambridge: Cambridge University Press, 2006.

Nauta, Lodi. *In Defense of Common Sense: Lorenzo Valla's Humanist Critique of Scholastic Philosophy.* Cambridge, MA: Harvard University Press, 2009.

Oberman, Heiko A., and Thomas A. Brady Jr., eds. *Itinerarium Italicum: The Profile of the Italian Renaissance in the Mirror of Its European Transformations.* Leiden: Brill, 1975.

Overfield, James H. *Humanism and Scholasticism in Late Medieval Germany.* Princeton, NJ: Princeton University Press, 1984.

Ozment, Steven. "Humanism, Scholasticism, and the Intellectual Origins of the Reformation." In *Continuity and Discontinuity in Church History,* edited by F. F. Church and T. George, 133–49. Leiden: Brill, 1957.

Petegree, Andrew. *The Book in the Renaissance.* New Haven, CT: Yale University Press, 2011.

Plumb, J. H. *The Italian Renaissance: A Concise Survey of Its History and Culture.* New York: Harper and Row, 1965.

Robb, Nesca A. *The Neoplatonism of the Italian Renaissance.* London: Octagon, 1968.

Rummel, Erika. *Biblical Humanism and Scholasticism in the Age of Erasmus.* Leiden: Brill, 2008.

———. *The Confessionalization of Humanism in Reformation Germany.* Oxford: Oxford University Press, 2000.

Schoeck, R. J. *Erasmus of Europe: The Making of a Humanist.* Edinburgh: Edinburgh University Press, 1990–93.

Skinner, Quentin, and Eckhard Kessler, eds. *Cambridge History of Renaissance Philosophy.* Cambridge: Cambridge University Press, 2008.

Southern, R. W. *Scholastic Humanism and the Unification of Europe.* 2 vols. New York: Blackwell, 1995–2000.

Spitz, Lewis W. *Luther and German Humanism.* Farnham, UK: Variorum, 1996.

———. *The Religious Renaissance of German Humanists.* Cambridge, MA: Harvard University Press, 1963.

———. *The Renaissance and Reformation Movements.* Vol. 2. Chicago: Rand McNally, 1971.

Trinkaus, Charles. *In Our Image and Likeness: Humanity and Divinity in Italian Humanist Thought.* Notre Dame: IN: University of Notre Dame Press, 1995.

———. *Renaissance Transformations of Late Medieval Thought.* Farnham, UK: Ashgate, 1999.

———. *The Scope of Renaissance Humanism.* Ann Arbor, MI: University of Michigan Press, 1983.

Weinstein, Donald. *Savonarola: The Rise and Fall of a Renaissance Prophet.* New Haven, CT: Yale University Press, 2011.

Witt, Ronald G. *In the Footsteps of the Ancients: The Origins of Humanism from Lovato to Bruni.* Leiden: Brill, 2000.

Chapter 7. The Ecclesiastical Watershed: Conciliarism, Curialism, and the Papacy on the Eve of the Reformation

Primary Sources

Gerson, John. *On the Unity of the Church*. In *Advocates of Reform, from Wyclif to Erasmus*, Matthew Spinka, 140–48. LCC 14. Philadelphia: Westminster, 1953.

Henry of Langenstein. *A Letter on Behalf of a Council of Peace*. In *Advocates of Reform, from Wyclif to Erasmus*, edited by Matthew Spinka, 106–39. LCC 14. Philadelphia: Westminster, 1953.

Hoeck, Jacob, and Wessel Gansfort. "Letter from Jacob Hoeck and Wessel Gansfort." In *Forerunners of the Reformation: The Shape of Late Medieval Thought*, edited by Heiko A. Oberman, 93–120. Cambridge: Clarke, 2002.

Hus, John. *The Letters of John Hus*. Translated and edited by Matthew Spinka. Manchester: Manchester University Press, 1972.

———. *On Simony*. In *Advocates of Reform, from Wyclif to Erasmus*, edited by Matthew Spinka, 196–280. LCC 14. Philadelphia: Westminster, 1953.

Nicholas of Clèmanges, *De studio theologico*. In Luc d'Archery, *Spicilegium*. Paris, 1723.

Major, John. *A Disputation on the Authority of a Council*. In *Advocates of Reform, from Wyclif to Erasmus*, ed. Matthew Spinka, 175–86. LCC 14. Philadelphia: Westminster, 1953.

Oberman, Heiko A., ed. *Forerunners of the Reformation: The Shape of Late Medieval Thought*. Philadelphia: Fortress, 1981. Reprint, Cambridge: T&T Clarke, 2002.

Spinka, Matthew, ed. *Advocates of Reform, from Wyclif to Erasmus*. LCC 14. Philadelphia: Westminster, 1953.

"The Twelve Conclusions of the Lollards, 1395." In *Creeds and Confessions of Faith in the Christian Tradition*, edited by Jaroslav Pelikan and Valerie R. Hotchkiss, 2:786–90. New Haven, CT: Yale University Press, 2003.

Valdes. "The Profession of Faith of Valdes, 1180." In *Creeds and Confessions of Faith in the Christian Tradition*, edited by Jaroslav Pelikan and Valerie R. Hotchkiss, 1:772–73. New Haven, CT: Yale University Press, 2003.

Wyclif, John. *The English Works of Wyclif Hitherto Unprinted*. Edited by F. D. Matthew. London: Early English Text Society, original series 74, 1880; rev. ed. 1902.

———. *English Wycliffite Sermons*. Edited by Anne Hudson and Pamela Gradon. 5 vols. Oxford: Clarendon, 1983–96.

———. *On the Pastoral Office*. In *Advocates of Reform, from Wyclif to Erasmus*, edited by Matthew Spinka, 32–60. LCC 14. Philadelphia: Westminster, 1953.

———. *On the Eucharist*. In *Advocates of Reform, from Wyclif to Erasmus*, edited by Matthew Spinka, 61–90. LCC 14. Philadelphia: Westminster, 1953.

———. *The Latin Writings of John Wyclyf*. Edited by Williell R. Thomson. Toronto: Pontifical Institute of Medieval Studies, 1983.

———. *Select English Works of John Wyclif*. Edited by T. Arnold. 3 vols. Oxford: Clarendon, 1869–71.

———. *Selections from English Wycliffe Writings*. Edited by Anne Hudson. Cambridge: Cambridge University Press, 1978.

———. *Wyclif's Latin Works*. 36 vols. London: Wyclif Society, 1882–1922.

Secondary Sources

Butler, Cuthbert. *The Vatican Council*. 2 vols. Longmans, Green: London, 1930.

Evans, Gillian R. *John Wyclif: Myth and Reality*. Downers Grove, IL: IVP Academic, 2005.

Fudge, Thomas A. "Hussite Theology and the Law of God." In *The Cambridge Companion to Reformation Theology*, edited by David Bagchi and David C. Steinmetz, 22–27. Cambridge: Cambridge University Press, 2004.

Haberkern, Phillip N. *Patron Saint and Prophet: Jan Hus in the Bohemian and German Reformations*. Oxford: Oxford University Press, 2016.

Hudson, Anne, and Michael Wilks. *From Ockham to Wyclif*. Oxford: Blackwell, 1987.

Kaminsky, Howard. *A History of the Hussite Revolution*. Berkeley: University of California Press, 1967.

Kenny, Anthony. *Wyclif*. Oxford: Oxford University Press, 1985.

———, ed. *Wyclif in His Times*. Oxford: Clarendon, 1986.

Maccarrone, Michele. "Una questione inedita dell'Olivi sull'infallibilità del papa." *Revista di storia della chiesa in Italia* 3 (1949): 309–43.

Ratzinger, Joseph. *Principles of Catholic Theology*. San Francisco: Ignatius, 1987.

Scales, Len. *The Shaping of German Identity: Authority and Crisis, 1245–1414*. Cambridge: Cambridge University Press, 2012.

Scase, Wendy. "Lollardy." In *The Cambridge Companion to Reformation Theology*, edited by David Bagchi and David C. Steinmetz, 15–21. Cambridge: Cambridge University Press, 2004.

Spinka, Matthew. *John Hus: A Biography*. Princeton, NJ: Princeton University Press, 1968.

Tierney, Brian. *The Crisis of Church and State 1050–1300*. Toronto: University of Toronto Press, 1988.

———. *Western Europe in the Middle Ages, 300–1475*. 6th ed. New York: McGraw-Hill, 1998.

PART 2: THE GENESIS OF REFORMATION

Primary Sources

Bartlett, Kenneth R., and Margaret McGlynn. *The Renaissance and Reformation in Northern Europe*. Toronto: University of Toronto Press, 2014.

Bruening, Michael W., ed. *A Reformation Sourcebook*. Toronto: University of Toronto Press, 2017.

Dennison, James T., Jr. *Reformed Confessions of the 16th and 17th Centuries in English Translation*. 4 vols. Grand Rapids: Reformation Heritage, 2014.

George, Timothy, Scott M. Manetsch, Gerald Lewis Bray, and Graham Tomlin, eds. *Reformation Commentary on Scripture*. 11 vols. Downers Grove, IL: InterVarsity Press, 2011–17.

Hillebrand, Hans E., ed. *The Protestant Reformation*. Rev. ed. New York: HarperCollins Perennial, 2009.

Janz, Denis, ed. *A Reformation Reader*. 2nd ed. Minneapolis: Augsburg Fortress, 2008.

———, ed. *Three Reformation Catechisms: Catholic, Anabaptist, Lutheran*. Lewiston, NY: Mellen, 1982.

Lindberg, Carter, ed. *The European Reformations Sourcebook*. 2nd ed. Oxford: Blackwell, 2014.

Littlejohn, Bradford, and Jonathan Roberts, eds. *Reformation Theology: A Reader of Primary Sources with Introduction*. Moscow, ID: Davenant, 2018.

McCain, Paul Timothy, W. H. T. Dau, and F. Bente. *Concordia, The Lutheran Confessions: A Reader's Edition of the Book of Concord*. St. Louis: Concordia, 2009.

Naphy, W. G., ed. *Documents on the Continental Reformation*. New York: Palgrave Macmillan, 1996.

Nestingen, James A., and Robert Kolb, eds. *Sources and Contexts of the Book of Concord*. Minneapolis: Fortress, 2001.

Spitz, Lewis W. *The Protestant Reformation: Major Documents*. St. Louis: Concordia, 1997.

Steinmetz, David C. *Reformers in the Wings*. 2nd ed. New York: Oxford University Press, 2001.

Secondary Sources

Atherstone, Andrew. *The Reformation: Faith and Flames*. Oxford: Lion, 2011.

Bagchi, David, and David C. Steinmetz, eds. *The Cambridge Companion to Reformation Theology.* Cambridge: Cambridge University Press, 2004.

Bainton, Roland Herbert. *The Reformation of the Sixteenth Century.* Boston, MA: Beacon, 1985.

Barrett, Matthew, ed. *The Doctrine on Which the Church Stands or Falls: Justification in Biblical, Theological, Historical, and Pastoral Perspective.* Wheaton, IL: Crossway, 2019.

——. *God's Word Alone, the Authority of Scripture: What the Reformers Taught and Why It Still Matters.* Grand Rapids: Zondervan, 2016.

——, ed. *Reformation Theology: A Systematic Summary.* Wheaton, IL: Crossway, 2017.

Brady, Thomas A., Jr., Heiko A. Oberman, James D. Tracy, eds. *Handbook of European History, 1400–1600: Late Middle Ages, Renaissance, and Reformation.* 2 vols. Grand Rapids: Eerdmans, 1994.

Bray, Gerald. *Doing Theology with the Reformers.* Downers Grove, IL: IVP Academic, 2019.

Burnett, Amy Nelson. *Debating the Sacraments: Print and Authority in the Early Reformation.* Oxford: Oxford University Press, 2019.

Chadwick, Owen. *The Penguin History of the Church 3: The Reformation.* London: Penguin Books. 1990.

Collinson, Patrick. *The Reformation: A History.* New York: Modern Library, 2006.

Duffy, Eamon. *Reformation Divided: Catholics, Protestants and the Conversion of England.* London: Bloomsbury, 2017.

Eire, Carlos M. N. *Reformations: The Early Modern World: 1450–1650.* New Haven, CT: Yale University Press, 2016.

——. *War against the Idols: The Reformation of Worship from Erasmus to Calvin.* Cambridge: Cambridge University Press, 1986.

Estep, William. *Renaissance & Reformation.* Grand Rapids: Eerdmans, 1986.

Evans, G. R. *Problems of Authority in the Reformation Debates.* Cambridge: Cambridge University Press, 1992.

George, Timothy. *Reading Scripture with the Reformers.* Downers Grover, IL: IVP Academic, 2011.

——. *Theology of the Reformers.* Rev. ed. Nashville: B&H Academic, 2013.

Grimm, Harold J. *The Reformation Era 1500–1650.* 2nd ed. New York: Macmillan, 1973.

Harline, Craig. *A World Ablaze: The Rise of Martin Luther and the Birth of the Reformation.* New York: Oxford University Press, 2017.

Hillerbrand, Hans J. *The Division of Christendom: Christianity in the Sixteenth Century.* Louisville: Westminster John Knox, 2007.

Jensen, De Lamar. *Reformation Europe: Age of Reform and Revolution.* 2nd ed. Lexington, MA: Heath, 2009.

Johnston, Pamela, and Bob Scribner. *The Reformation in Germany and Switzerland.* Cambridge: Cambridge University Press, 1993.

Levi, Anthony. *Renaissance and Reformation: The Intellectual Genesis.* New Haven, CT: Yale University Press, 2002.

Lindberg, Carter. *The European Reformations.* 2nd ed. Oxford: Blackwell, 2021.

——, ed. *The Reformation Theologians.* Oxford: Blackwell, 2002.

Lortz, Joseph, and Ronald Walls. *The Reformation in Germany.* 2 vols. London: Darton, Longman and Todd, 1968.

Maag, Karin. *Worshiping with the Reformers.* Downers Grove, IL: InterVarsity Press, 2021.

MacCulloch, Diarmaid. *All Things Made New: Writings on the Reformation.* New York: Penguin, 2017.

——. *The Reformation: A History.* New York: Viking Penguin, 2005.

Marshall, Peter. *The Oxford Illustrated History of the Reformation.* Oxford: Oxford University Press, 2015.

Massing, Michael. *Fatal Discord: Erasmus, Luther, and the Fight for the Western Mind.* New York: HarperColllins, 2018.

McGrath, Alister. *Iustitia Dei.* 3rd ed. Cambridge: Cambridge University Press, 2020.

———. *Reformation Thought: An Introduction.* Fourth edition. Oxford: Wiley-Blackwell, 2012.

Oberman, Heiko. *Masters of the Reformation: The Emergence of a New Intellectual Climate in Europe.* Cambridge: Cambridge University Press, 1981.

Ozment, Steven. *Protestants: The Birth of a Revolution.* New York: Doubleday, 1992.

———. *The Reformation in the Cities.* New Haven, CT: Yale University Press, 1975.

Oberman, Heiko A. *Werden und Wertung der Reformation.* Tübingen: Mohr Siebeck, 1989.

Payton, James R., Jr. *Getting the Reformation Wrong: Correcting Some Misunderstandings.* Downers Grove, IL: IVP Academic, 2010.

Pettegree, Andrew. *Brand Luther: How an Unheralded Monk Turned His Small Town into a Center of Publishing, Made Himself the Most Famous Man in Europe—and Started the Protestant Reformation.* New York: Penguin, 2017.

———. *The Early Reformation in Europe.* Cambridge: Cambridge University Press, 1992.

Provan, Iain. *The Reformation and the Right Reading of Scripture.* Waco, TX: Baylor University Press, 2017.

Raitt, Jill, ed. *Shapers of Religious Traditions in Germany, Switzerland, and Poland, 1560–1600.* New Haven, CT: Yale University Press, 1981.

Rupp, E. Gordon. *Patterns of Reformation.* Philadelphia: Fortress, 1969.

Ryrie, Alec. *Protestants: The Faith That Made the Modern World.* New York: Viking, 2017.

Taylor, Larissa, ed. *Preachers and People in the Reformations and Early Modern Period.* Leiden: Brill, 2003.

Trueman, Carl R. *Grace Alone: Salvation as a Gift of God.* Five Solas. Edited by Matthew Barrett. Grand Rapids: Zondervan, 2017.

Ullmann, Carl. *Reformatoren vor der Reformation.* 2 vols. Hamburg: Perthes, 1841–42.

Chapters 8–11 (The German Reformation)
Primary Sources

Arand, Charles P., and Robert Kolb, eds. *The Book of Concord: The Confessions of the Evangelical Lutheran Church.* Minneapolis: Fortress, 2005.

Arand, Charles P., James A. Nestingen, and Robert Kolb, eds. *Lutheran Confessions: History and Theology of the Book of Concord.* Minneapolis: Fortress, 2012.

The Augsburg Confession: A Collection of Sources. Edited by Johann Michael Reu. Fort Wayne, IN: Concordia Theological Seminary Press, 1966.

Chemnitz, Martin. *Loci Theologici.* Translated by J. A. O. Preus. 2 vols. St. Louis: Concordia, 1989.

Karlstadt, Andreas Bodenstein von. *De Legis Litera Sive Carne & Spiritu . . . Enarratio.* Wittenberg 1521. BSB 4 Asc. 186 (digital version).

———. *Dialogus oder ein gesprechbüchlin Von dem grewlichen vnnd abgöttischen mißbrauch des hochwirdigsten sacraments Jesu Christi.* Basel, 1524.

———. *The Eucharistic Pamphlets of Andreas Bodenstein von Karlstadt.* Translated and edited by Amy Nelson Burnett. University Park, PA: Penn State University Press, 2011.

———. *Karlstadt und Augustin: Der Kommentar des Andreas Bodenstein von Karlstadt zu Augustins Schrift De Spiritu et Litera.* Edited by E. Kahler. Halle: Max Niemeyer, 1952.

———. *Schriften aus den Jahren 1523–1525.* Parts 1 and 2. Edited by Erich Hertzsch. Halle: Max Niemeyer, 1956 and 1957.

Kolb, Robert, and James A. Nestingen, eds. *Sources and Contexts of the Book of Concord.* Minneapolis: Fortress, 2001.

Kolb, Robert, and Timothy J. Wengert, eds. *The Book of Concord (New Translation): The Confessions of the Evangelical Lutheran Church.* Minneapolis: Fortress, 2000.

Lund, Eric, ed. *Documents from the History of Lutheranism 1517–1750.* Minneapolis: Fortress, 2002.

Luther, Martin. *The Annotated Luther.* Edited by Hans Joachim Hillerbrand, Kirsi Irmeli Stjerna, Timothy J. Wengert, Euan Cameron, et al. 6 vols. Minneapolis: Fortress, 2015–17.

———. *Archiv zur Weimarer Ausgabe der Werke Martin Luthers: Texte und Untersuchungen.* 9 vols. Cologne, Weimar, and Vienna: Böhlau, 1981–.

———. *D. Martini Lutheri opera Latina varii argumenti ad Reformationis hisoriam imprimis pertinentia.* 7 vols. Frankfurt and Erlangen: Heyderi & Zimeri, 1865–73.

———. *Dokumente zur Luthers Entwicklung.* Edited by O. Scheel. 2nd ed. Tübingen: Mohr Siebeck 1929.

———. *D. Martin Luthers sämmtliche Schriften.* Edited by J. G. Walch. Rev. ed. 23 vols. St. Louis: Concordia, 1880–1910.

———. *Luther's Correspondence and Other Contemporary Letters.* Edited by Preserved Smith and Charles Jacobs. 2 vols. Philadelphia: Lutheran Publication Society, 1913, 1918.

———. *Luthers Werke in Auswahl.* Edited by Helmut T. Lehmann, Jaroslav Pelikan, et al. Vols. 1–55. St. Louis: Concordia; Philadelphia and Minneapolis: Fortress, 1955–86.

———. *Luther's Works.* Edited by Helmut Lehmann, Jaroslav Pelikan, et al. Vols. 1–55. St. Louis: Concordia; Philadelphia and Minneapolis: Fortress, 1955–86.

———. *Luther's Works.* Edited by Christopher Boyd Brown et al. Vols. 56–75. St. Louis: Concordia, 2006–.

———. *Martin Luther Lateinisch-Deutsche Studienausgabe: Die Kirche und ihre Amter.* Edited by W. Harle et al. 3 vols. Leipzig: Evangelische Verlagsanstalt, 2006–9.

———. *Martin Luther Studienausgabe.* Edited by Hans-Ulrich Delius et al. 6 vols. Berlin: Evangelische Verlagsanstalt, 1979–99.

———. *Martin Luther's Basic Exegetical Writings.* Edited by Carl L. Beckwith. St. Louis: Concordia, 2017.

———. *Martin Luther's Basic Theological Writings.* Edited by Timothy F. Lull and William R. Russell. Philadelphia: Fortress, 2012.

Melanchthon, Philip. "Die Apologie der Konfession." In *Die Bekenntnisschriften der Evangelisch-Lutherischen Kirche*, 141–404. Göttingen: Vandenhoeck & Ruprecht, 1967.

———. *Commentary on Romans.* Translated by Fred Kramer. St. Louis: Concordia, 1992.

———. *Corpus Reformatorum. Philippi Melanchthonis Opera quae supersunt omnia.* Edited by C. G. Bretschneider and H. E. Bindseil. Halle: Schwetschke, 1834–60.

———. *Loci Communes 1521.* St. Louis: Concordia, 2017.

———. *Loci Communes 1543.* Translated by J. A. O. Preus. St. Louis: Concordia, 1992.

———. *The Loci Communes of Philip Melanchthon.* Translated by Charles Leander Hill. Boston, MA: Meador, 1944.

———. *Melanchthon: Orations on Philosophy and Education.* Edited by Kusukawa, Sachiko. Translated by Christine F. Salazar. Cambridge: Cambridge University Press, 1999.

———. *Melanchthon: Selected Writings.* Translated by Charles Leander Hill. Minneapolis: Augsburg, 1962.

———. *Melanchthon and Bucer.* Edited by Wilhelm Pauck. LCC 19. Philadelphia: Westminster, 1969.

———. *Melanchthon on Christian Doctrine.* Edited by Clyde L. Manschreck. Library of Protestant Thought. New York: Oxford University Press, 1965.

———. *A Melanchthon Reader.* Translated by Ralph Keen. New York: Lang, 1988.

———. *Melanchthons Briefwechsel: Texte.* Edited by C. Mundhenk, H. Scheible, R. Wetzel, et al. 14 vols. Stuttgart–Bad Cannstatt: Frommann-Holzboog, 1977–.

———. *Melanchthons Werke (Studienausgabe).* Edited by Robert Stupperich et al. 6 vols. Gütersloh: Bertelsmann, 1951–83.

———. *Melanchthons Werke in Auswahl.* Edited R. Stupperich et al. 7 vols. Gütersloh: 1951–83.

Tetzel, Johann. *Johann Tetzel's Rebuttal against Luther's Sermon on Indulgence and Grace.* Translated by Dewey Weiss Kramer. Atlanta: Pitts Theology Library, 2012.

Vajta, Vilmos, ed. *Luther and Melanchthon.* Philadelphia: Muhlenberg, 1961.

———. *Luther on Worship.* Philadelphia: Muhlenberg, 1958.

Von Staupitz, Johannes. *Constitutiones Fratrum Heremitarum sancti Augustini ad apostolicorum privilegiorum formam pro Reformatione Alemanie.* Nuremberg: n.p., 1504.

———. *Decisio quaestionis de audientia misse in parochiali ecclesia dominicis et festivis diebus.* Tübingen: n.p., 1500.

———. *Johannis Staupiti: Opera quae reperiri potuerunt omnia edidit: Deutsche Schriften.* Edited by J. F. K. Knaake. Vol. 1. Potsdam, n.p., 1867.

———. *Libellus de executione eterne predestinationis.* Nuremberg, n.p., 1517.

———. *Sämtliche Schriften: Abhandlungen, Predigten, Zeugnisse, Lateinische Schriften.* Edited by Lothar Graf zu Dohna and Richard Wetzel. Spätmittelalter und Reformation, Texte und Untersuchungen, vols. 13–14. Berlin: de Gruyter, 1987.

———. *Sermones.* Codex Hs: b V 8, Saint Peter; Codex Hs: b II 11, Saint Peter; Codex Hs: 23 E 16, Nonnberg. Codices located in the Library of the Benedictine Abbey, Salzburg, Austria.

———. *Tübinger Predigten.* Edited by Georg Buchwald and Ernst Wolf. Quellen und Forschungen zur Reformationsgeschichte 8. Leipzig: Heinzius, 1927.

Secondary Sources

Althaus, Paul. *The Ethics of Martin Luther.* Translated by Robert C. Schultz. Philadelphia: Fortress, 1972.

———. *The Theology of Martin Luther.* Translated by Robert C. Schultz. Philadelphia: Fortress, 1966.

Arand, Charles P. *That I May Be His Own: An Overview of Luther's Catechisms.* St. Louis: Concordia, 2000.

Arnold, Brian J. *Justification in the Second Century.* Waco, TX: Baylor University Press, 2018.

Atkinson, James. *Martin Luther and the Birth of Protestantism.* London: Marshall, Morgan & Scott, 1982.

———. *The Trial of Luther.* New York: Stein and Day, 1971.

Bagchi, David. *Luther's Earliest Opponents: Catholic Controversialists, 1518–1525.* Minneapolis: Fortress, 1991.

Bainton, Roland H. *Here I Stand: A Life of Martin Luther.* New York: Penguin, 2002.

Bollinger, Daniel. *Infiniti contemplatio: Grudzüge der Scotus- und Scotismusrezeption im Werk Huldrych Zwinglis.* Leiden: Brill, 2003.

Bornkamm, Heinrich. *Luther and the Old Testament.* Translated by Eric W. and Ruth C. Gritsch. Edited by Victor I. Gruhn. Minneapolis: Fortress, 1969.

———. *Luther in Mid-Career, 1521–1530.* Philadelphia: Fortress, 1983.

———. *Luther's Doctrine of the Two Kingdoms in the Context of His Theology.* Philadelphia: Fortress, 1966.

———. *Luther's World of Thought*. St. Louis: Concordia, 2005.

Braaten, Carl E., and Robert W. Jenson. *Union with Christ: The New Finnish Interpretation of Luther*. Grand Rapids: Eerdmans, 2000.

Brecht, Martin. *Martin Luther: His Road to Reformation, 1483–1521*. Philadelphia: Fortress, 1985.

———. *Martin Luther: The Preservation of the Church, 1532–1546*. Minneapolis: Fortress, 1993.

———. *Martin Luther 1521–1532: Shaping and Defining the Reformation*. Philadelphia: Fortress, 1990.

Brendler, Gerhard. *Martin Luther, Theology and Revolution*. Oxford: Oxford University Press, 1991.

Cross, Richard. *Communicatio Idiomatum: Reformation Christological Debates*. Oxford: Oxford University Press, 2019.

Dickens, A. G. *The German Nation and Martin Luther*. New York: Harper and Row, 1974.

———. *Martin Luther and the Reformation*. London: English Universities Press, 1967.

Dieter, Theodor. "Luther as Late Medieval Theologian: His Positive and Negative Use of Nominalism and Realism." In *The Oxford Handbook of Martin Luther's Theology*, edited by Robert Kolb, Irene Dingel, and L'ubomír Batka, 31–48. Oxford: Oxford University Press, 2014.

Dingel, Irene, Robert Kolb, Nicole Kuropka, and Timothy J. Wengert. *Philip Melanchthon: Theologian in Classroom, Confession, and Controversy*. Göttingen: Vandenhoeck & Ruprecht, 2012.

Ebeling, Gerhard. *Luther: An Introduction to His Thought*. Minneapolis: Fortress, 1970.

Edwards, Mark U., Jr. *Luther's Last Battles: Politics and Polemics, 1531–1546*. Ithaca, NY: Cornell University Press, 1983.

Erikson, Erik. *Young Man Luther: A Study in Psychoanalysis and History*. New York: Norton, 1993.

Estes, James M. Peace. *Order and the Glory of God: Secular Authority and the Church in the Thought of Luther and Melanchthon, 1518–1559*. Leiden: Brill, 2005.

Forde, Gerhard O. *Christ Present in Faith: Luther's View of Justification*. Translated and edited by Kirsi Irmeli Stjerna. Minneapolis: Fortress, 2005.

———. *On Being a Theologian of the Cross: Reflections on Luther's Heidelberg Disputation, 1518*. Grand Rapids and Cambridge: Eerdmans, 1997.

———. *The Captivation of the Will: Luther vs. Erasmus on Freedom and Bondage*. Edited by Steven Paulson. Grand Rapids and Cambridge: Eerdmans, 2005.

Fraenkel, Pierre. *Testimonia Patrum: The Function of the Patristic Argument in the Theology of Philip Melanchthon*. Geneva: Droz, 1961.

Graybill, Gregory B. *Evangelical Free Will: Phillipp Melanchthon's Doctrinal Journey on the Origins of Faith*. Oxford: Oxford University Press, 2010.

Gregory, Brad S. *Rebel in the Ranks: Martin Luther, the Reformation, and the Conflicts That Continue to Shape Our World*. New York: HarperOne, 2017.

Gritsch, Eric W. *A History of Lutheranism*. 2nd ed. Minneapolis: Fortress, 2010.

———. *Martin, God's Court Jester: Luther in Retrospect*. Minneapolis: Fortress, 1983.

Grosshans, Hans-Peter. *Luther*. New York: Fount, 1997.

Hägglund, Bengt. *The Background of Luther's Doctrine of Justification in Late Medieval Theology*. Minneapolis: Fortress, 1971.

Haile, H. G. *Luther: An Experiment in Biography*. Princeton, NJ: Princeton University Press, 1983.

Hamm, Berndt. *The Early Luther: Stages in a Reformation Reorientation*. Translated by Martin J. Lohermann. Grand Rapids: Eerdmans, 2014.

Harran, Marilyn. *Luther on Conversion: The Early Years*. Ithaca, NY: Cornell University Press, 1983.

Heckel, Johannes. *Lex Charitatis: A Juristic Disquisition on Law in the Theology of Martin Luther*. Grand Rapids: Eerdmans, 2010.

Hendrix, Scott H. *Luther and the Papacy: Stages in a Reformation Conflict*. Minneapolis: Fortress, 1981.

————. *Martin Luther: Visionary Reformer.* New Haven, CT: Yale University Press, 2015.

Hermann, Rudolf. *Luthers Theologie.* Edited by Horst Beintker. Göttingen: Vandenhoeck & Ruprecht, 1967.

Herrmann, Erik. "Luther's Absorption of Medieval Biblical Interpretation." In *The Oxford Handbook of Martin Luther's Theology*, edited by Robert Kolb, Irene Dingel, and L'ubomír Batka, 71–90. Oxford: Oxford University Press, 2014.

Hildebrandt, Franz. *Melanchthon: Alien or Ally?* Cambridge: Cambridge University Press, 1946.

Hoffman, Bengt. *Luther and the Mystics.* Minneapolis: Augsburg, 1976.

Janz, Denis R. *The Westminster Handbook to Martin Luther.* Louisville: Westminster John Knox, 2010.

Jones, Rosemary Devonshire. *Erasmus and Luther.* Oxford: Oxford University Press, 1968.

Kärkkäinen, Veli-Matti. "Justification as Forgiveness of Sins and Making Righteous: The Ecumenical Promise of a New Interpretation of Luther." *One in Christ* 37, no. 2 (2002): 32–45.

Kerr, Hugh T., ed. *A Compend of Luther's Theology.* Philadelphia: Westminster, 1974.

Kilcrease, Jack D. *Justification by the Word: Restoring Sola Fide.* Bellingham, WA: Lexham, 2022.

Kirchner, Hubert. *Luther and the Peasants' War.* Minneapolis: Fortress, 1972.

Kittelson, James M. *Luther the Reformer: The Story of the Man and His Career.* Minneapolis: Fortress, 1986.

Kolb, Robert. *Bound Choice, Election, and Wittenberg Theological Method: From Martin Luther to the Formula of Concord.* Grand Rapids: Eerdmans, 2005.

————. "Confessional Lutheran Theology." In *The Cambridge Companion to Reformation Theology*, edited by David Bagchi and David C. Steinmetz, 68–79. Cambridge: Cambridge University Press, 2004.

————. *Luther and the Stories of God: Biblical Narratives as a Foundation for Christian Living.* Grand Rapids: Baker Academic, 2012.

————. *Luther's Wittenberg World: The Reformer's Family, Friends, Followers, and Foes.* Minneapolis: Fortress, 2018.

————. *Martin Luther: Confessor of the Faith.* Oxford: Oxford University Press, 2009.

————. *Martin Luther and the Enduring Word of God: The Wittenberg School and Its Scripture-Centered Proclamation.* Grand Rapids: Baker, 2016.

————. *Martin Luther as Prophet, Teacher, and Hero.* Grand Rapids: Baker, 1999.

————. *Nikolaus von Amsdorf: Champion of Martin Luther's Reformation.* St. Louis: Concordia, 2019.

Kolb, Robert, and Charles P. Arand. *The Genius of Luther's Theology: A Wittenberg Way of Thinking for the Contemporary Church.* Grand Rapids: Baker Academic, 2008.

————. *The Way of Concord: From Historic Text to Contemporary Witness.* St. Louis: Concordia Seminary Press, 2017.

Kusukawa, Sachiko. "Melanchthon." In *The Cambridge Companion to Reformation Theology*, edited by David Bagchi and David C. Steinmetz, 57–67. Cambridge: Cambridge University Press, 2004.

————. *The Transformation of Natural Philosophy: The Case of Philip Melanchthon.* Cambridge: Cambridge University Press, 1995.

Leppin, Volker. "Luther's Roots in Monastic-Mystical Piety." In *The Oxford Handbook of Martin Luther's Theology*, edited by Robert Kolb, Irene Dingel, and L'ubomír Batka, 49–61. Oxford: Oxford University Press, 2014.

————. "Luther's Transformation of Medieval Thought." In *The Oxford Handbook of Martin Luther's Theology*, edited by Robert Kolb, Irene Dingel, and L'ubomír Batka, 115–24. Oxford: Oxford University Press, 2014.

———. *Martin Luther: A Late Medieval Life*. Grand Rapids: Baker, 2017.

Loewenich, Walther von. *Luther's Theology of the Cross*. Minneapolis: Augsburg, 1976.

Lohse, Bernhard. *Martin Luther: An Introduction to His Life and Work*. Minneapolis: Fortress, 1986.

———. *Martin Luther's Theology: Its Historical and Systematic Development*. Translated and edited by Roy A. Harrisville. Minneapolis: Fortress, 1999.

Lull, Timothy F., and Derek R. Nelson. *Resilient Reformer: The Life and Thought of Martin Luther*. Minneapolis: Fortress, 2015.

Luy, David J. *Dominus Mortis: Martin Luther on the Incorruptibility of God in Christ*. Minneapolis: Fortress, 2014.

Maag, Karin, ed. *Melanchthon in Europe: His Work and Influence beyond Wittenberg*. Grand Rapids: Baker, 1999.

Mannermaa, Tuomo. *Christ Present in Faith: Luther's View of Justification*. Minneapolis: Fortress, 2005.

———. *Two Kinds of Love: Martin Luther's Religious World*. Minneapolis: Fortress, 2010.

Manschreck, Clyde L. *Melanchthon: The Quiet Reformer*. New York: Abingdon, 1968.

Marius, Richard. *Martin Luther: The Christian between God and Death*. Cambridge, MA: Belknap, 1999.

Marty, Martin. *Martin Luther*. New York: Penguin, 2004.

Mattes, Mark C. *Martin Luther's Theology of Beauty: A Reappraisal*. Grand Rapids: Baker Academic. 2017.

Maurer, Wilhelm. *Der junge Melanchthon*. Vol. 1. Göttingen: Vandenhoeck & Ruprecht, 1967.

———. *Historical Commentary of the Augsburg Confession*. Philadelphia: Fortress, 1986.

———. "Melanchthon as Author of the Augsburg Confession." *Lutheran World* 7 (1960): 153–67.

———. *Melanchthon-Studien*. Gütersloh: Gütersloher Verlagshaus / Mohn, 1964.

McGrath, Alister E. *Luther's Theology of the Cross: Martin Luther's Theological Breakthrough*. Oxford: Blackwell, 1985.

McKim, Donald K., ed. *The Cambridge Companion to Martin Luther*. Cambridge: Cambridge University Press, 2003.

McLelland, Joseph C. "Translator's Introduction." In Peter Martyr Vermigli, *The Oxford Treatise and Disputation on the Eucharist*, edited by Joseph C. McLelland, xvii–xlvi. Sixteenth Century Essays and Studies LVI. Truman State University Press, 2000. Reprint, Peter Martyr Library 7. Moscow, ID: Davenant, 2018.

McSorley, Harry J. *Luther: Right or Wrong?* Minneapolis: Fortress, 1969.

Meijering, E. P. *Melanchthon and Patristic Thought: The Doctrines of Christ and Grace, the Trinity, and the Creation*. Leiden: Brill, 1983.

Miller, Gregory J. "Luther on the Turks and Islam." *Lutheran Quarterly* 14 (200): 79–97.

Minnich, Nelson H., and Michael Root, eds. *Martin Luther and the Shaping of the Catholic Tradition*. Washington, DC: Catholic University of America Press, 2021.

Mullett, Michael A. *Martin Luther*. New York: Routledge, 2004.

Nestingen, James A. *Martin Luther: A Life*. Minneapolis: Fortress, 2003.

Oberman, Heiko A. *Luther: Man between God and the Devil*. New Haven, CT: Yale University Press, 2006.

Ozment, Steven. *Homo Spiritualis: A Comparative Study of the Anthropology of Johannes Tauler, Jean Gerson and Martin Luther (1509–16) in the Context of Their Theological Thought*. Leiden: Brill, 1969.

———. *The Serpent and the Lamb: Cranach, Luther, and the Making of the Reformation*. New Haven, CT: Yale University Press, 2011.

Pelikan, Jaroslav. *Spirit versus Structure: Luther and the Institutions of the Church.* New York: Harper and Row, 1968.

Pereira, Jairzinho Lopes. *Augustine of Hippo and Martin Luther on Original Sin and Justification of the Sinner.* Bristol, CT: Vandenhoeck & Ruprecht, 2013.

Posset, Franz. *The Real Luther: A Friar at Erfurt and Wittenberg.* St. Louis: Concordia, 2011.

Preus, Jacob A. O. *The Second Martin: The Life and Theology of Martin Chemnitz.* St. Louis: Concordia, 1994.

Quere, Ralph Walter. *Melanchthon's Christum Cognoscere: Christ's Efficacious Presence in the Euchartistic Theology of Melanchthon.* Nieuwkoop: De Graaf, 1977.

Rex, Richard. *The Making of Martin Luther.* Princeton, NJ: Princeton University Press, 2017.

Rittgers, Ronald. *The Reformation of the Keys: Confession, Conscience, and Authority in Sixteenth Century Germany.* Cambridge, MA: Harvard University Press, 2004.

Ruokanen, Miikka. *Trinitarian Grace in Martin Luther's The Bondage of the Will.* Oxford: Oxford University Press, 2021.

Rupp, E. Gordon. *Luther's Progress to the Diet of Worms.* New York: Harper and Row, 1964.

———. *The Righteousness of God: Luther Studies.* London: Hodder & Stoughton, 1953.

Russell, Wiliam R. *The Schmalkald Articles: Luther's Theological Testament.* Minneapolis: Fortress, 1995.

Schilling, Heinz. *Martin Luther: Rebel in an Age of Upheaval.* Oxford: Oxford University Press, 2017.

Schofield, John. *Philip Melanchthon and the English Reformation.* Farnham, UK: Ashgate, 2006.

Schwarz, Hans. *True Faith in the True God: An Introduction to Luther's Life and Thought.* Minneapolis: Fortress, 1996.

Shepherd, Victor A. *Interpreting Martin Luther: An Introduction to His Life and Thought.* Vancouver: Regent College, 2008.

Siggins, Ian D. K. *Martin Luther's Doctrine of Christ.* New Haven, CT: Yale University Press, 1970.

Smith, Ralph F. *Luther, Ministry, and Ordination Rites in the Early Reformation Church.* Frankfurt: Lang, 1996.

Spitz, Lewis W., and Wenzel Lohff, eds. *Discord, Dialogue, and Concord: Studies in the Lutheran Reformation's Formula of Concord.* Minneapolis: Fortress, 1977.

Steinmetz, David C. *Luther and Staupitz: An Essay in the Intellectual Origins of the Protestant Reformation.* Monographs in Medieval and Renaissance Studies 4. Durham, NC: Duke University Press, 1980.

———. *Luther in Context.* 2nd ed. Grand Rapids: Baker, 2002.

———. *Misericordia Dei: The Theology of Johannes von Staupitz in Its Late Medieval Setting.* Studies in Medieval and Reformation Thought 4. Leiden: Brill, 1968.

———. *Der unbekannte Melanchthon.* Stuttgart: Kohlhammer, 1961.

Stupperich, Robert. "The Development of Melanchthon's Theological-Philosophical World View." *Lutheran World* 7 (1960): 168–80.

———. *Melanchthon.* Translated by Robert H. Fischer. Philadelphia: Westminster, 1965.

Thompson, Mark D. *A Sure Ground on Which to Stand: The Relation of Authority and Interpretive Method of Luther's Approach to Scripture.* Eugene, OR: Wipf & Stock, 2004.

Trueman, Carl R. "Is The Finnish Line a New Beginning? A Critical Assessment of the Reading of Luther Offered by the Helsinki Circle." *WTJ* 65, no. 2 (2003): 231–44.

———. *Luther of the Christian Life.* Wheaton, IL: Crossway, 2015.

———. *Luther's Legacy.* Oxford: Oxford University Press, 1994.

Von Loewenich, Walther. *Luther's Theology of the Cross.* Minneapolis: Augsburg, 1976.

――――. *Martin Luther: The Man and His Work*. Minneapolis: Augsburg, 1986.

Wengert, Timothy J. *Defending Faith: Lutheran Responses to Andreas Osiander's Doctrine of Justification, 1551–1559*. Tübingen: Mohr Siebeck, 2012.

――――, ed. *Harvesting Martin Luther's Reflections on Theology, Ethics, and the Church*. Minneapolis: Fortress, 2017.

――――. *Human Freedom, Christian Righteousness: Philip Melanchthon's Exegetical Dispute with Erasmus of Rotterdam*. New York: Oxford University Press, 1998.

――――. *Law and Gospel: Philip Melanchthon's Debate with John Agricola of Eisleben*. Grand Rapids: Baker, 1997.

――――. *Martin Luther's 95 Theses: With Introduction, Commentary, and Study Guide*. Minneapolis: Fortress, 2015.

――――, ed. The *Pastoral Luther: Essays on Martin Luther's Practical Theology*. Grand Rapids: Eerdmans, 2009.

――――. *Philip Melanchthon, Speaker of the Reformation: Wittenberg's Other Reformer*. Farnham, UK: Ashgate Variorum, 2010.

――――. *Philip Melanchthon's Annotationes in Johannem in Relation to Its Predecessors and Contemporaries*. Geneva: Droz, 1987.

――――. *Reading the Bible with Martin Luther: An Introductory Guide*. Grand Rapids: Baker, 2013.

Wengert, Timothy J., et al, eds. *Dictionary of Luther and the Lutheran Traditions*. Grand Rapids: Baker Academic, 2017.

Wernisch, Martin. "Luther and Medieval Reform Movements, Particularly the Hussites." In *The Oxford Handbook of Martin Luther's Theology*, edited by Robert Kolb, Irene Dingel, and L'ubomír Batka, 62–70. Oxford: Oxford University Press, 2014.

Wicks, Jared. *Man Yearning for Grace: Luther's Early Spiritual Teaching*. Moscow, ID: Corpus, 1968.

Wilson, Derek. *Out of the Storm: The Life and Legacy of Martin Luther*. New York: St. Martin's, 2008.

Yeago, David. "The Catholic Luther." In *The Catholicity of the Reformation*, edited by Carl E. Braatan and Robert Jensen, 13–34. Grand Rapids: Eerdmans, 1996.

Zachman, Randall C. *Assurance of Faith: Conscience in the Theology of Martin Luther and John Calvin*. Minneapolis: Fortress, 1993.

PART 3: THE FORMATION OF REFORMED CATHOLICITY

Chapter 12. The Renewal of a Catholic Heritage: The Reformation among the Swiss

Primary Sources

Bullinger, Heinrich. *De Origine Erroris Libri Duo*. Zurich: Froschauer, 1539.

――――. *Bullinger's Decades*. Parker Society ed. 5 vols. Cambridge: Cambridge University Press, 1849–52.

――――. *Heinrich Bullinger Briefwechsel*. Vol. 12, *Briefe des Jahres 1543*. Edited by Rainer Henrich et al. Zurich: Theologischer, 2008.

――――. *In Apocalypsim Iesu Christi*. Basel: Oporinus, 1557.

――――. *In Piam et Eruditam Pauli ad Hebraeos epistolam*. Zurich: Froschauer, 1532.

――――. *Of the Holy Catholic Church*. In *Zwingli and Bullinger*, edited by G. W. Bromiley, 283–326. Louisville: Westminster John Knox, 2006.

――――. *Werke*. Edited by Fritz Büsser. Zürich: Theologischer, 1972–.

The First Helvetic Confession, 1536 and *The Second Helvetic Confession, 1566*. In *Creeds and Confessions of Faith in the Christian Tradition*, edited by Jaroslav Pelikan and Valerie R. Hotchkiss, 2:280–91 and 2:458–525. New Haven, CT: Yale University Press, 2003.

The Ten Theses of Bern, 1528. In *Creeds and Confessions of Faith in the Christian Tradition*, edited by Jaroslav Pelikan and Valerie R. Hotchkiss, 2:215–17. New Haven, CT: Yale University Press, 2003.

The Tetrapolitan Confession, 1530. In *Creeds and Confessions of Faith in the Christian Tradition*, edited by Jaroslav Pelikan and Valerie R. Hotchkiss, 2:218–48. New Haven, CT: Yale University Press, 2003.

Zwingli, Ulrich. *An Exposition of the Faith.* In *Zwingli and Bullinger*, edited by G. W. Bromiley, 239–82. Louisville: Westminster John Knox, 2006.

———. *Huldrych Zwingli Writings.* Translated by H. Wayne Pipkin. 2 vols. Allison Park, PA: Pickwick, 1984.

———. *The Latin Works.* Edited by S. M. Jackson. 3 vols. New York: Putnam, 1912–29.

———. *On Baptism.* In *Zwingli and Bullinger*, edited by G. W. Bromiley, 119–75. Louisville: Westminster John Knox, 2006.

———. *On the Clarity and Certainty of the Word of God.* In *Zwingli and Bullinger*, edited by G. W. Bromiley, 49–95. Louisville: Westminster John Knox, 2006.

———. *On the Lord's Supper.* In *Zwingli and Bullinger*, edited by G. W. Bromiley, 176–238. Louisville: Westminster John Knox, 2006.

———. *A Reckoning of the Faith, 1530.* In *Creeds and Confessions of Faith in the Christian Tradition*, edited by Jaroslav Pelikan and Valerie R. Hotchkiss, 2:249–71. New Haven, CT: Yale University Press, 2003.

———. *The Sixty-Seven Articles, 1523.* In *Creeds and Confessions of Faith in the Christian Tradition*, edited by Jaroslav Pelikan and Valerie R. Hotchkiss, 2:207–14. New Haven, CT: Yale University Press, 2003.

———. *Ulrich Zwingli: Early Writings.* Edited by Samuel M. Jackson. Durham, NC: Labyrinth, 1986.

———. *Ulrich Zwingli: Selected Works.* Edited by Samuel M. Jackson. Philadelphia: University of Pennsylvania Press, 1972.

———. *Writings in Search of True Religion.* Edited by H. Wayne Pipkin. 2 vols. Pickwick, 1984.

———. *Zwingli: Commentary on True and False Religion.* Samuel M. Jackson and C. N. Heller. Durham, NC: Labyrinth, 1981.

———. *Zwingli: On Providence and Other Essays.* Edited by William J. Hinke. Durham, NC: Labyrinth, 1983.

Secondary Sources

Baker, Wayne J. *Heinrich Bullinger and the Covenant: The Other Reformed Tradition.* Athens, OH: Ohio University Press, 1980.

Drake, K. J. *The Flesh of the Word: The Extra Calvinisticum from Zwingli to Early Orthodoxy.* New York: Oxford University Press, 2021.

Gäbler, Ulrich. *Huldrych Zwingli: His Life and Work.* Minneapolis: Fortress, 1986.

Gordon, Bruce. *The Swiss Reformation.* Manchester: Manchester University Press, 2002.

———. *Zwingli: God's Armed Prophet.* New Haven, CT: Yale University Press, 2021.

Gordon, Bruce, and Emidio Campi. *Architect of Reformation: An Introduction to Heinrich Bullinger, 1504–1575.* Grand Rapids: Baker Academic, 2004.

Hollweg, Walter. *Heinrich Bullingers Hausbuch.* Neukirchen: Kreis Moers, Verlag der Buchhandlung de Erziehungsvereins, 1956.

Kirby, W. J. Torrance. *The Zurich Connection and Tudor Political Theology.* Leiden: Brill, 2007.

Locher, Gottfried W. *Zwingli's Thought: New Perspectives.* Leiden: Brill, 1981.

McCoy, Charles S., and J. Wayne Becker. *Fountainhead of Federalism: Heinrich Bullinger and the Covenantal Tradition.* Louisville: John Knox, 1991.

Potter, G. R. *Zwingli*. Cambridge: Cambridge University Press, 1976.

Purcha, Leiden, and H. Wayne Pipkin, eds. *Prophet, Pastor, Protestant: The Work of Huldrych Zwingli after Five Hundred Years*. Pittsburgh, PA: Pickwick, 1984.

Rilliet, Jean. *Zwingli: Third Man of the Reformation*. Philadelphia: Westminster, 1964.

Staedke, Joachim. *Die Theologie des jungen Bullinger*. Zurich: Zwingli-Verlag, 1962.

———, ed. *Glauben und Bekennen: Vierhundert Jahre Confessio Helvetica Posterior*. Zurich: Zwingli-Verlag, 1966.

Stephens, W. Peter. *The Theology of Huldrych Zwingli*. Oxford: Oxford University Press, 1986.

———. "The Theology of Huldrych Zwingli." In *The Cambridge Companion to Reformation Theology*, edited by David Bagchi and David C. Steinmetz, 80–99. Cambridge: Cambridge University Press, 2004.

———. *Zwingli: An Introduction to His Thought*. Oxford: Oxford University Press, 1992.

Taplin, Mark. *Italian Reformers and the Zurich Church, 1540–1620*. Farnham, UK: Ashgate, 2003.

Venema, Cornelis P. *Heinrich Bullinger and the Doctrine of Predestination: Author of the Other Reformed Tradition*. Grand Rapids: Baker Academic, 2002.

Walser, Peter. *Die Prädestination bei Bullinger*. Zurich: Zwingli-Verlag, 1957.

Wandel, Palmer Lee. *Voracious Idols and Violent Hands: Iconoclasm in Reformation Zurich, Strasbourg, and Basel*. Cambridge: Cambridge University Press, 1995.

Chapter 13. Abandoning Catholicity for Primitive Christianity: Radicals and Revolutionaries

Primary Sources

Amsdorf, Nikolaus von. *Nikolaus von Amsdorf: Ausgewählte Schriften*. Edited by Otto Lerche. Gütersloh: Bertelsmann, 1938.

Baylor, Michael G., ed. *The Radical Reformation*. Cambridge: Cambridge University Press, 1991.

Denck, Hans. *Confession before the Nuremberg Council, 1525*. In *Creeds and Confessions of Faith in the Christian Tradition*, edited by Jaroslav Pelikan and Valerie R. Hotchkiss, 2:665–72. New Haven, CT: Yale University Press, 2003.

———. *Schriften*. Quellen zur Geschichte der Täufer 6. Gütersloh: Bertelsmann, 1955–56.

———. *Selected Writings of Hans Denck*. Translated by Edward J. Furcha with Ford Lewis Battles. Pittsburgh Original Texts and Translations, series 1. Pittsburgh, PA: Pickwick, 1975.

———. *Selected Writings of Hans Denck 1500–1527*. Texts and Studies in Religion 44. Edited by E. J. Furcha. Lewiston, NY: Mellen, 1989.

———. "Whether God Is the Cause of Evil." In *Spiritual and Anabaptist Writers*, edited by George H. Williams and Angel M. Mergal, 88–111. LCC 25. Philadelphia: Westminster, 1957.

———. *The Writings of Dirk Philips*. Edited by Cornelius J. Dyck, William E. Keeney, and Alvin J. Beachy. Scottdale, PA: Herald, 1992.

Grebel, Conrad, and Friends. "Letters to Thomas Müntzer (1524)." In *Spiritual and Anabaptist Writers*, edited by George H. Williams and Angel M. Mergal, 73–85. Louisville: Westminster John Knox, 1957.

Harder, Leland, ed. *The Sources of Swill Anabaptism: The Grebel Letters and Related Documents*. Scottdale, PA: Herald, 1985.

Hill, Kat. *Baptism, Brotherhood, and Belief in Reformation Germany: Anabaptism and Lutheranism, 1525–1558*. Oxford: Oxford University Press, 2015.

Hubmaier, Balthasar. *Balthasar Hubmaier, Theologian of Anabaptism*. Translated and edited by Wayne Pipkin and John H. Yoder. Scottdale, PA: Herald, 1989.

————. *A Christian Catechism, 1526.* In *Creeds and Confessions of Faith in the Christian Tradition,* edited by Jaroslav Pelikan and Valerie R. Hotchkiss, 2:673–93. New Haven, CT: Yale University Press, 2003.

————. "On Free Will." In *Spiritual and Anabaptist Writers,* edited by George H. Williams and Angel M. Mergal, 112–35. LCC 25. Philadelphia: Westminster, 1957.

————. *Schriften.* Edited by Gunnar Westin and Torsten Bergsten. Quellen zur Geschichte der Täufer 9. Gütersloh: Mohn, 1962.

Karlstadt, Andreas Bodenstein von. *Karlstadt und Augustin.* Edited by Ernst Kähler. Halle: Niemeyer, 1952.

————. *Karlstadts Schriften aus den Jahren 1523–25.* Edited by Erich Hertzsch. 2 vols. Halle: Niemeyer, 1956.

————. *A Reformation Debate: Karlstadt, Emser, and Eck on Sacred Images.* Translated and edited by Bryan Mangrum and Giuseppe Scavizzi. Toronto: Centre for Reformation and Renaissance Studies, 1998.

————. *Von Abtuhung der Bilder und das keyn Bedtler unther den Christen seyn sollen.* Edited by Hans Lietzmann. Kleine Texte für Vorlesungen und Übungen 74. Bonn: A. Marcus und E. Weber, 1911.

Osiander, Andreas. *De unico mediatore Iesu Christo et iustificatione fidei: Confessio Andreae Osiandri.* Königsberg, n.p., 1551.

————. *Ein Disputation von der Rechtfertigung des Glaubens.* Königsberg, n.p., 1551.

————. *Gesamtausgabe.* Edited by G. Müller. Gütersloh: Gütersloher Verlagshaus / Mohn, 1975.

The Schleitheim Confession, 1527. In *Creeds and Confessions of Faith in the Christian Tradition,* edited by Jaroslav Pelikan and Valerie R. Hotchkiss, 2:694–703. New Haven, CT: Yale University Press, 2003.

Schwenckfeld, Caspar. "An Answer to Luther's Malediction." In *Spiritual and Anabaptist Writers,* edited by George H. Williams and Angel M. Mergal, 163–81. LCC 25. Philadelphia: Westminster, 1957.

————. *Commentary on the Augsburg Confession.* Translated by Fred A. Grater. Pennsburg, PA: Schwenkfelder Library, 1982.

————. *Corpus Schwenckfeldianorum.* Edited by C. D. Hartranft, E. S. Johnson, and S. G. Schultz. Vols. 1–15.1 Leipzig: Breitkopf and Härtel, 1907–39. Vols. 15–19. Pennsburg, PA: Board of Publication of the Schwenkfelder Church, 1959–61.

Sider, Ronald J., ed. *Karlstadt's Battle with Luther: Documents in a Liberal-Radical Debate.* Philadelphia: Fortress, 1978.

Simons, Menno. *The Complete Works.* Elkhart, IN: 1871.

————. *The Complete Writings of Menno Simons.* Edited by J. C. Wenger. Translated by Leonard Verduin. Scottdale, PA: Herald, 1956, 1984.

Secondary Sources

Augsburger, Myron S. *The Fugitive: Menno Simons, Spiritual Leader in the Free Church Movement.* Scottdale, PA: Herald, 2008.

Bainton, Roland H. *Hunted Heretic: The Life and Death of Michael Servetus, 1511–1553.* Boston, MA: Beacon, 1953.

Balke, Willem. *Calvin and the Anabaptist Radicals.* Grand Rapids: Eerdmans, 1981.

Barge, Hermann. *Andreas Bodenstein von Karlstadt.* 2 vols. Leipzig: Friedrich Brandstetter, 1905.

Bauman, Clarence. *The Spiritual Legacy of Hans Deck: Interpretation and Translation of Key Texts.* Studies in Medieval and Reformation Thought 47. Leiden: Brill, 1991.

Bender, Harold S. *Conrad Grebel, c. 1498–1526: The Founder of the Swiss Brethren Sometimes Called Anabaptists*. Eugene, OR: Wipf & Stock, 1998.

———. "The Zwickau Prophets, Thomas Müntzer and the Anabaptists." *Mennonite Quarterly Review* 27, no. 1 (January 1953): 3–16.

Bollinger, Dennis E. *First-Generation Anabaptist Ecclesiology, 1525–1561: A Study of Swiss, German, and Dutch Sources*. Lewiston, NY: Mellen, 2008.

Brewer, Brian C., ed. *T&T Clark Handbook of Anabaptism*. London and New York, T&T Clark: 2022.

Brunk, Gerald R. ed. *Menno Simons, a Reappraisal: Essays in Honor of Irvin B. Horst*. Harrisonburg, VA: Eastern Mennonite College, 1992.

Brunner, Peter. *Nikolaus von Amsdorf als Bischof von Naumburg*. Schriften des Vereins für Reformationsgeschichte 179. Gütersloh: Mohn, 1961.

Burnett, Amy Nelson. *Karlstadt and the Origins of the Eucharistic Controversy: A Study in the Circulation of Ideas*. Oxford: Oxford University Press, 2011.

Cameron, Euan. *The Reformation of the Heretics: The Waldenses of the Alps, 1480–1580*. Oxford: Oxford University Press, 1984.

Davis, Kenneth Ronald. *Anabaptism and Asceticism: A Study in Intellectual Origins*. Scottdale, PA: Herald, 1974.

Deppermann, Klaus. *Melchior Hoffman: Social Unrest and Apocalyptic Visions in the Age of Reformation*. London: T&T Clark, 1987.

Ecke, Karl. *Fortsetzung der Reformation: Kaspar von Schwenckfelds: Schau einer apostolischen Reformation*. Gladbeck, Germany: Schriftenmissions-Verlag, 1978.

Edwards, Mark U. *Luther and the False Brethren*. Redwood City, CA: Stanford University Press, 1975.

Estep, William. *The Anabaptist Story*. Grand Rapids: Eerdmans, 1963.

Friedman, Jerome. *Michael Servetus: A Case Study in Total Heresy*. Geneva: Droz, 1978.

Friedmann, Robert. "The Doctrine of Original Sin as Held by the Anabaptists of the Sixteenth Century." In *Essays in Anabaptist Theology*, edited by H. Wayne Pipkin, 147–56. Elkart, IN: Institute for Mennonite Studies, 1994.

———. *The Theology of Anabaptism: An Interpretation*. Scottdale, PA: Herald, 1973.

Friesen, Abraham. *Thomas Muentzer, a Destroyer of the Godless: The Making of a Sixteenth Century Religious Revolutionary*. Berkeley: University of California Press, 1990.

Furcha, Edward J. *Schwenckfeld's Concept of the New Man*. Pennsburg, PA: Board of Publication of the Schwenkfelder Church, 1970.

Goertz, Hans Jürgen. *Thomas Müntzer: Apocalyptic Mystic and Revolutionary*. London: T&T Clark, 1993.

Gritsch, Eric W. *Reformer without a Church: The Life and Thought of Thomas Muentzer*. Philadelphia: Fortress, 1967.

Guggisberg, Hans R. *Sebastian Castellio, 1515–1563: Humanist and Defender of Religious Toleration in a Confessional Age*. Farnham, UK: Ashgate, 2003.

Hall, Thor. "The Possibilities of Erasmian Influence on Denck and Hubmaier in Their Views on the Freedom of the Will." *Mennonite Quarterly Review* 35 (1961): 149–70.

Hayden-Roy, Patrick. *The Inner Word and the Outer World: A Biography of Sebastian Franck*. Frankfurt: Lang, 1994.

Hillerbrand, Hans J. "Andreas Bodenstein of Carlstadt, Prodigal Reformer." *Church History* 35 (1966): 379–98.

———, ed. *Radical Tendencies in the Reformation: Divergent Perspectives*, in Sixteenth Century Essays and Studies 9. Kirksville, MO: Sixteenth Century Journal Publishers, 1988.

Jones, Rufus M. *Spiritual Reformers in the Sixteenth and Seventeenth Centuries*. London: Macmillan, 1914.

Klaassen, Walter. *Anabaptism: Neither Catholic nor Protestant*. Waterloo, ON: Conrad, 1973.

———, ed. *Anabaptism Revisited: Essays on Anabaptist/Mennonite Studies in Honor of C. J. Dyck*. Scottdale, PA: Herald, 1992.

———. *Living at the End of the Ages: Apocalyptic Expectations in the Radical Reformation*. New York: University Press of America, 1992.

Kolb, Robert. *Nikolaus von Amsdorf (1483–1565). Popular Polemics in the Preservation of Luther's Legacy. Bibliotheca Humanistica et Reformatorica* 24. Nieuwkoop: De Graaf, 1978.

Liechty, Daniel. *Early Anabaptist Spirituality: Selected Writings*. Mahwah, NJ: Paulist, 1994.

Littell, Franklin H. *The Origins of Sectarian Protestantism: A Study of the Anabaptist View of the Church*. New York: Macmillan, 1964.

Loetscher, Frederick William. *Schwenckfeld's Participation in the Eucharistic Controversy of the Sixteenth Century*. Philadelphia: MacCalla, 1906.

Maier, Paul L. "Caspar Schwenckfeld: A Quadricentennial Evaluation." *ARG* 54 (1963): 89–97.

McClendon, James William. "Balthasar Hubmaier, Catholic Anabaptist." *Mennonite Quarterly Review* 65 (1991): 20–33.

McLaughlin, R. Emmet. *Caspar Schwenckfeld, Reluctant Reformer: His Life to 1540*. New Haven, CT: Yale University Press, 1986.

———. *Freedom of Spirit, Social Privilege, and Religious Dissent: Caspar Schwenckfeld and the Schwenckfelders*. n.p.: V. Koerner, 1996.

Nebe, Otto Henning. *Reine Lehre: Zur Theologie des Niklas von Amsdorff*. Göttingen: Vandenhoeck & Ruprecht, 1935.

Oyer, John S. *Lutheran Reformers against Anabaptists: Luther, Melanchthon, and Menius, and the Anabaptists of Central Germany*. The Hague: Nijhoff, 1964.

Ozment, Steven E. *Mysticism and Dissent: Religious Ideology and Social Protest in the Sixteenth Century*. New Haven, CT: Yale University Press, 1973.

Packull, Werner O. "An Introduction to Anabaptist theology." In *The Cambridge Companion to the Reformation*, edited by David Bagchi and David C. Steinmetz, 194–219. Cambridge: Cambridge University Press, 2004.

———. *Mysticism and the Early South German-Austrian Anabaptist Movement 1525–1531*. Scottdale, PA: Herald, 1977.

Packull, Werner O., and Geoffrey L. Dipple, eds. *Radical Reformation Studies: Essays Presented to James M. Stayer*. Farnham, UK: Ashgate, 1999.

Pater, Calvin Augustine. *Karlstadt as the Father of the Baptist Movements: The Emergence of Lay Protestantism*. Toronto: University of Toronto Press, 1984.

Pearse, Meic. *The Great Restoration: The Religious Radicals of the 16th and 17th Centuries*. Cumbria, UK: Paternoster, 1998.

Pipkin, Wayne H. "The Baptismal Theology of Balthasar Hubmaier." *Mennonite Quarterly Review* 65 (1991): 34–53.

Pipkin, Wayne H., and John H. Yoder, eds. and trans. *Balthasar Hubmaier: Theologian of Anabaptism*. Scottdale, PA: Herald, 1989.

Preus, James S. *Carlstadt's Ordinaciones and Luther's Liberty: A Study of the Wittenberg Movement, 1521–22*. HTS 26. Cambridge, MA: Harvard University Press, 1974.

Rempel, John D. *The Lord's Supper in Anabaptism: A Study in the Christology of Balthasar Hubmaier, Pilgram Marpeck, and Dirk Philips*. Studies in Anabaptist and Mennonite History. Waterloo, ON: Herald, 1993.

Roth, John D., and James M. Stayer, eds. *A Companion to Anabaptism and Spiritualism, 1521–1700.* Leiden: Brill, 2007.

Rotondò, Antonio. *Calvin and the Italian Anti-Trinitarians.* St. Louis: Foundation for Reformation Research, 1968.

Rupp, E. Gordon. "Andrew Karlstadt and Reformation Puritanism." *JTS* 10 (1959): 308–26.

———. "Word and Spirit in the First Years of the Reformation." *ARG* 49 (1958): 13–26.

Ruth, John L. *Conrad Grebel, Son of Zurich.* Scottdale, PA: Herald, 1975.

Schultz, Selina Gerard. *Caspar Schwenckfeld von Ossig.* Pennsburg, PA: Board of Publication of the Schwenkfelder Church, 1946.

Séguenny, André. *The Christology of Caspar Schwenckfeld: Spirit and Flesh in the Process of Life Transformation.* Translated by Peter C. Erb and Simone Nienwoldt. Texts and Studies in Religion 35. Lewiston, NY: Mellen, 1987.

Sider, Ronald J. *Andreas Bodenstein von Karlstadt: The Development of His Thought, 1517–1525.* Studies in Medieval and Reformation Thought 11. Leiden: Brill, 1974.

Snyder, C. Arnold. *The Life and Thought of Michael Sattler.* Scottdale, PA: Herald, 1984.

Stayer, James M. *Anabaptists and the Sword.* Lawrence, KS: Coronado Press, 1972.

———. *The German Peasants' War and Anabaptist Community of Goods.* Montreal-Kingston: McGill-Queen's University Press, 1991.

Steinmetz, David C. "The Baptism of John and the Baptism of Jesus in Huldrych Zwingli, Balthasar Hubmaier and Late Medieval Theology." In *Continuity and Discontinuity in Church History.* Festschrift for George H. Williams. Edited by F. F. Church and T. George, 169–81. Leiden: Brill, 1979.

———. "Luther und Hubmaier im Streit um die Freiheit de menschlichen Willens." *EvT* 43 (1983): 512–26.

———. "Scholasticism and Radical Reform: Nominalist Motifs in the Theology of Balthasar Hubmaier." *Mennonite Quarterly Review* 45 (1972): 123–44.

Vedder, Henry C. *Balthasar Hubmaier: The Leader of the Anabaptists.* New York: Putnam, 1905.

von Kerssenbrock, Herman. *Narrative of the Anabaptist Madness: The Overthrow of Münster, the Famous Metropolis of Westphalia.* Translated by Christopher S. Mackay. Leiden: Brill, 2007.

Voolstra, Sjouke, *Menno Simons: His Image and Message.* Newton, KS: Mennonite Press, 1996.

Weaver, J. Denny. *Becoming Anabaptist: The Origin and Significance of Sixteenth-Century Anabaptism.* 2nd ed. Scottdale, PA: Herald, 2005.

Weingart, Richard E. "The Meaning of Sin in the Theology of Menno Simons." In *Essays in Anabaptist Theology*, edited by H. Wayne Pipkin, 157–73. Elkart, IN: Institute for Mennonite Studies, 1994.

White, Gary K. *David Jaris and Dutch Anabaptism, 1524–1543.* Waterloo, ON: Wilfrid Laurier University Press, 1990.

Williams, George H. *The Radical Reformation.* Philadelphia: Westminster, 1962.

Yoder, John H. "The Hermeneutics of the Anabaptists." *Mennonite Quarterly Review* 41 (1967): 291–308.

Chapters 14–15 (The Reformed Church)

Primary Sources

Bucer, Martin. *Common Places of Martin Bucer.* Edited and translated by David F. Wright. Courtenay Library of Reformation Classics 4. Abingdon: Sutton Courtenay, 1972.

———. *Concerning the True Care of Souls.* Translated by Peter Beale. Carlisle, PA: Banner of Truth. 2013.

———. *De Regno Christi*. Edited by François Wendel. Opera Latina 15. Paris: Presses Universitaires de France, 1955.

———. "De Regno Christi." In *Melanchthon and Bucer*, edited by Wilhelm Pauck, 155–394. LCC 19. Philadelphia: Westminster, 1969.

———. *De vera ecclesiarum in doctrina, ceremoniis, et disciplina reconciliationis and compositione.* Strasbourg: Wendelin Rihel, 1542.

———. *Deutsche Schriften*. Edited by Robert Stupperich. Vols. 1, 2, 3, 7. Gütersloh: Gütersloher Verlagshaus / Mohn, 1960–.

———. *Disputata Ratisbonae (sine loco)*. 1548.

———. *Enarratio in evangelium Iohannis*. Edited by Irena Backus. Martini Buceri Opera Omnia 2. Leiden: Brill, 1988.

———. *Gratulatio Martini Buceri ad ecclesiam anglicanam, de religionis Christi restitution.* Basel: Johannes Oporinus, 1548.

———. *Instruction in Christian Love*. Translated by Paul T. Fuhrmann. Richmond: John Knox, 1952.

———. *Metaphrasis et enarratio in epist. D. Pauli apostoli ad Romanos.* Basel: n.p., 1562.

———. *Metaphrases et enarrationes perpetuae Epistolarum D. Pauli Apostoli.* Vol. 1, *Metaphrasis et ennarratio in Epist. D. Pauli Apostoli ad Romanos.* Strasbourg: Wendelin Rihel, 1536.

———. *Opera Latina*. Leiden: Brill, 1982.

———. *Praelectiones doctiss. in epistoloam D.P. ad Ephesios.* Basel: Petrus Namus, 1562.

———. *S. Psalmorum libri quinque.* Strasbourg, n.p., 1529.

Calvin, John. *Acts of the Council of Trent with the Antidote.* Translated by Henry Beveridge. Edinburgh: Calvin Translation Society, 1851.

———. "Antidote to Trent." In *Acts of the Council of Trent: With the Antidote*, 17–188. In *Selected Works of John Calvin: Tracts and Letters*, vol. 3, edited by Henry Beverage and Jules Bonnet, trans. Henry Beveridge. Grand Rapids: Baker, 1983.

———. *The Bondage and Liberation of the Will: A Defense of the Orthodox Doctrine of Human Choice against Pighius.* Edited by A. N. S. Lane. Translated by Graham I. Davies. Grand Rapids: Baker, 2012.

———. *Calvin's Commentaries*. Translated by the Calvin Translation Society. Edinburgh, 1847–55. Reprint, 22 vols. Grand Rapids: Baker, 1984.

———. *Calvin's New Testament Commentaries*. Edited by D. W. Torrance and T. F. Torrance. Grand Rapids: Eerdmans, 1959–72.

———. *Institutes of the Christian Religion*. Edited by John T. McNeill. Translated by Ford Lewis Battles. 2 vols. LCC 20–21. Louisville: Westminster John Knox, 1960.

———. *Institutes of the Christian Religion: 1541 French Edition.* Translated by Elsie Anne McKee. Grand Rapids: Eerdmans, 2009.

———. *Institution of the Christian Religion (1536)*. Edited and translated by Ford Lewis Battles. Grand Rapids: Eerdmans, 1985; 1987.

———. *Ioannis Calvini opera omnia, denuo recognita et adnotazione critica instructa notisque illustrate.* Edited by W. H. Neuser et al. Geneva: Droz, 1992–.

———. *Ioannis Calvini opera quae supersunt omnia.* Edited by Johann-Wilhelm Baum, Edouard Cunitz, and Eduard Reuss. 59 vols. *Corpus Reformatorum* 29–87. Brunswick and Berlin, 1863–1900.

———. *Ioannis Calvini Opera Selecta.* Edited by Peter Barth and Wilhelm Niesel. 5 vols. Munich: Kaiser, 1926–52.

———. *John Calvin: Tracts and Letters.* Translated by Henry Beveridge. 7 vols. Edinburgh: Calvin Translation Society, 1849. Reprint, Edinburgh: Banner of Truth Trust, 2009.

——. *Letters of John Calvin*. Edited by Jules Bonnet. Translated by David Constable and Marcus Robert Gilchrist. 4 vols. Philadelphia: n.p., 1858. Reprint, Grand Rapids: Baker, 1983, as vols. 4–7 of *Calvin's Selected Works*.

——. *A Reformation Debate: John Calvin and Jacopo Sadoleto*. Edited by John C. Olin. Grand Rapids: Baker, 1966.

——. *The Secret Providence of God*. Edited by Paul Helm. Wheaton, IL: Crossway, 2010.

——. *Supplementa Calviniana. Sermons inédits*. Neukirchen-Vluyn: Neukirchener, 1936.

——. *Tracts and Treatises in Defense of the Reformed Faith*. Translated by Henry Beveridge. Historical notes by T. F. Torrance. 3 vols. Grand Rapids: Baker, 1983.

Pauck, Wilhelm, ed. *Melanchthon and Bucer*. LCC 19. Philadelphia: Westminster, 1969.

Vermigli, Girolamo. *De religione christiana fides—Confession of Christian Religion*. 2 vols. Edited by Luca Baschera and Christian Moser. Leiden and Boston: Brill, 2007.

——. *Locus on Justification*. In *Predestination and Justification: Two Theological Loci*. Translated and edited by Frank A. James III. Peter Martyr Library 8. Kirksville, MO: Sixteenth Century Essays & Studies, 2013.

Secondary Sources

Balke, Willem. *Calvin and the Anabaptist Radicals*. Translated by William J. Heynen. Grand Rapids: Eerdmans, 1981.

Backus, Irena, and Philip Benedict, eds. *Calvin and His Influence, 1509–2009*. Oxford: Oxford University Press, 2011.

Balserak, Jon. *Establishing the Remnant Church in France: Calvin's Lectures on the Minor Prophets, 1556–1559*. Leiden: Brill, 2011.

——. *John Calvin as Sixteenth-Century Prophet*. Oxford: Oxford University Press, 2014.

Barth, Karl. *The Theology of John Calvin*. Grand Rapids: Eerdmans, 1995.

Benedict, Philip. *Christ's Churches Purely Reformed: A Social History of Calvinism*. New Haven, CT: Yale University Press, 2004.

Bierma, Lyle D. *The Doctrine of the Sacraments in the Heidelberg Catechism: Melanchthonian, Calvinist, or Zwinglian*. Princeton, NJ: Princeton Theological Seminary, 1999.

——. *The Theology of the Heidelberg Catechism: A Reformation Synthesis*. Louisville: Westminster John Knox, 2013.

Bierma, Lyle D., with Charles D. Gunnoe, Karin Maag, and Paul W. Fields. *Introduction to the Heidelberg Catechism: Sources, History, and Theology*. Grand Rapids: Baker Academic, 2005.

Billings, J. Todd. *Calvin, Participation, and the Gift: The Activity of Believers in Union with Christ*. Oxford: Oxford University Press, 2007.

——. "The Catholic Calvin." *Pro Ecclesia* 20, no. 2 (2011): 120–34.

——. "Reformed Catholicity." In *Christian Doctrine*, edited by Michael Allen, 330–52. Cambridge: Cambridge University Press, 2022.

Billings, J. Todd, and I. John Hesselink. *Calvin's Theology and Its Reception: Disputes, Developments, and New Possibilities*. Louisville: Westminster John Knox, 2012.

Bouwsma, William J. *John Calvin: A Sixteenth Century Portrait*. Oxford: Oxford University Press, 1988.

Breen, Quirinus. *John Calvin: A Study in French Humanism*. Hamden, CT: Archon, 1968.

Bruening, Michael W. *Refusing to Kiss the Slipper: Opposition to Calvinism in the Francophone Reformation*. Oxford: Oxford University Press, 2021.

Burnette, Amy Nelson. *The Yoke of Christ: Martin Bucer and Christian Discipline*. Sixteenth Century Essays and Studies 26. Kirksville, MO: Truman State University, 1994.

Canlis, Julie. *Calvin's Ladder: A Spiritual Theology of Ascent and Ascension*. Grand Rapids: Eerdmans, 2010.

Chrisman, Miriam Usher. *Strasbourg and the Reform*. New Haven, CT: Yale University Press, 1967.

Cottret, Bernard. *Calvin: A Biography*. Grand Rapids: Eerdmans, 2000.

Davis, Thomas J. *This Is My Body: The Presence of Christ in Reformation Thought*. Grand Rapids: Baker, 2008.

De Greef, Wulfert. *The Writings of John Calvin: An Introductory Guide*. Translated by Lyle D. Bierma. Grand Rapids: Eerdmans, 2008.

Diefendorf, Barbara B. *The Saint Bartholomew's Day Massacre: A Brief History with Documents*. Boston, MA: Bedford/St. Martin's, 2009.

Douglas, Richard M. *Jacopo Sadoleto, Humanist and Reformer*. Cambridge, MA: Harvard University Press, 1959.

Dowey, Edward A., Jr. *The Knowledge of God in Calvin's Theology*. 3rd ed. Grand Rapids: Eerdmans, 1994.

Drake, K. J. *The Flesh of the Word: The Extra Calvinisticum from Zwingli to Early Orthodoxy*. New York: Oxford University Press, 2021.

Duffield, Gervase E. *John Calvin*. Grand Rapids: Eerdmans, 1968.

Eells, Hastings. *Martin Bucer*. New Haven, CT: Yale University Press, 1931.

Edmondson, Stephen. *Calvin's Christology*. Cambridge: Cambridge University Press, 2004.

Ellis, Brannon. *Calvin, Classical Trinitarianism, and the Aseity of the Son*. Oxford: Oxford University Press, 2012.

Elwood, Christopher. *The Body Broken: The Calvinist Doctrine of the Eucharist and the Symbolization of Power*. Oxford: Oxford University Press, 1998.

Fesko, John V. *Beyond Calvin: Union with Christ and Justification in Early Modern Reformed Theology (1517–1700)*. Göttingen: Vandenhoeck & Ruprecht, 2012.

Ganoczy, Alexandre. *The Young Calvin*. Louisville: Westminster John Knox, 1987.

George, Timothy, ed. *John Calvin and the Church: A Prism of Reform*. Louisville: Westminster John Knox, 1990.

Gerrish, B. A. *Grace and Gratitude: The Eucharistic Theology of John Calvin*. Minneapolis: Fortress, 1993.

Gordon, Bruce. *Calvin*. New Haven, CT: Yale University Press, 2009.

———. *John Calvin's Institutes of the Christian Religion: A Biography*. Princeton, NJ: Princeton University Press, 2017.

Greschat, Martin. *Martin Bucer: A Reformer and His Times*. Translated by Stephen E. Buckwalter. Louisville: Westminster John Knox, 2014.

Helm, Paul. *Calvin and the Calvinists*. Carlisle, PA: Banner of Truth, 1998.

———. *Calvin at the Centre*. Oxford: Oxford University Press, 2011.

———. *John Calvin's Ideas*. Oxford: Oxford University Press, 2005.

Holder, R. Ward. *John Calvin in Context*. Cambridge: Cambridge University Press, 2020.

Hopf, Constantin. *Martin Bucer and the English Reformation*. New York: Macmillan, 1947.

Huijgen, Arnold. *Divine Accommodation in John Calvin's Theology*. Göttingen: Vandenhoeck & Ruprecht, 2011.

Jenkins, Gary W. *Calvin's Tormentors: Understanding the Conflicts That Shaped the Reformer*. Grand Rapids: Baker Academic, 2018.

Jones, Serene. *Calvin and the Rhetoric of Piety*. Louisville: Westminster John Knox, 1995.

Kendall, R. T. *Calvin and English Calvinism to 1649*. Oxford: Oxford University Press, 1979.

Lane, Anthony N. S. *John Calvin: Student of the Church Fathers*. London: T&T Clark, 1999.

——. *Regensburg Article 5 on Justification: Inconsistent Patchwork or Substance of True Doctrine?* Oxford: Oxford University Press, 2020.

Lee, Daniel Y. K. *The Holy Spirit as Bond in Calvin's Thought.* Frankfurt: Lang, 2011.

Lillback, Peter A. *The Binding of God: Calvin's Role in the Development of Covenant Theology.* Grand Rapids: Baker, 2001.

Littell, Franklin H. "New Light on Butzer's Significance." In *Reformation Studies*, edited by Franklin H. Littell, 145–67. Richmond: John Knox, 1962.

Lugioyo, B. *Martin Bucer's Doctrine of Justification: Reformation Theology and Early Modern Irenicism.* New York: Oxford University Press, 2010.

Manetsch, Scott M. *Calvin's Company of Pastors: Pastoral Care and the Emerging Reformed Church, 1536–1609.* Oxford: Oxford University Press, 2012.

McDonnell, Kilian. *John Calvin, the Church, and the Eucharist.* Princeton, NJ: Princeton University Press, 1967.

McGinnis, Andrew M. *The Son of God Beyond the Flesh: A Historical and Theological Study of the extra Calvinisticum.* T&T Clark Studies in Systematic Theology 29. London: Bloomsbury T&T Clark, 2014.

McGrath, Alister. *A Life of John Calvin: A Study in the Shaping of Western Culture.* Oxford: Blackwell, 1990.

McKim, Donald K., ed. *Calvin and the Bible.* Cambridge: Cambridge University Press, 2006.

——, ed. *Cambridge Companion to John Calvin.* Cambridge: Cambridge University Press, 2004.

McNeill, John T. *The History and Character of Calvinism.* Oxford: Oxford University Press, 1954.

Muller, Richard A. *After Calvin: Studies in the Development of a Theological Tradition.* Oxford: Oxford University Press, 2003.

——. *Christ and the Decree: Christology and Predestination in Reformed Theology from Calvin to Perkins.* Grand Rapids: Baker Academic, 2008.

——. "John Calvin and later Calvinism: The Identity of the Reformed Tradition." In *The Cambridge Companion to the Reformation*, edited by David Bagchi and David C. Steinmetz, 130–49. Cambridge: Cambridge University Press, 2004.

——. "Not Scotist." *Reformation & Renaissance Review* 14, no. 2 (2012): 127–50.

——. *The Unaccommodated Calvin: Studies in the Foundation of a Theological Tradition.* Oxford: Oxford University Press, 2000.

Mullett, Michael A. *John Calvin.* London: Routledge, 2011.

Naphy, William G. *Calvin and the Consolidation of the Genevan Reformation.* Louisville: Westminster John Knox, 2003.

Neuser, Wilhelm H., ed. *Calvinus Sacrae Scripturae Professor: Calvin as Confessor of Holy Scripture.* Grand Rapids: Eerdmans, 1994.

Neuser, Wilhelm H., and Brian G. Armstrong, eds. *Calvinus Sincerioris Religionis Vindex: Calvin as Protector of the Purer Religion.* Kirksville, MO: Sixteenth Century Journal Publishers, 1997.

Niesel, Wilhelm. *The Theology of Calvin.* Philadelphia: Westminster, 1956.

Oberman, Heiko A. *Initia Calvini: The Matrix of Calvin's Reformation.* Amsterdam: Noord Hollandsche, 1991.

Parker, T. H. L. *Calvin: An Introduction to His Thought.* Louisville: Westminster John Knox, 1995.

——. *Calvin's Preaching.* Edinburgh: T&T Clark, 2002.

——. *John Calvin: A Biography.* Louisville: Westminster John Knox, 2007.

——. *The Oracles of God: An Introduction to the Preaching of John Calvin.* London: T&T Clark, 2002.

Partee, Charles. *Calvin and Classical Philosophy.* Louisville: Westminster John Knox, 2005.

——. *The Theology of John Calvin.* Louisville: Westminster John Knox, 2008.

Pettegree, Andrew, Alastair Duke, and Gillian Lewis, eds. *Calvinism in Europe, 1540–1620.* Cambridge, MA: Cambridge University Press, 1997.

Pitkin, Barbara. *Calvin, the Bible, and History: Exegesis and Historical Reflection in the Era of Reform.* Oxford: Oxford University Press, 2020.

———. *What Pure Eyes Could See: Calvin's Doctrine of Faith in Its Exegetical Context.* Oxford: Oxford University Press, 1999.

Puckett, D. L. *John Calvin's Exegesis of the Old Testament.* Louisville: Westminster John Knox, 1995.

Randell, Keith. *John Calvin and the Later Reformation.* London: Hodder & Stoughton, 1990.

Reid, W. Stanford. *John Calvin: His Influence in the Western World.* Grand Rapids: Zondervan, 1982.

Rorem, Paul. *Calvin and Bullinger on the Lord's Supper.* New York: Grove, 1989.

Schreiner, Susan E. *The Theater of His Glory: Nature and the Natural Order in the Thought of John Calvin.* Studies in Historical Theology 3. Durham, NC: Labyrinth, 1990.

———. *Where Shall Wisdom Be Found? Calvin's Exegesis of Job from Medieval and Modern Perspectives.* Chicago: University of Chicago Press, 1994.

Selderhuis, Herman J., ed. *The Calvin Handbook.* Grand Rapids: Eerdmans, 2009.

———. *John Calvin: A Pilgrim's Life.* Downers Grove, IL: IVP Academic, 2009.

Steinmetz, David C. "Calvin and the Irrepressible Spirit." *Ex Auditu* 12 (1996): 94–107.

———. *Calvin in Context.* Oxford: Oxford University Press, 1995.

———. "The Scholastic Calvin." In *Protestant Scholasticism*, edited by Carl R. Trueman and R. Scott Clark. Carlisle: Paternoster, 1999.

———. "The Theology of John Calvin." In *The Cambridge Companion to the Reformation*, edited by David Bagchi and David C. Steinmetz, 113–29. Cambridge: Cambridge University Press, 2004.

Stephens, Peter. *The Holy Spirit in the Theology of Martin Bucer.* Cambridge: Cambridge University Press, 1970.

Stroup, George. *Calvin.* Nashville: Abingdon, 2009.

Torrance, Thomas F. *Calvin's Doctrine of Man.* Cambridge: Lutterworth, 1949.

———. *The Hermeneutics of John Calvin.* Edinburgh: Scottish Academic Press, 1988.

Tuininga, Matthew J. *Calvin's Political Theology and the Public Engagement of the Church.* Cambridge: Cambridge University Press, 2017.

van den Belt, Henk, ed. *Restoration through Redemption: John Calvin Revisited.* Leiden: Brill, 2013.

van Vliet, Jason. *Children of God: The Imago Dei in John Calvin and His Context.* Göttingen: Vandenhoeck & Ruprecht, 2009.

Van't Spijker, Willem. *Calvin: A Brief Guide to His Life and Thought.* Louisville: Westminster John Knox, 2009.

———. *The Ecclesiastical Offices in the Thought of Martin Bucer.* Studies in Medieval and Reformation Thought 57. Leiden: Brill, 1996.

Wallace, Ronald. *Calvin's Doctrine of the Word and Sacrament.* Grand Rapids: Eerdmans, 1957.

Wendel, François. *Calvin: Origins and Development of His Religious Thought.* Grand Rapids: Baker Academic, 1963, 1997.

Willis, David. *Calvin's Catholic Christology: The Function of the So-Called Extra Calvinisticum in Calvin's Theology.* Leiden: Brill, 1966.

Wright, David F., ed. *Martin Bucer: Reforming Church and Community.* Cambridge: Cambridge University Press, 1994.

Zachman, Randall C. "Calvin as Analogical Theologian." *SJT* 51, no. 2 (1998): 162–87.

———. *Image and Word in the Theology of John Calvin.* Notre Dame, IN: University of Notre Dame Press, 2009.

———, ed. *John Calvin and Roman Catholicism: Critique and Engagement, Then and Now*. Grand Rapids: Baker Academic, 2008.

———. *John Calvin as Teacher, Pastor, and Theologian*. Grand Rapids: Baker Academic, 2006.

———. *Reconsidering John Calvin*. Cambridge: Cambridge University Press, 2012.

Zuidema, Jason, and Theodore Van Raalte. *Early French Reform: The Theology and Spirituality of Guillaume Farel*. Farnham, UK: Ashgate, 2011.

Chapter 16. An Apology for the Universal Church: The Reformation in England and Scotland
Primary Sources

Bray, Gerald Lewis, ed. *The Books of Homilies: A Critical Edition*. Cambridge: James Clarke, 2015.

———, ed. *Documents of the English Reformation 1526–1701*. 3rd ed. Cambridge: James Clarke, 2019.

Brewer, J. S., et al. *Letters and Papers of the Reign of Henry VIII*. 22 vols. London, 1862–1932.

Cameron, James K., ed. *The First Book of Discipline*. Edinburgh: St. Andrew Press, 1972.

Cranmer, Thomas. "Cranmer's Preface to the Great Bible, 1540." In *Documents of the English Reformation 1526–1701*, edited by Gerald Bray, 205–14. 3rd ed. Cambridge: James Clarke, 2019.

———. *Miscellaneous Writings and Letters of Thomas Cranmer*. Edited by John E. Cox. Parker Society ed. Cambridge: Cambridge University Press, 1846.

———. "A Sermon on the Salvation of Mankind by Only Christ Our Saviour, From Sin and Death Everlasting." In *The Books of Homilies: A Critical Edition*, edited by Gerald Bray, 22–30. Cambridge: James Clarke, 2015.

———. *Writings and Disputations of Thomas Cranmer Relative to the Sacrament of the Lord's Supper*. Edited by John E. Cox. Parker Society ed. Cambridge: Cambridge University Press, 1844.

Cummings, Brian, ed. *The Book of Common Prayer: The Texts of 1549, 1559, and 1662*. Oxford: Oxford University Press, 2011.

"Forty-Two Articles of the Church of England (1552/53)." In *Documents of the English Reformation 1526–1701*, edited by Gerald Bray, 253–80. 3rd ed. Cambridge: James Clarke, 2019.

Foxe, John. *Foxe's Book of Martyrs: Select Narratives*. Edited by John N. King. Oxford: Oxford University Press, 2009.

———. *To the True and Faithfull Congregation of Christ's Universal Church*. In *English Reformers*, edited by T. H. L. Parker, 61–88. LCC 26. Philadelphia: Westminster, 1966.

Gatiss, Lee, ed. *The First Book of Homilies: The Church of England's Official Sermons in Modern English*. London: Lost Coin, 2021.

Henderson, G. D., ed. *The Scots Confession 1560*. Edinburgh: St. Andrew Press, 1960.

Hooper, John. *A Declaration of Christ and His Office*. In *English Reformers*, edited by T. H. L. Parker, 193–218. LCC 26. Philadelphia: Westminster, 1966.

———. *Early Writings*. Parker Society ed. Cambridge: Cambridge University Press, 1848.

———. *Early Writings of John Hooper*. Edited by Samuel Carr. Cambridge: Cambridge University Press, 1843.

———. *Later Writings*. Edited by C. Nevinson. Parker Society ed. Cambridge: Cambridge University Press, 1852.

Jewel, John. *An Apologie of the Church of England*. In *English Reformers*, edited by T. H. L. Parker, 3–60. LCC 26. Philadelphia: Westminster, 1966.

———. *An Apology of the Church of England*. Edited by Robin Harris and Andre Gazal. Moscow, ID: Davenant, 2020.

Ketly, Joseph, ed. *Liturgies of Edward VI*. Parker Society ed. Cambridge: Cambridge University Press, 1844.

Knox, John. *John Knox's History of the Reformation in Scotland*. Edited by W. C. Dickinson. 2 vols. Edinburgh: Nelson, 1949.

———. *On Rebellion*. Edited by Roger A. Mason. Cambridge: Cambridge University Press, 1994.

———. *The Works of John Knox*. Edited by David Lang. 6 vols. Edinburgh: Bannatyne Society, 1846–64.

More, Sir Thomas. *The Complete Works of St. Thomas More*. 15 vols. Edited by V. J. M. Headley. New Haven, CT: Yale University Press, 1963–97.

———. *The Essential Works of Thomas More*. Edited by Gerard B. Wegemer and Stephen W. Smith. Yale University Press, 2020.

Pole, Reginald. *De Concilio*. Rome, 1562.

———. *Epistolae*. Edited by A. M. Quirini. 5 vols. Brescia, 1744–57.

———. *Pole's Defense of the Unity of the Church*. Translated by Joseph G. Dwyer. Westminster, MD: Newman, 1965.

———. *A Treatise of Justification*. Rome: Reformatio Angliae, Rome, 1562. Ilkley, UK: Scolar, 1976.

Robinson, Hastings, ed. *Original Letters Relative to the English Reformation*. 2 vols. Cambridge: Cambridge University Press, 1846–47.

The Thirty-Nine Articles, 1571. In *Creeds and Confessions of Faith in the Christian Tradition*, edited by Jaroslav Pelikan and Valerie R. Hotchkiss, 2:526–40. New Haven, CT: Yale University Press, 2003.

"The Act of the Six Articles, 1539." In *Documents of the English Reformation 1526–1701*, edited by Gerald Bray, 195–204. 3rd ed. Cambridge: James Clarke, 2019.

"The Act of Supremacy, 1534." In *Documents of the English Reformation 1526–1701*, edited by Gerald Bray, 97–98. 3rd ed. Cambridge: James Clarke, 2019.

"The Act of Supremacy, 1559." In *Documents of the English Reformation 1526–1701*, edited by Gerald Bray, 284–93. 3rd ed. Cambridge: James Clarke, 2019.

"The Act of Uniformity, 1549." In *Documents of the English Reformation 1526–1701*, edited by Gerald Bray, 2345–40. 3rd ed. Cambridge: James Clarke, 2019.

"The Act of Uniformity, 1552." In *Documents of the English Reformation 1526–1701*, edited by Gerald Bray, 250–52. 3rd ed. Cambridge: James Clarke, 2019.

"The Act of Uniformity, 1559." In *Documents of the English Reformation 1526–1701*, edited by Gerald Bray, 294–99. 3rd ed. Cambridge: James Clarke, 2019.

"The Edwardian Injunctions, 1547." In *Documents of the English Reformation 1526–1701*, edited by Gerald Bray, 218–26. 3rd ed. Cambridge: James Clarke, 2019.

"The Elizabethan Injunctions, 1559." In *Documents of the English Reformation 1526–1701*, edited by Gerald Bray, 300–12. 3rd ed. Cambridge: James Clarke, 2019.

"The First Henrician Injunctions, 1536." In *Documents of the English Reformation 1526–1701*, edited by Gerald Bray, 153–94. 3rd ed. Cambridge: James Clarke, 2019.

"The Forty-two Articles, 1553; The Thirty-Eight Articles, 1563; The Thirty-Nine Articles, 1571." In *Documents of the English Reformation 1526–1701*, edited by Gerald Bray, 251–78. 3rd ed. Cambridge: James Clarke, 2019.

"The Preface to the Book of Common Prayer, 1549." In *Documents of the English Reformation 1526–1701*, edited by Gerald Bray, 241–45. 3rd ed. Cambridge: James Clarke, 2019.

"The Marian Injunctions, 1554." In *Documents of the English Reformation 1526–1701*, edited by Gerald Bray, 281–83. 3rd ed. Cambridge: James Clarke, 2019.

"The Sacrament Act, 1547." In *Documents of the English Reformation 1526–1701*, edited by Gerald Bray, 227–31. 3rd ed. Cambridge: James Clarke, 2019.

"The Ten Articles, 1536." In *Documents of the English Reformation 1526–1701*, edited by Gerald Bray, 141–52. 3rd ed. Cambridge: James Clarke, 2019.

"The Wittenberg Articles, 1536." In *Documents of the English Reformation 1526–1701*, edited by Gerald Bray, 102–56. 3rd ed. Cambridge: James Clarke, 2019.

Torrance, T. F., trans. and ed. *The School of Faith: The Catechisms of the Reformed Church.* London: James Clarke, 1959.

Tyndale, William. *The New Testament: 1526 Edition.* British Library. Peabody, MA: Hendrickson, 2008.

———. *Tyndale's New Testament. 1534 edition.* Edited by Daniel Daniell. New Haven: Yale University Press, 1989.

———. *The Works of William Tyndale.* 2 vols. Carlisle, PA: Banner of Truth, 2010.

Secondary Sources

Ackroyd, Peter. *The Life of Thomas More.* London: Chatto & Windus, 1998.

Alford, Stephen. *Kingship and Politics in the Reign of Edward VI.* Cambridge: Cambridge University Press, 2002.

Bernard, G. W. *The King's Reformation: Henry VIII and the Remaking of the English Church.* New Haven, CT: Yale University Press, 2005.

———. *The Late Medieval English Church: Vitality and Vulnerability before the Break with Rome.* New Haven, CT: Yale University Press, 2012.

Bray, Gerald. *The Faith We Confess: An Exposition of the Thirty-Nine Articles.* London: Latimer Trust, 2009.

———. *A Fruitful Exhortation: A Guide to the Homilies.* London: Latimer Trust, 2014.

———. *Translating the Bible: From William Tyndale to King James.* London: Latimer Trust, 2010.

Brigden, Susan. *New Worlds, Lost Worlds: The Rule of the Tudors, 1485–1603.* New York: Viking, 2000.

Brooks, Peter Newman. *Thomas Cranmer's Doctrine of the Eucharist.* London: Macmillan, 1992.

Cameron, Nigel M. de S., David F. Wright, et al., eds. *Dictionary of Scottish Church History and Theology.* Edinburgh: T&T Clark, 1993.

Clebsch, William A. *England's Earliest Protestants.* New Haven, CT: Yale University Press, 1964.

Collinson, Patrick. *The Birthpangs of Protestant England.* New York: St. Martin's, 1988.

Constant, G. *The Reformation in England.* Vol. 2, *Introduction of the Reformation into England: Edward VI (1547–1553).* London: Sheed and Ward, 1942.

Cowan, Ian B. *The Scottish Reformation: Church and Society in Sixteenth-Century Scotland.* New York: St. Martin's, 1982.

Daniell, David. *William Tyndale: A Biography.* New Haven, CT: Yale University Press, 1994.

Dawson, Jane. *John Knox.* New Haven, CT: Yale University Press, 2015.

———. *The Politics of Religion in the Age of Mary, Queen of Scots: The Earl of Argyll and the Struggle for Britain and Ireland.* Cambridge: Cambridge University Press, 2002.

Dent, C. M. *Protestant Reformers in Elizabethan Oxford.* Oxford: Oxford University Press, 1983.

Dickens, A. G. *The English Reformation.* 2nd ed. University Park: Pennsylvania State University Press, 1991.

Donaldson, Gordon. *The Scottish Reformation.* Cambridge: Cambridge University Press, 1960.

Doran, Susan, and Thomas S. Freeman, eds. *Mary Tudor: Old and New Perspectives.* London: Macmillan, 2011.

Dugmore, C. W. *The Mass and the English Reformers.* London: Macmillan, 1958.

Duffy, Eamon. *Fires of Faith: Catholic England under Mary Tudor.* New Haven, CT: Yale University Press, 2009.

———. *Saints, Sacrilege and Sedition: Religion and Conflict in the Tudor Reformations.* New York: Bloomsbury, 2012.

————. *The Stripping of the Altars: Traditional Religion in England, 1400–1580.* New Haven, CT: Yale University Press, 1992.

Duffy, Eamon, and David Loades, eds. *The Church of Mary Tudor.* Burlington, VT: Ashgate, 2005.

Edwards, John. *Mary I: England's Catholic Queen.* New Haven, CT: Yale University Press, 2011.

Edwards, John, and Ronald Truman, eds. *Reforming Catholicism in the England of Mary Tudor: The Achievement of Friar Bartolomé Carranza.* Farnham, UK: Ashgate, 2005.

Evenden, Elizabeth, and Thomas S. Freeman. *Religion and the Book in Early Modern England: The Making of Foxe's "Book of Martyrs."* Cambridge: Cambridge University Press, 2011.

Fenlon, Dermot. *Heresy and Obedience in Tridentine Italy: Cardinal Pole and the Counter Reformation.* Cambridge: Cambridge University Press, 1972.

Gunther, Karl. *Reformation Unbound: Protestant Visions of Reform in England.* Cambridge: Cambridge University Press, 2014.

Guy, John. *Thomas More.* Oxford: Oxford University Press, 2000.

Haugaard, William. *Elizabeth and the English Reformation.* Cambridge: Cambridge University Press, 1968.

Hazlett, W. Ian P. *The Reformation in Britain and Ireland: An Introduction.* London: T&T Clark, 2003.

Heal, Felicity. *The Reformation in Britain and Ireland.* Oxford: Oxford University Press, 2003.

High, Christopher. *English Reformations: Religion, Politics, and Society under the Tudors.* Oxford: Oxford University Press, 1993.

Hornbeck, J. Patrick *What Is a Lollard? Dissent and Belief in Late Medieval England.* Oxford: Oxford University Press, 2010.

Hughes, Philip E. *The Reformation in England.* 3 vols. New York: Macmillan, 1963.

————. *Theology of the English Reformers.* London: Hodder and Stoughton, 1965.

Hunt, F. W. *The Life and Times of John Hooper (c. 1500–1555): Bishop of Gloucester.* Lewiston, NY: Mellen, 1992.

Jones, Norman. *The Birth of the Elizabethan Age.* Oxford: Blackwell, 1993.

————. *The English Reformation: Religion and Cultural Adaptation.* Oxford: Blackwell, 2002.

Kellar, Clare. *Scotland, England and the Reformation, 1523–1561.* Oxford: Oxford University Press, 2003.

Kenny, Anthony. *Thomas More.* Oxford: Oxford University Press, 1983.

Kyle, Richard G. *Theology and Revelation in the Scottish Reformation.* Grand Rapids: Baker, 1980.

Lahey, Stephen E. *John Wyclif.* Oxford: Oxford University Press, 2009.

Levin, Carole. *The Reign of Elizabeth I.* London: Palgrave, 2002.

Levy, Ian Christopher. *John Wyclif: Scriptural Logic, Real Presence, and the Parameters of Orthodoxy.* Milwaukee, WI: Marquette University Press, 2003.

Loach, Jennifer. *Edward VI.* New Haven, CT: Yale University Press, 2002.

Loades, David. *Mary Tudor: A Life.* Basil Oxford: Blackwell, 1989.

Logan, George M., ed. *The Cambridge Companion to Thomas More.* Cambridge: Cambridge University Press, 2011.

MacCulloch, Diarmaid. *The Boy King: Edward VI and the Protestant Reformation.* New York: St. Martin's, 1999.

————. *The Later Reformation in England, 1547–1603.* New York: St. Martin's, 1990.

————. *Thomas Cranmer.* New Haven, CT: Yale University Press, 1998.

Maltby, Judith. *Prayer Book and People in Elizabethan and Early Stuart England.* Cambridge: Cambridge University Press, 1998.

Marshall, Peter. *Beliefs and the Dead in Reformation England.* Oxford: Oxford University Press, 2002.

———. *Heretics and Believers: A History of the English Reformation*. New Haven, CT: Yale University Press, 2017.

———. *Reformation England, 1480–1642*. Oxford: Oxford University Press, 2003.

Marshall, Peter, and Alec Ryrie, eds. *The Beginnings of English Protestantism*. Cambridge: Cambridge University Press, 2002.

Mason, Roger A., ed. *John Knox and the British Reformations*. St. Andrews Studies in Reformation History. Farnham, UK: Ashgate, 1998.

McEwen, James S. *The Faith of John Knox*. London: Lutterworth Press, 1961.

Milton, Anthony, ed. *The Oxford History of Anglicanism*. Vol. 1, *Reformation and Identity, c. 1520–1662*. Oxford: Oxford University Press, 2017.

Moynahan, Brian. *God's Bestseller: William Tyndale, Thomas More, and the Writing of the English Bible*. New York: St. Martin's, 2003.

Newton, Diana. *Papists, Protestants, and Puritans, 1559–1714*. Cambridge: Cambridge University Press, 1998.

Null, Ashley. *Thomas Cranmer's Doctrine of Repentance*. Oxford: Oxford University Press, 2000.

Packer, J. I., and Roger T. Beckwith. *The Thirty-Nine Articles: Their Place and Use Today*. London: Latimer House, 2007.

Porter, Linda. *The First Queen of England: The Myth of Bloody Mary*. New York: St. Martin's, 2008.

Prescott, H. F. M. *Mary Tudor*. New York: Macmillan, 1953.

Rex, Richard. *Henry VIII and the English Reformation*. 2nd ed. London: Palgrave, 2006.

———. *The Theology of John Fisher*. Cambridge: Cambridge University Press, 1991.

Richards, Judith M. *Elizabeth I*. Abingdon: Routledge, 2012.

———. *Mary Tudor*. London: Routledge, 2008.

Ridley, Jasper. *John Knox*. Oxford: Clarendon, 1968.

Ronald, Susan. *Heretic Queen: Queen Elizabeth I and the Wars of Religion*. New York: St. Martin's, 2012.

Rupp, E. Gordon. *Studies in the Making of the English Protestant Tradition*. Cambridge: Cambridge University Press, 1949.

Ryrie, Alec. *The Gospel and Henry VIII: Evangelicals in the Early English Reformation*. Cambridge: Cambridge University Press, 2003.

———. *The Origins of the Scottish Reformation*. Manchester: Manchester University Press, 2006.

Scarisbrick, J. J. *Henry VIII*. New Haven, CT: Yale University Press, 1997.

———. *The Reformation and the English People*. Oxford: Blackwell, 1984.

Schaefer, Carol. *Mary Queen of Scots*. Hertford, NC: Crossroad, 2002.

Schenk, Wilhelm. *Reginald Pole, Cardinal of England*. London: Longmans, Green, 1950, 1977.

Shagan, Ethan H. *Popular Politics and the English Reformation*. Cambridge: Cambridge University Press, 2003.

Skidmore, Chris. *Edward VI: The Lost King of England*. New York: St. Martin's, 2007.

Tittler, Robert, and Norman Jones, eds. *A Companion to Tudor Britain*. Oxford: Blackwell, 2004.

Tittler, Robert, and Judith Richards. *The Reign of Mary I*. 3rd ed. London: Routledge, 2014.

Todd, Margo. *The Culture of Protestantism in Early Modern Scotland*. New Haven, CT: Yale University Press, 2002.

Trueman, Carl R. "The Theology of the English Reformers." In *The Cambridge Companion to the Reformation*, edited by David Bagchi and David C. Steinmetz, 161–73. Cambridge: Cambridge University Press, 2004.

Tyacke, Nicholas. *England's Long Reformation, 1500–1800*. London: UCL Press, 1998.

Wabuda, Susan. *Preaching during the English Reformation*. Cambridge: Cambridge University Press, 2002.

Warnicke, Retha M. *Mary Queen of Scots*. London: Routledge, 2006.

Werrell, Ralph S. *The Roots of William Tyndale's Theology*. Cambridge: James Clarke, 2013.

Whiting, Robert. *The Blind Devotion of the People: Popular Religion and the English Reformation*. Cambridge: Cambridge University Press, 1989.

Williams, Leslie. *Emblem of Faith Untouched: A Short Life of Thomas Cranmer*. Grand Rapids: Eerdmans, 2016.

Wright, David F. "The Scottish Reformation: Theology and Theologians." In *The Cambridge Companion to the Reformation*, edited by David Bagchi and David C. Steinmetz, 174–93. Cambridge: Cambridge University Press, 2004.

Wooding, L. E. C. *Henry VIII*. London: Routledge, 2009.

Zuck, Lowell H., ed. *Christianity and Revolution: Radical Christian Testimonies 1520–1650*. Philadelphia: Temple University Press, 1975.

PART 4: COUNTER-RENEWAL
Chapter 17. Roman but Catholic? Counter-Reformation, Catholic Renewal, and Antidotes to Trent
Primary Sources

Calvin, John. *Acta synodi tridentini cum antidoto*. In *Calvini Opera, VII*, 365–506. Braunschweig: Schwetschke und Sohn, 1868.

Chemnitz, Martin. *Examen Concilii Tridentini*. Berlin: Gustav Schlawitz, 1861.

———. *Examination of the Council of Trent*. Edited by Fred Kramer. 4 vols. St. Louis: Concordia, 1971.

Concilium Tridentinum: diariorum, actorum, epistolarum, tractatuum nova collectio. 13 vols. Fribourg: Societas Goerrsiana, 1901–85.

Dogmatic Decrees of the Council of Trent, 1545–63. In *Creeds and Confessions of Faith in the Christian Tradition*, edited by Jaroslav Pelikan and Valerie R. Hotchkiss, 2:819–71. New Haven, CT: Yale University Press, 2003.

Ignatius of Loyola. *The Spiritual Exercises of St. Ignatius: A Literal Translation and a Contemporary Reading*. Translated by David L. Fleming. St. Louis: Institute of Jesuit Sources, 1978.

———. *Spiritual Exercises and Selected Works*. The Classics of Western Spirituality. New York: Paulist, 1999.

Secondary Sources

Alberigo, Giuseppe. "The Council of Trent." In *Catholicism in Early Modern History: A Guide to Research*, edited by John O'Malley, 211–26. St. Louis: Center for Reformation Research, 1988.

Anderson, Marvin W. "Trent and Justification (1546): A Protestant Reflection." *SJT* 21 (1968): 385–406.

Bagchi, David. "Catholic theologians of the Reformation period before Trent." In *The Cambridge Companion to the Reformation*, edited by David Bagchi and David C. Steinmetz, 220–22. Cambridge: Cambridge University Press, 2004.

———. *Luther's Earliest Opponents: Catholic Controversialist, 1518–1525*. Minneapolis: Fortress, 1991.

Bamji, Alexandra, Geert H. Janssen, and Mary Laven, eds. *The Farnham, UK: Ashgate Research Companion to the Counter-Reformation*. Farnham, UK: Ashgate, 2013.

Bedouelle, Guy. *The Reform of Catholicism, 1480–1620*. Rome: Pontifical Institute of Medieval Studies, 2008.

Bireley, Robert. *The Refashioning of Catholicism, 1450–1700: A Reassessment of the Counter Reformation*. Washington, DC: Catholic University of America Press, 1999.

Blackwell, Richard J. *Galileo, Bellarmine, and the Bible.* Notre Dame, IN: University of Notre Dame Press, 1991.

Brodrick, James. *Robert Bellarmine, Saint and Scholar.* London: Burns & Oates, 1961.

Caraman, Philip. *Ignatius Loyola: A Biography of the Founder of the Jesuits.* New York: Harper and Row, 1990.

Conrod, Frédéric. *Loyola's Greater Narrative: The Architecture of the Spiritual Exercises in Golden Age and Enlightenment Literature.* Frankfurt: Lang, 2008.

Davidson, N. S. *The Counter-Reformation.* Oxford: Blackwell, 1987.

Denlinger, Aaron C. *Omnes in Adam Ex Pacto Dei: Ambrogio Catarino's Doctrine of Covenantal Solidarity and Its Influence on Post-Reformation Reformed Theologians.* Göttingen: Vandenhoeck & Ruprecht, 2010.

Dickens, A. G. *The Counter Reformation.* New York: Harcourt, Brace & World, 1969.

Eire, Carlos M. N. "Early Modern Catholic Piety in Translation." In *Cultural Translation in Early Modern Europe,* edited by Peter Burke and R. Po-chia Hsia, 83–100. Cambridge: Cambridge University Press, 2007.

Evennett, H. Outram. "Counter-Reformation Spirituality." In *The Counter-Reformation: The Essential Readings,* edited by David Luebke, 47–64. Hoboken, NJ: Wiley-Blackwell, 1999.

———. *The Spirit of the Counter-Reformation.* Notre Dame, IN: University of Notre Dame Press, 1970.

Funk, R. W., ed. *Distinctive Protestant and Catholic Themes Reconsidered.* New York: Harper and Row, 1967.

Geiselmann, J. R. "Scripture, Tradition, and the Church: An Ecumenical Problem." In *Christianity Divided,* edited by D. J. Callahan, H. A. Obermann, and D. J. O'Hanlon, 39–72. London: Sheed and Ward, 1962.

Gleason, Elizabeth G. "Sixteenth-Century Italian Spirituality and the Papacy." In *Anticlericalism in Late Medieval and Early Modern Europe,* edited by Peter Dykema and Heiko Oberman, 299–307. Leiden: E. J. Brill, 1993.

Heinz, Johann. *Justification and Merit: Luther vs. Catholicism.* Eugene, OR: Wipf & Stock, 2002.

Hsia, R. Po-chia. *The World of Catholic Renewal, 1540–1770.* Cambridge: Cambridge University Press, 1999.

Idígoras, J. Ignacio Tellechea. *Ignatius of Loyola: The Pilgrim Saint.* Chicago: Loyola University Press, 1994.

Iserloh, Erwin, Josef Glazik, and Hubert Jedin. *History of the Church.* Vol. 5, *Reformation and Counter Reformation.* New York: Seabury, 1980–82.

Jedin, Hubert. *A History of the Council of Trent.* 2 vols. St. Louis: Herder, 1957–61.

Jones, Martin D. W. *The Counter Reformation: Religion and Society in Early Modern Europe.* Cambridge: Cambridge University Press, 1995.

Kamen, Henry. *The Spanish Inquisition: A Historical Revision.* 4th ed. New Haven, CT: Yale University Press, 2014.

McGinness, Frederick J. *Right Thinking and Sacred Oratory in Counter-Reformation Rome.* Princeton, NJ: Princeton University Press, 1995.

McNally, Robert E. *The Council of Trent, the Spiritual Exercises, and the Catholic Reform.* Minneapolis: Fortress, 1970.

Meissner, W. W. *Ignatius of Loyola: The Psychology of a Saint.* New Haven, CT: Yale University Press, 1992.

Mullet, Michael A. *The Catholic Reformation.* London: Routledge, 1999.

O'Malley, John. *Trent: What Happened at the Council.* Cambridge, MA: Belknap, 2013.

————. *Trent and All That: Renaming Catholicism in the Early Modern Era*. Cambridge, MA: Harvard University Press, 2000.

Olin, John C. *Catholic Reform: From Cardinal Ximenes to the Council of Trent, 1495–1563*. New York: Fordham University Press, 1990.

Pattenden, Miles. *Pius IV and the Fall of the Carafa: Nepotism and Papal Authority in Counter-Reformation Rome*. Oxford: Oxford University Press, 2013.

Perez, Joseph. *The Spanish Inquisition: A History*. New Haven, CT: Yale University Press, 2005.

Posset, Franz. *Front-Runner of the Catholic Reformation: The Life and Works of Johann von Staupitz*. Farnham, UK: Ashgate, 2003.

Randell, Keith. *The Catholic and Counter Reformations*. London: Hodder & Stoughton, 2000.

Ravier, André. *Ignatius of Loyola and the Founding of the Society of Jesus*. San Francisco, CA: Ignatius, 1987.

Rawlings, Helen. *The Spanish Inquisition*. Oxford: Blackwell, 2006.

Worcester, Thomas, ed. *The Cambridge Companion to the Jesuits*. Cambridge: Cambridge University Press, 2008.

SUBJECT INDEX

SCRIPTURE INDEX

AUTHOR INDEX